17e

American Government

Institutions and Policies

James Q. Wilson
University of California, Los Angeles, emeritus
Pepperdine University
Boston College

John J. DiIulio, Jr.
University of Pennsylvania

Meena Bose
Hofstra University

Matthew Levendusky
University of Pennsylvania

Australia • Brazil • Canada • Mexico • Singapore • United Kingdom • United States

***American Government: Institutions and Policies*, Seventeenth Edition**
James Q. Wilson, John J. DiIulio Jr., Meena Bose, Matthew Levendusky

SVP, Higher Education & Skills Product: Erin Joyner

VP, Higher Education & Skills Product: Thais Alencar

Product Director: Laura Ross

Product Manager: Lauren Gerrish

Product Assistant: Martina Umunna

Content Manager: Dan Saabye

Senior Marketing Manager: Valerie Hartman

Senior Subject Matter Expert: Emily Hickey

Learning Designer: Erika Hayden

IP Analyst: Deanna Ettinger

IP Project Manager: Kelli Besse

Production Service: MPS Limited

Compositor: MPS Limited

Art Director: Sarah Cole

Text and Cover Designer: Sarah Cole

Cover Image: Bettman/Getty Images and SDI Productions/E+/Getty Images

For product information and technology assistance, contact us at **Cengage Customer & Sales Support, 1-800-354-9706** or **support.cengage.com**.

For permission to use material from this text or product, submit all requests online at **www.cengage.com/permissions**.

Library of Congress Control Number: 2020914195

Student Edition:
ISBN: 978-0-357-45965-2

Loose-leaf Edition:
ISBN: 978-0-357-45966-9

Cengage
200 Pier 4 Boulevard
Boston, MA 02210
USA

Cengage is a leading provider of customized learning solutions with employees residing in nearly 40 different countries and sales in more than 125 countries around the world. Find your local representative at **www.cengage.com**.

To learn more about Cengage platforms and services, register or access your online learning solution, or purchase materials for your course, visit **www.cengage.com**.

Printed at CLDPC, USA, 12-20

Brief Contents

Contents

Letter to Instructors

Dear American Government Instructor:

We wrote *American Government: Institutions and Policies, 17th edition,* not only to explain to students how the federal government works, but also to examine how its institutions have developed over time and evaluate their effects on public policy. Within this distinguishing framework, we explain the history of Congress, the presidency, the judiciary, and the bureaucracy because the politics we see today are different from those we would have seen in earlier generations. Likewise, we also explain how public opinion, elections, interest groups, and the media shape and contribute to policy, and how that influence has evolved over time.

American Government: Institutions and Policies, 17th edition, is grounded in certain key ideas that help students understand not simply American government, but also the reasons why the national government in this country is different from those in other democracies. These ideas include the principles of the U.S. Constitution and American constitutionalism, America's adversarial political culture, and a commitment to freedom and limited government. This book is an attempt to explain and discuss the historical and practical reasons for these differences.

New to This Edition

And as always, the book is thoroughly revised to excite students' interest about the latest in American politics and encourage critical thinking. Updates reflect the latest scholarship and current events, including the Trump administration, the 2020 election, the COVID-19 pandemic, and the protests following the death of George Floyd while in police custody. We also continue our discussion of ongoing debates about the federal budget, immigration, taxes, and other key issues in American politics; and foreign-policy issues in the Middle East, Europe, and elsewhere. Reworked Learning Objectives open, organize, and close each chapter, serving as a road map to key concepts and helping students assess their comprehension. Each chapter now contains a "Constitutional Connections" box to help students connect the topic to the nation's founding, "What Would You Do?" to deal with a real-life controversy, "Policy Dynamics: Inside/Outside the Box" to apply our framework for understanding public policy to various issues, and Infographic Questions to help students learn to reason from data.

MindTap: Your Course Stimulus Package

As an instructor, MindTap is here to simplify your workload, organize and immediately grade your students' assignments, and allow you to customize your course as you see fit. Through deep-seated integration with your Learning Management System, grades are easily exported and analytics are pulled with just the click of a button. MindTap provides you with a platform to easily add in current events videos and article links from national or local news sources.

We hope this book helps your students grapple with the fundamental questions of American government, and understand who governs and to what ends. And we also hope it inspires them to continue their engagement with the exciting and dynamic world of American politics.

Sincerely,

John J. DiIulio, Jr.

Meena Bose
Meena.Bose@hofstra.edu

Matthew S. Levendusky
mleven@sas.upenn.edu

Letter to Students

Dear Student:

Welcome to *American Government: Institutions and Policies, 17th ed*! We wrote the textbook to help you grapple with two of the fundamental questions of American government and politics: who governs and to what ends? The textbook will help you to answer these questions, and to better understand how the structure of American government determines the policies that we see. The features we include—from learning objectives, to constitutional connections, to policy dynamics, and what would you do—will help you to master key concepts and topics, and apply them from the classroom to everyday political life. Much has changed these last few years in American politics, especially in light of the COVID-19 pandemic and the protests following the death of George Floyd while in police custody. Our goal is to help you understand these important events, as well more long-standing features of American politics.

- **Learning Objectives** open and close each chapter, serving as a road map to the book's key concepts and helping you to assess your understanding.
- **Then and Now** chapter-opening vignettes offer attention-grabbing looks at a particular topic in the past and in the present, reinforcing the historical emphasis of the text and applying these experiences to the world around you today.
- **Constitutional Connections** features raise analytical issues from the constitutional debates that remain relevant today.
- **Policy Dynamics: Inside/Outside the Box** features present policy dynamics and encourage you to think about where they belong within *American Government*'s classic politics of policymaking framework, which is introduced in Chapter 1.
- **Infographic Questions** help you learn to reason from data.
- **Landmark Cases** provide brief descriptions of important Supreme Court cases.
- **What Would You Do?** features place you in the role of a decision maker on realistic contemporary policy debates.
- **To Learn More** sections close each chapter with carefully selected Web resources and classic and contemporary suggested readings to further assist you in learning about American politics.

The Benefits of Using MindTap as a Student

As a student, the benefits of using MindTap with this book are endless. With automatically graded practice quizzes and activities, an easily navigated learning path, and an interactive eBook, you will be able to test yourself inside and outside of the classroom with ease. The accessibility of current events coupled with interactive media makes the content fun and engaging. On your computer, phone, or tablet, MindTap is there when you need it, giving you easy access to flashcards, quizzes, readings, and assignments.

We hope all of these resources help you to master the material in the course and have a richer understanding of American government and democracy. We also hope that this textbook encourages you to continue your intellectual journey in American politics, and that understanding how the political process functions will inspire you to become involved in some way. How will you shape who governs and to what ends?

Sincerely,

John J. DiIulio, Jr.

Meena Bose
Meena.Bose@hofstra.edu

Matthew S. Levendusky
mleven@sas.upenn.edu

Resources

Students…

Cengage Unlimited
Cengage Unlimited saves students money, time and hassle when accessing course materials. One student subscription includes access to every Cengage etextbook, online homework platform, print rental benefits, study tools, and more — in one place, for one price. Cengage Unlimited eTextbooks is an option for courses that use textbooks only. Available for students in bookstores and online.

Details at **www.cengage.com/unlimited**. Available in select markets only.

Access your *American Government: Institutions and Policies, 17th ed.* resources by visiting **www.cengage.com**. If you purchased MindTap access with your book, click on "Register a Product" and then enter your access code.

The Cengage Mobile App
Complete course work on the go with the *Cengage Mobile App*, which delivers a seamless course experience on a smartphone or tablet. Read or listen to your textbook whether online or offline and study with the help of flashcards, practice quizzes and instant feedback from your instructor. You can receive due date reminders and complete assignments from the convenience of your mobile device!

Instructors…

Access *American Government: Institutions and Policies, 17e* resources via **www.cengage.com/login**. Log in using your Cengage Learning single sign-on user name and password, or create a new instructor account by clicking on "**New Faculty User**" and following the instructions.

Enhanced MindTap for *American Government: Institutions & Policies*

ISBN for Instant Access Code: 9780357459683
ISBN for Printed Access Card: 9780357459690

MindTap for *American Government: Institutions & Policies* 17e is an immersive, online learning experience built upon Cengage Learning content and correlated to a core set of learning outcomes. MindTap gives you complete control of your course—to provide engaging content, to challenge every individual, and to build their confidence. MindTap introduces students to core concepts from the beginning of your course using a simplified learning path that progresses from understanding to application. Concepts are presented using a blend of engaging narrative and media while minimizing distraction with assignments that pair learning content with assessments in a visually appealing side-by-side format. These activities engage students with a variety of content types—including graphs, infographics, and explanation videos—that extend learning beyond the textbook. Assignable, auto-graded assessments, quizzes, and brief writing activities enable students to flex their critical thinking muscles while soaking in key concepts. Students are encouraged to read with close attention, write persuasively with logic, interpret data, and analyze information presented.

MindTap provides students with ample opportunities to check themselves for where they need extra help, as well as allowing faculty to measure and assess student progress. The Cengage Mobile App enables greater flexibility for students to fit learning into their day, wherever they are, and allows instructors create polls to foster engagement and activate learning in the classroom.

As an instructor, MindTap is here to simplify your workload, organize and immediately grade your students' assignments, and allow you to customize your course with current events videos and news sources as you see fit. Through deep-seated integration with your learning management system (LMS), grades are easily exported, and analytics are pulled with the click of a button. MindTap can be used fully online with its interactive eBook for *American Government: Institutions & Policies* 17e, or in conjunction with the printed text.

Instructor Companion Website for *American Government: Institutions & Policies, 17e—for instructors only*

ISBN: 9780357459744

This Instructor Companion Website is an all-in-one resource for class preparation, presentation, and testing. Accessible through Cengage.com/login with your faculty account, you will find available for download: book-specific Microsoft® PowerPoint® presentations, a Test Bank compatible with multiple learning management systems (LMSs), an Instructor's Manual, and more.

The Test Bank, offered in Blackboard, Moodle, Desire2Learn and Canvas formats, contains learning objective-specific multiple-choice and essay questions for each chapter. Import the test bank into your LMS to edit and manage questions, and to create tests.

The Instructor's Manual includes information about all of the activities and assessments available for each chapter and their correlation to specific learning objectives, an outline, key terms with definitions, a chapter summary, and several ideas for engaging with students with discussion questions, ice breakers, case studies, and social learning activities that may be conducted in an on-ground, hybrid, or online modality.

The Microsoft® PowerPoint® presentations are closely tied to the Instructor's Manual, providing ample opportunities for generating classroom discussion and interaction. They offer ready-to-use, visual outlines of each chapter, which may be easily customized for your lectures. A guide to teaching online presents technological and pedagogical considerations and suggestions for teaching the Introduction to American Government course when you can't be in the same room with students. Access the Instructor Companion Website for these resources and more at www.cengage.com/login.

Cognero for *American Government: Institutions & Policies, 17e*

ISBN: 9780357459706

Cengage Learning Testing Powered by Cognero is a flexible, online system that allows you to author, edit, and manage test bank content from multiple Cengage Learning solutions; create multiple test versions in an instant; and deliver tests from your LMS, your classroom, or wherever you want. The Test Bank for *American Government: Institutions & Policies, Enhanced 17e,* contains learning objective-specific multiple-choice and essay questions for each chapter.

Acknowledgments

Special thanks go to Marc Siegal, Jesse Crosson, and Taylor Nefussy for their research assistance; Rosalyn Crain for her revision of the Instructor's Manual, and PowerPoint lecture; and Daniel Larsen and Andrew Conneen, of Adlai E. Stevenson H.S. for their work on the AP supplements.

We would also like to thank our team at Cengage: Dan Saabye, Content Manager; Valerie Hartman, Senior Marketing Manager; Sarah Cole, Senior Designer; Erika Hayden, Learning Designer; Emily Hickey, Senior Subject Matter Expert, Associate Product Manager Lauren Gerrish.

Reviewers

We would also like to thank the instructors who have contributed their valuable feedback through reviews of this text:

New Reviewers

Dr. Dovie D. Dawson Central Texas College
Dr. Kim Farley Western Wyoming Community College
James Goss Tarrant County College-Trinity River
Tally Payne Casper College

Previous Edition Reviewers

Philip Aka, *Chicago State University*
Lucas Allen, *Michigan State University*
Roger Ashby, *Peace College*
Michael Baranowski, *Northern Kentucky University*
James Brent, *Arkansas State University–Beebe*
Chuck Brownson, *Stephen F. Austin High School*
Dr. Robert Carroll, *East-West University*
Jonathan Culp, *University of Dallas*
Jack Citrin, *University of California, Berkeley*
Zach Courser, *Boston College*
Albert Cover, *Stony Brook University*
Stan Crippen, *Riverside County Office of Education*
Gregory Culver, *University of Southern Indiana*
Nicholas Damask, *Scottsdale Community College*
Teddy Davis, *Arkansas State University–Beebe*
Justin DePlato, *Robert Morris University*
Virgil H. Davis, *Pellissippi State Community College*
Jenna P. Duke, *Lehigh Carbon Community College*
Matthew Eshbaugh-Soha, *University of North Texas*
Terri Fine, *University of Central Florida*
Ethan Fishman, *University of South Alabama*
Glenn David Garrison, *Collin County Community College–Spring Creek Campus*
Cyril Ghosh, *Wagner College*
Mark Griffith, *University of West Alabama*
Richard Grubbs, *R.L. Paschal High School*
Thomas Harrington, *Santa Fe College*
Jeff Harmon, *University of Texas at San Antonio*
Kathleen C. Hauger, *Abington Senior High School*
James Hite, *Clackamas Community College*
Stephen Kerbow, *Southwest Texas Junior College*
David Kershaw, *Slippery Rock University of Pennsylvania*
Halima Asghar Khan, *Massasoit Community College*
Young-Choul Kim, *University of Evansville*
Junius H. Koonce, *Edgecombe Community College*
Vanessa Lal, *Adlai E. Stevenson High School*
William Lester, *Jacksonville State University*
Brad Lockerbie, *University of Georgia*
Randall McKeever, *Forney ISD*
Angela Narasimhan, *Keuka College*
Marvin Overby, *University of Missouri*
Anne F. Presley, *McKinney High School*
Elizabeth Prough, *Madonna University*
Greg Rabb, *Jamestown Community College*
Gayle Randolph, *Neosho County Community College*
Donald Ranish, *Antelope Valley College*
Kenneth Rivera, *Brandywine High School*
Jonathan Roberts, *Portland, Oregon, schools*
Lelia Roeckell, *Molloy College*
P. S. Ruckman, *Rock Valley College*
Cathy Ruffing, *Fairfax County Public Schools; Centreville High School*
Erich Saphir, *Pima Community College*
Sean Savage, *Saint Mary's College—Notre Dame*
Rebecca Small, *Herndon High School*
Randall Smith, *Naperville Central High School*
Greg Snoad, *Mauldin High School*
Brian Stevens, *Coldwater High School*
Matthew Szlapak, *Lord Fairfax Community College*
Linda Trautman, *Ohio University–Lancaster*
Jennifer Walsh, *Azusa Pacific University*
Peter Wielhouwer, *Western Michigan University*
David Wigg, *St. Louis Community College*
Teresa Wright, *California State University–Long Beach*
Adam Zucconi, *Richard Bland College*

About the Authors

James Q. Wilson

James Q. Wilson most recently taught at Boston College and Pepperdine University. He was Professor Emeritus of Management and Public Administration at the University of California, Los Angeles and was previously Shattuck Professor of Government at Harvard University. He wrote more than a dozen books on the subjects of public policy, bureaucracy, and political philosophy. Dr. Wilson was president of the American Political Science Association (APSA), and he is the only political scientist to win three of the four lifetime achievement awards presented by the APSA. He received the Presidential Medal of Freedom, the nation's highest civilian award, in 2003. Dr. Wilson passed away in March 2012 after battling cancer. His work helped shape the field of political science in the United States. His many years of service to his *American Government* book remain evident on every page and will continue for many editions to come.

John J. DiIulio, Jr.

John J. DiIulio, Jr. is Professor of Political Science at the University of Pennsylvania and has won each of Penn's most prestigious teaching awards. He was previously Professor of Politics and Public Affairs at Princeton University. Dr. DiIulio received his Ph.D. in Political Science from Harvard University. He has been a senior fellow and directed research programs at several leading think tanks, including the Brookings Institution, and has won awards from the Association of Public Policy Analysis and Management, the APSA, and other bodies. Dr. DiIulio has advised presidential candidates in both parties, served on bipartisan government reform commissions, and worked as a senior staff member in the White House.

Meena Bose

Meena Bose is Executive Dean of Public Policy and Public Service Programs in Hofstra University's Peter S. Kalikow School of Government, Public Policy and International Affairs, and Director of Hofstra's Peter S. Kalikow Center for the Study of the American Presidency. She received her Ph.D. (1996) from Princeton University. Dr. Bose teaches courses on the American Presidency, Presidential Leadership and Policy Making, and American Politics. She is the author or editor of several volumes in presidency studies and American politics. Dr. Bose taught for six years at the United States Military Academy at West Point.

Matthew S. Levendusky

Matthew S. Levendusky is Professor of Political Science at the University of Pennsylvania. He received his Ph.D. from Stanford University (2006). Dr. Levendusky teaches courses in public opinion, campaigns and elections, policymaking, and political polarization. He has written two books on political polarization and the mass media, both published by the University of Chicago Press.

PART 1

The American System

In framing a government which is to be administered by men over men, the great difficulty lies in this: You must first enable the government to control the governed; and in the next place oblige it to control itself.

— *FEDERALIST NO. 51*

Tony Savino/Corbis Historical/Getty Images

CHAPTER 1

The Study of American Government

Learning Objectives

1-1 Explain how politics drives democracy.

1-2 Discuss five views of how political power is distributed in the United States.

1-3 Explain why "who governs?" and "to what ends?" are fundamental questions in American politics.

1-4 Summarize the key concepts for classifying the politics of different policy issues.

Today, Americans and their elected leaders are hotly debating the federal government's fiscal responsibilities, for both spending and taxation.

Some things never change.

« Then In 1786, a committee of Congress reported that since the Articles of Confederation were adopted in 1781, the state governments had paid only about one-seventh of the monies requisitioned by the federal government. The federal government was broke and sinking deeper into debt, including debt owed to foreign governments. Several states had financial crises, too.

In 1788, the proposed Constitution's chief architect, James Madison, argued that while the federal government needed its own "power of taxation" and "collectors of revenue," its overall powers would remain "few and defined" and its taxing power would be used sparingly.[1] In reply, critics of the proposed Constitution, including the famous patriot Patrick Henry, mocked Madison's view and predicted that if the Constitution were ratified, there would over time be "an immense increase of taxes" spent by an ever-growing federal government.[2]

*** Now** The federal budget initially proposed for 2021 called for spending more than $4.8 trillion, with a budget deficit close to $1 trillion (i.e., spending that much more than projected government revenues). An expected national debt of more than $25 trillion, much of it borrowed from foreign nations, was projected to balloon to more than $30 trillion by 2030. Projected interest on the national debt in 2021 would be near $400 billion and was expected to top $600 billion by 2028.[3]

The Budget Control Act of 2011 had called for long-term deficit reduction, but when the White House and Congress could not reach agreement in 2013, automatic spending cuts—known as "sequestration"—went into effect, and the federal government even shut down for 16 days in October. The two branches ultimately reached agreement, but could not find common ground on questions about long-term revenue and spending goals—a problem that recurred in late 2018 and into 2019, when the government closed for five weeks over a debate about immigration and funding for border security.

So, in the 1780s, as in the 2010s, nearly everyone agreed that government's finances were a huge mess and that bold action was required, and soon; but in each case, then and now, there was no consensus about what action to take, or when.

issue A conflict, real or apparent, between the interests, ideas, or beliefs of different citizens.

1-1 Politics and Democracy

This might seem odd. After all, it may seem that the government's financial problems, including big budget deficits and revenue shortfalls, could be solved by simple arithmetic: either spend and borrow less, or tax more, or both. But now ask: Spend or borrow less for what, and raise taxes on whom, when, how, and by how much? For example, should we cut the defense budget but continue to fund health care programs, or the reverse? Or should we keep defense and health care funding at current levels but reduce spending on environmental protection or homeland security? Should we perhaps increase taxes on the wealthy (define *wealthy*) and cut taxes for the middle class (define *middle class*), or … what?

Then, as now, the fundamental government finance problems were *political*, not mathematical. People disagreed not only over how much the federal government should tax and spend, but also over whether it should involve itself at all in various endeavors. For example, in 2011, the federal government nearly shut down, not mainly over disagreements between the two parties about how much needed to be cut from the federal budget (in the end, the agreed-to cuts totaled $38.5 billion), but primarily over whether any federal funding at all should go to certain relatively small-budget federal health, environmental, and other programs.

Fights over taxes and government finances; battles over abortion, school prayer, and LGBTQ+ rights; disputes about where to store nuclear waste; competing plans on immigration, international trade, welfare reform, environmental protection, or gun control; and contention surrounding a new health care proposal. Some of these matters are mainly about money and economic interests; others are more about ideas and personal beliefs. Some people care a lot about at least some of these matters; others seem to care little or not at all.

Regardless, all such matters and countless others have this in common: each is an **issue**, defined as a conflict, real or apparent, between the interests, ideas, or beliefs of different citizens.[4]

An issue may be more apparent than real; for example, people might fight over two tax plans that, despite superficial differences, would actually distribute tax burdens on different groups in exactly the same way. Or an issue may be as real as it seems to the conflicting parties, as,

politics *The activity by which an issue is agitated or settled.*

power *The ability of one person to get another person to act in accordance with the first person's intentions.*

authority *The right to use power.*

for example, with matters that pose clear-cut choices (high tariffs or no tariffs; abortion legal in all cases or illegal in all cases).

And an issue might be more about conflicts over means than over ends. For example, on health care reform or other issues, legislators who are in the same party and have similar ideological leanings (like a group of liberal Democrats, or a group of conservative Republicans) might agree on objectives but still wrangle bitterly with each other over different means of achieving their goals. Or they might agree on both ends and means but differ over priorities (which goals to pursue first), timing (when to proceed), or tactics (how to proceed).

Whatever form issues take, they are the raw materials of politics. By **politics** we mean "the activity—negotiation, argument, discussion, application of force, persuasion, etc.—by which an issue is agitated or settled."[5] Any given issue can be agitated (brought to attention, stimulate conflict) or settled (brought to an accommodation, stimulate consensus) in many different ways. And government can agitate or settle, foster or frustrate political conflict in many different ways.

As you begin this textbook, this is a good time to ask yourself which issues matter to you. In general, do you care a lot, a little, or not at all about economic issues, social issues, or issues involving foreign policy or military affairs? Do you follow any particular, ongoing debates on issues such as tightening gun control laws, expanding health insurance, regulating immigration, or funding antipoverty programs?

As you will learn in Part II of this textbook, some citizens are quite issue-oriented and politically active. They vote and try to influence others to vote likewise; they join political campaigns or give money to candidates; they keep informed about diverse issues, sign petitions, advocate for new laws, or communicate with elected leaders; and more.

But such politically attentive and engaged citizens are the exception to the rule, most especially among young adult citizens under age 30. According to many experts, ever more young Americans are closer to being "political dropouts" than they are to being "engaged citizens" (a fact that is made no less troubling by similar trends in the United Kingdom, Canada, Scandinavia, and elsewhere).[6] Many high school and college students believe getting "involved in our democracy" means volunteering for community service, but not voting.[7] Most young Americans do not regularly read or closely follow political news; and most know little about how government works and exhibit no "regular interest in politics."[8] In response to such concerns, various analysts and study commissions have made proposals ranging from compulsory voting to enhanced "civic education" in high schools.[9]

The fact that you are reading this textbook tells us that you probably have some interest in American politics and government. Our goal in this textbook is to develop, enliven, and inform that interest through examining concepts, interests, and institutions in American politics from a historical perspective as well as through current policy debates.

Power, Authority, and Legitimacy

Politics, and the processes by which issues are normally agitated or settled, involves the exercise of power. By **power** we mean the ability of one person to get another person to act in accordance with the first person's intentions. Sometimes an exercise of power is obvious, as when the president tells the Air Force that it cannot build a new bomber, or orders soldiers into combat in a foreign land. Other times an exercise of power is subtle, as when the president's junior speechwriters, reflecting their own evolving views, adopt a new tone when writing about controversial issues such as education policy. The speechwriters may not think they are using power—after all, they are the president's subordinates and may see their boss face-to-face infrequently. But if the president speaks the phrases that they craft, then they have used power.

Power is found in all human relationships, but we are concerned here only with power as it is used to affect who will hold government office and how government will behave. We limit our view here to government, and chiefly to the American federal government. However, we repeatedly pay special attention to how things once thought to be "private" matters become "public"—that is, how they manage to become objects of governmental action. Indeed, as we discuss more later, one of the most striking transformations of American politics has been the extent to which, in recent decades, almost every aspect of human life has found its way onto the political agenda.

People who exercise political power may or may not have the authority to do so. By **authority** we mean the right to use power. The exercise of rightful power—that is, of authority—is ordinarily easier than the exercise of power not supported by any persuasive claim of right. We accept decisions, often without question, if they are made by people who we believe have the right to make them; we may bow to naked power because we cannot resist it, but by our recalcitrance or our resentment we put the users of naked power to greater trouble than the wielders of authority. In this book, we on occasion speak of "formal authority." By this we mean that the right to exercise power is vested in a governmental office. A president, a senator, and a federal judge have formal authority to take certain actions.

What makes power rightful varies from time to time and from country to country. In the United States, we usually say a person has political authority if the right to act in a certain way is conferred by a law or by a state or national constitution. But what makes a law or constitution a source of right? That is the question of **legitimacy**. In the United States, the Constitution today is widely, if not unanimously, accepted as a source of legitimate authority, but that was not always the case.

Defining Democracy

On one matter, virtually all Americans seem to agree: no exercise of political power by government at any level is legitimate if it is not in some sense democratic. That wasn't always the prevailing view. In 1787, as the Framers drafted the Constitution, Alexander Hamilton worried that the new government he helped create might be too democratic, whereas George Mason, who refused to sign the Constitution, worried that it was not democratic enough. Today, however, almost everyone believes that democratic government is the only proper kind. Most people believe that American government is democratic; some believe that other institutions of public life—schools, universities, corporations, trade unions, churches—also should be run on democratic principles if they are to be legitimate; and some insist that promoting democracy abroad ought to be a primary purpose of U.S. foreign policy.

Democracy is a word with at least two different meanings. First, the term *democracy* is used to describe those regimes that come as close as possible to Aristotle's definition—the "rule of the many."[10] A government is democratic if all, or most, of its citizens participate directly in either holding office or making policy. This often is called **direct or participatory democracy**. In Aristotle's time—Greece in the 4th century B.C.—such a government was possible. The Greek city-state, or *polis*, was quite small, and within it citizenship was extended to all free adult male property holders. (Slaves, women, minors, and those without property were excluded from participation in government.) In more recent times, the New England town meeting approximates the Aristotelian ideal. In such a meeting, the adult citizens of a community gather once or twice a year to vote directly on all major issues and expenditures of the town. As towns have become larger and issues more complicated, many town governments have abandoned the pure town meeting in favor of either the representative town meeting (in which a large number of elected representatives, perhaps 200–300, meet to vote on town affairs) or representative government (in which a small number of elected city councilors make decisions).

Ryan Rahman/Alamy Stock Photo

Image 1.1 In September 2019, thousands of students marched in lower Manhattan as part of a global protest against climate change.

Q How can students make a difference in American politics and policy making?

legitimacy *Political authority conferred by law or by a state or national constitution.*

democracy *The rule of the many.*

direct or participatory democracy *A government in which all or most citizens participate directly.*

representative democracy *A government in which leaders make decisions by winning a competitive struggle for the popular vote.*

The second definition of *democracy* is the principle of governance of most nations that are called democratic. It was most concisely stated by the economist Joseph Schumpeter: "The democratic method is that institutional arrangement for arriving at political decisions in which individuals [i.e., leaders] acquire the power to decide by means of a competitive struggle for the people's vote."[11] Sometimes this method is called, approvingly, **representative democracy**; at other times it is referred to, disapprovingly, as the elitist theory of democracy. It is justified by one or both of two arguments. First, it is impractical, owing to limits of time, information, energy, interest, and expertise, for the public at large to decide on public policy, but it is not impractical to expect them to make reasonable choices among competing leadership groups. Second, some people (including, as we shall see in the next chapter, many of the Framers of the Constitution) believe direct democracy is likely to lead to bad decisions because people often decide large issues on the basis of fleeting passions and in response to popular demagogues, or leaders who appeal to emotions, not reason, to gain support. This concern about direct democracy persists today, as evidenced by the statements of leaders who disagree with voter decisions. For example, voters in many states have rejected referenda that would have increased public funding for private schools. Politicians who oppose the defeated referenda speak approvingly of the "will of the people," but politicians who favor them speak disdainfully of "mass misunderstanding."

Whenever we refer to that form of democracy involving the direct participation of all or most citizens, we use the term *direct* or *participatory* democracy. Whenever the word *democracy* is used alone in this book, it will have the meaning Schumpeter gave it. Schumpeter's definition usefully implies basic benchmarks that enable us to judge the extent to which any given political system is democratic.[12] A political system is nondemocratic to the extent that it denies equal voting rights to part of its society and severely limits (or outright prohibits) "the civil and political freedoms to speak, publish, assemble, and organize,"[13] all of which are necessary to a truly "competitive struggle for the people's vote." A partial list of nondemocratic political systems would include absolute monarchies, empires, military dictatorships, authoritarian systems, and totalitarian states.[14]

Scholars of comparative politics and government have much to teach about how different types of political systems—democratic and nondemocratic—arise, persist, and change. For our present purposes, however, it is most important to understand that America itself was once far less democratic than it is today and that it was so not by accident but by design. As we discuss in the next chapter, the men who wrote the Constitution did not use the word *democracy* in that document. They wrote instead of a "republican form of government," but by that they meant what we call "representative democracy." And, as we emphasize when discussing civil liberties and civil rights (see Chapters 5 and 6), and again when discussing political participation (see Chapter 8), the United States was not born as a full-fledged representative democracy; and, for all the progress of the past half-century or so, the nation's representative democratic character is still very much a work in progress.

Image 1.2 The January 2017 Women's March on Washington to protest the Trump presidency became an annual event in subsequent years.

For any representative democracy to work, there must, of course, be an opportunity for genuine competition for leadership. This requires in turn that individuals and parties be able to run for office, that communications (through speeches or the press, in meetings, and on the Internet) be free, and that the voters perceive that a meaningful choice exists. But what, exactly, constitutes a "meaningful choice"? How many offices should be elective and how many appointive? How many candidates or parties can exist before the choices become hopelessly confused? Where will the money come from to finance electoral campaigns? Such questions have many answers. In some European democracies, for example, very few offices—often just those in the national or local legislature—are elective, and much of the money for campaigning for these offices comes from the government. In the United States, many offices—executive and judicial as well as legislative—are elective, and most of the money the candidates use for campaigning comes from industry, labor unions, and private individuals.

Some people have argued that the virtues of direct or participatory democracy can and should be reclaimed even in a modern, complex society. This can be done either by allowing individual neighborhoods in big cities to govern themselves (community control) or by requiring those affected by some government program to participate in its formulation (citizen participation). In many states, a measure of direct democracy exists when voters can decide on issues through a referendum—that is, policy choices that appear on the ballot. The proponents of direct democracy defend it as the only way to ensure that the "will of the people" prevails.

As we discuss in the nearby Constitutional Connections feature, and as we explore more in Chapter 2, the Framers of the Constitution did not think that the "will of the people" was synonymous with the "common interest" or the "public good." They strongly favored representative democracy over direct democracy, and they believed that elected officials could best ascertain what was in the public interest.

1-2 Political Power in America: Five Views

Scholars differ in their interpretations of the American political experience. Where some see a steady march of democracy, others see no such thing; where some emphasize how voting and other rights have been

Constitutional Connections | Deciding What's Legitimate

Much of American political history has been a struggle over what constitutes legitimate authority. The Constitutional Convention in 1787 was an effort to determine whether a new, more powerful federal government could be made legitimate; the succeeding administrations of George Washington, John Adams, and Thomas Jefferson were in large measure preoccupied with disputes over the kinds of decisions that were legitimate for the federal government to make. The Civil War was a bloody struggle over slavery and the legitimacy of the federal union; the New Deal of Franklin Roosevelt was hotly debated by those who disagreed over whether it was legitimate for the federal government to intervene deeply in the economy. Not uncommonly, the federal judiciary functions as the ultimate arbiter of what is legitimate in the context of deciding what is or is not constitutional (see Chapter 16). For instance, in 2012, amidst a contentious debate over the legitimacy of the federal health care law that was enacted in 2010, the U.S. Supreme Court decided that the federal government could require individuals to purchase health insurance but could not require states to expand health care benefits for citizens participating in the federal-state program known as Medicaid. In the spring and summer of 2017, the Trump White House and the Republican-led Congress tried unsuccessfully to repeal the 2010 law, though they did end the tax penalty, or mandate, for people who do not have health coverage.

steadily expanded, others stress how they were denied to so many for so long, and so forth. Short of attempting to reconcile these competing historical interpretations, let us step back now for a moment to our definition of representative democracy and five competing views about how political power has been distributed in America.

Representative democracy is defined as any system of government in which leaders are authorized to make decisions—and thereby to wield political power—by winning a competitive struggle for the popular vote. It is obvious then that very different sets of hands can control political power, depending on what kinds of people can become leaders, how the struggle for votes is carried on, how much freedom to act is given to those who win the struggle, and what other sorts of influence (besides the desire for popular approval) affect the leaders' actions.

The actual distribution of political power in a representative democracy depends on the composition of the political elites who are involved in the struggles for power and over policy. By **elite** we mean an identifiable group of persons who possess a disproportionate share of some valued resource—in this case, political power.

At least five views exist about how political power is distributed in America: (1) the **class view** (wealthy capitalists and other economic elites determine most policies), (2) the **power elite view** (a group of business, military, labor union, and elected officials controls most decisions), (3) the **bureaucratic view** (appointed bureaucrats ultimately run everything); (4) the **pluralist view** (representatives of a large number of interest groups are in charge), and (5) the **creedal passion view** (morally impassioned elites drive political change).

The first view began with the theories of Karl Marx, who, in the 19th century, argued that governments were dominated by business owners (the "bourgeoisie") until a revolution replaced them with rule by laborers (the "proletariat").[15] But strict Marxism has collapsed in most countries. Today, a class view, though it may derive inspiration from Marx, is less dogmatic and emphasizes the power of "the rich" or the leaders of multinational corporations.

The second view ties business leaders together with other elites whose perceived power is of concern to the view's adherents. These elites may include top military officials, labor union leaders, mass media executives, and the heads of a few special-interest groups. Derived from the work of sociologist C. Wright Mills, this power elite view argues that American democracy is dominated by a few top leaders, many of them wealthy or privately powerful, who do not hold elective office.[16]

The third view is that appointed officials run everything despite the efforts of elected officials and the public to control them. The bureaucratic view was first set forth

elite Persons who possess a disproportionate share of some valued resource, such as money, prestige, or expertise.

class view View that the government is dominated by capitalists.

power elite view View that the government is dominated by a few top leaders, most of whom are outside of government.

bureaucratic view View that the government is dominated by appointed officials.

pluralist view View that competition among all affected interests shapes public policy.

creedal passion view View that morally impassioned elites drive important political changes.

by German scholar Max Weber (1864–1920). He argued that the modern state, in order to become successful, puts its affairs in the hands of appointed bureaucrats whose competence is essential to the management of complex affairs.[17] These officials, invisible to most people, have mastered the written records and legislative details of the government and do more than just implement democratic policies; they actually make those policies.

The fourth view holds that political resources—such as money, prestige, expertise, and access to the mass media—have become so widely distributed that no single elite, no social class, no bureaucratic arrangement, can control them. Many 20th-century political scientists, among them David B. Truman, adopted a pluralist view.[18] In the United States, they argued, political resources are broadly shared in part because there are so many governmental institutions (cities, states, school boards) and so many rival institutions (legislatures, executives, judges, bureaucrats) that no single group can dominate most, or even much, of the political process.

The fifth view maintains that while each of the other four views is correct with respect to how power is distributed on certain issues or during political periods of "business as usual," each also misses how the most important policy decisions and political changes are influenced by morally impassioned elites who are motivated less by economic self-interest than they are by an almost religious zeal to bring government institutions and policies into line with democratic ideals. Samuel P. Huntington articulated this creedal passion view, offering the examples of Patrick Henry and the revolutionaries of the 1770s, the advocates of Jackson-style democracy in the 1820s, the progressive reformers of the early 20th century, and the leaders of the civil rights and antiwar movements in the mid-20th century.[19]

1-3 Who Governs? To What Ends?

So, which view is correct? At one level, all are correct, at least in part: Economic class interests, powerful cadres of elites, entrenched bureaucrats, competing pressure groups, and morally impassioned individuals have all at one time or another wielded political power and played a part in shaping our government and its policies.

But, more fundamentally, understanding any political system means being able to give reasonable answers to each of two separate but related questions about it: Who governs, and to what ends?

We want to know the answer to the first question because we believe that those who rule—their personalities and beliefs, their virtues and vices—will affect what they do to and for us. Many people think they already know the answer to the question, and they are prepared to talk and vote on that basis. That is their right, and the opinions they express may be correct. But they also may be wrong. Indeed, many of these opinions must be wrong because they are in conflict. When asked, "Who governs?" some people will say "the unions" and some will say "big business"; others will say "the politicians," "the people," or "the special interests." Still others will say "Wall Street," "the military," "crackpot liberals," "the media," "the bureaucrats," or "white males." Not all these answers can be correct—at least not all of the time.

The answer to the second question is important because it tells us how government affects our lives. We want to know not only who governs, but what difference it makes who governs. In our day-to-day lives, we may not think government makes much difference at all. In one sense that is right because our most pressing personal concerns—work, play, love, family, health—essentially are private matters on which government touches but slightly. But in a larger and longer perspective, government makes a substantial difference. Consider that in 1935, 96 percent of all American families paid no federal income tax, and for the 4 percent or so who did pay, the average rate was only about 4 percent of their incomes. Today almost all families pay federal payroll taxes, and the average rate is about 21 percent of their incomes. Or consider that in 1960, in many parts of the country, African Americans could ride only in the backs of buses, had to use washrooms and drinking fountains that were labeled "colored," and could not be served in most public restaurants. Such restrictions have almost all been eliminated, in large part because of decisions by the federal government.

It is important to bear in mind that we wish to answer two different questions, and not two versions of the same question. You cannot always predict what goals government will establish by knowing only who governs, nor can you always tell who governs by knowing what activities government undertakes. Most people holding national political office are economically secure, middle-aged, white, Protestant males, but we cannot then conclude that the government will adopt only policies that are to the narrow advantage of the economically secure, the middle-aged, whites, Protestants, or men. If we thought that, we would be at a loss to explain why the rich are taxed more heavily than the poor, why the War on Poverty was declared, why constitutional amendments giving rights to African Americans and women passed Congress by large majorities, or why Catholics and Jews have been appointed to so many important governmental posts.

This book is chiefly devoted to answering the question, who governs? It is written in the belief that this question cannot be answered without looking at how government makes—or fails to make—decisions about a large variety of concrete issues. Thus, in this book we inspect government policies to see what individuals, groups, and institutions seem to exert the greatest power in the continuous struggle to define the purposes of government.

Expanding the Political Agenda

No matter who governs, the most important decision that affects policymaking is also the least noticed one: deciding what to make policy *about*, or in the language of political science, deciding what belongs on the **political agenda**. The political agenda consists of issues that people believe require governmental action. We take for granted that politics is about certain familiar issues such as taxes, energy, welfare, civil rights, and homeland security. We forget that there is nothing inevitable about having these issues—rather than some other ones—on the nation's political agenda.

For example, at one time, it was unconstitutional for the federal government to levy income taxes; energy was a nonissue because everyone (or at least everyone who could chop down trees for firewood) had enough; welfare was something for cities and towns to handle; civil rights were supposed to be a matter of private choice rather than government action; "homeland security" was not in the political lexicon, and a huge federal cabinet department by that name was nowhere on the horizon.

At any given time, what is on the political agenda is affected by at least four things as follows:

- *Shared political values*—for example, if people believe that poverty is the result of social forces rather than individual choices, then they have a reason to endorse enacting or expanding government programs to combat poverty.
- *The weight of custom and tradition*—people usually will accept what the government customarily does, even if they are leery of what it proposes to do.
- *The importance of events*—wars, terrorist attacks, and severe or sustained economic downturns can alter our sense of the proper role of government.
- *Terms of debate*—the way in which political elites discuss issues influences how the public views political priorities.

Because many people believe that whatever the government now does it ought to continue doing, and because changes in attitudes and the impact of events tend to increase the number of things that government does, the political agenda is always growing larger. Thus, today there are far fewer debates about the legitimacy of a proposed government policy than there were in the 1920s or the 1930s.

political agenda *Issues that people believe require governmental action.*

For instance, in the 1930s, when what became the Social Security program was first proposed, the debate was largely about whether the federal government should have any role whatsoever in providing financial support for older adults or disabled citizens. In stark contrast, today, not a single member of Congress denies that the federal government should have a *major* role in providing financial support for older adults or disabled citizens, or advocates ending Social Security. Instead, today's debates about the program are largely over competing plans to ensure its longterm financial solvency.

Popular views regarding what belongs on the political agenda often are changed by events. During wartime or after a terrorist attack on this country, many people expect the government to do whatever is necessary to win, whether or not such actions are clearly authorized by the Constitution. Economic depressions or deep recessions, such as the ones that began in 1929, 2007, and 2020, also lead many people to expect the government to take action. A coal mine disaster leads to an enlarged role for the government in promoting mine safety. A series of airplane hijackings leads to a change in public opinion so great that what once would have been unthinkable—requiring all passengers at airports to be searched before boarding their flights—becomes routine. A global pandemic makes face masks routine in air travel and other contained public spaces.

But sometimes the government enlarges the political agenda, often dramatically, without any crisis or widespread public demand. This may happen even at a time when the conditions at which a policy is directed are improving. For instance, there was no mass public demand for government action to make automobiles safer before 1966, when a law was passed imposing safety standards on cars. Though the number of auto fatalities (per

Steve Wood/Shutterstock.com

Image 1.3 Seeing first responders in action in the immediate aftermath of 9/11, Americans felt powerfully connected to their fellow citizens.

100 million miles driven) had gone up slightly just before the law was passed, in the long term, highway deaths had been more or less steadily trending downward.

It is not easy to explain why the government adds new issues to its agenda and adopts new programs when little public demand exists and when, in fact, the conditions to which the policies are addressed have improved. In general, the explanation may be found in the behavior of groups, the workings of institutions, the media, and the action of state governments.

Groups

Many policies are the result of small groups of people enlarging the scope of government by their demands. Sometimes these are organized interests that negotiate with public officials (e.g., corporations or unions); sometimes they are groups of people that coalesce around an issue such as climate change or racial justice. The organized groups often work quietly, behind the scenes; groups that focus on a specific issue may try to influence public officials through rallies and protests.

For example, organized labor favored a tough federal safety law governing factories and other workplaces, not because it was unaware that factory conditions had been improving, but because the standards by which union leaders and members judged working conditions had risen even faster. As people became better off, conditions that once were thought normal suddenly became intolerable.

On occasion, a group expresses in violent ways its dissatisfaction with what it judges to be intolerable conditions. The riots in American cities during the mid-1960s had a variety of causes, and people participated out of a variety of motives. For many, rioting was a way of expressing pent-up anger at what they regarded as an unresponsive and unfair society. A sense of relative deprivation—of being worse off than one thinks one *ought* to be—helps explain why so large proportion of the rioters were not uneducated, unemployed recent migrants to the city, but rather young men and women born in the North, educated in its schools, and employed in its factories.[20] Life under these conditions turned out to be not what they had come to expect or what they were prepared to tolerate.

The new demands of such groups need not result in an enlarged political agenda, and they often do not produce such results when society and its governing institutions are confident of the rightness of the existing state of affairs. Unions could have been voted down on the occupational safety bill; rioters could have been jailed and ignored. At one time, this is exactly what would have happened. But society itself had changed: Many people who were not workers sympathized with the plight of the injured worker and distrusted the good intentions of business in this matter. Many well-off citizens felt a constructive, not just a punitive, response to the urban riots was required and thus urged the formation of commissions to study—and the passage of laws to deal with—the problems of inner-city life. Such changes in the values and beliefs of people generally—or at least of people in key government positions—are an essential part of any explanation of why policies not demanded by public opinion nonetheless become part of the political agenda.

Government Institutions

Among the set of institutions whose influence on agenda-setting has become especially important are the courts, the bureaucracy, and the Senate.

The courts can make decisions that force the hand of the other branches of government. For example, when in 1954 the Supreme Court ordered schools desegregated, Congress and the White House could no longer ignore the issue. Local resistance to implementing the order led President Dwight D. Eisenhower to send troops to Little Rock, Arkansas, despite his dislike for using force against local governments. Similarly, when the Supreme Court ruled in 1973 that the states could not ban abortions during the first trimester of pregnancy, abortion suddenly became a national political issue. Right-to-life activists campaigned to reverse the Court's decision or, failing that, to prevent federal funds from being used to pay for abortions. Pro-choice activists fought to prevent the Court from reversing course and to get federal funding for abortions. In these and many other cases, the courts act like trip wires: When activated, they set off a chain reaction of events that alters the political agenda and creates a new constellation of political forces.

Indeed, the courts can sometimes be more than trip wires. As the political agenda has expanded, the courts have become the favorite method for effecting change for which there is no popular majority. Little electoral support may exist for allowing abortion on demand, eliminating school prayer, ordering school busing, or attacking tobacco companies, but in the courts elections do not matter. The courts are the preferred vehicles for the advocates of unpopular causes.

The bureaucracy has acquired a new significance in American politics not simply because of its size or power but also because it is now a source of political innovation. At one time, the federal government *reacted* to events in society and to demands from segments of society; ordinarily it did not itself propose changes and new ideas. Today, the bureaucracy is so large and includes within it so great a variety of experts and advocates, that it has become a *source* of policy proposals as well as an implementer of those that become law. The late U.S. Senator Daniel Patrick Moynihan called this the "professionalization of reform," by which he meant, in part, that the government bureaucracy had begun to think up problems for government to solve rather than simply to respond to the problems identified by others.[21] In the 1930s, many of the key elements of the New Deal—Social Security, unemployment compensation, public housing, old-age benefits—were ideas devised by nongovernment experts and intellectuals here and abroad and then, as the crisis of the depression deepened, taken up by the federal government. In the 1960s, by contrast, most of the measures that became known as part of Lyndon Johnson's "Great Society"—federal aid to education, manpower development and training, Medicare and Medicaid, the War on Poverty, the Crime Control and Safe Streets Act providing federal aid to local law enforcement agencies—were developed, designed, and advocated by government officials, bureaucrats, and their political allies.

Chief among these political allies are U.S. senators and their staffs. Once the Senate was best described as a club that moved slowly, debated endlessly, and resisted, under the leadership of conservative Southern Democrats, the plans of liberal presidents. With the collapse of the one-party South and the increase in the number of liberal activist senators, the Senate became, in the 1960s, an incubator for developing new policies and building national constituencies.[22] (In chapter 13, we will explore whether the Senate still fits this description in the 21st century.)

Media

The national press can either help place new matters on the agenda or publicize those matters placed there by others. There was a close correlation between the political attention given in the Senate to proposals for new safety standards for industry, coal mines, and automobiles and the amount of space devoted to these questions in the pages of the *New York Times*. Newspaper interest in the matter, low before the issue was placed on the agenda, peaked at about the time the bill was passed.[23]

It is difficult, of course, to decide which is the cause and which the effect. The press may have stimulated congressional interest in the matter or merely reported on what Congress had already decided to pursue. Nonetheless, the press must choose which of thousands of proposals it will cover. The beliefs of editors and reporters led it to select the safety issue.

Action by the States

National policy is increasingly being made by the actions of state governments. You may wonder how. After all, a state can only pass laws that affect its own people. Of course, the national government may later adopt ideas pioneered in the states, as it did when Congress passed a "Do Not Call" law in 2003 to allow you to reduce phone calls from salespeople, on land lines or cell phones. The states had taken the lead on this issue.

But there is another way in which state governments can make national policy directly without Congress ever voting on the matter. The attorneys general of states may sue a business firm and settle the suit with an agreement that binds the industry throughout the country. The effect of one suit was to raise prices for consumers and create a new set of regulations. This is what happened in 1998 with the tobacco agreement negotiated between cigarette companies and some state attorneys general. The companies agreed to raise their prices, pay more than $240 billion to state governments (to use as they wished) and several billion dollars to private lawyers, and comply with a massive regulatory program. A decade later, the federal government passed laws that reinforced the state's regulations, culminating in the Family Smoking Prevention Tobacco Control Act of 2009. More recently, in 2019, a judge in Oklahoma ordered a pharmaceutical company to pay close to $600 million for treatment and other services to address the state's opioid crisis, and four drug companies in Ohio reached a $260 million settlement agreement for the same issue.

cost A burden that people believe they must bear if a policy is adopted.

benefit A satisfaction that people believe they will enjoy if a policy is adopted.

1-4 The Politics of Different Policy Issues

Once an issue is on the political agenda, its nature affects the kind of politicking that ensues. Some issues provoke intense conflict among interest groups; others allow one group to prevail almost unchallenged. Some issues involve ideological appeals to broad national constituencies; others involve quiet bargaining in congressional offices. We all know that private groups try to influence government policies; we often forget that the nature of the issues with which government is dealing influences the kinds of groups that become politically active.

One way to understand why government handles a given issue as it does is to examine what seem to be the costs and benefits of the proposed policy. The **cost** is any burden, monetary or nonmonetary, that some people must bear, or believe they must bear, if the policy is adopted. The costs of a government spending program are the taxes it entails; the cost of a foreign policy initiative may be the increased chance of having the nation drawn into war.

The **benefit** is any satisfaction, monetary or nonmonetary, that people believe they will enjoy if the policy is adopted. The benefits of a government spending program

majoritarian politics A policy in which almost everybody benefits and almost everybody pays.

are the payments, subsidies, or contracts received by some people; the benefits of a foreign policy initiative may include the enhanced security of the nation, the protection of a valued ally, or the vindication of some important principle such as human rights.

Two aspects of these costs and benefits should be borne in mind. First, it is the *perception* of costs and benefits that affects politics. People may think the cost of an auto emissions control system is paid by the manufacturer, when it is actually passed on to the consumer in the form of higher prices and reduced performance. Political conflict over pollution control will take one form when people think that the polluting industries pay the costs and another form when they think that the consumers pay.

Second, people take into account not only who benefits but also whether it is legitimate for that group to benefit. When programs providing financial assistance to women with dependent children were first developed in the early part of the 20th century, they were relatively noncontroversial because people saw the money as going to widows and orphans who deserved such aid. Later, giving aid to mothers with dependent children became controversial because some people now perceived the recipients not as deserving widows but as irresponsible women who had never married. Whatever the truth of the matter, the program had lost some of its legitimacy because the beneficiaries were no longer seen as "deserving." By the same token, groups once thought undeserving, such as men out of work, were later thought to be entitled to aid, and thus the unemployment compensation program acquired a legitimacy that it once lacked.

Politics is in large measure a process of raising and settling disputes over who *will* benefit or pay for a program and who *ought* to benefit or pay. Because beliefs about the results of a program and the rightness of those results are matters of opinion, it is evident that ideas are at least as important as interests in shaping politics. In recent years, ideas have become especially important with the rise of issues whose consequences are largely intangible, such as abortion, school prayer, and LGBTQ+ rights.

Though perceptions about costs and benefits change, most people most of the time prefer government programs that provide substantial benefits to them at low cost. This rather obvious fact can have important implications for how politics is carried out. In a political system based on some measure of popular rule, public officials have a strong incentive to offer programs that confer—or seem to confer—benefits on people with costs either small in amount, remote in time, or borne by "somebody else." Policies that seem to impose high, immediate costs in return for small or remote benefits will be avoided, enacted with a minimum of publicity, or proposed only in response to a real or apparent crisis.

Ordinarily, no president would propose a policy that would immediately raise the cost of fuel, even if he were convinced that future supplies of oil and gasoline were likely to be exhausted unless higher prices reduced current consumption. But when a crisis occurs, such as the Arab oil cartel's price increases beginning in 1973, it becomes possible for the president to offer such proposals—as did Richard Nixon, Gerald Ford, and Jimmy Carter in varying ways. Even then, however, people are reluctant to bear increased costs, and thus many are led to dispute the president's claim that an emergency actually exists.

Four Types of Politics

These entirely human responses to the perceived costs and benefits of proposed policies can be organized into a simple theory of politics.[24] It is based on the observation that the costs and benefits of a policy may be *widely distributed* (spread over many, most, or even all citizens) or *narrowly concentrated* (limited to a relatively small number of citizens or to some identifiable, organized group).

For instance, a widely distributed cost would include an income tax, a Social Security tax, or a high rate of crime; a widely distributed benefit might include retirement benefits for all citizens, clean air, national security, or low crime rates. Examples of narrowly concentrated costs include the expenditures by a factory to reduce its pollution, government regulations imposed on doctors and hospitals participating in the Medicare program, or restrictions on freedom of speech imposed on a dissident political group. Examples of narrowly concentrated benefits include subsidies to farmers or merchant ship companies, the enlarged freedom to speak and protest afforded a dissident group, or protection against competition given to an industry because of favorable government regulation.

The perceived distribution of costs and benefits shapes the *kinds of political coalitions that will form*—but it does not necessarily determine *who wins*. Four types of politics exist, and a given popular majority, interest group, client, or entrepreneur may win or lose depending on its influence and the temper of the times.

Majoritarian Politics: Distributed Benefits, Distributed Costs

Some policies promise benefits to large numbers of people at a cost that large numbers of people will have to bear (see Figure 1.1). For example, almost everyone will sooner or later receive Social Security benefits, and almost everyone who works has to pay Social Security taxes.

Such **majoritarian politics** are usually not dominated by pulling and hauling among rival interest groups;

Figure 1.1 **A Way of Classifying and Explaining the Politics of Different Policy Issues**

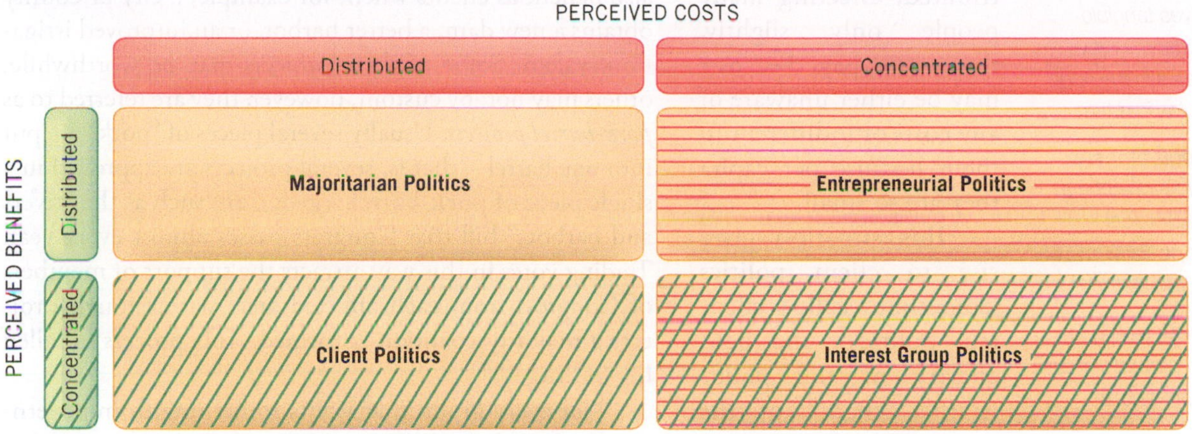

Q What are some factors that might influence how people perceive costs and benefits for a policy issue, and why?

instead, they involve making appeals to large segments of voters and their representatives in hopes of finding a majority. The reason why interest groups are not so important in majoritarian politics is that citizens rarely will have much incentive to join an interest group if the policy that such a group supports will benefit everybody, whether or not they are members of the group. This is the "free rider" problem. Why join the Committee to Increase (or Decrease) the Defense Budget when what you personally contribute to that committee makes little difference in the outcome and when you will enjoy the benefits of more (or less) national defense even if you stay on the sidelines?

Majoritarian politics may be controversial, but the controversy is usually over matters of cost or ideology, not between rival interest groups. For example, intense controversy ensued over the health care plan that President Barack Obama signed into law, but the debate was not dominated by interest groups, and many different types of politics were at play (see Policy Dynamics: Inside/Outside the Box on page 17). The military budget went up during the early 1980s, down in the late 1980s, up after 2001, and down again after 2010. These changes reflected different views on how much we need to spend on our military operations abroad.

Interest Group Politics: Concentrated Benefits, Concentrated Costs

In **interest group politics**, a proposed policy will confer benefits on some relatively small, identifiable group and impose costs on another small, equally identifiable group. For example, when Congress passed a bill requiring companies to give 60 days' notice of a plant closing or a large-scale layoff, labor unions (whose members would benefit) backed the bill, and many business firms (which would pay the costs) opposed it.

Issues of this kind tend to be fought out by organized interest groups. Each side will be so powerfully affected by the outcome that it has a strong incentive to mobilize: Union members who worry about layoffs will have a personal stake in favoring the notice bill; business leaders who fear government control of investment decisions will have an economic stake in opposing it.

interest group politics *A policy in which one small group benefits and another small group pays.*

client politics *A policy in which one small group benefits and almost everybody pays.*

Interest group politics often produces decisions about which the public is uninformed. For instance, bitter debates have occurred between television broadcasters and cable companies over who may send what kind of signals to which homes. But these debates hardly draw any public notice—until after a law is passed and people see their increased cable charges.

Though many issues of this type involve monetary costs and benefits, they can also involve intangible considerations. If the American Nazi party wants to march through a predominantly Jewish neighborhood carrying flags with swastikas on them, the community may organize itself to resist out of revulsion due to the horrific treatment of Jews by Nazi Germany. Each side may hire lawyers to debate the issue before the city council and in the courts. (We discuss how the courts ruled on this issue in Chapter 5.)

Client Politics: Concentrated Benefits, Distributed Costs

With **client politics** some identifiable, often small group will benefit, but everybody—or at least a large part of society—will pay the costs. Because the benefits are concentrated, the group to receive those benefits has an incentive to organize and work to get them. But because

pork-barrel legislation *Legislation that gives tangible benefits to constituents in several districts or states in the hope of winning their votes in return.*

log-rolling *A legislator supports a proposal favored by a colleague with reciprocal support for a proposal endorsed by the legislator.*

entrepreneurial politics *A policy in which almost everybody benefits and a small group pays.*

the costs are widely distributed, affecting many people only slightly, those who pay the costs may be either unaware of any costs or indifferent to them because per capita they are so small.

This situation gives rise to client politics (sometimes called clientele politics); the beneficiary of the policy is the "client" of the government. For example, many farmers benefit substantially from agricultural price supports, but the far more numerous food consumers have no idea what these price supports cost them in taxes and higher food prices. Similarly, for some time airlines benefited from the higher prices they were able to charge on certain routes as a result of government regulations that restricted competition over prices. But the average passenger was either unaware that costs were higher or did not think the higher prices were worth making a fuss about.

Image 1.4 During the Great Depression, depositors besieged a bank, hoping to get their savings out.

Not all clients have economic interests. Localities can also benefit as clients when, for example, a city or county obtains a new dam, a better harbor, or an improved irrigation system. Some of these projects may be worthwhile, others may not; by custom, however, they are referred to as *pork-barrel projects.* Usually several pieces of "pork" are put into one barrel—that is, several projects are approved in a single piece of **pork-barrel legislation**, such as the "rivers and harbors" bill that Congress passes almost every year. Trading votes in this way attracts the support of members of Congress from each affected area; with enough projects a majority coalition is formed. This process is called **log-rolling**.

Not every group that wants something from government at little cost to the average citizen will get it. Welfare recipients cost the typical taxpayer a small amount each year, yet there was great resistance to increasing these benefits. The homeless have not organized themselves to get benefits; indeed, most do not even vote. Yet benefits are being provided (albeit in modest amounts). These examples illustrate the importance of popular views concerning the legitimacy of client claims as a factor in determining the success of client demands.

By the same token, groups can lose legitimacy that they once had. People who grow tobacco once were supported simply because they were farmers, and were thus seen as both "deserving" and politically important. But when people began worrying about the health risks associated with using tobacco, farmers who produce tobacco lost some legitimacy compared with those who produce corn or cotton. As a result, it became harder to get votes for maintaining tobacco price supports and easier to slap higher taxes on cigarettes.

Entrepreneurial Politics: Distributed Benefits, Concentrated Costs

In **entrepreneurial politics**, society as a whole or some large part of it benefits from a policy that imposes substantial costs on some small, identifiable segment of society. The antipollution and safety requirements for automobiles were proposed as ways of improving the health and well-being of all people at the expense (at least initially) of automobile manufacturers.

It is remarkable that policies of this sort are ever adopted, and in fact many are not. After all, the American political system creates many opportunities for checking and blocking the actions of others. The Founders deliberately arranged things so that it would be difficult to pass a new law; a determined minority therefore has an excellent chance of blocking a new policy. And any organized group that fears the loss of some privilege or the imposition of some burden will become a very determined minority indeed. The opponent has every incentive to work hard; the large group of prospective beneficiaries may be unconvinced of the benefit or regard it as too small to be worth fighting for.

Nonetheless, policies with distributed benefits and concentrated costs are in fact adopted, and in recent decades they have been adopted with increasing frequency. A key element in the adoption of such policies has been the work of people who act on behalf of the unorganized or indifferent majority. Such people, called **policy entrepreneurs**, are those both in and out of government who find ways of pulling together a legislative majority on behalf of interests that are not well represented in the government. These policy entrepreneurs may or may not represent the interests and wishes of the public at large, but they do have the ability to dramatize an issue in a convincing manner. Ralph Nader is perhaps the best-known example of a policy entrepreneur, or as he might describe himself, a "consumer advocate." But there are other examples from both ends of the political spectrum, conservative as well as liberal.

Entrepreneurial politics can occur without the leadership of a policy entrepreneur if voters or legislators in large numbers suddenly become disgruntled by the high cost of some benefit that a group is receiving (or become convinced of the urgent need for a new policy to impose such costs). For example, voters may not care about government programs that benefit the oil industry when gasoline costs only one dollar a gallon, but they might care very much when the price rises to three dollars a gallon, even if the government benefits had nothing to do with the price increase. By the same token, legislators may not worry much about the effects of smog in the air until a lot of people develop burning eyes and runny noses during an especially severe smog attack.

In fact, most legislators did not worry very much about toxic or hazardous wastes until 1977, when the Love Canal dump site near Buffalo, New York, spilled some of its toxic waste into the backyards of an adjacent residential neighborhood and people were forced to leave their homes. Five years later, anyone who had forgotten about the Love Canal was reminded of it when the town of Times Beach, Missouri, had to be permanently evacuated because it had become contaminated with the chemical dioxin. Only then did it become widely known that more than 30,000 toxic waste sites nationwide posed public safety risks. The Superfund program was born in 1980 of the political pressure that developed in the wake of these and other highly publicized tales of toxic waste dangers. Superfund was intended to force industries to clean up their own toxic waste sites. It also authorized the Environmental Protection Agency (EPA) to act speedily, with or without cooperation from industries, in identifying and cleaning up any sites that posed a large or imminent danger.

policy entrepreneurs
Activists in or out of government who pull together a political majority on behalf of unorganized interests.

Superfund suffered a number of political and administrative problems, and only a few of the 1,300 sites initially targeted by the EPA had been cleaned up a dozen years after the program went into effect.[25] Regardless, Superfund is a good illustration of entrepreneurial politics in action. Special taxes on once largely unregulated oil and chemical companies funded the program. These companies once enjoyed special tax breaks, but as the politics of the issue changed, they were forced to shoulder special tax burdens. In effect, the politics of the issue changed from client politics to entrepreneurial politics.

Policy Dynamics: Inside/Outside the Box

Superfund also thereby illustrates how dynamic the politics of policymaking can be. Once an issue makes its way on to the political agenda, the politics of the issue can remain stable, change a little or a lot, and change very slowly or quite suddenly. And policy issues can "migrate" from one type of politics (and one of the four boxes) to another.

By the same token, the policy dynamics of some issues are simply harder to categorize and explain than the policy dynamics of others. For instance, in the mid-2000s, 13 states amended their state constitutions to prohibit or further restrict same-sex marriage. In 2008, California voters approved a ballot measure, Proposition 8, banning same-sex marriage. But virtually all of these policies were enacted at a time when popular acceptance of a person's sexual orientation, including same-sex marriage, was rising. In 2001, by a margin of 57 percent to 35 percent, Americans opposed same-sex marriage; but, by 2013, a 49 percent to 44 percent plurality favored same-sex marriage. In 2012, President Barack Obama, having previously ordered an end to the "Don't Ask, Don't Tell" policy that had banned people in the military who were not heterosexual from revealing their sexual orientation, publicly declared his support for legalizing same-sex marriage. Surveys indicated that the only groups still harboring wide majorities opposed to same-sex marriage were evangelical Christians and adults born in 1945 or earlier.[26] In 2013, the U.S. Supreme Court struck down a

1996 law that allowed the federal government to discriminate against same-sex married couples, and two years later, the Court declared that same-sex marriages are constitutional.

So, how best can we categorize or explain the politics of this issue? Which type of politics—majoritarian, client, interest group, or entrepreneurial—were most important to policymaking? Why did state laws become more restrictive at the very time that both mass public opinion and elite opinion were trending toward greater acceptance? Do the still-unfolding policy dynamics of this issue fit neatly (or fit at all) in any of our four boxes? Start thinking about these questions; we revisit them in Chapters 3 and 6.

Finally, while the politics of some issues do fit neatly into one box or another, the politics of other issues reflect several different types of politics.

For example, most major pieces of social legislation reflect *majoritarian* politics—Social Security remains a prime example—but health care issues often have played out within all four boxes—majoritarian, client, interest group, and entrepreneurial—at once. This was certainly true of the politics of the Patient Protection and Affordable Care Act of 2010, better known as "Obamacare." As we illustrate in our first Policy Dynamics: Inside/Outside the Box feature, the perceived costs and benefits of the Obama plan affected the political coalitions that formed around it and involved all four types of politics.

Understanding Politics

Whether pondering one's own positions on given issues, attempting to generalize about the politics of different policy issues, or tackling questions about American government, institutions, and policies, an astute student will soon come to know what Aristotle meant when he wrote that it is "the mark of the educated person to look for precision in each class of things just so far as the nature of the subject admits."[27]

Ideally, political scientists ought to be able to give clear answers, amply supported by evidence, to the questions we have posed about American democracy, starting with "who governs?" In reality they can (at best) give partial, contingent, and controversial answers. The reason is to be found in the nature of our subject. Unlike economists, who assume that people have more or less stable preferences and can compare ways of satisfying those preferences by looking at the relative prices of various goods and services, political scientists are interested in how preferences are formed, especially for those kinds of services, such as national defense or pollution control, that cannot be evaluated chiefly in terms of monetary costs.

Understanding preferences is vital to understanding power. Who did what in government is not hard to find out, but who wielded power—that is, who made a difference in the outcome and for what reason—is much harder to discover. *Power* is a word that conjures up images of deals, bribes, power plays, and arm-twisting. In fact, most power exists because of shared understanding, common friendships, communal or organizational loyalties, and different degrees of prestige. These are hard to identify and almost impossible to quantify.

Nor can the distribution of political power be inferred simply by knowing what laws are on the books or what administrative actions have been taken. The enactment of a consumer protection law does not mean that consumers are powerful, any more than the absence of such a law means that corporations are powerful. The passage of such a law could reflect an aroused public opinion, the lobbying of a small group claiming to speak for consumers, the ambitions of a senator, or the intrigues of one business firm seeking to gain a competitive advantage over another. A close analysis of what the law entails and how it was passed and administered is necessary before much of anything can be concluded.

This book avoids sweeping claims that we have an "imperial" presidency (or an impotent one), an "obstructionist" Congress (or an innovative one), or "captured" regulatory agencies. Such labels do an injustice to the different roles that presidents, members of Congress, and administrators play in different kinds of issues and in different historical periods.

The view taken in this book is that judgments about institutions and interests can be made only after one has seen how they behave on a variety of important issues or potential issues, such as economic policy, the regulation of business, social welfare, civil rights and liberties, and foreign and military affairs. The policies adopted or blocked, the groups heeded or ignored, the values embraced or rejected—these constitute the raw material from which

Image 1.5 Protestors decry efforts to repeal the Affordable Care Act.

Policy Dynamics: Inside/Outside the Box | Obamacare: All Four Boxes?

When Medicare was enacted in 1965, Democrats in the House and Senate voted for it by a wide margin, but roughly half of the Republicans in each chamber also supported it. But the 2010 health care bill was passed without any Republican support. In other words, the 1965 Medicare bill that President Lyndon Johnson signed into law had broad bipartisan backing, but the 2010 health care bill that President Obama signed into law had none. Using the model of the policy process explained in this chapter, here is a summary of how the costs and benefits of the Obama plan affected the political coalitions that formed around health care.

Majoritarian Politics: The bill was opposed by a majority of Americans for a variety of reasons. Many thought it too expensive ($940 billion over 10 years) or worried about the government regulations the law contained.

Client Politics: Drug manufacturers looked forward to having many new customers as more people owned health insurance. To get this benefit, the pharmaceutical companies agreed to pay up to $85 billion in higher taxes. Many hospitals thought they would be helped by having more patients who could pay their bills with health insurance.

Interest Group Politics: Labor unions wanted health care coverage, but business firms were upset by the higher taxes and fees they would have to pay. Poorer people liked it, but those earning $200,000 a year or more would see their taxes escalate. Older adults on Medicare and many doctors worried that the new law promised to cut payments to physicians, but the American Medical Association and the AARP (the largest organization representing senior citizens) endorsed the law.

Policy Entrepreneurs: In early 2010, the winners were President Obama and the Democratic leaders in the House who got a bill passed over popular and interest group opposition. In the latter half of 2010, however, the winners were the Republicans who opposed "Obamacare" and used the issue on the way to sweeping GOP* victories in the November 2010 elections. When the 112th Congress was seated in 2011, Republicans in the House made good on a pledge to vote for the outright repeal of the new law (the symbolic bill died in the Senate), and several state attorneys general challenged the law's constitutionality in the federal courts (focusing mainly on the provision mandating that individuals purchase health insurance). In 2012, the U.S. Supreme Court upheld the constitutionality of the law's individual mandate, but ruled against certain other provisions of the law, including ones pertaining to changes in the federal-state program known as Medicaid, a program that was created in 1965 alongside Medicare (see Chapter 17).

The Medicare law and the new health care law mobilized very different coalitions, in part because, between 1965 and 2010, Congress became a far more polarized institution (see Chapter 13). The Obamacare policy was based on a combination of majoritarian, client, interest group, and entrepreneurial politics. The politics of the issue was neither inside nor outside any one of the four boxes, but spread across all four.

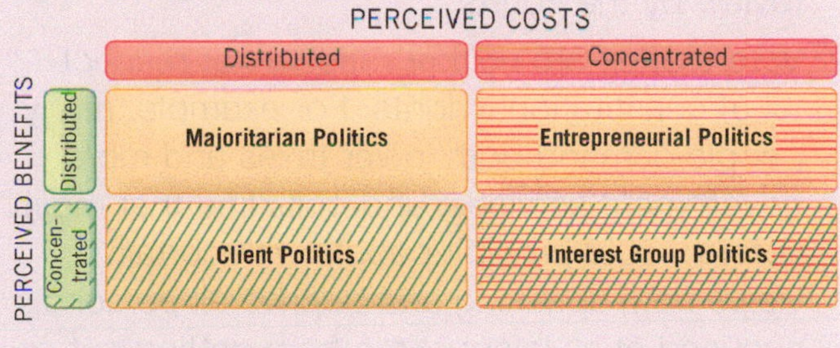

*"GOP" refers to "Grand Old Party," a widely used synonym for the Republican Party.

one can fashion an answer to the central questions we have asked: Who governs, and to what ends?

The way in which our institutions of government handle social welfare, for example, differs from the way other democratic nations handle it, and it differs as well from the way our own institutions once treated it. The description of our institutions in Part III will therefore include not only an account of how they work today but also a brief historical background on their workings and a comparison with similar institutions in other countries. We tend to assume that how we do things today is the only way they could possibly be done. In fact, a government can operate in other ways, based on some measure of popular rule. History, tradition, and belief weigh heavily on all that we do.

Although political change is not always accompanied by changes in public laws, the policy process is arguably one of the best barometers of changes in who governs. Our way of classifying and explaining the politics of different policy issues has been developed, refined, and tested over more than four decades (longer than most of our readers have been alive!). Our own students and others have valued it mainly because they have found it helps to answer such questions about

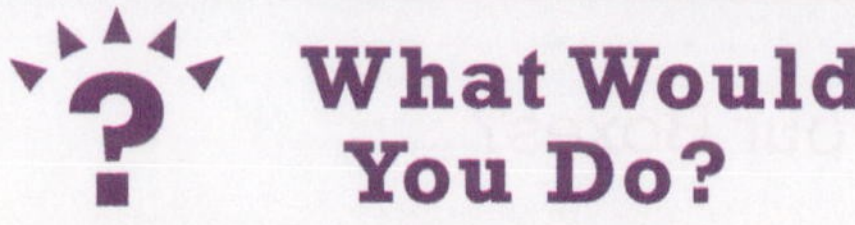

What Would You Do? | Will You Favor or Oppose the Ban on Initiatives?

To: *Governor Lucy Avery*
From: *Professor Ella Nicole*
Subject: *Initiative repeal*

You have supported several successful initiatives (life imprisonment for thrice-convicted violent felons, property tax limits), but you have never stated your views on the actual initiative process, and the repeal proposal likely will surface during tomorrow's news briefing.

To Consider:

A report released yesterday and signed by more than 100 law and public policy professors statewide urges that the state's constitution be amended to ban legislation by initiative. The initiative allows state voters to place legislative measures directly on the ballot by getting enough signatures. The initiative "has led to disastrous policy decisions on taxes, crime, and other issues," the report declared.

Arguments for:

1. Ours is a representative, not a direct, democracy in which voters elect leaders and elected leaders make policy decisions subject to review by the courts.
2. Voters often are neither rational nor respectful of constitutional rights. For example, many people demand both lower taxes and more government services, and polls find that most voters would prohibit people with certain views from speaking and deprive all persons accused of a violent crime from getting out on bail while awaiting trial.
3. Over the past 100 years, hundreds of statewide ballot initiatives have been passed in 24 states. Rather than giving power to the people, special interest groups have spent billions of dollars manipulating voters to pass initiatives that enrich or benefit their own interests, not those of the public at large.

Arguments against:

1. When elected officials fail to respond to persistent public majorities favoring tougher crime measures, lower property taxes, and other popular concerns, direct democracy via the initiative is legitimate, and the courts can still review the law.
2. More Americans than ever have college degrees and easy access to information about public affairs. Studies find that most average citizens are able to figure out which candidates, parties, or advocacy groups come closest to supporting their own economic interests and personal values.
3. All told, the 24 states that passed laws by initiative also passed thousands more laws by the regular legislative process (among the tens of thousands of bills they considered). Studies find that special interest groups are severely limited in their ability to pass new laws by initiative, whereas citizens' groups with broad-based public support are behind most initiatives that pass.

What Will You Decide? Enter **MindTap** to make your choice.

Your decision: ☐ Favor ban ☐ Oppose ban

who governs: How do political issues get on the public agenda in the first place? How, for example, did sexual harassment, which was hardly ever discussed or debated by Congress, burst onto the public agenda? Once on the agenda, how does the politics of issues like income security for older Americans—for example, the politics of Social Security, a program that has been on the federal books since 1935 (see Chapter 17)—change over time? And if, today, one cares about expanding civil liberties (see Chapter 5) or protecting civil rights (see Chapter 6), what political obstacles and opportunities will one likely face? What role will public opinion, organized interest groups, the media, the courts, political parties, and other institutions likely play in frustrating or fostering one's particular policy preferences, whatever they might be?

Peek ahead, if you wish, but understand that the place to begin a search for how power is distributed in national politics and what purposes that power serves is with the founding of the federal government in 1787: the Constitutional Convention and the events leading up to it. Though the decisions of that time were not made by philosophers or professors, the practical men who made them had a philosophic and professorial cast of mind, and thus they left behind a fairly explicit account of what values they sought to protect and what arrangements they thought ought to be made for the allocation of political power.

Learning Objectives

1-1 Explain how politics drives democracy.

Politics is the activity by which an issue is agitated or settled. Politics occurs because people disagree and the disagreement must be managed. Disagreements over many political issues, including disputes over government budgets and finances, are often fundamentally disagreements over what government should or should not do at all. Democracy can mean either that everyone votes on all government issues (direct or participatory democracy) or that the people elect representatives to make most of these decisions (representative democracy).

1-2 Discuss five views of how political power is distributed in the United States.

Some believe that political power in America is monopolized by wealthy business leaders, by other powerful elites, or by entrenched government bureaucrats. Others believe that political resources such as money, prestige, expertise, organizational position, and access to the mass media are so widely dispersed in American society, and the governmental institutions and offices in which power may be exercised so numerous and varied, that no single group truly has all or most political power. In this view, political power in America is distributed more or less widely. Still others suggest that morally impassioned leaders have at times been deeply influential in our politics. No one, however, argues that political resources are distributed equally in America.

1-3 Explain why "who governs?" and "to what ends?" are fundamental questions in American politics.

The political agenda consists of those issues that people with decision-making authority believe require government action. The behavior of groups, the workings of institutions, the media, and the actions of state governments have all figured in the expansion of America's political agenda, and understanding how those actors have expanded the agenda—that is, "who governs?"—is necessary to understand the nature of American politics. Similarly, the great shifts in the character of American government—its size, scope, institutional arrangements, and the direction of its policies—have reflected complex and sometimes sudden changes in elite or mass beliefs about what government is supposed to do—that is, "to what ends?" The federal government now has policies on street crime, the environment, homeland security, and many other issues that were not on the federal agenda a half-century (or, in the case of homeland security, just two decades) ago.

1-4 Summarize the key concepts for classifying the politics of different policy issues.

One way to classify and explain the politics of different issues is in relation to the perceived costs and benefits of given policies and how narrowly concentrated (limited to a relatively small number of identifiable citizens) or widely distributed (spread over many, most, or all citizens) their perceived costs and benefits are. This approach gives us four types of politics: *majoritarian* (widely distributed costs and benefits), *interest group* (narrowly concentrated costs and benefits), *client* (widely distributed costs and narrowly concentrated benefits), and *entrepreneurial* (narrowly concentrated costs and widely distributed benefits). Different types of coalitions are associated with each type of politics. Issues can sometimes "migrate" from one type of politics to another. Some policy dynamics involve more than one type of politics. And the politics of some issues is harder to classify and explain than the politics of others.

To Learn More

Huntington, Samuel P. *American Politics: The Promise of Disharmony.* Cambridge, MA: Harvard University Press, 1981. A fascinating analysis of the American political experience as shaped by recurring "creedal passion" periods.

Marx, Karl, and Friedrich Engels. "The Manifesto of the Communist Party." In *The Marx-Engels Reader*, 2nd ed. Edited by Robert C. Tucker, 469–500. New York: Norton, 1978. The classic and historic statement suggesting that government is a mere instrument of the economic elite (wealthy capitalists in the modern world).

Meyerson, Martin, and Edward C. Banfield. *Politics, Planning, and the Public Interest*. New York: Free Press, 1955. An understanding of issues and politics comparable to the approach adopted in this book.

Schumpeter, Joseph A. *Capitalism, Socialism, and Democracy,* 3rd ed. New York: Harper Torchbooks, 1950 (chaps. 20–23). A lucid statement of the theory of representative democracy and how it differs from participatory democracy.

Truman, David B. *The Governmental Process: Political Interests and Public Opinion.* New York: Knopf, 1951. A pluralist interpretation of American politics.

Weber, Max. *Max Weber: Essays in Sociology.* Translated and edited by H. H. Gerth and C. Wright Mills. London: Routledge & Kegan Paul, 1948 (chap. 8). A theory of bureaucracy and its power.

Wilson, James Q. *Political Organizations.* New York: Basic Books, 1973. It is from a theory originally developed in this treatise that the four-box model of how to classify and explain the politics of different issues that is presented in this chapter was derived.

CHAPTER 2

The Constitution

Learning Objectives

2-1 Explain how evolving debates about liberty led from the Revolutionary War to the Constitutional Convention.

2-2 Discuss the major proposals for and compromise over representation in the Constitutional Convention.

2-3 Summarize the key issues presented by Federalists and Antifederalists in ratification debates for the Constitution

2-4 Discuss continuing debates about democracy and the Constitution.

« Then When the Constitutional Convention was held in Philadelphia in 1787, its members were all white men. They were not chosen by popular election, and a few famous men, such as Patrick Henry of Virginia, refused to attend. One state, Rhode Island, sent no delegates at all. They assembled in secret and there was no press coverage. The delegates met to remedy the defects of the Articles of Confederation, under which the rebellious colonies had been governed; but instead of fixing the Articles, they wrote an entirely new constitution. Then they publicized it and said that it would go into effect once it had been ratified—not by state legislatures, but by popular conventions in at least nine states.

*** Now** Suppose you think we should have a new constitutional convention to remedy what you and others view as defects in the present document. As you will see later in this chapter, opinions about how our Constitution might be improved are quite diverse. Some critics want the Constitution to create an American version of the parliamentary system of government one finds in the United Kingdom. Others would rather that it weaken the federal government—for example, by requiring that the budget be balanced each year, or by cutting funds and staff from national programs, such as housing and education assistance, with the expectation that states or private organizations will take on those responsibilities.

Now try to imagine your answers to these questions: How would delegates be picked? How many would there be? Is there any way to limit what the new convention does? Should the meeting be covered by live television, and should delegates be free to publicize proceedings through social media posts?

2-1 The Problem of Liberty

The goal of the American Revolution was liberty. It was not the first revolution with that object (nor was it the last), but it was perhaps the clearest case of a people violently altering the political order, simply to protect their liberties. Subsequent revolutions had more complicated or utterly different objectives. The French Revolution in 1789 sought not only liberty, but also "equality and fraternity." The Russian Revolution (1917) and the Chinese Revolution (culminating in 1949) chiefly sought equality and were scarcely concerned with liberty as we understand it.

In signing the Declaration of Independence in 1776, the American colonists sought to protect the traditional liberties to which they thought they were entitled as British subjects. These liberties included the right to bring their legal cases before judges who were truly independent, rather than subordinate to the king; to be free of the burden of having British troops quartered in their homes; to engage in trade without burdensome restrictions; and, of course, to pay no taxes levied by a British Parliament in which they had no direct representation. During the 10 years or more of agitation and argument leading up to the War for Independence, most colonists believed their liberties could be protected while they remained a part of the British Empire.

Slowly but surely opinion shifted. By the time war broke out in 1775, a large number of colonists (though perhaps not a majority) had reached the conclusion that the colonies would have to become independent of Great Britain if their liberties were to be assured. The colonists had many reasons for regarding independence as the only solution, but one is especially important: they no longer had confidence in the English constitution. This constitution was not a single document, but rather a collection of laws, charters, and traditional understandings that proclaimed the liberties of British subjects. In the eyes of the colonists, these liberties were violated regularly, despite their constitutional protection. Clearly, then, the English constitution was an inadequate check on the abuses of political power. The revolutionary leaders sought an explanation of the constitution's insufficiency, and they found it in human nature.

The Colonial Mind

"A lust for domination is more or less natural to all parties," one colonist wrote.[1] Men will seek power, many colonists believed, because they are ambitious, greedy, and easily corrupted. John Adams denounced the "luxury, effeminacy, and venality" of English politics; Patrick Henry spoke scathingly of the "corrupt House of Commons"; and Alexander Hamilton described England as "an old, wrinkled, withered, worn-out hag."[2] This was in part flamboyant rhetoric designed to whip up enthusiasm for the conflict, but it was also deeply revealing of the colonial mindset. Their belief that English politicians—and, by implication, most politicians in general—tended to be corrupt was the colonists' explanation of why the English constitution was not an adequate guarantee of the liberty of the citizens. This opinion was to persist and, as we shall see, profoundly affect the way the Americans went about designing their own governments.

The liberties the colonists fought to protect were, they thought, widely understood. They were based not on the generosity of the king or the language of statutes but on a "higher law" embodying "natural rights" that were ordained by God, discoverable in nature and history, and essential to human progress. These rights, John Dickinson wrote, are "born with us; exist with us; and cannot be taken away from us by any human power."[3] There was general agreement that the essential rights included life, liberty, and property long before Thomas Jefferson wrote them into the Declaration of Independence. (Jefferson changed "property" to "the pursuit of happiness," but almost everybody else went on talking about property.)

This emphasis on property did not mean the American Revolution was thought up by the rich and wellborn to protect their interests or that there was a struggle between property owners and the propertyless. In late-18th-century America, most people (except the black slaves) had property of some kind. The overwhelming majority of citizens were self-employed—as farmers or artisans—and rather few people benefited financially by gaining independence from England. Taxes were higher during and after the war than they were before it, trade was disrupted by the conflict, and debts mounted perilously as various expedients were invented to pay for the struggle. There were, of course, war profiteers and those who tried to manipulate the currency to their own advantage, but most Americans at the time of the war saw the conflict in terms of political rather than economic issues. It was a war of ideology.

We all recognize the glowing language with which Jefferson set out the case for independence in the second paragraph of the Declaration:

> We hold these truths to be self-evident, that all men are created equal, that they are endowed by their Creator with certain unalienable Rights, that among these are Life, Liberty, and the pursuit of Happiness.—That to secure these rights, Governments are instituted among Men, deriving their just powers from the consent of the governed—that whenever any Form of Government becomes destructive of these ends, it is the Right of the People to alter or to abolish it, and to institute new Government, having its foundation on such principles, and organizing its powers in such form, as to them shall seem most likely to effect their Safety and Happiness.

unalienable *A human right based on nature or God.*

What almost no one recalls, but which are an essential part of the Declaration, are the next 27 paragraphs, in which Jefferson listed, item by item, the specific complaints the colonists had against George III and his ministers. None of these items focused on social or economic conditions in the colonies; all spoke instead of specific violations of political liberties. The Declaration was in essence a lawyer's brief, prefaced by a stirring philosophical claim that the rights being violated were **unalienable**—that is, based on nature and Providence, and not on the whims or preferences of people. Jefferson, in his original draft, added another complaint—that the king had allowed the slave trade to continue *and* was inciting slaves to revolt against their masters. Congress, faced with so contradictory a charge, instead decided to include a muted reference to slave insurrections and omit all reference to the slave trade.

The Real Revolution

The Revolution was more than the War of Independence. It began before the war, continued after it, and involved

De Agostini/Dea Picture Library/Getty Images

Image 2.1 Signing the Declaration of Independence, painted by John Trumbull.

more than driving out the British army by force. The *real* Revolution, as John Adams explained afterward in a letter to a friend, was the "radical change in the principles, opinions, sentiments, and affections of the people."[4] This radical change had to do with a new vision of what could make political authority legitimate and personal liberties secure. Government by royal prerogative was rejected; instead, legitimate government would require the consent of the governed. Political power could not be exercised on the basis of tradition, but only as a result of a direct grant of power contained in a written constitution. Human liberty existed before government was organized, and government must respect that liberty. The legislative branch of government, in which the people were directly represented, should be superior to the executive branch.

These were indeed revolutionary ideas. No government at the time had been organized on the basis of these principles. To the colonists, such notions were not empty words, but rules to be put into immediate practice. In 1776, eight states adopted written constitutions. Within a few years, every former colony had adopted one except Connecticut and Rhode Island, two states that continued to rely on their colonial charters. Most state constitutions had detailed bills of rights defining personal liberties, and most placed the highest political power in the hands of elected representatives.

Written constitutions, representatives, and bills of rights are so familiar to us now that we don't realize how bold and unprecedented those innovations were in 1776 for the original thirteen colonies identified in the map below (Figure 2.1). Indeed, many Americans did not think they would succeed; such arrangements either would be so strong that they would threaten liberty or so weak that they would permit chaos.

The 11 years that elapsed between the Declaration of Independence and the signing of the Constitution in 1787 were years of turmoil, uncertainty, and fear. George Washington headed a bitter, protracted war effort without anything resembling a strong national government to

Figure 2.1 **North America in 1787**

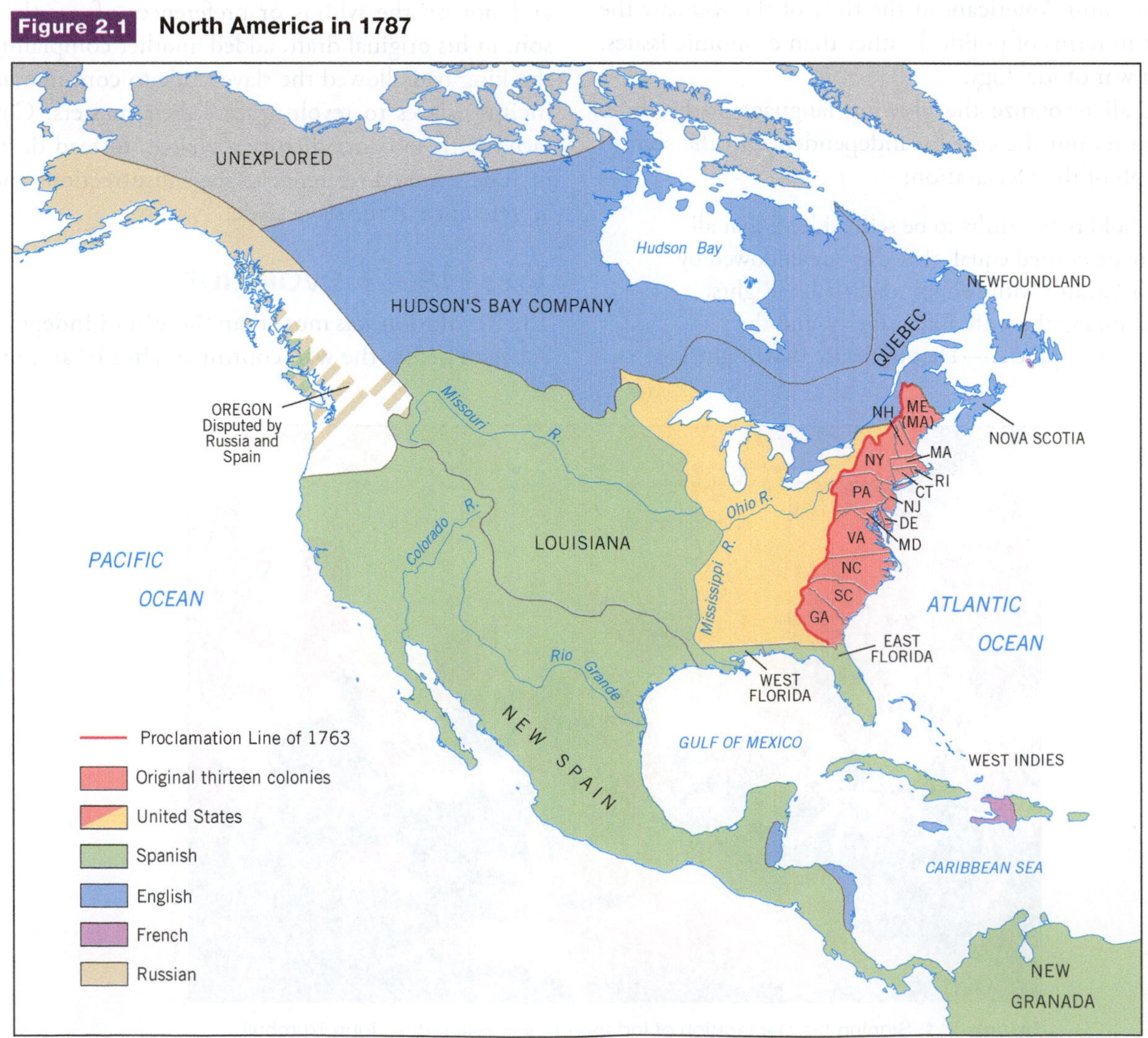

Figure 2.2 Articles of Confederation

Congressional Powers:

- Congress could borrow money from the people
- Congress could settle disputes between states on state petition
- Congress could enter into treaties and alliances
- Congress could establish and control the armed forces, declare war, and make peace
- Congress could create a postal system, admiralty courts, create government departments, and regulate Indian affairs
- Congress could regulate coinage and set standards for weights and measures

Weaknesses:

- Congress could not regulate commerce
- Congress could not directly tax the people
- Congress could not compel states to pay their share of government costs
- Congress lacked power to enforce its laws
- Congress could not enforce foreign treaties with the states and states entered into treaties independent of Congress
- Congress could not draft soldiers
- Approval of nine of thirteen states needed to enact legislation
- Amendments to the Articles required the consent of all thirteen states
- No permanent executive branch
- No permanent judicial branch
- Congress could not issue paper money and a single currency

support him. The supply and financing of his army were based on a series of hasty improvisations, most administered badly and few supported adequately by the fiercely independent states. When peace came, many parts of the nation were a shambles. At least a quarter of New York City was in ruins, and many other communities were nearly devastated. Though the British lost the war, they still were powerful on the North American continent, with an army available in Canada (where many Americans loyal to Britain had fled) and a large navy at sea. Spain claimed the Mississippi River Valley and occupied what are now Florida and California. Men who had left their farms to fight came back to discover themselves in debt with no money and heavy taxes. The paper money printed to finance the war was now virtually worthless.

Weaknesses of the Confederation

The 13 states had formed only a faint semblance of a national government with which to bring order to the nation. The **Articles of Confederation**, which went into effect in 1781, created little more than a "league of friendship" that could not levy taxes or regulate commerce. As summarized in the above chart (Figure 2.2), each state retained its sovereignty and independence, each state (regardless of size) had one vote in Congress, 9 (of 13) votes were required to pass any measure, and the delegates who cast these votes were picked and paid for by the state legislatures. Congress did have the power to make peace, and thus it was able to ratify a treaty with England in 1783. It could coin money, but there was precious little to coin; it could appoint key army officers, but the army was small and depended for support on independent state militias; it was allowed to run the post office, then, as now, a thankless job that no one else wanted. In 1785, John Hancock was elected to the meaningless office of "president" under the Articles and never showed up to take the job. Several states claimed the unsettled lands in the West, and they occasionally pressed those claims with

Articles of Confederation
A weak constitution that governed America during the Revolutionary War.

Hulton Archive/Stringer/Getty Images

Image 2.2 In 1775, British and American troops exchanged fire in Lexington, Massachusetts, the first battle of the War of Independence.

Constitutional Convention *A meeting in Philadelphia in 1787 that produced a new constitution.*

guns. Pennsylvania and Virginia went to war near Pittsburgh, and Vermont threatened to become part of Canada. There was no national judicial system to settle these or other claims among the states. To amend the Articles of Confederation, all 13 states had to agree.

Many of the leaders of the Revolution, such as George Washington and Alexander Hamilton, believed a stronger national government was essential. They lamented the disruption of commerce and travel caused by the quarrelsome states and deeply feared the possibility of foreign military intervention, with England or France playing one state off against another. A small group of men, conferring at Washington's home at Mount Vernon in 1785, decided to call a meeting to discuss trade regulation. That meeting, held at Annapolis, Maryland, in September 1786, was not well attended (no delegates arrived from New England), and so another meeting, this one in Philadelphia, was called for the following spring—in May 1787—to consider ways of remedying the defects of the Confederation.

2-2 The Constitutional Convention

The delegates assembled at Philadelphia at the **Constitutional Convention**, for what was advertised (and authorized by Congress) as a meeting to revise the Articles; they adjourned four months later, having written a wholly new constitution. When they met, they were keenly aware of the problems of the confederacy, but far from agreement as to what should be done about those problems. The protection of life, liberty, and property was their objective in 1787, as it had been in 1776, but they had no accepted political theory that would tell them what kind of national government, if any, would serve that goal.

The Lessons of Experience

They had read ancient and modern political history, only to learn that nothing seemed to work. James Madison spent a good part of 1786 studying books sent to him by Thomas Jefferson, then in Paris, in hopes of finding some model for a workable American republic. He took careful notes on various confederacies in ancient Greece and on the more modern confederacy of the United Netherlands. He reviewed the history of Switzerland and Poland and the ups and downs of the Roman republic. He concluded that there was no model; as he later put it in one of the *Federalist* papers, history consists only of beacon lights "which give warning of the course to be shunned, without pointing out that which ought to be pursued."[5] The problem seemed to be that confederacies were too weak to govern and tended to collapse from internal dissension, whereas all stronger forms of government were so powerful as to trample the liberties of the citizens.

State Constitutions

Madison and the others did not need to consult history, or even the defects of the Articles of Confederation, for illustrations of the problem. These could be found in the government of the American states at the time. Pennsylvania and Massachusetts exemplified two aspects of the problem.

The Pennsylvania constitution, adopted in 1776, created the most radically democratic of the new state regimes. All power was given to a one-house (unicameral) legislature, the Assembly, the members of which were elected annually for one-year terms. No legislator could serve more than four years. There was no governor or president, only an Executive Council that had few powers. Thomas Paine, whose pamphlets had helped precipitate the break with England, thought the Pennsylvania constitution was the best in America, and in France philosophers hailed it as the very embodiment of the principle of rule by the people. Though popular in France, it was a good deal less popular in Philadelphia. The Assembly disenfranchised the Quakers, persecuted conscientious objectors to the war, ignored the requirement of trial by juries, and manipulated the judiciary.[6] To Madison and his friends, the Pennsylvania constitution demonstrated how a government, though democratic, could be tyrannical as a result of concentrating all powers into one set of hands.

The Massachusetts constitution, adopted in 1780, was a good deal less democratic. There was a clear separation of powers among the various branches of government, the directly elected governor could veto acts of the legislature, and judges served for life. Both voters and elected officials had to be property owners; the governor, in fact, had to own at least £1,000 worth of property. The principal officeholders had to swear they were Christians.

Shays's Rebellion

But if the government of Pennsylvania was thought too strong, that of Massachusetts seemed too weak despite

Image 2.3 The Framers drafted the Constitution in Philadelphia during the summer of 1787.

GraphicaArtis/Archive Photos/Getty Images

its "conservative" features. In January 1787, a group of ex-Revolutionary War soldiers and officers, plagued by debts and high taxes and fearful of losing their property to creditors and tax collectors, forcibly prevented the courts in western Massachusetts from sitting. This became known as **Shays's Rebellion**, after one of the officers, Daniel Shays. The governor of Massachusetts asked the Continental Congress to send troops to suppress the rebellion, but it could not raise the money or the manpower. Then he turned to his own state militia, but discovered he did not have one. In desperation, private funds were collected to hire a volunteer army, which marched on Springfield and, with the firing of a few shots, dispersed the rebels, who fled into neighboring states.

Shays's Rebellion, occurring between the Annapolis and Philadelphia Conventions, had a powerful effect on opinion. Delegates who might have been reluctant to attend the Philadelphia meeting, especially those from New England, were galvanized by the fear that state governments were about to collapse from internal dissension. George Washington wrote a friend despairingly: "For God's sake, if they [the rebels] have real grievances, redress them; if they have not, employ the force of government against them at once."[7] Thomas Jefferson, living in Paris, took a more detached view: "A little rebellion now and then is a good thing," he wrote. "The tree of liberty must be refreshed from time to time with the blood of patriots and tyrants."[8] Though Jefferson's detachment might be explained by the fact that he was in Paris and not in Springfield, others, like Governor George Clinton of New York, shared the view that no strong central government was required. (Whether Clinton would have agreed about the virtues of spilled blood, especially his, is another matter.)

The Framers

Shays's Rebellion *A 1787 rebellion in which ex-Revolutionary War soldiers attempted to prevent foreclosures of farms as a result of high interest rates and taxes.*

The Philadelphia Convention attracted 55 delegates, of whom only about 30 participated regularly in the proceedings. One state, Rhode Island, refused to send anyone. The convention met during a miserably hot Philadelphia summer, with the delegates pledged to keep their deliberations secret. The talkative and party-loving Benjamin Franklin was often accompanied by other delegates to make sure that neither wine nor his delight in telling stories would lead him to divulge delicate secrets.

Those who attended were for the most part young (Hamilton was 30; Madison, 36) but experienced. Eight delegates had signed the Declaration of Independence, 7 had been governors, 34 were lawyers and reasonably well-to-do, a few were wealthy. They were not "intellectuals," but men of practical affairs. Thirty-nine had served in the ineffectual Congress of the Confederation; a third of all delegates were veterans of the Continental Army.

Some names made famous by the Revolution were conspicuously absent. Thomas Jefferson and John Adams were serving as ministers abroad; Samuel Adams was ill; Patrick Henry was chosen to attend but refused, commenting that he "smelled a rat in Philadelphia, tending toward monarchy."

The key men at the convention were an odd lot. George Washington was a very tall, athletic man who was the best horseman in Virginia and who impressed everyone with his dignity, despite decaying teeth and big eyes. James Madison was the very opposite: quite short with a frail body, and not much of an orator, but possessed of one of the best minds in the country. Benjamin Franklin, though old and ill, was the most famous American in the world as a scientist and writer, and always displayed shrewd judgment, at least when sober. Alexander Hamilton, the son of a French woman and a Scottish merchant who were not married, had so strong a mind and so powerful a desire that he succeeded in everything he did, from being Washington's aide during the Revolution to serving as a splendid secretary of the treasury during Washington's presidency.

The convention produced not a revision of the Articles of Confederation, as it had been authorized to do, but instead a wholly new written constitution creating a true national government unlike any that had existed before. That document is today the world's oldest written national constitution. Those who wrote it were neither saints nor schemers, and the deliberations were not always lofty or philosophical—much hard bargaining, more than a little confusion, and the accidents of personality and

Virginia Plan *Proposal to create a strong national government.*

time helped shape the final product. The delegates were split on many issues—what powers should be given to a central government, how the states should be represented, what was to be done about slavery, the role of the people—each of which was resolved through compromise. The speeches of the delegates (known to us from the detailed notes kept by Madison) did not explicitly draw on political philosophy or quote from the writings of philosophers. Everyone present was quite familiar with the traditional arguments and, on the whole, well read in history. Though the leading political philosophers were only rarely mentioned, the debate was profoundly influenced by philosophical beliefs, some formed by the revolutionary experience and others by the 11-year attempt at self-government.

From the debates leading up to the Revolution, the delegates had drawn a commitment to liberty, which, despite the abuses sometimes committed in its name, they continued to share. Their defense of liberty as a natural right was derived from the writings of the 17th-century English philosopher John Locke.

Unlike his English rival, Thomas Hobbes, Locke did not believe that an all-powerful government was necessary or that democracy was impossible. Hobbes had argued that in any society without an absolute, supreme ruler there is bound to be ceaseless violent turmoil—a "war of all against all." Locke disagreed. In a "state of nature," Locke argued, all men cherish and seek to protect their life, liberty, and property. But in a state of nature—that is, a society without a government—the strong can use their liberty to deprive the weak of their own liberty. The instinct for self-preservation leads people to want a government that will prevent this exploitation. But if the government is not itself to deprive its subjects of their liberty, it must be limited. The chief limitation, he said, should derive from the fact that it is created, and governs, by the consent of the governed. People will not agree to be ruled by a government that threatens their liberty; therefore, the government to which they freely choose to submit themselves must be a limited government designed to protect liberty.[9]

The Pennsylvania experience as well as the history of British government led the Framers to doubt whether popular consent alone would be a sufficient guarantor of liberty. A popular government may prove too weak (as in Massachusetts) to prevent one faction from abusing another, or a popular majority can be tyrannical (as in Pennsylvania). In fact, the tyranny of the majority can be an even graver threat than rule by the few. In the former case, the individual may have no defenses—one lone person cannot count on the succor of public opinion or the possibility of popular revolt.

The problem, then, was a delicate one: how to devise a government strong enough to preserve order but not so strong that it would threaten liberty. The answer, the delegates believed, was not "democracy" as it was then understood. To many conservatives in the late 18th century, democracy meant mob rule—it meant, in short, Shays's Rebellion (or, if they had been candid about it, the Boston Tea Party). On the other hand, *aristocracy*—the rule of the few—was no solution, since the few were likely to be self-serving. Madison, writing later in the *Federalist Papers*, put the problem this way:

> If men were angels, no government would be necessary. If angels were to govern men, neither external nor internal controls on government would be necessary. In framing a government which is to be administered by men over men, the great difficulty lies in this: you must first enable the government to control the governed; and in the next place oblige it to control itself.[10]

Striking this balance could not be done, Madison believed, simply by writing a constitution that set limits on what government could do. The example of British rule over the colonies proved that laws and customs were inadequate checks on political power. As he expressed it, "A mere demarcation on parchment of the constitutional limits [of government] is not a sufficient guard against those encroachments which lead to a tyrannical concentration of all the powers of government in the same hands."[11]

The Challenge

The resolution of political issues, great and small, often depends crucially on how the central question is phrased. The delegates came to Philadelphia in general agreement that the Articles of Confederation contained defects that ought to be remedied. Had they, after convening, decided to make their business that of listing these defects and debating alternative remedies for them, the document that emerged would in all likelihood have been very different from what in fact was adopted. But immediately after the convention had organized itself and chosen Washington to be its presiding officer, the Virginia delegation, led by Governor Edmund Randolph but relying heavily on the draftsmanship of James Madison, presented to the convention a comprehensive plan for a wholly new national government. The plan quickly became the major item of business at the meeting, and little else was debated for the next two weeks.

The Virginia Plan

When the convention decided to make the **Virginia Plan** its agenda, it had fundamentally altered the nature of its task. The business at hand was not to be the Articles and their defects, but rather how one should go about designing a true national government. The Virginia Plan called for a strong national union organized into three governmental branches: the legislative, executive, and judicial. The legislature was to comprise two houses, the first elected directly by the people and the second chosen by the first house from among the candidates nominated by state legislatures. The executive was to be chosen by the national legislature, as were members of a national judiciary. The executive and some members of the judiciary were to constitute a "council of revision" that could veto acts of the legislature; that veto, in turn, could be overridden by the legislature. There were other interesting details, but the key features of the Virginia Plan were two: (1) a national legislature would have supreme powers on all matters on which the separate states were not competent to act, as well as the power to veto any and all state laws; and (2) at least one house of the legislature would be elected directly by the people.

The New Jersey Plan

As the debate continued, the representatives of New Jersey and other small states became increasingly worried that the convention was going to write a constitution in which the states would be represented in both houses of Congress on the basis of population. If this happened, the smaller states feared they would always be outvoted by the larger ones, and so, with William Paterson of New Jersey as their spokesman, they introduced a new plan. The **New Jersey Plan** proposed to amend, not replace, the old Articles of Confederation. It enhanced the power of the national government (though not as much as the Virginia Plan), but it did so in a way that left the states' representation in Congress unchanged from the Articles—each state would have one vote. Thus not only would the interests of the small states be protected, but Congress itself would also remain to a substantial degree the creature of state governments.

Andre Jenny/Alamy Stock Photo

Image 2.4 The Declaration of Independence and the U.S. Constitution were developed and signed in Independence Hall in Philadelphia.

If the New Jersey resolutions had been presented first and taken up as the major item of business, it is quite possible they would have become the framework for the document that finally emerged. But they were not. Offered after the convention had been discussing the Virginia Plan for two weeks, the resolutions encountered a reception very different from what they may have received if introduced earlier. The debate had the delegates already thinking in terms of a national government that was more independent of the states, and thus it had accustomed them to proposals that, under other circumstances, might have seemed quite radical. On June 19, the first decisive vote of the convention was taken: seven states preferred the Virginia Plan, three states the New Jersey Plan, and one state was split.

New Jersey Plan *Proposal to create a weak national government.*

Great Compromise *Plan to have a popularly elected House based on state population and a state-selected Senate, with two members for each state.*

With the tide running in favor of a strong national government, the supporters of the small states had to shift their strategy. They now began to focus their efforts on ensuring that the small states could not be outvoted by the larger ones in Congress. One way was to have the members of the lower house elected by the state legislatures rather than the people, with each state getting the same number of seats rather than seats proportional to its population.

The debate was long and feelings ran high, so much so that Benjamin Franklin, the oldest delegate present (at 81 years of age), suggested that each day's meeting begin with a prayer. It turned out that the convention could not even agree on this: Hamilton is supposed to have objected that the convention did not need "foreign aid," and others pointed out that the group had no funds with which to hire a minister. And so the argument continued.

The Compromise

Finally, a committee was appointed to meet during the Fourth of July holidays to work out a compromise, and the convention adjourned to await its report. Little is known of what went on in that committee's session, though some were later to say that Franklin played a key role in hammering out the plan that finally emerged. That compromise, the most important one reached at the convention, and later called the **Great Compromise** (or sometimes the Connecticut Compromise), was submitted to the full convention on July 5 and debated for another week and a half. The debate might have gone on even longer, but suddenly the hot weather moderated, and Monday, July 16, dawned cool and fresh after a month of misery. On that day, the plan was adopted: five states were in favor, four opposed, and two

Figure 2.3 **The Virginia Plan Versus the New Jersey Plan and the Great (Connecticut) Compromise**

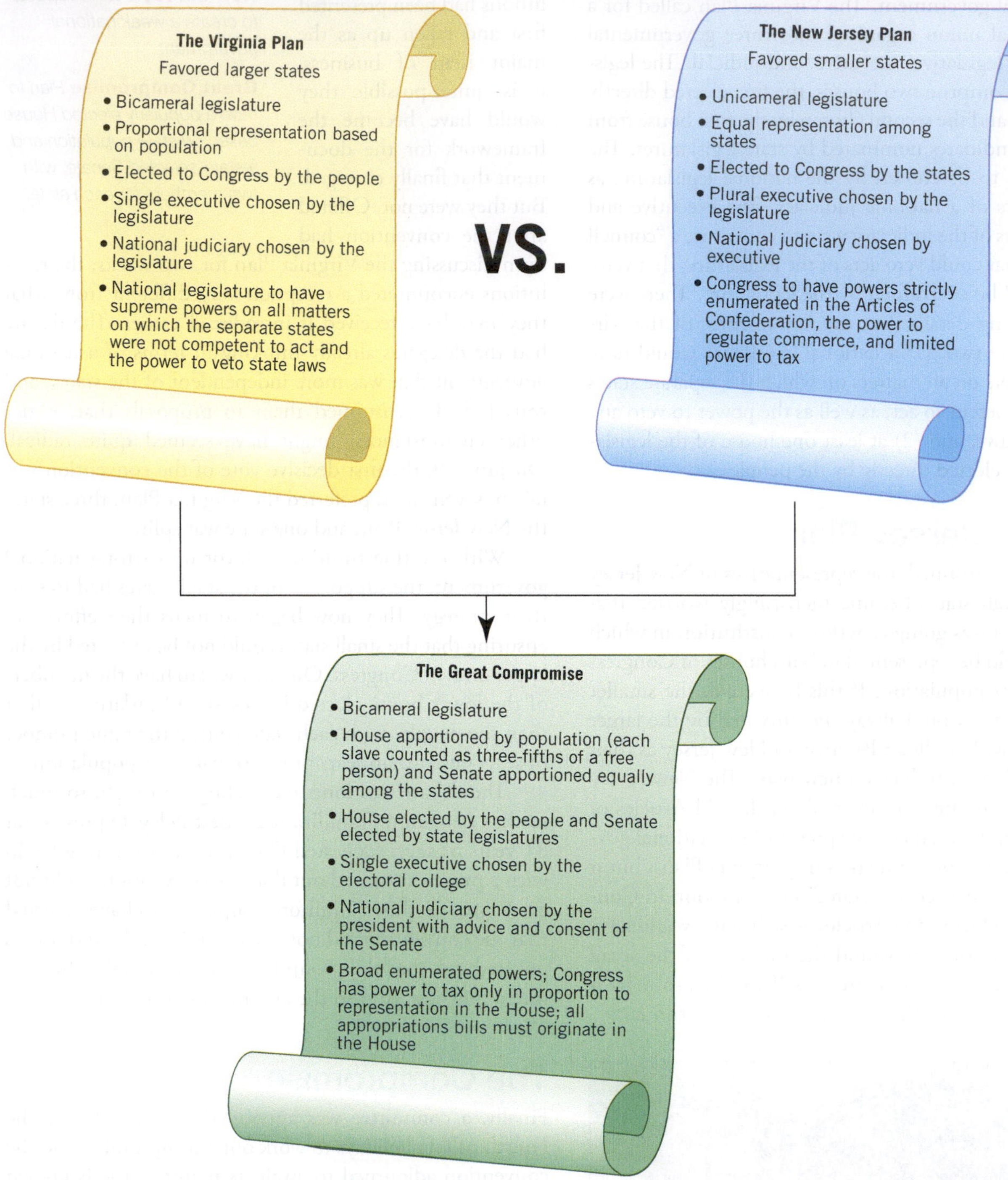

Q **How did the Great Compromise address interests of both large and small states, and how relevant are those interests to national governance and policy making today?**

did not vote.* Thus, by the narrowest of margins, the structure of the national legislature was decided, drawing upon both the Virginia Plan and the New Jersey Plan, as illustrated in Figure 2.3. Its key features included the following:

- A House of Representatives consisting initially of 65 members apportioned among the states roughly on the basis of population and elected by the people.
- A Senate consisting of two senators from each state to be chosen by the state legislatures.

The Great Compromise reconciled the interests of small and large states by allowing the former to predominate in

*The states in favor were Connecticut, Delaware, Maryland, New Jersey, and North Carolina. Those opposed were Georgia, Pennsylvania, South Carolina, and Virginia. Massachusetts was split down the middle; the New York delegates had left the convention. New Hampshire and Rhode Island were absent.

the Senate and the latter in the House. This reconciliation was necessary to ensure that a strong national government would receive support from small as well as large states. It represented major concessions on the part of several groups. Madison, for one, was deeply opposed to the idea of having the states equally represented in the Senate. He saw in that a way for the states to hamstring the national government and much preferred some measure of proportional representation in both houses. Delegates from other states worried that representation on the basis of population in the House of Representatives would enable the large states to dominate legislative affairs. Although the margin by which the compromise was accepted was razor-thin, it held firm. In time, most of the delegates from the dissenting states accepted it.

After the Great Compromise, many more issues had to be resolved, but by now a spirit of accommodation had developed. When one delegate proposed having Congress choose the president, another, James Wilson, proposed that the president be elected directly by the people. When neither side of that argument prevailed, a committee invented a plan for an "electoral college" that would choose the president. When some delegates wanted the president chosen for a life term, others proposed a seven-year term, and still others wanted the term limited to three years without eligibility for reelection. The convention settled on a four-year term with no bar to reelection. Some states wanted the Supreme Court picked by the Senate; others wanted it chosen by the president. They finally agreed to let the justices be nominated by the president and then confirmed by the Senate.

Finally, on July 26, the proposals that were already accepted, together with a bundle of unresolved issues, were handed over to the Committee of Detail, consisting of five delegates. This committee included Madison and Gouverneur Morris, who was to be the chief drafter of the document that finally emerged. The committee hardly contented itself with mere "details," however. It inserted some new proposals and made changes in old ones, drawing for inspiration on existing state constitutions and the members' beliefs as to what the other delegates might accept. On August 6, the report—the first complete draft of the Constitution—was submitted to the convention. There it was debated item by item, revised, amended, and finally, on September 17, approved by all 12 states in attendance. Not all *delegates* approved, however; three, including Edmund Randolph, who first submitted the Virginia Plan, refused to sign. (The full approved Constitution and subsequent amendments are reprinted at the end of this book and summarized in Figure 2.4.)

2-3 Ratification Debates

A debate continues to rage over whether the Constitution created, or was even intended to create, a democratic government. The answer is complex.

republic *A government in which elected representatives make the decisions.*

The Framers did not intend to create a "pure democracy"—one in which the people rule directly. For one thing, the size of the country and the distances between settlements would have made that physically impossible. But more importantly, the Framers worried that a government in which all citizens directly participate, as in the New England town meeting, would be a government excessively subject to temporary popular passions and one in which minority rights would be insecure. They intended instead to create a **republic**, by which they meant a government in which a system of representation operates.

The Framers favored a republic over a direct democracy because they believed that government should mediate, not mirror, popular views and that elected officials should represent, not register, majority sentiments. They supposed that most citizens did not have the time, information, interest, and expertise to make reasonable choices among competing policy positions. They suspected that even highly educated people could be manipulated by demagogic leaders who played on their fears and prejudices. They knew that representative democracy often proceeds slowly and prevents sweeping changes in policy, but they cautioned that a government capable of doing great good quickly can also do great harm quickly. They agreed that majority opinion should figure in the enactment of many or most government policies, but they insisted that protection of civil rights and civil liberties—the right to a fair trial; the freedom of speech, press, and religion; or the right to vote itself—ought never to hinge on a popular vote. Above all, they embraced representative democracy because they saw it as a way of minimizing the chances that power would be abused either by a tyrannical popular majority or by self-serving officeholders.

The Framers were influenced by philosophers who had discussed democracy. Aristotle defined *democracy* as the rule of the many; that is, rule by ordinary people, most of whom would be poor. But democracy, he suggested, can easily decay into an oligarchy (rule of the rich) or a tyranny (the rule of a despot). To prevent this, a good political system must be a mixed regime, combining elements of democracy and oligarchy: most people will vote, but talented people will play a large role in managing affairs.

But, as we noted earlier in this chapter, the Framers were strongly influenced by John Locke, the 17th-century English writer who argued against powerful kings and in favor of popular dissent. In Locke's *Second Treatise of Civil Government* (1690), he argued that people can exist in a state of nature—that is, without any ruler—so long as they can find enough food to eat and a way to protect themselves. But food may not be plentiful and, as a result, life may be poor and difficult.

Figure 2.4 **Overview of the Constitution of the United States**

PREAMBLE

ARTICLE I.	**The Legislative Branch**
Section 1.	Bicameral Congress
Section 2.	Membership of the House
Section 3.	Membership of the Senate
Section 4.	Laws governing elections
Section 5.	Rules of Congress
Section 6.	Salaries and immunities of members
Section 7.	Passing laws
Section 8.	Powers of Congress
Section 9.	Restrictions on powers of Congress
Section 10.	Restrictions on powers of states
ARTICLE II.	**The Executive Branch**
Section 1.	President and vice-president
Section 2.	Powers of the president
Section 3.	Relations of the president with Congress
Section 4.	Impeachment
ARTICLE III.	**The Judicial Branch**
Section 1.	Federal Courts
Section 2.	Jurisdiction of courts
Section 3.	Treason
ARTICLE IV.	**Relations among States**
Section 1.	Full faith and credit
Section 2.	Privileges and immunities
Section 3.	New states and territories
Section 4.	Federal protection of states
ARTICLE V.	**Amending the Constitution**
ARTICLE VI.	**National Supremacy**
ARTICLE VII.	**Ratification procedure**

Amendments to the Constitution

Amendment		Subject
First (1791)	Bill of Rights	Free speech, press, religion, assembly
Second (1791)	Bill of Rights	Right to bear arms
Third (1791)	Bill of Rights	No quartering of troops in homes
Fourth (1791)	Bill of Rights	No unreasonable searches/seizures
Fifth (1791)	Bill of Rights	Right to due process, grand jury, no double jeopardy, self-incrimination
Sixth (1791)	Bill of Rights	Right to speedy and public trial, counsel
Seventh (1791)	Bill of Rights	Right to trial by jury in civil cases
Eighth (1791)	Bill of Rights	No excessive bail, fines, cruel/unusual punishment
Ninth (1791)	Bill of Rights	Rights not enumerated retained by people
Tenth (1791)	Bill of Rights	Powers not delegated to Congress or prohibited to states belong to states or people
Eleventh (1798)		No federal cases between state, citizen of other state
Twelfth (1804)		Modification of electoral college rules
Thirteenth (1865)		Abolition of slavery
Fourteenth (1868)		States can't deprive right to due process, equal protection, privileges and immunities
Fifteenth (1870)		Right to vote can't be denied by race
Sixteenth (1913)		Congress can levy individual income taxes
Seventeenth (1913)		Direct election of senators
Eighteenth (1919)		Prohibition of liquors
Nineteenth (1920)		Women's right to vote
Twentieth (1933)		Dates for inauguration, Congress's session
Twenty-first (1933)		Repeal of prohibition
Twenty-second (1951)		Presidential term limits
Twenty-third (1961)		D.C. residents' vote for president
Twenty-fourth (1964)		Ban on poll taxes
Twenty-fifth (1967)		Appointment of new vice president, presidential incompetence
Twenty-sixth (1971)		Eighteen-year-olds' right to vote
Twenty-seventh (1992)		Congressional pay raises effective only after election

The human desire for self-preservation will lead people to want a government that will enable them to own property and thereby to increase their supply of food. But unlike his English rival, Thomas Hobbes, Locke argued for a government with defined and limited powers. In *Leviathan* (1651), Hobbes had argued that people live in a "war of all against all" and so an absolute, supreme ruler was essential to prevent civil war. Locke disagreed: People can get along with one another if they can securely own their farms and live off what they produce. But for that to happen a decent

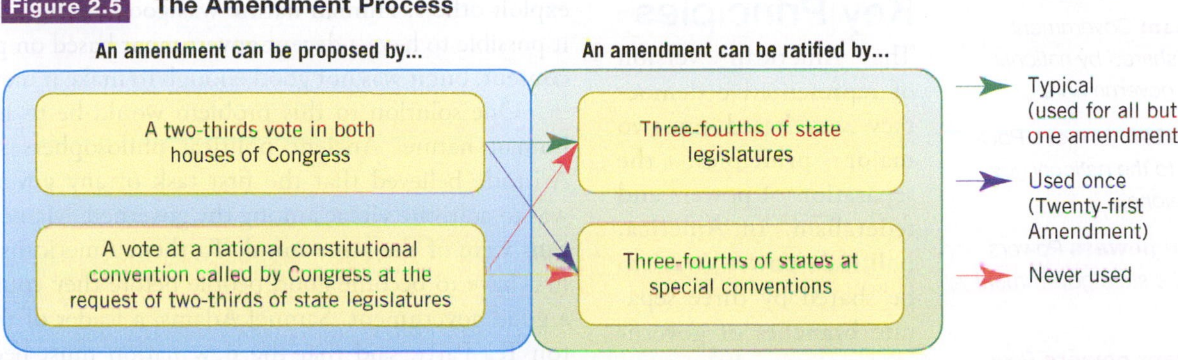

Figure 2.5 **The Amendment Process**

Q **Why do you think the second constitutional provision for ratifying an amendment has never been used?**

government must exist with the consent of the governed and be managed by majority rule. To prevent a majority from hurting a minority, Locke wrote, the government should separate its powers, with different and competing legislative and executive branches.

Thus, in 1787 the Framers tried to create a republic that would protect freedom and private property, a moderate regime that would simultaneously safeguard people and leave them alone. In designing that republic, the Framers chose, not without argument, to have the members of the House of Representatives elected directly by the people. Some delegates did not want to go even that far. Elbridge Gerry of Massachusetts, who refused to sign the Constitution, argued that though "the people do not want [i.e., lack] virtue," they often are the "dupes of pretended patriots." Roger Sherman of Connecticut agreed. But George Mason of Virginia and James Wilson of Pennsylvania carried the day when they argued that "no government could long subsist without the confidence of the people," and this required "drawing the most numerous branch of the legislature directly from the people."[12] Popular elections for the House were approved: six states were in favor, two opposed.

But though popular rule was to be one element of the new government, it was not to be the only one. State legislatures, not the people, would choose the senators; electors, not the people directly, would choose the president. As we have seen, without these arrangements there would have been no Constitution at all, for the small states adamantly opposed any proposal that would have given undue power to the large ones. And direct popular election of the president would clearly have made the populous states the dominant ones. In short, the Framers wished to observe the principle of majority rule, but they felt that, on the most important questions, two kinds of majorities were essential: a majority of the voters and a majority of the states.

The power of the Supreme Court to declare an act of Congress unconstitutional—**judicial review**—is also a way of limiting the power of popular majorities. It is not clear whether the Framers intended that there be judicial review, but there is little doubt that in the Framers' minds the fundamental law, the Constitution, had to be safeguarded against popular passions. They made the process for amending the Constitution easier than it had been under the Articles but still relatively difficult.

judicial review *The power of the courts to declare laws unconstitutional.*

An amendment can be proposed either by a two-thirds vote of both houses of Congress *or* by a national convention called by Congress at the request of two-thirds of the states.† Once proposed, an amendment must be ratified by three-fourths of the states, either through their legislatures or through special ratifying conventions in each state. (Figure 2.5 summarizes the amendment process outlined in Article V of the Constitution.) Twenty-seven amendments have survived this process, all of them proposed by Congress and all but one (the Twenty-First Amendment) ratified by state legislatures rather than state conventions.

In short, the answer to the question of whether the Constitution brought into being a democratic government is yes, if by *democracy* one means a system of representative government based on popular consent. The degree of that consent has changed since 1787, and the institutions embodying that consent can take different forms. One form, rejected in 1787, gives all political authority to one set of representatives, directly elected by the people. (That is the case, for example, in most parliamentary regimes, such as the United Kingdom, and in some city governments in the United States.) The other form of democracy is one in which different sets of officials, chosen directly or indirectly by different groups of people, share political power. (That is the case with the United States and a few other nations where the separation of powers is intended to operate.)

†Many attempts have been made to assemble a new constitutional convention. In the 1960s, 33 states, one short of the required number, requested a convention to consider the reapportionment of state legislatures. In the 1980s, efforts were made to call a convention to consider amendments to ban abortions and to require a balanced federal budget.

federalism *Government authority shared by national and local governments.*

enumerated powers *Powers given to the national government alone.*

reserved powers *Powers given to the state government alone.*

concurrent powers *Powers shared by the national and state governments.*

separation of powers *Sharing of constitutional authority by multiple branches of government.*

checks and balances *Constitutional ability of multiple branches of government to limit each other's power.*

Key Principles

The American version of representative democracy was based on two major principles: the separation of powers and federalism. In America, political power was to be shared by three separate branches of government; in parliamentary democracies, that power was concentrated in a single, supreme legislature. In America, political authority was divided between a national government and several state governments—**federalism**—whereas in most European systems authority was centralized in the national government. Neither of these principles was especially controversial at Philadelphia.

The delegates began their work in broad agreement that separated powers and some measure of federalism were necessary, and both the Virginia and New Jersey Plans contained a version of each. How much federalism should be written into the Constitution was quite controversial, however.

Under these two principles, governmental powers in this country can be divided into three categories. The powers given to the national government exclusively are the delegated or **enumerated powers**. They include the authority to print money, declare war, make treaties, conduct foreign affairs, and regulate commerce among the states and with foreign nations. Those given exclusively to the states are **reserved powers** and include the power to issue licenses and to regulate commerce wholly within a state. Those shared by both the national and the state governments are called **concurrent powers** and include collecting taxes, building roads, borrowing money, and maintaining courts.

Government and Human Nature

The desirability of separating powers and leaving the states equipped with a broad array of rights and responsibilities was not controversial at the Philadelphia Convention because the Framers' experiences with British rule and state government under the Articles had shaped their view of human nature—that people would seek their own advantage in and out of politics, and that this pursuit of self-interest, unchecked, would lead some people to exploit others. Human nature was good enough to make it possible to have a decent government based on popular consent, but it was not good enough to make it inevitable.

One solution to this problem would be to improve human nature. Ancient political philosophers such as Aristotle believed that the first task of any government was to cultivate virtue among the governed. Many Americans were of the same mind. To them Americans would first have to become good people before they could have a good government. Samuel Adams, a leader of the Boston Tea Party, said that the new nation must become a "Christian Sparta." Others spoke of the need to cultivate frugality, industry, temperance, and simplicity.

But to James Madison and the other architects of the Constitution, the deliberate cultivation of virtue would require a government too strong and thus too dangerous to liberty, at least at the national level. Self-interest, freely pursued within reasonable limits, was a more practical and durable solution to the problem of government than any effort to improve the virtue of the citizenry. He wanted, he said, to make republican government possible "even in the absence of political virtue."

Madison argued that the very self-interest that leads people toward factionalism and tyranny might, if properly harnessed by appropriate constitutional arrangements, provide a source of unity and a guarantee of liberty.

This harnessing was to be accomplished by dividing the offices of the new government among many people and giving to the holder of each office the "necessary means and personal motives to resist encroachments of the others." In this way, "ambition must be made to counteract ambition" so that "the private interest of every individual may be a sentinel over the public rights."[13]

If men were angels, all this would be unnecessary. But Madison and the other delegates pragmatically insisted on taking human nature pretty much as it was, and therefore they adopted "this policy of supplying, by opposite and rival interests, the defect of better motives."[14] The **separation of powers** would work not in spite of the imperfections of human nature, but because of them, through requiring the three political institutions to work together. And through **checks and balances**, each branch of government would ensure that the others did not exceed their constitutional powers. (See examples of how the three branches check each other in Table 2.1.)

So it also is with federalism. By dividing power between the states and the national government, one level of government can serve as a check on the other. This should provide a "double security" to the rights of the people: "The different governments will control each other, at the same time that each will be controlled by itself."[15] This was especially likely to happen in America, Madison thought, because it was a large country filled with diverse interests—rich and

TABLE 2.1 | Checks and Balances

The Constitution creates a system of *separate* institutions that *share* powers. Because the three branches of government share powers, each can (partially) check the powers of the others. This is the system of *checks and balances*. The major checks possessed by each branch are listed below.

I. Congress	1. Can check the president in these ways:
	(a) By refusing to pass a bill the president wants
	(b) By passing a law over the president's veto
	(c) By using the impeachment powers to remove the president from office
	(d) By refusing to approve a presidential appointment (Senate only)
	(e) By refusing to ratify a treaty the president has signed (Senate only)
	2. Can check the federal courts in these ways:
	(a) By changing the number and jurisdiction of the lower courts
	(b) By using the impeachment powers to remove a judge from office
	(c) By refusing to approve a person nominated to be a judge (Senate only)
II. The President	1. Can check Congress by vetoing a bill it has passed
	2. Can check the federal courts by nominating judges
III. The Courts	1. Can check Congress by declaring a law unconstitutional
	2. Can check the president by declaring actions by him or his subordinates unconstitutional or not authorized by law

In addition to these checks specifically provided for in the Constitution, each branch has informal ways of checking the others. For example, the president can try to withhold information from Congress (on the grounds of "executive privilege"), and Congress can try to get information by mounting an investigation. The exact meaning of the various checks is explained in Chapter 13 on Congress, Chapter 14 on the presidency, and Chapter 16 on the courts.

poor, Protestant and Catholic, Northerner and Southerner, farmer and merchant, creditor and debtor. Each of these interests would constitute a **faction** that would seek its own advantage. One faction might come to dominate government, or a part of government, in one place, and a different and rival faction might dominate it in another. The pulling and hauling among these factions would prevent any single government—say, that of New York—from dominating all of government. The division of powers among several governments would provide virtually every faction an opportunity to gain some—but not full—power.

The Constitution and Liberty

A more difficult question is whether the Constitution created a system of government that would respect personal liberties. In fact, that is the question that was debated in the states when the document was presented for ratification. The proponents of the Constitution called themselves the **Federalists** (though they might more accurately have been called "nationalists"). The opponents came to be known as the **Antifederalists** (though they might more accurately have been called "states' rights advocates").‡

‡ To the delegates a truly "federal" system was one, like the New Jersey Plan, that allowed for very strong states and a weak national government. When the New Jersey Plan lost, the delegates who defeated it began using the word federal to describe their plan even though it called for a stronger national government. Thus men who began as "Federalists" at the convention ultimately became known as "Antifederalists" during the struggle over ratification.

faction *A group with a distinct political interest.*

Federalists *Those who favor a stronger national government.*

Antifederalists *Those who favor a weaker national government.*

To be put into effect, the Constitution had to be approved at ratifying conventions in at least nine states. This was perhaps the most democratic feature of the Constitution: It had to be accepted, not by the existing Congress (still limping along under the Articles of Confederation), nor by the state legislatures, but by special conventions elected by the people.

Though democratic, the process established by the Framers for ratifying the Constitution was technically illegal. The Articles of Confederation, which still governed, could be amended only with the approval of all 13 state legislatures. The Framers wanted to bypass these legislatures because they feared that, for reasons of ideology or out of a desire to retain their powers, the legislators would oppose the Constitution. The Framers wanted ratification with less than the consent of all 13 states because they knew that such unanimity could not be attained. And indeed the conventions in North Carolina and Rhode Island did initially reject the Constitution. (Figure 2.6 shows which states initially supported or opposed the Constitution.)

Figure 2.6 **Ratification of the Federal Constitution by State Constitutional Conventions, 1787–1790**

The Antifederalist View

The great issue before the state conventions was liberty, not democracy. The opponents of the new Constitution, the Antifederalists, had a variety of objections but were in general united by the belief that liberty could be secure only in a small republic in which the rulers were physically close to—and closely checked by—the ruled. Their central objection was stated by a group of Antifederalists at the ratifying convention in an essay published just after they had lost: "a very extensive territory cannot be governed on the principles of freedom, otherwise than by a confederation of republics."[16]

These dissenters argued that a strong national government would be distant from the people and would use its powers to annihilate or absorb the functions that properly belonged to the states. Congress would tax heavily, the Supreme Court would overrule state courts, and the president would come to head a large standing army. (Since all these things have occurred, we cannot dismiss the Antifederalists as cranky obstructionists who opposed without justification the plans of the Framers.) These critics argued that the nation needed, at best, a loose confederation of states, with most of the powers of government kept firmly in the hands of state legislatures and state courts.

coalition *An alliance of groups.*

But if a stronger national government was to be created, the Antifederalists argued, it should be hedged about with many more restrictions than those in the constitution then under consideration. They proposed several such limitations, including narrowing the jurisdiction of the Supreme Court, checking the president's power by creating a council that would review his actions, leaving military affairs in the hands of the state militias, increasing the size of the House of Representatives so that it would reflect a greater variety of popular interests, and reducing or eliminating the power of Congress to levy taxes. And some of them insisted that a *bill of rights* be added to the Constitution.

James Madison gave his answer to these criticisms in *Federalist* No. 10 and No. 51 (reprinted in the Appendix with a reading guide). It was a bold answer, for it flew squarely in the face of widespread popular sentiment and much philosophical writing. Following the great French political philosopher Montesquieu, many Americans believed liberty was safe only in small societies governed either by direct democracy or by large legislatures with small districts and frequent turnover among members.

Madison argued quite the opposite—that liberty is safest in *large* (or as he put it, "extended") republics. People in a small community, he said, will have relatively few differences in opinion or interest; they will tend to see the world in much the same way. Anyone who dissents or pursues an individual interest will be confronted by a massive majority and will have few, if any, allies. But a large republic will include people with many opinions and interests; as a result, it will be hard for a tyrannical majority to form or organize, and anyone with an unpopular view will find it easier to acquire allies. If Madison's argument seems strange or abstract, ask yourself the following question: if I have an unpopular opinion, an exotic lifestyle, or an unconventional interest, will I find greater security living in a small town or a big city?

By favoring a large republic, Madison was not trying to stifle democracy. Rather, he was attempting to show how democratic government really works, and what can make it work better. To rule, different interests must come together and form a **coalition**—that is, an alliance. In *Federalist* No. 51, he argued that the coalitions that formed in a large republic would be more moderate than those that formed in a small one because the bigger the republic, the greater the variety of interests, and thus the more a coalition of the majority would have to accommodate a diversity of interests and opinions if it hoped to succeed. He concluded that in a nation the size of the United States, with its enormous variety of interests, "a coalition of a majority of the whole society could seldom take place on any other principles than those of justice and the general good." Whether he was right in that prediction is a matter to which we return repeatedly.

The implication of Madison's arguments was daring, for he was suggesting that the national government should be at some distance from the people and insulated from their momentary passions, because the people did not always want to do the right thing. Liberty was threatened as much (or even more) by public passions and popularly based factions as by strong governments. Now the Antifederalists themselves had no very lofty view of human nature, as is evidenced by the deep suspicion with which they viewed "power-seeking" officeholders. What Madison did was take this view to its logical conclusion, arguing that if people could be corrupted by office, they could also be corrupted by factional self-interest. Thus, the government had to be designed to prevent both the politicians and the people from using it for ill-considered or unjust purposes.

To argue in 1787 against the virtues of small democracies was like arguing against motherhood. Moreover, the Federalists' counterargument involved many steps: representative democracy over direct democracy; a large republic over a small republic; diversity of economic, religious, and other interests over homogeneity of such interests; and barriers, not boosts, to majority group formation and influence. Still, the Federalists prevailed, probably because many citizens were convinced that a reasonably strong national government was essential if the nation were to stand united against foreign enemies, facilitate commerce among the states, guard against domestic insurrections, and keep one faction from oppressing another. The political realities of the moment and the recent bitter experiences with the Articles probably counted for more in ratifying the Constitution than Madison's arguments. His cause was helped by the fact that, for all their legitimate concerns and their uncanny instinct for what the future might bring, the Antifederalists could offer no agreed-upon alternative to the new Constitution. In politics, then as now, you cannot beat something with nothing.

But this does not explain why the Framers failed to add a bill of rights to the Constitution. If they were so preoccupied with liberty, why didn't they take this most obvious step toward protecting liberty, especially since the Antifederalists were demanding it? Some historians have suggested that this omission was evidence that liberty was not as important to the Framers as they claimed. In fact, when one delegate suggested that a bill of rights be drawn up, the state delegations at the convention unanimously voted the idea down. They did this for several reasons.

First, the Constitution, as written, *did* contain a number of specific guarantees of individual liberty, including the right of trial by jury in criminal cases and the privilege of the writ of **habeas corpus**. The following list identifies some of the liberties guaranteed in the Constitution (before the Bill of Rights was added):

- Writ of habeas corpus may not be suspended (except during invasion or rebellion).
- No **bill of attainder** may be passed by Congress or the states.
- No **ex post facto law** may be passed by Congress or the states.
- Right of trial by jury in criminal cases is guaranteed.
- The citizens of each state are entitled to the privileges and immunities of the citizens of every other state.
- No religious test or qualification for holding federal office is imposed.
- No law impairing the obligation of contracts may be passed by the states.

habeas corpus *An order to produce an arrested person before a judge.*

bill of attainder *A law that declares a person, without a trial, to be guilty of a crime.*

ex post facto law *A law that makes an act criminal even though the act was legal when it was committed.*

Second, most states in 1787 had bills of rights. When Elbridge Gerry proposed to the convention that a federal bill of rights be drafted, Roger Sherman rose to observe that it was unnecessary because the state bills of rights were sufficient.[17]

But third, and perhaps most important, the Framers thought they were creating a government with specific, limited powers. It could, they thought, do only what the Constitution gave it the power to do, and nowhere in that document was it given permission to infringe on freedom of speech or of the press or to impose cruel and unusual punishments. Some delegates probably feared that if any serious effort were made to list the rights that were guaranteed, later officials might assume that they had the power to do anything not explicitly forbidden.

Need for a Bill of Rights

Whatever their reasons, the Framers made at least a tactical and perhaps a fundamental mistake. It quickly became clear that without at least the promise of a bill of rights, the Constitution would not be ratified. Though the small states, pleased by their equal representation in the Senate, quickly ratified (in Delaware, New Jersey, and Georgia, the vote in the conventions was unanimous), the battle in the large states was intense and the outcome uncertain. In Pennsylvania, Federalist

Bill of Rights *First 10 amendments to the Constitution.*

supporters dragged boycotting Antifederalists to the legislature in order to ensure a quorum was present so a convention could be called. There were rumors of other rough tactics.

In Massachusetts, the Constitution was approved by a narrow majority, but only after key leaders promised to obtain a bill of rights. In Virginia, James Madison fought against the fiery Patrick Henry, whose climactic speech against ratification was dramatically punctuated by a noisy thunderstorm outside. The Federalists won by 10 votes. In New York, Alexander Hamilton argued the case for six weeks against the determined opposition of most of the state's key political leaders; he carried the day, but only by three votes, and then only after New York City threatened to secede from the state if it did not ratify. By June 21, 1788, the ninth state—New Hampshire—had ratified, and the Constitution was law.

Many people think that the first Congress moved quickly to adopt a **Bill of Rights**—that is, the first 10 amendments to the Constitution (summarized in Table 2.2)—in order to satisfy demands made in state ratifying conventions that this be done. Unfortunately, that is not quite right. Of the many criticisms of the proposed Constitution, hardly any referred to civil liberties. Take, for example, the Massachusetts Convention. Several critics, including John Hancock, said they would vote to ratify the document if the new members of Congress did all they could to get nine amendments adopted. But these amendments had nothing to do with free speech or a free press. Instead, they involved the size of the House of Representatives, congressional influence on local elections, the power of Congress to impose taxes, and the need for grand juries in criminal cases.[18] Other speakers wanted an amendment that would have House members stand for election every year. Critics in other states made the same arguments.

Despite the bitterness of the ratification struggle, the new government that took office in 1789–1790, headed by President Washington, was greeted enthusiastically. By the spring of 1790, all 13 states had ratified. There remained, however, the task of fulfilling the promise of amending the document. To that end, James Madison introduced into the first session of the First Congress a set of proposals, 12 of which were approved by Congress; 10 of these were ratified by the states and went into effect in 1791. But with only a few exceptions, these bore no relationship to the criticisms made in the state conventions. On what, then, did Madison base them? Probably on the Virginia Declaration of Rights, written by George Mason and Madison, and unanimously approved by the Virginia legislature in 1776. These amendments, which no one called a Bill of Rights as late as 1792, did not limit the power of state governments over citizens, only the power of the federal government. Later, the Fourteenth Amendment, as interpreted by the Supreme Court, extended many of the guarantees of the Bill of Rights to cover state governmental action.

The Constitution and Slavery

Though slaves amounted to one-third of the population of the five Southern states, nowhere in the Constitution can one find the word *slave* or *slavery.*

To some, the failure of the Constitution to address the question of slavery was a great betrayal of the promise of the Declaration of Independence that "all men are created

TABLE 2.2 | The Bill of Rights

The First Ten Amendments to the Constitution Grouped by Topic and Purpose	
Protections afforded citizens to participate in the political process	• **Amendment 1:** Freedom of religion, speech, press, and assembly; the right to petition the government.
Protections against arbitrary police and court action	• **Amendment 4:** No unreasonable searches or seizures.
	• **Amendment 5:** Grand jury indictment required to prosecute a person for a serious crime; no "double jeopardy" (being tried twice for the same offense); prohibition on forced self-incrimination no loss of life, liberty, or property without due process.
	• **Amendment 6:** Right to speedy, public, impartial trial with defense counsel and right to cross-examine witnesses.
	• **Amendment 7:** Jury trials in civil suits where value exceeds $20.
	• **Amendment 8:** No excessive bail or fines, no cruel and unusual punishments.
Protections of states' rights and unnamed rights of people	• **Amendment 9:** Unlisted rights are not necessarily denied.
	• **Amendment 10:** Powers not delegated to the United States or denied to states are reserved to the states.
Other Amendments	• **Amendment 2:** Right to bear arms.
	• **Amendment 3:** Troops may not be quartered in homes in peacetime.

Image 2.5 In 1852, abolitionist Frederick Douglass delivered a historic Independence Day speech calling for the end of slavery and the guarantee of the principles in the Declaration of Independence for all Americans.

equal." For the Constitution to be silent on the subject of slavery, and thereby to allow that odious practice to continue, was to convert, by implication, the wording of the Declaration to "all white men are created equal."

It is easy to accuse the signers of the Declaration and the Constitution of hypocrisy. They knew of slavery, many of them owned slaves, and yet they were silent. Indeed, British opponents of the independence movement took special delight in taunting the colonists about their complaints of being "enslaved" to the British Empire while ignoring the slavery in their very midst.

Increasingly, revolutionary leaders during this period spoke to this issue. Thomas Jefferson had tried to get a clause opposing the slave trade put into the Declaration of Independence. James Otis of Boston had attacked slavery and argued that black as well as white men should be free. As revolutionary fervor mounted, so did Northern criticism of slavery. The Massachusetts legislature and then the Continental Congress voted to end the slave trade; Delaware prohibited the importation of slaves; Pennsylvania voted to tax slavery out of existence; and Connecticut and Rhode Island decided that all slaves brought into those states would automatically become free.

Slavery continued unabated in the South, defended by some whites because they thought it right, by others because they found it useful. But even in the South there were opponents, though rarely conspicuous ones. George Mason, a Virginia slaveholder and a delegate to the convention, warned prophetically that "by an inevitable chain of causes and effects, providence punishes national sins [slavery] by national calamities."[19]

The blunt fact, however, was that any effort to use the Constitution to end slavery would have meant the end of the Constitution. The Southern states would never have signed a document that seriously interfered with slavery. Without the Southern states, the Articles of Confederation would have continued, which would have left each state entirely sovereign and thus entirely free of any prospective challenge to slavery.

Thus, the Framers compromised with slavery; the late political scientist Theodore Lowi called this their Greatest Compromise.[20] Slavery is dealt with in three places in the Constitution, though never by name. In determining the representation each state was to have in the House, "three-fifths of all other persons" (i.e., of slaves) are to be added to "the whole number of free persons."[21] The South originally wanted slaves to count fully even though, of course, none would be elected to the House; they settled for counting 60 percent of them. The Great (or Connecticut) Compromise favored smaller states, which were mostly Northern, by giving each state two senators; but the three-fifths compromise even more strongly favored the South's slaveholding states. For example, apportioned according to its free population, the Southern states would have had a combined total of 33 House seats rather than the 47 they claimed. The three-fifths compromise is the primary reason why Southern-born presidents, House leaders, and Supreme Court justices generally dominated antebellum American national government.[22]

The convention also agreed not to allow the new government—by law or even constitutional amendment—to prohibit the importation of slaves until 1808.[23] The South thus had 20 years in which it could acquire more slaves from abroad; after that, Congress was free (but not required) to end the importation. Finally, the Constitution guaranteed that if a slave escaped to a free state, then the slave would be returned by that state to "the party to whom . . . service or labour may be due."[24]

The unresolved issue of slavery was to prove the most explosive question of all. Allowing slavery to continue was a fateful decision, one that led to the worst social and political catastrophe in the nation's history—the Civil War. The Framers chose to sidestep the issue in order to create a union that, they hoped, would eventually be strong enough to deal with the problem when it could no longer be postponed. The legacy of that choice reverberates to this day.

2-4 Democracy and the Constitution: Post-Ratification Debates

The Framers were not saints or demigods. They were men with political opinions who also had economic interests and human failings. It would be a mistake to conclude that everything they did in 1787 was motivated by a disinterested commitment to the public good. But it would be an equally great mistake to think that what they did was nothing but an effort to line their pockets by producing a government that would serve their own narrow interests. As in almost all human endeavors, the Framers acted out of a mixture of motives. What is truly astonishing is that economic interests played only a modest role in their deliberations.

Economic Interests

Some of the Framers were wealthy; some were not. Some owned slaves; some had none. Some were creditors (having loaned money to the Continental Congress or to private parties); some were deeply in debt. For nearly a century, scholars have argued over just how important these personal interests were in shaping the provisions of the Constitution.

In 1913, historian Charles Beard published *An Economic Interpretation of the Constitution,* which argued that the better-off urban and commercial classes, especially those members who held the IOUs issued by the government to pay for the Revolutionary War, favored the new Constitution because they stood to benefit from it.[25] But in the 1950s, that view was challenged by historians who, after looking carefully at what the Framers owned or owed, concluded that one could not explain the Constitution exclusively or even largely in terms of the economic interests of those who wrote it.[26] Some of the richest delegates, such as Elbridge Gerry of Massachusetts and George Mason of Virginia, refused to sign the document, while many of its key backers—James Madison and James Wilson, for example—were men of modest means or heavy debts.

In the 1980s, a new group of scholars, primarily economists applying more advanced statistical techniques, found evidence that some economic considerations influenced how the Framers voted on some issues during the Philadelphia Convention. Interestingly, however, the economic position of the *states* from which they came had a greater effect on their votes than did their *own* monetary condition.[27]

We have already seen how delegates from small states fought to reduce the power of large states and how those from slave-owning states made certain that the Constitution would contain no provision that would threaten slavery.

But contrary to what Beard asserted, the economic interests of the Framers themselves did not dominate the convention. Some delegates owned a lot of public debt they had purchased for low prices. A strong national government of the sort envisaged by the Constitution was more likely than the weak Continental Congress to pay off this debt at face value, thus making the delegates who owned it much richer. Despite this, the ownership of public debt had no significant effect on how the Framers voted in Philadelphia. Nor did the big land speculators vote their interests. Some, such as George Washington and Robert Morris, favored the Constitution, whereas others, such as George Mason and William Blount, opposed it.[28]

In sum, the Framers tended to represent their states' interests on important matters. Since they were picked by the states to do so, this is exactly what one would expect. If they had not met in secret, perhaps they would have voted even more often as their constituents wanted. With the grave and enormous exception of slavery, the Framers usually did not vote their own respective economic interests.

At the popularly elected state ratifying conventions, economic factors played a larger role. Delegates who were merchants, who lived in cities, who owned large amounts of western land, who held government IOUs, and who did not own slaves were more likely to vote to ratify the new Constitution than delegates who were farmers, who did not own public debt, and who did own slaves.[29] There were plenty of exceptions, however. Small farmers dominated the conventions in some states where the vote to ratify was unanimous.

Though interests made a difference, they were not simply elite interests. In most states, the great majority of adult white males could vote for delegates to the ratifying conventions. This means that women and blacks were excluded from the debates, but by the standards of the time—standards that did not change for over a century—the ratification process was remarkably democratic.

The Constitution and Equality

Ideas counted for as much as interests. At stake were two views of the public good. One, espoused by the Federalists, was that a reasonable balance of liberty, order, and progress required a strong national government. The other, defended by the Antifederalists, was that liberty would not be secure in the hands of a powerful, distant government; freedom required decentralization.

Today that debate has a new focus. The defect of the Constitution, to some contemporary critics, is not that the government it created is too strong but that it is too weak. In particular, the national government is too weak to resist the pressures of special interests that reflect and perpetuate social inequality.

Income Tax Rates: Majoritarian, Client, or Entrepreneurial Politics?

As we noted in Chapter 1, in 1788, the proposed Constitution's chief architect, James Madison, argued that the federal government needed its own "power of taxation," whereas critics of the proposed Constitution, including Patrick Henry, opposed giving the federal government this power. Madison's view prevailed, but it was not until 1913, with the passage of the Sixteenth Amendment to the Constitution, that the federal government acquired "the power to lay and collect taxes on incomes."

The federal income tax system is progressive, meaning that tax rates rise with income levels. In 2020, there were seven federal "tax brackets": 10, 12, 22, 24, 32, 35, and 37 percent. A single person would pay 10 percent in federal income taxes on the first $9,700 earned that year, all the way up to 37 percent on every dollar above $510,301 earned that year. Thus, in 2020, 37 percent was the "top marginal tax rate."

Every year Congress debates proposals to change the federal income tax system. Depending on the proposal, the politics may be viewed as majoritarian, client, or entrepreneurial.

Majoritarian Politics: Some advocates for tax reform say the system needs to be simplified, with fewer income brackets, credits, and deductions. At the same time, they argue that everyone needs to pay taxes because everyone benefits from the federal government's activities, thereby presenting their case as majoritarian politics.

Client Politics: Some politicians argue for a "flat tax," which would be one tax rate for everybody, with no credits or deductions. Advocates say this system would be more efficient, with tax returns potentially being no larger than a postcard, and fair, as everyone would pay the same tax rate. From this perspective, the proposal is viewed as majoritarian politics, as everyone has the same tax percentage levied on their income. Critics, however, contend that a flat tax would be, in effect, client politics, as the wealthy would no longer be taxed on capital gains and other investments, and therefore would shoulder less of the overall tax burden than people who do not have such income.

Entrepreneurial Politics: Some advocates for tax reform say the system needs to be even more steeply progressive, with wealthier people paying a higher percentage of income tax. After all, today's top marginal federal income rate is low by historical standards. During World War I, the rate peaked at 77 percent. During World War II, it peaked at 91 percent. For most of the period from 1945 to 1985, it was above 50 percent. Advocates for higher tax rates contend that the top percent (one, two, or slightly more, depending on your view) of people who earn more should contribute more through taxes to help the vast majority who are not able to contribute as much, thereby arguing for entrepreneurial politics. (The proposal also could be viewed as interest-group politics, with wealthy people paying more, so people with less income may receive certain benefits and services, but it typically is presented as providing benefits for society at large.)

How elected officials, lobbyists, and voters discuss tax reform depends on how they think income tax rates need to be changed (if at all), and how they perceive the consequences, both the costs and the benefits.

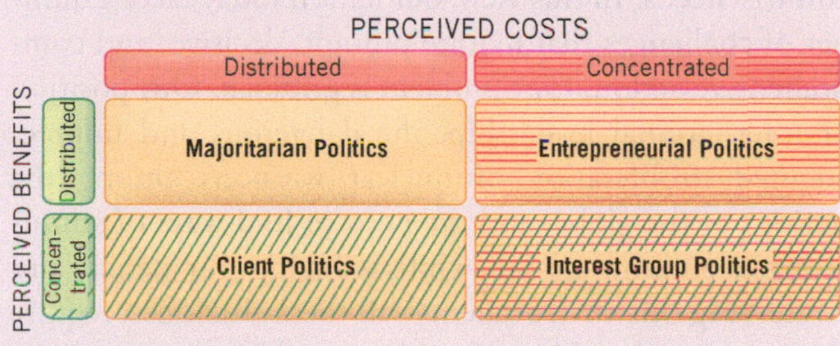

This criticism reveals how our understanding of the relationship between liberty and equality has changed since the Founding. To Jefferson and Madison, citizens naturally differed in their talents and qualities. What had to be guarded against was the use of governmental power to create unnatural and undesirable inequalities. This might happen, for example, if political power was concentrated in the hands of a few people (who could use that power to give themselves special privileges) or if it was used in ways that allowed some private parties to acquire exclusive charters and monopolies. To prevent the inequality that might result from having too strong a government, its powers must be kept strictly limited.

Today, some people think of inequality quite differently. To them, it is the natural social order—the marketplace and the acquisitive talents of people operating in that marketplace—that leads to undesirable inequalities, especially in economic power. The government should be powerful enough to restrain these natural tendencies and produce, by law, a greater degree of equality than society allows when left alone.

To the Framers, liberty and (political) equality were not in conflict; to some people today, these two principles are deeply in conflict. To the Framers, the task was to keep government so limited as to prevent it from creating the worst inequality—political privilege. To some modern observers, the task is to make government strong enough to reduce what they believe is the worst inequality— differences in wealth.

Constitutional Reform: Modern Views

Almost from the day it was ratified, the Constitution has been the object of debate over ways in which it might be improved. These debates have rarely involved average citizens, who tend to revere the document even if they cannot recall all of its details. Because of this deep and broad popular support, scholars and politicians have been wary of attacking the Constitution or suggesting many wholesale changes. But such attacks have occurred. During the 1980s—the decade in which we celebrated the bicentennial of its adoption—we heard a variety of suggestions for improving the Constitution, ranging from particular amendments to wholesale revisions. In general, today, as in the 18th century, critics typically align with one of two categories: those who think the federal government is too weak, and those who think it is too strong.

Reducing the Separation of Powers

To the first kind of critic, the chief difficulty with the Constitution is the separation of powers. By making every decision the uncertain outcome of the pulling and hauling between the president and Congress, the Constitution precludes the emergence—except perhaps in times of crisis—of the kind of effective national leadership the country needs. In this view, our nation today faces a number of challenges that require prompt, decisive, and comprehensive action. Our problem is gridlock. Our position of international leadership, the dangerous and unprecedented proliferation of nuclear weapons among the nations of the globe, and the need to find ways of stimulating economic growth while reducing our deficit and conserving our environment—all these situations require the president be able to formulate and carry out policies free of some of the pressures and delays from interest groups and members of Congress tied to local interests.

Not only would this increase in presidential authority make for better policies, these critics argue, it would also help voters hold presidents and their political parties accountable for their actions. As matters now stand, nobody in government can be held responsible for policies: Everyone takes the credit for successes and no one is willing to take the blame for failures. Typically, the president, who tends to be the major source of new programs, cannot get policies adopted by Congress without long delays and much bargaining, the result of which often is some watered-down compromise that neither the president nor Congress really likes but that each must settle for if anything is to be done at all.

Finally, critics of the separation of powers complain that the government agencies responsible for implementing a program are exposed to undue interference from legislators and special interests. In this view, the president is supposed to be in charge of the bureaucracy but in fact must share this authority with countless members of Congress and congressional committees.

Not all critics of the separation of powers agree with all these points, nor do they all agree on what should be done about the problems. But they all have in common a fear that the separation of powers makes the president too weak and insufficiently accountable. Their proposals for reducing the separation of powers include the following:

- Allow the president to appoint members of Congress to serve in the cabinet (the Constitution forbids members of Congress from holding any federal appointive office while in Congress).
- Allow the president to dissolve Congress and call for a special election (elections now can be held only on the schedule determined by the calendar).
- Allow Congress to require a president who has lost its confidence to face the country in a special election before his term would normally end.
- Require the presidential and congressional candidates to run as a team in each congressional district; thus a presidential candidate who carries a given district could be sure the congressional candidate of his party would also win in that district.
- Have the president serve a single six-year term instead of being eligible for up to two four-year terms; this would presumably free the president to lead without having to worry about reelection.
- Lengthen the terms of members of the House of Representatives from two to four years so that the entire House would stand for reelection at the same time as the president.[30]

Some of these proposals are offered by critics out of a desire to make the American system of government work more like the British parliamentary system, in which, as we will see in Chapters 13 and 14, the prime minister is the undisputed leader of the majority in the British Parliament. The parliamentary system is the major alternative in the world today to the American separation-of-powers system.

Both the diagnoses and the remedies proposed by these critics of the separation of powers have been challenged. Many defenders of our present constitutional system believe that nations, such as the United Kingdom, with a different, more unified political system have done no better than the United States in dealing with the problems of economic growth, national security, and environmental protection. Moreover, they argue, close congressional scrutiny of presidential proposals has improved these policies more often than it has weakened them. Finally, congressional "interference" in the work of government agencies is a good way of ensuring that the average citizen can fight back against the bureaucracy; without that so-called interference, citizens and interest groups might be helpless before big and powerful agencies.

Each of the specific proposals, defenders of the present constitutional system argue, would either make matters worse or have, at best, uncertain effects. Adding a few members of Congress to the president's cabinet would not provide much help in getting his program through Congress; there are 535 senators and representatives, and probably only about half a dozen would be in the cabinet. Giving either the president or Congress the power to call a special election in between the regular elections (every two or four years) would cause needless confusion and great expense; the country would live under the threat of being in a perpetual political campaign with even weaker political parties. Linking the fate of the president and congressional candidates by having them run as a team in each district would reduce the stabilizing and moderating effect of having them elected separately. A Republican presidential candidate who wins in the new system would have a Republican majority in the House; a Democratic candidate winner would have a Democratic majority. We might as a result expect dramatic changes in policy as the political pendulum swung back and forth. Giving presidents a single six-year term would indeed free them from the need to worry about reelection, but it is precisely that worry that keeps presidents reasonably concerned about what the American people want.

Limiting the National Government

The second kind of critic of the Constitution thinks the government does too much, not too little. Though the separation of powers at one time may have slowed the growth of government and moderated the policies it adopted, in the past few decades government has grown helter-skelter. The problem, these critics argue, is not that democracy is a bad idea but that democracy can produce bad—or at least unintended—results if the government caters to the special-interest claims of the citizens rather than to their long-term values.

To see how these unintended results might occur, imagine a situation in which every citizen thinks the government grows too big, taxes too heavily, and spends too much. Each citizen wants the government made smaller by reducing the benefits other people get—but not by reducing their own benefits. In fact, such citizens may even be willing to see their own benefits cut, provided everyone else's benefits are cut as well, and by a like amount.

But the political system attends to individual wants, not general preferences. It gives aid to farmers, contracts to industry, grants to professors, pensions to older adults, and loans to students. As someone once said, the government is like an adding machine: During elections, candidates campaign by promising to do more for whatever group is dissatisfied with what the incumbents are doing for it. As a result, most elections bring to office men and women committed to doing more for somebody. The grand total of all these additions is more for everybody. Few politicians have an incentive to do less for anybody.

line-item veto *An executive's ability to block a particular provision in a bill passed by the legislature.*

To remedy this state of affairs, these critics suggest various mechanisms, but principally a constitutional amendment that would either set a limit on the amount of money the government could collect in taxes each year or require that each year the government have a balanced budget (i.e., not spend more than it takes in in taxes), or both. In some versions of these plans, an extraordinary majority (say, 60 percent) of Congress could override these limits, and the limits would not apply in wartime.

The effect of such amendments, the proponents claim, would be to force Congress and the president to look at the big picture—the grand total of what they are spending—rather than just to operate the adding machine by pushing the "add" button over and over again. If they could spend only so much during a given year, they would have to allocate what they spend among all rival claimants. For example, if more money were to be spent on the poor, less could then be spent on the military, or vice versa.

Some critics of an overly powerful federal government think these amendments will not be passed or may prove unworkable; instead, they favor enhancing the president's power to block spending with a **line-item veto**. Most state governors can veto a particular part of a bill and approve the rest using a line-item veto. The theory is that such a veto would better equip the president to stop unwarranted spending without vetoing the other provisions of a bill. In 1996, President Bill Clinton signed the Line Item Veto Act, passed by the 104th Congress. But despite its name, the new law did not give the president full line-item veto power (only a change in the Constitution could confer that power). Instead, the law gave the president authority to selectively eliminate individual items in large appropriations bills, expansions in certain income-transfer programs, and tax breaks (giving the president what budget experts call *enhanced rescission authority*). But it also left Congress free to craft bills in ways that would give the president few opportunities to veto (or *rescind*) favored items. For example, Congress could still force the president to accept or reject an entire appropriations bill simply by tagging on this sentence: "Appropriations provided under this act (or title or section) shall not be subject to the provisions of the Line Item Veto Act." In *Clinton et al. v. New York*

Constitutional Connections | Women and the Constitution

Women were mentioned nowhere in the Constitution when it was written in 1787. Moreover, Article I, which set forth the provisions for electing members of the House of Representatives, granted the vote to those people who were allowed to vote for members of the lower house of the legislature in the states in which they resided. In no state at the time could women participate in those elections. In no state could they vote in any elections or hold any offices. Furthermore, wherever the Constitution uses a pronoun, it uses the masculine form—*he* or *him*.

Wherever the Constitution or the Bill of Rights defines a right that people are to have, it either grants that right to "persons" or "citizens," not to "men," or it makes no mention at all of people or gender. For example:

- "The *citizens* of each State shall be entitled to all privileges and immunities of citizens of the several States."

  [Art. I, sec. 9]

- "No *person* shall be convicted of treason unless on the testimony of two witnesses to the same overt act, or on confession in open court."

  [Art. III, sec. 3]

- "No bill of attainder or ex post facto law shall be passed."

  [Art. I, sec. 9]

- "The right of the *people* to be secure in their persons, houses, papers, and effects, against unreasonable searches and seizures, shall not be violated."

  [Amend. IV]

- "No *person* shall be held to answer for a capital, or otherwise infamous crime, unless on presentment or indictment of a grand jury … nor shall any *person* be subject for the same offense to be twice put in jeopardy of life or limb; … nor be deprived of life, liberty, or property, without due process of law."

  [Amend. V]

- "In all criminal prosecutions the *accused* shall enjoy the right to a speedy and public trial, by an impartial jury."

  [Amend. VI]

Moreover, when the qualifications for elective office are stated, the word *person*, not *man*, is used.

- "No *person* shall be a Representative who shall not have attained to the age of twenty-five years."

  [Art. I, sec. 2]

- "No *person* shall be a Senator who shall not have attained to the age of thirty years."

  [Art. I, sec. 3]

- "No *person* except a natural born citizen … shall be eligible to the office of President; neither shall any *person* be eligible to that office who shall not have attained to the age of thirty-five years."

  [Art. II, sec. 1]

In places, the Constitution and the Bill of Rights used the pronoun *he*, but always in the context of referring back to *a person* or *citizen*. At the time, and until quite recently, the male pronoun was often used in legal documents to refer generically to both men and women.

Thus, though the Constitution did not give women the right to vote until the Nineteenth Amendment was ratified in 1920, it did use language that extended fundamental rights, and access to office, to women and men equally.

Of course, what the Constitution permitted did not necessarily occur. State and local laws denied women rights that in principle they ought to have enjoyed. Except for a brief period in New Jersey, no women voted in statewide elections until, in 1869, they were given the right to cast ballots in territorial elections in Wyoming.

When women were first elected to Congress, there was no need to change the Constitution; nothing in it restricted officeholding to men.

- When women were given the right to vote by constitutional amendment, it was not necessary to amend any existing language in the Constitution because nothing in the Constitution itself denied women the right to vote; the amendment simply added a new right: "The right of citizens of the United States to vote shall not be denied or abridged by the United States or any state on account of sex."

  [Amend. XIX]

Source: Adapted from Robert Goldwin, "Why Blacks, Women and Jews Are Not Mentioned in the Constitution," *Commentary* (May 1987): 28–33.

et al. (1998), the Supreme Court struck down the 1996 law, holding six to three that the Constitution does not allow the president to cancel specific items in tax and spending legislation. Clinton's successor, President George W. Bush, championed the line-item veto, but to no avail; when asked about the line-item veto in early 2009, President Barack Obama's press secretary, Robert Gibbs, quipped that the new president would "love to take that for a test drive."

Finally, some critics of a powerful government feel that the real problem arises not from an excess of "adding-machine" democracy but from the growth in the power of the federal courts, as described in Chapter 16. These critics would like to devise a set of laws or constitutional amendments that would narrow the authority of federal courts.

The opponents of these suggestions argue that constitutional amendments to restrict the level of taxes or to require a balanced budget are unworkable, even assuming—which they do not—that a smaller government is desirable. There is no precise, agreed-upon way to measure how much the government spends or to predict in advance how much it will receive in taxes during the year; thus, defining and enforcing a "balanced budget" is no easy matter. Since the government can always borrow money, it might easily evade any spending limits. It has also shown great ingenuity in spending money in ways that never appear as part of the regular budget.

The line-item veto may or may not be a good idea. Unless the Constitution is amended to permit it, future presidents will have to do without it. The states, where some governors have long had the veto, are quite different from the federal government in power and responsibilities. Whether a line-item veto would work as well in Washington, DC, as it does in many state capitals is something that we may simply never know.

Finally, proposals to curtail judicial power are thinly veiled attacks, the opponents argue, on the ability of the courts to protect essential citizens' rights. If Congress and the people do not like the way the Supreme Court has interpreted the Constitution, they can always amend the Constitution to change a specific ruling; there is no need to adopt some across-the-board limitation on court powers.

Who Is Right?

Some of the arguments of these two sets of critics of the Constitution may strike you as plausible or even entirely convincing. Whatever you may ultimately decide, make no decision now. One cannot make or remake a constitution based entirely on abstract reasoning or unproven factual arguments. Even when the Constitution was first written in 1787, it was not an exercise in abstract philosophy but rather an effort to solve pressing, practical problems in light of a theory of human nature, the lessons of past experience, and a close consideration of how governments in other countries and at other times had worked.

Just because the Constitution is more than 200 years old does not mean it is out of date. The crucial questions are these: How well has it worked over the long sweep of American history? How well has it worked compared with the constitutions of other democratic nations?

The only way to answer these questions is to study American government closely—with special attention to its historical evolution and to the practices of other nations. That is what this book is about. Of course, even after close study, people will still disagree about whether our system should be changed. People want different things and evaluate human experience according to different beliefs. But if we first understand how, in fact, the government works and why it has produced the policies it has, we can then argue more intelligently about how best to achieve our wants and give expression to our beliefs.

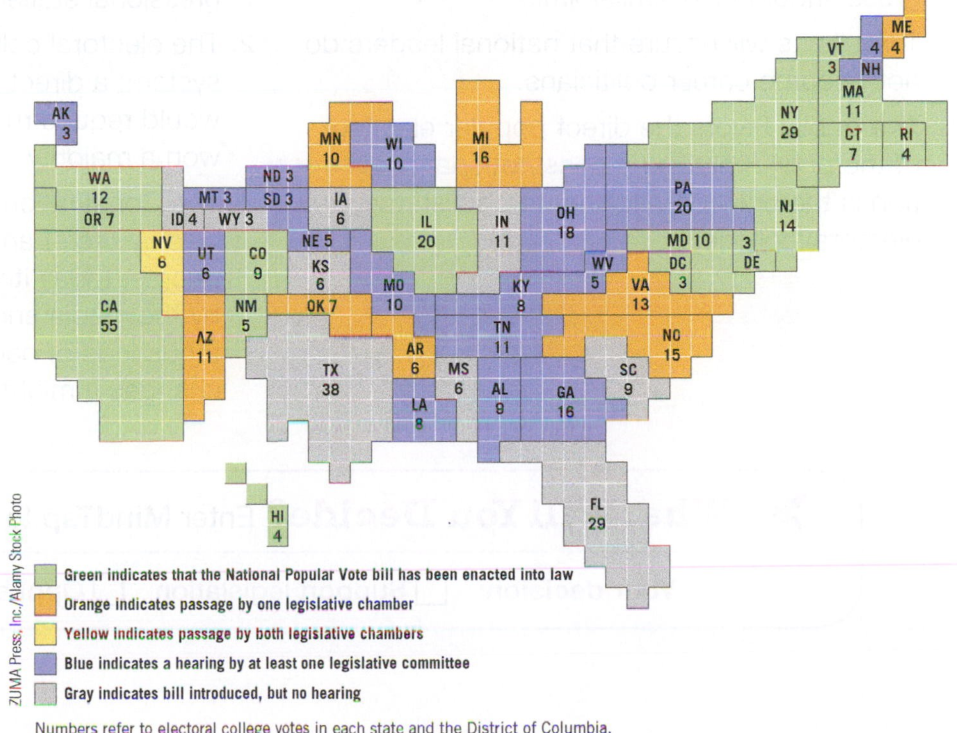

ZUMA Press, Inc./Alamy Stock Photo

Image 2.6 The National Popular Vote organization proposes effectively replacing the electoral college without abolishing it by having all states award their electoral college votes to the winner of the popular vote. In recent years, it has steadily gained support in states—as of the summer of 2020, 15 states and the District of Columbia had approved the plan. (See "How Things Work: The Electoral College" in Chapter 14, pp. 346, and www.nationalpopularvote.com.)

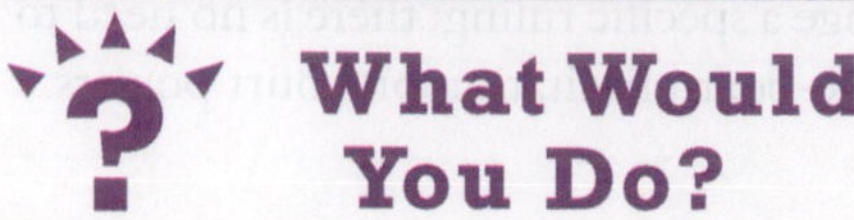

Should Pennsylvania Back Proposal for Constitutional Convention?

To: *Brian Arjun, Pennsylvania state senate majority leader*
From: *Amaia Grace, chief of staff*
Subject: *Proposal for a new constitutional convention*

In the 1990s, several states approved term limits for their members of Congress, but the Supreme Court ruled in 1995 that states do not have this authority. Now term-limit advocates are pursuing a broader strategy, calling for states to approve legislation that would require Congress to convene a special convention to consider several amendment proposals. Recommendations include enacting term limits for members of Congress and abolishing the electoral college to permit the direct popular election of the president. The Pennsylvania House of Representatives passed such a bill last week, and several senators in your party have declared their support.

To Consider:

Yesterday Pennsylvania's House of Representatives approved a proposal for a constitutional convention, and now the proposal goes to the State Senate. The Constitution states that Congress shall hold a convention for proposing amendments at the request of two-thirds of the state legislatures, but it has never happened in U.S. history. Pennsylvania could become the twenty-eighth state to endorse the proposal, and then only six more states would have to approve for Congress to take action.

Arguments for:

1. The Twenty-Second Amendment restricts presidents to two terms, so members of Congress should face similar limits.
2. Term limits will ensure that national leaders do not become career politicians.
3. The public favors the direct popular election of the president, and a constitutional convention is the only realistic way to abolish the electoral college.

Arguments against:

1. Limiting members of Congress to two terms would increase the power of lobbyists, congressional staffers, and administrative officials.
2. The electoral college encourages a two-party system; a direct popular vote for the president would require runoff elections if no candidate won a majority.
3. The Constitutional Convention of 1787 was held in secret and involved only a few dozen people; today it would be heavily covered by the media and involve hundreds, perhaps thousands of people. No one knows what changes it might make.

What Will You Decide? Enter **MindTap** to make your choice.

Your decision: ☐ Support legislation ☐ Oppose legislation

Learning Objectives

2-1 Explain how evolving debates about liberty led from the Revolutionary War to the Constitutional Convention.

The 13 colonies declared independence from Great Britain to protect their liberty, that is, their freedom to pursue their interests without undue and unfair interference from the monarch. After the Revolutionary War, the Articles of Confederation established a national government with limited powers in the new republic. But those powers did not ensure sufficient authority for governmental action, so the Constitutional Convention was called to strengthen the national political system while protecting states' rights and individual liberty.

2-2 Discuss the major proposals for and compromise over representation in the Constitutional Convention.

The delegates to the Constitutional Convention debated two major plans over representation in the national legislature. The Virginia Plan proposed allocating seats based on population, whereas the New Jersey Plan proposed allocating equal seats to each state. The Connecticut Compromise created a bicameral legislature with seats allocated by population in one chamber (House) and two seats given to each state in the other chamber (Senate).

2-3 Summarize the key issues presented by Federalists and Antifederalists in ratification debates for the Constitution.

The Federalists argued for a strong national government that would control factions, limit public participation in governance primarily to voting, and empower elected officials to decide which policies would be in the public interest. The Antifederalists were concerned about giving too much power to the national government and favored increased political participation in state and local governance, as well as a Bill of Rights to ensure that the national government did not encroach upon individual rights.

2-4 Discuss continuing debates about democracy and the Constitution.

From the time the Constitution was drafted, people have debated how effectively it promotes democratic governance. In the twenty-first century, critics typically have two overarching, and opposing, perspectives: the American political system does too little, or the system does too much. Some critics argue for reducing the separation of powers in the American political structure to make the government more efficient and effective. Other critics say the federal government needs to reevaluate priorities and sharply reduce spending to focus only on policies that clearly are in the national interest.

To Learn More

To find historical and legal documents: **http://teachingamericanhistory.org**

National Constitution Center: **https://constitutioncenter.org**

Congress: **www.congress.gov**

To look at court cases about the Constitution: Cornell University: **www.law.cornell.edu/supct**

Bailyn, Bernard. *The Ideological Origins of the American Revolution*. Cambridge, MA: Harvard University Press, 1967. A brilliant account of how the American colonists formed and justified the idea of independence.

Becker, Carl L. *The Declaration of Independence*. New York: Vintage, 1942. The classic account of the meaning of the Declaration.

Federalist papers. By Alexander Hamilton, James Madison, and John Jay. The definitive edition, edited by Jacob E. Cooke, was published in Middletown, CT, in 1961, by the Wesleyan University Press.

Maier, Pauline. *Ratification: The People Debate the Constitution*, 1787–1788. New York: Simon and Schuster, 2010. Not only is this a marvelous study of ratification, but it also is virtually the only one in existence. A splendid, comprehensive account.

McDonald, Forrest. *Novus Ordo Seclorum*. Lawrence: University of Kansas Press, 1985. A careful study of the intellectual origins of the Constitution. The Latin title means "New World Order," which is what the Framers hoped they were creating.

Sheldon, Garrett W. *The Political Philosophy of James Madison*. Baltimore: Johns Hopkins University

Press, 2001. Masterful account of Madison's political thought and its roots in classical republicanism and Christianity.

Storing, Herbert J. *What the Anti-Federalists Were For*. Chicago: University of Chicago Press, 1981. Close analysis of the political views of those opposed to the ratification of the Constitution.

Sundquist, James L. *Constitutional Reform and Effective Government*. Rev. ed. Washington, DC: Brookings Institution Press, 1992. Systematic evaluation of proposals to incorporate features of parliamentary democracy in the American political system.

Wood, Gordon S. *The Creation of the American Republic*. Chapel Hill: University of North Carolina Press, 1969. A detailed study of American political thought before the Philadelphia Convention.

__________. *The Radicalism of the American Revolution*. New York: Knopf, 1992. Magisterial study of the nature and effects of the American Revolution and the relationship between the socially radical Revolution and the Constitution.

CHAPTER 3

Federalism

Learning Objectives

3-1 Discuss the historical origins of federalism, and explain how it has evolved over time.

3-2 Summarize the pros and cons of federalism in the United States.

3-3 Describe how funding underlies federal–state interactions and how this relationship has changed over time.

3-4 Discuss whether the devolution of programs to the states beginning in the 1980s really constitutes a revolution in federal–state relations.

« Then When the Framers drafted the Constitution, the Antifederalists opposed it primarily on the grounds that it gave too much power to national government. The Antifederalists recognized the limitations of the Articles of Confederation, but they feared that the Constitution sacrificed liberty and civic responsibility with its expansion of the power of the national government.

*** Now** The Federalists prevailed over the Antifederalists with the ratification of the Constitution. Amended only 27 times in more than 225 years, the Constitution is still the law of the land today. However, much as the Antifederalists predicted, the federal government has taken on responsibilities that traditionally were the province of state governments, such as social welfare policy, education, health care, and a minimum wage. States have some flexibility in implementing policies, but the national government sets the direction in many more policy areas today than it did originally; and, as the Antifederalists feared, we now have a large standing army and powerful federal courts.

These changes between then and now do not mean that the Constitution was wrong. (If we were forced to take sides, we would have sided with the Federalists—would you?) But there is no denying that the federal government has grown far beyond anything that even the most ardent Federalists had envisioned. Much of that growth has occurred in just the past half-century or so. In recent years, the federal government has spent roughly $4 trillion every year. Adjusted for inflation, this is more than five times what it spent in 1960.

But that is only about half of the story. Over the past half-century, state and local government spending has risen steeply, too. Today, state and local governments spend more than $3 billion per year, every year. Adjusted for inflation, that was more than six times what they spent in 1960.

No less telling has been the growth in the number of government employees. As we can see in Figure 3.1, the number of government employees has expanded dramatically since 1960. But nearly all of that growth has come at the state and local level. The number of federal civilian (non-military) employees has remained at approximately 2 million individuals since President Eisenhower left office in 1960. During this time, the country's population increased considerably, so the fraction of the workforce

Figure 3.1 Government Employment, 1960–2018

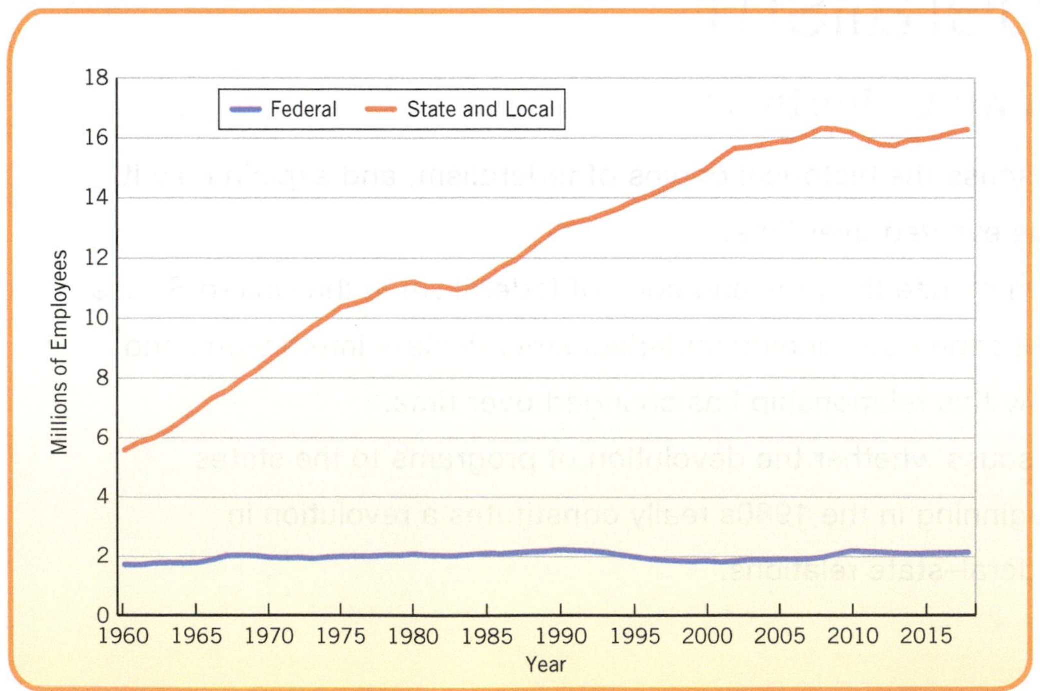

Source: U.S. Bureau of Economic Analysis. Data on federal government employment comes from the series "Full-time equivalent employees: Federal general government: Civilian [B4379C0A173NBEA]"; data on state and local employment comes from the series "Full-time equivalent employees: State and local government [A4382C0A173NBEA]," both retreived from FRED, Federal Reserve Bank of St. Louis, January 2020.

employed directly by the federal government has actually *shrunk* over time.[1] But the number employed by state and local governments has skyrocketed to roughly 16 million in 2018, nearly three times what they employed in 1960. Today, most of those employed by government work in state capitals and city halls, not Washington, D.C.

Back when the Federalists and the Antifederalists debated the Constitution, neither side anticipated that what today we call "big government" would encompass all three levels of government: federal, state, and local. Then, they fussed and fought over how vast the federal government might someday become. Now the reality is that, apart from military affairs and international diplomacy, most "national" laws, policies, and programs are shaped, administered, or funded in whole or in part through a complex, and often contentious, system of federal–state relations.

3-1 Why Federalism Matters

The heated controversies that surrounded the enactment of the federal health reform law in 2010, and the ensuing legal challenges to that law, are in large part battles over how the federal government should relate to the states. To be sure, not all of the debate over Obamacare (also known as the Patient Protection and Affordable Care Act) centers on federal–state relations: For example, a contentious debate ensued over the individual mandate, which requires everyone to have health insurance or pay a penalty. But much of the ongoing controversy over the law centers on federal–state relations. For instance, states had to expand Medicaid or risk losing funding for the program. (Medicaid assists low-income women, children, families, and the disabled in obtaining medical care; we discuss this program more in Chapter 17.)

Many federal–state conflicts have ended up before the U.S. Supreme Court (for a short list, see the Landmark Cases feature on page 59), and this one did, too. In *National Federation of Business v. Sebelius* (2012), the Court, by a five-to-four majority led by Chief Justice John Roberts, held that the individual mandate was constitutional because it could be construed as a "tax," and it is clearly within the power of Congress to levy taxes. But the Court also held the law's Medicaid expansion—which forced states to expand Medicaid or lose *all* of their Medicaid funding—was overly coercive and unconstitutional. Since then, some states have chosen to expand Medicaid under the Affordable Care Act, whereas others have not.

In 2015, the Supreme Court once again took up how the states and federal government relate to one another under the Affordable Care Act. In *King v. Burwell* (2015), the court ruled on whether the federal government could issue subsidies only for health insurance purchased on state-run exchanges, or whether it could also provide them for the federally run exchange as well. Because all citizens must have health insurance due to the individual mandate, the federal government authorized states to set up exchanges where citizens could go to purchase health insurance. Furthermore, the federal government provides subsidies to individuals purchasing insurance through these exchanges (to make insurance more affordable for lower- and middle-income Americans). As of 2020, twelve states and the District of Columbia have set up their own exchanges, but for citizens in the other thirty-eight states, the federal government fully or partially runs an exchange for them.[2]

federalism *Government authority shared by national and local governments.*

sovereignty *The ultimate political author in a system.*

unitary system *A system of government where sovereignty is fully vested in the national government, not the states.*

As written, the Affordable Care Act only allows the government to provide subsidies to those purchasing insurance through the state-level exchanges, and the plaintiffs in the case argued that providing the subsidies to those using the federally run exchanges is illegal. The Court decided that the government could provide subsidies to those using either type of exchange.

These are just two of the most recent of a series of cases stretching back to the start of the republic in which the Court, in effect, refereed disputes relating to "federalism." **Federalism** can be defined as a political system in which the national government shares power with local governments (state governments in the case of the United States, but other subnational governments in the case of federal systems including Australia, India, and Switzerland). Constitutionally, in America's federal system, state governments have a specially protected existence and the authority to make final decisions over many governmental activities. Even today, despite considerable expansion of federal authority over time, state and local governments are not mere junior partners in deciding important public policy matters. The national government can pass laws to protect the environment, store nuclear waste, expand low-income housing, guarantee the right to an abortion, provide special services for the handicapped, or toughen public-school graduation standards. But whether and how such federal laws are followed or funded often involves decisions by diverse state and local government officials, both elected and appointed. Policy passed in Washington, D.C., must be implemented in state capitals—and local governments—across the country.

The study of federalism involves the study of **sovereignty**, the supreme (ultimate) political authority. A sovereign government is one that is legally and politically independent of any other government. A system can be either unitary, confederal, or federal. A **unitary system** is one in which sovereignty is wholly in the hands of the national government, so

confederation or confederal system *A system of government where state governments are sovereign, and the national government can do only what the states permit.*

federal system *A system of government where the national and state governments share sovereignty.*

that the states and localities are dependent on its will. An example of a unitary system would be a nation like France: The central government makes all formal decisions, and local decisions are effectively simply enacting central government mandates. A **confederation or confederal system** is one in which the states are sovereign and the national government is allowed to do only that which the states permit. This was the case under the Articles of Confederation. A **federal system** is one in which sovereignty is shared, so that in some matters the national government is supreme and in other matters the states are supreme. As we will see throughout the chapter, that is true of the United States, though what comprises the spheres of federal and state supremacy have shifted over time. Figure 3.2 shows the differences between unitary, confederal, and federal systems.

The Founding Fathers often took *confederal* and *federal* to mean much the same thing. Rather than establishing a government in which sovereign authority was clearly divided between the national and state governments, they saw themselves as creating a government that combined some characteristics of a unitary regime with some of a confederal one. Or, as James Madison expressed the idea in *Federalist* No. 39, the Constitution "is, in strictness, neither a national nor a federal Constitution, but a composition of both." Where sovereignty is located in this system is a matter that the Founders did not clearly answer.

In this text, a federal regime is defined in the simplest possible terms—as one in which local units of government have a specially protected existence and can make some final decisions over some governmental activities.

Federalism or federal–state relations may seem like an arcane or boring subject until you realize that it is behind many things that matter to many people: how much you pay in certain taxes, whether you can drive faster than 55 miles per hour on certain roadways, whether or where you can buy liquor, how strictly pollution is regulated, how much money gets spent on schools, whether all or most children have health insurance coverage, and much more. For instance, as summarized in the Constitutional Connections feature on page 53, federalism is at the heart of many of the controversies surrounding the Affordable Care Act. By the same token, federalism affects almost every aspect of crime and punishment in America: Persons convicted of murder are subject to the death penalty in some states but not in others; penalties for illegal drug sales vary widely from state to state; and, as you can explore in the Policy Dynamics: Inside/Outside the Box on page 71, an unresolved conflict exists between national law and certain states' laws regarding the use of marijuana. Perhaps most importantly, federalism is critical to how certain civil liberties (Chapter 5) and civil rights (Chapter 6) are defined and protected: for instance, some state constitutions mention God, and some state laws specifically prohibit funding for religious schools.

Federalism matters, but how it matters has changed over time. In 1908, Woodrow Wilson observed that the relationship between the national government and the states "is the cardinal question of our constitutional system," a question that cannot be settled by "one generation, because it is a question of growth, and every successive stage of our political and economic development gives it a new aspect, makes it a new question."[3]

Figure 3.2 **Lines of Power in Three Systems of Government**

UNITARY SYSTEM

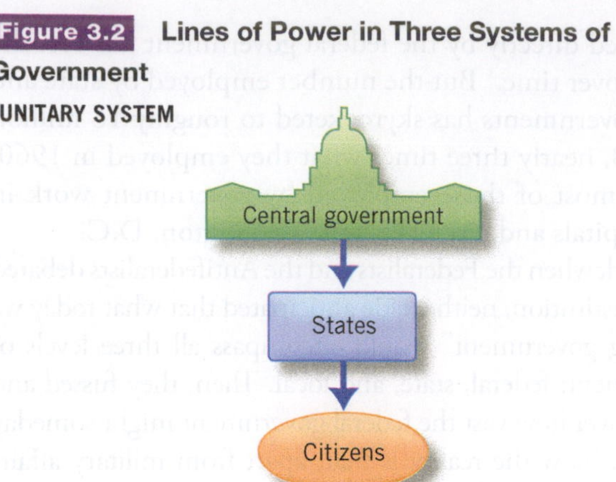

Power centralized.
State or regional governments derive authority from central government. Examples: the United Kingdom, France.

FEDERAL SYSTEM

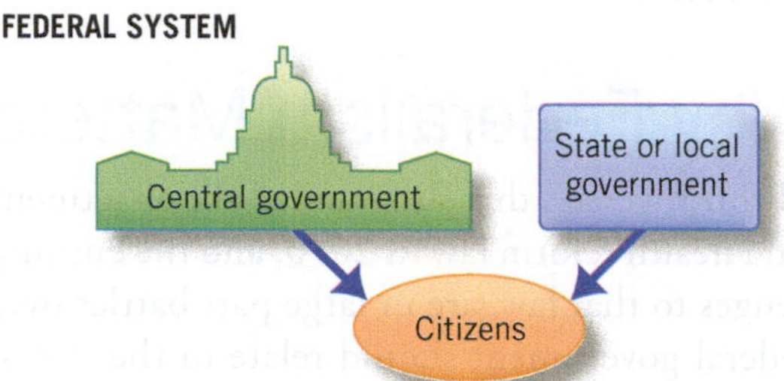

Power divided between central and state or local governments.
Both the government and constituent governments act directly upon the citizens.
Both must agree to constitutional change.
Examples: Canada, the United States since adoption of Constitution.

CONFEDERAL SYSTEM (or CONFEDERATION)

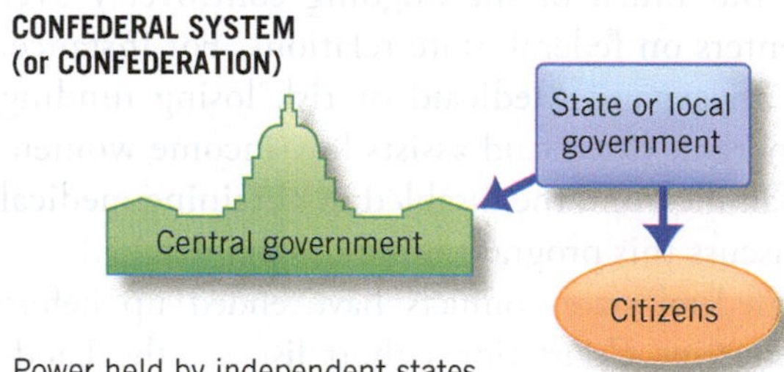

Power held by independent states.
Central government is a creature of the constituent governments.
Example: the United States under the Articles of Confederation.

Constitutional Connections | Obamacare, the Individual Mandate, and Medicaid Expansion

The Patient Protection and Affordable Care Act (Obamacare) is one of the most fundamental transformations of American health care in recent decades. But it is also one of the most controversial policies in recent years and has generated several key constitutional rulings from the Supreme Court.

For example, in *National Federation of Business v. Sebelius* (2012), the Court ruled that Congress did not have the power to impose the individual mandate under the commerce clause, but did have that power under the Constitution's tax and spending clause (the first clause of Article 1, Section 8). Because Congress has the power to tax under the Constitution, the Court argued, it has the power to force people to buy insurance or pay a tax (the heart of the individual mandate).

In that same decision, however, the Court ruled that the federal government did not have the power to force states to expand Medicaid. Under Obamacare, the states had to expand Medicaid (the federal–state joint program to provide health care to the poor and disabled) or lose all of their Medicaid funds. The Court held this was not constitutional. The Court argued (based on previous decisions) that the same spending clause of the Constitution gives Congress the power to attach conditions to the receipt of federal funds. But it also held that such conditions must not be coercive, and it argued that this condition—expand Medicaid or lose all Medicaid funds—was coercive (and hence prohibited). The court did not, however, establish a clear standard for what constitutes coercive; it merely held that this law was coercive.

In *King v. Burwell* (2015), the Court held that citizens using both the state-level and the federally run exchanges were eligible to receive subsidies. While this ruling left the insurance subsidies in place, it did not settle the debate over the Affordable Care Act—far from it. And it's not just the courts that have debated the Affordable Care Act, so has Congress. In 2017, Congress passed the Tax Cut and Jobs Act, which reduced the penalty for noncompliance with the individual mandate to $0. While the law still requires individuals to purchase health insurance, there is no financial penalty for failing to do so. The debate over the Act, and how best to provide health care, will continue into the future, as we discuss in later chapters.

Since the adoption of the Constitution in 1787, the single most persistent source of political conflict has been the relations between the national and state governments. The political conflict over slavery, for example, was intensified because some state governments condoned or supported slavery, while others took action to discourage it. The proponents and opponents of slavery were thus given territorial power centers from which to carry on the dispute. Other issues, such as the regulation of business and the provision of social welfare programs, were in large part fought out, for well over a century, in terms of "national interests" versus "states' rights." While other nations, such as Great Britain, were debating the question of whether the national government *ought* to provide old-age pensions or regulate the railroads, the United States debated a different question—whether the national government *had the right* to do these things.

AP Images/Eric Risberg

Image 3.1 Prison systems and other aspects of the criminal justice system vary considerably from state to state. This is just one example of how federalism shapes public policy.

The Founding

The goal of the Founders seems clear: Federalism was one device whereby personal liberty was to be protected. (The separation of powers was another.) The Founders feared that placing final political authority in any one set of hands, even in the hands of persons popularly elected, would so concentrate power as to risk tyranny. But they had seen what happened when independent states tried to form a compact, as under the Articles of Confederation; what the states put together, they could also take apart. The alliance that existed among the states from 1776 to 1787 was a confederation, that is, a system of government in which the people create state governments, which in turn create and operate a national government (see Figure 3.2 on page 51). Since the national government in a confederation derives its powers from the states, it is dependent on their continued cooperation for its survival. By 1786, that cooperation was barely forthcoming.

A Bold, New Plan

A federation—or a "federal republic," as the Founders called it—derives its powers directly from the people, as do the state governments. As the Founders envisioned it, both levels of government, the national and the state, would have certain powers, but neither would have supreme authority over the other. James Madison, writing in *Federalist* No. 46, said that both the state and federal governments "are in fact but different agents and trustees of the people, constituted with different powers." In *Federalist* No. 28, Alexander Hamilton explained how he thought the system would work: The people could shift their support between state and federal levels of government as needed in order to keep the two in balance. "If their rights are invaded by either, they can make use of the other as the instrument of redress."

It was an entirely new plan, for which no historical precedent existed. Nobody came to the Philadelphia Convention with a clear idea of what a federal (as opposed to a unitary or a confederal) system would look like, and there was not much discussion at Philadelphia of how the system would work in practice. Few delegates then used the word *federalism* in the sense in which we now use it (it was originally used as a synonym for *confederation* and only later came to stand for something different).[4] The Constitution does not spell out the powers that the states are to have, and until the Tenth Amendment was added at the insistence of various states, it did not even include a clause saying (as did the amendment) that "the powers not delegated to the United States by the Constitution, nor prohibited by it to the states, are reserved to the states respectively, or to the people." The Founders assumed from the outset that the federal government would have only those powers given to it by the Constitution; the Tenth Amendment was an afterthought, added to make that assumption explicit and allay fears that something else was intended.[5]

The Tenth Amendment has rarely had much practical significance, however. From time to time, the Supreme Court has tried to interpret that amendment as putting certain state activities beyond the reach of the federal government, but usually the Court has later changed its mind and allowed Washington to regulate such matters. For example, while the Court initially ruled that the federal government could not regulate the hours worked by employees of a city-owned mass transit system, it later reversed course and decided that the federal government could do that. The Court reasoned that running such a transportation system was not one of the powers "reserved to the states," and hence could be regulated by the federal government.[6] But, as we explain later in this chapter, the Court has recently begun to give new life to the Tenth Amendment and the doctrine of state sovereignty.

Elastic Language

The need to reconcile the competing interests of various factions at the convention—large versus small states, southern versus northern states—was difficult enough without trying to spell out the exact relationship between the state and national governments. For example, Congress was given the power to regulate commerce "among the several states." The Philadelphia Convention would have gone on for four years rather than four months if the Founders had decided that it was necessary to describe, in clear language, how one was to tell where commerce *among* the states ended and commerce wholly *within* a single state began. The Supreme Court, as we shall see, devoted more than a century to that task before giving up.

Though some clauses bearing on federal–state relations were reasonably clear (see the How Things Work feature box on page 57), other clauses were quite vague. The Founders realized, correctly, that they could not make an exact and exhaustive list of everything the federal government was empowered to do—circumstances would change, and new exigencies would arise. Thus they added the following elastic language to Article I: Congress shall have the power to "make all laws which shall be necessary and proper for carrying into execution the foregoing powers."

The Founders themselves carried away from Philadelphia different views of what federalism meant. One view was championed by Hamilton. Since the people had created the national government, since the laws and treaties made pursuant to the Constitution were "the supreme law of the land" (Article VI), and since the most pressing needs were the development of a national economy and the conduct of foreign affairs, Hamilton thought that the national government was the superior and leading force in political affairs and that its powers ought to be broadly defined and liberally construed.

The other view, championed by Thomas Jefferson, was that the federal government, though important, was the product of an agreement among the states; and though "the people" were the ultimate sovereigns, the principal threat to their liberties was likely to come from the national government. (Madison, a strong supporter of national supremacy at the convention, later became a champion of states' rights.) Thus the powers of the federal government should be narrowly construed and strictly limited. As Madison put it in *Federalist* No. 45, in language that probably made Hamilton wince, "The powers delegated by the proposed Constitution to the federal government are few and defined. Those which are to remain in the State governments are numerous and indefinite."

Hamilton argued for national supremacy, Jefferson for states' rights. Though their differences were greater in theory than in practice (as we shall see in Chapter 14, Jefferson while president sometimes acted in a positively Hamiltonian manner), the differing interpretations they offered of the Constitution continue to shape political debate even today.

Stock Montage/Archive Photos/Getty Images

Image 3.2 Benjamin Franklin, Thomas Jefferson, Livingston Adams, and Roger Sherman writing the Declaration of Independence.

The Debate on the Meaning of Federalism

Since Hamilton and Jefferson fought over states' rights more than two centuries ago, this question of state versus federal supremacy has remained at the core of American politics. Indeed, the Civil War was fought, in part, over this question. That bloody conflict, however, only settled one part of the federalism question: the national government was supreme, its sovereignty derived directly from the people, and thus the states could not lawfully secede from the Union. Virtually every other aspect of the national-supremacy issue has continued to be contested throughout time. As we will see below, the Courts have generally given the federal government more power over time, but they have also recently begun to place some important restrictions on federal power as well.

The Supreme Court Speaks

As arbiter of what the Constitution means, the Supreme Court became the focal point of the debate over whether state or national power should reign supreme. In Chapter 16, we shall see in some detail how the Court made its decisions. For now it is enough to know that during the formative years of the new Republic, the Supreme Court was led by a staunch and brilliant advocate of Hamilton's position, Chief Justice John Marshall. In a series of decisions, he and the Court powerfully defended the national-supremacy view of the newly formed federal government.

The *Landmark Cases* feature box on page 59 lists some landmark cases in the history of federal–state relations. Perhaps the most important decision was in a case, seemingly trivial in its origins, that arose when James McCulloch, the cashier of the Baltimore branch of the Bank of the United States—which had been created by Congress—refused to pay a tax levied on that bank by the state of Maryland. He was hauled into state court and convicted of failing to pay the tax. In 1819, McCulloch appealed all the way to the Supreme Court in a case known as *McCulloch v. Maryland.* The Court, in a unanimous opinion, answered two questions in ways that expanded the powers of Congress and confirmed the supremacy of the federal government in the exercise of those powers.

The first question was whether Congress had the right to set up a bank, or any other corporation, since such a right is nowhere explicitly mentioned in the Constitution. Marshall said that, though the federal

"necessary and proper" clause *Section of the Constitution allowing Congress to pass all laws "necessary and proper" to its duties, and that has permitted Congress to exercise powers not specifically given to it (enumerated) by the Constitution.*

nullification *The doctrine that a state can declare null and void a federal law that, in the state's opinion, violates the Constitution.*

dual federalism *Doctrine holding that the national government is supreme in its sphere, the states are supreme in theirs, and the two spheres should be kept separate.*

government possessed only those powers enumerated in the Constitution, the "extent"—that is, the meaning—of those powers required interpretation. Though the word *bank* is not in that document, one finds there the power to manage money: to lay and collect taxes, issue a currency, and borrow funds. To carry out these powers, Congress may reasonably decide that chartering a national bank is "necessary and proper." Marshall's words were carefully chosen to endow the **"necessary and proper" clause** with the widest possible sweep:

> Let the end be legitimate, let it be within the scope of the Constitution, and all means which are appropriate, which are plainly adapted to that end, which are not prohibited, but consistent with the letter and spirit of the Constitution, are constitutional.[7]

The second question was whether a federal bank could lawfully be taxed by a state. To answer it, Marshall went back to first principles. The government of the United States was not established by the states, but by the people, and thus the federal government was supreme in the exercise of those powers conferred upon it. Having already concluded that chartering a bank was within the powers of Congress, Marshall then argued that the only way for such powers to be supreme was for their use to be immune from state challenge and for the products of their use to be protected against state destruction. Since "the power to tax involves the power to destroy," and since the power to destroy a federal agency would confer upon the states supremacy over the federal government, the states may not tax any federal instrument. Hence the Maryland law was unconstitutional.

McCulloch won, and so did the federal government. Half a century later, the Court decided that what was sauce for the goose was sauce for the gander. It held that just as state governments could not tax federal bonds, the federal government could not tax the interest people earn on state and municipal bonds. In 1988, the Supreme Court reversed course and decided that Congress was now free, if it wished, to tax the interest on such state and local bonds.[8] Municipal bonds, which for nearly a century were a tax-exempt investment protected (so their holders thought) by the Constitution, were now protected only by politics. So far, Congress hasn't tried to tax them.

Nullification

The Supreme Court can decide a case without settling the issue. The struggle over states' rights versus national supremacy continued to rage in Congress, during presidential elections, and ultimately on the battlefield. The issue came to center on the doctrine of **nullification**. When Congress passed laws (in 1798) to punish newspaper editors who published stories critical of the federal government, James Madison and Thomas Jefferson opposed the laws, suggesting (in statements known as the Virginia and Kentucky Resolutions) that the states had the right to "nullify" (i.e., declare null and void) a federal law that, in the states' opinion, violated the Constitution. The laws expired before the claim of nullification could be settled in the courts.

Later, John C. Calhoun of South Carolina revived the doctrine of nullification, first in opposition to a tariff enacted by the federal government and later in opposition to federal efforts to restrict slavery. Calhoun argued that if Washington attempted to ban slavery, the states had the right to declare such acts unconstitutional and thus null and void. This time the issue was settled—by war. The northern victory in the Civil War determined once and for all that the federal union is indissoluble and that states cannot declare acts of Congress unconstitutional, a view later confirmed by the Supreme Court.[9]

Dual to Cooperative Federalism

After the Civil War, the debate about the meaning of federalism focused on the interpretation of the commerce clause of the Constitution. Out of this debate emerged the doctrine of **dual federalism**, which held that though the national government was supreme in its sphere, the states were equally supreme in theirs, and that these two spheres of action should and could be kept separate. Applied to commerce, the concept of dual federalism implied that there were such things as *interstate* commerce, which Congress could regulate, and *intrastate* commerce, which only the states could regulate, and that the Court could determine which was which.

For a long period the Court tried to decide what was interstate commerce based on the kind of business that was conducted. Transporting things between states was obviously interstate commerce, and so subject to federal regulation. Thus federal laws affecting the interstate shipment of lottery tickets,[10] prostitutes,[11] liquor,[12] and harmful foods and drugs[13] were upheld. On the other hand, manufacturing,[14] insurance,[15] and farming[16] were in the

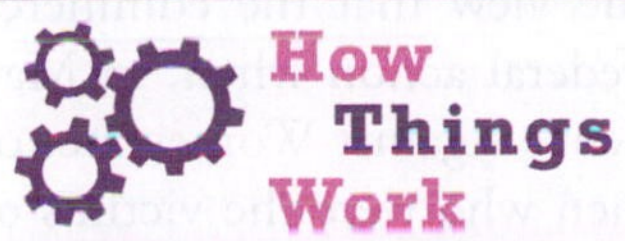

The States and the Constitution

The Framers made some attempt to define the relations between the states and the federal government and how the states were to relate to one another. The following points were made in the original Constitution—before the Bill of Rights was added.

Restrictions on Powers of the States

States may not make treaties with foreign nations, coin money, issue paper currency, grant titles of nobility, pass a bill of attainder or an ex post facto law, or, without the consent of Congress, levy any taxes on imports or exports, keep troops and ships in time of peace, or enter into an agreement with another state or with a foreign power.

[Art. I, sec. 10]

Guarantees by the Federal Government to the States

The national government guarantees to every state a "republican form of government" and protection against foreign invasion and (provided the states request it) protection against domestic insurrection.

[Art. IV, sec. 4]

An existing state will not be broken up into two or more states or merged with all or part of another state without that state's consent.

[Art. IV, sec. 3]

Congress may admit new states into the Union.

[Art. IV, sec. 3]

Taxes levied by Congress must be uniform throughout the United States: they may not be levied on some states but not others.

[Art. I, sec. 8]

The Constitution may not be amended to give states unequal representation in the Senate.

[Art. V]

Rules Governing How States Deal with Each Other

"Full faith and credit" shall be given by each state to the laws, records, and court decisions of other states. (For example, a civil case settled in the courts of one state cannot be retried in the courts of another.)

[Art. IV, sec. 1]

The citizens of each state shall have the "privileges and immunities" of the citizens of every other state. (No one is quite sure what this is supposed to mean.)

[Art. IV, sec. 2]

If a person charged with a crime by one state flees to another, that person is subject to extradition—that is, the governor of the state that finds the fugitive is obliged to return the person to the original state.

[Art. IV, sec. 2]

past considered *intra*state commerce, and so only the state governments were allowed to regulate them.

Such product-based distinctions turned out to be hard to sustain. For example, if you ship a case of whiskey from Kentucky to Kansas, how long is it in interstate commerce (and thus subject to federal law), and when does it enter intrastate commerce and become subject only to state law? For a while, the Court's answer was that the whiskey was in interstate commerce so long as it was in its "original package,"[17] but that only precipitated long quarrels as to what was the original package and how one is to treat things, like gas and grain, which may not be shipped in packages at all. And how could one distinguish between manufacturing and transportation when one company did both or when a single manufacturing corporation owned factories in different states? And if an insurance company sold policies to customers both inside and outside a given state, were there to be different laws regulating identical policies that happened to be purchased from the same company by persons in different states?

In time, the effort to find some clear principles that distinguished interstate from intrastate commerce was pretty much abandoned. Commerce was like a stream flowing through the country, drawing to itself contributions from thousands of scattered enterprises and depositing its products in millions of individual homes. The Court began to permit the federal government to regulate almost anything that affected this stream, so that by the 1940s not only had farming and manufacturing been redefined as part of interstate commerce,[18] but even the janitors and window washers in buildings that housed companies engaged in interstate commerce were now said to be part of that stream.[19]

More generally, over time, the power of the federal government expanded and intruded on areas once thought solely to be the province of the states. Today, unlike in the 19th century, it is more difficult to define many areas of clearly national or state dominance. The example of interstate commerce discussed above is one, but other areas, such as school policy and highways, also illustrate the point. For example, at one time, highways

cooperative federalism
Idea that the federal and state governments share power in many policy areas.

were the responsibility of state governments, but with the establishment of the interstate highway system in the 1950s, the federal government took on a large role in transportation policy. Likewise, while education has long been considered primarily a state and local government concern, over time the federal government has become more involved through the Elementary and Secondary Education Act, the No Child Left Behind Act, the Every Student Succeeds Act, and President Barack Obama's Race to the Top initiative. Today, some speak of a program of **cooperative federalism**, where the national and state governments share responsibilities in most policy areas. If dual federalism is a layer cake with the state and federal governments having separate spheres of sovereignty (hence separate layers), cooperative federalism is a marble cake where the two blend together. Table 3.1 shows areas of state power, areas of federal power, and areas where the states and federal government share powers in the contemporary United States.

State Sovereignty

It would be a mistake to think that the doctrine of dual federalism is entirely dead, however. Until recently, Congress—provided that it had a good reason—could pass a law regulating almost any kind of economic activity anywhere in the country, and the Supreme Court would call it constitutional. But in *United States v. Lopez* (1995), the Court held that Congress had exceeded its commerce clause power by prohibiting guns in a school zone. This marked the first in a series of decisions in which the court began to reassert a greater role for state (as opposed to national) power.

The Court reaffirmed the view that the commerce clause does not justify any federal action when, in May 2000, it overturned the Violence Against Women Act of 1994. This law allowed women who were the victims of a crime of violence motivated by gender to sue the guilty party in federal court. In *United States v. Morrison*, the Court, in a five-to-four decision, said that attacks against women are not, and do not substantially affect, interstate commerce, and hence Congress cannot constitutionally pass such a law. Chief Justice William Rehnquist said that "the Constitution requires a distinction between what is truly national and what is truly local." The states, of course, can pass such laws, and many have.

The Court has moved to strengthen states' rights on other grounds as well. In *Printz v. United States* (1997), the Court invalidated a federal law that required local police to conduct background checks on all gun purchasers. The Court ruled that the law violated the Tenth Amendment by commanding state governments to carry out a federal regulatory program. Writing for the five-to-four majority, Justice Antonin Scalia declared, "The Federal government may neither issue directives requiring the states to address particular problems, nor command the states' officers, or those of their political subdivisions, to administer or enforce a Federal regulatory program. . . . Such commands are fundamentally incompatible with our constitutional system of dual sovereignty."

The Court has also given new life to the Eleventh Amendment, which protects states from lawsuits by citizens of other states or foreign nations. In 1999, the Court shielded states from suits by copyright owners who claimed infringement of copyrights issued by state agencies, and immunized states from lawsuits by people who argued that state regulations create unfair economic competition. In *Alden v. Maine* (1999), the Court held that state employees could not sue to force state compliance with

TABLE 3.1 | Government Powers: Federal, State, and Both

Powers of the Federal Government	Powers of the State Government	Powers Exercised by Both the Federal and State Governments
• Subject to Article V of the Constitution, deciding on the process by which amendments to the Constitution are to be proposed and ratified • Declaring war • Maintaining and deploying military forces • Making foreign policy, international treaties, and trade deals • Printing money • Regulating interstate commerce • Maintaining postal offices and services	• Ratifying amendments to the Constitution through state legislatures or ratifying conventions • Conducting elections for public offices, initiatives, and referenda • Establishing local governments • Regulating intrastate commerce • Licensing occupations and land uses • Enacting laws to promote public safety, health, and morals (the "police power")	• Taxing citizens and businesses • Chartering banks and corporations • Building and maintaining roads • Borrowing money and managing public debts • Administering criminal justice institutions • Regulating Native American gaming (casino) businesses

federal fair-labor laws. In the Court's five-to-four majority opinion, Justice Anthony M. Kennedy stated, "Although the Constitution grants broad powers to Congress, our federalism requires that Congress treat the states in a manner consistent with their status as residuary sovereigns and joint participants in the governance of the nation." A few years later, in *Federal Maritime Commission v. South Carolina Ports Authority* (2002), the Court further expanded states' sovereign immunity from private lawsuits. Writing for the five-to-four majority, Justice Clarence Thomas declared that dual sovereignty "is a defining feature of our nation's constitutional blueprint," adding that the states "did not consent to become mere appendages of the federal government" when they ratified the Constitution.

Not all Court decisions, however, support greater state sovereignty. In 1999 in *Saenz v. Roe*, for example, the Court ruled seven to two that state welfare programs may not restrict new residents to the welfare benefits they would have received in the states from which they moved. Likewise, in *Gonzales v. Raich* (2005), the Court ruled that Congress can criminalize marijuana even in states where it is approved for medicinal purposes. Furthermore, in 2012 in *Arizona v. United States*, the Court held that only the federal government—and not state governments—had the right to regulate immigration laws and enforcement. More generally, to empower states is not to disempower Congress, which, as it has done since the late 1930s, can still make federal laws regarding almost anything as long as it does not go too far in "commandeering" state resources or gutting states' rights.

The Court's 2015 ruling on same-sex marriage offers another illustration of federal law trumping state ones.

Federal–State Relations

- ***McCulloch v. Maryland* (1819):** The Constitution's "necessary and proper" clause permits Congress to take actions (in this case, to create a national bank) when it is essential to a power that Congress has (in this case, managing the currency).
- ***Gibbons v. Ogden* (1824):** The Constitution's commerce clause gives the national government exclusive power to regulate interstate commerce.
- ***Wabash, St. Louis and Pacific Railroad v. Illinois* (1886):** The states may not regulate interstate commerce.
- ***United States v. Lopez* (1995):** The national government's power under the commerce clause does not permit it to regulate matters not directly related to interstate commerce (in this case, banning firearms in a school zone).
- ***Printz v. United States* (1997):** The national government's authority to require state officials to administer or enforce a federal regulation is limited.
- ***Alden v. Maine* (1999):** Congress may not act to subject nonconsenting states to lawsuits in state courts.
- ***Reno v. Condon* (2000):** The national government's authority to regulate interstate commerce extends to restrictions on how states gather, circulate, or sell certain information about citizens.
- ***United States v. Morrison* (2000):** The national government's power to regulate interstate commerce does not extend to giving female victims of violence the right to sue perpetrators in federal court.
- ***Federal Maritime Commission v. South Carolina Ports Authority* (2002):** States "did not consent to become mere appendages of the federal government" when they ratified the Constitution. Expanded states' sovereign immunity from private lawsuits.
- ***Kelo v. City of New London* (2005):** The Constitution allows a local government to seize property, not only for "public use" such as building highways, but also to "promote economic development" in a "distressed" community.
- ***National Federation of Independent Business v. Sebelius* (2010):** The national government's authority to "alter" or "amend" programs that it jointly funds and administers with the states is limited.
- ***Arizona v. United States* (2012):** Only the federal government may regulate immigration laws and enforcement.
- ***King v. Burwell* (2015):** Individuals using both the state-run and federally run health insurance exchanges may receive health insurance subsidies from the federal government.
- ***Obergefell v. Hodges* (2015):** People have a constitutional right to same-sex marriage in the United States.

Traditionally, marriage has been a state matter, not a federal one. As LGBTQ+ individuals began to push for greater equality, including the right to marry (see Chapter 6), many states responded by banning same-sex marriage. In *Obergefell v. Hodges,* the Court ruled that such bans were unconstitutional, and established a right to marriage for same-sex couples under the Constitution. While marriage laws are generally a state matter, such laws cannot contravene the Constitution.

This ongoing debate about state versus national sovereignty calls to mind President Wilson's quote from earlier in the chapter: Federalism really is at the heart of American politics, and cannot be resolved definitively, but rather is contested again and again. Over time, the spheres of activity of the state and national governments have shifted, and will continue to do so moving forward.

Finally, we would note that not only the Court shapes federalism. As we discuss in later chapters, American national institutions have recently become more characterized by gridlock and the inability to produce new policies. In response, many interest groups and activists have turned to state houses to press their agendas. As a result, policy debates that once raged in the halls of Congress—on issues such as abortion, gun control, environmental protection, the minimum wage, and so forth—are now largely fought at the state level.[20] This ensures that federalism will remain a relevant topic in the years to come.

3-2 Governmental Structure

Federalism refers to a political system that comprises local (territorial, regional, provincial, state, or municipal) units of government, as well as a national government, that can make final decisions with respect to at least some governmental activities and whose existence is specially protected. Almost every nation in the world has local units of government of some kind, if for no other reason than to decentralize the administrative burdens of governing. But these governments are not federal unless the local units exist independent of the preferences of the national government and can make decisions on at least some matters without regard to those preferences.

The United States, Canada, Australia, India, Germany, and Switzerland are federal systems, as are a few other nations. France, Great Britain, Italy, and Sweden are not; they are unitary systems because such local governments as they possess can be altered or even abolished by the national government and cannot plausibly claim to have final authority over any significant governmental activities.

The special protection that subnational governments enjoy in a federal system derives in part from the constitution of the country, but also from the habits, preferences, and dispositions of the citizens and the actual distribution of political power in society. The constitution of the former Soviet Union in theory created a federal system, as claimed by that country's full name—the Union of Soviet Socialist Republics—but for most of their history, none of these "socialist republics" were in the slightest degree independent of the central government. Were the American Constitution the only guarantee of the independence of the American states, they would long since have become mere administrative subunits of the government in Washington. Their independence results in large measure from the commitment of Americans to the idea of local self-government and from the fact that Congress consists of people who are selected by and responsive to local constituencies.

"The basic political fact of federalism," writes David B. Truman, "is that it creates separate, self sustaining centers of power, prestige, and profit."[21] Political power is locally acquired by people whose careers depend for the most part on satisfying local interests. As a result, though the national government has come to have vast powers, it exercises many of those powers through state governments. What many of us forget when we think about "the government in Washington" is that it spends much of its money and enforces most of its rules not directly on citizens, but on other, local units of government. A large part of the welfare system, all of the interstate highway system, virtually every aspect of programs to improve cities, the largest part of the effort to supply jobs to the unemployed, the entire program to clean up our water, and even much of our military manpower (in the form of the National Guard) are enterprises in which the national government does not govern so much as it seeks, by regulation, grant, plan, argument, and cajolery, to get the states to govern in accordance with nationally (though often vaguely) defined goals.

Sometimes, however, confusion or controversy about which government is responsible for which functions surfaces at the worst possible moment and lingers long after attempts have been made to sort it all out. Sadly, this has been what federalism has meant to some citizens after natural disasters, such as Hurricanes Katrina and Rita in 2005, or amidst health crises, such as the COVID-19 outbreak in 2020.

Before, during, and after Hurricanes Katrina and Rita struck in 2005, federal, state, and local officials could be found fighting among themselves over everything from who was supposed to maintain and repair the levees to who should lead disaster-relief initiatives. In the weeks after the hurricanes hit, it was widely reported that the main first responders and disaster-relief workers came not from government, but from myriad religious and other charitable organizations. Not only that, but government agencies, such as the Federal Emergency Management Agency (FEMA), often acted in ways that made it harder, not easier, for these volunteers and groups to deliver help when and where it was most badly needed. Similarly, amidst the COVID-19 outbreak, there were debates between the federal and state governments about who had the responsibility to obtain medical equipment, such as ventilators and personal protective equipment, for hospitals and health care workers.

Federalism needs to be viewed dispassionately through a historical lens wide enough to encompass both its worst legacies (for instance, state and local laws that once legalized racial discrimination against African Americans) and its best (for instance, African Americans winning mayors' offices and seats in state legislatures when there were very few African Americans in Congress).

Federalism, it is fair to say, has the virtues of its vices and the vices of its virtues. To some, federalism means allowing states to block action, prevent progress, upset national plans, protect powerful local interests, and cater to the self-interest of hack politicians. Harold Laski, a British observer, described American states as "parasitic and poisonous,"[22] and William H. Riker, an American political scientist, argued that "the main effect of federalism since the Civil War has been to perpetuate racism."[23] By contrast, another political scientist, Daniel J. Elazar, argued that the "virtue of the federal system lies in its ability to develop and maintain mechanisms vital to the perpetuation of the unique combination of governmental strength, political flexibility, and individual liberty, which has been the central concern of American politics."[24]

So diametrically opposed are the views of Riker and Elazar that one wonders whether they are talking about the same subject. They are, of course, but they each stress different aspects of the same phenomenon. Whenever the opportunity to exercise political power is widely available (as among the 50 states, more than 3,000 counties, and many thousands of municipalities in the United States), it is obvious that in different places different people will make use of that power for different purposes. There is no question that allowing states and cities to make autonomous, binding political decisions will allow some people in some places to make those decisions in ways that maintain racial segregation, protect vested interests, and facilitate corruption. It is equally true, however, that this arrangement also enables other people in other places to pass laws that attack segregation, regulate harmful economic practices, and purify politics, often long before these ideas gain national support or become national policy.

The existence of independent state and local governments means that different political groups pursuing different political purposes will come to power in different places. The smaller the political unit, the more likely it is to be dominated by a single political faction. James Madison understood this fact perfectly and used it to argue (in *Federalist* No. 10) that it would be in a large (or "extended") republic, such as the United States as a whole, that one would find the greatest opportunity for all relevant interests to be heard. When William Riker condemns federalism, he is thinking of the fact that in some places the ruling factions in cities and states have opposed granting equal rights to African Americans. When Daniel Elazar praises federalism, he is recalling that, in other states and cities, the ruling factions have taken the lead (long in advance of the federal government) in developing measures to protect the environment, extend civil rights, and improve social conditions. If you live in California, whether you like federalism depends in part on whether you like the fact that California has, independent of the federal government, cut property taxes, strictly controlled coastal land use, heavily regulated electric utilities, and increased (at one time) and decreased (at another time) its welfare rolls.

Increased Political Activity

Federalism has many effects, but its most obvious effect has been to facilitate the mobilization of political activity. Unlike Don Quixote, average citizens do not tilt at windmills. They are more likely to become involved in organized political activity if they feel a reasonable chance exists of producing a practical effect. The chances of having such an effect are greater where there are many elected officials and independent governmental bodies, each with a relatively small constituency, than where there are few elected officials, most of whom have the nation as a whole for a constituency. In short, a federal system, by virtue of the decentralization of authority, lowers the cost of organized political activity; a unitary system, because of the centralization of authority, raises the cost. We may disagree about the purposes of organized political activity, but the fact of widespread organized activity can scarcely be doubted—or if you do doubt it, that is only because you have not yet read Chapters 8 and 11.

It is impossible to say whether the Founders, when they wrote the Constitution, planned to produce such widespread opportunities for political participation. Unfortunately, they were not very clear (at least in writing) about how the federal system was supposed to work, and thus most of the interesting questions about the jurisdiction and powers of our national and state governments had to be settled by a century and a half of protracted and often bitter conflict.

Different States, Different Policies

The states play a key role in many, if not most, policy areas, such as social welfare, public education, law enforcement, criminal justice, health care and hospitals, roads and highways, and managing water supplies.

laboratories of democracy *Idea that different states can implement different policies, and the successful ones will spread.*

initiative *Process that permits voters to put legislative measures directly on the ballot.*

referendum *Procedure enabling voters to reject a measure passed by the legislature.*

recall *Procedure whereby voters can remove an elected official from office.*

On these and many other matters, state constitutions and laws are far more detailed and sometimes confer more rights than the federal one. For example, the California constitution includes an explicit right to privacy, says that noncitizens have the same property rights as citizens, and requires the state to use "all suitable means" to support public education.

This diversity is a benefit of federalism: that different states can construct different policies that better fit with their local needs. This is the classic idea of "**laboratories of democracy**": States can try out different policies, and if they are successful, others states can copy them.[25] This is indeed a benefit to federalism: Many successful policies are first adopted in one place (such as health care reforms, welfare reforms, and so forth), and then copied in other states (or even in the federal government) when they prove to be successful.[26]

But this sort of experimentation generates a cost as well. Because different states have different policies, different citizens will be treated differently depending on their state of residence. For example, as we explained in the Constitutional Connections box, part of Obamacare called for states to expand Medicaid to provide health insurance to the working poor. Some states have chosen to expand Medicaid under Obamacare (such as California, North Dakota, and West Virginia), whereas others (such as Texas, Oklahoma, and Florida) have not. So an otherwise similar low-income citizen would qualify for Medicaid in some states, but not others. Likewise, in some states, those convicted of certain crimes are subject to the death penalty, but not in others. The benefit of policy differences means that we pay a price in terms of equality.

More generally, this variation in federalism highlights the two competing values at stake here: equality and participation. On the one hand, federalism, by allowing states to design different policies for health care, education, criminal justice, and so forth, means that citizens in different jurisdictions will be treated differently (and hence pay a cost in terms of equality). But on the other hand, federalism allows for participatory input: for more say in how schools are governed, where roads are built, how criminal justice policies are set, and so forth. Indeed, the differences in policy discussed above are largely (though not completely) a function of the differences in participation. So we cannot have more equality without having less participation, and vice versa. Having the benefit of "laboratories of democracy" means that not all citizens will be treated equally.

Stock Montage/Archive Photos/Getty Images

Image 3.3 Federalism has permitted experimentation. Women were able to vote in the Wyoming Territory in 1888, long before they could do so in most states.

Why do these various policies differ so much across states? The most fundamental answer is that participation is different: Different people, with different preferences, participate in the decision-making process in different states. But they can also differ because different states have different institutions as well, especially in terms of direct democracy. As we saw in Chapter 2, the federal Constitution is based on a republican, not a democratic, principle: Laws are to be made by the representatives of citizens, not by the citizens directly. But many state constitutions open one or more of three doors to direct democracy. About half of the states provide for some form of legislation by initiative. The **initiative** allows voters to place legislative measures (and sometimes constitutional amendments) directly on the ballot by getting enough signatures (usually between 5 and 15 percent of those who voted in the last election) on a petition. About half of the states permit the **referendum**, a procedure that enables voters to reject a measure adopted by the legislature. Sometimes the state constitution specifies that certain kinds of legislation (e.g., tax increases) must be subject to a referendum whether the legislature wishes it or not. The **recall** is a procedure, in effect in more than 20 states, whereby voters can remove an elected official from office. If enough signatures are gathered on a petition, the official must go before voters, who can vote to keep the person in office, remove the person from office, or remove the person and select someone else. In 2003, California voters recalled then governor Gray Davis and replaced him with Arnold Schwarzenegger, and in 2012, Wisconsin governor Scott Walker faced a recall election, but survived and remained in office.

The existence of the states is guaranteed by the federal Constitution: no state can be divided without its consent, each state must have two representatives in the Senate (the only provision of the Constitution that may not be amended), every state is assured of a republican form of government, and the powers not granted to Congress are reserved for the states. By contrast, cities, towns, and counties enjoy no such protection; they exist at the pleasure of the states. Indeed, states have frequently abolished certain kinds of local governments, such as independent school districts.

This explains why there is no debate about city sovereignty comparable to the debate about state sovereignty. The constitutional division of power between them is settled: The state is supreme. But federal–state relations can be complicated because the Constitution invites elected leaders to struggle over sovereignty. Which level of government has the ultimate power to decide where nuclear waste gets stored, how much welfare beneficiaries are paid, what rights prisoners enjoy, or whether supersonic jets can land at local airports? American federalism answers such questions, but on a case-by-case basis through intergovernmental politics and court decisions.

3-3 Federal Money, State Programs

As we discussed above, over time, we have moved to a system where both the national and state governments contribute to most policy areas. One key way this occurs is via various federal grant programs, where the federal government provides the money—and accompanying rules—for programs implemented at the state level. To understand contemporary federalism, we need to understand how national monies help to shape policy at all levels of government.

Grants-In-Aid

Perhaps the oldest example of national funds being used at the state level is federal **grants-in-aid**. The first of these programs began even before the Constitution was adopted, in the form of land grants made by the national government to the states in order to finance education. (State universities all over the country were built with the proceeds from the sale of these land grants; hence the name *land-grant colleges*.) Land grants were also made to support the building of wagon roads, canals, railroads, and flood-control projects. These measures were hotly debated in Congress (President Madison thought some were unconstitutional), even though the use to which the grants were put was left almost entirely to the states.

grants-in-aid *Money given by the national government to the states.*

Cash grants-in-aid began almost as early. In 1808, Congress gave $200,000 to the states to pay for their militias, with the states in charge of the size, deployment, and command of these troops. However, grants-in-aid programs remained few in number and small in price until the 20th century, when scores of new ones came into being. Today, federal grants go to hundreds of programs, including such giant federal–state programs as Medicaid (see Table 3.2). Overall, in fiscal year 2019 (the most recent data available), the federal government spent $721.1 billion on federal grants-in-aid, representing 16.2 percent of federal outlays in that year.[27]

The grants-in-aid system, once under way, grew quickly because it helped state and local officials resolve a dilemma. On the one hand, they wanted access to the superior taxing power of the federal government. On the other hand, prevailing constitutional interpretation, at least until the late 1930s, held that the federal government could only spend money for purposes authorized by the Constitution. The solution was obviously to have federal money put into state hands: Washington would pay the bills; the states would run the programs.

TABLE 3.2 | Federal Grants to State and Local Governments (2019)

The federal government spent more than $721 billion on grants to states in 2019.	
Among the biggest categories	
Health care (including Medicaid)	$442.3 billion
Income security	$112.6 billion
Transportation	$65.6 billion
Education, training, employment, and social services	$63.1 billion
Community and regional development	$15.6 billion

Source: Office of Management and Budget, FY2021 Budget, Historical Table 12.2, Totatl Outlays for Grants to State and Local Governments, by Function and Fund Group: 1940–2025.

Johnny Stockshooter/Alamy Stock Photo

Image 3.4 Some of the nation's top academic institutions, such as Penn State, began as land-grant colleges.

To state officials, federal money seemed so attractive for several reasons. First, the money was there. Thanks to the high-tariff policies of the Republicans, Washington in the 1880s had huge budget surpluses. Second, in the early 20th century, as those surpluses dwindled, Washington inaugurated the federal income tax. It automatically brought in more money as economic activity (and thus personal income) grew. Third, the federal government, unlike the states, managed the currency and could print more at will. (Technically, it borrowed this money, but it was under no obligation to pay it all back because, as a practical matter, it had borrowed from itself.) States could not do this; if they borrowed money (and many could not), they had to pay it back, in full.

These three economic reasons for the appeal of federal grants were probably not as important as a fourth reason: politics. Federal money seemed to a state official to be "free" money. Governors did not have to propose, collect, or take responsibility for federal taxes. Instead, governors could denounce the federal government for being profligate in its use of the people's money. Meanwhile, they could claim credit for a new public works or other projects funded by Washington and, until recent decades, expect little or no federal supervision in the bargain.[28]

That every state had an incentive to ask for federal money to pay for local programs meant, of course, that it would be very difficult for one state to get money for a given program without every state getting it. The Senators from Alabama who vote for the project to improve navigation on the Tombigbee River will have to vote in favor of projects improving navigation on every other river in the country if they expect their Senate colleagues to support such a request. Federalism as practiced in the United States means that when Washington wants to send money to one state or congressional district, it must send money to many states and districts.

Shortly after September 11, 2001, for example, President George W. Bush and congressional leaders in both parties pledged new federal funds to help prevent future terror attacks. Since then, New York City and other big cities have received tens of millions of federal dollars for such purposes, but so have scores of smaller cities and towns. The grants allocated by the Department of Homeland Security were based on so-called fair-share formulas mandated by Congress, which are basically the same formulas the federal government uses to allocate certain highway and other funds among the states. These funding formulas not only spread money around but also generally skew funding toward states and cities with low populations. For example, Grand Forks County, North Dakota (population 70,000), received $1.5 million to purchase biochemical suits, a semi-armored van, decontamination tents, and other equipment to deal with weapons of mass destruction.[29]

Other local governments similarly received federal funds through other programs. For example, the St. Louis Area Regional Response System (which administers these grants for the St. Louis area) has spent $9.4 million on equipment for area police departments since 2003, including a Bearcat armored truck, two helicopters, night-vision goggles, and body armor. Such equipment was used in the clashes between police and protesters in 2014 following the death of Michael Brown in Ferguson, Missouri (a suburb of St. Louis).[30] In the wake of Brown's death, such programs were put under the spotlight with calls for tighter regulation on the provision of military-grade equipment to local police forces. The Obama administration imposed some limits on these transfers, but those restrictions were lifted by the Trump administration.[31] Such transfers came to the fore again in 2020 when police across the country used similar equipment to quell the protests that erupted after the death of George Floyd while in police custody.

CHANDAN KHANNA/AFP/Getty Images

Image 3.5 Police armed with military gear clashed with protesters following the death of George Floyd in 2020. The military gear was provided to police departments by federal grants.

Meeting National Needs

Until the 1960s, most federal grants-in-aid were conceived by or in cooperation with the states and were designed to serve essentially state purposes. Large blocs of voters and a variety of organized interests would press for grants to help farmers, build highways, or support vocational education. During the 1960s, however, an important change occurred: the federal government began devising grant programs based less on what states were demanding and more on what federal officials perceived to be important *national* needs (see Figure 3.3). Federal officials, not state and local ones, were the principal proponents of grant programs to aid the urban poor, combat crime, reduce pollution, and deal with drug abuse.

This change in these programs had two significant effects. First, it changed the amount of money flowing from the federal government to states and localities. Whereas federal aid amounted to less than 2 percent of state general revenue in 1927, by 2017 federal aid accounted for slightly more than one-third of state general revenue.[32] Since 1960, the amount going to states and localities through grants has increased (adjusting for inflation) more than 10.5 fold, growing from 7.6 percent of federal outlays to over 16 percent.[33]

Second, not only did the amounts increase, but what programs these grants supported also changed. Figure 3.3 shows the changing purposes of federal grants to state and local governments from 1960 to the present. The chart tracks the percentage of all federal grant monies going to four major types of programs: transportation (funds for roads, bridges, and so forth), education, training, employment, and social services (funds for schools, job training programs, and so forth), income security (funds for the Women, Infants, and Children program, the Temporary Assistance for Needy Families program, and so forth), and health care (largely, but not exclusively, funds for Medicaid, the joint federal-state health care program for the poor). While these are not the only types of grants, they make up the lion's share of them; other categories never amount to more than 15 percent of the overall total, and today make up only about 5 percent.

Over time, we see a quite dramatic shift. In 1960, more than 40 percent of grants went to fund transportation, and just slightly less than that went to income security. Health care amounted to only 3 percent of federal grants. Today transportation and education funding each account for less than 10 percent of grants, and income security only about 15 percent. What has replaced them? Health care—more than 60 percent of all federal grants to state and local governments go to fund health care, largely to fund the Medicaid program. This is partially due to the Medicaid expansion provided by the Affordable Care

Figure 3.3 **The Changing Purpose of Federal Grants to State and Local Governments, 1960–2019**

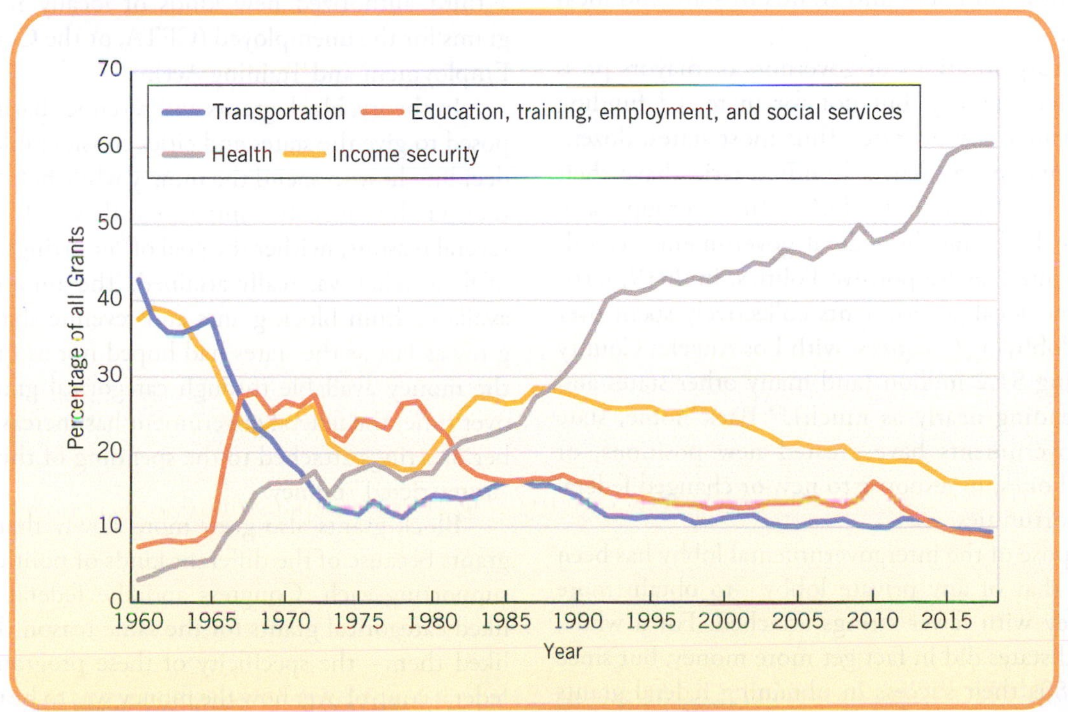

Source: Office of Management and Budget, FY2021 Budget, Historical Table 12.2, Totatl Outlays for Grants to State and Local Governments, by Function and Fund Group: 1940–2025.

categorical grants *Federal grants for specific purposes, such as building an airport.*

Act—note that there is a sharp rise after 2010, when the law was passed. But this alone does not account for the trend, rather it is a product of the decades-long rise in health care costs. How this changes—and the implications this has for both health care and other programs—will be an important development to watch in the years to come.

The Intergovernmental Lobby

State and local officials, both elected and appointed, began to form an important new lobby—the "intergovernmental lobby," made up of mayors, governors, superintendents of schools, state directors of public health, county highway commissioners, local police chiefs, and others who had come to depend on federal funds.[34] Today, federal agencies responsible for health care, criminal justice, environmental protection, and other programs have people on staff who specialize in providing information, technical assistance, and financial support to state and local organizations, including the "Big 7": the U.S. Conference of Mayors, the National Governors Association, the National Association of Counties, the National League of Cities, the Council of State Governments, the International City/County Management Association, and the National Conference of State Legislatures. Reports by these groups are read routinely by many federal officials to keep a handle on issues and trends in state and local government.

National organizations of governors or mayors press for more federal money, but not for increased funding for any particular city or state. Thus most states, dozens of counties, and more than a hundred cities have their own offices in Washington, D.C. These groups also spend big on lobbying the federal government: according to the Center for Responsive Politics, in 2019, territory, state, and local governments collectively spent over $76 million lobbying Congress, with Los Angeles County alone spending $1.2 million (and many other states and localities spending nearly as much).[35] Back home, state and local governments have created new positions, or redefined old ones, in response to new or changed federal funding opportunities.

The purpose of the intergovernmental lobby has been the same as that of any private lobby—to obtain more federal money with fewer strings attached. For a while, the cities and states did in fact get more money, but since the early 1980s their success in obtaining federal grants has been more checkered, though this has not stopped their lobbying efforts.

Categorical Grants

The effort to loosen the strings took the form of shifting, as much as possible, federal aid from **categorical grants** to block grants. A categorical grant is one for a specific purpose defined by federal law: to build an airport or a college dormitory, for example, or to make welfare payments to low-income mothers. Such grants usually require that the state or locality put up money to "match" some part of the federal grant, though the amount of matching funds can be quite small (sometimes only 10 percent or less). Governors and mayors complained about these categorical grants because their purposes were often so narrow that it was impossible for a state to adapt federal grants to local needs. A mayor seeking federal money to build parks might have discovered that the city could get money only if it launched an urban-renewal program that entailed bulldozing several blocks of housing or small businesses.

One response to this problem was to consolidate several categorical or project grant programs into a single block grant devoted to some general purpose and with fewer restrictions on its use. Block grants began in the mid-1960s, when such a grant was created to fund health care programs. Though many block grants were proposed between 1966 and 1980, only five were enacted. Of the three largest, one consolidated various categorical grant programs aimed at cities (Community Development Block Grants), another created a program to aid local law enforcement (Law Enforcement Assistance Act), and a third authorized new kinds of locally managed programs for the unemployed (CETA, or the Comprehensive Employment and Training Act).

In theory, block grants and revenue sharing were supposed to give the states and cities considerable freedom in deciding how to spend the money while helping to relieve their tax burdens. To some extent they did. However, for several reasons, neither the goal of "no strings" nor the one of fiscal relief was really attained. The amount of money available from block grants and revenue sharing did not grow as fast as the states had hoped nor as quickly as did the money available through categorical grants. Further, over time, the federal government has increased the number of strings attached to the spending of this supposedly "unrestricted" money.

Block grants also grew more slowly than categorical grants because of the different kinds of political coalitions supporting each. Congress and the federal bureaucracy liked categorical grants for the same reason the states disliked them—the specificity of these programs enhanced federal control over how the money was to be used. Federal officials, joined by liberal interest groups and organized labor, tended to distrust state governments. Whenever

Congress wanted to address some national problem, its natural inclination was to create a categorical grant program so that it, and not the states, would decide how the money would be spent.

Fourth, even though governors and mayors like block grants, these programs cover such a broad range of activities that no single interest group has a vital stake in pressing for their enlargement. Categorical grants, on the other hand, often are a matter of life and death for many agencies—state departments of welfare, of highways, and of health, for example, are utterly dependent on federal aid. Accordingly, the administrators in charge of these programs will press strenuously for their expansion. Moreover, categorical programs are supervised by special committees of Congress, and as we shall see in Chapter 13, many of these committees have an interest in seeing their programs grow.

Rivalry Among the States

The more important federal money becomes to the states, the more likely the states are to compete among themselves for the largest share of it. For a century or more, the growth of the United States—in population, business, and income—was concentrated in the industrial Northeast. In recent decades, however, that growth—at least in population and employment, if not in income—has shifted to the South, Southwest, and Far West. This change has precipitated an intense debate over whether the federal government, by the way it distributes its funds and awards its contracts, is unfairly helping some regions and states at the expense of others. Journalists and politicians have dubbed the struggle as one between Snowbelt (or Frostbelt) and Sunbelt states.

Whether there is in fact anything worth arguing about is far from clear: The federal government has had great difficulty in figuring out where it ultimately spends what funds for what purposes. For example, a $1 billion defense contract may go to a company with headquarters in California, but much of the money may actually be spent in Connecticut or New York, as the prime contractor in California buys from subcontractors in the other states. It is even less clear whether federal funds actually affect the growth rate of the regions. The uncertainty about the facts has not prevented a debate about the issue, however. That debate focuses on the formulas written into federal laws by which block grants are allocated. These formulas take into account such factors as a county's or city's population, personal income in the area, and housing quality. A slight change in a formula can shift millions of dollars in grants in ways that favor either the older, declining cities of the Northeast or the newer, stillgrowing cities of the Southwest.

With the advent of grants based on distributional formulas (as opposed to grants for a particular project), the results of the census, taken every 10 years, assume monumental importance. A city or state shown to be losing population may, as a result, forfeit millions of dollars in federal aid. Senators and representatives now have access to data that can tell them instantly the effect on their states

SAUL LOEB/AFP/Getty Images

Q What are some of the ways in which federalism shaped how the U.S. government responded to the COVID-19 pandemic and other emergencies, such as natural disasters?

Image 3.6 California Governor Gavin Newsom and President Trump tour areas damaged by wildfires.

conditions of aid *Terms set by the national government that states must meet if they are to receive certain federal funds.*

mandates *Terms set by the national government that states must meet whether or not they accept federal grants.*

waiver *A decision by an administrative agency granting some other party permission to violate a law or rule that would otherwise apply to it.*

and districts of even minor changes in a formula by which federal aid is distributed. These formulas rely on objective measures, but the exact measure is selected with an eye toward its political consequences. There is nothing wrong with this in principle, since any political system must provide some benefits for everybody if it is to stay together. Given the competition among states in a federal system, however, the struggle over allocation formulas becomes especially acute.

Federal Aid and Federal Control

So important has federal aid become for state and local governments that mayors and governors, along with others, began to fear that Washington was well on its way to controlling other levels of government. "He who pays the piper calls the tune," they muttered. In this view, the constitutional protection of state government to be found in the Tenth Amendment was in jeopardy as a result of the strings attached to the grants-in-aid on which the states were increasingly dependent.

Block grants were an effort to reverse this trend by allowing the states and localities freedom to spend money as they wished. But as we have seen, the new device did not in fact reverse the trend. Categorical grants—those with strings attached—continued to grow even faster.

Two kinds of federal controls are applied to state governmental activities. The traditional control tells the state government what it must do if it wants to get some grant money. These strings often are called **conditions of aid**. A newer form of control tells the state government what it must do, period. These rules are called **mandates**. Most mandates have little or nothing to do with federal aid—they apply to all state governments whether or not they accept grants.

Mandates

Most mandates concern civil rights and environmental protection. States may not discriminate in the operation of their programs, no matter who pays for them. Initially the antidiscrimination rules applied chiefly to distinctions based on race, sex, age, and ethnicity, but of late they have broadened to include physical and mental disabilities as well. Various pollution control laws require the states to comply with federal standards for clean air, pure drinking water, and sewage treatment.[36]

Stated in general terms, these mandates seem reasonable enough. It is hard to imagine anyone arguing that state governments should be free to discriminate against people because of their race or national origin. In practice, however, some mandates create administrative and financial problems, especially when the mandates are written in vague language, thereby giving federal administrative agencies the power to decide for themselves what state and local governments are supposed to do.

But not all areas of public law and policy are equally affected by mandates. Federal–state disputes about who governs on such controversial matters as minors' access to abortion and medical uses for banned narcotics make headlines. It is mandates that fuel everyday friction in federal–state relations, particularly those levied by Washington but paid for by the states. One study concluded that "the number of unfunded federal mandates is high in environmental policy, low in education policy, and moderate in health policy."[37] But why?

Some think that how much Washington spends in a given policy area is linked to how common federal mandates, funded or not, are in that same area. There is some evidence for that view. For instance, annual federal grants to state and local governments for environmental protection—a policy area where unfunded mandates are pervasive—have been about $6 billion, whereas federal grants for health care—an area where unfunded mandates have been less pervasive—amounted to over $400 billion. The implication is that when Washington itself spends less on something it wants done, it squeezes the states to spend more for that purpose. Washington is more likely to grant state and local governments waivers in some areas than in others. A **waiver** is a decision by an administrative agency granting some other party permission to violate a law or administrative rule that would otherwise apply to it. For instance, in general, education waivers have been easy for state and local governments to get, but environmental protection waivers have proven almost impossible to acquire.[38]

However, caution is in order. Often, the more one knows about federal–state relations in any given area, the harder it becomes to generalize about present-day federalism's fiscal, administrative, and regulatory character, the conditions under which "permissive federalism" prevails, or whether new laws or court decisions will considerably tighten or further loosen Washington's control over the states.

Mandates are not the only way in which the federal government imposes costs on state and local governments. Certain federal tax and regulatory policies make it difficult or expensive for state and local governments to raise revenues, borrow funds, or privatize public functions. Other federal laws expose state and local governments to financial liability, and numerous federal court decisions and administrative regulations require state and local governments to do or not do various things, either by statute or through an implied constitutional obligation.[39]

It is clear that the federal courts have helped fuel the growth of mandates. As interpreted by the U.S. Supreme Court, the Tenth Amendment provides state and local officials no protection against the march of mandates. Indeed, many of the more controversial mandates result not from congressional action but from court decisions. For example, many state prison systems have been, at one time or another, under the control of federal judges who required major changes in prison construction and management in order to meet standards the judges derived from their reading of the Constitution.

The Supreme Court has of late made it much easier for citizens to control the behavior of local officials. A federal law, passed in the 1870s to protect newly freed slaves, makes it possible for a citizen to sue any state or local official who deprives that citizen of any "rights, privileges, or immunities secured by the Constitution and laws" of the United States. A century later, the Court decided that this law permitted a citizen to sue a local official if the official deprived the citizen of *anything* to which the citizen was entitled under federal law (and not just those federal laws protecting civil rights). For example, citizens can now use the federal courts to obtain from a state welfare office a payment to which they may be entitled under federal law.

Conditions of Aid

By far the most important federal restrictions on state action are the conditions attached to the grants the states receive. In theory, accepting these conditions is voluntary—if you don't want the strings, don't take the money. But when the typical state depends for a quarter or more of its budget on federal grants, many of which it has received for years and on which many of its citizens depend for their livelihoods, it is not clear exactly how "voluntary" such acceptance is. During the 1960s, some strings were added, the most important of which had to do with civil rights. But beginning in the 1970s, the number of conditions began to proliferate and has expanded since.

Some conditions are specific to particular programs, but most are not. For instance, if a state builds something with federal money, it must first conduct an environmental impact study, it must pay construction workers the "prevailing wage" in the area, it often must provide an opportunity for citizen participation in some aspects of the design or location of the project, and it must ensure that the contractors who build the project have nondiscriminatory hiring policies. The states and the federal government, not surprisingly, disagree about the costs and benefits of such rules. Members of Congress and federal officials feel they have an obligation to develop uniform national policies with respect to important matters and to prevent states and cities from misspending federal tax dollars. State officials, on the other hand, feel these national rules fail to take into account diverse local conditions, require the states to do things that the states must then pay for, and create serious inefficiencies.

What state and local officials discovered, in short, was that "free" federal money was not quite free after all. In the 1960s, federal aid seemed entirely beneficial; what mayor or governor would not want such money? But just as local officials found it attractive to do things that another level of government then paid for, in time federal officials learned the same thing. Passing laws to meet the concerns of national constituencies—leaving the cities and states to pay the bills and manage the problems—began to seem attractive to Congress.

Because they face different demands, federal and local officials find themselves in a bargaining situation in which each side is trying to get some benefit (solving a problem, satisfying a pressure group) while passing on to the other side most of the costs (taxes, administrative problems). The bargains struck in this process used to favor the local officials, because members of Congress were essentially servants of local interests: they were elected by local political parties, they were part of local political organizations, and they supported local autonomy. Beginning in the 1960s, however, changes in American politics that will be described in later chapters shifted the orientation of many in Congress toward favoring Washington's needs over local needs.

3-4 A Devolution Revolution?

In 1981, President Ronald Reagan tried to reverse this trend. He asked Congress to consolidate scores of categorical grants into just six large block grants. Congress obliged. Soon state and local governments started getting less federal money, but with fewer strings attached to such grants. During the 1980s and into the early 1990s, however, many states also started spending more of their own money and replacing federal rules on programs with state ones.

With the election of Republican majorities in the House and Senate in 1994, a renewed effort was led by Congress to cut total government spending, roll back federal regulations, and shift important functions back to the states. The first key issue was welfare—that is, Aid to Families with Dependent Children (AFDC).

devolution *The transfer of power from the national government to state and local governments.*

Since 1935, there had been a federal guarantee of cash assistance to states that offered support to low-income, unmarried mothers and their children. In 1996, President Bill Clinton signed a new federal welfare law that ended any federal guarantee of support and, subject to certain rules, turned the management of the program entirely over to the states, aided by federal block grants.

These and other Republican initiatives were part of a new effort called **devolution**, which aimed to pass on to the states many federal functions. It is an old idea, but one that actually acquired new vitality because Congress, rather than the president, was leading the effort. Members of Congress traditionally liked voting for federal programs and categorical grants; that way they could take credit for what they were doing for particular constituencies. Under its new conservative leadership, Congress, especially the House, was looking for ways to scale back the size of the national government. President Clinton seemed to agree when, in his 1996 State of the Union address, he proclaimed that the era of big national government was over.

But was it over? No. Today, the federal government spends roughly $31,000 per year per household, which, adjusted for inflation, is much higher than it was just a few decades ago.[40] Adjusted for inflation, total spending by state and local governments has also increased rapidly in recent years, reaching about $3.6 trillion in 2017, with total revenues of approximately $3.9 trillion.[41]

Rachael Warriner/Alamy Stock Photo

Image 3.7 Protesters march in support of sanctuary cities. This has been a point of tension between federal immigration authorities and local governments in recent years.

Devolution did not become a revolution. AFDC was ended and replaced by a block grant program called Temporary Assistance for Needy Families (TANF). But other federal–state programs were not turned into block grant programs. While the Trump administration did propose allowing states to opt into a Medicaid block grant program in 2020, the program is voluntary, and opponents are almost certain to challenge the program in court.[42] Moreover, both federal and state spending on most programs, including the block-granted programs, increased after 1996. Although by no means the only new or significant block grant, TANF now looked like the big exception that proved the rule. The devolution revolution was curtailed by public opinion. Today, as in 1996, most Americans favor "shifting responsibility to the states," but not if that also means cuts in government programs that benefit most citizens (not just low-income families), uncertainty about who is eligible to receive benefits, or new hassles associated with receiving them.

Devolution seems to have resulted in more, not fewer, government rules and regulations. In response to the federal effort to devolve responsibility to state and local governments, states have not only enacted new rules and regulations of their own, but also prompted Washington to issue new rules and regulations on environmental protection and other matters.[43] For example, several states and cities successfully sued the Environmental Protection Agency to force it to regulate carbon dioxide and other greenhouse gases as pollutants.[44]

Still, where devolution did occur, it has had some significant consequences. The devolution of welfare policy has been associated with dramatic decreases in welfare rolls. Scholars disagree about how much the reductions were due to the changes in law and how much they were caused by economic conditions and other factors. Substantial debate also exists over whether new benefits are adequate, or whether the jobs most recipients have gotten through welfare-to-work programs are adequate.[45] But few now doubt that welfare devolution has made a measurable difference in how many people receive benefits and for how long (we discuss these debates more extensively in Chapter 17).

Subject to state discretion, scores of local governments are now designing and administering welfare programs (job placement, child care, and others) through

Brian van der Brug/Los Angeles Times/Getty Images

Image 3.8 Many governors activated their national guard during the protests following the death of George Floyd. Federal troops were also sent to some cities, such as Portland, Oregon.

for-profit firms and a wide variety of nonprofit organizations, including local religious congregations. In some big cities, more than a quarter of welfare-to-work programs have been administered through public–private partnerships that have included various local community-based organizations as grantees.[46]

Funding is perhaps the main challenge states face today when assuming more responsibility for public programs. Today, most states have budget shortfalls and face mounting debts for the foreseeable future. While this is due in part to the 2008 financial crisis and other economic downturns, a longer-term factor is the role of public sector unions, especially members' pensions.[47] Many such pensions are severely underfunded and could pose serious limits to states' future spending levels unless changes are made.[48] Consequently, several states (most notably Wisconsin) limited collective bargaining rights for public employees, though it remains to be seen how widely such proposals will spread or how states will manage these challenges more generally.

As states look to reduce costs, they need to consider which responsibilities are theirs to shoulder and which ones the federal government must bear. Each year, the Government Accountability Office releases a study that identifies ways to reduce fragmentation, duplication, and overlap both within the federal government, as well as between the federal and state governments. Every year, this report finds a number of different areas where changes could generate large cost savings.[49] But identifying bureaucratic overlap is easier than eliminating it (as we will see in Chapter 15), and federal public officials typically have very different views than their state counterparts about what qualifies as "wasteful" spending. Consequently, how states will address their long-term debt, and the implications for further devolution in policymaking, remains to be seen. And, as noted in a 2013 study by the Congressional Budget Office, intergovernmental programs involve administrative costs at multiple levels of government; any major cost-cutting efforts have to be coordinated between Washington and the states, and that never proves easy.[50]

Congress and Federalism

Just as it remains to be seen whether the Supreme Court will continue to revive the doctrine of state sovereignty, so it is not yet clear whether the devolution movement will regain momentum, stall, or be reversed. But whatever the movement's fate, the United States will not become a wholly centralized nation. There remains more political and policy diversity in America than one is likely to find in any other large, industrialized nation. The reason is not only that state and local governments have retained certain constitutional protections but also that members of Congress continue to think of themselves as the representatives of localities **to** Washington and not as the representatives **of** Washington to the localities. As we shall see in Chapter 13, American politics, even at the national level, often remains local in its orientation.

But if this is true, why do these same members of Congress pass laws that create so many problems for—and stimulate so many complaints from—mayors, governors, and other state and local officials? Members of Congress represent different constituencies from the same localities. For example, one member of Congress from Los Angeles may think of the city as a collection of businesspeople, homeowners, and taxpayers, whereas another may think of it as a group of African Americans, Hispanics, and nature lovers. If Washington wants to simply send money to Los Angeles, these two representatives could be expected to vote together. But if Washington wants to impose mandates or restrictions on the city, these representatives might very well vote on opposite sides, each voting as their constituents would most likely prefer.

When somebody tries to speak "for" a city or state in Washington, that person has little claim to any real authority. The mayor of Philadelphia may favor one program, the governor of Pennsylvania may favor another, and individual local and state officials—school superintendents, the insurance commissioner, public health administrators—may favor still others. In

Policy Dynamics: Inside/Outside the Box | Marijuana Legalization: Entrepreneurial, Not Majoritarian, Politics

In 1996, California citizens passed Proposition 215, a ballot measure permitting the "compassionate use" of marijuana for medicinal purpose, making it the first state to allow for any sort of legal marijuana use. Since then, other states have allowed various forms of legalized marijuana. 15 states allow for the recreational use of marijuana, others have decriminialized the possession of small amounts of the drug, and most states now allow for medicinal marijuana. Despite these steps, marijuana remains illegal under the federal Controlled Substances Act of 1970, setting up a conflict between state and federal authorities.

On the surface, marijuana legalization seems to be an example of majoritarian politics—the costs and the benefits are both widely distributed. By this logic, the debate should be over which side has the most compelling argument. For example, over time, support for marijuana legalization has grown considerably, from only 12 percent in 1969 to two-thirds of Americans today—with more than three-quarters of young people supporting legalization. Much of this growth in support likely comes from recognition that many of the fears of legalization opponents have not come to pass where medicinal and/or recreational marijuana has been legalized, thereby suggesting that legalization proponents have the stronger argument.

But this shift in popular support has not translated into broader action for marijuana legalization at the federal level. Why? It is because powerful interests oppose legalization, and hence this issue is better categorized as entrepreneurial politics. Police departments receive millions of dollars annually to fight the war on drugs, and some of that money would likely evaporate if marijuana were legalized. Prison guards—and private prison companies—also have a vested interest in ensuring that drug users are imprisoned. Furthermore, the federal government itself can act to complicate state-level legalization by, for example, forcing banks not to accept money from legalized marijuana (the federal government could charge banks under federal drug-trafficking laws), imposing stiff federal taxes on marijuana dispensaries, or enforcing federal laws (the Supreme Court ruled that federal authorities could enforce federal laws banning marijuana even where states have legalized it). These are significant hurdles for legalization supporters to overcome.

As is typically the case for entrepreneurial politics, supporters need to find an entrepreneur to help them overcome these hurdles, and finding one nationally has been difficult. Some liberal and libertarian politicians may well be sympathetic to the cause, but they have chosen to invest their energies on other issues they see as more pressing, such as bank regulation or criminal justice reform. The other path to broader passage would be for the issue to be more salient, but while the issue has majority support, it is a very low priority for most voters, suggesting that this is not likely to become a particularly salient issue absent some significant shift.

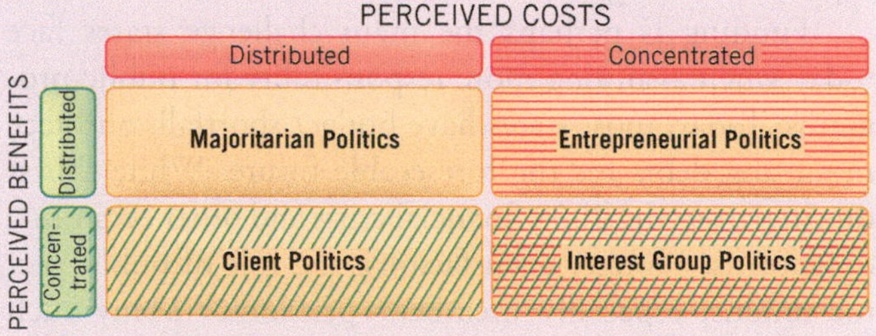

Source: Andrew Danniller, "Two Thirds of Americans Support Marijuana Legalization," Prew Research Center Fact Tank, 14 November 2019; Kendell Benson, "Money, Not Morals, Drives Marijuana Prohibition Movement, OpenSecrets Blog, 5 August 2014; German Lopez, "How Marijuana Legalization Became a Majority Movement," *Vox*, 1 October 2014; "The Trouble with Marijuana Legalization: Banks," *Governing*, 5 January 2015; Jack Healy, "Legal Marijuana Faces Another Federal Hurdle: Taxes," *New York Times*, 9 May 2015.

bidding for federal aid, those parts of the state or city that are best organized often do the best, and increasingly these groups are not the political parties but rather specialized occupational groups such as doctors or schoolteachers. If one is to ask, therefore, why members of Congress do not listen to their states anymore, the answer is, "What do you mean by *the state*? Which official, which occupational group, which party leader speaks for the state?"

Finally, Americans differ in the extent to which we prefer federal as opposed to local decisions. When people are asked which level of government gives them the

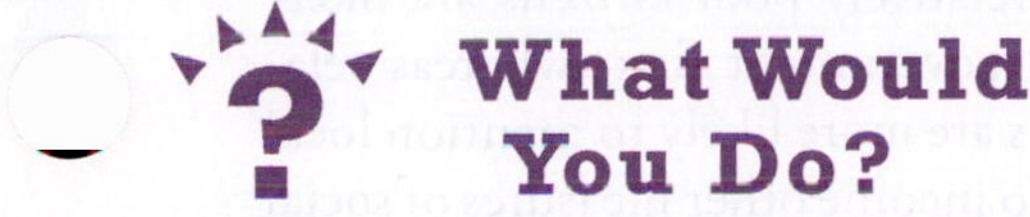

What Would You Do? | Should States Adopt the Common Core National Education Standards?

To: *Secretary of Education Lucy Sadie*
From: *White House Special Assistant Talya Ili*
Subject: *National curricular standards for elementary and secondary schools*

There has been a large debate in recent years about whether states should adopt the Common Core Educational Standards. The Common Core standards seek to set uniform national benchmarks for student achievement in every grade level in English/language arts and mathematics. The goal is to help students be prepared for college and the workforce in the 21st century.

The president is making a push for national standards, and the major arguments for and against this proposal follow. Will you present the initiative and address states' concerns at the National Governors Association meeting next week?

To Consider:

The president seeks a national curriculum for all kindergarten through grade 12 schoolchildren. Supporters argue that such standards will prepare students for the jobs of the 21st century, but opponents argue that federally mandated standards will do more harm than good.

Arguments for:

1. American jobs in the 21st century will require advanced skills in literacy, mathematics, and information technology that all schools must teach.
2. Variations in state curriculum standards leave students ill-prepared for high-paying jobs and for college.
3. If the national government does not invest in creating a uniform school curriculum now, then increased funding will be needed for remedial instruction later.

Arguments against:

1. States are better able to determine educational standards that will prepare their diverse populations for the workforce than the federal government.
2. Imposing a national curriculum will stifle state and local creativity in education and will be so basic that it will make little difference in college preparation.
3. The national government has a history of imposing educational mandates on states with insufficient funding, and governors are skeptical of receiving sufficient funding to successfully implement a national curriculum for students with varying needs.

What Will You Decide? Enter **MindTap** to make your choice.

Your decision: ☐ Support bill ☐ Oppose bill

ZUMA Press, Inc./Alamy Stock Photo

Image 3.9 A marijuana dispensary in Colorado. While legal in some states, marijuana remains illegal under federal law.

How do the debates over legalized marijuana reflect broader debates over federalism we have seen elsewhere in the chapter?

most for their money, relatively poor citizens are likely to mention the federal government first, whereas relatively well-to-do citizens are more likely to mention local government. If we add to income other measures of social diversity—race, religion, and region—there emerge even sharper differences of opinion about which level of government works best. It is this social diversity—and the fact that it is represented not only by state and local leaders but also by members of Congress—that keeps federalism alive and makes it so important. Americans simply do not agree on enough things, or even on which level of government ought to decide on those things, to make possible a unitary system.

Learning Objectives

3-1 Discuss the historical origins of federalism, and explain how it has evolved over time.

The Framers of the Constitution created a federal system of government for the United States because they wanted to balance the power of the central government with states that would exercise independent influence over most areas of people's lives, outside of national concerns such as defense, coining money, and so forth. Since the Founding, the balance of power between the national government and the states has shifted over time. Overall, the federal government's power and responsibilities have increased, particularly with the expansion of programs in the 20th and 21st centuries. Still, states exercise broad latitude in implementing policies, and they frequently provide models for the federal government to consider in creating national policies.

3-2 Summarize the pros and cons of federalism in the United States.

Debates over federalism come down to debates over equality versus participation. Federalism means that citizens living in different parts of the country will be treated differently, not only in spending programs, such as welfare, but also in legal systems that assign in different places different penalties to similar offenses or that differentially enforce civil rights laws. But federalism also means that more opportunities exist for participation in making decisions—in influencing what is taught in schools and in deciding where highways and government projects are to be built. Indeed, differences in public policy—that is, unequal treatment—are in large part the result of participation in decision making. It is difficult, perhaps impossible, to have more of one of these values without having less of the other.

3-3 Describe how funding underlies federal–state interactions and how this relationship has changed over time.

Funding is perhaps the key link between federal and state governments: In fiscal year 2019, the federal government provided approximately $721 billion in grants to state and local governments. Many of these grants fund programs designed in Washington but implemented at the state level. Such programs can be contentious because of the mandates and requirements imposed by the federal government on the states.

3-4 Discuss whether the devolution of programs to the states beginning in the 1980s really constitutes a revolution in federal–state relations.

Devolution was not a revolution, but it did generate important changes in programs like welfare. More generally, it continued the shift toward federal programs administered by states.

To Learn More

National Conference of State Legislators: **https://www.ncsl.org**

State news: **www.stateline.org**

Council of State Governments: **www.csg.org**

National Governors Association: **www.nga.org**

Supreme Court decisions: **www.findlaw.com/casecode/supreme.html**

Beer, Samuel H. *To Make a Nation: The Rediscovery of American Federalism.* Cambridge, Mass.: Harvard University Press, 1993. The definitive study of the philosophical bases of American federalism.

Conlan, Timothy. *From New Federalism to Devolution.* Washington, DC: Brookings Institution, 1998.

A masterful overview of the politics of federalism from Richard Nixon to Bill Clinton.

Daniel, Ronald, Donald F. Kettl, and Howard Kureuther, eds. *On Risk and Disaster: Lessons from Hurricane Katrina.* Philadelphia: University of Pennsylvania Press, 2006. Several experts evaluate the government response.

Derthick, Martha N. *Keeping the Compound Republic.* Washington, D.C.: Brookings Institution, 2001. A masterful analysis of trends in American federalism from the Founding to end of the 20th century.

Diamond, Martin. "The Federalist's View of Federalism." In *Essays in Federalism,* edited by George C. S. Benson, 21–64. Claremont, Calif.: Institute for Studies in Federalism of Claremont Men's College, 1961. A profound analysis of what the Founders meant by federalism.

Grodzins, Morton. *The American System.* Chicago: Rand McNally, 1966. Argues that American federalism has always involved extensive sharing of functions between national and state governments.

Melnick, R. Shep. *Between the Lines: Interpreting Welfare Rights.* Washington, D.C.: Brookings Institution, 1994. An examination of how trends in statutory interpretation have affected broader policy developments, including the expansion of the agenda of national government, the persistence of divided government, and the resurgence and decentralization of Congress.

Riker, William H. *Federalism: Origin, Operation, Significance.* Boston: Little, Brown, 1964. A classic explanation and critical analysis of federalism here and abroad.

Rozell, Mark and Clyde Wilcox. 2019. *Federalism: A Very Short Introduction*. New York, NY: Oxford University Press. A readable introduction to the politics of federalism in the U.S. and abroad.

Teske, Paul. *Regulation in the States*. Washington, D.C.: Brookings Institution, 2004. States have responded to devolution by adding new regulations of their own.

CHAPTER 4

American Political Culture

Learning Objectives

4-1 Explain the concept of political culture and its key components in the United States.

4-2 Discuss how the political culture of the United States differs from that in other countries.

4-3 Identify the key sources of political culture in the United States.

4-4 Evaluate how conflicts in American political culture affect public confidence in government and tolerance of different political views.

« Then In 1831, a French political official, Alexis de Tocqueville, visited the United States to conduct research on its prison systems. Based on two years of travel across the country, de Tocqueville wrote a two-volume study titled *Democracy in America* that continues to be one of the defining texts of American political culture. De Tocqueville argued that democracy endured in the United States because of geography, laws, and "the manners and customs of the people."[1] He concluded that the attitude of Americans about the merits of democracy was fundamental to its success here.

*** Now** In the 21st century, a number of issues divide Americans: reducing the rapidly growing national debt, combating terrorism, providing health care, determining the appropriate scope of responsibility and power for the federal government, and so forth. But the political parties and interest groups (both of which we will discuss later in this textbook) that disagree about these issues share a common belief in preserving the principles of American constitutionalism-liberty, equality of opportunity, and so on-even if they differ over how to put those principles into practice. The Tea Party movement in the past decade, for example, derived its name from a historic event in American politics, and its adherents say they seek to return American democracy to its founding principles. People in the United States today may have very different views of what democracy means for policymaking, but they continue to display the same veneration for democracy that de Tocqueville identified more than 175 years ago.

The United States, the United Kingdom, and France are all western nations with well-established representative democracies. Millions of people in each country (maybe including you) have been tourists in one or both of the other two countries. Ask any American who has spent time in either country what it is like and you will probably hear generalizations about the "culture"—"friendly" or "cold," "very different" or "surprisingly like home," and so on.

But "culture" also counts when it comes to politics and government. Politically speaking, at least three major differences exist among and between countries: constitutional, demographic, and cultural. Each difference is important, and the differences tend to feed each other. Arguably, however, the cultural differences are not only the most consequential but also often the trickiest to analyze. As we will see, that holds true not only for cross-national differences between America and other countries but also when it comes to deciphering political divides within America itself. And the differences usually endure over time.

political culture *A patterned and sustained way of thinking about how political and economic life ought to be carried out.*

4-1 Political Culture

Constitutional differences tend to be fairly obvious and easy to summarize. The United States and France each have a written constitution, whereas the United Kingdom does not. The United States separates powers between three equal branches of its national government. By contrast, the United Kingdom has a parliamentary system in which the legislature chooses a prime minister from within its own ranks. And France has a semi-presidential or quasi-parliamentary system in which the president selects a prime minister from the majority party in the lower house of the parliament, and the prime minister exercises most executive powers.

Demographic differences are also straightforward. America is a large land with close to 330 million inhabitants. The dominant language is English, but millions of people also speak Spanish. About one-sixth of its population is Hispanic. More than 80 percent of its adults identify themselves as Christians, but they are divided between Catholics (about a quarter) and more than a dozen different Protestant denominations. By comparison, France and the United Kingdom are each home to about 60 million people and have small but growing immigrant and foreign-born subpopulations. Most French (more than 80 percent) are Catholic; most British belong to the Church of England (Anglican, the official state religion) or the Church of Scotland. But in neither country do many people go to church.

The differences among these three democracies go much deeper. Each country has a different **political culture**—a patterned and sustained way of thinking about how political and economic life ought to be carried out. Most Americans, British, and French think that democracy is good, favor majority rule, and believe in respecting minority rights. And few in each nation would say that a leader who loses office in an election has any right to retake office by force. Even so, their political cultures differ. Crossnational surveys consistently find that Americans are far more likely than the French or British to believe that everybody should be equal politically, but far less likely to think it important that everybody should be equal economically. For example, in one large survey in the early post–Cold War era, the French and British were more than twice as likely as Americans to agree that "it is government's responsibility to take care of the very poor," and less than a third as likely as Americans to agree that "government should **not** guarantee every citizen food and basic shelter."[2]

When it comes to ensuring political equality or equality before the law, Americans are more committed from an early age. For instance, a classic study compared how children aged 10 to 14 in the United States, Great Britain, and France responded to a series of questions about democracy and the law. They were asked to imagine the following:

> One day the President (substitute the Queen in England, President of the Republic in France) was driving his car to a meeting. Because he was late, he was driving very fast. The police stopped the car. Finish the story.[3]

The children from each country ended the story quite differently. French children declared that the president would not be reprimanded. British children said the queen would not be punished. But American children were most likely to say that the president would be fined or ticketed, just like any other person should be.

The Granger Collection, NYC

Image 4.1 Alexis de Tocqueville (1805–1859) was a young French aristocrat who came to the United States to study the American prison system. He wrote the brilliant *Democracy in America* (2 volumes, 1835–1840), a profound analysis of our political culture.

Cross-national differences wrought by political culture seem to be even sharper between the United States and such countries as Argentina, Brazil, Mexico, and the Philippines. Why have these countries, whose constitutions are very much like the American one, had so much trouble with corruption, military takeovers, and the rise of demagogues? Each of these nations has had periods of democratic rule, but only for a short period of time, despite having an elected president, a separately elected congress, and an independent judiciary.

Some have argued that democracy took root in the United States but not in other countries that copied its constitution because America offered more abundant land and greater opportunities for people. No feudal aristocracy occupied the land, taxes remained low, and when one place after another filled up, people kept pushing west to find new opportunities. America became a nation of small, independent farmers with relatively few landless peasants or indentured servants.

However, as Alexis de Tocqueville, the perceptive French observer of American politics, noted in the 1830s, much of South America contains fertile land and rich resources, but democracy has not flourished there. The constitution and the physical advantages of the land cannot by themselves explain the persistence of any nation's democratic institutions. Nor can they account for the fact that American democracy survived a Civil War and thrived as wave after wave of immigrants became citizens and made the democracy more demographically diverse. What can begin to account for such differences are the customs of the people—what de Tocqueville called their "moral and intellectual characteristics,"[4] and what social scientists today call political culture.

Japan, like the United States, is a democracy. But while America is an immigrant nation that has often favored open immigration policies, Japan remains a Japanese nation in which immigration policies are highly restrictive and foreign-born citizens are few. America, like Saudi Arabia, is a country in which most people profess religious beliefs, and many people identify themselves as orthodox believers. But America's Christian majority favors religious pluralism and church–state separation, whereas Saudi Arabia's Muslim majority supports laws that maintain Islam as the state religion. In Germany, courts have held that non-Christian religious symbols and dress, but not Christian ones, may be banned from schools and other public places. In France, the government forbids wearing face-covering headwear in public schools. In the United States, such rulings or restrictions would violate First

Amendment guarantees of free speech and free exercise of religion.

The Political System

The American view of the political system contains at least five important elements as follows:

- ***Liberty:*** Americans are preoccupied with their rights. They believe they should be free to do pretty much as they please, with some exceptions, as long as they don't hurt other people.
- ***Equality:*** Americans believe everybody should have an equal vote and an equal chance to participate and succeed.
- ***Democracy:*** Americans think government officials should be accountable to the people.
- ***Civic duty:*** Americans generally believe people ought to take community affairs seriously and help out when they can.[5]
- ***Individual responsibility:*** A characteristically American view is that, barring some disability, individuals are responsible for their own actions and well-being.

By vast majorities, Americans believe that every citizen should have an equal chance to influence government policy and to hold public office, and they oppose the idea of letting people have titles such as "Lord" or "Duke," as in England. By somewhat smaller majorities, they believe people should be allowed to vote even if they can't read or write or vote intelligently.[6] Though Americans recognize that people differ in their abilities, they overwhelmingly agree with the statement, "Teaching children that all people are really equal recognizes that all people are equally worthy and deserve equal treatment."[7]

At least three questions can be raised about this political culture. First, how do we know that the American people share these beliefs? For most of our history there were no public opinion polls, and even after they became commonplace, they were rather crude tools for measuring the existence and meaning of complex, abstract ideas. There is in fact no way to prove that values such as those listed above are important to Americans. But neither is there good reason for dismissing the list out of hand. One can infer, as have many scholars, the existence of certain values by a close study of the kinds of books Americans read, the speeches they hear, the slogans to which they respond, and the political choices they make, as well as by noting the observations of insightful foreign visitors. Personality tests, as well as opinion polls—particularly those asking similar questions in different countries—also supply useful evidence, some of which will be reviewed in the following paragraphs.

Enigma/Alamy Stock Photo

Image 4.2 Despite differences in ethnic backgrounds, ideological views, religious beliefs, and more, Americans historically have demonstrated strong popular support for a shared political culture. All schoolchildren, for example, are taught to say the Pledge of Allegiance.

Second, if these values are important to Americans, how can we explain the existence in our society of behavior that is obviously inconsistent with them? For example, if white Americans believe in equality of opportunity, why did so many of them for so long deny that equality to African Americans? That people act contrary to their professed beliefs is an everyday fact of life: People believe in honesty, yet they steal from their employers and sometimes under-report their taxable income. In addition to values, self-interest and social circumstances also shape behavior. Gunnar Myrdal, a Swedish observer of American society, described race relations in this country as "an American dilemma" resulting from the conflict between the "American creed" (a belief in equality of opportunity) and American behavior (denying African Americans full citizenship).[8] But the creed remains important because it is a source of change: as more and more people become aware of the inconsistency between their values and their behavior, that behavior slowly changes.[9]

Race relations in this country would take a very different course if instead of an abstract but widespread belief in equality there were an equally widespread belief that one race is inherently inferior to another. The late political scientist Samuel P. Huntington put it this way: "Critics say that America is a lie because its reality falls so far short of its ideals. America is not a lie, it is a disappointment. And it can be a disappointment only because it is also a hope."[10]

Third, if Americans agree on certain political values, why has there been so much political conflict in our history? How could a people who agree on such fundamentals fight a bloody civil war, engage in violent labor–management disputes, take to the streets in riots and demonstrations, and sue each other in countless court battles? Conflict, even violent struggles, can occur over specific policies even among those who share, at some level of abstraction, common beliefs. Many political values may be irrelevant to specific controversies: No abstract value, for example, would settle the question of whether steelworkers ought to organize unions. More important, much of our conflict has occurred precisely because we have strong beliefs that happen, as each of us interprets them, to be in conflict. Equality of opportunity seems an attractive idea, but sometimes it can be pursued only by curtailing another value that most people hold dear: personal liberty. The states went to war in 1861 over one aspect of that conflict—the rights of slaves versus the rights of slave-owners.

Indeed, the Civil War illustrates the way certain fundamental beliefs about how a democratic regime ought to be organized have persisted despite bitter conflict over the policies adopted by particular governments. When the southern states seceded from the Union, they formed not a wholly different government but one modeled, despite some important differences, on the U.S. Constitution. Even some of the language of the Constitution was duplicated, suggesting that the southern states believed not that a new form of government or a different political culture ought to be created, but rather that the South was the true repository of the existing constitutional and cultural order.[11]

Perhaps the most frequently encountered evidence that Americans believe themselves bound by common values and common hopes is the persistence of the word *Americanism* in our political vocabulary. From the 19th century onward, *Americanism* and *the American dream* have been familiar terms not only in Fourth of July speeches but also in everyday discourse. For many years, the House of Representatives had a committee called the House Un-American Activities Committee. Hardly any example of such a way of thinking can be found abroad: There is no "Britishism" or "Frenchism," and when Britons and French people become worried about subversion, they call it a problem of internal security, not a manifestation of "un-British" or "un-French" activities.

The United States has ended slavery, endorsed civil rights, and expanded the scope of free discussion, but these gains have not ended political conflict. We argue about abortion, morality, religion, immigration, and affirmative action. Some people believe that core moral principles are absolute, whereas others feel they are relative to the situation. Some people believe all immigrants should become like every other American, whereas

Topham/The Image Works

Image 4.3 In the 1950s Senator Joseph McCarthy of Wisconsin was the inspiration for the word *McCarthyism* after his highly publicized attacks on alleged communists working in the federal government.

others argue that we should, in the name of diversity and multiculturalism, celebrate group differences.

The 2016 presidential campaign illustrated these divisions in the sharply contrasting candidacies of Hillary Clinton and Donald Trump. Upon taking office after his surprise election victory, President Trump moved quickly to enact several of his campaign promises by executive order, such as a travel ban from several countries with large Muslim populations, which the Supreme Court narrowly upheld. Throughout the Trump administration, highly polarized ideological debates between the president's supporters and opponents tested the resilience of American political institutions to address deep policy conflicts. Historic voter turnout in the November 2020 elections—about two-thirds of eligible voters, representing the highest percentage since the early twentieth century—demonstrated clear public awareness of the choices and issues at stake, particularly in the presidential race between Trump and Joe Biden. But Trump's allegations (widely refuted) of corruption with mail-in ballots and vote counts in several battleground states raised troubling questions about sustaining the legitimacy of political participation in American politics.

Much depends on how we define a good citizen. Some people define a good citizen as a person who votes, pays taxes, obeys the law, and supports the military; others describe a good citizen as skeptical of government and ready to join protest movements, boycott products, and take other actions to press for change. These competing opinions sometimes reflect differences in age and education. Older people are more likely to take the first view, whereas younger people who are college educated are more likely to take the second.[12] But these conflicts, though they affect every American, should not obscure the enduring principles of American political culture, which can incorporate multiple perspectives.

The Economic System

Americans judge the economic system using many of the same standards by which they judge the political system, albeit with some very important differences. As it is in American politics, liberty is important in the U.S. economy. Thus Americans support the idea of a free-enterprise economic system, calling the nation's economy "generally fair and efficient" and denying that it "survives by keeping the poor down."[13] However, there are limits to how much freedom they think should exist in the marketplace. People support government regulation of business in order to keep some firms from becoming too powerful and to correct specific abuses.[14]

Americans are more willing to tolerate economic inequality than political inequality. They believe in maintaining "equality of opportunity" in the economy but not "equality of results." If everyone has an equal opportunity to get ahead, then it is all right for people with more ability to earn higher salaries and for wages to be set based on how hard people work rather than on their economic needs. Classic studies found that although Americans were quite willing to support education and training programs to help disadvantaged people get ahead, they were strongly opposed to anything that looks like preferential treatment (e.g., hiring quotas) in the workplace.[15]

Those studies also found that leaders of more liberal political groups typically are more willing than the average American to support preferential treatment in the hiring and promotion of minorities and women. They do so because, unlike most citizens, they believe that whatever disadvantages minorities and women face are the result of failures of the economic system rather than the fault of individuals. Even so, these leaders still strongly support the idea that earnings should be based on ability and oppose the idea of having any top limit on what people can earn.[16]

This popular commitment to economic individualism and personal responsibility may help explain how Americans think about particular public policies, such as welfare and affirmative action. Polls show that Americans are willing to help people "truly in need" (this includes older adults and the disabled) but not those deemed "able to take care of themselves" (this includes, in the public's mind, people "on welfare"). Also, Americans dislike preferential hiring programs and the use of quotas to address racial inequality.

At the core of these policy attitudes is a widely (but not universally) shared commitment to economic individualism and personal responsibility. Some scholars, among them Donald Kinder and David Sears, have interpreted these individualistic values as "symbolic racism"—a kind of plausible camouflage for anti-black attitudes.[17] But other scholars, such as Paul M. Sniderman and Michael Gray Hagen, have argued that these views are not a smokescreen for bigotry or insensitivity but a genuine commitment to the ethic of self-reliance.[18] Since many Americans fall on both sides of this issue, debates about welfare and racial justice tend to be especially intense. What is striking about the American political culture is that in this country the individualist view of public policy historically has been by far the most popular.[19]

In the 2020 presidential race, "income inequality" sparked major political debates, though people disagreed about its sources and relative importance compared to other policy issues.[20] Several political elites, including leading contenders for the Democratic presidential nomination, were strong advocates for policies to reduce the "wealth gap," such as a public health care system for all. But other candidates argued for more moderate approaches to improving people's economic conditions through modifying instead of replacing the 2010 health care law. This policy conflict and others may prompt shifts in public views in the coming years; we also take up debates over income inequality in Chapter 18.

In the United States, we have seen public attitudes about economic and social policies change over time. Americans are now much more inclined than they once were to believe that the government should help the needy and regulate business. But the commitment to certain underlying principles has been remarkably enduring. In 1924, almost half of the high school students in Muncie, Indiana, said that "it is entirely the fault of the man himself if he cannot succeed" and disagreed with the view that differences in wealth showed that the system was unjust. More than half a century later, the students in this same high school were asked the same questions again, with the same results.[21] And an early 2020 Pew survey found that while a majority of Americans agreed that economic inequality was a problem, they ranked it lower than other issues such as health care, combating terrorism, and reducing gun violence. Democrats and Republicans alike also agreed that some economic inequality is part of American democracy, though they differed on how much is acceptable.[22]

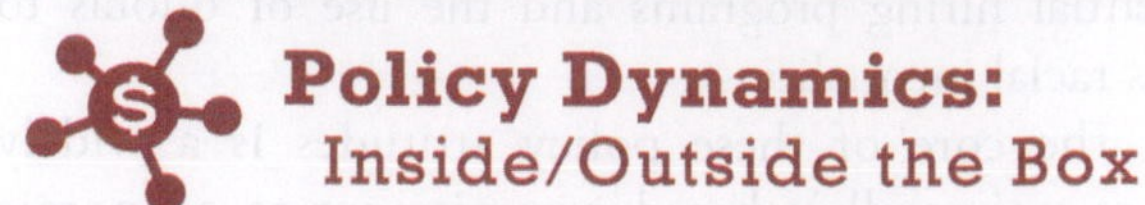

Bilingual Education: Majoritarian or Client Politics?

Hispanics are the largest and fastest-growing minority group in America. The nation's almost 60 million Hispanics represent about 18 percent of the total U.S. population. They comprise more than a third of the population in several states, including California, New Mexico, and Texas. By 2050, it is estimated that about one in four U.S. residents will be Hispanic.

Some analysts have asserted that Hispanic immigrants, the vast majority of whom come from Mexico, will remain strangers to American political culture. But all the evidence suggests that, if anything, Hispanic immigrants over time are far more likely to embrace and emulate, rather than to reject or refashion, American political culture.

To assist immigrants in their transition, the federal government began in the late 1960s to promote bilingual education, or teaching children in their native language as well as in English. Proponents of bilingual education make a case for majoritarian politics: Everyone supports the education system through taxes (primarily state and local), and everyone benefits from bilingual schooling in the long run because it helps immigrants to succeed professionally and advance American productivity.

Critics of bilingual education programs, however, say they benefit only the groups who participate, and that even those benefits are questionable, if people do not learn English quickly. In 1998, California voters approved Proposition 227, which removed bilingual education from most public schools in the state. Nearly two decades later, though, voters overturned the law with Proposition 58, which ended English-only instruction, in 2016. Nationally, the 2002 No Child Left Behind law encouraged English instruction and testing over time. The future of bilingual education in the United States will depend largely on whether the programs are viewed as having a narrow or broad public interest.

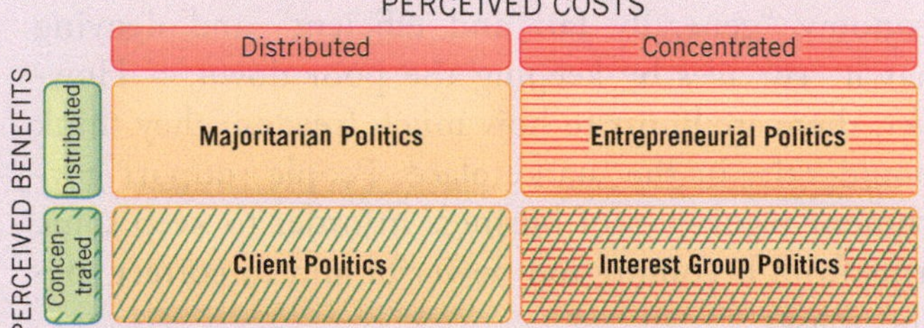

Source: Luis Noe-Bustamante and Antonio Flores, "Facts on Latinos in the U.S.," Pew Research Center: Hispanic Trends, 16 September 2019, https://www.pewresearch.org/hispanic/fact-sheet/latinos-in-the-u-s-fact-sheet/; Jack Citrin, et al., "Testing Huntington: Is Hispanic Immigration a Threat to American Identity?" *Perspectives on Politics,* vol. 5, no. 1, March 2007, 31–48; Samuel P. Huntington, *Who Are We? The Challenges to America's National Identity.* New York: Simon & Shuster, 2004; David Nieto, "A Brief History of Bilingual Education in the United States," *Perspectives on Urban Education,* Spring 2009, 61–72.

4-2 How the United States Compares With Other Nations

Americans' attitudes toward politics and public life differ from those of people in European democracies in some important ways. In Figure 4.1, we see that more than 70 percent of Americans think working hard is important to get ahead in life, compared with 49 percent of Germans and 25 percent of French. A majority of people in Germany, Italy, and Poland think success in life is determined by forces outside an individual's control; Americans disagree. Americans also think religion is very important in their lives, but fewer people in the United Kingdom, Germany, and Spain say the same. Following are some examples from politics, the economy, and religion that further illustrate different attitudes among Americans and people in other democracies.

The Political System

Sweden has a well-developed democratic government, with a constitution, free speech, an elected legislature, competing political parties, and a reasonably honest and nonpartisan bureaucracy. But the Swedish political culture is significantly different from ours; it is more deferential than participatory. Though almost all adult Swedes vote in national elections, few participate in politics in any other way. They defer to the decisions of experts and specialists who work for the government, rarely challenge governmental decisions in court, believe leaders and legislators ought to decide issues on the basis of "what is best" more than on "what the people want," and value equality as much as (or more than) liberty.[23] Whereas Americans are contentious, Swedes value harmony; while Americans tend to assert their rights, Swedes tend to observe their obligations.

Figure 4.1 Attitudes in the United States and Other Democracies

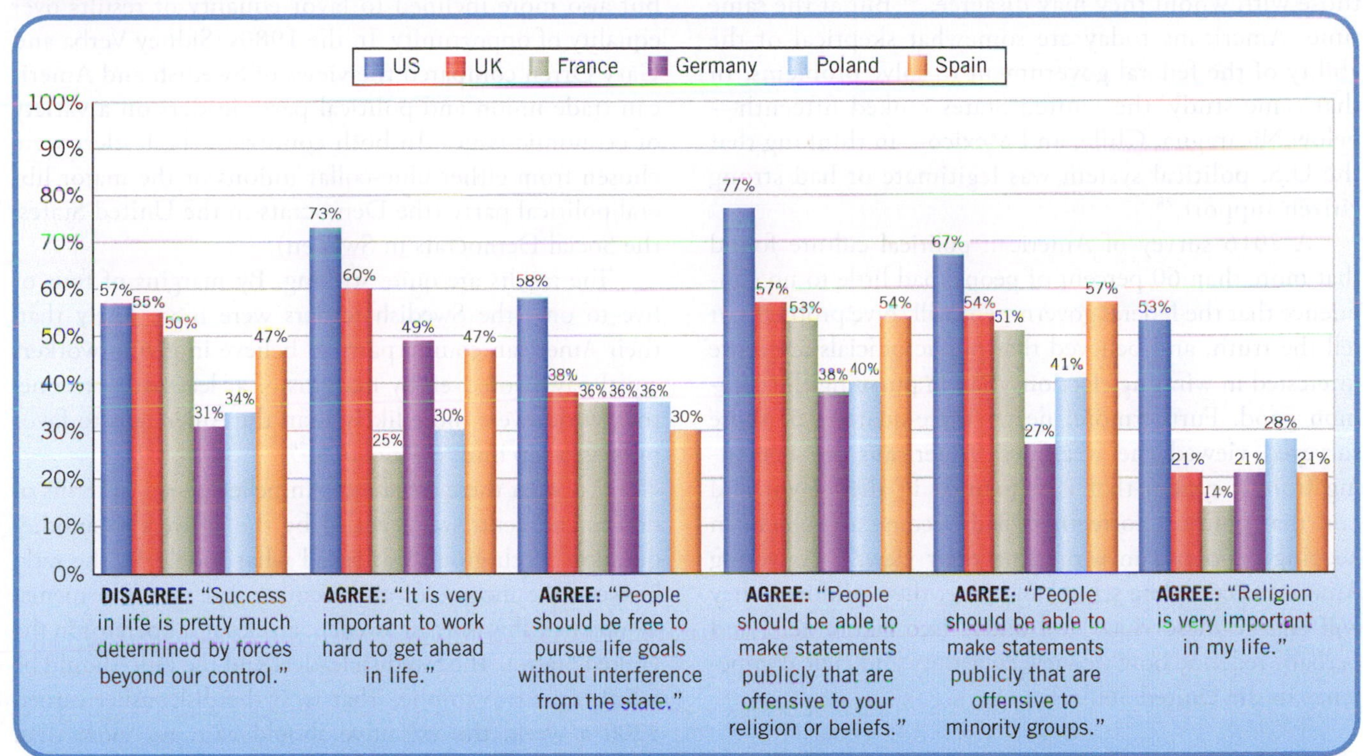

Source: Richard Wike, "5 Ways Americans and Europeans Are Different," *Fact Tank: News in the Numbers,* Pew Research Center, 19 April 2016, www.pewresearch.org/fact-tank/2016/04/19/5-ways-americans-and-europeans-are-different/; Angelina E. Theodorou, "Americans Are in the Middle of the Pack Globally When It Comes to Importance of Religion," Pew Research Center, 23 December 2015, www.pewresearch.org/fact-tank/2015/12/23/americans-are-in-the-middle-of-the-pack-globally-when-it-comes-to-importance-of-religion/.

The contrast in political cultures is even greater when one looks at a nation such as Japan, with a wholly different history and set of traditions. One study compared the values expressed by a small number of upper-status Japanese with those of some similarly situated Americans. Whereas the Americans emphasized the virtues of individualism, competition, and equality in their political, economic, and social relations, the Japanese attached greater value to maintaining good relations with colleagues, having decisions made by groups, preserving social harmony, and displaying respect for hierarchy. The Americans were more concerned than the Japanese with rules and with treating others fairly but impersonally, with due regard for their rights. The Japanese, on the other hand, stressed the importance of being sensitive to the personal needs of others, avoiding conflict, and reaching decisions through discussion rather than the application of rules.[24]

A classic study of political culture in five nations found that Americans, and to a lesser degree citizens of the United Kingdom, had a stronger sense of **civic duty** (a belief that one has an obligation to participate in civic and political affairs) and a stronger sense of **civic competence** (a belief that one can affect government policies) than the citizens of Germany, Italy, and Mexico. More than half of all Americans and one-third of all Britons in the early 1960s believed the average citizen ought to "be active in one's community," compared with only a tenth in Italy and a fifth in Germany.

civic duty *A belief that one has an obligation to participate in civic and political affairs.*

civic competence *A belief that one can affect government policies.*

Moreover, many more Americans and Britons than Germans, Italians, or Mexicans believed they could "do something" about an unjust national law or local regulation.[25] Some thirty years later, a study of citizen participation in politics found that while America lagged behind Austria, the Netherlands, Germany, and the United Kingdom in voter participation, when it came to campaigning, attending political meetings, becoming active in the local community, and contacting government officials, Americans were as active—or substantially more active—than citizens elsewhere.[26]

More recently, a 2014 study of democratic attitudes in countries in the Western Hemisphere found that the United States ranked highest among some two dozen nations for political tolerance, defined as "the respect by citizens for the political rights of others, especially those with whom they may disagree."[27] But at the same time, Americans today are somewhat skeptical of the ability of the federal government to solve problems. In that same study, the United States ranked fifteenth—below Nicaragua, Chile, and Mexico—in thinking that the U.S. political system was legitimate or had strong citizen support.[28]

A 2016 survey of American political culture found that more than 60 percent of people had little to no confidence that the federal government will solve problems or tell the truth, and believed that public officials are more interested in winning elections than in pursuing the common good. Furthermore, nearly three-quarters of those surveyed viewed the wealthiest Americans are benefiting from a system that is structured in their favor and said that political correctness had become a problem in keeping people from expressing their views.[29] As young Americans complete school and enter the workforce, they will engage these views and others (see Figure 4.2), and perhaps redefine how we view civic duty and civic competence in the United States.

The Economic System

In American political culture, equality for most people refers to equality of opportunity. But not all democracies define equality this way. For example, the political culture of Sweden is not only more deferential than ours but also more inclined to favor equality of results over equality of opportunity. In the 1980s, Sidney Verba and Gary Orren compared the views of Swedish and American trade union and political party leaders on a variety of economic issues. In both countries, the leaders were chosen from either blue-collar unions or the major liberal political party (the Democrats in the United States, the Social Democrats in Sweden).

The results are quite striking. By margins of four or five to one, the Swedish leaders were more likely than their American counterparts to believe in giving workers equal pay. Moreover, by margins of at least three to one, the Swedes were more likely than the Americans to favor putting a top limit on incomes.[30]

Just what these differences in beliefs mean in terms of dollars and cents was revealed by the answers to another question. Each group was asked what should be the ratio between the income of an executive and that of a menial worker (a dishwasher in Sweden, an elevator operator in the United States). The Swedish leaders said the ratio should be a little over two to one. That is, if the dishwasher earned \$200 a week, the executive should earn no more than \$440 to \$480 a week. But the American leaders were ready to let the executive earn between \$2,260 and \$3,040 per week when the elevator operator was earning \$200.

Americans, compared with people in many other countries, are more likely to think that freedom is more

Figure 4.2 **How the American Public Views Political Leaders**

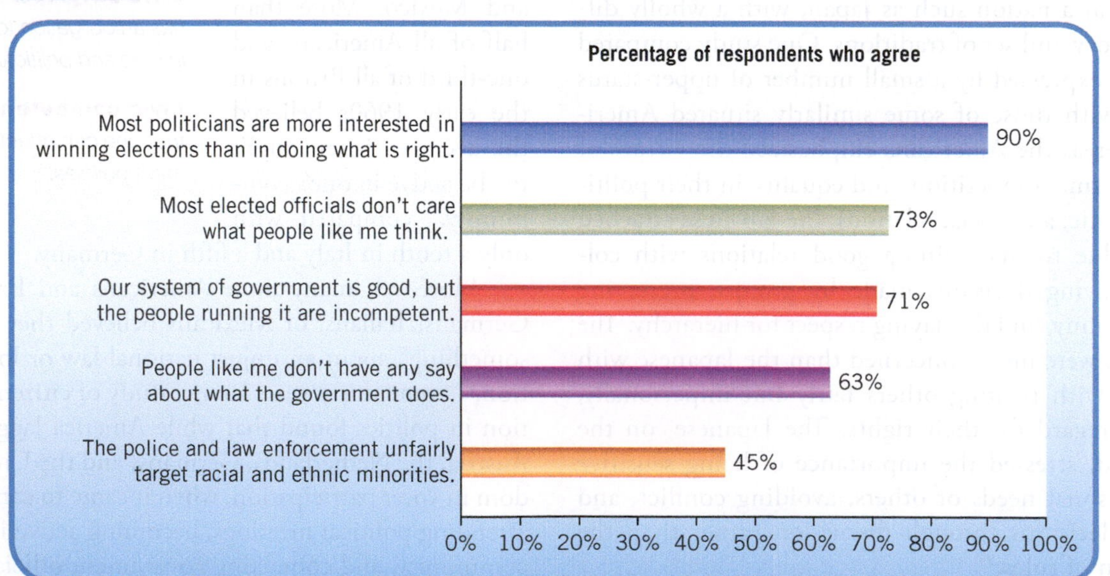

Source: James Davison Hunter and Carl Desportes Bowman, "The Vanishing Center of American Democracy," Figure 2: Opinions of Political Leaders (University of Virginia: Advanced Studies in Culture Foundation, 2016), p. 20; www.iasc-culture.org/survey_archives/VanishingCenter.pdf.

Q **How does the American public view civic competence in the twenty-first century?**

important than equality and less likely to think that hard work goes unrewarded or that the government should guarantee citizens a basic standard of living. These cultural differences make a difference in politics. In fact, there is less income inequality in Sweden than in the United States—the Swedish government sees to that.

The Civic Role of Religion

In the 1830s, de Tocqueville was amazed at how religious Americans were in comparison to his fellow Europeans. From the first days of the new Republic to the present, America has been among the most religious countries in the world. The average American is more likely than the average European to believe in God, to pray on a daily basis, and to acknowledge clear standards of right and wrong.[31]

Religious people donate more than three times as much money to charity as secular people, even when the incomes of the two groups are the same, and they volunteer their time twice as often. And this is true whether religious people go to a church, mosque, synagogue, temple, or other places of organized worship regularly. Moreover, religious people are more likely to give money and donate time to nonreligious organizations, such as the Red Cross, than secular people.[32] It is clear that religion in America has a large effect on our culture.

Religion also affects our politics. The religious revivalist movement of the late 1730s and early 1740s (known as the First Great Awakening) transformed the political life of the American colonies. Religious ideas fueled the break with England, a country that had, in the words of the Declaration of Independence, violated "the laws of nature and nature's God." Religious leaders were central to the struggle over slavery in the 19th century and the temperance movement of the early 20th century.

AP Images/J. Scott Applewhite

Image 4.4 Congress traditionally convenes a new session with an opening prayer, as the U.S. House of Representatives did on the first day of the 116th Congress on January 3, 2019.

Both liberals and conservatives have used the pulpit to promote political change. The civil rights movement of the 1950s and 1960s was led mainly by black religious leaders, most prominently Martin Luther King, Jr. In the 1980s, a conservative religious group known as the Moral Majority advocated constitutional amendments that would allow prayer in public schools and ban abortion. In the 1990s, another conservative religious group, the Christian Coalition, attracted an enormous amount of media attention and became a prominent force in many national, state, and local elections.

Candidates for national office in most contemporary democracies mention religion rarely, if they mention it at all. Not so in America. During the 2000 presidential campaign, for example, both Democratic candidate Al Gore and Republican candidate George W. Bush gave major speeches extolling the virtues of religion and advocating the right of religious organizations that deliver social services to receive government funding on the same basis as all other nonprofit organizations. President Barack Obama opted to keep the White House "faith-based" office that Bush had established, expanded the office to cabinet centers at every federal cabinet department, and made frequent references to religion in public addresses. Soon after taking office, President Donald Trump signed an executive order permitting tax-exempt religious organizations to participate in some political activity, though the change from existing policy was limited.

The general American feeling about religion became apparent when a federal appeals court in 2002 tried to ban the Pledge of Allegiance because it contained the phrase "under God." There was an overwhelming and bipartisan condemnation of the ruling. To a degree that would be almost unthinkable in many other democracies, religious beliefs will probably continue to shape political culture in America for many generations to come. The Supreme Court, by deciding that the man who brought the case was not entitled to do so, left the Pledge intact without deciding whether it was constitutional.

Finally, although the number has declined in the past decade, just over three-fourths of Americans declare a religious affiliation. Two-thirds of Americans born before the end of World War II say religion is very important in their lives, as do more than half of people

Constitutional Connections | "A Religious People"

Justice William O. Douglas was the U.S. Supreme Court's longest-serving member, beginning his term in 1939 and ending it in 1975. When Douglas died in 1980, he was widely remembered as the Court's most consistently liberal voice, a major force in legalizing abortion rights, and a proponent of the "wall-of-separation" doctrine regarding church-state relations (see Chapter 5). In *Zorach v. Clauson* (1952), however, Douglas held that a New York City policy permitting public school students to be released during the school day to receive religious instruction off school grounds was not only constitutional but consistent with Americans' best "traditions" as "a religious people":

> *We are a religious people whose institutions presuppose a Supreme Being. We guarantee the freedom to worship . . . . We make room for a wide variety of beliefs . . . . When the state encourages religious instruction or cooperates with religious authorities, it follows the best of our traditions.*

Source: *Zorach v. Clauson*, 343 U.S. 306 (1952).

born between 1946 and 1980. But the number drops below 50 percent for people born in the 1980s, and just under 40 percent of people born in the early to mid-1990s say religion is very important to them (see Figure 4.3). More recent surveys indicate that these trends are continuing, which could affect American politics in coming years if decreased religious affiliation affects civic participation.[33]

Figure 4.3 **Americans' Beliefs About Religion**

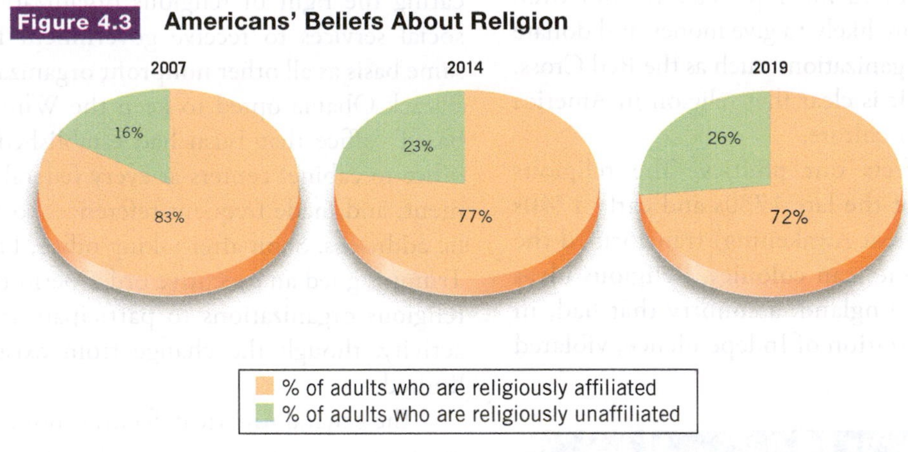

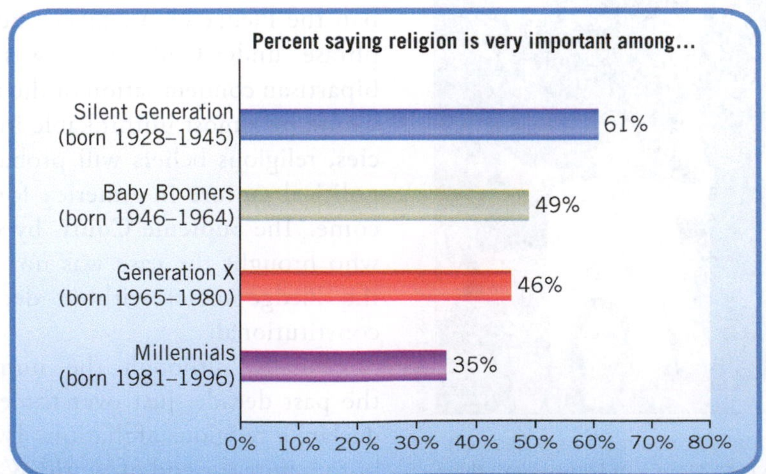

Sources: Pew Research Center Religious Landscape Studies (2007 and 2014); 2018 and 2019 Aggregated Pew Research Center political surveys. Note: Figures may not add up to 100% because some respondents said they don't know or refused to answer.

4-3 Sources of Political Culture

That Americans bring a distinctive way of thinking to their political life is easier to demonstrate than to explain. But even a brief, and necessarily superficial, effort to understand the sources of our political culture can help make its significance clearer.

The American Revolution, as we discussed in Chapter 2, was essentially a war fought over liberty: an assertion by the colonists of what they took to be their rights. Though the Constitution, produced 11 years after the Revolution, had to deal with other issues as well, its animating spirit reflected the effort to reconcile personal liberty with the needs of social control. These founding experiences, and the political disputes that followed, have given to American political thought and culture a preoccupation with the assertion and maintenance of rights. This tradition has imbued the daily conduct of U.S. politics with a kind of adversarial spirit quite foreign to the political life of countries that did not undergo a libertarian revolution or that were formed out of an interest in other goals, such as social equality, national independence, or ethnic supremacy.

The adversarial spirit of the American political culture reflects not only our preoccupation with rights but also our long-standing distrust of authority and of people wielding power. The experiences of the American colonies with British rule were one source of that distrust. But another, older source was the religious belief of many Americans, which saw human nature as fundamentally depraved. To the colonists, all of humankind suffered from original sin, symbolized by Adam and Eve eating the forbidden fruit in the Garden of Eden. Since no one was born innocent, no one could be trusted with power. Thus, the Constitution had to be designed in such a way as to curb the darker side of human nature. Otherwise, everyone's rights would be in jeopardy.

The contentiousness of a people animated by a suspicion of government and devoted to individualism could easily have made democratic politics so tumultuous as to be impossible. After all, one must be willing to trust others with power if there is to be any kind of democratic government, and sometimes those others will be people not of one's own choosing. The first great test case took place around 1800 in a battle between the Federalists, led by John Adams and Alexander Hamilton, and the Democratic Republicans, led by Thomas Jefferson and James Madison. The two factions deeply distrusted each other: the Federalists had passed laws designed to suppress Jeffersonian journalists, Jefferson suspected the Federalists were out to subvert the Constitution, and the Federalists believed Jefferson intended to sell out the country to France. But as we shall see in Chapter 9, the threat of civil war never materialized, and the Jeffersonians came to power peacefully. Within a few years, the role of an opposition party became legitimate, and people abandoned the idea of making serious efforts to suppress their opponents. By happy circumstance, people came to accept that liberty and orderly political change could coexist.

The Constitution, by creating a federal system and dividing political authority among competing institutions, provided ample opportunity for widespread—though hardly universal—participation in politics. The election of Jefferson in 1800 produced no political catastrophe, and those who had predicted one were, to a degree, discredited. But other, more fundamental features of American life contributed to the same end. One of the most important of these was religious diversity.

The absence of an established or official religion for the nation as a whole, reinforced by a constitutional prohibition of such an establishment and by the migration to this country of people with different religious backgrounds, meant that religious diversity was inevitable. Since there could be no orthodox or official religion, it became difficult for a corresponding political orthodoxy to emerge. Moreover, the conflict between the Puritan tradition, with its emphasis on faith and hard work, and the Catholic Church, with its devotion to the sacraments and priestly authority, provided a recurrent source of cleavage in American public life. The differences in values between these two groups showed up not only in their religious practices but also in areas involving the regulation of manners and morals, and even in people's choice of political party. For more than a century, candidates for state and national offices were deeply divided over whether the sale of liquor should be prohibited, a question that ultimately arose out of competing religious doctrines.

Even though there was no established church, there was certainly a dominant religious tradition—Protestantism, and especially Puritanism. The Protestant churches provided people with both a set of beliefs and an organizational experience that had profound effects on American political culture. Those beliefs encouraged, or even required, a life of personal achievement as well as religious conviction: a believer had an obligation to work, save money, obey the secular law, and do good works. Max Weber explained the rise of capitalism in part by what he called the *Protestant ethic*—what we now sometimes call the *work ethic*.[34] Such values had political consequences, as people holding them were motivated to engage in civic and communal action.

Churches offered ready opportunities for developing and practicing civic and political skills. Since most

class-consciousness *A belief that one is a member of an economic group whose interests are opposed to people in other such groups.*

orthodox *A belief that morality and religion ought to be of decisive importance.*

progressive *A belief that personal freedom and solving social problems are more important than religion.*

Protestant churches were organized along congregational lines—that is, the church was controlled by its members, who put up the building, hired the preacher, and supervised the finances—they were, in effect, miniature political systems with leaders and committees, conflict and consensus. Developing a participatory political culture was undoubtedly made easier by the existence of a participatory religious culture. Even some Catholic churches in early America were under a degree of lay control. Parishioners owned the church property, negotiated with priests, and conducted church business.

All aspects of culture, including the political, are preserved and transmitted to new generations primarily by the family. Though some believe that the weakening of the family unit has eroded the extent to which it transmits anything, particularly culture, and has enlarged the power of other sources of values—the mass media and the world of friends, fashion, leisure, and entertainment—there is still little doubt that the ways in which we think about the world are largely acquired within the family. In Chapter 7, we shall see that the family is the primary source of one kind of political attitude: identification with one or another political party. Even more important, the family shapes in subtle ways how we think and act on political matters. Psychologist Erik Erikson noted certain traits that are more characteristic of American than of European families—the greater freedom enjoyed by children, for example, and the larger measure of equality among family members. These familial characteristics promote a belief, carried through life, that every person has rights deserving protection and that a variety of interests have a legitimate claim to consideration when decisions are made.[35]

The combined effect of religious and ethnic diversity, an individualistic philosophy, fragmented political authority, and the relatively egalitarian American family can be seen in the absence of a high degree of class-consciousness among Americans. **Class-consciousness** means thinking of oneself as a worker whose interests are in opposition to those of management, or vice versa. In this country, most people, whatever their jobs, think of themselves as "middle class."

Though the writings of Horatio Alger are no longer popular, Americans still seem to believe in the message of those stories—that the opportunity for success is available to people who work hard. This may help explain why the United States is the only large industrial democracy without a significant socialist party and why the nation has been slower than other advanced industrialized democracies to adopt certain social-welfare programs.

4-4 The Culture War

Almost all Americans share some elements of a common political culture. Why, then, is there so much cultural conflict in American politics? For many years, the most explosive political issues have included abortion, LGBTQ+ rights, drug use, school prayer, and pornography. Viewed from a Marxist perspective, politics in the United States is utterly baffling: instead of two economic classes engaged in a bitter struggle over wealth, we have two cultural classes locked in a war over values.

As first formulated by sociologist James Davison Hunter, the idea is that there are, broadly defined, two cultural classes in the United States: the orthodox and the progressive. On the **orthodox** side are people who believe that morality is as important as, or more important than, self-expression and that moral rules derive from the commands of God or the laws of nature—commands and laws that are relatively clear, unchanging, and independent of individual preferences. On the **progressive** side are people who think that personal freedom is as important as, or more important than, certain traditional moral rules and that those rules must be evaluated in light of the circumstances of modern life—circumstances that are quite complex, changeable, and dependent on individual preferences.[36]

Most conspicuous among the orthodox are fundamentalist Protestants and evangelical Christians, and so critics who dislike orthodox views often dismiss them as the fanatical expressions of "the Religious Right." But many people who hold orthodox views are not fanatical or deeply religious or right-wing on most issues: they simply have strong views about drugs, pornography, and sexual morality. Similarly, the progressive side often includes members of liberal Protestant denominations (e.g., Episcopalians and Unitarians) and people with no strong religious beliefs, and so their critics often denounce them as immoral, anti-Christian radicals who have embraced the ideology of secular humanism, the belief that moral standards do not require religious justification. But few progressives are immoral or anti-Christian, and most do not regard secular humanism as their defining ideology.

Examples of the culture war abound in many areas of public policy. Groups supporting and opposing the right to abortion have had many angry confrontations since the 1973 Supreme Court ruling that legalized abortion (see

Chapter 6). The latter have been arrested while attempting to block access to abortion clinics; some clinics have been fire-bombed and several physicians and clinic workers have been killed. In the early 1990s, a controversy over what schoolchildren should be taught about sexual orientation was responsible, in part, for the firing of the head of the New York City school system; in other states, there have been fierce arguments in state legislatures and before the courts over whether LGBTQ+ couples should be allowed to marry or adopt children. (We take up the question of same-sex marriage in Chapter 6.) Although most Americans want to keep heroin, cocaine, and other drugs illegal, a significant number of people want to legalize (or at least decriminalize) use of certain substances (such as marijuana; see the Policy Dynamics Box in Chapter 3). The Supreme Court has ruled that there cannot be state-sponsored prayer in public schools, but this has not stopped many parents and school authorities from trying to reinstate school prayer, or at least prayer-like moments of silence. The discovery that a federal agency, the National Endowment for the Arts, had given money to support exhibitions and performances that many people thought were obscene led to a furious congressional struggle over the future of the agency.

The culture war differs from other political disputes (over such matters as taxes, business regulations, and foreign policy) in several ways: money is not always at stake, compromises are almost impossible to arrange, and the conflict is more profound. It is animated by deep differences in people's beliefs about private and public morality—that is, about the standards that ought to govern individual behavior and social arrangements. It is about what kind of country we ought to live in, not just about what kinds of policies our government ought to adopt.

Two opposing views exist about the importance of the culture war. One view, developed by Morris Fiorina and others, holds that politically, the culture war is a myth. While political leaders are polarized, most Americans occupy a middle position. Journalists write about the split between "blue states" (those that vote Democratic) and "red states" (those that vote Republican), but in fact popular views on many policy issues are similar across both kinds of states.[37]

The rival view, developed by Alan Abramowitz and others, holds that more and more people are choosing their party affiliations on the basis of the party's position on moral issues. Moreover, a growing percentage of the public is politically engaged; that is, they do more to express their political views than simply vote.[38] Choosing between these two theories (which are discussed more fully in Chapter 7) will take time, as we watch what happens in future elections.

Mistrust of Government

One aspect of public opinion worries many people. Since the late 1950s there has been a more or less steady decline in the proportion of Americans who say they trust the government in Washington to do the right thing. In the past, polls showed that about three-quarters of Americans said they trusted Washington most of the time or just about always. The percentage of people who say they trust the government has on occasion gone up (e.g., during the first term of the Reagan presidency, and again just after the 9/11 terrorist attacks), but by and large trust has been waning since at least the mid-1960s. Since 2008, trust in government has remained consistently below 30 percent (see Figure 4.4).

In interpreting this data, we should remember that people often are talking about government officials, not the system of government. Americans historically have been much more supportive of the country and its institutions than Europeans are of theirs. Even so, the decline in public confidence in our officials is striking and of concern. There are all sorts of explanations for why it has happened.

In the 1960s, there was our unpopular war in Vietnam; in the 1970s, President Richard Nixon had to resign because of his involvement in the Watergate scandal; in the 1990s, President Bill Clinton went through scandals that led to his impeachment by the House of Representatives (but he was not convicted of that charge by the Senate). Beginning in 2003, President George W. Bush presided over a divisive war in Iraq. President Barack Obama faced great difficulty in winning bipartisan support for his policies, and in his last year in office, Washington had become so polarized that the Republican-led Senate refused to consider the president's Supreme Court nomination. President Trump's time in office was marked with numerous partisan debates, including his impeachment.

But there is another way of looking at the matter. Maybe in the 1950s we had an abnormally *high* level of confidence in government, one that could never be expected to last no matter what any president did. After all, when President Dwight Eisenhower took office in 1952, we had won a war against fascism, overcome the Depression of the 1930s, possessed a near monopoly of the atom bomb, had a currency that was the envy of the world, and dominated international trade. Moreover, in those days not much was expected out of Washington. Many people questioned whether the federal government should address major issues such as civil rights, crime, environmental policy, harassment, highway safety, illegal drugs, and other policy areas that clearly are on the national agenda in the twenty-first century.

Paul Taggart/Bloomberg/Getty Images

Image 4.5 Demonstrators from the Occupy Wall Street movement protested income inequality for several weeks in New York City in the fall of 2011, before New York City police cleared their camp area in lower Manhattan.

Figure 4.4 **Trust in the Federal Government, 1958–2019**

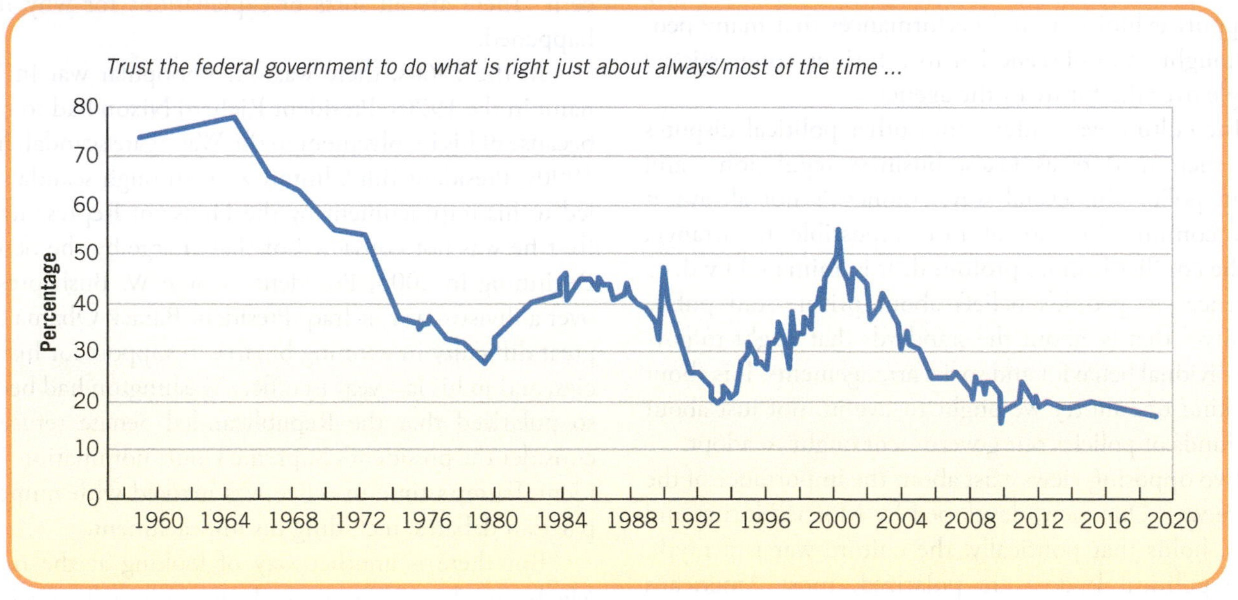

Source: Pew Research Center, "Public Trust in Government: 1958-2019," 11 April 2019, https://www.people-press.org/2019/04/11/public-trust-in-government-1958-2019/

The 1960s and 1970s changed all of that. Domestic turmoil, urban riots, a civil rights revolution, the war in Vietnam, economic inflation, and a new concern for the environment dramatically increased what we expected Washington to do. And since these problems are very difficult ones to solve, many people became convinced that our politicians couldn't do much.[39]

Those events also pushed the feelings Americans had about their country—that is, their patriotism—into the background. We liked the country, but there weren't many occasions when expressing that approval seemed to make much sense. But on September 11, 2001, when terrorists crashed hijacked airliners into the World Trade Center in New York City and the Pentagon in Washington, all of that changed. There was an extraordinary outburst of patriotic fervor; flags were displayed everywhere, fire and police heroes were widely celebrated, and there was strong national support for our going to war in Afghanistan to find the key terrorist, Osama bin Laden, and destroy the tyrannical Taliban regime that he supported. By November of that year, about half of all Americans of both political parties said they trusted

Washington officials to do what is right most of the time, the highest level in many years.

Those who had hoped or predicted that this new level of support would last, not ebb and flow, have been disappointed. In October 2001, more than half of Americans surveyed said they trusted the federal government to do what is right always or most of the time. But by the summer of 2002, about 40 percent expressed such trust in the federal government. In the fall of 2006, the fraction that said they trusted the federal government to do what is right always or most of the time had fallen below 30 percent, and as of March 2019, the figure had dropped to 17 percent (with an all-time low of 15 percent in the fall of 2011).[40]

Less than 20 percent of all Americans have a lot of confidence in Congress, but it—and the rest of the government—should not feel lonely. With few exceptions, Americans have lost confidence in many institutions. As Figure 4.5 shows, churches, public schools, the media, and American national political institutions have all suffered a big drop in public confidence during the past three decades. Only the military has gained support (73 percent of us say we have "a great deal" or "a lot" of confidence in it). This support may have implications for politics. One recent study of people who endorsed President Trump's candidacy found that they showed authoritarian characteristics, that is, support for and obedience to strong leaders, as well as aggressive responses to perceived threats from outsiders.[41] But another study finds that Trump supporters are populist, not authoritarian, with strong nationalist sentiments and opposition to elites.[42]

Because Americans are less likely than they once were to hold their leaders in high esteem, to have confidence in government policies, and to believe the system will be responsive to popular wishes, some observers like to say that Americans today are more "alienated" from politics. Perhaps this is true, but careful studies of the subject have not yet been able, for example, to demonstrate any relationship between overall levels of public trust in government or confidence in leaders, on the one hand, and the rates at which people come out to vote, on the other. There is, however, some evidence that the less voters trust political institutions and leaders, the more likely they are to support candidates from the nonincumbent major party (in two-candidate races) and third-party candidates.[43]

civil society *Voluntary action that makes cooperation easier.*

Civil Society

Distrust of governmental and other institutions makes more important the role of **civil society**, the collection of private, voluntary groups that—independent of the government and the commercial market—make human cooperation easier and provide ways of holding the government accountable for its actions.

The individualism of the American political culture makes civil society especially important. As we shall see in Chapter 11, Americans are more likely than people in other democracies to join voluntary groups. These organizations teach people how to cooperate, develop community service skills, and increase social capital. This last phrase refers to the connections people have with each other through friendship, personal contact, and group efforts.

Several scholars, such as Robert Putnam, argue that the more social capital a community has, the greater the level of trust among its members. And the more trust that exists, the easier it is to achieve common goals such as improving a neighborhood, combating intolerance, and producing useful projects outside of government. Putnam

Figure 4.5 Confidence in American Institutions

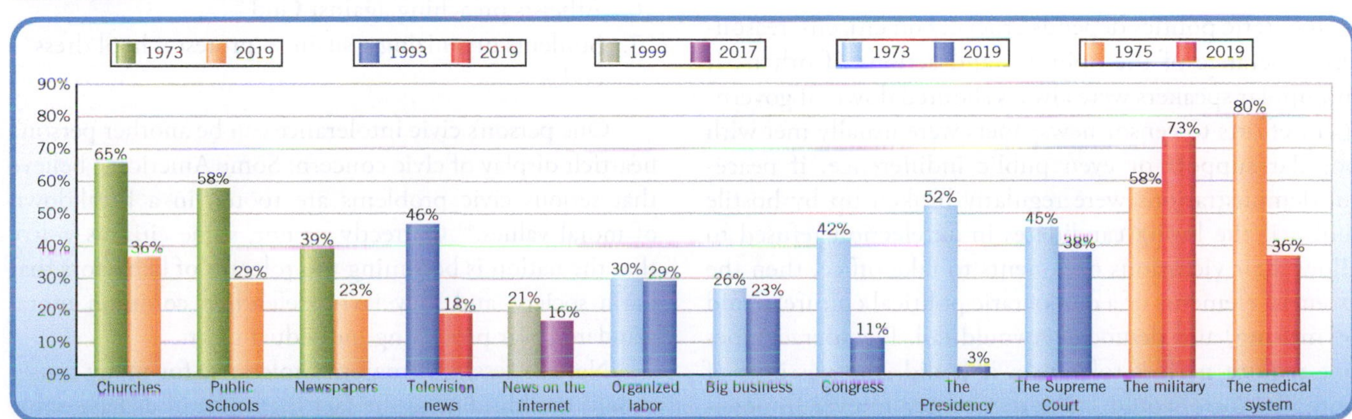

Source: Gallup Poll, "Confidence in American Institutions," https://news.gallup.com/poll/1597/confidence-institutions.aspx

Q Which institutions in the United States have had the sharpest declines in public confidence since the 1970s? What factors might explain why some institutions have seen sharper declines in confidence than others?

worries that our social capital may be decreasing because people are less and less likely to join voluntary associations. In Putnam's famous phrase, we once bowled in leagues; now we bowl alone. We once joined organizations such as the Parent Teacher Association, the National Association for the Advancement of Colored People, or the Veterans of Foreign Wars; now we are more likely to stay home and watch television or spend time on our computers.[44]

There are three qualifications to this argument. First, Americans still join more groups than people in most other democracies. Second, young Americans today are more likely to say volunteering is an important civic duty than this group was some 30 years ago.[45] Third, in ethnically and racially diverse communities, we "hunker down"—that is, we don't trust our neighbors, contribute to charities, cooperate with others, or join voluntary groups.[46] Just where we most need social capital, we do not have as much as we would like.

Furthermore, in the post-9/11 world, young people in the United States have demonstrated increased interest in public affairs and civic engagement. But this heightened involvement seems to be most pronounced for people with high incomes; Putnam describes this division as "a growing civic and social gap in the United States between upper-middle-class young white people and their less affluent counterparts."[47] In his 2015 book *Our Kids: The American Dream in Crisis,* Putnam examines how children in economically well-off families are far more likely to experience social capital in their homes, schools, and activities than children whose families face severe economic difficulties.[48] Without social capital, economic and social mobility become daunting, not realistic, goals. A major societal challenge for the 9/11 generation will be to expand opportunities for making the American dream a reality and keeping public confidence in American political culture.

Political Tolerance

Democratic politics depends crucially on citizens' reasonable tolerance of the opinions and actions of others. If unpopular speakers were always shouted down, if government efforts to censor newspapers were usually met with popular support or even public indifference, if peaceful demonstrations were regularly broken up by hostile mobs, if the losing candidates in an election refused to allow their victorious opponents to take office, then the essential elements of a democratic political culture would be missing, and democracy would fail. Democracy does not require perfect tolerance; if it did, the passions of human nature would make democracy forever impossible. But at a minimum, citizens must have a political culture that allows the discussion of ideas and the selection of rulers in an atmosphere reasonably free of oppression.

Andrew Cullen/The Washington Post/Getty Images

Image 4.6 Many communities in the United States offer English language lessons, tutoring, and other services for immigrants.

Public opinion surveys show that the overwhelming majority of Americans agree with concepts such as freedom of speech, majority rule, and the right to circulate petitions—at least in the abstract. But when we get down to concrete cases, a good many Americans are not very tolerant of groups they dislike. Suppose you must decide which groups will be in a community public auditorium. Which of these groups would *you* say should be permitted to hold a meeting?

1. A religious group hosting a revival meeting
2. A parent organization that opposes mandatory annual testing in schools
3. Concerned citizens protesting the building of a cell phone tower near their homes
4. A women's rights organization campaigning for stronger legislation to punish sexual harassment in the workplace
5. A civil rights group that advocates for transgender rights
6. Atheists preaching against God
7. Students organizing a sit-in to protest school dress codes

One person's civic intolerance can be another person's heartfelt display of civic concern. Some Americans believe that serious civic problems are rooted in a breakdown of moral values.[49] Correctly or not, some citizens worry that the nation is becoming too tolerant of behaviors that harm society, and they favor defending common moral standards over protecting individual rights.

Nonetheless, this majority tolerance for many causes should not blind us to the fact that most of us have some group or cause from which we are willing to withhold political liberties—even though we endorse those liberties in the abstract.

If most people dislike one or another group strongly enough to deny it certain political rights that we usually take for granted, how is it that such groups (and such rights) survive? The answer, in part, is that most of us don't act on our beliefs. We rarely take the trouble—or have the chance—to block another person from making a speech or teaching school. Some scholars have argued that among people who are in a position to deny other people rights—officeholders and political activists, for example—the level of political tolerance is somewhat greater than among the public at large, but that claim has been strongly disputed.[50]

But another reason may be just as important. Most of us are ready to deny *some* group its rights, but we usually can't agree on which group that should be. Sometimes we can agree, and then the disliked group may be in for real trouble. There have been times (1919–1920, and again in the early 1950s) when socialists and communists were disliked by most people in the United States. On each occasion the government took strong actions against them. Today, fewer people agree that these left-wing groups are a major domestic threat, and so their rights are now more secure.

Finally, the courts are sufficiently insulated from public opinion that they can act against majority sentiments and enforce constitutional protections (see Chapter 16). Most of us are not willing to give all rights to all groups, but most of us are not judges.

These facts should be a sober reminder that political liberty cannot be taken for granted. Men and women are not, it would seem, born with an inclination to live and let live, at least politically, and many—possibly most—never acquire that inclination. Liberty must be learned and protected. Happily, the United States, during much of its recent history, has not been consumed by revulsion for any one group, at least not revulsion strong enough to place the group's rights in jeopardy.

Nor should any part of society pretend that it is always more tolerant than another. In the 1950s, for example, ultraconservatives outside the universities were attacking the rights of professors to say and teach certain things. In the 1960s and 1970s, ultraliberal students and professors inside the universities were attacking the rights of other students and professors to say certain things.

The American system of government is supported by a political culture that fosters a sense of civic duty, takes pride in the nation's constitutional arrangements, and provides support for the exercise of essential civil liberties. In recent decades, mistrust of government officials (though not of the system itself) has increased, and confidence in their responsiveness to popular feelings has declined.

Although Americans value liberty in both the political system and the economy, they believe equality is important in the political realm. In economic affairs, they wish to see equality of opportunity but accept inequality of results.

Not only is our culture generally supportive of democratic rule, it also has certain distinctive features that make our way of governing different from what one finds in other democracies. Americans are preoccupied with their rights, and this fact, combined with a political system that (as we shall see) encourages the vigorous exercise of rights and claims, gives to our political life an *adversarial* style. Unlike Swedes or Japanese, we do not generally reach political decisions by consensus, and we often do not defer to the authority of administrative agencies. American politics, more than that of many other nations, is shot through at every stage with protracted conflict.

But as we shall learn in the next chapter, that conflict is not easily described as, for example, always pitting liberals against conservatives. Not only do we have a lot of conflict, it is often messy conflict, a kind of political Tower of Babel. Foreign observers sometimes ask how we stand the confusion. The answer, of course, is that we have been doing it for more than 200 years. Maybe our Constitution is two centuries old, not in spite of this confusion, but because of it. We shall see.

Learning Objectives

4-1 Explain the concept of political culture and its key components in the United States.

Political culture refers to long-standing patterns in how people view government, politics, and the economy. Key components of American political culture include liberty, equality (of opportunity), democracy, civic duty, and individual responsibility.

4-2 Discuss how the political culture of the United States differs from that in other countries.

The question of whether the United States is "exceptional" among democracies sparks much debate among social scientists and historians. While characteristics of American exceptionalism are difficult to identify and measure, surveys discussed in this chapter do show that Americans

What Would You Do? | Will You Support the Creation of Required Civics Courses for all U.S. High Schools?

To: *Jae Luce, White House Chief of Staff*
From: *Ella Sophia, Secretary of Education*
Subject: *Civics education in schools*

The decline in political knowledge that Americans have about our governmental system is alarming. We need to work in partnership with Congress and the states to promote civic education in secondary schools. In her upcoming State of the Union message, the president needs to make a case for high school civics education and endorse the creation of a bipartisan task force to develop guidelines for such classes.

To Consider:

A recent survey shows that only 24 percent of twelfth graders scored proficient or higher in civics, a statistic that does not bode well for an informed and engaged U.S. citizenry.

Arguments for:

1. A recent survey finds that only about 6 in 10 Americans can name the vice president, and more than half believe incorrectly that the Supreme Court prohibits public school classes that compare world religions.
2. Schools have a responsibility to teach students the principles of American constitutionalism, such as federalism and separation of church and state.
3. If the federal government does not take the initiative in promoting civics education, then states will develop their own standards, which will weaken understanding of our shared political principles.

Arguments against:

1. Civics education needs to be incorporated into existing courses, not taught separately, so students understand how public activity affects their education, career paths, and lives.
2. Individuals need to take responsibility for understanding the political system in which they live.
3. Based on their individual historical experiences, states are better prepared than the federal government to determine how the underlying principles of American politics should be taught in their classrooms.

What Will You Decide? Enter **MindTap** to make your choice.

Your decision: ☐ Support ☐ Oppose

view government, politics, religion, and economics differently than citizens of other advanced industrialized democracies.

American political culture has imbued people with more tolerance and a greater respect for orderly procedures and personal rights than can be found in nations with constitutions like ours. Americans are willing to let whoever wins an election govern without putting up a fuss, and the U.S. military does not intervene.

4-3 Identify the key sources of political culture in the United States.

People learn the concepts of political culture from their families, schools, organizations (including religious groups), and interactions with the government-federal, state, and local.

4-4 Evaluate how conflicts in American political culture affect public confidence in government and tolerance of different political views.

Compared to the 1950s, we are much less likely to think the government does the right thing or cares about what we think. But when we look at our system of government-the Constitution and our political culture-we are very pleased with it. Americans are much more patriotic than people in many other democracies. And we display a great deal of support for churches in large measure because we are more religious than most Europeans.

To Learn More

Polling organizations that frequently measure aspects of political culture

www.ropercenter.cornell.edu

www.gallup.com

U.S. Census Bureau: **www.census.gov**

Almond, Gabriel, and Sidney Verba. *The Civic Culture*. Princeton, NJ: Princeton University Press, 1963. Classic study of the political cultures of five nations—the United States, Germany, Great Britain, Italy, and Mexico—as they were in 1959.

Hartz Louis. *The Liberal Tradition in America*. New York: Harcourt Brace Jovanovich, 1955. A stimulating interpretation of American political thought since the Founding, emphasizing the notion of a liberal consensus.

Lipset, Seymour Martin. *The First New Nation*. Rev. ed. New York: Norton, 1979. How the origins of American society gave rise to the partially competing values of equality and achievement, and the ways in which these values shape political institutions.

McClosky, Herbert, and John Zaller. *The American Ethos: Public Attitudes toward Capitalism and Democracy*. Cambridge, MA: Harvard University Press, 1984. Study of the ways in which Americans evaluate political and economic arrangements.

Nivola, Pietro S., and David W. Brady, eds. *Red and Blue Nation? Characteristics and Causes of America's Polarized Politics*. Washington, D.C.: Brookings Institution, 2006. Compares the arguments of those who do and do not believe that a culture war exists.

Putnam, Robert D. *Bowling Alone: The Collapse and Revival of American Community.* New York: Simon & Schuster, 2000. An important argument that American political culture has been harmed by the decline in membership in organizations that bring people together for communal activities.

Putnam, Robert D., and David E. Campbell. *American Grace: How Religion Unites and Divides Us*. New York: Simon & Schuster, 2010. State-of-the-art study of Americans' religious identities and how they matter to civic life.

Tocqueville, Alexis de. *Democracy in America*, edited by Phillip Bradley. 2 vols. New York: Knopf, 1951. First published in 1835–1840, this was and remains the greatest single interpretation of American political culture.

Verba, Sidney, Kay Lehman Schlozman, and Henry E. Brady. *Voice and Equality: Civic Voluntarism in American Politics.* Cambridge, Ma.: Harvard University Press, 1995. Extensive survey analysis of how Americans engage in civil society.

Wilson, James Q., and Peter Schuck, eds. *Understanding America: Anatomy of an Exceptional Nation*. New York: Public Affairs, 2008. Topical essays on American political culture by leading experts.

CHAPTER 5

Civil Liberties

Learning Objectives

5-1 Discuss why the courts are so important in defining civil liberties, for both the national government and the states.

5-2 Describe which forms of expression are not protected by the Constitution, and why.

5-3 Explain how the Constitution protects religious freedom.

5-4 Evaluate how, in the 21st century, the Constitution protects civil liberties for people accused of a crime or designated as "enemy combatants."

5-5 Summarize the evolution of civil liberties in the United States.

« Then in 1803, President Thomas Jefferson wrote to the governor of Pennsylvania complaining about the "licentiousness" of newspapers and urging him and other state leaders to bring about "a few prosecutions of the most prominent offenders." This would, Jefferson said, have a "wholesome effect in restoring the integrity of the presses."[1]

*** Now** Today, such a recommendation likely would spark much public criticism. Prosecuting publishers who had attacked the government would strike many people as outrageous.

There are two key differences between then and now. First, as you will see later in this chapter, the Supreme Court decided in 1833 that the Bill of Rights restricted only the federal government. The only limits on state governments with regard to free speech, a free press, and religious freedom were those found in state constitutions. This law changed after the ratification of the Fourteenth Amendment in 1868 and was (slowly) interpreted by the Supreme Court to mean that the states must also honor freedom for speech, publications, and churches.

The second change occurred in the minds of the American people. Gradually, but especially in the 20th century, they acquired a libertarian view of personal freedom. According to this perspective, the government at every level ought to leave people alone with respect to what they say, write, read, or worship.

If you think that civil liberties are an issue only for people who make inflammatory speeches, think again. Imagine, for a moment, that you are a high school student. Dogs trained to sniff out drugs go down your high school corridors and detect marijuana in some lockers. The school authorities open and search your locker without permission or a court order. You are expelled from school without any hearing. Have your liberties been violated?

Angry at what you consider unfair treatment, you decide to wear a cloth American flag sewn to the seat of your pants, and your fellow students decide to wear black armbands to class to protest how you were treated. The police arrest you for wearing a flag on your seat, and the school punishes your classmates for wearing armbands contrary to school regulations. Have your liberties, or theirs, been violated?

You file suit in federal court to find out. We cannot be certain how the court would decide the issues in this particular case, but in similar cases in the past, the courts have held that school authorities can use dogs to detect drugs in schools and that these officials can conduct a "reasonable" search of you and your effects if they have a "reasonable suspicion" that you are violating a school rule. But they cannot punish your classmates for wearing black armbands, they cannot expel you without a hearing, and the state cannot make it illegal to treat the flag "contemptuously" (by sewing it to the seat of your pants, for example). In 2007, however, the Supreme Court allowed a school principal to punish a student for displaying a flag saying "Bong Hits 4 Jesus" that the official felt endorsed drug use during a school-supervised event. So a student's free-speech rights (and a school's authority to enforce discipline) now lie somewhere between disgracing a flag (okay) and encouraging drug use (not okay).[2]

Civil liberties *Rights—chiefly, rights to be free of government interference—accorded to an individual by the Constitution: free speech, free press, and so on.*

Your claim that these actions violated your constitutional rights would have astonished the Framers of the Constitution. They thought they had written a document that stated what the federal government *could* do, not one that specified what state governments (such as school systems) *could not* do. And they thought they had created a national government of such limited powers that it was not even necessary to add a list—a bill of rights—stating what that government was forbidden from doing. It would be enough, for example, that the Constitution did not authorize the federal government to censor newspapers; an amendment prohibiting censorship would be superfluous.

The people who gathered in the state ratifying conventions weren't so optimistic. They suspected—rightly, as it turned out—that the federal government might well try to do things it was not authorized to do, and so they insisted that the Bill of Rights be added to the Constitution. But even they never imagined that the Bill of Rights would affect what *state* governments could do. Each state would decide that for itself, in its own constitution. And if by chance the Bill of Rights did apply to the states, surely its guarantees of free speech and freedom from unreasonable search and seizure would apply to big issues—the freedom to attack the government in a newspaper editorial, for example, or to keep the police from breaking down the door of your home without a warrant. The courts would not be deciding who could wear what kinds of armbands or under what circumstances a school could expel a student.

Civil liberties are the rights—chiefly, rights to be free of government interference—accorded to an individual by the Constitution: free exercise of religion, free speech, and so on. Civil rights, to be discussed in the next chapter, usually refer to protecting certain groups from discrimination based on characteristics such as their sex, sexual orientation, race, or ethnicity.

In practice, however, there is no clear line between civil liberties and civil rights. For example, is the right to an abortion a civil liberty or a civil right? In this chapter, we take a look at free speech, free press, religious freedom, and the rights of the accused. In the next chapter, we look at discrimination and abortion.

5-1 The Courts and Conflicts over Civil Liberties

We often think of "civil liberties" as a set of principles that protect the freedoms of all of us all of the time. That is true—up to a point. But in fact, the Constitution and the Bill of Rights contain a list of *competing* rights and duties. Clashes over civil liberties often end up in the courts.

Rights in Conflict

Political struggles over civil liberties follow much the same pattern as interest group politics involving economic issues, even though the claims in question are made by individuals. Indeed, formal, organized interest groups are concerned with civil liberties. The Fraternal Order of the Police complains about restrictions on police powers, whereas the American Civil Liberties Union defends and seeks to expand those restrictions. Catholics have pressed for public support of parochial schools; Protestants and Jews have argued against it. Sometimes the opposing groups are entirely private; sometimes one or both are government agencies.

Competition over civil liberties becomes obvious when one person asserts one constitutional right or duty and another person asserts a different one. For example:

- At the funeral of a Marine killed in Iraq, Fred Phelps and others from a church picketed it with signs saying "Thank God for Dead Soldiers" and other outrageous remarks. (The opening photo for this chapter shows such picketers outside the Supreme Court.) The Marine's father sued the church, saying the picketers caused him suffering. Free speech versus extreme emotional distress.
- The U.S. government has an obligation to "provide for the common defense" and, in pursuit of that duty, has claimed the right to keep secret certain military and diplomatic information. The *New York Times* claimed the right to publish such secrets as the "Pentagon Papers" without censorship, citing the Constitution's guarantee of freedom of the press. A duty and a right in conflict.
- Carl Jacob Kunz delivered inflammatory anti-Jewish speeches on the street corners of a Jewish neighborhood in New York City, suggesting, among other things, that Jews be "burned in incinerators." The Jewish people living in that area were outraged. The New York City police commissioner revoked Kunz's license to hold public meetings on the streets. When he continued to air his views on the public streets, Kunz was arrested for speaking without a permit. Freedom of speech versus the preservation of public order.

Even a disruptive high school student's right not to be a victim of arbitrary or unjustifiable expulsion is in partial conflict with the school's obligation to maintain an orderly environment in which learning can take place. To address these conflicts, courts must weigh which constitutional protection merits higher protection, and those judgments may change over time. (When the Supreme Court decided the cases given earlier, Phelps, the *New York Times,* and Kunz all won.[3])

War has usually been the crisis that has restricted the liberty of some minority. For example:

- The Sedition Act of 1798, declared that to write, utter, or publish "any false, scandalous, and malicious writing" with the intention of defaming the president, Congress, or the government, or of exciting against the government "the hatred of the people" was a crime. The occasion was a kind of half-war between the United States and France, stimulated by fear in this country of the violence following the French Revolution of 1789. The policy entrepreneurs were Federalist politicians who believed that Thomas Jefferson and his followers were supporters of the French Revolution and would, if they came to power, encourage here the kind of anarchy that seemed to be occurring in France.
- The Espionage and Sedition Acts of 1917–1918 made crimes of uttering false statements that would interfere with the American military; sending through the mail material "advocating or urging treason, insurrection, or forcible resistance to any law of the United States"; or uttering or writing any disloyal, profane, scurrilous, or abusive language intended to incite resistance to the United States or to curtail war production. The occasion was World War I, and the impetus was the fear that Germans in this country were spies and also that radicals were seeking to overthrow the government. Under these laws, more than 2,000 persons were prosecuted (about half were convicted), and thousands of aliens were rounded up and deported. The policy entrepreneur leading this massive crackdown (the so-called Red Scare) was Attorney General A. Mitchell Palmer.
- The Smith Act was passed in 1940, the Internal Security Act in 1950, and the Communist Control Act in 1954. These laws made it illegal to advocate the overthrow of the U.S. government by force or violence (Smith Act), required members of the Communist Party to register with the government (Internal Security Act), and declared the Communist Party to be part of a conspiracy to overthrow the government (Communist Control Act). The occasion was World War II and the Korean War, which, like earlier wars, inspired

fears that foreign agents (Nazi and Soviet) were trying to subvert the government. For the latter two laws, the policy entrepreneur was Senator Joseph McCarthy, who attracted a great deal of attention with his repeated (and sometimes inaccurate) claims that Soviet agents were working inside the U.S. government.

These laws had in common an effort to protect the nation from threats, real and imagined, posed by people who claimed to be exercising their freedom to speak, publish, organize, and assemble. In each case, a real threat (a war) led the government to narrow the limits of permissible speech and activity. Almost every time such restrictions were imposed, the Supreme Court was called upon to decide whether Congress (or sometimes state legislatures) had drawn those limits properly. In most instances, the Court tended to uphold the legislatures. But as time passed and the war or crisis ended, popular passions abated and many of the laws proved unimportant.

Though uncommon, some use is still made of the sedition laws. In the 1980s, various white supremacists and Puerto Rican nationalists were charged with sedition. In each case, the government alleged that the accused had not only spoken in favor of overthrowing the government but had actually engaged in violent actions such as bombings. Later in this chapter, we shall see how the Court has increasingly restricted the power of Congress and state legislatures to outlaw political speech; to be found guilty of sedition now, it usually is necessary to do something more serious than just talk about it.

Image 5.1 A Hispanic girl studies both English and Spanish in a bilingual classroom.

Cultural Conflicts

In the main, the United States was originally the creation of white European Protestants. Blacks were, in most cases, slaves, and American Indians were not citizens. Catholics and Jews in the colonies composed a small minority, often a persecuted one. The early schools tended to be religious—that is, Protestant—ones, many of which received state aid. It is not surprising that under these circumstances a view of America arose that equated "Americanism" with the values and habits of white Anglo-Saxon Protestants.

But immigration to this country brought a flood of new settlers, many of whom came from very different backgrounds (see Figure 5.1). In the mid-19th century, the potato famine led millions of Irish Catholics to migrate here. At the turn of the century, religious persecution and economic disadvantage brought more millions of people, many Catholic or Jewish, from southern and eastern Europe.

In recent decades, political conflict and economic want have led Hispanics (mostly from Mexico but increasingly from all parts of Latin America), Caribbeans, Africans, Middle Easterners, Southeast Asians, and Asians to come to the United States—most legally, but some illegally. Among them have been Buddhists, Catholics, Muslims, and members of many other religious and cultural groups.

Ethnic, religious, and cultural differences have given rise to different views as to the meaning and scope of certain constitutionally protected freedoms. For example:

- Many Jewish groups find it offensive for a crèche (i.e., a scene depicting the birth of Christ in a manger) to be displayed in front of a government building such as city hall at Christmastime, whereas many Catholics and Protestants regard such displays as an important part of our cultural heritage. Does a religious display on public property violate the First Amendment requirement that the government pass no law "respecting an establishment of religion"?
- Many English-speaking people believe that the public schools ought to teach all students to speak and write English because the language is part of our nation's cultural heritage. Some Hispanic groups argue that schools should teach pupils in both English and Spanish, since Spanish is part of the Hispanic cultural heritage. Is bilingual education constitutionally required?
- The Boy Scouts of America once refused to allow LGBTQ+ men to become scout leaders even though several states and localities prohibit discrimination based on sexual orientation. Many civil libertarians challenged this policy as discriminatory, while the Boy Scouts defended it because their organization was a private association free to make its own rules. When are private organizations

Figure 5.1 **People Granted Permanent Resident Status in the United States, 1850–2018**

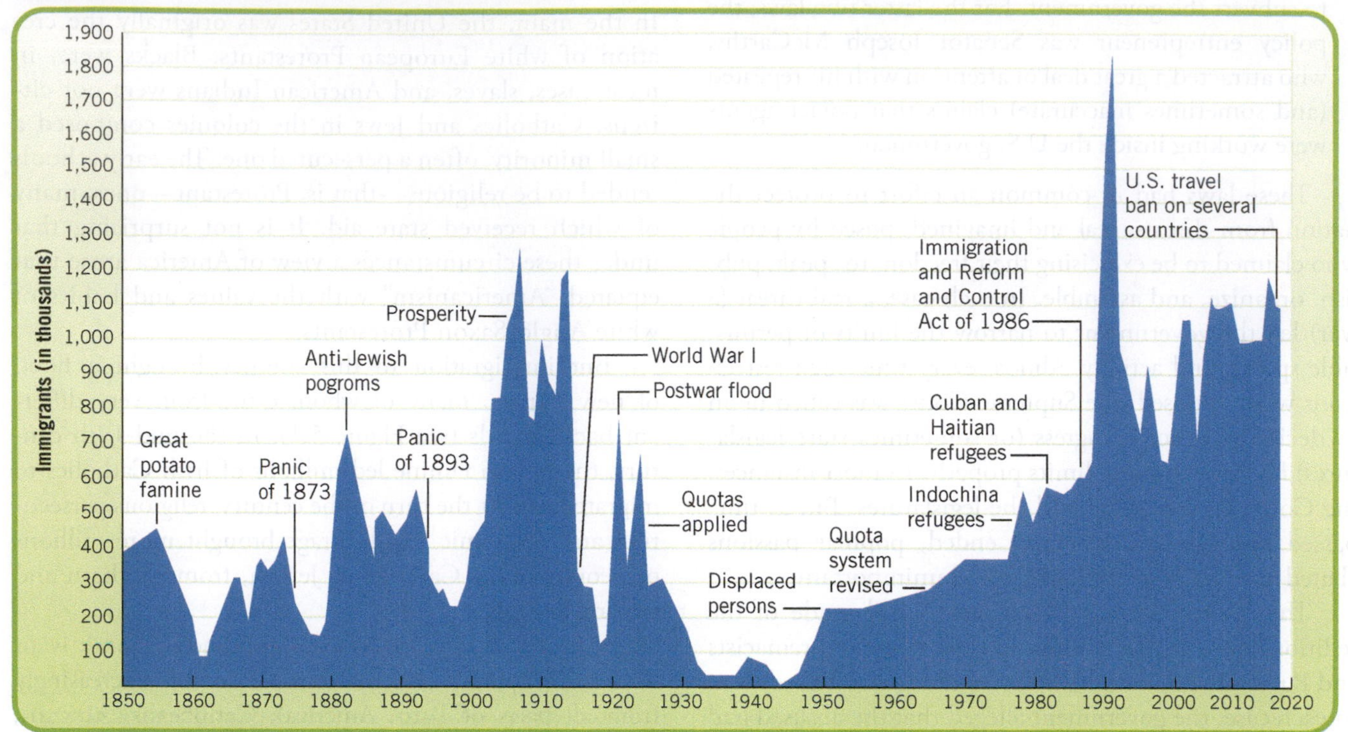

Source: Office of Immigration Statistics, *2018 Yearbook of Immigration Statistics* (Washington, DC: U.S. Department of Homeland Security, 2020), Table 1, "Persons Obtaining Lawful Permanent Resident Status: Fiscal Years 1820 to 2018," https://www.dhs.gov/immigration-statistics/yearbook/2018/table1.

Q **How might the events listed here influence the number of people who become legal permanent residents of the United States?**

due process of law *Denies the government the right, without due process, to deprive people of life, liberty, and property.*

equal protection of the laws *A standard of equal treatment that must be observed by the government.*

subject to public laws? In this case, in 2000 the Supreme Court upheld the Boy Scouts' defense on the grounds of their right to associate freely, but in 2015, the organization announced that it would lift the ban. And in 2017, the Scouts announced that children would be permitted to join troops based on their gender identity, thus opening the organization to transgender boys.

Even within a given cultural tradition there are important differences of opinion as to the balance between community sensitivities and personal self-expression. To some people, the sight of a store carrying pornographic books or a theater showing a pornographic movie is deeply offensive; to others, pornography is offensive but such establishments ought to be tolerated to ensure that laws restricting them do not also restrict politically or artistically important forms of speech; to still others, pornography itself is not especially offensive. What forms of expression are entitled to constitutional protection?

Applying the Bill of Rights to the States

For many years after the Constitution was signed and the Bill of Rights was added to it as amendments, the liberties these documents detailed applied only to the federal government. The Supreme Court made this clear in a case decided in 1833.[4] Except for Article I, which, among other things, banned ex post facto laws and guaranteed the right of habeas corpus, the Constitution was silent on what the states could not do to their residents.

This began to change after the Civil War, when new amendments were ratified in order to ban slavery and protect newly freed slaves. The Fourteenth Amendment, ratified in 1868, was the most important addition. It said that no state shall "deprive any person of life, liberty, or property without **due process of law**" (a phrase now known as the "due process clause") and that no state shall "deny to any person within its jurisdiction the **equal protection of the laws**" (a phrase now known as the "equal protection clause").

Beginning in 1897, the Supreme Court started to use these two phrases as a way of applying certain rights to state governments. It first said that no state could take private property without paying just compensation, and then in 1925 held, in the *Gitlow* case, that the federal guarantees of free speech and free press also applied to the states. In 1937, it went much further and said in *Palko v. Connecticut* that certain rights should be applied to the states because, in the Court's words, they "represented the very essence of a scheme of ordered liberty" and were "principles of justice so rooted in the traditions and conscience of our people as to be ranked fundamental."[5]

The Supreme Court began the process of selective incorporation by which most, but not all, federal rights also applied to the states. But which rights are so "fundamental" that they ought to govern the states? There is no entirely clear answer to this question, but in general the entire Bill of Rights is now applied to the states except for the following:

- The right not to have soldiers forcibly quartered in private homes (Third Amendment)
- The right to be indicted by a grand jury before being tried for a serious crime (Fifth Amendment)
- The right to a jury trial in civil cases (Seventh Amendment)
- The ban on excessive bail and fines (Eighth Amendment)

The Second Amendment that protects "the right of the people to keep and bear arms" may or may not apply to the states. In 2008, the Supreme Court in *District of Columbia v. Heller* held for the first time that this amendment did not allow the federal government to ban the private possession of firearms. But the case arose in the District of Columbia, which is governed by federal law. The decision raised two questions. First, will this ruling be incorporated so that it also applies to state governments? In 2010, the Supreme Court said in *McDonald v. Chicago* that the decision in the Heller case also applied to the states.[6] Second, will it still be possible to regulate gun purchases and gun use even if the government cannot ban guns? In late 2019, the Supreme Court heard arguments in a case that challenged a New York City ordinance that barred residents from taking their guns outside the city. After the Supreme Court agreed to hear the case, the city amended the law so individuals with permits could take their guns to specific places, such as second homes and shooting ranges, outside the city, and New York State passed a similar law.[7] The Supreme Court subsequently dismissed the case.

5-2 The First Amendment and Freedom of Expression

The First Amendment contains the language that has been at issue in most of the cases to which we have thus far referred. It has roughly two parts: one protecting **freedom of expression** ("Congress shall make no law . . . abridging the freedom of speech, or of the press, or the right of people peaceably to assemble, and to petition the government for a redress of grievances") and the other protecting **freedom of religion** ("Congress shall make no law respecting an establishment of religion; or abridging the free exercise thereof").

freedom of expression *Right of people to speak, publish, and assemble.*

freedom of religion *People shall be free to exercise their religion, and government may not establish a religion.*

prior restraint *Censorship of a publication.*

Speech and National Security

The traditional view of free speech and a free press was expressed by William Blackstone, the great English jurist, in his *Commentaries*, published in 1765. A free press is essential to a free state, he wrote, but the freedom that the press should enjoy is the freedom from **prior restraint**—that is, freedom from censorship, or rules telling a newspaper in advance what it can publish. Once a newspaper has published an article or a person has delivered a speech, that paper or speaker has to take the consequences if what was written or said proves to be "improper, mischievous, or illegal."[8]

The U.S. Sedition Act of 1798 was in keeping with traditional English law. Like it, the act imposed no prior restraint on publishers; it did, however, make them liable to punishment after the fact. The act was an improvement over the English law, however, because unlike the British model, it entrusted the decision to a jury, not a judge, and allowed defendants to be acquitted if they could prove the truth of what had been published. Although several newspaper publishers were convicted under the act, none of these cases reached the Supreme Court. When Jefferson became president in 1801, he pardoned the people who had been imprisoned under the Sedition Act. Though Jeffersonians objected vehemently to the law, their principal objection was not to the idea of holding newspapers accountable for what they published but to letting the *federal* government do this. Jefferson was perfectly prepared to have the *states* punish what he called the "overwhelming torrent of slander" by means of "a few prosecutions of the most prominent offenders."[9]

It would be another century before the federal government would attempt to define the limits of free speech and writing. Perhaps recalling the widespread opposition to the sweep of the 1798 act, Congress in 1917–1918 placed restrictions not on publications that were critical of the government but only on those that advocated

selective incorporation process *The process whereby the Court has applied most, but not all, parts of the Bill of Rights to the states.*

"treason, insurrection, or forcible resistance" to federal laws or attempted to foment disloyalty or mutiny in the armed services.

In 1919, this new law was examined by the Supreme Court when it heard the case of Charles T. Schenck, who had been convicted of violating the Espionage Act because he had mailed circulars to men eligible for the draft, urging them to resist. At issue was the constitutionality of the Espionage Act and, more broadly, the scope of Congress's power to control speech. One view held that the First Amendment prevented Congress from passing *any* law restricting speech; the other held that Congress could punish dangerous speech. For a unanimous Supreme Court, Justice Oliver Wendell Holmes announced a rule by which to settle the matter.

Constitutional Connections | Selective Incorporation

The **selective incorporation process**—the process by which the Supreme Court has applied most, but not all, parts of the Bill of Rights to the states—began in earnest in 1925 and has continued ever since, most recently with the Supreme Court's decision in the Second Amendment case of *McDonald v. Chicago*.

The selective incorporation process has never been straightforward or simple. For instance, in *Palko v. Connecticut* (1937), the Supreme Court held that states must observe all "fundamental" rights, but declared that the Fifth Amendment's protection against "double jeopardy" (being tried, found innocent, and then tried again for the same crime), which was the issue at hand in the case, was *not* among those rights. It was only about three decades later, in its decision in *Benton v. Maryland* (1969), that the Court partially incorporated the double jeopardy provision of the Fifth Amendment. Still, to this day no provision of the Fifth Amendment has been fully incorporated, and the provision regarding the right to be indicted by a grand jury has not been incorporated at all.

Similarly, in *Powell v. Alabama* (1932), the Supreme Court incorporated the right to counsel bestowed by the Sixth Amendment, but only in capital punishment cases. In *Gideon v. Wainwright* (1962), the Court extended that right to all felony defendants that might, if convicted, go to prison for years or for life. In the decade thereafter, the Court issued six more Sixth Amendment selective incorporation decisions. In the last of these, *Argersinger v. Hamlin* (1972), the Court extended the right to legal counsel to any defendant facing a sentence that might result in incarceration.

The Third Amendment, which establishes the right not to have soldiers forcibly "quartered in any home without the consent" of the homeowner, and the Seventh Amendment, which establishes the right to a trial in civil cases, each remains wholly unincorporated. The Eighth Amendment's prohibition against "cruel and unusual punishment" is partially incorporated, whereas its provision forbidding excessive bail or fines remains wholly unincorporated.

Year	Amendment	Provision	Case
1925	First	Free speech	*Gitlow v. New York*
1931	First	Free press	*Near v. Minnesota*
1932	Sixth	Legal counsel	*Powell v. Alabama*
1937	First	Free assembly	*De Jonge v. Oregon*
1937	Fifth	Double jeopardy	*Palko v. Connecticut*
1947	First	No religious establishment	*Everson v. Board of Education*
1948	Sixth	Public trial	*In re Oliver*
1949	Fourth	Unreasonable searches and seizures	*Wolf v. Colorado*
1958	First	Free association	*NAACP v. Alabama*
1961	Fourth	Warrantless searches and seizures	*Mapp v. Ohio*
1963	First	Free petition	*NAACP v. Button*
1963	Sixth	Legal counsel	*Gideon v. Wainwright*
1965	Sixth	Confront witnesses	*Pointer v. Texas*
1966	Sixth	Impartial jury	*Parker v. Gladden*
1967	Sixth	Speedy trial	*Klopfer v. North Carolina*
1967	Sixth	Compel witnesses	*Washington v. Texas*
1968	Sixth	Jury trial	*Duncan v. Louisiana*
1972	Sixth	Legal counsel	*Argersinger v. Hamlin*
2010	Second	Keep and bear arms	*McDonald v. Chicago*

It soon became known as the **clear-and-present-danger test**:

> The question in every case is whether the words used are used in such circumstances and are of such a nature as to create a clear and present danger that they will bring about the substantive evils that Congress has a right to prevent.[10]

clear-and-present-danger test *Law should not punish speech unless there was a clear and present danger of producing harmful actions.*

The Court held that Schenck's leaflets did create such a danger, and so his conviction was upheld. In explaining why, Holmes said that not even the Constitution protects a person who has been "falsely shouting fire in a theatre and causing a panic." In this case, things that might safely be said in peacetime may be punished in wartime.

The clear-and-present-danger test may have clarified the law, but it kept no one out of jail. Schenck went, and so did the defendants in five other cases in the period 1919–1927, even though during this time Holmes, the author of the test, shifted his position and began writing dissenting opinions in which he urged that the test had not been met and so the defendant should go free.

Bettmann/Getty Images

Image 5.2 Women picketed in front of the White House, urging President Warren Harding to release political radicals arrested during his administration.

In 1925, Benjamin Gitlow was convicted of violating New York's sedition law—a law similar to the federal Sedition Act of 1918—by passing out some leaflets, one of which advocated the violent overthrow of our government. The Supreme Court upheld his conviction but added, as we have seen, a statement that changed constitutional history: Freedom of speech and of the press were now among the "fundamental personal rights" protected by the due process clause of the Fourteenth Amendment from infringements by *state* action.[11] Thereafter, state laws involving speech, the press, and peaceful assembly were struck down by the Supreme Court for being in violation of the freedom-of-expression guarantees of the First Amendment, made applicable to the states by the Fourteenth Amendment.[12]

The clear-and-present-danger test was a way of balancing the competing demands of free expression and national security. As the memory of World War I and the ensuing Red Scare evaporated, the Court began to develop other tests, ones that shifted the balance more toward free expression. Some of these tests are listed in Table 5.1 on page 106.

But when a crisis reappears, as it did in World War II and the Korean War, the Court has tended to defer, up to a point, to legislative judgments about the need to protect national security. For example, it upheld the conviction of 11 leaders of the Communist Party for having advocated the violent overthrow of the U.S. government, a violation of the Smith Act of 1940.

This conviction once again raised the hard question of the circumstances under which words can be punished. Hardly anybody would deny that actually *trying* to overthrow the government is a crime; the question is whether *advocating* its overthrow is a crime. In the case of the 11 communist leaders, the Court said that the government

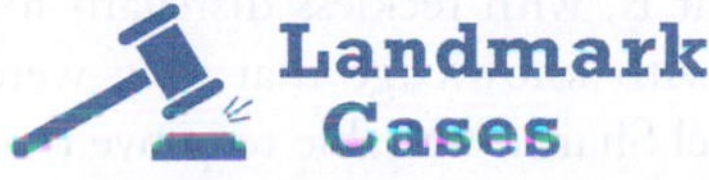

Incorporation

- ***Gitlow v. New York* (1925):** The Supreme Court says the First Amendment applies to states.
- ***Palko v. Connecticut* (1937):** The Supreme Court says that states must observe all "fundamental" liberties.
- ***McDonald v. Chicago* (2010):** The Second Amendment that allows the people to keep and bear arms applies to state governments as well as the federal government.

libel *Writing that falsely injures another person.*

did not have to wait to protect itself until "the *putsch* [rebellion] is about to be executed, the plans have been laid and the signal is awaited." Even if the communists were not likely to be successful in their effort, the Court held that specifically advocating violent overthrow could be punished. "In each case," the opinion read, the courts "must ask whether the gravity of the 'evil,' discounted by its improbability, justifies such invasion of free speech as is necessary to avoid the danger."[13]

But as the popular worries about communists began to subside and the membership of the Supreme Court changed, the Court began to tip the balance even further toward free expression. By 1957, the Court made it clear that for advocacy to be punished, the government would have to show not just that a person believed in the overthrow of the government but also that the person was using words "calculated to incite" that overthrow.[14]

By 1969, the pendulum had swung to the point where the speech would have to be judged likely to incite "imminent" unlawful action. When Clarence Brandenburg, a Ku Klux Klan leader in Ohio, made a speech before Klan members in which he called for "revengeance [sic]" against blacks and Jews (described with racial slurs) and called for a march on Washington, he was arrested and convicted for "advocating" violence. The Supreme Court reversed the conviction, holding that the First Amendment protects speech that abstractly advocates violence unless that speech will incite or produce "imminent lawless action."[15] While the Supreme Court ruled in 1942 that "fighting words" did not have constitutional protection, it narrowed the definition of that concept significantly in subsequent cases, though it has not overturned the ruling to date.[16]

This means that no matter how offensive or provocative some forms of expression may be, they nevertheless have powerful constitutional protections. In 1977, a group of American Nazis wanted to parade through the streets of Skokie, Illinois, a community with a large Jewish population. The residents, outraged, sought to ban the march. Many feared violence if it occurred. But the lower courts, under prodding from the Supreme Court, held that, noxious and provocative as the anti-Semitic slogans of the Nazis may be, the Nazi party had a constitutional right to speak and parade peacefully.[17]

Similar reasoning led the Supreme Court in 1992 to overturn a Minnesota statute that made it a crime to display symbols or objects, such as a Nazi swastika or a burning cross, that are likely to cause alarm or resentment among an ethnic or racial group, such as Jews or African Americans.[18] On the other hand, if you are convicted of actually hurting someone, you may be given a tougher sentence if it can be shown that you were motivated to assault them by racial or ethnic hatred.[19] To be punished for such a hate crime, your bigotry must result in some direct and physical harm, and not just the display of an odious symbol.

What Is Speech?

If most political speaking or writing is permissible, save that which actually incites someone to take illegal actions, what *kinds* of speaking and writing qualify for this broad protection? Though the Constitution says that the legislature may make "no law" abridging freedom of speech or the press, and although some justices have argued that this means literally *no* law, the Court has held that at least four forms of speaking and writing are not automatically granted full constitutional protection: libel, obscenity, symbolic speech, and commercial and youthful speech.

Libel

A **libel** is a written statement that defames the character of another person. (If the statement is spoken, it is called a *slander*.) The libel or slander must harm the person being attacked. In some countries, such as the United Kingdom, it is easy to sue another person for libel and to collect. In this country, it is much harder. For one thing, you must show that the libelous statement was false. If it was true, you cannot collect no matter how badly it harmed you.

A beauty contest winner was awarded $14 million (later reduced on appeal) when she proved that *Penthouse* magazine had libeled her. Actress Carol Burnett collected a large sum from a libel suit brought against a gossip newspaper. But when Theodore Roosevelt sued a newspaper for falsely claiming that he was a drunk, the jury awarded him damages of only six cents.[20]

If you are a public figure, it is much harder to win a libel suit. A public figure such as an elected official, a candidate for office, an army general, or a well-known celebrity must prove not only that the publication was false and damaging but also that the words were published with "actual malice"—that is, with reckless disregard for their truth or falsity or with knowledge that they were false.[21] Israeli General Ariel Sharon was able to prove that the statements made about him by *Time* magazine were false and damaging but not that they were the result of "actual malice."

For a while, people who felt they had been libeled would bring suit in the United Kingdom against an American author. One Saudi leader sued an American author who had accused him of financing terrorism, even though

Tim Boyle/Newsmakers/Hulton Archive/Getty Images

Image 5.3 A Ku Klux Klan member used the constitutional right to free speech to utter "white power" chants in Skokie, Illinois.

she had not sold her book in the United Kingdom (but word about it had been on the Internet). This strategy, called "libel tourism," was ended in 2010 when Congress unanimously passed and the president signed a bill that bars enforcement in U.S. courts of libel actions against Americans if what they published would not be libelous under American law.

Obscenity

Obscenity is not protected by the First Amendment. The Court has always held that obscene materials, because they have no redeeming social value and are calculated chiefly to appeal to one's sexual rather than political or literary interests, can be regulated by the state. The problem, of course, arises with the meaning of *obscene.* In the period from 1957 to 1968, the Court decided 13 major cases involving the definition of obscenity, which resulted in 55 separate opinions.[22] Some justices, such as Hugo Black, believed that the First Amendment protected all publications, even wholly obscene ones. Others believed that obscenity deserved no protection and struggled heroically to define the term. Still others shared the view of former Justice Potter Stewart, who objected to "hardcore pornography" but admitted that the best definition he could offer was "I know it when I see it."[23]

It is unnecessary to review in detail the many attempts by the Court to define obscenity. The justices have made it clear that nudity and sex are not, by definition, obscene and that they will provide First Amendment protection to anything that has political, literary, or artistic merit, allowing the government to punish only the distribution of "hardcore pornography." Their most recent definition of this is as follows: to be obscene, the work, taken as a whole, must be judged by "the average person applying contemporary community standards" to appeal to the "prurient interest" or to depict "in a patently offensive way, sexual conduct specifically defined by applicable state law" and to lack "serious literary, artistic, political, or scientific value."[24]

After Albany, Georgia decided that the movie *Carnal Knowledge* was obscene by contemporary local standards, the Supreme Court overturned the distributor's conviction on the grounds that the authorities in Albany failed to show that the film depicted "patently offensive hardcore sexual conduct."[25]

It is easy to make sport of the problems the Court has faced in trying to decide obscenity cases (one conjures up images of black-robed justices leafing through the pages of *Hustler* magazine, taking notes), but these problems reveal, as do other civil liberties cases, the continuing problem of balancing competing claims. One part of the community wants to read or see whatever it wishes; another part wants to protect private acts from public degradation. The first part cherishes liberty above all; the second values decency above liberty. The former fears that *any* restriction on literature will lead to *pervasive* restrictions; the latter believes that reasonable people can distinguish (or reasonable laws can require them to distinguish) between patently offensive and artistically serious work.

Anyone strolling today through an "adult" bookstore must suppose that no restrictions at all exist on the distribution of pornographic works. This condition does not arise simply from the doctrines of the Court. Other factors operate as well, including the priorities of local law enforcement officials, the political climate of the community, the procedures that must be followed to bring a viable court case, the clarity and workability of state and local laws on the subject, and the difficulty of changing the behavior of many people by prosecuting one person. The current view of the Court is that localities can decide for themselves whether to tolerate hard-core pornography; but if they choose not to, they must meet some fairly strict constitutional tests.

The protections given by the Court to expressions of sexual or erotic interest have not been limited to books, magazines, and films. Almost any form of visual or auditory communication can be considered "speech" and thus protected by the First Amendment. In one case, even nude dancing was given protection as a form of "speech,"[26] although in 1991 the Court held that nude dancing was only "marginally" within the purview of First Amendment protections, and so it upheld an Indiana statute that banned *totally* nude dancing.[27]

Some feminist organizations have attacked pornography on the grounds that it exploits and degrades women. They persuaded Indianapolis, Indiana, to pass an ordinance that defined pornography as portrayals of the "graphic, sexually explicit subordination of women" and allowed people to sue the producers of such material. Sexually explicit portrayals of women in positions of equality were not defined as pornography. The Court disagreed. In 1986, it affirmed a lower-court ruling that such an ordinance was a violation of the First Amendment because it represented a legislative preference for one form of expression (women in positions of equality) over another (women in positions of subordination).[28]

One constitutionally permissible way to limit the spread of pornographic materials has been to establish rules governing where in a city they can be sold. When one city adopted a zoning ordinance prohibiting an "adult" movie theater from locating within 1,000 feet of any church, school, park, or residential area, the Court upheld the ordinance, noting that the purpose of the law was not to regulate speech but to regulate the use of land. And in any case, the adult theater still had much of the city's land area in which to find a location.[29]

With the advent of the Internet, it has become more difficult for the government to regulate obscenity. The Internet spans the globe. It offers an amazing variety of materials—some educational, some entertaining, some sexually explicit. But it is difficult to apply the Supreme Court's standard for judging whether sexual material is obscene—the "average person" applying "contemporary community standards"—to the Internet because there is no easy way to tell what "the community" is. Is it the place where the recipient lives or the place where the material originates? And since no one is in charge of the Internet, who can be held responsible for controlling offensive material? Since anybody can send anything to anybody else without knowing the age or location of the recipient, how can the Internet protect children?

When Congress tried to ban obscene, indecent, or "patently offensive" materials from the Internet, the Supreme Court struck down the law as unconstitutional. The Court went even further with child pornography. Though it has long held that child pornography is illegal even if it is not obscene because of the government's interest in protecting children, it would not let Congress ban pornography involving computer-designed children. Under the 1996 law, it would be illegal to display computer simulations of children engaged in sex even if no real children were involved. The Court said "no." It held that Congress could not ban "virtual" child pornography without violating the First Amendment because, in its view, the law might bar even harmless depictions of children and sex (e.g., in a book on child psychology).[30]

Symbolic Speech

Ordinarily, you cannot claim that an illegal act should be protected because that action is meant to convey a political message. For example, if you burn your draft card in protest against the foreign policy of the United States, you can be punished for the illegal act (burning the card), even

TABLE 5.1 | Testing Restrictions on Expression

The Supreme Court has used various standards and tests to decide whether a restriction on freedom of expression is constitutionally permissible.

1. **Preferred position** The right of free expression, though not absolute, occupies a higher, or more preferred, position than many other constitutional rights, such as property rights. This is still a controversial rule; nonetheless, the Court always approaches a restriction on expression skeptically.
2. **Prior restraint** With scarcely any exceptions, the Court will not tolerate a prior restraint on expression, such as censorship, even when it will allow subsequent punishment of improper expressions (such as libel).
3. **Imminent danger** Punishment for uttering inflammatory sentiments will be allowed only if there is an imminent danger that the utterances will incite an unlawful act.
4. **Neutrality** Any restriction on speech, such as a requirement that parades or demonstrations not disrupt other people in the exercise of their rights, must be neutral—that is, it must not favor one group more than another.
5. **Clarity** If you must obtain a permit to hold a parade, the law must set forth clear (as well as neutral) standards to guide administrators in issuing that permit. Similarly, a law punishing obscenity must contain a clear definition of obscenity.
6. **Least-restrictive means** If it is necessary to restrict the exercise of one right to protect the exercise of another, the restriction should use the least-restrictive means to achieve its end. For example, if press coverage threatens a person's right to a fair trial, the judge may only do what is minimally necessary to achieve that end, such as transferring the case to another town rather than issuing a "gag order."

Cases cited, by item: (1) *United States v. Carolene Products*, 304 U.S. 144 (1938); (2) *Near v. Minnesota*, 283 U.S. 697 (1931); (3) *Brandenburg v. Ohio*, 395 U.S. 444 (1969); (4) *Kunz v. New York*, 340 U.S. 290 (1951); (5) *Hynes v. Mayor and Council of Oradell*, 425 U.S. 610 (1976); (6) *Nebraska Press Association v. Stuart*, 427 U.S. 539 (1976).

Q **What pattern do you see in the Supreme Court's tests to determine whether expression may constitutionally be restricted?**

if your intent was to communicate your beliefs. The Court reasoned that giving such **symbolic speech** the same protection as real speech would open the door to permitting all manner of illegal actions—murder, arson, rape—if the perpetrator meant thereby to send a message.[31]

On the other hand, a statute that makes it illegal to burn the American flag is an unconstitutional infringement of free speech.[32] Why is there a difference between a draft card and the flag? The Court argues that the government has a right to run a military draft and so can protect draft cards, even if this incidentally restricts speech. But the only motive that the government has in banning flag burning is to restrict this form of speech, and that would make such a restriction improper.

The American people were outraged by the flag-burning decision, and in response the House and Senate passed by huge majorities (380 to 38 and 91 to 9) a law making it a federal crime to burn the flag. But the Court struck this law down as unconstitutional.[33] Now that it was clear that only a constitutional amendment could make flag-burning illegal, Congress was asked to propose one. But it would not. Earlier members of the House and Senate had supported a law banning flag-burning with more than 90 percent of their votes, but when asked to make that law a constitutional amendment, they could not muster the necessary two-thirds majorities. The reason is that Congress is much more reluctant to amend the Constitution than to pass new laws. Several members decided that flag-burning was wrong, but not so wrong or so common as to justify an amendment.

Commercial and Youthful Speech

If people have a right to speak and publish, do corporations, interest groups, and children have the same right? By and large the answer is yes, though there are some exceptions.

When the attorney general of Massachusetts tried to prevent the First National Bank of Boston from spending money to influence votes in a local election, the Court stepped in and blocked him. The Court held that a corporation, like a person, has certain First Amendment rights. Similarly, when the federal government tried to limit the spending of a group called Massachusetts Citizens for Life (an antiabortion organization), the Court held that such organizations have First Amendment rights.[34] The Court has also told states that they cannot forbid liquor stores from advertising their prices and informed federal authorities that they cannot prohibit casinos from plugging gambling.[35]

When the California Public Utility Commission tried to compel one of the utilities it regulates (the Pacific Gas and Electric Company) to enclose in its customers' monthly bills statements written by groups attacking the utility, the Supreme Court blocked the agency and said that forcing it to disseminate political statements violated the firm's free-speech rights. "The identity of the speaker is not decisive in determining whether speech is protected," the Court said. "Corporations and other associations, like individuals, contribute to the discussion, debate, and the dissemination of information and ideas that the First Amendment seeks to foster." In this case, the right to speak includes the choice of what *not* to say.[36]

symbolic speech *An act that conveys a political message.*

Even though corporations have some First Amendment rights, the government can place more limits on commercial than on noncommercial speech. The legislature can place restrictions on advertisements for cigarettes, liquor, and gambling; it can even regulate advertising for some less harmful products provided that the regulations are narrowly tailored and serve a substantial public interest.[37] If the regulations are too broad or do not serve a clear interest, then ads are entitled to some constitutional protection. For example, the states cannot bar lawyers from advertising or accountants from personally soliciting clients.[38]

A big exception to the free-speech rights of corporations and labor unions groups was imposed by the McCain-Feingold campaign finance reform law passed in 2002. Many groups, ranging from the American Civil Liberties Union and the AFL-CIO to the National Rifle Association and the Chamber of Commerce, felt that the law banned legitimate speech. Under its terms, organizations could not pay for "electioneering communications" on radio or television that "refer" to candidates for federal office within 60 days before the election. But the Supreme Court temporarily struck down these arguments, upholding the law in *McConnell v. Federal Election Commission.* The Court said ads that only mentioned but did not "expressly advocate" a candidate were ways of influencing the election. Some dissenting opinion complained that a Court that had once given free-speech protection to nude dancing ought to give it to political speech.[39] But seven years later, the Court, in *Citizens United v. Federal Election Commission*, decided that the part of the McCain-Feingold law that denied corporations and labor unions the right to run ads (independent of a political party's or candidate's campaign) about the election violated their rights to free speech under the Constitution.

Under certain circumstances, young people may have less freedom of expression than adults. In 1988, the Supreme Court held that the principal of Hazelwood High School could censor articles appearing in the student-edited newspaper. The newspaper was published using school funds and was part of a journalism class.

Robert Pearce/The Sydney Morning Herald/Fairfax Media/Getty Images

Image 5.4 "Symbolic speech." When young men burned their draft cards during the 1960s to protest the Vietnam War, the Supreme Court ruled that it was an illegal act for which they could be punished.

Landmark Cases | Free Speech and Free Press

- ***Schenck v. United States*** **(1919):** Speech may be punished if it creates a clear and present danger of illegal acts.
- ***Chaplinksy v. New Hampshire*** **(1942):** "Fighting words" are not protected by the First Amendment.
- ***New York Times v. Sullivan*** **(1964):** To libel a public figure, there must be "actual malice."
- ***Tinker v. Des Moines*** **(1969):** Public school students may wear armbands to class protesting against America's war in Vietnam when such display does not disrupt classes.
- ***Miller v. California*** **(1973):** Obscenity defined as appealing to prurient interests of an average person with materials that lack literary, artistic, political, or scientific value.
- ***Texas v. Johnson*** **(1989):** There may not be a law to ban flag-burning.
- ***Reno v. ACLU*** **(1997):** A law that bans sending "indecent" material to minors over the Internet is unconstitutional because "indecent" is too vague and broad a term.
- ***FEC v. Wisconsin Right to Life*** **(2007):** Prohibits campaign finance reform law from banning political advocacy.
- ***Citizens United v. FEC*** **(2010):** The part of the McCain-Feingold campaign finance reform law that prevents corporations and labor unions from spending money on advertisements (independent of political candidates or parties) in political campaigns is unconstitutional.

The principal ordered the deletion of stories dealing with student pregnancies and the impact of parental divorce on students. The student editors sued, claiming their First Amendment rights had been violated. The Court agreed that students do not "shed their constitutional rights to freedom of speech or expression at the schoolhouse gate" and that they cannot be punished for expressing on campus their personal views. But students do not have exactly the same rights as adults if the exercise of those rights impedes the educational mission of the school. Students may lawfully say things on campus, as individuals, that they cannot say if they are part of school-sponsored activities (such as plays or school-run newspapers) that are part of the curriculum. School-sponsored activities can be controlled so long as the controls are "reasonably related to legitimate pedagogical concerns."[40]

5-3 The First Amendment and Freedom of Religion

Everybody knows, correctly, the language of the First Amendment that protects freedom of speech and the press, though most people are not aware of how complex the legal interpretations of these provisions have become. But many people also believe, wrongly, that the language of the First Amendment clearly requires the "separation of church and state." It does not.

What that amendment actually says is quite different and maddeningly unclear. It has two parts. The first, often referred to as the **free-exercise clause**, states that Congress shall make no law prohibiting the "free exercise" of religion. The second, which is called the **establishment clause**, states that Congress shall make no law "respecting an establishment of religion."

free-exercise clause *First Amendment requirement that law cannot prevent free exercise of religion.*

establishment clause *First Amendment ban on laws "respecting an establishment of religion."*

The Free-Exercise Clause

The free-exercise clause is the clearer of the two, though by no means is it lacking in ambiguity. It obviously means that Congress cannot pass a law prohibiting Catholics from celebrating Mass, requiring Baptists to become Episcopalians, or preventing Jews from holding a bar mitzvah. Since the First Amendment has been applied to the states via the due process clause of the Fourteenth Amendment, it means that state governments cannot pass such laws either. In general, the courts have treated religion like speech: You can pretty much do or say what you want so long as it does not cause some serious harm to others.

Even some laws that do not seem on their face to apply to churches may be unconstitutional if their enforcement imposes particular burdens on churches or greater burdens on some churches than others. For example, a state cannot apply a license fee on door-to-door solicitors when the solicitor is a Jehovah's Witness selling religious tracts.[41] By the same token, the courts ruled that the city of Hialeah, Florida, cannot ban animal sacrifices by members of an Afro-Caribbean religion called Santeria. Since killing animals generally is not illegal (if it were, there could be no hamburgers or chicken sandwiches served in Hialeah's restaurants, and rat traps would be unlawful), the ban in this case was clearly directed against a specific religion and hence was unconstitutional.[42]

Having the right to exercise your religion freely does not, however, mean that you are exempt from laws binding other citizens, even when the law goes against your religious beliefs. A man cannot have more than one wife, even if (as once was the case with Mormons) polygamy is thought desirable on religious grounds.[43] For religious reasons, you may oppose being vaccinated or having blood transfusions, but if the state passes a compulsory vaccination law or orders that a blood transfusion be given to a sick child, the courts will not block it on grounds of religious liberty.[43] Similarly, if you belong to an Indian tribe that uses a drug, such as peyote, in religious ceremonies, you cannot claim that your freedom was abridged if the state decides to ban the use of that drug, provided the law applies equally to all.[44] Since airports have a legitimate need for tight security measures, begging can be outlawed in them even if some of the people doing the begging are part of a religious group (in this case, the Hare Krishnas).[46]

In 1993, Congress passed the Religious Freedom Restoration Act, which stated that a law that attempted to be religiously neutral might still violate the free exercise clause if it interfered with a religious practice. (The law was passed in response to the ruling about the use of peyote by Indian tribes, as many religious groups opposed the decision.) Four years later, the Supreme Court ruled that the act did not apply to state and local laws, leading several states to pass their own comparable legislation.[47]

In 2014, the Supreme Court applied the federal law to find that some companies may be exempt from the Affordable Care Act's "contraceptive mandate," which had required health insurance provided by companies to include birth-control coverage for female employees.[48] The Obama administration, which had spearheaded health care reform, subsequently stated that health insurance for companies that objected to the mandate would provide contraceptive coverage without additional cost either for employers or employees.[49] In 2017, the Trump White House issued an executive order allowing religious organizations and other employers with religious objections to seek exemption from the contraceptive mandate, and the Supreme Court upheld the Trump administration's position in 2020. (See Landmark Cases box on p. 112.) In another 2020 case, the Court ruled that religious organizations have broad protections to classify employees as performing religious duties, which restricts those employees from filing some anti-discrimination lawsuits.

Many conflicts between religious belief and public policy are difficult to settle definitively. What if you believe on religious grounds that war is immoral? The draft laws have always exempted a conscientious objector from military duty, and the Court has upheld such exemptions. But the Court has gone further: It has said that people cannot be drafted even if they do not believe in a Supreme Being or belong to any religious tradition, so long as their "consciences, spurred by deeply held moral, ethical, or religious beliefs, would give them no rest or peace if they allowed themselves to become

wall of separation *Court ruling that government cannot be involved with religion.*

part of an instrument of war."[50] Do exemptions on such grounds create an opportunity for some people to evade the draft because of their political preferences? In trying to answer such questions, the courts often have had to try to define religion—no easy task.

And even when there is no question about your membership in a bona fide religion, the circumstances under which you may claim exemption from laws that apply to everybody else are unclear. What if you, a member of the Seventh-Day Adventists, are fired by your employer for refusing on religious grounds to work on Saturday, and then it turns out that you cannot collect unemployment insurance because you refuse to take an available job—one that also requires you to work on Saturday? Or what if you are a member of the Amish sect, which refuses, contrary to state law, to send its children to public schools past the eighth grade? The Court has ruled that the state must pay you unemployment compensation and cannot require you to send your children to public schools beyond the eighth grade.[51]

These decisions show that even the "simple" principle of freedom of religion gets complicated in practice and can lead to the courts giving, in effect, preference to members of one church over members of another.

The Establishment Clause

What in the world did the members of the First Congress mean when they wrote into the First Amendment language prohibiting Congress from making a law "respecting" an "establishment" of religion? The Supreme Court has more or less consistently interpreted this vague phrase to mean that the Constitution erects a "**wall of separation**" between church and state.

That phrase, so often quoted, is not in the Bill of Rights nor in the debates of the First Congress that drafted the Bill of Rights; it comes from the pen of Thomas Jefferson, who was opposed to having the Church of England as the established church of his native Virginia. (At the time of the Revolutionary War, there were established churches—that is, official, state-supported churches—in at least 8 of the 13 former colonies.) But it is not clear that Jefferson's view was the majority view.

dmac/Alamy Stock Photo

Image 5.5 Public schools cannot organize prayers, but private ones can.

During much of the debate in Congress, the wording of this part of the First Amendment was quite different and much plainer than what finally emerged. Up to the last minute, the clause was intended to read "no religion shall be established by law" or "no national religion shall be established." The meaning of those words seems quite clear: Whatever the states may do, the federal government cannot create an official, national religion or give support to one religion in preference to another.[52]

But Congress instead adopted an ambiguous phrase, and so the Supreme Court had to decide what it meant. It has declared that these words do not simply mean "no national religion" but mean as well no government involvement with religion at all, even on a nonpreferential basis. They mean, in short, erecting a "wall of separation" between church and state.[53] Though the interpretation of the establishment clause remains a topic of great controversy among judges and scholars, the Supreme Court has more or less consistently adopted this wall-of-separation principle.

Its first statement of this interpretation was in 1947. The case involved a New Jersey town that reimbursed parents for the costs of transporting their children to school, including parochial (in this case Catholic) schools. The Court decided that this reimbursement was constitutional, but it made it clear that the establishment clause of the First Amendment applied (via the Fourteenth Amendment) to the states and that it meant, among other things, that the government cannot require a person to profess a belief or disbelief in any religion; it cannot aid one religion, some religions, or all religions; and it cannot spend any tax money, however small the amount might be, in support of any religious activities or institutions.[54] The reader may wonder, in view of the Court's reasoning, why it allowed the town to pay for busing children to Catholic schools. The answer it gave is that busing is a religiously neutral activity, akin to providing fire and police protection to Catholic schools. Busing, available to public and private schoolchildren alike, does not breach the wall of separation.

Since 1947, the Court has applied the wall-of-separation theory to strike down as unconstitutional most efforts to have any officially conducted or sponsored prayer in public schools, even if it is nonsectarian,[55] voluntary,[56] or limited to reading a passage of the Bible.[57] Since 1992, it has been unconstitutional for a public school to ask a rabbi or minister to offer a prayer—an invocation or a benediction—at the school's graduation ceremony. Since 2000, it has been unconstitutional for a student to lead a prayer at a public high school football game because it was done "over the school's public address system, by a speaker representing the student body, under the supervision of the school faculty, and pursuant to school policy."[58] The Court made clear, however, that public school students could pray voluntarily during school provided that the school or the government did not sponsor that prayer. But in 2012, a federal district court ruled that a prayer banner that had hung in a public high school auditorium for nearly 50 years had to be removed because its presence in that setting was unconstitutional.[59]

Moreover, the Court has held that laws prohibiting teaching the theory of evolution or requiring giving equal time to "creationism" (the biblical doctrine that God created humankind) are religiously inspired and thus unconstitutional.[60] A public school may not allow its pupils to take time out from their regular classes for religious instruction if this occurs within the schools, though "released-time" instruction is all right if it is done outside the public school building.[61] The school prayer decisions in particular have provoked a storm of controversy, but efforts to get Congress to propose to the states a constitutional amendment authorizing such prayers have failed.

Almost as controversial have been Court-imposed restrictions on public aid to parochial schools, though here the wall-of-separation principle has not been used to forbid any and all forms of aid. For example, it is permissible for the federal government to provide aid for constructing buildings on denominational (as well as nondenominational) college campuses[62] and for state governments to loan free textbooks to parochial school pupils,[63] grant tax-exempt status to parochial schools,[64] allow parents of parochial schoolchildren to deduct their tuition payments on a state's income tax returns,[65] and pay for computers and deaf children's sign language interpreters at private and religious schools.[66] But the government cannot pay a salary supplement to teachers who teach secular subjects in parochial schools,[67] reimburse parents for the cost of parochial school tuition,[68] supply parochial schools with services such as counseling,[69] give money with which to purchase instructional materials, require that "creationism" be taught in public schools, or create a special school district for Hasidic Jews.[70]

The Court sometimes changes its mind on these matters. In 1985, it said the states could not send teachers into parochial schools to teach remedial courses for needy children, but 12 years later it decided they could. "We no longer presume," the Court wrote, "that public employees will inculcate religion simply because they happen to be in a sectarian environment."[71]

Perhaps the most important establishment-clause decision in recent times was the Court ruling that vouchers may be used to pay for children being educated at religious and other private schools. The case began in Cleveland, Ohio, where the state offered money to any family (especially poor ones) whose children attended a school that had done so badly that it was under a federal court order requiring it to be managed directly by the state superintendent of schools. The money, a voucher, could be used to send a child to any other public or private school, including one run by a religious group. The Court held that this plan did not violate the establishment clause because the aid went not to the school, but to the families who were to choose a school.[72] In 2020, the Supreme Court similarly ruled that a Montana program that had provided financial aid for students to attend private schools had to permit religious schools to participate in the program.

If you find the twists and turns of Court policy in this area confusing, you are not alone. The wall-of-separation principle has not been easy to apply, and in the post-World War II era, the Court has faced numerous questions about church–state matters. The Court tried to sort out the confusion in the early 1970s by developing a three-pronged test to decide under what circumstances government involvement in religious activities is improper[73]:

1. It has a strictly secular purpose.
2. Its primary effect neither advances nor inhibits religion.
3. It does not foster an excessive government entanglement with religion.

No sooner had the test been developed than the Court decided that it was all right for the government of Pawtucket, Rhode Island, to erect a Nativity scene as part of a Christmas display in a local park.[74] But five years later, it said Pittsburgh could not put a Nativity scene in front of the courthouse, but could display a menorah (a Jewish symbol of Chanukah) next to a Christmas tree and a sign extolling liberty. The Court ruled that the crèche had to go (because, being too close to the courthouse, a government endorsement was implied) but the menorah could stay (because, being next to a Christmas tree, it would not lead people to think that Pittsburgh was endorsing Judaism).

When the Ten Commandments are displayed in or near a public building, a deeply divided Court has made some complicated distinctions. It held that two Kentucky counties putting up the Ten Commandments in their courthouses was unconstitutional because the purpose was religious. Even though one Kentucky courthouse surrounded the Ten Commandments with displays of the Declaration

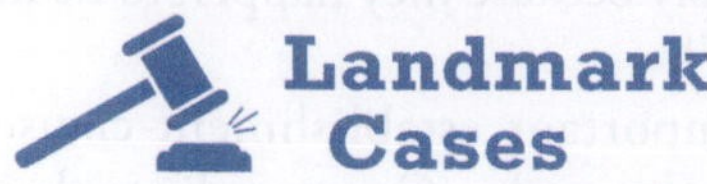

Landmark Cases | Religious Freedom

- ***Pierce v. Society of Sisters* (1925):** Though states may require public education, they may not require that students attend only public schools.
- ***Everson v. Board of Education* (1947):** The wall-of-separation principle is announced.
- ***Zorach v. Clauson* (1952):** States may allow students to be released from public schools to attend religious instruction.
- ***Engel v. Vitale* (1962):** There may not be a prayer, even a nondenominational one, in public schools.
- ***Lemon v. Kurtzman* (1971):** Three tests are described for deciding whether the government is improperly involved with religion.
- ***Lee v. Weisman* (1992):** Public schools may not have clergy lead prayers at graduation ceremonies.
- ***Santa Fe Independent School District v. Doe* (2000):** Students may not lead prayers before the start of a football game at a public school.
- ***Zelman v. Simmons-Harris* (2002):** Voucher plan to pay school bills is upheld.
- ***Town of Greece v. Galloway* (2014):** Local legislative session may begin with a prayer.
- ***Burwell v. Hobby Lobby* (2014):** Certain companies may be exempt from providing contraceptive coverage in health insurance if that violates their owners' religious beliefs.
- ***Espinoza v. Montana Department of Revenue* (2020):** State programs that provide financial aid for students to attend private schools may not exclude religious schools.
- ***Little Sisters of the Poor v. Commonwealth of Pennsylvania* (2020):** Employers with religious or moral objections may be exempt from contraceptive mandate in Affordable Care Act.

of Independence and the Star Spangled Banner so as to make the Commandments part of America's political heritage, the Court said it was still a religious effort. (The Court did note that there was a frieze containing Moses in the Supreme Court's own building, but said this was not religious.) But when the Ten Commandments were put up outside the Texas state capitol, this was upheld. Justice Stephen Breyer, who forbid the Kentucky display but allowed the Texas one, wrote that in Texas the Commandments now revealed a secular message, and, besides, no one had sued to end this display until 40 years after it was erected.[75]

Though the Court has struck down prayer in public schools, it has upheld prayer in Congress. (Since 1789, the House and Senate have opened each session with a prayer).[76] In 2014, the Court ruled that beginning a town legislative session with a prayer does not violate the Constitution's establishment clause.[77] Furthermore, while a public school cannot have a chaplain, the armed services can. The Court has said that the government cannot "advance" religion, but it has not objected to the printing of the phrase "In God We Trust" on the back of every dollar bill.

These distinctions show that the Court tends to use the wall-of-separation test for public schools but that it tries to strike a reasonable balance for Congress or state office buildings, perhaps because schools have a young and captive population, whereas public forums have adult and voluntary membership.

It is obvious that despite its efforts to set forth clear rules governing church–state relations, the Court's actual decisions are hard to summarize. It is deeply divided—some would say deeply confused—on these matters, and so the efforts to define the "wall of separation" will continue to prove to be as difficult as the Court's earlier efforts to decide what is interstate and what is local commerce (see Chapter 3).

5-4 Crime and Due Process

While the central problem in interpreting the religion clauses of the First Amendment has been to decide what they mean, the central problem in interpreting those parts of the Bill of Rights that affect people accused of a crime has been to decide not only what they mean but also how to put them into effect. It is not obvious what constitutes an "unreasonable search," but even if we settle that question, we still must decide how best to protect people against such searches in ways that do not unduly hinder criminal investigations.

That protection can be provided in at least two ways. One is to let the police introduce in court evidence relevant to the guilt or innocence of a person, no matter how it was obtained, and then, after the case is settled, punish the police (or their superiors) if the evidence was gathered improperly (e.g., by an unreasonable search). The other way is to exclude improperly gathered evidence from the trial in the first place, even if it is relevant to determining the guilt or innocence of the accused.

Most democratic nations, including the United Kingdom, use the first method; the United States uses the second. Because of this, many of the landmark cases decided by the Supreme Court have been bitterly controversial. Opponents of these decisions have argued that a guilty person should not go free just because the police officer blundered, especially if the mistake was minor. Supporters rejoin that there is no way to punish errant police officers effectively other than by excluding tainted evidence; moreover, nobody should be convicted of a crime except by evidence that is above reproach.[78]

The Exclusionary Rule

The American method relies on what is called the **exclusionary rule**. That rule holds that evidence gathered in violation of the Constitution cannot be used in a trial. The rule has been used to implement two provisions of the Bill of Rights: the right to be free from unreasonable searches and seizures (Fourth Amendment) and the right not to be compelled to give evidence against oneself (Fifth Amendment).*

exclusionary rule *Improperly gathered evidence may not be introduced in a criminal trial.*

Not until 1949 did the Supreme Court consider whether to apply the exclusionary rule to the states. In a case decided that year, the Court made it clear that the Fourth Amendment prohibited the police from carrying out unreasonable searches and obtaining improper confessions, but held that it was not necessary to use the exclusionary rule to enforce those prohibitions. It noted that other nations did not require that evidence improperly gathered had to be excluded from a criminal trial. The Court said that the local police should not improperly gather and use evidence, but if they did, the remedy was to sue the police department or punish the officer.[79]

* We shall consider here only two constitutional limits—those bearing on searches and confessions. Thus we omit many other important constitutional provisions affecting criminal cases, such as rules governing wiretapping, prisoner rights, the right to bail and to a jury trial, the bar on ex post facto laws, the right to be represented by a lawyer in court, the ban on "cruel and unusual" punishment, and the rule against double jeopardy.

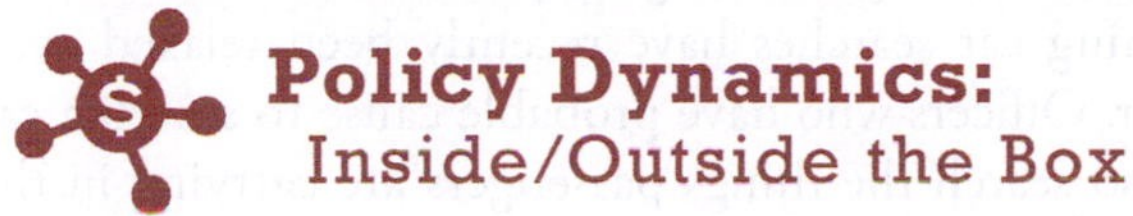

Creating the White House Office of Faith-Based and Community Initiatives: Majoritarian or Interest-Group Politics?

After taking office in 2001, President George W. Bush created the Office of Faith-Based and Community Initiatives by executive order. The office was responsible for linking religious groups and social services; as originally enacted in the 1996 welfare reform law, religious organizations would be eligible for public funds to provide nonreligious programs, such as after-school activities, mentoring programs, and other social services. Such programs would be well within constitutional boundaries for religion and public life. As John J. DiIulio Jr., the first director of the office, later wrote, "Faith-friendly federal neutrality unto religious pluralism—neither a Christian nation nor a secular state—is precisely what [James] Madison and most of the other framers wanted for America."[80]

Advocates for these initiatives presented them as majoritarian politics—everyone pays for government funding through taxes, and American society at large benefits from the success of people who participate in the programs, all without encroaching on the First Amendment's protections for religious freedom. A case also could be made for client politics, with everyone paying and only program participants directly benefiting. The legitimacy of such initiatives was not in question, though, given strong support at the time for having the federal government facilitate participation in nonreligious social programs run by organizations with religious affiliations.

Implementation of these goals raised several challenges that illustrate interest-group politics at work. Some religious organizations proposed program requirements that posed potential conflicts with state laws, such as prohibitions on employer discrimination based on sexual orientation. Critics, in turn, declared that such requirements intruded upon the separation of church and state guaranteed in the First Amendment. With both sides passionately arguing their case, and limited broad public attention to the debate, interest-group concerns dominated the discussion. President Barack Obama renamed the office in 2009, calling it the Office of Faith-Based and Neighborhood Partnerships, to emphasize the community-service component of the program over religious affiliations of participating groups. In May 2018, the Trump administration issued an executive order that established the White House Faith and Opportunity Initiative to support religious freedom and help faith-based groups seeking government funding.[81]

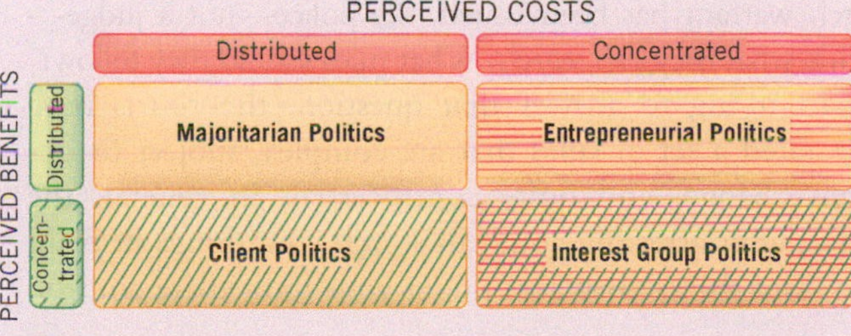

search warrant *A judge's order authorizing a search.*

probable cause *Reasonable cause for issuing a search warrant or making an arrest; more than mere suspicion.*

But in 1961, the Supreme Court changed its mind about the use of the exclusionary rule. It all began when the Cleveland police broke into the home of Dollree Mapp in search of a suspect in a bombing case. Not finding him, they instead arrested her for possessing some obscene pictures found there. The Court held that this was an unreasonable search and seizure because the police had not obtained a search warrant, though they had had ample time to do so. Furthermore, such illegally gathered evidence could not be used in the trial of Mapp.[82] Beginning with this case—*Mapp v. Ohio—the* Supreme Court required the use of the exclusionary rule as a way of enforcing a variety of constitutional guarantees.

Search and Seizure

After the Court decided to exclude improperly gathered evidence, the next problem was to decide what evidence was improperly gathered. What happened to Dollree Mapp was an easy case; hardly anybody argued that it was reasonable for the police to break into someone's home without a warrant, ransack their belongings, and take whatever they could find that might be incriminating. But that left a lot of hard choices still to be made.

When can the police search you without it being unreasonable? Under two circumstances: when they have a search warrant or when they have lawfully arrested you. A **search warrant** is an order from a judge authorizing the search of a place; the order must describe what is to be searched and seized, and the judge can issue it only if persuaded by the police that good reason (**probable cause**) exists to believe that a crime has been committed and that the evidence bearing on that crime will be found at a certain location. (The police can also search a building if the occupant gives them permission.)

In addition, you can be searched if the search occurs when you are lawfully arrested. When can you be arrested? You can be arrested if a judge has issued an arrest warrant for you, if you commit a crime in the presence of a police officer, or if the officer has probable cause to believe you have committed a serious crime (usually a felony). If you are arrested and no search warrant has been issued, the police—not a judge—decide what they can search. What rules should they follow?

In trying to answer that question, the courts have elaborated a set of rules that are complex, subject to frequent change, and quite controversial. In general, the police, after arresting you, can search you, things in plain view, and things or places under your immediate control. As a practical matter, things "in plain view" or "under your immediate control" mean the room in which you are arrested but not other rooms of the house.[83] If the police want to search the rest of your house or a car parked in your driveway, they will first have to go to a judge to obtain a search warrant. But if the police arrest a college student on campus for underage drinking and then accompany the student back to a dormitory room to see proof of legal drinking age, then, the police can seize drugs in plain view in that room.[84] And if marijuana is growing in plain view in an open field, the police can enter and search that field even though it is fenced off with a locked gate and a "No Trespassing" sign.[85]

What if you are arrested while driving your car—how much of it can the police search? The answer to that question has changed almost yearly. In 1979, the Court ruled that the police could not search a suitcase taken from a car of an arrested person, and in 1981 it extended this protection to any "closed, opaque container" found in the car.[86] But the following year, the Court decided that all parts of a car, closed or open, could be searched if the officers had probable cause to believe they contained contraband (i.e., goods illegally possessed). And the rules governing car searches have recently been relaxed even further. Officers who have probable cause to search a car can also search the things passengers are carrying in the car. And if the car is stopped for a traffic infraction, the car can be searched if the officer develops a "reasonable, articulable suspicion" that the car is involved in other illegal activity.[87]

In this confusing area of the law, the Court is attempting to protect those places in which a person has a "reasonable expectation of privacy." Your body is one such place, and so the Court has held that the police cannot compel you to undergo surgery to remove a bullet that might be evidence of your guilt or innocence in a crime.[88] But the police can require you to take a Breathalyzer test to determine whether you have been drinking while driving.[89] Your home is another place where you have an expectation of privacy, but a barn next to your home is not, nor is your backyard viewed from an airplane, nor is your home if it is a motor home that can be driven away, and so the police need not have a warrant to look into these places.[90]

If you work for the government, you have an expectation that your desk and files will be private; nonetheless, your supervisor may search the desk and files without a warrant, so long as the search is for something related to your work.[91] But bear in mind that the Constitution protects you only from *the government*; a private employer has a great deal of freedom to search your desk and files.

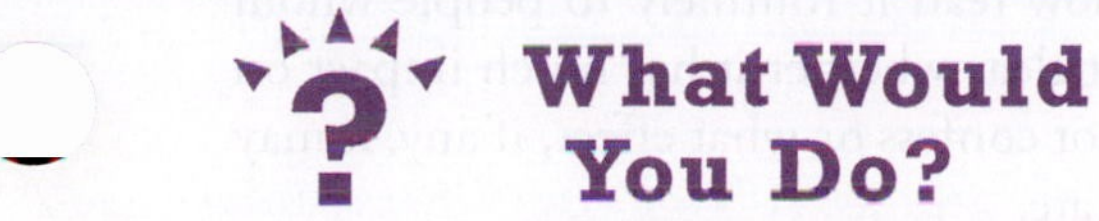

Will You Support the Patriot Act Provision on Library Records?

To: *Nicole Maxwell, Supreme Court justice*
From: *Benjamin Andrew, law clerk*
Subject: *Patriot Act and libraries*

The Patriot Act allows the Federal Bureau of Investigation (FBI) to seek the records of possible terrorists from banks, businesses, and libraries. Many libraries claim this will harm the constitutional rights of Americans. You support these rights, but are also aware of the need to protect national security.

To Consider:

Two public libraries have asked the Supreme Court to strike down provisions of the Patriot Act that allow the FBI to see the borrowing records of persons who are under investigation.

Arguments for:

1. The Patriot Act does not target individuals who have not violated a criminal law and who do not threaten human life.
2. For the FBI to collect information about borrowers, it must first obtain permission from a federal judge.
3. Terrorists may use libraries to study and plan activities that threaten national security.

Arguments against:

1. Freedom of speech and expression are fundamental constitutional guarantees that should not be infringed.
2. The law might harm groups engaged in peaceful protests.
3. The law allows the government to delay notifying people that their borrowing habits are being investigated.

What Will You Decide? Enter **MindTap** to make your choice.

Your decision: ☐ Uphold this provision ☐ Overturn this provision

good faith exception *An error in gathering evidence sufficiently minor that it may be used in a trial.*

public safety exception *The police can question a non-Mirandized suspect if there is an urgent concern for public safety.*

inevitable discovery *The police can use evidence if it would inevitably have been discovered.*

Confessions and Self-Incrimination

The constitutional ban on being forced to give evidence against oneself was originally intended to prevent the use of torture or "third-degree" police tactics to extract confessions. But it has since been extended to cover many kinds of statements uttered not out of fear of torture but from a lack of awareness of one's rights, especially the right to remain silent, whether in the courtroom or in the police station.

For many decades, the Supreme Court had held that involuntary confessions could not be used in federal criminal trials but had not ruled that they were barred from state trials. But in the early 1960s, it changed its mind in two landmark cases: *Escobedo* and *Miranda*.[92] The story of the latter and of the controversy that it provoked is worth telling.

Ernesto A. Miranda was convicted in Arizona of the rape and kidnapping of a young woman. The conviction was based on a written confession that Miranda signed after two hours of police questioning. (The victim also identified him.) Two years earlier, the Court had decided that the rule against self-incrimination applied to state courts.[93] Now the question arose of what constitutes an "involuntary" confession. The Court decided that a confession should be presumed involuntary unless the person in custody had been fully and clearly informed of the right to be silent, to have an attorney present during any questioning, and to have an attorney provided free of charge if the person could not afford one. The accused could waive these rights and offer to talk, but the waiver must be truly voluntary. Since Miranda did not have a lawyer present when he was questioned and had not knowingly waived his right to a lawyer, the confession was excluded from evidence in the trial and his conviction was overturned.[94]

Miranda was tried and convicted again, this time on the basis of evidence supplied by his girlfriend, who testified that he had admitted to her that he was guilty. Nine years later, he was released from prison; four years after that, he was killed in a barroom fight. When the Phoenix police arrested the prime suspect in Ernesto Miranda's murder, they read him his rights from a "*Miranda* card."

Everyone who watches cops-and-robbers shows on television probably knows the "Miranda warning" by heart. The police now read it routinely to people whom they arrest. It is not clear whether it has much impact on who does or does not confess or what effect, if any, it may have on the crime rate.

In time, the *Miranda* rule was extended to mean that you have a right to a lawyer when you appear in a police lineup[95] and when you are questioned by a psychiatrist to determine whether you are competent to stand trial.[96] The Court threw out the conviction of a man who had killed a child because the accused, without being given the right to have a lawyer present and having undergone harsh questioning, had led the police to the victim's body.[97] You do not have a right to a *Miranda* warning, however, if while in jail you confess a crime to another inmate who turns out to be an undercover police officer.[98]

Some police departments have tried to get around the need for a Miranda warning by training their officers to question suspects before giving them a Miranda warning and then, if the suspect confesses, giving the warning and asking the same questions over again. But the Supreme Court has not allowed this and has struck the practice down.[99]

Relaxing the Exclusionary Rule

Cases such as *Miranda* were highly controversial and led to congressional efforts, mostly unsuccessful, to modify or overrule the decisions by statute. But as the rules governing police conduct became increasingly more complex, pressure mounted to find an alternative. Some thought that any evidence should be admissible, with the question of police conduct left to lawsuits or other ways of punishing official misbehavior. Others said that the exclusionary rule served a useful purpose but had simply become too technical to be an effective deterrent to police misconduct (the police cannot obey rules that they cannot understand). And still others maintained that the exclusionary rule was a vital safeguard to essential liberties and should be kept intact. The Court has refused to let Congress abolish *Miranda* because it is a constitutional rule.[100]

The courts began to decide some cases in ways that modified—but retained—the exclusionary rule. The police were given greater freedom to question juveniles.[101] If the police got a warrant they thought was valid but the judge had used the wrong form, they could use it under the **good faith exception**.[102] The Supreme Court has allowed the police to question a suspect without first issuing a *Miranda* warning if the questions were motivated by overriding considerations of public safety, referred to as a **public safety exception**.[103] And the Court changed its mind about the killer who led the police to the victim's body. Under the **inevitable discovery** rule, the Court decided that if a victim will be discovered anyway, the evidence will not be excluded.[104]

A related issue to confessions and self-incrimination that has gained increased public attention in recent years is **civil forfeiture**, or the practice of law-enforcement officers taking assets (such as money or property) from people suspected of involvement with legal activity, but not charged with a crime. In modern American politics, civil forfeiture developed in the 1980s as a tool in the war on drugs, as it allowed governments to collect funds quickly from suspected criminals and use that money for fighting crime or providing restitution to victims. More recently, though, people who have been pulled over for traffic stops have been asked to turn over cash in their cars (sometimes thousands of dollars, often for alleged purposes such as buying a used car) or face arrest. Others who have family members who have drug problems or legal infractions sometimes have been ordered to turn over their cars or even their homes. The courts may weigh in on this highly controversial issue in the near future.[105]

Terrorism and Civil Liberties

The horrific terrorist attacks of September 11, 2001, raised important questions about how far the government can go in investigating and prosecuting individuals. Americans have hotly debated civil liberties questions about both information gathering and prosecuting suspected terrorists.

Information Gathering and Surveillance

A little more than one month after the attacks, Congress passed a new law, the USA Patriot Act, designed to increase federal powers to investigate terrorists.† Its main provisions are as follows:

- *Telephone taps.* The government may, if it has a court order, tap any telephone a suspect uses instead of having to get a separate order for each telephone.
- *Internet taps.* The government may, if it has a court order, tap Internet communications.
- *Voice mail.* The government may, with a court order, seize voice mail.
- *Grand jury information.* Investigators can now share with other government officials things learned in secret grand jury hearings.
- *Immigration.* The attorney general may hold any noncitizen who is thought to be a national security risk for up to seven days. If the person cannot be charged with a crime or deported within that time, then the government may still detain the person by certifying a security risk.
- *Money laundering.* The government gets new powers to track the movement of money across U.S. borders and among banks.
- *Crime.* This provision eliminates the statute of limitation on terrorist crimes and increases the penalties.

civil forfeiture *A procedure in which law-enforcement officers take assets from people who are suspected of illegal activity, but have not been charged with a crime.*

When it was first passed in October 2001, the Patriot Act made certain provisions temporary to allay concerns of civil libertarians. The law was renewed in March 2006 and again in May 2011, after extensive debate each time, but ultimately with only a few changes. Controversial parts of the law included the use of secret "national security letters" by the Federal Bureau of Investigation to gain access to records from banks, libraries, and telephone companies. One of the most heavily scrutinized parts of the law was Section 215, which allowed the National Security Agency (NSA)—the U.S. intelligence agency responsible for code-breaking and electronic surveillance—to conduct domestic surveillance through bulk collection of telephone metadata.[106]

The Patriot Act had some historical precedent. For much of the 20th century, presidents of both parties authorized telephone taps without warrants when they believed the person being tapped was a foreign spy. Some presidents also did so to collect information about their political enemies. In 1978, Congress decided to bring this practice under legislative control. It passed the Foreign Intelligence Surveillance Act (FISA), which required the president to go before a special court, comprising seven judges selected by the chief justice, to obtain approval for electronic eavesdropping on persons who were thought to be foreign spies. The FISA court would impose a standard lower than that which governs the issuance of warrants against criminals. For criminals, a warrant must be based on showing "probable cause" that the person is engaged in a crime; for FISA warrants, the government need show only that the person is likely to be working for a foreign government.

In late 2005, the *New York Times* revealed that the NSA had a secret program to intercept telephone calls and email messages, without seeking a warrant, between certain people abroad and Americans in the United States. (The *Times* had known about the program for

† The name of the law is an acronym derived from the official title of the bill, drawn from the first letters of the following capitalized words: Uniting and Strengthening America by Providing Appropriate Tools Required to Intercept and Obstruct Terrorism (USA Patriot).

a year, but waited to collect additional information before publishing, in part because administration officials expressed concern that making the program public would hinder national security.) The Bush administration, which had secretly authorized the program in 2002, argued that the intercepts were designed not to identify criminals or foreign spies, but to alert the country to potential terrorist threats. It could not rely on FISA because its procedures took too long and its standards of proof were too high.[107]

In 2002, the court that hears appeals from the FISA court had noted that the president, as commander in chief, has the "inherent authority" to conduct warrantless searches to obtain foreign intelligence information. When the NSA's secret program became public in 2005, critics said it imperiled Americans' civil liberties by conducting domestic surveillance without court approval. The Bush administration argued that after 9/11, Congress's authorization for the president to exercise "all necessary and appropriate" uses of military force included warrantless intercepts of terrorist communications.[108]

Public debate about the domestic surveillance program spurred Congress to pass a bill in 2008 that allowed the government to intercept foreign communications with people in the United States, provided the FISA court had approved the surveillance methods. But the administration could begin the surveillance before a FISA ruling was issued if it declared the need to be urgent. However, if Americans living overseas were the target of surveillance, then there must first be a FISA warrant. In addition, private telephone and Internet companies that aided in the surveillance were exempt from lawsuits so long as they had received "substantial evidence" that the program was authorized by the president.[109]

In 2013, controversy erupted again when news organizations revealed that nine U.S. Internet companies had collaborated with the NSA and British intelligence agencies on a secret and extensive surveillance program. This information became public through the unauthorized release of thousands of classified government documents by NSA contractor Edward Snowden, who asserted that leaking files to journalists was necessary to make the American people aware of the agency's alleged constitutional violations. Under risk of arrest in the United States for spying, Snowden eventually was granted temporary asylum in Russia, while an intense public debate weighed whether his actions had harmed national security or provided much-needed scrutiny of government surveillance.[110]

In the aftermath of the Snowden controversy and continuing questions about NSA surveillance, certain provisions of the Patriot Act expired on June 1, 2015. Many members of Congress—both Democrats and Republicans—objected to the mass collection of telephone records that the law had permitted. On June 2, 2015, President Obama signed into law the USA Freedom Act, which addressed congressional concerns by requiring the federal government to get special judicial approval (by the Foreign Intelligence Surveillance Court) to receive data collections from telephone companies.[111]

Prosecuting Suspected Terrorists

Another significant legal issue for the United States as it has waged war and captured suspected terrorists is whether those suspects may be detained without access to the courts. The traditional view, first announced during World War II, was that spies sent to this country by the Nazis could be tried by a military tribunal instead of by a civilian court. They were neither citizens nor soldiers, but "unlawful combatants."[112] The Bush administration relied on this view when it authorized the detention at the U.S. military base in Guantanamo Bay, Cuba, of people captured by American forces in Afghanistan.

In November 2001, President Bush issued an executive order stating that any noncitizen believed to be a terrorist or to have harbored a terrorist would be tried by a military, rather than a civilian, court. But the detainees at Guantanamo Bay included American citizens, who demanded access to U.S. courts. In 2004, the Supreme Court issued two rulings that said that suspected terrorists, both Americans and noncitizens, had the right to challenge their detention before a neutral decision maker.[113] The Bush administration subsequently created military tribunals to review the status of the alleged "enemy combatants" at Guantanamo Bay, but the Supreme Court ruled in 2006 that the executive branch could not create military commissions unilaterally—that is, without congressional approval.[114] Congress then passed the Military Commissions Act of 2006, which authorized the use of military commissions to try alien enemy combatants.

The Military Commissions Act of 2006 stated that each commission must comprise at least five military officers and must allow the defendant certain fundamental rights (such as to see evidence and to testify). Decisions could be appealed to the U.S. Court of Military Commission Review, whose members are selected by the secretary of defense, in Washington, DC. Further appeals could be made to the federal appeals court for the District of Columbia and the Supreme Court.[115] The law had

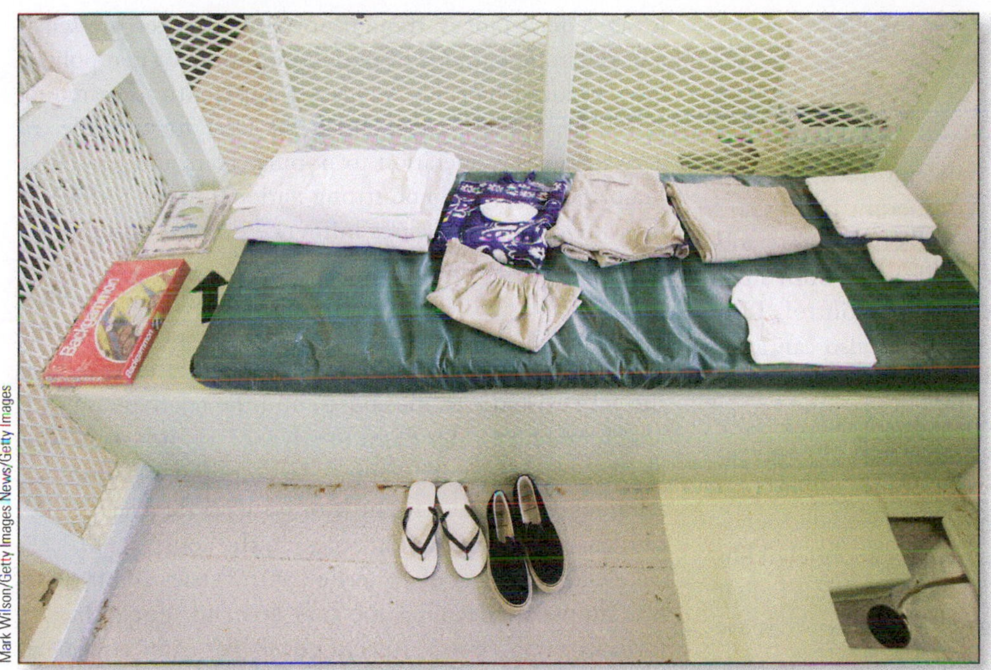
Mark Wilson/Getty Images News/Getty Images

Image 5.6 Inside a cell at the terrorist prison in Guantanamo, where Muslim inmates received a copy of the Koran, a chess set, and an arrow pointing toward Mecca.

Criminal Charges

- ***Mapp v. Ohio* (1961):** Evidence illegally gathered by the police may not be used in a criminal trial.
- ***Gideon v. Wainwright* (1964):** Persons charged with a crime have a right to an attorney even if they cannot afford one.
- ***Miranda v. Arizona* (1966):** The Supreme Court describes warning that police must give to arrested persons.
- ***United States v. Leon* (1984):** Illegally obtained evidence may be used in a trial if it was gathered in good faith without violating the principles of the *Mapp* decision.
- ***Dickerson v. United States* (2000):** The *Mapp* decision is based on the Constitution and cannot be altered by Congress passing a law.
- ***Rasul v. Bush and Hamdi v. Rumsfeld* (2004):** Terrorist detainees must have access to a neutral court to decide whether they are legally held.
- ***Hamdan v. Rumsfeld* (2006):** The executive branch cannot unilaterally set up military commissions to try suspected terrorists; Congress must authorize their creation.
- ***Boumedine v. Bush* (2008):** Congress may not suspend the writ of habeas corpus for suspected terrorists held at Guantanamo Bay.

prohibited defendants from challenging their detention in federal court, but the Supreme Court ruled in 2008 that the constitutional writ of habeas corpus applies to detainees.[116] Subsequent reforms were incorporated into the law in 2009.[117]

Of the nearly 800 individuals who have been held at the Guantanamo Bay detention camp, more than half were released during the Bush administration, and another quarter were released during the Obama administration. Upon taking office in 2009, President Obama issued an executive order to close the Guantanamo prison within one year. The administration subsequently announced that some detainees would be tried in the United States, but strong congressional and public opposition stymied this plan. When Obama left office in 2017, 41 detainees remained in the prison.[118] The Trump White House expressed interest in keeping Guantanamo Bay open and detaining more suspected terrorists there.

5-5 Civil Liberties and American Democracy

In some ways, civil liberties questions are both like and unlike ordinary policy debates. Like most issues, civil liberties problems often involve competing interests—in this case, conflicting rights or conflicting rights and duties—and so we have groups mobilized on both sides of issues involving free speech and crime control. Like some other issues, civil liberties problems also can arise from the successful appeals of a policy entrepreneur, and so we have periodic reductions in liberty resulting from popular fears, usually aroused during or just after a war.

But civil liberties are unlike many other issues in at least one regard: More than struggles over welfare spending or defense or economic policy, debates about civil liberties reach down into our fundamental political beliefs and political culture, challenging us to define what we mean by religion, Americanism, and decency. The most important of these challenges focuses on the meaning of the First Amendment: What is "speech"? How much of it should be free? How far can the state go in aiding religion? How do we strike a balance between national security and personal expression? The zigzag course followed by the courts in judging these matters has, on balance, tended to enlarge freedom of expression.

Almost as important has been the struggle to strike a balance between the right of society to be protected from criminals and terrorists, and the right of people (including criminals and terrorists) to have constitutional guarantees of due process. As with free speech cases, the courts generally have broadened the rights of individuals at some expense to the power of the police. But in recent years, the Supreme Court has pulled back from some of its more sweeping applications of the exclusionary rule.

The resolution of these issues by the courts is political in the sense that differing opinions about what is right or desirable compete, with one side or another prevailing (often by a small majority). In this competition of ideas, federal judges, though not elected, often are sensitive to strong currents of popular opinion. When politics has produced new action against apparently threatening minorities, judges are inclined, at least for a while, to give serious consideration to popular fears and legislative majorities. And when no strong national mood is discernible, the opinions of elites influence judicial thinking (as described in Chapter 16).

At the same time, courts resolve political conflicts in a manner that differs in important respects from the resolution of conflicts by legislatures or executives. First, the very existence of the courts, and the relative ease with which one may enter them to advance a claim, facilitates challenges to accepted values. An unpopular political or religious group may have little or no access to a legislature, but it will have substantial access to the courts.

Second, judges often settle controversies about rights not simply by deciding the case at hand, but rather by formulating a general rule to cover like cases elsewhere. This has an advantage (the law tends to become more consistent and better known) but a disadvantage as well: a rule suitable for one case may be unworkable in another. Judges reason by analogy and sometimes assume two cases are similar when in fact important differences exist. For example, a definition of "obscenity" or "fighting words" may suit one situation but be inadequate in another.

Third, judges interpret the Constitution, whereas legislatures often consult popular preferences or personal convictions. However much their own beliefs influence what judges read into the Constitution, almost all of them are constrained by its language.

Taken together, the desire to find and announce rules, the language of the Constitution, and the personal beliefs of judges have led to a general expansion of civil liberties. As a result, even allowing for temporary reversals and frequent redefinitions, any value thought to hinder freedom of expression and the rights of the accused has generally lost ground to the claims of the First, Fourth, Fifth, and Sixth Amendments.

Learning Objectives

5-1 Discuss why the courts are so important in defining civil liberties, for both the national government and the states.

The courts are independent of the executive and legislative branches, both of which respond to public pressures. In wartime or in other crisis periods, people want "something done." The president and members of Congress know this. The courts usually are a brake on the people's demands. Of course, the courts can make mistakes or get things confused, as many people believe they have with the establishment clause and the rights of criminal defendants. Still, when it comes to government respecting civil liberties like the freedom to express unpopular beliefs, the courts are often citizens' last best hope.

After the Fourteenth Amendment was adopted in 1868, the Supreme Court began the slow but steady process of "Incorporation" by which federal rights deemed "fundamental" also applied to the states. Today, the entire Bill of Rights is now applied to the states except the Third Amendment right not to have soldiers forcibly quartered in private homes, the Fifth Amendment right to be indicted by a grand jury before being tried for a serious crime, the Seventh Amendment right to a jury trial in civil cases, and the Eighth Amendment ban on excessive bail and fines. Although states still may regulate gun purchases and gun use, the latest incorporated right is the Second Amendment right to own and "bear arms," which the Court applied to the states in a 2010 decision.

5-2 Describe which forms of expression are not protected by the Constitution, and why.

Forms of expression not protected by the Constitution include: threats of "imminent, lawless action" (speech that incites others to commit illegal acts or that directly and immediately provokes another person to violent behavior); libel (injurious written statements about another person); obscenity (writing or pictures that the average person, applying community standards, believes appeal to the prurient interest and lack literary, artistic, political, or scientific value); and certain types of symbolic (actions that convey a political message) or commercial and youthful (expression by corporations, interest groups, and children) speech.

5-3 Explain how the Constitution protects religious freedom.

The First Amendment bans the federal government, but not the states, from having an "established," tax-supported church. Some states had tax-funded churches well into the 19th century, but the Supreme Court has long since outlawed state-sponsored churches. The First Amendment also prohibits the federal government from interfering with people's religious activities.

5-4 Evaluate how, in the 21st century, the Constitution protects civil liberties for people accused of a crime or designated as "enemy combatants."

The Constitution includes several due-process protections for people accused of committing a crime: the exclusionary rule (evidence gathered in violation of the Constitution cannot be used in a trial), the need for a search warrant (an order from a judge authorizing the search of a place), the *Miranda* rules (warnings that police must give to a person being arrested regarding the rights of the accused), and others. The Supreme Court has ruled that terrorist detainees and enemy combatants (persons who are neither citizens nor prisoners of war) have constitutionally guaranteed due-process protections.

5-5 Summarize the evolution of civil liberties in the United States.

The Bill of Rights guarantees to the people certain freedoms upon which the national government may not infringe, and the courts have extended many of those protections at the state level as well. While freedoms from government must be balanced against public interests, such as national security, the courts over time generally have ruled in favor of broad interpretations of civil liberties, requiring the government to meet a high standard to justify restrictions.

To Learn More

Court cases: **www.law.cornell.edu**

Civil Rights Division of the Department of Justice: **www.usdoj.gov**

American Civil Liberties Union: **www.aclu.org**

American Center for Law and Justice: **https://aclj.org**

Americans United for Separation of Church and State: **www.au.org**

Institutional Religious Freedom Alliance: **www.irfalliance.org**

Abraham, Henry J., and Barbara A. Perry. *Freedom and the Court,* 7th ed. New York: Oxford University Press, 1998. Analysis of leading Supreme Court cases on civil liberties and civil rights.

Amar, Akhil Reed. *The Constitution and Criminal Procedure: First Principles*. New Haven, CT: Yale

University Press, 1997. A brilliant critique of how the Supreme Court has interpreted those parts of the Constitution bearing on search warrants, the exclusionary rule, and self-incrimination.

Berns, Walter. *The First Amendment and the Future of American Democracy.* New York: Basic Books, 1976. A look at what the Founders intended by the First Amendment that takes issue with contemporary Supreme Court interpretations of it.

Clor, Harry M. *Obscenity and Public Morality.* Chicago, IL: University of Chicago Press, 1969. Argues for the legitimacy of legal restrictions on obscenity.

Levy, Leonard W. Legacy of Suppression: Freedom of Speech and Press in Early American History. Rev. ed. New York: Oxford University Press, 1985. Careful study of what the Founders and the early leaders meant by freedom of speech and press.

SAUL LOEB/AFP/Getty Images

CHAPTER 6

Civil Rights

Learning Objectives

6-1 Explain how Supreme Court rulings and federal legislation have attempted to end racial discrimination in the United States.

6-2 Explain how Supreme Court rulings and federal legislation have attempted to advance women's rights in the United States.

6-3 Discuss the evolution of affirmative action programs after the Supreme Court and Congress ended racial segregation.

6-4 Discuss how Court doctrine and public opinion on LGBTQ+ rights have changed in the 21st century.

6-5 Summarize how American political institutions and public opinion have expanded civil rights.

civil rights *The rights of people to be treated without unreasonable or unconstitutional differences.*

« Then

In 1830, Congress passed a law requiring all Indians (as they were then called in the law) east of the Mississippi River to move to the Indian Territory west of the river, and the army set about implementing it. In the 1850s, a major political fight broke out in Boston over whether the police department should be obliged to hire an Irish officer. Until 1920, women could not vote in most elections. In the 1930s, the Cornell University Medical School had a strict quota limiting the number of Jewish students who could enroll. In the 1940s, President Franklin D. Roosevelt ordered that all Japanese Americans be removed from their homes in California and placed in relocation centers far from the coast. Until 1954, public schools in many states were required by law to be segregated by race. Until 1967, 16 states outlawed marriages between white people and non-white people. Until 2003, 14 states outlawed consensual sexual relations between same-sex partners.

* Now

Now it would be inconceivable that the army would forcibly relocate Native Americans. No one can be denied entry into a police department by reason of race, ethnicity, or religion. Women not only have long had the right to vote, but actually now vote at higher rates than men do. Unlike during World War II, today no group of people can be forcibly relocated or held against their will en masse, and even suspected terrorists and "enemy combatants" cannot be detained indefinitely without having their day in court. The quotas that once limited Jews' access to colleges and universities are history. State laws requiring segregated public schools and banning interracial marriage are history, too. And, within just the past decade, state laws forbidding consensual sexual relations between same-sex partners have been eliminated, as have restrictions on same-sex marriage.

Still, then, as now, if the government passes a law that treats different groups of people differently, that law is not necessarily unconstitutional.

Civil rights refer to cases in which some group, usually defined along racial or ethnic lines, is denied access to facilities, opportunities, or services that are available to other groups. The pertinent question regarding civil rights is not whether the government has the authority to treat different people differently; it is whether such differences in treatment are reasonable. Many laws and policies make distinctions among people—for example, the tax laws require people with higher incomes to pay taxes at a higher rate than those with lower incomes—but not all such distinctions are defensible. The courts have long held that classifying people on the basis of their income and taxing them at different rates is quite permissible because such classifications are not arbitrary or unreasonable and are related to a legitimate public need (i.e., raising revenue). Increasingly, however, the courts have said that classifying people on the basis of their race or ethnicity is unreasonable.[1] The tests the courts use are summarized in Table 6.3 on page 138.

Robert W. Kelley/The LIFE Picture Collection/Getty Images

Image 6.1 Reverend Dr. Martin Luther King, Jr. and other civil rights leaders participated in the March on Washington for Jobs and Freedom, popularly known as the March on Washington, on August 28, 1963.

To explain the victimization of certain groups and the methods by which they have begun to overcome it, we start with racial classifications and the case of African Americans. The strategies used by or on behalf of African Americans have typically set the pattern for the strategies used by other groups. At the end of this chapter, we look at the issues of women's rights and LGBTQ+ rights.

6-1 Race and Civil Rights

In July 2013, the National Urban League (NUL), led by its president, Marc H. Morial, the former mayor of New Orleans, came to Philadelphia for its annual conference. With the National Association for the Advancement of Colored People (NAACP), the NUL is among the nation's most historic and important civil rights organizations. Its 2013 conference theme was "Redeem the Dream." Fifty years earlier, in 1963, Reverend Dr. Martin Luther King, Jr. delivered his historic "I Have a Dream" speech in Washington, D.C. In its 2013 *State of Black America* report, the NUL credited civil rights laws (see Table 6.1 on page 127) for the progress made over the past half-century or so in closing white-black gaps in education and standards of living:

- The white-black high school completion rate gap has closed by 57 points; whereas only 25 percent of blacks graduated from high school in 1963, by 2013 the fraction had risen to 85 percent, and there had been a threefold increase in the number of blacks enrolled in college.
- The white-black poverty rate gap fell by 23 points; whereas 48 percent of blacks lived in poverty in 1963, by 2013 the fraction had fallen to 28 percent.
- The number of black homeowners increased by 14 percent.

But the same report also documented numerous racial gaps and disparities in housing, education, health care, employment, and overall economic opportunity:

AFP/Getty Images

Image 6.2 Reverend Dr. Martin Luther King, Jr. delivered his historic "I Have a Dream" speech on the Washington, D.C. mall during the March on Washington.

Shannon Finney/Getty Images Entertainment/Getty Images

Image 6.3 U.S. Supreme Court Justice Ruth Bader Ginsburg, the second woman to hold that position, was appointed in 1993 and served on the Court until her death at age 87 in 2020.

- In 2013, as in 1963, the black-white unemployment ratio was still 2 to 1, regardless of education, gender, region, or income level.
- In 2013, as in 1963, more than a third of all black children (38 percent) still lived in poverty.
- In 2013, as in 1963, blacks employed in the public sector earned less than whites in the same jobs, and a still-wider black-white wage disparity persisted in the private sector.

Citing the history surrounding Reverend Dr. King's "I Have a Dream" speech, Morial and other leaders called on all citizens to come together to eliminate these and other racial gaps and disparities in housing, education, employment, and other areas. As late as the mid-20th century, African Americans in many parts of the country could not vote, attend integrated schools, ride in the front seats of buses, or buy homes in white neighborhoods. Conditions were especially oppressive in those parts of the country, notably the Deep South, where blacks were often in the majority. There, the politically dominant white minority felt keenly the potential competition for jobs, land, public services, and living space posed by large numbers of people of another race. But even in the North, black gains often seemed to be at the expense of lower-income whites who lived or worked near them, not at the expense of upper-status whites who lived in suburbs.

African Americans were not allowed to vote at all in many areas; they could vote only with great difficulty in others; and even in those places where voting was easy, they often lacked the material and institutional support for effective political organization. If your opponent feels deeply threatened by your demands and can deny you access to the political system that will decide the fate of those demands, you are, to put it mildly, at a disadvantage. Yet from the end of Reconstruction to the 1960s—for nearly a century—many blacks in the South found themselves in just such a position.

To the dismay of those who prefer to explain political action in terms of economic motives, people often attach greater importance to the intangible costs and benefits of policies than to the tangible ones. Thus, even though the average black represented no threat to the average white, antiblack attitudes—racism—produced some appalling actions. Between 1882 and 1946, 4,715 people, about three-fourths of them African Americans, were lynched in the United States.[2] Some of these brutalities were perpetrated by small groups of vigilantes acting with much ceremony, but others were the actions of frenzied mobs. In the summer of 1911, a black man charged with murdering a white man in Livermore, Kentucky, was dragged by a mob to the local theater, where he was hanged. The audience, which had been charged admission, was invited to shoot the swaying body (those in the orchestra seats could empty their revolvers; those in the balcony were limited to a single shot).[3]

Though the public in other parts of the country was shocked by such events, little was done because lynching was a local, not a federal, crime. It obviously would not require many such horrific killings for African Americans in these localities to decide it would be foolhardy to try to vote or enroll in a white school. And even in those states where black Americans did vote, popular attitudes were not conducive to blacks buying homes or taking jobs on an equal basis with whites.

Even among those professing to support equal rights, a substantial portion opposed African Americans' efforts to obtain them and federal action to secure them. In 1942, a national poll showed that only 30 percent of white people thought black and white children should attend the same schools; in 1956, the proportion had risen, but only to 49 percent, still less than a majority. (In the South, white support for school integration was even lower—14 percent favored it in 1956, about 31 percent in 1963.) As late as 1956, a majority of Southern whites were opposed to integrated public transportation facilities. Even among whites who generally favored integration, there was in 1963 (*before* the inner-city riots that occurred later in the decade) considerable opposition to the black civil rights movement: nearly half of the whites classified in a survey as moderate integrationists thought demonstrations hurt the black cause, nearly two-thirds disapproved of actions taken by the civil rights movement, and more than a third felt civil rights should be left to the states.[4]

In short, the political position in which African Americans found themselves until the 1960s made it difficult for them to advance their interests through a feasible legislative strategy; their opponents were aroused, organized, and powerful. Thus, if black interests were to be championed in Congress or state legislatures, blacks would have to have white allies. Though some such allies could be found, they were too few to make a difference in a political system that gives a substantial advantage to strongly motivated opponents of any new policy. For that to change, one or both of two things would have to happen: additional allies would have to be recruited (a delicate problem, given that many white integrationists disapproved of aspects of the civil rights movement), or the struggle would have to be shifted to a policymaking arena in which the opposition enjoyed less of an advantage.

Partly by plan, and partly by accident, black leaders followed both of these strategies simultaneously. By publicizing their grievances and organizing a civil rights movement that (at least in its early stages) concentrated on dramatizing the denial to blacks of essential and widely accepted liberties, African Americans were able to broaden their base of support both among political elites and among the general public, thereby elevating the importance of civil rights issues on the political agenda. By waging a patient, prolonged, but carefully planned legal struggle, black leaders shifted decision-making power on key civil rights issues from Congress, where they had been stymied for generations, to the federal courts.

After this strategy had achieved some substantial successes—once black Americans had become enfranchised and legal barriers to equal participation in political and economic affairs had been lowered—the politics of civil rights became more conventional. African Americans were able to assert their demands directly in the legislative and executive branches of government with reasonable (though scarcely certain) prospects of success. Civil rights became less a matter of gaining entry into the political system and more one of waging interest-group politics within that system. (See Table 6.1 for a summary of major civil-rights laws.)

At the same time, the goals of civil rights politics broadened. The struggle to gain entry into the system had

Everett Collection Historical/Alamy Stock Photo

Image 6.4 Segregated water fountain in Oklahoma City (1939).

TABLE 6.1 | Key Provisions of Major Civil Rights Laws

1957	Voting	Made it a federal crime to try to prevent a person from voting in a federal election. Created the Civil Rights Commission.
1960	Voting	Authorized the attorney general to appoint federal referees to gather evidence and make findings about allegations that African Americans were deprived of their right to vote. Made it a federal crime to use interstate commerce to threaten or carry out a bombing.
1964	Voting	Made it more difficult to use devices such as literacy tests to bar African Americans from voting.
	Public accommodations	Barred discrimination on grounds of race, color, religion, or national origin in restaurants, hotels, lunch counters, gasoline stations, movie theaters, stadiums, arenas, and lodging houses with more than five rooms.
	Schools	Authorized the attorney general to bring suit to force the desegregation of public schools on behalf of citizens.
	Employment	Outlawed discrimination in hiring, firing, or paying employees on grounds of race, color, religion, national origin, or sex.
	Federal funds	Barred discrimination in any activity receiving federal assistance.
1965	Voter registration	Authorized appointment by the Civil Service Commission of voting examiners who would require registration of all eligible voters in federal, state, and local elections, general or primary, in areas where discrimination was found to be practiced or where less than 50 percent of voting-age residents were registered to vote in the 1964 election.
	Literacy tests	Suspended use of literacy tests or other devices to prevent African Americans from voting.
1968	Housing	Banned, by stages, discrimination in sale or rental of most housing (excluding private owners who sell or rent their homes without the services of a real-estate broker).
	Riots	Made it a federal crime to use interstate commerce to organize or incite a riot.
1972	Education	Prohibited sex discrimination in education programs receiving federal aid.
	Discrimination	Declared that if any part of an organization receives federal aid, no part of that organization may discriminate on the basis of race, sex, age, or physical disability.
1991	Discrimination	Made it easier to sue over job discrimination and collect damages; overturned certain Supreme Court decisions. Made it illegal for the government to adjust, or "norm," test scores by race.

Q How have civil rights laws aimed to enact the Fourteenth Amendment's guarantee of "equal protection of the laws"?

focused on the denial of fundamental rights (to vote, to organize, to obtain equal access to schools and public facilities); since then, dominant issues have included economic progress, professional advancement, and improvement of housing and neighborhoods. But these battles can reveal denial of fundamental legal rights as well. With housing, for example, both government agencies, such as the Federal Housing Authority, and private lenders have pursued strategies to make home ownership more difficult for black Americans, such as "redlining" neighborhoods, that is, either denying loans or making them more expensive.

Among the most visible and devastating examples of civil-rights violations for black Americans in recent years are the horrific deaths from police brutality or by individuals who claim to have acted in self-defense. In 2013, the Black Lives Matter movement started after an acquittal in the fatal shooting of unarmed teenager Trayvon Martin by a civilian in the Florida community where he was staying. The following year, Michael Brown in Ferguson, Missouri, and Eric Garner in Staten Island, New York, were killed in police altercations, and their deaths resulted in massive public protests. In 2015, Baltimore resident Freddie Gray died of fatal injuries received in police custody. Of subsequent tragedies, one of the most shocking is the death of George Floyd in Minneapolis in 2020, after a police officer pressed a knee on Floyd's neck for almost nine minutes. Repeated public protests called for addressing longstanding racism in police departments and other institutions in American politics.[5]

The Campaign in the Courts

The Fourteenth Amendment was both an opportunity and a problem for black activists. Adopted in 1868, it seemed to guarantee equal rights for all: "No state shall make or enforce any law which shall abridge the privileges or immunities of citizens of the United States; nor shall any state deprive any person of life, liberty, or property, without due process of law; nor deny to any person within its jurisdiction the equal protection of the laws."

The key phrase was "equal protection of the laws." Read broadly, it might mean that the Constitution should be regarded as color-blind: No state law could have the effect of treating whites and blacks differently. Thus, a law segregating blacks and whites into separate schools or neighborhoods would be unconstitutional. Read narrowly, "equal protection" might mean only that blacks and whites had certain fundamental legal rights in common (such as the right to sign contracts, to serve on juries,

separate-but-equal doctrine *The doctrine established in* Plessy v. Ferguson *(1896) that African Americans could constitutionally be kept in separate but equal facilities.*

or to buy and sell property), but otherwise they could be treated differently.

In a series of decisions beginning in the 1870s, the Supreme Court took the narrow view, albeit often by narrow majorities. Adopted in 1870, the Fourteenth Amendment had been proposed as a means to reinforce the Civil Rights Act of 1866. That Act was intended by Congress to ensure that former slaves' citizenship rights would be respected not only by the federal government but also by the state governments, both North and South. But in its 5-to-4 majority decision in the *Slaughter-House Cases* (1873), the Court ruled that the "privileges and immunities" clause of the Fourteenth Amendment did not protect citizens from discriminatory actions by state governments.

Though in 1880 it declared unconstitutional a West Virginia law requiring juries to comprise only white men,[6] the Court decided in 1883 that it was unconstitutional for Congress to prohibit racial discrimination in public accommodations such as hotels.[7] The difference between the two cases seemed, in the eyes of the Court, to be this: Serving on a jury was an essential right of citizenship that the state could not deny to any person on racial grounds without violating the Fourteenth Amendment, but registering at a hotel was a convenience controlled by a private person (the hotel owner), who could treat black and white guests differently.

The major decision that determined the legal status of the Fourteenth Amendment for more than half a century was *Plessy v. Ferguson.* Louisiana had passed a law requiring blacks and whites to occupy separate cars on railroad trains operating in that state. When Adolph Plessy, who was seven-eighths white and one-eighth black, refused to obey the law, he was arrested. He appealed his conviction to the Supreme Court, claiming that the law violated the Fourteenth Amendment. In 1896, the Court rejected his claim, holding that the law treated both races equally even though it required them to be separate. The equal protection clause guaranteed political and legal but not social equality. "Separate-but-equal" facilities were constitutional because if "one race be inferior to the other socially, the Constitution of the United States cannot put them on the same plane."[8]

"Separate but Equal"

Thus began the **separate-but-equal doctrine**. Three years later, the Court applied it to schools as well, declaring in *Cumming v. Richmond County Board of Education* that a decision in a Georgia community to close the black high school while keeping open the white high school was not a violation of the Fourteenth Amendment because blacks could always go to private schools. Here the Court seemed to be saying that not only could schools be separate, they could even be unequal.[9]

What the Court has made, the Court can unmake. But to get it to change its mind requires a long, costly, and uncertain legal battle. The NAACP was the main organization that waged that battle against the precedent of *Plessy v. Ferguson.* Formed in 1909 by a group of whites and blacks in the aftermath of a race riot, the NAACP did many things, including lobbying in Washington and publicizing black grievances (especially in the pages of *The Crisis*, a magazine edited by W. E. B. Du Bois). But its most influential role was played in the courtroom.

It was a rational strategy. Fighting legal battles does not require forming broad political alliances or changing public opinion, tasks that would have been very difficult for a small and unpopular organization. A court-based approach also enabled the organization to remain nonpartisan. But it was a slow and difficult strategy. The Court had adopted a narrow interpretation of the Fourteenth Amendment. To get the Court to change its mind would require the NAACP to bring before it cases involving the strongest possible claims that a black had been unfairly treated—and under circumstances sufficiently different from those of earlier cases, so that the Court could find some grounds for changing its mind.

The steps in that strategy were these: First, persuade the Court to declare unconstitutional laws creating schools that were separate but obviously unequal. Second, persuade it to declare unconstitutional laws supporting schools that were separate but unequal in not-so-obvious ways. Third, persuade it to rule that racially separate schools were inherently unequal and hence unconstitutional.

Can Separate Schools Be Equal?

The first step was accomplished in a series of court cases stretching from 1938 to 1948. In 1938, the Court held that Lloyd Gaines had to be admitted to an all-white law school in Missouri because no black law school of equal quality existed in that state.[10] In 1948, the Court ordered the all-white University of Oklahoma Law School to admit Ada Lois Sipuel, a black woman, even though the state planned to build a black law school later. For education to be equal, it had to be equally available.[11] It still could be separate, however: The university admitted Ms. Sipuel but required her to attend classes in a section of the state capitol, roped off from other students, where she could meet with her law professors.

The second step was taken in two cases decided in 1950. Heman Sweatt, an African American man, was treated by the University of Texas Law School much as Ada Sipuel had been treated in Oklahoma: "admitted" to the all-white school but relegated to a separate building. Another African American man, George McLaurin, was allowed to study for his Ph.D. in a "colored section" of the all-white University of Oklahoma. The Supreme Court unanimously decided that these arrangements were unconstitutional because, by imposing racially based barriers on the black students' access to professors, libraries, and other students, they created unequal educational opportunities.[12]

The third step, the climax of the entire drama, began in Topeka, Kansas, where Linda Brown wanted to enroll in her neighborhood school but could not because she was black and the school was by law reserved exclusively for whites. When the NAACP took her case to the federal district court in Kansas, the judge decided the black school Linda could attend was substantially equal in quality to the white school she could not attend and, therefore, denying her access to the white school was constitutional. To change that, the lawyers would have to persuade the Supreme Court to overrule the district judge on the grounds that racially separate schools were unconstitutional even if they were equal. In other words, the separate-but-equal doctrine would have to be overturned by the Court.

It was a risky and controversial step to take. Many states, Kansas among them, were trying to make their all-black schools equal to those of whites by launching expensive building programs. If the NAACP succeeded in getting separate schools declared unconstitutional, the Court might well put a stop to the building of these new schools. Blacks could win a moral and legal victory but suffer a practical defeat—the loss of these new facilities. Despite these risks, the NAACP decided to go ahead with the appeal.

Brown v. Board of Education

On May 17, 1954, a unanimous Supreme Court, speaking through an opinion written and delivered by Chief Justice Earl Warren, found that "in the field of public education the doctrine of 'separate but equal' has no place" because "separate educational facilities are inherently unequal."[13] *Plessy v. Ferguson* was overruled, and "separate but equal" was dead.

The ruling was a landmark decision, but the reasons for it and the means chosen to implement it were as important and as controversial as the decision itself. There were at least three issues. First, how would the decision be implemented? Second, on what grounds were racially separate schools unconstitutional? Third, what test would a school system have to meet in order to be in conformity with the Constitution?

Implementation

The *Brown* case involved a class-action suit; that is, it applied not only to Linda Brown but to all others similarly situated. This meant that black children everywhere now had the right to attend formerly all-white schools. This change would be one of the most far-reaching and conflict-provoking events in modern American history. It could not be effected overnight or by the stroke of a pen. In 1955, the Supreme Court decided it would let local federal district courts oversee the end of segregation by giving them the power to approve or disapprove local desegregation plans. This was to be done "with all deliberate speed."[14]

In the South, "all deliberate speed" turned out to be a snail's pace. Massive resistance to desegregation broke out in many states. Some communities simply defied the Court;

AP images/Douglas Martin

Image 6.5 Dorothy Counts, the first black student to attend Harding High School in Charlotte, North Carolina, maintained her poise as she was taunted by shouting, gesticulating white students in September 1957.

de jure segregation
Racial segregation that is required by law.

de facto segregation
Racial segregation that occurs not as a result of the law, but as a result of patterns of residential settlement.

some sought to evade its edict by closing their public schools. In 1956, more than 100 Southern members of Congress signed a "Southern Manifesto" that condemned the *Brown* decision as an "abuse of judicial power" and pledged to "use all lawful means to bring about a reversal of the decision."

In the late 1950s and early 1960s, the National Guard and regular army paratroopers were used to escort black students into formerly all-white schools and universities. It was not until the 1970s that resistance collapsed and most Southern schools were integrated. The use of armed force convinced people that resistance was futile, the disruption of the politics and economy of the South convinced leaders that it was imprudent, and the voting power of blacks convinced politicians that it was suicidal. In addition, federal laws began providing financial aid to integrated schools and withholding it from segregated ones. By 1970, only 14 percent of Southern black schoolchildren still attended all-black schools.[15]

The Rationale

As the struggle to implement the *Brown* decision continued, the importance of the rationale for that decision became apparent. The case was decided in a way that surprised many legal scholars.

The Court could have said that the equal protection clause of the Fourteenth Amendment makes the Constitution, and thus state laws, color-blind. Or it could have said that the authors of the Fourteenth Amendment meant to ban segregated schools. It did neither. Instead, it said segregated education is bad because it "has a detrimental effect upon the colored children" by generating "a feeling of inferiority as to their status in the community" that may "affect their hearts and minds in a way unlikely ever to be undone."[16] This conclusion was supported by a footnote reference to social science studies of the apparent impact of segregation on black children.

MPI/Archive Photos/Getty Images

Image 6.6 In 1963, Governor George Wallace of Alabama stood in the doorway of the University of Alabama to block the entry of black students. Facing him was U.S. Deputy Attorney General Nicholas Katzenbach.

Why did the Court rely on social science as much as or more than the Constitution in supporting its decision? Apparently for two reasons. One was the justices' realization that the authors of the Fourteenth Amendment may *not* have intended to outlaw segregated schools. The schools in Washington, DC, were segregated when the amendment was proposed, and when this fact was mentioned during the debate, it seems to have been made clear that the amendment was not designed to abolish this segregation. When Congress debated a civil rights act a few years later, it voted down provisions that would have ended segregation in schools.[17] The Court could not easily base its decision on a constitutional provision that had, at best, an uncertain application to schools. The other reason grew out of the first. On so important a matter, the chief justice wanted to speak for a unanimous court. Some justices did not agree that the Fourteenth Amendment made the Constitution color-blind. In the interests of harmony, the Court found an ambiguous rationale for its decision.

Desegregation Versus Integration

That ambiguity led to the third issue. If separate schools were inherently unequal, what would "unseparate" schools look like? Since the Court had not said race was irrelevant, an "unseparate" school could be either one that blacks and whites were free to attend if they chose or one that blacks and whites in fact attended whether they wanted to or not. The first might be called a desegregated school, and the latter an integrated school. Think of the Topeka case. Was it enough that there was now no barrier to Linda Brown's attending the white school in her neighborhood? Or was it necessary that there be black children (if not Linda, then some others) actually going to that school together with white children?

As long as the main impact of the *Brown* decision lay in the South, where laws had prevented blacks from attending white schools, this question did not seem important. Segregation by law (**de jure segregation**) was now clearly unconstitutional. But in the North, laws had not kept black and white people apart; instead, all-black and all-white schools were the result of residential segregation, preferred living patterns, informal social forces, and administrative practices (such as drawing school district lines so as to produce single-race schools). This often was called segregation in fact (**de facto segregation**).

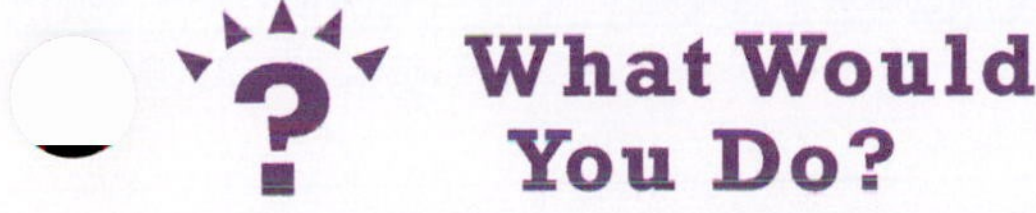

What Would You Do? | Should Affirmative Action Programs in Higher Education Continue to Be Supported?

To: *Justice Roberta Wilson*
From: *Robert Gilbert, law clerk*
Subject: *Affirmative action in higher education*

Affirmative-action programs in higher education in the 21st century face strong political scrutiny. In the 1970s, the Supreme Court said such programs could be instituted as a means of overcoming institutional problems of past discrimination, but the Court has wrestled with the specifics of doing so. For example, it has said that diversity goals are permissible, but not quotas. In recent years, the Court has questioned whether the need for affirmative-action programs still exists. The Court needs to decide whether affirmative-action programs are constitutional, so schools operate uniformly, and constitutionally, in making decisions about admissions.

To Consider:

The Supreme Court has announced that it will decide whether affirmative-action programs in colleges and universities are necessary in the 21st century as a means of redress for past discrimination against racial minorities and women.

Arguments for:

1. Diversity is an important goal in higher education, as numerous schools, including military academies, have said in briefs for earlier cases.
2. The effects of segregation and discrimination continue in American politics today, and affirmative-action programs provide a necessary means of countering those problems.
3. Institutions of higher education grant preference to applicants for several reasons, including family ties to the school. Taking race, ethnicity, or gender into account has the same goal of incorporating a range of interests and perspectives into an entering class.

Arguments against:

1. Colleges and universities focus on higher learning and should seek intellectual, not individual, diversity.
2. Race is a suspect classification, and no state program that chiefly serves one race can be allowed.
3. Institutions of higher education should make admissions decisions on merit criteria, not on other considerations.

What Will You Decide? Enter **MindTap** to make your choice.

Your decision:
☐ Continue affirmative-action programs in higher education
☐ Ban affirmative-action programs in higher education

Constitutional Connections | Suspect Classifications

Beginning with the *Brown* case, virtually every form of racial segregation imposed by law has been struck down as unconstitutional. Race has become a **suspect classification** such that any law making racial distinctions is now subject to **strict scrutiny**. To be upheld as constitutional, a suspect classification must be related to a "compelling government interest," be "narrowly tailored" to achieve that interest, and use the "least restrictive means" available. But the Court has also determined that though race is a suspect classification, the Constitution is not "color-blind," and so the government may make racial distinctions for the purpose of remedying past racial discrimination. Later in this chapter we discuss affirmative action—the laws or administrative regulations that require a business firm, government agency, labor union, school, college, or other organization to take positive steps to increase the number of African Americans, other minorities, or women in its membership.

suspect classification *Classifications of people based on their race or ethnicity; laws so classifying people are subject to "strict scrutiny."*

strict scrutiny *The standard by which "suspect classifications" are judged. To be upheld, such a classification must be related to a "compelling government interest," be "narrowly tailored" to achieve that interest, and use the "least restrictive means" available.*

In 1968, the Supreme Court settled the matter. In New Kent County, Virginia, the school board had created a "freedom-of-choice" plan under which every pupil would be allowed without legal restriction to attend the school of that student's choice. As it turned out, all the white children chose to remain in the all-white school, and 85 percent of the black children remained in the all-black school. The Court rejected this plan as unconstitutional because it did not produce the "ultimate end," which was a "unitary, nonracial system of education."[18] In the opinion written by Justice William Brennan, the Court seemed to be saying that the Constitution required actual racial mixing in the schools, not just the repeal of laws requiring racial separation.

This impression was confirmed three years later when the Court considered a plan in North Carolina under which pupils in Mecklenburg County (which includes Charlotte) were assigned to the nearest neighborhood school without regard to race. As a result, about half the black children now attended formerly all-white schools, with the other half attending all-black schools. The federal district court held that this was inadequate and ordered some children to be bused into more distant schools in order to achieve a greater degree of integration. The Supreme Court, now led by Chief Justice Warren Burger, upheld the district judge on the grounds that the court plan was necessary to achieve a "unitary school system."[19] This case—*Swann v. Charlotte-Mecklenburg Board of Education*—pretty much set the guidelines for all subsequent cases involving school segregation. The essential features of those guidelines are as follows:

- To violate the Constitution, a school system, by law, practice, or regulation, must have engaged in discrimination. Put another way, a plaintiff must show intent to discriminate on the part of the public schools.
- The existence of all-white or all-black schools in a district with a history of segregation creates a presumption of intent to discriminate.
- The remedy for past discrimination will not be limited to freedom of choice, or what the Court called "the walk-in school." Remedies may include racial quotas in the assignment of teachers and pupils, redrawn district lines, and court-ordered busing.
- Not every school must reflect the social composition of the school system as a whole.

Relying on *Swann,* district courts supervised redistricting and busing plans in localities all over the nation, often in the face of bitter opposition from the community. In Boston, the control of the city schools by a federal judge, W. Arthur Garrity, lasted for more than a decade and involved him in every aspect of school administration. One major issue not settled by *Swann* was whether busing and other remedies should cut across city and county lines. In some places, the central-city schools had become virtually all black. Racial integration could be achieved only by bringing black pupils to white suburban schools or moving white pupils into central-city schools.

In a series of split-vote decisions, the Court ruled that court-ordered intercity busing could be authorized only if it could be demonstrated that the suburban areas as well as the central city had in fact practiced school segregation. Where that could not be shown, such intercity busing would not be required. The Court was not persuaded that intent had been proved in Atlanta, Detroit, Denver, Indianapolis, and Richmond, but it was persuaded that intent had been proved in Louisville and Wilmington.[20]

The importance the Court attaches to intent means that if a school system that was once integrated develops a majority population of black students as a result of white residents moving to the suburbs, the Court will not require that district lines constantly be redrawn or new busing plans be adopted to adjust to the changing distribution of the population.[21] This in turn means that as long as black people and white people live in different neighborhoods for whatever reason, there is a good chance that some schools in both areas will be heavily of one race.

If mandatory busing plans or other integration measures cause white people to move out of a city at a faster rate than they otherwise would (a process often called "white flight"), then efforts to integrate the schools may in time create more single-race schools. Ultimately, integrated schools will exist only in integrated neighborhoods or where the quality of education is so high that both black and white students will enroll in the school, even at some cost for travel and inconvenience.

Mandatory busing to achieve racial integration has been a deeply controversial program and has generated considerable public opposition. Surveys show that a majority of people oppose it.[22] A 1992 poll showed that 48 percent of whites in the Northeast and 53 percent of Southern whites felt it was "not the business" of the federal government to ensure "that black and white children go to the same schools."[23] Presidents Richard Nixon, Gerald Ford, and Ronald Reagan opposed busing; all three supported legislation to prevent or reduce it, and Reagan petitioned the courts to reconsider busing plans. The courts refused to reconsider, and Congress has passed only minor restrictions on busing.

The reason why Congress has not followed public opinion on this matter is complex. It has been torn between the desire to support civil rights and uphold the courts and the desire to represent the views of its constituents.

Str/FILE UPI Photo Service/Newscom

Image 6.7 In the 1970s, antibusing protestors picketed against sending children out of neighborhoods to desegregate schools.

Because it faces a dilemma, Congress has taken both sides of the issue simultaneously. By the late 1980s, busing was a dying issue in Congress, in part because no meaningful legislation seemed possible and in part because popular passion over busing had somewhat abated.

Then, in 1992, the Supreme Court made it easier for local school systems to reclaim control over their schools from the courts. In DeKalb County, Georgia (a suburb of Atlanta), the schools had been operating under court-ordered desegregation plans for many years. Despite this effort, full integration had not been achieved, largely because the county's neighborhoods had increasingly become either all black or all white. The Court held that local schools could not be held responsible for segregation caused solely by segregated living patterns and so the courts would have to relinquish their control over the schools. In 2007, the Court said race could not be the decisive factor in assigning students to schools that had either never been segregated (as in Seattle) or where legal segregation had long since ended (as in Jefferson County, Kentucky).[24]

The Campaign in Congress

The campaign in the courts for desegregated schools, though slow and costly, was a carefully managed effort to alter the interpretation of a constitutional provision. But to get new civil rights laws out of Congress required a far more difficult and decentralized strategy, one that was aimed at mobilizing public opinion and overcoming the many congressional barriers to action.

The first problem was to get civil rights on the political agenda by convincing people that something had to be done. This could be achieved by dramatizing the problem in ways that tugged at the conscience of white people who were not racist but were ordinarily indifferent to black people's problems. Brutal lynchings of black people had shocked many white people, but the practice of lynching was on the wane in the 1950s.

Civil rights leaders could, however, arrange for dramatic confrontations between black people claiming some obvious right and white people who denied it to them. Beginning in the late 1950s, these confrontations began to occur in the form of sit-ins at segregated lunch counters and "freedom rides" on segregated bus lines. At about the same time, efforts were made to get blacks registered to vote in counties where whites had used intimidation and harassment to prevent it.

The best-known campaign occurred in 1955–1956 in Montgomery, Alabama, where blacks, led by a young minister named Martin Luther King, Jr., boycotted the local bus system after it had a black woman, Rosa Parks, arrested because she refused to surrender her seat on a bus to a white man. These early demonstrations were based on the philosophy of

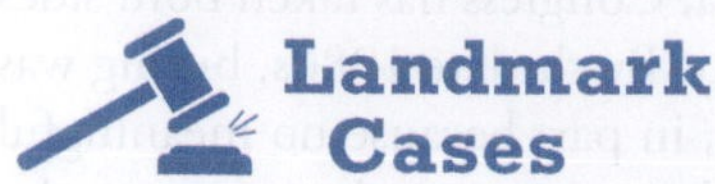

Landmark Cases | Civil Rights

- ***Dred Scott* case, *Scott v. Sanford* (1857):** Congress had no authority to ban slavery in a territory. A slave was considered a piece of property.
- ***Plessy v. Ferguson* (1896):** Upheld separate-but-equal facilities on railroad cars for people based on their race.
- ***Brown v. Board of Education* (1954):** Said separate public schools are inherently unequal, thus starting racial desegregation.
- ***Green v. County School Board of New Kent County* (1968):** Banned a freedom-of-choice plan for integrating schools, suggesting students must actually attend racially mixed schools.
- ***Swann v. Charlotte-Mecklenburg Board of Education* (1971):** Approved busing and redrawing district lines as ways of integrating public schools.
- ***Parents Involved in Community Schools v. Seattle School District #1 and Meredith v. Jefferson County Board of Education* (2007):** Overturned voluntary desegregation plans in public schools without evidence of past discrimination.

civil disobedience
Opposing a law one considers unjust by peacefully disobeying it and accepting the resultant punishment.

civil disobedience—that is, peacefully violating a law, such as one requiring blacks to ride in a segregated section of a bus, and allowing oneself to be arrested as a result.

But the momentum of protest, once unleashed, could not be centrally directed or confined to nonviolent action. A rising tide of anger, especially among younger blacks, resulted in the formation of more militant organizations and the spontaneous eruption of violent demonstrations and riots in dozens of cities across the country. From 1964 to 1968, there were in the North as well as the South several "long, hot summers" of racial violence.

The demonstrations and rioting succeeded in getting civil rights on the national political agenda, but at a cost: many white people, opposed to the demonstrations or appalled by the riots, dug in their heels and fought against making any concessions to "lawbreakers," "troublemakers," and "rioters." In 1964 and again in 1968, more than two-thirds of white people interviewed in opinion polls said the civil rights movement was pushing too fast, had hurt the cause, and was too violent.[25]

In short, a conflict existed between the agenda-setting and coalition-building aspects of the civil rights movement. This was especially a problem since conservative Southern legislators still controlled many key congressional committees that had for years been the graveyard of civil rights legislation. The Senate Judiciary Committee was dominated by a coalition of Southern Democrats and conservative Republicans, and the House Rules Committee was under the control of a chairman hostile to civil rights bills, Howard Smith of Virginia. Any bill that passed the House faced an almost certain filibuster in the Senate. Finally, President John F. Kennedy was reluctant to submit strong civil rights bills to Congress.

Several developments made breaking the deadlock possible. First, public opinion was changing. From the mid-1950s to the mid-1990s, surveys found that the proportion of whites who were willing to have their children attend a school that was half black increased sharply (though the proportion of white people willing to have their children attend a school with a predominantly black student population increased by much less). About the same change could be found in white people's attitudes toward allowing black people equal access to hotels and buses.[26] Of course, support in principle for these civil rights measures was not necessarily the same as support in practice; nonetheless, clearly a major shift was occurring in popular approval of at least the principles of civil rights. At the leading edge of this change were young, college-educated people.[27]

Second, certain violent reactions by white segregationists to black demonstrators were vividly portrayed by the media (especially television) in ways that gave the civil rights cause a powerful moral force. In May 1963, the head of the Birmingham police, Eugene "Bull" Connor, ordered his men to use attack dogs and high-pressure fire hoses to repulse a peaceful march by African Americans demanding desegregated public facilities and increased job opportunities. The pictures of that confrontation (such as the one on page 136) created a national sensation and contributed greatly to the massive participation—by white and black people alike—in the "March on Washington" that summer. About a quarter of a million people gathered in front of the Lincoln Memorial to hear the Reverend Dr. Martin Luther King, Jr. deliver the aforementioned "I Have a Dream" speech, which is now widely regarded as one of the most significant public addresses in American history, and which today is read, studied, or memorized in whole or in part by millions of schoolchildren each year.

The following summer in Neshoba County, Mississippi, three young civil rights workers (two white men and one black man) were brutally murdered by Klansmen aided by the local sheriff. When the FBI identified the murderers, the effect on national public opinion was galvanic; no white Southern leader could any longer offer persuasive opposition to federal laws protecting voting rights when white law enforcement officers had killed students working to protect those rights. And the next year, a white woman, Viola Liuzzo, was shot and killed while driving a car used to transport civil rights workers. Her death was the subject of a presidential address.

Third, President John F. Kennedy was assassinated in Dallas, Texas, in November 1963. Many people originally (and wrongly) thought he had been killed by a right-wing conspiracy. Even after the assassin had been caught and shown to have left-wing associations, the shock of the president's murder—in a Southern city—helped build support for efforts by the new president, Lyndon B. Johnson (a Texan), to obtain passage of a strong civil rights bill as a memorial to the slain president.

Fourth, the 1964 elections not only returned Johnson to office with a landslide victory but also sent a huge Democratic majority to the House and retained the large Democratic margin in the Senate. This made it possible for Northern Democrats to outvote or outmaneuver Southerners in the House.

The cumulative effect of these forces, as well as other significant events, led to the enactment of five civil rights laws between 1957 and 1968. Three (1957, 1960, and 1965) were chiefly directed at protecting the right to vote; one (1968) was aimed at preventing discrimination in housing; and one (1964), the most far-reaching of all, dealt with voting, employment, schooling, and public accommodations.

The passage of the 1964 act was the high point of the legislative struggle. Liberals in the House had drafted a bipartisan bill, but it was now in the House Rules Committee, where such proposals had often disappeared without a trace. In the wake of Kennedy's murder, a discharge petition was filed—with President Johnson's support—to take the bill out of committee and bring it to the floor of the House. But the Rules Committee, without waiting for a vote on the petition (which it probably realized it would lose), sent the bill to the floor, where it passed overwhelmingly. In the Senate, an agreement between Republican minority leader Everett Dirksen and President Johnson smoothed the way for passage in several important respects. The House bill was sent directly to the Senate floor, thereby bypassing the Southern-dominated Judiciary Committee. Nineteen Southern senators began an eight-week filibuster against the bill. On June 10, 1964, by a vote of 71 to 29, cloture (the Senate rule to end a filibuster—see Chapter 13) was invoked to end the filibuster—the first time in history this happened for a filibuster aimed at blocking civil rights legislation.

Since the 1960s, congressional support for civil rights legislation has grown. Indeed, while once calling a bill a civil rights measure would have been the kiss of death, today that is no longer the case. For example, in 1984 the Supreme Court decided the federal ban on

Library of Congress Prints and Photographs Division [LC-DIG-ppmsca-08095]

AP Images/Bob Jordan

Image 6.8 and Image 6.9 In 1960, black students from North Carolina Agricultural and Technical College staged the first "sit-in" when they were refused service at a lunch counter in Greensboro (left). Twenty years later, graduates of the college returned to the same lunch counter (right). Though prices had risen, the service had improved.

AP Images/Bill Hudson

Image 6.10 This picture of a police dog lunging at a black man during a racial demonstration in Birmingham, Alabama, in May 1963 was one of the most influential photographs ever published. It was widely reprinted throughout the world and was frequently referred to in congressional debates on the Civil Rights Act of 1964.

discrimination in education applied only to the "program or activity" receiving federal aid and not to the entire school or university.[28] In 1988, Congress passed a bill to overturn this decision by making it clear that antidiscrimination rules applied to the entire educational institution and not just to that part (say, the physics lab) receiving federal money.

When President Reagan vetoed the bill (because, in his view, it would diminish the freedom of church-affiliated schools), Congress overrode the veto. In the override vote, every Southern Democrat in the Senate and almost 90 percent of those in the House voted for the bill. This was a dramatic change from 1964, when more than 80 percent of the Southern Democrats in Congress voted against the civil rights act (see Figure 6.1). This change partly reflected the growing political strength of Southern black voters. In 1960, less than one-third of voting-age black people in the South were registered to vote; by 1971 more than half were, and by 1984 two-thirds were.

In 2008, Barack Obama was elected president and became the first African American to hold the nation's highest elected office. That monumental historic

Figure 6.1 **Increase in Support Among Southern Democrats in Congress for Civil Rights Bills, 1957–1991**

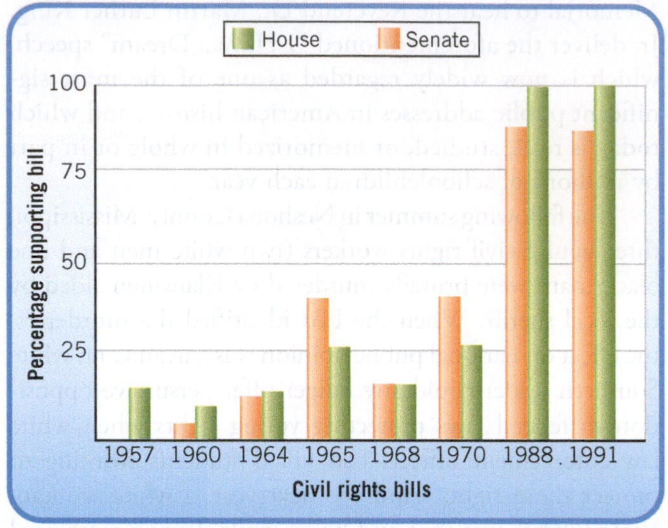

Source: Congressional Quarterly, *Congress and the Nation*, vols. 1, 2, 3, 7, 8.

TABLE 6.2 | Increase in Number of Black Elected Officials

	1970	2010
Federal Office	10	43
State Office	169	642
Local Office	1,290	9,800

Source: "A Time to Reflect: Charting the Quality of Life for Black Americans: Politics," *USA Today*, 21 February, 2011.

What factors might explain why in this table local office shows the greatest increase in black elected officials compared to state and national office?

moment, which included Obama winning two Southern states, was preceded by four decades of growth in the number of black elected officials at all levels of government. Between 1970 and 2010, the total number of black elected officials rose from fewer than 1,500 to more than 9,500 (see Table 6.2). In the presidential elections of 2008 and 2012, turnout rates among African American voters equaled or exceeded that of white voters. Such parity in voter turnout rates and the aforementioned increase in the number of black elected officials could not have happened without civil rights laws like the Voting Rights Act (VRA) of 1965.

In 2006, following more than 20 public hearings, and with support from then President George W. Bush, Congress reauthorized the VRA's key provisions for another quarter-century, including the section (Section 4) designating the "preclearance" formula used to determine which state or local jurisdictions must have any major changes to their voting laws or procedures approved in advance by the U.S. Department of Justice or by a federal court. Along with the need to remain vigilant in checking any recurrence of old methods of discrimination, the bill's bipartisan backers also cited concerns about "racial gerrymandering," the proliferation of "voter identification" laws, and other measures that could adversely and disproportionately affect minority participation in the electoral process.

But, in 2013, in the case of *Shelby County v. Holder*, the Supreme Court struck down the VRA's preclearance formula as unconstitutional. Writing for the Court's five-to-four majority, Chief Justice John Roberts declared that "things have changed dramatically" in the South since 1965; he also issued a statement from the bench indicating that Congress "may draft another formula based on current conditions."[29] Writing for the four dissenting justices, Justice Ruth Bader Ginsburg declared that the majority had "failed to grasp why the VRA has proven effective." Issuing a summary of her dissent from the bench—a move that indicated the deep division in the Court on this ruling—Ginsburg noted that Congress had approved an extension of the VRA in 2006 because it found that "40 years has not been a sufficient amount of time to eliminate the vestiges of discrimination following 100 years of disregard for the dictates of the 15th amendment."[30] (See Chapter 8 for more discussion of this case.)

In response to the ruling, President Obama issued a statement in which he observed that the decision "upsets decades of well-established practices that help to make sure voting is fair, especially in places where voting discrimination has been historically prevalent."[31] He also called on Congress to pass voting rights legislation with a new formula for determining which jurisdictions required federal preclearance for changes in voting procedures.

While Congress has not acted, several states have passed legislation to enact changes such as online voter registration, voter-identification requirements, and restrictions on early voting and the number of places where voters may cast ballots. In 2016, federal courts overturned such laws in Kansas, North Carolina, North Dakota, Texas, and Wisconsin, declaring that they disproportionately affected racial minorities and thus were racially discriminatory. (In overturning the North Carolina law, the U.S. Court of Appeals for the Fourth Circuit stated that the state legislature acted for partisan reasons, namely, to restrict voting for people who likely would oppose the majority party. Nevertheless, "even if done for partisan ends, that constituted racial discrimination.")[32] In 2017, the Supreme Court declined to hear appeals to reinstate voter-identification laws in North Carolina and Texas. (See Chapter 8, page 178, for further discussion of voter-identification laws.)

6-2 Women and Equal Rights

The political and legal efforts to secure civil rights for African Americans were accompanied by efforts to expand the rights of women. There was an important difference between the two movements, however: whereas African Americans were arguing against a legal tradition that explicitly aimed to keep them in a subservient status, women had to argue against a tradition that claimed to be protecting them. For example, in 1908 the Supreme Court upheld an Oregon law that limited female laundry workers to a 10-hour workday against the claim that it violated the Fourteenth Amendment. The Court justified its decision with this language:

> The two sexes differ in structure of body, in the functions to be performed by each, in the amount of physical strength, in the capacity for long-continued labor, particularly when done standing . . . the self-reliance which enables one to assert full rights, and in the capacity to maintain the struggle for subsistence. This difference justifies a difference in legislation and upholds that which is designed to compensate for some of the burdens which rest upon her.[33]

The origin of the movement to give more rights to women was probably the Seneca Falls Convention held in 1848. Its leaders began to demand the right to vote for women. Though this was slowly granted by several states, especially in the West, it was not until 1920 that the Nineteenth Amendment made it clear that no state may deny the right to vote on the basis of sex. The great change in the status of women, however, took place during World War II when the demand for workers in our defense plants led to the employment of millions of women, such as "Rosie the Riveter," in jobs they had rarely held before. After the war, the feminist movement took flight with the publication in 1963 of *The Feminine Mystique* by Betty Friedan.

Congress responded by passing laws that required equal pay for equal work, prohibited discrimination on the basis of sex in employment and among students in any school or university receiving federal funds, and banned discrimination against pregnant women on the job.[34]

At the same time, the Supreme Court was altering the way it interpreted the Constitution. The key passage was the Fourteenth Amendment, which prohibits any state from denying to "any person" the "equal protection of the laws." For a long time the traditional standard, as we saw in the 1908 case, was a kind of protective paternalism. By the early 1970s, however, the Court had changed its mind. In deciding whether the Constitution bars all, some, or no sexual discrimination, the Court had a choice among three standards. (See Table 6.3 for a summary and examples of the three standards.)

The first standard is the *rational basis* standard. This says that when the government treats some classes of people differently from others—for example, applying statutory rape laws to men but not to women—the different treatment must be reasonable and not arbitrary.

The second standard is *intermediate scrutiny.* When women complained that some laws treated them unfairly, the Court adopted a standard somewhere between the reasonableness and strict scrutiny tests. Thus, a law that treats men and women differently must be more than merely reasonable, but the allowable differences need not meet the strict scrutiny test.

And so, in 1971, the Court held that an Idaho statute was unconstitutional because it required that males be preferred over females when choosing people to administer the estates of deceased children. To satisfy the Constitution, a law treating men and women differently "must be reasonable, not arbitrary, and must rest on some ground of difference having a fair and substantial relation to the object of legislation so that all persons similarly circumstanced shall be treated alike."[35]

The third standard is *strict scrutiny.* This says that some instances of drawing distinctions between different groups of people—for example, by treating white and black people differently—are inherently suspect; thus, the Court will subject them to strict scrutiny to ensure they are clearly necessary to attain a legitimate state goal. Over time, some members of the Court have wanted to make classifications based on sex inherently suspect and subject to the strict scrutiny test, but no majority has yet embraced this position.[36]

Federal legislation also has addressed sex discrimination. The Civil Rights Act of 1964 prohibits sex discrimination in the hiring, firing, and compensation of employees. Legislation passed in 1972, popularly known as Title IX (which is part of the Education Amendments of 1972), bans sex discrimination in local education programs receiving federal aid. These laws apply to *private*, and not just government, actions. The Lilly Ledbetter Fair Pay Act of 2009 extends the time period for workers to file a lawsuit against their employer alleging pay discrimination.[37]

In recent years, public officials and the courts have debated whether Title IX applies to protections for transgender students in schools. The Obama administration announced in 2016 that it did, and specifically that schools should recognize a student's gender identity. The issue sparked controversy when North Carolina passed legislation requiring people to use public bathrooms that match the gender on their birth certificate. After several states filed suit against the new federal guidelines, a federal court issued a nationwide injunction, which the Obama administration appealed. In early 2017, the Trump administration dropped the appeal and then rescinded Title IX guidelines for transgender students, saying the

TABLE 6.3 | How the Court Decides Whether You Discriminate

The Supreme Court has produced three different tests to decide whether a government policy produces unconstitutional discrimination. Don't be surprised if you find it a bit hard to tell them apart.

Test	Description	Examples
Rational basis	If the policy uses reasonable means to achieve a legitimate government goal, it is constitutional.	If the government says you can't buy a drink until you are age 21, this meets the rational basis test: the government wants to prevent children from drinking, and age 21 is a reasonable means to define when a person is an adult. And a state can ban advertising on trucks unless the ad is about the truck owner's own business.
Intermediate scrutiny	If the policy "serves an important government interest" and is "substantially related" to serving that interest, it is constitutional.	Men can be punished for statutory rape even if women are not punished because men and women are not "similarly situated." And men can be barred from entering hospital delivery rooms even though (obviously) women are admitted.
Strict scrutiny	To be constitutional, the discrimination must serve a "compelling government interest," it must be "narrowly tailored" to attain that interest, and it must use the "least restrictive means" to attain it.	Distinctions based on race, ethnicity, religion, or voting must pass the strict scrutiny test. You cannot bar black children from a public school or black adults from voting, and you cannot prevent one religious group from knocking on your door to promote its views.

federal government should not decide the issue for states. Soon after, the Supreme Court declined to hear a Virginia lawsuit about whether a transgender student may choose which bathroom to use. A federal district court judge then decided that the school district's policy requiring students to use bathrooms based on their biological gender violated Title IX and the Constitution's equal protection clause.[38] In 2019, the Supreme Court declined to hear a case challenging a Pennsylvania school district that allows students to use bathrooms in accordance with their gender identity, thereby leaving the policy in place.[39]

Another way to combat sex discrimination is to ban it in the Constitution. In 1972, Congress approved the Equal Rights Amendment (ERA), which states that "Women shall have equal rights in the United States and every place subject to its jurisdiction. Equality of rights under the law shall not be denied or abridged by the United States or by any State on account of sex."[40] Thirty-five states ratified the amendment in the next five years, but it failed to reach the required threshold of 38 states by the 1982 ratification deadline. In the last few years, however, three states—Nevada, Illinois, and most recently, Virginia in 2020—ratified the amendment, sparking debate over whether Congress could establish a new deadline so the amendment would be enacted. As with most hotly contested constitutional issues, this battle likely will have to be resolved in the courts.[41]

Women's Rights and the Supreme Court

Over the years, the Court has decided many cases involving sexual classification. The following lists provide several examples of illegal sexual discrimination (violating either the Constitution or a civil rights act) and legal sexual distinctions (violating neither).

Illegal Discrimination

- A state cannot set different ages at which men and women legally become adults.[42]
- A state cannot set different ages at which men and women are allowed to buy beer.[43]
- Women cannot be barred from jobs by arbitrary height and weight requirements.[44]
- Employers cannot require women to take mandatory pregnancy leaves.[45]
- Girls cannot be barred from Little League baseball teams.[46]
- Business and service clubs, such as the Junior Chamber of Commerce and Rotary Club, cannot exclude women from membership.[47]
- Though women as a group live longer than men, an employer must pay them monthly retirement benefits equal to those received by men.[48]
- High schools must pay the coaches of girls' sports the same as they pay the coaches of boys' sports.[49]

Decisions Allowing Differences Based on Sex

- A law that punishes males but not females for statutory rape is permissible; men and women are not "similarly situated" with respect to sexual relations.[50]
- All-boy and all-girl public schools are permitted if enrollment is voluntary and quality is equal.[51]
- States can give widows a property-tax exemption not given to widowers.[52]
- The navy may allow women to remain officers longer than men without being promoted.[53]

The lower federal courts and state courts have been especially busy in the area of sexual distinctions. They have said that public taverns may not cater to men only and that girls may not be prevented from competing against boys in noncontact high school sports; on the other hand, hospitals may bar fathers from the delivery room. Women do not have to change their last names after marriage.[54]

In 1996, the Supreme Court ruled that women must be admitted to the Virginia Military Institute, until then an all-male state-supported college that had for many decades supplied what it called an "adversative method" of training to instill physical and mental discipline in cadets. In practical terms, this meant the school was very tough on students. The Court said that for a state to justify spending tax money on a single-sex school, it must supply an "exceedingly persuasive justification" for excluding the other gender. Virginia countered by offering to support an all-female training course at another college, but this was not enough.[55] This decision came close to imposing the strict scrutiny test, and so it has raised important questions about what could happen to all-female or historically black colleges and universities that accept state money.

Perhaps the most far-reaching cases defining the rights of women have involved the draft and abortion. In 1981, the Court held in *Rostker v. Goldberg* that Congress may require men but not women to register for the draft without violating the due-process clause of the Fifth Amendment.[56] In the area of national defense, the Court will give great deference to congressional policy. For many years, women could be pilots and sailors but not on combat aircraft or combat ships. The issue played a role in the debate at the time about the proposed Equal Rights Amendment to the Constitution because of fears that it would reverse *Rostker*

Women's Rights

- ***Reed v. Reed* (1971):** Gender discrimination violates the equal protection clause of the Constitution.
- ***Craig v. Boren* (1976):** Gender discrimination can be justified only if it serves "important governmental objectives" and is "substantially related to those objectives."
- ***Rostker v. Goldberg* (1981):** Congress can draft men without drafting women.
- ***United States v. Virginia* (1996):** State may not finance an all-male military school.

police powers *State power to effect laws promoting health, safety, and morals.*

v. Goldberg. But in 1993, the secretary of defense opened air and sea combat positions to all persons regardless of gender; only ground-troop combat positions were still reserved for men. Two decades later the ban on women serving in combat was lifted as well, and in the summer of 2015, for the first time, two women graduated from Ranger School, the Army's elite combat training and leadership course.

Sexual Harassment

When Paula Corbin Jones accused President Bill Clinton of sexual harassment, the judge threw the case out of court because she had not submitted enough evidence such that, if the jury believed her story, she would have made a legally adequate argument that she had been sexually harassed.

What, then, is sexual harassment? Drawing on rulings by the Equal Employment Opportunities Commission, the Supreme Court has held that harassment can take one of two forms. First, it is illegal for someone to request sexual favors as a condition of employment or promotion. This is the "quid pro quo" rule. If a person does this, the employer is "strictly liable." Strict liability means the employer can be found at fault even if he or she did not know a subordinate was requesting sex in exchange for hiring or promotion.

Second, it is illegal for an employee to experience a work environment that has been made hostile or intimidating by a steady pattern of offensive sexual teasing, jokes, or obscenity. But employers are not strictly liable in this case; they can be found at fault only if they were "negligent"—that is, they knew about the hostile environment but did nothing about it.

In 1998, the Supreme Court decided three cases that made these rules either better or worse, depending on your point of view. In one, it determined that a school system was not liable for the conduct of a teacher who seduced a female student because the student never reported the actions. In a second, it held that a city was liable for a sexually hostile work environment confronting a female lifeguard even though she did not report this to her superiors. In the third, it decided that a female employee who was not promoted after having rejected the sexual advances of her boss could recover financial damages from the firm. But, it added, the firm could have avoided paying this bill if it had put in place an "affirmative defense" against sexual exploitation, although the Court never said what such a policy might be.[57]

Sexual harassment is a serious matter, but because few federal laws govern it, we are left with somewhat vague and often inconsistent court and bureaucratic rules to guide us. The issue sparked a national outcry in 2017, starting with reports of numerous women alleging decades of sexual harassment and assault by movie mogul Harvey Weinstein. Similar reports about celebrities in many professions—including business, Hollywood, the media industry, politics, and sports—followed, as did the #MeToo movement, in which people shared experiences of sexual harassment or assault on social media. As a result, several states and businesses have established prevention training programs in the workplace, and states have passed laws to expand protections for victims of sexual violence, but the national government has not enacted legislation to date.[58]

Privacy and Sex

Regulating sexual matters has traditionally been left up to the states, which do so by exercising their **police powers**. These powers include more than the authority to create police departments; they include all laws designed to promote public order and secure the safety and morals of the citizens. Some have argued that the Tenth Amendment to the Constitution, by reserving to the states all powers not delegated to the federal government, meant that states could do anything not explicitly prohibited by the Constitution. But that changed when the Supreme Court began expanding the power of Congress over business and when it started to view sexual matters under the newly discovered right to privacy.

Until that point, it had been left up to the states to decide whether and under what circumstances a woman could obtain an abortion. For example, New York allowed abortions during the first 24 weeks of pregnancy, whereas Texas banned it except when the mother's life was threatened. That began to change in 1965 when the Supreme Court held that the states could not prevent the sale of contraceptives because by so doing it would invade a "zone of privacy." Privacy is nowhere mentioned in the Constitution, but the Court argued that it could be inferred from "penumbras" (literally, shadows) cast off by various provisions of the Bill of Rights.[59]

Eight years later the Court, in its famous *Roe v. Wade* decision, held that a "right to privacy" is "broad enough to encompass a woman's decision whether or not to terminate a pregnancy."[60] The case, which began in Texas, produced this view: During the first three months (or trimester) of pregnancy, a woman has an unfettered right to an abortion. During the second trimester, states may regulate abortions but only to protect the mother's health. In the third trimester, states might ban abortions.

In reaching this decision, the Court denied that it was trying to decide when human life began—at the moment of conception, at the moment of birth, or somewhere in between. But that is not how critics of the decision saw things. To them, life begins at conception, and so the human fetus is a "person" entitled to the equal protection of the laws guaranteed by the Fourteenth Amendment. People having this view began to use the slogans "right to life" and "pro-life." Supporters of the Court's action saw matters differently. In their view, no one can say for certain when human life begins; what one *can* say, however, is that a woman is entitled to choose whether or not to have a baby. These people took the slogans "right to choose" and "pro-choice."

Almost immediately, the congressional allies of prolife groups introduced constitutional amendments to overturn *Roe v. Wade*, but none passed Congress. Nevertheless, abortion foes did persuade Congress, beginning in 1976, to bar the use of federal funds to pay for abortions except when the life of the mother is at stake. The chief effect of the provision, known as the Hyde Amendment (after its sponsor, former U.S. Representative Henry Hyde), has been to deny the use of Medicaid funds to pay for abortions for low-income women.

Despite pro-life opposition, the Supreme Court for 16 years steadfastly reaffirmed and even broadened its decision in *Roe v. Wade*. It struck down laws requiring, before an abortion could be performed, a woman to have the consent of her husband, an "emancipated" but underage girl to have the consent of her parents, and a woman to be advised by her doctor as to the facts about abortion.[61]

But in 1989, under the influence of justices appointed by President Reagan, the Court began in the *Webster* case to uphold some state restrictions on abortions. When that happened, many people predicted that in time *Roe v. Wade* would be overturned, especially if President George H. W. Bush was able to appoint more justices. He appointed two (Souter and Thomas), but *Roe* survived. The key votes were cast by Justices O'Connor, Souter, and Kennedy. In 1992, in its *Casey* decision, the Court by a vote of five-to-four explicitly refused to overturn *Roe*, declaring that there was a right to abortion.

At the same time, however, it upheld a variety of restrictions imposed by the state of Pennsylvania on women seeking abortions. These included a mandatory 24-hour waiting period between the request for an abortion and the performance of it, the requirement that teenagers obtain the consent of one parent (or, in special circumstances, of a judge), and a requirement that women contemplating an abortion be given pamphlets about alternatives to it. Similar restrictions had been enacted in many other states, all of which looked to the Pennsylvania case for guidance as to whether they could be enforced. In allowing these restrictions, the Court overruled some of its own

Privacy and Abortion

- ***Griswold v. Connecticut* (1965):** Found a "right to privacy" in the Constitution that would ban any state law against selling contraceptives.
- ***Roe v. Wade* (1973):** State laws prohibiting abortion were unconstitutional.
- ***Webster v. Reproductive Health Services* (1989):** Allowed states to ban abortions from public hospitals and permitted doctors to test to determine whether fetuses were viable.
- ***Planned Parenthood v. Casey* (1992):** Reaffirmed *Roe v. Wade* but upheld certain limits on its use.
- ***Gonzales v. Carhart* (2007):** Federal law may ban certain forms of partial-birth abortion.
- ***Whole Women's Health v. Hellerstedt* (2016):** Overturned Texas law requiring hospital standards at abortion clinics and admitting privileges for clinic doctors at nearby hospitals, for creating an "undue burden" upon women seeking the procedure.
- ***June Medical Services L.L.C. v. Russo (2020):*** Overturned Louisiana law requiring doctors who perform abortions to have admitting privileges at nearby hospitals, for imposing a "substantial obstacle" and "undue burden" upon women seeking the procedure.

equality of results Making certain that people achieve the same result.

equality of opportunity Giving people an equal chance to succeed.

affirmative action Laws or administrative regulations that require a business firm, government agency, labor union, school, college, or other organization to take positive steps to increase the number of African Americans, other minorities, or women in its membership.

earlier decisions.[62] On the other hand, the Court did strike down a state law that would have required married women to obtain the consent of their husbands before having an abortion.

After a long political and legal struggle, the Court in 2007 upheld a federal law that bans certain kinds of partial-birth abortions. The law does not allow an abortion in which the fetus, still alive, is withdrawn until its head is outside the mother and then it is killed. But the law does not ban a late-term abortion if it is necessary to protect the physical health of the mother or if it is performed on an already dead fetus, even if the doctor has already killed it.[63]

The debate over abortion continues today, especially at the state level, as we mentioned in Chapter 3. Between 2011 and 2013, 205 new abortion laws were passed, many of them seeking to restrict access to abortion (in contrast, between 2001 and 2010, only 189 new laws were passed).[64] Many of these laws put restrictions on the facilities where abortions can be performed, though others restrict how and when doctors and other health care providers can perform abortions.

In 2016, an eight-member Supreme Court (following the death of Justice Antonin Scalia) decided five to three to overturn a Texas law that had required abortion clinics to provide hospital-standard low-risk surgical facilities, and to give doctors hospital admitting privileges within 30 miles of the clinic. The law had led to the closing of the majority of clinics in the state, and the Court ruled that the restrictions created an "undue burden" (a test created in the 1992 *Casey* case) for women seeking to have an abortion. This issue was raised again a few years later, when the Supreme Court agreed to hear a challenge to a Louisiana law that required hospital admitting privileges similar to what Texas had required for doctors performing abortions. In 2020, the Court overturned the Louisiana law in a 5-4 decision, following the precedent set in the Texas case. (See Landmark Cases: Privacy and Abortion box on p. 141.)

The Court also has debated several times in recent years whether employers with religious affiliations should have to follow the "contraceptive mandate" in the Affordable Care Act. In 2014, the Court ruled in *Burwell v. Hobby Lobby Stores* that businesses could not be forced to pay for contraceptive coverage for employees if doing so substantially interfered with their free exercise of religion. Employees of organizations who objected to the mandate on these grounds instead would have insurance companies or the government pay for contraceptive coverage through an exemption filed by their employer. But religious nonprofit organizations and hospitals objected to this process and filed multiple lawsuits. In 2016, the Court ruled in *Zubik v. Burwell* that seven cases with conflicting decisions would be returned to appeals courts (eight cases had ruled in favor of the mandate and one was opposed; not all of the rulings were appealed) to work out a compromise, with no taxes or penalties imposed on groups opposing the exemption provision in that time. Then in 2020 the Supreme Court heard a new challenge by the Trump administration, which had issued regulations permitting employers that opposed contraception on religious or moral grounds to opt out of the contraceptive mandate.[65] In a 7-2 decision, the Court upheld the exemption from the contraceptive mandate for any employer who objects for moral or religious reasons. (See Landmark Cases: Religious Freedom box in Chapter 5, p. 112.)

The woman who started the suit that became Roe v. Wade, using the pseudonym "Jane Roe," actually never had an abortion and was not active in the lawsuit. Many years later, using her real name, Norma McCorvey, she became an evangelical Christian and participated in antiabortion demonstrations. Testifying before the U.S. Senate in 1998, she declared her commitment to "undoing the law that bears my name."[66] But in a 2020 documentary that was filmed shortly before she died in 2017, McCorvey stated that anti-abortion groups had paid her to express their views, which did not reflect her own beliefs.

6-3 Affirmative Action

A common thread running through the politics of civil rights is the argument between **equality of results** and **equality of opportunity**. These concepts are central to the debate over affirmative action as a means of attaining equal rights for Americans regardless of race or gender. They also apply to civil-rights battles for people with disabilities, as discussed in Table 6.4 in page 143.

Equality of Results

One view, expressed by many civil rights and feminist organizations, is that the burdens of racism and sexism can be overcome only by taking race or sex into account in designing remedies. It is not enough that people be given rights; they also must be given benefits. If life is a race, everybody must be brought up to the same starting line (or possibly even to the same finish line). This means that the Constitution is not and should not be color-blind or sex-neutral.

TABLE 6.4 | The Rights of the Disabled

In 1990, the federal government passed the Americans with Disabilities Act (ADA), a sweeping law that extended many of the protections enjoyed by women and racial minorities to disabled persons.

Who Is a Disabled Person?	Anyone who *has* a physical or mental impairment that substantially limits one or more major life activities (e.g., holding a job), anyone who has a *record* of such impairment, or anyone who is *regarded* as having such an impairment is considered disabled.
What Rights Do Disabled Persons Have?	
Employment	Disabled persons may not be denied employment or promotion if, with "reasonable accommodation," they can perform the duties of that job. (Excluded from this protection are people who currently use illegal drugs, gamble compulsively, or are homosexual or bisexual.) Reasonable accommodation need not be made if this would cause "undue hardship" on the employer.
Government Programs and Transportation	Disabled persons may not be denied access to government programs or benefits. New buses, taxis, and trains must be accessible to disabled persons, including those in wheelchairs.
Public Accommodations	Disabled persons must enjoy "full and equal" access to hotels, restaurants, stores, schools, parks, museums, auditoriums, and the like. To achieve equal access, owners of existing facilities must alter them "to the maximum extent feasible"; builders of new facilities must ensure they are readily accessible to disabled persons, unless this is structurally impossible.
Telephones	The ADA directs the Federal Communications Commission to issue regulations to ensure telecommunications devices for hearing-and speech-impaired people are available "to the extent possible and in the most efficient manner."
Congress	The rights under this law apply to employees of Congress.
Rights Compared	The ADA does not enforce the rights of disabled persons in the same way as the Civil Rights Act enforces the rights of African Americans and women. Racial or gender discrimination must end *regardless of cost;* denial of access to disabled persons must end unless "undue hardship" or excessive costs would result.

In education, this implies that the races must actually be mixed in the schools, by busing if necessary. In hiring, it means that **affirmative action** must be used in the hiring process. Affirmative action refers to laws or administrative regulations that require a business firm, government agency, labor union, school, college, or other organization to take positive steps to increase the number of African Americans, other minorities, or women in its membership. It means that increasing the number of women in the workforce means more than giving them the opportunity to do so; they may require resources such as family leave time (which of course today is widely recognized as a necessary benefit for all employees). On payday, workers' checks should reflect not just the results of competition in the marketplace, but the results of plans designed to ensure that people earn comparable amounts for comparable jobs. Of late, affirmative action has been defended in the name of diversity or multiculturalism—the view that every institution (firm, school, or agency) and every college curriculum should reflect the cultural and ethnic diversity of the nation.

Equality of Opportunity

Another view holds that if it is wrong to discriminate *against* African Americans and women, it is equally wrong to give them preferential treatment over other groups. The Constitution and laws should be color-blind and sex-neutral.[67]

In this view, allowing children to attend the school of their choice is sufficient; busing them to attain racial integration is wrong. Eliminating barriers to job opportunities is right; using numerical "targets" and "goals" to place minorities and women in specific jobs is wrong. If people wish to compete in the market, they should be satisfied with the market verdict concerning the worth of their work.

Take, for example, the question of affirmative action. Both advocates of equality of opportunity and those of equality of results would object to employer discrimination against hiring African American or women employees, and both likely would expect an employer to demonstrate fair hiring practices. Affirmative action in this case can mean *either* looking hard for qualified women and minorities and giving them a fair shot at jobs *or* setting a numerical goal for the number of women and minorities that should be hired and insisting that that goal be met. Persons who defend the second course of action call these goals "targets"; persons who criticize that course call them "quotas."

The issue has largely been fought in the courts. Between 1978 and 1990, about a dozen major cases involving affirmative-action policies were decided by the Supreme Court; in about half the policies were upheld, and in the other half they were overturned. The different outcomes reflect two things: the differences in the facts of the cases and the arrival on the Court of three justices (Kennedy, O'Connor, and Scalia) appointed by a president, Ronald Reagan, who was opposed to (at least) the broader interpretation of affirmative action. As a result of these decisions, the law governing affirmative action is now complex and confusing.

Consider one issue: Should the government be allowed to use a quota system to select workers, enroll students, award contracts, or grant licenses? In the *Bakke* decision in 1978, the Court said the medical school of the University of California at Davis could not use an explicit numerical quota in admitting minority students but could "take race into account."[68] So no numerical quotas, right?

Wrong. Two years later, the Court upheld a federal rule that set aside 10 percent of all federal construction contracts for minority-owned firms.[69] All right, maybe quotas can't be used in medical schools, but they can be used in the construction industry?

Not exactly. In 1989, the Court overturned a Richmond, Virginia, law that set aside 30 percent of its construction contracts for minority-owned firms.[70] Well, maybe the Court just changed its mind between 1980 and 1989.

No. One year later it upheld a federal rule that gave preference to minority-owned firms in the awarding of broadcast licenses.[71] Then in 1993, it upheld the right of white contractors to challenge minority set-aside laws in Jacksonville, Florida.[72]

Making sense of these twists and turns is challenging because a deeply divided Court is still wrestling with the issues, and Congress (as with the Civil Rights Act of 1991) is modifying or superseding earlier Court decisions. But a few general standards seem to be emerging. In simplified form, they are as follows:

- The courts will subject any quota system created by state or local governments to "strict scrutiny" and will look for a "compelling" justification for it.
- Quotas or preference systems cannot be used by state or local governments without first showing that such rules are needed to correct an actual past or present pattern of discrimination.[73]
- In proving there has been discrimination, it is not enough to show that African Americans (or other minorities) are statistically underrepresented among employees, contractors, or union members; the actual practices that have had this discriminatory impact must be identified.[74]
- Quotas or preference systems created by *federal* law will be given greater deference, in part because Section 5 of the Fourteenth Amendment gives to Congress powers not given to the states to correct the effects of racial discrimination.[75]
- It may be easier to justify in court a voluntary preference system (e.g., one agreed to in a labor-management contract) than one that is required by law.[76]
- Even when you can justify special preferences in *hiring* workers, the Supreme Court is not likely to allow racial preferences to govern who gets *laid off*. A worker laid off to make room for a minority worker loses more than a worker not hired in preference to a minority applicant.[77]

Complex as they are, these rulings still generate a great deal of passion. Supporters of the decisions barring certain affirmative action plans hail these decisions as steps back from an emerging pattern of reverse discrimination. In contrast, civil rights organizations have denounced those decisions that have overturned affirmative action programs.

In thinking about these matters, most Americans distinguish between compensatory action and preferential treatment. They define *compensatory action* as "helping disadvantaged people catch up, usually by giving them extra education, training, or services." A majority of the public supports this. They define preferential treatment as "giving minorities preference in hiring, promotions, college admissions, and contracts." Large majorities oppose this.[78] These views reflect an enduring element in American political culture—a strong commitment to individualism ("nobody should get something without deserving it") coupled with support for help for the disadvantaged ("people who are suffering through no fault of their own deserve a helping hand"). Polls have suggested that if affirmative action is defined as "helping," people will support it, but if it is defined as "using quotas," they will oppose it.[79]

A small construction company named Adarand tried to get a contract to build guardrails along a highway in Colorado. Though it was the low bidder, it lost the contract because of a federal government program that favored small businesses owned by "socially and economically disadvantaged individuals"—that is, by racial and ethnic minorities. Adarand filed suit against the U.S.

Department of Transportation, saying the program violated constitutional guarantees of due process and equal protection of the laws. In a five-to-four decision, the Court agreed with Adarand and sent the case back to Colorado for a new trial.

The essence of the Court's decision was that *any* discrimination based on race must be subject to strict scrutiny, even if its purpose is to help, not hurt, a racial minority. Strict scrutiny means two things:

- Any racial preference must serve a "compelling government interest."
- The preference must be "narrowly tailored" to serve that interest.[80]

To serve a compelling governmental interest, it is likely that any racial preference will have to remedy a clear pattern of past discrimination. No such pattern had been shown in Colorado.

This decision prompted a good deal of political debate about affirmative action. In California, an initiative was put on the 1996 ballot to prevent state authorities from using "race, sex, color, ethnicity, or national origin as a criterion for either discriminating against, or granting preferential treatment to, any individual or group" in public employment, public education, or public contracting. When the votes were counted, it passed. Michigan, Nebraska, and Washington have adopted similar measures, and other states may do so.

But the *Adarand* case and the passage of the California initiative did not mean affirmative action was dead. Though the federal Court of Appeals for the Fifth Circuit had rejected the affirmative action program of the University of Texas Law School,[81] the Supreme Court did not take up that case. It waited for several more years to rule on a similar matter arising from the University of Michigan. In 2003, the Supreme Court overturned the admissions policy of the University of Michigan that had given to every African American, Hispanic, and Native American applicant a bonus of 20 points out of the 100 needed to guarantee admission to the University's undergraduate program.[82] This policy was not "narrowly tailored." In rejecting the bonus system, the Court reaffirmed its decision in the 1978 *Bakke* case in which it had rejected a university using a "fixed quota" or an exact numerical advantage to the exclusion of "individual" considerations.

But that same day, the Court upheld the policy of the University of Michigan Law School that used race as a "plus factor" but not as a numerical quota.[83] It did so even though using race as a plus factor increased by threefold the proportion of minority applicants who were admitted. In short, admitting more minorities serves a "compelling state interest," and doing so by using race as a plus factor is "narrowly tailored" to achieve that goal. But, in 2006, Michigan voters approved a ballot measure banning the use of race as a consideration in academic admissions,

Affirmative Action

- ***Regents of the University of California v. Bakke* (1978):** In a confused set of rival opinions, the decisive vote was cast by Justice Powell, who said that a quota-like ban on Bakke's admission was unconstitutional but that "diversity" was a legitimate goal that could be pursued by taking race into account.
- ***United Steelworkers v. Weber* (1979):** Despite the ban on racial classifications in the 1964 Civil Rights Act, this case upheld the use of race in an employment agreement between the steelworkers union and a steel plant.
- ***Richmond v. Croson* (1989):** Affirmative action plans must be judged by the strict scrutiny standard that requires any race-conscious plan to be narrowly tailored to serve a compelling interest.
- ***Grutter v. Bollinger and Gratz v. Bollinger* (2003):** Numerical benefits cannot be used to admit minorities into college, but race can be a "plus factor" in making those decisions.
- ***Parents v. Seattle School District* (2007):** Race cannot be used to decide which students may attend especially popular high schools because this was not "narrowly tailored" to achieve a "compelling" goal.
- ***Schuette v. Coalition to Defend Affirmative Action* (2014):** Public institutions of higher education may not give preference in admission based on race, sex, color, ethnicity, or national origin.
- ***Fisher v. University of Texas at Austin et al* (2016):** A university may consider race as one of many factors in admissions decisions to create a diverse group of students.

public employment, and government contracting. In 2012, a U.S. Circuit Court struck down the ban, but only in relation to academic admissions; two years later, the U.S. Supreme Court upheld the ban for academic admissions.[84]

In *Fisher v. University of Texas* (2013), the Court, in a seven-to-one decision, sent another affirmative action case involving college admissions back to the Fifth Circuit Court of Appeals for reconsideration. Invoking the *Bakke* (1978) and *Grutter* (2003) decisions (see the Landmark Cases box above), the majority declared that the lower court had failed to apply the strict scrutiny test. But in 2016, the Supreme Court upheld the University of Texas's admissions program (by a four-to-three vote, because of one vacancy and one recusal on the Court), ruling that consideration of race as one of several factors to ensure diversity among students was constitutionally permissible.

6-4 Sexual Orientation and Civil Rights

In the 1980s, the Supreme Court was willing to let states make decisions about people's sex lives. Georgia, for example, passed a law banning sodomy (i.e., any sexual contact involving the sex organs of one person and the mouth or anus of another). In *Bowers v. Hardwick* (1986), the Supreme Court decided, by a five-to-four majority, that the Constitution indicated no reason to prevent a state from having such a law. There was a right to privacy, but it was designed simply to protect "family, marriage, or procreation."[85]

But 10 years later, the Court seemed to take a different position. The voters in Colorado had adopted a state constitutional amendment that made it illegal to pass any law to protect persons based on their "homosexual, lesbian, or bisexual orientation." The law did not penalize LGBTQ+ people based on their sexual orientation; instead, it said they could not become the object of specific legal protection of the sort that had traditionally been given to racial or ethnic minorities. (Ordinances to give specific protection to gay people had been adopted in some Colorado cities.) The Supreme Court struck down the Colorado constitutional amendment because it violated the equal protection clause of the federal Constitution.[86]

Now we faced a puzzle: a state can pass a law banning some types of sex, as Georgia did, but a state cannot adopt a rule preventing cities from protecting people from harm based on their sexual orientation, as Colorado did. The matter was finally put to rest in 2003. In *Lawrence v. Texas,* the Court, again by a five-to-four vote, overturned a Texas law that banned sexual contact between persons of the same sex. The Court repeated the language it had used earlier in cases involving contraception and abortion. If "the right to privacy means anything, it is the right of the individual, married or single, to be free from unwanted governmental intrusion" into sexual matters. The right of privacy means the "right to define one's own concept of existence, of meaning, of the universe, and of the mystery of human life." It specifically overruled *Bowers v. Hardwick.*[87]

In 2003, the same year as the *Lawrence* decision, the Massachusetts Supreme Judicial Court decided, by a four-to-three vote, that LGBTQ+ people must be allowed to be married in the state.[88] In response, the Massachusetts legislature passed a bill that would amend that state's constitution to ban same-sex marriage. But that amendment required another ratification vote, which took place in 2007, and the amendment was defeated. In the mid-2000s, while Massachusetts legalized same-sex marriage and officials in other states considered doing the same, 13 states amended their state constitutions to prohibit or further restrict it. State by state, a complicated set of political and legal actions and counteractions had begun.

For instance, in California, the mayor of San Francisco began issuing marriage licenses to hundreds of same-sex couples. In 2004, the California Supreme Court overturned the mayor's decisions. The next year, the state legislature voted to make same-sex marriages legal, but Governor Arnold Schwarzenegger vetoed the bill. In 2008, the state's voters approved a ballot measure, Proposition 8, banning same-sex marriage. But, in 2010, a federal district judge overturned that vote. After a federal appeals court put the lower federal court's decision on hold, a case concerning Proposition 8 made its way before the U.S. Supreme Court.

In March 2013, the Court heard oral arguments in each of two same-sex marriage cases. In *Hollingsworth v. Perry,* the central issue was the constitutionality of California's Proposition 8: Does the Proposition 8 ban on same-sex marriage violate the Constitution's "equal protection" or other provisions? In *United States v. Windsor,* the central issue was the constitutionality of the Defense of Marriage Act (DOMA), a 1996 federal law that bars the federal government from recognizing same-sex marriage couples in relation to health, tax, and other benefits that it affords to heterosexual married couples: Does the DOMA violate the Constitution by depriving all persons who are legally married under the laws of their respective states the same recognition, benefits, and rights, and is same-sex marriage a fundamental right that all states must respect?

In June 2013, the Court issued opinions that in each case were widely understood as victories for same-sex marriage proponents, but that also in each case left the central constitutional questions for another day. In the Proposition 8 case, the Court held, by a five-to-four majority, that the private parties who brought the suit did not have standing to defend the law in federal court after California state officials had declined to do so. The practical effect was to let stand the lower federal court's decision striking down Proposition 8 as unconstitutional and thereby overturn the ban on same-sex marriage in California without, however, affecting laws in other states that prohibit same-sex marriage. In the more significant DOMA case, the Court held, by a five-to-four majority, that the 1996 law was unconstitutional because it deprived LGBTQ+ couples married in states where same-sex marriage is legal of the same federal health, tax, and other benefits that heterosexual married couples receive. But the Court stopped far short of declaring that same-sex marriage is a fundamental right that all states must respect. Still, in the months following the Court's decisions on Proposition 8 and the DOMA, new legal challenges to laws banning same-sex marriage were launched in a half-dozen states. In 2015, the Court ruled, five to four, in *Obergefell v. Hodges* that same-sex marriage is constitutional.

Thus far, the Court has continued to treat sexual orientation cases involving private groups differently from the way that it has treated such cases involving government agencies or benefits. The Court has

LGBTQ+ Rights

- ***Boy Scouts of America v. Dale* (2000):** A private organization may ban LGBTQ+ people from its membership.
- ***Lawrence v. Texas* (2003):** State law may not ban sexual relations between same-sex partners.
- ***United States v. Windsor* (2013):** LGBTQ+ couples married in states where same-sex marriage is legal must receive the same federal health, tax, and other benefits that heterosexual married couples receive.
- ***Obergefell v. Hodges* (2015):** Same-sex couples have a constitutional right to marry.
- ***Masterpiece Cakeshop v. Colorado Civil Rights Commission* (2018):** Baker with a religious objection does not have to make a wedding cake for a same-sex couple.
- ***Bostock v. Clayton County, Ga.* (2020):** Prohibition of employment discrimination on the basis of sex in Title VII of Civil Rights Act of 1964 applies to LGBTQ+ employees.

Justin Sullivan/Getty Images News/Getty Images

Image 6.11 Proposition 8 opponents celebrated a ruling to overturn the initiative, which had denied same-sex couples the right to marry in the state of California.

maintained that private groups are free to exclude people from their membership based on their sexual orientation. For example, in 2000 the Court decided, by a five-to-four vote, that the Boy Scouts of America could exclude LGBTQ+ men and boys because that group had a right to determine its own membership.[89] In May 2013, following more than a decade of controversy over the decision and the policy, the Boy Scouts of America announced that it would admit openly LGBTQ+ boys but continue to exclude openly LGBTQ+ men from leadership and membership in the organization. Two years later, the organization lifted this ban, and in 2017, it announced that transgender boys may participate in Scout programs. Then in 2018, the Supreme Court ruled in favor of a Colorado baker who objected on religious grounds to baking a wedding cake for a same-sex couple.

Overall, such changes reflect not only an evolving understanding of the Constitution and other laws but also broad shifts in social norms and mores. A generation ago, the American Psychological Association classified homosexuality as a mental disorder (that practice was ended in 1973), and openly LGBTQ+ individuals were extremely rare in most parts of the country. Today, society has become far more accepting of people's sexual orientation in nearly all walks of life. As we will discuss in Chapter 7, there has been a sea change in public opinion on sexual orientation, and now many rights for people of different sexual orientations—including the right to marry—have majority support among the U.S. public. (See the Policy Dynamics box in this chapter on page 149.) While the Supreme Court does not always respond to public opinion, it does reflect these sorts of broad social shifts in norms and attitudes. In 2020, for example, the Supreme Court decided that the longstanding legal protection against employment discrimination on the basis of sex, provided by Title VII of the Civil Rights Act of 1964, applied to LGBTQ+ employees – a position with overwhelming public support.[90]

6-5 Looking Back—and Ahead

The civil rights movement in the courts and in Congress profoundly changed the nature of African American participation in politics by bringing Southern black voters into the political system so they could become an effective interest group. The decisive move was to enlist Northern opinion in this cause, a job made easier by the Northern perception that civil rights involved simply an unfair contest between two minorities: Southern whites and Southern blacks. That perception changed when it became evident the court rulings and legislative decisions would apply to the North as well as the South, leading to the emergence of Northern opposition to court-ordered busing and affirmative action programs.

By the time this reaction developed, the legal and political system had been changed sufficiently to make it difficult—if not impossible—to limit the application of civil rights laws to the special circumstances of the South or to alter by legislative means the decisions of federal courts. Though the courts can accomplish little when they have no political allies (as revealed by the massive resistance to early school-desegregation decisions), they can accomplish a great deal, even in the face of adverse public opinion, when they have some organized allies. The feminist movement has paralleled in organization and tactics many aspects of the black civil rights movement, but with important differences. Women sought to repeal or reverse laws and court rulings that in many cases were ostensibly designed to protect rather than subjugate them. The conflict between protection and liberation was sufficiently intense to defeat the effort to ratify the Equal Rights Amendment in the 1970s (though in 2020 it passed the threshold of required states for ratification, as discussed earlier).

Among the most divisive civil rights issues in American politics are abortion and affirmative action. From 1973 to 1989, the Supreme Court seemed committed to giving constitutional protection to all abortions within the first trimester; since 1989, it has approved various state restrictions on the circumstances under which abortions can be obtained.

There has been a similar shift in the Court's view of affirmative action. Though it will still approve some quota plans, it now insists they pass strict scrutiny to ensure they are used only to correct a proven history of discrimination, they place the burden of proof on the party alleging discrimination, and they are limited to hiring and not extended to layoffs. Congress has modified some of these rulings with new civil rights legislation.

Finally, while it remains to be seen whether both court doctrines and legislative initiatives on LGBTQ+ rights will follow patterns like those that expanded civil rights protections for African Americans, other minorities, and women, it is clear that the policy dynamics surrounding same-sex marriage are quite different from what they were only a dozen years ago (see Policy Dynamics: Inside/Outside the Box on page 149).

Policy Dynamics: Inside/Outside the Box | Support for LGBTQ+ Rights: On the Way to Majoritarian?

Some ideas about public policy grab media attention, garner political support, and go on to become public laws; other ideas never even make it on to the "public agenda." Political scientists have many different theories, taxonomies, and models about the policy process. In Chapter 1, we outlined our way of classifying and explaining the politics of different issues: majoritarian politics, client politics, interest group politics, and entrepreneurial politics (see Chapter 1, pages 13–17). First, take a moment now to reflect on what you have learned so far in this chapter about the policy dynamics surrounding the civil rights laws that have affected all Americans, most especially African-Americans, other racial and ethnic minorities, and women. How might you begin to characterize the politics of the changes in law and policy that expanded civil rights for each group?

Next, how might you explain the still-unfolding politics of LGBTQ+ rights? This much seems clear: the politics of the issue have changed in recent years. For example, in 1993, President Clinton tried lifting the ban on LGBTQ+ individuals serving openly about their sexual orientation in the military. But the political reaction among both the public at large and leaders in both parties caused him in the first instance to back off the plan, and in the next instance to support not only the "Don't Ask, Don't Tell" (DADT) policy for the military but also the Defense of Marriage Act (DOMA) of 1996. When he came to office in 2009, President Obama supported both DADT and DOMA. But by 2013 he had lifted the ban on LGBTQ+ soldiers serving openly in the military and supported the repeal of DOMA. In June 2013, the Supreme Court declared that DOMA was unconstitutional, and in June 2015, it declared that same-sex marriage was legal (see pages 146–147).

In the past 20 years, public opinion has flipped completely on this issue. In 1996, only 27 supported same-sex marriage, but that figure climbed steadily to reach 67 percent by 2018. As we will discuss in Chapter 7, younger voters are more supportive, but even older Americans now support same-sex marriage. In 2012, Tammy Baldwin (D-WI), a seven-term member of the U.S. House of Representatives, became the first openly LGBTQ+ politician elected to the U.S. Senate. Baldwin was reelected in 2018, and Arizona's Kyrsten Sinema also became the first openly bisexual person to win a Senate seat in that same year. In the 116th Congress, there are 11 openly LGBTQ+ individuals serving in Congress.

Chip Somodevilla/Getty Images News/Getty Images

Image 6.12 U.S. Senator Tammy Baldwin (D-Wisconsin) is the first openly LGBTQ+ person to win election to Congress in both chambers. She served in the U.S. House of Representatives for seven terms, from 1999–2013, and she ran successfully for the U.S. Senate in 2012 and 2018.

Public opinion data on other LGBTQ+ rights issues show a similar, but less marked, shift over time. Are these issues now becoming less like "culture war" issues featuring battles between diametrically opposed interest groups and more like majoritarian issues such as Social Security or Medicare? What role will the public, the mass media, and policy entrepreneurs play in the debates over other LGBTQ+ issues in the years to come?

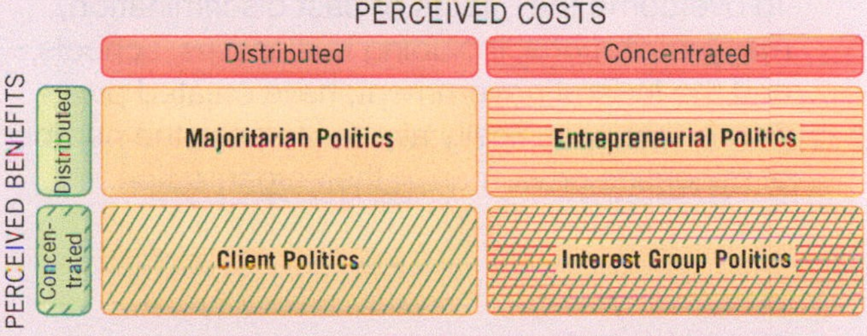

Sources: Emanuella Grinberg, "Wisconsin's Tammy Baldwin Is First Openly Gay Person Elected to Senate," CNN.com, November 7, 2012; Justin McCarthy, "Two in Three Americans Support Same-Sex Marriage," Gallup, May 23, 2018.

Learning Objectives

6-1 Explain how Supreme Court rulings and federal legislation have attempted to end racial discrimination in the United States.

After the Supreme Court ruled that school segregation was unconstitutional, Congress and the executive branch debated over how they would implement the decision. But in time, these institutions began spending federal money and using federal troops and law enforcement officials in ways that greatly increased the rate of integration.

6-2 Explain how Supreme Court rulings and federal legislation have attempted to advance women's rights in the United States.

While court rulings and laws state that treating men and women differently in several areas, such as pay and membership in professional organizations, is discrimination, the Supreme Court also says a difference in treatment can be justified constitutionally if the difference is fair, reasonable, and not arbitrary. Sex differences need not meet the "strict scrutiny" test. It is permissible to punish men for statutory rape to create single-sex public schools (so long as they meet certain requirements), and to draft men without drafting women.

6-3 Discuss the evolution of affirmative action programs after the Supreme Court and Congress ended racial segregation.

To overcome the effects of past discrimination, many institutions, including businesses, schools, and the federal government, have created programs that specifically aim to increase the number of minorities or women in their organization. In some cases, the Supreme Court has upheld affirmative action programs, but more recent Court rulings have overturned such programs or said they may not be necessary in the near future.

6-4 Discuss how Court doctrine and public opinion on sexual orientation have changed in the 21st century.

As late as 1986, the Supreme Court upheld a state law forbidding certain sexual acts. But in 2003 the Court struck down state laws banning consensual sexual relations between same-sex partners. In the 2000s, while some states legalized same-sex marriage and other states outlawed it, public opinion shifted in favor of allowing LGBTQ+ people to marry, rising from 35 percent, a minority, in favor in 2001 to 47 percent, a plurality, in favor in 2012.

In 2013, the Court struck down as unconstitutional the federal Defense of Marriage Act, declaring that the federal government must provide LGBTQ+ couples married in states where same-sex marriage is legal with the same health, tax, and other benefits that heterosexual married couples receive. In 2015, the Supreme Court ruled that same-sex marriage is constitutional.

6-5 Summarize how American political institutions and public opinion have expanded civil rights.

American civil rights have expanded through the joint efforts of political institutions and public opinion. In some areas, public opinion has mobilized the national government to act, whereas in other areas, court rulings and legislation have spurred public reaction.

To Learn More

Court cases: **www.law.cornell.edu**

Department of Justice: **www.usdoj.gov**

Martin Luther King, Jr., "I Have a Dream" speech, Lincoln Memorial, Washington, D.C., 28 August 1963 **www.archives.gov/press/exhibits/dream-speech.pdf**

Civil rights organizations:

National Association for the Advancement of Colored People: **www.naacp.org**

National Organization for Women: **www.now.org**

National LGBTQ Task Force: **www.thetaskforce.org**

National Council of La Raza: **www.nclr.org**

National Urban League: **http://nul.iamempowered.com**

American Arab Anti-Discrimination Committee: **www.adc.org**

Anti-Defamation League: **www.adl.org**

Branch, Taylor. *Parting the Waters: America in the King Years.* New York: Simon and Schuster, 1988. A vivid account of the civil rights struggle.

Flexner, Eleanor. Century of Struggle: The Women's Rights Movement in the United States. Rev. ed. Cambridge, MA: Harvard University Press, 1975. A historical account of the feminist movement and its political strategies.

Foreman, Christopher A. The African-American Predicament. Washington, D.C.: Brookings Institution, 1999. Thoughtful essays on challenges and problems for African Americans in the late twentieth century.

Franklin, John Hope. *From Slavery to Freedom,* 5th ed. New York: Knopf, 1980. A survey of black history in the United States.

Friedan, Betty. *The Feminine Mystique.* New York: Norton, 1963. Tenth anniversary edition, 1974. A well-known call for women to become socially and culturally independent.

Kluger, Richard. *Simple Justice.* New York: Random House/Vintage Books, 1977. Detailed and absorbing account of the school-desegregation issue, from the Fourteenth Amendment to the Brown case.

Kull, Andrew. The Color-Blind Constitution. Cambridge, MA: Harvard University Press, 1992. A history of efforts, none yet successful, to make the Constitution color-blind.

Mansbridge, Jane J. *Why We Lost the ERA.* Chicago, IL: University of Chicago Press, 1986. Explains why the Equal Rights Amendment did not become part of the Constitution.

Thernstrom, Stephan, and Abigail Thernstrom. *America in Black and White.* New York: Simon and Schuster, 1997. Detailed history and portrait of African Americans.

Wilhoit, Francis M. *The Politics of Massive Resistance.* New York: George Braziller, 1973. The methods—and ultimate collapse—of all-out Southern resistance to school desegregation.

Woodward, C. Vann. *The Strange Career of Jim Crow.* New York: Oxford University Press, 1957. Brief, lucid account of the evolution of Jim Crow practices in the South.

PART 2

Opinions, Interests, and Organizations

The latent causes of faction are thus sown in the nature of man; and we see them everywhere brought into different degrees of activity, according to the different circumstances of civil society.

— FEDERALIST NO. 10

CHAPTER 7

Public Opinion

Learning Objectives

7-1 Discuss what "public opinion" is and how we measure it.

7-2 Outline the major factors that shape public opinion.

7-3 Summarize the arguments for and against the claim that low levels of political knowledge among ordinary voters affect American democracy.

7-4 Discuss the relationship between public opinion and public policy.

Defined simply, **public opinion** refers to how people think or feel about particular things. In this chapter, we take a close look at what "public opinion" is, how it is formed, and how public opinion influences government policy. In later chapters, we examine the workings of political parties, interest groups, and government institutions and consider what effect they have on whether public opinion affects government policy. Let's begin this journey by recognizing how perspectives on the role public opinion is supposed to play in the country's representative democracy have changed since the nation was founded.

« Then The Founding Fathers believed that most average citizens lacked the time, information, energy, interest, and experience to decide on public policy. The Constitution's chief architect, James Madison, argued that direct popular participation in the decisions of government was a recipe for disaster, and that "it is the reason, alone, of the public that ought to control and regulate the government."[1] Madison and the other Framers looked to "the representatives of the people," most particularly the U.S. Senators who were not directly elected until 1913, "as a defense to the people against their own temporary errors and delusions."[2]

*** Now** Try imagining candidates for the U.S. Senate or, for that matter, for any federal, state, or local office, winning election or reelection, or maintaining high public approval ratings after they questioned "rule by the people" or doubted the majority's opinions the way that the Framers routinely, matter-of-factly, and publicly did.

Ironically, today, about the only circumstances under which elected leaders can get away with sounding the least bit that way is when public opinion polls get the public talking about how little most people know about government or civics. For example, in 2019, a study from the Annenberg Public Policy Center at the University of Pennsylvania found that only 39 percent of Americans could name the three branches of government, and almost one-quarter of the public—22 percent—could not name a single one. Only roughly one-half of Americans know that it takes a two-thirds majority of the House and Senate to override a Presidential veto, or which party had a majority in the House of Representatives. Commenting on the results, one scholar called this level of civics knowledge "dismal."[3] This study is only the latest to show that most Americans know little about the basic functions and figures

Image 7.1 Exit polls are conducted on Election Day to collect data on what voters think about candidates, issues, and other related topics.

Steve Debenport/E+/Getty Images

of American democracy. Later in the chapter, we'll consider whether this lack of information matters for politics and policy.

public opinion *How people think or feel about particular things.*

In the Gettysburg Address, Abraham Lincoln said the United States has a government "of the people, by the people, and for the people." That suggests the government should do what the people want. If that is the case, it is puzzling that:

- Today, the federal government is running budget deficits of over a trillion dollars a year, but many people want a balanced budget.
- Large majorities have called for stricter gun control legislation in the wake of repeated school shootings, yet no such national reforms have passed.
- Most people want to limit the role of money in politics, but each election cycle, more and more is spent on campaigns.

As we will see later in the chapter, public policy typically follows public opinion, but not always, as these examples attest. Some people, reflecting on these gaps between what the government does and what the people want, may become cynical and think our system is democratic in name only. That would be a mistake. Government policy often seems to be at odds with public opinion for several very good reasons.

First, it bears repeating that the Framers of the Constitution did not try to create a government that would do from day to day "what the people want." They created a government for the purpose of achieving certain substantive goals. The Preamble to the Constitution lists six of these: "to form a more perfect Union, establish Justice, ensure domestic Tranquility, provide for the common defense, promote the general Welfare, and secure the Blessings of Liberty."

poll *A survey of public opinion.*

random sampling *Method of selecting from a population in which each person has an equal probability of being selected.*

One means of achieving these goals was popular rule, as provided for by the right of the people to vote for members of the House of Representatives (and later for senators and presidential electors). But other means were provided as well: representative government, federalism, the separation of powers, a Bill of Rights, and an independent judiciary. These were all intended to be checks on public opinion. In addition, the Framers knew that in a nation as large and diverse as the United States, any such thing as "public opinion" would be rare; rather, there would be many "publics" (i.e., factions) holding many opinions. The Framers hoped the struggle among these many publics would protect liberty (no one "public" would dominate) while at the same time permit the adoption of reasonable policies that commanded the support of many factions.

Second, it is not easy to know what the public thinks. These days we are so inundated with public opinion polls that we may imagine that they tell us what the public believes. That may be true on a few rather simple, clear-cut, and widely discussed issues, but it is not true with respect to most matters on which the government must act. The best pollsters know the limits of their methods, and citizens should know them as well.

7-1 What Is Public Opinion?

Some years ago, researchers at the University of Cincinnati asked 1,200 local residents whether they favored passage of the Monetary Control Bill. About 21 percent said they favored the bill, 25 percent said they opposed it, and the rest said they hadn't thought much about the matter or didn't know. But there was no such thing as the Monetary Control Bill. The researchers made it up. About 26 percent of the people questioned in a national survey also expressed opinions on the same nonexistent piece of legislation.[4] In many surveys, large majorities favor expanding most government programs *and* paying less in taxes (see the discussion in Chapter 18). On some issues, the majority in favor one month gives way to the majority opposed the next, often with no obvious basis for the shift. This raises an important question: How much confidence should we place in surveys that presumably tell us "what the American people think" about legislation and other issues?

The first major academic studies of public opinion and voting, published in the 1940s, painted a distressing picture of American democracy. The studies found that, while a small group of citizens knew a lot about government and had definite ideas on many issues, the vast majority knew next to nothing about government and had only vague notions of even much-publicized public policy matters that affected them directly.[5] In the ensuing decades, however, other studies painted a somewhat more reassuring picture. These studies suggested that, while most citizens are poorly informed about government and care little about most public policy issues, they are nonetheless pretty good at using limited information (or cues) to figure out what policies, parties, or candidates most nearly reflect their values or favor their interests, and then acting (or voting) accordingly.[6]

The more closely scholars have studied public opinion on particular issues, the less uniformed, indifferent, or fickle it has seemed to be. For example, a study by political scientist Terry M. Moe analyzed public opinion concerning whether the government should provide parents with publicly funded grants, or vouchers, that they can apply toward tuition at private schools. He found that although most people are unfamiliar with the voucher issue, "they do a much better job of formulating their opinions than skeptics would lead us to expect." When supplied with basic information, average citizens adopt "their positions for good substantive reasons, just as the informed do."[7] As this example suggests, and as we will see in this chapter, while there are important limits to what public opinion can tell us, it is less fickle and transient than it seems at first glance.

How Do We Measure Public Opinion?

If properly conducted, a survey of public opinion—popularly called a **poll**—can capture the opinions of 330 million Americans by interviewing as few as 1,500 of them. To draw valid conclusions from such a poll, two particular ingredients are needed: a properly drawn sample and carefully worded questions.

No poll, whatever it asks and however it is worded, can provide us with a reasonably accurate measure of how people think or feel unless the persons polled are selected via **random sampling**, a process through which any given voter or adult has an equal chance of being interviewed. Through a process called stratified or multistage area sampling, the pollster makes a list of all the geographical units in the country—say, all the counties—and groups (or "stratifies") them by the size of their population. The pollster then selects at random units from each group or stratum in proportion to its total population. Within each selected county, smaller and smaller geographical units (down to particular blocks or streets) are chosen, and then, within the smallest unit, individuals are

Constitutional Connections | Majority Opinion and Public Policy

For the most part, the Framers of the Constitution thought that public opinion should play only a limited and indirect role in making public policy (see Chapters 1 and 2). They favored representative democracy over direct democracy. They doubted that most people would have the time, energy, interest, information, or expertise to deliberate and decide well on policy matters. They worried that majority opinion would often be fickle, factious, and overly influenced by short-term thinking. Thus, in *Federalist* No. 63, James Madison reflected on the need to defend "the people against their own temporary errors and delusions" and the "tyranny of their own passions." On the other hand, however, the Framers believed that while the opinions held by a temporary or "transient" majority should carry little weight with elected policymakers, the opinions expressed by a persistent majority—for example, a majority that persists over the staggered terms of House and Senate and over more than a single presidential term—should be heard and, in many (though not in all) cases heeded. When it came to civil liberties and civil rights, Madison and the other Framers were not willing to empower even persistent majorities or subject fundamental freedoms to a popular vote. Still, they believed that, on most public policy issues, a truly representative democratic government would and should enact the policies persistently favored by most people.

selected at random (by, for example, choosing the oldest occupant of every fifth house). These methods were initially developed to conduct in-person polls. Such polls are extremely expensive and time-intensive to conduct, so pollsters gradually shifted to interviewing respondents by telephone. At first, telephone interviews meant calling land lines, but over time, cell phones have replaced land lines, though the basic idea of random sampling remains the same.

If this process is repeated using equally randomized methods, the pollster might get slightly different results. The difference between the results of two surveys or samples is called **sampling error**. For example, if one random sample shows that 70 percent of all Americans approve of the way the president is handling the job, and another random sample taken at the same time shows that 65 percent do, the sampling error is 5 percent.

When properly conducted, polls are quite accurate, though certainly not infallible. Since 1952, most major polls have in fact picked the winner of the presidential election. In 2016, nearly all of the polls predicted that Hillary Clinton would win the popular vote—as she did by almost 2.9 million votes—though they did not foresee that she would lose the election by not winning 270 electoral votes (we will return to this point in Chapter 10). Likewise, **exit polls**—interviews with randomly selected voters conducted at polling places on election day in a representative sample of voting districts—have proven to be quite accurate. While errors in prediction occasionally occur, especially in close elections, in general, polling reflects what the public actually thinks.

For any sizable population, pollsters need to interview a large number of respondents to ensure that the opinions of the sample differ only slightly from what the results would have been had they interviewed the entire population from which the sample was drawn (this difference is known as the margin of error). For example, for the margin of error to be only 3 percent, a pollster must interview approximately 1,100 randomly selected individuals. That can be very expensive to do. As a result, firms have begun to investigate other methods of conducting polls, such as recruiting volunteers online. Such methods have worked well in some instances, but not in others. Whether such techniques can be shown to be as high quality as standard random sampling remains to be seen.[8]

sampling error *The difference between the results of random samples taken at the same time.*

exit polls *Polls based on interviews conducted on election day with randomly selected voters.*

question wording *The way in which survey questions are phrased, which influences how respondents answer them.*

How Do We Ask Questions?

The first step to obtaining quality information from a poll is to draw the sample correctly. The second is to ask the questions correctly. Pollsters aim to write their questions clearly and plainly, so as to avoid ambiguity and loaded language. They do so because how they ask the questions determines the answers they get.

Survey researchers spend considerable time worrying about **question wording**: the specific phrases used to describe policies in survey questions. For example, in one

political socialization
Process by which one's family influences one's political views.

canonical study, researchers conducted an experiment. Half of the respondents were asked how much they supported government welfare programs, and half were asked how much they supported government aid to the poor. Researchers expected the two items to give very similar results, as welfare programs are the government's efforts to aid the poor. However, when they conducted the study, the two items gave very different results, with many more respondents supporting aid to the poor.[9] When researchers did a follow-up study to investigate this discrepancy, they found a surprising result: while researchers saw welfare and aid to the poor as the same thing, respondents did not. For respondents, government welfare programs meant policies such as food stamps or public housing. But aid to the poor included not only those items, but also other policies such as homeless shelters, soup kitchens, and food banks. Respondents viewed these latter programs more positively, and hence were more supportive of aid to the poor.[10] By equating welfare and aid to the poor, researchers had set up a misleading comparison.

The debate over abortion rights provides another example of how question wording can yield flawed conclusions. Imagine that we wanted to answer a seemingly basic question about abortion attitudes: Are more Americans pro-life or pro-choice? Many surveys purport to answer this question. In a recent one, 68 percent of Americans said the phrase "pro-choice" described them "very well" or "somewhat well." In that same survey, just a few questions later, 71 percent said the same thing about the phrase "pro-life."[11] As these numbers make clear, many respondents consider themselves *both pro-life and pro-choice.* Ordinary Americans' views on abortion are complex and not easily captured by these sorts of simplistic terms: Americans generally support abortion rights, but want them to be limited to particular circumstances.[12] Americans are both pro-choice and pro-life, and do not fit neatly into one category or the other. To actually understand where the public stands on this issue—or any other one—we need to avoid asking questions that oversimplify difficult policy issues.

Not only can the wording of a question influence the results, but so can the order in which we ask the items. For example, in one study, researchers wanted to understand public support for LGBTQ+ rights, and asked about both same-sex marriage and civil unions. If they asked about civil unions before same-sex marriage, 49 percent supported civil unions. But if they asked about same-sex marriage first, support for civil unions increased to 56 percent.[13] Why the shift? Some respondents seem to be uneasy with allowing same-sex marriage, but could support civil unions as a middle ground. By asking about same-sex marriage first, and then asking about civil unions, it allowed respondents to see civil unions as a compromise position. But when civil unions were asked first, respondents lacked this contrast effect, and hence support for them was lower. Asking the questions in a different order affected the results.[14]

You might be thinking at this point that we can never trust public opinion data, but that fear is unwarranted. Public opinion data can offer us very valuable insights into what the public wants from its leaders and its government, but to do that, a survey needs to be conducted with care. When you see a poll reported in the news, carefully scrutinize the questions and look for particular wordings or order effects that could affect the results. Look for other high-quality polls conducted around the same time, and see whether they offer similar results. If you find multiple polls using different, well-worded questions that yield similar results, then you have found something you can trust. In contrast, if just one poll with an oddly worded question shows support for a particular policy, then you should be more skeptical of that result.

7-2 What Drives Opinion?

To understand public opinion and how it shapes government policy, we need to understand why it differs across individuals. What factors make people hold different attitudes and beliefs? A complete answer to that question is beyond the scope of this book (and is not really even knowable), but political scientists focus on three main factors that shape attitudes: political socialization and the family, demographic factors, and individuals' partisanship and ideology. While these are not the only factors that explain why people believe what they do (e.g., the mass media also matters, as we will discuss in Chapter 12), they are among the most important.

Political Socialization and the Family

For a long time, scholars have known that people acquire their political views from their families. The great majority of high school students know the party affiliation of their parents, and only a tiny minority of children supports a party opposite that of their parents.[15] Likewise, children's views on the issues tend to be broadly similar to those of their parents. Children do not automatically adopt the views of their parents, but rather, just as parents influence a child's religion or general outlook on life, they influence a child's political views as well. We refer to this process as **political socialization**. A child's first experience with politics is in the home, and so it should not be surprising that the parents' views shape the child's views.

This happens via two mechanisms. First, some evidence shows that some political attitudes can be passed genetically from parents to child, just like height or eye color.[16] We should note that while some political scientists accept this evidence, others dispute it.[17] The fairest thing to say is that there is suggestive evidence for the genetic transmission of political traits, but more work is needed to definitively establish it. Second, and much less controversially, scholars argue that children learn from the political cues provided by their parents. If the parents sit around the dinner table—or the evening television—and discuss politics and global affairs, the children learn where their parents stand on the issues of the day (and where the children think they themselves should stand). Such effects are especially pronounced in highly politicized families where politics is a more frequent topic of conversation.[18]

Of course, to say that parents and the family greatly shape one's political outlook is not to say that they determine it completely. The political environment in which they come of age also heavily influences children's attitudes. Political scientists call this the **impressionable years hypothesis**: Young people's political attitudes are very strongly influenced by what happens during their formative years (roughly their mid-teens through their mid-20s, when they are in high school and college).[19] For most people, this period is the first time they really notice politics, and these initial events shape how they see the political world. Those who came of age in the 1960s, during the Civil Rights movement, the protests against the Vietnam War, and student unrest, saw the political world fundamentally differently from their parents, who came of age during the years immediately after World War II. Likewise, today's students, who do not remember a world before 9/11, see the political world differently from their parents (who came of age during the end of the Cold War). Early experiences shape political attitudes and persist throughout the life cycle.

impressionable years hypothesis *Argument that political experiences during the teens and early 20s powerfully shape attitudes for the rest of the life cycle.*

Scott Olson/Getty Images News/Getty Images

Image 7.2 Young people and their parents watch a speech by Senator Elizabeth Warren (D-MA) during the 2020 Democratic Primary. Exposure to politics as a young person has a strong effect on one's political attitudes.

Q Think about your own political socialization. What events have been particularly important to you as you have formed your political beliefs?

We can examine political attitudes over the life cycle to see this. Americans who were born in 1941, and who would be 80 in 2021, came of age during the presidency of Dwight Eisenhower, a popular Republican. As a result, these voters are consistently more Republican than Democratic, even today. However, those born 11 years later in 1952 (and would be age 69 in 2021) are somewhat more Democratic, having grown up during the Great Society with President Lyndon Johnson. Likewise, those who came of age during the Ronald Reagan and George H. W. Bush years (the parents of today's young adults) are more Republican.[20] The early experiences during our formative years powerfully shape our political views.

What about young people today, the so-called "Generation Z" voters born in 1997 or later? It is true that, on balance, these individuals are more likely to identify as liberals, and to support Democrats,[21] than previous generations. They are also considerably more racially and ethnically diverse than older generations, and are on track to become better educated as well.[22] But we should not assume that younger voters are more liberal on every issue—as we can see in Figure 7.1, the reality is more complex than you might suppose. On some issues—like marijuana legalization—younger voters are more liberal than their older counterparts. But on many other issues, the differences are small to nonexistent. For example, voters of all ages overwhelmingly support Social Security and Medicare (as we discuss more in Chapter 17),[23] and younger voters are not (generally speaking) in favor of increased government spending across the board.[24] Further, despite the salience of the Parkland students and the March for Our Lives movement, younger voters are no more supportive of gun control than older ones.[25]

The largest gaps between younger and older voters come from their different attitudes toward government's regulation of appropriate behavior. Such differences stem from broad changes in society. For example, when today's senior citizens were growing up, interracial marriage was much more taboo, and racial and ethnic diversity was much less salient, in part because a larger share of Americans were white and fewer Americans were immigrants. Today, as America has become more racially and ethnically diverse, the stigma around inter-racial marriage has subsided, and younger voters are more likely to see this as a good thing, and to think more generally that growing diversity is good for society as well.

We see a similar shift with respect to sexual orientation and gender identity. A generation ago, homosexuality was criminalized and seen as a mental disorder, but today it is broadly accepted. Likewise, even a few years ago, most Americans had never heard the term transgender and had never used a gender-neutral pronoun to refer to someone, but today, this is increasingly routine. It should not be terribly surprising, then, to learn that support for LGBTQ+ rights, including support for same-sex marriage, as well as comfort with gender-neutral pronouns, is markedly higher among younger voters (see Figure 7.1). Both of these examples highlight the importance of the impressionable years and socialization: Because today's teens and seniors grew up in vastly different environments, they have vastly different attitudes on certain topics.

This same pattern of higher youth support holds true even in subgroups opposed to same-sex marriage. For example, overall white evangelical Protestants are the religious group most strongly opposed to same-sex marriage, with only 34 percent in favor. Yet even among this group, support among the young is much higher. More than twice as many young white evangelical Protestants favor same-sex marriage as senior citizens (53 percent versus 25 percent).[26] As younger voters continue to replace older voters in the electorate, attitudes on same-sex marriage and similar issues will continue to evolve.

Demographic Factors

The family, however, is not the only factor that shapes why we believe what we believe. Our demographic traits—our race and ethnicity, gender, age, social class/

Figure 7.1 **Opinion Gaps Between Young Adults and Senior Citizens**

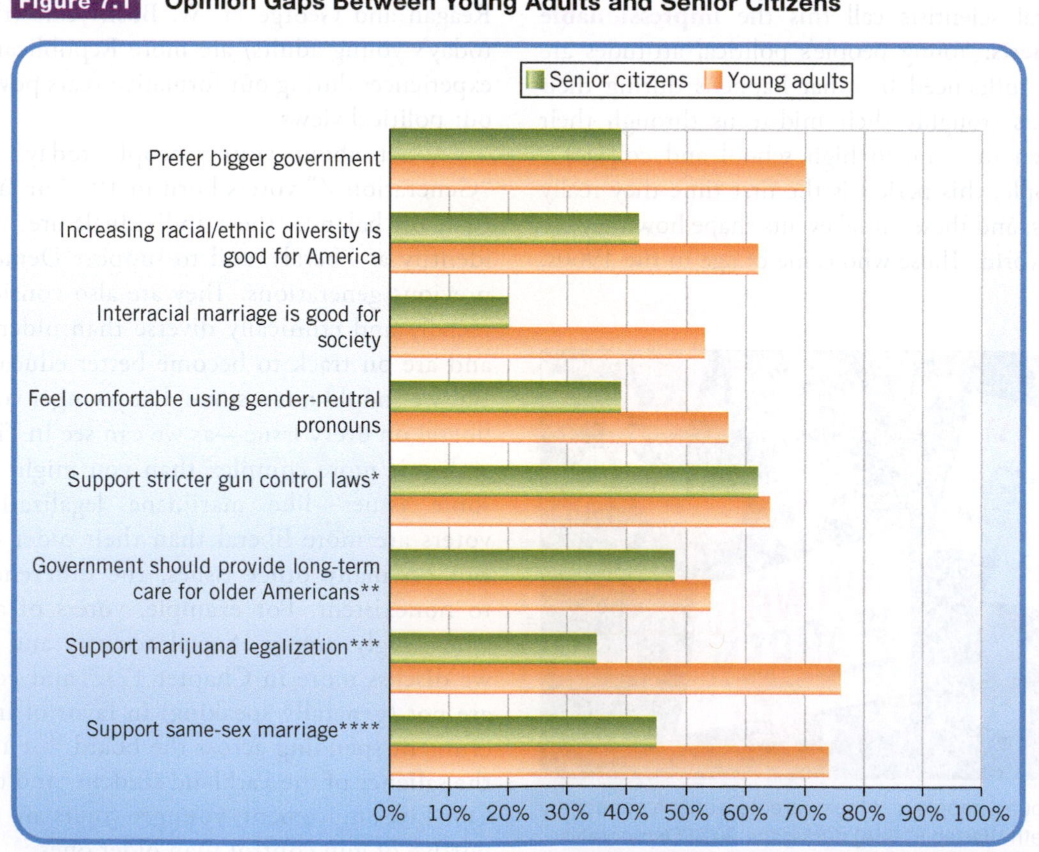

Source: Pew Research Center, "Generation Z Looks a Lot Like Millennials on Key Social and Political Issues," January 2019: *From: Pew Research Center, "Share of Americans Who Favor Stricter Gun Laws Has Increased Since 2017," October 2019; **From: Pew Research Center, "Looking to the Future, Public Sees an America in Decline on Many Fronts," March 2019; ***From: Pew Research Center, "Two-Thirds of Americans Support Marijuana Legalization," November 2019; ****From: Pew Research Center, "Fact Sheet: Attitudes on Same-Sex Marriage," May 2019.

income, religion, and so forth—also powerfully shape and influence our political attitudes. While many different demographic factors shape political attitudes, we consider only a few of the most salient ones here in the interest of space: gender, race and ethnicity, religion, and social class/income. Together, these demographic factors highlight how who we are shapes what we believe.

The Gender Gap

Journalists often point out that women have "deserted" Republican candidates to favor Democratic ones. In some cases, this is true. But it would be equally correct to say that men have "deserted" Democratic candidates for Republican ones. The **gender gap** is the difference in political views between men and women. As we see in Chapters 9 and 10, women are more likely than men to identify as Democrats and to vote for Democratic candidates.

gender gap *Difference in political views between men and women.*

Behind the gender gap in partisan self-identification and voting are differences between men and women over prominent political issues and which issues matter most. Many initially assumed that abortion drove the gender gap, but this turns out to be incorrect. On average, there have consistently been only very modest differences between men and women on abortion over time. Instead, two other factors drive the gender gap: women hold more liberal social welfare and foreign policy attitudes than men, and they are more likely to see social welfare issues as more important.[27] Women are more likely than men to favor activist government, universal health care, environmental protection regulations, antipoverty programs, and laws supporting same-sex marriage, and are less likely than men to favor cutting taxes at the expense of social services or to support military interventions. Figure 7.2 shows these trends graphically.

Race and Ethnicity

Perhaps the most striking political difference between African Americans and whites is that African Americans are overwhelmingly Democratic, and have been so since the Civil Rights movement in the 1960s;[28] we return to this point more in Chapters 9 and 10.

African Americans and whites hold many similar political attitudes. Both African Americans and whites support same-sex marriage[29] and marijuana legalization[30] at similar rates, oppose the idea of making abortion legal in all cases, agree that government is typically wasteful, and think that everyone has it in their own power to succeed.[31] Similarly, African Americans and whites both strongly agree that all races can get along in America.[32]

There are, however, sharp differences between whites and African Americans on other public policy questions. For example, African Americans are much more likely than whites to oppose the death penalty, and are more supportive of efforts to help the poor and disadvantaged, including supporting reparations for the descendants of slaves. African Americans are also likely to believe that not enough attention has been paid to race, and that to achieve racial equality, the country will have to do more.

But some of the largest racial opinion gaps concern attitudes toward the criminal justice system. African Americans are much more likely to think that the criminal justice system is unfair and is biased against minorities, as we can see in Figure 7.3. This gap stems from their differential experiences with it. African Americans are more likely to have had negative interactions with the criminal justice system, as have their African American friends and family.[33]

The fact that numerous African Americans have been killed by police or died in police custody in recent years—such as Michael Brown, Eric Garner, Freddie Gray, Tamir Rice, Sandra Bland, Walter Scott, Breonna Taylor, George Floyd and numerous others—has brought this issue to the forefront of national discussions. These deaths helped to spark the Black Lives Matter movement and have led to numerous calls for reforms to policing and the criminal justice system. As we discuss in Chapter 11, the death of George Floyd sparked a nation-wide series of protests. These events changed public opinion. In 2014, 43 percent of Americans felt that African Americans and other minorities were treated equally in the criminal justice system. In July 2020, that fell to 26 percent. Similarly, all racial groups became more supportive of the Black Lives Matter movement in the summer of 2020.[34] This underlines an important truth about public opinion: it is dynamic, and it changes in response to changes in society.

Image 7.3 After the death of George Floyd, record numbers of citizens protested police brutality across the country.

Figure 7.2 **The Gender Gap in Public Opinion**

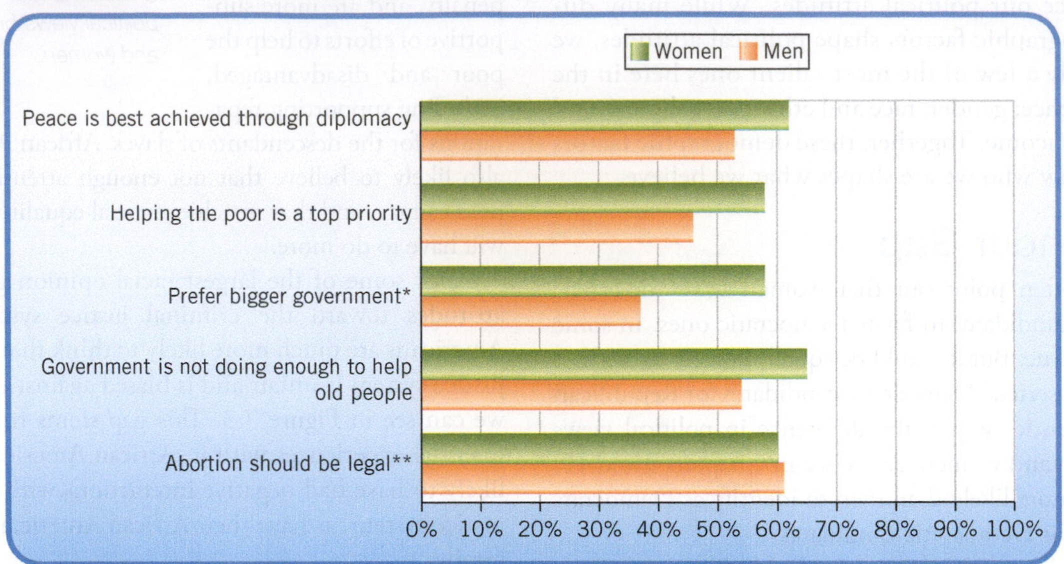

Source: Pew Research Center, "The Gender Gap: Three Decades Old, As Wide As Ever," March 2012; *From Pew Research Center, "Gender Gap Widens in Views of Government's Role—And of Trump," April 2019; **From Pew Research Center, "U.S. Public Continues to Favor Legal Abortion, Oppose Overturning *Roe v. Wade*," August 2019.

Figure 7.3 **Public Opinion in Black and White**

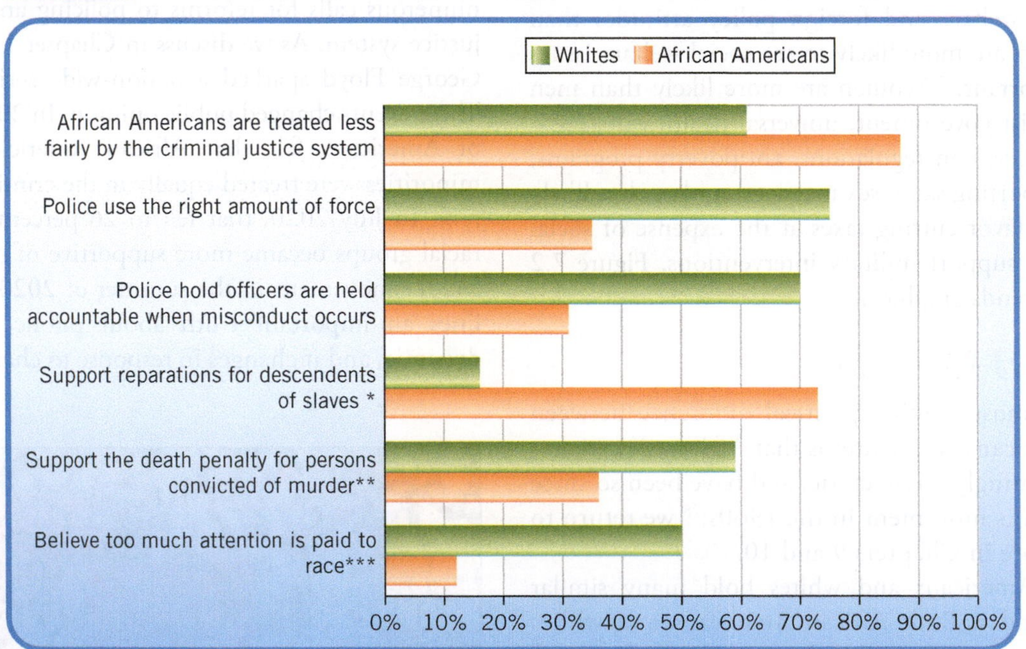

Source: Pew Research Center, "From Police to Parole, Black and White Americans Differ Widely in their Views of Criminal Justice System," May 2019; *From: Gallup, "Race Relations," January 2020, **From: Pew Research Center, "Public Support for the Death Penalty Ticks Up," June 2018; ***From: Pew Research Center, "Race in America 2019," April 2019.

But contemporary America is not simply limited to African Americans and whites; the country contains a multitude of ethnic groups from around the world. Most notably, Latinos are now the largest minority group in America, numbering roughly 60 million people. While research on Latino public opinion is still an emerging field, today a growing body of research explores how Latinos differ—and how they do not—from other Americans.

We note that it is difficult to speak of "Latino" public opinion as a monolith. With tens of millions Latinos coming from a diverse array of countries throughout Central and South America, from many different backgrounds, one cannot say that all Latinos share a particular point of view. Important generational differences also exist, with second and third generation Latinos, who were born in the United States, being more similar to other Americans than first generation Latino immigrants, who came here from other nations.[35] If anything, we should speak about Latino "opinions" rather than a singular opinion shared by this large, and diverse, group.

That said, some broad patterns do emerge. On issues that most directly speak to the concerns and experiences of Latinos—issues such as immigration reform or bilingual education—Latinos' attitudes are distinct from those of other Americans, though the differences are smaller than one might expect, as we can see in Figure 7.4. But on a wide range of other issues, such as abortion, jobs, education, and foreign policy, Latinos' views look very similar to those of other Americans.

G. Ronald Lopez/Alamy Stock Photo

Image 7.4 Representative Alexandria Ocasio-Cortez, a Democrat from New York City, is the youngest woman ever to serve in the U.S. House of Representatives.

Figure 7.4 **Latino Public Opinion**

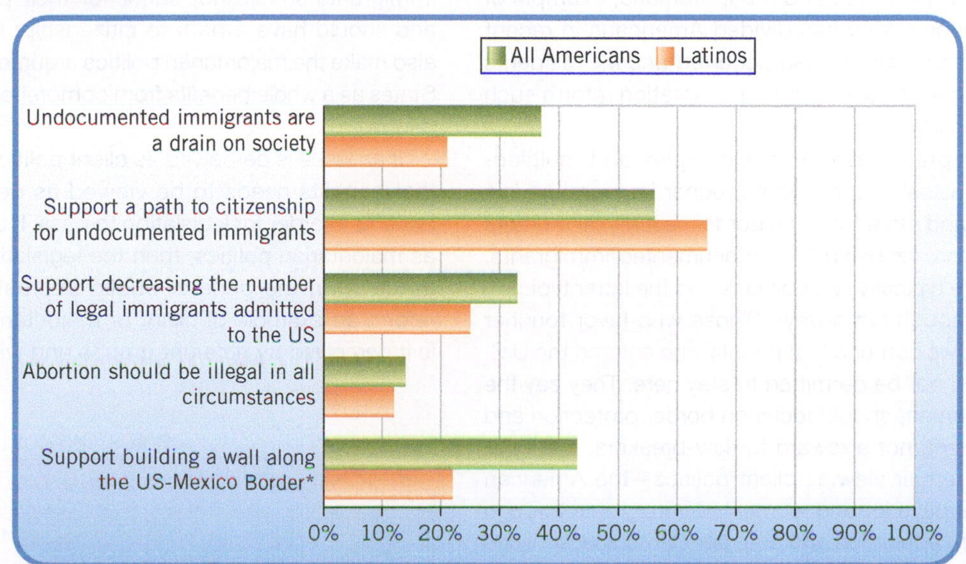

Source: Authors' analysis of the 2018 Views of the Electorate Research (VOTER) Study data; *From: Pew Research Center, "On Immigration Policy, Partisan Differences but also Some Common Ground," August 2016.

Review the data in Figures 7.1 through 7.4. What patterns do you notice? Are there ones that surprise you?

Religion

As we discussed in Chapter 4, Americans are a religious people, especially compared with the more secular nations of Western Europe. Given this religiosity, it is perhaps not surprising that religion shapes public opinion on many political issues. While we typically think that religious people are all on the conservative end of the spectrum, that is not in fact the case—the relationship between religion and public opinion is more nuanced than this stereotype would suggest.

Fifty years ago, discussions of religion and politics focused more on differences between denominations, which at that time largely meant Protestants, Catholics, and Jews. Such divisions remain useful: In general, Jewish Americans, as well as African American Protestants, tend to remain on the left, evangelical (or born-again) Protestants are more on the right, and Catholics and mainline Protestants fall more in the middle of the ideological spectrum.

But in recent years, scholars have noticed another important division: the divide between those who are more religious and those who are less so. Those who are more religious are more conservative—often considerably more conservative—on issues of sex and the family, such as abortion and same-sex marriage.[36] For example, among Christians who attend church weekly (and hence are more religious), 39 percent support banning abortion in all circumstances, but among those who seldom or never attend worship services, that figure is only 11 percent.[37] As we saw above, evangelicals (most of whom take a conservative view on social issues) are strongly opposed to same-sex marriage. Such links are not terribly surprising: Many religious traditions, especially Christian traditions, take a conservative position on issues of reproduction and the family, so it is not surprising that religious individuals adopt them. Indeed, when asked, those who are highly religious say that their faith drives their position on these types of issues.[38] This suggests that the stereotype that highly religious people are more conservative is true at least some of the time.

Yet on other issues, we see a quite different pattern. How religious one is has no effect on attitudes toward

Policy Dynamics: Inside/Outside the Box | Immigration Reform: Client or Majoritarian Politics?

Immigration reform has been one of the most contentious issues in recent years. During the 2016 election, Clinton and Trump took sharply different positions on this issue, and once in office, President Trump shut down the government and then declared a national emergency to get funding for his wall along the border with Mexico. This conflict is only the latest, and most dramatic, example of how immigration policy has divided Americans in recent decades; similar debates also occurred under Presidents Obama and Bush as well. Why is immigration reform such a politically charged topic?

While immigration reform is a complex and multifaceted issue, basically some want tougher immigration law enforcement and more focus on border security, and others want a path to citizenship for undocumented immigrants. The former are typically Republicans and the latter typically Democrats, though not always. Those who favor tougher immigration laws contend that people who entered the U.S. illegally should not be permitted to stay here. They say the federal government should focus on border protection and law enforcement, not a reward for law-breakers. Immigration reform, in their view, is client politics—the American public at large pays for undocumented immigrants through providing them education and emergency medical services (pursuant to Supreme Court decisions). Providing a path to citizenship also means that people lose confidence that the federal government will uphold the law, so the long-term health of American democracy suffers to benefit a few.

Supporters of a "path to citizenship" present it as majoritarian politics—everyone, including undocumented immigrants, pays for this opportunity through hard work and taxes, and everyone benefits by ensuring an economically productive, just, and humane society. They also make a client politics case that the children of undocumented immigrants should not suffer for their parents' mistakes and should have a path to citizenship; but these groups also make the majoritarian politics argument that the United States as a whole benefits from comprehensive immigration reform.

If an issue is perceived as client politics, then the group that benefits needs to be viewed as deserving of those benefits in order for legislation to pass. If an issue is viewed as majoritarian politics, then the legislation must be seen as being in the general public interest. Is immigration reform an example of client or majoritarian politics? How is it perceived by different groups and why?

PERCEIVED BENEFITS \ PERCEIVED COSTS	Distributed	Concentrated
Distributed	Majoritarian Politics	Entrepreneurial Politics
Concentrated	Client Politics	Interest Group Politics

immigration (controlling for other relevant demographics). And on the death penalty and support for environmental spending, those who are more religious are more *liberal* (i.e., more opposed to the death penalty and more supportive of environmental spending).[39] This stands in sharp contrast to the stereotype that religious individuals are always more conservative. But such findings should not surprise us: Many of these same faith traditions speak out against the death penalty and support greater environmental stewardship. For example, in 2010, the Southern Baptist Convention—the largest evangelical Christian denomination—denounced the government's handling of the Deepwater Horizon oil spill and called for greater efforts at environmental stewardship and conservation.[40] Likewise, some evangelical pastors have also begun promulgating a message more focused on helping the poor and feeding the sick than on abortion, same-sex marriage, and school prayer.[41] Such efforts suggest that the relationship between religion and public opinion will continue to evolve in the 21st century.

Social Class and Income

Americans speak of "social class" with embarrassment. The norm of equality tugs at our consciences, urging us to judge people as individuals, not as parts of some social group (such as "the lower class"). Social scientists speak of "class" with confusion. They know it exists but quarrel constantly about how to define it: by income? occupation? wealth? schooling? prestige? personality?

Let's face up to the embarrassment and skip over the confusion. Truck drivers and investment bankers look differently, talk differently, and vote differently. There is nothing wrong with saying that the first group consists of "working-class" (or "blue-collar") people and the latter of "upper-class" (or "white-collar") people. Moreover, though different definitions of class produce slightly different groupings of people, most definitions overlap to such an extent that it does not matter too much which we use.

However defined, public opinion and voting have been less determined by class in the United States than in Europe, and these cleavages have weakened everywhere in recent years. In the 1950s, V. O. Key found that differences in political opinion were closely associated with occupation. He noted that people holding managerial or professional jobs had distinctly more conservative views on social welfare policy and more internationalist views on foreign policy than manual workers.[42] During the next decade, this pattern changed greatly. Opinion surveys done in the late 1960s showed that business and professional people had views quite similar to those of manual workers on matters such as the poverty program, health insurance, American policy in Vietnam, and government efforts to create jobs.[43]

Similar patterns have continued to hold over time: differences between social classes and incomes are relatively modest on a wide variety of public policy questions.[44] There are, however, some important differences on certain economic issues, especially between the very rich (the "1 percent" or the "0.1 percent") and everyone else. In general, the very wealthy are (relative to the general public) less supportive of the social safety net, government health insurance, government regulation, and redistribution (especially via taxes).[45] As we will see, these differences can have important consequences for public policy.

partisanship *An individual's identification with a party; whether they consider themselves a Democrat, Republican, or an Independent.*

The Limits of Demographics

As we have seen throughout this section, various groups in America hold different opinions, as race, ethnicity, gender, social class, and other demographic factors influence our beliefs. But such patterns are, at best, averages, and do not describe everyone. Plumbers and professors may have similar incomes, but they rarely have similar views, and businesspeople in New York City often take a very different view of government than businesspeople in Houston or Birmingham. Your best friend may be a conservative African American Republican, or your wealthy neighbor may be far to the left on economic issues. In short, knowing someone's demographics gives us a good guess as to their views on the issues, but it is just that: a good guess. To really understand their views, we need to know more than just their demographic attributes.

Political Partisanship and Ideology

After familial socialization, the largest influence on what citizens believe is their political partisanship and their ideological beliefs. When we talk about **partisanship** or partisan identity, we mean people's attachment to their political party: Do they think of themselves as a Democrat or a Republican? We address partisanship in more detail in Chapter 9, but here, we consider its influence on citizens' attitudes.

Simply put, partisanship has a powerful, even fundamental, influence on citizens' attitudes. On issue after issue—taxes, spending on social programs, gun control, and many others—Democrats and Republicans have different opinions. Identifying with a party powerfully shapes an individual's beliefs.[46]

party sorting *The alignment of partisanship and issue positions so that Democrats tend to take more liberal positions and Republicans tend to take more conservative ones.*

Such differences between ordinary Democrats and Republicans are driven by differences among elected officials. Ordinary Democrats and Republicans look to Democratic and Republican officials to know where to stand on the issues.[47] When people watch a media report about a political issue, the media typically use elected officials from the parties to represent the various positions,[48] meaning that the political parties define the competing perspectives on the issues for most people. Because Democratic and Republican elected officials diverge on these issues, so do ordinary voters (though the differences between ordinary voters are much more muted, as we will see).

This is not just blind obedience. Rather, it reflects the fact that people identify with a party because it shares their values, and as a result, they will follow the lead of their party's officials. So, if you are a Democrat, you might look to, say, Elizabeth Warren or Bernie Sanders to see where they stand on the issue, and follow suit. Likewise, a Republican might do the same with Donald Trump or Mike Pence. The attitudes of ordinary Democrats and Republicans reflect the opinions of elite Democrats and Republicans.

If ordinary Americans' attitudes reflect the attitudes of political elites, then this raises an important question: Are ordinary voters now polarized? Over the past 50 years or so, elected Democrats and Republicans (especially in Congress) have become much more sharply divided.[49] As we see in Chapter 13, Democratic members of Congress are essentially all on the left, and elected Republicans are essentially all on the right. Is the same thing true of ordinary Democrats and Republicans? The answer is no. The most careful analysis of the attitudes of ordinary Democrats and Republicans indicates that they are relatively moderate on most issues.[50] Elites may be polarized, but ordinary voters are not.

But how can this be: If ordinary Americans' attitudes reflect those of elites, and elites are polarized, how is the mass public not? The answer is that ordinary voters have sorted, but they have not polarized.[51] **Party sorting** is the process of aligning issue positions and party. So today, unlike 40 years ago, ordinary Democrats tend to take the liberal position on the issues, and ordinary Republicans, the conservative one. We can see this happen visually in Figure 7.5 using data from the Pew Research Center: since 1994, Democrats have moved to the left, and Republicans have moved to the right, across a variety of different issues.

While Americans have sorted, they have not gone all the way to the ideological poles. There is still a great deal of heterogeneity among the mass public: a large segment of each party takes positions that are centrist or on the opposite ideological side from their party, and as we discuss below, many Americans are best described as not terribly ideological. Sorted, rather than polarized, best describes ordinary Americans.

But one might logically ask: If sorting continues, will ordinary Americans come to be deeply polarized? It certainly is possible. If everyone sorted, then the country would

Figure 7.5 **Growing Ideological Consistency, 1994–2017**

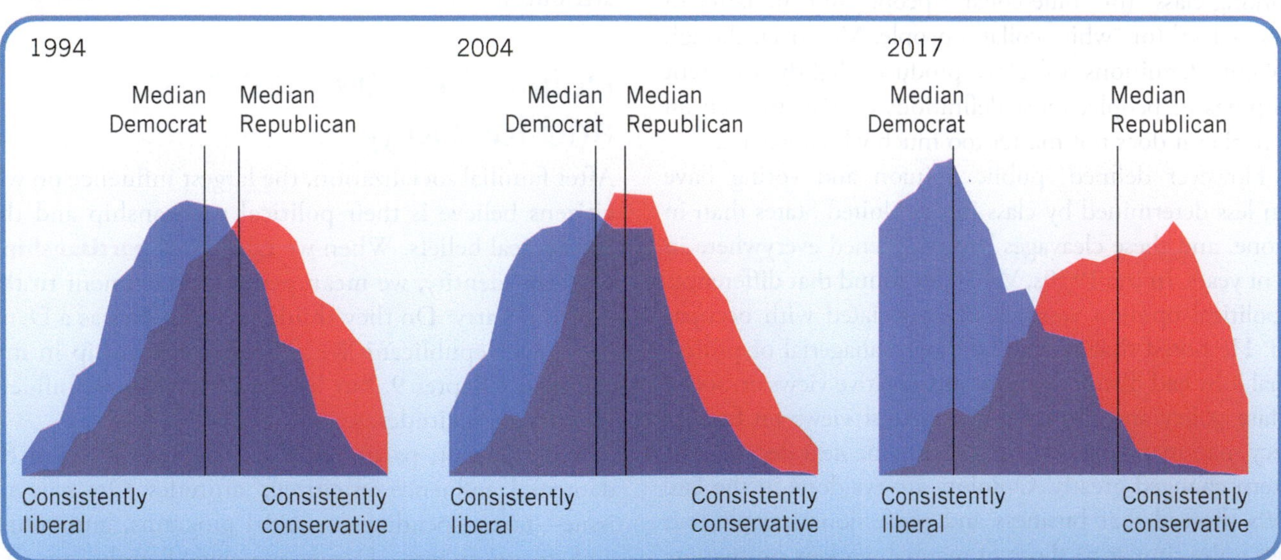

Source: Pew Research Center, "The Partisan Divide on Political Values Grows Even Wider," October 2017.

certainly be more polarized. However, such a situation is unlikely. While people now take more consistent positions on the issues (i.e., Democrats are on the left, Republicans are on the right), they are largely just to the left or right of the center. They are "slightly liberal" or "slightly conservative" more than "very liberal" or "very conservative."[52] Furthermore, as we see below, most Americans are not terribly well informed about politics, nor are they especially interested in it. Given this, they are unlikely to adopt the sort of extreme positions that would be required to generate extensive mass polarization. Sorting does increase mass polarization, but only very slightly. We can say the electorate has become quite a bit better sorted, but not really very polarized.

While ordinary voters have not polarized, the same is not true for those who are most active in politics. Among those who are politically active and participate in campaigns, polarization is a more accurate description of what has happened.[53] They have moved to the extremes, and as we see in later chapters, this has important consequences for elected officials.

But in recent years, another dimension to polarization has emerged. Even if ordinary Democrats and Republicans are not very far apart on the issues, they have come to increasingly dislike and distrust one another, a phenomenon known as **affective polarization**.[54] For example, Democrats and Republicans alike think that those from the other party are close-minded, unintelligent, and lazy, and a majority of both parties say that they have "very unfavorable" feelings toward those from across the political aisle.[55] Partisans today are uninterested in dating those from the other party,[56] in working with them,[57] or even talking to them about apolitical topics![58]

Do Americans really feel so much animosity toward those from the other party? It is certainly true that there is more animosity and anger in politics today than there was a generation ago. But these studies show that Americans are not quite as affectively polarized as it may seem. When Americans are asked whether they trust someone from the other political party, they think about polarized activists or political elites, not their friends, neighbors, and co-workers from the other party.[59] When you ask them about ordinary citizens from the other party—most of whom are not terribly political interested or ideological, as we saw above—they have far lower levels of distrust.[60] So while most Americans do not like the political elites and activists from the other party, they have much warmer feelings toward that party's ordinary voters. Much as most voters are not very polarized on the issues, they are also not all that affectively polarized as well.

Political Ideology

Partisanship is not the only core fundamental identity that shapes public opinion: so does one's ideology, whether one is a liberal or a conservative. Up to now the words *liberal* and *conservative* have been used as though everyone agrees on what they mean and as if they accurately describe general sets of political beliefs held by large segments of the population. Neither of these assumptions is correct. Like many useful words—*love, justice, happiness*—they are as vague as they are indispensable.

affective polarization *Tendency of partisans to dislike and distrust those from the other party*

political ideology *A more or less consistent set of beliefs about what policies government ought to pursue.*

When we refer to people as liberals, conservatives, socialists, or radicals, we are implying that they have a patterned set of beliefs about how government and other important institutions in fact operate and how they ought to operate, and in particular about what kinds of policies government ought to pursue. These groups are said to display to some degree a **political ideology**—that is, a more or less consistent set of beliefs about what policies government ought to pursue.

Political scientists measure the extent to which people have a political ideology in two ways. The first is by determining how frequently people use broad political categories (such as "liberal," "conservative," "radical") to describe their own views, which is referred to as symbolic ideology. The second method involves a simple mathematical procedure: measuring how accurately one can predict peoples' views on a subject at one time based on their view on that subject at an earlier time, or measuring how accurately one can predict peoples' views on one issue based on their view on a different issue. The higher the accuracy of such predictions (or correlations), the more we say a person's political opinions display "constraint" or ideology.

Looking at the first method (can Americans identify themselves as liberal, moderate, or conservative), it seems as though many Americans can select an ideological orientation for themselves. For example, in 2017, 26 percent identified as liberals, 38 percent as conservatives, and 36 percent as moderates, and those patterns have been roughly stable for over a decade.[61] Yet that simple question belies a host of complexity. When we dig slightly deeper, we find that many people adopt those labels without having much of an understanding of what they mean. When given an option to say they "don't know" which label best describes them, many Americans choose that option—indeed, it is often the plurality response. Furthermore, many people's views on the issues (what they think of taxes and spending, gun control, abortion, and so forth) are only weakly correlated with the label (liberal, conservative, or moderate) they use to describe themselves.[62] Ordinary Americans know where they stand on the issues, but they do not necessarily deeply comprehend the ideological labels used in politics. Except when asked by pollsters, most Americans do not actually use the words *liberal, conservative,* or *moderate* in explaining or justifying their preferences for parties, candidates, or policies, and not many more than half can give plausible definitions of these terms.

What about the second method of measuring ideology? Here, the evidence is—as it has been for 60 years—that most Americans are not deeply ideological.[63] Most people's views are not tightly aligned into neat liberal or conservative bundles, unlike elites. The vast majority of Americans simply do not think about politics in an ideological or very coherent manner. Partly in recognition of these and related limitations, pollsters have increasingly taken a fresh approach to documenting and analyzing average Americans' ideological cast and character. Essentially, rather than asking people to identify themselves as "liberal," "conservative," or "moderate," they ask people multiple questions about politics and government, and then use the answers to sort them into a half-dozen or more different groups.

One prominent example, conducted by the Pew Research Center, began in 1987 and has been updated several times since, most recently in 2017. To see where you fit, you can take the survey at https://www.people-press.org/quiz/political-typology/. Americans, it finds, are divided into eight different groups, each defined by certain key characteristics (see Table 7.1). Table 7.1 ranks the groups from top to bottom in how Republican they are; so the most Republican groups are at the top, and the most Democratic groups are at the bottom.

By this measure, approximately one-third of Americans—and 45 percent of the politically engaged—are ideologically consistent and are consistently liberal or conservative on the issues. Note too that these individuals have almost completely sorted themselves into political parties as well: 97 percent of core conservatives are Republicans, and 99 percent of solid liberals are Democrats.[64]

But most Americans are not so ideologically consistent. They are somewhere in the middle, taking conservative positions on some issues but liberal positions on others. For example, the group "Market Skeptical Republicans" are generally conservative, but think business has too much power and should be more tightly regulated (a more liberal economic position). And 8 percent of Americans are bystanders, largely removed from the political process.

Dig deeper into the data on these groups (also available via the same website cited above), such as the related survey findings regarding each group's socioeconomic status and views on religion and other matters that affect politics, and you will see that the old three-way (liberal-conservative-moderate) self-identification surveys probably obscured more than they revealed regarding most Americans' opinions about many different political issues. Analyses of other survey data support the same conclusion.[65] This underlines what we said above about polarization. The politically active and engaged—the steadfast liberals and conservatives—are divided and ideological. But most Americans, even if they have sorted and now take the party's views on some issues, are moderate, centrist, and less ideological. Ideology is more for elites than for ordinary voters.

TABLE 7.1 | Political Ideology: Eight Types

	General Public (%)	Registered Voters (%)	Politically Engaged (%)
Core Conservatives	13	15	20
Country-First Conservatives	6	7	6
Market Skeptic Republicans	12	12	10
New Era Enterprisers	11	11	9
Bystanders	8	--	--
Devout and Diverse	9	9	6
Disaffected Democrats	14	14	11
Opportunity Democrats	12	13	13
Solid Liberals	16	19	25

Source: Pew Research Center, "Political Typology Reveals Deep Fissures on the Right and the Left," October 2017.

Liberal and Conservative Elites

Although the terms *liberal* and *conservative* do not adequately describe the political views held by most average Americans, they do capture the views held by many, perhaps most, people who are in the country's political elite. As we discussed in Chapter 1, every society has an elite because in every society government officials have more power than the general public, some people make more money than others, and some people are more popular than others. The former Soviet Union even had an official name for the political elite—the *nomenklatura.*

In America, we often refer to **political elites** more casually as "activists"—people who hold office, run for office, work in campaigns or on newspapers, lead interest groups and social movements, and speak out on public issues. Being an activist is not an all-or-nothing proposition: People display differing degrees of activism, from full-time politicians to persons who occasionally get involved in a campaign (see Chapter 8). It is these activists—especially the most committed—who are most likely to display ideological consistency on the conventional liberal-conservative spectrum.

The reasons for this greater consistency seem to be information and peers. First, consider information. In general, the better-informed people are about politics and the more interest they take in politics, the more likely they are to have consistently liberal or conservative views.[66] This higher level of information and interest may lead them to find relationships among issues that others don't see and to learn from the media and elsewhere what are the "right" things to believe. This does not mean no differences exist among liberal elites (or among conservative ones), only that the differences occur within a liberal (or conservative) consensus that is more well defined, more consistent, and more important to those who share it than would be the case among ordinary citizens.

Second is the matter of peers. Politics does not make strange bedfellows. On the contrary, politics is a process of like attracting like. The more active you are in politics, the more you will associate with people who agree with you on some issues; the more time you spend with those people, the more your other views will shift to match theirs.

The greater ideological consistency of political elites can be seen in Congress. As we note in Chapter 13, Democratic members of Congress tend to be consistently liberal, and Republican members of Congress tend to be consistently conservative—far more consistently than Democratic voters and Republican voters. By the same token, the delegates to presidential nominating conventions are far more ideological (liberal in the Democratic convention, conservative in the Republican one) than is true of voters who identify with the Democratic or Republican parties. For elites and activists, ideology is more central to their political world view than for ordinary voters.

political elites Persons with a disproportionate share of political power.

heuristics Informational shortcuts used by voters to make a decision.

7-3 Political Information and Public Opinion

As we mentioned at the beginning of this chapter, considerable evidence shows that Americans don't know much about politics. A litany of studies have shown that Americans do not know basic facts about civics (i.e., the three branches of government, which branch can declare war, etc.), nor can they answer current events types of questions that ask, for example, the identity of the Speaker of the House, the party in control of the Senate, and so forth.[67] Such results are nothing new: Dating back to the dawn of modern survey research, political scientists have shown that Americans know little about politics. By any measure, most Americans are woefully ignorant of the details of American political life, and have been for some time.

Many scholars and political reformers are troubled by this lack of knowledge about the basic dimensions of American government and politics. They argue that if Americans do not know much about politics, they will be hard-pressed to guide politicians and select good representatives at the ballot box. The opinions we discussed previously will be based on ephemera and will not reflect a real understanding of the underlying issues. This concern is nothing new in American politics—it goes all the way back to the Founding Fathers. The Founders were suspicious of too much popular control, and they consequently set up a system in which many of the decisions of government were removed from direct popular control (recall that only the House of Representatives was directly elected before the 20th century).

But is this in fact the case? While there is no disputing that Americans are ill informed, does this information deficit harm American democracy? Some scholars say no: Americans may not know much about the specific details of politics and public life, but that does not mean they cannot make reasonable decisions. After all, what does knowing the identity of the chief justice of the Supreme Court have to do with casting a ballot for president or Congress? These skeptics argue that citizens can use information shortcuts, or **heuristics**, to make well-informed decisions.

Such heuristics seem to work well in at least some cases. In the late 1980s, California voters were asked to vote on a series of ballot propositions that would have changed the rates for automobile insurance. Surveys showed that many voters did not understand the details of the various proposals, yet many still voted in ways that were consistent with their underlying interests. How? They knew (largely from advertising) where key groups, such as the insurance industry and trial lawyers, stood on the measures. They used those group endorsements to figure out how they should vote.[68] Likewise, an analysis of voters in recent presidential elections suggests that many (though not all) voters vote the way they would vote if they were fully informed (i.e., knew where the candidates stood in great detail on every issue).[69] While these examples concern voting in elections, the same logic would apply equally well to forming opinions on particular policies: Even if citizens do not understand the intricacies of, say, tax policy, they can reasonably deduce what their position "should" be by knowing where the relevant political actors stand on it.[70]

Before we become too sanguine, however, it is important to note that other scholarship suggests there are important limits to heuristics, and they can sometimes lead voters astray and result in making worse decisions, not better ones.[71] For example, voters assume that politicians from working-class backgrounds will be more hospitable to working-class interests (using a heuristic that the politician's class background will be an indicator of their behavior), but this is not the case.[72] Furthermore, when voters lack information, this affects their political attitudes. Some argue that at least some of the public support for the 2001 and 2003 Bush tax cuts was due to low (or incorrect) information on the part of many voters.[73] Perhaps even more tellingly, when given additional information about various policies, citizens' preferences change, sometimes quite dramatically, even among those who are generally well informed about politics.[74] It seems that information about policies can have a large and consequential impact on people's political attitudes. Heuristics and shortcuts are a partial substitute, but just that: a partial one. At least in some circumstances, a lack of information about politics can be detrimental to the political process.

7-4 Public Opinion and Public Policy

So far, we have spent the chapter delving into the origins and measurement of public opinion. But we have not said anything about the consequences of public opinion: Does public opinion matter? In particular, does public opinion shape public policy?

Happily, the answer to that question is yes, at least most of the time. An encyclopedic study looked at every law for which there were relevant public opinion polls over several decades. It found that when public opinion changed, policy change usually followed. Furthermore, such changes were almost always congruent: When opinion became more liberal (conservative), the policy itself moved to the left (right). This was especially true for more salient policies, or for particularly large shifts in opinion.[75] This seems to be a "good" outcome for democratic theory: Government decisions do, in fact, reflect the will of the people.

But as we suggested at the outset of the chapter, policies do not always follow the majority's will. Sometimes, to understand why, we need to understand the role of parties, interest groups, the media, and political institutions, as we will see in later chapters. But sometimes policy does not reflect majority will because the minority is more politically powerful.

This typically occurs because the minority is more politically engaged and active, and pressures politicians accordingly. Gun control is perhaps the best-known example of this situation. Surveys consistently show that a majority of Americans favors gun control. However, among the minority who oppose action, the issue is a much higher priority. For example, gun-control opponents weigh the issue more heavily when choosing a candidate and were more likely to have given money to relevant interest groups.[76] A study of the members of the leading anti-gun-control organization (the National Rifle Association) found that they were more politically engaged and active than other Americans (and more so than gun-control proponents).[77] In this setting, politicians will respond to the better-organized minority rather than the apathetic majority.

Another example—and a deeply troubling one—is that several studies have shown that government policy is often more responsive to the preferences of the economic elite than to the views of other citizens.[78] Those at the top of the economic ladder are more likely to participate in politics[79] and, as a result, these studies suggest, politicians heed their views more fully. Given that the economic elite have divergent preferences on some issues (notably, issues of regulation, taxes, and so forth; see our discussion of social class earlier in the chapter), this inequality in responsiveness has real consequences. Put more directly, both examples highlight that government policy responds to those who participate in politics. To understand policy, we need to understand who participates. We turn to that task in the next chapter.

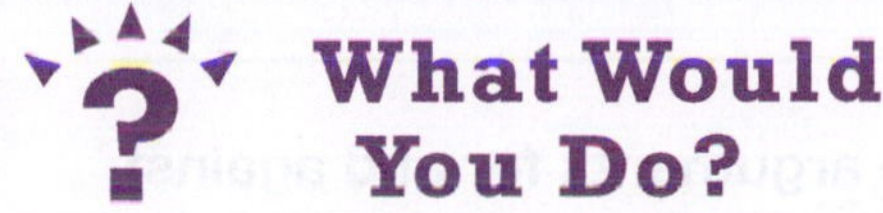

What Would You Do? | Should You Support the Comprehensive Immigration Reform Bill?

To: *Senator Matthew Joseph*
From: *Rachel N. James, legislative assistant*
Subject: *Vote on "path-to-citizenship" immigration bill*

Your state has only a small undocumented immigration population, but voters have concerns about both maintaining law and order, and providing economic opportunities and a pathway to citizenship for people who have resided in this country for many years, especially those brought here as children. While there have been many proposals to address this issue in recent years, none have been enacted into law, hence the need for a new bill. As you contemplate both your vote on the bill and your possible presidential bid as a Republican, note that public opinion on the subject is complex. While support for building a border wall is highly divided along party lines (with Democrats opposed and Republicans supporting), both Democrats and Republicans think that both tougher border security and a pathway to citizenship are important dimensions of immigration reform. You might also consider whether the issue better fits into majoritarian or client politics (see the "Policy Dynamics: Inside/Outside the Box " feature on page 164).

To Consider:

The U.S. House of Representatives is weighing a bill that would result in the most comprehensive immigration reform in more than a decade. Proponents say it will both improve border security and provide opportunities for legal residency for the roughly 11 million undocumented immigrants in the United States. The bill received a mixed reception, however, as critics denounced the provisions for undocumented immigrants, saying they amount to "amnesty" for law breakers.

Arguments for:

1. Your state contains a small but slowly growing proportion of first-generation Americans who favor a "path to citizenship" for immigrants who have lived in this country for years, regardless of their legal status.
2. Some argue that undocumented immigrants often take jobs that nobody else wants, and they contribute to the U.S. economy by paying taxes and buying goods and services.
3. A path to citizenship, with fines and other penalties for being in the country illegally, is the most realistic option for individuals who have family and other long-term ties in the United States.

Arguments against:

1. Your party leaders oppose comprehensive immigration reform, saying that enhanced border security must be a higher priority.
2. Some argue that undocumented immigrants take jobs away from native-born Americans and cost more in public services, such as education and emergency health care, than they contribute to the economy.
3. People who entered the country illegally must not be rewarded for breaking the law, and enforcement can be effective with sufficient resources.

Source: Pew Research Center, "On Immigration Policy, Partisan Differences but Also Common Ground," August 2016; Pew Research Center, "Americans' Immigration Priorities: Divisions Between—And Within—The Two Parties," November 2019.

What Will You Decide? Enter **MindTap** to make your choice.

Your decision: ☐ Vote for bill ☐ Vote against bill

Learning Objectives

7-1 Discuss what "public opinion" is and how we measure it.

Public opinion refers to how people think or feel about particular things, including but not limited to politics and government. Today, it is commonly measured by means of scientific survey research or polls based on random samples of given populations and carefully worded questions.

7-2 Outline the major factors that shape public opinion.

Many different factors shape public opinion, but three key ones are political socialization and the family, demographics, and partisanship and political ideology. Political socialization refers to the influence of one's family on one's political views. Demographics refer to our underlying characteristics (race, gender, age, etc.) that shape our political beliefs. Finally, political partisanship and ideology are core values that shape and guide what people want from government, and hence influence their views on the issues.

7-3 Summarize the arguments for and against the claim that low levels of political knowledge among ordinary voters affect American democracy.

In general, Americans don't know much about politics and government. Some argue that this is not a terrible limitation, as citizens can use heuristics (information shortcuts) to substitute for low levels of knowledge. However, shortcuts are not a perfect substitute for information, and when citizens have more information about a policy, their preferences can change. This suggests that a lack of information does affect American democracy in at least some settings.

7-4 Discuss the relationship between public opinion and public policy.

Generally speaking, public opinion drives policy: When opinion changes, so does policy, especially on salient issues or when the opinion change is especially large. But when a minority group is particularly politically consequential (typically because they are more politically engaged on the issue), government policy follows the minority view, rather than the majority one.

To Learn More

Gallup Polls: **www.gallup.com**

Pew Research Center: **https://www.pewresearch.org**

Rasmussen Reports: **www.rasmussenreports.com**

Roper Center for Public Opinion Research: **https://ropercenter.cornell.edu**

Wall Street Journal/NBC News polls: **http://graphics.wsj.com/wsjnbcpoll/**

Five Thirty Eight Pollster Ratings: **https://projects.fivethirtyeight.com/pollster-ratings/**

Erikson, Robert S., and Kent L. Tedin. *American Public Opinion: It's Origins, Content, and Impact*, 10th ed. New York: Pearson, 2019. An excellent summary of how opinion is measured, what it shows, and how it affects politics.

Fiorina, Morris. 2017. *Unstable Majorities: Polarization, Party Sorting and Political Stalemate*. Stanford, CA: Hoover Institution Press. An update to his earlier classic *Culture War?*, this shows that most Americans have sorted but not polarized.

Gilens, Martin. *Affluence and Influence: Economic Inequality and Political Power in America.* Princeton, NJ: Princeton University Press, 2012. An argument that the wealthy have greater sway over policy than other Americans.

Jennings, M. Kent, and Richard G. Niemi. *Generations and Politics.* Princeton, NJ: Princeton University Press, 1981. A classic study of political socialization.

Kinder, Donald and Nathan Kalmoe. *Neither Liberal Nor Conservative*. Chicago: University of Chicago Press, 2017. An excellent summary of the decades of evidence showing that most Americans are not terribly ideology.

Key, V. O., Jr. *The Responsible Electorate.* Cambridge, MA: Harvard University Press, 1966. An argument, with evidence, that American voters are not fools.

Moe, Terry M. Schools, *Vouchers, and the American Public*. Washington, D.C.: Brookings Institution Press, 2001. A masterful study of how public opinion matters to education policy, suggesting that most people, with only slight information, form reasonable views.

Weissberg, Robert. *Polling, Policy, and Public Opinion.* New York: Palgrave Macmillan, 2002. A critique of what we think we know from opinion polling, showing the many ways in which polls can give us misleading answers.

Zaller, John. *The Nature and Origins of Mass Opinion.* Cambridge, England: Cambridge University Press, 1992. A pathbreaking study of how the public forms an opinion, illustrating the ways in which elite views help shape mass views.

Rob Crandall/Shutterstock.com

CHAPTER 8

Political Participation

Learning Objectives

8-1 Discuss how American voter turnout compares to other advanced industrialized democracies.

8-2 Describe the historical expansion of suffrage in America and how this affected voter participation.

8-3 Outline what factors explain who participates in politics.

political participation *The many different ways that people take part in politics and government.*

voting-age population (VAP) *Residents who are eligible to vote after reaching the minimum age requirement.*

Defined simply, **political participation** refers to the many different ways that people take part in politics and government: voting or trying to influence others to vote, joining a political party or giving money to a candidate for office, keeping informed about government or debating political issues with others, signing a petition, attending a political protest, advocating for a new law, or writing a letter to an elected leader. Some scholars argue that, in addition to these activities, almost any form of civic engagement, such as helping out at a local homeless shelter or attending a school board meeting, should also count as political participation. And some believe that the rise of the Internet, especially social media, make traditional ideas about what constitutes political participation obsolete (we will have more to say about how the Internet and social media have, and have not, changed politics in Chapter 12).

But no matter how they define it, most academics who study political participation pay close attention to voting and begin with a puzzle: Despite successive legal and other changes that might be expected to increase electoral participation, voter turnout rates in America today are lower than they were for previous generations, and scores of millions of Americans now sit out each presidential and midterm national election.

« Then In most states, well into the 19th century, only property-owning white men could vote. After the Civil War and into the mid-20th century, many states used all manner of stratagems to keep African Americans from voting. Women did not receive the right to vote until 1920, when the Nineteenth Amendment to the Constitution was ratified. Before 1961, residents of the District of Columbia could not vote in presidential elections; the Twenty-third Amendment to the Constitution gave them that right. Into the 1960s, most white people had only limited formal education; women and many minority groups faced legal, social, and other barriers or disincentives to voting; and there was nothing resembling today's steady stream of political news via multiple media outlets.

*** Now** National laws extend voter eligibility to all persons age 18 or older (courtesy of the Twenty-sixth Amendment to the Constitution, ratified in 1971). No state may restrict voting based on discriminatory tests, taxes, or residency requirements. In areas where many non-English speakers live, election authorities must supply ballots written in the appropriate native languages. People in all 50 states can register to vote when applying for a driver's license, and most states now allow voters to vote by absentee ballot before Election Day, even if they are not residing outside their home state. Many states also permit people to register on the same day that they vote, and some states now conduct their elections entirely through the mail.

Over the past half-century, formal education levels have risen among all groups, and news, information, and opinions about politics and government are just about everywhere one turns (or clicks).

And yet, voter turnout in presidential elections was typically higher in the 19th century than it is today. In the 2020 presidential election, voter turnout surged to levels not seen since that period, and more than 66 percent of eligible voters cast a ballot. But even then, more than 80 million Americans did not vote. Over the last few decades, voter turnout in midterm national elections has typically been around 40 percent, and it hit a 70-year low in 2014 when only about one-third of Americans turned out to vote.[1] Young voters, despite averaging more years of formal education, facing fewer legal barriers, and enjoying more access to information than any previous generation could have imagined, are nonetheless mostly nonvoters; for example, in the six midterm national elections since 1998, only 20 to 30 percent of 18-to 24-year-olds cast a ballot.

What explains nonvoting? Are voter turnout rates in America today really as bad as they seem, either in historical terms or relative to rates in other modern democracies? And what about other forms of political participation in America today?

8-1 A Close Look at Nonvoting

Start with the fact that voter turnout can be measured in at least two different ways, and they give different answers about the prevalence of nonvoting.[2] All U.S. residents age 18 or older constitute the **voting-age population (VAP)**. But many residents of the United States who are of voting age (18 or older) are not, in fact, eligible to vote. Two such groups are noncitizens who reside in America and convicted felons who in some states are disenfranchised by state laws. Unlike the VAP, the **voting-eligible population (VEP)** measure excludes from the calculation U.S. residents age 18 or older who are not legally permitted to cast a ballot. For example, in 2018 the VAP numbered approximately 255 million, but that included about 20 million noncitizens, prisoners, and disenfranchised felons. Measured by the VAP, the national voter turnout rate was 46.4 percent in 2018, but measured by the VEP it was 50.3 percent; and since 1948, as the percentage of the population age 18 and older that consists of noncitizens and disenfranchised convicted felons has increased, the gap between the VAP and the VEP measures of voter turnout has also grown (see Figure 8.1).

voting-eligible population (VEP)
Residents who have reached the minimum age to be eligible to vote, excluding those who are not legally permitted to cast a ballot.

Another important nuance about nonvoting concerns registered versus unregistered voters. Take a look at Table 8.1. Column A compares democratic nations in terms of the percentage of their VAP who went to the polls in their most recent national elections. The United States ranks dead last, with 55.7 percent voter turnout (that was the VAP turnout in 2016). From this perspective, U.S. turnout looks not like other developed nations like France or Germany, but rather like former communist countries such as Estonia, Poland, or Slovenia.

Now, however, look at Column B. It compares the same nations in terms of percentage of registered voters (those eligible voters who have completed a registration form by a set date) who went to the polls in the same elections. The United States looks much better, landing near the top of the pack, with 86.8 percent of registered voters having voted in 2016. Here, our voter turnout appears much more like the voter turnout in other advanced, industrialized democracies.

Although we vote at lower rates in the United States than people do abroad, the meaning of our voting is different. For one thing, we elect far more public officials than the citizens of any other nation do. There are more than a half million elective offices in the United States, and just about every other week of the year there is an election going on somewhere in this country.

A citizen of Massachusetts, for example, votes not only for the U.S. president but also for two senators, the state governor, the member of the House of Representatives, a state representative, a state senator, the state attorney general, the state auditor, the state treasurer, the secretary of state, a county commissioner, a sheriff, and clerks of various courts, as well as (in the cities) for the mayor, the city councilor, and school committee members and (in towns) for selectmen, town meeting members, a town moderator, library trustees, health board members, assessors, water commissioners, the town clerk, housing authority members, the tree warden, and the commissioner of the public burial ground. (We have probably forgotten others.)

Figure 8.1 Two Methods of Calculating Turnout in Presidential Elections, 1948–2020

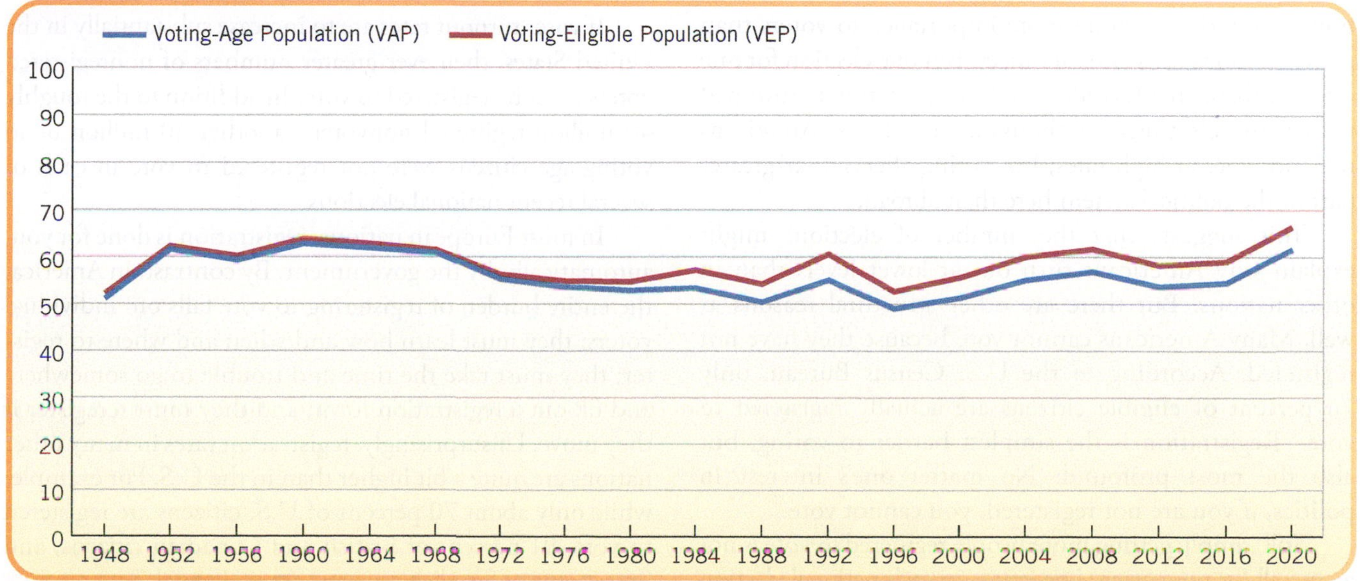

Source: Data until 2000 from Michael P. McDonald and Samuel L. Popkin, "The Myth of the Vanishing Voter," *American Political Science Review* 95 (December 2001): 966. Data from 2004 forward are from Michael McDonald, United States Election Project, Voter Turnout Data, www.electproject.org.

TABLE 8.1 | Two Ways of Calculating Voting Turnout, Here and Abroad

A		B	
	Turnout as Percentage of Voting-Age Population		Turnout as Percentage of Registered Voters
Belgium	87.2	Australia	91
Sweden	82.6	Belgium	89.4
Denmark	80.3	**United States**	**86.8**
Australia	79	Denmark	85.9
South Korea	77.9	Sweden	85.8
The Netherlands	77.3	The Netherlands	81.9
Israel	76.1	South Korea	77.2
New Zealand	75.7	Israel	72.3
Finland	73.1	New Zealand	79.0
Germany	69.1	Germany	76.2
France	67.9	France	74.6
United Kingdom	63.3	United Kingdom	69.3
Canada	62.1	Canada	68.3
United States	**55.7**	Finland	66.9

Source: Drew DeSilver, "U.S. Voter Turnout Trails Most Developed Countries," Pew Research Center Fact Tank, 21 May 2018.

Q **Compare the different countries in Table 8.1. What patterns do you notice? Are there other factors (like region of the world or having a presidential versus a parliamentary system) that might help to explain these differences?**

In many European nations, by contrast, voters get to make just one choice once every four or five years: they can vote for or against a member of parliament. When only one election for one office occurs every several years, that election is bound to assume more importance to voters than many elections for scores of offices. But one election for one office probably has less effect on how the nation is governed than many elections for thousands of offices. Americans may not vote at high rates, but voting affects a far greater part of the political system here than abroad.

This suggests that the number of elections might explain why Americans turn out at lower levels than in other nations. But there are other structural reasons as well. Many Americans cannot vote because they have not registered: According to the U.S. Census Bureau, only 70 percent of eligible citizens are actually registered to vote.[3] Registration is the simplest barrier to voting, but also the most profound: No matter one's interest in politics, if you are not registered, you cannot vote.

Still, simply getting more people registered to vote is not a cure-all for nonvoting, however—in each national election since 2006, about half of all nonvoters were registered. When registered nonvoters were asked why they did not vote, two of the most common reasons were that they were not interested or did not like the candidates or campaign issues, suggesting a lack of interest. Many others said that they had scheduling conflicts or were simply too busy, suggesting a lack of time.[4]

Because many people are too busy to vote on one day during the work week, some have proposed making Election Day a national holiday or holding national elections on weekends. Such proposals, though popular, remain only proposals, though several states—such as Virginia—have made Election Day a holiday.[5] States have taken steps, however, to make voting easier for citizens. As of 2020, 40 states allow early voting (that is, voting before Election Day), and 29 states and the District of Columbia afforded voters the option of "no-fault" absentee voting, meaning that voters can vote absentee without having to demonstrate they are residing outside their home state or giving any other explanation. Five states—Washington, Oregon, Colorado, Hawaii, and Utah—conduct their elections entirely via mail, and in 2020, voters in King County, Washington could vote in a local election via their smartphones[6] (see the Constitutional Connections box on page 179 for more information). While reformers had hoped that such reforms would dramatically increase voter turnout, the evidence suggests that their effect is very modest, on the order of a few percentage points at most.[7]

In 2020, due to the coronavirus pandemic, many states permitted more voters to vote by mail. 20 states and the District of Columbia made it easier to vote by mail, and as a result 83 percent of Americans had the ability to vote by mail in that election.[8] While some officials—including President Trump—argued that vote-by-mail favored Democrats, careful academic studies showed that this reform does not favor either political party.[9]

If voter turnout rates are to increase substantially in the United States, then ever greater numbers of nonregistered voters must be registered to vote. In addition to the roughly 40 million registered nonvoters, another 40 million or so voting-age citizens were not registered to vote in each of several recent national elections.

In most European nations, registration is done for you, automatically, by the government. By contrast, in America, the entire burden of registering to vote falls on individual voters: they must learn how and when and where to register; they must take the time and trouble to go somewhere and fill out a registration form; and they must reregister if they move. Unsurprisingly, registration rates in many other nations are quite a bit higher than in the U.S. For example, while only about 70 percent of U.S. citizens are registered to vote, 91 percent of British and Canadian citizens, and 96 percent of Swedish citizens, are registered.[10]

But would making it less burdensome to register necessarily result in higher percentages of Americans becoming registered voters and voting? In 1993, Congress passed a law designed to make it easier to register to vote. Known as the National Voter Registration Act, it is typically called the "motor-voter law" because it allows people in all 50 states to register to vote when applying for driver's licenses. The law also requires states to provide mail-based registration, and to offer registration at some state offices, such as those that serve the disabled or low-income families.

As with early, mail-in, and absentee balloting (see the Constitutional Connections feature on page 179), the evidence regarding the impact of the motor-voter law on voter participation remains hard to interpret definitively. Millions of citizens have registered to vote via state motor vehicle bureaus or other state offices, but a study found "that those who register when the process is costless are less likely to vote."[11] In recent years, including 2018, motor-voter law-related means of registration were the single most widely used method (see Figure 8.2). While the motor-voter law has certainly increased registration, there is little evidence it has led to a substantial increase in voter participation. Other studies of efforts to facilitate registration have come to similar conclusions: increasing registration increases turnout only modestly.[12]

Recently, however, several states have begun to adopt a reform that might have a larger effect on voter turnout: automatically registering all eligible citizens to vote unless they explicitly opt out of doing so (typically, using driver's licenses and other state records). As of early in 2020, 19 states and the District of Columbia have enacted automatic voter registration. Oregon—the first to adopt such a law in 2015—found that in 2016, they automatically registered more than 225,000 residents based on interactions with the state's department of motor vehicles. Of those, nearly 100,000 individuals voted in the November presidential election, a turnout rate of 43 percent, an impressive rate for the newly registered.[13] Preliminary analyses of the 2018 election suggest that automatic voter registration also boosted both registration and turnout in at least some states where it was used.[14] How these patterns evolve in 2020 and beyond will be an important topic of study to determine the long-term effects of this reform.

Campaigns have recently begun to invest more heavily in old-fashioned get-out-the-vote (GOTV) drives to boost voter turnout. Many careful studies have found that such efforts do increase participation, though the exact amount depends on many different factors, including the type of message used, how the campaign makes contact with the voter (e.g., through a mailer, a phone call, or an in-person visit from a canvasser), the salience of the election, and so forth.[15]

Arguably the most effective GOTV message is the "social pressure" message. In this message, subjects are told before the election that whether they vote in the election is a matter of public record (as it is in nearly all states), and after the election, the campaign will inform their neighbors whether or not they voted (they send a mailer indicating who voted on the block, and who did not). This message is powerful: People do not want their nonvoting revealed to their neighbors! Those who received this message were more than 8 percent more likely to turn out and vote.[16] This may not sound like much in the abstract, but in a close election, it could well make the difference between who wins and who loses.

Such efforts, replicated on a large scale, can help to reshape the electorate. For example, in 2008 and 2012, the Obama campaign conducted a massive GOTV effort. The Obama campaign organized 2.2 million volunteers to have 24 million conversations with Americans and register 1.8 million additional voters.[17] While Republican operations were not quite as large, they, too, were impressive. One estimate suggests that the 2012 Romney and Obama campaigns together generated over 400 million voter contacts (obviously contacting many voters multiple times), with a net increase of almost 2.6 million voters as a result.[18] Perhaps even more importantly, these studies found that being involved in such activities helps to bring many new people into the political process, integrating them into their communities more fully, illustrating that the effects of GOTV efforts extend beyond the ballot box.[19]

But such efforts are not a panacea. While Obama's effort was especially successful, others have been less effective, including those by Hillary Clinton's campaign in 2016.[20] Furthermore, political scientists have shown that GOTV efforts often heighten participatory inequalities by targeting those who are already most likely to vote, rather than those who are less likely to cast a ballot (we consider what factors drive political participation later in the chapter).[21] While particular efforts have targeted infrequent voters to increase their participation,[22] such efforts are relatively rare. This suggests that while GOTV drives can help to reshape the electorate, they are not likely to significantly expand U.S. voter turnout. In 2020, due to the coronavirus pandemic, there was somewhat less in-person GOTV and more via phone, text messaging, and online. What effects this had on turnout will be an important topic of study in the years to come.

Of course, voting is only one way of participating in politics. It is important—we could hardly be considered a democracy if nobody voted—but it is not all-important. Joining civic associations, supporting social movements, writing to legislators, fighting city hall—all these and other activities are ways of participating in politics. It is possible that, through these measures, Americans participate in politics more than most Europeans—or anybody else, for that matter. Moreover, low rates of registration may indicate that people are reasonably well satisfied with how the country is governed. If 100 percent of all adult Americans registered and voted (especially under a system that makes registering relatively difficult), it could mean that people were deeply upset about how things were run. In short, it is not at all clear whether low voter turnout is a symptom of political disease or a sign of political good health.

Figure 8.2 **Method of Voter Registration, 2018**

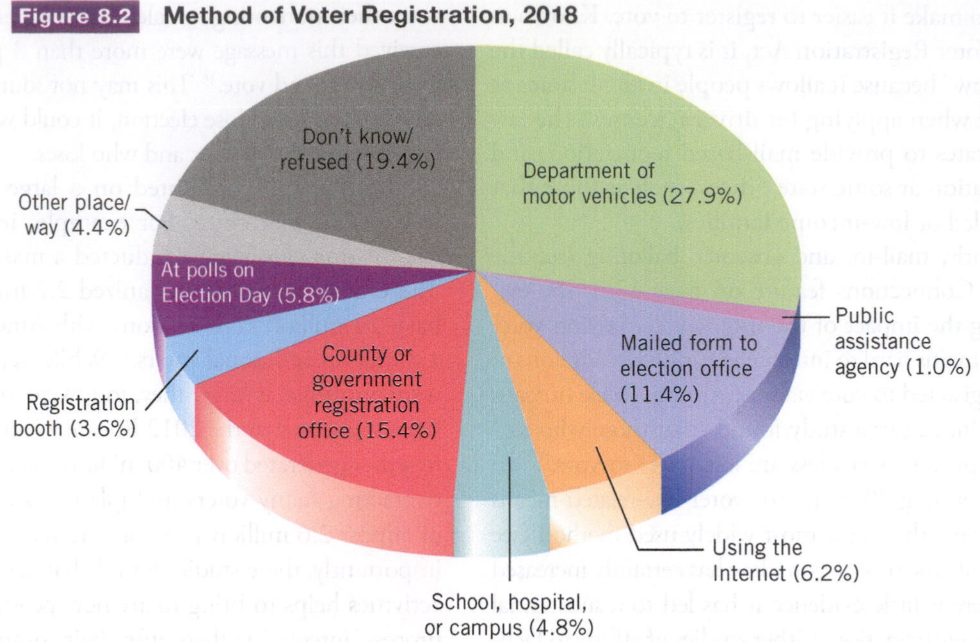

Source: U.S. Bureau of the Census, "Voting and Registration In the Election of 2018," April 2019.

The important question about participation is not how much participation there is but how different kinds of participation affect the kind of government we get. This question cannot be answered just by looking at voter turnout, the subject of this chapter; it also requires us to look at the composition and activities of political parties, interest groups, and the media (the subjects of later chapters).

Nonetheless, voting is important. To understand why participation in American elections takes the form that it does, we must first understand how laws have determined who shall vote and under what circumstances.

8-2 The Rise of the American Electorate

It is ironic that relatively few citizens vote in American elections, since it was in this country that the mass of people first became eligible to vote. At the time the Constitution was ratified, the vote was limited to property owners or taxpayers, but by the administration of Andrew Jackson (1829–1837) it had been broadened to include virtually all white male adults. Only in a few states did property restrictions persist: they were not abolished in New Jersey until 1844 or in North Carolina until 1856. And, of course, African American males could not vote in many states, in the North as well as in the South, even if they were not slaves. Women could not vote in most states until the 20th century; Chinese Americans were widely denied the vote; and being in prison is grounds for losing the franchise in many states even today. Foreign nationals on the other hand, often were allowed to vote if they had at least begun the process of becoming citizens. By 1880, only an estimated 14 percent of all adult men in the United States could not vote; in England in the same period, about 40 percent of adult men were disenfranchised.[23]

From State to Federal Control

Initially, it was left entirely to the states to decide who could vote and for what offices. The Constitution gave Congress the right to pick the day on which presidential electors would gather and to alter state regulations regarding congressional elections. The only provision of the Constitution requiring a popular election was the clause in Article I stating that members of the House of Representatives be chosen by the "people of the several states."

Because of this permissiveness, early federal elections varied greatly. Several states picked their members of the House at large (that is, statewide) rather than by district; others used districts but elected more than one representative from each. Some had their elections in odd-numbered years, and some even required that a congressional candidate win a majority, rather than simply a plurality, of votes to be elected (when that requirement was in effect, runoff elections—in one case, as many as 12—were necessary). Furthermore, presidential electors and senators were at first picked by state legislatures rather than directly by voters.

Congress, by law and constitutional amendment, has steadily reduced state prerogatives in these matters. In 1842, a federal law required that all members of the House be elected by districts; other laws over the years required that all federal elections be held in even-numbered years on the Tuesday following the first Monday in November.

Constitutional Connections | State Voting Laws and Procedures

"The Times, Places and Manner of holding Elections for Senators and Representatives, shall be prescribed in each State by the Legislature thereof ..." Thus begins Article I, Section 4, of the Constitution. The United States is unique among modern democracies in the extent to which the laws and procedures under which its citizens vote vary according to where in the nation they reside. As discussed elsewhere in this chapter, the states are no longer as free as they once were to decide who could vote for what office, but the shift to federal control has not eliminated differences in state voting laws and procedures. With few exceptions, the federal courts, including the U.S. Supreme Court, have let present-day differences in states' voting laws and procedures stand.

Currently, in addition to the traditional Election Day trek to a polling place or "voting booth" in one's home voting district, voting-age Americans can cast ballots in three other ways.

- ***Early Voting:*** 40 states and the District of Columbia permit people to cast ballots before Election Day without requiring that they furnish any excuse for doing so. Delaware passed a law in 2019 permitting early voting beginning in 2022, which will make it the 41st state to allow this. The early voting periods range from 4 days to 45 days before Election Day. The average early voting period was 19 days in 2020.
- ***Absentee Voting:*** All states permit absentee voting by mail for military personnel, their voting-age dependents, and U.S. citizens living overseas. All states also mail absentee ballots to certain other voters; normally in 16 states, an excuse is required to vote absentee, but in 2020 due to COVID-19, only 6 states kept this requirement. (As noted earlier, voting in five states is done by mail, so absentee ballots are not required.)
  In eight states, certain citizens receive "permanent absentee ballot" privileges; in most, the citizens granted this status must give evidence of a chronic illness or disability. In Alaska, this status is also afforded to citizens who live in remote parts of the state.
- ***Mail Voting:*** A ballot is automatically mailed to every eligible citizen, no request required. While there are no traditional Election-Day precincts, states do provide locations for voters to turn in ballots on Election Day. Five states—Oregon, Washington, Colorado, Hawaii, and Utah—conduct their elections this way.

It happens that the states with the most restrictive voting laws and procedures—no early voting, and an excuse required for absentee voting—are all located in the eastern half of the country. Constitutionally, states have also been permitted to decide whether to deny voting rights to voting-age citizens who have been convicted of felony crimes. There continue to be wide state-by-state disparities in felon disenfranchisement laws and procedures. For instance, some states allow currently incarcerated prisoners to vote, others permit convicted felons to vote once they have served their prison sentence, whereas yet others permanently disenfranchise convicted felons. The Sentencing Project estimates that nearly 6 million Americans cannot vote because of a felony conviction.

Source: National Conference of State Legislatures, "Voting Outside the Polling Place: Absentee, All-Mail and other Voting at Home Options" April 2020; National Conference of State Legislatures, "State Laws Governing Early Voting," August 2019; Jean Chung, "Felony Disenfranchisement: A Primer," The Sentencing Project, May 2016.

The most important changes in elections have been those that extended suffrage to women, African Americans, and 18-year-olds, and made mandatory the direct popular election of U.S. senators. The Fifteenth Amendment, adopted in 1870, said that the "right of citizens of the United States to vote shall not be denied or abridged by the United States or by any state on account of race, color, or previous condition of servitude." Reading those words today, one would assume they gave African Americans the right to vote. That is not what the Supreme Court of the 1870s thought they meant. By a series of decisions, it held that the Fifteenth Amendment did not necessarily confer the right to vote on anybody; it merely asserted that if someone was denied that right, the denial could not be explicitly on the grounds of race. And the burden of proving that it was race that led to the denial fell on the African American citizen who was turned away at the polls.[24]

This interpretation opened the door to three especially notorious but then-legal devices to keep African Americans from voting. One was a **literacy test** (a large proportion of former slaves were illiterate); another was a requirement that a **poll tax** be paid (most former slaves were poor); and the third was the practice of keeping African Americans from voting in primary elections (in the one-party South, the only meaningful election was the Democratic primary). To allow whites who were illiterate

literacy test *A requirement that citizens show that they can read before registering to vote.*

poll tax *A requirement that citizens pay a tax in order to register to vote.*

grandfather clause *A clause in registration laws allowing people who do not meet registration requirements to vote if they or their ancestors had voted before 1867.*

white primary *The practice of keeping African Americans from voting in the southern states' primaries through arbitrary use of registration requirements and intimidation.*

or poor to vote, a **grandfather clause** was added to the law, saying that a person could vote, even without meeting the legal requirements, if the person's ancestors voted before 1867 (African Americans, of course, could not vote before 1867). When all else failed, African Americans were intimidated, threatened, or harassed if they showed up at the polls.

There began a long, slow legal process of challenging in court each of these restrictions in turn. One by one, the Supreme Court set most of them aside. The grandfather clause was declared unconstitutional in 1915,[25] and the **white primary** finally fell in 1944.[26] Some of the more blatantly discriminatory literacy tests also were overturned.[27] The practical result of these rulings was slight: only a small proportion of voting-age African Americans were able to register and vote in the South, and they were found mostly in the larger cities. A dramatic change did not begin until 1965, with the passage of the Voting Rights Act. This act suspended the use of literacy tests, authorized the appointment of federal examiners who could order the registration of African Americans in states and counties (mostly in the South) where fewer than 50 percent of the voting-age population were registered or had voted in the last presidential election, and prevented areas with a history of racial discrimination from changing their voting rules without first obtaining permission from the federal government. It also provided criminal penalties for interfering with the right to vote.

Though implementation in some places was slow, the number of African Americans voting rose sharply throughout the South. For example, in Mississippi the proportion of voting-age African Americans who registered rose from 5 percent to over 70 percent from 1960 to 1970. These changes had a profound effect on the behavior of many white southern politicians, such as Alabama Governor George Wallace, who stopped making pro-segregation speeches and began courting the African American vote. The act also helped to elect more racial and ethnic minorities to office.[28]

In 2013, the Supreme Court made a significant change in the implementation of the Voting Rights Act with *Shelby County v. Holder*. The case challenged the way in which the federal government decided which states and

Expanding Voting: Majoritarian Politics

As we discussed in the text, in recent decades, a number of states have expanded access to the ballot. A few states now allow all-mail balloting, whereas others allow no excuse absentee balloting or early voting before Election Day (see the Constitutional Connections box on page 179 for more information). Such efforts to broaden access to the ballot are best thought of as majoritarian politics. Benefits are dispersed to all citizens from expanded access to the ballot, since it makes it easier for everyone to take part in elections. Citizens no longer need to go to a polling place on Election Day and stand in line to cast a ballot; rather, they can vote in a more convenient manner. However, as we noted in the body of the chapter, such reforms have done little to boost turnout.

At the same time, costs are dispersed among all voters as well. Voters who vote early may vote differently than voters who cast their ballot on Election Day. Those who vote early necessarily miss some of the campaign, and hence may have voted differently if important information comes out after they have cast their ballot. Furthermore, some have raised concerns about the security of vote by mail in particular (for both all-mail and absentee ballots). When voting in person, safeguards are in place to protect the integrity of the ballot, but many of them are gone when voting by mail, leading to the potential for abuse.

As is typically the case with majoritarian politics, the ultimate debate has come down to which side has the more compelling argument (since the costs and benefits are so widely dispersed). In the end, in most places, the arguments about increasing the ease of voting have carried the day. To respond to criticisms, some states have put in place systems to try and reduce fraud, though it is unclear how serious a problem it is or how to best stop it.

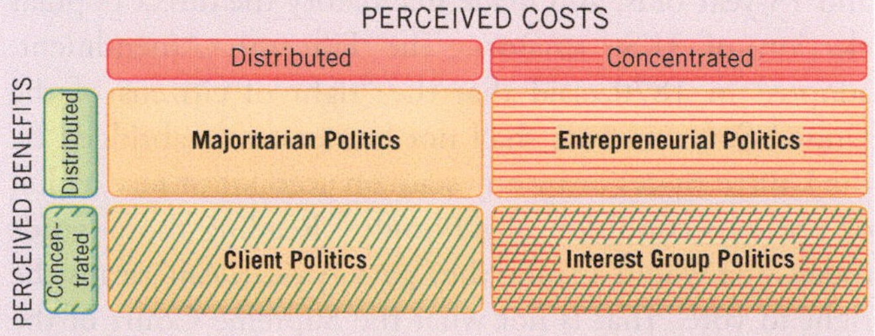

Sources: Adam Liptak, "Error and Fraud at Issue as Absentee Voting Rises," New York Times, 7 October, 2012.

localities needed to receive approval before changing their voting laws. The original rules were based on whether a state or locality had used discriminatory practices before the law's passage in 1965. The Court, in a 5-4 ruling, argued that the rules could no longer use historical practices, but needed to consider current patterns of discrimination. As a result, Congress would need to pass a new formula to decide which states are subject to these rules; so far, they have failed to do so. In a 2018 review, the U.S. Commission on Civil Rights, a bipartisan independent commission designed to investigate civil rights issues, argued that since this decision, many states—including those previously covered by the original formulas—have enacted laws that make it harder to vote.[29] The debate over the effects of this decision, and subsequent laws, will no doubt continue into the future.

Women were kept from the polls by law more than by intimidation, and when the laws changed, women almost immediately began to vote in large numbers. By 1915, several states, mostly in the West, had begun to permit women to vote. But it was not until the Nineteenth Amendment to the Constitution was ratified in 1920, after a struggle lasting many decades, that women generally were allowed to vote. At one stroke, the size of the eligible voting population almost doubled. Contrary to the hopes of some and the fears of others, no dramatic changes occurred in the conduct of elections, the identity of the winners, or the substance of public policy. Initially, at least, women voted more or less in the same manner as men, though not quite as frequently.

The political impact of the youth vote was also less than expected. The Voting Rights Act of 1970 gave 18-year-olds the right to vote in federal elections beginning January 1, 1971. It also contained a provision lowering the voting age to 18 in state elections, but the Supreme Court declared this unconstitutional. As a result, the Twenty-Sixth Amendment, which made the voting age 18 in all U.S. elections, was proposed by Congress and ratified by the states in 1971. The 1972 elections became the first in which all people between the ages of 18 and 21 could cast ballots (before then, four states had allowed those under 21 to vote). About 25 million people suddenly became eligible to participate in elections, but their turnout (42 percent) was lower than for the population as a whole, and they did not flock to any particular party or candidate.

Image 8.1 After the Civil Rights Act of 1964 was passed, African Americans and whites voted together in a small Alabama town.

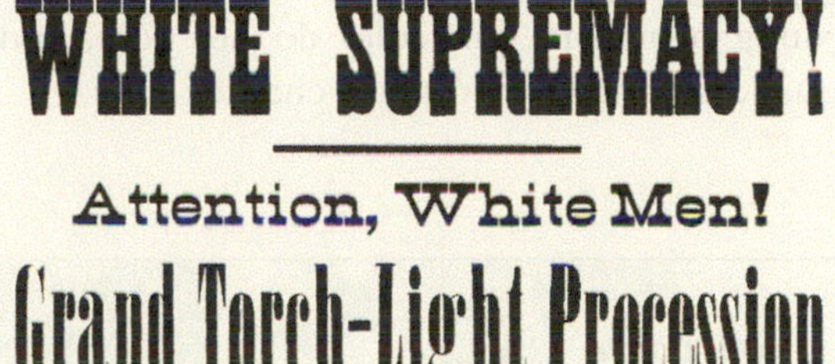

Image 8.2 After Reconstruction ended in 1876, black voting shrank under the attacks of white supremacists.

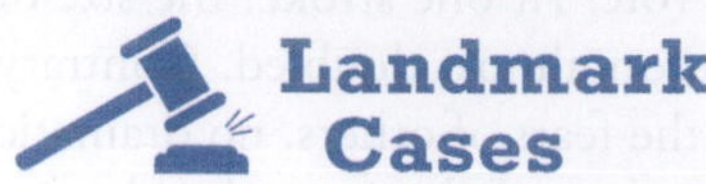

Landmark Cases | Right to Vote

- ***Smith v. Allwright* (1944):** Because political parties select candidates for public office, they may not exclude African Americans from voting in their primary elections.
- ***Shelby County v Holder* (2013):** Congress must consider present-day, rather than historical, discrimination when determining which states and localities require federal permission to change their voting laws.

Every presidential election year since 1972 has been accompanied by predictions that the "youth vote" is likely to surge. Such predictions were especially prevalent in 2008, when 23 million citizens under age 30, representing 52 percent of the 18-to 29-year-old voting population, voted. That was a higher fraction than in 1996 (37 percent), 2000 (41 percent), and 2004 (48 percent), but lower than 1972 (55 percent) and the same as 1992 (52 percent). Preliminary analyses of the 2020 election suggest that turnout increased to 53 percent among young people.[30] We return to the questions of why young people in particular do not vote, and the consequences of that, later in the chapter.

Image 8.3 The campaign to win the vote for women nationwide succeeded with the adoption of the Nineteenth Amendment in 1920.

Voter Turnout

The proportion of the voting-age population that has gone to the polls in presidential elections has remained about the same—between 50 and 63 percent of those eligible—at least since 1928, and appears today to be much smaller than it was in the latter part of the 19th century (see Figure 8.3). In every presidential election between 1860 and 1900, at least 70 percent of the eligible population apparently went to the polls, and in some years (1860 and 1876) almost 80 percent seem to have voted. Since 1900, in not a single presidential election has turnout reached 70 percent, and on two occasions (1920 and 1924), it did not even reach 50 percent.[31] Even outside the South, where efforts to disenfranchise African Americans make data on voter turnout especially hard to interpret, turnout seems to have declined: Over 85 percent of the voting-age population participated in presidential elections in non-Southern states between 1884 and 1900, but only 68 percent participated between 1936 and 1960, and even fewer have done so since then.[32]

Scholars have vigorously debated the meaning of these figures. One view is that this decline in turnout, even allowing for the shaky data on which the estimates are based, has been real and is the result of a decline of popular interest in elections and a weakening of the competitiveness of the two major parties. During the 19th century, according to this theory, the parties fought hard, worked strenuously to get as many voters as possible to the polls, afforded the mass of voters a chance to participate in party politics through caucuses and conventions, kept the legal barriers to participation (such as complex registration procedures) low, and looked forward to close, exciting elections. After 1896, by which time the South had become a one-party Democratic region and the North heavily Republican, both parties became more conservative, national elections usually resulted in lopsided victories for the Republicans, and citizens began to lose interest in politics because it no longer seemed relevant to their needs. The parties ceased functioning as organizations to mobilize the mass of voters and fell under the control of leaders, mostly conservative, who resisted mass participation.[33]

There is another view, however. It argues that the decline in voter turnout has been more apparent than real. Though elections were certainly more of a popular sport in the 19th century than they are today, the parties were no more democratic then than now, and voters then may have been more easily manipulated. Until around the beginning of the 20th century, voting fraud was commonplace because it was easy to pull off. The political parties, not the government, printed the ballots; they often were cast in public, not private, voting booths; few serious efforts were made to decide who was eligible to vote, and the rules that did operate were easily evaded.

Under these circumstances, it was easy for a person to vote more than once, and the party machines made heavy use of these repeat voters, or "floaters." "Vote early and often" was not a joke; it was a fact. The parties often controlled the counting of votes, padding the totals whenever they feared losing. As a result of these machinations, the number of votes counted was often larger than the number cast, and often the number cast was in turn larger than the number of individuals eligible to vote.

Around 1890, the states began adopting the **Australian ballot**. This was a government-printed ballot of uniform size and shape that was cast in secret, created to replace the old party-printed ballots cast in public. By 1910, only three states were without the Australian ballot. Its use cut back on (but certainly did not eliminate) vote buying and fraudulent vote counts.

In short, if votes had been legally cast and honestly counted in the 19th century, the statistics on election turnout might well be much lower than the inflated figures we now have.[34] To the extent that this is true, voter participation may not have declined as much as some have suggested. Nevertheless, most scholars believe that turnout probably did actually decline somewhat after the 1890s. One reason was that voter registration regulations became more burdensome: there were longer residency requirements; foreign nationals who had begun but not completed the process of becoming citizens could no longer vote in most states; it became harder for African Americans to vote; educational qualifications for voting were adopted by several states; and voters had to register long in advance of the elections. These changes, designed to "purify" the electoral process, were aspects of the progressive reform impulse (as described in Chapter 9) and served to cut back on the number of people who could participate in elections.

Australian ballot
A government-printed ballot of uniform dimensions to be cast in secret that many states adopted around 1890 to reduce voting fraud associated with party-printed ballots cast in public.

Figure 8.3 Voter Participation in Presidential Elections, 1860–2020

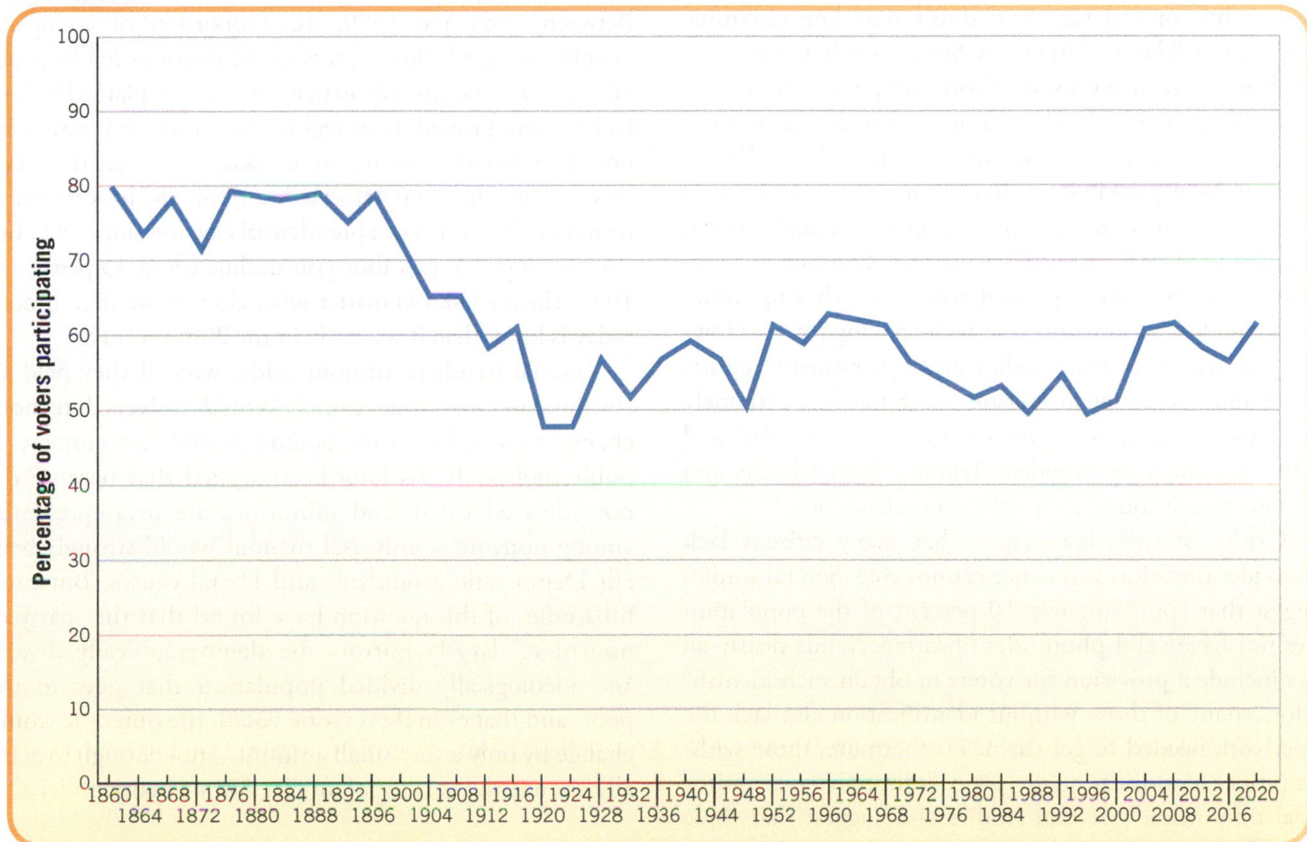

Note: Several southern states did not participate in the 1864 and 1868 elections.

Source: For 1860–1928: Bureau of the Census, *Historical Statistics of the United States, Colonial Times to 1970*, part 2, 1071; 1932–1944: *Statistical Abstract of the United States*, 1992, 517; for 1948–2000: Michael P. McDonald and Samuel L. Popkin, "The Myth of the Vanishing Voter," *American Political Science Review* 95 (December 2001): 966; for 2004–2012: American National Election Studies (ANES); for 2016 and onward: U.S. Election Project.

voter identification laws
Laws requiring citizens to show a government-issued photo ID in order to vote.

Strict voter registration procedures, like most reforms in American politics, had unintended as well as intended consequences. These changes not only reduced fraudulent voting but also reduced voting in general because they made it more difficult for certain groups of perfectly honest voters—those with little education, for example, or those who had recently moved—to register and vote. This was not the first time, and it will not be the last, that a reform designed to cure one problem created another.

Following the controversy over Florida's vote count in the 2000 presidential election, many proposals were made to overhaul the nation's voting system. In 2002, Congress passed the Help America Vote Act, which requires each state to have in place a system for counting the provisional (disputed) ballots of voters whose names were left off official registration lists. In addition, the law provides federal funds for upgrading voting equipment and procedures and for training election officials. But it stops short of creating a uniform national voting system. Paper ballots, lever machines, and punch-card voting systems will still be used in some places, while optical scan and direct recording electronic equipment will be used in others. Since then, however, there have been fewer such calls to reform voting technology.

In the past decade, the major legal challenge to voter laws has been the rise of **voter identification laws**. Thirty-six states have passed laws that require voters to show a government-issued photo identification to vote, and 35 such laws were in place for the 2020 election.[35] Proponents claim such laws are needed to prevent voter fraud (having someone pretend to be someone else at the polling place). However, numerous careful studies and government reports have found that such in-person voter fraud is extremely rare.[36] Indeed, despite claims of voter fraud in 2016 and 2020—including by President Trump—both scholars and election officials found essentially no evidence of it.[37]

Critics of such laws argue that many citizens lack photo identification and hence cannot vote: Several studies suggest that approximately 10 percent of the population does not have valid photo identification. While nearly all laws include a provision for voters to obtain such identification, many of those without identification also lack the paperwork needed to get them. Furthermore, those without proper identification are overwhelmingly poor and/or racial minorities.[38] Several studies also suggest that these voter ID laws may not be enforced uniformly: Minority voters are more likely to be asked to show an ID, even after relevant demographic factors are taken into account.[39]

Given this, many such laws have been challenged in court. While the Supreme Court ruled in 2008 that such laws are not necessarily unconstitutional,[40] subsequent court challenges have struck down some laws, while leaving others

Image 8.4 Supports of Donald Trump and Joe Biden attend a political event during the 2020 election.

intact, depending on the specifics of the law. There is no doubt there will continue to be legal challenges to these laws into the future. Regardless of their legal status, however, such laws do not seem to have much impact on overall turnout. The best evidence shows that if these laws affect aggregate turnout at all, they reduce it by at most a few percentage points.[41]

Even after all the legal changes are taken into account, citizen participation in elections seems to have declined. Between 1960 and 1980, the proportion of voting-age people casting a ballot in presidential elections fell by about 10 percentage points, a drop that cannot be explained by how ballots were printed, how registration rules were rewritten, nor the other changes reviewed above. Nor can these factors explain why 1996 witnessed not only the lowest level of turnout (49 percent) in a presidential election since 1924 but also the single steepest four-year decline (from 55 percent in 1992) since 1920. No matter what election we use, turnout today is lower than it was early in the 20th century.

Actual trends in turnout aside, what if they held an election and everyone came? Would universal turnout change national election outcomes and the content of public policy? It has long been argued that because the poor, less educated, and minorities are overrepresented among nonvoters, universal turnout would strongly benefit Democratic candidates and liberal causes. But careful studies of this question have found that the "party of nonvoters" largely mirrors the demographically diverse and ideologically divided population that goes to the polls, and that even if everyone voted, the outcome would change by only a very small amount—not enough to actually change the balance of an election or many policies.[42]

8-3 Who Participates in Politics?

To understand better why voter turnout declined and what, if anything, that decline may mean, we must first determine who participates in politics.

Forms of Participation

While voting is perhaps the quintessential form of political participation, citizens can be involved in the political process in many other ways. For example, people can be involved in a campaign: they can volunteer to staff a phone bank or participate in a get-out-the-vote drive, or they can write a check to a candidate or a party. They can also participate by attending community meetings; contacting public officials to direct their attention to a particular problem; working through an interest group; participating in a protest, demonstration, or social movement; and so forth. Some scholars argue that even purchasing decisions can be a form of political participation, such as when individuals buy or boycott products that support or oppose particular political causes.[43] When political scientists think of participation, we think of any method that citizens engage in to try to influence politics.

As we saw above approximately 50–60 percent of the public has voted in recent presidential elections. Other types of political participation are less common. For example, in most election years, approximately 20 percent display a yard sign, bumper sticker, or button; 15 percent give money to a candidate or party; 10 percent attend a political meeting or rally; and only 5 to 6 percent volunteer for a campaign or party. Such patterns have been quite consistent for more than 50 years, suggesting that it is not simply that today's citizens participate less than those of yesteryear.[44]

Such numbers perhaps should not surprise us: After all, political participation is a costly activity, requiring resources (time, money, and so forth) as well as interest in politics. That said, however, we should not conclude that Americans are not interested in their communities, as studies have found that Americans frequently participate in apolitical ways, for example, by volunteering with a religious or charitable organization. Furthermore, relative to citizens from other nations, Americans are more involved in politics and community affairs (even though fewer of us turn out to vote, as we saw in Table 8.1).[45]

In one study, scholars analyzed the ways in which people participate in politics and came up with six forms of participation that are characteristic of six different kinds of U.S. citizens. About one-fifth (22 percent) of the population is completely inactive: they rarely vote, they do not get involved in organizations, and they probably do not even talk about politics very much. These inactive citizens typically have little education and low incomes and are relatively young. Many are African American. At the opposite extreme are the complete **activists**, constituting about one-ninth of the population (11 percent). These people are highly educated, have high incomes, and tend to be middle-aged rather than young or old. They tend to participate in all forms of politics.

activists *People who tend to participate in all forms of politics.*

Between these extremes are four categories of limited forms of participation. The *voting specialists* are people who vote but do little else; they tend not to have much schooling or income and to be substantially older than the average person. *Campaigners* not only vote but also like to get involved in campaign activities. They are better educated than the average voter, but what seems to distinguish them most is their interest in the conflicts, passions, and struggles of politics; their clear identification with a political party; and their willingness to take strong positions. *Communalists* have a social background much like that of campaigners but have a very different temperament: They do not like the conflict and tension of partisan campaigns. They tend to reserve their energy for community activities of a more nonpartisan nature, forming and joining organizations to deal with local problems and contacting local officials about these problems. Finally, there are *parochial participants,* who do not vote and stay out of election campaigns and civic associations but are willing to contact local officials about specific, often personal, problems.[46]

What Drives Participation?

But who participates in politics? The characterizations above suggest that some people are deeply involved, whereas others are content to sit on the political sidelines. What groups actually participate most in elections? Figure 8.4 shows what percentages of various demographic groups voted in several recent presidential elections.

Several interesting patterns immediately jump out. First, education has an enormous effect on voter turnout: Those who have more education are much more likely to participate in politics, and the same is true of those who are employed. Likewise, while there are effectively no black–white differences in turnout, we find large effects for Hispanics, who are more than 20 percent less likely to vote. Why do these differences occur? Political scientists have identified many factors that increase political participation; here we focus on several of the most important.

Chip Somodevilla/Getty Images News/Getty Images

Image 8.5 During the COVID-19 pandemic, many citizens volunteered to help those affected by virus and the subsequent economic slowdown.

Figure 8.4 **Voter Turnout in Presidential Elections by Schooling, Employment, and Race, 2004–2016**

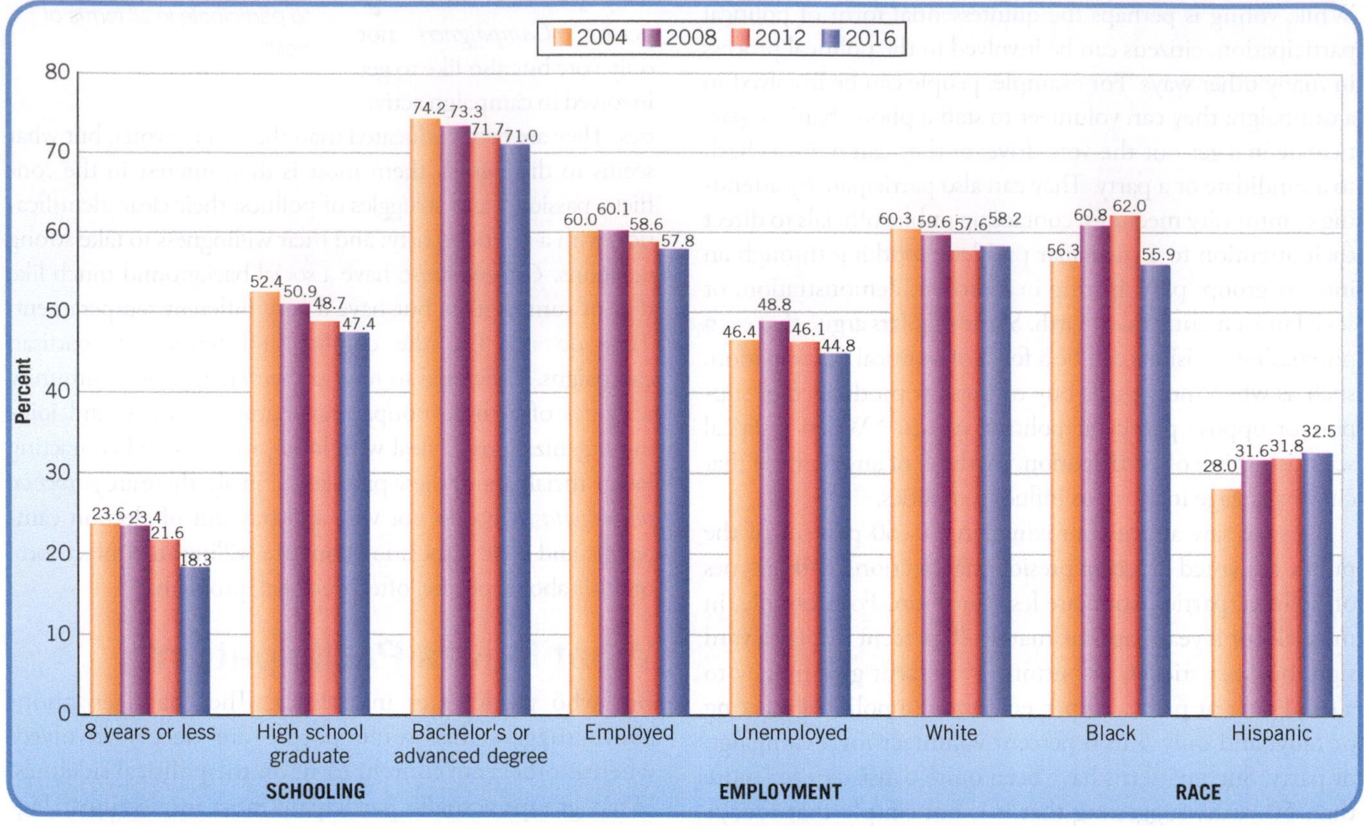

Source: Adapted from U.S. Bureau of the Census, Historical CPS Time Series Tables.

First, and perhaps most importantly, citizens need the resources necessary to participate in politics, which include factors such as time, money, and civic skills. Time is an obvious prerequisite to participating in politics: If you do not have the free time to be politically active, you cannot participate. Likewise, if you are going to donate to a campaign, you need the financial resources to make the contribution. With more money, you can also afford to have a stable residence and avoid the need to reregister because you changed your address. Finally, civic skills are the communication and organization abilities that help people participate in politics. These include factors such as comfort with public speaking, experience organizing meetings, the ability to speak and understand English (and American politics/culture), and so forth. So if you are a strong public speaker, can write well, and frequently organize people into meetings (setting the agenda, running the meeting, etc.), then you may find it easier to do these tasks in politics as well.[47] Resources are, in effect, the "raw ingredients" of political participation; without these background characteristics, it is difficult to participate.

Differences in resources help to explain differences across these groups, especially with factors such as employment and education. Those with more education (or who are employed) have more of the resources necessary to participate in politics. For example, those with more education have higher levels of civic skills, and they typically have higher incomes as well. Likewise, those who are employed have the opportunity to develop civic skills (running meetings, being organized, etc.) through their jobs. As a result, these groups participate more.

Differences in resources also help to explain why voting-eligible Hispanics participate at lower levels than voting-eligible whites or African Americans. Scholars have found that once they adjust for relevant resource-related factors (such as age, education, residential mobility, income, and employment), the gaps become smaller.[48]

Steve Cukrov/Alamy Stock Photo

Image 8.6 Young people attend a rally in support of Senator Bernie Sanders during the 2020 Democratic Primary.

For example, some Hispanics have limited English proficiency, which is often a barrier to participating in politics. Likewise, those who are second-or third-generation Latinos—those who grew up in America and hence are more familiar with American culture and politics, and who have family members who already vote in America—are more likely to participate. Put slightly differently, Hispanic citizens tend to have fewer political resources than other Americans, but conditional on that, their participation is similar to that of other groups.[49]

But resources alone do not explain who participates in politics. After all, some people with advanced degrees always vote, while others never come to the polls. Resources are only a start in fully understanding participation. Engagement with politics also matters. To participate, you must believe your voice matters in the political process, and you have to be interested in politics. Absent these, you are unlikely to participate, no matter what your level of resources.[50]

This interest in politics can come from many places, but schools are a particularly important source. Education helps foster civic norms in students, and helps them realize that their participation in government matters. Such effects are especially strong among those who take government and/or civics classes, where they are instilled with the importance of political participation. As a result, these individuals participate more later in life.[51] Thus education increases participation in two ways: by providing civic skills and by increasing political interest. Given this, education is one of the most important pathways to participation in America.

Third, for many people, being mobilized is a key step to participation: When asked why they participated, many politically active citizens said they did so because they were asked.[52] We saw above that political parties and campaigns (via get-out-the-vote efforts) are key mobilizing factors in contemporary elections. But so too are other organizations. For example, it has long been noted that more religious citizens are more likely to participate in politics. Scholars have found that the reason why is that churches foster social networks that encourage participation. Many people at a place of worship are involved in their community more broadly, and they encourage their friends there to participate politically as well. As a result, more religious people participate more not because of resources, but because of mobilization.[53] Likewise, churches have provided a valuable mechanism for bringing Latino voters into the political system.[54] Such mobilization also takes place through the Kiwanis Club, a bowling league, or even just among friends.

Mobilization becomes even more important when we realize that participation is habit-forming. Those who are mobilized by a get-out-the-vote message in one election are more likely to vote in future elections, even without receiving another get-out-the-vote message.[55] Likewise, young voters who participate in one election are more likely to participate in future elections,[56] and, more generally, for most citizens, voting is a habit: Once they begin to vote, they are likely to continue, as with any habit.[57] Being mobilized in one election can have important spillover consequences for future elections as well.

Fourth, some people become politically active because they care deeply about a particular issue. For example, they may be upset at drug dealers using a corner park in their neighborhood and organize a local neighborhood watch, partnering with the police to drive the drug dealers out. In so doing, they learn valuable skills about how to organize their neighbors, how to work with local officials, and so forth. These skills are directly transferable to other types of political participation. Indeed, many who first become involved with politics or community life because of a particular issue often then become more broadly politically involved.[58] Such pathways to participation are especially important for those who lack the types of political resources discussed above. Lacking resources, passion and motivation can inspire some voters to participate.

Finally, experiences with government programs can also shape political participation. For example, before the creation of the Social Security program, senior citizens participated far less than other Americans, but today, seniors are among the most politically involved Americans. Why did Social Security increase participation among the aged? The program gave seniors income security and meant that many of them no longer had to work. This gave them free time to become politically engaged, and they focused much of their attention on the program most directly relevant to their lives: Social Security. Seniors, in the wake of the program's passage, became more involved in politics and argued on behalf of the program, thereby strengthening it. Thus citizens create programs (by participating in government), but programs also create citizens by giving them valuable political skills.[59]

Political Participation Among Young People

Above, we saw how some groups participate more, while others participate less. One of the most striking inequalities in participation occurs with respect to age. Older voters are more likely to be registered to vote and are more likely to actually show up to the polls on Election Day. For example, in midterm and presidential elections alike, Americans ages 18 to 24 register at much lower rates and also fail to vote at much higher rates than do Americans age 65 and older, as we see in Figure 8.5. Even in 2018, which had high turnout for young people in a midterm election (32.4 percent), their turnout still lagged behind the participation of senior citizens (66.1 percent).

Yet while young people participate much less in politics, they are no less engaged with their communities than older voters. What explains this disconnect? Why do young people eschew politics but not community and civic life more generally? These younger voters think community service is important, but they do not feel the same way about politics. They are more cynical about politics, and many think that political participation does not matter.[60]

Does this lower youth political participation matter? Some argue that it does not. They say that younger voters traditionally have voted at lower levels and, over time, as these voters mature, they will participate more, as their parents and grandparents did. But even if this is true, there is still an important reason to be concerned with low levels of youth turnout and participation. Quite simply, politicians respond to those who vote far more than those who do not. Above, we saw the example that Social Security helped senior citizens become more involved with politics by providing them with political skills and resources. And as seniors became more involved, the government strengthened Social Security. But it is critical to note this second step: Government responded because seniors were politically involved. Governments are generally responsive to public opinion (as we saw in Chapter 7), but they are particularly responsive to those who participate more. So, to the extent that younger people do not vote or participate in politics, politicians have less incentive to respond to their concerns. Therefore programs that largely benefit young people—things like expanded Pell grants and student loan debt relief—receive less attention from policymakers than they likely would if young people voted at the same level as senior citizens. If you want government to respond to your demands, you must take part in the political process.

Figure 8.5 **Voter Registration and Turnout by Age**

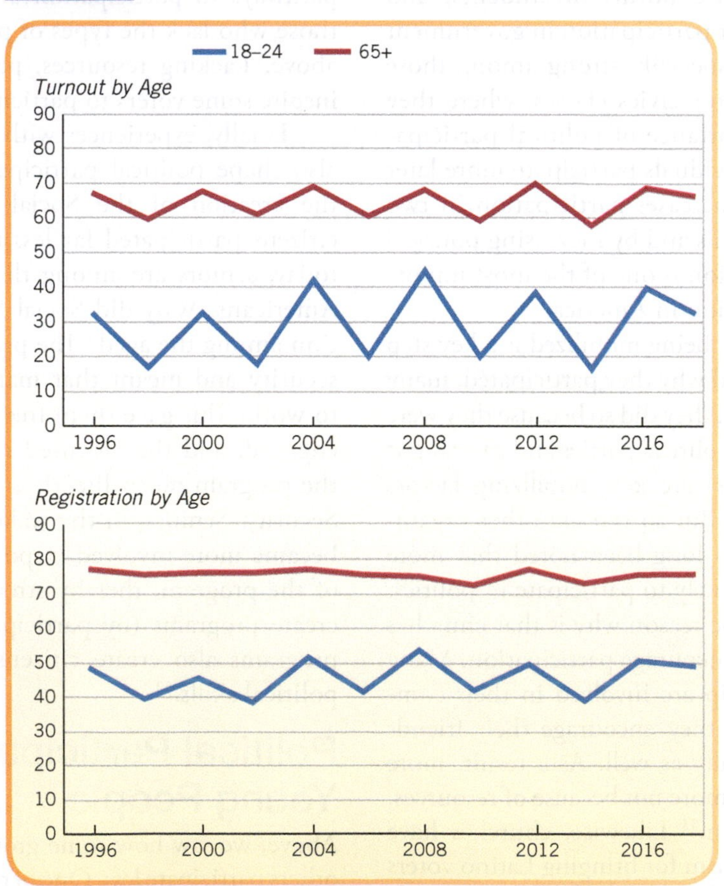

Source: Adapted from U.S. Bureau of the Census, Historical CPS Time Series Tables, Table A-1, Reported Voting and Registration by Race, Hispanic Origin, Sex, and Age Groups, 1964–2018

Compare the differences between youth and senior citizen voter turnout. Why does young people's participation vary more? What factors might explain these differences?

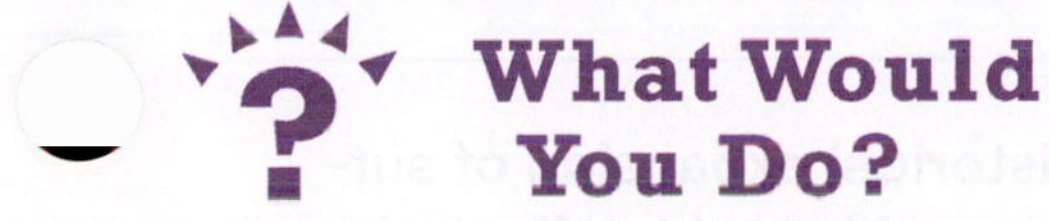

Will You Make Election Day a Holiday?

To: *Senator Lily Jae Lucy*
From: *Luke Brian, legislative analyst*
Subject: *Voting reform legislation*

In recent years, only 6 in 10 Americans voted in presidential elections, and only a third or so cast ballots for congressional elections. In a few recent presidential primaries and statewide special elections, turnout has run 10 percent or less. Studies show that often citizens miss the opportunity to vote because of complications with work or child care. To address this problem, legislators from both parties support celebrating Veterans Day on Election Day, which would create a national holiday for voting. Eligible voters who do not go to the polls would be fined.

To Consider:

With bipartisan concern about maximizing voter turnout for upcoming elections, both the House and the Senate are considering bills to combine Veterans Day with Election Day and/or impose fines on nonvoters. Members of Congress declare that increasing turnout is vital to the continued health of American democracy.

Arguments for:

1. This proposal honors veterans by recognizing their service with the fundamental requirement of representative democracy, rule by the people through voting.
2. A voting holiday ensures that people who cannot take time off from work to vote or have other responsibilities have the opportunity to exercise their democratic right.
3. Imposing a fine for nonvoting sends a moral message that voting is a civic duty in a democracy. More citizens will feel morally obliged to vote if all citizens are legally obliged to do so.

Arguments against:

1. Just as veterans volunteer their service, so too should citizens volunteer to exercise their democratic responsibilities.
2. Voting is a right, but citizens have a civic duty to exercise that right, and the government should not, in effect, exercise that duty on their behalf. Moreover, people can vote by absentee ballot at their convenience.
3. Compulsory voting does not guarantee informed voting. It is both unwise and undemocratic to legally oblige people to vote.

What Will You Decide? Enter **MindTap** to make your choice.

Your decision: ☐ Vote for bill ☐ Vote against bill

Learning Objectives

8-1 Discuss how American voter turnout compares to other advanced industrialized democracies.

American voter turnout is generally lower than in other advanced industrialized democracies. But it is important to note that American elections differ from their European counterparts across many dimensions. Americans elect far more officials, have far more frequent elections, and are required to register to vote (rather than being automatically enrolled). Efforts to increase registration, such as the motor-voter law, have gotten more names onto the voting rolls, but often these new additions do not vote as frequently as other registered voters. Most states now permit people to vote early, as an absentee, and by mail, but neither these measures, nor various "get-out-the-vote" tactics, have yet been shown to increase voter turnout in ways that result in most eligible citizens voting in most elections.

8-2 Describe the historical expansion of suffrage in America and how this affected voter participation.

Initially, only white male property holders could vote, but over time, those barriers were lifted. Today, nearly all citizens can vote, though there have been heated debates in recent years about voter identification laws.

8-3 Outline what factors explain who participates in politics.

Many factors determine participation, but we identified several key ones: having the resources (such as time, income, and civic skills), being psychologically engaged with politics, being mobilized, being motivated, and having experiences with government programs.

To Learn More

Information for voters:

Registering to Vote: **www.vote.gov**

National Mail Voter Registration Form: **https://www.eac.gov/voters/national-mail-voter-registration-form**

League of Women Voters: **www.lwv.org**

Voter Information Services: **www.vis.org**

Issues on the Ballot: **www.vote411.org**

Voter turnout statistics: **www.electproject.org**

Burnham Walter Dean. *Critical Elections and the Mainsprings of American Politics.* New York: Norton, 1970. A classic argument about the decline of voter participation, linking it to changes in the economic system.

Eisner, Jane. *Taking Back the Vote: Getting American Youth Involved in Our Democracy*. Boston: Beacon Press, 2004. Highly readable account of why young Americans volunteer a lot but vote little, with recommendations for getting young people more interested in politics.

Green, Donald P., and Alan S. Gerber. *Get Out the Vote: How to Increase Voter Turnout,* 4th ed. Washington, D.C.: Brookings Institution Press, 2019. Excellent review of the evidence on what works—and what doesn't—to get more people to the polls.

D. Sunshine Hillygus and John Holbein. *Making Young Voters: Converting Civic Attitudes into Civic Action*. New York: Cambridge University Press, 2020. An argument that non-cognitive skills, such as grit and fortitude, are crucial to turnout, especially among young people.

Niemi, Richard, Herbert F. Weisberg, and David C. Kimball, eds. *Controversies in Voting Behavior,* 5th ed. Washington, D.C.: Congressional Quarterly Press, 2010. Essays on voting and related topics that summarize the most advanced empirical research and offer competing perspectives on what the data show.

Shaw, Daron and John Petrocik. *The Turnout Myth: Voting Rates and Partisan Outcomes in American National Elections*. New York: Oxford University Press, 2020. Argues that high voter turnout does not systematically favor one party or the other.

Verba, Sidney, Norman H. Nie, and Jae-on Kim. *Participation and Political Equality*. Cambridge, England: Cambridge University Press, 1978. Classic comparative study of political participation in seven nations.

Wattenberg, Martin P. *Is Voting for Young People?* 4th ed. New York: Pearson, 2015. An account of why youth voter turnout in America has been so low and a case for compulsory voting.

CHAPTER 9

Political Parties

Learning Objectives

9-1 Describe the roles of American political parties and how they differ from parties in other democracies.

9-2 Summarize the historical evolution of the party system in America.

9-3 Explain the major functions of political parties.

9-4 Explain how parties are organized in America.

9-5 Define partisan identification, and explain how it shapes the political behavior of ordinary Americans.

9-6 Summarize the arguments for why America has a two-party system.

political party *A group that seeks to elect candidates to public office.*

In recent years, partisan control of the elected branches of government has flipped back and forth between the two major political parties. In 2006, Democrats had reason to smile. They won control of the House and the Senate that year, and then they achieved unified government after Barack Obama won the 2008 presidential election. Democrats were less happy in 2010 when Republicans won back control of the House; Republicans would later win back control of the Senate in 2014. In 2016, it was Republicans who were smiling, when Donald Trump's surprise victory in the presidential election gave Republicans unified control of government for the first time since the George W. Bush administration. In 2018, Democrats retook the House of Representatives, returning the country once again to a state of divided government. Divided government is also likely in the 117th Congress: while Joe Biden won the presidency, Republicans will remain in control of the Senate unless Democrats win both run-off elections in Georgia in early January 2021.

With all of these shifts in party control, you might think that voters' underlying party loyalties also shifted a great deal, but you would be wrong. Over this period, party loyalty among voters stayed basically the same. For instance, in the spring of 2020, Gallup polls found that about 30 percent of voters self-identified as Republicans, 38 percent as Independents, and 30 percent as Democrats. This is basically the same breakdown that existed 14 years earlier under the Bush administration.[1] As we will see later in the chapter, partisan identities remain quite stable over time, even if the party in control of the presidency or Congress changes more frequently.

Today, parties are central to the way we think about politics in the United States. But this is far from inevitable: the very existence and endurance of political parties in the United States is significant, given how the Framers of the Constitution opposed them.

« Then The Founders disliked parties, thinking of them as "factions" motivated by ambition and self-interest. George Washington, dismayed by the quarreling between Alexander Hamilton and Thomas Jefferson in his cabinet, devoted much of his farewell address to condemning parties. Indeed, in that address, Washington remarked: "the common and continual mischiefs of the spirit of party are sufficient to make it the interest and duty of a wise people to discourage and restrain it. It serves always to distract the public councils and enfeeble the public administration. It agitates the community with ill-founded jealousies and false alarms, kindles the animosity of one part against another, foments occasionally riot and insurrection."[2] Clearly, Washington viewed parties with a deep and abiding disdain.

This hostility toward parties was understandable: the legitimacy and success of the newly created federal government were still very much in doubt. When Jefferson organized his followers to oppose Hamilton's policies, it seemed to Hamilton and his followers that Jefferson was opposing not just a policy or a leader but also the very concept of a national government. Jefferson, for his part, thought Hamilton was not simply pursuing bad policies but was subverting the Constitution itself. Before political parties could become legitimate, it was necessary for people to separate in their minds quarrels over policies and elections from disputes over the legitimacy of the new government itself. The ability to make that distinction was slow in coming; thus, parties were objects of profound suspicion, at first defended only as temporary expedients.

*** Now** American political parties are the oldest in the world, dating back to the first decade of the republic. In the late 20th century, many claimed they were in decline, but today they have resurged in many ways. New parties and affiliated movements (like the Green Party launched in 2000 by consumer advocate Ralph Nader, or the Tea Party movement that emerged in 2009) may come and go, but two parties, the Democratic and Republican, still dominate the country's campaigns and elections. Nor have party leaders been replaced by media consultants, pollsters, or others whose profession is raising money or devising strategies for whichever candidates bid highest for their services. What distinguishes political parties from other groups, and why are they a fundamental feature of American politics? This chapter aims to explain what parties are, what they do, and why they have remained such an important part of American politics for over 200 years.

9-1 What Is a Party?

A **political party** is a group that seeks to elect candidates to public office by supplying them with a label—a "party identification"—by which they are known to the electorate.[3] This definition is purposefully broad so that it includes both familiar parties (Democratic and Republican) and unfamiliar ones (Whig, Libertarian, and Socialist Workers) and covers periods in which a party is very strong (having an elaborate and well-disciplined organization that provides money and workers to its candidates) as well as periods in which it is quite weak (supplying nothing but the label to candidates).

Political scientists think of parties as having three parts. A party exists as an *organization* that recruits and campaigns for candidates, as a *label* in the minds of voters, and as a *set of leaders* who try to organize and control the legislative and executive branches of government.[4] Parties help candidates get elected (by nominating and recruiting candidates, and then giving signals to voters about which candidates to support), and then organize and run government once they are in office.

First, parties recruit and support candidates in elections. Party leaders work to find potential candidates and recruit them to run for office, and then help them win the party's nomination. They then help these candidates raise money, conduct polls and focus groups, and develop advertisements to win the general election as well.

Second, parties exist in the heads of voters. When Americans walk into a polling place, many of them identify as either a Democrat or a Republican. As we will see later in the chapter, this label—whether voters consider themselves Democrats or Republicans—powerfully shapes how they evaluate political leaders, how they vote in elections, and even how they perceive the political world.

Third, parties coordinate behavior among elite politicians in office. As we will see in Chapter 13, the majority party in the House and the Senate has the responsibility of organizing the chamber. Furthermore, party leaders in Congress work with the president to try to enact a legislative agenda. Sometimes, the president and congressional parties are in near-complete agreement on an issue. For example, nearly all Democrats supported—and nearly all Republicans opposed—the Affordable Care Act when it was passed in 2010. In 2019, we saw similarly high levels of party unity when the House of Representatives voted to impeach President Trump and when he was acquitted in the Senate. Indeed, only one Senate Republican—Utah's Mitt Romney—voted in favor of either article of impeachment. But at other times, the president and the party diverge greatly on what they want. For example, both parties have been divided internally in recent years about whether to expand free trade, and several prominent Republican defections killed the effort to repeal the Affordable Care Act in 2017.

In this chapter, we discuss the first two dimensions of party politics: how parties help elect candidates and how they shape the behavior of ordinary voters. We defer the third aspect of parties—parties as coordination devices among elected politicians—to later chapters (see especially Chapter 13 on Congress and Chapter 14 on the presidency).

What makes a party powerful? A powerful party is one whose label has a strong appeal for voters, whose organization can decide who will be candidates and how their campaigns will be managed, and whose leaders can dominate one or all branches of government. In the late 19th century, political parties in America reached their zenith in all three areas: voters were very loyal to their parties (largely because of patronage and other factors), party leaders dominated the Congress, and party bosses controlled who ran for office. In the 20th century, parties weakened considerably along all three dimensions. But in more recent decades, parties have regained some of their strength, though they are not as powerful as they were in the 19th century. As we will see throughout this chapter, the reasons for the decay and resurgence of parties are deeply rooted in political factors.

Political Parties at Home and Abroad

While American parties have been weaker or stronger over time, in general, they have been weaker than parties in many other advanced industrialized democracies, especially parliamentary democracies. Several important reasons account for this disparity in power.

First, in many other systems, parties control access to the ballot. In the great majority of American states, the party leaders do not select people to run for office; by law, those people are chosen by the voters in primary elections. Though sometimes the party can influence who will win a primary contest, it is ultimately up to the voters to decide. In Europe, by contrast, there is no such thing as a primary election—the only way to become a candidate for office is to persuade party leaders to put your name on the ballot. This obviously gives party leaders much more sway over their members: if ordinary members get out of line, the party can threaten to remove their name from the ballot in the next election.

Second, in a parliamentary system, the legislative and executive branches are unified, rather than divided as they are in America. If an American political party wins control of Congress, it does not—as in most European nations with a parliamentary system of government—also win the right to select the chief executive of the government. The American president, as we have seen, is independently elected; this means that the president will choose principal subordinates not from among members of Congress but from among persons outside of Congress. Should the president pick a representative or senator for the cabinet, the Constitution requires that person to resign from Congress in order to accept the job. Thus, an opportunity to be a cabinet secretary is not an important reward for members of Congress, and so the president cannot use the prospect of that reward as a way of controlling congressional action, as the prime minister could in a parliamentary system.

Guillaume Destombes/Shutterstock.com

Image 9.1 Eleven candidates competed in the first round of the 2017 French presidential election. France, like many European countries, has a multi-party system, rather than a two-party system like the United States.

Third, the federal system of government in the United States decentralizes political authority and thus decentralizes political party organizations. For nearly two centuries, most important governmental decisions were made at the state and local levels—decisions regarding education, land use, business regulation, and public welfare—and thus it was at the state and local levels that the important struggles over power and policy occurred. Moreover, most people with political jobs—either elective or appointive—worked for state and local governments, and thus a party's interest in obtaining these jobs for its followers meant it had to focus attention on who controlled city hall, the county courthouse, and the state capitol. While power has increasingly been concentrated in Washington, D.C., many important decisions are still made at the state and local levels.

Federalism, in short, meant American political parties would acquire jobs and money from local sources and fight local contests. This, in turn, meant the national political parties would be coalitions of local parties, and though these coalitions would have a keen interest in capturing the presidency (with it, after all, came control of large numbers of federal jobs), the national party leaders rarely had as much power as the local ones. The Republican leader of Cuyahoga County, Ohio, for example, could often ignore the decisions of the Republican national chair and even the Ohio state chair. All of these factors help explain why American parties are (generally) weaker than parties in other nations.

9-2 The Rise and Decline of the Political Party

Our nation began without parties and, over time, their power has waxed and waned. Today, while parties are powerful in some respects, they are weaker in others. We can see this process in five broad periods of party history: (1) when political parties were created (roughly from the Founding to the 1820s); (2) when the more or less stable two-party system emerged (roughly from the time of President Andrew Jackson to the Civil War); (3) when parties developed a comprehensive organizational form and appeal (roughly from the Civil War to the 1930s); (4) when party "reform" began to alter the party system (beginning in the early 1900s but taking effect chiefly from the New Deal until the late 1960s); and (5) the period of polarization and resurgence (from the late 1960s through to today).

The Founding

The first organized political party in American history was made up of the followers of Thomas Jefferson, who, beginning in the 1790s, called themselves *Republicans* (hoping to suggest thereby that their opponents were secret monarchists).* The followers of Alexander Hamilton kept the label *Federalist*, which once referred to all supporters of the new Constitution (hoping to imply that their opponents were "Antifederalists," or enemies of the Constitution).

These early parties were loose caucuses of political notables in various localities, with New England strongly Federalist and much of the South passionately Republican. Jefferson and his ally James Madison thought their Republican Party was a temporary arrangement designed to defeat John Adams, a Federalist, in his bid to succeed Washington in 1796. (Adams narrowly defeated Jefferson, who, under the system then in effect, became vice president because he had the second most electoral votes.) In 1800, Adams's bid to succeed himself intensified party activity even more, but this time Jefferson won and the Republicans assumed office. The Federalists feared that Jefferson would dismantle the Constitution, but Jefferson adopted a conciliatory posture, saying in his inaugural address that "we are all Republicans, we are all Federalists."[5] It was not true, of course: the Federalists detested Jefferson, and some were planning to have New England secede from the Union. But it was good politics, expressive of the need that every president has to persuade the public that, despite partisan politics, the presidency exists to serve all the people.

So successful were the Republicans that the Federalists virtually ceased to exist as a party. Jefferson was reelected in 1804 with almost no opposition; Madison easily won two terms; James Monroe carried 16 of 19 states in 1816 and was reelected without opposition in 1820. Political parties had seemingly disappeared, just as Jefferson had hoped. The parties that existed in these early years were essentially small groups of local notables. Political participation was limited, and nominations for most local offices were arranged rather casually.

*The Jeffersonian Republicans were not the party that today we call Republican. In fact, present-day Democrats consider Jefferson to be the founder of their party; see Figure 9.1 for more on the evolution of the parties over time.

The Jacksonians

What often is called the second party system emerged around 1824 with Andrew Jackson's first run for the presidency and lasted until the Civil War became inevitable. Its distinctive feature was that political participation became a mass phenomenon. For one thing, the number of voters to be reached had become quite large. Only about 365,000 popular votes were cast in 1824. But as a result of laws that enlarged the number of people eligible to vote and an increase in the population, by 1828 well over a million votes were tallied. By 1840, the figure was well over 2 million. (In England at this time, there were only 650,000 eligible voters.) In addition, by 1832 presidential electors were selected by popular vote in virtually every state. (As late as 1816, electors were chosen by the state legislatures, rather than by the people, in about half the states.) Presidential politics had become a truly national, genuinely popular activity; in many communities, election campaigns had become the principal public spectacle.

The party system of the Jacksonian era was built from the bottom up rather than from the top down, as it had been since the Founding. No change better illustrates this transformation than the abandonment of the system of having caucuses comprising members of Congress nominate presidential candidates. The caucus system was an effort to unite the legislative and executive branches by giving the former some degree of control over who would have a chance to capture the latter. The caucus system became unpopular when the caucus candidate for president in 1824 ran third in a field of four in the general election. It was completely discredited that same year when Congress denied the presidency to Jackson, the candidate with the greatest share of the popular vote.

To replace the caucus, the party convention was invented. The first convention in American history was held by the Anti-Masonic Party in 1831; the first convention of a major political party was held by the anti-Jackson Republicans later that year (it nominated Henry Clay for president). The Democrats held a convention in 1832 that ratified Jackson's nomination for reelection and picked Martin Van Buren as his running mate. The first convention to select a man who would be elected president and who was not already the incumbent president was held by the Democrats in 1836; they chose Van Buren.

The Civil War and Sectionalism

Though the party system created in the Jacksonian period was the first truly national system, with Democrats (followers of Jackson) and Whigs (opponents of Jackson) fairly evenly balanced in most regions, it could not withstand the deep split in opinion created by the agitation over slavery. Both parties tried, naturally, to straddle the issue, since neither wanted to divide its followers and thus lose the election to its rival. But slavery and sectionalism were issues that could not be straddled. The old parties divided and new ones emerged. The modern Republican Party (not the old Democratic-Republican Party of Thomas Jefferson) began as a third party. As a result of the Civil War, it became a major party (the only third party ever to gain major-party status) and dominated national politics, with only occasional interruptions, for three-quarters of a century.

Republican control of the White House, and to a lesser extent Congress, was in large measure the result of two events that gave to Republicans a marked advantage in the competition for the loyalties of voters. The first of these was the Civil War. This bitter, searing crisis deeply polarized popular attitudes. Those who supported the Union became Republicans for generations; those who supported the Confederacy, or who had opposed the war, became Democrats.

"The Spirit of Party"

Noted historian Richard Hofstadter wrote about the Constitution as "A Constitution against Parties." That was the title Hofstadter gave to the second chapter of his 1969 book, *The Idea of a Party System: The Rise of Legitimate Opposition in the United States, 1780–1840.* For the republic's first half-century, most national leaders did not accept the idea that parties were a necessary and desirable feature of American government. For example, near the end of his second term as president, George Washington wrote a letter that later became known as his "Farewell Address." It reads in part:

Let me now take a more comprehensive view, and warn you in the most solemn manner against the baneful effects of the spirit of party generally. This Spirit, unfortunately, is inseparable from our nature, having its root in the strongest passions of the human mind. . . . The alternate domination of one faction over another, sharpened by the spirit of revenge natural to party dissension . . . is itself a frightful despotism. . . . [The] common and continual mischiefs of the spirit of party are sufficient to make it the interest and the duty of a wise people to discourage and restrain it.

Image 9.2 When Andrew Jackson ran for president in 1828, more than a million votes were cast for the first time in American history. This poster, from the 1832 election, was part of the emergence of truly mass political participation.

mugwumps *or* **progressives** *Republican Party faction of the 1890s to the 1910s, comprising reformers who opposed patronage.*

As it turned out, this partisan division was nearly even for a while: Though the Republicans usually won the presidency and the Senate, they often lost control of the House. There were many northern Democrats. In 1896, however, another event—the presidential candidacy of William Jennings Bryan—further strengthened the Republican Party. Bryan, a Democrat, alienated many voters in the populous northeastern states while attracting voters in the South and Midwest. The result was to confirm and deepen the split in the country, especially North versus South, begun by the Civil War. From 1896 to the 1930s, with rare exceptions, northern states were solidly Republican, southern ones solidly Democratic.

This split had a profound effect on the organization of political parties, for it meant that most states were now one-party states. As a result, competition for office at the state level had to go on *within* a single dominant party (the Republican Party in Massachusetts, New York, Pennsylvania, Wisconsin, and elsewhere; the Democratic Party in Georgia, Mississippi, South Carolina, and elsewhere). Consequently, there emerged two major factions within each party, but especially within the Republican Party. One comprised the party regulars—the professional politicians, the "stalwarts," the Old Guard. They were preoccupied with building up the party machinery, developing party loyalty, and acquiring and dispensing patronage—jobs and other favors—for themselves and their faithful followers. Their great skills were in organization, negotiation, bargaining, and compromise; their great interest was in winning.

The other faction, variously called **mugwumps** or **progressives** (or "reformers"), was opposed to the heavy emphasis on patronage; disliked the party machinery because it permitted only bland candidates to rise to the top; was fearful of the heavy influx of immigrants into American cities and of the ability of the party regulars to organize them into "machines"; and wanted to see the party take unpopular positions on certain issues (such as free trade). Their great skills lay in the areas of advocacy and articulation; their great interest was in principle.

At first the mugwumps tried to play a balance-of-power role, sometimes siding with the Republican Party (of which they were members), at other times defecting to the Democrats (as when they bolted from the Republican Party to support Grover Cleveland, the Democratic nominee, in 1884). But later, as the Republican strength grew throughout the nation, progressives within that party became increasingly less able to play a balance-of-power role, especially at the state level. If the progressives were to have any power, they came to believe, it would require an attack on the very concept of partisanship itself.

The Era of Reform

Progressives began to espouse measures to curtail or even abolish political parties. They favored primary elections to replace nominating conventions because the latter were viewed as manipulated by party bosses; they favored nonpartisan elections at the city level and in some cases at the state level as well; they argued against corrupt alliances between parties and businesses. They wanted strict voter registration requirements that would reduce voting fraud (but would also, as it turned out, keep ordinary citizens who found the requirements cumbersome from voting); they pressed for civil service reform to eliminate patronage; and they made heavy use of the mass media as a way of attacking the abuses of partisanship and of promoting their own ideas and candidacies.

The progressives were more successful in some places than in others. In California, for example, progressives led by Governor Hiram Johnson in 1910–1911 were able to institute the direct primary and to adopt procedures—called the *initiative* and the *referendum*—so citizens could vote directly on proposed legislation, thereby bypassing the state legislature. Governor Robert La Follette brought about similar changes in Wisconsin.

Figure 9.1 **Cleavages and Continuity in the Two-Party System**

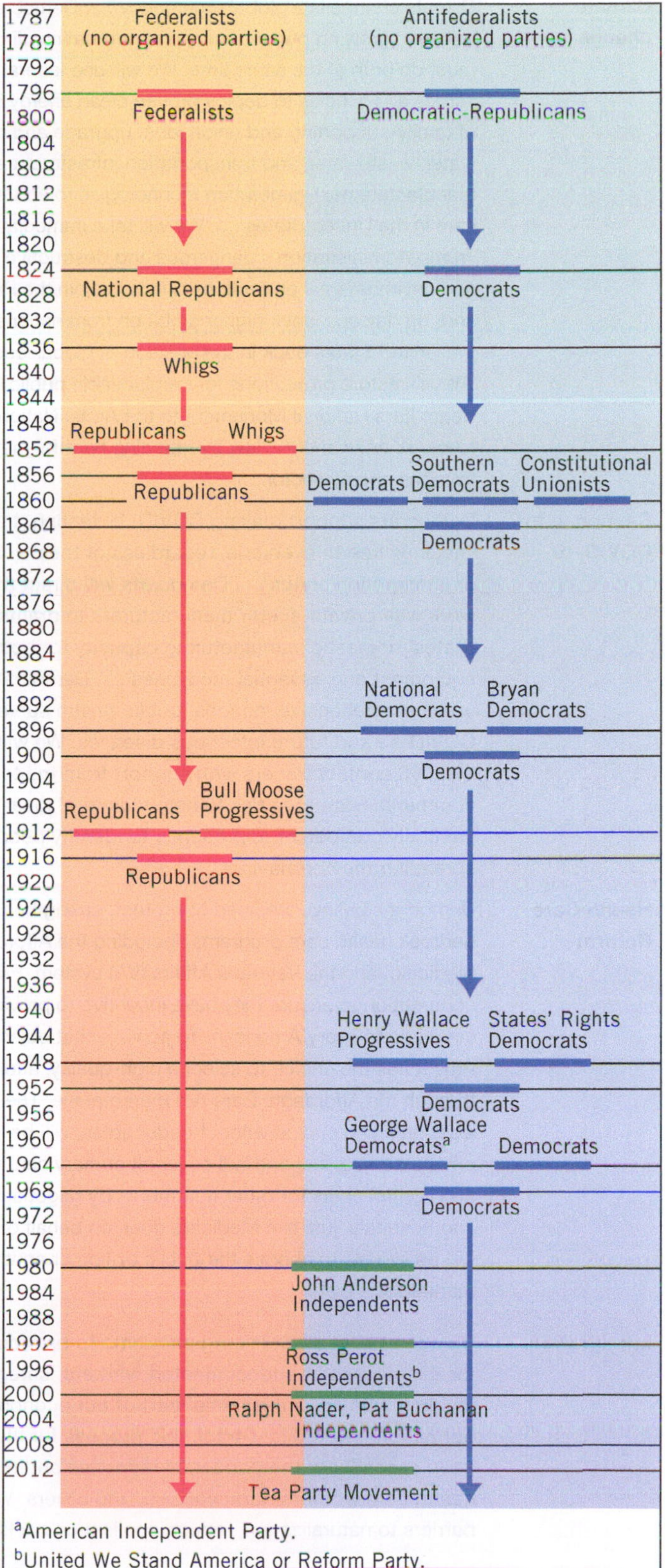

[a]American Independent Party.
[b]United We Stand America or Reform Party.

The effect of these changes was to reduce substantially the worst forms of political corruption and ultimately to make boss rule in politics difficult if not impossible. But they also had the effect of making political parties, whether led by bosses or by statesmen, weaker, less able to hold officeholders accountable, and less able to assemble the power necessary for governing the fragmented political institutions created by the Constitution. In Congress, party lines began to grow fainter, as did the power of congressional leadership. Above all, the progressives did not have an answer to the problem first faced by Jefferson: If there is not a strong political party, by what other means will candidates for office be found, recruited, and supported?

Polarization and Resurgence

By the mid-to late-20th century, political parties reached their nadir in America. In Congress, levels of party voting were quite low, and congressional Democrats were divided into Northern and Southern wings, which disagreed vociferously on segregation and civil rights for African Americans. Parties as organizations were weakened by the progressive-era reforms discussed previously, and voters' attachments to their parties weakened as well (see Figure 9.2 later in the chapter). Elections came to be much more about the candidates than the party, with the candidates responsible for their own fate (in sharp contrast to earlier eras of strong parties). Many scholars argued that parties were in a state of decline.[6]

But slowly, this situation began to change. In the aftermath of major civil rights fights in Congress, segregation was outlawed, and the parties began to gradually take their modern positions on race, with Democrats more supportive of government efforts to address racial inequalities, and Republicans less so. This helped to transform the South—which had been solidly Democratic since the Civil War 100 years earlier—into a competitive, two-party region (and today, one that more strongly favors Republicans).[7]

At the same time, the parties began to diverge not just on race, but on a whole host of issues, taking more distinct stands on taxes, abortion, women's rights, and so forth. As we discuss later, this change was due in part to the increasing importance of activists: as the party machines died, they were replaced with issue activists motivated by positions on particular issues. This helped to drive apart the parties on the major issues of the day and make ideology—rather than patronage—the glue that holds the parties together. Today, at the elite level, the parties are fairly characterized as polarized, with Democrats on the left and Republicans on the right. We will see this in Chapter 13 when we examine congressional roll-call voting—congressional elites today are nearly as divided as they were in the late 19th century. We also see evidence of this division in the party's recent platforms. In 2016, the parties clashed over a number of issues, including climate change, abortion, health care reform, immigration, financial regulation, and same-sex marriage. In 2020, while the Democratic Party adopted a new platform, the Republican Party did not, becoming the first party in modern history to fail to do so. Instead, the

TABLE 9.1 | Party Platform Differences, 2016 and 2020

Policy	Democratic Position (2020)	Republican Position (2016)
Climate change	Climate change is a global emergency . . . Democrats reject the false choice between growing our economy and combating climate change; we can and must do both at the same time. We will use federal resources and authorities across all agencies to deploy proven clean energy solutions; create millions of family-supporting and union jobs; upgrade and make resilient our energy, water, wastewater, and transportation infrastructure; and develop and manufacture next-generation technologies to address the climate crisis right here in the United States . . . We will take immediate action to reverse the Trump Administration's dangerous and destructive rollbacks of critical climate and environmental protections. We will rejoin the Paris Climate Agreement and, on day one, seek higher ambition from nations around the world, putting the United States back in the position of global leadership where we belong. We will restore protections for irreplaceable public lands and waters, from Bears Ears National Monument to the Arctic National Wildlife Refuge. We will follow science and the law by reducing harmful methane and carbon pollution from the energy sector.	The United Nations' Intergovernmental Panel on Climate Change is a political mechanism, not an unbiased scientific institution. Its unreliability is reflected in its intolerance toward scientists and others who dissent from its orthodoxy. . . . We reject the agendas of both the Kyoto Protocol and the Paris Agreement.
Response to COVID-19	Democrats support making COVID-19 testing, treatment, and any eventual vaccines free to everyone, regardless of their wealth, insurance coverage, or immigration status . . . Democrats will direct the federal government to work with private-sector manufacturers to dramatically scale up the United States' domestic manufacturing capacity for both personal protective equipment and essential medicines . . . Democrats will act swiftly to stand up a comprehensive, national public health surveillance program for COVID-19 and future infectious diseases. We will recruit at least 100,000 contact tracers with support from trusted local organizations in the communities most at risk to help state and local health departments use culturally competent approaches to identify people at risk of contracting or spreading the coronavirus.	[Not discussed]
Health Care Reform	Democrats believe we need to protect, strengthen, and build upon our bedrock health care programs, including the Affordable Care Act, Medicare, Medicaid, and the Veterans Affairs (VA) system. Private insurers need real competition to ensure they have incentive to provide affordable, quality coverage to every American. To achieve that objective, we will give all Americans the choice to select a high-quality, affordable public option through the Affordable Care Act marketplace. The public option will provide at least one plan choice without deductibles; will be administered by CMS, not private companies; and will cover all primary care without any co-payments and control costs for other treatments by negotiating prices with doctors and hospitals, just like Medicare does on behalf of older people. Everyone will be eligible to choose the public option or another Affordable Care Act marketplace plan.	It [The Affordable Care Act] must be removed and replaced with an approach based on genuine competition, patient choice, excellent care, wellness, and timely access to treatment. To that end, a Republican president, on the first day in office, will use legitimate waiver authority under the law to halt its advance and then, with the unanimous support of Congressional Republicans, will sign its repeal.
Immigration	Democrats believe it is long past time to provide a roadmap to citizenship for the millions of undocumented workers, caregivers, students, and children who are an essential part of our economy and of the fabric of our nation. We will fast-track this process for those workers who have been essential to the pandemic response and recovery efforts, including health care workers, farmworkers, and others. We will also eliminate unfair barriers to naturalization, reduce application backlogs, and make our	The executive amnesties of 2012 and 2014 [about immigration] are a direct violation of federal law and usurp the powers of Congress as outlined in Article I of the Constitution. These unlawful amnesties must be immediately rescinded by a Republican president. . . .

	immigration processes faster, more efficient, and less costly . . . Democrats oppose President Trump's illegal, chaotic, and reckless changes to the legal immigration system, including decisions to slash family-based immigration as well as H-1B and other visa programs that can help our economy.	We support building a wall along our southern border and protecting all ports of entry. The border wall must cover the entirety of the southern border and must be sufficient to stop both vehicular and pedestrian traffic.
Police Reform	Democrats will reinvigorate community policing approaches, so officers on the beat better serve the neighborhoods they work in, and make smart investments to incentivize departments to build effective partnerships with social workers and mental health and substance use counselors to help respond to public health challenges . . . Democrats believe weapons of war have no place on our streets, and will once again limit the sale and transfer of surplus military weapons to domestic law enforcement agencies—a policy President Trump reversed immediately upon taking office. We cannot create trust without holding those in power accountable for their actions. Democrats will reinvigorate pattern-or-practice investigations into police misconduct at the Department of Justice, and strengthen them through new subpoena powers and expanded oversight to address systemic misconduct by prosecutors . . . We will also act to ensure that victims of federal, state, or local law enforcement abuses of power can seek justice through civil litigation by reining in the doctrine of qualified immunity.	[Not addressed]

Source: 2020 Democratic Party Platform. In 2020, the Republican Party chose not to enact a platform, so we include their 2016 positions here.

Q Compare and contrast the positions of Democrats and Republicans on these issues. What differences do you notice? How did these differences play out during the 2020 presidential election?

Republicans said that the party would "continue to enthusiastically support the President's America-first agenda." In Table 9.1, we present contrasts between the 2020 Democratic Party Platform and the 2016 Republican Party Platform on several salient issues.

We also can see today's stronger parties reflected in the resurgent strength of parties as nominating bodies. In the era of party bosses, the party itself selected the nominee, but as we discussed above, the progressives dismantled this system and replaced it with a system of primary elections. The weakened state and local parties that followed from progressive reforms meant that members of Congress needed to develop their own personal organizations to win reelection. At the presidential level, a series of reforms (described below) similarly weakened the power of party bosses to select the nominee in the 1970s. But in the ensuing decades, parties have returned to become more important. Parties now help to shape the field of candidates and influence who wins.[8] To be clear, party bosses can no longer pick candidates, and the elite cannot simply choose the candidate they like—take Hillary Clinton in 2008 or Jeb Bush in 2016, for example. But party leaders have reasserted themselves in the candidate selection process, as we will see below.

The rise of such polarized parties has led some to bemoan this development and call for a weakening of parties. However, it is important to remember that stronger parties come with some benefits as well. In 1950, a committee of political scientists published a famous report arguing that we needed stronger parties to give voters clear and distinct policy alternatives.[9] Today, we arguably have parties that can do this for voters, and as a result, it is easier for them to make such choices.[10] But at the same time, such divided parties can generate gridlock and division. Polarized parties generate benefits, but they also come at a real cost as well.

critical or **realignment periods** *A period when a major, lasting shift occurs in the popular coalition supporting one or both parties.*

Party Realignments

The strength of the major parties has clearly experienced important turning points, when we have had an alternation of dominance by one party and then the other. To help explain these major shifts in the tides of politics, scholars have developed the theory of **critical** or **realignment periods**. During such periods a sharp, lasting shift occurs in the popular coalition supporting one or both parties. The issues that separate the two parties change, and so the kinds of voters supporting each party change. This shift may occur at the time of an election or just after, as the new administration draws in new supporters.[11]

There seem to have been five major realignments in American politics: 1800, when the Jeffersonian Republicans defeated the Federalists; 1828, when the Jacksonian Democrats came to power; 1860, when the

Whig Party collapsed and the Republicans under Lincoln came to power; 1896, when the Republicans defeated William Jennings Bryan; and 1932, when the Democrats under Roosevelt came into office.

At least two kinds of realignment occur: one in which a major party is so badly defeated that it disappears and a new party emerges to take its place (this happened to the Federalists in 1800 and to the Whigs in 1856–1860), and another in which the two existing parties continue but voters shift their support from one to the other (this happened in 1896 and 1932).

The year 1860 offers a clear case of realignment. By 1860, the existing parties could no longer straddle the fence on the slavery issue. The Republican Party was formed in 1856 on the basis of clear-cut opposition to slavery; the Democratic Party split in half in 1860, with one part (led by Stephen A. Douglas and based in the North) trying to waffle on the issue and the other (led by John C. Breckinridge and drawing its support from the South) categorically denying that any government had any right to outlaw slavery. The remnants of the Whig Party, renamed the Constitutional Union Party, tried to unite the nation by writing no platform at all, thus remaining silent on slavery. Lincoln and the antislavery Republicans won in 1860; Breckinridge and the proslavery Southern Democrats came in second. From that moment on, the two major political parties acquired different sources of support and stood (at least for a decade) for different principles. The parties that had tried to straddle the fence were eliminated. The Civil War fixed these new party loyalties deep in the popular mind, and the structure of party competition was set for nearly 40 years.

While such examples are still quite useful historically (and help to demarcate the different party systems in American politics), many scholars question the idea of realignment today.[12] They note that while parties have changed dramatically in recent decades, there is no single realigning election. Instead, the process has occurred gradually.[13] Furthermore, it is not that one issue replaced another, but rather that the parties have been divided on multiple salient issues: abortion, LGBTQ+ rights, the size of the economy, and so on.[14] While it is clear that parties will continue to change and evolve over time, the exact process of that change is less clear.

9-3 The Functions of Political Parties

Previously, we saw that parties exist primarily to help elect particular candidates to office. To actually achieve this goal, parties need to recruit candidates to run for office, nominate them, and then work to help them get elected in the general election by appealing to voters. All three activities are vital for parties to actually hold power.

Recruiting Candidates

The first step to selecting candidates to office is convincing them to run. In the last chapter, we saw that most people do not get involved in politics on their own: they need to be asked. Political candidates are no different: many of them did not think about running until someone asked them to consider doing so. Party leaders are typically the people doing the asking.[15] Recruiting the right candidates is crucial to winning elections.

Party leaders often work tirelessly to recruit candidates. For example, before the 2006 election, Rahm Emanuel (then the chair of the Democratic Congressional Campaign Committee) worked for months to recruit good candidates to run for Congress. He held meetings with many members of Congress to enlist their help in identifying good potential candidates, and then asked them to make appeals to convince these candidates to run. Similarly, Democrats worked hard to recruit high-quality candidates in 2018.[16]

Party leaders expend this effort to recruit candidates because the right candidates greatly increase the chances that their party will win close elections. Having the right candidate is not the only factor, but it is certainly an important one. For example, in both 2006 and 2018, Democrats worked hard to recruit candidates with military backgrounds to help overcome Republicans' traditional advantage on national security issues.[17]

One of the best examples of the importance of candidate quality in recent years came in the special 2017 Alabama Senate race. Everyone expected Republicans to hold onto this seat easily, as no Democrat had won a Senate election in Alabama since 1992, and President Trump carried the state with 62 percent of the vote in 2016. (The seat became vacant after Senator Jeff Sessions resigned to become President Trump's first attorney general.) Roy Moore, the controversial former chief justice of the Alabama Supreme Court, won the Republican primary, but then several young women came forward and claimed Moore had made unwanted sexual advances toward them when they were teenagers. Democrat Doug Jones, a former prosecutor, narrowly defeated Moore in the election. President Trump endorsed Moore, but that did not overcome the accusations.

While state and local parties run many of these efforts, the national parties are also increasingly involved in this process, as the example of Rahm Emanuel illustrates. In the late 1960s and early 1970s, Republicans began to convert their national party into a well-financed, highly staffed organization devoted to finding and electing Republican candidates, especially to Congress. Money went to recruit and train Republican candidates, give them legal and financial advice, study issues and analyze voting trends, and conduct national advertising campaigns on behalf of the party as a whole. Shortly thereafter, Democrats followed suit, and also began having the national party work to recruit and train candidates.

Which candidates the parties recruit matters not just to who wins, but what happens to policy afterward. For example, Nebraska had a long tradition of centrism and a lack of polarization in its state legislature; indeed, the legislature is officially nonpartisan. But in recent years, the chamber has polarized quickly, as party leaders have recruited quite extreme candidates to run.[18] So party leaders' recruitment decisions shape policy in important ways.

Nominating Candidates

Once a party has recruited candidates, it needs to decide which candidates will run under the party's label in the general election. Historically, parties did this via party caucuses and conventions (see the discussion above). But since the progressive era, most such nominations have occurred via **primary elections**.

Two main types of primary elections exist: closed primaries and open primaries. In a **closed primary**, only registered members of a political party may vote to select the nominee. Before the primary, voters must register with either the Democratic or the Republican Party. When they go to the polls to vote in the primary, they are given the ballot only for their party. The primary is closed to those outside the party. In this sort of primary system, Independent voters (those who are not registered with either major party) typically do not get to vote in the primary election.

In contrast, in an **open primary**, voters do not need to declare their party affiliation before going to the polls (indeed, in some states with open primaries, voters do not declare a party affiliation when they register). Citizens can vote in the primary of either party, but they can only vote in one party's primary (i.e., you can vote in the Democratic or the Republican primary, but not the Democratic *and* the Republican primary). One concern with open primaries is that there can be crossover voting: Voters from one party can vote in the other party's primary, and this may affect the outcome. While such crossover voting does occur, however, it typically does not decide the election outcomes.[19]

Both open and closed primaries are used widely throughout the United States. Somewhat more states use open primary systems, but closed primaries are by no means uncommon. To find out exactly what type of primary system your state uses, you can consult the National Conference of State Legislators, which records (among many other things) the type of primary system used in each state (see www.ncsl.org).

Some states have also recently experimented with the "top-two" primary election system. In these types of systems, all candidates compete on one primary election ballot, and the top two candidates—regardless of party—advance to the general election. Thus in this type of primary, a voter could vote for a Democrat for one office but a Republican for another, giving voters even more freedom than in an open primary. This system is used in California and Washington, as well as for the Nebraska state legislature. A similar procedure is used in Louisiana: All candidates appear on the same primary ballot, and if a candidate receives 50 percent of the vote, they are directly elected to the office. If not, a runoff election chooses between the top two finishers.

primary elections *An election held to determine the nominee from a particular party.*

closed primary *A primary election where only registered party members may vote for the party's nominee.*

open primary *A primary election where all voters (regardless of party membership) may vote for the party's nominee.*

Scholars of primary systems argue that two consequences flow from a state's choice of primary system. First, states with closed primaries tend to have stronger parties. The primary system is probably both a cause and an effect of the strength of the parties. Having strong parties means that the parties can mobilize in the state to prevent opening the primary process. A closed primary is also beneficial to party leaders: Because voters register with a party, party leaders know which voters will be most receptive to their political messages. Unsurprisingly, many party leaders favor closed primaries for just this reason.

Second, many reformers argue that open or top-two primaries favor moderate candidates. They claim that because all voters—rather than just members of one party—vote in these primaries, candidates will adopt more centrist positions. While intuitively appealing, there is little empirical support for this claim. It seems that the types of voters who actually vote in open (or top-two) primaries is not much different than in closed primaries, so the candidates they produce are not very different.[20] Hence, the type of primary system (open vs. closed vs. top two) does not really affect candidate polarization.

Nominations via Convention

As we discussed above, in most places, nominations occur through primary elections (though a few places, such as Utah, do make some use of conventions). But there is one major election where the nomination occurs via a convention: the national conventions to nominate candidates for president.

The national committee selects the time and place of the next national convention and issues a "call" for the convention that sets forth the number of delegates each state and territory is to have and the rules under which delegates must be chosen. These delegates then select the party's nominee at the convention.

There are two main types of delegates. First, there are the so-called pledged delegates. These are the delegates awarded through the presidential primaries and caucuses, with the understanding that they will support a particular candidate at the convention. So, when you vote in a presidential primary or a caucus, you are actually voting

Will You Support a Closed or Open Primary?

To: *Brian Dillon, state senator*
From: *Jake Matthew, legislative assistant*
Subject: *Open vs. Closed Primary Elections*

Some in your state have proposed changing the primary election from a closed primary (where only those registered with the party can vote in the primary) to an open primary (where all registered voters, regardless of party, could vote in the primary).

To Consider:

State legislators are currently debating a measure to change the state's electoral system from a closed primary (where only registered party members can vote) to an open primary (where any registered voter can vote). Supporters claim this allows more voters a voice in the process and supports moderate candidates, but opponents claim this is unfair to party members, who should decide their party's nominee, and opens the possibility for mischief from party "raiding."

Arguments for:

1. An open primary lets all voters—not just party members—decide which candidates run in the general election.
2. By appealing to all voters, not just voters from one party, open primaries might produce more moderate candidates.

Arguments against:

1. The party members themselves should decide who runs under the party's label in the general election.
2. Members of the other party can "raid" a party's primary to support the least appealing candidate, unfairly helping their own party.

What Will You Decide? Enter **MindTap** to make your choice.

Your decision: ☐ Keep closed primary ☐ Support open primary for delegates pledged to one candidate or another. Each party has a formula for awarding delegates based on the results of the election: Democrats award delegates proportionately, Republicans use a mix of proportional representation and winner-take-all systems.

Each party has a given number of pledged delegates and uses complex formulas to determine how many come from each state (and territory). For the Democrats, this takes into account the vote each state cast for Democratic candidates in past elections and the number of electoral votes of each state; for the Republicans, this takes into account the number of representatives in Congress and whether the state in past elections cast its electoral votes for the Republican presidential candidate and elected Republicans to the Senate, the House, and the governorship. Thus, the Democrats give extra delegates to large states, whereas the Republicans give extra ones to loyal states.

But pledged delegates are not the only type of delegates. Second, there are unpledged delegates, who are party leaders and elected officials; they are often called "**super-delegates.**" These super-delegates typically are not bound to vote for one candidate or another (as pledged delegates are), but can choose which candidate to support. To win the nomination, a candidate must have support from both pledged delegates and super-delegates, though super-delegates typically follow the lead of the pledged delegates. Super-delegates can be crucial, however, if the pledged delegate count is very close, as it was in 2008 between Barack Obama and Hillary Clinton, or as it was in 2016 between Hillary Clinton and Bernie Sanders. In both cases, the eventual nominee—Obama in 2008 and Clinton in 2016—needed super-delegate support to clinch the nomination. Partially in response to critiques from Bernie Sanders's supporters, Democrats weakened the power of super-delegates beginning in 2020.[21]

Reformers designed this system to weaken the power of party bosses. If delegates chosen through primaries and caucuses largely elect the candidate, party bosses implicitly have less power. Previously, party leaders chose the nominees in the proverbial smoke-filled rooms. Adlai Stevenson in 1952 and Hubert Humphrey in 1968 won the Democratic presidential nominations without even entering a single primary—party bosses chose them. Reformers wanted to weaken the power of the party bosses, so both parties designed reforms to reshape how delegates were chosen in the 1970s and 1980s. These reforms were designed to give power to the people, rather than to party elites.

While these reforms did make the nomination process more democratic, they had an unintended consequence: they empowered activists. Candidates choose the people who will serve as their pledged delegates at the convention, and they often choose people who are active in local politics and will be loyal to them. Many of these people are activists who are deeply involved with particular issues. Their views are not like the views of ordinary voters. Since 1972, scholars have done extensive surveys of convention delegates, and they have uncovered a consistent pattern of results: Democratic delegates are more liberal than Democratic voters, and Republican delegates are more conservative than Republican voters. Activists, unlike ordinary voters, are deeply divided.

super-delegates *Party leaders and elected officials who become delegates to the national convention without having to run in primaries or caucuses.*

invisible primary *Process by which candidates try to attract the support of key party leaders before an election begins.*

The fact that these activists are more polarized pushes candidates to take more polarized positions to win and maintain their support.[22] By moving away from party bosses (who prioritize winning) to activists (who prioritize purity), the current system pushes candidates away from the center. While activists want to nominate a candidate who is electable, they also want someone who takes the "right" position on the issues.

This creates a tension for party leaders: They too want a candidate who will excite activists, but they also want a candidate who can win in November. To avoid nominating a candidate outside the mainstream, party leaders have worked to reassert themselves in the process. One way is by using super-delegates, which give party leaders and elected officials some say at the convention. Another is through the so-called invisible primary. Candidates who hope to win elected office, especially the presidency, must survive the **invisible primary**, the process of attracting key party and interest group figures to your camp.[23] The idea is that key party elites—elected party officials, state and local party chairpersons, key interest group leaders, party fundraisers,

Sean Rayford/Getty Images News/Getty Images

Image 9.3 Candidates competing in the 2020 Democratic Primary election march in a Martin Luther King Jr. Day parade in South Carolina.

national convention *A meeting of party delegates held every four years, which nominates the party's candidate for president.*

national committee *Delegates who run party affairs between national conventions.*

congressional campaign committee *A party committee in Congress that provides funds to members and would-be members.*

senior staffers, and so forth—are trying to settle on which candidate they think will be the best nominee. They work to recruit that person, and then tilt resources toward them so they have an advantage in the actual primaries and caucuses. Those resources certainly include money, but they are also the best fundraisers and staffers, key interest group leaders who will help supply volunteers, and so forth.

Of course, we should be careful not to push this argument too far: Elites play an important role in winnowing down the list of candidates, but what elites want is not always what happens. For instance, Hillary Clinton—the clear choice of many party insiders headed into 2008—was not the eventual nominee that year. And in 2016, few—if any—Republican elites wanted Donald Trump to be the party's nominee. Party leaders certainly try to influence the process, but the voters ultimately decide.

Helping Candidates Win Elections

Finally, once candidates have been recruited to run, and they have been nominated, the party has to help them win in the general election. First, parties help their candidates by giving them a party label. As we will discuss, voters overwhelmingly vote for the candidate who shares their party label: In recent years, more than 90 percent of Democratic (Republican) voters have supported the Democratic (Republican) nominee for president. This means that candidates typically can count on their party's supporters to vote for them if they show up to the polls.

Image 9.4 Volunteers conduct a voter registration drive before the 2018 election. Voter turnout was higher in 2018 than in any midterm election since 1914.

But not all of a party's supporters get to the polls, however. The second way parties help candidates win elections is to engage in get-out-the-vote campaigns. In Chapter 8, we discussed the Obama campaign's groundbreaking efforts to mobilize volunteers to register and then turn out voters for President Obama. While other campaigns have not been as large or as sophisticated, conducting get-out-the-vote campaigns has become a key role played by parties and affiliated groups in recent years.

Third, parties also provide a variety of services to their candidates. One important service is the get-out-the-vote drives discussed above, but they also gather additional resources to share with candidates: lists of supporters (say, from the lists of those who declare a party affiliation in order to vote in a closed primary), polling and other public opinion data, campaign staffers, and so forth. Parties are in service to their candidates.

Given the escalating cost of campaigns, perhaps the most important resource campaigns can provide candidates is money. While rules limit how much money a party can contribute directly to candidates (in federal elections, the national parties may donate only $5,000 per candidate per election), these donations have value beyond the amount given. When a party gives a donation to a candidate, they are signaling to other donors—individuals, interest groups, political action committees (see Chapter 10), and so forth—that this is a high-quality candidate whom they should support. A donation from a party, while not much in dollar amounts, can be a powerful signal to other donors.[24]

9-4 Parties as Organizations

Because political parties exist at the national, state, and local levels, you might suppose they are arranged like a big corporation, with a national board of directors giving orders to state managers who in turn direct the activities of rank-and-file workers at the county and city levels. For better or for worse, that is not the case. The various levels are independent of one another, and while they do coordinate for some activities, as we have seen, there is nothing like a top-down, hierarchical system in place.

The national Democratic and Republican Parties are structured quite similarly. In both parties, ultimate authority is in the hands of the **national convention** that meets every four years to nominate a presidential candidate. Between these conventions, party affairs are managed by a **national committee** made up of delegates from each state and territory. In Congress, each party has a **congressional campaign committee** that helps members of Congress running for reelection or would-be members running for an open seat or challenging a candidate from the opposition party. The day-to-day work of the party is managed by a full-time, paid **national chair** elected by the committee.

Beneath them are the state parties, and then the local parties. In every state, a Democratic and a Republican state party is organized under state law. Each typically consists of a state central committee, below which are county committees and sometimes city, town, or even precinct committees. The members of these committees are chosen in a variety of ways—sometimes in primary elections, sometimes by conventions, sometimes by a building-block process whereby people elected to serve on precinct or town committees choose the members of county committees, who in turn choose state committee members.

The National Parties

The main responsibility for national parties is to call the national party convention, which we have discussed in detail. Apart from the convention, the national party primarily serves to represent the party in the media and to raise money. As mentioned earlier, the party's fundraising apparatus is an important component of candidate success. And given changes in the political environment, parties now raise large sums of money. During the 2018 election cycle, all congressional candidates raised $2.77 billion, and the parties raised an additional $1.55 billion.[25] Some of this party money is transferred to specific candidates, but other parts are distributed to state and local parties as well.

The resurgent strength of the national party has also strengthened state and local parties, a point we return to below.[26]

State and Local Parties

One of the difficulties in writing about state and local parties is that there is not just one state party but 100 (one for each party in each of the 50 states), and there are literally thousands of local parties, and no two are exactly alike. Some states and locales have strong parties, whereas others are weak and more a party in name than anything else.

But regardless of the exact form of state and local parties, they have all undergone a fundamental change from earlier generations. Before, state and local parties were often **political machines** (see the earlier discussion of the historical evolution of the party system). Political machines are party organizations that recruit their members by using tangible incentives—money, political jobs, an opportunity to get favors from government—and are characterized by a high degree of leadership control over member activity. At one time, many local party organizations were machines, and the struggle over political jobs—patronage—was their chief concern.

Such machines were long a core component of American party politics, especially in the 19th century. For example, the famous Tammany Hall machine in New York City wielded patronage as a powerful tool: During the 1870s, it was estimated that one of every eight voters in New York City had a federal, state, or city job.[27] The federal bureaucracy was one important source of those jobs. The New York Custom House alone employed thousands of people, virtually all of whom were replaced if their party lost the presidential election. The postal system was another source, and it was frankly recognized as such. When James N. Tyner became postmaster general in 1876, he was "appointed not to see that the mails were carried, but to see that Indiana was carried."[28] Elections and conventions were so frequent and the intensity of party competition so great that being a party worker was for many a full-time paid occupation.

national chair *Day-to-day party manager elected by the national committee.*

political machines *A party organization that recruits members by dispensing patronage.*

Well before the arrival of vast numbers of poor immigrants from Ireland, Italy, and elsewhere, old-stock Americans had perfected the machine, run up the cost of government, and systematized voting fraud. Kickbacks on contracts, payments extracted from officeholders, and funds raised from businesspeople made some politicians rich but also paid the huge bills of the elaborate party organization. When immigrants began flooding the eastern cities, the party machines were there to provide them with all manner of services in exchange for their support at the polls: the machines were a vast welfare organization operating before the creation of the welfare state.

The abuses of the machine were well known and gradually curtailed. Stricter voter registration laws reduced fraud, civil service reforms cut down the number of patronage jobs, and competitive bidding laws made it harder to award overpriced contracts to favored businesses. The Hatch Act (passed by Congress in 1939) made it illegal for federal civil service employees to take an active part in political management or political campaigns by serving as party officers, soliciting campaign funds, running for partisan office, working in a partisan campaign, endorsing partisan candidates, taking voters to the polls, counting ballots, circulating nominating petitions, or being delegates to a party convention. (They may still vote and make campaign contributions.)

These restrictions gradually took federal employees out of machine politics, but they did not end the machines. Many cities—Chicago, Philadelphia, and Albany—found ways to maintain the machines even though city employees were technically under the civil service. Far more

partisan identification *A voter's long-term, stable attachment to one of the political parties.*

partisanship *Another name for partisan identity.*

important than the various progressive reforms that weakened the machines were changes among voters. As voters grew in education, income, and sophistication, they depended less and less on the advice and leadership of local party officials. And as the federal government created a bureaucratic welfare system, the parties' welfare systems declined in value.

It is easy either to scorn the political party machine as a venal and self-serving organization or to romanticize it as an informal welfare system. In truth, it was a little of both. Above all, it was a frank recognition of the fact that politics requires organization; the machine was the supreme expression of the value of organization. Even allowing for voting fraud, in elections where party machines were active, voter turnout was huge: More people participated in politics when mobilized by a party machine than when appealed to via television or good-government associations.[29]

By the mid-1980s, the traditional party organization (one based on machine-style politics with strong, hierarchical organization) existed in only a few places.[30] In the intervening years, even those have largely died out, though vestiges survive in a few places, such as the Democratic machine in Cook County, Illinois (Chicago), or the Republican machine in Nassau County, New York.

Today, most state and local parties take a far different form. Without the staffing of the machines, they have come to be dominated by intense policy advocates, particularly those from social movements such as civil rights, peace, feminism, environmentalism, libertarianism, abortion, and so forth. The result is that in many places the party has become a collection of people drawn from various social movements.[31] For candidates to win the party's support, they typically must satisfy the "litmus test" demands of the ideological activists in the party. Former Democratic Senator Barbara Mikulski noted that social movements have become an important source of candidates for the parties, effectively become their modern-day farm clubs. People who feel intensely about particular issues have replaced machines in most places.

By permission of the Houghton Library/Harvard University

Image 9.5 Former Senator George Washington Plunkitt of Tammany Hall explains machine politics from atop the bootblack stand in front of the New York County Courthouse around 1905.

In the years following the decline of the machine parties, many argued that state and local parties were effectively dead, and could exert little influence. Yet more recent research suggests that today's parties are actually quite effective and powerful, albeit not to the same extent as political machines of the previous era. This is largely due to the influence of money. As the national parties have become more adept at fundraising, they (and their donors) have channeled money to help boost state parties, and state parties themselves have become more adept fundraisers (and as we discuss in the next chapter, recent campaign finance rule changes have helped to make this shift possible).[32] State and local parties have used this increased money to build stronger infrastructures and provide more services to candidates.[33] As a result, today's state and local parties have become important political players.

9-5 Parties in the Electorate: Partisanship

Above, we saw how parties are organized, how they recruit candidates, and so forth. Our three-part categorization of parties from the beginning of the chapter described parties as organizations. But parties also exist as powerful symbols in the minds of voters. Voters have a **partisan identification**: a stable, long-term attachment to a political party (this is sometimes also called a voter's **partisanship**).

As we discussed in Chapter 7, two major factors help explain who is a Democrat and who is a Republican: parents' partisanship and the political environment as one comes of age politically (refer back to the discussion of socialization in Chapter 7). First, voters' partisanship is heavily influenced by their parents' partisanship: Parents who are Republicans (typically) have children who are Republicans.[34] Second, the political environment as one comes of age politically also powerfully shapes one's partisanship: Voters who came of age under Ronald Reagan and George H. W. Bush are more Republican than those who first experienced politics under Bill Clinton. Such partisanship is remarkably stable: Voters who were Democratic at age 18 tend to be Democratic at age 75, despite all that happened in between.[35] Partisanship is akin to being part of a like-minded group or political team.[36]

Policy Dynamics: Inside/Outside the Box | The Auto Industry Bailout: Party-Based Client Politics?

Chrysler, Ford, and General Motors are known as the "Big Three" American auto companies. When the Big Three ran into big financial trouble in 2008, they asked the federal government for billions of dollars in loans. Most Americans opposed the bailout, but the majorities against helping the auto industry were not as wide as those against bailing out the "too big to fail" banks, insurance companies, and investment firms.

Reactions to various auto industry bailout bills broke down along party lines. Most Big Three blue-collar employees have been represented by the United Auto Workers, a labor union that has favored Democrats. Many Republican leaders, and most self-identified GOP voters, opposed any auto industry bailout by Washington. Instead, they favored having the Big Three enter bankruptcy proceedings. By contrast, many Democratic leaders, and most self-identified Democratic voters, favored the federal government loaning money to the Big Three to tide them over, provided that executive bonuses were curtailed and that taxpayers, functioning as shareholders, were paid back fully once the economy recovered and car sales improved.

But the pro-bailout policy had one supremely important Republican ally: President George W. Bush. Several top Republicans in Congress insisted that any bailout would cost taxpayers billions and benefit "the unions" without either saving the industry or benefitting most consumers. Rejecting such claims, in 2008 Bush directed that $17.4 billion from the antirecession Troubled Asset Relief Program go to bail out Chrysler and General Motors; and, in December 2008, he supported various bills in Congress that succeeded his own initial plan.

In 2009, President Barack Obama, a Democrat, made $60 billion more available to the companies. In the end, the companies ended up repaying much of what the government loaned them, though the bailout did cost the public about $12.3 billion. Public opinion toward the bailout remained starkly different by party: While 63% of Democrats approved of the bailout, only 25% of Republicans did. A decade on, while some debate still continues, many economists argue that the bailout was necessary to help stabilize the auto industry, and with it, the broader U.S. economy.

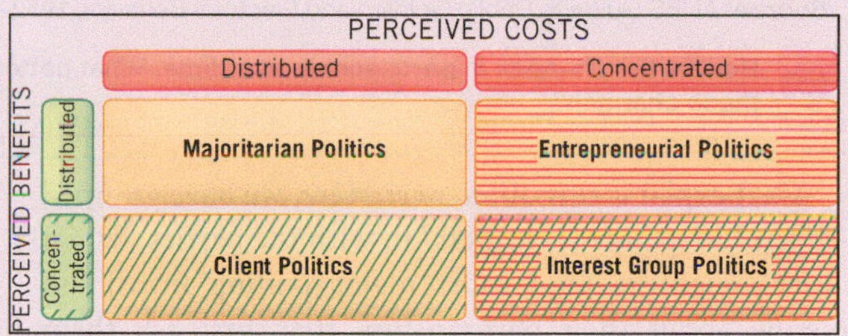

Source: ProPublica, "Failed Bailout Investments," http://projects.propublica.org/bailout/list/losses, accessed February 2015; Gallup, "Republicans, Democrats Differ Over U.S. Automaker Bailout," February 2012; "The Auto Bailout 10 Years Later: Was It the Right Call?" Knowledge at Wharton, https://knowledge.wharton.upenn.edu/article/auto-bailout-ten-years-later-right-call/

Of course, to say that partisanship is stable is not to say that it never changes. Partisanship is a stable identity, but in response to major events, it can—and does—change.[37] In response to the economic boom of the 1990s, voters moved toward the Democratic Party. In response to the 9/11 attacks and the ensuing focus on terrorism and national security—two issues where voters think Republicans are more competent than Democrats—more voters identified as Republicans.[38]

If we look at the distribution of partisanship in the electorate over time, we see this same pattern: underlying stability with changes in response to major events. Figure 9.2 shows the rise and fall of partisan identification from the 1950s to 2016.

Several patterns stand out. First, in the 1950s, the Democrats had a substantial partisan advantage over Republicans: While almost 60 percent of the population identified as Democrats, only about 40 percent identified as Republicans. Over time, as the party coalitions shifted, that edge has declined sharply. Today, that gap in identification is only a few percentage points, much less than what it was some 60 years ago. There are many reasons for this shift, but perhaps the most important one is the decline of the solid South. In the 1950s, nearly all white Southerners would have identified as Democrats (as they'd done since the Civil War, see the historical discussion above). As the parties moved apart on the issues, most notably civil rights, white Southerners gradually became Republicans.[39]

Second, and more striking, is the relatively modest number of Independents. In the popular press, we hear reports of how Independents are the largest group in the electorate; in recent years, roughly 40 percent of Americans have identified as Independents.[40] However, Figure 9.2 shows considerably fewer Independents, and their numbers have declined from their high of approximately 20 percent in the early 1970s (they have stabilized in recent years at around 10 percent of the public).

Figure 9.2 **Voter Partisanship, 1952–2016**

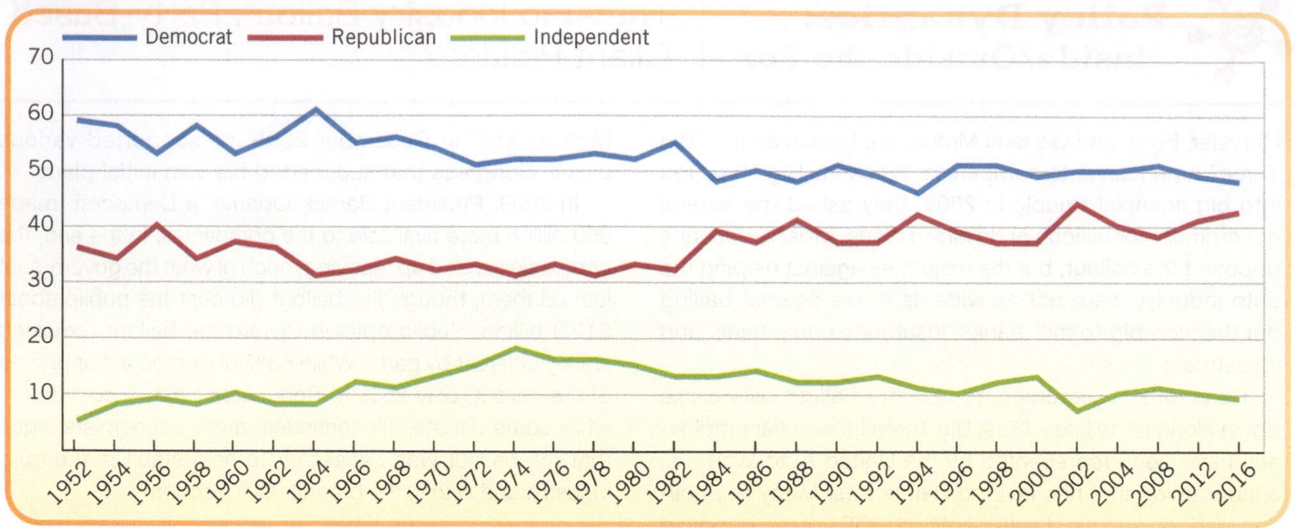

Source: ANES Guide to Public Opinion and Electoral Behavior, 1952–2008; 2012–2016 provided by the authors' analysis of the ANES data.

Q **Review the changes in partisanship over time. What patterns do you notice? What factors do you think contributed to these changes?**

What explains this difference? Here, we have grouped so-called Independent "leaners" in with the parties. When political scientists (and most major polling firms) ask someone about their partisanship, they first ask them whether they are a Democrat, a Republican, or an Independent. If they identify as an Independent, they are asked whether they lean toward either the Democratic or the Republican party. It turns out that most Independents lean toward one party or the other. In the 2016 American National Election Study, 40 percent of Americans initially identified as Independents. But when asked the followup leaner item, 15 percent leaned toward the Democrats, 16 percent leaned toward the Republicans, and the remaining 9 percent leaned toward neither party. Most Independents actually are closer to one party or the other.

Why do we group such leaners with partisans? When political scientists study their behavior, these Independent leaners look a great deal like partisans in attitudes and vote choice.[41] If they look and act so much like partisans, why do Independent leaners call themselves Independent? For many, calling oneself an "Independent" seems to signal that they are moderate and not beholden to a particular party (even if they consistently vote for one party or the other). It reflects the positive valence of the word "Independent" as much as anything about their political beliefs.[42] It turns out that most Independents aren't really that Independent, so here we treat them as partisans.

What about partisanship during the Trump era? While the most recent data from the National Election Study used to produce Figure 9.2 was collected in 2016, we can use other surveys to learn about more recent trends in partisanship. One might think that there had been big shifts in partisanship during the period: President Trump has been a polarizing figure, and Democrats retook the House in 2018, gaining 41 seats. This assumption, however, would be wrong. While there are modest fluctuations, there is no clear pattern of change.[43] Indeed, even if we look at the same individuals interviewed several times throughout the Trump administration (a so-called panel study), we find that most voters stick to their same partisan identity over time, despite all that has happened in recent years.[44] From this perspective, the Trump administration looks much the same as earlier eras, with little change in the distribution of voters' partisan identities.[45]

If this partisanship was only a label that voters applied to themselves but did not affect their behavior, we would not need to worry ourselves with it. But as political scientists have shown, a voter's partisanship powerfully shapes their attitudes and behavior. As we saw in Chapter 7, partisanship has a powerful effect on one's opinions. This same power extends to vote choice as well. In Figure 9.3, we see that in recent years partisanship has become an extremely powerful predictor of vote choice for president. For simplicity, we include only the presidential vote here, but other votes—for Congress, governor, state legislator, and so on—would follow very similar patterns as well.

Until the 1990s, Republican voters were more loyal than Democratic ones, sometimes considerably so. But since the 1990s, both parties have been (roughly) equally loyal to their party's presidential nominee, and today, party voting hovers around 90 percent; that is, about 90 percent of Democrats support the Democratic nominee, and about 90 percent of Republicans support the Republican nominee for president (again, party loyalty levels for other offices would be similar).

Figure 9.3 **Party Voting in Presidential Elections, 1952–2016**

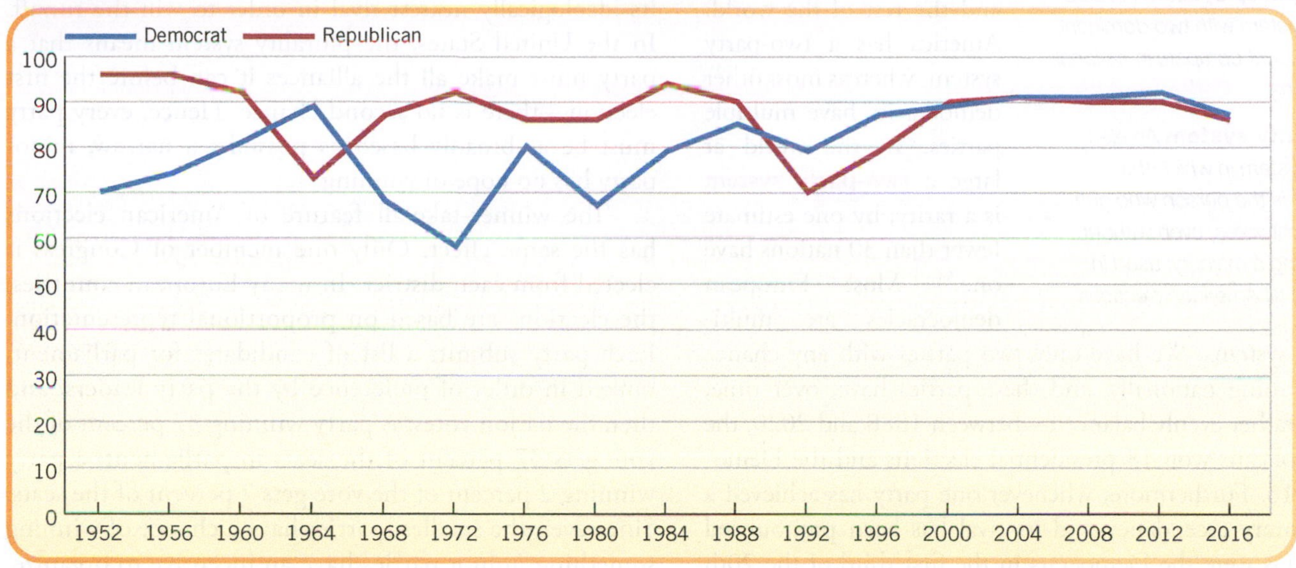

Source: Authors' analysis of ANES Data.

As we will see in Chapter 10, other factors (such as the economy and issues) also shape vote choice, but partisanship is the dominant factor.[46]

Partisanship also colors how partisans evaluate the political world. On the eve of the 2016 election, with President Obama still in power, Republicans were quite pessimistic about the economy: only 16 percent thought the economy was getting better, but 81 percent thought it was getting worse. But in the days after Trump's upset victory in 2016, their attitudes shifted dramatically: 49 percent now said it was getting better, and only 44 percent said it was getting worse (Democrats became more pessimistic after the election, though to a smaller degree).[47] While the fundamentals of the economy did not shift in this brief interval, the party of the incoming president did, which makes all the difference.[48] Similarly, in 2006, during the bird flu scare—or in 2020 during the COIVD-19 pandemic—Republicans were much more confident than Democrats that the government could respond appropriately to the issue. But in 2014 during the Ebola scare, it was Democrats who had greater confidence in the government to respond appropriately.[49] The difference between them was the party of the president: Republicans trusted the government with a Republican in the oval office, and Democrats did the same when their party was in power. The same is true of trust in government more generally: We trust the government to do what is right when "our" party is in power, but not when the opposing party is in power.[50] Partisans see the world through partisan-colored lenses.

This partisan slant in interpreting the political world is most obvious in how Democrats and Republicans evaluate objective facts. In 1988, at the end of the Reagan presidency, researchers asked voters whether the unemployment rate and the inflation rate had gotten better, gotten worse, or stayed about the same while Reagan was in office. During Reagan's tenure, unemployment had gone from a high of 9.7 percent in 1982 to 5.5 percent in 1988,[51] and inflation fell from 13.5 in 1980 to 4 percent in 1988.[52] Clearly, both inflation and unemployment got better during Reagan's tenure in office. While only about 25 percent of strong Democrats said inflation had gotten "much better" or "somewhat better," about 70 percent of Republicans said that was the case (with-similar results on unemployment). Almost as many strong Democrats said inflation got "much worse" as said it got "much better" or "somewhat better," despite the clear improvement in the actual inflation rate. In 2000, at the end of the Clinton presidency, researchers repeated a similar exercise, asking about the budget deficit and crime rate (both of which had fallen sharply since Clinton took office). Here, we see the same pattern of partisan bias, but in the opposite direction: Democrats were accurate, Republicans were not.[53] Some interpret these sorts of patterns to mean that ordinary voters are stupid, but this is not correct. Instead, it is correct to say that such patterns reflect partisans' engagement with the political world: They see important differences between the parties and are engaged in the process. They cheer when their side wins, and weep when it loses. Parties powerfully shape how ordinary Americans interpret the political world.

9-6 The Two-Party System

So far, we have seen how the U.S. political parties function, and how they differ from political parties elsewhere. But we have not really touched on the most striking difference

two-party system An electoral system with two dominant parties that compete in national elections.

plurality system An electoral system in which the winner is the person who gets the most votes, even without receiving a majority; used in almost all American elections.

between the United States and the rest of the world: America has a two-party system, whereas most other democracies have multiple parties. In the world at large a **two-party system** is a rarity; by one estimate fewer than 30 nations have one.[54] Most European democracies are multi-party systems. We have only two parties with any chance of winning nationally, and these parties have, over time, been rather evenly balanced—between 1888 and 2020, the Republicans won 18 presidential elections and the Democrats 16. Furthermore, whenever one party has achieved a temporary ascendancy and its rival has been pronounced dead (as were the Democrats in the first third of the 20th century and the Republicans during the 1930s and the 1960s), the "dead" party has displayed remarkable powers of recuperation, coming back to win important victories.

At the state and congressional district levels, however, the parties are not evenly balanced. For a long time, the South was so heavily Democratic at all levels of government as to be a one-party area, whereas upper New England and the Dakotas were strongly Republican. All regions are more competitive today than once was the case, though important divisions exist between the parties at smaller levels (i.e., with Democrats doing better in major cities, and Republicans doing better in rural areas).[55]

Scholars do not entirely agree on why the two-party system should be so permanent a feature of American political life, but two explanations are of major importance. The first has to do with the system of elections, the second with the distribution of public opinion.

Elections at every level of government are based on the plurality, winner-take-all method. The **plurality system** means that in almost all elections in the United States from president on down to city council, the winner gets the *most* votes, even if that person does not get a *majority* of all votes cast. We are so familiar with this system that we sometimes forget there are other ways of running an election. For example, one could require that the winner get a majority of the votes, thus producing runoff elections if nobody got a majority on the first try. France does this in choosing its national legislature. In the first election, candidates for parliament who win an absolute majority of the votes cast are declared elected. A week later, remaining candidates who received at least one-eighth, but less than one-half, of the vote go into a runoff election; those who then win an absolute majority are also declared elected.

The French method encourages many political parties to form, each hoping to win at least one-eighth of the vote in the first election and then to enter into an alliance with its ideologically nearest rival in order to win the runoff. In the United States, the plurality system means that a party must make all the alliances it can before the first election—there is no second chance. Hence, every party must be as broadly based as possible; a narrow, minor party has no hope of winning.

The winner-take-all feature of American elections has the same effect. Only one member of Congress is elected from each district. In many European countries, the elections are based on proportional representation. Each party submits a list of candidates for parliament, ranked in order of preference by the party leaders, and then the nation votes. A party winning 37 percent of the vote gets 37 percent of the seats in parliament; a party winning 2 percent of the vote gets 2 percent of the seats. Since even the smallest parties have a chance of winning something, minor parties have an incentive to organize. Indeed, some reformers have advocated for changing our electoral rules in the hope of creating more viable parties in the U.S.,[56] and still others have advanced proposals to reform or abolish the Electoral College (see Chapter 14).

The most dramatic example of the winner-take-all principle is the electoral college (see Chapter 14). In every state but Maine and Nebraska, the candidate who wins the most popular votes in a state wins *all* of that state's electoral votes. In 2016, Donald Trump won Utah's six electoral college votes by winning only 45 percent of the votes cast in that state; the remaining votes were divided primarily between Hillary Clinton and Independent candidate Evan McMullin. Even prominent minor party candidates—like Ross Perot in 1992, Ralph Nader in 2000, and McMullin, Gary Johnson, or Jill Stein in 2016—have been unable to win electoral college votes. Voters often are reluctant to "waste" their votes on a minor-party candidate who cannot win.

The presidency is the great prize of American politics; to win it, you must form a party with as broad appeal as possible. As a practical matter, this means there will be, in most cases, only two serious parties—one made up of those who support the party already in power, and the other made up of everybody else. Only one third party ever won the presidency—the Republican Party in 1860—and it had by then pretty much supplanted the Whig Party. No third party is likely to win, or even come close to winning, the presidency anytime soon.

Voters' opinions also help to explain why we have a two-party system. This might seem puzzling, as polls often show that voters want a third party: for example, one 2018 poll found that 68 percent of Americans supported having a third party. But voters do not agree on what positions that party should take. In that same poll, voters were split about whether they wanted the new party to be more centrist, more left-wing, or more right-wing.[57]

When you look at this data, voters want a third party that adopts *their* issue positions. But because Americans are not terribly ideological (see Chapter 7), there is no obvious set of positions for a third party to take and win.

There is another reason why voters' opinions help to maintain a two-party system. Most voters think they are better represented by one party or the other,[58] and this reflects the fact that the parties take positions on the issues. National surveys have found that most Americans see "a difference in what Democratic and Republican parties stand for." This percentage has increased in recent years as the parties have moved apart ideologically.[59] The public sees the two parties as having different platforms and issues, with different policy specialties. For the most part, the majority has deemed Democrats better at handling such issues as poverty, the environment, and health care and the Republicans better at handling such issues as national defense, foreign trade, and crime; but voters generally have split on which party is best at handling the economy and taxes.[60] The strength of these different issues brings multiple, and broad, coalitions of voters into each party, and that helps to maintain a two-party system.

While there have been periods of division in American politics, citizens still come together under the umbrella of the two major parties. There has not been a massive and persistent body of opinion that has rejected the prevailing economic system (and thus we have not had a Marxist party with mass appeal); there has not been in our history an aristocracy or monarchy (and thus no party has sought to restore aristocrats or monarchs to power). Churches and religion have almost always been regarded as matters of private choice that lie outside politics (and thus no party has sought to create or abolish special government privileges for one church or another). In some European nations, the organization of the economy, the prerogatives of the monarchy, and the role of the church have been major issues with long and bloody histories. In these countries, these issues have been so divisive that they have helped prevent the formation of broad coalition parties.

But Americans have had other deep divisions—between African Americans and white Americans, for example, and between North and South—and yet the two-party system has endured. This suggests that our electoral procedures are of great importance—the winner-take-all, plurality election rules have made it useless for anyone to attempt to create an all-white or an all-African American national party except as an act of momentary defiance or in the hope of taking enough votes away from the two major parties to force the presidential election into the House of Representatives. (That may have been George Wallace's strategy in 1968.)

For many years, there was an additional reason for the two-party system: The laws of many states made it difficult, if not impossible, for third parties to get on the ballot. In 1968, for example, the American Independent Party of George Wallace found that it would have to collect 433,000 signatures (15 percent of the votes cast in the last statewide election) in order to get on the presidential ballot in Ohio. Wallace took the issue to the Supreme Court, which ruled, six to three, that such a restriction was an unconstitutional violation of the equal protection clause of the Fourteenth Amendment.[61] Wallace got on the ballot. In 1980, John Anderson, running as an Independent, was able to get on the ballot in all 50 states; in 1992, Ross Perot did the same. But for the reasons already indicated, the two-party system will probably persist even without the aid of legal restrictions.

Minor Parties

The electoral system may prevent minor parties from winning, but it does not prevent them from forming. Minor parties—usually called, erroneously, "third parties"—have been a permanent feature of American political life.

Broadly speaking, four types of minor parties exist. Most notable are the ideological parties, ones that have a comprehensive view of American society and government that is radically different from that of the mainstream parties. Many of these, though not all, have been left-wing parties, such as the Socialist Party (1901 to the 1960s), Socialist Labor Party (1888 to 2009), and the Communist Party (1920s to the present). They usually are not interested in immediate electoral success and thus persist despite their poor showing at the polls. One such party, however, the Socialist Party of Eugene Debs, won nearly 6 percent of the popular vote in the 1912 presidential election. During its heyday, 1,200 candidates were elected to local offices, including 79 mayors. Part of the Socialist appeal arose from its opposition to municipal corruption, its opposition to American entry into World War I, and its critique of American society. No ideological party has ever carried a state in a presidential election.

The other three types of minor parties have focused more on short-term issues or divisions in the electorate. For example, single-issue parties focus their energies primarily on one issue. The most notable examples include the Free Soil Party, which opposed the spread of slavery (1848–1852), the American ("Know Nothing") Party, which opposed immigrants and Catholics (1856), and the Woman's Party, which fought for the right to vote for women (1913–1920). Third, economic protest parties typically focus on the economic grievances of a particular group, such as farmers; the Greenback Party (1876–1884) and the Populist Party (1892–1908) are the most prominent examples. Finally, the factional parties have split from a major party over some difference with them. Famous examples include the "Bull Moose" Progressive Party, which split from the Republican Party in 1912, and the States' Rights ("Dixiecrat") Party, which split from the Democratic Party in 1948.

None of these minor parties, however, has had much electoral success. Apart from the Republicans, who quickly became a major party, the only minor parties to carry states and thus win electoral votes were one party of economic protest (the Populists, who carried five states in 1892) and several factional parties (most recently, the States' Rights Democrats in 1948 and the American Independent Party of George Wallace in 1968). Though factional parties may hope to cause the defeat of the party from which they split, they have not always been able to achieve this. Harry Truman was elected in 1948 despite the defections of both the leftist progressives, led by Henry Wallace, and the right-wing Dixiecrats, led by J. Strom Thurmond. It seems likely that Hubert Humphrey would have lost in 1968 even if George Wallace had not been in the race (Wallace voters would probably have switched to Nixon rather than to Humphrey, though of course one cannot be certain). It is quite possible, on the other hand, that a Republican might have beaten Woodrow Wilson in 1912 if the Republican Party had not split in two (the regulars supporting William Howard Taft, the progressives supporting Theodore Roosevelt).

What is striking is not that we have had so many minor parties but that we have not had more. Several major political movements did not produce a significant third party: the Civil Rights movement of the 1960s, the antiwar movement of the same decade, and, most important, the labor movement of the 20th century. African Americans were part of the Republican Party after the Civil War and part of the Democratic Party after the New Deal (even though the southern wing of that party for a long time kept them from voting). The antiwar movement found candidates with whom it could identify within the Democratic Party (Eugene McCarthy, Robert F. Kennedy, George McGovern), even though a Democratic president, Lyndon B. Johnson, was chiefly responsible for the U.S. commitment in Vietnam. After Johnson only narrowly won the 1968 New Hampshire primary, he withdrew from the race. Unions have not tried to create a labor party—indeed, they were for a long time opposed to almost any kind of national political activity. Since labor became a major political force in the 1930s, the largest industrial unions have been content to operate as a part (a very large part) of the Democratic Party.

One reason some potential sources of minor parties never formed such parties, in addition to the dim chance of success, is that the direct primary and the national convention made it possible for dissident elements of a major party—unless they become completely disaffected—to remain in the party and influence the choice of candidates and policies. The antiwar movement had a profound effect on the Democratic Conventions of 1968 and 1972; African-Americans have played a significant role in the Democratic Party, especially with the candidacy of Jesse Jackson in 1984 and 1988 and Barack Obama in 2008 and 2012; only in 1972 did the unions feel that the Democrats nominated a presidential candidate (McGovern) unacceptable to them.

The impact of minor parties on American politics is hard to judge. One bit of conventional wisdom holds that minor parties develop ideas that the major parties later come to adopt. The Socialist Party, for example, supposedly called for major social and economic policies that the Democrats under Roosevelt later embraced and termed the New Deal. It is possible the Democrats did steal the thunder of the Socialists, but it hardly seems likely that they did it because the Socialists had proposed these things or proved them popular. (In 1932, the Socialists received only 2 percent of the vote and in 1936 less than one-half of 1 percent.) Roosevelt probably adopted the policies in part because he thought them correct and in part because dissident elements within his *own* party—leaders such as Huey Long of Louisiana—were threatening to bolt the Democratic Party if it did not move to the left. Even Prohibition was adopted more as a result of the efforts of interest groups such as the Anti-Saloon League than as the consequence of its endorsement by the Prohibition Party.

The minor parties that have probably had the greatest influence on public policy have been the factional parties. Mugwumps and liberal Republicans, by bolting the regular party, may have made that party more sensitive to the issue of civil service reform; the Bull Moose and La Follette Progressive Parties probably helped encourage the major parties to pay more attention to issues of business regulation and party reform; the Dixiecrat and Wallace movements probably strengthened the hands of those who wished to go slow on desegregation. The threat of a factional split is a risk that both major parties must face,

Image 9.6 Tea Party members at a rally. The Tea Party is not truly a minor party, but has influenced the Republican Party in recent years.

and it is in the efforts that each makes to avoid such splits that one finds the greatest impact of minor parties—or at least that was the case in the 20th century.

The Tea Party movement is not a single national party, but it does share characteristics with minor parties. It emerged in 2009, organized by voters and groups opposed to government spending, as well as to President Obama.[62] The group did have some notable successes, getting tough spending limits put it place in a 2011 budget deal, and helping to defeat some long-standing Republican elected officials, such as former House majority leader Eric Cantor, who lost in a 2014 primary election to a Tea Party-backed candidate. But with the removal of those spending caps in a budget deal in 2019, and the return of trillion-dollar plus yearly budget deficits, Senator Rand Paul—and many observers—declared the group dead.[63]

Some have argued that the Tea Party was a temporary aberration with little lasting effect, but this is not correct. First, the group exerted—and continues to exert—an influence over policy. While the Tea Party Caucus is now defunct, the House Freedom Caucus—joined by many of the same members—continues to push for conservative policies on a wide variety of topics. Further, many of those who came into Congress through the Tea Party have become important leaders in the Republican Party.[64] Finally, and most importantly, the Tea Party paved the way for Donald Trump's election as president—many of his strongest supporters were initially Tea Party supporters.[65]

Learning Objectives

9-1 Describe the roles of American political parties and how they differ from parties in other democracies.

A political party is an organization that works to elect candidates to public office and identifies candidates by a clear name or label. American parties tend to be somewhat weaker than their counterparts elsewhere for several structural reasons (control of access to the ballot, divided legislative/executive power, and federalism).

9-2 Summarize the historical evolution of the party system in America.

Initially, there were no parties in America: George Washington called parties "factions." But as soon as it was time to select his replacement, the republic's first leaders realized they had to organize their followers to win the election, and parties were born. They gradually strengthened during the 19th century, before progressive reforms weakened their power in the early to mid-20th century. More recently, however, the parties have become both stronger and more polarized.

9-3 Explain the major functions of political parties.

Parties help candidates win office, and then coordinate their behavior once in office. To win office, they recruit candidates, nominate them (either via primaries or conventions), and then help them win the general election.

9-4 Explain how parties are organized in America.

The parties have a federalized structure: there is a national party, and state and local parties organized beneath them. While the different levels operate independently of one another, there are important areas of collaboration between them.

9-5 Define partisan identification, and explain how it shapes the political behavior of ordinary Americans.

Partisan identification refers to Americans' attachment to a political party. For most people, it is like belonging to a political team. Party identification powerfully shapes vote choice in elections: more than 90 percent of partisans supported their party's candidate in recent elections. It also influences their evaluation of political leaders and institutions, with partisans more trusting of the government when their party is in control.

9-6 Summarize the arguments for why America has a two-party system.

The United States has a two-party political system because of two structural features in American politics: single-member districts and winner-take-all elections, as well as the distribution of voter opinions. These features encourage the existence of two major parties, as smaller parties face great difficulty in winning elective office.

To Learn More

Democratic National Committee: **www.democrats.org**

Republican National Committee: **www.gop.com**

Green Party: **www.gp.org**

Libertarian Party: **www.lp.org**

Aldrich, John H. *Why Parties? The Origin and Transformation of Political Parties in America.* Chicago, IL: University of Chicago Press, 1995. Explains why parties emerged and continue in American politics.

Cohen, Martin, David Karol, Hans Noel, and John Zaller. *The Party Decides: Presidential Nominations Before and After Reform*. Chicago, IL: University of Chicago Press, 2008. Argues that party elites have reclaimed the presidential nomination process via the invisible primary process.

Drutman, Lee. *Breaking the Two-Party Doom Loop: The Case for Multiparty Democracy in America.* New York: Oxford University Press, 2020. Argues for different electoral systems to promote multi-party democracy and reduce polarization.

Hershey, Marjorie. *Party Politics in America*, 17th ed. New York: Routledge, 2017. Discusses the ways parties shape American politics.

Hofstadter, Richard. *The Idea of a Party System: The Rise of Legitimate Opposition in the United States*, 1780–1840. Berkeley: University of California Press, 1969. Brilliant history of how political parties came to be viewed by most leaders as necessary and desirable political institutions.

Key, V. O., Jr. *Southern Politics*. New York: Knopf, 1949. A classic account of the one-party South.

Klar, Samara, and Yanna Krupnikov. *Independent Politics: How American Disdain for Parties Leads to Political Inaction*. New York: Cambridge University Press, 2016. Argues that Americans identify as Independents largely because they dislike political conflict, and this in turn limits political activity.

Nader, Ralph. *Crashing the Party: Taking on the Corporate Government in an Age of Surrender*. New York: St. Martin's Press, 2002. An impassioned attack on the two-party system by a well-known activist who ran for president as a minor-party candidate in 2000 and 2004.

Riordan, William L. *Plunkitt of Tammany Hall*. New York: Knopf, 1948. (First published in 1905.) Insightful account of how an old-style party boss operated.

Schattschneider, E. E. *Party Government*. New York: Holt, Rinehart and Winston, 1942. An argument for a more disciplined and centralized two-party system.

Wilson, James Q. *The Amateur Democrat*. Chicago, IL: University of Chicago Press, 1962. Analysis of the issue-oriented political clubs that rose in the 1950s and 1960s.

Kevin Dietsch/UPI/Bloomberg/Getty Images

CHAPTER 10

Elections and Campaigns

Learning Objectives

10-1 Describe the factors that influence the presidential primaries.

10-2 Explain how campaigns shape the outcome of presidential elections.

10-3 Summarize how voters learn about the candidates in elections.

10-4 Explain which social groups have been most loyal to the parties over time.

10-5 Describe the key differences between presidential and congressional elections.

10-6 Summarize the history of campaign finance reform efforts, and explain the current state of campaign finance regulation.

10-7 Describe how elections shape public policy.

National elections in the United States in the 21st century would be virtually unrecognizable to politicians from the early republic. As we saw in Chapter 9, political parties once determined, or powerfully influenced, who got nominated. In the 19th century, the members of Congress from a given caucus would meet to pick their presidential candidate. After the caucuses were replaced by the national nominating conventions, the real power was wielded by local party leaders, who came together (sometimes in the legendary "smoke-filled rooms") to choose the candidate, whom the rest of the delegates would then endorse. Congressional candidates were also often hand-picked by local party bosses. Most people voted a straight party ticket. This system endured until well into the 20th century.

« Then In 1968, Vice President Hubert Humphrey won the Democratic presidential nomination without competing in a single state primary. His party's bosses pretty much delivered the nomination to him. He competed in a three-way race for president without having to raise nearly as much money as candidates routinely do today. (He lost in a close race to Republican Richard M. Nixon.)

*** Now** In 2020, President Donald Trump was seeking his second term in office. Though Trump lost the 2016 popular vote to former Secretary of State Hillary Clinton by almost 3 million votes, he won the election by securing enough Electoral College votes. The Democratic primary was wide open, with more than 2 dozen candidates seeking the nomination. The field was especially notable for having a wide variety of candidates of different races and genders, and was among the most diverse fields of any presidential nominating contest. Many people assumed that former Vice President Joe Biden would be an also-ran after finishing a disappointing fouth in the Iowa caucus and fifth in the New Hampshire primary. But after an unexpectedly strong win in the South Carolina primary, Biden surged in subsequent primaries and became the party's nominee. In the general election, Biden and Trump clashed over the economy, the coronavirus pandemic, and issues of racial justice, with Biden winning enough Electoral College votes to become the 46th president.

In both the primary and general election, all of the candidates raised money at a feverish pace. In just 2019 alone—before the primary process had even begun—the presidential candidates raised over $1.1 billion, which does not include the considerable amounts raised and spent by the parties or outside groups (let alone the money spent on other races).[1]

Within the lifetimes of many living national political leaders, campaigns and elections have changed rather dramatically: parties went from being important to unimportant and (partially) back again, mass media—especially television and the Internet—have become more important, polling has become ubiquitous, and money—and the nonstop fundraising that keeps it coming—now matters more than ever.

Perhaps the most striking finding about contemporary elections is how much money candidates must raise and spend to compete. As Figure 10.1 shows, for the last two decades, congressional candidates have raised over $1 billion each election cycle; in 2018, that figure jumped to a record $2.77 billion. In the 2016 election, candidates for president raised $1.5 billion, candidates for Congress raised $1.6 billion, the party committees raised $1.6 billion, and political action committees (PACs) raised $4 billion, for a combined total of approximately $8.7 billion.

Thus, we have entered the era of the $8 billion presidential election cycle. The climb there has been steep but steady. For instance, in 1980, all presidential candidates raised about $162 million. Adjusted for inflation, the 2016 total is over three times the 1980 total. Even in the last decade and a half, the amount of money raised in presidential elections has increased sharply. In 2000, all presidential candidates raised about $578 million; adjusted for inflation, the 2016 figure is 1.8 times as much; congressional fundraising tells much the same tale. Whether we will witness $9 billion, or more, national election cycles in the future remains to be seen, but the amounts of money that candidates, parties, and PACs collect have been increasing exponentially.

Many people lament the fact that so much money is spent on elections, arguing that the consultants, media ads, and modern campaign techniques end up emphasizing ephemera and avoiding the real issues. While it is true that media reports of elections leave much to be desired (as we will discuss in Chapter 12), campaigns do stress the issues, and voters respond to their messages in reasonable ways. While they are far from perfect, campaigns are ultimately the most important pathway linking voters' preferences to government policy. In this chapter we show what campaigns do, how voters respond, and what this tells us about the link between voters and government.

Here and Abroad

Unlike elections in many other democratic nations, elections in America have not one but two crucial phases: getting nominated and getting elected. Getting nominated means getting your name on the ballot. In the great majority of states, winning your party's nomination for either the presidency or Congress requires effort

Figure 10.1 Campaign Receipts, 2000–2018

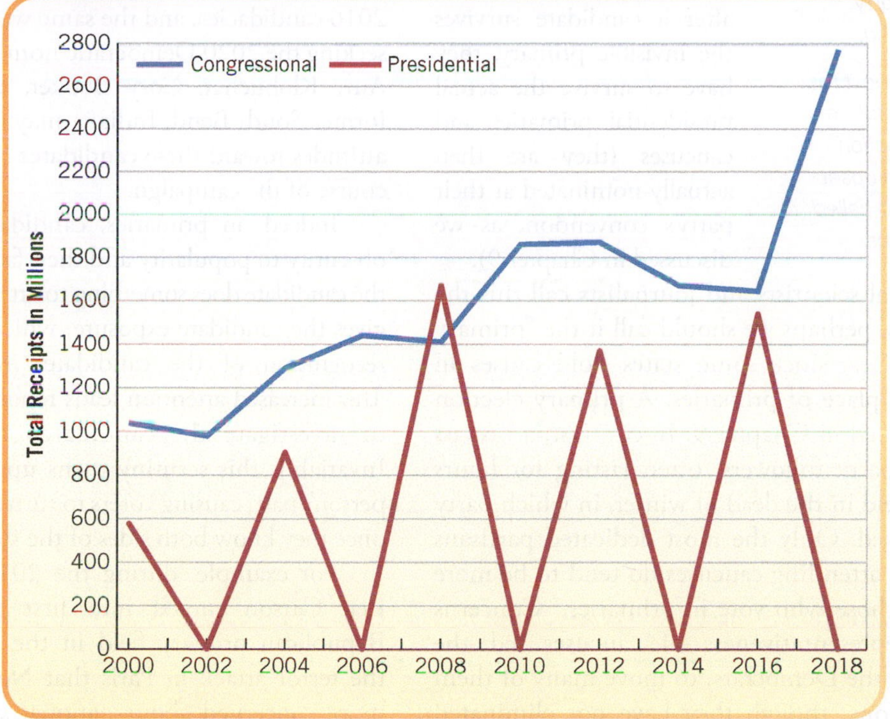

Source: Federal Election Commission, FEC Statistical Summaries of the Various Election Cycles.

Note: Cell entries are in millions of dollars, not adjusted for inflation.

on your part. As we discussed in the previous chapter, the party may help to recruit you (and may even provide other services), but the candidates themselves need to staff and run their own campaigns. By contrast, in most European parliamentary democracies, winning a party's nomination for parliament involves an *organizational* decision—*the party* looks you over, *the party* decides whether to allow you to run, and *the party* puts your name on its list of candidates.

American political parties do play a role in determining the outcome of the final election, but both the candidates themselves and the party matter. By contrast, many other democratic nations conduct campaigns almost entirely as a contest between parties. In Israel and the Netherlands, the names of the candidates for the legislature do not even appear on the ballot; only the party names are listed there. And even where candidate names are listed, as in Great Britain, voters tend to vote "Conservative" or "Labour" more than they vote for Smith or Jones. European nations (except France) do not have a directly elected president; instead, the party that has won the most seats in parliament selects the head of the government, termed the *prime minister*. As we saw in the last chapter, American parties are quite different from their European counterparts, and these differences spill over into their elections as well.

Chip Somodevilla/Getty Images News/Getty Images

Image 10.1 After working in the Obama administration to create the Consumer Financial Protection Bureau, Elizabeth Warren won election to the U.S. Senate from Massachusetts in 2012, and won reelection in 2018. In 2020, she ran for the Democratic nomination for president, when she became known for taking selfies with voters.

10-1 Presidential Elections: Winning the Nomination

No office in American politics is more important than the presidency, and the first step to winning it is to survive the primary process. We discussed in Chapter 9 the invisible primary, the process party elites use to narrow down the field

caucus *A meeting of party followers in which party delegates are selected.*

momentum *The boost that a candidate gains in future contests after an election victory (especially an upset win). Sometimes also called the bandwagon effect.*

to the candidates that they find acceptable. But even after a candidate survives the invisible primary, they have to survive the actual presidential primaries and caucuses (they are then actually nominated at their party's convention, as we discussed in Chapter 9).

While political scientists and journalists call this the "primary" process, perhaps we should call it the "primary and caucus" process, since some states hold causes in addition to or in place of primaries. A primary election operates as described in Chapter 9. In contrast, a **caucus** is a meeting of party followers, often lasting for hours and sometimes held in the dead of winter, in which party delegates are picked. Only the most dedicated partisans attend, and those attending caucuses do tend to be more ideological than those who vote in primaries.[2] Concerns about the un-representativeness of caucuses led the parties, especially the Democrats, to move many of them to primary elections, though they have not eliminated them completely.[3] To win the nomination, a candidate needs to succeed in both primaries and caucuses.

For most candidates, the biggest challenge in the primary is that they are largely unknown to the public, so voters' attitudes about them are quite malleable. When an incumbent president runs for reelection—as President Obama did in 2012, or President Trump did in 2020—voters have a relatively fixed opinion of the incumbent, since that person has been president for four years. But many voters will never even have heard of most other candidates. For example, many Americans had no idea who Ted Cruz, Ben Carson, and Bernie Sanders were before their 2016 candidacies, and the same was true for many of those seeking the 2020 Democratic nomination, such as Senators Amy Klobuchar, Cory Booker, and Kamala Harris, or former South Bend, Indiana mayor Pete Buttigieg. Voters' attitudes toward these candidates changed rapidly over the course of the campaign.

CHRIS CARLSON/AFP/Getty Images

Image 10.2 New Jersey Senator Corey Booker gives a speech during his campaign for the Democratic Party's 2020 nomination.

Indeed, in primaries, candidates frequently go from obscurity to popularity and then fade away again.[4] Initially, the candidate does something to attract media attention. This gives the candidate exposure, which in turn increases their recognition of the candidate's name and favorability.[5] This increased attention leads reporters—and opponents—to investigate the candidate's record more carefully. Invariably, this scrutiny turns up negative aspects of the person's past, causing voters to turn away from the candidate once they know both sides of the story.

For example, during the 2016 Republican primary, Ben Carson surged into first place in the crowded Republican primary field in the fall of 2015. But after the terror attack in Paris that November, voters became more concerned about national security, an issue where Carson was weak.[6] After that, Carson's numbers fell and never recovered, and he dropped out the race in March of 2016, though he would later serve as President Trump's Secretary of Housing and Urban Development. Similarly, in the 2020 Democratic primary, Senator Elizabeth Warren surged to first place in the fall of 2019. But she then faced scrutiny about how she would pay for her universal health care plan, driving down her poll numbers and leading her to drop out of the race in March of 2020.

This pattern highlights the crucial role of media in campaigns. One core finding (as we will discuss in Chapter 12) is that media influence is greatest when people have the least knowledge about an issue.[7] In a primary election, when voters are just getting to know a candidate, the media have a large effect. For example, one of several factors explaining Donald Trump's success in the 2016 primary season is that he received nearly $2 billion in free media coverage during the winter and spring months.[8] Trump was nearly always in the news while other candidates struggled to get airtime, giving him an advantage. By the time of the general election, when voters have a stronger impression of the candidates, the media's effect is less significant, though still very important.

But media coverage is not the only factor that matters in a primary election. Another key factor is **momentum** or the *bandwagon effect.* A candidate's win, especially in an upset victory, generates favorable press coverage, which increases name recognition and approval of the candidate. Winning once convinces voters that you can do it again, which changes the dynamics of an election.[9] President

Obama's 2008 campaign offers a striking example of this phenomenon. Before the 2008 campaign began, pundits and politicians alike assumed Hillary Clinton would easily walk away with the Democratic nomination. But then, early in the year, Barack Obama won a surprising upset victory in the Iowa Caucuses, and the momentum swung his way. Though Clinton won the next primary in New Hampshire, and the primary process went on for months, Obama's victory in Iowa convinced voters that he was electable. Similarly, in 2020, while Joe Biden had been expected to win the South Carolina primary, few expected him to win it as overwhelmingly as he did—he carried every single county in the state, garnering nearly 2.5 times as many votes as his nearest rival, Senator Bernie Sanders. That win—along with the consolidation of the party behind him—helped propel him to victory in subsequent primaries, and eventually he became the presumptive nominee when his last remaining rival, Senator Sanders, suspended his campaign in early April.

Any discussion of momentum points to another concern about the primary process: the front-loading of the primary calendar. Every state wants their primary to "matter," and state leaders all think the way to make that happen is to move their state's primary to the beginning of the calendar. In 1968, it took 12 weeks for the parties to award 50 percent of the delegates in the party's national conventions, but by 2004, it took only five weeks (for Republicans) and six weeks (for Democrats) to award 50 percent of the delegates.[10]

Concerned about the shortened length of the campaign, the parties have pushed back somewhat on frontloading in the last few election cycles, issuing rules about when parties can hold primaries. As a result of these changes, in 2012, it took closer to 10 weeks for 50 percent of the delegates to be awarded.[11]

Some Republicans concluded that the lengthy 2012 primary hurt Mitt Romney, the party's nominee. Therefore they voted to change the rules for 2016 to again frontload the process and make it easier for a candidate to capture the nomination early on.[12] Indeed, they put nearly half of the delegates required to win the nomination up for grabs on a single day (March 1, Super Tuesday). While Donald Trump did not clinch the nomination until late in the process, more than half of the delegates had been awarded by mid-March, six weeks after the primary season began in Iowa. While many Republicans had hoped that these rules would allow an establishment favorite to capture the nomination early—someone like, say, Jeb Bush—they actually helped Donald Trump.[13] As is often the case in politics, reforms have unintended consequences.

Such front-loading may benefit state parties, but it harms voters: they have less time to learn about the candidates. Furthermore, because so much of the campaign happens early in the season, fewer voters get to participate in the process: If the key events are the first few primaries, then those in the later states have effectively no say in the nominees.[14] That said, because states want greater say in the process, front-loading is unlikely to reverse completely—though the rules issued by the parties have limited its growth.

Adam Glanzman/Bloomberg/Getty Images

Image 10.3 Candidates for the 2020 Democratic presidential nomination competed in a primary election debate.

10-2 How Does the Campaign Matter?

Once the candidates secure their party's nomination via the primary process, the general election begins. The modern general election campaign takes place roughly from Labor Day (or the conventions, if they come first) to Election Day.

While we like to think that the president is elected on Election Day in November, according to the Constitution, the Electoral College actually selects the president when it meets in December. Indeed, although Hillary Clinton received more popular votes than Donald Trump did in 2016—almost 3 million more—Trump became president by winning more Electoral College votes. We discuss the Electoral College in more detail in Chapter 14; for now, we note that it has enormous implications for campaign strategy. With the exception of Maine and Nebraska, states award their Electoral College votes in a winner-take-all format, so that even if one candidate receives barely more voters than the other, that candidate wins all of the state's Electoral College votes. For example, in 2016, Donald Trump beat Hillary Clinton in Michigan by just over 10,000 votes of nearly 5 million ballots cast, a margin of victory of 0.2 percent. Despite this razor-thin margin, Trump won *all* of the state's 16 Electoral College votes.

battleground states *The most competitive states in the presidential election that either candidate could win; also called swing states.*

retrospective voting *Voting for a candidate because you like their past actions in office.*

prospective voting *Voting for a candidate because you favor their ideas for handling issues.*

Given this winner-take-all allocation rule, campaigns have a large incentive to focus on the most competitive states—the so-called swing or **battleground states**—where either candidate can win the state (and hence its electoral votes). For example, although California has more electoral votes than any other state (55), few candidates spend much time there because it is so heavily Democratic. Instead, most candidates spend their time in more competitive states. In recent election cycles, those have been states such as Pennsylvania, Florida, Michigan, North Carolina, and Wisconsin, though they can change from election to election. The candidates and their surrogates blanket these states with campaign ads and appearances, and as a result, voters in these states are better informed about the issues and the candidates.[15] This highlights a point to which we will return below: campaigns do help to inform and educate voters!

It is a truism to say that "campaigns matter." But how do they matter? How do campaigns convince voters to select a particular candidate? We argue that campaigns do this primarily through three related forces: by assigning credit or blame for the state of the nation, by activating latent partisanship, and by allowing voters to judge the qualities of the candidates' character. We take up each one below in turn.

Assigning Credit or Blame for the State of the Nation

The first thing campaigns do is help voters assign credit or blame for the state of the nation. Voters hold the president responsible for the overall state of the country: Is the economy doing well? Are we at war? Are we facing a global health pandemic? Americans may have hazy, even erroneous, views about monetary policy, business regulation, and defense policy, but they likely have a very good idea about whether unemployment is up or down, grocery prices are stable or rising, or Americans are dying in a foreign war. In short, the voters know whether the country is (in general) headed on the right track or the wrong track.

If things are going well, the incumbent candidate (or if the incumbent is not running, the candidate from the incumbent's party) tries to claim credit for the peace and prosperity the country is experiencing. In contrast, if the country is doing poorly, the challenger tries to pin the blame for the poor state of affairs on the incumbent. Campaigns help voters connect the state of the nation with the party in power—reelect me (or my party) because we have been good stewards, or vote out the incumbent for not being one.[16] This is why incumbent Ronald Reagan spoke of "Morning in America" in 1984 when the economy was doing well, but challenger Bill Clinton spoke of "It's the Economy, Stupid!" during a recession in 1992.

This idea—that elections are decided based on punishment or reward for the health of the nation—is known as **retrospective voting**. It is retrospective because voters look back on the previous administration and make a judgment about whether or not they deserve another term in office.[17] In contrast, other voters vote prospectively. *Prospective* means "forward-looking"—we vote prospectively when we examine the rival candidates' views on the issues of the day and then cast our ballots for the person we think has the best ideas for handling these matters. **Prospective voting** requires a lot of information about issues and candidates, and most who do it are political junkies who are deeply engaged in politics. As a result, prospective voting is a relatively minor factor in most elections, whereas retrospective voting is much more common.

The quintessential summary of retrospective voting came from Ronald Reagan during the 1980 election: "Are you better off than you were four years ago?" The economy had soured under Carter, and things seemed to be getting worse overseas. In that election, voters decided that they were no better off in 1980 than they were in 1976, and they voted Carter out of office. In contrast, making that same comparison in 2012, voters decided they were better off in 2012 than they were in 2008, and they reelected President Obama.

These same contrasts played out in 2020 as well. President Trump lost (as we explain in the "How Things Work" feature on page 225) because of voter's assessment of his handling of the economy and related issues like the coronavirus pandemic.

This retrospective effect is so strong that political scientists can use the fundamentals to predict election outcomes reasonably well in advance of the campaign. Figure 10.2 shows the relationship between the health of the economy in the election year (measured by the change in gross domestic product [GDP]) and the incumbent's vote share.

Each dot in Figure 10.2 represents a presidential election (19 in all, from 1948 to 2020), and the solid line shows the relationship between the two (this is the so-called regression line). Note that the two are strongly related: incumbents (or their party) do much better when the economy is doing better. Voters reward incumbents for a good economy and punish them for a bad one.

Figure 10.2 **The Economy and the Presidential Vote, 1948–2020**

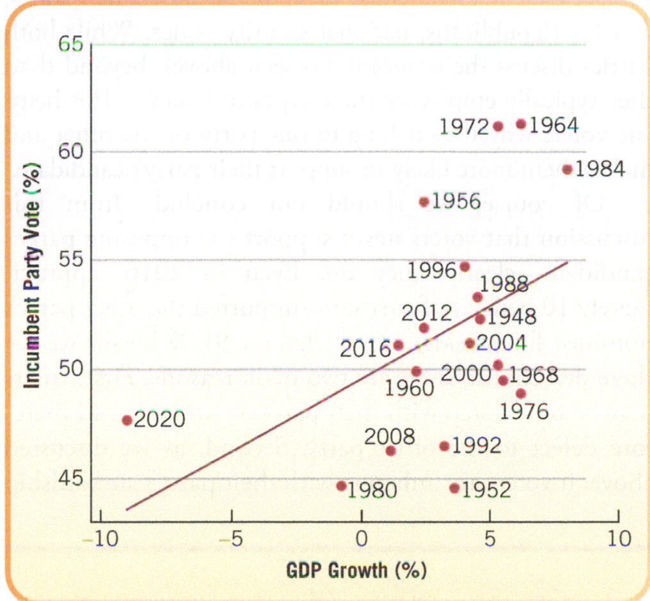

Source: GDP growth data from the Federal Reserve Bank of St. Louis, https://fred.stlouisfed.org/, as published in February 2017; election returns come from Dave Leip's Atlas of U.S. Presidential Elections, http://uselectionatlas.org.

We should not interpret Figure 10.2 to mean that no other issues matter to the campaign beyond the economy. Other issues matter a great deal: crime, foreign policy, health care, immigration, and many others are hotly debated in elections. Foreign policy and terrorism in particular have long been central to many election campaigns: how the candidate would address the threat of communism was a staple of nearly every election during the Cold War, and since 9/11, how the candidates would address the threat of terrorism has similarly been a perennial debate (especially in 2004, shortly after the U.S. decision to invade Iraq). In 2016, while the economy was a key issue dividing voters between Clinton and Trump, just as important were attitudes toward immigration and other salient issues.[18] In 2020, the candidates sparred not only over the economy but about how to best address to the coronavirus pandemic, as well as how to respond to ongoing calls for racial justice. The issues matter in campaigns.

But in most years, for most voters, the economy is the central issue. For many years, the Gallup organization has been asking respondents to identify the most important problem facing the nation. When asked during an election year, Americans typically say the economy is the most important problem, often by a substantial margin.[19] Just before the 2012 election, for example, 72 percent said the economy (including the economy broadly, unemployment, the budget deficit, and so on) was the most important problem; similarly, 69 percent named the economy in 2008.[20] In the cases where the economy is not the major issue, it is either typically because the economy is booming (as it was in 2000) or because we face a major foreign policy challenge (going back to the Cold War). Because the economy is so central to people's lives, and the president is seen as the primary economic steward of the nation, the economy is the core issue in almost every presidential campaign.

In 2020, the candidates clashed over how much credit Trump deserved for the strong economy pre-COVID and how much blame he deserved for the pandemic-related slowdown.

The power of retrospective voting highlights an essential truth about elections: the fundamentals matter a great deal. A simple indicator of the health of the economy allows us to predict, with reasonable accuracy, the outcome of the election before the main part of the general election campaign even begins. The underlying health of the nation—the economy, whether we are at war or peace, the popularity of the incumbent (which is tied to the economy)—drives the election.[21]

But do not interpret this to mean that campaigns do not matter. If campaigns were irrelevant, all of the points in Figure 10.2 would lie along the solid line (the regression line), and this chapter would be much shorter. Instead, we see that in some years, the points are quite close to the line, whereas in others, they are farther away, suggesting the outcomes diverged from the predictions based on the fundamentals. Just as the fundamentals matter, so does the campaign. After all, the campaign is what helps voters know how to assign credit or blame for the fundamentals. Furthermore, a well-run campaign, especially in a close election, can make the difference between winning and losing.[22] The fundamentals get us in the ballpark of the final outcome, but we need to study the campaigns to understand the eventual outcome.

Image 10.4 Joe Biden and Dr. Jill Biden meet with voters during their train tour of PA and OH during the 2020 campaign.

Activating Latent Partisanship

Campaigns do more than help voters assign credit and blame for the state of the nation. They also activate voters' latent partisanship. As we saw in Chapter 9, in recent presidential elections, approximately 90 percent of voters supported their party's nominee. This is not just blind obedience. Rather, it reflects a process of the campaign helping voters understand *why* they should support their party's nominee. As Professor James Campbell put it, "campaigns remind Democrats why they are Democrats rather than Republicans and remind Republicans why they are Republicans rather than Democrats."[23]

Campaigns do this through a variety of methods, such as campaign appearances, advertisements, debates, and so forth; we discuss these methods later in the chapter.[24] Through all of these methods, however, candidates stress the issues that appeal to, and activate, their partisans. These are typically the issues for which the public sees them as being more competent than the other party. As we discussed in Chapter 9, for Democrats, these are social welfare issues, and for Republicans, national security issues. While both parties discuss the economy (as seen above), beyond that, they typically emphasize these types of issues.[25] This helps cue voters why they belong to one party or the other and makes them more likely to support their party's candidate.

Of course, we should not conclude from this discussion that voters never support the opposing party's candidate—clearly, they do. Even in 2016, approximately 10 percent of partisans supported the other party's nominee for president (see Chapter 9). Why do we see these defections? There are two main reasons. First, voters may be out of step with their party on an issue and therefore defect to the other party. Second, as we discussed above, if voters are unhappy with their party's stewardship

Can We Trust Pre-Election Polling?

In the run-up to the 2016 election, most polls had Hillary Clinton ahead—narrowly—of Donald Trump in the race for the presidency, and many polling-based forecasts predicted a near-certain Clinton win. In the aftermath of Trump's victory, many questioned whether such polls were still reliable. Can we trust election polling?

The answer is at least partially yes, though there obviously are important lessons to learn from 2016 and 2020. First, it is important to note that national polls are an estimate of the national popular vote, not the Electoral College vote. On that basis, the 2016 polls were accurate: the polls had Secretary Clinton up very slightly in the race for the White House, and she did win the popular vote by approximately 2 percent. Indeed, the polls in 2016 were *more* accurate than they were in 2012, and had similar levels of accuracy to those from 2008 and 2004. A recent study across many countries and elections concluded that election polling today is no less accurate than it has been in the past.

But that does not explain why 2016 polling missed the actual result in several key states, most notably Pennsylvania, Michigan, and Wisconsin. In the aftermath of the election, the American Association for Public Opinion Research convened a panel of leading pollsters and academics to study this issue. They identified several factors that help to explain these polling errors. First, an unusually large number of voters were undecided and broke at the last minute to disproportionately favor President Trump. While some attribute this shift to FBI Director James Comey's letter to Congress on October 28th, there is no definitive proof that it was the key factor—it undoubtedly played *some* role, but there were many other factors as well.

Second, those with more education were both more willing to participate in pre-election polls, and were more likely to support Secretary Clinton. Unless pollsters correct for this bias—and in 2016, many did not—their polls would have systematically over-stated her true support. This "education gap" has been increasing in recent years, so in previous elections, this was a less serious issue (we discuss this point in section 10-4 later in the chapter). But in 2016, this turned out to be an especially important issue, particularly in those key swing states.

In 2020, while the polls correctly predicted a Biden win, they did again over-estimate his support, especially in several key swing states. Pollsters will need to do a deep dive to understand why they missed the mark again. One special challenge in 2020 may have been that the COVID-19 pandemic changed which voters were at home and willing to answer pre-election polls, but more data will be needed to know for sure.

In the end, the most important points to remember when analyzing election polls are the ones we discussed in Chapter 7 about looking at multiple polls from different pollsters, examining the sample size, the wording, and so forth. Much as good polling can tell us what the public thinks about the candidates, it can also help us learn about what the public is likely to do in an election.

Source: Courtney Kennedy et al., "An Evaluation of the 2016 Presidential Election Polls in the United States," *Public Opinion Quarterly* 82(April 2018): 1–33; Will Jennings and Christopher Wlezien, "Election Polling Errors Across Time and Space," *Nature Human Behavior* 2 (2018): 276–83.

of the nation, they are likely to vote for the other party. For example, one of the keys to Donald Trump's victory in 2016 was convincing many voters to switch from supporting President Obama in 2012 to supporting him four years later.[26]

Understanding how campaigns activate partisanship also helps to clarify two other dynamics of electoral campaigns. First, the number of undecided voters declines over the course of a campaign. Much of this decline comes from partisans returning home to their party: Watching the campaign, they are reminded of why they are a Democrat or a Republican, and they move to support their candidate.[27] Many who are undecided early in the campaign just have not had their latent partisanship activated.

Second, this also reminds us that some voters do not identify with a party—they are Independents. As we saw in Chapter 9, in contemporary American presidential elections, both parties will win approximately 90 percent of their party's supporters. But we also saw that neither party has enough supporters to win by just appealing to its own base. Both parties also need to court Independent voters if they want to win elections.

Judging the Candidates' Character

A third major component of a campaign is helping voters judge the character of the candidates. Voters care about the issues, but they also care about a candidate's character. Voters not only want a candidate who takes the right positions on the issues; they also want someone who has the right traits as well—someone who provides strong leadership, has integrity and honesty, and displays empathy (i.e., cares about people like them).[28] Voters rely on these sorts of judgments because they provide clues as to how a president will behave in office. No one can know all the issues that a new president will face once in office. But if a candidate has these broad traits, then he or she will be more likely to be up to the challenge.

Contemporary campaigns often invoke these traits. Indeed, in 2016, much of the campaign focused on the candidates' character, both in the news media and in the advertisements and messages from the candidates themselves. For example, nearly 75 percent of Secretary Clinton's television ads, and nearly one-half of President Trump's, were about the candidates' character (and as we will see

Constitutional Connections | The "Natural Born" Presidents Clause

Article II, section 1, clause 5 of the Constitution states that "no person except a natural born Citizen, or a Citizen of the United States, at the time of the Adoption of this Constitution, shall be eligible to the Office of the President." During the Constitutional Convention, there was little debate on this clause. In Federalist No. 3, John Jay wrote of possible "dangers from foreign arms and influence" (emphasis in the original), but he did not specifically mention the Constitution's "natural born" presidents clause.

Eight of the 55 delegates to the Constitutional Convention were themselves foreign-born. Among them was Alexander Hamilton, born in the West Indies. In Federalist No. 67, the first of Hamilton's essays on the "constitution of the executive department," he answers critics who he says have depicted future presidents as "seated on a throne ... giving audience to the envoys of foreign potentates," and have associated the office with "images of Asiatic despotism and voluptuousness." But Hamilton, like Jay, makes no specific mention of the clause requiring that all save those foreign-born citizens alive when the Constitution is ratified must be born on American soil to be eligible to serve as president. However, in the 19th century, persons associated with anti-immigrant, anti-Catholic "Nativist" groups sometimes invoked the natural born presidents clause.

The clause has come to wide public attention twice more recently. In 2003, Arnold Schwarzenegger, the Austrian-born action-movie star and former champion bodybuilder, was elected as California's governor. In 2004, persons supporting Schwarzenegger for a possible run for the presidency launched websites and rallied to repeal the clause. But the "Amend for Arnold" movement (advocating repeal of the clause through a new constitutional amendment) was short-lived.

Second, Barack Obama, during his 2008 and 2012 campaigns, was subject to claims by various "birther" groups asserting that he was not born in Hawaii but in Kenya, or that he once held citizenship in Indonesia. There was no evidence in support of the claim, but that did not stop news about it from spreading. Donald Trump was among those questioning the president's Hawaiian birth in 2011, though the debate seemingly was settled when President Obama released a copy of his birth certificate that year. The issue resurfaced during the 2016 campaign, where Hillary Clinton used it to attack Trump's character. In the exchange, Trump falsely accused Hillary Clinton's 2008 campaign of starting the birther rumor, but he did admit that President Obama had been born in the United States. Afterward, the issue—and the clause—faded from public view.

Source: Thomas Beaumont, "AP Fact Check: Trump's Bogus Birtherism Claim about Clinton," PBS News Hour: The Rundown Blog, 21 September 2016.

valence issue *An issue on which everyone agrees, but the question is whether the candidate embraces the same view.*

positional issues *Issues in which rival candidates have opposing views and that also divide voters.*

in Chapter 12, the media were similarly focused on character, rather than the issues).[29] Secretary Clinton's ads argued that Mr. Trump lacked the temperament to be president, and 63 percent of voters agreed with her that he did not. Among this group, Clinton won 79 percent to 19 percent. Similarly, many of President Trump's messages stressed that Secretary Clinton was dishonest; he often called her "crooked Hillary" in his speeches. Around 61 percent of voters said that Hillary Clinton was not honest or trustworthy, and Trump won these voters 72 percent to 20 percent.[30] Campaign messages emphasizing the candidates' character (and especially their character flaws) had a strong effect on voters in 2016. Even controlling for other factors (such as the health of the economy, issues, and partisanship), assessments of a candidate's character matter.[31]

These sorts of character evaluations are an example of a **valence issue**.[32] A valence issue is one where everyone agrees; the question is whether or not the candidate embraces that view. For example, everyone wants the president to be a strong leader, to have integrity, and to display empathy; the question is whether a particular candidate has those qualities. Likewise, everyone wants a robust economy and a strong national defense, the question is whether a particular candidate's plan will help us get there. In contrast, there are also **positional issues**—ones in which the rival candidates have opposing views on a question that also divides the voters. Many of the issues we think about are positional issues: gun control, abortion, same-sex marriage, and tax cuts, to name a few. As this section has made clear, both types of issues matter in elections.

Which Factors Matter Most?

Throughout this section, we explained how campaigns do three important things: help assign credit or blame for the state of the nation, activate voters' latent partisanship, and allow voters to judge the character of the candidates. But which of these are most important? Obviously, all three are important, but ultimately partisanship probably takes the most important ranking, with the health of the nation second and character third. Partisanship is arguably the most central factor, and it anchors most voters to a party election after election. The health of the nation is almost equally important: voters, except for the strongest partisans, are unlikely to support their party's candidate if he or she has performed poorly in office. And for voters with weaker partisan ties, or Independent voters, the health of the nation is paramount. These are the "fundamentals" we discussed earlier that primarily drive elections. Finally, character evaluations also matter, but less so than these other two factors. Ultimately, however, it is important to remember that all of these factors matter.

10-3 How Do Voters Learn About the Candidates?

We just reviewed what campaigns do for voters. But how do campaigns actually convey this information to voters? How do voters learn which candidate should be credited for a booming economy, or which one they don't like because he or she lacks integrity? They do so through campaign communication. This can take many forms, but we can think of them as usefully falling into two broad classes: campaign-created communications (e.g., advertisements, speeches) and campaign events (e.g., debates and conventions). They both help inform voters, but in somewhat different ways.

Campaign Communications

As we learned at the outset of the chapter, presidential campaigns now cost in the billions of dollars—several times what they cost even a few decades ago. In every recent election, advertising has typically been the single biggest expense for both candidates. Most notably, this would be television advertisements, though it would also include other methods such as direct mail, social media platforms, and so forth.

In every recent presidential election, both campaigns have spent lavishly on television advertisements, especially in key battleground states. In 2016, Clinton and Trump advertised heavily in states such as Florida, Ohio, Pennsylvania, Iowa, Wisconsin, and Colorado. For example, during the 2016 election, Clinton and Trump spent over $110 million dollars in the state of Florida alone.[33] Indeed, in many areas, one cannot watch TV during an election year without being bombarded by television advertisements. To see the ads that were aired in 2020, as well as in previous elections, visit the Living Room Candidate (www.livingroomcandidate.org).

Anyone who has seen campaign advertisements on television knows that many of them, if not most, share two features: they appeal to emotions, and they make negative attacks. Emotional appeals have become ubiquitous. A comprehensive study carefully analyzed thousands

How Things Work | The 2020 Election

The 2020 election was certainly one for the textbooks! After a hard-fought campaign, Joe Biden secured the 270 Electoral College votes needed to win the presidency, making Donald Trump the first incumbent to lose a reelection bid since George. H. W. Bush lost to Bill Clinton in 1992. While the election took place during a global pandemic, this did not stop approximately 159 million voters from casting a ballot in this election, giving the U.S. the highest voter turnout in a presidential election since the early 20th century. This election also marks the first time a woman or a person of color has become the vice president, with U.S. Senator Kamala Harris elected to that position on the Democratic ticket.

Despite all of the upheaval in the country over the course of the year—from impeachment, to COVID-19, to protests over racial injustice and police brutality—polling data throughout the campaign showed little change over time, with former Vice President Biden holding a modest lead over President Trump for most of the year. While some states were still counting (or recounting) votes at the time this textbook was published, as of late November 2020, Joe Biden was on track to win an Electoral College majority similar to Donald Trump's in 2016, though Biden also was expected to win the national popular vote by about 4-5 percentage points (as we note below, this is somewhat less than what pre-election polls predicted he would receive). While the world was tumultuous in 2020, the presidential race was not.

What variables best explain this stability, as well as why Biden won? The first is that partisanship, and views of President Trump, were especially crucial in 2020. As in other recent elections, more than 9 in 10 Democrats backed Joe Biden, and Republicans supported Donald Trump at similar levels (as is typical, the winning candidate, Joe Biden, won Independent voters). Similarly, pollsters ask voters whether their vote is primarily *for* their own candidate, or more *against* their opponent. In 2020, among those who said that their vote was primarily for their candidate, Trump and Biden fared similarly. But among those whose vote was more against the opposing candidate, President Trump did quite poorly. For many voters, this election was much more about President Trump than it was about former Vice President Biden. Love him or hate him, President Trump elicited strong feelings throughout his White House tenure, meaning there were fewer persuadable voters at the presidential level (there were far more persuadable voters down-ballot, however, as discussed below).

Second, while President Trump won voters who thought the economy was the most important issue, an equally sized group of voters saw the coronavirus pandemic or racial injustice as the most important issues in the election, and former Vice President Biden overwhelmingly won these individuals. Of course, in the context of 2020, it is very difficult to separate out these three issues, because how the United States addresses the coronavirus pandemic is directly related to the economy, as well as ongoing conversations about racial justice (as racial and ethnic minorities suffered disproportionately from the COVID-19 pandemic and subsequent economic fallout). Voters were persuaded that President Trump's management of these issues meant he did not deserve a second term.

Third, as in 2016, we saw large gaps among white voters with and without college degrees. In 2020, white voters with college degrees favored Vice President Biden, but non-college-educated white voters broke strongly for President Trump. Fascinatingly, however, these same college-educated white voters did not necessarily support Democrats down-ballot, which meant that House Democrats saw their majority shrink and Democrats made few gains in state-level races. Whether this education gap among white voters is a durable shift, or was largely a reaction to President Trump, will be an important issue moving forward.

Interestingly, according to the exit polls, while men's support for President Trump stayed the same from 2016 to 2020, women shifted away from President Trump over this time. In 2016, Secretary Clinton won the support of 54 percent of women, but Vice President Biden won 57 of their support in 2020. But as in past years, this masks large differences among married versus unmarried people. Among married men and women alike, President Trump won a majority of voters, whereas Vice President Biden won those who were not married. This is partially due to an age effect, as unmarried voters are disproportionately younger, and Vice President Biden handily won younger voters.

Finally, as we discussed in the How Things Work box on page 222, as in 2016, the polls over-estimated support for the Democratic nominee. As of late November 2020, former Vice President Biden was likely to win the national popular vote by 4-5 percentage points (the final figure was not known, as several states were still counting mail-in ballots), but the pre-election polling average showed him winning it by approximately 7 points. State-level polls similarly over-estimated his support in several key states, such as Florida and Wisconsin. While it is too soon to say for sure, one important issue (in addition to those raised earlier in the chapter) is that it may have been difficult to estimate how many voters would turn out to vote by mail versus in person during a pandemic. An unprecedented numbers of Americans voted through the mail in 2020, and these voters, perhaps due to President Trump's false claims about voting by mail and fraud, skewed heavily Democratic. In contrast, those who showed up to vote in person skewed heavily Republican. If pollsters mis-estimated the share of in-person vs. mail ballots in the race, given this partisan split, that would skew their results. Pollsters and academics will be closely studying the polls to understand why they've now been wrong in two straight elections.

Scholars, pundits, and all Americans will continue to debate and dissect these issues in the years to come. Based on these results, what would you recommend candidates, political parties, the national government, and states do to prepare for elections in 2022, 2024, and beyond?

Figure 10.3 **2020 Presidential Election Results**

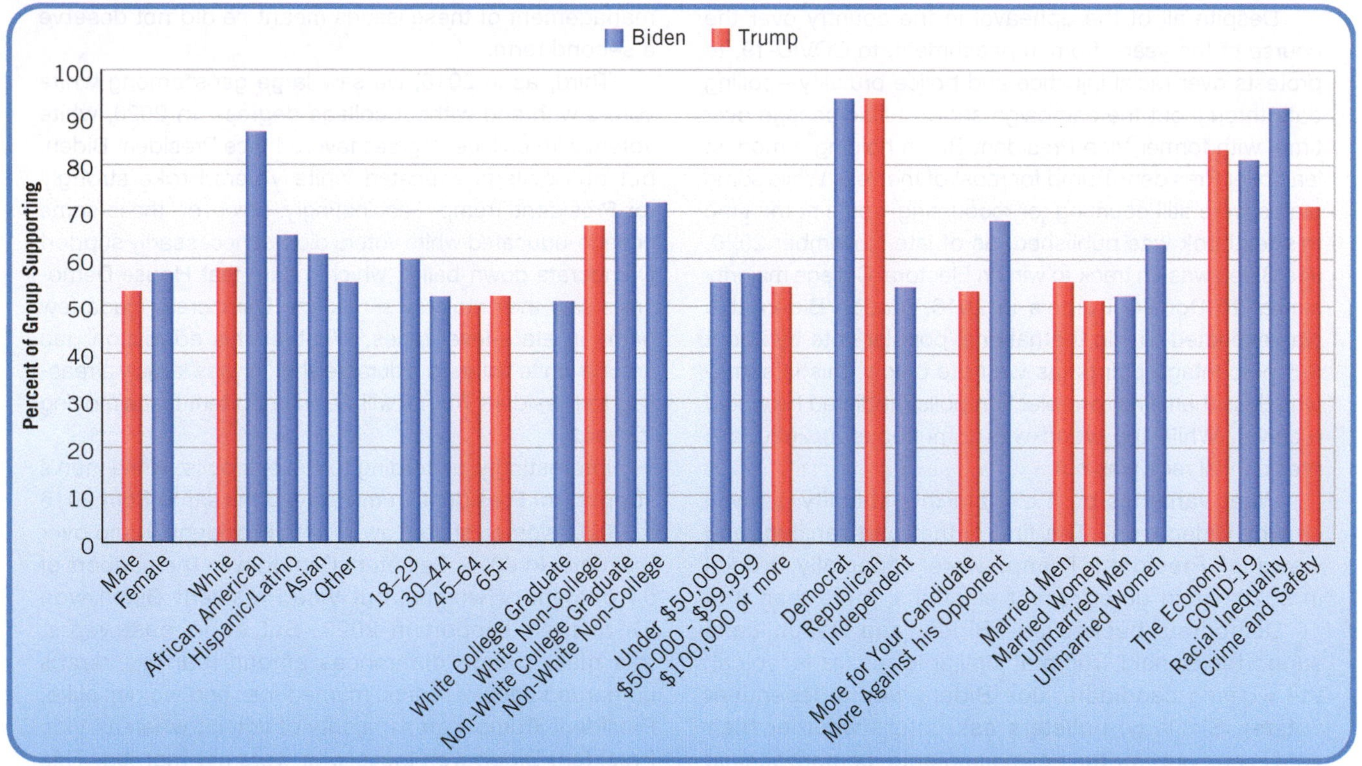

Source: 2020 Exit Polls, as reported by NBC News.

Q Looking at these patterns above, what would you suggest that the parties do to prepare for 2022, 2024, and beyond?

of political ads.[34] A plurality, it found, was purposely designed (everything from the images used to the music playing in the background) to appeal mainly to voters' fears (impending war, losing a job, etc.). A smaller but significant fraction was more focused on stirring positive emotions (patriotism and community pride). Interestingly, such ads do not simply work on the uninformed. Instead, they have larger effects on those who are the most informed and engaged with politics, suggesting that even the most "sophisticated" among us can fall prey to such ads.[35]

Second, most political ads are negative. Simply put, a negative advertisement is an advertisement that directs viewers' attention to the downsides of a candidate (rather than their beneficial qualities); such ads are sometimes called attack ads. In 2016, negative ads from Secretary Clinton questioned President Trump's fitness for the office by attacking his character, often by repeating some of his more inflammatory comments. Negative ads from the Trump campaign suggested that Clinton was an out-of-touch elitist, one who looked down on hard-working, ordinary voters. Such ads dominated the airwaves: nearly 80 percent of ads aired in 2016 were negative. While this was down very slightly from 2012, the level in 2016 was much higher than in earlier elections like 2000 or 2004.[36]

Are such advertisements harmful? Many implicitly assume so. But this is perhaps premature because it conflates a negative ad—one that highlights a candidate's shortcomings on the issues—with a deceptive or dirty ad that distorts the truth or engages in personal attacks on a candidate. Just because an ad is negative does not mean it is dirty or deceptive: one can present a truthful critique.[37] While some negative advertisements devolve into personal attacks and falsehoods, many are ads that criticize an opponent's stance on the issues or record in office.[38] Mudslinging is not helpful, but ads that portray where the candidates stand on the issues are.

As a result, negative advertisements (at least those that focus on issues) are typically more informative than positive advertisements. Positive advertisements tend to traffic in happy platitudes with little substantive detail, whereas negative ads tend to offer actual critiques on the issues.[39] Negative advertisements can be a valuable tool for learning about the issues.

Image 10.5 Many blame negative campaign ads for voters' unhappiness with campaigns, but the scholarly evidence suggests they can help voters learn about the candidates.

But whether an ad appeals to our emotions, and whether it is positive or negative, the real question is, Do advertisements work? In particular, we can ask three questions: Do advertisements change who turns out to vote? Do they inform voters? Do they change voters' assessments of the candidates?

First, advertisements do not affect turnout very much.[40] As we discussed in Chapter 8, many other factors determine whether someone turns out to vote, and political advertising contributes little beyond these factors. Second, as we saw above, ads, especially when they discuss substantive issues, can inform voters and help them learn where the candidates stand on the issues of the day.[41] Finally, advertisements also shape how voters think about the candidates. Advertisements shape people's assessments of the candidates' traits (factors such as strong leadership, integrity, and empathy, discussed earlier), and they also seem to affect a candidate's overall likability.[42] It is fair to say that advertising works.

But it is important to point out, however, that advertising does not determine election outcomes. This is true for two reasons. First, these effects are modest, not massive. The studies cited above find that advertisements change the outcome by a few percent at most, and these effects decay very quickly. Scholars can detect the effects of an ad for a day or two after it airs, but it fades away after that.[43] Even ads that are repeated again and again have relatively small effects in the end. Simply running more advertisements will not fundamentally reshape an election. Second, at the presidential level, because the campaigns are relatively evenly matched, the effects from one campaign's advertisements cancel out the effects from the other campaign's advertisements.[44] Candidates spend so many millions of dollars on ads partly because they need to match their opponent's ads. This quickly escalates the cost without necessarily changing the outcome very much, as the ads cancel each other out. Neither side can back down, however, because that would give their opponent an edge (ads from one side that are not answered by the other side could have a larger effect). The end result is a great deal of spending without much of an effect on the overall outcome.

Campaign Events

Beyond advertisements and other forms of communication from the campaigns, voters also learn about the candidates from the campaign events themselves. In particular, two campaign events are particularly important to voters: the parties' nominating conventions and the presidential debates. These events matter because they are the way in which most people actually encounter the candidates in their own words, beyond 30-second television ads. For many voters, these events are their longest sustained interactions with the candidates.

As we reviewed in Chapter 9, a party's convention is the formal mechanism used to nominate that party's candidate for president (though the decision effectively is made by the voters months earlier in the primaries). The convention is the party's chance to make its case to the voters for why their nominee should win the election. The convention culminates with the nominee giving an acceptance speech, but in the days leading up to it, other party luminaries and rising stars also make the case for the nominee and the party. Such events are especially valuable for the party because they get to speak directly to voters, without any rebuttal from the other side. Furthermore, not only does the party get to broadcast its message, it typically also gets highly favorable press coverage during the event, which also moves voters toward the party's nominee in the days and weeks following the convention.[45]

As a result of this sustained one-sided and favorable coverage, candidates traditionally got a sustained "bump" from the convention: their poll numbers went up following the convention (though this boost quickly dissipated in most years). Figure 10.4 shows that convention bump over time.

As we can see in Figure 10.4, in some years, there have been truly large convention bumps of 10 and even 15 points. Interestingly, however, the average size of the convention bump has decreased over time. This could be due to many factors, but one likely factor is the timing of the convention. The conventions were at one time held almost a month apart. But starting in 2000, they have occurred much closer together, and since 2008, the conventions have occurred in back-to-back weeks. When the conventions were a month apart, each party's message had time to sink in and be absorbed by voters. But having the conventions take place in such rapid succession limits their potential effectiveness.[46]

The general-election debates also serve as an important source of voter information about the candidates. They typically are viewed by the largest audience a candidate reaches during the campaign: in 2016, over 80 million Americans watched the first presidential debate—more than double the audience for either candidate's acceptance speech. The debates also give the candidates an opportunity to show how they function under pressure, as they have to tackle questions from the moderator and audience and still get their message across.

Much like the conventions, the media's coverage of a debate strongly colors how people respond to it. While millions do tune in to watch the debate itself, they also see pundits discuss it in the hours, days, and weeks that follow. Indeed, the post-debate commentary can often be just as influential for voters as the actual debate itself.[47] The media typically declare one candidate to be the winner, and then that candidate's standing in the polls rises.

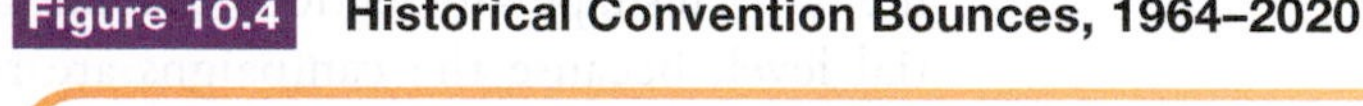
Figure 10.4 **Historical Convention Bounces, 1964–2020**

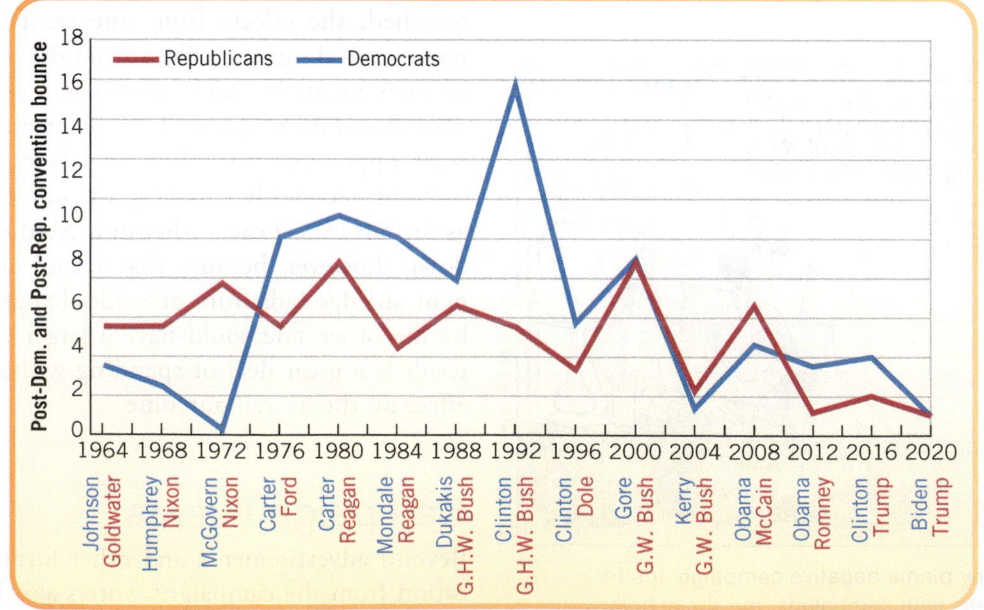

Source: 1964–2012, data from various Gallup Polls; 2016: data from Alan Rappeport, "New Poll Reflects a Post-Convention Bounce for Hillary Clinton," New York Times, 1 August 2016; 2020: data from FiveThirtyEight Polling Averages.

This bump to the winner's poll numbers is typically quite modest, however—only a few points at most. Why do debates move opinion less than the conventions? The debates take place much later in the election season (usually in October), and by that point most viewers have made a decision and are unlikely to be swayed. Indeed, for many Americans who have picked a candidate, debates are mostly an opportunity to cheer for that person.[48]

That does not mean, however, that debates do not matter. The evidence suggests that debates can matter for any remaining undecided voters and for wavering partisans (those who are not currently supporting their party's nominee).[49] For example, in the first debate in 2012, Mitt Romney had a stronger than expected performance and was the consensus winner according to the post-debate commentary. Perhaps not surprisingly, then, Romney's standing in the polls jumped by about four points after the debate. But much of this shift was due to undecided Republicans coming back to Romney.[50] This debate, like many other campaign events, activated latent partisanship and helped to bring wavering partisans back into the fold; it no doubt also helped undecided voters make up their minds as well.

Beyond the debates and conventions, journalists always try to claim that various events are "game changers": this rally or that speech will be the one that fundamentally alters the dynamics of an election. One study of a recent election found that over the course of the campaign, journalists called 68 different events "game changers," when most were anything but.[51] In the end, most campaign events do not really change the dynamics of the race because the dynamics are driven by the underlying fundamentals. Campaigns—and campaign events—certainly matter, but they matter more at the margins.

Brian Snyder/Reuters

Image 10.6 Vice presidential nominees Kamala Harris and Mike Pence square off in the 2020 vice presidential debate.

10-4 Building a Winning Coalition

Earlier in the chapter, we argued that campaigns primarily focus on three factors to persuade voters: assigning credit and blame for the state of the nation, activating voters' latent partisanship, and helping voters judge the candidates' character. As a result, these factors largely shape a voter's decision in the ballot box. If we want to understand how voters will cast their ballot, these are the factors to understand.

While valuable, however, this sort of analysis does not tell us how the parties each construct a winning coalition. Which groups are the base of support for each party? Which groups divide their support more evenly between them? Women? Young voters? Someone else? To answer these sorts of questions, we need to examine the level of support for the parties from different demographic groups over time. Figure 10.5 shows how various salient social groups have voted over the previous 60 years, broken down into several demographic categories.

In the upper-left hand panel, we see the pattern of support among different racial and ethnic groups. We immediately see that African Americans have been extremely loyal to the Democratic party, especially since the 1964 election. Indeed, since then, more than 85 percent of African Americans have supported the Democratic Party in every election. While a majority of Hispanics have supported the Democratic nominee in every election since 1980 (when the National Election Study first asked about Hispanic identification), their support is considerably lower than among African Americans, given differences among Latinos based on generation, age, and religion (see the discussion in Chapter 7). White voters, by contrast, have given less than 50 percent of their ballots to the Democratic candidate in every election since 1964, with their support currently hovering around 40 percent.

But when we break down the racial patterns by education in the upper-right hand panel, we see some important differences. Here, we group all non-white respondents together so that we have enough data to say something credible about the trends. We see that it used to be the case that college-educated non-white voters were much less Democratic than non-white voters who had not graduated from college: in 1980, the gap was nearly 30 percentage points! But over time, that difference has shrunk, as all non-white voters have increasingly supported Democratic candidates. For white voters, however, the pattern is the opposite. It used to be the case that in the 1950s and 1960s that non-college educated whites were more loyal to Democrats. Those differences shrank over time, but in the last few elections, especially 2016, there was a large education gap, where college-educated

Figure 10.5 **Group Support for the Democratic Nominee, 1952–2016**

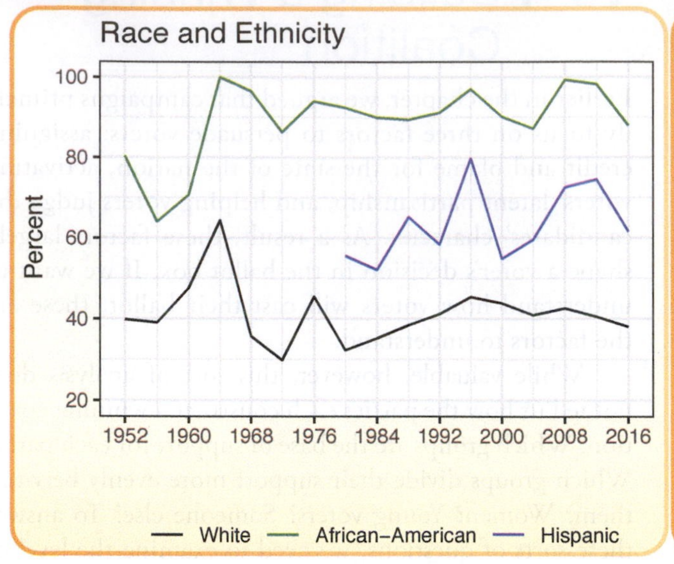

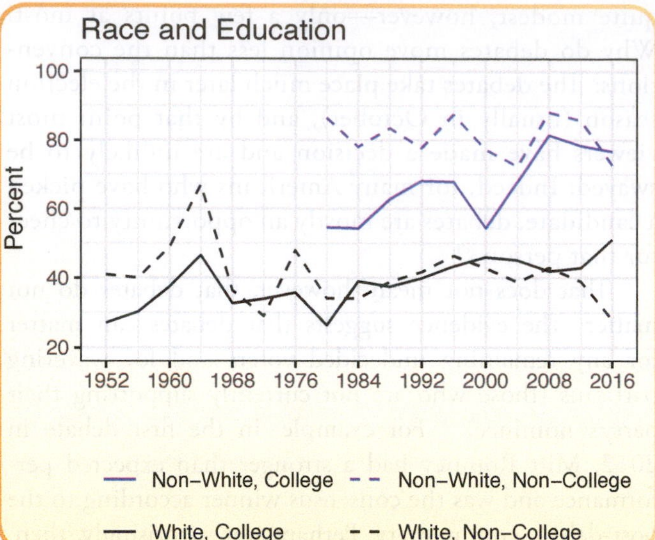

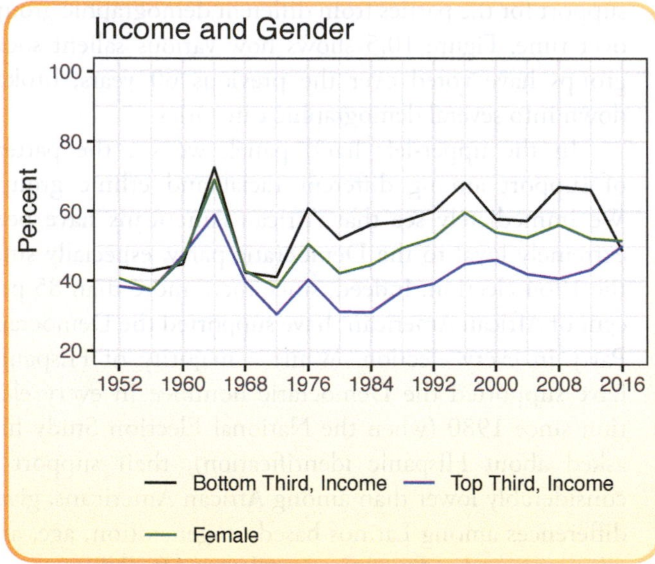

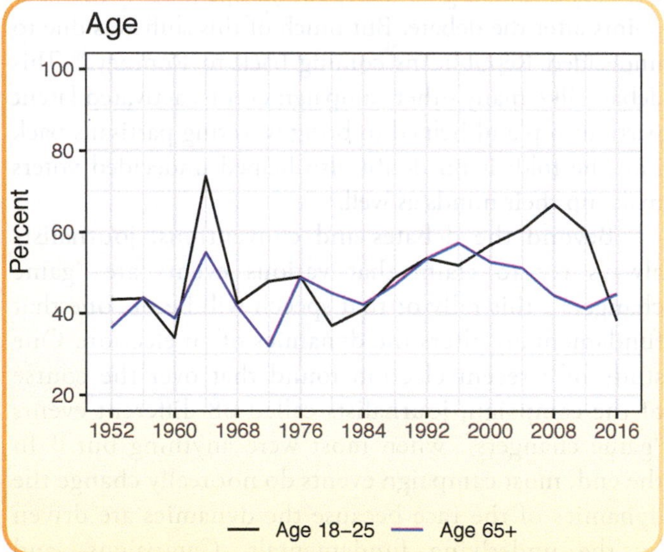

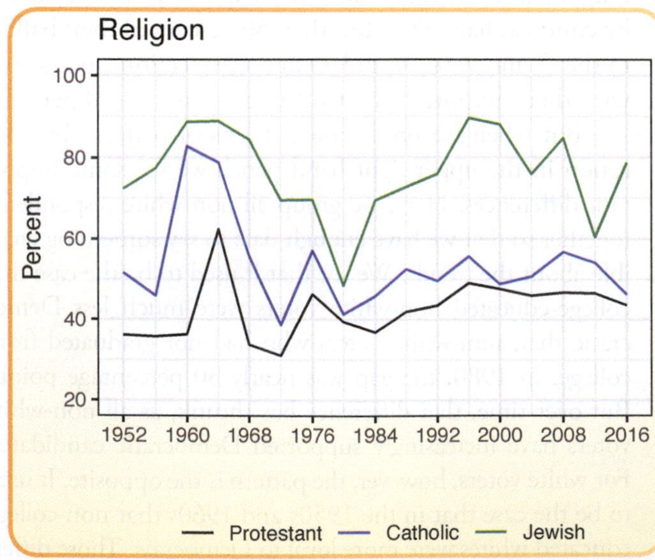

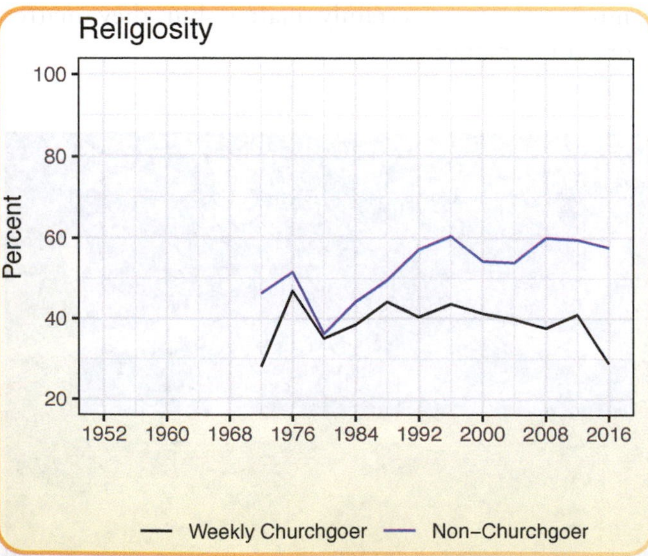

Source: Authors' analysis of the American National Election Study Cumulative Data File.

Q **Studying these patterns, what are the implications for 2020 and beyond for both parties? If you were advising one of the parties, which voters would you instruct them to target and why?**

white voters were considerably more supportive of Hillary Clinton (a similar gap emerged in the 2018 midterm elections). If this trend continues, that will have important implications for each party's base of electoral support.

The parties also divide along income lines (see the middle panel on the left-hand side). Those in the bottom third of the income distribution tend to favor Democrats, whereas those in the top third favor Republicans (those in between have swung between the parties). This same general pattern held in 2016, though lower-income voters were somewhat less supportive of the Democratic nominee than in previous years; this is due in part to the education gap noted above.

Over time, women and young people have become more important Democratic constituencies as well. Since the 1980s, women have been trending toward the Democratic Party, and in recent years they have tended to favor Democrats by a several-point margin, whereas men are increasingly Republican (see the middle panel on the left-hand side). Young people used to split their votes more evenly between the parties, but since the 1990s they have favored Democratic candidates (see the middle panel on the right-hand side). The age gap became especially large during the Obama years, though it dropped in 2016. This, however, was due to young people being more likely to support third-party candidates, rather than an embrace of President Trump by young voters.

Traditionally, the parties used to divide along religious lines, with Catholic and Jewish voters supporting Democrats, and Protestants supporting Republicans (see the bottom panel on the left-hand side). While Jewish voters still largely support the Democrats, Catholics and Protestants now split their votes almost evenly between the parties. What's now more important is one's level of religiosity, or how committed one is to that faith. Starting in 1980, we see a growing divide between those who regularly attend church and those who do not attend church (the latter group includes those with no religious affiliation); in 2016 this gap was almost 30 points!

incumbent *The person already holding an elective office.*

Image 10.7 President Trump campaigns for reelection in 2020.

Looking across these various divides, however, what becomes clear is that few demographic groups overwhelmingly favor one party or the other. Yes, African Americans and Jews heavily favor the Democrats in most elections, but most other groups favor one party or the other by a relatively modest amount, often less than five percentage points. This suggests that neither party can afford to write off any demographic group, and that either party's candidate needs a broad coalition to capture the presidency.

10-5 Congressional Elections

So far in the chapter, we have focused almost exclusively on the presidential election. But this is not the only election in American politics: We also go to the polls to elect members of the House and Senate (not to mention dozens of state and local officials). Congressional elections are very similar to presidential elections in many ways, and many of the factors we reviewed earlier—the health of the economy, partisanship, and judgments about the candidates' character—matter a great deal here as well. But a number of important differences also exist. Here we focus on three particularly key ones that give congressional elections their own unique dynamics.

The Incumbency Advantage

In presidential elections, the **incumbent** (i.e., the sitting president) typically receives 50 to 55 percent of the vote—most presidential elections are close, hard-fought contests, as we mentioned above. In contrast, in congressional elections, many incumbents win with an overwhelming share (often more than 60 percent) of the vote. In most election years, the vast majority of incumbents—often more than 90 percent—are reelected to Congress. In 2020, this same pattern held as well.

Even when party control changes, the vast majority of incumbents are reelected. For example, in 2018 when Democrats recaptured the House of Representatives, 91 percent of House incumbents who sought reelection won it. Since the mid-1960s, the incumbent reelection rate has never dropped below 80 percent in the House or 60 percent in the Senate (see Figure 13.2 in Chapter 13

incumbency advantage *The tendency of incumbents to do better than otherwise similar challengers, especially in congressional elections.*

gerrymandering *Drawing the boundaries of legislative districts in bizarre or unusual shapes to favor one party.*

for a depiction of the incumbent reelection rate over time). Not only are incumbents more likely to be reelected, they do better than an otherwise similar challenger would. Scholars estimate that House candidates today get several percent more of the vote than would a challenger who is otherwise similar (with Senate candidates getting a similar, albeit smaller, boost).[52] Clearly, incumbents do quite well in legislative elections.

Political scientists have studied this phenomenon extensively and argue that this **incumbency advantage** reflects a number of factors that favor incumbents over challengers in congressional elections. We discuss these factors in more detail in Chapter 13 on Congress, but several of the main factors are briefly reviewed here. One important factor is the members' ability to serve their constituency. Members of Congress—unlike the president—are very likely to actively provide services to those whom they represent. Members can help a constituent track down a lost Social Security check, help apply for a small business loan, or, more generally, intervene on a constituent's behalf with a federal agency. Indeed, almost every member of Congress has a section on their website to encourage constituents to reach out and contact them if they need help with some aspect of the federal government. Members of Congress want to be of service to those they represent.

Second, members of Congress also are able to claim credit for every bridge, road, and project in their district. They can point to their ability to help secure funds for the district as a reason to reelect them year after year. In both cases, this helps members build a reservoir of support that is not tied to partisanship, but rather to the members themselves. If a Democratic member helps a Republican constituent apply for a government program, then that constituent is more likely to vote for that member of Congress despite their partisan differences.[53]

Members of Congress also have an important name recognition advantage: they are much better known than most challengers. After all, the incumbent congressperson has already been elected once, and can more easily command media attention. Furthermore, they can use the franking privilege (the ability of members of Congress to send mail to constituents) to communicate their accomplishments in office to their constituents. Such efforts boost the name recognition and standing of incumbent members of Congress.

Finally, members enjoy an enormous fundraising advantage over challengers. Sitting members of Congress have the ability to raise funds throughout their term, and often have much more cash than their potential opponents (who typically struggle to raise money). Despite efforts to limit the influence of money in politics (discussed below), members of Congress almost always out-spend their challengers. All of these reasons—and many more—help to explain why members of Congress are so frequently reelected.

Redistricting and Gerrymandering

Since 1911, the size of the House has been fixed at 435 members, except for a brief period when it had 437 members owing to the admission of Alaska and Hawaii to the Union in 1959. Once the size was decided, it was necessary to find a formula for performing the painful task of apportioning seats among the states as they gained and lost population. The Constitution requires such reapportionment every 10 years (a process also known as redistricting). A more or less automatic method was selected in 1929 based on a complex statistical system that has withstood decades of political and scientific testing. Since 1990, under this system 18 states have lost representation in the House and 11 have gained it. In general, states in the South and West have tended to gain seats, while states in the Midwest and Northeast have tended to lose representatives.

When such reapportionment and redistricting takes place, many complain there has been **gerrymandering**, which means drawing a district boundary in some bizarre or unusual shape to make it easy for the candidate of one party to win election in that district. This would seem to make it much easier for incumbents to win reelection: One district can be made heavily Democratic by packing many Democratic voters into it, thereby making it easier for a Democrat to win reelection in that district. There is some truth to this claim, but only some, as many competing pressures are put on drawing districts. Many states (and the courts) mandate that districts be of roughly equal population, follow natural political boundaries (like towns), be contiguous (i.e., be able to travel from any point in the district to any other), and so forth. This puts significant constraints on what districts can be drawn. So while gerrymandering affects congressional elections, the effects are less than many claim.[54]

On-Year and Off-Year Elections

The U.S. holds presidential elections every four years, but congressional elections every two years. In general, the president's party loses seats in the midterm election. As we can see in Figure 10.6, the president's party has lost seats in every midterm election since 1938, except for 1998 and 2002.

What explains this striking pattern? Political scientists call this pattern **surge and decline**. In a presidential election year, the president's supporters show up at the polls to vote for the president. They also vote for other candidates from the president's party (such as members of Congress), a phenomenon known as **coattails**.[55] This generates a surge in support for the president's fellow partisans. As a result, when a new president is elected, typically he brings in to Congress more members of his own party. For example, after the 2008 elections, 21 more Democrats joined the House, and after 2012, the Democrats gained 8 more seats.

But in the subsequent midterm election, without the appeal of the president at the top of the ticket, many of those voters stay home, and support for the party's candidates declines. With the president at the top of the ticket, partisans flock to the polls, and the president's party does better with Independents. But in the midterm elections, without the president running, partisans stay home, especially those who are more marginal voters.[56] The surge in the on-year election means that the president's party picks up seats normally held by the other party, but in the off-year election, without the president at the top of the ticket, those seats are more difficult to hold. So while Obama helped bring more Democrats into office in 2008 and 2012, in the two midterm elections of 2010 and 2014, his party's fortunes declined: Democrats lost 63 seats in the House of Representatives in 2010 and 13 seats in 2014. Relative to the 2008 and 2012 electorates, those in 2010 and 2014 were more conservative and Republican, older, whiter, and more male.[57] As we discussed earlier, these groups tend to favor Republicans somewhat (see Figure 10.5), so Republicans did better in Obama's two

surge and decline *Tendency for the president's party to do better in presidential election years when the president is at the top of the ticket (the surge), but to do worse in midterm election years when the president is not because many voters are less enthusiastic and stay home (the decline).*

coattails *The tendency of candidates to win more votes in an election because of the presence at the top of the ticket of a better-known candidate, such as the president.*

Figure 10.6 House Seats Won or Lost by the President's Party in Midterm Elections, 1946–2018

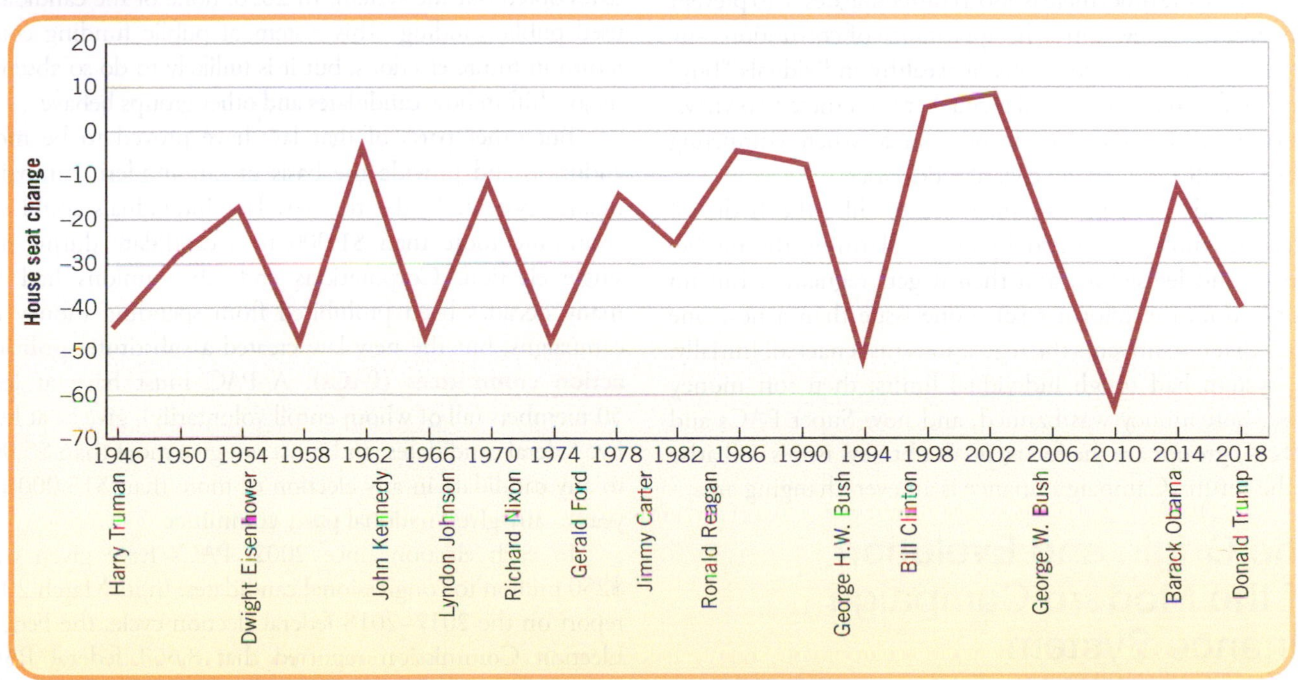

Source: The American Presidency Project, "Seats in Congress Gained/Lost by the President's Party in Mid-Term Elections." https://www.presidency.ucsb.edu/statistics/data/seats-congress-gainedlost-the-presidents-party-mid-term-elections (accessed January 2020).

political action committees (PACs) *Committees set up by a corporation, labor union, or interest group that raise and spend campaign money from voluntary donations.*

midterm elections. In the 2018 midterm elections, with Trump in the White House, Democrats had the energy on their side, and they gained 40 House seats and retook control of that chamber. Because of this pattern of surge and decline, the party controlling the White House typically loses seats in the midterm election.

10-6 Campaign Finance: Regulating the Flow of Political Money

We opened the chapter by noting the vast sums of money that now flow through presidential and congressional elections, and throughout the chapter we have explained what this money buys and how that matters to election outcomes. But it does not explain the history of our campaign finance system, and how the government regulates the flow of money in elections. We take up that task here.

We will note at the outset that campaign finance is a difficult problem for two related reasons. First, there are two important conflicting values at stake. On the one hand, courts have ruled that campaign donations are a form of free speech, which is protected by the Constitution (see Chapter 5). But at the same time, there is also a competing desire to prevent corruption—or even just the appearance of corruption—by seeming to have corporations or wealthy individuals "buy" their preferred outcome. Balancing between these two views, is not easy, just as we saw in other areas where competing values conflict, like many civil liberties cases.

Second, campaign finance is a bit like the hydra of Greek mythology. An activity arises, alarming the public, courts, and legislators, and then it gets regulated. But no sooner does the reform resolve one issue than a new one arises that circumvents the regulations just enacted! Initially, the system had tough individual limits, then soft money arose. Soft money was banned, and now Super PACs and 501c(4) groups are the focus; no doubt new issues will arise in the future. Campaign finance is an ever-changing area.

The Origin and Evolution of the Modern Campaign Finance System

During the 1972 presidential election, men hired by President Nixon's campaign staff broke into the headquarters of the Democratic National Committee in the Watergate office building. They were caught by an alert security guard. The subsequent investigation disclosed that Nixon's people had engaged in dubious or illegal money-raising schemes, including taking large sums from wealthy contributors in exchange for appointing them to ambassadorships. Many individuals and corporations were indicted for making illegal donations—since 1925, it had been against the law for corporations or labor unions to contribute money to candidates, but the law had been unenforceable. Some of the accused had given money to Democratic candidates as well as to Nixon.

When the break-in was discovered, the Watergate scandal unfolded. It had two political results: President Nixon was forced to resign, and a new campaign finance law was passed.

The law put in place a system of public financing to help pay for campaigns (designed as a way for candidates not to need to raise so much money from corporations and wealthy donors). The system funded presidential primary campaigns, the major-party candidate general election campaigns, and a fraction of the minor-party candidate general election campaigns. (This system also initially covered the costs of the major parties' presidential nominating conventions, but President Obama signed a law ending the convention funding in 2014.) In order to receive this public funding, however, candidates had to agree to abide by strict spending limits, so over time, more and more candidates began to withdraw from the system (if you do not accept the public money, you do not have to accept the spending limits). In 2016, the only candidate who accepted public funding was Martin O'Malley, who competed for the Democratic nomination; all other candidates opted out the system. In 2020, none of the candidates used public funding. This system of public funding could return in future elections, but it is unlikely to do so absent a major shift in how candidates and other groups behave.

But other parts of that law have proved to be more enduring and provide the basis of our modern campaign finance system. Under the new law, individuals could not contribute more than $1,000 to a candidate during any single election. Corporations and labor unions had for many decades been prohibited from spending money on campaigns, but the new law created a substitute: **political action committees (PACs)**. A PAC must have at least 50 members (all of whom enroll voluntarily), give to at least five federal candidates, and must not give more than $5,000 to any candidate in any election or more than $15,000 per year to any given national party committee.

In each election since 2002, PACs have given over $250 million to congressional candidates. In its March 2019 report on the 2017–2018 federal election cycle, the Federal Election Commission reported that 8,663 federal PACs raised $4.7 billion and spent $4.6 billion on that cycle's elections. This included significant spending from corporate PACs ($404.8 million), labor PACs ($342.2 million), and super PACs, which spent $1.5 billion.

The 1974 campaign finance law produced two problems. The first was **independent expenditures**. A PAC, a corporation, or a labor union could spend whatever it wanted supporting or opposing a candidate, so long as this spending was "independent," that is, not coordinated with or made at the direction of the candidate's wishes. Simply put, independent expenditures are ordinary advertising directed at or against candidates.

The second was **soft money**. Under the law, individuals, corporations, labor unions, and other groups could give unlimited amounts of money to political parties provided the money was not used to back candidates by name. But the money could be used in ways that helped candidates, for example, by financing voter registration and get-out-the-vote drives. Many, however, saw such activities as de facto spending on candidates (for example, by showing people a photo of a candidate, encouraging people to vote for that candidate's party, but not naming that candidate, the ad could be paid for with soft money). Such activities therefore became controversial.

A Second Campaign Finance Law

Reform is a tricky word. We like to think it means fixing something gone wrong. But some reforms can make matters worse. For example, the campaign finance reforms enacted in the early 1970s helped matters in some ways by ensuring that all campaign contributors would be identified by name. But they made things worse in other ways, for example, by requiring candidates to raise small sums from many donors. This made it harder for challengers to run (incumbents are much better known and raise more money) and easier for wealthy candidates to run because, under the law as interpreted by the Supreme Court, candidates can spend as much of their own money as they want.

After the 2000 campaign, a strong movement developed in Congress to reform the reforms of the 1970s. The result was the Bipartisan Campaign Reform Act of 2002, which passed easily in the House and Senate and was signed by President Bush. After the 1970s laws were passed, the Supreme Court, in *Buckley v. Valeo* (424 U.S. 1, 1976), upheld federal limits on campaign contributions even as it ruled that spending money to influence elections is a form of constitutionally protected free speech (hence candidates were free to give unlimited amounts of money to their own campaigns). That precedent had pretty much held, but the new law made three important changes.

First, it banned soft-money contributions to national political parties from corporations and unions. After the federal elections in 2002, no national party or party committee could accept soft money. Any money the national parties get must come from "hard money"—that is, individual donations or PAC contributions as limited by federal law. Many feared this would substantially weaken parties, as they had become dependent on soft-money donations to fund their operations. But, as we discussed in Chapter 9, the parties changed their tactics and are raising more money today than ever before.

independent expenditures *Spending by political action committees, corporations, or labor unions to help a party or candidate but done independent from the party or candidate.*

soft money *Funds obtained by political parties that are spent on party activities, such as get-out-the-vote drives, but not on behalf of a specific candidate.*

Second, the limit on individual contributions was raised from $1,000 per candidate per election to $2,000 (and indexed in order to rise with inflation; the limit for the 2019–2020 election cycle is $2,800). And third, independent expenditures by corporations, labor unions, trade associations, and (under certain circumstances) non-profit organizations are sharply restricted. Now none of these organizations can use their own money to refer to a clearly identified federal candidate in any advertisement during the 60 days preceding a general election or the 30 days preceding a primary contest. (PACs can still refer to candidates in their ads, but of course PACs are restricted to hard money—that is, the amount they can spend under federal law.)

Immediately after the law was signed, critics filed suit in federal court, claiming it was unconstitutional. The suit brought together a number of organizations that rarely work together, such as the American Civil Liberties Union and the National Right to Life Committee. The suit claimed that the ban on independent spending that "refers to" clearly identified candidates 60 days before an election is unconstitutional because it is an abridgement of the right of free speech. Under the law, an organization need not even endorse or oppose a candidate; it is enough that it mention a politician. This means that 60 days before an election, an organization cannot say, for example, that it "supports (or opposes) a bill proposed by Congresswoman Pelosi."

Newspapers, magazines, and radio and television stations are not affected by the law, so they can say whatever they want for or against a candidate. One way of evaluating the law is to observe that it shifts influence away from businesses and unions and toward the media.

In *McConnell v. Federal Election Commission* (2002), the Supreme Court decided to uphold almost all of the law. As we saw in Chapter 5, it rejected the argument of those who claimed that speech requires money and decided it was no violation of the free speech provisions of the First Amendment to eliminate the ability of corporations and labor unions (and the organizations that use their money) to even *mention* a candidate for federal office for 60 days before the national election. In 2007, however, the Court backed away from this view. An ad by a right-to-life group urged people to write to Senator Russell Feingold to convince him to vote for certain

527 organizations *Organizations under section 527 of the Internal Revenue Code that raise and spend money to advance political causes.*

super PAC *A group that raises and spends unlimited amounts of money from corporations, unions, and individuals but cannot coordinate its activities with campaigns in any way.*

501(c)4 group *A social welfare organization that can devote no more than 50 percent of its funds to politics. Sometimes referred to as "dark money" groups because they do not have to disclose their donors.*

judicial nominees, but it did not tell people how to vote. The Court decided this was "issue advocacy" protected by the First Amendment and so could not be banned by the McCain-Feingold law (*Federal Election Commission v. Wisconsin Right to Life*).

Two more recent decisions have further relaxed campaign finance rules. In the 2010 *Citizens United* decision (*Citizens United v. Federal Election Commission*), the Court narrowly decided, in a five-to-four decision, to overturn the ban on corporate and union funding of campaign ads. The decision kept in place the limits on donations to candidates, but allows corporations, unions, and other groups to spend unlimited funds calling for the support or defeat of particular candidates (and also helped to give rise to so-called super PACs, as we explain below).

In 2014, in *McCutcheon v. Federal Election Commission,* the Court overturned the aggregate biennial limits on contributions to national parties and candidates. By law, individuals were limited in how much they can give in total to candidates, parties, and other political committees. So, before the McCutcheon ruling, individuals could give no more than $48,600 in total to all candidates, and could give no more than $2,600 to any candidate—any individual could give the federal limit to only 18 candidates. *McCutcheon* kept the limits on how much anyone could give to a particular candidate, but overturned the limit on the aggregate rules. So now an individual may give the federal limit ($2,800 in 2019–2020) to as many candidates as he or she likes. (The decision made a parallel set of rulings with respect to parties.)

If the past is any guide, neither recent changes nor the existing legal maze will do much to keep individuals, PACs, party leaders, and others from funding the candidates they favor.

New Sources of Money

Because money is, indeed, the mother's milk of politics, efforts to make the money go away are not likely to work. The Bipartisan Campaign Reform Act, once enforced, immediately stimulated people to find other ways to spend political money.

One way people did so immediately after passage of the act was through **527 organizations**. These groups, named after a provision of the Internal Revenue Code, are designed to permit the kind of soft-money expenditures once made by political parties. In 2004, the Democrats created the Media Fund, America Coming Together, America Votes, and many other groups. The Republicans responded by creating Progress for America, the Leadership Forum, America for Job Security, and other groups. Under the law as it is now interpreted, 527 organizations can spend their money on politics so long as they do not coordinate with a candidate or lobby directly for that person.

While such 527 organizations still exist, they have largely been supplanted by other groups in recent years. First are the "**super PACs**" (technically known as "independent expenditure-only political committees"). These super PACs were born after the *Citizens United* decision and several other related decisions and rule changes. Super PACs can raise and spend unlimited amounts of money from corporations, labor unions, individuals, and other groups, whereas traditional PACs have strict limits on how much they can accept from any individual. Super PACs must operate independently of campaigns and candidates; they may not be "in concert or cooperation with" the candidate and their campaign organization, or a political party. So, for example, a super PAC's television ad for a given candidate must be funded and fashioned without that candidate, the campaign managers, or the candidate's party leaders being involved in any way.

Super PACs have become major sources of campaign dollars in recent elections. Super PACs raised and spent a little over $1.5 billion in the 2017–2018 election cycle, roughly the same as the Democratic and Republican Party committees raised.[58] In the 2015–2016 election cycle, super PACs spent $1.8 billion, which was more than presidential candidates or parties raised in that election year!

Second, **501(c)4 groups** (also called social welfare organizations) have also emerged as important political funders. 501(c)4 groups, named after the section of the tax code that created them, are groups that are dedicated to promoting social welfare and have existed for many years. Many community and civic groups fall into this category, such as civic leagues and many local volunteer fire departments, not to mention groups like the Sierra Club, the AARP, and the National Rifle Association. Such groups are allowed to engage in politics so long as politics is not their focus: No more than 50 percent of their money can be spent on politics. Such groups have an attractive feature that super PACs do not. Super PACs (like regular PACs) must disclose their donors, but a 501(c)4 group does not. Such groups are therefore sometimes called "dark money" groups, since the identity of the donors is not known. Such groups do spend on campaigns, but estimating the amount on politics is tricky, because unlike a traditional PAC, not all of their activity is political, and defining what is political, and what is not, can be very complicated. According to the Center for Responsive Politics, spending by these groups grew from only about

Landmark Cases | Financing Elections

- ***Buckley v. Valeo* (1976):** Held that a law limiting contributions to political campaigns was constitutional but that one restricting candidates' expenditures of their own money was not.
- ***McConnell v. Federal Election Commission* (2002):** Upheld 2002 Bipartisan Campaign Reform Act (popularly known as the McCain-Feingold law) prohibiting corporations and labor unions from running ads that mention candidates and their positions for 60 days before a federal general election.
- ***Federal Election Commission v. Wisconsin Right to Life, Inc.* (2007):** Held that issue ads may not be prohibited before a primary or general election.
- ***Citizens United v. Federal Election Commission* (2010):** Overturned part of a 2002 law that had prohibited corporate and union funding of campaign ads.
- ***McCutcheon et al. v. Federal Election Commission* (2014):** Overturned aggregate limits on individual contributions to candidates and national parties

$5 million in 2006 to more than $300 million in 2012 and $181 million in 2016.[59] While some groups have pushed for efforts to regulate these types of organizations more tightly, so far they have not been successful.

All of this emphasizes what we said above: campaign finance is an ever-evolving system, and reforms designed to cure one ill (soft money) then create others (527s, Super PACs, etc.). No doubt there will be other types of groups that arise in future elections as well.

Where Does the Money Come From?

The discussion above tracked the twists and turns that regulate the flow of money into elections. But it does not answer a fundamental question: where does this money come from? Most people might think that PACs provide most of the money, but that would be incorrect. PACs obviously matter, but among the most important sources of fundraising are individual donors. As we saw above, the amount of money any one person can give is capped, so candidates need to raise money from many different individuals. Looking at the 2018 election cycle, the Campaign Finance Institute estimated that individual donors provided 65 percent of the funds raised by candidates for the House of Representatives, with PACs providing 27 percent (the remainder came from self-financing and other sources).[60] The Senate numbers look, if anything, even more slanted, with individual donors there making up almost 80 percent of Senate campaign funds in 2018.[61] Because the rules sharply limit how much any individual can give directly to candidates (see our discussion above), most donations are relatively modest amounts ($100 or $200) given by ordinary people, rather than a few rich plutocrats.[62]

At the presidential level, the patterns are similar (though given the complexity of financing these races, we cannot speak with quite as much precision). In particular, a candidate's ability to raise money from small donors is especially important. Typically, when campaigns refer to small donors, they mean those individuals giving less than $200, which means that the campaign does not have to disclose the name of the person giving the money (anyone giving more than that must be disclosed by the campaign). In 2016, according to the Center for Responsive Politics, 26 percent of Trump's fundraising total, and 19 percent of Clinton's total, came from donations of $200 or less.[63] For Bernie Sanders's 2016 campaign—which had a particular focus on small donors—34 percent of his campaign's fundraising came from small donors, and he had 7 small donors for every large one.[64]

The story was much the same in 2020, with small donors being an especially important factor for many candidates. The exceptions were both billionaires who spent lavishly on their own campaigns: businessman Tom Steyer and former New York City Mayor Michael Bloomberg. While Steyer spent "only" $342 million on his bid for the White House, Bloomberg spent over $1 billion on his. As we note below, however, these vast sums of money did not ultimate garner either of them very much, suggesting that money alone may not be enough for a candidate to break through—they also need to resonate with voters.

Money and Winning

But does all of this money matter? Does money change who is elected president? At the presidential level, the answer is not really. In the primary process, it does not change the winner; Jeb Bush's campaign and affiliated groups spent almost $130 million on his unsuccessful 2016 run for the White House,[65] and as we noted above, both Bloomberg and Steyer spent hundreds of millions of dollars, to no avail. The ability of wealthy donors to keep a campaign afloat, however, could change the dynamics of a race in the future.

What Would You Do? | Would Banning Super PACs Enhance Democracy?

To: *Senator Brian Paul*
From: *Jacob S. Dylan, legislative analyst*
Subject: *Vote on bill to eliminate super PACs*

In the wake of the 2010 *Citizens United* and several other decisions, super PACs (independent expenditure-only committees) have become a major source of campaign financing in recent years, spending almost $1.6 billion in the 2018 election—as much as the Democratic and Republican Parties' campaign committees combined. Concerns over this record spending have led your colleagues to introduce a bill to ban such super PACs.

To Consider:

Given record levels of spending by super PACs in recent elections, some in Congress are calling for a ban on super PACs. Some argue that banning these organizations would reduce public concerns about corruption and lessen the role of the wealthy in the political process, but critics charge that such restrictions would violate the First Amendment and harm voters.

Arguments for:

1. These groups allow the wealthy (and corporations and unions) to have too much say in the political process. They can outspend other groups and shape the messages voters hear in the election.
2. There is no evidence that super PACs cause corruption, but they produce the *appearance* of corruption or a quid pro quo. This weakens citizens' trust in our government.

Arguments against:

1. Political spending is a form of political speech and is protected by the First Amendment. This includes spending by super PACs.
2. By sponsoring political ads, super PACs can inform voters and provide them with information they need to make a choice between candidates.

What Will You Decide? Enter **MindTap** to make your choice.

Your decision: ☐ Vote to ban super PACs ☐ Vote not to ban super PACs

In the general election for president, money is typically not an issue: Both candidates are usually relatively evenly matched, and their spending tends to track one another. For example, the single largest campaign expenditure for presidents is television advertisements and, as we discussed earlier, one party's advertisements largely cancel out the other's (generating a small, but important, net effect). As we have seen, three main factors typically shape presidential elections: political party affiliation, the state of the economy, and the character of the candidates. While the candidate who spends more money typically wins, that need not be the case. In 2016, Clinton spent more than twice as much as Trump but still lost the election.

At the congressional level, however, money matters a great deal more. In many congressional elections, spending is highly uneven. As we discussed above, incumbents can raise money much more easily than challengers can, and this sets up an asymmetry. And of course there's an irony here: Challengers, not incumbents, need money if they are to be competitive. Challengers are not well known and need to spend money to spread their message to the voters. While there is some debate about how much spending more helps the incumbent, the literature is clear that spending more greatly benefits challengers.[66] If challengers are to win, they need access to money.

Given these concerns about funding, some states have passed laws to have public financing of state legislative elections. The idea is that the state provides funding for elections, which means that potential candidates do not need to raise money on their own to be competitive candidates (and in some states, candidates are prohibited from raising private funds if they take the public money).[67] According to the National Conference of State Legislatures, 14 states offer at least some public monies, and several states such as Connecticut and Arizona offer public funding to candidates for all statewide offices and the state legislature. Studies of these systems suggest they have some important benefits; in particular, legislators and others freed from the need to raise money spend more time interacting with constituents and otherwise doing their jobs.[68] This suggests there may be upsides to public financing, though such a system is very unlikely to be implemented at the federal level.

Image 10.8 President Trump meets with political donor and businessman Stephen Schwarzman.

10-7 Effects of Elections on Policy

To the candidates, and perhaps to the voters, the only interesting outcome of an election is who wins. To a political scientist, the interesting outcomes are the broad trends in winning and losing and what they imply about the attitudes of voters, the operation of the electoral system, the fate of political parties, and the direction of public policy.

Figure 10.7 shows the trend in the popular vote for president since before the Civil War. From 1876 to 1896, the Democrats and Republicans were hotly competitive. The Republicans won three times, the Democrats twice in close contests. Beginning in 1896, the Republicans became the dominant party, and except for 1912 and 1916, when Woodrow Wilson, a Democrat, was able to win owing to a split in the Republican Party, the Republicans carried every presidential election until 1932. Then Franklin Roosevelt put together what has since become known as the "New Deal coalition," and the Democrats became the dominant party. They won every election until 1952, when Eisenhower, a Republican and a popular military hero, was elected for the first of his two terms. In the presidential elections since 1952, power has frequently switched hands between the parties.

Still, cynics complain that elections are meaningless: No matter who wins, crooks, incompetents, or self-serving politicians still hold office. The more charitable argue that elected officials usually are decent enough, but that public policy remains more or less the same no matter which official or party is in office.

This cynical view is, in our opinion, wrong. American public policy does change in response to the pressure of elections.

In a parliamentary system with strong parties, such as that in the United Kingdom, an election often can have a major effect on public policy. When the Labour Party won office in 1945, it put several major industries under public ownership and launched a comprehensive set of social services, including a nationalized health care plan. Its ambitious and controversial campaign platform was converted, almost item by item, into law. When the

Figure 10.7 **Partisan Division of the Presidential Vote in the Nation, 1856–2020**

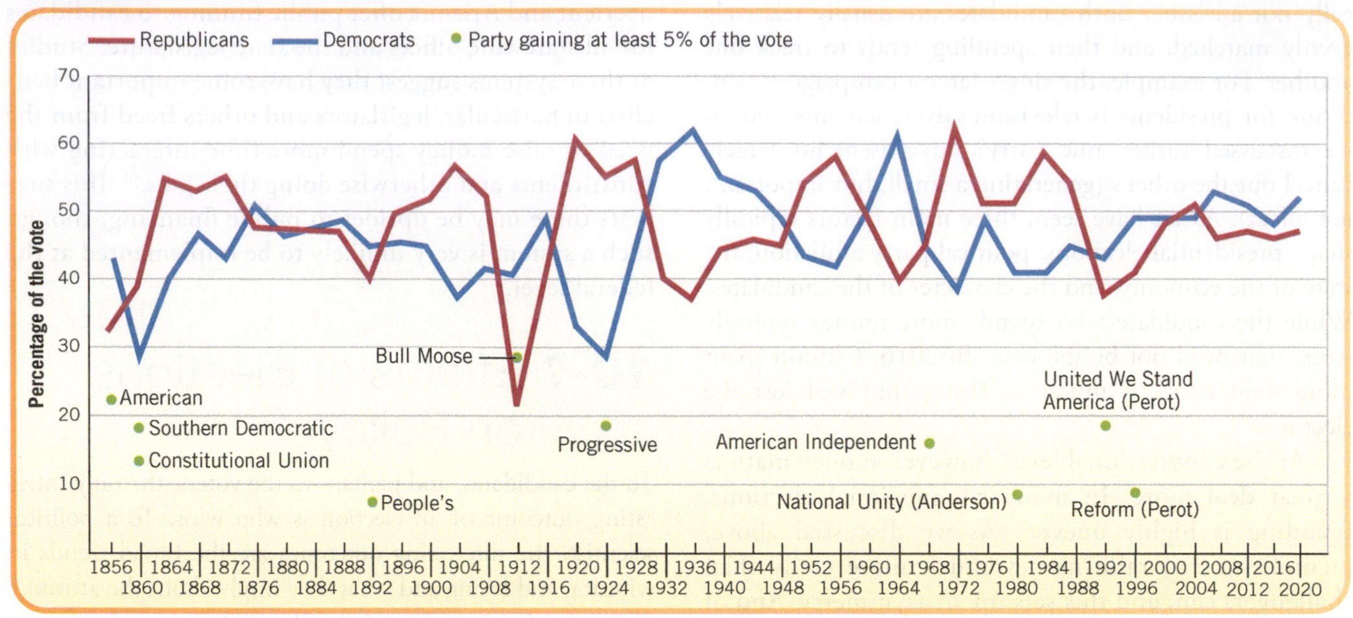

Sources: William H. Flanigan and Nancy H. Zingale, *Political Behavior of the American Electorate; World Almanac and Book of Facts 1994*; Dave Leip's Atlas of U.S. Presidential Elections.

Conservative Party returned to power in 1951, it accepted some of these changes but rejected others (e.g., it denationalized the steel industry).

American elections, unless accompanied by a national crisis such as a war or a depression, rarely produce changes of the magnitude of those that occurred in Britain in 1945. The constitutional system within which our elections take place was designed to moderate the pace of change—to make it neither easy nor impossible to adopt radical proposals. Elections do produce changes in policy, though they are often quite modest ones in normal circumstances.

Yet with dramatic elections, even the American system can produce dramatic changes. The election of 1860 brought to national power a party committed to opposing the extension of slavery and Southern secession; it took a bloody war to vindicate that policy. The election of 1896 led to the dominance of a party committed to high tariffs, a strong currency, urban growth, and business prosperity—a commitment that was not significantly altered until 1932. The election of that year led to the New Deal, which produced the greatest single enlargement of federal authority since 1860. The election of 1964 gave the Democrats such a large majority in Congress (as well as control of the presidency) that there began to issue forth an extraordinary number of new policies of sweeping significance—Medicare and Medicaid, federal aid to education and to local law enforcement, two dozen environmental and consumer protection laws, the Voting Rights Act of 1965, a revision of the immigration laws, and a new cabinet-level Department of Housing and Urban Development.

In view of all these developments, it is hard to argue that the pace of change in our government is always slow or that elections never make a difference. Studies by scholars confirm that elections generate significant shifts in public policy. Many promises from campaigns are actually put into action, both at the presidential and congressional levels.[69] While many think that politicians do not keep their promises, this is partially a function of the fact that the media tends to focus on cases where candidates do not implement their promises (and often does not report when they do; we return to this point in Chapter 12).[70] Even in "ordinary" times, elections shape the policies produced by the government.

Another study examined the party platforms of the Democrats and Republicans from 1844 to 1968 and all the laws passed by Congress between 1789 and 1968. Through use of a complex statistical method, the author of the study was able to show that during certain periods the differences between the platforms of the two parties were especially large (1856, 1880, 1896, and 1932) and that there was at about the same time a high rate of change in the kinds of laws being passed.[71] This study supports the general impression conveyed by history that elections often can be central to important policy changes.

Why then do we so often think elections make little difference? It is because public opinion and the political parties enter a phase of consolidation and continuity between periods of rapid change. During this phase, the changes are digested, and party leaders adjust to the new popular consensus, which may (or may not) evolve around the merits of these changes. During the 1870s and 1880s, Democratic politicians had to come to terms with the failure of the Southern secessionist

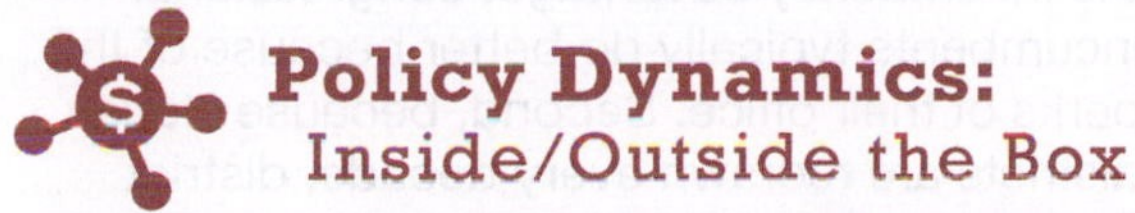

Campaign Finance Reform: Entrepreneurial Politics

In recent years, the role of money in politics has once again come to the fore, especially in light of the record-breaking spending of super PACs and other groups in recent elections. Some reformers have called for legislation to either outlaw or more tightly regulate such groups (and to regulate the flow of money in politics more generally). One such proposed reform was H.R. 1, the "For the People Act," which would implement a number of election reforms, including requiring additional documentation for donors to 501(c)4 and measures to encourage campaigns to seek more small donors. The bill passed the House in 2019, but has not been taken up by the Senate.

Such efforts are examples of entrepreneurial politics. Reforming the system imposes concentrated costs on those who are large contributors in the status quo, since their activity is what would be most strongly limited. Furthermore, such efforts would also impose costs on political parties. As we discussed in Chapter 9, the parties have broken fundraising records in recent years in part by relying on the donations of wealthy individuals who contribute large sums. Both of these groups are well positioned to oppose reform.

In contrast, the primary benefit of reform would be to all Americans, who would benefit from a decreased perception of corruption and a greater sense of fairness. As we will discuss in Chapter 11, there is little evidence that money in politics directly leads to corruption, but many Americans think it does, which threatens their trust in the government. However, as we discussed in Chapter 1, reforming this area would take a policy entrepreneur to mobilize the public, which has not yet happened.

The other way (as we discussed in Chapter 1) for entrepreneurial politics to succeed is for the salience of the issue to change. While many Americans report they are dissatisfied with the current system and think there is too much money in politics, few want Congress to make it a top priority. This suggests that unless opinion changes significantly, or an entrepreneur appears, the status quo is likely to remain in place.

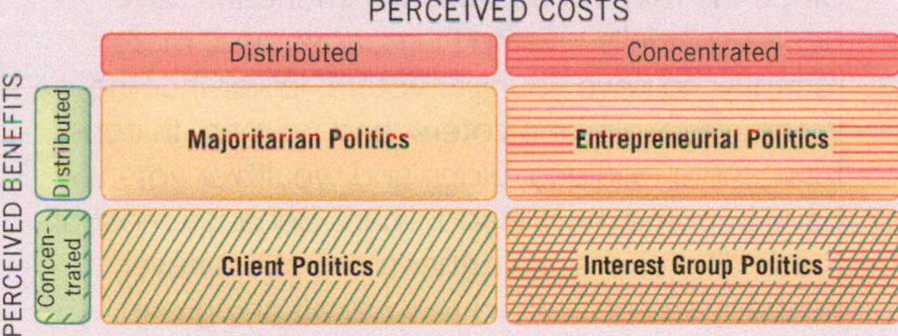

Source: Lydia Saad, "Half in U.S. Support Publicly Financed Federal Campaigns," Gallup, June 2013.

movement and the abolition of slavery; during the 1900s, the Democrats had to adjust again, this time to the fact that national economic policy was going to support industrialization and urbanization, not farming; during the 1940s and 1950s, the Republicans had to learn to accept the popularity of the New Deal.

Elections in ordinary times are not "critical"—they do not produce any major party realignment, they are not fought out over a dominant issue, and they provide the winners with no clear mandate. In most cases, an election is little more than a retrospective judgment on the record of the incumbent president and the existing congressional majority. If times are good, incumbents win easily; if times are bad, incumbents may lose—even though their opponents may have no clear plans for change. But even a "normal" election can produce dramatic results if the winner is a person such as Ronald Reagan, who helped give his party a distinctive political philosophy, or Barack Obama, the nation's first African American president.

Learning Objectives

10-1 Describe the factors that influence the presidential primaries.

In primaries, candidates are much less well known, and many briefly surge in the polls and then fade away just as quickly. Because voters do not know much about the candidates yet, media coverage plays a large role. Momentum also matters a great deal: Candidates who win early in the process often (but not always) have an advantage in later contests.

10-2 Explain how campaigns shape the outcome of presidential elections.

Campaigns shape outcomes by focusing on three key factors for voters: assigning credit or blame for the state of the nation (especially the state of the national economy), activating voters' latent partisanship, and allowing voters to judge the character of the candidates. These three factors—the state of the nation, the voters' partisanship, and the candidates' character—are three of the most important elements in shaping a voter's decision at the ballot box.

10-3 Summarize how voters learn about the candidates in elections.

Much of what voters learn about candidates comes through the media, especially through campaign advertisements (which are the single largest expense for most national campaigns). Such advertisements affect what voters know and feel about the candidates. In most elections, because advertisements are roughly equally balanced, the net effect is rather small. Citizens also learn from various campaign events, in particular, party conventions and debates.

10-4 Explain which social groups have been most loyal to the parties over time.

Since the mid-1960s, African Americans have been especially loyal to Democrats and, more recently, so have younger voters, lower-income voters, less religious voters, and women. In contrast, more religious, older, and wealthier voters have become more Republican. Because most of these differences are rather modest, however, neither party can afford to write off any group.

10-5 Describe the key differences between presidential and congressional elections.

Congressional elections have three key differences from presidential elections. First, there's the incumbency advantage: congressional incumbents typically do better because of the perks of their office. Second, because House districts are redrawn every decade, district boundaries can change, with implications for how members behave (though with fewer implications than many believe). Finally, because of the surge and decline in voter turnout, the president's party almost always does worse in midterm elections.

10-6 Summarize the history of campaign finance reform efforts, and explain the current state of campaign finance regulation.

The modern campaign finance system dates to the aftermath of the Watergate era and put in place strict limits on donations. Numerous reform efforts have been proposed and passed, but none have significantly altered the role of money in politics. Today, much of the concern centers around outside groups (such as super PACs) and their role in the process.

10-7 Describe how elections shape public policy.

When a dramatic shift occurs as a result of an election (such as 1860, 1932, or 1964), policy can change dramatically as a result. But even in more normal times, who wins elections has important implications for the policies they enact.

To Learn More

Federal Election Commission: **www.fec.gov**

Candidates' Positions on the Issues, from Project Vote Smart: **www.votesmart.org**

Election history: **http://clerk.house.gov**

Electoral College: **www.archives.gov/federal-register/electoral-college/**

Data on campaign finance: **www.opensecrets.org**

Black, Earl, and Merle Black. *Divided America: The Ferocious Power Struggle in American Politics*. New York: Simon and Schuster, 2007. Detailed account of how evenly balanced the two parties are in all parts of the country.

Burnham, Walter Dean. *Critical Elections and the Mainsprings of American Politics*. New York: Norton, 1970. An argument about the decline in voting participation and the significance of the realigning election of 1896.

Fowler, Erika Franklin, Michael Franz, and Travis Ridout. 2016. *Political Advertising in the United States*. Boulder, CO: Westview Press. An excellent overview of the data on political advertising and its effects.

Sides, John, Lynn Vavreck, and Michael Tessler. *Identity Crisis: The 2016 Presidential Campaign and the Battle for the Meaning of America.* Princeton, NJ: Princeton University Press, 2018. An excellent summary of what political scientists know about elections and how that helps us understand the dynamics of 2016.

Sundquist, James L. *Dynamics of the Party System: Alignment and Realignment of Political Parties in the United States,* rev. ed. Washington, D.C.: Brookings Institution, 1983. Historical analysis of realigning elections from 1860 to the nonrealignment of 1980.

Vavreck, Lynn. *The Message Matters: The Economy and Presidential Campaigns.* Princeton, NJ: Princeton University Press, 2009. Explains why the economy drives presidential elections (because campaigns work to assign credit/blame for the economy).

Cory Clark/NurPhoto/Getty Images

CHAPTER 11

Interest Groups

Learning Objectives

11-1 Explain what an interest group is, and identify the main factors that led to their rise in America.

11-2 Detail the various types of interest groups in America, and explain the types of people who join interest groups.

11-3 Summarize the ways interest groups relate to social movements.

11-4 Explain the various ways interest groups try to influence the policymaking process.

11-5 Describe the ways in which interest groups' political activity is limited.

interest group *An organization of people sharing a common interest or goal that seeks to influence public policy.*

lobbyist *A person who tries to influence legislation on behalf of an interest group.*

You probably do not think of yourself or of people you know as belonging to an "interest group." But are you or your friends part of an effort to improve the environment? Do you have family or friends who build houses, teach school, or practice law? If the answer to any of these questions is yes, then you likely know someone who belongs to the Sierra Club or the Audubon Society, a labor union, the American Federation of Teachers, or the American Bar Association. In short, if you examine your own activities and affiliations and those of at least some people you know well, chances are that you or they belong to one or more interest groups.

An **interest group** is an organization of people sharing a common interest or goal that seeks to influence public policy. The size and diversity of our country, the decentralizing effects of our Constitution, and the vast number of nonprofit organizations make it certain that interest groups will be an important way for people to have their voices heard. But while interest groups are as old as the republic itself, the number of interest groups has grown rapidly since 1960, and today record numbers of interest groups are active in politics through a variety of different means from protests, to voter registration, to political donations, to lobbying. In this chapter, we explore the rise of such groups, and explain how they influence the political process.

« Then During the 1770s, many groups arose to agitate for American independence; during the 1830s and 1840s, the number of religious associations increased sharply, and the antislavery movement began. In the 1860s, craft-based trade unions emerged in significant numbers, farmers formed the Grange, and various fraternal organizations were born. In the 1880s and 1890s, business associations proliferated.

The great era of organization-building, however, was in the first two decades of the 20th century. Within this 20-year period, many of the best-known and largest associations with an interest in national politics were formed: the Chamber of Commerce, the National Association of Manufacturers, the American Medical Association, the National Association for the Advancement of Colored People (NAACP), the Urban League, the American Farm Bureau Federation, the Farmers' Union, the National Catholic Welfare Conference, the American Jewish Committee, and the Anti-Defamation League.

*** Now** The wave of interest group formation that occurred in the 1960s led to the emergence of a wide variety of new groups and social movement. In the 1970s, campaign finance laws allowed for the development of Political Action Committees (see Chapter 10), and to a growth in lobbying. But these activities do not tell the whole story of interest group activity in recent years. A wide range of groups have organized important political protests, from the March for our Lives on gun control, to the Sunrise Movement on climate change, to the Women's March, to the Black Lives Matter protests that emerged in the wake of the death of George Floyd. Indeed, the Floyd protests are the broadest in U.S. history—taking place in all 50 states and Washington D.C.—and are also among the largest.[1] In this chapter, we will explore how all of these interest group activities shape politics.

A **lobbyist** is someone who lobbies; that is, someone who tries to influence legislation on behalf of a client, often an interest group. When Americans think of lobbying, they usually think of ideological groups like the National Rifle Association or the Sierra Club. But businesses actually conduct the majority of lobbying. For instance, between 1981 and 2005, the number of full-time and part-time lobbyists in Washington representing just the S&P 500 corporations increased from 1,475 to 2,765.[1] As we will see later in the chapter, while business groups tend to dominate lobbying, they are not the only important interest groups. For example, many citizen movements—such as the Tea Party, Black Lives Matter, and the Women's March on Washington—have shaped our politics in recent years.

Why are associations in general and political interest groups in particular created more rapidly in some periods than in others? After all, there have always been farmers in this country, but there were no national farm organizations until the latter part of the 19th century. African Americans were victimized by many white-supremacist groups and policies after the Civil War, but the NAACP did not emerge until 1910. People worked in factories for decades before industrial unions were formed. Every political era featured activists who believed strongly in liberal or conservative ideology, but only in recent decades have ideological groups become so pervasive. Organized business interests have battled organized labor interests over public policy for more than a hundred years, but only recently has the big-business lobbying presence in Washington expanded so dramatically both in absolute terms and relative to big labor.

Four factors have helped shape how and when given interest groups arose in America. We now turn to a consideration of them.

11-1 The Rise of Interest Groups

At least four factors help explain the rise of interest groups. The first consists of broad economic developments that create new interests and redefine old ones. Farmers had little reason to become organized for political activity so long as most of them consumed what they produced. The importance of regular political activity became evident only after most farmers began to produce cash crops for sale in markets that were unstable or affected by forces (the weather, the railroads, foreign competition) that those farmers could not control. Similarly, for many decades most workers were craftspeople working alone or in small groups. Such unions as existed were little more than craft guilds interested in protecting members' jobs and in training apprentices. The impetus for large, mass-membership unions did not exist until there arose mass-production industry operated by large corporations.

Second, government policy itself helps to create interest groups. Wars create veterans, who in turn demand pensions and other benefits. The first large veterans' organization, the Grand Army of the Republic, was made up of Union veterans of the Civil War. By the 1920s, these former soldiers were receiving about a quarter of a billion dollars a year from the government, and naturally they created organizations to watch over the distribution of this money. The federal government encouraged the formation of the American Farm Bureau Federation (AFBF) by paying for county agents who would serve the needs of farmers under the supervision of local farm organizations; these county bureaus eventually came together as the AFBF. The Chamber of Commerce was launched at a conference attended by President William Howard Taft. Professional societies, such as those made up of lawyers and doctors, became important in part because state governments gave to such groups the authority to decide who was qualified to become a lawyer or a doctor.

Workers had a difficult time organizing as long as the government, by the use of injunctions enforced by the police and the army, prevented strikes. Unions, especially those in mass-production industries, began to flourish after Congress passed laws in the 1930s prohibiting the

JEFF KOWALSKY/AFP/Getty Images

Image 11.1 Citizens protested at several state capitals in response to stay-at-home orders during the COVID-19 pandemic.

use of injunctions in private labor disputes, requiring employers to bargain with unions, and allowing a union representing a majority of the workers in a plant to require all workers to join it.[2]

Third, political organizations do not emerge automatically, even when government policy permits them and social circumstances seem to require them. Somebody must exercise leadership, often at substantial personal cost. These organizational entrepreneurs are found in greater numbers at certain times than at others. Often they are young, caught up in a social movement, drawn to the need for change, and inspired by some political or religious doctrine.

Antislavery organizations were created in the 1830s and 1840s by enthusiastic young people influenced by a religious revival sweeping the country. The period from 1890 to 1920, when so many national organizations were created, was a time when the college-educated middle class was growing rapidly: The number of people who received college degrees each year has tripled between 1890 and 1920.[3] During this era, natural science and fundamentalist Christianity were locked in a bitter contest, with the Gospels and Darwinism offering competing ideas about personal salvation and social progress. The 1960s, when many new organizations were born, was a decade in which the civil rights and antiwar movements powerfully influenced young people and college enrollments are more than doubled.

Finally, the more government does, the more interest groups will arise or expand and try to influence public policy.[4] Most Washington offices representing corporations, labor unions, and trade and professional associations were established before 1960—in some cases many decades before—because it was during the 1930s or even earlier that the government began making policies important to business and labor. The great majority of "public-interest" lobbies (those concerned with the environment or consumer protection), social welfare associations, and organizations concerned with civil rights, older adults, and people with disabilities established offices in Washington after major new federal laws in these respective areas were enacted.

A particularly dramatic example is what happened in the post-9/11 years, after the USA Patriot Act was enacted in 2001 and the Department of Homeland Security (DHS) was created in 2002.[5] With billions of dollars a year in federal funding, more than 500 new private companies specializing in work related to security and counterterrorism emerged in the subsequent decade, and 1,400 or so existing companies expanded into this domain.[6] New lobbies quickly formed to represent those firms and keep their homeland security grants and contracts coming; for example, the "full-body scanner" lobby represents firms that sell body-scanning equipment used in airports to a DHS subunit, the Transportation Security Administration.[7] Moreover, many local governments, from big cities to small towns, have hired lobbyists to work on getting or sustaining their fair share of federal homeland security money (recall the discussion of these grant programs in Chapter 3). As government expands, so do lobbyists.

11-2 Kinds of Organizations

When we think of an organization, we usually think of something like the Boy Scouts or the League of Women Voters—a group consisting of individual members. In Washington, however, many organizations do not have individual members at all but are offices—corporations, law firms, public relations firms, or "letterhead" organizations that get most of their money from other organizations or from the government—out of which a staff operates. It is important to understand the differences between the two kinds of interest groups: institutional and membership.[8]

Institutional Interests

Institutional interests are individuals or organizations representing other organizations. For example, long before the government bailed it out in 2008, General Motors had representatives in Washington, and it is now not uncommon for even midsized corporations to have one or more full-time representatives plus part-time lawyers or public relations consultants working for them in Washington. Another kind of institutional interest is the trade or governmental association, such as the National Independent Retail Jewelers and the National Association of Counties.

Individuals or organizations that represent other organizations tend to be interested in bread-and-butter issues of vital concern to their clients. Some of the people who specialize in this work can earn very large fees. Top public relations experts and Washington lawyers can charge $500 an hour or more for their time. Since they earn a lot, they are expected to deliver a lot.

Just what they are expected to deliver, however, varies with the diversity of the groups making up the organization. The Manufactured Housing Institute represents those who make prefabricated (modular) homes. This group has a relatively narrow and cohesive agenda: they want to ensure policies that encourage homebuilding, especially modular homebuilding. It should come as no surprise, then, that the group has an active lobbying presence in Washington, D.C., and spent $1.25 million on

Constitutional Connections | A "Faction" or "Special Interest"?

While the Constitution does not explicitly discuss interest groups (though the First Amendment does guarantee their rights of assembly and speech), the Framers were very concerned about "factions" undermining the new republic. James Madison warned in *Federalist* No. 10 of the dangers of factions, arguing that republican (i.e., representative) democracy would control the effects of factions through elected officials and a large republic, in which groups would compete to influence policy, forcing compromise and preventing the domination of any single group. But what is a faction? Madison said any individual or group, whether a minority or majority of the whole, is a faction if it has interests that are opposed to the "permanent and aggregate interests of the community." Who defines those interests? The Framers thought our elected officials had the knowledge and expertise to do so, and those officials depend on interest groups for many resources, including information, campaign funds, and votes. A "faction" for one person may be a "special interest" for another. Madison's point about the need to limit the influence of factions remains true, but those groups also play an integral part in American democracy.

lobbying in 2019, according to the Center for Responsive Politics. Sometimes the institute is successful, sometimes not, but it is never hard to explain what it is doing.

By contrast, the U.S. Chamber of Commerce represents thousands of different businesses in hundreds of different communities. Year in and year out, the Chamber spends more on lobbying than any other group. Over the last two decades, the Chamber has spent over $1.5 billion on lobbying (see Figure 11.1), a figure much larger than what was spent by any other organization over the same period, including corporate giants such as Exxon Mobil and membership giants such as AARP. Indeed, in 2019 alone, the Chamber spent $77.2 million on lobbying, more than the total combined spending of companies like Blue Cross/Blue Shield, Facebook, Amazon, and Boeing.[9] Its membership is so large and diverse that the Chamber in Washington can speak out clearly and forcefully on only those relatively few matters in which all, or most, businesses take the same position. Since all businesses would like lower taxes, the Chamber favors that. On the other hand, since some businesses (those that import goods) want lower tariffs and other businesses (those that face competition from imported goods) want higher tariffs, the Chamber says little or nothing about tariffs.

Institutional interests do not just represent business firms; they also represent governments, foundations, and universities. For example, the American Council on Education speaks for most institutions of higher education, the American Public Transportation Association represents local mass-transit systems, and the National Association of Counties argues on behalf of county governments.

Membership Interests

It often is said that America is a nation of joiners, and so we take for granted the many organizations around us supported by the activities and contributions of individual citizens. But we should not take this multiplicity of organizations for granted; in fact, their existence is something of a puzzle.

Americans join only certain kinds of organizations more frequently than citizens of other democratic countries. We are no more likely than the British, for example, to join social, business, professional, veterans', or charitable organizations, and we are *less* likely to join labor unions. Our reputation as a nation of joiners arises chiefly out of our unusually high tendency to join religious and civic or political associations.

Figure 11.1 **What the Top Lobby Spent, 1998–2019**

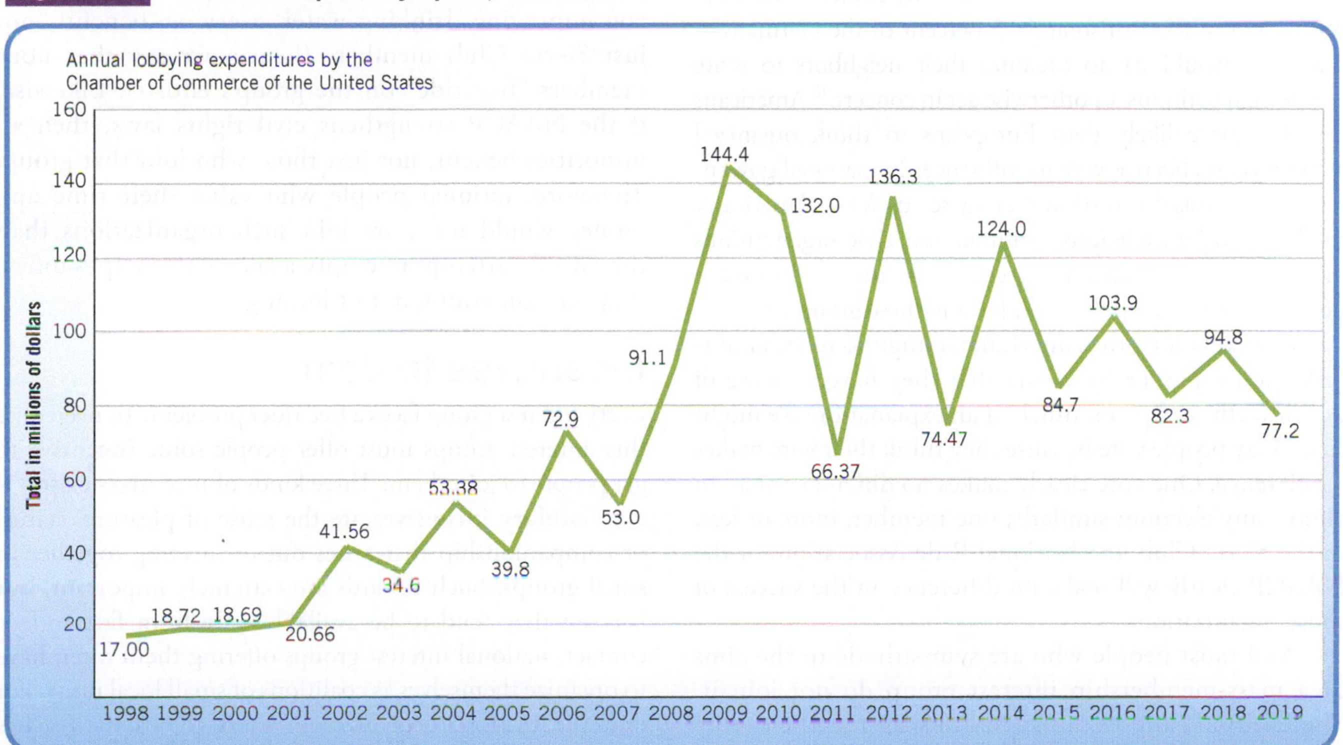

Source: Center for Responsive Politics, Lobbying: Top Spenders, www.opensecrets.org/lobby/top.php?indexType=s, Accessed February 2020.

Q Study the over-time pattern in the amount spent on lobbying by the Chamber of Commerce. Can you think of reasons why they spent more in some years than in others?

Landmark Cases | Lobbying Congress

- ***United States v. Harriss* (1954):** The Constitution protects the lobbying of Congress, but the government may require information from groups that try to influence legislation.

free rider problem *The tendency of individuals to avoid contributing to public goods.*

public good *Something of value that all individuals share, whether or not they contribute to it (such as clean air or water).*

incentive *Something of value one cannot get without joining an organization.*

solidary incentives *The social rewards (sense of pleasure, status, or companionship) that lead people to join political organizations.*

This proclivity of Americans to get together with other citizens to engage in civic or political action apparently reflects a greater sense of political efficacy and a stronger sense of civic duty than that found in some nations. In a classic study of political culture (See Chapter 4), Gabriel Almond and Sidney Verba asked citizens of five nations what they would do to protest an unjust local regulation; 56 percent of the Americans—but only 34 percent of the British and 13 percent of the Germans—said they would try to organize their neighbors to write letters, sign petitions, or otherwise act in concert.[10] Americans are also more likely than Europeans to think organized activity is an effective way to influence the national government, remote as that institution may seem. While Americans' tendency to join religious, cultural, and civic organizations has declined somewhat in recent years, they still outpace people in other democracies in joining these groups.[11]

But explaining the American willingness to join politically active groups by saying that they have a "sense of political efficacy" is not much of an explanation; we might as well say people vote because they think their vote makes a difference. One vote clearly makes no difference at all in almost any election; similarly, one member, more or less, in the Sierra Club, the National Rifle Association, or the NAACP clearly will make no difference in the success of those organizations.

And most people who are sympathetic to the aims of a mass-membership interest group do not join it. The NAACP, for example, enrolls as members only a tiny fraction of all African Americans. This is not because people are selfish or apathetic but because they are rational and numerous. A single African American individual, for example, knows that making a difference in the success of the NAACP alone is difficult, just as a single nature enthusiast knows that one individual will not enhance the power of the Sierra Club. Moreover, if the NAACP or the Sierra Club succeeds, African Americans and nature lovers will benefit even if they are not members. This tendency is known as the **free rider problem**.[12] The free rider problem arises because these groups are pursuing a **public good**: something valuable for which one person's consumption does not affect another person's consumption. For example, if the Sierra Club gets passed by the legislature a law improving drinking water, everyone benefits, not just Sierra Club members (hence, we say that nonmembers "free ride" on the group's efforts). Likewise, if the NAACP strengthens civil rights laws, then all minorities benefit, not just those who join that group. Therefore, rational people who value their time and money would no more join such organizations than they would attempt to empty a lake with a cup—unless they got something out of joining.

Samuel Corum/Anadolu Agency/Getty Images

Image 11.2 Young people participate in a pro-life rally in Washington, D.C.

Incentives to Join

Every interest group faces a free rider problem. To overcome this, interest groups must offer people some **incentive** to get people to join them. Three kinds of incentives exist.

Solidary incentives are the sense of pleasure, status, or companionship that arises out of meeting together in small groups. Such rewards are extremely important, but because they tend to be available only from face-to-face contact, national interest groups offering them often have to organize themselves as coalitions of small local units. For example, the League of Women Voters, the Parent Teacher Association (PTA), the NAACP, the Rotary Club, and the American Legion all consist of small local chapters that support a national staff. It is the task of the local chapters to lure members and obtain funds from them; the state or national staff can then use these funds to pursue political objectives.

Forming organizations made up of small local chapters is probably easier in the United States than in Europe because of the great importance of local government in our federal system. There is plenty for a PTA, an NAACP, or a League of Women Voters to do in its own community, and so its members can be kept busy with local affairs while the national staff pursues larger goals.

A second kind of incentive consists of **material incentives**—that is, money, or things and services readily valued in monetary terms. Farm organizations have recruited many members by offering a wide range of services. The Illinois Farm Bureau, for example, offers to its members—and *only* to its members—a chance to buy farm supplies at discount prices, market their products through cooperatives, and purchase low-cost insurance. These material incentives help explain why the Illinois Farm Bureau has been able to enroll nearly every farmer in the state as well as many nonfarmers who also value these rewards.

Similarly, the AARP has recruited tens of millions of members by supplying them with everything from low-cost life insurance and mail-order discount drugs to tax advice and group travel plans. Almost half of the nation's population aged 50 and older—one of every four registered voters—belongs to the AARP. With an annual operating budget of several hundred million dollars and a yearly cash flow of several billion dollars, the AARP seeks to influence public policy in many areas, from health and housing to taxes and transportation. To gain additional benefits for members, interest groups like the AARP also seek to influence how public laws are administered and who gets government grants.

The third—and most difficult—kind of incentive is the *purpose* of the organization. Many associations rely chiefly on this **purposive incentive**—the appeal of their stated goals—to recruit members. If the attainment of those goals will also benefit people who do not join, individuals who do join will have to be those who feel passionately about the goal, who have a strong sense of duty (or who cannot say no to a friend who asks them to join), or for whom the cost of joining is so small that they are indifferent to joining or not. Organizations that attract members by appealing to their interest in a coherent set of (usually) controversial principles are sometimes called **ideological interest groups**.

Bill Pugliano/Getty Images News/Getty Images

Image 11.3 Union members hold a rally in Michigan to protest against right-to-work legislation.

material incentives Money or things valued in monetary terms.

purposive incentive A benefit that comes from serving a cause or principle.

ideological interest groups Political organizations that attract members by appealing to their political convictions or principles.

public-interest lobby A political organization whose goals will principally benefit nonmembers.

When the purpose of the organization, if attained, will principally benefit nonmembers, it is customary to call the group a **public-interest lobby**. (Whether the public at large will really benefit is, of course, a matter of opinion, but at least the group members think they are working selflessly for the common good.)

One common type of public-interest lobby is an organization that advances its cause by bringing lawsuits to challenge existing practices or proposed regulations. Such a public-interest law firm will act in one of two ways. First, it will find people who have been harmed by some public or private policy and bring suit on their behalf. Second, it will file a brief with a court supporting somebody else's lawsuit (this is called an amicus curiae brief; it is explained in Chapter 16). While some of these groups are more liberal—such as the American Civil Liberties Union, National Resources Defense Council, and the NAACP Legal Defense and Education Fund—others are more conservative, such as the Center for Individual Rights, the American Center for Law & Justice, and the Atlantic Legal Foundation.

Though some public-interest lobbies may pursue relatively noncontroversial goals (e.g., persuading people to vote or raising money to house orphans), the most visible of these organizations are highly controversial. It is precisely the controversy that attracts the members, or at least those members who support one side of the issue. Many of these groups can be described as having a markedly liberal or decidedly conservative outlook.

Such ideological groups tend to be the dominant examples of purposive interest groups. For example, groups like NARAL Pro-Choice America (which supports abortion rights) and Operation Rescue (which opposes them) are good examples: The members work for these goals because they believe in them and the organization's mission. Likewise, many other ideological groups can best be characterized this way, including broad, umbrella ideological groups like the Public Interest Research Group on the left, and the American Conservative Union on the right.

Think Tanks—public-interest organizations that do research on policy questions and disseminate their findings in books, articles, conferences, op-ed essays for newspapers, and (occasionally) testimony before Congress—are another such example. While some are nonpartisan and strive for neutrality, many—including some of the most important ones—are more partisan and ideological. For example, organizations like the Center for American Progress or the Center for Budget and Policy Priorities try to advance liberal and Democratic causes, whereas groups like the Heritage Foundation and the American Enterprise Institute advocate for conservative and Republican causes.

Membership organizations that rely on purposive incentives, especially appeals to deeply controversial purposes, tend to be shaped by the mood of the times. When an issue is hot—in the media or with the public—such organizations can grow quickly. When the spotlight fades, the organization may lose support. Thus, such organizations have a powerful motive to stay in the public eye. To remain visible, public-interest lobbies devote a lot of attention to generating publicity by developing good contacts with the media and issuing dramatic press releases about crises and scandals.

Because of their need to take advantage of a crisis atmosphere, public-interest lobbies often do best when the government is in the hands of an administration that is *hostile*, not sympathetic, to their views. Conservative interest groups were able to raise more money with the Democrats Barack Obama or Bill Clinton in the White House than with the Republicans George W. Bush or Donald Trump there (and vice versa for liberal groups). For example, during the first year and half of the Trump administration, the ACLU saw its membership jump from 400,000 members to 1.84 million members, and yearly online donations increase from $5 million to $120 million.[13] These groups actively make the case that their preferred policy outcome is under threat in order to motivate people to join and contribute to the group.[14]

The Influence of the Staff

We often make the mistake of assuming that, politically, an interest group simply exerts influence on behalf of its members. That is indeed the case when all the members have a clear and similar stake in an issue. But many issues affect different members differently. In fact, if the members joined to obtain solidary or material benefits, they may not care at all about many of the issues with which the organization gets involved. In such cases, what the interest group does may reflect more what the staff wants than what the members believe.

For example, a classic survey of the white members of a large labor union showed that one-third of them believed the desegregation of schools, housing, and job opportunities had gone too fast; only one-fifth thought it had gone too slowly. But among the staff members of the union, *none* thought desegregation had gone too fast, and over two-thirds thought it had gone too slowly.[15] As a result, the union staff aggressively lobbied Congress for the passage of tougher civil rights laws, even though most of the union's members did not feel they were needed. The members stayed in the union for reasons unrelated to civil rights, giving the staff the freedom to pursue its own goals.

Upper-Class Bias?

Observers often believe that interest groups active in Washington reflect an upper-class bias. There are two reasons for this belief: first, well-off people are more likely than poor people to join and be active in interest groups; second, interest groups representing business and the professions are much more numerous and better financed than organizations representing minorities, consumers, or the disadvantaged.

Many scholars have shown that people with higher incomes, those whose schooling went through college or beyond, and those in professional or technical jobs are much more likely to belong to a voluntary association than people with the opposite characteristics. Just as we would expect, higher-income people can afford more organizational memberships than lower-income ones; people in business and the professions find it easier to attend meetings (they have more control over their own work schedules) and attach more importance to doing so than people in blue-collar jobs; and people with college degrees often have a wider range of interests than those without.

One study found that between 1981 and 2006, the ratio of business lobbyists to union plus public-interest lobbyists prone to oppose business interests rose from about 12 to 1 to nearly 16 to 1.[16] Some now argue that the nation's 2007–2010 economic crises were due in part to the disproportionate political influence wielded during the preceding decade by rich Wall Street executives and related business interests. There is some truth to this view. In 1999, corporate lawyers and lobbyists won a long legislative battle to repeal the Banking Act of 1933, better known as the Glass-Steagall Act, which strictly separated investment from commercial banking and imposed many other restrictions on financial companies. The repeal permitted the home mortgage business to change in ways that made it easier to offer risky loans to people with poor credit histories, and it gave birth to new financial products and services that were weakly regulated by government and incomprehensible to most consumers.

But note that the 1933 law, albeit with certain changes made in subsequent decades, remained on the books for more than 60 years before it was repealed. And, strongly opposed though it was by myriad powerful business interests, today the Wall Street Reform and Consumer Protection Act of 2010 is law. Better known as Dodd-Frank, this law did not restore the Glass-Steagall Act's strict separation between depository banking and financial trading, but it did tighten regulations on virtually all financial companies and broaden consumer protections for all, including first-time mortgage-seekers and small investors.

As this example suggests, even if it is true that financial moguls, big-business executives, and other wealthy people typically have more (high-priced) lobbyists looking out for their interests than other citizens do, the question of an upper-class bias is by no means entirely settled. Business may operate from a privileged position of wealth and power, but they only sometimes—not always—get what they want.[17]

In the first place, lobbyists represent certain *inputs* into the political system; what matters are the *outputs*—that is, who wins and who loses on particular issues. For instance, even if scores and scores of groups inside the Capital Beltway are pushing to protect the oil industry and those who benefit financially from it the most, this is important only if the oil industry in fact gets protected. Sometimes it does; sometimes it does not. At one time, when oil prices were low, oil companies were able to get Congress to pass a law that sharply restricted the importation of foreign oil. A few years later, after oil prices had risen and people were worried about energy issues, these restrictions were ended.

social movement *A widely shared demand for change in some aspect of the social or political order.*

In the second place, business-oriented interest groups often are divided among themselves. Take one kind of business: farming. Once, farm organizations seemed so powerful in Washington that scholars spoke of an irresistible "farm bloc" in Congress that could get its way on almost anything. Today, dozens of agricultural organizations operate in the capital, with some (such as the Farm Bureau) attempting to speak for all farmers and others (such as the Tobacco Institute and Mid-America Dairymen) representing particular commodities and regions.

Whenever American politics is described as having an upper-class bias, it is important to ask exactly what this bias is. Most major conflicts in American politics—over foreign policy, economic affairs, environmental protection, and equal rights for women—are conflicts *within* the upper class; that is, they are conflicts among politically active elites. As we saw in earlier chapters, profound cleavages of opinion exist among these elites. Interest-group activity reflects these cleavages.

It would be a mistake to ignore the overrepresentation of business in Washington. A student of politics should always take differences in the availability of political resources as an important clue to possible differences in the outcomes of political conflicts. Nonetheless, the differences are only clues, not conclusions, and in any given case, we need to consider many other factors to understand what happens.

Image 11.4 After the horrific school shooting in Newtown, Connecticut, in December 2012, thousands of people participated in the March on Washington for Gun Control.

11-3 Interest Groups and Social Movements

Because it is difficult to attract people with purposive incentives, interest groups using them tend to arise out of social movements. A **social movement** is a widely shared demand for change in some aspect of the social or political order. The Civil Rights movement of the 1960s was such an event, as was the environmentalist movement of the 1970s.

A social movement need not have liberal goals. In the 19th century, for example, various nativist movements sought to reduce immigration to this country or to keep Catholics or Masons out of public office. Broad-based religious revivals are social movements. During the Obama presidency, the conservative

Tea Party movement played a role in both local and national elections (see our discussion of this movement in Chapter 9), and likewise pro-life and pro-gun rights groups are important political groups today.

No one is quite certain why social movements arise. At one moment, people are largely indifferent to some issue; at another moment, many of these same people care passionately about religion, civil rights, immigration, or conservation. A social movement may be triggered by a tragedy (such as the death of many African Americans while in police custody), the dramatic and widely publicized activities of a few leaders (lunch counter sit-ins helped stimulate the Civil Rights movement), or the coming of age of a new generation that takes up a cause advocated by eloquent writers, teachers, or evangelists.

Whatever its origin, the effect of a social movement is to increase the value some people attach to purposive incentives. As a consequence, new interest groups are formed that rely on these incentives for participation and support and many have important policy consequences.[18]

Scott Heins/Getty Images News/Getty Images

Image 11.5 Young people participate in the Climate Strike movement to protest for action on climate change.

The Environmental Movement

The environmental movement provides a good example of how a social movement gives rise to interest groups formed from reliance on purposive incentives. In the 1890s, as a result of the emergence of conservation as a major issue, the Sierra Club was organized. In the 1930s, conservation once again became popular, and the Wilderness Society and the National Wildlife Federation were created. In the 1960s and 1970s, environmental issues again had high public interest, and we saw the emergence of the Environmental Defense Fund and Environmental Action.

The smallest of these organizations (Environmental Action and the Environmental Defense Fund) tend to have the most liberal members. This often is the case with organizations that arise from social movements. A movement will spawn many organizations. The most passionately aroused people will be the fewest in number, and they will gravitate toward the organizations that take the most extreme positions; as a result, these organizations are small but vociferous. The more numerous and less passionate people will gravitate toward more moderate, less vociferous organizations, which tend to be larger.

As happens over the years to most politically successful movements, the environmental movement has become more fragmented than it was in the 1970s. Different leading voices and organizations within it have begun to advocate somewhat different policy approaches to achieving the same basic (in this case, environmental protection and sustainability) goals.[19]

Environmental activists have recently been particularly active in two areas: climate change and domestic oil and gas production, particularly with respect to new pipelines. We discuss the politics of climate change in Chapter 17, but it is important to know that many environmental interest groups are active on this issue, pressing for action at the federal and state levels, and trying to raise public awareness on the issue. Younger people have been especially involved in movements surrounding climate change, both through groups such as the Sunrise Movement, as well as through various student "climate strikes," in which students take a day off from school to protest and demand action on climate change. The 2019 Climate Strike in New York City had an estimated 60,000, if not more, participants.[20]

Environmentalists have also been active in debates over increased oil and natural gas production, particularly with respect to proposed pipelines to transport this oil and natural gas. The Dakota Access Pipeline project, which would transport oil from North Dakota to other states, has proved to be especially controversial, as it would cross lands considered sacred by the Standing Rock Indian Tribe. In 2016, tribe members and environmental activists staged a lengthy protest to try to block the pipeline's construction. While President Obama blocked the pipeline's completion before leaving office, President Trump overturned this decision, allowing the pipeline to open in 2017, though various lawsuits surrounding it are still being litigated.

The Feminist Movement

Several feminist social movements have occurred in this country's history—in the 1830s, the 1890s, the 1920s, and the 1960s. Each period brought about new organizations, some of which have endured to the present. For example, the League of Women Voters was founded in 1920 to educate and organize women for the purpose of effectively using their newly won right to vote. As we discussed in Chapter 6 on civil rights, many women's rights groups have been important through American history for pressing for gender equality.

Though a strong sense of purpose may lead to the creation of organizations, each will strive to find some incentive that will sustain it over the long haul. These permanent incentives affect how the organization participates in politics.

At least three kinds of feminist organizations exist. First, there are those that rely chiefly on solidary incentives, primarily enroll upper-/middle-class women with relatively high levels of schooling, and tend to support those causes that command the widest support among women generally. The League of Women Voters and the Federation of Business and Professional Women are examples. Both supported the campaign in the 1970s to ratify the Equal Rights Amendment (ERA), but as Jane Mansbridge observed in her history of the ERA, they were uneasy with the kind of intense, partisan fighting displayed by some other women's organizations and with the tendency of more militant groups to link the ERA to other issues, such as abortion. The reason for their uneasiness is clear: to the extent they relied on solidary incentives, they had a stake in avoiding issues and tactics that would divide their membership or reduce the extent to which membership provided camaraderie and professional contacts.[21]

Second, some women's organizations attract members with purposive incentives. The National Organization for Women (NOW) and NARAL Pro-Choice America are two of the largest such groups, though many smaller ones exist. Because they rely on purposes, these organizations must take strong positions, tackle divisive issues, and use militant tactics. Anything less would turn off the committed feminists who make up the rank and file and contribute the funds. But because these groups take controversial stands, they are constantly embroiled in internal quarrels between those who think they have gone too far and those who think they have not gone far enough. Moreover, purposive organizations often cannot make their decisions stick at the local level (local chapters will do pretty much as they please, despite the directives of the central organization).[22]

The third kind of women's organization is groups that take on issues that have material benefits for women. For example, many professional associations of women, such as the U.S. Women's Chamber of Commerce, aim to provide networking and career advancement for women, but also advocate on various political issues important to women. Likewise, legal advocacy groups such as Legal Momentum (formerly the NOW Legal Defense Fund) work through the political system to press for outcomes that will help women politically and economically.

Still other groups work to try to elect women to political office, providing a combination of multiple types

Anna Watson/Alamy Stock Photo

Image 11.6 The Women's March began in 2017, and has continued to attract many participants in subsequent years.

of incentives. For example, the National Women's Political Caucus, the National Federation of Republican Women, and EMILY's List all work to elect more women to government. These groups provide solidary incentives, in that members could work together on an issue of interest (electing women to office), as well as purposive incentives (working for the goal of electing more women legislators). Like many groups, these groups offer members multiple rationales to join.

The day after President Trump's inauguration, there was a Women's March on Washington, responding to the rhetoric of the 2016 election and some of the proposed policies of the new administration. Several hundred thousand people joined the march in Washington, and hundreds of marches took place around the nation and the world, with an estimated 2.6 million people participating.[23] Since then, the march has become an annual event, with a smaller, but highly passionate, audience in subsequent years.

The women's movement had two successes in recent years. First, a record number of women ran for Congress and won in 2018; women are now approximately one-quarter of both the House and the Senate.[24] Many argue that this was due to the mobilization inspired by the women's march.[25] Second, while many had assumed the Equal Rights Amendment was dead, in 2020 Virginia became the 38th state to ratify it, potentially clearing the way for the amendment to be added to the Constitution. Whether the amendment actually will be added, however, is unclear as some claim the timeline to do so expired in the 1980s. (See the discussion in Chapter 6.)

The Union Movement

When social movements run out of steam, they leave behind organizations that continue the fight. But with the movement dead or dormant, the organizations often must struggle to stay alive. This has happened to labor unions.

The major union movement in this country occurred in the 1930s when the Great Depression, popular support, and a sympathetic administration in Washington led to a rapid growth in union membership. In 1945, union membership peaked; at that time, nearly 36 percent of all non-farm workers were union members.

Since then, union membership has declined more or less steadily. Today, unions cover only about 10 percent of all workers. Between 1983 and 2018, the number of union members fell by 3 million (from 17.7 million to 14.6 million). But because the nation's population grew considerably over that time period, the fraction of workers belonging to a labor union fell by almost one-half, from 20.1 percent in 1983 to 10.3 percent today.

This decline was caused by several factors. The nation's economic life has shifted away from industrial production (where unions have traditionally been concentrated) and toward service delivery (where unions have usually been weak). But accompanying this decline, and perhaps contributing to it, has been a decline in popular approval of unions. Approval has moved down side by side with a decline in membership and declines in union victories in elections held to see whether workers in a plant want to join a union. The social movement that supported unionism has faded.

But unions will persist because most can rely on incentives other than purposive ones to keep them going. In many states, unions can require workers to join if they wish to keep their jobs; in other places, workers believe they get sufficient benefits from the union to make even voluntary membership worthwhile. And in a few industries, such as teaching and government, membership has grown as some white-collar workers have turned to unions to advance their interests.

While private-sector unions have declined, public-sector unions—unions of government employees—have not. Indeed, according to the U.S. Bureau of Labor Statistics, in 2019, the union membership rate for public-sector workers (33.6 percent) was more than five times that for private-sector workers (6.2 percent).[26] In recent years, however, some elected officials and their supporters have pushed back against the expansion of public-sector unions. Several states, most notably Wisconsin, have passed legislation to limit public-sector unions.

In 2018, the Supreme Court made an important change to how public-sector unions can finance themselves in *Janus v. American Federation of State, County, and Municipal Employees*.[27] Prior to this decision, non-members who were covered by collective bargaining agreements—the contracts that unions negotiate with employers to spell out salary and benefits for workers—were required to pay a fee to the union to cover the cost of negotiating these agreements. In *Janus*, the Court ruled that public-sector unions could no longer collect these fees from non-members. Many commentators expected the decision to cripple public sector unions, as it would effectively allow people to free ride on the union's efforts. So far, this has not really happened,[28] but undoubtedly the politics of public sector unions will continue to be a political issue into the future.

Public-sector unions, led by groups like the American Federation of State County and Municipal Employees and the American Federation of Teachers (AFT), remain robust, relatively well funded, and significant sources of campaign contributions. For example, in the 2017–2018 election cycle, the AFT gave over $2 million to candidates, making it among the largest PAC contributors to candidates in that election cycle.

Unions can more or less reliably raise at least a portion of the funds they need by charging their members dues, but many interest groups struggle with raising money; some cannot easily predict what their budget will be from one quarter to the next. This is especially true for membership organizations that rely on appeals to purpose—to accomplishing stated goals. As a result, the Washington office of a public-interest lobbying group is likely to be small, stark, and crowded, whereas that of an institutional lobby, such as the AFL-CIO or the American Council on Education, will be rather lavish.

To make ends meet and maintain such influence as they each may have, diverse interest groups attempt to fund themselves through some combination of private foundation grants, government grants, direct-mail solicitation, and online appeals and donations, often tied in to the group social media sites.

11-4 The Activities of Interest Groups

Size and wealth are no longer accurate measures of an interest group's influence—if indeed they ever were. Depending on the issue, the key to political influence may be the ability to generate a dramatic newspaper headline, mobilize a big letter-writing campaign, stage a protest demonstration, file a suit in federal court to block (or compel) some government action, or supply information to key legislators. All of these things require organization, but few of them require big or expensive organizations.

Lobbying and Providing Information

Of all these tactics, the single most important one—in the eyes of virtually every lobbyist and every academic student of lobbying—is supplying credible information.

Indeed, if one were to ask what is the core of lobbying and interest-group influence, it would be providing information. Information is so valuable because to busy legislators and bureaucrats, information is in short supply. Legislators in particular must take positions on a staggering number of issues about which they cannot possibly become experts.

Much of the information lobbyists and their affiliated interest groups provide is about the consequences of a particular piece of legislation, either the policy consequences (How will this bill affect health care policy?) or the political consequences (How will this bill affect my next reelection campaign?).[29] Because legislators want to craft good policy and win reelection (see Chapter 13), both types of information are highly valuable.

The kind of information lobbyists provide is not easily accessible online or by other means (if it was, lobbying would not be necessary). Instead, it is highly specialized, often quite technical information, which only someone with a strong stake in an issue would gather.[30] Lobbyists, for the most part, are not flamboyant, party-giving arm-twisters; they are specialists who gather information (favorable to their clients, naturally) and present it in as organized, persuasive, and factual a manner as possible.

All lobbyists no doubt exaggerate, but few can afford to misrepresent the facts or mislead a legislator, and for a very simple reason: Almost every lobbyist must develop and maintain the confidence of a legislator over the long term, with an eye on tomorrow's issues as well as today's.[31] Because lobbyists want to develop long-term relationships with legislators, they have a strong incentive to be at least mostly truthful.

Dennis Brack-Pool/Getty Images News/Getty Images

Image 11.7 Former Vice President Joe Biden chats with former Senator John Kerry at a dinner in Washington, D.C. Such events are often opportunities for lobbyists or donors to meet with politicians.

Lobbying has become ubiquitous in American politics. A vast panoply of groups lobby: interest groups ranging from the National Rifle Association to the American Automobile Association, as well as unions, businesses, and other branches of government (recall our discussion of the intergovernmental lobby in Chapter 3). It may even surprise you to learn that universities—from major private universities such as Harvard and Yale, to state universities like the University of Texas and the University of California, to for-profit colleges—also lobby the federal government. These schools lobby about regulations governing student financial aid, education policy, and for funds for research projects.

While all of these groups lobby, the dominant players in the lobbying market are business organizations. One study found that business groups and trade associations account for approximately three-quarters of all lobbying activity.[32] Why? Businesses dominate lobbying primarily because they are seeking private goods. If the Sierra Club is lobbying for a particular policy, it is most likely a public good, like cleaner drinking water or tighter air pollution rules. In contrast, much of what firms lobby for are private goods: they want a particular tax break, or a policy that will benefit their industry. If they do not lobby, they will not receive that benefit, so they have the strongest incentive to lobby (and hence are over-represented in the lobbying community).

When most people think of lobbying, they think of lobbying on highly salient issues, such as Obamacare, immigration reform, gun control, or the Keystone XL pipeline. Lobbying certainly happens on these sorts of highly visible issues, but it is not the norm. A careful study of lobbying efforts found that lobbying was extremely skewed: Hundreds of lobbyists were active on a handful of significant bills, but on most issues, only one or two lobbyists were active.[33] The typical example of lobbying is a small, niche effort to change some small area of government policy that is relevant only to a few actors.

Furthermore, these two types of lobbying look very different. On highly salient bills with lobbyists on both sides of the issue, lobbying is unlikely to affect the outcome very much. Advocates for both sides make their case to legislators, and their lobbying is only one of many inputs to how a legislator decides. Lobbyists can of course affect the outcome, but they are constrained by these other factors. On these salient issues, other elements—most notably, members' own ideology and what their constituents want—are likely to be decisive.

However, on more narrow niche bills, far from the spotlight, lobbyists may be more influential. Typically only one side lobbies on these narrow issues, and this

political cue *A signal telling a legislator what values are at stake in a vote, and how the issue fits into the legislator's own political views or party agenda.*

ratings *Assessments of a representative's voting record on issues important to an interest group.*

will be the side with more resources and advantages. Many of these issues are examples of client politics, such as when a firm tries to obtain a particularistic exemption from a regulation or tariff (recall from Chapter 1 that client politics involves a group seeking concentrated benefits at the expense of a diffuse majority). No one lobbies for those bearing the dispersed costs in these cases, but there are lobbyists for the concentrated benefits. We cannot know that lobbyists have undue influence here, but it certainly suggests that lobbyists are likely more powerful on these narrow issues.

Beyond lobbying, groups can also provide another type of valuable information: political cues. A **political cue** is a signal telling the official what values are at stake in an issue—who is for, and who is against, a proposal—and how that issue fits into the legislator's own political beliefs. Some legislators feel comfortable when they are on the liberal side of an issue, and others feel comfortable when they are on the conservative side, especially when they are not familiar with the details of the issue. A liberal legislator will look to see whether the AFL-CIO, the NAACP, the Americans for Democratic Action, the Farmers' Union, and various consumer organizations favor a proposal; if so, that is often all the legislator has to know. If liberal groups are split, then the legislator will worry about the matter and try to look into it more closely. Similarly, a conservative legislator will feel comfortable taking a stand on an issue if the Chamber of Commerce, the National Rifle Association, the American Medical Association, various business associations, and Americans for Constitutional Action are in agreement about it; but the legislator may feel less comfortable if such conservative groups are divided. As a result of this process, lobbyists often work together in informal coalitions based on general political ideology.

One important way in which these cues are made known is by **ratings** that interest groups make of legislators. These are regularly compiled by dozens of interest groups; some of the most prominent ones include the AFL-CIO (on who is pro-labor), by the Americans for Democratic Action (on who is liberal), by the Americans for Constitutional Action (on who is conservative), by the Consumer Federation of America (on who is pro-consumer), and by the League of Conservation Voters (on who is pro-environment). These ratings are designed to generate public support for (or opposition to) various legislators. They can be helpful sources of information to both legislators and their constituents.

Figure 11.2 shows part of the ratings produced by the League of Conservation Voters (LCV) for the second session of the 115th Congress (2018). The LCV is an environmental organization, so its ratings capture which members it thinks are more pro-environment. In that year, the LCV picked 14 votes where they took a position and scored members of the Senate. For example, the second vote was to confirm Andrew Wheeler as deputy administrator of the Environmental Protection Agency (this was Senate roll call vote 71). The LCV opposed this nomination, so here those voting against the nomination receive a higher score. Likewise, vote 14 was a vote to approve the 2018 Farm Bill, which the LCV supported, so those for vote for the bill receive a higher score from the LCV (this was Senate roll call vote 259). To generate the final score, the LCV totals the number of times the Senator voted the way favored by the LCV. So a score of 100 percent means the Senator took the LCV's preferred position on every bill (i.e., the position it says is more pro-environment), and a 0 percent means the Senator took the LCV's preferred position on no bills.

Looking at these first few states, we see a pattern that repeats itself throughout the Senate: most members score either quite high (above, say, 70 percent) or quite low (below 20 percent), with few people in the middle. For example, Senator Jones of Alabama scored a 79, while every other Senator from Alabama, Alaska, Arizona, and Arkansas was a 14 or below. This is because groups use these ratings to identify their supporters and opponents, so they pick bills strategically that allow them to make this differentiation.[34] Note that the LCV also includes a lifetime score, which totals across all previous years in which a member has served, and that too follows this same pattern of very high or very low scores.

Second, the scores are also sharply differentiated by party. Indeed, only two Democratic Senators receive a score from the LCV below 70—Senator Manchin of West Virginia received a 43, and Senator Heitkamp of North Dakota received a score of 50. Likewise, the highest score awarded to a Republican was a 21, given to Senator Collins of Maine. If we went back a generation, we would not necessarily see this pattern, as there would be some Republicans who were rated as being more pro-environment, and some Democrats as more anti-environment. But as we discuss in Chapter 13, members of Congress have polarized across many issues, including the environment.

Figure 11.2 **League of Conservation Voters Scorecard, 115th Congress**

SENATE VOTES

KEY

- ✓ = Pro-environment action
- ✖ = Anti-environment action
- ⓘ = Ineligible to vote
- ? = Absence (counts as negative)

		LCV SCORES: 2018 %	115th Congress %	Lifetime %	1 Border Wall Funding & Anti-Immigrant Policy	2 Wheeler Confirmation (EPA Deputy Administrator)	3 Exposing Waterways to Invasive Species	4 Bridenstine Confirmation (NASA Administrator)	5 Pompeo Confirmation (Secretary of State)	6 Anti-Environmental Rescission Package	7 Oldham Confirmation (Fifth Circuit Court of Appeals)	8 Grant Confirmation (Eleventh Circuit Court of Appeals)	9 Kavanaugh Cloture Vote (Supreme Court)	10 Kavanaugh Confirmation (Supreme Court)	11 Clark Confirmation (Asst. Att. General, DOJ Environment and Natural Resources Division)	12 Nelson Confirmation (Ninth Circuit Court of Appeals)	13 McNamee Confirmation (Federal Energy Regulatory Commission)	14 Farm Bill Conference Report
ALABAMA																		
Jones	D	79	N/A	79	✓	✓	✖	✓	✖	✓	✓	✓	✓	✓	✓	✖	✓	✓
Shelby	R	7	3	13	✖	✖	✖	✖	✖	✖	✖	✖	✖	✖	✖	✖	✖	✓
ALASKA																		
Murkowski	R	14	6	17	✓	✖	✖	✖	✖	✖	✖	✖	✓	?	✖	✖	✖	✖
Sullivan	R	7	3	7	✖	✖	✖	✖	✖	✖	✖	✖	✖	✖	✖	✖	✖	✓
ARIZONA																		
Flake	R	7	3	8	✓	✖	✖	✖	✖	✖	✖	?	✖	✖	✖	✖	✖	✖
Kyl*	R	0	N/A	8	ⓘ	ⓘ	ⓘ	ⓘ	ⓘ	ⓘ	ⓘ	ⓘ	✖	✖	✖	✖	✖	✖
McCain*	R	0	N/A	19	?	?	?	?	?	?	?	?	ⓘ	ⓘ	ⓘ	ⓘ	ⓘ	ⓘ
ARKANSAS																		
Boozman	R	7	3	7	✖	✖	✖	✖	✖	✖	✖	✖	✖	✖	✖	✖	✖	✓
Cotton	R	0	0	2	✖	✖	✖	✖	✖	✖	✖	✖	✖	✖	✖	✖	✖	✖

Source: 2018 Environmental LCV Scorecard, Second Session of the 115th Congress.

Look at the interest group ratings for an organization of your choice. Look at the votes they picked, and how they scored members. Does the scoring reflect what you know about members and their positions on that issue?

Earmarks

Information can be linked to influence. Lobbyists not only tell members of Congress facts, they also learn from these members what Washington is doing and then look for ways to sell that information to their clients. What often results is an **earmark**, that is, a provision in a law that provides a direct benefit to a client without the benefit having been reviewed on the merits by all of Congress.

earmark *A provision in a law that provides a direct benefit to a client without the benefit having been reviewed on the merits by all of Congress.*

Earmarks have always existed, but they became much more common in the 1970s and later. There are two reasons for this. First, the federal government was doing much more and thus affecting more parts of society. Second, lobbying organizations figured out that clients would pay for information about how to convert some bit of federal activity to their benefit.

One study showed how a new kind of lobbying firm was born. Cassidy and Associates prospered by helping clients get earmarks. The firm charged a flat fee ($10,000 or more per month) and devoted its energy to studying

grassroots lobbying Using the general public (rather than lobbyists) to contact government officials about a public policy.

congressional laws in order to find opportunities for its clients.[35] Its first big client was a university that wanted federal money to pay for a nutrition center it hoped to build. The Cassidy firm discovered that Congress had authorized a "national" nutrition center and then set about persuading key congressional leaders that such a center should be located at the university that was paying Cassidy a fee. Soon many more universities pushed for earmarks for their pet ideas (a foreign-service school, defense software institutes, and computer centers). Not long after that, business firms joined the hunt.

In 2008, the Office of Management and Budget estimated that Congress had approved more than 11,000 earmarks at a cost of more than $16 billion. Many see earmarks as a classic example of wasteful spending, and they focus on the most flagrant abuses, such as the famous "Bridge to Nowhere" in Alaska. But not all earmarks are really wasteful spending: many earmarks support programs important to a particular community, such as a nutrition center, a job-training program, a program to hire additional police officers, or a program to pave new roads.

In 2011, amid criticism of the earmarks process, Congress agreed to ban earmarks. The desire of groups—and legislators—to direct funding to particular projects, however, was great, and they developed a way to at least partially sidestep this ban. Since the earmark ban, some spending bills have contained special funds not attached to a particular program. It is up to the government agencies to decide where and how to spend these funds. While the agencies make these decisions, members of Congress try to influence them: members send letters and make telephone calls to push for projects in their own districts (hence these funds are often called "lettermarking" or "phonemarking").[36] The requests from members are not binding on the agency (unlike earmarks), but agencies are usually eager to avoid antagonizing powerful members of Congress.

Public Support: Rise of the New Politics

Once upon a time, when the government was small, Congress was less individualistic, and television was nonexistent, lobbyists mainly used an *insider strategy:* they worked closely with a few key members of Congress, meeting them privately to exchange information and (sometimes) favors. Matters of mutual interest could be discussed at a leisurely pace, over dinner or while playing golf. Public opinion was important on some highly visible issues, but there were not many of these.

Following an insider strategy is still valuable, but interest groups have increasingly turned to an *outsider strategy.* The newly individualistic nature of Congress has made this tactic useful, and modern technology has made it possible. Websites, email, and social media allow groups to direct citizens to contact their members of Congress to make their opinions known. Online public opinion polls can be done virtually overnight to measure (and help generate) support for or opposition to proposed legislation. Mail can be automatically directed to people already known to have an interest in a particular matter.

This kind of **grassroots lobbying** is central to the outsider strategy. It is designed to generate public pressure directly on government officials. The "public" that exerts this pressure is not every voter or even most voters; it is that part of the public (sometimes called an *issue public*) directly affected by or deeply concerned with a government policy. What modern technology has made possible is the overnight mobilization of specific issue publics.

Not every issue lends itself to an outsider strategy. It is hard to get many people excited about, for example, complex tax legislation affecting only a few firms. But as the government does more and more, and as its policies affect more and more people, many more will join in grassroots lobbying efforts over matters such as abortion, Medicare, Social Security, environmental protection, same-sex marriage, and affirmative action. Grassroots lobbying is most common on these sorts of highly salient issues that have the potential to mobilize and appeal to a broad swath of the public.[37] For example, in 2010, both sides of the debate over the Affordable Care Act made extensive use of grassroots lobbying,[38] a pattern that has continued to today.

Money and PACs

Contrary to popular suspicions, money is probably one of the less effective ways by which interest groups advance their causes. That was not always the case. Only a few decades ago, powerful interests used their bulging wallets to buy influence in Congress. The passage of campaign finance legislation in the early 1970s changed that. The laws had two effects. First, they sharply restricted the amount any interest group could give to a candidate for federal office. Second, they allowed the formation of political action committees (PACs) that could make political contributions (we discussed these points in some detail in Chapter 10).

Once PACs became legal, their numbers grew rapidly. More than 8,000 PACs were active in the 2018 election, up from just over 4,000 in 2004 (a 100 percent increase in less than fifteen years). As we can see in Figure 11.3, the number of corporate and labor PACs have been (more or less) steady for the past 30 years, but other types of PACs—such as nonconnected PACs and super PACs—have grown rapidly (for more on the rise of super PACs, see our discussion in Chapter 10).

Figure 11.3 **Growth in the Number of PACs, 1986–2018**

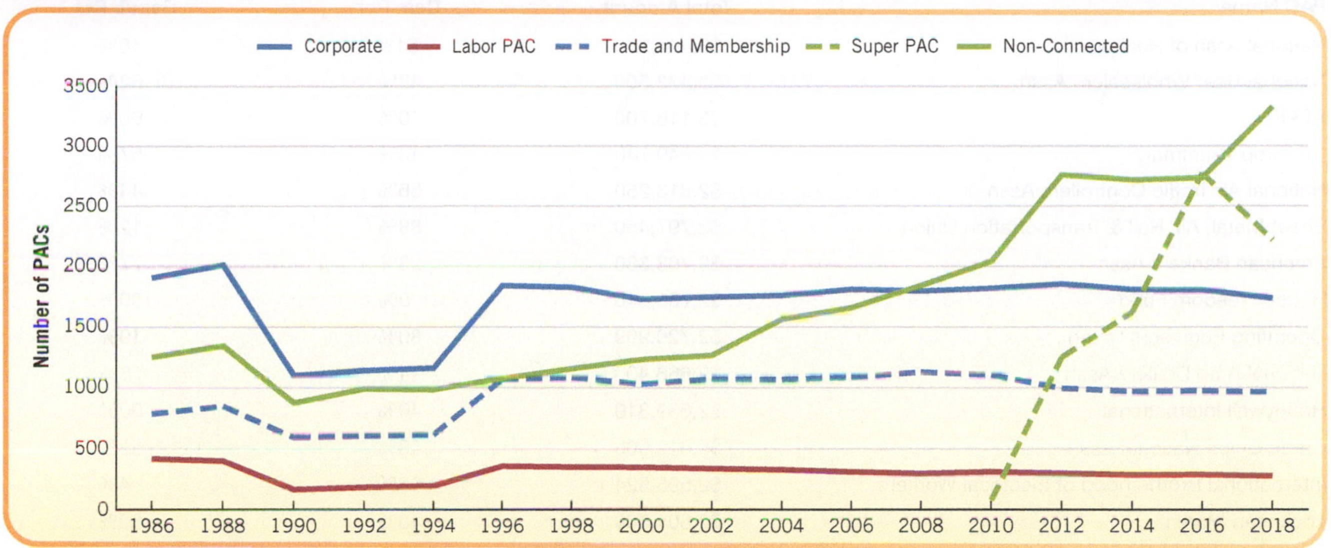

Source: FEC summaries of the various election cycles.

Most PACs are connected to a particular corporation, labor union, trade association, or membership organization, and can only solicit voluntary contributions from individuals associated with said organization. Because these PACs are connected to a particular organization, they are referred to as connected PACs. In contrast, nonconnected PACs are organized around particular ideological views or a particular personality. Unlike other PACs, nonconnected PACs can solicit contributions from the general public (though all PACs are subject to certain rules, as we explained in Chapter 10).

One of the most prominent types of nonconnected PAC is a leadership PAC, which is a PAC associated with a particular member of Congress, such as Speaker of the House Nancy Pelosi or Senate Majority Leader Mitch McConnell. For example, in the 2017–2018 cycle, Pelosi's Leadership PAC, named PAC to the Future, raised $1.4 million dollars, which it then distributed to Democrats running for Congress. Setting up such a PAC is now practically required to rise up in the congressional leadership hierarchy in either party.[39]

Not only has the number of PACs increased, they are also spending more on elections. For example, in the 2000 election cycle, PACs spent $611 million; by the 2017–2018 election cycle, they spent $4.6 billion, a nearly seven-fold increase. But there is a huge variation in how much each PAC spends. In the 2017–2018 election cycle, there were roughly 3,100 connected PACs who spent a total of $1.03 billion, for an average spending of roughly $331,000 per PAC. But this figure is highly misleading: as we can see in Table 11.1 on page 260, the top 20 spending PACs each spent over $2.3 million dollars, and many other PACs only raised and spent a few thousand dollars.

A chart like this might suggest that all of this political money has resulted in our having, as the late Senator Edward Kennedy put it, "the finest Congress that money can buy." More likely, the increase in the number of PACs has had just the opposite effect. The reason is simple: With PACs so numerous and so easy to form, it is now probable that money will be available on every side of almost every conceivable issue. As a result, members of Congress can take money and still decide for themselves how to vote. As we shall see, there is not much scholarly evidence that money buys votes in Congress.

Further, when we dig deeper into the data in Table 11.1, we see a few important points that might change how we interpret this data. First, if you look at the average donation from these PACs to members of Congress, they are typically quite modest and far below the legal limits. These groups also overwhelmingly favor incumbents over challengers, and they (with the exception of labor unions and a few ideological groups) split their funds pretty evenly between Democrats and Republicans, giving slightly more to the party in power. Before the 2018 elections, Republicans controlled the House of Representatives, and so most groups gave more to Republicans than Democrats, but only slightly. But with Democrats in control after 2018, that pattern reversed for the 2020 election.

TABLE 11.1 | Top 20 PAC Contributors to Candidates, 2017–2018

PAC Name	Total Amount	Dem Pct	Repub Pct
National Assn of Realtors	$3,444,276	51%	48%
National Beer Wholesalers Assn	$3,433,500	48%	52%
AT&T Inc	$3,116,700	40%	60%
Northrop Grumman	$2,849,740	43%	57%
National Air Traffic Controllers Assn	$2,813,250	56%	44%
Sheet Metal, Air, Rail & Transportation Union	$2,797,450	88%	12%
American Bankers Assn	$2,768,330	23%	77%
House Freedom Fund	$2,733,340	0%	100%
Operating Engineers Union	$2,726,909	80%	19%
National Auto Dealers Assn	$2,666,400	24%	76%
Honeywell International	$2,639,310	49%	50%
Credit Union National Assn	$2,619,000	48%	52%
International Brotherhood of Electrical Workers	$2,595,524	96%	4%
Lockheed Martin	$2,504,500	40%	60%
American Crystal Sugar	$2,470,000	54%	46%
United Parcel Service	$2,441,597	33%	66%
American Assn for Justice	$2,402,000	94%	5%
Blue Cross/Blue Shield	$2,394,300	41%	59%
Boeing Co	$2,391,499	43%	57%
Deloitte LLP	$2,380,000	44%	56%

Source: Center for Responsive Politics, "PACS: Top PACs, 2017–2018" https://www.opensecrets.org/pacs/toppacs.php. Accessed May 2020.

Q Look over these top-spending PACs. What do they have in common? What does that tell you about the behavior of PACs?

Why do PACs behave this way: giving modest donations to many incumbents from both parties? Most PAC contributions are a means of gaining access to members.[40] Members have busy schedules and receive far more requests for meetings than they could ever possibly grant. A PAC contribution is a way that the organization can get its foot in the door: if a PAC has given money to a member's campaign, then the member will be more likely to take their call and meet with them.[41]

Tom Williams/CQ-Roll Call Group/Getty Images

Image 11.8 Citizens meet with members of Congress to promote particular programs, an example of grassroots lobbying.

While considerable evidence shows that contributions provide access, there is little evidence that PAC donations (or other types of political money) affect how legislators vote.[42] On most issues, a legislator's vote is primarily explained by their general party and ideology, as well as their constituents' preferences; factors like the amount of PAC money received are very minor considerations. This also reflects the fact that PACs tend to donate more to their friends than to fence-sitters or their opponents—PAC contributions are a form of subsidy to friendly legislators.[43] The PAC contribution is a way to help reelect a member with whom the organization has a good relationship. For example, many defense contractors give their largest contributions to members of Congress who have factories located in their districts. If we see that those members supported a bill to award that firm a contract for a new weapons system, it was likely not the PAC donation that drove their vote, but rather the prospect of new jobs in their district. In the end, a PAC donation is almost certainly not enough to sway a member of Congress's vote one way or the other.

In any event, if interest-group money makes a difference at all, it probably affects certain kinds of issues more than others. Much as with lobbying, interest-group money probably matters most on narrow issues that are best characterized as client politics (concentrated benefits but dispersed costs). While PAC contributions do not seem to matter much in the aggregate, they may well matter more on these sorts of narrow policies.[44]

The "Revolving Door"

Every year, hundreds of people leave important jobs in the federal government to take more lucrative positions in private industry. Some go to work as lobbyists, others as consultants to businesses, still others as key executives in corporations, foundations, and universities. Many people worry that this "revolving door" may give private interests a way of improperly influencing government decisions. If federal officials uses their positions to do something for a corporation in exchange for a cushy job after leaving government, or if people who who have left government use their personal contacts in Washington to get favors for private parties, then the public interest may suffer.

From time to time, certain incidents stir these fears. For instance, as the *Washington Post* reported, following the attempted bombing of a U.S. airliner on Christmas Day 2009, Michael Chertoff, the former secretary of the Department of Homeland Security (DHS), "gave dozens of media interviews touting the need for the federal government to buy more full body-scanners for airports"; but in that media blitz Chertoff did not always make clear what his security consulting firm, the Chertoff Group, had disclosed in a statement issued before he made the media rounds, namely, that the former DHS chief represented a client that manufactured the machines and sold them to a DHS subunit, the Transportation Safety Administration.[45]

Over the years, more than a few scandals have emerged concerning corrupt dealings between federal department officials and industry executives. Many have involved contractors or their consultants bribing procurement officials. Far more common, however, have been major breakdowns in the procurement process itself. For example, in 2006, DHS revealed the results from an internal audit.[46] In the previous year, the department had spent $17.5 billion on contracts for airport security, radiation detectors, and other goods and services. But records for nearly three dozen contracts were completely missing, and records for many other contracts lacked evidence that the department had followed federal rules in negotiating best prices. (The internal audit itself was performed by private consultants, presumably in compliance with all relevant rules.) However, while there are various examples like these, we lack full and systematic data on the problem more broadly, so it is difficult to draw firm conclusions about it more generally.

Agencies differ in their vulnerability to outside influences. If the Food and Drug Administration is not vigilant, people in that agency who help decide whether a new drug should be placed on the market may have their judgment affected by the possibility that, if they approve the drug, the pharmaceutical company that makes it will later offer them a lucrative position. On the other hand, lawyers in the Federal Trade Commission who prosecute businesses that violate the antitrust laws may decide that their chances for getting a good job with a private law firm later on will increase if they are particularly vigorous and effective prosecutors. The firm, after all, wants to hire competent people, and winning a case is a good test of competence.[47]

In response to concerns of undue influence, recent administrations have put new limits on the ability of former executive branch officials to work as lobbyists. Both Presidents Obama and Trump have put certain restrictions in place, including blocking former officials from serving as lobbyists for several years after leaving office. [48] Whether they will be effective at limiting such concerns remains to be seen.

Civil Disobedience

Public displays and disruptive tactics—protest marches, sit-ins, picketing, and violence—have always been a part of American politics. Indeed, they were among the favorite tactics of the American colonists seeking independence in 1776.

Both ends of the political spectrum have used display, disruption, and violence. On the left feminists, LGBTQ+ rights activists, civil rights activists, coal miners, auto workers, welfare mothers, environmentalists, antinuclear power groups, public housing tenants, Native American movements, the Students for a Democratic Society, and the Weather Underground have created "trouble" ranging from peaceful sit-ins at segregated lunch counters to bombings and shootings. On the right, the Ku Klux Klan has used terror, intimidation, and murder; parents opposed to forced busing of schoolchildren have demonstrated; business firms have used strong-arm squads against workers; right-to-life groups have blockaded abortion clinics; and an endless array of "anti-" groups (anti-Catholics, anti-Masons, anti-Jews, anti-immigrants, anti-saloons, anti-African Americans, anti-protesters, and probably even anti-antis) have taken their disruptive turns on stage. The Tea Party and affiliated groups have used protests and rallies to help spread their message. These various activities are not morally the same—a sit-in demonstration is quite different from a lynching—but politically they constitute a similar problem for a government official.

Policy Dynamics: Inside/Outside the Box | Gun Control: Contentious Entrepreneurial Politics

In December 2012, Adam Lanza fatally shot 20 children and 6 adult staff members at Sandy Hook Elementary School in Newtown, Connecticut. The incident ranked as one of the deadliest mass shootings in U.S. history, and afterward, numerous politicians, including President Barack Obama, called for tougher gun control legislation. Large majorities of Americans supported specific reforms, such as tougher background checks, in the aftermath of the attack. Legislation was introduced in Congress, but it did not pass. Other subsequent mass shootings similarly did not lead to tougher gun laws. If the public and many political elites support tougher gun control measures, why are they so difficult to enact?

The answer lies (in part) in the nature of the policy. Gun control is best characterized as entrepreneurial politics. If gun control measures are enacted, then all of society will benefit from increased safety (though it is important to note that some gun control opponents doubt this claim). But gun owners will pay the costs because it will be more difficult and expensive to own a gun. This means there are dispersed benefits but concentrated costs, which generates entrepreneurial politics.

Those opposed to gun control are well organized in interest groups, most notably, the National Rifle Association, which has been strongly opposed to gun control in recent years. Furthermore, as we discussed in Chapter 7, gun control opponents are also highly politically active on this issue, making them a potent constituency for members of Congress.

Consistent with our expectations of entrepreneurial politics, gun control supporters, by contrast, have not been as well organized. Gun control advocates have struggled to build effective organizations and have not found effective policy entrepreneurs, a struggle Kristin Goss documents in her book *Disarmed.* As we discussed in Chapter 1, a change in the salience of an issue can bring about change even in the absence of an entrepreneur. While Newtown did make gun control more salient, and it did increase public support for gun control, such support was temporary. By May 2013, gun control opinion had returned to its pre-Newtown levels.

While there has been little legislative or policy change nationally, gun control advocates have been far more successful at the state level. In 2018, state legislatures passed 69 gun control measures, more than any other year since 2012. This was due to both the increased salience of gun control, especially after the Parkland, FL mass shooting, and more activity by gun control supporters. This reinforces a point we made in Chapter 3: one consequence of a federal system is that different actors may have more success in pressing their case with different government bodies.

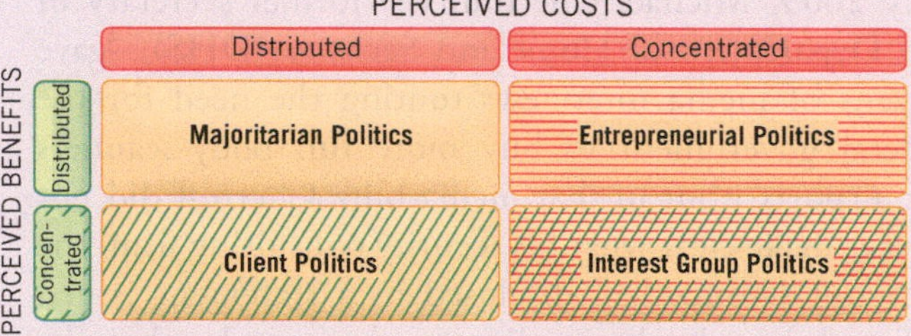

Source: Caroll Doherty, "Did Newtown Really Change Public Opinion About Gun Control?" CNN.com, 6 December, 2013; Kristen Goss, *Disarmed: The Missing* Movement for Gun Control in America. Princeton, NJ: Princeton University Press, 2006; Maggie Astor & Karl Russell, "After Parkland, A New Surge in State Gun Control Laws," *New York Times*, 14 December 2018.

An explanation of why and under what circumstances disruption occurs is beyond the scope of this book. To understand interest-group politics, however, it is important to remember that making trouble has, since the 1960s, become a quite conventional political resource and is no longer simply the last resort of extremist groups. Making trouble is now an accepted political tactic of ordinary middle-class citizens as well as the disadvantaged or disreputable.

Of course, the use of disruptive methods by "proper" people has a long history. For example, in a movement that began in England at the turn of the 20th century and then spread to America, feminists would chain themselves to lampposts or engage in what we now call "sit-ins" as part of a campaign to win the vote for women. The object then was much the same as the object of similar tactics today: to disrupt the working of some institution so that it is forced to negotiate with you; or, failing that, to enlist the sympathies of third parties (the media, other interest groups) who will come to your aid and press your target to negotiate with you; or, failing that, to goad the police into making attacks and arrests so that martyrs are created.

The civil rights and antiwar movements of the 1960s gave experience in these methods to thousands of young people and persuaded others of the effectiveness of such methods under certain conditions. Though these movements have abated or disappeared, their veterans and emulators have put such tactics to new uses—trying to block the construction of a pipeline or nuclear power plant, for

Image 11.9 Same-sex marriage supporters celebrate after the Supreme Court ruled in their favor in 2015.

example, or occupying the office of a cabinet secretary to obtain concessions for a particular group. As a result, today such techniques are common on both the left and the right. They can sometimes affect policy,[49] which helps to explain their use by groups across the political spectrum.

Which Groups and Strategies Are Most Effective?

Reviewing the various strategies interest groups use to influence the policy process, one might naturally ask two questions about interest-group power. First, which strategies are most effective? And second, which interest groups are most influential? Consider the question of strategy first. Unfortunately, this kind of question does not have an easy answer. The best strategy depends on the group and the issue in question. For some issues—especially highly salient ones that would generate significant public support—a grassroots lobbying strategy and a media campaign would be most effective. For other issues, especially more niche client politics issues, an insider lobbying campaign of key legislators would be the most efficacious strategy. Furthermore, on many issues, the best strategy isn't any one choice, it's a multitude of choices: it is not grassroots or insider lobbying, it is both.[50] For example, the Civil Rights movement not only used protests and civil disobedience, they also used a strategic series of lawsuits, as well as both insider and grassroots lobbying. Most groups use many of the tactics described in this section.

Can we say, then, which groups are most effective? Such a question is, at its core, effectively impossible to answer, as different groups will be influential for different reasons. However, one common thread connecting many of these groups is that they have the power to demonstrate clear electoral consequences to opposing their policies. For example, the Dodd-Frank reform bill put in place the Consumer Financial Protection Bureau (CFPB) to regulate lenders (among other tasks). But one group of lenders was initially largely unregulated by the CFPB: automobile lenders, especially automobile dealerships (while automobile dealers do not typically make loans themselves, they often serve as the middleman, connecting buyers with financing). Why did this group get this exemption? They got it because they engaged in a vigorous grassroots lobbying campaign. Theirs was a particularly potent grassroots campaign because there are approximately 18,000 automobile dealerships across the country that employ close to 1 million Americans.[51] Hence every congressional district in America has a number of people employed in connection with automobile dealerships and loans, and they could make a powerful case to legislators: regulating us would harm the economy. While the CFPB did issue some regulations about these lenders under the Obama administration, the Trump administration reversed many of these restrictions in 2018.[52] Similarly, one reason why the National Rifle Association (NRA) has long been seen as a powerhouse interest group is that NRA members are highly politically engaged and will vote against—and campaign against—members who oppose their policy positions (see the Policy Dynamics: Inside/Outside the Box feature on page 262 in this chapter).[53] It is this activism—more than their PAC contributions—that makes them a potent force in Washington. The AARP is also widely seen as powerful because its core demographic—senior citizens—is highly politically engaged (see the discussion in Chapter 8). We can say these groups are "important" because they represent large, geographically dispersed constituencies who can impose electoral costs on members of Congress. In short, one key part of "importance" or "influence" is being able to generate electoral reward or punishment for members.

Furthermore, as we have discussed throughout the chapter, the political context also matters. Interest groups are most effective when they pursue issues best characterized as client politics. Groups that advocate for change on broad-based entrepreneurial or majoritarian politics (things like regulating the environment) face a more uphill battle because of the nature of the issue.

This highlights an important truth about American politics. Many assume that money determines policy outcomes, but the logic above shows that this is not really correct: organization, political consequences, and political context matter just as much, if not more. Studies find that the side with the most money (or that spends the most money) is only weakly correlated with policy success, and a majority of lobbying efforts—even those from well-connected, high-profile groups—fail.[54] If all it took to change the status quo was money, then neither tobacco nor oil drilling would be regulated at all (instead, both are heavily regulated). As we discussed earlier in the chapter, business often, but not always, gets what it wants in a pluralistic system like ours. To ultimately understand interest-group success and failure, we need to consider organizations and the political context in which groups operate.

11-5 Regulating Interest Groups

Interest-group activity is a form of political speech protected by the First Amendment to the Constitution: it cannot lawfully be abolished or even much curtailed. In 1946, Congress passed the Federal Regulation of Lobbying Act, which requires groups and individuals seeking to influence legislation to register with the secretary of the Senate and the clerk of the House and to file quarterly financial reports. The Supreme Court upheld the law but restricted its application to lobbying efforts involving direct contacts with members of Congress.[55] More general "grassroots" interest-group activity may not be restricted by the government. The 1946 law had little practical effect. Not all lobbyists took the trouble to register, and there was no guarantee that the financial statements were accurate. There was no staff in charge of enforcing the law.

After years of growing popular dissatisfaction with Congress, prompted in large measure by the (exaggerated) view that legislators were the pawns of powerful special interests, Congress unanimously passed in late 1995 a bill that tightened up the registration and disclosure requirements. Signed by the president, the law restated the obligation of lobbyists to register with the House and Senate, but it broadened the definition of a lobbyist to include the following:

- People who spend at least 20 percent of their time lobbying
- People who are paid at least $5,000 in any six-month period to lobby
- Corporations and other groups that spend more than $20,000 in any six-month period on their own lobbying staffs

The law covered people and groups who lobbied the executive branch and congressional staffers as well as elected members of Congress, and it included law firms that represent clients before the government. Twice a year, all registered lobbyists were required to report the names of their clients, their income and expenditures, and the issues on which they worked.

The registration and reporting requirements did not, however, extend to grassroots lobbying. Nor was any new enforcement organization created, although congressional officials could refer violations to the Justice Department for investigation. Fines for breaking the law could amount to $50,000. In addition, the law barred tax-exempt, nonprofit advocacy groups that lobby from getting federal grants.

Just as the Republicans moved expeditiously to pass new regulations on interest groups and lobbying when they regained majorities in Congress in the November 1994 elections, the Democrats' first order of business after retaking Congress in the November 2006 elections was to adopt sweeping reforms. Beginning March 1, 2007, many new regulations took effect, including the following:

- No gifts of any value may be accepted from registered lobbyists or firms that employ lobbyists
- Travel costs may not be reimbursed by registered lobbyists or firms that employ lobbyists
- Travel costs may not be reimbursed, no matter the source, if the trip is in any part organized or requested by a registered lobbyist or firm that employs lobbyists

Strictly speaking, these and related new rules mean that a House member cannot go on a "fact-finding" trip to a local site or a foreign country and have anyone associated with lobbying arrange to pay for it. Even people who are not themselves registered lobbyists, but who work for a lobbying firm, are not permitted to take members of Congress to lunch or give them any other "thing of value," no matter how small.

But if past experience is any guide, "strictly speaking" is not how the rules will be followed or enforced. For instance, buried in the fine print of the new rules are provisions that permit members of Congress to accept reimbursement for travel from lobbyists if the travel is for "one-day trips," so long as the lobbyists themselves do not initiate the trip, make the reservations, or pick up incidental expenses unrelated to the visit. Moreover, these rules have not yet been adopted in precisely the same form by the Senate; and neither chamber has yet clarified language or closed loopholes related to lobbying registration and reporting.

Do not suppose, however, that such remaining gaps in lobbying laws render the system wide open to abuses or evasions. For one thing, the lobbying laws, loopholes and all, are now tighter than ever. For another, the most significant legal constraints on interest groups come not from the current federal lobbying law (though that may change) but from the tax code and the campaign finance laws. Nonprofit organizations—which include not only charitable groups but also almost all voluntary associations that have an interest in politics—need not pay income taxes, and financial contributions to it can be deducted on the donor's income tax return, provided that the organization does not devote a "substantial part" of its activities to "attempting to influence legislation."[56]

Many tax-exempt organizations do take public positions on political questions and testify before congressional

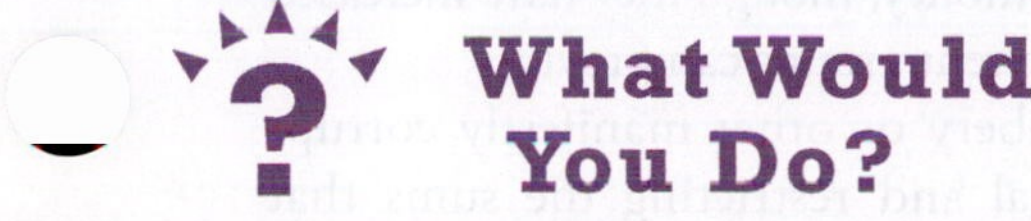

What Would You Do? | Will You Support or Oppose Full Federal Financing of Presidential Campaigns?

To: *Chandra Enakshi, Senate majority leader*
From: *Brian Luce, chief of staff*
Subject: *Full federal financing of presidential campaigns*

In recent years, more and more candidates have opted out of the public funding system, with only one candidate participating in 2016, and none participating in 2020. Elections have also become vastly more expensive, with presidential candidates alone raising over $1.5 billion in 2016 (not counting party committees, PACs, or outside groups). Congress needs to decide whether elections are a public investment or a political free market for citizens and candidates. We support a bill that would fully fund all major-party presidential candidates.

To Consider:

A bipartisan group of senators has proposed that Congress control campaign expenses by fully funding and setting an upper limit on financing for presidential campaigns. Presidential contenders so far have refrained from taking a position on the legislation.

Arguments for:

1. Legal precedents are promising. For the both the primary and general elections, candidates are already eligible for federal funding if they agree to abide by strict spending requirements. This bill would simply require that everyone participate in that system.
2. The funding required would be small. Even if it cost $1 billion, that is hardly a fiscal drain in a nearly $4.1 trillion annual budget.
3. The effects would be pervasive. Candidates and party leaders would stop covertly courting big donors with phone calls, lunches, and personal visits, and would focus instead on the needs of average citizens.

Arguments against:

1. Constitutional precedent for requiring political candidates to accept public funds is weak. In *Buckley v. Valeo* (1976), the Supreme Court upheld limits on campaign contributions for candidates who accept public money, but it also defined spending money for political purposes as expression protected by the First Amendment, thereby giving individuals the right to raise and spend as much of their own money as they choose, if they forego federal funds.
2. Campaign spending would soon spiral once again. The federal government may not restrict spending by individuals or organizations working independently from the political parties, and federal funds would merely supplement, not supplant, private fundraising.
3. Less than 10 percent of taxpayers currently support public financing through voluntary federal income tax check-offs, and voters would likely view bankrolling elections as serving politicians, not the people.

What Will You Decide? Enter **MindTap** to make your choice.

Your decision: ☐ Support legislation ☐ Oppose legislation

committees. If the organization does any serious lobbying, however, it will lose its tax-exempt status (and thus find it harder to solicit donations and more expensive to operate). This happened to the Sierra Club in 1968, when the Internal Revenue Service revoked its tax-exempt status because of its extensive lobbying activities. Some voluntary associations try to deal with this problem by setting up separate organizations to collect tax-exempt money—for example, the NAACP lobbies and must pay taxes, but the NAACP Legal Defense and Education Fund, which does not lobby, is tax-exempt.

Finally, the campaign finance laws, described in detail in Chapter 10, limit to $5,000 the amount any political action committee can spend on a given candidate in a given election. These laws have sharply curtailed the extent to which any *single* group can give money, though they have increased the *total* amount that different groups can provide.

Beyond making bribery or other manifestly corrupt forms of behavior illegal and restricting the sums that campaign contributors can donate, there is probably no system for controlling interest groups that would both make a useful difference and leave important constitutional and political rights unimpaired. Ultimately, the only remedy for imbalances or inadequacies in interest-group representation is to devise and sustain a political system that gives all affected parties a reasonable chance to be heard on matters of public policy. That, of course, is exactly what the Founders thought they were doing. Whether they succeeded or not is a question to which we shall return at the end of this book.

Learning Objectives

11-1 Explain what an interest group is, and identify the main factors that led to their rise in America.

An interest group is an organization of people sharing a common interest or goal that seeks to influence public policy. Several factors help to explain the rise of these groups, including the growth of the market economy in America, government policy itself (by creating constituencies that receive benefits from the government), political movements that create political entrepreneurs, and the growing scope of government policy.

11-2 Detail the various types of interest groups in America, and explain the types of people who join interest groups.

Two kinds of interest groups exist: institutional and membership. Institutional groups represent other organizations (like lobbying firms that represent corporations or trade groups in Washington, D.C.), whereas membership groups represent their own members and their members' policy preferences and beliefs (like the National Association for the Advancement of Colored People, a historic civil rights membership organization). People join groups for the same basic reasons that they join any organization. There are three kinds of incentives: solidary, material, and purposive.

11-3 Summarize the ways interest groups relate to social movements.

Social movements are mass movements that push for a particular type of policy change. Groups that use purposive benefits are especially likely to be linked to broad social movements.

11-4 Explain the various ways interest groups try to influence the policymaking process.

Groups use a variety of strategies, including lobbying (and more generally providing information), earmarking (though it is currently banned, there are some ways around it), donations to legislators, and civil disobedience. The most effective strategies in any given instance depend on the type of group and its goals. Whether a group is successful is determined at least in part by its organization and the political environment.

11-5 Describe the ways in which interest groups' political activity is limited.

Interest groups' activities are restricted by literally scores of laws. For example, Washington lobbyists must register with the House or Senate. All registered lobbyists must publicly divulge their client list and expenditures. There are legal limits on PAC contributions. Every new wave of campaign finance laws (see Chapter 10) has resulted in more rules regulating interest groups. The Internal Revenue Service has tightly restricted political activity by religious groups, private schools, and other organizations as a condition for their exemption from federal income tax. Finally, states and cities have their own laws regulating interest groups, and some places are more restrictive than others.

To Learn More

Conservative interest groups:

American Conservative Union: **www.conservative.org**

Christian Coalition: **www.cc.org**

Liberal interest groups:

American Civil Liberties Union: **www.aclu.org**

Americans for Democratic Action: **www.adaction.org**

Environmental groups:

Environmental Defense Fund: **www.edf.org**

National Resources Defense Council: **www.nrdc.org**

Civil rights groups:

NAACP: **www.naacp.org**

Center for Equal Opportunity: **www.ceousa.org**

Baumgartner, Frank R., Jeffrey M. Berry, Marie Hojnacki, David C. Kimball, and Beth L. Leech. *Lobbying and Policy Change: Who Wins, Who Loses, and Why.* Chicago, IL: University of Chicago Press, 2009. Thorough empirical assessment of which interest groups exercise influence in Washington.

Cigler, Allan J., and Burdett A. Loomis, eds. *Interest Group Politics.* 8th ed., Washington, D.C.: Congressional Quarterly Press, 2011. Essays on interest groups active in American politics today.

Gillion, Daniel. 2020. *The Loud Minority: Why Protests Matter in American Democracy*. Princeton, NJ: Princeton University Press, 2020. A study of how protests affect both voters and elected officials and help to produce policy change.

Grossman, Matt. *The Not-So-Special Interests: Interest Groups, Public Representation, and American Governance.* Stanford, CA: Stanford University Press, 2012. A comprehensive study of which interest groups become more influential in American politics and why.

Lowi, Theodore J. *The End of Liberalism.* New York: Norton, 1969. A critique of the role of interest groups in American government.

Olson, Mancur. *The Logic of Collective Action.* Cambridge, MA: Harvard University Press, 1965. An economic analysis of interest groups, especially the "free rider" problem.

Truman, David B. *The Governmental Process*. 2nd ed., New York: Knopf, 1971. First published in 1951, this was the classic analysis—and defense—of interest-group pluralism.

Wilson, James Q. *Political Organizations*. Revised ed., Princeton, NJ: Princeton University Press, 1995. A theory of interest groups, emphasizing the incentives they use to attract members.

Shiiko Alexander/Alamy Stock Photo

CHAPTER 12

The Media

Learning Objectives

12-1 Trace the evolution of the press in America, and explain how media coverage of politics has changed over time.

12-2 Describe how the rise of the Internet and social media have influenced the media's effect on politics.

12-3 Explain the main political functions of the media in America, and discuss how the media both enhance and detract from American democracy.

12-4 Discuss the reasons behind lower levels of media trust today, and summarize the arguments for and against media bias.

12-5 Explain how the government controls and regulates the media.

For much of the 20th century, Americans mostly got the same news. Into the 1980s, when someone sat down to watch the news on television—back then, how the majority of Americans got their news—they could really only watch one of three choices: the nightly news on CBS, ABC, and NBC (PBS also had a nightly news broadcast, but it has never attracted as many viewers). There was no cable TV or Internet. While there were many local newspapers, their national political coverage probably came from a set of wire services. Everyone could get the same basic facts about issues, because the number of sources was more limited.

Today, the world of news is quite different. If you wanted to get the news, what would you do? You could still turn on the TV, but you would be confronted with a whole range of choices. You would not only have the broadcast networks, but also numerous shows on cable and satellite television, not to mention streaming programs. If you didn't want to watch television, then you could go online, and not only to the websites of major news outlets like *The New York Times* or CNN, but to many websites and other outlets from every conceivable point of view. You could listen to a podcast, or turn to social media sites like Instagram, TikTok, and Twitter to see content from your friends and those you follow. Indeed, it is hard to speak about "the media" conveying a particular set of facts at all today.

And sadly, we need to be concerned about not just real news, but fake news as well. Such concerns became particularly acute in the aftermath of the 2016 election, when nefarious actors, some linked to Russia and other foreign governments, posted false stories on social media. For example, a story on Facebook about Pope Francis endorsing Donald Trump for president was shared, liked, or commented on more than 960,000 times in 2016, and a story about Hillary Clinton selling weapons to ISIS generated nearly as many likes, shares, and comments.[1] Neither story was true, but these fake news stories may have influenced some voters (we return to the effects of fake news, and efforts to combat it, later in the chapter).

« Then In 1972–1974, the Nixon administration's efforts to cover up the burglary of Democratic National Committee headquarters at the Watergate Hotel in Washington, DC, were revealed through a series of articles published in the *Washington Post,* which gained national fame for its riveting news coverage by journalists Bob Woodward and Carl Bernstein.[2] In the summer of 1987, Congress held live, televised hearings about the Iran-Contra scandal, which captivated viewers.

*** Now** Television is still an important source of news, but more and more Americans are getting their news online. And when we talk about getting news online, it is not simply reading the electronic version of *The Washington Post*, but also getting the news from social media outlets like Facebook, Instagram, and Twitter. The media landscape is shifting dramatically every year, and no doubt it will look quite different in the years to come.

As we will learn throughout this chapter, the mass media play a vital role in politics, but many people misunderstand that role and have a variety of misconceptions about what the media can—and cannot—do. In this chapter, we will help you better understand the media's political powers, but—just as important—we will help you to understand their limitations as well.

12-1 The Media and Politics

The Internet is an important new venue for politics, but it presents similar challenges for politicians as earlier technological advances in communication did. From the beginning of the Republic, public officials have tried to get the media on their side while knowing that, because the media love controversy, they are as likely to attack as to praise. The Internet may strike some politicians as the solution to this problem, since they can connect directly with voters via email, Twitter, Facebook, YouTube, TikTok, and many other websites and social media platforms, thereby allowing them to sidestep the media. This is, of course, correct—politicians today can directly reach voters in a way their predecessors could not. For example, as of May 2020, 79.3 million people around the globe follow President Trump on Twitter, so whenever he sends a tweet, all of those individuals see it (and even more people learn about the tweet on the news and see it via likes and retweets). And the president does use this unfiltered medium a lot—in his first 33 months in office, President Trump sent more than 11,000 tweets. Many of these tweets are used to attack his opponents (both at home and abroad), or to demand action on particular policy issues, such as immigration.[3]

For example, in July 2019, President Trump took to Twitter to attack a group of 4 Democratic members of Congress—Ayanna Pressley of Massachusetts, Rashida Tlaib of Michigan, Alexandria Ocasio-Cortez of New York, and Ilhan Omar of Minnesota—who have been

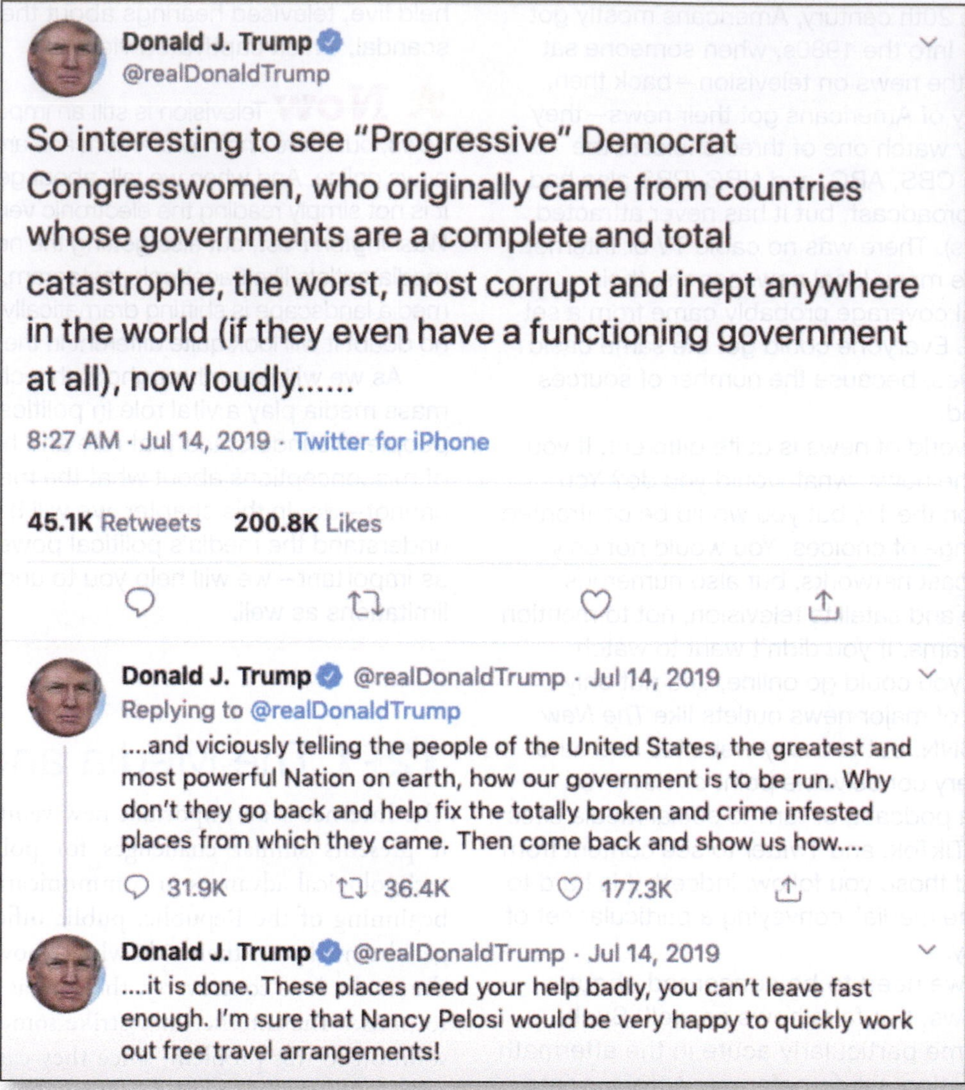

Image 12.1 President Trump frequently uses Twitter to communicate with the public. In these tweets, he attacks a group of Democratic members of Congress who have been critical of his policies.

Source: Twitter, Inc.

critical of his policies (see Image 12.1). Trump told them to go home and fix their own countries rather than criticizing the U.S., but three of the four were born in the United States, and the fourth (Representative Omar) came here as a refugee from war-torn Somalia.

These tweets, however, illustrate some of the limitations of using social media to communicate with the public. First, especially when using these media to attack an opponent, the opponent can push back. Not only did these members of Congress respond to Trump in the media, the House of Representatives formally admonished the president for sending those tweets.[4] The Internet is a two-way street, and whenever politicians use it to send a message, their opponents can use it to push their own as well.

Second, and perhaps more importantly, most Americans are not paying attention to what happens in any media source, including social media. While those who are politically interested track Trump's use of Twitter, many Americans do not. Nearly a quarter of Americans do not think about or even hear about Trump's use of Twitter, and only 4 percent of Americans use Twitter, follow President Trump, and read his tweets.[5] This particular tweet generated a great deal of attention, but even for this sort of tweet, most Americans are unaware that it was sent. This general pattern—that many Americans are relatively politically uninterested and do not carefully follow the news—is an important limitation to the media's power, as we discuss below.

All of this takes place in a country so committed to a free press that the government can do little to control the process. As we shall see, efforts have been made to control radio and television via the government's right to license broadcasters, but most of these attempts have evaporated. Today, regulators struggle to understand how to regulate firms like Facebook, Google, and Twitter who are not traditional broadcasters at all, but yet are key sources of news for many Americans.

Even strongly democratic nations restrict the press more than the United States. For example, the laws governing libel are much stricter in the United Kingdom than in the United States. As a result, it is easier in the United Kingdom for politicians to sue newspapers for publishing articles that defame or ridicule them. In this country, the libel laws make it almost impossible to prevent press criticisms of public figures. Moreover, England has an Official Secrets Act that can be used to punish any past or present public officials who leak information to the press.[6] In this country, information is leaked all the time, and our Freedom of Information Act makes it relatively easy for the press to extract documents from the government.

European governments can be much tougher on people who make controversial statements than the American political system. In 2006, an Austrian court sentenced a man to three years in prison for denying that the Nazi death camp at Auschwitz killed its inmates. A French court convicted a distinguished American historian for telling a French newspaper that the slaughter of Armenians may not have been the result of planned effort. An Italian journalist stood trial for writing things "offensive to Islam." In the United States, however, such statements would be protected by the Constitution even if, as with the man who denied the existence of the Holocaust, they were profoundly wrong.[7]

America has a long tradition of privately owned media. By contrast, private ownership of television has come only recently to other nations, such as France. And the Internet is not owned by anybody: Here, and in most nations, people can say or read (more or less) whatever they want on their computers, tablets, and smart phones. Newspapers in this country require no government permission to operate, but radio and television stations need licenses granted by the Federal Communications Commission (FCC), which must be renewed periodically. On occasion, the White House has made efforts to use license renewals as a way of influencing station owners who were out of political favor, but in recent decades, the level of FCC control over what is broadcast has decreased.

Two potential issues limit the freedom of privately owned newspapers and broadcast stations. First, they must make a profit. Some critics believe the need for profit will lead media outlets to distort the news in order to satisfy advertisers or to build an audience. Though there is some truth to this argument, it is too simple. Every media outlet must satisfy a variety of people—advertisers, subscribers, listeners, reporters, and editors—and balancing those demands is complicated and will be done differently by different owners. (We return to this point below.)

The second problem is media bias. If most reporters and editors have similar views about politics, and if they act on those views, then the media would give us only one side of many stories. Later in this chapter, we take a close look at whether the media are actually biased. (The answer might surprise you!)

Journalism in American Political History

Important changes in the nature of American politics have gone hand in hand with major changes in the organization and technology of the press. It is the nature of politics, essentially a form of communication, to respond to changes in how communications are carried on. This can be seen by considering five important periods in journalistic history.

The Party Press

In the early years of American democracy, politicians of various factions and parties created, sponsored, and controlled newspapers to further their interests. This was possible because circulation was of necessity small (newspapers could not easily be distributed to large audiences, owing to poor transportation) and newspapers were expensive (the type was set by hand and the presses printed copies slowly). Furthermore, few large advertisers existed to pay the bills. These newspapers circulated chiefly among the political and commercial elites who could afford the high subscription prices. Even with high prices, the newspapers often required subsidies that frequently came from the government or a political party.

During the Washington administration, the Federalists, led by Alexander Hamilton, created the *Gazette of the United States.* The Republicans, led by Thomas Jefferson, retaliated by creating the *National Gazette* and made its editor, Philip Freneau, "clerk for foreign languages" in the State Department at $250 a year (more than $6,000 in today's dollars) to help support him. After Jefferson became president, he introduced another publisher, Samuel Harrison Smith, to start the *National Intelligencer,* subsidizing him by giving him a contract to print government documents. Andrew Jackson, when he became president, aided in the creation of the *Washington Globe.* By some estimates, more than 50 journalists were on the government payroll during this era. Naturally, these newspapers were relentlessly partisan in their views. Citizens could choose among different party papers, but only rarely could they find a paper that presented both sides of an issue.

The Popular Press

Changes in society and technology made possible the rise of a self-supporting daily newspaper with a mass readership. The development of the high-speed rotary press enabled publishers to print thousands of copies of a newspaper cheaply and quickly. The invention of the telegraph in the 1840s meant that news from Washington could be flashed almost immediately to New York, Boston, Philadelphia, and Charleston, thus providing local papers with access to information that once only the Washington papers enjoyed. The creation in 1846 of the Associated Press (AP) allowed telegraphic and systematic dissemination of information to newspaper editors. Since the AP provided stories that had to be brief and that went to newspapers of every political hue, it could not afford to be partisan or biased; to attract as many subscribers as possible, it had to present the facts objectively.

Meanwhile, the nation was becoming more urbanized, with large numbers of people brought together in densely settled areas. These people could support a daily newspaper by paying only a penny per copy and by patronizing merchants who advertised in its pages—indeed, this was a major factor in establishing an independent press.[8] Newspapers no longer needed political patronage to prosper, and soon such subsidies began to dry up. In 1860, the Government Printing Office was established, thereby putting an end to most of the printing contracts that Washington newspapers had once enjoyed.

The mass-readership newspaper was scarcely nonpartisan, but the partisanship it displayed arose from the convictions of its publishers and editors rather than from the influence of its party sponsors. And these convictions blended political beliefs with economic interests. The way to attract a large readership was with sensationalism: violence, romance, and patriotism, coupled with exposés of government, politics, business, and society. As practiced by Joseph Pulitzer and William Randolph Hearst, founders of large newspaper empires, this editorial policy had great appeal for the average citizen and especially for immigrants flooding into the large cities.

Strong-willed publishers could often become powerful political forces. Hearst used his papers to agitate for war with Spain when Cubans rebelled against Spanish rule. Conservative Republican political leaders were opposed to the war, but a steady diet of newspaper stories about real and imagined Spanish brutalities whipped up public opinion in favor of intervention. At one point, Hearst sent noted artist Frederic Remington to Cuba to supply paintings of the conflict. Remington cabled back: "Everything is quiet.... There will be no war." Hearst supposedly replied: "Please remain. You furnish the pictures and I'll furnish the war."[9] When the battleship *USS Maine* blew up in Havana Harbor, President William McKinley felt helpless to resist popular pressure, and the United States declared war in 1898.

For all their excesses, mass-readership newspapers began to create a common national culture, to establish the feasibility of a press free of government control or subsidy, and to demonstrate how exciting (and profitable) the criticism of public policy and the revelation of public scandal could be.

Magazines of Opinion

The growing middle class often was repelled by what it called "yellow journalism" and around the turn of the century developed a taste for political reform and a belief in the doctrines of the progressive movement. To satisfy this market, a variety of national magazines appeared that—unlike those devoted to manners and literature—discussed issues of public policy. Among the first of these were *The Nation,* the *Atlantic Monthly,* and *Harper's,* founded in the 1850s and 1860s; later came the more broadly based mass-circulation magazines such as *McClure's, Scribner's,* and *Cosmopolitan.* They provided the means for developing a national constituency for certain issues such as regulating business (or, in the language of the times, "trust-busting"), purifying municipal politics, and reforming the civil service system. Lincoln Steffens and other so-called muckrakers were frequent contributors to the magazines, setting a pattern for what we now call "investigative reporting."

The national magazines of opinion provided an opportunity for individual writers to gain a nationwide following. The popular press, though initially under the heavy influence of founder-publishers, made certain reporters and columnists household names. In time, the great circulation wars between the big-city daily newspapers started to wane as the more successful papers bought up or otherwise eliminated their competition. This reduced the need for the more extreme forms of sensationalism, a change reinforced by the growing sophistication and education of America's readers. And the founding publishers gradually were replaced by less flamboyant managers. All of these changes—in circulation needs, audience interests, managerial style, and the emergence of nationally known writers—helped increase the power of editors and reporters.

Though writers may have been identified with social causes during the muckraking era, they became less identified with political parties. During the late 19th and early 20th centuries, overt partisanship in journalism largely

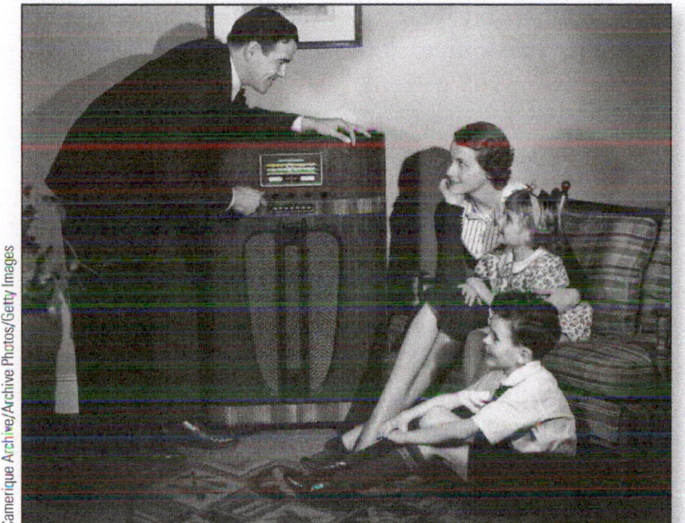

Image 12.2 and 12.3 News used to come by radio, but today many people read news on iPads, smart phones, and other electronic devices.

faded away, as journalists and editors sought to be objective and neutral in their coverage of politics (we discuss later in the chapter whether they actually live up to that ideal). The partisan press gradually was replaced by a more mainstream nonpartisan press.[10]

Electronic Journalism

Radio came on the national scene in the 1920s, television in the late 1940s. They represented a major change in the way news was gathered and disseminated, though few politicians at first understood the importance of this change. A broadcast permits public officials to speak directly to audiences without their remarks being filtered through editors and reporters. This was obviously an advantage to politicians, provided they were skilled enough to use it; they could in theory reach the voters directly on a national scale without the services of political parties, interest groups, or friendly editors.

But there was an offsetting disadvantage—people could easily ignore a speech broadcast on a radio or television station, either by not listening at all or by tuning to a different station. By contrast, the views of at least some public figures would receive prominent and often unavoidable display in newspapers, and a growing number of cities had only one daily paper. Moreover, space in a newspaper is cheap compared to time on a television broadcast.

Adding one more story, or one more name to an existing story, costs a newspaper little. By contrast, fewer stories can be carried on radio or television, and each news segment must be quite brief to avoid boring the audience. As a result, the number of political personalities that can be covered by radio and television news is much smaller than is the case with newspapers, and the cost (to the station) of making a news item or broadcast longer often is prohibitively large.

Thus, to obtain the advantages of electronic media coverage, public officials must do something sufficiently bold or colorful to gain free access to radio and television news—or they must find the money to purchase radio and television time. The president of the United States, of course, is routinely covered by radio and television and can ordinarily get free time to speak to the nation on matters of importance. All other officials must struggle for media attention, often by doing something "newsworthy." For example, one study found that those who are more ideologically extreme, and therefore are more likely to make inflammatory pronouncements, are more likely to appear on television, as their fiery rhetoric makes them more provocative and more likely to draw in viewers.[11] Others get time on air by acquiring a national reputation on particular issues, and still others find ways to purchase expensive air time.

Until the 1980s, the "big three" television networks (ABC, CBS, and NBC) together claimed 80 percent or more of all viewers. This was, in large part, because they were effectively the only game in town. Before the rise of cable television, most Americans had only a handful of television stations: the three broadcast networks, PBS, and maybe 1–2 other local or public access stations. As a result, evening newscasts from the major broadcast networks dominated media coverage of politics and government affairs, with roughly 50 million Americans regularly watching them, more than 20 percent of the population at the time. When it came to presidential campaigns, the three networks were likewise the main television news source—they reported on the primaries, broadcast the party conventions, and covered the general election campaigns, including any presidential debates.

But starting in the 1980s with the rise of cable television, the dominance of these major broadcasters waned. Now viewers could not only watch one of these major network's newscasts, they could also watch cable channels like CNN, Fox News, or MSBNC, not to mention news magazines, Sunday talk shows, early morning television programs, late-night comedy programs, and many others. This proliferation of choices ended the dominance of the big three networks. While 50 million Americans watched the nightly broadcast news on one of those 3 outlets in 1980, by 2019, that had slipped to only 16 million people, a decline of 70 percent.[12] Further, because the audience for these programs is older than the average American, this decline is likely to accelerate in the future. While the major TV networks still play a key role in today's media environment, their importance has diminished considerably from even just a few years ago.

The Internet Age

Of course today, we not only have radio, newspapers, and television, we also have the Internet and social media. These new technologies have dramatically increased the diversity and complexity of the media landscape. Indeed, the Internet and social media are today among the most important sources of news for many Americans today. In Figure 12-1, we show the sources where Americans say they often get their news (note that they can select more than one source, so the figures in any category will not add up to 100 percent).

You may be surprised that television is still the most commonly used source for news by Americans overall: nearly half (49 percent) of Americans often get their news from television. But as we can see, this is largely because television is the overwhelming choice for Americans over the age of 50. Likewise, almost all of those getting their news from a print newspaper are over the age of 50 (we return to the decline of print newspapers, and its broader significance, below). This suggests that even if younger and older people get similar news, they often get it via different media.

What has replaced television and newspapers? News websites and social media. Note that if we combine websites and social media together, then they—not television—become the largest source of news for *all* Americans (30 percent of Americans often use news websites, and another 20 percent use social media). For the young, the figures are even more dramatic. Nearly two-thirds of those under the age of 50 often get their news online, either from news websites or from social media. For younger people, the Internet has become the default source of news and information. While older Americans also consult these sources, they do so at lower levels, primarily due to habit, as well as less familiarity and comfort with them.

But it is a bit amorphous just to say that Americans, especially young Americans, get the news online. Which

Figure 12.1 **Americans Sources for News, Overall and By Age**

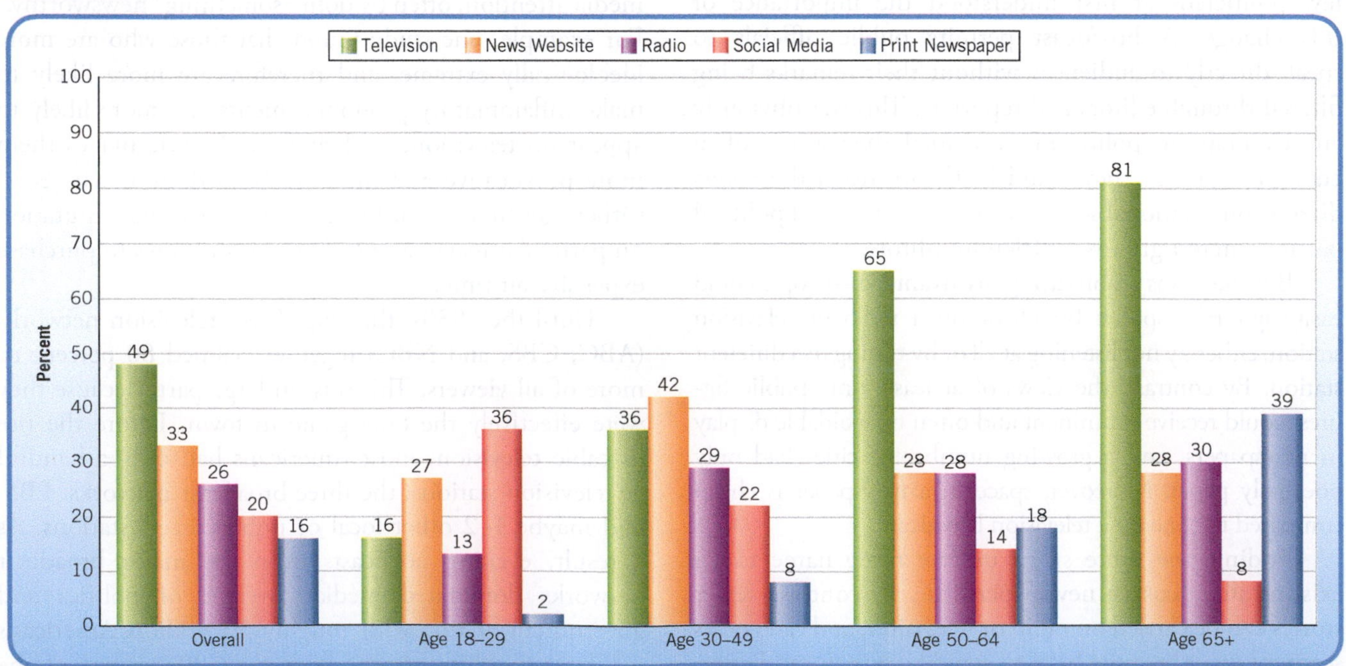

Source: Elisa Shearer, "Social Media Outpaces Print Newspapers in the U.S. as a News Source," Pew Research Center, 10 December 2018.

Q **Compare the data above to your own sources for news—how do you compare to other Americans? Are some of these outlets better or worse sources for news and political information?**

Figure 12.2 **Social Media Websites Americans Use to Follow the News**

Site	Use site (Percent)	Get news on site (Percent)
Facebook	71	52
Twitter	23	17
LinkedIn	27	8
Snapchat	23	6
Tumblr	4	1
TikTok	3	<1
YouTube	74	28
Instagram	38	14
Reddit	13	8
WhatsApp	18	4
Twitch	5	1

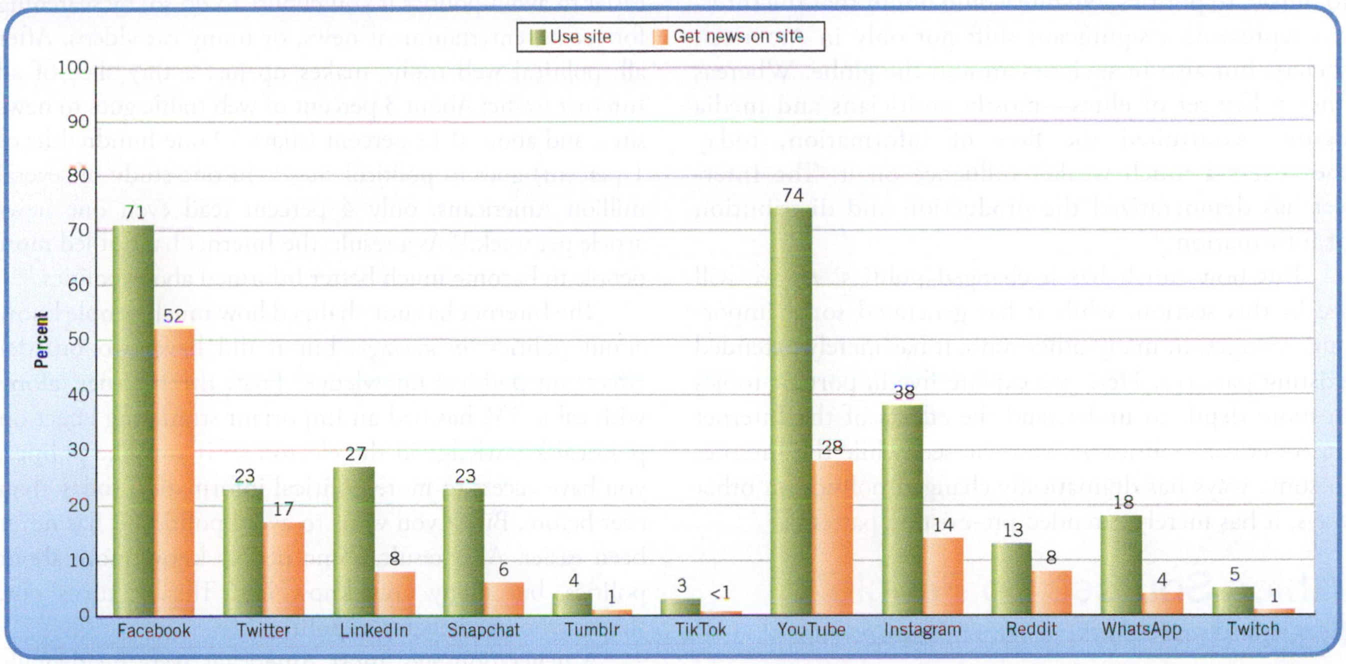

Source: Elisa Shearer and Elizabeth Grieco, "Americans Are Wary of the Role Social Media Sites Play in Delivering the News," Pew Research Center, 2 October 2019.

news websites do they use, and what do we mean when we say Americans use "social media" to get the news? As we explain in detail below, when Americans go online to look for news, most visit either large news aggregators, like Yahoo! News or Google News, or they visit the website of a leading mainstream outlet like *USA Today, The Washington Post*, or *The New York Times*. More partisan websites, like Daily Kos, Breitbart, or Gateway Pundit, have audiences that are only a tiny fraction of the mainstream outlets.

What about social media—what sources are Americans using for news there? Figure 12.2 breaks down the social media platforms Americans use to follow the news.

At the moment, for most Americans, Facebook is still the dominant platform, especially for news: 71 percent of American adults use Facebook, and 52 percent get at least some of their news from Facebook. Fascinatingly, just as many Americans use YouTube (74 percent), though only 28 percent get political news and information from it, likely preferring to watch music, sports, or how-to videos. Other platforms are also popular sources for news, such as Twitter (17 percent of Americans), Instagram (14 percent), as well as LinkedIn (8 percent), Reddit (8 percent), Snapchat (6 percent), and WhatsApp (4 percent). These patterns may well change in the future, however. In that same report, the Pew Research Center broke down the data by age, and younger Americans are the ones using Snapchat, Reddit, and Instagram for news, so in the future, these are likely to become even more prominent. Politicians, recognizing that this is an important way of reaching out to voters, now work to carefully craft their social media presence. President Trump is a prolific Twitter user, and many candidates and officeholders are on Snapchat, Instagram, and other platforms (indeed, they go to any platform where they think they can reach voters). Politics, like every other activity in the 21st century, has entered the digital age.

Clearly, the Internet age has ushered in a fundamentally new era in how Americans get their news. Many have claimed that it has also fundamentally transformed politics. As we will see below, while the Internet has changed politics in some important ways, in many others it fundamentally has not.

12-2 Have the Internet and Social Media Changed Everything?

Ever since the emergence of wide-spread access to the Internet in the 1990s and 2000s, scholars, activists, and ordinary citizens have claimed that the Internet would radically change all aspects of our society from movies, to music, to politics. No one would doubt that the Internet represents a significant shift not only in American society, but also in societies around the globe. Whereas once a key set of elites—mostly politicians and media figures—controlled the flow of information, today they exert a much weaker influence on it. The Internet has democratized the production and distribution of information.

But how much has it changed politics? As we will see in this section, while it has generated some important changes, in many other ways, it has merely extended existing patterns. Here, we explore five important topics in more depth to understand the effects of the Internet on American politics. As you will see, while the Internet in some ways has dramatically changed politics, in other ways, it has merely extended pre-existing patterns.

Which Sources Do People Read and What Do They Know about Politics?

Clearly, the Internet has changed the medium through which people get the news: today, people can use their smartphones to check Facebook or Twitter rather than reading a newspaper or watching the evening news broadcast. Has this led people to consult a broader array of sources or to know more about politics? The evidence, perhaps surprisingly, is somewhat more mixed than you might expect.

First, many had hoped that the Internet would let people get access to a wider range of political information than ever before. At some level, this is no doubt true: If you can write it down, you can post it online—a few minutes scrolling through your Facebook or Instagram feed will convince you that people believe the most seemingly implausible theories. However, this democratizing impact has been quite muted in practice. Most people find political news online through major search engines or by visiting leading news sites, such as Yahoo! News, Google News, or the websites of major news organizations like the *New York Times*. Many of the links shared on Facebook and other social media outlets are also to these dominant sites. While people can search out different or alternative voices online, most do not. As a result, online news largely looks like offline news, just in a different format.[13]

Second, many had hoped that the Internet would transform how much people know about politics, especially young people. But the effect has again been relatively modest. The Internet makes a world of political information available to you: If you love politics, then you have never had access to more information about politics and public affairs than you do now. However, it has also never been easier to avoid politics if you choose to do so, by searching for sports, entertainment news, or funny cat videos. After all, political web traffic makes up just a tiny slice of all Internet traffic: About 3 percent of web traffic goes to news sites, and about 0.12 percent (that's 12 one-hundredths of 1 percent) goes to political sites.[14] In one study of several million Americans, only 4 percent read even one news article per week.[15] As a result, the Internet has not led most people to become much better informed about politics.[16]

The Internet has not changed how much people know about politics *on average*, but it did have two broader effects on political knowledge. First, the Internet, along with cable TV, has had an important stratifying effect on political knowledge in the electorate. If you like politics, you have access to more political information today than ever before. But if you want to avoid politics, it has never been easier. As a result, some people know more about politics, but many now know less. This, it turns out, shapes who participates in politics.[17]

A generation ago, most Americans were incidentally exposed to political news and information. There were a limited number of TV channels, and if you wanted to watch television in the early evening hours, you had to watch the news (because every channel broadcast the news then). Similarly, when the president came on television to give a prime-time address, you had to watch it if you turned on the TV—every network would have covered it.[18] This meant that most Americans got some news about politics. As a result, they were more likely to participate in politics.

But today, far fewer Americans receive such incidental exposure. If you do not want to watch the news, you can flip to a cable channel and catch a rerun of *Modern Family*, a basketball game, a cooking show, a travel show, entertainment news, or any of the hundreds of other options available (or you can watch programming saved on your DVR or log in to Netflix, Hulu, Amazon Prime, Apple TV, or many other streaming services). The same is true of presidential speeches, such as the State of the Union address, or even presidential debates. Those who do not like politics are less likely to be informed about it because so many other options are available to them. Because they don't know the candidates and the issues, they are less likely to show up to the polls.[19] So, increased media choice reduces some people's propensity to participate in politics.

Ironically, then, by giving people more choice, the Internet and cable TV have helped to lead some people to be *less* politically informed and engaged. There is no easy solution to this, as it is a by-product of modern technology. While we generally view our array of modern entertainment choices favorably, it can have some unintended negative consequences for politics.

Second, the Internet has also led people to become less informed about *local* politics. A generation ago, newspapers were second only to TV as a source of political information, and almost half of Americans regularly read their local newspaper.[20] Today, however, newspaper readership has fallen precipitously, and less than 10 percent of those under the age of 50 often read the newspaper (see Figure 12.1). Even among senior citizens—where newspaper readership is considerably higher—the levels today are less than they were in previous years. This has particular importance for how citizens learn about state and local politics. The vast variety of sources on television and the Internet ensures that citizens can—if they seek out that information—learn a great deal about *national* politics. Television, however, rarely gives much attention to state and local politics except when it is particularly salacious. Given its national scope, there simply is not enough time to cover politics in all 50 states, let alone the thousands of municipalities in the United States.

Even during election season, few gubernatorial or Senate races (and almost no House races) receive national TV attention, and very little attention from major online sources. Local TV news gives little coverage to state and local politics, and even during election season, their coverage is largely superficial (reporting on poll results rather than substantive issues).[21] If you want to learn about state and local politics and campaigns, you largely need to do so through a newspaper.

Unfortunately, local newspapers are in decline, both because of declining and aging readership (see Figure 12.1) and declining advertising revenue. The number of newspapers in the United States has shrunk by almost 20 percent in the past 25 years, and almost half of that loss has occurred since 2007.[22] A number of large cities—such as New Orleans and Birmingham—no longer have a daily print newspaper (and many other notable papers have also closed). Even where newspapers have remained in business, layoffs have been plentiful and journalistic budgets have shrunk. For example, the number of reporters devoted to covering state politics has declined by 35 percent since 2004.[23] While some have suggested using online sources to replace local newspapers, so far, this has not worked.[24]

As we explore later, the decline of local news sources has implications for the press's role as a political watchdog. But it has other consequences as well. Local newspapers are vital to promoting political engagement, especially in state and local politics. In places where a local paper has closed, citizens know less about the issues and are less politically active.[25] This suggests that the substitution of the Internet for newspapers demonstrated in Figure 12.1 does matter politically. So far, Internet news sources have not provided the same depth of coverage, especially of subnational politics, as newspapers, and that, as a result, changes how citizens participate.

Image 12.4 While newspapers have long been an important source for news, fewer Americans read them today than in the past.

Did the Internet Increase Political Participation?

Many scholars and activists also had hoped that the Internet, and especially social media platforms, would increase political participation and activism. Here, there is stronger evidence that the Internet has changed politics in the way people had hoped. For example, grassroots organizing for many groups, especially on the political left, has been greatly aided by the Internet.[26] The classic example is MoveOn.org, which since its founding in 1998 has used online tools to organize for political causes, often generating significant offline activism. Other groups have used similar online techniques to facilitate organizing and mobilizing voters. This is true not only here in the U.S., but around the globe—by making it possible for individuals to communicate directly with one another, it is easier for protests and other social movements to spread, even in repressive regimes.

This electronic mobilization has also helped to increase voter participation and engagement. For example, showing people a simple message in their Facebook feed—which of their friends report having voted—increases voter turnout.[27] Such techniques are likely to be especially effective among young people. For example, in Chapter 8 we discussed how get-out-the-vote operations—especially in-person operations—can effectively boost turnout. But some groups are especially hard to reach through such in-person visits, especially young people, who are more likely to live in apartment buildings (where canvassers cannot gain entry) or have evening plans or jobs and so are not at home when canvassers knock on the door. Sending these voters text messages, however, can increase their turnout.[28]

Similarly, many groups are turning to online tools to mobilize young people politically, often with positive success.[29] For example, the phrase *Black Lives Matter* first emerged in a Facebook post, then spread to

selective exposure *Consuming only those news stories with which one already agrees.*

echo chamber *Media environment in which people only hear messages they already agree with; they are also called filter bubbles*

Twitter, and eventually became a broad-based social movement.[30] In short, the Internet may not have transformed what people know about politics, but it has changed political activism and activity.

Does The Internet Create Echo Chambers?

A generation ago, when most Americans got their news from either newspapers or broadcast television, it was clear they would get multiple perspectives on political news. Most journalists strived to be objective and politically neutral (at least in theory), and they worked to present both sides of the story. Those same tendencies are true today for journalists working at mainstream media outlets like ABC News, National Public Radio, *The New York Times*, or *USA Today*.

But today, not all news comes from journalists dedicated to these norms of objectivity and balance. For example, some cable news networks slant the news in favor of one side or the other. Various studies have shown that Fox News generally leans right and favors Republicans, whereas MSNBC generally leans left and favors Democrats.[31] Similarly, many talk radio hosts like Rush Limbaugh, Sean Hannity, and Randi Rhodes favor one side or the other. And of course, ordinary people posting on social media may feel no such need to be objective whatsoever, and as a result post often outlandish claims about politics.

With the return of such partisan outlets, as well as the rise of social media, there is a concern about **selective exposure**, where citizens can choose to hear only one side of the issue—their side. Do people consciously avoid opposing points of view? If so, they're said to live in an **echo chamber**, whereby they only hear arguments from their own side (i.e., they hear only the echo of their pre-existing beliefs; these are also sometimes called filter bubbles, since they filter our dissonant views). If this is true, this has important consequences for American politics. Hearing both sides of the issue is an important part of being a well-informed citizen, and of knowing—and respecting—other people's beliefs and values.[32]

Al Drago/Bloomberg/Getty Images

Image 12.5 Mark Zuckerberg, the CEO of Facebook, testifies before Congress.

On the one hand, the is some evidence that people do engage in selective exposure, at least in some domains. For example, of those who watch MSNBC, 48 percent call themselves liberals and only 18 percent call themselves conservatives. For Fox News, the figures are reversed (18 percent call themselves liberals and 46 percent call themselves conservatives).[33] Likewise, certain highly partisan news websites do have fairly segregated audiences (i.e., one set of websites is read by liberals, another by conservatives).[34] At least some of the time, people do select media outlets based on their ideology.[35]

But these examples are the exceptions, not the rule. Looking across a wide variety of news outlets online, as well as social media sites, scholars have found that most people actually get a balanced media diet.[36] As we noted above, most people's media consumption online, are driven largely by mainstream news websites and news aggregators like Google News. Likewise, most of the links posted on social media sites come from mainstream news outlets like CNN or *USA Today*.[37] Large studies of the individuals people follow on Twitter suggest that most people follow few political accounts, but to the extent that they do, they tend to follow those from both sides of the political aisle.[38] Indeed, social media typically *increases* exposure to diverse viewpoints, largely because individuals join them primarily to keep up with friends and family, many of whom hold different political beliefs.[39] For example, in a study of 10.1 million U.S. Facebook users, scientists found that nearly one-quarter of the average user's friends are from a different political party, and 29 percent of the stories in their news feed came from the opposing point of view.[40] While many have claimed that Facebook and other platforms use algorithms that create echo chambers (by simply showing people content from their own point of view), that same study found that Facebook's algorithms showed people more diverse content than they otherwise would have encountered, likely by showing people content from those in their network with a different point of view.

These results might surprise you, as we all know someone who only reads right-wing or left-wing websites, shares crazy stories with you on Facebook or Instagram, and unfriends those with opposing points of view. Just because most people do not live in filter bubbles does not mean that no one does. The best research suggests that there is a small but significant segment of the public who consumes news and information from only one side of the aisle.[41] These people's views look quite different from ordinary Americans, and they are strong partisans and typically quite ideologically extreme.[42]

But the key point to emphasize is that this is a small set of Americans. The audience for most partisan websites is very modest; many more Americans go online to read CNN than to read Breitbart or DailyKos. Likewise, even the most popular programs on Fox News or MSNBC attract tiny audiences—a few million people at most—much smaller even than the audience for the nightly broadcast news. While most people have the option to select into narrow "echo chambers," the reality is that they do not.

Why then do we hear so much about filter bubbles? Those who are in them are more politically engaged and active, and they yield disproportionate influence in the system. So there is a parallel to the findings we saw in Chapter 7: just as most Americans are relatively moderate and centrist, most Americans get a balanced media diet. But just as activists tended to be more ideologically extreme, so too do these individuals tend to cocoon themselves in echo chambers.

Fake News and Social Media

Even if the Internet and social media do not create echo chambers, they have had one pernicious effect in recent years—an increase in fake news stories and more generally, misinformation (broadly speaking, **fake news** is news that is made up, typically to support a particular candidate or point of view).[43] Such stories long predate the Internet—during his presidency, John Adams noted that "there has been more new error propagated by the press in the last ten years than in a hundred years before 1789."[44] But the spread of social media has greatly accelerated the spread of such misinformation, by making it possible for anyone to create a "news" outlet and post stories online that can be shared and liked. Bots—fake accounts that simply repost content—can help to spread this misinformation widely in a short period of time.

The 2016 election brought many of these issues into the public consciousness. As noted at the beginning of this chapter, many such stories were posted online during the campaign, for example, alleging that Pope Francis endorsed Donald Trump, that Hillary Clinton sold weapons to ISIS, or that Mike Pence called Michelle Obama vulgar (none of these are even the least bit true). Such stories spread rapidly: one report showed that in the final three months of the campaign, the top 20 fake news stories on Facebook were liked, shared, and commented on more times than the top 20 genuine news stories from outlets like the *New York Times* or the *Washington Post*.[45]

fake news *Manufactured stories typically designed to support a particular point of view or candidate.*

But what effect did such stories have? Did they sway voters in the election? Shortly after Trump's upset victory, some commentators claimed that they helped to swing the election, especially since much of the fake news prior to the 2016 election favored Donald Trump, rather than Hillary Clinton. Estimating the effect of fake news on the election is extremely difficult, but the best evidence suggest that its effect on the outcome was likely small. The reason why is that a small slice of the population consumed most of the fake news—by some estimates, only 1 percent of individuals accounted for 80 percent of exposure to fake news.[46] Further, these individuals tended to be extremely ideological and partisan, and hence the fake news seems to have reinforced, rather than changed, their beliefs.[47] Even for these individuals, fake news represented a small fraction of their overall media exposure, so claims that these sources swung the election are probably incorrect.[48]

Nevertheless, such stories are deeply troubling, as they suggest that voters may be subject to misinformation online: indeed, many Americans report being confused by fake news,[49] and partially as a result, many Americans say they distrust the news, especially the new that they find on social media.[50] Indeed, this is perhaps the most pernicious effect of fake news: it makes people think that all news is suspect (this is likely the intent of the malicious actors who create much of this content).[51]

What can be done in response to fake news? In the aftermath of the 2016 election, Facebook and other online companies have announced numerous steps to combat fake news,[52] and such efforts do seem to be reducing its prevalence.[53] Journalists and various social networks have also begun experimenting with issuing corrections to fake news, either by telling people these stories are fake or by posting corrections to them. These do make people believe fake news is fake, but they have the pernicious effect of making people distrust even true stories.[54] This may explain why users feel frustrated and confused by these stories, as we noted above.

More generally, perhaps the most important lesson of fake news is that readers need to adopt a critical eye toward news stories they see online. Remember that much of the fake news online is there because nefarious foreign actors are attempting to sow discord in American politics and interfere in our elections. Robert Muller indicted 13 Russians for doing exactly that as part of his

trial balloon *Information leaked to the media to test public reaction to a possible policy.*

investigation into the 2016 elections,[55] and FBI director Christopher Wray testified before Congress that foreign governments are looking to try to do the same things in 2020 and beyond.[56] Readers should investigate the source, determine whether it is credible, and check that the information can be verified with another source, such as a third-party fact-checking website or a major news source. They should look at the language and consider whether it is balanced, or if it favors one side or the other. As with so many things in life, if something seems too good to be true, it probably is.

Has The Internet Changed How Politicians Interact with the Media?

Over time, as the media environment has changed—from a partisan press to circulation-driven papers to broadcast outlets to the Internet and social media—so has how political actors interact with the media. As we will see, these changes have transformed how the press treats politicians (and perhaps just as important, how politicians treat the press).

No office illustrates this shift more than the presidency. Initially, the president was rather remote and removed from the public eye, but no longer. Theodore Roosevelt was the first president to raise the systematic cultivation of the press to an art form. From the day he took office, he made it clear that he would give inside stories to friendly reporters and withhold them from hostile ones. He made sure that scarcely a day passed without his doing something newsworthy.

In 1902, Roosevelt built the West Wing of the White House and included in it, for the first time, a special room for reporters near his office; he invited the press to view, and become fascinated by, the antics of his children. In return, the reporters adored him. Teddy's nephew Franklin Roosevelt institutionalized this system by making his press secretary (a job created by Herbert Hoover) a major instrument for cultivating and managing, as well as informing, the press.

Today, the press secretary heads a large staff that meets with reporters, briefs the president on questions likely to be asked, attempts to control the flow of news from cabinet departments to the press, and arranges briefings for out-of-town editors (to bypass what many presidents think are the biases of the White House press corps). All this effort is directed primarily at the White House press corps, journalists who have dedicated space in the White House where they wait for a story to break, attend the daily press briefing, or take advantage of a "photo op"—an opportunity to photograph the president with some newsworthy person.

No other nation in the world has brought the press into such close physical proximity to the head of its government. The result is that the actions of our government are personalized to a degree not found in most other democracies. Whether the president rides a horse, comes down with a cold, greets a school group, or takes a trip, the press is there. And given the press's tendency to critique those in power, the press corps is always ready to leap on the president's gaffes and malapropisms.

While every president has a somewhat confrontational relationship with the White House press corps (since all presidents feel the corps is too hard on them), President Trump's stands out. President Trump has repeatedly attacked both the White House press corps and the press more generally, claiming that they spread mistruths. In 2019 alone, President Trump called the press "the enemy of the people" in 21 tweets, and he used the phrase "fake news" 273 times on Twitter.[57] Yet at the same time, President Trump is extremely accessible to media, and consumes media content voraciously. So even while he attacks the press, he continues to engage with them.

Of course, the president and his advisors are not fools—they give this access because they understand there are political benefits to doing so. Giving reporters access to the chief executive gets the president's name in the press and may promote the White House's agenda. For example, the president or other officials may strategically leak a policy to the media to see how it plays with the public; this is called floating a **trial balloon**. If the policy is a success, the president rolls it out officially; if not, it dies a quiet death. More generally, as we will see in Chapter 14, the president can use the media strategically to appeal to public opinion to try and win support for policies.

Other political actors in Washington, DC, have learned the same lesson: cultivating the press can allow them to promulgate their messages. In every agency and cabinet department, in every House and Senate office, staff are trained to deal with the media. Even the Supreme Court—which famously bans cameras in its courtroom and works to present an image of itself as above politics—has a press office that works with the media to disseminate information about its rulings.

Members of Congress are classic exemplars of how to use the media to promulgate a message and increase one's visibility, a lesson members first learned 70 years ago. Estes Kefauver was initially a little-known senator from Tennessee, but then he chaired a Senate committee

Image 12.6 and 12.7 In 1939, White House press conferences were informal affairs, as when reporters gathered around Franklin Roosevelt's desk in the Oval Office. Today, they are huge gatherings held in a special conference room, as shown on the right.

investigating organized crime. When these dramatic hearings were televised, Kefauver became a household name. In 1952, he ran for the Democratic nomination for president and won a lot of primary votes before losing to Adlai Stevenson.

Since then, members of Congress have realized that appearing in the media—especially on TV—can help them further their careers. While television cameras were not permitted on the House and Senate floors until the late 1970s, today C-SPAN provides extensive coverage of both chambers. Even more importantly, members of Congress—especially those with presidential ambitions—seek to appear on the panoply of television news programs to increase their name recognition and profile.

Social media have further changed the relationship between the press and politicians. Today, unlike in the past, political leaders can speak directly to voters without going through the mass media. At least in theory, this allows politicians a more direct route to the public. But as we saw earlier in the chapter, a key limitation is that most voters are not paying attention to these channels. Only 4 percent of Americans closely follow President Trump's tweets on Twitter, and the figure for other politicians would be even lower. While social media offer the possibility of directly communicating with the public, it is more potential than reality at this point.

Instead, most of the effects of social media—including President Trump's Twitter feed—come about because the mass media discuss it in news stories. When President Trump tweets about something, the media cover it, thereby promulgating his ideas. The president's 2016 campaign was an excellent example of how a candidate can use social media, especially Twitter, to drive media coverage, which helped to fuel his campaign.[58] And of course, politicians try to carefully craft and control their images in the media without the interference of journalists. As we will see below, there is a tension between what politicians present to the press and what the press wants to cover. In short, politicians are not simply passive figures being covered by the media; they actively try to shape their media image. The Internet changed the mechanism through which politicians communicate with the public, but it did not change this fundamental truth.

Looking back over this entire section on the effects of the Internet, we can see that it has generated some significant changes in politics, but in other ways, it has merely extended other pre-existing trends. Like many other technological developments, we should avoid assuming that it either did nothing or did everything.

12-3 Media Effects

So far, we have learned how the media developed over time in American politics, and have reviewed how the Internet and social media have—and have not—changed politics. But what, exactly, is the media's role in politics? How do the media affect politics? At the broadest level, the media serve to inform the public about politics and public affairs. While this entails many components, three in particular are noteworthy. First, the mass media help to set the political agenda—that is, they shape what people think about. Second, they frame political issues and influence how people understand them. Finally, they serve as a watchdog to guard against corruption and to hold politicians accountable.

agenda-setting (gatekeeping) *The ability of the news media, by printing stories about some topics and not others, to shape the public agenda.*

priming *The ability of the news media to influence the factors individuals use to evaluate political elites.*

Setting the Public Agenda

One vital role of the media is agenda-setting. In any given day, far more happens than any particular paper or news outlet could report. Part of the job of journalists is to decide what stories are important enough to report. This process is known as **agenda-setting** or **gatekeeping**. By covering some issues but not others, the mass media shapes the issues that are being discussed at any given point in time.[59]

How do journalists decide which stories to cover? That is not easy to answer, as journalists use a variety of different criteria to select them. But many of the stories they report on include familiar people, focus on conflict or scandal, and are timely.[60] This helps to explain why political stories often attract a great deal of attention, as they feature all of those characteristics.

Some people argue that the mass media can manipulate the agenda and cause individuals to care about problems that are not especially important. This can happen, but it is relatively uncommon. More typically, the mass media's attention to problems is largely dictated by important real-world events. For example, when the government foils a terrorist plot, there are many stories about it in the news, and people become more concerned about terrorism. Likewise, as droughts, hurricanes, and other natural disasters resulting from climate change have become more frequent, these topics have received more news coverage, and voters view climate change as a more important problem. The media do set the agenda, and that agenda is heavily influenced by what is happening in the real world.

Some people read about theories like agenda-setting and assume that scholars think ordinary people are just pawns of a powerful media: If the media tells people that issue X is important, then they think it's important. This somewhat cynical view, however, is too simplistic. Rather, ordinary people are making a subtler judgment. They assume that if the mass media is talking about a story, then it must be important (otherwise, the media would talk about something else).[61] People use the media's discussion of a topic as a cue that said topic is important. Agenda setting reflects engagement with the news more than blind obedience to the media.

Not only does the media help to set the political agenda, they also influence which issues the public uses to

Dabig/ZUMA Press/Newscom

Image 12.8 News stories about terrorist groups such as ISIS have increased the salience of terrorism in recent years. This is an example of agenda setting.

assess political leaders. This process is known as **priming**. The basic logic of priming is an extension of agenda-setting. When the mass media covers an issue, viewers assume it is important. As a result, they rely on that issue more heavily when evaluating political elites.[62] For example, imagine you are trying to decide whether you approve of the job President Trump is doing in office. To do that, you would think about how well the president has handled all of the various issues he faces. But what issues will you consider and weigh most heavily? You will be most likely to consider the issues that have been covered in the news. For example, if the economy has been doing poorly and there have been more stories on the economy lately, you may weigh Trump's handling of the economy more heavily. Likewise, if there have been more stories about scandals and corruption in his administration in the news, you may weigh those issues more heavily.[63] That is the idea of priming: By the media covering a story, citizens use that issue to judge politicians.

We saw a potent example of priming during the George W. Bush presidency. Before 9/11, approval of President Bush was closely tied to perceptions of how well he was handling the economy: those who approved (disapproved) of Bush's handling of the economy tended to approve (disapprove) of him overall. But after the 9/11 attacks—and the ensuing spike in media attention to terrorism—evaluations of how well Bush handled terrorism became much more important. Similarly, after the 2008 financial crisis, evaluations of the president were much more closely tied to evaluations of his management of the economy.[64]

Much as with agenda-setting, the point of priming is not to suggest that voters are fools led by the media. Rather, viewers use the media's coverage of an issue to infer that it is important (and hence should be the basis of political judgments). In fact, it is the more informed viewers who are most susceptible to priming effects.[65] More informed viewers are the ones who understand how to take what they learned in media reports and apply it to evaluate a particular politician. Priming is not a consequence of voter ignorance; rather, it comes from voter knowledge.

Framing

Framing refers to the way in which the media presents a particular story. By presenting some aspects of an issue and ignoring others, the media influences how people think about that issue.[66] For example, suppose you are undecided about whether the United States should expand domestic production of oil and natural gas. If you watched one news report that emphasized the large number of high-paying jobs that would be created, you might be more likely to support more oil and gas production. In contrast, if you instead saw a report suggesting more drilling for oil and gas would seriously damage the environment, you might be more strongly opposed to it. The way in which the media frames the issue—as one of job creation versus environmental damage—shapes your opinion.

This makes framing a particularly important type of media effect—by influencing the way people understand an issue, framing shapes their attitudes. Framing is a key way the media works to change attitudes. But in most cases, framing effects are more modest than massive. Why? Because typically, media outlets present both sides of the story (remember the journalistic norms of balance discussed earlier). So, in our example of oil drilling, they would present both the increased jobs and the risk to the environment at the same time. As a result, the frames partially cancel each other out, and the overall effect is rather modest. Most people end up close to where they would be without the frame.[67]

But framing need not be so innocuous. In particular, some cases where the media presents a lopsided frame that favors one side of the issue, and here, larger, and more pernicious, effects can occur. For example, few issues have received more media coverage since 9/11 than the fight against terrorism, particularly how to balance the need for security with American civil liberties. This tension became especially acute in 2013, after Edward Snowden leaked classified documents detailing extensive domestic surveillance programs conducted by the National Security Agency (as discussed in Chapter 5).

A large-scale analysis of media coverage of this issue finds that the frames used lead to greater support for government surveillance. Many stories about these programs stress the successes of the programs and indicate that they have helped to keep Americans safe. Fewer stories offer a more critical take and focus more on the cases where civil liberties have been harmed. As a result, Americans tend to support expansive government surveillance more than they otherwise might.[68]

Framing *The way in which the news media, by focusing on some aspects of an issue, shapes how people view that issue.*

watchdog *The press's role as an overseer of government officials to ensure they act in the public interest.*

That said, of course, this argument has limits. In response to Snowden's revelations, and the ensuing public debate, Congress passed the USA Freedom Act in 2015, which did curtail the collection of phone and other records (see the discussion in Chapter 5). And public opinion has shifted on this issue over time, demonstrating that the media is merely one input into what people believe. Framing is a real effect, but as we have seen throughout the chapter, the media is not all-powerful.

Similarly, media frames for public assistance programs also weaken support for them. Media reports on these programs discuss waste and fraud in the system, and focus on individuals who abuse such programs. Such abuses are less common, however, than one would suspect from many media reports. But because the media report on the abuses in these programs (consistent with its watchdog role), people suspect waste, fraud, and abuse are more widespread than they are in reality.[69]

The point of these examples is not to suggest that there are no legitimate security threats that justify surveillance, or that there is no abuse of public assistance programs. Obviously, there needs to be some surveillance to protect against terrorism, and there is fraud in public assistance programs. But the problem in both cases is that the media is giving us only part of the story—they are privileging one frame over another. We need to hear both sides of the story to make an informed decision. We wanted to hear about both the economic gains and the environmental risk of more drilling to make an informed decision, and these other cases are no different. When you hear news stories discussing particular issues, think carefully about what is being presented and, equally important, what is not.

The Media as Watchdog: Political Accountability

Another core function for the media is to serve as a **watchdog** to guard against fraud and abuse, and to hold politicians to account for their campaign promises. Americans see this as a vital role for the media. While they are critical of the media in many respects (especially with respect to question of bias), nearly three-quarters of Americans think the media keeps leaders from doing

fact checking *Efforts by news organizations to evaluate the veracity of statements by politicians and other public actors*

things that should not be done.[70] As we discussed above, the idea of the journalist as watchdog has a long history in American politics, and it continues to be important today.

One of the most critical parts of this task is to fight against corruption in government. As we discussed in Chapter 11, there is not much evidence that interest groups "buy" policy through campaign donations. However, there is always a concern that politicians will be tempted to enter into corrupt deals, trading their political power for personal financial gain. For example, in 2014, former Virginia governor Bob McDonnell was convicted of corruption, as was former Illinois governor Rod Blagojevich in 2011. One study of corruption found that corruption was the least likely in states and localities with a vigorous press, especially investigative journalism.[71] The rationale is relatively straightforward: With more (and better) investigative journalists, politicians are more likely to be caught when they engage in misconduct. While the press presence is obviously not the only factor, it does suggest that the press serves as a critical watchdog.

The press also serves as a watchdog via fact checking. **Fact checking** is when journalists or nonprofit organizations evaluate the veracity of the claims made by politicians and state whether they are true or false. Some of the most prominent examples include Politifact (https://www.politifact.com) and FactCheck.Org (https://www.factcheck.org), both of which evaluate hundreds of claims by politicians, media reports, pundits, and various other sources every year.

For example, Image 12-9 below presents part of a fact check from FactCheck.Org of President Trump's 2020 State of the Union Address. The authors researched the points Trump raised in his speech on the economy, trade, energy, immigration, and other issues, and then evaluated the truth or falsehood of such claims.

This is another example of the press's watchdog role. All politicians stretch the truth; the goal of fact checking is to get them not to push it past the breaking point. Such fact checking makes politicians more truthful,[72] and it also helps ordinary citizens hold more accurate beliefs.[73] Ensuring that political elites tell the truth—and calling them out when they do not—is an important part of this watchdog role.

The press also helps to ensure that politicians respond to public opinion. Several studies have found that when newspapers report more frequently on their local members of Congress, members are more likely to follow their constituent's wishes on legislative votes.[74] When the media reports on what politicians are doing in office, voters have more information about politicians' decisions. This makes it easier for voters to hold politicians

FACTCHECK.ORG® *A Project of The Annenberg Public Policy Center* DONATE

HOME ARTICLES ▾ ASK A QUESTION ▾ DONATE TOPICS ▾ ABOUT US ▾ SEARCH MORE ▾

ARTICLES › FEATURED POSTS

FactChecking the State of the Union

The president's address included false and misleading claims on jobs, wages, energy, immigration and more.

By Eugene Kiely, Brooks Jackson, Lori Robertson, Robert Farley, D'Angelo Gore, Jessica McDonald and Isabella Fertel

Posted on February 5, 2020

Summary

In his 2020 address to Congress, President Donald Trump stretched and distorted the facts:

- Trump claimed the economy is "the best it has ever been." But GDP growth fell to 2.3% last year and economists predict further slowing this year.
- He said he brought about low unemployment by reversing "years of economic decay" and "failed economic policies," when in fact over 1 million more jobs were added in the 35 months before he took office than in the first 35 months since.
- Trump boasted that the "unemployment rate for women reached the lowest level in almost 70 years." That's true, but it had been trending down for several years before he took office.
- The president wrongly said, "After decades of flat and falling incomes, wages are rising

Ask FactCheck

Q: Are hospitals inflating the number of COVID-19 cases and deaths so they can be paid more?

A: Recent legislation pays hospitals higher Medicare rates for COVID-19 patients and treatment, but there is no evidence of fraudulent reporting.

Read the full question and answer
View the Ask FactCheck archives
Have a question? Ask us.

Image 12.9 Many journalists now work to fact check speeches by politicians and other figures so that the public knows when they are telling the truth, and when they are not. Such efforts help to keep politicians more honest, and serve as part of the press's watchdog role.

Source: Factcheck.org

Visit one of the major fact-checking websites and evaluate one of their fact checks. What evidence did the authors present? What other information would you have liked to have known to evaluate their efforts?

accountable for their decisions, and hence politicians respond accordingly. Press coverage of politics helps to promote political accountability.

Of course, the challenge to this finding is that local newspapers are in decline. Local television news gives scant attention to members of Congress, and national papers and television do not have the space or time to cover individual members, so it is unclear whether online venues will have the resources to investigate members' records in this way. The decline of local news not only affects political participation, as we saw above, it also makes it more difficult to hold politicians accountable.

Can the Media Lead Us Astray?

The functions of the mass media we discussed above—setting the public agenda, framing issues, and serving as a watchdog—suggest a (relatively) positive role for the media. But the ways in which the media covers some issues can also sometimes lead us astray. In this section, we discuss several different ways in which media coverage can mislead and distort the truth. We do this to help readers become more informed consumers of the news media.

Political Campaigns as a Political Game

In Chapter 10, we explained how the media contributes to helping inform citizens about the candidates and issues in elections. To the extent that the media report on the substantive issues of the day, the public becomes better informed. And generally speaking, as a result of such coverage, the public does learn about the issues of the day through the media. But one dimension of campaign reporting is more harmful than helpful: a focus on elections as a political game. This "**game frame**" for political reporting has two elements. First, there is a focus on where the candidates stand in the polls: who is up, and who is down? This type of poll-based coverage is known as **horse-race (or scorekeeper) journalism.** Second, there's a focus on tactics and strategy rather than substance: why did candidate X say Y? What does the trailing candidate need to do to get ahead? Together, they suggest to voters that style and strategy—not substance—decide elections.

game frame *The tendency of media to focus on political polls and strategy rather than on the issues.*

horse-race (scorekeeper) journalism *News coverage that focuses on who is ahead rather than on the issues.*

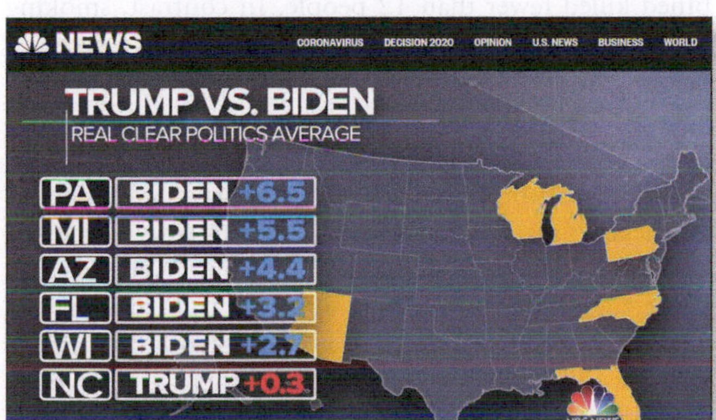

Image 12.10 News media coverage of elections frequently centers around polls such as these, rather than discussion of substantive campaign issues.

Source: NBCNEWS.COM

Coverage of polls in elections is nothing new; it even predates the birth of modern public opinion polling. But over time, especially in the past few decades, stories about polls—and politicians' efforts to get ahead in the polls—have become strikingly more common. Over time, there has been less reporting on the substantive issues in elections.[75] In its place, journalists have substituted reports on the horse-race and candidate strategy.[76]

Such stories dominated coverage of the 2016 election. According to data gathered by Harvard University's Shorenstein Center, coverage of both the primaries and the general election focused largely on horse-race coverage. In the primary period, 56 percent of stories focused on politics as a game, versus only 11 percent that focused directly on the substantive issues of the campaign.[77] Looking at the general election, the figures improve slightly, but not by much: "only" 42 percent of stories focused on the horse race, and just 10 percent focused on the candidates' policy positions.[78]

We see one such example of 2020 horse race coverage in Image 12-10, where NBC News reported on polls showing that Joe Biden was leading President Trump in the polls in many key states, including Pennsylvania, Michigan, and Arizona. Even "elite" media outlets are not immune to these trends. An analysis of the *New York Times'* coverage of the 2016 campaign found that in one several-week stretch, a full three-quarters of the stories they published focused on the horse race.[79] Similar analyses of earlier elections show the same pattern: most election coverage focuses on the horse race.

Why do journalists devote so much time and attention to these types of stories? They do so for three main reasons. First, readers like them. Reading about strategy and such is exciting, and suggests to readers that they're getting the "real scoop" behind the campaigns. Why understand what candidates said when you can understand *why* they said it? Furthermore, most readers find substantive reporting rather dull. If you doubt this, sit down and read the candidates' position papers on various issues (you'll likely find it rather soporific). Unsurprisingly, given the choice, most voters opt for the horse-race and strategy coverage over detailed, issue-focused coverage.[80]

Second, reporting on strategy—especially polling—is relatively easy, so it simplifies journalists' task in an era of shrinking resources. A poll result has a clear message and does not require in-depth reporting the way a detailed piece on candidates' substantive positions would.[81]

Finally, this sort of coverage reflects the press's desire to be seen as independent of political elites. Because politicians carefully control their substantive message, reporters do not want to simply report on that, as it would make them seem like patsies being duped by politicians. Instead, they want to uncover the "real" story about why a candidate does what he does, so they write stories about candidates' strategies and motives.[82]

Such coverage matters because it tends to make ordinary citizens more cynical about the political process.[83] It's not hard to see why: by promoting the idea that elections (and politics more generally) is all about strategy and tactics—and not substance—the media make politics out to be just another game. This focus makes ordinary people think elections are not about the major issues. As we discussed in Chapter 10, major issues—especially the health of the economy—are really the driver of the election, even if that message does not always come through in the media.

Luckily, there is a simple solution to combat these sorts of effects. When you see the media discussing strategy and tactics, just ignore it. When you see the media obsessing over polling data, remember the lesson from Chapter 10 that the daily fluctuation in the polls reflects noise more than true movement. Instead, seek out substantive coverage and focus there. It might be less entertaining, but it is far more helpful for casting an informed ballot.

Sensationalism and Negativity

The media also tends to focus on the negative in stories, rather than on the positive. This fits with the media's understanding of itself as a "watchdog," and the ensuing belief that they should be on the lookout for corruption and scandal. Furthermore, such stories attract more attention: finding evidence of fraud and abuse is more newsworthy than finding that government programs function effectively.

Such patterns are true of the media generally,[84] but this tendency has become especially pronounced in reporting on recent elections. In 2016, more than 70 percent of stories about Clinton and Trump were negative. Trump's coverage was slightly more negative than Clinton's was, but not by much: 77 percent of his stories were negative, versus "only" 64 percent for Clinton. These figures were even more lopsided when it came to stories about Trump and Clinton's fitness for office, where nearly 90 percent were negative.[85] Much like the example of horse-race coverage above, 2016 is the continuation of a long-term trend. In every election since 1988, negative coverage outpaced positive coverage, and that trend shows no sign of reversing any time soon.[86]

Another example of this bias toward negativity is how journalists report on campaign promises. Overall, politicians, once in office, generally *do* try to enact their campaign promises. Indeed, they often enact the vast majority of them, at least in part.[87] For example, during his eight years in office, President Obama fully or partially implemented approximately three-quarters of his campaign promises.[88] Why then do most voters think that politicians frequently break their promises? Part of the explanation is that the media—in keeping with its watchdog role—focuses on the cases where politicians break them.

More generally, focusing on waste, fraud, and abuse—and any area where government is not performing effectively—helps to expose corruption and abuse (as we saw above), but it also makes citizens more negative and cynical about government.[89] If citizens hear stories suggesting that government is not functioning effectively, they take those stories to heart. While trying to root out waste, fraud, and abuse is generally a good thing, too much focus here can turn off voters and make them cynical about the process.

Similarly, sensationalistic stories—ones that focus on salacious topics such as sex, drugs, or public health scares—also are overreported in the mass media. The level of coverage of these stories is grossly out of proportion to their importance to the general public. For example, in 2003, the media published more than 100,000 news articles discussing SARS and bioterrorism, though both combined killed fewer than 12 people. In contrast, smoking and physical inactivity—which killed millions—received little attention.[90] This one year was not an aberration, more generally, the media under-report on the real dangers to most Americans, and over-report on sensationalistic topics like terrorism, Ebola, or the Zika virus. Stories about politicians' sex lives are similarly frequently discussed ad nauseam—see, for example, Anthony Weiner, Larry Craig, and, perhaps most famous of all, Bill Clinton.

The media focus on such stories because they attract viewers and readers.[91] The fact that there are so many more news outlets now only increases the pressure to publish salacious stories. No longer do just the three major broadcast networks (NBC, CBS, and ABC) broadcast politics, now so do several cable news channels, dozens of talk radio stations, and thousands of websites. Given this

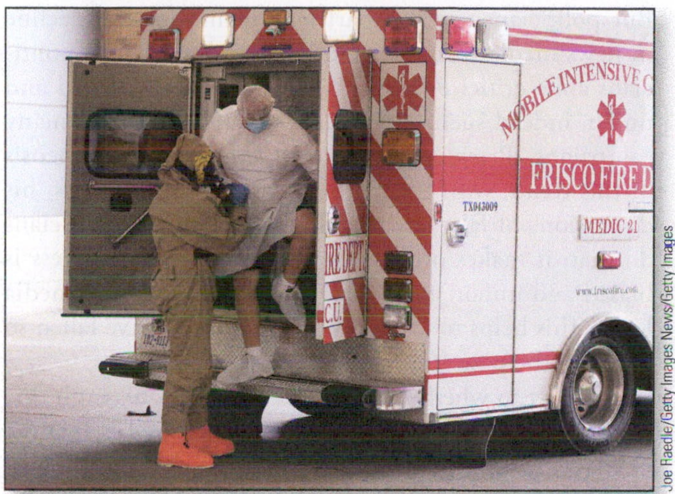

Joe Raedle/Getty Images News/Getty Images

Image 12.11 Extensive media coverage of the Ebola outbreak in the United States in 2014 is an example of sensationalism, as relatively few people were affected and there was little danger for most Americans.

intense competition for viewers, each program has a big incentive to air salacious stories to attract viewers. Even elite news outlets—like the *New York Times*—are not immune and succumb to sensationalism to grab readers.[92] While voters like these stories, they do little to inform the public. When you see the media covering a sensationalistic or salacious topic, ask yourself how relevant it actually is to becoming a better-informed citizen. The danger to this sort of reporting becomes clear when we face an actual crisis, such as the COVID-19 pandemic. Some people initially under-estimated the seriousness of the problem, as they assumed it was just another health scare being over-hyped by the media. When stories are routinely over-sensationalized, it becomes harder to tell the real threats from the over-hyped ones.

After reading this section on the ways in which media can lead one astray, you might think that you can never trust the media, but that is not correct. We wrote this section not to make you cynical about the media, but rather to help point out some ways in which the media can distort your understanding of politics. Become a skeptical news consumer, but not a cynical one.

Are There Limits to Media Power?

After reading this section, you might think the media are quite powerful: they can shape the agenda, frame issues to influence opinions, and make viewers cynical with their focus on strategy and negativity. All of these effects are real, but it is important to understand that there is a very important limit to the media's effect on attitudes: people's experiences in everyday life.

In general, the media is most powerful when people know the least about an issue. As people know more and more about an issue, the media's effect gets smaller and smaller.[93] We discussed this phenomenon in Chapter 10. Early in the primary season, when voters do not know the candidates, the media's portrayal of them has a big effect. After all, the public is just being introduced to the candidates, so the media's depiction of them matters a great deal. But over the course of the campaign, as voters learn more about the candidates, how the media depicts them matters less because there is less room for the media to influence voters' attitudes.

The same pattern is true of issues more generally. For example, the media typically have less ability to move people on issues where they have more personal experience, such as the economy. If you see many of your neighbors lose their jobs—or if you lose your own—you do not need the media to tell you that the economy is struggling. By contrast, most people have less direct experience with ISIS, Ebola, or America's role in Afghanistan. On these sorts of issues more removed from voters' everyday lives, the media have a larger effect on attitudes.

But people's level of information about an issue is not the only constraint, so is their overall attention to the media and politics. As we discussed in Chapter 7, most people are not very knowledgeable about politics, and likewise, most people are not terribly interested in political news. In January 2020, a poll by CNN found that nearly a quarter of Americans were not paying much attention to President Trump's impeachment trial, one of the most significant political events of the year.[94] This is not an isolated event; many Americans are simply not that interested in politics, and do not pay much attention to political news. This, in many ways is the key constraint on the media's power: if people are not paying attention to the media and political news, it is unlikely to affect their attitudes and beliefs—those who engage closely with the media are the ones who are most affected by it (see our discussion of priming and agenda setting above).

Furthermore, in many situations, the media are constrained by elites. This might seem odd—we have just discussed ways, such as serving as a watchdog, that the media can act as a check on elites and prevent them from abusing power. This is certainly true. But in many cases, the media are also dependent on information from elites. For example, on foreign policy and terrorism, the media often cannot gather information on its own. Because of issues of national security, the government restricts what reporters can know, and information is leaked—typically strategically, as we will see below—by people who are trying to advance a particular political position.

Likewise, on technical or complex scientific issues such as Internet security, nuclear power, or global warming, the media typically depends on elites to explain and clarify the issues at hand. As a result, much of the time, media reports reflect the elite debate—that is, elites set the terms of the debate, and the media just pass along that debate to the mass public.[95] In short, while the media are powerful, they are often constrained in their ability to shape public opinion and public policy.

12-4 Are the Media Trustworthy and Unbiased?

Do Americans have confidence in the press? Do they think they can reliably depend on the press to get the information they need to be informed about politics and public affairs? Since the early 1970s, political scientists have been asking survey questions to gauge how much confidence individual citizens have in the press. We present these data in Figure 12.3.

The data are clear: Over time, Americans have become less confident in the press. In 1973 (the first year this question was asked), 23 percent of respondents had a great deal of confidence in the press, 62 percent had some confidence in the press, and 15 percent had hardly any confidence in the press. In 2018 (the most recent data available), respondents were far less confident in the press. Now only 13 percent have a great deal of confidence, 41 percent have some confidence, and 45 percent have hardly any confidence. Since the 1970s, the number of people with a great deal of confidence in the press has declined sharply, and the number with no confidence has risen sharply (and there has been a similar, albeit less steep, decline in those with some confidence in the press). Americans trust the press less today than they did 40 years ago.

While the data in Figure 12.3 provide the best information available over time, other data show the same pattern of declining confidence in trust in the media. For example, the Gallup Organization has been asking about trust in the media since the 1970s as well, and finds that media trust has fallen over time.[96] While people do trust the sources they use themselves more than "the media" in general,[97] even evaluating specific sources, trust is often not terribly high.[98] No matter what data you use, it seems that Americans do not trust the press very much.

But why do Americans distrust the media? Part of the reason is undoubtedly the sorts of issues we discussed in the previous section: the emphasis on strategy and polls in election coverage, negativity, and so forth. But politicians are also partly to blame for the decline in news media trust. Democratic and Republican politicians alike criticize the press and attack it as biased and unfair, indeed such criticisms are a regular part of many campaigns. President Trump is perhaps the apotheosis of this trend, with his frequent attacks on the press, his discussions of fake news, and so forth. When politicians do that, it makes ordinary voters think that the press is biased and unfair, and hence Americans trust the media less.[99] This helps to explain why trust levels have fallen so much in the past 40 years.

We get to whether the media is actually biased in the next section, but the research suggests that by labeling the media as biased, politicians decrease trust in the media. There is, however, another lesson here in how to be an informed consumer of the news. Remember that whenever politicians accuse the media of bias, or of spreading fake news, they typically have an incentive to do so. Taking that into account is important as you decide for yourself whether media are actually biased in a particular instance.

Are the Media Biased?

Above, we saw that Americans do not trust the media. Is this because the media are actually biased? Most Americans certainly *think* so. In one study from the Pew Research Center, only 26 percent of Americans thought the press gets its facts straight and only 20 percent thought it was pretty independent.[100] In another study, sixty-eight percent of Americans said the press tends to favor one side rather than treating both sides fairly.[101] But are Americans' beliefs accurate? The answer, as we will see in this section, is subtler and less obvious than you probably think.

In any discussion of media bias, one of the first facts that most people mention is that journalists tend to be overwhelmingly liberal and Democratic. Many studies, dating back to the early 1980s, have concluded that members of the national press are more liberal than the average citizen.[102]

The public certainly believes that members of the media are liberals and that they favor Democratic candidates. A Gallup Poll done in 2019 found that 42 percent of Americans believe the media are "too liberal," versus only 14 percent who thought they were "too conservative."[103] In a poll taken in 2016 by Suffolk University and *USA Today,* nearly 8 in 10 respondents thought that the media favored Hillary Clinton over Donald Trump.[104]

While most journalists are liberals, not all are, especially in recent years with the rise of conservative hosts on talk radio (like Rush Limbaugh or Sean Hannity), on Fox News, and in newspapers like the *Washington Times.*

Figure 12.3 **Confidence in the Press, 1973–2018**

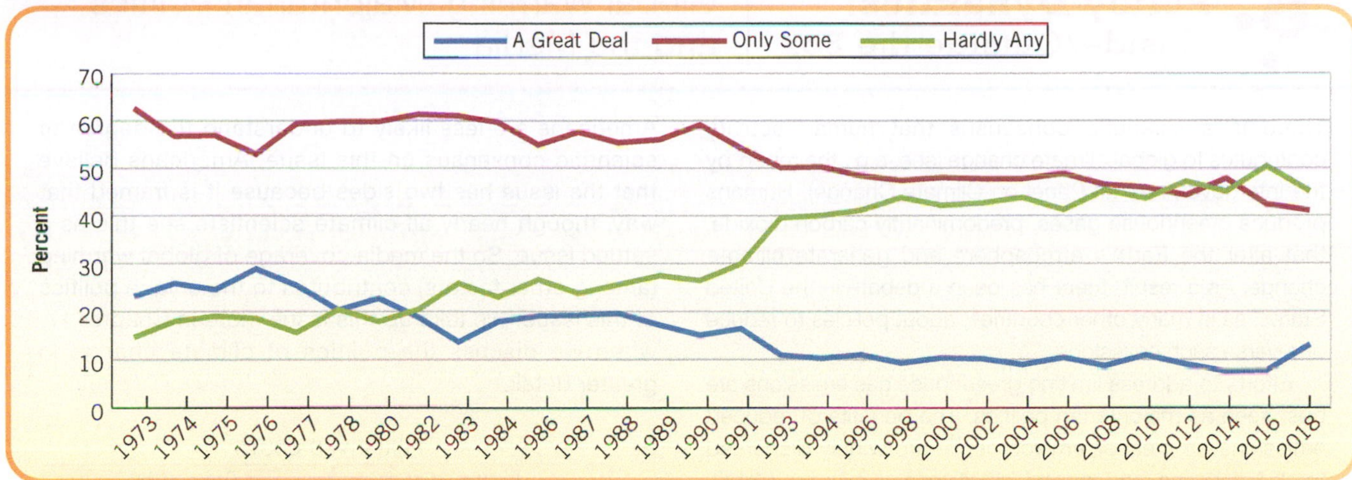

Source: Authors' analysis of the General Social Survey, 1973–2018.

That said, by all accounts, it seems like most journalists do favor Democrats.

The liberal and Democratic bent of journalists, however, is not in and of itself enough evidence to conclude that the media are biased. A recent large-scale study found no evidence that journalists are biased for or against liberals or conservatives, instead striving to cover the news in a balanced fashion.[105] While journalists are typically liberal, they are also committed to journalistic norms of objectivity and balance, which will counteract their personal biases.[106]

The best way to study media bias is to look at detailed content analyses of the media's coverage of politicians to determine whether any bias exists in favor of one party or another. Some studies have found evidence of a liberal, pro-Democratic bias in the media. The best of these is the work by Professor Tim Groseclose, who does identify examples of pro-Democratic media slant on some issues.[107] However, many more studies find that overall, media coverage is not biased in favor of one party or another.

Scholars have come to this conclusion studying patterns of coverage in campaigns,[108] as well as coverage of politicians outside of campaigns.[109] Studies find that, if anything, media outlets tend to favor incumbents, regardless of party. News outlets (especially newspapers) that endorse candidates are much more likely to endorse the incumbent,[110] and endorsed candidates receive more positive coverage in those outlets (and in turn are better liked by voters).[111] In general, then, there does not seem to be much overall evidence indicating the media slants in favor of one party or the other.

This overall lack of clear bias stems not just from journalistic norms of balance and objectivity but also from economics. Media outlets need to attract viewers and advertisers to stay in business. If media outlets are too biased or slanted, they will lose audience share.[112] Given that most Americans are relatively centrist (see Chapter 7), mainstream outlets want to cater to typical Americans. If these outlets lose viewers, they will be less attractive to advertisers, who want to reach as many people as possible.[113] Given this, it makes economic sense for most outlets to be relatively politically balanced.

Image 12.12 Many claim that the media have a liberal bias. For example, many claim that most mainstream news outlets support Democratic candidates.

Policy Dynamics: Inside/Outside the Box | Global Warming: Majoritarian Politics and the Media

There is a scientific consensus that human activity contributes to global climate change (see, e.g., the report by the Intergovernmental Panel on Climate Change). Humans produce greenhouse gases, predominantly carbon dioxide, that alter the Earth's atmosphere and generate climate change. As a result, there has been a debate in the United States, as in many other countries, about policies to reduce or reverse such emissions.

Efforts to address limiting greenhouse gas emissions are best seen as majoritarian politics. The benefits of reduced emissions—a cleaner environment—are widely dispersed to all Americans (and indeed, all citizens all over the globe). Similarly, the costs would be borne by all Americans as well: According to the Environmental Protection Agency, more than two-thirds of carbon dioxide emissions come from electricity generation and transportation, which all Americans use.

A large part of the debate in the United States, however, has centered on whether the scientific consensus about global warming is correct. The majoritarian debate has not been over what policy to pursue, but whether any policy at all is needed. There are many reasons why this debate takes this form in the United States, but one reason is how the mass media cover the issue of climate change.

While climate scientists almost all agree that human activity contributes to global warming (via greenhouse gases), the mass media portray this as a debate, rather than an area of scientific consensus. As a result, Americans are less likely to understand the degree of scientific consensus on this issue. Americans believe that the issue has two sides because it is framed that way, though nearly all climate scientists see this as a settled issue. So the media coverage of global warming (among other factors) contributes to the unique politics of this issue. We take up this issue more in Chapter 17, when we discuss the politics of climate change in greater detail.

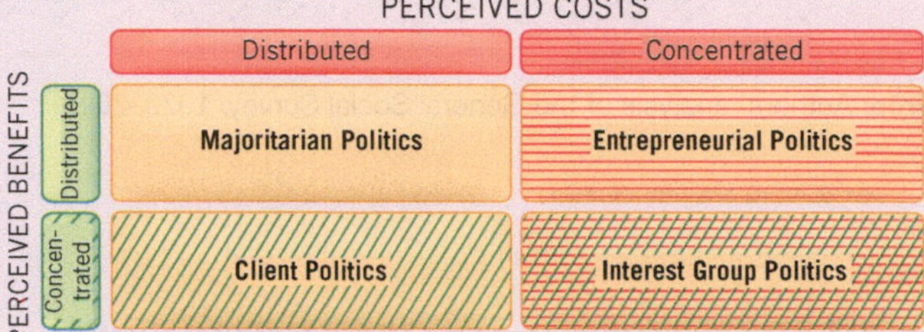

Source: Ariel Malka et al., "Featuring Skeptics in News Media Stories about Global Warming Reduces Public Beliefs in the Seriousness of Global Warming" (unpublished manuscript, Stanford University, June 2009); Maxwell Boykoff and Jules Boykoff, "Balance as Bias: Global Warming and the U.S. Prestige Press," *Global Environmental Change* 14, no. 2 (2004): 125–136; Eric Merkley, "Are Experts (News)Worthy? Balance, Conflict, and Mass Media Coverage of Expert Consensus," *Political Communication*, Forthcoming.

12-5 Government Regulation of the Media

Ironically, the least competitive media outlets—newspapers—are almost entirely free from government regulation, whereas the most competitive ones—radio and television stations—must have a government license to operate and must adhere to a variety of government regulations. And while the Internet has effectively no *content* regulations, regulators are beginning to grapple with how we might regulate Internet companies such as Facebook and Twitter.

Newspapers and magazines need no license to publish, their freedom to publish may not be restrained in advance, and they are liable for punishment for what they do publish only under certain highly restricted circumstances. The First Amendment has been interpreted as meaning that no government, federal or state, can place "prior restraints" (i.e., censorship) on the press except under very narrowly defined circumstances.[114] When the federal government sought to prevent the *New York Times* from publishing the Pentagon Papers, a set of secret government documents stolen by an antiwar activist, the Supreme Court held that the paper was free to publish them.[115]

Once something is published, a newspaper or magazine may be sued or prosecuted if the material is libelous or obscene, or if it incites someone to commit an illegal act. But these usually are not very serious restrictions because the courts have defined *libelous, obscene,* and *incitement* so narrowly as to make it more difficult here than in any other nation to find the press guilty of such conduct. For example, for a paper to be found guilty of libeling a public official or other prominent person, the person must not only show that what was printed was wrong and damaging but also must show, with "clear and convincing evidence," that it was printed maliciously—that is, with "reckless disregard" for its truth or falsity.[116] When in 1984 Israeli general Ariel Sharon sued *Time* magazine for libel, the jury decided the story *Time* printed was false and defamatory but that *Time* had not published it as the result of malice, and so Sharon did not collect any damages. (See Chapter 5 for more discussion of freedom of the press.)

There are also laws intended to protect the privacy of citizens, but they do not really inhibit newspapers. In general, your name and picture can be printed without your consent if they are part of a news story of some conceivable public interest. And if a paper attacks you in print, it has no legal obligation to give you space for a reply.[117] It is illegal to use printed words to advocate the violent overthrow of the government if by your advocacy you incite others to action, but this rule has only rarely been applied to newspapers.[118]

Confidentiality of Sources

Reporters believe they should have the right to keep confidential the sources of their stories. Some states agree and have passed laws to that effect. Most states and the federal government do not agree, so the courts must decide in each case whether the need of a journalist to protect confidential sources does or does not outweigh the interest of the government in gathering evidence in a criminal investigation. In general, the Supreme Court has upheld the right of the government to compel reporters to divulge information as part of a properly conducted criminal investigation, if it bears on the commission of a crime.[119]

This conflict arises not only between reporters and law enforcement agencies but also between reporters and persons accused of committing a crime. In the 1970s, Myron Farber, a *New York Times* reporter, wrote a series of stories that led to the indictment and trial of a physician on charges he had murdered five patients. The judge ordered Farber to show him his notes to determine whether they should be given to the defense lawyers. Farber refused, arguing that revealing his notes would infringe upon the confidentiality he had promised to his sources. Farber was sent to jail for contempt of court. On appeal, the New Jersey Supreme Court and the U.S. Supreme Court decided against Farber, holding that the accused person's right to a fair trial includes the right to compel the production of evidence, even from reporters.

In another case, the Supreme Court upheld the right of the police to search newspaper offices, so long as they have a warrant. But Congress then passed a law forbidding such searches (except in special cases), requiring instead that the police subpoena the desired documents.[120]

In 2005, two reporters were sentenced to jail when they refused to give prosecutors information about who in the Bush administration had told them that a woman was in fact a CIA officer. A federal court decided they were not entitled to any protection for their sources in a criminal trial. *New York Times* reporter Judith Miller spent 85 days in jail; she was released after a government official authorized her to talk about their conversation. There is no federal shield law that protects journalists, though such laws exist in 34 states.

In recent years, discussions of source confidentiality and shield laws have once again come back into the news, particularly in the context of the War on Terror. Several major stories about the fight against terrorism—from Abu Ghraib, to CIA black site prisons, to the NSA domestic surveillance programs—have been broken by whistleblowers from inside the government. In rare cases, the person has been willing to come forward—most notably Edward Snowden—but more have wanted to remain anonymous, as if their identities are disclosed, they will face prosecution (see the case of Chelsea Manning). This highlights a fundamental tension in a democratic society between freedom of the press (and freedom to investigate government abuses) and the protection of government secrets. We consider this issue more in the What Would You Do? box on page 294.

Why Do We Have So Many News Leaks?

This tension over source confidentiality and shield laws raises an important question: why are there so many leaks in American government? Why do so many insiders go to the press with their story to try to generate change? The answer lies in the Constitution. Because we have separate institutions that must share power, each branch of government competes with the others to get power. One way to compete is to try to use the press to advance your pet projects and to make the other side look bad. For example, one argument for why there were so many leaks in the early days of the Trump administration is that bureaucrats (and even some officials within the Trump administration) were unhappy with certain policies, so they strategically leaked things to the press to help press their case.[121]

Image 12.13 Activists urge Congress to pass a law shielding reporters from being required to testify about their sources.

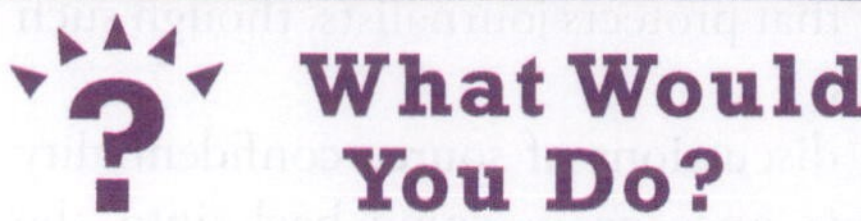

Will You Support or Oppose a Shield Law Bill?

To: *Senator Brian Dillon*
From: *Lucy Rae, political communication strategist*
Subject: *Protecting Journalists*

The Supreme Court has held that forcing a reporter to testify does not violate the First Amendment to the Constitution. But Congress could pass a law, similar to that in many states, banning such testimony if it reveals a confidential source.

To Consider:

Efforts by the White House to find out who is the "high-ranking official" cited in recent news stories about possible ethics violations have renewed calls by media groups for a "shield law" for journalists. Congress may hold hearings later this week.

Arguments for:

1. Thirty-four states now have shield laws similar to the one proposed by Congress.
2. Effective journalism requires protecting sources from being identified; without protection, many important stories would not be written.
3. The government should be able to collect sufficient information to prosecute cases without relying on journalists to do this work for them.

Arguments against:

1. Persons accused in a criminal trial have the right to know all of the evidence against them and to confront witnesses. A shield law would deprive people of this right.
2. A shield law would allow any government official to leak secret information with no fear of being detected.
3. The Supreme Court has already imposed a high barrier to forcing reporters to reveal confidential information, but that barrier should not be absolute, as situations can and do arise where a reporter is the only person who has the information necessary to investigate alleged criminal activity that threatens national security.

What Will You Decide? Enter **MindTap** to make your choice.

Your decision: ☐ Support bill ☐ Oppose bill

Constitutional Connections | Journalism, Secrecy, and Politics

The role of the media in American politics was not a high priority in drafting the Constitution. The First Amendment (added as part of the Bill of Rights in 1791) guaranteed freedom of the press, and the Framers appreciated the need for independent journalism in a democracy, but they did not pay significant attention to how journalists would affect governance. Yet the very ratification of the Constitution depended partly on cooperation from journalists, first in the secrecy surrounding the constitutional convention debates in Philadelphia in the summer of 1787, and second in the publication in New York newspapers of the *Federalist Papers* endorsing ratification of the Constitution (though newspapers at the time were party presses rather than independent organizations).

With the 24-hour news cycle, politicians today have fewer opportunities to engage in policymaking without media scrutiny. While media coverage provides an essential check on elected officials, it also can hinder prospects for decision making and compromise.

Nevertheless, a free press is crucial to a well-functioning democracy. Thomas Jefferson famously remarked that "were it left to me to decide whether we should have a government without newspapers, or newspapers without a government, I should not hesitate a moment to prefer the latter."[122] Both the public and political scientists agree: as we learned above, the public views journalists as a vital watchdog on government, and a recent survey of political scientists found that nearly all see a free press as essential to a democracy.[123] Most politicians, in general, agree, though they also often critique the press as well. Perhaps no contemporary figure exemplifies this more than President Trump, who courts the press while also saying he is at "war" with it, as we discussed elsewhere in the chapter. While others in the Trump White House—including the vice president—have sometimes tried to walk back some of Trump's critique of the press, Trump continues to frequently critique the media.[124]

Far fewer leaks occur in other democratic nations in part because power is centralized in the hands of a prime minister, who does not need to leak in order to get the upper hand over the legislature, and because the legislature has too little information to be a good source of leaks. In addition, we have no Official Secrets Act of the kind that exists in the United Kingdom; except for a few matters, it is not against the law for the press to receive and print government secrets.

Even if the press and the politicians loved each other, the competition between the various branches of government would guarantee plenty of news leaks. But since the Vietnam War, the Watergate scandal, and the Iran-Contra Affair, the press and the politicians have come to distrust one another. As a result, journalists today are far less willing to accept at face value the statements of elected officials and are far more likely to try to find somebody who will leak "the real story." We have, in short, come to have an **adversarial press**—that is, one that (at least at the national level) is suspicious of officialdom and eager to break an embarrassing story that will win for its author honor, prestige, and (in some cases) a lot of money.

This cynicism and distrust of government and elected officials have led to an era of attack journalism—seizing on any bit of information or rumor that might call into question the qualifications or character of a public official. Media coverage of gaffes—misspoken words, misstated ideas, clumsy moves—has become a staple of political journalism. At one time, such "events" as Vice President Quayle misspelling the word potato, President Obama saying he had visited 57 U.S. states, or President Trump staring at an eclipse would have been ignored, but now they are hot news items. Attacking public figures has become a professional norm, where once it was a professional taboo, reinforcing the norm of negativity we discussed earlier in the chapter.

adversarial press *The tendency of the national media to be suspicious of officials and eager to reveal unflattering stories about them.*

Regulating Broadcasting and Ownership

Although newspapers and magazines by and large are not regulated, broadcasting is regulated by the government. No one may operate a radio or television station without a license from the Federal Communications Commission, renewable every seven years for radio and every five for television stations. An application for renewal is rarely refused, but until recently the FCC required the broadcaster to submit detailed information about its programming and how it planned to serve "community needs" in order to get a renewal. Based on this information or on the complaints of some group, the FCC could use its powers of renewal to influence what the station put on the air. For example, it could induce stations to reduce the amount of violence shown, increase the proportion of "public service" programs on the air, or alter the way it portrayed various ethnic groups.

equal time rule *An FCC rule that if a broadcaster sells time to one candidate, it must sell equal time to other candidates.*

Of late a movement has arisen to deregulate broadcasting, on the grounds that so many stations are now on the air that competition should be allowed to determine how each station defines and serves community needs. In this view, citizens can choose what they want to hear or see without the government shaping the content of each station's programming. For example, since the early 1980s, a station can simply submit a postcard requesting that its license be renewed, a request automatically granted unless some group formally opposes the renewal. In that case, the FCC holds a hearing. As a result, some of the old rules—for instance, that each hour on TV could contain only 16 minutes of commercials—are no longer rigidly enforced.

Radio broadcasting has been deregulated the most. Before 1992, one company could own one AM and one FM station in each market. In 1992, this number was doubled. And in 1996, the Telecommunications Act allowed one company to own as many as eight stations in large markets (five in smaller ones) and as many as it wished nationally. This trend has had two results. First, a few large companies now own most of the big-market radio stations. Second, the looser editorial restrictions that accompanied deregulation mean that a greater variety of opinions and shows can be found on the radio. There are many more radio talk shows now than would have been heard when content was more tightly controlled.

More generally, over time, the federal government has loosened rules on ownership, so that large corporations now control a larger share of media outlets (for the current rules, visit the FCC's website).[125] indeed, media ownership has become strikingly concentrated. In the 1980s, more than 50 companies controlled the majority of American media outlets. Today, only six companies control more than 90 percent of media outlets.[126] So while there are hundreds of television stations and thousands of newspapers and radio stations, they are owned by a relatively small set of actors.

RosaireneBetancourt 1/Alamy Stock Photo

Image 12.14 Fox News and similar outlets arose after the end of the fairness doctrine.

This raises concerns about owners biasing the content that their stations broadcast. While studies have found that owners typically do not bias content in favor of one party or the other,[127] owners can bias reporting in other ways. For example, studies have found that when media outlet owners stand to benefit from a policy, that shifts the outlet's coverage in favor of that policy.[128] This sort of finding raises concerns that ownership concentration affects what gets reported, though more research is needed on this topic.

Deregulation changes not only the ownership structure of media but also government regulation of what media say. At one time, for example, a "fairness doctrine" required broadcasters that air one side of a story to give time to opposing points of view. But there are now so many radio and television stations that the FCC relies on competition to manage differences of opinion. The abandonment of the fairness doctrine permitted the rise of controversial talk radio shows and partisan cable TV news—if the doctrine had stayed in place, there would be no programs from Rush Limbaugh or Michael Savage, no MSNBC or Fox News.[129] The FCC decided that competition among news outlets protected people by giving them many different sources of news.

There still exists an **equal time rule** that obliges stations that sell advertising time to one political candidate to sell equal time to that person's opponents. When candidates wish to campaign on radio or television, the equal time rule applies.

Regulating Campaigning

During campaigns, a broadcaster must provide equal access to candidates for office and charge them rates no higher than the cheapest rate applicable to commercial advertisers for comparable time. At one time, this rule meant that a station or network could not broadcast a debate between the Democratic and Republican candidates for an office without inviting all other candidates as well—Libertarian, Prohibitionist, or whatever. Thus, a presidential debate in 1980 could be limited to the major candidates, Reagan and Carter (or Reagan and Anderson), only by having the League of Women Voters sponsor it and then allowing radio and TV to cover it as a "news event." Now stations and networks can themselves sponsor debates limited to major candidates.

Though laws guarantee that candidates can buy time at favorable rates on television, not all candidates take advantage of this. The reason is that television is not always an efficient way to reach voters. A television message is literally "broad cast"—spread out to a mass audience without regard to the boundaries of the district in which a candidate is running. Presidential candidates, of course, always use television because their constituency is the whole nation. Candidates for senator or representative, however, may or may not use television, depending on whether the boundaries of their state or district conform well to the boundaries of a television market.

A *media market* is an area easily reached by a television signal; there are about 200 such media markets in the country. if you are a member of Congress from South Bend, Indiana, you come from a television market based there. You can buy ads on the TV stations in South Bend at a reasonable fee. But if you are a member of Congress from northern New Jersey, the only television stations are in nearby New York City. in that market, the costs of a TV ad are very high because they reach a lot of people, most of whom are not in your district and so cannot vote for you. Buying a TV ad would be a waste of money. As a result, a much higher percentage of Senate than House candidates use television ads.

Regulating the Internet and Social Media Platforms

In principle, the Internet is a space free of regulation, and with some notable exceptions, people can say and do more or less whatever they like online. Recently, however, there have been efforts to regulate Internet firms as they relate to politics. In particular, there have been concerns both about privacy, especially as it relates to social media, as well as about online advertising, specifically with respect to campaign advertisements.

First, consider the role of online privacy. Social media networks gather some of the most intimate details of our lives: they know our names and birthdays, where we work, the identities of our children, friends, and family members, and often have access to our photos and other information. In theory, at least, such data is supposed to be closely guarded, but in some instances, that turns out not to be correct. In the aftermath of the 2016 election, *The New York Times* and several other media outlets discovered that Cambridge Analytica, a firm which had worked with the Trump campaign, had gathered information from some 50 million Facebook users without their consent, in violation of Facebook's own rules (as well as the terms of an 2011 agreement with the Federal Trade Commission, which resulted from earlier concerns about how the firm handled user's privacy).[130] The Federal Trade Commission investigated, and found that Facebook misled users about their privacy, and so fined the company $5 billion and required them to create new privacy practices, including a third-party auditor of their practices.[131]

Second, there are increasing concerns about how online companies such as Google, Facebook, and Twitter treat political advertisements. Campaigns and interest groups not only run advertisements on television and radio, they also put them online—you might see them as part of a Google search result, or in your Facebook, Twitter, or Instagram feed. Such advertising can represent a sensible investment for a campaign, because they could direct the ad only to those in a particular geographic location, making it more cost effective than a TV or radio ad. Further, at least in theory, the campaigns could target the advertisement to each voter, sending one ad to voters concerned about abortion and another ad to those concerned about climate change, for example. Spending on these digital ads has increased rapidly in recent election cycles, and in the 2018 election cycle, campaigns and other groups spent $950 million on them.[132] Equivalent advertisements run on television and radio are regulated by the FEC, but whether such rules apply online is less clear. (The FEC has proposed such rules, but they have not been enacted.)

Some firms have moved to ban or limit such advertisements—in 2019, Twitter announced that it would ban political advertisements altogether,[133] and Google banned targeting specific groups of individuals with ads.[134] Facebook permits political ads, but requires that advertisers verify their identities before purchasing political ads, and has created a database of such ads. Many have called on Facebook and other platforms to fact check the ads before they appear online, but the firm has so far declined to do this.[135] As the importance of the Internet and social media continues to expand in our lives into the future, no doubt such debates will continue as well.

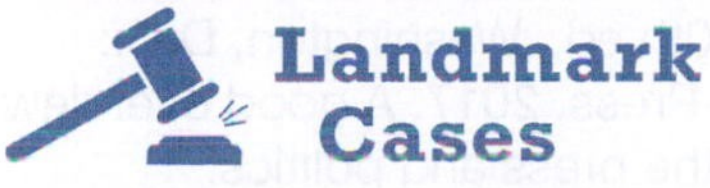

The Rights of the Media

- ***Near v. Minnesota* (1931):** Freedom of the press applies to state governments, so that they cannot impose prior restraint on newspapers.
- ***Miami Herald v. Tornillo* (1974):** A newspaper cannot be required to give someone a right to reply to one of its stories.
- ***New York Times v. Sullivan* (1964):** Public officials may not win a libel suit unless they can prove that the statement was made knowing it to be false or with reckless disregard of its truth.

Learning Objectives

12-1 Trace the evolution of the press in America, and explain how media coverage of politics has changed over time.

Over time, the press evolved from a partisan mouthpiece to an independent political actor. While many Americans still get their news from television, today, many young people get their news via the Internet and social media.

12-2 Describe how the rise of the Internet and social media have influenced the media's effect on politics.

The Internet and social media have changed how people receive information, but their effects on politics are less than many suspected. Most Americans continue to consume a relatively balanced selection of news, with information from largely mainstream sources. While the Internet makes a great deal more information available, it is mostly those who like politics who consume it. It has, however, facilitated certain kinds of online mobilization.

12-3 Explain the main political functions of the media in America, and discuss how the media both enhance and detract from American democracy.

The mass media serves to help educate the public in a democracy. Two particular ways this happens are by setting the public agenda and by serving as a watchdog to maintain political accountability. The media can also lead viewers astray, through framing, covering campaigns as a game, or relying too much on sensationalism and negativity. Viewers should be on guard to protect themselves from these tendencies.

12-4 Discuss the reasons behind lower levels of media trust today, and summarize the arguments for and against media bias.

Overall levels of trust in the media have declined sharply in recent years, both in general and for nearly all specific media outlets. Part of the reason is that politicians from both parties attack the media as biased, leading ordinary citizens to think the media is biased (and hence less trustworthy). Overall, the evidence suggests that there is not much systematic bias in favor of one party or the other in the media.

12-5 Explain how the government controls and regulates the media.

Government regulations control both media ownership and media content, though the First Amendment prohibits many stricter sorts of interference.

To Learn More

To search many news sources: **https://dp.la** (Digital Public Library of America)

Analyses of the press:

Nonpartisan view: **www.cmpa.com** (Center for Media and Public Affairs)

Liberal view: **www.fair.org** (Fairness & Accuracy in Reporting)

Conservative view: **www.mrc.org** (Media Research Center)

Public opinion about the press:

Pew Research Center: **www.pewresearch.org**

National media:

New York Times: **www.nytimes.com**

Wall Street Journal: **www.wsj.com**

Washington Post: **www.washingtonpost.com**

Compilation of major daily news sources: **www.realclearpolitics.com**

Graber, Doris A and Johanna Dunaway. *Mass Media and American Politics,* 10th ed., Washington, D.C.: Congressional Quarterly Press, 2017. A good overview of what we know about the press and politics.

Groseclose, Tim. *Left Turn: How Liberal Media Bias Distorts the American Mind.* New York: St. Martin's Press, 2011. The best evidence documenting several examples of pro-liberal/Democratic media bias.

Iyengar, Shanto, and Donald R. Kinder. *News That Matters.* Chicago, IL: University of Chicago Press,

1987. A report of experiments testing the effect of television news on public perceptions of politics.

Ladd, Jonathan. *Why Americans Hate the News and How It Matters.* Princeton, NJ: Princeton University Press, 2012. An exploration of growing public distrust of the mass media.

Lichter, S. Robert, Stanley Rothman, and Linda S. Lichter. *The Media Elite.* Bethesda, MD: Adler and Adler, 1986. A study of the political beliefs of elite journalists and how those beliefs influence what we read and hear.

Patterson, Thomas E. *Out of Order.* New York: Alfred Knopf, 1993. A study of the decline of substantive coverage of campaigns, and the rise of the game frame.

Prior, Markus. *Post-Broadcast Democracy.* New York: Cambridge University Press, 2006. An explanation of how media choice decreases knowledge of and participation in politics.

Schudson, Michael. 2018. *Why Journalism Still Matters*. Cambridge, UK: Polity. An argument that journalism is more relevant than ever to help voters separate fact from fiction.

Stroud, Natalie Jomini. *Niche News: The Politics of News Choice.* New York: Oxford University Press, 2011. Extensive empirical analysis of how political partisanship shapes the news sources that people use.

PART 3

Institutions of Government

But the great security against a gradual concentration of the several powers in the same department consists in giving to those who administer each department the necessary constitutional means and personal motives to resist encroachments of the others.

— FEDERALIST NO. 51

Chip Somodevilla/Getty Images News/Getty Images

CHAPTER 13

Congress

Learning Objectives

13-1 Contrast congressional and parliamentary systems.

13-2 Trace the evolution of Congress in American politics.

13-3 Discuss who serves in Congress and what influences their votes.

13-4 Summarize the organization of Congress.

13-5 Explain how a bill becomes a law.

13-6 Discuss possibilities for congressional reform.

If you are like most Americans, you trust the Supreme Court, respect the presidency—whether or not you like the president—and dislike Congress, even if you like your own representative and senators. Congress is the most unpopular branch of government, but it is also the most important one: you cannot understand the national government without first understanding Congress. Glance at the Constitution and you will see why Congress is so important: the first four and a half pages are about Congress, while the presidency gets only a page and a half and the Supreme Court about three-quarters of a page.

To the Framers of the Constitution, the bicameral (two-chamber) Congress was "the first branch." They expected Congress to wield most of the national government's powers, including its most important ones like the "power of the purse" (encompassing taxation and spending decisions) and the ultimate authority to declare war. They understood Congress as essential to sustaining federalism (guaranteeing two senators to each state without regard to state population) and maintaining the separation of powers (ensuring that no lawmaker would be allowed to serve in either of the other two branches while in Congress). They also viewed Congress as the linchpin of the system of checks and balances, constitutionally empowered as it was both to override presidential vetoes and to determine the structure and the jurisdiction of the federal judiciary, including the Supreme Court. We delineate the constitutional powers of Congress in Table 13.1, and spell out the requirements to serve in Congress in Table 13.2.

Most contemporary Americans and many experts, however, think of Congress not as the first branch but as "the broken branch," unable to address the nation's most pressing domestic, economic, and international problems in an effective way; unduly responsive to powerful organized special interests; awash in nonstop campaign fundraising and other activities that many believe border on political corruption; and unlikely to fix itself through real reforms.[1]

Consistent with this "broken branch" view, in recent decades, less than one-third of Americans typically have approved of Congress. In the late 1990s and early 2000s, ratings in the 30s and 40s were the norm. In recent years, however, ratings have typically been one-half that earlier level (around 20 percent), and have sometimes even dipped below 10 percent, as they did in 2013 after the government shutdown.

Many academic analysts and veteran Washington journalists echo the popular discontent with Congress as the broken branch, but the experts focus on two more things, the first a paradox and the second a puzzle. The paradox is that most Americans consistently disapprove of Congress yet routinely reelect their own members to serve in it. In political scientist Richard F. Fenno's famous phrase, if "Congress is the broken branch then how come we love our congressmen so much more than our Congress?"[2] Despite public approval ratings that are frequently dismal, almost all congressional incumbents who have sought reelection have won it, most by comfortable margins.

partisan polarization
Heightened conflict between elected Democrats and Republicans

Even in elections in which "anti-incumbent" public sentiment seems rife and voters effect a change in party control of one or both chambers of Congress, incumbents prevail and dominate the institution. For example, in the 2018 midterm elections, Republicans lost their Congressional majority, but still 91 percent of House members who sought reelection won it (senators seeking reelection won at just slightly lower levels). This is the rule, not the exception: in election after election, the vast majority of incumbents—typically more than 90 percent—win reelection. Americans may dislike Congress, but they rarely vote out their member of Congress. Later in the chapter, we will explore several different answers to the paradox, although none of them fully resolve it.

The puzzle is why the post-1970 Congress has become even more polarized by partisanship and divided by ideology, and whether this development reflects ever-widening political cleavages among average Americans, or instead, constitutes a disconnect between the people and their representatives on Capitol Hill.

« Then During 1890–1910, about two-thirds of all votes in Congress evoked a party split, and in several sessions more than half the roll calls found about 90 percent of each party's members opposing the other party.[3] But such polarization faded over the first few decades of the 20th century, and by the 1970s, such **partisan polarization** in Congress was very much the exception to the rule. Well into the 1960s, Congress commonly passed major legislation on most issues on a bipartisan basis, and liberal members and conservative members held leadership positions in both parties and in both chambers.

Such liberal and conservative voting blocs as existed typically crossed party lines, like the mid-20th-century conservative bloc featuring Republicans and Southern Democrats. Leaders in Congress in each party were usually veteran politicians interested mainly in winning elections, dispensing patronage, obtaining tangible benefits for their own districts or states and constituents, and keeping institutional power and perks. Even members with substantial seniority did not get the most coveted committee chairmanships unless they were disposed to practice legislative politics as the art of the possible and the art of the deal. This meant forging interparty coalitions and approaching interbranch (legislative–executive) relations in ways calculated to result ultimately in bipartisan bargains and compromises, and doing so even on controversial issues and even when congressional leaders and the president were not all in the same party.

*** Now** When the 91st Congress ended in 1970, the more liberal half of the House had 29 Republicans and the more conservative half of the House had 59 Democrats.[4] By the time the 105th Congress ended in 1998, the more liberal half of the House had only 10 Republicans while the more conservative half of the House had zero Democrats.[5] (Zero!) In recent years, liberal Republicans and conservative Democrats became virtually extinct in both the House and the Senate—even the most liberal Republican is now to the right of the most conservative Democrat. As a result, party-line votes are increasingly common. For example, in 2010, the Patient Protection and Affordable Care Act (better known as Obamacare) proposed by Democrats passed in Congress without a single Republican voting for it, and the 2017 Tax Cut and Jobs Act passed without a single Democrat voting for it.

These are not the only examples of this sort of deep partisan division in Congress. In 2011, congressional partisanship hit an all-time high: Republicans in the House voted with their party's caucus 91 percent of the time, which was a new record for party unity. Sadly, the record was short-lived: in 2013, that figure crept up to 92 percent. Democrats are no less united: 94 percent of Democrats in the Senate voted with their party's caucus in 2013,[6] and party unity for both political parties has remained high since then. All of this makes it clear that members of Congress are deeply polarized. While we saw in Chapter 7 that the mass public has sorted but not polarized, the same cannot be said for our elected officials.

We will explore the reasons for this congressional polarization later in the chapter. But three things are clear. First, Congress has never perfectly embodied the Founders' fondest hopes for the first branch—not when the First Congress met in 1789–1791 (and wrangled endlessly over the Bill of Rights); not during the decades before, during, and just after the Civil War; not during the late 19th century through 1970; and certainly not since.

TABLE 13.1 | The Powers of Congress (Article 1, Section 8)

- To lay and collect taxes, duties, imposts, and excises
- To borrow money
- To regulate commerce with foreign nations and among the states
- To establish rules for naturalization (i.e., becoming a citizen) and bankruptcy
- To coin money, set its value, and punish counterfeiting
- To fix the standard of weights and measures
- To establish a post office and post roads
- To issue patents and copyrights to inventors and authors
- To create courts inferior to (below) the Supreme Court
- To define and punish piracies, felonies on the high seas, and crimes against the law of nations
- To declare war
- To raise and support an army and navy and make rules for their governance
- To provide for a militia (reserving to the states the right to appoint militia officers and to train the militia under congressional rules)
- To exercise exclusive legislative powers over the seat of government (the District of Columbia) and other places purchased to be federal facilities (forts, arsenals, dockyards, and "other needful buildings")
- To "make all laws which shall be necessary and proper for carrying into execution the foregoing powers, and all other powers vested by this Constitution in the government of the United States." (*Note:* This "necessary and proper," or "elastic," clause has been generously interpreted by the Supreme Court, as explained in Chapter 16.)

TABLE 13.2 | Qualifications for Entering Congress and Privileges of Serving in Congress

Representative	• Must be 25 years of age (when seated, not when elected) • Must have been a citizen of the United States for seven years • Must be an inhabitant of the state from which elected *(Note:* Custom, but *not* the Constitution, requires that representatives live in the district that they represent.)
Senator	• Must be 30 years of age (when seated, not when elected) • Must have been a citizen of the United States for nine years • Must be an inhabitant of the state from which elected
Judging Qualifications	• Each house is the judge of the "elections, returns, and qualifications" of its members. Thus, Congress alone can decide disputed congressional elections. On occasion, it has excluded a person from taking a seat on the grounds that the election was improper. Either house can punish a member—by reprimand, for example—or, by a two-thirds vote, expel a member.
Privileges	• Members of Congress have certain privileges, the most important of which, conferred by the Constitution, is that "for any speech or debate in either house they shall not be questioned in any other place." This doctrine of " privileged speech" has been interpreted by the Supreme Court to mean that members of Congress cannot be sued or prosecuted for anything that they say or write in connection with their legislative duties. • When Senator Mike Gravel read the Pentagon Papers—some then-secret government documents about the Vietnam War—into the *Congressional Record* in defiance of a court order restraining their publication, the Court held that this was "privileged speech" and beyond challenge *(Gravel v. United States,* 408 U.S. 606, 1972). But when Senator William Proxmire issued a press release critical of a scientist doing research on monkeys, the Court decided the scientist could sue him for libel because a press release was not part of the legislative process *(Hutchinson v. Proxmire,* 443 U.S. 111, 1979).

James Madison envisioned members of Congress as "proper guardians of the public weal"—public-spirited representatives of the people who would govern by intelligently mediating and dispassionately resolving conflicts among the nation's competing financial, religious, and other interests.[7] Representatives or senators who might instead fan partisan passions and refuse to compromise were disparaged by Madison as selfish, unenlightened, or "theoretic politicians" (what today we might call "extremists," "hyper-partisans," or "ideologues").[8] At least if judged by the Founders' highest aspirations for the first branch and its members, Congress has always been something of a broken branch.

Second, Congress is now home to ideologically distinct political parties that seem more unified than ever with respect to how their respective members vote, but the body still does not come close to matching the near-total party unity that has been typical in the national legislatures of the United Kingdom and other parliamentary democracies.

Third, Madison and the other Framers expressly rejected a parliamentary system like Great Britain's in favor of a system featuring both a separation of powers and checks and balances. They understood the fundamental differences between a "congress" and a "parliament," and so must every present-day student who hopes to really understand the U.S. Congress.

13-1 Congress Versus Parliament

The United States (along with many Latin American nations) has a congress; the United Kingdom (along with most Western European nations) has a parliament. A hint as to the difference between the two kinds of legislatures can be found in the original meanings of the words. *Congress* derives from a Latin term that means "a coming together," a meeting, as of representatives from various places. *Parliament* comes from a French word, *parler,* which means "to talk."

There is of course plenty of talking—some critics say there is nothing *but* talking—in the U.S. Congress, and certainly members of a parliament represent to a degree their local districts. But the differences implied by the names of the lawmaking groups are real ones, with profound significance for how laws are made and how the government is run. These differences affect two important aspects of lawmaking bodies: how one becomes a member and what one does as a member.

Ordinarily, candidates become members of a parliament (such as the British House of Commons) by persuading a political party to put their names on the ballot. Though usually a local party committee selects a person to be its candidate, that committee often takes suggestions from national party headquarters. The local group selects as its candidate someone willing to support the national party program and leadership. In the election, voters in the district choose not between two or three personalities running for office, but between two or three national parties.

By contrast, a person becomes a candidate for representative or senator in the U.S. Congress by running in a primary election. As we discussed in Chapter 9, parties may try to influence the outcome of primary elections, but they cannot determine them.

As a result of these different systems, a parliament tends to be made up of people loyal to the national party leadership who meet to debate and vote on party issues. A congress, on the other hand, tends to be made up of people who think of themselves as independent representatives of their districts or states and who, while willing to support their party on many matters, expect to vote as their (or their constituents') beliefs and interests require.

Once they are in the legislature, members of a parliament discover they can make only one important decision—whether or not to support the government. The government in a parliamentary system such as that of the United Kingdom consists of a prime minister and various cabinet officers selected from the party that has the most seats in parliament. As long as the members of that party vote together, that government will remain in power. Should members of a party in power in parliament decide to vote against their leaders, the leaders lose office, and a new government must be formed. With so much at stake, the leaders of a party in parliament have a powerful incentive to keep their followers in line. They insist that all members of the party vote together on almost all issues. If someone refuses, the penalty is often drastic: The party does not renominate the offending member in the next election.

Members of the U.S. Congress do not select the head of the executive branch of government—that is done by the voters when they choose a president. Far from making members of Congress less powerful, this makes them more powerful. Representatives and senators can vote on proposed laws without worrying that their votes will cause the government to collapse and without fearing that a failure to support their party will lead to their removal from the ballot in the next election.

Indeed, despite record levels of party unity in recent years, members of both parties have rebuked their leaders and yet remained in office. For example, conservative Republicans effectively forced Republican John Boehner to resign as Speaker of the House in 2015. While Boehner—and his successor as Speaker, Paul Ryan—may have been unhappy with this behavior, they could not remove these Republicans from office (or really do all that much to punish them).

Congress has independent powers, defined by the Constitution, that it can exercise without regard to presidential preferences. Political parties do not control nominations for office, and thus they cannot discipline members of Congress who fail to support the party leadership. Because Congress is constitutionally independent of the president, and because party discipline is highly imperfect, individual members of Congress are free to express their views and vote as they wish. They are also free to become involved in the most minute details of law-making, budget making, and supervising the administration of laws. They do this through an elaborate set of committees and subcommittees.

A real parliament, such as that in Britain, is an assembly of party representatives who choose a government and discuss major national issues. The principal daily work of a parliament is debate. A congress, such as that in the United States, is a meeting place of the representatives of local constituencies—districts and states. Members of the U.S. Congress can initiate, modify, approve, or reject laws, and they share with the president supervision of the administrative agencies of the government. The principal work of a congress is representation and action, most of which takes place in committees.

What this means in practical terms to the typical legislator is easy to see. Because members of the British House of Commons have little independent power, they get rather little in return. They are provided a modest salary, have a small staff, are allowed only limited sums to buy stationery, and can make a few free local telephone calls. Each is given a desk, a filing cabinet, and a telephone, but not always in the same place.

By contrast, a member of the U.S. House of Representatives, even a junior one, has power and is rewarded accordingly. For example, in 2020, each member earned a substantial base salary ($174,000) plus generous health care and retirement benefits, and was entitled to a large office (or "clerk-hire") allowance, to pay for about two dozen staffers. (Each chamber's majority and minority leaders earned $193,400 a year, and the Speaker of the House earned $223,500.) Each member also received individual allowances for travel, computer services, and the like. In addition, each member could mail newsletters and certain other documents to constituents for free using the "franking privilege." Senators, and representatives with seniority, received even larger benefits. Each senator is entitled to a generous office budget and legislative

Images 13.1, 13.2, and 13.3 Three powerful Speakers of the House: Thomas B. Reed (1889–1891, 1895–1899) (left), Joseph G. Cannon (1903–1911) (center), and Sam Rayburn (1941–1947, 1949–1953, 1955–1961) (right). Reed put an end to a filibuster in the House by refusing to allow dilatory motions and by counting as "present"—for purposes of a quorum-members in the House even though they were not voting. Cannon further enlarged the Speaker's power by refusing to recognize members who wished to speak without Cannon's approval and by increasing the power of the Rules Committee, over which he presided. Cannon was stripped of much of his power in 1910. Rayburn's influence rested more on his ability to persuade than on his formal powers.

assistance allowance and is free to hire as many staff members as needed with the money. These examples are not given to suggest that members of Congress are over-rewarded, but only that their importance as individuals in our political system can be inferred from the resources they command.

Because the United States has a congress made up of people chosen to represent their states and districts, rather than a parliament that represents competing political parties, no one should be surprised to learn that members of the U.S. Congress are more concerned with their own constituencies and careers than with the interests of any organized party or program of action. Because Congress does not choose the president, members of Congress know that worrying about the voters they represent is much more important than worrying about whether the president succeeds with his programs. These two factors taken together mean that Congress tends to be a decentralized institution, with members more interested in their own views and those of their voters than with the programs proposed by the president.

Indeed, the Founders designed Congress in ways that almost inevitably make it unpopular with voters. Americans want government to act clearly and decisively. Americans dislike political arguments, the activities of special-interest groups, and the endless pulling and hauling that often precede any congressional decision. But the people who feel this way are deeply divided about what government should do: Be liberal? Be conservative? Spend money? Cut taxes? Support abortions? Stop abortions? Because they are divided, and because members of Congress must worry about how voters feel, it is inevitable that on controversial issues Congress will engage in endless arguments, worry about what interest groups (who represent different groups of voters) think, and work out compromise decisions. When it does those things, however, many people are disappointed and say they have a low opinion of Congress.

Of course, a member of Congress might explain all these constitutional facts to the people, but not many members are eager to tell their voters that they do not really understand how Congress was created and organized. Instead, they run for reelection by promising voters they will go back to Washington and "clean up that mess."

13-2 The Evolution of Congress

The Framers chose to place legislative powers in the hands of a congress rather than a parliament for philosophical and practical reasons. They did not want to have all powers concentrated in a single governmental institution, even one that was popularly elected because they feared such a concentration could lead to rule by an oppressive or impassioned majority. At the same time, they knew the states were jealous of their independence and would never consent to a national constitution if it did not protect their interests and strike a reasonable balance between large and small states. Hence, they created a

bicameral legislature A lawmaking body made up of two chambers or parts.

bicameral (two-chamber) **legislature**—with a House of Representatives, whose members are elected directly by the people, and a Senate, consisting of two members from each state who are chosen by the legislatures of each state. Though "all legislative powers" were vested in Congress, those powers would be shared with the president (who could veto acts of Congress), limited to powers explicitly conferred on the federal government, and, as it turned out, subject to the power of the Supreme Court to declare acts of Congress unconstitutional.

For decades, critics of Congress complained that the body cannot plan or act quickly. They are right, but two competing values are at stake: centralization versus decentralization. If Congress acted quickly and decisively as a body, then there would have to be strong central leadership, restrictions on debate, few opportunities for stalling tactics, and minimal committee interference. If, on the other hand, the interests of individual members—and the constituencies they represent—were protected or enhanced, then there would have to be weak leadership, rules allowing for delay and discussion, and many opportunities for committee activity.

Though there have been periods of strong central leadership in Congress, the general trend for much of the 20th century was toward decentralizing decision making and enhancing the power of the individual member at the expense of the congressional leadership. That said, the recent rise in polarization has somewhat reversed that trend, though leaders today are less powerful than those of the late 19th and early 20th centuries (the apogee of the speaker's power).

This decentralization may not have been inevitable. Most American states have constitutional systems quite similar to the federal one, yet in many state legislatures, such as those in New York, Massachusetts, and Indiana, the leadership is quite powerful. In part, the position of these strong state legislative leaders may be the result of the greater strength of political parties in some states than in the nation as a whole. In large measure, however, it is a consequence of permitting state legislative leaders to decide who shall chair what committee and who shall receive what favors.

The House of Representatives, though always powerful, often has changed the way in which it is organized and led. In some periods, it has given its leader, the Speaker, a lot of power. In other periods, it has given much of that power to the chairs of the House committees. In still other periods, it has allowed individual members to acquire great influence. To simplify a complicated story, the How Things Work box starting on page 308 outlines six different periods in the history of the House.

The House faces fundamental problems: it wants to be big (it has 435 members) and powerful, and its members want to be powerful as individuals and as a group. But being big makes it hard for the House to be powerful unless some small group is given the authority to run it. If a group runs the place, however, then individual members lack much power. Individuals can gain power, but only at the price of making the House harder to run and thus reducing its collective power in government. There is no lasting solution to these dilemmas, and so the House will always be undergoing changes.

The Senate does not face any of these problems (we review important House/Senate differences in Table 13.3). It is small enough (100 members) that it can be run without giving much authority to any small group of leaders. In addition, it has escaped some of the problems the House once faced. During the period leading up to the Civil War, it was carefully balanced so that the number of senators from slave-owning states exactly equaled the number from free states. Hence, fights over slavery rarely arose in the Senate.

From the first, the Senate was small enough that no time limits had to be placed on how long a senator could speak. This meant there never was anything like a Rules Committee that controlled the amount of debate.

Finally, senators were not elected by the voters until the 20th century. Before that, they were picked instead by state legislatures. Thus senators often were the leaders of local party organizations, with an interest in funneling jobs back to their states.

The big changes in the Senate came not from any fight about how to run it (nobody ever really ran it), but from a dispute over how its members should be chosen. For more than a century after the Founding, members of the Senate were chosen by state legislatures. Though often these legislatures picked popular local figures to be senators, just as often there was intense political maneuvering among the leaders of various factions, each struggling to win (and sometimes buy) the votes necessary to become senator. By the end of the 19th century, the Senate was known as the Millionaires' Club because of the number of wealthy party leaders and businessmen in it. There arose a demand for the direct, popular election of senators.

Naturally the Senate resisted, and without its approval the necessary constitutional amendment could not pass Congress. When some states threatened to demand a new constitutional convention, the Senate feared that such a convention would change more than just the way in which senators were chosen. A protracted struggle ensued, during which many state legislatures devised ways to ensure that the senators they picked would already have won a popular election. The Senate finally agreed

TABLE 13.3 | Comparing the House of Representatives and the Senate

House		Senate
• At least 25 years of age (when seated, not elected) • Citizen of the United States for at least seven years • Inhabit the state from which elected (it is customary but *not* required by the Constitution, that representatives live in the district they represent)	← Qualifications →	• At least 30 years of age (when seated, not elected) • Citizen of the United States for at least nine years • Inhabit the state from which elected
435	← Number of Members →	100
2 Years	← Length of Terms →	6 Years
• Legislative authority • Impeach • Power of the purse • Elect the president in the case of a tie in the Electoral College • Approve appointments to the vice presidency • Approve treaties that involve foreign trade • Investigation and oversight • Declare war	← Special Powers →	• Legislative authority • Conduct impeachment trials • Review and approve presidential nominees • Approve treaties made by the president (by a two-thirds vote) and amend treaties • Investigation and oversight • Declare war • Elect the vice president in case of a tie in the electoral college
• Many rules, more formal • May expel members of the House with a two-thirds vote • May censure members of the House • Decide disputed House elections	← Procedures →	• Few rules, less formal • May expel members of the Senate with a two-thirds vote • May censure members of the Senate • Filibuster and cloture • Decide disputed Senate elections
• "Privileged speech"—members of Congress cannot be sued or prosecuted for anything they say or write in connection with their legislative duties	← Privileges →	• "Privileged speech"—members of Congress cannot be sued or prosecuted for anything they say or write in connection with their legislative duties

Constitutional Connections | From Convention to Congress

Article I of the Constitution (on Congress) is several times longer than Article II (on the presidency and executive branch) and Article III (on the federal judiciary) combined. The Framers treated Congress as "the first branch" of American national government. As evidenced by the records of the debates among the 55 men who convened the Constitutional Convention, the Framers had good philosophical reasons for treating the new republic's new legislature with special care. Besides, most of the delegates were themselves former legislators: 41 of the 55 had served, or at the time of the Convention were still serving, as members of the Continental Congress. Moreover, 28 of the 55 delegates would go on to serve in the new Congress created by Article I: four served in both the House and the Senate; nine served in the House only; and 15 served in the Senate only. Among those who went on to serve in the House was the Constitution's chief intellectual architect, James Madison. Madison would also go on to serve as secretary of state (under President Thomas Jefferson) and, of course, as the nation's fourth president (succeeding Jefferson).

Source: Adapted from the U.S. National Archives and Records Administration, "The Founding Fathers: A Brief Overview," 2013.

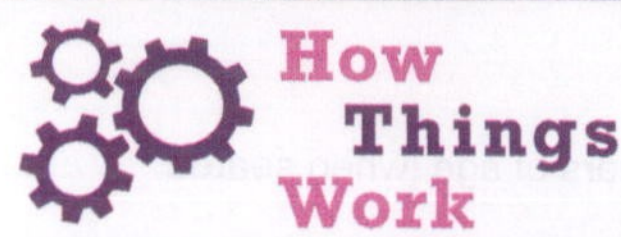

House History: Six Phases

Phase One: The Powerful House

During the first three administrations—of George Washington, John Adams, and Thomas Jefferson—leadership in Congress often was supplied by the president or his cabinet officers. Rather quickly, however, Congress began to assert its independence. The House of Representatives was the preeminent institution, overshadowing the Senate.

Phase Two: The Divided House

In the late 1820s, the preeminence of the House began to wane. Andrew Jackson asserted the power of the presidency by vetoing legislation he did not like. The party unity necessary for a Speaker, or any leader, to control the House was shattered by the issue of slavery. Of course, representatives from the South did not attend during the Civil War, and their seats remained vacant for several years after it ended. A group called the Radical Republicans, led by men such as Thaddeus Stevens of Pennsylvania, produced strong majorities for measures aimed at punishing the defeated South. But as time passed, the hot passions generated by the war began to cool, and it became clear that the leadership of the House remained weak.

Phase Three: The Speaker Rules

Toward the end of the 19th century, the Speaker of the House gained power. When Thomas B. Reed of Maine became Speaker in 1889, he obtained by vote of the Republican majority more authority than any of his predecessors, including the right to select the chairs and members of all committees. He chaired the Rules Committee and decided what business would come up for a vote, any limitations on debate, and who would be allowed to speak and who would not. In 1903, Joseph G. Cannon of Illinois became Speaker. He tried to maintain Reed's tradition, but he had many enemies within his Republican ranks.

Phase Four: The House Revolts

In 1910–1911, the House revolted against "Czar" Cannon, voting to strip the Speaker of his right to appoint committee chairs and to remove him from the Rules Committee. The powers lost by the Speaker flowed to the party caucus, the Rules Committee, and the chairs of the standing committees. It was not, however, until the 1960s and 1970s that House members struck out against all forms of leadership.

Phase Five: The Members Rule

Newly elected Democrats could not get the House to vote on a meaningful civil rights bill until 1964 because powerful committee chairs, most of them from the South, kept such legislation bottled up. In response, Democrats changed the rules so that chairpersons lost much of their authority.

Library of Congress Prints and Photographs Division (LC-DIG-ppmsca-09398)

Image 13.4 One of the most powerful Speakers of the House, Henry Clay, is shown here addressing the U.S. Senate around 1850.

Beginning in the 1970s, committee chairs would no longer be selected simply on the basis of seniority: they had to be elected by the members of the majority party. Chairpersons could no longer refuse to call committee meetings, and most meetings had to be public. Committees without subcommittees had to create them and allow their members to choose subcommittee chairs. Individual members' staffs were greatly enlarged, and half of all majority-party members were chairs of at least one committee or subcommittee.

Phase Six: The Leadership Returns

Because every member had power, it was harder for the House to get anything done. By slow steps, culminating in some sweeping changes made in 1995, there were efforts to restore some of the power the Speaker had once had. The number of committees and subcommittees was reduced. Republican Speaker Newt Gingrich dominated the choice of committee chairs, often passing over more senior members for more agreeable junior ones. But Gingrich's demise was as quick as his rise. Following the 1995 government shutdown, several other scandals, and losses in the 1998 midterms, Gingrich—who resigned—was replaced by a more moderate Speaker, Republican Dennis Hastert of Illinois.

When the 110th Congress began in 2007, Democrat Nancy Pelosi of California held the Speaker's gavel. Pelosi was the 60th Speaker in House history and the first woman to lead the House. Pelosi's most significant legislative achievement was securing enough votes to pass the Affordable Care Act. Following heavy Democratic losses in the 2010 midterm elections, Pelosi was succeeded as Speaker by Republican John Boehner of Ohio in January 2011. Following unrest in his caucus, largely from conservatives, Boehner stepped down as Speaker in 2015, and was replaced by Paul Ryan of Wisconsin. Republicans lost 40 seats and their majority in 2018 (Ryan announced earlier in the year he was retiring from Congress). In 2019, Nancy Pelosi once again became Speaker, becoming only the seventh person to serve as Speaker in nonconsecutive terms.

to a constitutional amendment that required the popular election of its members, and in 1913 the Seventeenth Amendment was approved by the necessary three-fourths of the states. Ironically, given the intensity of the struggle over this question, no great change in the composition of the Senate resulted; most of those members who had first been chosen by state legislatures managed to win reelection by popular vote.

The other major issue in the development of the Senate was the filibuster. A **filibuster** is a prolonged speech, or series of speeches, made to delay action in a legislative assembly. It had become a common—and unpopular—feature of Senate life by the end of the 19th century. It was used by liberals and conservatives alike and for lofty as well as self-serving purposes. The first serious effort to restrict the filibuster came in 1917, after an important foreign policy measure submitted by President Wilson had been talked to death by, as Wilson put it, "eleven willful men." Rule 22 was adopted by a Senate fearful of tying a president's hands during a wartime crisis. The rule provided that debate could be cut off if two-thirds of the senators present and voting agreed to a "cloture" motion (it has since been revised to allow 60 senators to cut off debate). Two years later, it was first invoked successfully when the Senate voted cloture to end, after 55 days, the debate over the Treaty of Versailles.

AP Images/Uncredited

Image 13.5 Several Senate Democrats led a filibuster in June 2016 to call for stronger gun control measures.

Despite the existence of Rule 22, the tradition of unlimited debate remains strong in the Senate, and examples of famous filibusters abound. One—by former South Carolina Senator Strom Thurmond—lasted for more than 24 hours (Thurmond was filibustering a proposed Civil Rights Act). We take up the filibuster's contemporary effects later in the chapter.

filibuster *An attempt to defeat a bill in the Senate by talking indefinitely, thus preventing the Senate from taking action on the bill.*

13-3 Who Is in Congress?

With power so decentralized in Congress, the kind of person elected to it is especially important. Since each member exercises some influence, the beliefs and interests of each individual affect policy. Viewed simplistically, most members of Congress seem the same: the typical representative or senator is a middle-aged white Protestant male lawyer. If all such persons usually thought and voted alike, that would be an interesting fact, but they do not, and so it is necessary to explore the great diversity of views among seemingly similar people.

Gender and Race

Congress has gradually become less male and less white. Between 1950 and 2019, the number of women in the House increased from 9 to 102 (plus 4 nonvoting delegates from Washington, DC, U.S. territories, and Puerto Rico) and the number of African Americans increased from 2 to 52 (plus 2 delegates). There are also 40 Latino members (plus 2 delegates), and 4 Native American members.[9]

Until recently, the Senate changed much more slowly (see Figure 13.1). Before the 1992 election, there were no African Americans and only two women in the Senate. But in 1992, four more women, including one African American woman, Carol Mosely Braun of Illinois, were elected. These numbers have continued to increase since then and today in the 116th Congress, 25 women, 3 African Americans, and 4 Latinos serve in the U.S. Senate.

Figure 13.1 **African Americans, Hispanics, and Women in Congress, 1971–2019**

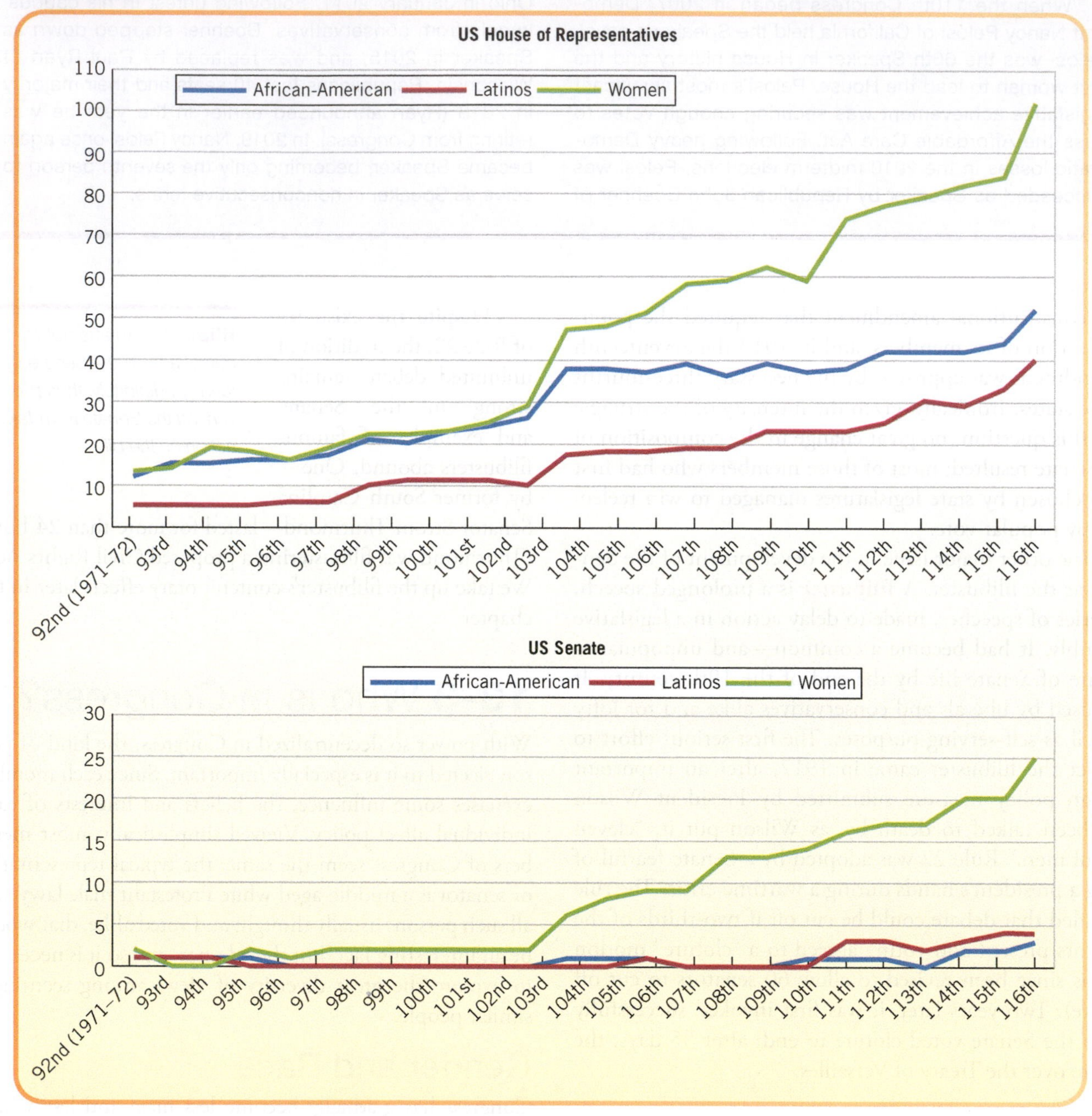

Source: Congressional Quarterly, various years.

Q **What consequences do you think these demographic changes will have? In what other ways have the demographics of members of Congress changed, and what are the implications of those changes?**

majority-minority districts
Congressional district where a majority of voters are racial/ethnic minorities.

descriptive representation
When citizens are represented by elected officials from their same racial/ethnic background.

Part of the increase in African American and Latino members of Congress comes from the creation of **majority-minority districts**. In such districts, a majority of residents are racial or ethnic minorities. These districts are designed to allow these groups to elect candidates of choice, and were created as a result of litigation surrounding the Voting Rights Act. Most often, the candidate of choice is someone from their racial or ethnic group: for example, districts with a majority of African American voters typically, though not always, elect an African American candidate. Such districts have played a key role in bringing more racial and ethnic minorities into Congress. As a result, such districts certainly increase **descriptive representation**, when a minority officeholder represents minority constituents. Such descriptive representation is valuable because someone from a minority group will typically be best positioned to understand and represent the needs of that group.[10]

Yet some scholars claim that such districts may inadvertently harm minority interests. To create majority-minority districts, many racial and ethnic minorities need to be packed into a single district, and as a result, surrounding districts typically have fewer racial and ethnic minorities. This has two consequences. First, members in surrounding districts, because they have fewer minority constituents, have less incentive to respond to the needs of minority voters.[11] Second, these surrounding districts become less likely to elect Democrats to office.[12] This follows because these districts have fewer racial and ethnic minorities, who typically strongly support Democratic candidates.

For example, evidence shows that the creation of new majority-minority districts following the 1990 census helped to elect more Republicans to Congress.[13] Because Democrats often, but not always, support policies that are more in line with the preferences of most racial and ethnic minorities, a Congress with fewer Democrats is less likely to pass legislation favored by racial and ethnic minorities (for example, on policies such as affirmative action). This suggests that while such districts increase symbolic representation, they might decrease **substantive representation**: the ability of voters (in this case, minority voters) to elect officials who will enact policies in line with their preferences.

In the end, then, which is preferable? Is it better to elect more racial and ethnic minorities to Congress, even if it means also passing fewer policies supported by racial and ethnic minorities? Or instead should we aim to elect fewer racial and ethnic minorities to Congress, but disperse minority voters across more districts to elect members who (on average) are more supportive of policies favored by minorities? The answer is unclear, and depends on how one views the relative importance of descriptive and substantive representation.

However one feels about descriptive versus substantive representation, majority-minority districts have increased the power of African American and Latino members in another way. Because such districts are typically quite electorally safe, their members often become senior leaders in Congress, especially on committees. For example, in 1994, African Americans chaired four House committees and Latinos chaired three. When the Democrats retook control of Congress in 2019, African Americans chaired five committees and Latinos chaired two more. Some of the committee chairpersons—such as Charles Rangel and Maxine Waters—have become powerful members of Congress.

substantive representation *Ability of citizens to elect officials who will enact into law policies that the citizens favor.*

Similarly, the first woman to become Speaker (Nancy Pelosi in 2007, and then again in 2019) is a Democrat, and the increase of women in Congress after 1970 has been led by Democrats: in the 116th Congress that began in 2019, 17 of the 25 women in the Senate, and 89 of the 102 women in the House, were Democrats (the four female delegates are split evenly by party).

The 2018 election was particularity notable because so many women, LGBTQ+ individuals, and people of color won election to Congress. While many of these individuals who won in 2018 are Democrats, Republicans are actively trying to recruit more women and minorities as candidates for future elections.[14]

Middle-aged white men with law degrees are still prevalent in Congress, but as Table 13.4 shows, compared with the makeup of the 102nd Congress that began in 1991, the 116th Congress that began in 2019 had not only more women, African Americans, and Latinos, but also fewer lawyers, fewer military veterans, more businesspeople, more people over the age of 55, and more members (about one in five overall) serving their first term.

Incumbency

The recent spike in first-termers in Congress is interesting, but the most important change that has occurred in the composition of Congress has been so gradual that most people have not noticed it. In the 19th century, a large fraction—often a majority—of congressmen served only one term. In 1869, for example, more than half the members of the House were serving their first term in Congress. Being a congressman in those days was not regarded as a career. This was in part because the federal government was not very important (most of the interesting political decisions were made by the states); in part because travel to Washington, DC, was difficult and the city was not a pleasant place in which to live; and in part because being a congressman did not pay well. Furthermore, many congressional districts were highly competitive, with the two political parties fairly evenly balanced in each.

TABLE 13.4 | Who's in Congress, 1991–1992 versus 2019–2020

	102nd Congress (1991–1992)	116th Congress (2019–2020)
Average Age		
House	53	58
Senate	57	63
Occupation		
Law	244	192
Business	189	212
Had served in the military	277	96
Serving a first term	44	99

Source: 102nd Congress data adapted from chart based on Congressional Research Service and Military Officers Association data in John Harwood, "For New Congress, Data Shows Why Polarization Abounds," *New York Times*, 6 March, 2011. 116th Congress data from Congressional Research Service, "Membership of the 116th Congress: A Profile," 7 March, 2019.

By the 1950s, however, serving in Congress had become a career. Between 1863 and 1969, the proportion of first-termers in the House fell from 58 percent to 8 percent.[15] As the public took note of this shift, people began to complain about "professional politicians" being "out of touch with the people," and some pushed for term limits. The issue had a brief burst of popularity in the mid-1990s, and numerous states passed laws to limits the terms of members of Congress. In 1995, however, the Supreme Court ruled that any such term limits on federal legislators could only be imposed by a constitutional amendment,[16] and efforts to pass one in Congress failed (some states do have term limits for state legislators, however). The issue largely vanished from popular discussion until Donald Trump resurrected the issue during the 2016 election. After Trump's win, several legislators introduced constitutional amendments to impose term limits, but the issue faces a long and uphill battle.[17]

Term limits remain popular with the public: a 2016 Quinnipiac poll found that 82 percent of the public would impose term limits if given the chance.[18] Scholars who have studied state legislative term limits have found that they have little effect on who gets elected to office (i.e., they do not increase citizen legislators).[19] Second, if anything, they find that term limits *decrease* politicians' responsiveness to public opinion (since term-limited legislators know they cannot run for reelection) and tend to shift power to the executive branch and the bureaucracy.[20] As in many areas, reforms designed to solve one problem can create others!

In more recent years, political forces did what legislation could not—they brought new faces to the capital. Since 2012, there have been at least 52 new members of the House elected in each election, with nearly 100 new members elected in 2018. In each of the last four Congresses, at least one-half of the House had six or fewer years of experience.[21]

But these periodic power shifts accompanied by the arrival of scores of new faces in Congress should not obscure an important fact that was documented decades ago by political scientists and is still true today: Even in elections that result in the out party regaining power, most incumbent House members who seek reelection not only win, but win big, in their districts.[22] And while Senators have been somewhat less secure than House members, most Senate incumbents who have sought reelection have won it by a comfortable margin.

Figure 13.2 shows the 1964–2018 reelection rates for incumbent House and Senate members who sought reelection. Over that span of more than two dozen elections, the average reelection rate for House incumbents was 93 percent and the average reelection rate for Senate incumbents was 82 percent. As Figure 13.2 demonstrates, reelection rates have been consistently high throughout this period. Even in years characterized by an anti-incumbent mood, the vast majority of House and Senate incumbents were typically reelected.

In the 2010 midterm election, despite polls showing mass disaffection with Congress and a strong "anti-incumbent" mood, 85 percent of House incumbents who sought reelection won it (53 House incumbents who sought reelection lost), and 84 percent of Senate

Image 13.6 Senator Tim Scott (R-SC) is one of three African Americans who served in the 116th Senate. He is the first African American to be elected to both the House and the Senate.

incumbents who sought reelection won it (4 Senate incumbents who sought reelection lost, 2 in primary elections and 2 in the general election). And 2014 was another year characterized by anti-incumbent sentiments. The largest-ever number of voters told pollsters that their own member did not deserve reelection (35 percent), which many took to mean a deeply dissatisfied electorate would vote many members out of office.[23] While some highly notable incumbents were defeated, such as Senator Kay Hagan in North Carolina, 95 percent of House members who sought reelection won, as did more than 80 percent of Senators. In 2018, 91 percent of House incumbents, and 84 percent of Senate incumbents, who sought reelection won. Year in and year out, most members of Congress are reelected.

House incumbents who seek reelection normally beat their opponents by 10 points or more. Political scientists call districts that have close elections (when the winner gets less than 55 percent of the vote) **marginal districts** and districts where incumbents win by wide margins (55 percent or more) **safe districts**. By this standard, in the 2016 election, only 7.6 percent of House seats were marginal.[24] But perhaps we should use a stricter definition of safety: winning with 60 percent or more of the vote. Even here, the majority of incumbents would be considered safe. Since the 1970s, more than 60 percent of House members—in some years as high as 80 percent—have been reelected with at least 60 percent of the major-party vote.[25] By contrast, over the same period, less than half of all Senate incumbents who won reelection did so by such a wide margin. Safe states are far less common than safe districts.

Why congressional seats have become less marginal—that is, safer—is not entirely clear, and a number of factors have been proposed. Some of the most prominent ones focus on the resources of incumbents. Incumbents, as we explained in Chapter 10, have a large fundraising advantage over challengers. Further, incumbents are simply much better known than challengers, so they have a built-in advantage in terms of name recognition. Incumbents also do much to deluge the voters with free mailings, travel frequently (and at public expense) to meet constituents, and get their names in the headlines by sponsoring bills or conducting investigations. Simply having a familiar name is important in getting elected, and incumbents find it easier than challengers to make their names known.

marginal districts *Districts in which candidates elected to the House of Representatives win in close elections (typically, less than 55 percent of the vote).*

safe districts *Districts in which incumbents win by a comfortable margin.*

Further, incumbents can use their power to get programs passed or funds spent to benefit their districts—and thereby to benefit themselves.[26] They can help keep an army base open, support the building of a new highway (or block the building of an unpopular one), take credit for federal grants to local schools and hospitals, make certain a particular industry or labor union is protected by tariffs against foreign competition, and so on.

They can also provide individual services to their constituents, helping them locate a lost Social Security check or provide help with a federal agency, such as the IRS or the Department of Veterans Affairs. If a member helps out a voter this way, then that voter is more likely to support the member in the next election.[27]

Figure 13.2 **Reelection Rates for House and Senate Incumbents, 1964–2018**

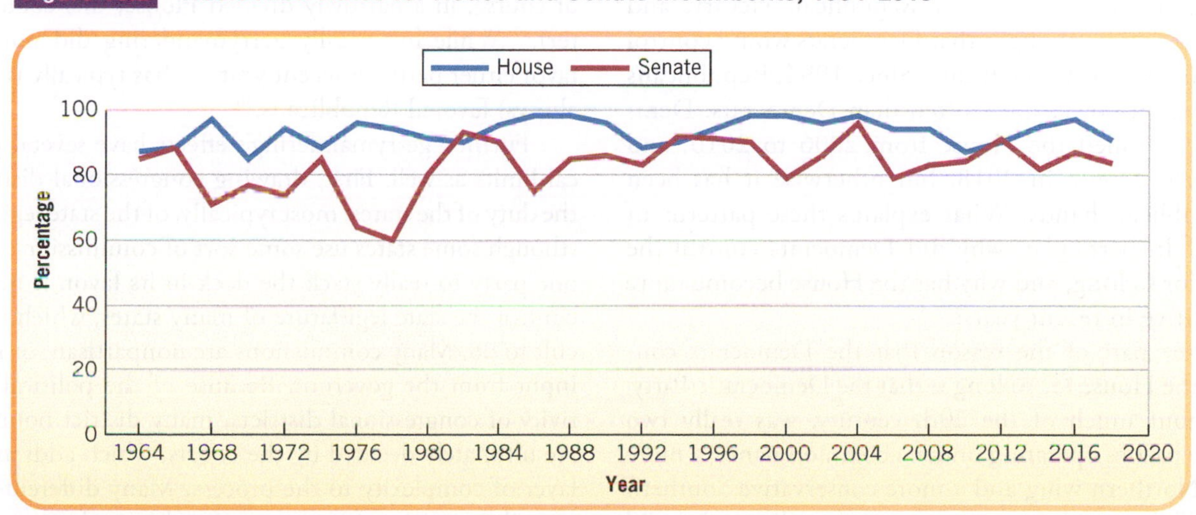

Source: Center for Responsive Politics, "Reelection Rates Over the Years," www.opensecrets.org/overview/reelect.php.

conservative coalition *An alliance between Republicans and conservative Democrats.*

Finally, incumbents over time have learned to behave as if they are at risk even when they are not.[28] No one thought that Joe Crowley, the fourth-ranking House Democrat, would lose his primary to a politically unknown challenger named Alexandria Ocasio-Cortez in 2018, but he did. While losses like Crowley's are relatively rare, close elections are not—many members have had an uncomfortably narrow election win, and even if they have not, they know someone who has. These sorts of unexpected losses and near-losses lead members to always be wary, and to act as if they are not safe, even if they are. So members work hard to raise money, increase their name recognition, and provide services to their constituents, which increases their safety.

Probably all of these factors make some difference and help to explain why districts are so safe today. This has two important implications. First, as we discussed in Chapter 10, there is an incumbency advantage, whereby incumbents do better than challengers (for all of the reasons we discussed above). Second, this incumbency advantage means that in ordinary times no one should expect any dramatic changes in the composition of Congress. Even when elections effect a change in party control in one or both chambers, even when new leaders are in charge and new members abound, many old hands will still be on hand in Congress.

Party

Forty-five Congresses convened between 1933 and 2021 (a new Congress convenes every two years). The Democrats controlled both houses in 27 of these Congresses and at least one house in 33 of them, and they controlled the House continuously from 1952 to 1994. Few scholars predicted the 1994 Republican victory, and many at the time thought that Democrats would control the House well into the future. Since 1994, Republicans have been in power more often than Democrats: Democrats controlled the House from 2006 to 2010, and retook the House in 2018, but otherwise it has been in Republican hands. What explains these patterns of control? In particular, why did Democrats control the House for so long, and why has the House become more competitive in recent years?

A key part of the reason that the Democrats controlled the House for so long is that the Democratic Party, throughout much of the 20th century, was really two separate parties operating under a common name: a more liberal Northern wing and a more conservative Southern wing. While they did not agree on many policies, they did share a common party label and hence formed a large partisan bloc, which allowed them to be the majority party in the House for many decades.

While Northern and Southern Democrats aligned to maintain majority control of the chamber (and with it, control of congressional committees and the legislative process), they typically parted ways when it came to policy. Southern Democrats often would vote with the Republicans in the House or Senate, thereby forming what came to be called the **conservative coalition**. During the 1960s and 1970s, that coalition came together in about one-fifth of all roll-call votes. When it did, it usually won, defeating Northern Democrats. But since the 1980s, and especially since the watershed election of 1994, the conservative coalition has become much less important. The reason is simple: Many Southern Democrats in Congress have been replaced by Southern Republicans, and the Southern Democrats who remain (many of them African Americans) are as liberal as Northern Democrats. This change was an important contributor to the growing levels of polarization we observe in Congress today.

But this factor alone does not explain why the Democrats controlled the House for so long, or why the process is now more competitive. One popular theory among the public, though not among scholars, is that gerrymandering is to blame. As we discussed in Chapter 10, gerrymandering is the process of drawing districts to favor one party or the other. Those who favor this explanation suggest that when Democrats are in power, they tend to draw districts favoring Democrats and vice versa when Republicans are in power. As we discussed in Chapter 10, gerrymandering does influence congressional elections, and it has contributed to electoral safety. But its effect is modest rather than massive. Studies show that gerrymandering affects Congressional election outcomes, but only to a limited degree, typically changing at most a few seats (though, of course, in a narrowly divided House, this could matter).[29] While historically gerrymandering did not really favor either party, in recent years, it has typically (but not always) favored Republicans.[30]

Further, gerrymandering's effects have several practical limits as well. First, drawing congressional districts is the duty of the states, most typically, of the state legislature (though some states use some sort of commission). So for one party to really stack the deck in its favor, it needs to control the state legislature of many states, which is difficult to do. Many commissions are nonpartisan, or receive input from the governor. Because of the political sensitivity of congressional districts, many district boundaries are ultimately decided by the courts, which adds another layer of complexity to the process. Many different actors contribute to drawing congressional boundaries, making it hard for one party to really gain an advantage solely due to redistricting.

The effects of gerrymandering are also constrained by relevant state and federal laws. Federal law requires that districts have equal population, and the courts have interpreted this rather strictly, rejecting even modest deviations in population across congressional districts.[31] Further, as we discussed above, the Voting Rights Act established majority-minority districts, which requires many states to have districts predominantly comprising racial/ethnic minorities. Many states also have relevant state laws that require districts to be contiguous and geographically compact, as well as to respect political boundaries and communities of interest. Even when legislators want to engage in gerrymandering, their ability to do so is constrained by other factors. Even if there were no gerrymandering, many members of Congress would easily be reelected to Congress.

While redistricting alone typically only nets one party or the other a few seats, the Republicans do have a small but persistent advantage in contemporary House elections that stems from geography. Simply put, Republican voters are more evenly spread across districts, whereas Democratic voters are more heavily concentrated in certain districts. Democrats win a large share of voters from racial and ethnic minorities, young people, and liberals, who tend to be clustered in cities. As a result, Democrats tend to carry overwhelmingly districts located in urban areas. While Republicans currently do better in mostly rural districts, those districts are not as skewed toward Republicans because even rural areas tend to have pockets of Democrats (in, say, a college town or a former industrial city). This gives Republicans an important, but certainly not insurmountable, advantage in the House.[32]

Regardless of the size of gerrymandering's effects, several recent lawsuits have challenged the practice. In 2019, the Supreme Court ruled, in a 5-4 decision, that *federal* courts cannot hear challenges to partisan gerrymandering (*Rucho et al. v. Common Cause et al.*). But state courts have been active on this issue. For example, in 2018, the Pennsylvania Supreme Court ruled that the state's congressional districts had been unlawfully gerrymandered to favor Republicans, and replaced the existing map with a new one. Plaintiffs in other states are pushing similar cases, and no doubt this will continue to be an area of active debate in the years to come.

Representation and Polarization

In a decentralized, individualistic institution such as Congress, it is not obvious how its members will behave. They could be devoted to doing whatever their constituents want or, because most voters are not aware of what their representatives do, act in accordance with their own beliefs, the demands of interest groups, or the expectations of congressional leaders. You may think it would be easy to figure out whether members are devoted to their constituents by analyzing how they vote, but that is not quite right. Members can influence legislation in many ways other than by voting: they can conduct hearings, help mark up bills in committee meetings, and offer amendments to the bills proposed by others. A member's final vote on a bill may conceal as much as it reveals; some members may vote for a bill that contains many things they dislike because it also contains a few things they value.

There are at least three theories about how members of Congress behave: representational, organizational, and attitudinal. The *representational* explanation is based on the reasonable assumption that members want to get reelected, and therefore they vote to please their constituents. The *organizational* explanation is based on the equally reasonable assumption that because most constituents do not know how their legislator has voted, it is not essential to please them. But it is important to please fellow members of Congress, whose goodwill is valuable in getting things done and in acquiring status and power in Congress. The *attitudinal* explanation is based on the assumption that the many conflicting pressures on members of Congress cancel one another out, leaving the members virtually free to vote on the basis of their own beliefs. Political scientists have studied, tested, and argued about these (and other) explanations for decades, and nothing like a consensus has emerged. Some facts have been established, however, in regard to these three views.

Representational View

The representational view has some merit under certain circumstances—namely, when constituents have a clear view on some issue and a legislator's vote on that issue is likely to attract their attention. Such is often the case for civil rights laws: representatives of districts with significant numbers of African American voters are unlikely to oppose civil rights bills; representatives of districts with few African Americans are comparatively free to oppose such bills. Prior to the Voting Rights Act, many Southern representatives were able to oppose civil rights measures because their African American constituents were systematically disenfranchised (see the discussion in Chapter 8). On the other hand, many representatives without many African American constituents have supported civil rights bills, partly out of personal belief and partly perhaps because certain white groups in their districts—organized liberals, for example—have insisted on such support.

From time to time, an issue arouses deep passions among voters, and legislators cannot escape the need either

Image 13.7 U.S. Representative Sharice Davids of Kansas is the first LGBTQ+ Native American to serve in Congress. She was first elected in 2018.

to vote as their constituents want, whatever their personal views, or to anguish at length about which side of a divided constituency to support. Gun control has been one such question and the use of federal money to pay for abortions has been another. Some fortunate members of Congress get unambiguous cues from their constituents on these matters, and no hard decision is necessary. Others get conflicting views, and they know that whichever way they vote, it may cost them dearly in the next election. Occasionally, members of Congress in this fix will try to be out of town when the matter comes up for a vote.

You might think that members of Congress who won a close race in the last election—who come from a "marginal" district—would be especially eager to vote the way their constituents want. Research has shown that is not generally the case, however, and there seem to be about as many independent-minded members of Congress from marginal as from safe districts.[33] Perhaps it is because opinion is so divided in a marginal seat that one cannot please everybody; as a result, the representative votes on other grounds.

The limit to the representative explanation is that public opinion is not strong and clear on most measures on which Congress must vote. Many representatives and senators face constituencies that are divided on key issues. Some constituents go to special pains to make their views known (these interest groups were discussed in Chapter 11). But as we indicated, the power of interest groups to affect congressional votes depends, among other things, on whether a legislator sees them as united and powerful or as disorganized and marginal.

But when public opinion is strong and clear, members do respond to it. A recent study nicely illustrates this point. The researchers gave some legislators—but not others—information about public opinion in their districts toward a proposed spending bill. Those who received the information were much more likely to support the position favored by their constituents.[34] This fits with broader studies that show that legislators are highly attuned to public sentiment in their districts, and try to vote in ways that reflect their constituents' views.[35]

Why does constituent opinion exert such a strong effect on member behavior? Because voting counter to the wishes of their constituents put members at grave risk of being voted out of office. If members are repeatedly out of step with public opinion in their districts, then challengers will leap on this pattern of votes in the next election. While most voters do not know how their member of Congress voted on various pieces of legislation, challengers will pounce and exploit votes taken by a member that many constituents would oppose. If a member is too liberal or conservative for their district, they will typically be defeated.[36] Indeed, even one vote against the constituency's wishes can be fatal, especially if it is on a highly salient piece of legislation such as Obamacare.[37] Those members who vote against the district's wishes typically find themselves out of a job.

Organizational View

When voting on matters where constituency interests or opinions are not vitally at stake, members of Congress respond primarily to cues provided by their colleagues. This is the organizational explanation of their votes. The principal cue is party—no other factor explains as much of a member's behavior in office. Even when a Democrat and a Republican represent the same district, with the exact same voters, they will often vote differently (note the parallel to the power of party in shaping voters' views, as we discussed in Chapter 7).

But do not think that members blindly adopt their party's position on the issues with little or no thought—far from it. Nor does the power of party simply reflect the power of party leaders to whip members into adopting the party line. While leaders do have some powers to reward and punish members,[38] those powers are relatively constrained.[39] Rather, the effect of party reflects different values of Democratic and Republican members. Members' party affiliations reflect their beliefs about how the government should be run—in today's Congress, those who want to see a more active role for government are by and large Democrats, and those who want to see the government do less are typically Republicans. Further, Democratic (Republican) members of Congress have similar constituencies to other Democratic (Republican) members, and similar interest groups support them. It is the power of these other influences—the constituents, supporting interest groups, and political values—that lead Democrats and Republicans to vote differently in Congress.

Another influence—closely related to party—could be the view of an important ideological group within the House. A number of groups on both sides of the aisle represent various points of view in the various ideological debates in Congress. On the left are groups like the Congressional Progressive Caucus, and on the right, the House Freedom Caucus.

But party and other organizations do not have clear positions on all matters. For the scores of votes that do not involve the "big questions," a representative or senator is especially likely to be influenced by party members on the sponsoring committee. It is easy to understand why. Suppose you are a Democratic representative from Michigan who is summoned to the floor of the House to vote on a bill to authorize a new weapons system. You may well not understand the bill in any detail, since you are not a member of the authorizing committee. There is no obvious liberal or conservative position on this matter. How do you vote? Simple. You take your cue from several Democrats on the House Armed Services Committee that handled the bill. Some are liberal; others are more moderate. If both liberals and moderates support the bill, you vote for it unhesitatingly. If they disagree, you vote with whichever Democrat is generally closest to your own political ideology. If the matter is one that affects your state, you can take your cue from members of your state's delegation to Congress.

Attitudinal View

Finally, members' own ideologies influence their behavior. This should hardly be surprising. As we saw in Chapter 7, political elites think more ideologically than the public. And as we saw above, it is a member's personal views—their ideology and values—that shapes why party is such a powerful influence. But, as we suggested at the start of this chapter, Congress has become an increasingly ideological organization, that is, its members are more sharply divided by political ideology than they once were. Today, all of Congress's most liberal members are Democrats, and all of its most conservative ones are Republicans.

Why attitudes have hardened along ideological and partisan lines in Congress is a topic of much scholarly debate. Many different factors have contributed to Congress becoming more polarized, and we lack the space to discuss all of them. We discussed a crucial factor above—conservative Southern Democrats gradually became conservative Southern Republicans over the second half of the 20th century. Another factor is that those who are the most involved in politics (the activists) tend to be those with the strongest views, as we discussed in Chapter 7. Most Americans, unlike members of Congress, remain relatively moderate and nonideological. But among those who participate the most, there tends to be more division and ideological thinking.

This division in the electorate supports congressional polarization. As we discussed in earlier chapters, members of Congress respond to those who participate. If those who vote, donate money, and volunteer for campaigns are more extreme, this influences the positions taken by members of Congress. Further, while most voters prefer compromise and bipartisanship, these activists do not; they instead want their members to stand firm for ideological principles,[40] adding further fuel to the polarization fire.

This stands in stark contrast to most ordinary Americans, who are moderate, are largely nonideological, and like compromise and consensus. Unfortunately, most ordinary Americans are also not terribly politically interested, and are less likely to turn out and vote or to participate in politics in other ways. For example, one study found that, of political moderates, only about 20 percent are politically attentive, while the rest are largely disengaged from politics.[41] Given this, members of Congress tend to pay these voters less heed, unless someone organizes them to make their voice heard. While overall district sentiment matters (as we discussed above), those who vote end up being the most influential—politicians respond to those who make their voices heard.

This helps us to understand the puzzle from the beginning of the chapter. We see that congressional polarization reflects both deep divisions in the public and a disconnect from ordinary Americans. The deep divisions are among political activists; the disconnect is from the rest of the electorate.[42]

13-4 The Organization of Congress: Parties and Interests

Congress is not a single organization; it is a vast and complex collection of organizations by which the business of Congress is carried on and through which members of Congress form alliances. Unlike the British Parliament, in which the political parties are the only important kind of organization, parties are only one of many important units in Congress (though they are one of the most important).

Party Organizations

The Democrats and Republicans in the House and the Senate are organized by party leaders, who in turn are elected by the full party membership within the House and Senate.

majority leader *The legislative leader elected by party members holding the majority of seats in the House or the Senate.*

minority leader *The legislative leader elected by party members holding a minority of seats in the House or the Senate.*

whip *A senator or representative who helps the party leader stay informed about what party members are thinking.*

Speaker *The presiding officer of the House of Representatives and the leader of the majority party in the House.*

The Senate

The majority party chooses one of its members—usually the person with the greatest seniority—to be president pro tempore of the Senate. This is usually an honorific position, required by the Constitution so that the Senate will have a presiding officer when the vice president of the United States (according to the Constitution, the president of the Senate) is absent. In fact, both the president pro tem and the vice president usually assign the tedious chore of presiding to a junior senator.

The real leadership is in the hands of the majority and minority leaders. The principal task of the **majority leader** is to schedule the business of the Senate, usually in consultation with the **minority leader**. A majority leader who has a strong personality and is skilled at political bargaining (such as Lyndon Johnson, the Democrats' leader in the 1950s) may also acquire much influence over the substance of Senate business.

A **whip**, chosen by each party, helps party leaders stay informed about what the party members are thinking, rounds up members when important votes are taken, and attempts to keep a count of how voting on a controversial issue is likely to go. Several senators assist each party whip.

Each party also chooses a policy committee comprising a dozen or so senators who help the party leader schedule Senate business, choosing what bills will be given major attention and in what order.

For individual senators, however, the key party organization is the group that assigns senators to the Senate's standing committees: for the Democrats, the Steering and Outreach Committee; for the Republicans, the Committee on Committees. For newly elected senators, their political careers, opportunities for favorable publicity, and chances for helping their states and constituents depend in great part on the committees to which they are assigned. Achieving ideological and regional balance is a crucial—and delicate—aspect of selecting party leaders, making up important committees, and assigning freshmen senators to committees.

The House of Representatives

The party structure is essentially the same in the House as in the Senate, though the titles of various posts are different. But leadership carries more power in the House than in the Senate because of the House rules. Being so large (435 members), the House must restrict debate and schedule its business with great care; thus leaders who manage scheduling and determine how the rules shall be applied usually have substantial influence.

The **Speaker**, who presides over the House, is the most important person in that body and is elected by whichever party has a majority. Unlike the president pro tem of the Senate, this position is anything but honorific, for the Speaker is also the principal leader of the majority party. Though Speakers as presiders are expected to be fair, Speakers as party leaders are expected to use their powers to help pass legislation favored by their party.

In helping the majority party, the Speaker has some important formal powers. The Speaker decides who shall be recognized to speak on the floor of the House, rules whether a motion is relevant and germane to the business at hand, and decides (subject to certain rules) the committees to which new bills shall be assigned. The Speaker influences what bills are brought up for a vote and appoints the members of special and select committees. Since 1975, the Speaker has been able to select the majority-party members of the Rules Committee, which plays an important role in the consideration of bills. The Speaker also has some informal powers, which include control over some patronage jobs in the Capitol building and assignment of extra office space. Though now far less powerful than some predecessors, the Speaker is still an important person to have on one's side.

In the House, as in the Senate, the majority party elects a floor leader, called the *majority leader*. The other party chooses the minority leader. Traditionally, the majority leader becomes Speaker when the person in that position dies or retires—provided, of course, that the leader's party

Image 13.8 Nancy Pelosi is the first female Speaker of the House. She previously served as Speaker from 2007–2011, and was re-elected as Speaker in 2019.

is still in the majority. Each party also has a whip, with several assistant whips in charge of rounding up votes. For the Democrats, committee assignments are made and the scheduling of legislation is discussed in a Steering and Policy Committee chaired by the Speaker (or minority leader, depending on which party is in the majority on the committee). The Republicans have divided responsibility for committee assignments and policy discussion between two committees. Each party also has a congressional campaign committee to provide funds and other assistance to party members running for election or reelection to the House.

Party Voting

The effect of this elaborate party machinery can be crudely measured by the extent to which party members vote together in the House and the Senate. A **party vote** can be defined in various ways; naturally, the more stringent the definition, the less party voting will occur.

Figure 13.3 shows party voting in the House of Representatives since the mid-1950s. Most scholars say a party vote occurs when at least 50 percent of the Democrats vote together against 50 percent of the Republicans; this is the definition we use in Figure 13.3 (though some insist on a stricter definition, when 90 percent of Democrats vote against 90 percent of Republicans; by this definition, there are obviously fewer party votes). Figure 13.3 shows a striking trend: since the 1970s, there have been more and more party unity votes as a fraction of all votes cast. That is, more votes (today, nearly 7 in 10 votes) are party unity votes.

party vote *A vote where most Democrats are on one side of the bill, and most Republicans are on the other.*

Given that political parties as organizations do not tightly control a legislator's ability to get elected, this high level of party voting is surprising. Congressional members of one party sometimes do vote together against a majority of the other party, for several reasons. First, members of Congress do not randomly decide to be Democrats or Republicans; at least for most members, these choices reflect some broad policy agreements. By tabulating the ratings that several interest groups give members of Congress for voting on important issues (see Chapter 11), it is possible to rank each member of Congress from most to least liberal in many policy areas, including economic affairs, social issues, and foreign and military affairs. Democrats in the House and Senate are much more liberal than Republicans across nearly all issues. This has been true for many years, and as we discussed elsewhere in the chapter, the gap between Democrats and Republicans on the issues has been increasing.

In addition to their personal views, members of Congress have other reasons for supporting their party's position at least some of the time. On many matters that come up for vote, members of Congress often have little information and no opinions. It is only natural that they look to fellow party members for advice. Furthermore, supporting the party position can work to the long-term

Figure 13.3 **Party Unity Votes in House and Senate, 1956–2018**

Percentage of votes in which a majority of voting Democrats opposed a majority of voting Republicans.

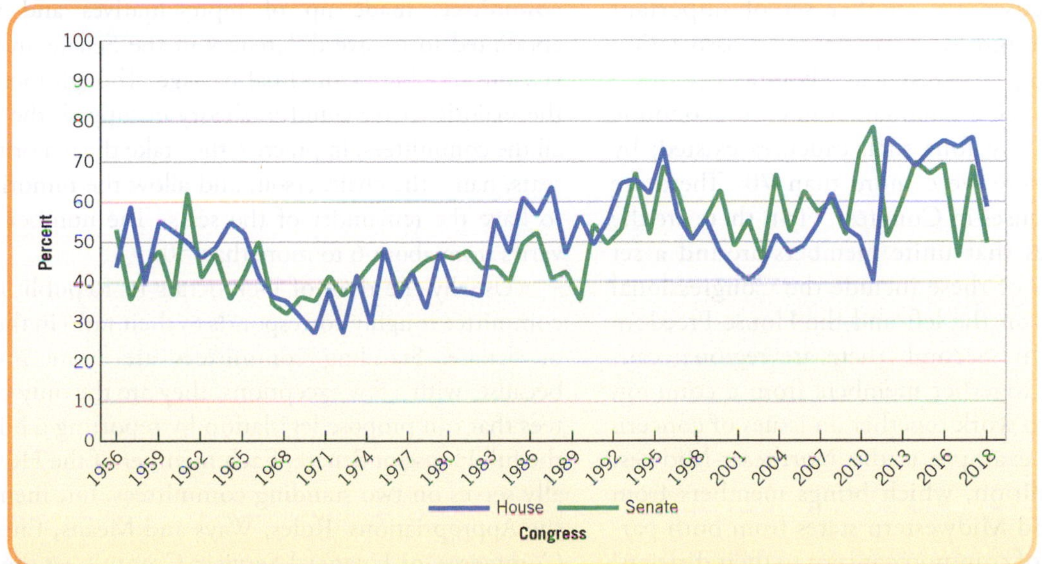

Source: CQ, "History: Party Unity Vote Studies," 25 February 2019.

Q **What factors do you think best explain the variation in the frequency of party unity votes over time?**

caucus *An association of congressional members created to advance a political ideology or a regional, ethnic, or economic interest.*

standing committees *Permanently established legislative committees that consider and are responsible for legislation within a certain subject area.*

select committees *Congressional committees appointed for a limited time and purpose.*

joint committees *Committees on which both senators and representatives serve.*

conference committee *Joint committees appointed to resolve differences in the Senate and House versions of the same bill.*

advantage of a member interested in gaining status and influence in Congress. Though party leaders are weaker today than in the past, they are hardly powerless. Sam Rayburn reputedly told new members of Congress that "if you want to get along, go along." That is less true today, but still good advice.

In short, party *does* make a difference—though not as much as it did at the turn of the 20th century and not as much as it does in a parliamentary system. Party affiliation is still the single most important thing to know about a member of Congress. Because party affiliation in the House today embodies strong ideological preferences, the mood of the House is often testy and strident. Members no longer get along with each other as well as they did 40 years ago. Many liberals and conservatives dislike each other intensely, despite their routine use of complimentary phrases.

Caucuses

Congressional caucuses are another set of important organizations in Congress. A **caucus** is an association of members of Congress created to advocate a political ideology or to advance a regional, ethnic, or economic interest. In 1959, only four such caucuses existed; by the early 1980s, there were more than 70. There are several types of caucuses in Congress. First, there are the ideological caucuses that unite members around a set of beliefs; examples of these include the Congressional Progressive Caucus on the left and the House Freedom Caucus on the right. Second, there are regional caucuses, which bring together members from a common geographic region to work together on issues of concern to that area. One example is the Northeast-Midwest Congressional Coalition, which brings members from 18 Northeastern and Midwestern states from both parties to discuss areas of common concern to their districts. Third, there are caucuses devoted to particular issues, such as the Congressional Diabetes Caucus, which seeks to address diabetes-related issues. Finally, there are caucuses that advocate for those from particular racial or ethnic groups; the most famous of these is the Congressional Black Caucus. The activity level of these caucuses varies widely, with some being very active and pressing an agenda on many issues, whereas others remain more behind the scenes.

The Organization of Congressional Committees

The most important organizational feature of Congress beyond the parties is the set of legislative committees of the House and Senate. Most of the power of Congress is found in the chairmanship of these committees, and their subcommittees. The number and jurisdiction of these committees are of the greatest interest to members of Congress because decisions on these subjects determine what groups of legislators with what political views will pass on legislative proposals, oversee the workings of agencies in the executive branch, and conduct investigations. A typical Congress has, in each chamber, about two dozen committees and well over 100 subcommittees.

Periodically, efforts have been made to cut the number of committees in order to give each a broader jurisdiction and to reduce conflict between committees over a single bill. But as the number of committees declined, the number of subcommittees rose, leaving matters much as they had been.

Three kinds of committees exist: **standing committees** (more or less permanent bodies with specific legislative responsibilities), **select committees** (groups appointed for a limited purpose, which do not introduce legislation and which exist for only a few years), and **joint committees** (on which both representatives and senators serve). An especially important kind of joint committee is the **conference committee**, made up of representatives and senators appointed to resolve differences in the Senate and House versions of a bill before final passage. Though members of the majority party could in theory occupy all the seats on all the committees, in practice they take the majority of the seats, name the chairperson, and allow the minority party to have the remainder of the seats. The number of seats varies from about 6 to more than 50.

Usually the ratio of Democrats to Republicans on a committee roughly corresponds to their ratio in the House or Senate. Standing committees are more important because, with a few exceptions, they are the only committees that can propose legislation by reporting a bill out to the full House or Senate. Each member of the House usually serves on two standing committees, but members of the Appropriations, Rules, Ways and Means, Energy and Commerce, or Financial Services Committees are limited to one committee. Each senator may serve on two major committees and one minor committee (see Table 13.5), but this rule is not strictly enforced.

TABLE 13.5 | Standing Committees of the House and Senate

House
Exclusive Committees: *Members may not serve on any other committee except for Budget.*
Appropriations
Rules
Ways and Means
Energy and Commerce*
Financial Services**
Major Committees: *Members may serve on only one major committee.*
Agriculture
Armed Services
Education and Labor
Foreign Affairs
Homeland Security
Judiciary
Transportation and Infrastructure
Nonmajor Committees: *Members may serve on one major and two nonmajor committees.*
Budget
House Administration
Natural Resources
Oversight and Reform
Science, Space, and Technology
Small Business
Ethics
Veterans' Affairs
Select Committees
Intelligence
Climate Crisis
Modernization of Congress

Senate
Major Committees: *No senator serves on more than two, though this rule may be ignored.*
Agriculture, Nutrition, and Forestry
Appropriations
Armed Services
Banking, Housing, and Urban Affairs
Budget
Commerce, Science, and Transportation
Energy and Natural Resources
Environment and Public Works
Finance
Foreign Relations
Health, Education, Labor, and Pensions
Homeland Security and Governmental Affairs
Judiciary
Minor Committees: *No senator is supposed to serve on more than one.*
Rules and Administration
Small Business and Entrepreneurship
Veterans' Affairs
Select Committees
Aging
Indian Affairs
Intelligence
Ethics
Joint Committees
Printing
Taxation
Library
Economic

*For Democrats, the Energy and Commerce Committee is an exclusive committee for those who first served on the committee in the 104th House or later.

**For Democrats, the Financial Services Committee is an exclusive committee for those who first served on the committee in the 109th Congress or later.

In the past, when party leaders were stronger, committee chairs were picked on the basis of loyalty to the leader. When this leadership weakened, seniority on the committee came to govern the selection of chairpersons. While the seniority system still largely governs which members become committee chairs, seniority is no longer sacrosanct. In 1971, House Democrats decided in their caucus to elect committee chairs by secret ballot; four years later, they used that procedure to remove three committee chairs who held their positions by seniority. Between 1971 and 1992, the Democrats replaced a total of seven senior Democrats with more junior ones as committee chairs. When Republicans took control of the House in 1995, Speaker Newt Gingrich ignored seniority in selecting several committee chairs, picking instead members who he felt would do a better job. In this and other ways, Gingrich enhanced the speaker's power to a degree not seen since 1910.

Throughout most of the 20th century, committee chairs dominated the work of Congress. In the early 1970s, their power came under attack, mostly from liberal Democrats upset at the opposition by conservative Southern Democratic chairs to civil rights legislation. The liberals succeeded in getting the House to adopt rules that weakened the chairs and empowered individual members. Some of the key changes included electing committee chairs by secret ballot within the majority party, banning committee chairs from blocking legislation by refusing to refer it to a subcommittee, requiring public meetings in all committees and subcommittees (unless the committee has voted to close them), and electing subcommittee chairs by a vote of committee members.

When the Republicans took control of the House in 1995, they made further changes. They eliminated some committees, and they also changed the powers of committee chairs. Some of these reforms strengthened the power of the committee chairs—for example, chairs were allowed to hire subcommittee staff—while others limited chairs in other significant ways, such as imposing term limits on committee and subcommittee chairs (three consecutive terms, or six years), and banning proxy voting (i.e., allowing the chair to cast an absent member's vote by proxy).

The Senate has seen fewer such changes, in large part because individual senators have always had more power than their counterparts in the House. That said, in 1995, senators also imposed six-year term limits on their committee chairs and voted to elect chairpersons by secret ballot of the committee members.

Despite these new rules, the committees remain the place where the real work of Congress is done. These committees tend to attract different kinds of members. Some, such as the committees that draft tax legislation (the Senate Finance Committee and the House Ways and Means Committee) or that oversee foreign affairs (the Senate and House Foreign Relations Committees), have been attractive to members who want to shape public policy, become experts on important issues, and have influence with their colleagues. Others, such as the House and Senate committees dealing with public lands, small business, and veterans' affairs, are attractive to members who want to serve particular constituency groups.[43]

dpa picture alliance/Alamy Stock Photo

Image 13.9 Secretary of State Mike Pompeo testifies before Congress.

For example, a member from a district with a great deal of agricultural land might want to serve on the House Committee on Agriculture, or a member from a district with a large military base might want to serve on the House Armed Services Committee. Doing so will allow those members to gain expertise on policy areas relevant to their districts, as well as to provide benefits to their constituents. Such knowledge and benefits in turn further a member's reelection chances.[44] Indeed, many members choose to serve on committees that are relevant to their districts' economic interests.

The Organization of Congress: Staffs and Specialized Offices

In 1900, representatives had no personal staff, and senators averaged fewer than one staff member each. By 1979, the average representative had 16 assistants and the average senator had 36. In total, Congress employed nearly 27,000 people, including members' personal staffs, plus committee staffs, the staff for support agencies, and other miscellaneous staff. Today, despite the growing complexity of the world, and the federal government, Congress has reduced its overall staff to around 19,600, a decline of more than one-quarter.[45] Starting in the mid-1990s, Congress began to reduce its staff as a cost-cutting measure. Later in the chapter, we will see that some have argued that was a penny wise but pound foolish decision.

Regardless of the number of staff, they perform a variety of important tasks. Some staff persons work in a member's home district, meeting with constituents and fulfilling requests for assistance with the government (this is a component of the incumbency advantage we discussed earlier in the chapter). The legislative function of congressional staff members is also important. With each senator serving on an average of more than two committees and seven subcommittees, it is virtually impossible for members of Congress to become familiar with the details of all the proposals that come before them or to write all the bills that they feel ought to be introduced.[46] The role of staff members has expanded in proportion to the tremendous growth in Congress's workload.

The orientation of committee staff members differs. Some think of themselves as—and to a substantial degree they are—politically neutral professionals whose job it is to assist members of a committee, whether Democrats or Republicans, in holding hearings or revising bills. Others see themselves as partisan advocates, interested in promoting Democratic or Republican causes, depending on who hired them.

Those who work for individual members of Congress, as opposed to committees, see themselves entirely as advocates for their bosses. They often assume an entrepreneurial function, taking the initiative in finding and selling a policy to their boss—a representative or senator—who can take credit for it. Lobbyists and reporters understand this completely and therefore spend a lot of time cultivating congressional staffers.

The increased reliance on staff has changed Congress, mainly because the staff has altered the environment within which Congress does its work. In addition to their role as entrepreneurs promoting new policies, staffers act as negotiators: Members of Congress today are more likely to deal with one another through staff intermediaries than through personal contact. Congress has thereby become less collegial, more individualistic, and less of a deliberative body.[47]

In addition to increasing the number of staff members, Congress also has created a set of staff agencies that work for Congress as a whole. These have come into being in large part to give Congress specialized knowledge equivalent to what the president has by virtue of being chief of the executive branch. One of these, the *Congressional Research Service (CRS)*, is part of the Library of Congress and employs about 600 people; it is politically neutral, responding to requests by members of Congress for information and giving both sides of arguments. The *Government Accountability Office (GAO)*, once merely an auditing agency, now has about 3,000 employees and investigates policies and makes recommendations on almost every aspect of government; its head, though appointed by the president for a 15-year term, is very much the servant of Congress rather than the president. The *Congressional Budget Office (CBO)*, created in 1974, advises Congress on the likely impact of different spending programs and attempts to estimate future economic trends.

13-5 How a Bill Becomes a Law

Some bills zip through Congress; others make their way painfully and slowly, sometimes emerging in a form very different from their original one. Congress is like a crowd, moving either sluggishly or, when excited, with great speed. While reading the following account of how a bill becomes law (see Figure 13.4), keep in mind that the complexity of congressional procedures ordinarily gives powerful advantages to the opponents of any new policy. Action can be blocked at many points. This does not mean that nothing gets done, but that to get something done, a member of Congress must *either* slowly and painstakingly assemble a majority coalition or take advantage of enthusiasm for some new cause that sweeps away the normal obstacles to change.

simple resolution *An expression of opinion either in the House or Senate to settle procedural matters in either body.*

concurrent resolution *An expression of opinion without the force of law that requires the approval of both the House and the Senate, but not the president.*

joint resolution *A formal expression of congressional opinion that must be approved by both houses of Congress and by the president; constitutional amendments need not be signed by the president.*

Introducing a Bill

Any member of Congress may introduce a bill—in the House by handing it to a clerk or dropping it in a box; in the Senate by being recognized by the presiding officer and announcing the bill's introduction. Bills are then numbered and printed. If a bill is not passed within one session of Congress, it is dead and must be reintroduced during the next Congress.

We often hear that legislation is initiated by the president and enacted by Congress. The reality is more complicated. Congress often initiates legislation (e.g., most consumer and environmental laws passed since 1966 originated in Congress), and even laws recommended by the president often have been incubated in Congress. Even as the principal author of a bill, a prudent president will submit only after careful consultation with key congressional leaders. In any case, the president cannot introduce legislation; only a member of Congress may do so.

In addition to bills, Congress can also pass resolutions. Either house can use a **simple resolution** for such matters as establishing operating rules. A **concurrent resolution** is used to settle housekeeping and procedural matters that affect both houses. Simple and concurrent resolutions are not signed by the president and do not have the force of law. A **joint resolution** requires approval by both houses and a presidential signature; it is essentially the same as a law. A joint resolution is also used to propose a constitutional amendment, in which case it must be approved by a two-thirds vote in each house, but does not require the signature of the president.

Study by Committees

A bill is referred to a committee for consideration by either the Speaker of the House or the Senate's presiding officer. If a chairperson or committee is known to be

Figure 13.4 How a Bill Becomes a Law

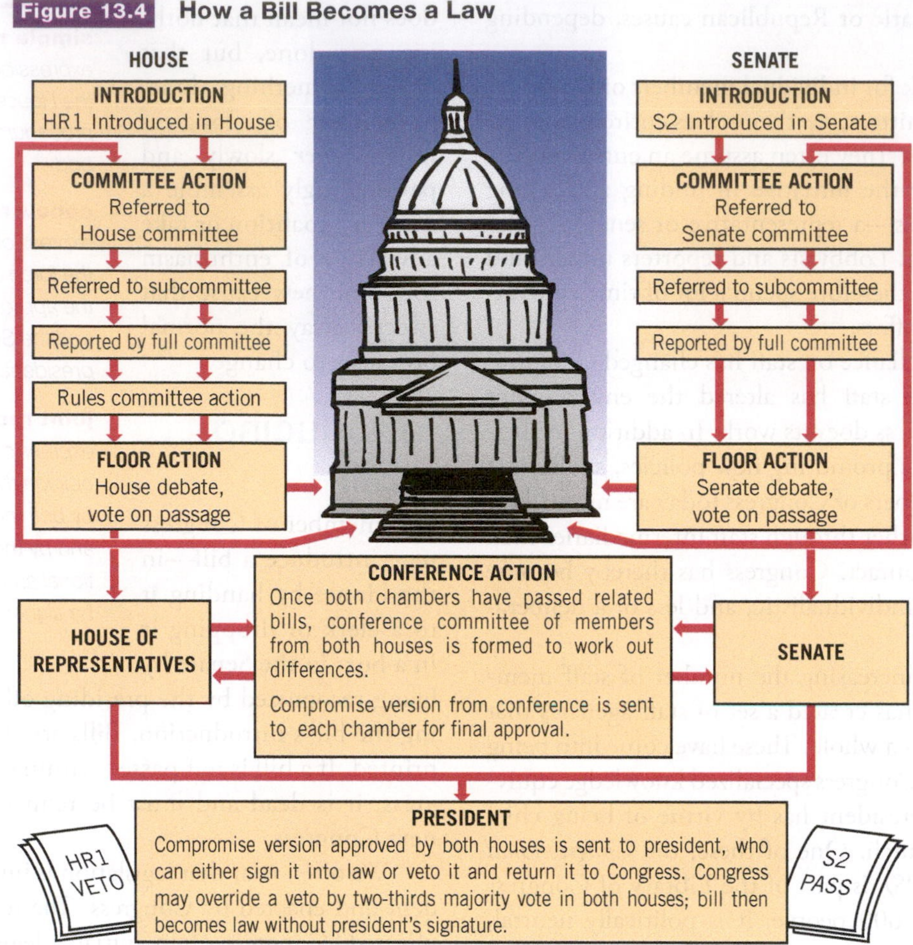

hostile to a bill, assignment can be a crucial matter. Rules govern which committee will get which bill, but sometimes a choice is possible. In the House, the Speaker's right to make such a choice (subject to appeal to the full House) is an important source of power.

The Constitution requires that "all bills for raising revenue shall originate in the House of Representatives." The Senate can and does amend such bills, but only after the House has acted first. Bills that are not for raising revenue—that is, that do not alter tax laws—can originate in either chamber. In practice, the House also originates *appropriations bills* (bills that direct the spending of money). Because of the House's special position on revenue legislation, the committee that handles tax bills—the Ways and Means Committee—is particularly powerful.

Most bills die in committee. They are often introduced only to get publicity for various members of Congress or to enable them to say to a constituent or pressure group that they "did something" on some matter. Bills of general interest—many of them drafted in the executive branch though introduced by members of Congress—are assigned to a subcommittee for a hearing where witnesses appear, evidence is taken, and questions are asked. These hearings are used to inform members of Congress, to permit interest groups to speak out (whether or not they have anything helpful to say), and to build public support for a measure favored by the majority on the committee.

Though committee hearings are necessary and valuable, they also fragment the process of considering bills dealing with complex matters. Both power and information are dispersed in Congress, and thus it is difficult to take a comprehensive view of matters cutting across committee boundaries. This has made it harder to pass complex legislation. For example, President George W. Bush's proposals to expand government support for religious groups that supply social services were dissected into small sections for the consideration of the various committees that had jurisdiction; after three years, no laws emerged. But strong White House leadership and supportive public opinion can push through controversial measures without great delay, as in the cases of Bush's tax cuts in 2001 and homeland security plans in 2002.

After the hearings, the committee or subcommittee makes revisions and additions (sometimes extensive) to the bill, but these changes do not become part of the bill unless they are approved by the entire house. If a majority of the committee votes to report a bill favorably to the House or Senate, it goes forward, accompanied by an explanation of why the committee favors it and why it wishes to see its amendments, if any, added; committee members who oppose the bill may include their dissenting opinions.

If the committee does not report the bill out to the House favorably, that ordinarily kills it, though there are complex procedures whereby the full House can get a bill that is stalled in committee out and onto the floor. The process involves getting a majority of all House members to sign a **discharge petition**. If 218 members sign, then the petition can be voted on; if it passes, then the stalled bill goes directly to the floor for a vote. These procedures are rarely attempted and even more rarely succeed—one study suggests that only about 2 percent of bills where a discharge petition is filed eventually become law.[48] That said, discharge petitions have been used on several important pieces of legislation that became law, such as the Bipartisan Campaign Reform Act of 2002, and the 2015 Reauthorization of the Export-Import Bank of the United States. Further, even a threat of a discharge petition can bring legislation to the floor, as in the case of the 1964 Civil Rights Act.

For a bill to come before either house, it must first be placed on a calendar. There are five of these in the House and two in the Senate. Though the bill goes onto a calendar, it is not necessarily considered in chronological order or even considered at all. In the House, the powerful Rules Committee—an arm of the party leadership, especially of the speaker—reviews most bills and sets the rule, that is, the procedures, under which they will be considered by the House. A **restrictive** or **closed rule** sets strict limits on debate and confines amendments to those proposed by the committee; an **open rule** permits amendments from the floor. The Rules Committee is no longer as mighty as it once was, but it can still block any House consideration of a measure and can bargain with the legislative committee by offering a helpful rule in exchange for alterations in the substance of a bill. In the 1980s, closed rules became more common.

The House needs the Rules Committee to serve as a traffic cop; without some limitations on debate and amendment, nothing would ever get done. The House can bypass the Rules Committee in a number of ways, but it rarely does so unless the committee departs too far from the sentiments of the House.

No such barriers to floor consideration exist in the Senate, where bills may be considered in any order at any time whenever a majority of the Senate chooses. In practice, bills are scheduled by the majority leader in consultation with the minority leader.

Floor Debate

Once on the floor, the bills are debated. In the House all revenue and most other bills are discussed by the *Committee of the Whole*—that is, whoever happens to be on the floor at the time, so long as at least 100 members are present. The Committee of the Whole can debate, amend, and generally decide the final shape of a bill but technically cannot pass it—that must be done by the House itself, for which the **quorum** is half the membership (218 representatives). The sponsoring committee guides the discussion, and normally its version of the bill is the version that the full House passes.

Procedures are a good deal more casual in the Senate. Measures that have already passed the House can be placed on the Senate calendar without a committee hearing. There is no Committee of the Whole and no rule (as in the House) limiting debate, so filibusters (lengthy speeches given to prevent votes from being taken) and irrelevant amendments, called **riders**, are possible. Filibusters can be broken if three-fifths of all senators resolve to invoke the **cloture rule**.

The sharp increase in Senate filibusters has been made easier by a new process called **double tracking**. When a senator filibusters against a bill, it is temporarily put aside so the Senate can move on to other business. Because of double tracking, senators no longer have to speak around

discharge petition *A device by which any member of the House, after a committee has had the bill for 30 days, may petition to have it brought to the floor.*

restrictive rule *An order from the House Rules Committee that permits certain kinds of amendments but not others to be made to a bill on the floor.*

closed rule *An order from the House Rules Committee that sets a time limit on debate; forbids a bill from being amended on the floor.*

open rule *An order from the House Rules Committee that permits a bill to be amended on the floor.*

quorum *The minimum number of members who must be present for business to be conducted in Congress.*

riders *Amendments on matters unrelated to a bill that are added to an important bill so that they will "ride" to passage through the Congress. When a bill has many riders, it is called a Christmas-tree bill.*

cloture rule *A rule used by the Senate to end or limit debate.*

double tracking *A procedure to keep the Senate going during a filibuster in which the disputed bill is shelved temporarily so that the Senate can get on with other business.*

voice vote *A congressional voting procedure in which members shout "yea" in approval or "nay" in disapproval, permitting members to vote quickly or anonymously on bills.*

division vote *A congressional voting procedure in which members stand and are counted.*

roll-call vote *A congressional voting procedure that consists of members answering "yea" or "nay" to their names.*

teller vote *A congressional voting procedure in which members pass between two tellers, the "yeas" first and the "nays" second.*

the clock to block a bill. Once they talk long enough, the bill is shelved. Indeed, some have argued that this practice is a key reason that filibusters have increased dramatically since the middle of the 20th century: if senators have to speak around the clock, filibustering is extremely costly and will be rare. If it requires much less effort, it will become more common.[49]

We can see the rise in filibustering by looking at the number of cloture votes cast in Congress: in the middle of the 20th century, only a handful occurred in each Congress, typically no more than three or four. Starting in the 1970s, it begins to increase rapidly, and in recent Congresses there have often been over a hundred; the record was 218 such votes in the 113th Congress (2013–2015).[50] Indeed, because of the threat of a filibuster, for all practical purposes, nearly all legislation in the Senate now requires 60 votes to pass.

The Senate has also changed the rules governing the nomination of judges and other officials. In 2005, seven Democrats and seven Republicans agreed not to filibuster judicial nominations except in "exceptional circumstances." A few nominees whose appointments had been blocked managed to get confirmed by this arrangement. While this truce held for several years, it did not last forever. In 2013, Democrats under Majority Leader Harry Reid used a parliamentary tactic to block filibusters of nominations, except for the Supreme Court and certain other offices. Even this compromise failed in 2017, when Republicans eliminated the filibuster for Supreme Court nominees to allow for a confirmation vote on Neil Gorsuch. While the filibuster is gone for nominations, it still exists on legislation, at least for now.[51]

One rule was once common to both houses: courtesy, often of the most exquisite nature, was required. Members always referred to each other as "distinguished" even if they were mortal political enemies. Personal or ad hominem criticism was frowned upon, but of late it has become more common. In recent years, members of Congress—especially of the House—have become more personal in their criticisms of one another, and human relationships have deteriorated.

Methods of Voting

There are several methods of voting in Congress, which can be applied to amendments to a bill as well as to the question of final passage. Some observers of Congress make the mistake of deciding who was for and who against a bill based on the final vote. This can be misleading. Often, a member of Congress will vote for final passage of a bill after having supported amendments that, if they had passed, would have made the bill totally different. To keep track of members' voting records, therefore, it is often more important to know how they voted on key amendments than how they voted on the bill itself.

Finding that out is not always easy, though it has become simpler in recent years. The House has three procedures for voting. A **voice vote** consists of the members shouting "yea" or "nay"; a **division vote** (or standing vote) involves the members standing and being counted. In neither case are the names recorded of who voted which way. This is done only with a **roll-call vote**. Since 1973, an electronic voting system has been in use that greatly speeds up roll-call votes, and the number of recorded votes has thus increased sharply. To ensure a roll-call vote, one-fifth of House members present must request it. Voting in the Senate is simpler; it votes by voice or by roll call; they do not use a **teller vote** or electronic counters.

If a bill passes the House and Senate in different forms, the differences must be reconciled if the bill is to become law. If they are minor, the last house to act may simply refer the bill back to the other house, which then accepts the alterations. Major differences must be ironed out in a conference committee, though only a minority of bills requires a conference. Each house must vote to form such a committee. The members are picked by the chairs of the standing committees that have been handling the legislation; the minority as well as the majority party is represented. No decision can be made unless approved by a majority of *each* delegation. Bargaining is long and hard; in the past it was also secret, but some sessions are now public. Often—as with Carter's energy bill—the legislation is substantially rewritten in conference. Theoretically nothing already agreed upon by both the House and Senate is to be changed, but in the inevitable give-and-take, even those matters already approved may be modified.

Conference reports on spending bills usually split the difference between the House and Senate versions. Overall, the Senate tends to do slightly better than the House.[52] But whoever wins, conferees report their agreement back to their respective houses, which usually consider the report immediately. The report can be accepted or rejected; it cannot be amended. In the great majority of cases, it is accepted—the alternative is to have no bill at all, at least for that Congress.

Image 13.10 President Trump signs the 2017 Tax Cut and Jobs Act into law.

The bill, now in final form, goes to the president for signature or **veto**. A vetoed bill returns to the house of origin, where an effort can be made to override the veto. Two-thirds of those present (provided there is a quorum) must vote, by roll call, to override. If both houses override, the bill becomes law without the president's approval.

Legislative Productivity

In recent years, political scientists have studied how productive Congress has been and whether the post-9/11 Congress has performed especially well or especially poorly. The first issue concerns how best to measure the body's major and minor "legislative productivity." It is clear that Congress passed and funded an enormous number of bills in response to the Great Depression in the 1930s and in the mid-1960s, mainly in conjunction with that era's "war on poverty." And most scholars agree that in recent decades the body's legislative output has often slowed or declined.[53] Indeed, the 112th (2011–2013) and 113th (2013–2015) passed the fewest bills of any Congress in the post–World War II era, making them the least productive Congresses of that period.[54] While productivity increased slightly in the 114th and 115th Congresses, it still remained below historical levels.

Some argue that **divided government** (one party in control of the presidency and the other in charge of one or both chambers of Congress) decreases legislative productivity. Although there are some exceptions, most studies of the subject suggest that divided party government reduces the passage of only the most far-reaching and costly legislation.[55] As we discuss in Chapter 14, divided party government does not lead inevitably to "policy gridlock" any more than having **unified government** (a single party in power in the White House and in both chambers of Congress) makes enacting ever more sweeping laws easy or inevitable.

Second, there is the issue of whether Congress, by cutting its staff, has hampered its ability to legislate and to oversee various agencies (indeed, this may be one of many factors related to the decline in legislative productivity in recent years).[56] As we noted earlier in the chapter, Congress has dramatically cut back on its staff in recent years, yet the federal government has grown ever-more complex, with a nearly $4 trillion budget and hundreds of agencies. As a result, some say that Congress has become too reliant on special interests and bureaucrats, and needs to strengthen itself to reassert its power.[57] The 116th Congress voted to establish the House Select Committee on the Modernization of Congress to study how best to update Congress, including making recommendations on staffing, legislative scheduling, and other issues. While the committee has made some recommendations that have been enacted into law, they have not yet addressed these staffing issues.

Finally, there is how the post-9/11 Congress has legislated on matters directly relevant to homeland security, especially its own. The Framers crafted Congress as an institution that favors deliberation over dispatch; to act boldly only when backed by a persistent popular majority or a broad consensus among its leaders, or both; and to be slow to change its time-honored procedures and structures.

But intelligence officials believe that a fourth plane involved in the 9/11 terrorist attacks was headed for the Capitol. In its June 2003 report, the bipartisan Continuity of Government Commission concluded that "the greatest hole in our constitutional system is the possibility of a terrorist attack that would kill or injure many members of Congress."[58]

This "hole" is relatively small with respect to the Senate. The Seventeenth Amendment allows the emergency replacement of senators by the governors of their states provided the state legislature allows it; otherwise, the governors must call for new elections. But the problem is greater for the House, where vacancies can be

veto *Literally, "I forbid"; it refers to the power of a president to disapprove a bill, and may be overridden by a two-thirds vote of each house of Congress.*

divided government *One party controls the White House and another party controls one or both houses of Congress.*

unified government *The same party controls the White House and both houses of Congress.*

Policy Dynamics: Inside/Outside the Box | National Service: A Bridge to Entrepreneurial Politics?

As you are learning in this chapter, the process by which a bill becomes law can be quite complicated. Most bills, in fact, never do become law. And even bills that are broadly popular often go nowhere unless there is at least one wise, well-positioned, and energetic policy entrepreneur, whether inside or outside the government, to get the idea on the policy agenda, sustain interest in it, and navigate the legislative process.

John M. Bridgeland, known widely in Washington, DC, as "Bridge," has been the policy entrepreneur behind successive recent federal national service initiatives. Before serving in the early 2000s as a senior White House assistant, Bridgeland, a Harvard-educated, moderate Republican from Ohio with a law degree, had spent a half-decade as a top legislative aide on Capitol Hill.

Working both within the West Wing and inside the halls of Congress, in 2002, Bridge got President George W. Bush, congressional leaders in both parties, diverse business and nonprofit leaders, and others to support an effort to expand existing national service programs including AmeriCorps, Senior Corps, and Peace Corps; encourage Americans to commit at least two years (4,000 hours) to volunteer service over their lifetime; and boost federal support for myriad other volunteer and community service projects. He created what became officially known as USA Freedom Corps and served as its founding director. Although he functioned as a classic policy entrepreneur, his case for the plan was steadfastly majoritarian in character: everybody contributes, everybody benefits.

After leaving the White House, Bridgeland founded a policy research and development organization and continued to develop national service proposals. For instance, in 2008, he co-led the "Service Nation" summit that brought together then-presidential candidates Barack Obama and John McCain. In 2009, with the summit's network behind it, a broadly bipartisan coalition of more than 100 organizations supported the Edward M. Kennedy Serve America Act. The bill passed with 79 votes in the Senate, and was signed into law by President Obama in April 2009.

The 2009 law authorized, and in some cases revitalized, many of the USA Freedom Corps initiatives that Bridgeland had crafted in 2002. Through the Aspen Institute's "Franklin Project," he led in developing a proposal for a million, full-time, year-round national service slots for the nation's 18-to 28-year-olds, including recently returned military veterans; he currently is the CEO of Civic, a policy firm based in Washington, D.C.

Image 13.11 John Bridgeland

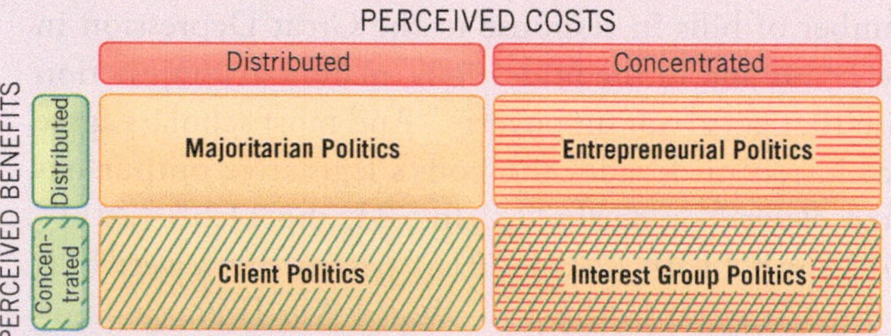

Source: John M. Bridgeland, *Heart of the Nation: Volunteering and America's Civic Spirit.* Lanham, MD: Rowman and Littlefield, 2013.

filled only by special elections, a process that can take many months.

Congress has enacted some, but by no means all, of the 9/11 Commission's recommendations.[59] But, as of early 2020, more than a decade and a half after the 9/11 attacks on the United States, it had failed to enact comprehensive legislation or proposals for constitutional amendments to ensure that "the first branch" can continue to function should a terrorist attack kill or incapacitate many or most of its members.

13-6 Reforming Congress

While most citizens are only vaguely familiar with the rules and procedures under which Congress operates, they do care whether Congress as an institution serves the public interest and fulfills its mission as a democratic body. Over the past several decades, many proposals have been made to reform and improve Congress—term limitations, new ethics and campaign finance laws, and organizational changes intended to reduce the power and perks of members while making it easier for Congress to pass needed legislation in a timely fashion (the proposal to rehire more Congressional staff discussed above would be another such proposal). Some of these proposals—for example, campaign finance reforms (see Chapter 10)—have recently become law, though most remain just proposals.

Many would-be reformers share the view that Congress is self-indulgent. It is, they complain, quick to impose new laws on states, cities, businesses, and average citizens but slow to apply those same laws to itself and its members. It is quick to pass **pork-barrel legislation**—bills that give tangible benefits (highways, dams, post offices) to constituents in the hope of winning their votes in return—but slow to tackle complex and controversial questions of national policy. The reformers' image of Congress is unflattering, but is it wholly unwarranted?

No perk is more treasured by members of Congress than the frank. Members of Congress are allowed by law to send material through the mail free of charge by substituting their facsimile signature (*frank*) for postage. But rather than using this **franking privilege** to keep their constituents informed about the government, most members use franked newsletters and questionnaires as campaign literature. That is why use of the frank soars in the months before an election. Thus, the frank amounts to a taxpayer subsidy of members' campaigns, a perk that bolsters the electoral fortunes of incumbents. While Congress has not removed the frank altogether, it has put limits on franking in recent years that have dramatically reduced the cost and extent of such mailings over time.[60]

For years, Congress routinely exempted itself from many of the laws it passed. In defense of this practice, members said that if members of Congress were subject to, for example, the minimum-wage laws, the executive branch, charged with enforcing these laws, would acquire excessive power over Congress. This would violate the separation of powers. But as public criticism of Congress grew and confidence in government declined, more and more people demanded that Congress subject itself to the laws that applied to everybody else. In 1995, the 104th Congress did this by passing a bill that obliges Congress to obey 11 important laws governing things such as civil rights, occupational safety, fair labor standards, and family leave.

The bipartisan Congressional Accountability Act of 1995 had to solve a key problem: under the constitutional doctrine of separated powers, it would have been unwise and perhaps unconstitutional for the executive branch to enforce congressional compliance with executive-branch regulations. So Congress created the independent Office of Compliance and an employee grievance procedure to deal with implementation. Now Congress, too, must obey laws such as the Civil Rights Act, the Equal Pay Act, the Age Discrimination Act, and the Family and Medical Care Leave Act. Further, in response to concerns about ethical lapses around campaign finance, Congress has also subjected itself to various ethics laws (see the discussion in Chapter 10).

pork-barrel legislation *Legislation that gives tangible benefits to constituents in several districts or states in the hope of winning their votes in return.*

franking privilege *The ability of members to mail letters to their constituents free of charge by substituting their facsimile signature for postage.*

As already mentioned, bills containing money for local dams, bridges, roads, and monuments are referred to disparagingly as pork-barrel legislation. Reformers complain that when members act to "bring home the bacon," Congress misallocates tax dollars by supporting projects with trivial social benefits in order to bolster their reelection prospects.

No one can doubt the value of trimming unnecessary spending, but pork is not necessarily the villain it is made out to be. For example, the main cause of the budget deficit was the increase in spending on entitlement programs (such as health care programs like Medicaid or Medicare) without a corresponding increase in taxes. Spending on pork is a small fraction of total annual federal spending (about 2.5 percent, on average, from 1993 to 2005).[61] By 2015, what most observers would count as pork spending was below 1 percent of total federal spending. Of course, one person's pork is another person's necessity. No doubt some congressional districts get an unnecessary bridge or highway, but others get bridges and highways that are long overdue. The notion that every bridge or road that members of Congress get for their districts is wasteful pork is tantamount to saying that no member attaches any importance to merit.

Even if all pork were bad, it would still be necessary. Congress is an independent branch of government, and members are, by constitutional design, the advocate of their districts and states. No member's vote can be won by coercion, and few can be had by mere appeals to party loyalty or presidential needs. Pork is a way of obtaining consent. The only alternative is bribery, but bribery, besides being wrong, would benefit only the member, whereas pork usually benefits voters in the member's district. If you want to eliminate pork, you must eliminate Congress, by converting it into a parliament under the control of a powerful party leader or prime minister. In a tightly controlled parliament, no votes need be bought; they can be commanded. But members of such a parliament can do little to help their constituents cope with government or to defend them against bureaucratic abuses, nor can they investigate the conduct of the executive branch. The price of a citizen-oriented Congress is a pork-oriented Congress.

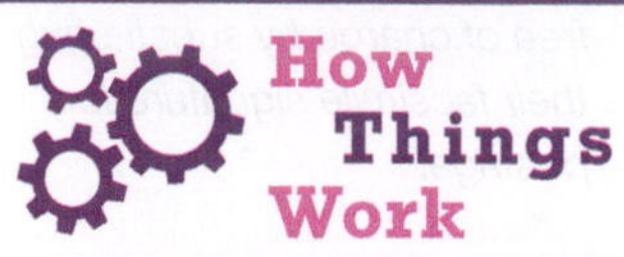

How Congress Raises Its Pay

For more than 200 years, Congress has tried to find a politically painless way to raise its own pay. It has managed to vote itself a pay increase 23 times in those two centuries, but usually at the price of a hostile public reaction. Twice during the 19th century, a pay raise led to a massacre of incumbents in the next election.

Knowing this, Congress has invented various ways to get a raise without actually appearing to vote for it. For example, members have voted for a tax deduction for expenses incurred as a result of living in Washington, or linking increases in pay to decreases in speaking fees and other honoraria. Another proposal would have created a citizens' commission that could recommend a pay increase that would take effect automatically, provided Congress did not vote against it.

In 1989, a commission recommended a congressional pay raise of over 50 percent (from $89,500 to $135,000) and a ban on honoraria. The House planned to let it take effect automatically. But the public wouldn't have it, demanding that Congress vote on the raise—and vote it down. It did.

Embarrassed by its maneuvering, Congress retreated. At the end of 1989, it voted itself (as well as most top executive and judicial branch members) a small pay increase (7.9 percent for representatives, 9.9 percent for senators) that also provided for automatic cost-of-living adjustments (up to 5 percent a year) in the future. Congress, however, has often rejected those automatic increases, typically because of fear of citizen reprisal. Congress last raised its pay in 2009, when it went from $169,300 to $174,000, where it stands today. The Twenty-Seventh Amendment—first proposed by James Madison in 1789 but not finally ratified by the necessary three-fourths of states until 1992—ensures that any pay change for members of Congress not take effect until the start of the following congressional term. The amendment had languished in obscurity for nearly two centuries, and might have remained there indefinitely, had it not been rediscovered by undergraduate Gregory Watson in 1982 while researching a class term paper. Watson began a campaign to ratify the amendment, and a decade later, it became the most recent amendment to the Constitution.[62]

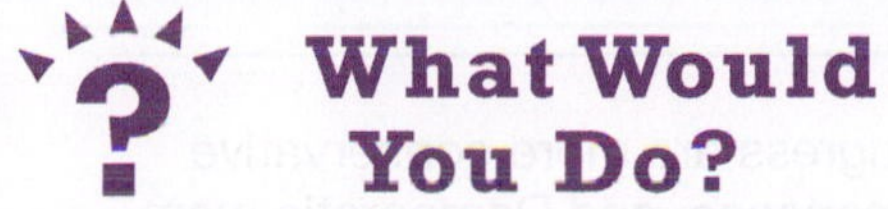

What Would You Do? | Will You Support an Increase in Size of the House of Representatives?

To: *U.S. Representative Hope Shelly*
From: *Jacki Julie, legislative aide*
Subject: *The size of the House of Representatives*

The House can decide how big it wishes to be. When it was created, there was one representative for every 30,000 people; now each House member typically represents almost 700,000 people. In most other democracies, each member of parliament represents far fewer people. Doubling the size of the House may be a way of avoiding term limits.

To Consider:

A powerful citizens' organization has demanded that the House of Representatives be made larger so that voters can feel closer to their members. Each representative now speaks for more than 700,000 Americans—far too many, the group argues, to make it possible for all points of view to be heard.

Arguments for:

1. Doubling the size of the House would reduce the huge demand for constituent services each member now faces.
2. A bigger House would represent more shades of opinion more fairly.
3. Each member could raise less money because the campaign would be smaller.

Arguments against:

1. A bigger House would be twice as hard to manage, and it would take even longer to pass legislation.
2. Campaigns in districts of 350,000 people would cost as much as ones in districts with 700,000 people.
3. Interest groups do a better job of representing public opinion than would a House with more members.

What Will You Decide? Enter **MindTap** to make your choice.

Your decision: ☐ Increase size of House ☐ Do not increase size of House

Learning Objectives

13-1 Contrast congressional and parliamentary systems.

A congress differs from a parliament in two basic ways: how one becomes a member and what one does as a member. To run for a seat in a parliament like the United Kingdom's, you first need a political party to put your name on a ballot, but to become a candidate for representative or senator in Congress, you first need to enter a primary election (political parties exercise relatively little control over who runs). In a parliament, the head of the executive branch (the prime minister) is selected by the majority party from among its members, and once in office a member of parliament has only one important decision to make—whether or not to support the government. By contrast, the voters, not the Congress, pick the president, and once elected, members of Congress have powers that they can exercise without regard to presidential preferences.

13-2 Trace the evolution of Congress in American politics.

The Framers of the Constitution created a bicameral legislature—the House and Senate—to ensure that power would be shared in the national government. Because of its larger size, the House has always been more centralized than the Senate, but since the 1950s, more power has devolved to individual members. The most significant change in the evolution of the Senate has been the change, with the Seventeenth Amendment in 1913, in election from state legislatures to voters. The rise of the filibuster, the tradition of unlimited debate in the Senate, also is an important development in the institution.

13-3 Discuss who serves in Congress and what influences their votes.

Demographically, members of Congress share few similarities with the American public. Most Americans, unlike most members of Congress, are not middle-aged white men with law degrees or past political careers. Some groups (e.g., women, African Americans, and Latinos) are much less prevalent in Congress than they are in the nation as a whole, whereas other groups (e.g., Catholics) constitute about the same fraction of Congress as they do of the American people. Ideologically, Republican members of Congress are more conservative than average Americans, and Democratic members of Congress are more liberal than average Americans. But many factors influence how legislators vote, including their constituents' interests, political party priorities, and their own political beliefs.

13-4 Summarize the organization of Congress.

Congress comprises numerous committees in each chamber, including standing committees, select committees, joint committees, and conference committees. Members of Congress also have their own staffs, as do congressional committees. Congress also has specialized agencies, such as the Congressional Budget Office and the Government Accountability Office, to assist in its operations.

13-5 Explain how a bill becomes a law.

A bill must undergo a lengthy policymaking process and overcome many hurdles to become a law. Briefly, a bill must be introduced in the House or Senate (all revenue-raising bills must originate in the House), be approved by each chamber—usually after undergoing extensive committee and subcommittee review—be reviewed by a conference committee and then approved again by both chambers, and then be signed by the president. If a bill is not passed in a congressional session (which lasts for two years), then it must be reintroduced in the next Congress and go through the entire process again.

13-6 Discuss possibilities for congressional reform.

The Framers of the Constitution knew that Congress would normally proceed slowly and err in favor of deliberative, not decisive, action. Congress was intended to check and balance strong leaders in the executive branch, not automatically cede its authority to them, not even during a war or other national crisis. Today, the increased ideological and partisan polarization among members has arguably made Congress even less capable than it traditionally has been of planning ahead or swiftly adopting coherent changes in national policies. Some people say Congress should function more like a parliamentary system, where the majority party selects the executive, and the political structure encourages executive-legislative cooperation. Others propose longer terms for members of the House and Senate, to permit more time for policymaking. Other democracies have such political systems, but they would fundamentally change the system of Madisonian democracy that has endured for more than 225 years.

To Learn More

House of Representatives: **www.house.gov**

Senate: **www.senate.gov**

Library of Congress: **www.loc.gov**

For news about Congress:

Roll Call magazine: **www.rollcall.com**

C-SPAN: **www.c-span.org**

Arnold, R. Douglas. *The Logic of Congressional Action.* New Haven, CT: Yale University Press, 1990. Masterful analysis of how Congress sometimes passes bills that serve the general public, not just special interests.

Fenno, Richard F., Jr. *Congressmen in Committees.* Boston: Little Brown 1973. Classic study of the styles of 12 standing committees.

Fiorina, Morris P. *Congress: Keystone of the Washington Establishment.* 2nd ed. New Haven, CT: Yale University Press, 1989. Argues that congressional behavior is aimed at guaranteeing the members' chances for reelection.

Jacobson, Gary and Jamie Carson. *The Politics of Congressional Elections.* 10th ed. New York: Pearson, 2019. Authoritative study of how members of Congress are elected.

Kaiser, Robert. *Act of Congress: How America's Essential Institution Works, and How It Doesn't.* New York: Vintage Books, 2014. An account of the passage of the 2008 Dodd-Frank Financial Reform bill.

Mann, Thomas E., and Norman J. Ornstein, *The Broken Branch: How Congress Is Failing America and How to Get It Back on Track.* 2nd ed. New York: Oxford University Press, 2008. Critically compares the post–1994 Congress to its predecessors and suggests several major reforms.

Poole, Keith T., and Howard Rosenthal. *Congress: A Political-Economic History of Roll Call Voting.* New York: Oxford University Press, 1997. Sophisticated study of why members of Congress vote as they do and how relatively stable congressional voting patterns have been throughout American history.

Sundquist, James L. *The Decline and Resurgence of Congress.* Washington, D.C.: Brookings Institution, 1981. A history of the fall and, after 1973, the rise of congressional power vis-à-vis the president.

Taylor, Andrew J. *Congress: A Performance Appraisal.* Boulder, CO: Westview Press, 2013. Offers evidence and arguments to suggest that the present-day Congress is not the dysfunctional body that the mass public and many scholars believe it to be.

CNP/AdMedia/SIPA/Newscom

CHAPTER 14

The Presidency

Learning Objectives

14-1 Explain how presidents differ from prime ministers and discuss the evolution of divided government in the United States.

14-2 Summarize how the constitutional and political powers of the presidency have evolved from the founding of the United States to the present.

14-3 Discuss how modern presidents influence policymaking.

14-4 Explain why presidential character and organization matter for policymaking.

14-5 Describe presidential transitions and their consequences for executive power.

14-6 Evaluate how powerful U.S. presidents are today.

« Then When the Framers wrote the Constitution in the summer of 1787, they did not have a ready consensus on how to select the chief executive or define the powers of the office. James Wilson of Pennsylvania wanted the president to be elected by the people, Roger Sherman of Connecticut wanted him elected by Congress. Wilson's view got almost no support because the size of the United States (in 1787 it was as large as England, Ireland, France, Germany, and Italy combined) made it unlikely that anybody save George Washington could obtain a popular majority. Sherman's view got a lot of support, but many delegates worried that the president would become nothing more than a tool of Congress.

The Committee on Postponed Matters, a small subset of the group, suggested creating an Electoral College to choose the president. The Framers approved the plan, but as they thought candidates would have difficulty winning a majority in the Electoral College, they expected that the U.S. House of Representatives ultimately would decide most elections.

*** Now** More than 200 years later, the Electoral College endures (for now), and the House has not chosen a president since 1824. The stability of this institution is surprising, given that the Framers settled on it as a last-minute compromise, and because twice in the 21st century, 2000 and 2016, the presidential candidate who won the election lost the popular vote. (Before 2000, this had not happened since 1888.) Nevertheless, the Electoral College is the only part of the presidential campaign process that the Framers would recognize in the 21st century.

The lengthy road to the nomination, the extensive fundraising required (the two major-party candidates, their political parties, and super PACs raised approximately $2.5 billion for the 2016 presidential race),[1] and 24-hour media coverage are all standard features of modern presidential selection. Furthermore, the weighty demands of winning the White House affect how the victorious candidate governs as president.

As you read this chapter, think about which features of the American presidency make sense today and which might merit change, keeping in mind that the Framers were not necessarily wedded to all aspects of the institution they created, nor could they have anticipated how technology and other factors would change it. The Constitution created an executive office with much leeway for action, which means that either of the following scenarios about teaching how the American presidency functions is possible.

First Scenario: Professor Reddy speaks to a political science class:

> The president of the United States occupies one of the most powerful offices in the world. Presidents John F. Kennedy and Lyndon B. Johnson sent American troops to Vietnam, President George H. W. Bush (41) sent them to Saudi Arabia, President Bill Clinton conducted air strikes in Kosovo, and President Donald Trump did the same in Syria, all without a declaration of war by Congress. In fact, Clinton continued the air attacks in Kosovo even after the House of Representatives rejected, in a mostly party-line vote, a resolution to authorize the bombing. President Barack Obama faced a similar situation when the House refused to authorize military operations in Libya (though the House also rejected a bill to limit funding for U.S. combat).
>
> President Richard M. Nixon imposed wage and price controls on the country. Presidents Clinton, George W. Bush (43), Barack H. Obama, and Donald J. Trump have selected most of the federal judges now on the bench, thus shaping the courts with their political philosophies. President Bush (43) created military tribunals to try captured terrorists and persuaded Congress to toughen counterterrorism laws. President Obama, within just months of taking office, got Congress to go along with his plans for giving the executive branch new and sweeping powers to regulate financial markets. After taking office, President Trump issued numerous executive orders, including a highly controversial ban on immigration from some countries, which the Supreme Court upheld as within the president's national security power (see p. 356 in this chapter). No wonder people talk about our having an "imperial presidency."

Second Scenario: A few doors down the hall, Professor Romero speaks to another political science class:

> The president, compared with the prime ministers of other democratic nations, is one of the weakest chief executives anywhere. President Carter signed an arms-limitation treaty with the Soviets, but the Senate wouldn't ratify it. President Reagan was not allowed even to test antisatellite weapons, and in 1986 Congress rejected his budget before the ink was dry. President Clinton's health care plan was ignored, and the House impeached him. The federal courts struck down several parts of President Bush (43)'s counterterrorism policies.

> Even with his party in control of both chambers of Congress, President Obama's first budget proposals were nixed on Capitol Hill, and his first health care reform plan was quickly recast by congressional committee chairpersons. President Trump has made several major decisions via executive order, but has had more difficulty enacting legislation with Congress, particularly after he was impeached in 2019 (and then acquitted) for abuse of power and obstruction of justice. Subordinates who are supposed to be loyal to the president regularly leak White House views to the press and undercut programs before Congress. No wonder people call the U.S. president a "pitiful, helpless giant."

Can Professors Reddy and Romero be talking about the same office? Who is correct? In fact, they both are. The American presidency is a unique office, with elements of great strength and profound weakness built into it by its constitutional origins.

14-1 Presidents and Prime Ministers

The indirect popular election of the president through an Electoral College (see the How Things Work: The Electoral College feature on page 346–47) is a uniquely American institution. Of the world's some 125 democracies, in which there is some degree of party competition and thus, presumably, some measure of free choice for the voters, just over 40, including the U.S. president, has substantive powers. The democratic alternative in almost 70 other countries is for the chief executive to be a prime minister, chosen by and responsible to the parliament. This system prevails in most Western European countries as well as in Israel and Japan. No nation in Europe has a purely presidential political system; France, for example, combines a directly elected president with a prime minister and parliament. About 15 democracies share executive power between a president and prime minister.[2]

In a parliamentary system, the prime minister is the chief executive. The prime minister is chosen not by the voters but by the legislature, and the prime minister in turn selects ministers for national departments from members of parliament. If the parliament has only two major parties, the ministers usually will be chosen from the majority party; if there are many parties (as in Israel), several parties may participate in a coalition cabinet.

Prime ministers remain in power as long as their party has a majority of seats in the legislature or as long as the coalition they have assembled holds together. The voters choose who is to be a member of parliament—usually by voting for one or another party—but cannot choose who is to be the chief executive officer. Whether a nation has a presidential or a parliamentary system makes a big difference in the identity and powers of the chief executive.

U.S. Presidents Are Often Outsiders

People become president by winning elections, and sometimes winning is easier if you can show the voters that you are not part of "the mess in Washington." Prime ministers are selected from among people already in parliament, and so they are always insiders.

Carter, Reagan, Clinton, Bush (43), and Trump did not hold national office before becoming president. Franklin D. Roosevelt (FDR) had been assistant secretary of the navy, but his real political experience was as governor of New York. Dwight D. Eisenhower was a general, not a politician. Kennedy, Lyndon B. Johnson, Nixon, Gerald R. Ford, Bush (41), and Obama had served in Congress, and four of them served as vice president as well (Johnson, Nixon, Ford, and Bush [41]).

In addition to his elected offices, Bush (41) had a great deal of executive experience in Washington—including U.S. representative to China, U.S. Permanent Representative to the United Nations, and director of the Central Intelligence Agency—whereas Clinton and Bush (43) both served as governors. Obama was the third president to be elected directly from the U.S. Senate to the White House; the other two were Warren G. Harding in 1920 and Kennedy in 1960. Trump was elected to political office for the first time when he won the 2016 presidential race.

Presidents Choose Cabinet Members from Outside Congress

Under the Constitution, no sitting member of Congress can hold office in the executive branch. The persons chosen by a prime minister to be in the cabinet are almost always members of parliament.

Of the 15 heads of cabinet-level departments in the first Bush (43) administration, only 4 had been members of Congress. The rest, as is customary with most presidents, were close personal friends or campaign aides, representatives of important constituencies (e.g., farmers, African Americans, or women), experts on various policy issues, or some combination of all three. The prime minister of the United Kingdom, by contrast, picks all cabinet ministers from members of Parliament. This is one way in which the prime minister exercises control over the legislature. If you are an ambitious member of Parliament,

FPG/Archive Photos/Getty Images

Image 14.1 The first cabinet: left to right, Secretary of War Henry Knox, Secretary of State Thomas Jefferson, Attorney General Edmund Randolph, Secretary of the Treasury Alexander Hamilton, and President George Washington.

eager to become prime minister yourself someday, and if you know your main chance of realizing that ambition is to be appointed to a series of ever more important cabinet posts, then you likely will not antagonize the person who appoints you.

Presidents Have No Guaranteed Majority in the Legislature

A prime minister's party (or coalition) always has a majority in parliament; if it did not, somebody else would be prime minister. A president's party often does not have a congressional majority; instead, Congress can be controlled by the opposite party, creating a divided government. Divided government means that cooperation between the two branches, hard to achieve under the best of circumstances, is often further reduced by partisan bickering. Even when one party controls both the White House and Congress, the two branches often work at cross-purposes. The U.S. Constitution created a system of separate branches sharing powers. The authors of the document expected there would be conflict between the branches, and they have not been disappointed.

When Kennedy was president, his party, the Democrats, held a large majority in the House and the Senate. Yet Kennedy was frustrated by his inability to get Congress to approve proposals to enact civil rights, supply federal aid for school construction, create a department of urban affairs and housing, or establish a program of subsidized medical care for older adults. Carter did not fare much better; even though the Democrats controlled Congress, many of his most important proposals were defeated or greatly modified. Only FDR (1933–1945) and Johnson (1963–1969) had even brief success in leading Congress, and for FDR, most of that success was confined to his first term or to wartime.

divided government *One political party controls the White House and another political party controls one or both chambers of Congress.*

unified government *The same political party controls the White House and both chambers of Congress.*

These differences in political position are illustrated by how Bush (43) and Tony Blair managed the war in Iraq. Once Bush decided to fight, he had to cajole Congress, even though it was controlled by his own party, to support him. Once Blair decided to fight, there could not be any meaningful political resistance in Parliament. When public opinion turned against Bush, he continued the fight because he could not be removed from office. When public opinion turned against Blair, he announced he would resign from office and turn over the job of prime minister to another member of his party.

The guaranteed majority that prime ministers have in their legislature may exist for American presidents, but it has become much less common since the mid-20th century. From 1952 through 2020 there were 35 congressional elections and 18 presidential elections. At least 60 percent of the 35 produced **divided government**—a government in which one party controls the White House and a different party controls one or both chambers of Congress. When Donald Trump became president in 2017, he was only the fifth president in almost 50 years to have party control of both chambers of Congress, creating a **unified government**—though this changed after 2018, when Democrats won control of the House. In 2020, Democratic presidential candidate Joe Biden won the White House, and Democrats maintained a smaller House majority. Party control of the Senate depended on the outcome of two runoff elections in Georgia.

Before the Trump presidency, the 2001 inauguration of President Bush (43) marked the first time since 1953 that the Republicans were fully in charge of both the executive and legislative branches of government (they controlled the White House and the Senate from 1981 to 1987). But not long after the Senate convened, one Republican, James Jeffords

gridlock *The inability of the government to act because rival parties control different parts of the government.*

of Vermont, announced that he was an independent and voted with the Democrats. Divided government returned until an additional Republican was elected to the Senate in 2002. But the Democrats retook control in 2007 and increased their majorities in both chambers two years later, even gaining the 60 votes necessary to halt filibusters in the Senate following a contested Minnesota race that ended with Democrat Al Franken being declared the winner and seated.

The Democrats lost their filibuster-proof majority in 2010, when Republican Scott Brown won a surprise victory to fill the seat of recently deceased Senator Ted Kennedy of Massachusetts. And President Obama faced a partially divided government after two years in office, with a Republican-led House and a narrowly Democratic Senate, a division of power that continued even after Obama won reelection in 2012. In 2014, Republicans increased their majority in the House and won control of the Senate as well, resulting in a fully divided government for the last two years of the Obama presidency. Divided government returned in 2019, when Democrats regained control of the House after 12 years (but Republicans kept control of the Senate). After the 2020 elections, as discussed above, Democrats kept control of the House, while the Senate majority leadership would be determined by two runoff elections in Georgia.

Americans say they don't like divided government. They, or at least the pundits who claim to speak for them, think divided government produces partisan bickering, political paralysis, and policy gridlock. During the 1990 budget battle between President Bush and a Democratic Congress, one magazine compared it to a movie featuring the Keystone Kops, characters from silent movies who wildly chased each other around while accomplishing nothing.[3] In the 1992 campaign, Bush, Clinton, and Ross Perot bemoaned the "stalemate" that had developed in Washington. When Clinton was sworn in as president, many commentators spoke approvingly of the "end of gridlock."

There are two things wrong with these complaints. First, it is not clear that divided government produces a gridlock that is any worse than that which exists with unified government. Second, it is not clear that, even if **gridlock** does exist, it is always, or even usually, a bad thing for the country.

Does Gridlock Matter?

Despite the well-publicized stories about presidential budget proposals being ignored by Congress (Democrats used to describe Reagan's and Bush's budgets as being "dead on arrival"), it is not easy to tell whether divided governments produce fewer or worse policies than unified ones. Scholars who have looked closely at the matter have, in general, concluded that divided governments do about as well as unified ones in passing important laws, conducting important investigations, and ratifying significant treaties.[4] Political scientist David Mayhew studied 267 important laws that were enacted between 1946 and 1990. These laws were as likely to be passed when different parties controlled the White House and Congress as when the same party controlled both branches.[5] For example, divided governments produced the 1948 Marshall Plan to rebuild war-torn Europe and the 1986 Tax Reform Act. Table 14.1 lists six examples of divided government in action.

Why do divided governments produce about as much important legislation as unified ones? The main reason is that "unified government" is something of a myth. Just because the Republicans control both the presidency and Congress does not mean that the Republican president and the Republican senators and representatives will see things the same way. For one thing, Republicans themselves are divided between conservatives (mainly from the South) and more moderate members (largely from the Midwest and West). They disagree about policy among themselves, though to a lesser degree than Democrats and Republicans do. For another thing, the Constitution ensures that the president and Congress will be rivals for power and thus rivals in policymaking. That's what the separation of powers and checks and balances are all about.

As a result, periods of unified government often turn out not to be so unified. Democratic president Johnson could not get many Democratic members of Congress to support his war policy in Vietnam. Democratic president Carter could not get the Democratic-controlled Senate to ratify his strategic arms-limitation treaty. President Clinton could not convince congressional Democrats even to vote on his health care plan, and it was Senate Democrats who demanded large changes to Obamacare. While Republican President Trump did pass the 2017 Tax Cut and Jobs Act, he could not get Congress to agree to "repeal and replace" Obamacare, as he—and congressional Republicans—had pledged to do.

The only time there really is a unified government is when not just the same party but the same *ideological wing* of that party is in effective control of both branches of government. This was true in 1933 when Franklin Roosevelt was president and change-oriented Democrats controlled Congress, and it was true again in 1965 when Johnson and liberal Democrats dominated Congress. Both were periods when many major policy initiatives became law: Social Security, business regulations, Medicare, and civil rights legislation. But these periods of ideologically unified government are very rare.

TABLE 14.1 | Divided Government at Work

President George W. Bush and the partly Democratic-controlled Congress (Senate) passed legislation to institute assessment requirements in primary and secondary education. (Several years later, President Barack Obama and the Republican Congress enacted new education legislation that gave more flexibility to states in testing.)
President Bill Clinton and the Republican-controlled Congress overhauled the nation's welfare system and balanced the federal budget.
President George H. W. Bush and the Democratic-controlled Congress enacted historic legislation to aid disabled persons.
President Ronald Reagan and the partly Democrat-controlled Congress (House) reformed the federal tax system.
President Richard Nixon and the Democrat-controlled Congress created many new federal environmental policies and programs.
President Dwight D. Eisenhower and the Democrat-controlled Congress established the interstate highway system.

Source: Eisenhower to Clinton examples adapted from Associated Press, "Major Laws Passed in Divided Government," 9 November 2006.

Is Policy Gridlock Bad?

An American president has less ability to decide what laws get passed than does a British prime minister. If you think the job of a president is to "lead the country," that weakness may worry you. The only cure for that weakness is either to change the Constitution so that our government resembles the parliamentary system in effect in the United Kingdom, or always to vote into office members of Congress who are of the same party as the president and also agree with the president on policy issues.

We suspect that even Americans who dislike gridlock and want more leadership are not ready to make sweeping constitutional changes or to stop voting for presidents and members of Congress from different parties. This unwillingness suggests they like the idea of national political institutions being able to block a policy if it lacks strong public support. Since all of us don't like something, we all have an interest in some degree of gridlock.

And we seem to protect that interest. In presidential elections, about one-fourth of all voters historically have voted for one party's candidate for president and the other party's candidate for Congress. More recently, this pattern of having about one-fourth of all House congressional districts represented by a person from a different party than the presidential candidate who carried that district is much smaller due to partisan sorting, as discussed in Chapter 7. Some scholars believe that voters split tickets deliberately in order to create divided government and thus magnify the effects of the checks and balances built into our system, but the evidence supporting this belief is not conclusive.

Gridlock, to the extent that it exists, is a necessary consequence of a system of representative democracy. Such a system causes delays, intensifies deliberations, forces compromises, and requires the creation of broad-based coalitions to support most policies. This system is the opposite of direct democracy. If you believe in direct democracy, you believe that what the people want on some issue should become law with as little fuss and bother as possible.

Political gridlocks are like traffic gridlocks—people get overheated, things boil over, nothing moves, and nobody wins except journalists who write about the mess and lobbyists who charge big fees to steer their clients around the tie-up. In a direct democracy, the president would be a traffic cop with broad powers to decide in what direction the traffic should move and to make sure that it moves that way.

But if unified governments are not really unified—if in fact they are split by ideological differences within each party and by the institutional rivalries between the president and Congress—then this change is less important than it may seem. What **is** important is the relative power of the president and Congress. That has changed greatly.

14-2 The Powers of the President

Though presidents, unlike prime ministers, cannot command an automatic majority in the legislature, they do have some formidable, albeit vaguely defined, powers. The Framers of the Constitution designed the executive office with limited powers, but over time, the presidency has evolved to assume increasing political responsibilities and to face heightened public expectations, even as the institution's constitutional powers have remained largely the same.

Constitutional Powers

The president's official powers are mostly set forth in Article II of the Constitution and are of two sorts: those the president can exercise without formal legislative approval, and those that require the consent of the Senate or of Congress as a whole.

Powers of the President Alone

- Serve as commander-in-chief of the armed forces
- Commission officers of the armed forces
- Grant reprieves and pardons for federal offenses (except impeachment)
- Convene Congress in special sessions
- Receive ambassadors
- Take care that the laws be faithfully executed
- Wield the "executive power"
- Appoint officials to lesser offices

Powers the President Shares with the Senate

- Make treaties
- Appoint ambassadors, judges, and high officials

Powers the President Shares with Congress as a Whole

- Approve legislation

Taken alone and interpreted narrowly, this list of powers is not very impressive. Obviously, the president's authority as commander-in-chief is important, but literally construed, most of the other constitutional grants seem to provide for little more than a president who is chief clerk of the country. Nearly one hundred years after the Founding, that is about how matters appeared to even the most astute observers. In 1884, Woodrow Wilson wrote a book about American politics titled *Congressional Government,* in which he described the business of the president as "usually not much above routine," mostly "*mere* administration." The president might as well be an officer of the civil service. Success required simply obeying Congress and staying alive.[6]

But even as Wilson wrote, he was overlooking some examples of enormously powerful presidents, such as Abraham Lincoln, and he was not sufficiently attentive to the potential for presidential power to be found in the more ambiguous clauses of the Constitution as well as in the political realities of American life. The president's authority as commander-in-chief has grown—especially, but not only, in wartime—to encompass not simply the direction of the military forces, but also the management of the economy and the direction of foreign affairs as well. A quietly dramatic reminder of the awesome implications of the president's military powers occurs at the precise instant that a new president assumes office. A military officer carrying a locked briefcase moves from the side of the outgoing president to the side of the new one. In the briefcase are the secret codes and orders that permit the president to authorize the launch of American nuclear weapons.

The president's duty to "take care that the laws be faithfully executed" has become one of the most elastic phrases in the Constitution. By interpreting this broadly, Grover Cleveland was able to use federal troops to break a labor strike in the 1890s, and Eisenhower was able to send troops to help integrate a public school in Little Rock, Arkansas, in 1957.

The greatest source of presidential power, however, is not found in the Constitution at all but in politics and public opinion. Increasingly since the 1930s, Congress has passed laws that confer on the executive branch broad grants of authority to achieve some general goals, leaving it up to the president and his deputies to define the regulations and programs that will actually be put into effect. In Chapter 15, we see how this delegation of legislative power to the president has contributed to the growth of the bureaucracy. Moreover, the American people—always in times of crisis, but increasingly as an everyday matter—look to presidents for leadership and hold them responsible for a large and growing portion of our national affairs. The public thinks, wrongly, of the presidency as the "first branch" of government.

The Evolution of the Presidency

Not surprisingly, given the preeminence of the presidency in American politics today, few issues inspired as much debate or concern among the Framers in 1787 as the problem of defining the chief executive. The delegates feared anarchy and monarchy in about equal measure. When the Constitutional Convention met, the existing state constitutions gave most, if not all, power to the legislatures. In 8 states, the governor actually was chosen by the legislature, and in 10 states, the governor could not serve more than one year. Only in New York, Massachusetts, and Connecticut did governors have much power or serve for any length of time.

Some of the Framers proposed a plural national executive (i.e., several people would each hold the executive power in different areas, or they would exercise the power as a committee). Others wanted the executive power checked, as it was in Massachusetts, by a council that would have to approve many of the chief executive's actions. Alexander Hamilton strongly urged the exact opposite: in a five-hour speech, he called for something very much like an elective monarchy, patterned in some respects after the British kind. No one paid much attention to this plan or even, at first, to the more modest (and ultimately successful) suggestion of James Wilson for a single, elected president.

BRENDAN SMIALOWSKI/AFP/Getty Images

Image 14.2 A military aide to the president carries a leather briefcase containing the classified nuclear war plan, popularly known as the "football," to Marine One.

In time, those who won out believed that the governing of a large nation, especially one threatened by foreign enemies, required a single president with significant powers. Their cause was aided, no doubt, by the fact that everybody assumed George Washington would be the first president, and confidence in him—and in his sense of self-restraint—was widely shared. Even so, several delegates feared the presidency would become, in the words of Edmund Randolph of Virginia, "the foetus of monarchy."

Concerns of the Founders

The delegates in Philadelphia, and later the critics of the new Constitution during the debate over its ratification, worried about aspects of the presidency that were quite different from those that concern us today. In 1787–1789, some Americans suspected that the president, by being able to command the state militia, would use the militia to overpower state governments. Others were worried that if presidents were allowed to share treaty-making power with the Senate, they would be "directed by minions and favorites" and become a "tool of the Senate."

But the most frequent concern was over the possibility of presidential reelection: Americans in the late 18th century were sufficiently suspicious of human nature and sufficiently experienced in the arts of mischievous government to believe that a president, once elected, would arrange to stay in office in perpetuity by resorting to bribery, intrigue, and force. This might happen, for example, every time the presidential election was thrown into the House of Representatives because no candidate had received a majority of the votes in the Electoral College, a situation that most people expected to happen frequently.

In retrospect, these concerns seem misplaced, even foolish. The power over the militia has had little significance, the election has gone to the House only twice (1800 and 1824), and though the Senate dominated the presidency off and on during the second half of the 19th century, it has not done so recently. The real sources of the expansion of presidential power—the president's role in foreign affairs, ability to shape public opinion, position as head of the executive branch, and claims to have certain "inherent" powers by virtue of the office—were hardly predictable in 1787.

There was nowhere in the world at that time, nor had there been at any time in history, an example of an American-style presidency. It was a unique and unprecedented institution, and the Framers and their critics can easily be forgiven for not predicting accurately how it would evolve. At a more general level, however, they understood the issue quite clearly. Gouverneur Morris of Pennsylvania put the problem of the presidency this way: "Make him too weak: the Legislature will usurp his powers. Make him too strong: he will usurp on the Legislature."[7]

The President: Qualifications and Benefits

Qualifications

- A natural-born citizen (can be born abroad to parents who are American citizens)
- 35 years of age
- A resident of the United States for at least 14 years (but not necessarily the 14 years just preceding the election)

Benefits

- A nice house
- A salary of $400,000 per year (taxable)
- An expense account of $50,000 per year (tax-free)
- Travel expenses of $100,000 per year (tax-free)
- A pension, upon retirement, equal to the pay of a cabinet member (taxable)
- Staff support and lifetime Secret Service protection after leaving the presidency
- A White House staff of approximately 400–500
- A country residence at Camp David
- A personal airplane, Air Force One
- A fine chef

Electoral College *The people chosen to cast each state's votes in a presidential election. Each state can cast one electoral vote for each senator and representative it has. The District of Columbia has three electoral votes, even though it cannot elect a representative or senator.*

The Framers knew very well that the relations between the president and Congress and the manner in which the president is elected were of profound importance, and they debated both at great length. The first plan was for Congress to elect the president—in short, for the system to be quasi-parliamentary. But if that were done, some delegates pointed out, Congress could dominate an honest or lazy president, whereas a corrupt or scheming president might dominate Congress.

After much discussion, it was decided that the president should be chosen directly by voters. But which voters? The emerging nation was large and diverse. It seemed unlikely that every citizen would be familiar enough with the candidates to cast an informed vote for a president directly. Worse, a direct popular election would give inordinate weight to the large, populous states, and no plan with that outcome had any chance of adoption by the smaller states.

The Electoral College

Thus the **Electoral College** was invented, whereby each of the states would select electors in whatever manner it wished. The electors would then meet in each state capital and vote for president and vice president. Many Framers expected that this procedure would lead to each state's electors voting for a home-state favorite, and thus no candidate would win a majority of the popular vote. In this event, it was decided, the House of Representatives should make the choice, with each state delegation casting one vote.

The plan seemed to meet every test: large states would have their say, but small states would be protected by having a minimum of three electoral votes no matter how tiny their population. The small states together could wield considerable influence in the House, where it was widely expected most presidential elections would ultimately be decided. Of course, it did not work out quite this way: The Framers did not foresee the role that political parties would play in producing nationwide support for a slate of national candidates.

Once the manner of electing the president was settled, the question of powers was much easier to decide. After all, if you believe the procedures are fair and balanced, then you are more confident in assigning larger powers to the president within this system. Accordingly, the right to make treaties and the right to appoint lesser officials, originally reserved for the Senate, were given to the president "with the advice and consent of the Senate."

The President's Term of Office

Another issue was put to rest soon thereafter. George Washington, the unanimous choice of the Electoral College to be the first president, firmly limited himself to two terms in office (1789–1797), and no president until FDR (1933–1945) dared to run for more (though

Constitutional Connections | Executive Checks and Balances

In *Federalist* No. 70, Alexander Hamilton famously wrote of the need for "energy in the Executive," which he defined as "unity" (a single president), "duration" (a term of office long enough for the executive to be effective), "adequate provision for its support" (a reasonable salary), and "competent powers" (the ability to fulfill the responsibilities of the office). Addressing fears that Article II of the Constitution made the executive too powerful, Hamilton said the president would be checked by "a due dependence on the people" (elections) and "a due responsibility" (commitment to the public good). Do these checks suffice to keep the Framers' system of separation of powers/checks and balances intact, and the president accountable, in the 21st century?

Source: Alexander Hamilton, The *Federalist* No. 70: The Executive Department Further Considered, March 15, 1788. Available online through the Avalon Project: Documents in Law, History and Diplomacy, Yale Law School.

Ulysses S. Grant tried). In 1951, the Twenty-Second Amendment to the Constitution was ratified, formally limiting all subsequent presidents to two terms.

The remaining issues concerning the nature of the presidency, and especially the relations between the president and Congress, have been the subject of continuing dispute. The pattern of relationships we see today is the result of an evolutionary process that has extended over more than two centuries. The first problem was to establish the legitimacy of the presidency itself, that is, to ensure, if possible, public acceptance of the office, its incumbent, and its powers, and to establish an orderly transfer of power from one incumbent to the next.

Today, we take this for granted. The Twentieth Amendment states that a president's (and vice president's) term ends at noon on January 20. An incumbent who has not been elected to another term (such as Obama, who was ineligible to run in 2016 after having won election twice), or loses a reelection campaign (as Trump did in 2020), will no longer be president at that time. In many nations, a new chief executive comes to power with the aid of military force or as a result of political intrigue, and a predecessor often leaves office disgraced, exiled, or dead.

At the time the Constitution was written, the Founders could only hope that an orderly transfer of power from one president to the next would occur. France had just undergone a bloody revolution; England in the not-too-distant past had beheaded a king; and in Poland the ruler was elected by a process so manifestly corrupt and so open to intrigue that Thomas Jefferson, in what may be the first example of ethnic humor in American politics, referred to the proposed American presidency as a "bad edition of a Polish king."

Yet by the time Lincoln found himself at the helm of a nation plunged into a bitter, bloody civil war, 15 presidents had been elected, served their time, and left office without a hint of force being used to facilitate the process and with the people accepting the process—if not admiring all the presidents. This orderly transfer of authority occurred despite passionate opposition and deeply divisive elections (such as that which brought Jefferson to power). And it did not happen by accident.

The First Presidents

Those who first served as president were among the most prominent men in the new nation, all active either in the movement for independence or in the Founding, or in both. Of the first five presidents, four (all but John Adams) served two full terms. Washington and Monroe were not even opposed. The first administration had at the highest levels the leading spokesmen for all of the major viewpoints: Alexander Hamilton was Washington's secretary of the treasury (and was sympathetic to urban commercial interests), and Jefferson was secretary of state (and more inclined toward rural, small-town, and farming views).

Washington spoke out strongly against political parties, and though parties soon emerged, there was a stigma attached to them: Many people believed that it was wrong to take advantage of divisions in the country, to organize deliberately to acquire political office, or to make legislation depend on party advantage. As it turned out, this hostility to party (or "faction," as it was more commonly called) was unrealistic; parties are as natural to democracy as churches are to religion.

Establishing the legitimacy of the presidency in the early years was made easier by the fact that the national government had relatively little to do. It had, of course, to establish a sound currency and to settle the debt accrued during the Revolutionary War. The Treasury Department inevitably became the principal federal office, especially under the strong leadership of Hamilton. Relations with England and France were important—and difficult—but otherwise government took little time and few resources.

In appointing people to federal office, a general rule of "fitness" emerged: Those appointed should have some standing in their communities and be well thought of by their neighbors. Appointments based on partisanship soon arose, but community stature could not be neglected. The presidency was kept modest. Washington clearly had not sought the office and did not relish the exercise of its then modest powers. He traveled widely so that as many people as possible could see their new president. His efforts to establish a semi-regal court etiquette were quickly rebuffed; the presidency was to be kept simple. Congress decided that not until after a president was dead might his likeness appear on a coin or on currency; no president until Eisenhower was given a pension upon his retirement.

The president's relations with Congress were correct but not close. Washington appeared before the Senate to ask its advice on a proposed treaty with some Indian tribes. He got none and instead was politely told that the Senate would like to consider the matter in private. He declared that he would be "damned if he ever went there again," and he never did. Thus ended the responsibility of the Senate to "advise" the president. Vetoes were sometimes cast by the president, but sparingly, and only when the president believed the law was not simply unwise but unconstitutional. Washington cast only two vetoes; Jefferson and Adams cast none.

The Jacksonians

At a time roughly corresponding to the presidency of Andrew Jackson (1829–1837), broad changes began to occur in American politics. These changes, together with the personality of Jackson himself, altered the relations between the president and Congress and the nature of presidential leadership. As so often happens, few people at the time Jackson took office had much sense of what his presidency would be like. Though he had been a member of the House of Representatives and of the Senate, he was elected as a military hero—and an apparently doddering one at that. Sixty-one years old and seemingly frail, he nonetheless used the powers of his office as no one before him had.

Jackson vetoed 12 acts of Congress, more than all his predecessors combined and more than any subsequent president until Andrew Johnson 30 years later. His vetoes were not simply on constitutional grounds but on policy ones: As the only official elected by the entire voting citizenry, he saw himself as the "Tribune of the People." None of his vetoes were overridden. He did not initiate many new policies, but he struck out against the ones he did not like. He did so at a time when the size of the electorate was increasing rapidly, and new states, especially in the West, had entered the Union. (There were then 24 states in the Union, nearly twice the original number.)

Jackson demonstrated what could be done by a popular president. He did not shrink from conflict with Congress, and the tension between the two branches of government that was intended by the Framers became intensified by the personalities of those in government: Jackson in the White House, and Henry Clay, Daniel Webster, and John Calhoun in Congress. These powerful figures walked the political stage at a time when bitter sectional

Library of Congress Prints and Photographs Division

Universal History Archive/Universal Images Group/Getty Images

Images 14.3 and 14.4 America witnessed peaceful transfers of power not only between leaders of different parties (such as Woodrow Wilson and William Howard Taft in 1913), but also after a popular leader was assassinated (Lyndon Johnson is sworn in after John F. Kennedy's death).

Image 14.5 President Andrew Jackson thought of himself as the "Tribune of the People," and he symbolized this by throwing a White House party that anyone could attend. Hundreds of people showed up and ate or carried away most of a 1,400-pound block of cheese.

conflicts—over slavery and commercial policies—were beginning to split the country. Jackson, though he was opposed to a large and powerful federal government and wished to return somehow to the agrarian simplicities of Jefferson's time, was nonetheless a believer in a strong and independent presidency. This view, though obscured by nearly a century of subsequent congressional dominance of national politics, was ultimately to triumph—for better or for worse.

The Reemergence of Congress

With the end of Jackson's second term, Congress quickly reestablished its power, and except for the wartime presidency of Lincoln and brief flashes of presidential power under James Polk (1845–1849) and Grover Cleveland (1885–1889, 1893–1897), the presidency for a hundred years was the subordinate branch of the national government. Of the eight presidents who succeeded Jackson, two (William H. Harrison and Zachary Taylor) died in office, and none of the others served more than one term. Schoolchildren, trying to memorize the list of American presidents, always stumble in this era of the "no-name" presidents. This is hardly a coincidence: Congress was the leading institution, struggling unsuccessfully with slavery and sectionalism.

It was also an intensely partisan era, a legacy of Jackson that lasted well into the 20th century. Public opinion was closely divided. In 9 of the 17 presidential elections between the end of Jackson's term in 1837 and Theodore Roosevelt's election in 1904, the winning candidate received less than half the popular vote. Only two candidates (Lincoln in 1864 and Ulysses S. Grant in 1872) received more than 55 percent of the popular vote.

During this long period of congressional—and usually senatorial—dominance of national government, only Lincoln broke new ground for presidential power. Lincoln's expansive use of that power, like Jackson's, was totally unexpected. He was first elected in 1860 as a minority president, receiving less than 40 percent of the popular vote among a field of four candidates. Though a member of the new Republican Party, he had been a member of the Whig Party, a group that had stood for limiting presidential power. He had opposed America's entry into the Mexican War and had been critical of Jackson's use of executive authority.

But as president during the Civil War, Lincoln made unprecedented use of the vague powers in Article II of the Constitution, especially those that he felt were "implied" or "inherent" in the phrase "take care that the laws be faithfully executed" and in the express authorization for him to act as commander-in-chief. Lincoln raised an army, spent money, blockaded Southern ports, temporarily suspended the writ of habeas corpus, and issued the Emancipation Proclamation to free the slaves—all without prior congressional approval. He justified this, as most Americans probably would have, by the emergency conditions created by civil war. In this he acted little differently from Thomas Jefferson, who while president waged undeclared war against various North African pirates.

After Lincoln, Congress reasserted its power and became, during Reconstruction and for many decades thereafter, the principal federal institution. But it had become abundantly clear that a national emergency could equip the president with great powers and that a popular and strong-willed president could expand political power even without an emergency.

Rise of the Modern Presidency

Except for the administrations of Theodore Roosevelt (1901–1909) and Woodrow Wilson (1913–1921), the president was, until the New Deal, at best a negative force—a source of opposition to Congress, not a source of initiative and leadership for it. Grover Cleveland was a strong personality, but for all his efforts he was able to do little more than veto bills that he did not like. He cast 414 vetoes—more than any other president until FDR. Frequent targets of his vetoes were bills to confer special pensions on Civil War veterans.

Today we are accustomed to thinking that the president formulates a legislative program to which Congress then responds, but until the 1930s the opposite was more the case. Congress ignored the initiatives of such presidents as Grover Cleveland, Rutherford Hayes, Chester Arthur, and Calvin Coolidge. Woodrow Wilson in 1913 was the first president since John Adams to deliver personally the

The Electoral College

Until November 2000, students and teachers alike spent little time talking about the Electoral College, as presidential election results typically showed a solid majority for the winning candidate. But in the 2000 presidential election, Florida's electoral votes hung in the balance for weeks, with George W. Bush finally winning them and (though he had fewer popular votes than Al Gore) the presidency. As this Electoral College-popular vote discrepancy had not happened since 1888, many people said 2000 was a historical anomaly—until it happened again in 2016, when Donald Trump won the presidential election with 304 Electoral College votes, but Hillary Clinton won nearly 3 million more popular votes. (In 2020, Joe Biden won both the popular vote and the electoral college vote.)

Here are the essential facts: each state gets electoral votes equal to the number of its senators and representatives (the District of Columbia also gets three, even though it has no representatives in Congress). There are 538 electoral votes today. To win, therefore, a candidate must receive over half, or 270.

In all but two states, the candidate who wins the most popular votes wins all of the state's electoral votes. Maine and Nebraska have a different system. They allow electoral votes to be split by awarding some votes on the basis of a candidate's statewide total and some on the basis of how the candidate did in each congressional district. In 2016, three of Maine's electoral votes went to Clinton; one went to Trump, who also won all five available in Nebraska. (In 2008, Barack Obama won one Electoral College vote in Nebraska, and Biden did the same in 2020.)

Electoral Votes per State

The distribution of Electoral College votes per state in the map below is for the 2020 presidential election, based on the 2010 census. The colors indicate which states voted Democratic and Republican in 2020.

The winning slates of electors assemble in their state capitals about six weeks after the election to cast their ballots. Ordinarily this is a pure formality. Occasionally, however, an elector will vote for a presidential candidate other than the one who carried the state. Such "faithless electors" have appeared in several elections since 1796. The 2016 presidential election had seven faithless electors—two pledged for Donald Trump and five pledged for Hillary Clinton—more than any other presidential election in nearly 200 years (apart from ones in which a presidential or vice-presidential candidate died before Electoral College votes were cast, and electors then voted for another candidate). After the election, lawsuits in Colorado and Washington, which respectively replaced and fined faithless electors, led to a unanimous Supreme Court ruling in 2020 that states may require electors to vote for the candidate who wins the state's popular vote, and that they may penalize or replace those who do not comply.

The state electoral ballots are opened and counted before a joint session of Congress during the first week of January. The candidate with a majority is declared elected. If no candidate wins a majority, the House of Representatives chooses the president from among the three leading candidates, with each state casting one vote. By House rules, each state's vote is allotted to the candidate preferred by a majority of the state's House delegation. If there is a tie within a delegation, that state's vote is not counted.

The House has had to decide two presidential contests. In 1800, Thomas Jefferson and Aaron Burr tied in the Electoral College because of a defect in the language of the Constitution—each state cast two electoral votes, without indicating which was for president and which for vice president. (Burr was supposed to be vice president and, after much maneuvering, he was.) This problem was corrected by the Twelfth Amendment, ratified in 1804. The only House decision under the modern system was in 1824, when it chose John Quincy Adams over Andrew Jackson and William H. Crawford, even though Jackson had more electoral votes (and probably more popular votes) than his rivals.

Today the winner-takes-all system in effect in 48 states makes it possible for a candidate to win at least 270 electoral votes without winning a majority of the popular votes. This happened in 2016, 2000, 1888, and 1876, and almost happened in 1960 and 1884. Today, a candidate who carries the 10 largest states wins 256 electoral votes, only 14 short of a presidential victory.

This means candidates have a strong incentive to campaign extensively in big states they have a chance of winning. In 2016, Hillary Clinton and Donald Trump worked hard in key swing states such as Florida, Pennsylvania, North Carolina, and Virginia, but they spent less time in states where their respective political party has a strong majority (such as California for the Democrats and Texas for the Republicans). But the Electoral College also gives power to small states. South Dakota, for example, has three electoral votes (about 0.5 percent of the total), even though it casts only about 0.3 percent of the popular vote. South Dakota and other small states are thus overrepresented in the Electoral College. In 2016, Clinton and Trump made multiple trips to highly competitive states such as New Hampshire and Nevada, which have four and six Electoral College votes, respectively, because the race was so close.

Sometimes states can have surprising results: In 2016, Hillary Clinton was expected to win Michigan and Wisconsin (her campaign's confidence in the latter was so high that she did not campaign there between the primary and general election). But Trump won both states and their combined 26 Electoral College votes, which, along with Pennsylvania's 20 Electoral College votes, were key to his victory in 2016. (Trump lost all three states in 2020.)

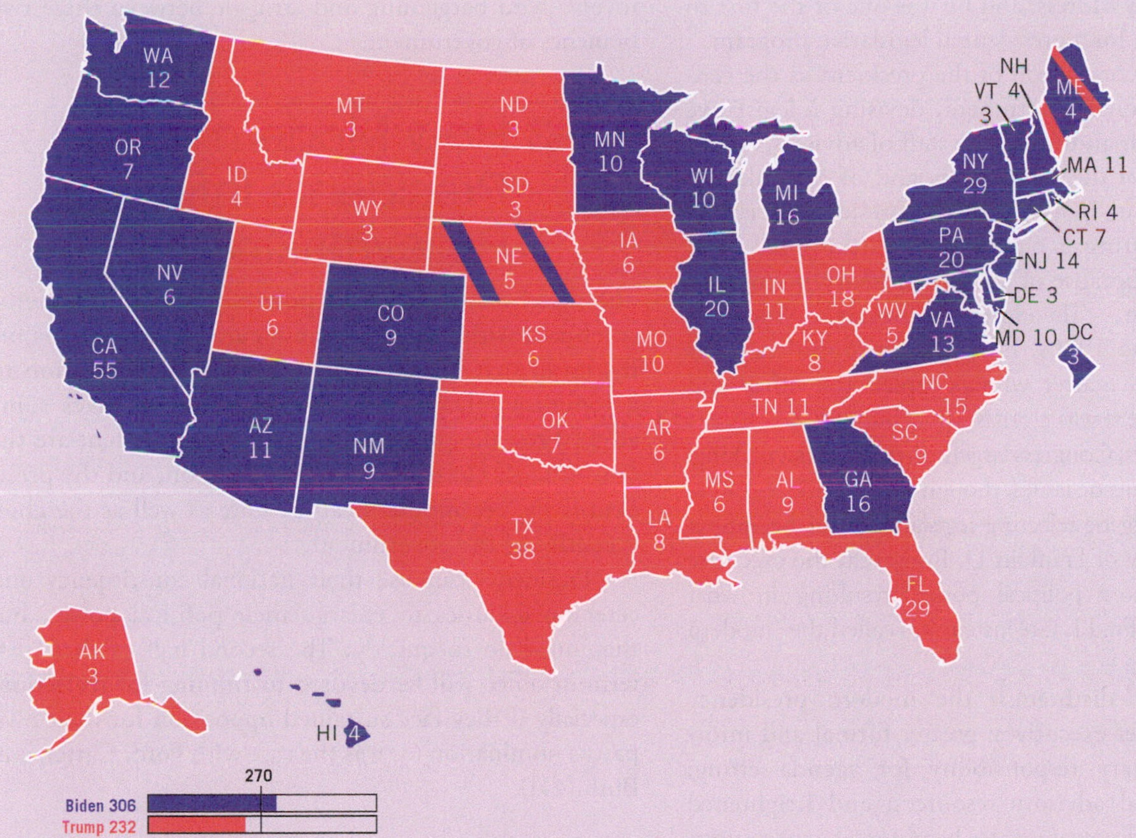

NOTE: As of November 2020, pending official electoral college results.

Given the conflict between the popular vote and the Electoral College vote in two of the last six elections, many Americans would like to abolish the Electoral College. But doing away with it entirely would present other issues about what constitutes victory. If we relied just on the popular vote, there might have to be a runoff election among the two leading candidates if neither gets a majority because third-party candidates won a lot of votes. This might encourage support for third parties (such as the Green Party or the Libertarian Party, both of which have fielded candidates in recent elections that received at least one percent of the popular vote). Each third party would then be in a position to negotiate with one of the two major parties between the first election and the runoff about favors it wanted in return for its support. American presidential politics might come to look like the multiparty systems in France and Italy.

Other changes could be made. One is for each state to allocate its electoral votes proportional to the popular vote the candidates receive in that state. Voters in Colorado acted on that measure in November 2004, but that proposal failed. If every state did that, several past elections would have been decided in the House of Representatives because no candidate got a majority of the popular vote. In the mid-2000s, the National Popular Vote organization began advocating for states to enact legislation that would award their electors to the presidential candidate who wins the most popular votes nationwide (a plurality, or the most votes, not a majority, which would require more than 50 percent). This reform would in effect establish a popular vote for presidential selection without a constitutional amendment to abolish the Electoral College. As of 2020, 15 states and the District of Columbia, with a combined total of 196 Electoral College votes, had approved legislation for a national popular vote—with the caveat that implementation will take place if enough states enact legislation to reach the 270-vote minimum threshold in the Electoral College.[8]

Given the discrepancy between the popular and Electoral College votes in 2000 and 2016, pressure to modify or abolish the Electoral College likely will increase in coming years. The Electoral College makes candidates think about carrying states as well as popular votes, and so heightens the influence of states in national politics. At the same time, the Electoral College is unique in American national elections for selecting a president based on a majority of state votes instead of a plurality of popular votes.

The Framers of the Constitution decided on the Electoral College toward the end of the Constitutional Convention in 1787 as a compromise between a very indirect popular vote (the public selects state legislators who select electors to vote for the president) and legislative selection (the House of Representatives selects the president if no candidate receives a majority of the Electoral College vote). More than two centuries later, the eligible voting public has expanded greatly, as we have discussed (see Chapter 8). Should the system of presidential selection change as well?

What are the strongest arguments in favor of keeping or abolishing the Electoral College? Which do you find more persuasive, and why?

State of the Union address, and he was one of the first to develop and argue for a presidential legislative program.

Our popular conception of the president as the central figure of national government, devising a legislative program and commanding a large staff of advisers, is very much a product of the modern era and of the enlarged role of government. In the past, the presidency became powerful only during a national crisis (the Civil War, World War I) or because of an extraordinary personality (Andrew Jackson, Theodore Roosevelt, Woodrow Wilson). Since the 1930s, however, the presidency has been powerful no matter who occupied the office and whether or not there was a crisis.

Until the 1930s, Congress largely directed policymaking, particularly for domestic issues, though some presidents were active in promoting or rejecting legislation. But beginning with the presidency of Franklin D. Roosevelt, the executive office acquired more political power, resulting in what presidency scholar Fred I. Greenstein has called the "modern presidency."[9]

Four features distinguish the modern presidency from previous chief executives: greater formal and informal power; primary responsibility for agenda-setting; increased staff and advisory resources; and heightened visibility. Increased power creates heightened expectations for leadership, which presidents cannot always meet. Even so, presidents today exercise far more initiative in setting the policy agenda and promoting legislation than the Framers envisioned.

Because government now plays such an active role in our national life, the president is the natural focus of attention and the titular head of a huge federal administrative system (whether the president is the real boss is another matter). But the popular conception of the president as the central figure of national government belies the realities of present-day legislative–executive relations. Even in the modern presidency, Congress still takes the lead in some areas to set the legislative agenda.[10] For example, the 1990 Clean Air Act, like the 1970 Clean Air Act before it, was born and bred mainly by congressional, not presidential, action. Administration officials played almost no role in the legislative process that culminated in these laws.[11]

When President George Bush (41) signed the 1990 Clean Air Act or President Clinton signed the 1996 Welfare Reform Act, each took credit for it, but in fact both bills were designed by members of Congress, not by the president.[12] Likewise, although presidents dominated budget policymaking from the 1920s into the early 1970s, they no longer do. Instead, the "imperatives of the budgetary process have pushed congressional leaders to center stage."[13] Thus, as often as not, Congress proposes, the president disposes, and legislative–executive relations involve hard bargaining and struggle between these two branches of government.

14-3 How Modern Presidents Influence Policymaking

The sketchy constitutional powers given to presidents, combined with the lack of an assured legislative majority, mean that they must rely heavily on persuasion to accomplish much. Here, the Constitution gives some advantages; the president and the vice president are the only officials elected by the whole nation, and the president is the ceremonial head of state as well as the chief executive of the government.

Presidents can use their national constituency and ceremonial duties to enlarge their political power, but they must do so quickly: The second half of their first term in office will be devoted to running for reelection, especially if they face sustained opposition for their own party's nomination (as was the case with Ford, Carter, and Bush [41]).

The Three Audiences

The president's persuasive powers are aimed at three audiences. The first, and often the most important, is the Washington, DC, audience of fellow politicians and leaders. As Richard Neustadt points out in his book *Presidential Power and the Modern Presidents,* a president's reputation among Washington colleagues is of great importance in affecting how much deference the chief executive's views receive and thus how much power the White House may wield.[14] If a president is thought to be "smart," "sure, " "cool, " "on top or things, " or "shrewd," and thus "effective," then the president likely *will* be effective. Franklin Roosevelt had that reputation, and so did Lyndon Johnson, at least for his first few years in office. Truman, Ford, and Carter often did not have that reputation, and they lost ground accordingly. Power, like beauty, exists largely in the eye of the beholder.

A second audience comprises party activists and officeholders outside Washington—the partisan grassroots. These persons want the president to exemplify their principles, trumpet their slogans, appeal to their fears and hopes, and help them get reelected. As we explained in Chapter 9, partisan activists increasingly have an ideological orientation toward national politics. Therefore, they will expect "their" president to make fire-and-brimstone speeches that confirm in them a shared sense of purpose and, incidentally, help them raise money from contributors to state and local campaigns.

The third audience is "the public." But of course that audience is really many publics, each with a different view or set of interests. A president or presidential candidate on the campaign trail speaks boldly of what will be accomplished; a president in office typically speaks quietly of problems that must be overcome. Citizens often are irritated at the apparent tendency of elected officials, including the president, to sound mealy-mouthed and equivocal. But it is easy to criticize the cooking when you haven't been the cook. A president learns quickly that every utterance will be scrutinized closely by the media and by organized groups here and abroad, and errors of fact, judgment, timing, or even inflection will be immediately and forcefully pointed out. Given the risks of saying too much, it is a wonder that presidents say anything at all.

Presidents have made fewer and fewer impromptu remarks in the years since FDR held office; they instead rely more and more on prepared speeches from which political errors can be removed in advance. Hoover and FDR held, on average, one or more press conferences per week, but no president since then has come close to that frequency.[15] (The White House press secretary traditionally meets daily with the media in formal briefings and informally as well, but the Trump administration halted that practice in 2019.)[16] Instead, modern presidents make formal speeches, or they communicate directly with the public through events or, more recently, social media. A president's use of public speeches is called the **bully pulpit**, a phrase that means taking advantage of the prestige and visibility of the presidency to try to guide or mobilize the American people.

Presidential public communication has become more important since the early 20th century. Woodrow Wilson resumed the custom started by the first two presidents of delivering state of the union messages in person to Congress. Presidential scholar Richard E. Neustadt wrote in 1960 of the need for presidents to appeal to multiple constituencies, and he emphasized the importance of "public prestige," for which a president must be "effective as a teacher to the public."[17]

Political scientists and communication scholars have identified the use of public rhetoric as a political strategy by presidents in modern American politics. Samuel Kernell shows how modern presidents routinely use a practice of "going public" to build popular support for their policies, and Jeffrey K. Tulis examines the development of the "rhetorical presidency," in which presidents use public speeches to exercise popular leadership. Mary E. Stuckey finds that advances in media technology shape what presidents say and how they say it, while Karlyn Kohrs Campbell and Kathleen Hall Jamieson evaluate how presidents use rhetorical opportunities to exercise political influence with other institutions of government.[18]

bully pulpit *The president's use of prestige and visibility to guide or mobilize the American public.*

Despite all the time and energy that presidents invest in their public communication, their efforts may not yield the results they seek. Based on extensive analysis of public opinion polls, George C. Edwards III argues that presidential speeches serve to bolster existing public views rather than to change them—the "bully pulpit," he says, falls "on deaf ears." Jeffrey E. Cohen examines media coverage of the presidency and finds that presidents can influence segments of the public through local news coverage, but that national strategies of "going public" are less successful.[19]

Popularity and Influence

Despite the limits of the bully pulpit, presidents communicate with the public to attempt to convert personal popularity into congressional support for the president's legislative programs (and to improve chances for reelection). It is not obvious, of course, why Congress should care about a president's popularity. After all, as we saw in Chapter 13, most members of Congress are secure in their seats, and few need fear any "party bosses" who might deny them renomination. Moreover, the president cannot ordinarily provide credible electoral rewards or penalties to members of Congress. By working for their defeat in the 1938 congressional election, President Franklin Roosevelt attempted to "purge" members of Congress who opposed his program, but he failed. Nor does presidential support help a particular member of Congress: Most representatives win reelection anyway, and the few who are in trouble are rarely saved by presidential intervention. When President Reagan campaigned hard for Republican senatorial candidates in 1986, he, too, failed to have much effect.

That said, as we discussed in Chapter 10, congressional candidates do benefit from the president's coattails; when a popular president is at the top of the ticket, more of that party's candidates win their races for Congress. It is true, as can be seen from Figure 14.1, that a winning president will often find that party strength in Congress increases. Of course, as we also discussed in Chapter 10, other factors affect legislative elections as well, so presidential coattails are just one of several factors that matter there. While coattails exist, they are more modest than earlier studies suggested.

In midterm election years, when the president is not running for office, the president's party typically fares less well than in presidential election years. The decay in the reputation of the president and party midterm is evident in Figure 14.2. Since 1934, in every off-year election but three, the president's party has lost seats in one or both chambers of Congress (see also the discussion in Chapter 10 of the surge-and-decline phenomenon). In 1934, during the Great Depression and Franklin D. Roosevelt's first term as president, the Democrats gained nine seats in the House and nine seats in the Senate. In 1998, during President Bill Clinton's second term in office and in the midst of a contentious and volatile inquiry into the president's affair with a White House intern (see page 369), the Democrats won five seats in the House and lost none in the Senate. In 2002, during the first term of President George W. Bush and just over a year after the devastating 9/11 terror attacks, the Republicans gained eight House seats and two in the Senate. Outside of crises, the ability of the president to persuade is important but limited.

Nonetheless, a president's personal popularity may have a significant effect on how many White House initiatives are enacted into law, even if those initiatives do not affect reelection chances for members of Congress. Though they do not fear a president who threatens to campaign against them (or cherish one who promises to support them), members of Congress do have a sense that it is risky to oppose too adamantly the policies of a popular president. Politicians share a sense of a common fate: they tend to rise or fall together. Statistically, a president's popularity, as measured by a Gallup poll (see Figure 14.3), is associated with the proportion of presidential legislative proposals approved by Congress (see Figure 14.4). Other things equal, the more popular the president, the higher the proportion of presidential bills that Congress will pass.

But use these figures with caution. How successful a president is with Congress depends not just on the numbers reported here, but on many other factors as well. First, the president can be "successful" on a big bill or on a trivial one. If the president is successful on a lot of small matters and never on a big one, the measure of presidential victories does not tell us much. Second, a president can keep the victory score high by not taking a position on any controversial measure. (President Carter made his views known on only 22 percent of House votes, whereas President Eisenhower made his views known on 56 percent of those votes.) Third, a president may seem successful if a few executive initiatives are passed, but then much of the president's legislative program may stall in Congress and never come to a vote. Given these problems, "presidential victories" are hard to measure accurately.

Figure 14.1 **Partisan Gains or Losses in Congress in Presidential Election Years**

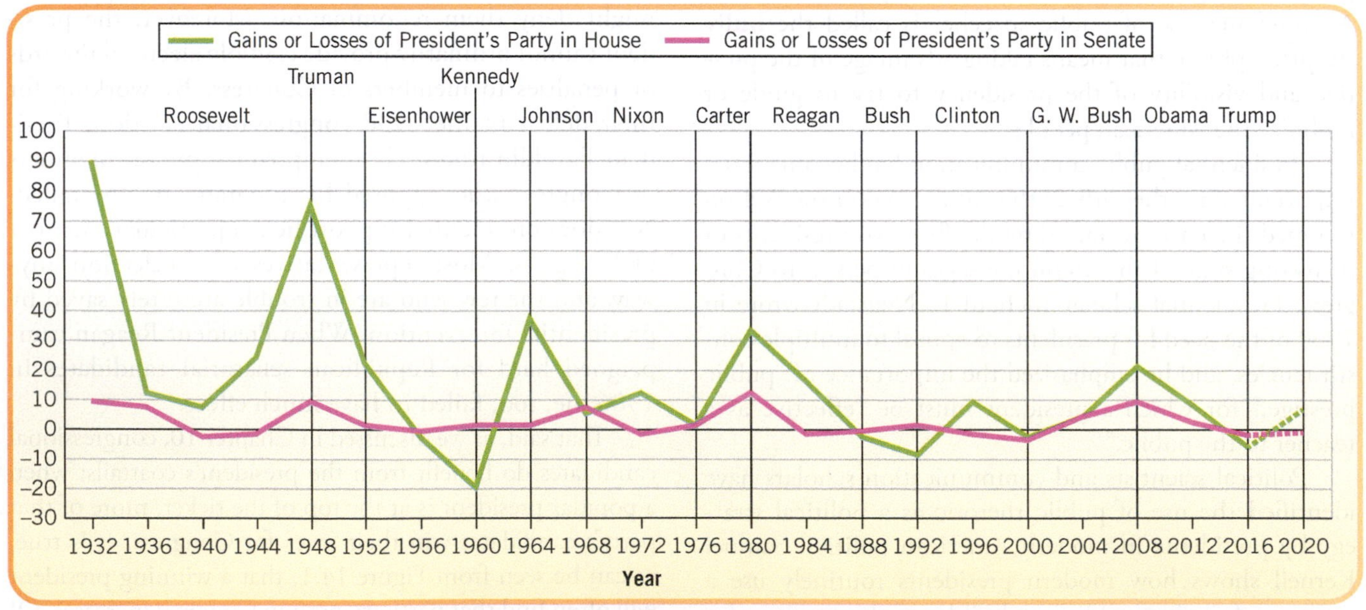

Source: Gerhard Peters, "Seats in Congress Gained or Lost by the President's Party in Presidential Election Years," *The American Presidency Project,* edited by John T. Woolley and Gerhard Peters, Santa Barbara, CA: University of California, 1999–2017. https://www.presidency.ucsb.edu/statistics/data/seats-congress-gained-or-lost-the-presidents-party-presidential-election-years. Updated by authors as of mid-November 2020, with final results pending vote counts in some House races and runoff elections in two Senate races.

Figure 14.2 **Partisan Gains or Losses in Congress in Off-Year Elections**

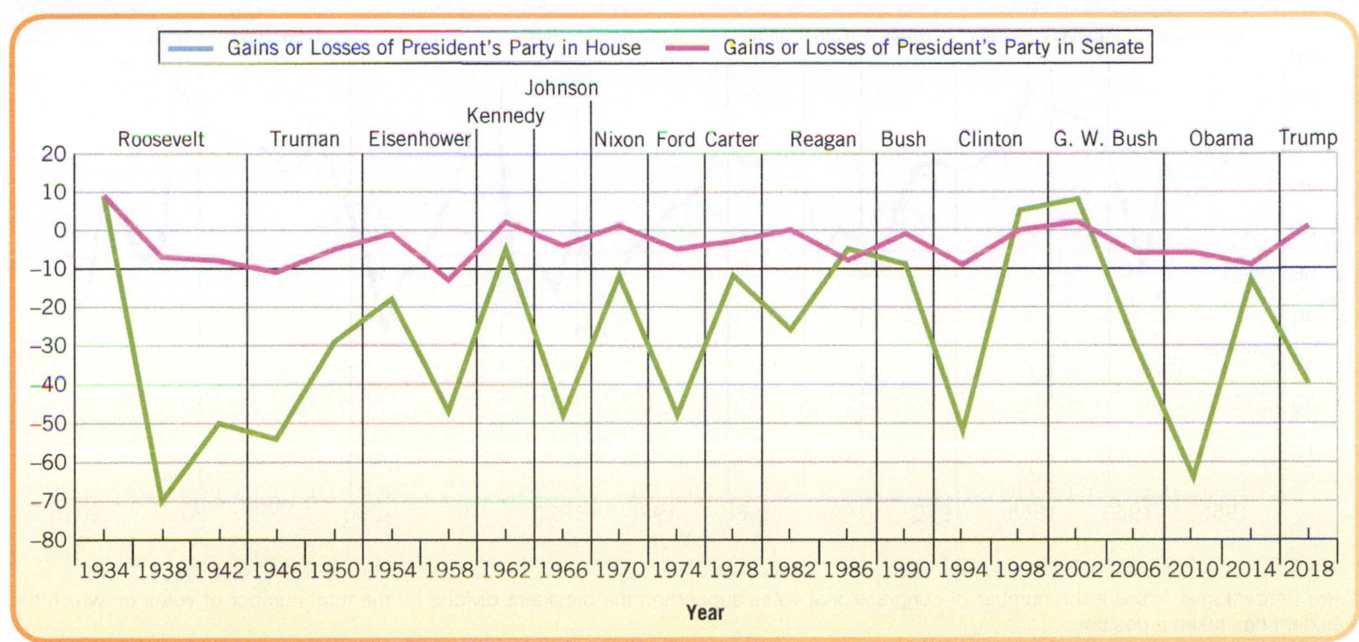

Source: The American Presidency Project. "Seats in Congress Gained/Lost by the President's Party in Mid-Term Elections." Santa Barbara, CA: University of California. Available from the World Wide Web: https://www.presidency.ucsb.edu/node/332343/.

Figure 14.3 **Presidential Popularity**

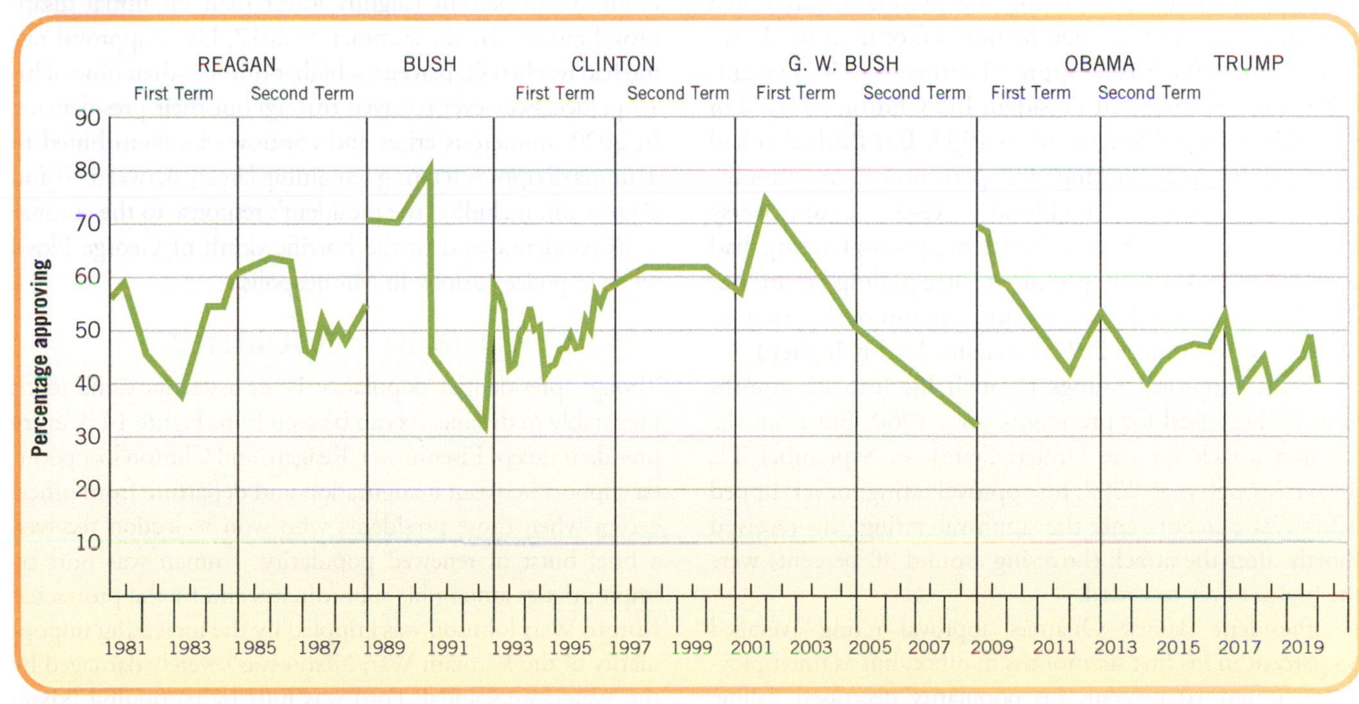

Note: Popularity is measured by asking "Do you approve of the way ________ is handling his job as president?" on a regular basis.

Source: Gallup, Presidential Job Approval Center. https://news.gallup.com/interactives/185273/presidential-job-approval-center.aspx

Q **Why do presidential approval ratings typically decline during a presidency, and what events or actions can help to improve those ratings?**

Figure 14.4 **Presidential Victories on Votes in Congress, 1953–2016**

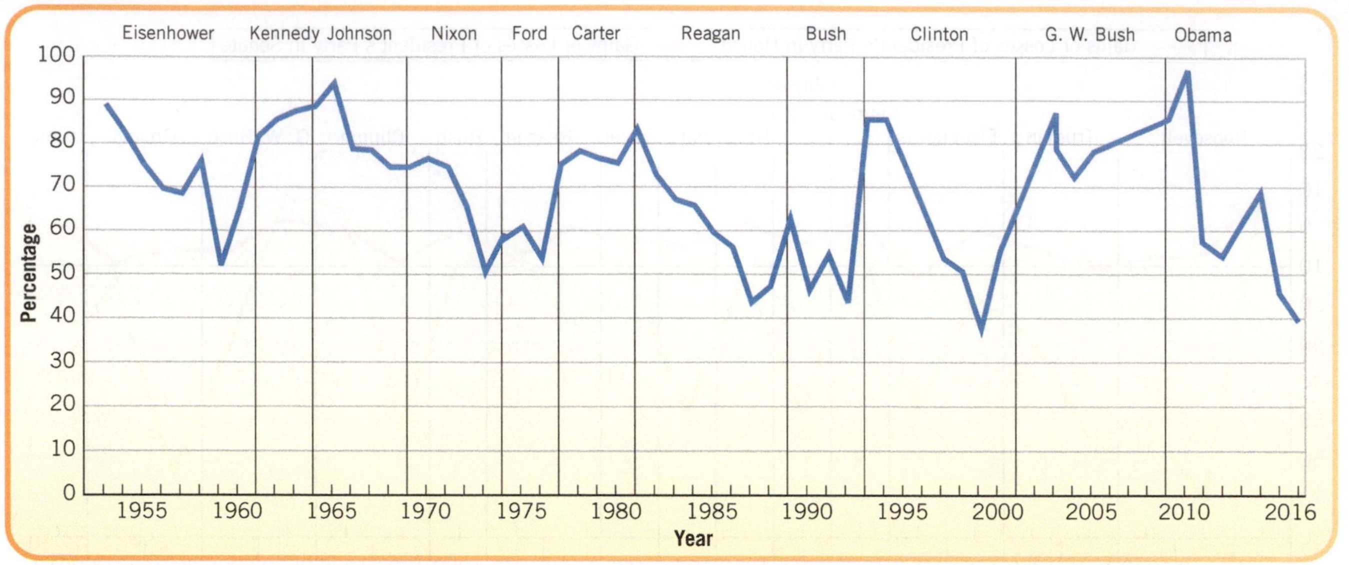

Note: Percentages indicate the number of congressional votes supporting the president divided by the total number of votes on which the president has taken a position.

Source: The Brookings Institution, "Presidential Victories on Votes in Congress, 1953–2016," in *Vital Statistics on Congress* (chapter 8, Table 8-1), https://www.brookings.edu/wp-content/uploads/2017/01/vitalstats_ch8_tbl1.pdf .

A fourth general caution: presidential popularity is hard to predict and can be greatly influenced by factors over which nobody, including the president, has much control. For example, when he took office in 2001, President George W. Bush's approval rating was 57 percent, nearly identical to what President Bill Clinton received in his initial rating (58 percent) in 1993. But Bush also had an initial *dis*approval rating of 25 percent, which undoubtedly was due partly to the Florida vote-count controversy (see Chapter 10). (Bush's initial disapproval rating had been the highest of any president since polling began, but President Donald Trump's initial disapproval rating of 47 percent in January 2017 was considerably higher.)

Bush's approval ratings through his first six months were fairly typical for presidents since 1960. But from the terrorist attack on the United States on September 11, 2001, through mid-2002, his approval ratings never dipped below 70 percent, and the approval ratings he received shortly after the attack (hovering around 90 percent) were the highest ever recorded.

President Barack Obama's approval rating averaged 63 percent in his first six months in office, but as unemployment neared 10 percent, his popularity decreased, falling below 45 percent by the 2010 midterm elections. In 2011 and 2012, Obama's approval ratings typically averaged between 45 and 50 percent, and they were above 50 percent when he won reelection. In his second term, Obama's approval ratings dropped to the low 40s, but they moved just above 50 percent before he left office. President Trump took office in 2017 with an historically low initial public approval rating of 45 percent (slightly lower than his initial disapproval rating). By the summer of 2017, his disapproval rating had reached 60 percent, a higher number than nine of his 13 predecessors ever received throughout their presidencies. In 2020, numerous crises and controversies contributed to Trump's disapproval rating remaining largely between 50 and 60 percent, including the president's response to the coronavirus pandemic and to the horrific death of George Floyd while in police custody in Minneapolis.

The Decline in Popularity

Though presidential popularity is an asset, its value tends inexorably to decline. As can be seen from Figure 14.3, every president except Eisenhower, Reagan, and Clinton lost popular support between inauguration and departure from office, except when those presidents who won reelection received a brief burst of renewed popularity. Truman was hurt by improprieties among his subordinates and by the protracted Korean War; Johnson was crippled by the increasing unpopularity of the Vietnam War; Nixon was severely damaged by the Watergate scandal; Ford was hurt by pardoning Nixon for his part in Watergate; Carter was weakened by continuing inflation, staff irregularities, and the Iranian kidnapping of American hostages; George H. W. Bush was harmed by an economic recession, as was Barack Obama. George W. Bush suffered from public criticism of the war in Iraq.

Because a president's popularity tends to be highest right after an election, political commentators like to speak of a "honeymoon," during which, presumably, the president's love affair with the people and with Congress can be consummated. Certainly, Roosevelt enjoyed such a honeymoon. In the legendary "first hundred days" of his presidency, from March to June 1933, FDR obtained from a willing Congress a vast array of new laws creating new agencies and authorizing new powers. But those were extraordinary times; the most serious economic depression of that century had put millions out of work, closed banks, impoverished farmers, and ruined the stock market. It would have been politically irresponsible for Congress to have blocked, or even delayed, action on measures that seemed to be designed to help the nation out of the crisis.

Other presidents, serving in more normal times, have not enjoyed such a honeymoon. Truman had little success with what he proposed; Eisenhower proposed little. Kennedy, Nixon, Ford, and Carter had some victories in their first year in office, but nothing that could be called a honeymoon. Only Lyndon Johnson enjoyed a highly productive relationship with Congress; until the Vietnam War sapped his strength, he rarely lost. Reagan began his administration with important victories in his effort to cut expenditures and taxes, but he then faced more challenges in his second year (though he recovered to win reelection resoundingly in 1984). Nevertheless, presidents do have other ways besides persuasion to influence policymaking.

Other Ways for Presidents to Influence Policymaking

The Constitution gives the president the power to veto legislation. In addition, most presidents have asserted the right of "executive privilege," or the right to withhold information that Congress may want to obtain from the president or subordinates, and some presidents have tried to impound funds appropriated by Congress. Presidents also may use their "executive power," as enumerated in Article II of the Constitution, to make policy pronouncements through executive orders and signing statements. These efforts by the president to say no are not only a way of blocking action but also a way of forcing Congress to bargain with the White House over the substance of policies.

Veto Power

If a president disapproves of a bill passed by both houses of Congress, then a veto is possible in one of two ways. One is by a **veto message**. This is a statement that the president sends to Congress accompanying the bill, within 10 days (not counting Sundays) after the bill has been passed. In it the president sets forth reasons for not signing the bill. The other is the **pocket veto**. If the president does not sign the bill within 10 days *and* Congress has adjourned within that time, then the bill will not become law.

veto message *A message from the president to Congress stating that that a bill passed in both chambers will not be signed. Must be produced within 10 days of the bill's passage.*

pocket veto *A bill fails to become law because the president did not sign it within 10 days before Congress adjourns.*

line-item veto *An executive's ability to block a particular provision in a bill passed by the legislature.*

Obviously, a pocket veto can be used only during a certain time of the year—just before Congress adjourns at the end of its second session. At times, however, presidents have pocket-vetoed a bill just before Congress recessed for a summer vacation or to permit its members to campaign during an off-year election. In 1972, Senator Edward M. Kennedy of Massachusetts protested that this was unconstitutional, since a recess is not the same thing as an adjournment. In a case brought to federal court, Kennedy was upheld, and it is now understood that the pocket veto can be used only just before the life of a given Congress expires.

A bill not signed or vetoed within 10 days while Congress is still in session becomes law automatically, without the president's approval. A bill returned to Congress with a veto message can be passed over the president's objections if at least two-thirds of each house votes to override the veto. A bill that has received a pocket veto cannot be brought back to life by Congress (since Congress has adjourned), nor does such a bill carry over to the next session of Congress. If Congress wants to press the matter, it will have to start all over again by passing the bill anew in its next session, and then hope the president will sign it or, if not, that they can override a veto.

The president must either accept or reject the entire bill. Presidents do not have the power, possessed by most governors, to exercise a **line-item veto**, with which the chief executive can approve some provisions of a bill and disapprove others. Congress could take advantage of this by putting items the president did not like into a bill otherwise favored, forcing the president to approve those provisions along with the rest of the bill or reject the entire legislation.

In 1996, Congress passed a bill, which the president signed into law, giving the president the power of "enhanced rescission." This means the president could cancel parts of a spending bill passed by Congress without vetoing the entire bill. The president had five days after signing a bill to send a message to Congress rescinding some parts of what had been signed. These rescissions would take effect unless

Congress, by a two-thirds vote, overturned them. Congress could choose which parts of the president's cancellations it wanted to overturn. But the Supreme Court has decided that this law is unconstitutional. The Constitution gives the president no such power to carve up a bill: the president must sign the whole bill, veto the whole bill, or allow it to become law without a presidential signature.

Nevertheless, the veto power is a substantial one, because Congress rarely has the votes to override it. From George Washington to Donald Trump, close to 2,600 presidential vetoes were cast (about 1,500 regular vetoes and more than 1,000 pocket vetoes); 111 were overridden. Cleveland, Franklin Roosevelt, Truman, and Eisenhower made the most extensive use of vetoes, accounting for almost 60 percent of all vetoes ever cast.[20]

George W. Bush (43) did not veto a single bill in his first term, though he issued 12 vetoes in his second term, of which 4 were overridden. In his first term in office, Barack Obama vetoed just 2 bills, with a total of 12 in his presidency, of which Congress overrode one. In his first two years in office, President Donald J. Trump did not veto any bills, but he did so six times in 2019.[21] Even without an override, vetoed legislation can be revised by Congress and passed in a form suitable to the president. There is no tally of how often this happens, but it is frequent enough so that both branches of government recognize that the veto, or even the threat of it, is part of an elaborate process of political negotiation in which the president has substantial powers.

Executive Privilege

The Constitution says nothing about whether the president is obliged to divulge private communications with principal advisers, but presidents have acted as if they do have that privilege of confidentiality. The presidential claim is based on two grounds. First, the doctrine of the separation of powers means that one branch of government does not have the right to inquire into the internal workings of another branch headed by constitutionally named officers. Second, the principles of statecraft and of prudent administration require that the president have the right to obtain confidential and candid advice from subordinates; such advice could not be obtained if it quickly would be exposed to public scrutiny.

For almost 200 years, the claim of presidential confidentiality was not seriously challenged. The Supreme Court did not require the disclosure of confidential communications to or from the president.[22] Congress was never happy with this claim but until 1973 did not seriously dispute it. Indeed, in 1962, a Senate committee explicitly accepted a claim by President Kennedy that his secretary of defense, Robert S. McNamara, was not obliged to divulge the identity of Defense Department officials who had censored certain speeches by generals and admirals.

In 1974, the Supreme Court for the first time met the issue directly. A federal special prosecutor sought tape recordings of White House conversations between President Nixon and his advisers as part of his investigation of the Watergate scandal. In the case of *United States v. Nixon*, the Supreme Court, by a vote of eight to zero, held that while there may be a sound basis for the claim of executive privilege, especially where sensitive military or diplomatic matters are involved, there is no "absolute unqualified Presidential privilege of immunity from judicial process under all circumstances."[23] To admit otherwise would be to block the constitutionally defined function of the federal courts to decide criminal cases.

Thus, Nixon was ordered to hand over the disputed tapes and papers to a federal judge so that the judge could decide which were relevant to the case at hand and allow those to be introduced into evidence. In the future, another president may well persuade the Court that a different set of records or papers is so sensitive as to require protection, especially if there is no allegation of criminal misconduct requiring the production of evidence in court. As a practical matter, it seems likely that presidential advisers will be able, except in unusual cases such as Watergate, to continue to give private advice to the president.

In 1997 and 1998, President Clinton was sued while in office by a private person, Paula Jones, who claimed he had solicited sex from her in ways that hurt her reputation. In defending him against that and other matters, Clinton's lawyers attempted to claim executive privilege for Secret Service officers and government-paid lawyers who worked with him. Federal courts held, however, that not only could a president be sued, but these other officials could not claim executive privilege.[24]

One consequence of this case is that the courts have greatly limited the number of officials with whom the president can speak in confidence. Presidents must be attentive to the possibility that the courts may later compel associates to testify about what the chief executive said to them. But this process can be lengthy, and often the executive and legislative branches will seek to resolve conflicts directly rather than through the judicial process, as a ruling may impose more restrictions than either branch desires. In the fall of 2019, for example, President Trump declared that current and former White House staff did not have to respond to congressional subpoenas about his efforts to pressure the Ukrainian government to investigate former Vice President Joe Biden and his son Hunter Biden in return for U.S. military assistance. Trump declared that White House staff had absolute immunity from congressional subpoenas, and consequently the House impeached him. The Senate conducted a trial without hearing from witnesses and then acquitted the president (as discussed later in this chapter), and an appeals court upheld the White House's position that the president's top advisers cannot be required to testify

Drew Angerer/Getty Images News/Getty Images

Image 14.6 People expressed support following the Supreme Court ruling in 2020 that blocked termination of the Deferred Action for Childhood Arrivals program.

before Congress.[25] But in 2020 the Supreme Court rejected a different claim of absolute immunity by Trump, ruling in a 7-2 decision that the president may not unilaterally refuse to comply with a subpoena for personal financial records (see Landmark Cases: Powers of the President box on p. 356). The Court also ruled in a related case that Congress had not made a sufficient case to see those records.

Impoundment of Funds

From time to time, presidents have refused to spend money appropriated by Congress. Truman did not spend all that Congress wanted spent on the armed forces, and Johnson did not spend all that Congress made available for highway construction. Kennedy refused to spend money appropriated for new weapons systems that he did not like. Indeed, the precedent for impounding funds goes back at least to the administration of Thomas Jefferson.

But what has precedent is not thereby constitutional. The Constitution is silent on whether the president *must* spend the money that Congress appropriates; all it says is that the president cannot spend money that Congress has *not* appropriated. The major test of presidential power in this respect occurred during the Nixon administration. Nixon wished to reduce federal spending. He proposed in 1972 that Congress give him the power to reduce federal spending so that it would not exceed $250 billion for the coming year. Congress, under Democratic control, refused. Nixon responded by pocket-vetoing 12 spending bills and then impounding funds appropriated under other laws that he had not vetoed.

Congress in turn responded by passing the Budget Reform Act of 1974, which, among other things, requires the president to spend all appropriated funds unless Congress is told what funds should not be spent, and then Congress agrees, within 45 days, to delete the items. If the president wishes simply to delay spending the money, then Congress need only be informed, but Congress then can refuse the delay by passing a resolution requiring the immediate release of the money. Federal courts have upheld the rule that the president must spend, without delay for policy reasons, money that Congress has appropriated.

executive order *A presidential directive that calls for action within the executive branch.*

Executive Orders

Article II of the Constitution states that "The executive Power shall be vested in a President of the United States of America." Executive power to sign or veto laws passed by Congress is clearly explained in the Constitution; but presidents historically have interpreted executive power more broadly in order to make decisions and take action unilaterally—that is, without seeking congressional approval. In so doing, presidents sometimes have issued **executive orders**, which are presidential directives that call for action within the executive branch. As one scholar wrote, "presidents have used executive orders to make momentous policy choices, creating and abolishing executive agencies, reorganizing administrative and regulatory processes, determining how legislation is implemented, and taking whatever action is permitted within the boundaries of their constitutional or statutory authority."[26]

Virtually every president has issued executive orders, though their number, type, and substance have varied considerably over time. George Washington's Neutrality Proclamation to keep the United States out of conflicts in Europe, Thomas Jefferson's Louisiana Purchase, Abraham Lincoln's Emancipation Proclamation, Franklin D. Roosevelt's relocation of Japanese Americans to internment camps during World War II, Harry S. Truman's desegregation of the armed forces and seizure of steel mills during the Korean War, and Dwight D. Eisenhower's decision to call the Arkansas National Guard into service to enforce a school desegregation in Little Rock all were actions taken by executive order.[27] Since the 1930s, most executive orders are numbered and published in the *Federal* Register.[28] Presidents also may issue proclamations, memoranda, and other executive actions that are comparable to executive orders but do not have the same requirements for numbering and publication.[29]

All of these executive statements have the force of law, but they remain in effect only as long as the president allows or the courts permit. For example, in 2012, Barack Obama unilaterally created the Deferred Action for Childhood Arrivals (DACA) program, which allowed people who entered the United States illegally as children to receive two-year work permits (which could be renewed), and have temporary relief from deportation procedures.[30] Obama did so because the White House and Congress could not come close to an agreement on comprehensive immigration reform. Two years later, Obama announced the Deferred Action for Parents of Americans and Lawful Permanent Residents

signing statement *A presidential document that reveals what the president thinks of a new law and how it ought to be enforced.*

(DAPA) program, which extended similar protections to illegal immigrants whose children are U.S. citizens. But when a federal court issued an injunction on the program in response to a lawsuit filed by several states, DAPA was halted, and the U.S. Citizenship and Immigration Services agency announced that it would not extend the DACA program either.[31]

The Trump administration announced in the fall of 2017 that it would end the DACA program because the use of executive power to create it was unconstitutional. But in 2020 the Supreme Court blocked the administration from doing so, declaring in a 5-4 decision that the administration had not met the procedural requirement of providing a sufficient rationale for terminating the program.

In his first seven weeks in office, President Trump issued some two dozen executive orders or comparable unilateral actions. Some were information-oriented, such as the creation of task forces to combat crime or to review military readiness or the 2010 Dodd-Frank financial regulations. Some were organizational, such as restructuring the National Security Council or moving the Historically Black Colleges and Universities offices back from the Department of Education to the White House. And some were highly controversial policy changes, most significantly a revised executive order that temporarily suspended the U.S. refugee program and banned immigration from several countries with majority Muslim populations, citing national security concerns about potential terrorist attacks. But federal courts blocked both the original order, issued one week after Trump took office, and the revised one. In 2018, the Supreme Court upheld the Trump administration's travel ban (which was issued for a third time in September 2017), stating in a 5-4 decision that control over the country's borders fell within executive power over national security.[32]

After several shocking and violent deaths of African Americans in conflicts with police officers in the spring of 2020, Trump issued an executive order calling for changes in police training, though it did not mandate specific actions.

Signing Statements

Since the presidency of James Monroe, the White House has issued statements at the time the president signs a bill that has been passed by Congress. These statements have had several purposes: to express presidential attitudes about the law, to tell the executive branch how to implement it, or to declare that the president thinks some part of the law is unconstitutional. President Andrew Jackson, for example, issued a statement in 1830 saying that a law designed to build a road from Chicago to Detroit should not cross the Michigan boundary (and so not get to Chicago). Congress complained, but Jackson's view prevailed and the road did not get to Chicago.

In the 20th century, these statements became common. President Reagan issued 71, President George H. W Bush signed 141, and President Clinton inked 105. By the late 1980s, they were published in legal documents as part of the legislative history of a bill.[33] During his two terms, President George W. Bush signed more than 150, and in so doing he challenged more than 1,200 sections of legislation, about double the number challenged by all of his predecessors. President Obama, who campaigned against the use of signing statements, signed more than three dozen.[34]

Naturally, members of Congress are upset by this practice. To them, a **signing statement** often blocks the enforcement of a law Congress has passed and is therefore equivalent to an unconstitutional line-item veto. But presidential advisers have defended these documents, arguing (as did an assistant attorney general in the Clinton administration) that they not only clarify how the law should be implemented but also allow the president to declare what part of the law is in his view unconstitutional and thus ought not to be enforced at all.[35]

While the Supreme Court has allowed signing statements to clarify the unclear legislative intent of a law, it has never given a clear verdict about the constitutional significance of such documents.[36] In 2007, the Democratic Congress considered a challenge to the practice, and President Obama issued a memo less than three months after taking office, stating that he would use signing statements only to protest unconstitutional provisions on legislation, not for policy disagreements. But even with unified government, Obama issued signing statements during his first year in office, and members of Congress criticized him for doing so. The struggle over signing statements is another illustration of what one scholar has called the "invitation to struggle" that the Constitution has created between the president and Congress.[37]

Powers of the President

- ***United States v. Nixon* (1974):** A president is entitled to receive confidential advice but can be required to reveal material related to a criminal prosecution.
- ***Nixon v. Fitzgerald* (1982):** The president may not be sued while in office.
- ***Clinton v. Jones* (1997):** The president may be sued for actions taken before becoming president.
- ***Trump v. Vance* (2020):** The president does not have absolute immunity to block release of personal financial records in response to a subpoena.

14-4 Presidential Character, Organization, and Policymaking

Although all presidents share certain constitutional and political powers, every president brings to the White House a distinctive personality; the way the White House is organized and run will reflect that personality. Moreover, the public will judge the president not only in terms of accomplishments but also in terms of perception of character. Thus, personality plays a more important role in explaining the presidency than it does in explaining Congress, as the selected examples of modern presidential leadership below illustrate.

Presidential Personality and Leadership Style

Dwight Eisenhower brought an orderly, military style to the White House. He was accustomed to delegating authority and to having careful and complete staff work done for him by trained specialists. Though critics often accused him of having a bumbling, incoherent manner of speaking, in fact much of that was a public disguise—a strategy for avoiding being pinned down in public on matters where he wished to retain freedom of action. His private papers reveal a very different Eisenhower—sharp, precise, deliberate.[38]

John F. Kennedy brought a very different style to the presidency. He projected the image of a bold, articulate, and amusing leader who liked to surround himself with talented amateurs. Instead of clear, hierarchical lines of authority, there was a pattern of personal rule and an atmosphere of improvisation. Kennedy did not hesitate to call very junior subordinates directly and tell them what to do, bypassing the chain of command.[39]

Lyndon Johnson was a master legislative strategist who had risen to be majority leader of the Senate on the strength of his ability to persuade other politicians in face-to-face encounters. He was a consummate deal maker who, having been in Washington for 30 years before becoming president, knew everybody and everything. As a result, he tried to make every decision himself. But the style that served him well in political negotiations did not serve him well in speaking to the country at large, especially when trying to retain public support for the war in Vietnam.[40]

Richard Nixon was a highly intelligent man with a deep knowledge of and interest in foreign policy, coupled with a deep suspicion of the media, his political rivals, and the federal bureaucracy. In contrast to Johnson, he disliked personal confrontations and tended to shield himself behind an elaborate staff system. Distrustful of the cabinet agencies, he tried first to centralize power in the White House and then to put into key cabinet posts former White House aides loyal to him. Like Johnson, his personality made it difficult for him to mobilize popular support. Eventually, he was forced to resign under the threat of impeachment arising out of his role in the Watergate scandal.[41]

Gerald Ford, before being appointed vice president, had spent his political life in Congress and was at home with the give-and-take, discussion-oriented procedures of that body. He was also a genial man who liked talking to people and encouraged an open system of White House organization. But this meant that many decisions were made in a disorganized fashion in which key people—and sometimes key problems—were not reviewed systematically.[42]

Jimmy Carter was an outsider to Washington and boasted of it. A former Georgia governor, he was determined not to be "captured" by Washington insiders. He also was a voracious reader with a wide range of interests and an appetite for detail. These dispositions led him to try to do many things and to do them personally. Like Ford, he began with an open system; unlike Ford, he based his decisions on reading countless memos and asking detailed questions. His advisers finally decided that he was trying to do too much in too great detail, and later in his presidency, he shifted toward a more structured advisory process.[43]

Ronald Reagan was also an outsider, a former governor of California. But unlike Carter, he wanted to set the broad directions of his administration and leave the details to others. He gave wide latitude to subordinates and to cabinet officers, within the framework of an emphasis on lower taxes, less domestic spending, a military buildup, and a tough line with the Soviet Union. He was a superb leader of public opinion, earning the nickname "The Great Communicator."[44]

George H. W Bush lacked Reagan's speaking skills and was much more of a hands-on manager. Drawing on his extensive experience in the federal government (he had been vice president, director of the CIA, ambassador to the United Nations, representative to China, and a member of the House), Bush made decisions on the basis of personal contacts with key foreign leaders and Washington officials.[45]

Bill Clinton, like Carter, brought gubernatorial experience to the White House, paid a lot of attention to public policy, and preferred informal, ad hoc arrangements for running his office. Unlike Carter, he was an effective speaker who could make almost any idea sound plausible. Consistent with his governing philosophy in his home state of Arkansas, he was elected president as a centrist Democrat but immediately pursued liberal policies such as comprehensive health insurance. When those failed and the Republicans won control of Congress in 1994, Clinton became a centrist again. His sexual affairs became the object of major investigations, and he was impeached by the House but acquitted by the Senate.[46]

George W. Bush, the 43rd president, entered office as an outsider from Texas, but he was an outsider with a difference: his father had served as the 41st president of the United States, his late paternal grandfather had served as a U.S. senator from Connecticut, and he won the presidency only after the U.S. Supreme Court halted a recount of ballots in Florida, where his brother was governor. Bush, who had earned an advanced degree in business administration from Harvard, ran a very tight White House ship, insisting that meetings run on time and that press contacts be strictly controlled. He turned back public doubts about his intellect through self-deprecating humor. Following the terrorist attack on America on September 11, 2001, his agenda shifted almost entirely to foreign and military affairs, the war on terror, and homeland security.[47]

Barack Obama was the first African American to win a major party's presidential nomination and only the third person elected to the presidency while a sitting U.S. Senator. In the 2008 presidential race, Obama campaigned as the candidate of change and hope ("Yes we can!" was his most popular mantra). He came to office in January 2009 amid a global economic crisis that included devastating losses in America's real-estate sector and financial markets. In his first term in office, he passed the largest budget in U.S. history and enacted legislation for comprehensive health insurance. Obama won reelection in 2012 but faced severe policymaking challenges in his second term, including a government shutdown in 2013 and a refusal by a Republican-led Senate to consider his Supreme Court nominee in 2016. While Obama's public popularity was above 50 percent when he left the White House, criticism of his leadership style included perceptions of aloofness and a dislike of the ongoing engagement and communication with political opponents required for policymaking.[48]

Donald Trump's unexpected victory in the 2016 presidential race was surprising for several reasons. A businessman who never mounted a full-fledged political campaign before the 2016 election, Trump did not follow the traditional path of fundraising, endorsements from party elites, and campaign staff with extensive expertise in presidential politics. He relied on social media, particularly Twitter, to convey ideas and attack political opponents, and he continued to rely on this tool as a means of governance from the White House. After taking office, President Trump issued executive orders to follow through on several campaign promises, such as a travel ban on immigration from certain countries (which the Supreme Court upheld in 2018) and a decision to withdraw from the Trans-Pacific Partnership trade agreement. He also enacted legislation on tax and criminal justice reform. His refusal to sign budgetary legislation in December 2018 led to a five-week partial government shutdown, the longest in U.S. history. In 2019, a congressional investigation into Trump's efforts to pressure Ukraine to investigate former Vice President Joe Biden and his son in return for military aid led to the president's impeachment.

Then in 2020, Trump resisted calls for a federally coordinated response to the coronavirus pandemic, castigated protestors calling for police reform and policies to address racial discrimination after several horrific deaths of African Americans in conflicts with police officers, and evinced little interest in using the office of the presidency to elevate discourse and build unity to address the country's multiple economic and social crises.

The Office of the President

It was not until 1857 that the president was allowed to have a private secretary paid with public funds, and it was not until after the assassination of President McKinley in 1901 that the president was given a Secret Service bodyguard. The president was not able to submit a single presidential budget until after 1921, when the Budget and Accounting Act was passed and the Bureau of the Budget (now called the Office of Management and Budget) was created. Grover Cleveland personally answered the White House telephone, and Abraham Lincoln often answered his own mail.

Today, of course, the president has hundreds of people who can assist, and the trappings of power—helicopters, guards, limousines—are plainly visible. The White House staff has grown enormously. (Just how big the staff is, no one knows. Presidents like to pretend that the White House is not the large bureaucracy that it in fact has become.) Add to this the opportunities for presidential appointments to the cabinet, the courts, and various agencies, and the resources at the disposal of the president would appear to be awesome. That conclusion is partly true and partly false, or at least misleading, and for a simple reason. If presidents were once helpless for lack of assistance, they now confront an army of assistants so large that it constitutes a bureaucracy that can be difficult to control.

The ability of a presidential assistant to affect the president is governed by the rule of propinquity: in general, power is wielded by people in the room when a decision is made. Presidential appointments can thus be classified in terms of their proximity, physical and political, to the president. There are three degrees of propinquity: the White House Office, the Executive Office, and the cabinet.

The White House Office

The president's closest assistants have offices in the White House, usually in the West Wing of the building. Their titles often do not reveal the functions that they actually perform: "counsel," "counselor," "assistant to the president," "special assistant," "special consultant," and so forth. The actual titles vary from one administration to another, but in general the people who hold them oversee the political and policy interests of the president. As part of the president's personal staff, these aides do not have to be confirmed by the Senate; the president can hire and fire them at will. The White House staff today typically includes about 400–500 people.[49]

Essentially, a president can organize personal staff in three ways—through the "pyramid," "circular," and "ad hoc" methods. In a **pyramid structure**, used by Eisenhower, Nixon, Reagan, both Presidents Bush, and (after a while) Clinton, most assistants report through a hierarchy to a chief of staff, who then deals directly with the president. In a **circular structure**, used by Carter, cabinet secretaries and assistants report directly to the president. In an **ad hoc structure**, used for a while by President Clinton, task forces, committees, and informal groups of friends and advisers deal directly with the president. For example, the Clinton administration's health-care policy planning was spearheaded not by the Health and Human Services secretary Donna E. Shalala, but by First Lady Hillary Rodham Clinton and a White House adviser, Ira Magaziner. Likewise, its initiative to reform the federal bureaucracy (the National Performance Review) was led not by the Office of Management and Budget director Leon E. Panetta, but by an adviser to Vice President Gore, Elaine Kamarck.[50] President Trump has had very high staff turnover in his administration and left many staff offices unfilled as well, illustrating an ad hoc advisory structure.[51]

It is common for presidents to mix methods. For example, Franklin Roosevelt alternated between the circular and ad hoc methods in the conduct of his domestic policy and sometimes used a pyramid structure when dealing with foreign affairs and military policy.

Taken individually, each method of organization has advantages and disadvantages. A pyramid structure provides for an orderly flow of information and decisions, but does so at the risk of isolating or misinforming the president. The circular method has the virtue of giving the president a great deal of information, but at the price of confusion and conflict among cabinet secretaries and assistants. An ad hoc structure allows great flexibility, minimizes bureaucratic inertia, and generates ideas and information from disparate channels, but it risks cutting the president off from the government officials who are ultimately responsible for translating presidential decisions into policy proposals and administrative action.

All presidents claim they are open to many sources of advice, and some presidents try to guarantee that openness by using the circular method of staff organization. President Carter liked to describe his office as a wheel, with himself as the hub and his several assistants as spokes. But most presidents discover, as did Carter, that the difficulty of managing the large White House bureaucracy and of conserving their own limited supply of time and energy makes it necessary for them to rely heavily on one or two key subordinates. Carter, in July 1979, dramatically altered the White House staff organization by elevating Hamilton Jordan to the post of chief of staff, with the job of coordinating the work of the other staff assistants.

pyramid structure *A president's subordinates report to him through a clear chain of command headed by a chief of staff.*

circular structure *Several of the president's assistants report directly to him.*

ad hoc structure *Several subordinates, cabinet officers, and committees report directly to the president on different matters.*

At first, President Reagan adopted a compromise between the circle and the pyramid, putting the White House under the direction of three key aides. At the beginning of his second term in 1985, however, the president shifted to a pyramid, placing all his assistants under a single chief of staff. Clinton began with an ad hoc system and then changed to one more like a pyramid. Each assistant has, of course, other assistants, sometimes a large number. At a slightly lower level of status, "special assistants to the president" serve various purposes. (Being "special" means, paradoxically, being less important.)

Typically, senior White House staff members are drawn from the ranks of the president's campaign staff—longtime associates in whom the president has confidence. A few members, however, will be experts brought in after the campaign; such was the case, for example, with Henry Kissinger, a former Harvard professor who became President Nixon's assistant for national security affairs. The offices these men and women occupy often are small and crowded (Kissinger's was not much bigger than the one he had while a professor at Harvard), but their occupants willingly put up with any discomfort in exchange for the privilege (and the power) of being *in* the White House. The arrangement of offices—their size, and especially their proximity to the president's Oval Office—is a good measure of the relative influence of the people in them.

To an outsider, the amount of jockeying among the top staff for access to the president may seem comical or even perverse. The staff attaches enormous significance to whose office is closest to the president's, who can see the president on a daily as opposed to a weekly basis, who can get an appointment with the president and who cannot, and who has a right to see documents and memoranda just before they go to the Oval Office. To be sure, there is ample grist here for Washington political novels. But there is also something important at stake: it is not simply a question of power plays and ego trips. Who can see the president and who sees and "signs off" on memoranda going to the president affect in important ways who influences policy and thus whose goals and beliefs become embedded in policy.

The Executive Office of the President

Agencies in the Executive Office of the President (EOP) report directly to the president and perform staff services, but are not located in the White House itself. Their members may or may not enjoy intimate contact with the president; some agencies are rather large bureaucracies. The top positions in these organizations are filled by presidential appointment, but unlike the White House staff positions, these appointments typically require Senate confirmation. Principal agencies in the EOP include the Council of Economic Advisers, Director of National Intelligence, National Security Council, Office of Management and Budget (OMB), Office of the U.S. Trade Representative, and Office of the Vice President.

Of all the EOP agencies, perhaps the most important in terms of the president's need for assistance in administering the federal government is the OMB. First called the Bureau of the Budget when it was created in 1921, it became OMB in 1970 to reflect its broader responsibilities. Today it does considerably more than assemble and analyze the figures that go each year into the national budget the president submits to Congress. It also studies the organization and operations of the executive branch, devises plans for reorganizing various departments and agencies, develops ways of getting better information about government programs, and reviews proposals that cabinet departments want included in the president's legislative program.

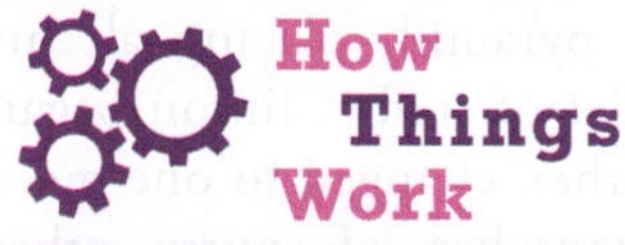

The Myth and Reality of the White House Office

The Myth

The White House Office was created in the 1930s following recommendations made by the President's Commission on Administrative Management. The principles underlying those recommendations have been endorsed by almost every presidential chief of staff since then. The key ones are:

1. *Small is beautiful.* The presidential staff should be small. At first, there were only six assistants.
2. *A passion for anonymity.* The president's personal assistants should stay out of the limelight.
3. *Honest brokers.* The presidential staff should not make decisions for the president; it should only coordinate the flow of information to the president.

The Reality

Increasingly, the operations of the White House Office seem to reflect almost the exact opposite of these principles.

1. *Big is better.* The White House staff has grown enormously in size. Hundreds now work there.
2. *Get out front.* Key White House staffers have become household words—Henry Kissinger (under Nixon and Ford), H. R. Haldeman (under Nixon), Hamilton Jordan (under Carter), Howard Baker (under Reagan), George Stephanopoulos (under Clinton), Karl Rove (under G. W. Bush), David Axelrod (under Obama), and Kellyanne Conway (under Trump).
3. *Be in charge.* Cabinet officers regularly complain that White House staffers are shutting them out and making all the important decisions. Congressional investigations have revealed the power of such White House aides as Haldeman, John Poindexter, and Lieutenant Colonel Oliver North.

Why the Gap Between Myth and Reality?

The answer is—the people and the government. The people expect much more from presidents today; no president can afford to say, "We're too busy here to worry about that." The government is much more complex, and so leadership requires more resources. Even conservatives such as Ronald Reagan and George W. Bush have been activist presidents.

Source: Adapted from Samuel Kernell and Samuel L. Popkin, editors, *Chief of Staff*. Berkeley: University of California Press, 1986, pp. 193–232.

The OMB has a staff of more than 500 people, almost all career civil servants, many of high professional skill and substantial experience. Traditionally, OMB has been a nonpartisan agency—experts serving all presidents, without regard to party or ideology. Starting with the Reagan administration, however, OMB has played a major role in advocating policies rather than merely analyzing them.[52] David Stockman, President Reagan's OMB director, was the primary architect of the 1981 and 1985 budget cuts proposed by the president and enacted by Congress. Stockman's proposals often were adopted over the objections of the affected department heads. In 2001, President George W. Bush's OMB director, Mitch Daniels, also participated fully in West Wing political strategy sessions; he later was elected governor of Indiana.

President Obama's first OMB director, Peter Orzag, was highly active in the administration's health care reform initiative. In President Obama's second term, he appointed Sylvia Mathews Burwell, a former executive in the Gates Foundation and former OMB staffer under President Clinton, to head OMB. Burwell also was active in promoting the president's policy agenda, and she became the administration's main official for implementing the Affordable Care Act upon her appointment as secretary of Health and Human Services in 2014. In 2017, South Carolina Congressman John Michael ("Mick") Mulvaney was appointed OMB Director in the Trump administration (and later acting White House chief of staff as well). A founding member of the Tea Party movement and the House Freedom Caucus (until he left Congress to take the OMB post), Mulvaney demonstrated clear determination to pursue major cuts in federal spending (though, as we discuss in Chapter 18, whether such cuts have actually emerged is less clear).

The Cabinet

The **cabinet** is a product of tradition and hope. At one time, the heads of the federal departments met regularly with the president to discuss matters, and some people, especially those critical of strong presidents, would like to see this kind of collegial decision making reestablished. But in fact this role of the cabinet is largely fiction. Indeed, the Constitution does not even mention the cabinet (though the Twenty-fifth Amendment implicitly defines it as consisting of "the principal offices of the executive departments").

When Washington tried to get his cabinet to work together, its two strongest members—Alexander Hamilton and Thomas Jefferson—spent most of their time feuding. The cabinet, as a presidential committee, did not work any better for John Adams or Abraham Lincoln, for Franklin Roosevelt or John Kennedy. Dwight Eisenhower is almost the only modern president who came close to making the cabinet a truly deliberative body; he gave it a large staff, held regular meetings, and listened to opinions expressed there. But even under Eisenhower, the cabinet did not have much influence over presidential decisions, nor did it help him gain more power over the government.

cabinet *The heads of the 15 executive branch departments of the federal government.*

By custom, cabinet officers are the heads of the 15 major executive departments. These departments, together with the dates of their creation and the approximate number of their employees, are given in Table 14.2. The order of their creation is unimportant except in terms of protocol: where one sits at cabinet meetings is determined by the age of the department that one heads. Thus, the secretary of state sits next to the president on one side and the secretary of the treasury sits next to him on the other. Down at the foot of the table are the heads of the newer departments.

The president appoints or directly controls vastly more members of cabinet departments than does the British prime minister. The reason is simple: the president must struggle with Congress for control of these agencies, whereas the prime minister has no rival branch of government that seeks this power. Presidents get more appointments than prime ministers to make up for what the separation of powers denies them.

This abundance of political appointments, however, does not give the president ample power over the departments. The secretary of Health and Human Services (HHS) reports to the president and has a few hundred political appointees to assist in responding to the president's wishes. But the secretary of HHS heads an agency with nearly 80,000 employees, 11 operating divisions, hundreds of grant-making programs, and a budget of more than $1 trillion (of which approximately 85 percent is for spending on Medicare and Medicaid).[53] Likewise, the secretary of Housing and Urban Development (HUD) spends the most time on departmental business and vastly less on talking to the president. It is hardly surprising that the secretary is largely a representative of HUD to the president, rather than the president's representative to HUD. And no one should be surprised that the secretary of HUD rarely finds much to talk about with the secretary of defense at cabinet meetings.

Having the power to make these appointments does give the president one great advantage, namely, a lot of opportunities to reward friends and political supporters. In the Education Department, for example, President Clinton found jobs for one-time mayors, senators, state legislators, and campaign aides.

TABLE 14.2 | The Cabinet Departments

Department	Year Created	Approximate Employees (2017)
State	1789	10,166
Treasury	1789	78,734
Defense*	1947	90,054
Justice	1789	111,778
Interior	1849	49,721
Agriculture†	1889	73,231
Commerce	1913	35,757
Labor	1913	14,424
Health and Human Services‡	1953	65,866
Housing and Urban Development	1965	7,697
Transportation	1966	53,568
Energy	1977	14,249
Education	1979	3,842
Veterans Affairs	1989	342,111
Homeland Security	2002	173,326

*Formerly the War Department, created in 1789. Figures are for civilians only.

†Agriculture Department was created in 1862; was made part of the cabinet in 1889.

‡Originally Health, Education and Welfare; reorganized in 1979.

Source: U.S. Office of Personnel Management, *Sizing Up the Executive Branch: Fiscal Year 2017*, Table 3: Federal Executive Branch Employment by Cabinet Level Agency.

Independent Agencies, Commissions, and Judgeships

The president also appoints people to four dozen or so agencies and commissions that are not considered part of the cabinet and that by law often have a quasi-independent status. The difference between an "executive" and an "independent" agency is not precise. In general, it means the heads of executive agencies serve at the pleasure of the president and can be removed at the president's discretion. On the other hand, the heads of many independent agencies serve for fixed terms of office and can be removed only "for cause."

The president can also appoint federal judges, subject to the consent of the Senate. Judges serve for life unless they are removed by impeachment and conviction. The reason for the special barriers to the removal of judges is that they represent an independent branch of government as defined by the Constitution, and limits on presidential removal powers are necessary to preserve that independence.

Who Gets Appointed

As we have seen, a president can make a lot of appointments but rarely knows more than a few of the appointees. Unlike cabinet members in a parliamentary system, the president's cabinet officers and their principal deputies usually have not served with the chief executive in the legislature. Instead, they come from private business, universities, think tanks, foundations, law firms, labor unions, and the ranks of former and present members of Congress as well as past state and local government officials. A president is fortunate to have agreement from most cabinet members on major policy questions. President Reagan made a special effort to ensure that his cabinet members were ideologically in tune with him, but even so, Secretary of State Alexander Haig soon got into a series of quarrels with senior members of the White House staff and had to resign.

The men and women appointed to the cabinet and to the subcabinet usually will have had some prior federal experience. One study of more than a thousand such appointments made by five presidents (Franklin Roosevelt through Lyndon Johnson) found that about 85 percent of the cabinet, subcabinet, and independent-agency appointees had some prior federal experience. In fact, most were in government service (at the federal, state, or local level) just before they received their cabinet or subcabinet appointment.[54] Clearly, the executive branch is not, in general, run by novices.

Many of these appointees are what Richard Neustadt has called "in-and-outers": people who alternate between jobs in the federal government and ones in the private sector, especially in law firms and in universities. Donald Rumsfeld, before becoming secretary of defense to President George W. Bush, had been secretary of defense and chief of staff under President Ford and before that a member of Congress. Between his Ford and Bush services, he was an executive in a large pharmaceutical company. This pattern is quite different from that of parliamentary systems, where all the cabinet officers come from the legislature and typically are full-time career politicians.

At one time, the cabinet had in it many people with strong political followings of their own—former senators and governors and powerful local party leaders. Under Franklin Roosevelt, Truman, and Kennedy, the postmaster general was the president's campaign manager. George Washington, Abraham Lincoln, and other presidents had to contend with cabinet members who were powerful figures in their own right: Alexander Hamilton and Thomas Jefferson worked with Washington; Simon Cameron (a Pennsylvania political boss) and Salmon P. Chase (formerly governor of Ohio) worked for—and against—Lincoln. Before 1824, the post of secretary of state was regarded as a stepping-stone to the presidency; and after that at least 10 people ran for president who had been either secretary of state or ambassador to a foreign country.[55]

Of late, however, a tendency has developed for presidents to place in their cabinets people known for their expertise or administrative experience rather than for their political following. This is in part because party leaders can no longer demand a place in the cabinet and in part because presidents want (or think they want) "experts." A remarkable illustration of this is the number of people with doctoral degrees who have entered the cabinet. President Nixon, who supposedly did not like Harvard professors, appointed two—Henry Kissinger and Daniel Patrick Moynihan—to important posts. President Clinton appointed Georgetown professor Madeleine Albright to serve as the U.S. permanent representative to the United Nations and then secretary of state; President George W. Bush appointed Stanford professor Condoleezza Rice to serve as national security adviser and then secretary of state. President Obama appointed former Harvard professor Ashton Carter to serve as secretary of defense. (Carter previously served in the Clinton administration's Defense Department.)

Additionally, presidents have become more attentive to recognizing politically important groups, regions, and organizations in their executive appointments. Robert Weaver became the first African American cabinet member when he served as secretary of HUD under President Johnson. The secretary of labor must be acceptable to the AFL-CIO, the secretary of agriculture to at least some organized farmers. In recent years, presidents such as Bill Clinton, George W. Bush, and Barack Obama appointed several women and members of traditionally under-represented racial and ethnic groups to cabinet positions.

Because political considerations must be addressed in making cabinet and agency appointments, and because any head of a large organization will tend to adopt the perspective of that organization, there is an inevitable tension—even a rivalry—between the White House staff and the department heads. Staff members see themselves as extensions of the president's personality and policies; department heads see themselves as repositories of expert knowledge (often knowledge of why something will not work as the president hopes).

White House staffers, many of them young men and women in their 20s or early 30s with little executive experience, will call department heads, often persons in their 50s with substantial executive experience, and tell them "the president wants" this or that or "the president asked me to tell you" one thing or another. Department heads try to conceal their irritation and then maneuver for some delay so they may develop counterproposals. On the other hand, when department heads call a White House staff person and ask to see the president, unless they are one of the privileged few in whom the president has special

Keystone-France/Gamma-Keystone/Getty Images

Chip Somodevilla/Getty Images News/Getty Images

Images 14.7 and 14.8 Secretary of Labor Frances Perkins (left), appointed by President Franklin Roosevelt, was the first woman cabinet member. When Condoleezza Rice was selected by President George W. Bush to be National Security Advisor, she became the first woman to hold that position (and later the first African American woman to be Secretary of State).

confidence, they often are told that "the president can't be bothered with that," or "the president doesn't have time to see you."

The President's Program

Imagine you have just spent three or four years running for president, during which time you have given essentially the same speech over and over again. You have had no time to study the issues in any depth. To reach a large television audience, you have couched your ideas largely in rather simple—if not simple-minded—slogans. Your principal advisers are political aides, not legislative specialists.

You win. You are inaugurated. Now you must *be* a president instead of just talking about it. You must fill hundreds of appointive posts, but you know personally only a handful of the candidates. You are expected to deliver an address to a joint session to Congress only two or three weeks after you are sworn in. It is quite possible you have never read, much less written, such a message before. You must submit a new budget; the old one is hundreds of pages long, much of it comprehensible only to experts. Foreign governments, as well as the stock market, hang on your every word, interpreting many of your remarks in ways that totally surprise you. What will you do?

The Constitution is not much help. It directs you to report on the state of the union and to recommend "such measures" as you shall judge "necessary and expedient." Beyond that, you are charged to "take care that the laws be faithfully executed."

At one time, of course, the demands placed on a newly elected president were not very great because the president was not expected to do very much. The president, upon assuming office, might speak of the tariff, or relations with England, or the value of veterans' pensions, or the need for civil service reform. In the 18th and 19th centuries, presidents were not expected to have something to say (and offer) to everybody, but they generally are expected to do so today.

Putting Together a Program

A president can develop a program in essentially two ways. One, exemplified by Presidents Carter and Clinton, is to have a policy on almost everything. To do this, they worked endless hours and studied countless documents, trying to learn something about and then state their positions on a large number of issues. The other method, illustrated by President Reagan, is to concentrate on three or four major initiatives or themes and leave everything else to subordinates.

But even when a president has a governing philosophy, as did Reagan, plunging ahead independently is risky. The president must judge public and congressional reaction to the proposed program before committing fully to it. Therefore, the president often will allow parts of the program to be "leaked" to the press, or "floated" as a trial balloon. Reagan's commitment to a 30 percent tax cut and larger military expenditures was so well known that it required no leaking, but he did have to float his ideas on Social Security and certain budget cuts to test popular reaction. His opponents in the bureaucracy did exactly the same thing, hoping for the opposite effect. They leaked controversial parts of the program in an effort to discredit the whole policy. This process of testing the winds by a president and his critics helps explain why so many news stories coming from Washington mention no person by name but only an anonymous "highly placed source."

In addition to the risks of adverse reaction, the president faces three other constraints on planning a program. One is the sheer limits of time and attention span. Every president works harder than ever before. A 90-hour week is typical. Even so, the president has great difficulty keeping up with everything to know and make decisions about. For example, Congress during an average year passes several hundred bills, each of which the president must sign, veto, or allow to take effect without a presidential signature. Scores of people wish to see the president. Hundreds of phone calls must be made to members of Congress and others in order to ask for help, to smooth ruffled feathers, or to get information. The president must receive all newly appointed ambassadors and visiting heads of state and in addition have pictures taken with countless people, from a Nobel Prize winner to a child whose likeness will appear on the Easter Seal.

The second constraint is the unexpected crisis. Franklin Roosevelt obviously had to respond to a depression and to the mounting risks of world war.[56] But most presidents get their crises when they least expect them. Kennedy faced the failure of the Bay of Pigs invasion in Cuba just three months after taking office, and then successfully resolved the Cuban missile crisis 18 months later.[57] Johnson wanted to focus on domestic policy, but his incremental escalation of U.S. involvement in the Vietnam War ultimately dominated his presidency.[58] Nixon had to contend with the Vietnam War, increasing oil prices, and the Watergate burglary and cover-up, which forced his resignation.[59] George H. W. Bush managed the U.S. response to the ending of the Cold War and the dissolving of the Soviet Union into independent republics, and then developed a multilateral coalition to repel Iraq's invasion of Kuwait.[60] George W. Bush led the nation after the devastating 9/11 terrorist attacks, waging war in both Afghanistan and Iraq.[61] Upon taking office, Obama enacted an economic stimulus package to combat the great recession. To combat the coronavirus pandemic in 2020—the most severe global health crisis in a century—Trump initially approved a $2 trillion economic assistance package, but resisted calls for a coordinated national plan of action.

The third constraint is that the federal government and most federal programs, as well as the federal budget, can be changed only marginally, except in special circumstances. The vast bulk of federal expenditures are beyond control in any given year; the money must be spent whether the president likes it or not. Many federal programs have such strong congressional or public support that they must be left intact, or modified only slightly. And this means that most federal employees can count on being secure in their jobs, whatever a president's views on reducing the bureaucracy.

The result of these constraints is that the president, at least in ordinary times, has to be selective about priorities. The president can be thought of as having a stock of influence and prestige comparable to a supply of money. To get the most "return" on resources, the president must "invest" that influence and prestige carefully in enterprises that promise substantial gains—in public benefits and political support—at reasonable costs.

Each president tends to speak in terms of changing everything at once, using overarching concepts such as a "New Deal," a "New Frontier," a "Great Society," the "New Federalism," or "Make America Great Again." But beneath the rhetoric, the president must identify a few specific proposals to pursue while remaining mindful of the need to leave a substantial stock of resources in reserve to handle the inevitable crises and emergencies. What a president manages to do beyond this will depend on personal views and a sense of what the nation, as well as reelection, requires.

And it will depend on one other source: opinion polls. The last president who never used polls was Herbert Hoover. Franklin Roosevelt began making heavy use of them, and every president since has relied on them. Bill Clinton had voters polled about almost everything—where he should go on vacation (the West) and how to deal with Bosnia (no ground troops). Once, when polls did not exist, politicians often believed they should do what they thought the public interest required. Now that polls are commonplace, some politicians act on the basis of what their constituents want. Scholars call the first view the trustee approach: do what the public good requires, even if the voters are skeptical. The second view is the delegate model: do what your constituents want you to do.

But there is another way of looking at polls. They may be a device not for picking a policy, but for deciding what language to use in explaining that policy. Choose a policy that helps you get reelected or that satisfies an interest group, but then explain it with poll-tested words. President Clinton wanted to keep affirmative action (described in Chapter 6), but knew that most voters disliked it. So he used a poll-tested phrase—"mend it but don't end it"—and then did nothing to mend it.

New York Times Co./Archive Photos/Getty Images

Image 14.9 During the Great Depression, the federal government created the Civilian Conservation Corps to provide employment through public works projects.

Finally, a president's program can be radically altered by a dramatic event or prolonged crisis. George W. Bush ran as a candidate interested in domestic issues and with little background in foreign affairs, but the terrorist attack of September 11, 2001, on the World Trade Center and the Pentagon dramatically changed his presidency into one preoccupied with foreign and military policy. Barack Obama campaigned against the war in Iraq but spent the first months of his presidency focused mainly on the country's sagging economy. Donald Trump planned to focus on a strong economy in his 2020 reelection campaign, but the COVID-19 pandemic unraveled those gains and prompted Trump to declare he would exercise wartime leadership to combat the national crisis precipitated by the virus.

Attempts to Reorganize

One item on the presidential agenda has been the same for almost every president since Herbert Hoover: reorganizing the executive branch of government. In the wake of the terrorist attack on the United States on September 11, 2001, the president, by executive order, created a new White House Office of Homeland Security, headed by his friend and former Pennsylvania governor, Tom Ridge. In the months that followed, it became clear to all, including the president, that he had given Ridge an impossible job. For one thing, despite its obvious importance, Ridge's office, like most units with the Executive Office of the President, had only a dozen or so full-time staff, little budgetary authority, and virtually no ability to make and enforce decisions regarding how cabinet agencies operated. Nobody could meaningfully coordinate the literally dozens of administrative units that the administration's new homeland security blueprint required Ridge's office to somehow manage.

To address this problem, President Bush called for a reorganization that would create the third-largest cabinet department: encompassing 22 federal agencies, nearly 180,000 employees, and an annual budget of close to $40 billion. Among the federal agencies placed under the new Department of Homeland Security are the Coast Guard, the Customs Service, the Federal Emergency Management Agency, and the Immigration and Naturalization Service. A law authorizing the new Department of Homeland Security was enacted in November 2002, but it has taken years and much effort for the new agency to become fully operational.

Important as it is, the ongoing attempt to reorganize the federal government around homeland security goals is neither the first, nor even the largest, reorganization effort made by a sitting president. With few exceptions, every president since 1928 has tried to change the structure of the staff, departments, and agencies that are theoretically subordinate to the White House. Every president has been appalled by the number of federal agencies and by the apparently helter-skelter manner in which they have grown. But this is only one—and often not the most important—reason for wanting to reorganize. If a president wants to get something done, put new people in charge of a program, or recapture political support for a policy, it often is easier to do so by creating a new agency or reorganizing an old one than by abolishing a program, firing a subordinate, or passing a new law. Reorganization serves many objectives and thus is a recurring theme.

Legally, the president can reorganize the personal White House staff anytime. To reorganize in any important way the larger Executive Office of the President or any of the executive departments or agencies, however, Congress must first be consulted. For more than 40 years, this consultation usually took the form of submitting to Congress a reorganization plan that would take effect provided that neither the House nor the Senate passed, within 60 days, a concurrent resolution disapproving the plan (such a resolution was called a legislative veto [discussed in Chapter 15]). This procedure, first authorized by the Reorganization Act of 1939, could be used to change, but not create or abolish, an executive agency. In 1981, authority under that act expired, and Congress did not renew it. Two years later, the Supreme Court declared all legislative vetoes unconstitutional (see Chapter 15), and so today any presidential reorganization plan would have to take the form of a regular law, passed by Congress and signed by the president.

What has been said so far may well give you the impression that the president is virtually helpless. That is not the case. The *actual* power that presidents exercise usually is measured in terms of what they can accomplish. What this chapter has described so far is the office as the president finds it—the burdens, restraints, demands, complexities, and resources that are present upon entering the Oval Office for the first time. Every president since Truman has remarked on how limited the powers of the president seem from the inside compared to what they appear to be from the outside. Franklin Roosevelt compared his struggles with the bureaucracy to punching a feather bed; Truman wrote that the power of the president was chiefly the power to persuade people to do what they ought to do anyway. After in office a year or so, Kennedy spoke to interviewers about how much more complex the world appeared than he had first supposed. Johnson and Nixon were broken by the office and the events that happened there.

Yet Franklin Roosevelt helped create the modern presidency, with its vast organizational reach, and directed a massive war effort. Truman ordered two atomic bombs dropped on Japanese cities. Eisenhower sent American troops to Lebanon; Kennedy supported an effort to invade Cuba. Johnson sent troops to the Dominican Republic and to Vietnam; Nixon ordered an invasion of Cambodia; Reagan launched an invasion of Grenada and sponsored an antigovernment insurgent group in Nicaragua; Bush invaded Panama and sent troops to the Persian Gulf to fight Iraq; Clinton sent troops to Haiti and Bosnia; George W. Bush ordered U.S. military operations in Afghanistan and Iraq; Obama approved air strikes in Libya. Obviously Europeans, Russians, Vietnamese, Panamanians, Iraqis, and others do not think the American president is "helpless."

14-5 Presidential Transition

No president but Franklin Roosevelt has ever served more than two terms, and since the ratification of the Twenty-second Amendment in 1951, no president will ever again have the chance. But more than tradition or the Constitution escorts presidents from office. Only about one-third of the presidents since George Washington have been elected to a second term. Of the 27 not reelected, four died in office during their first term. But the remainder either did not seek or (more usually) could not obtain reelection.

Of the eight presidents who died in office, four were assassinated: Lincoln, Garfield, McKinley, and Kennedy. At least six other presidents were the objects of unsuccessful assassination attempts: Jackson, Theodore Roosevelt, Franklin Roosevelt, Truman, Ford, and Reagan. (There may have been attempts on other presidents that never came to public notice; the attempts mentioned here involved public efforts to fire weapons at presidents.)

The presidents who served two or more terms fall into certain periods, such as the Founding (Washington, Jefferson, Madison, Monroe), wartime or economic crisis (Lincoln, Wilson, Franklin D. Roosevelt, George W. Bush, Obama), relatively tranquil times (Monroe, McKinley, Eisenhower, Clinton), or some combination of the above. When the country is deeply divided, as during the years just before the Civil War and during the period of Reconstruction afterward, presidential reelection is much more difficult.

Michael Evans/The White House/National Archives and Records Administration

Image 14.10 President Reagan waved to onlookers moments before he was shot on March 30, 1981, by a would-be assassin. The Twenty-fifth Amendment addresses the issue of presidential disability by providing for an orderly transfer of power to the vice president.

The Vice President

Eight times a vice president has become president because of the death of his predecessor. It first happened to John Tyler, who became president in 1841 when William Henry Harrison died peacefully after only one month in office. The question for Tyler and for the country was substantial: Was Tyler simply to be the acting president and a kind of caretaker until a new president was elected, or was he to be *president* in every sense of the word? Despite criticism and despite what might have been the contrary intention of the Framers of the Constitution, Tyler decided on the latter course and was confirmed in that opinion by a decision of Congress. Ever since, the vice president has automatically become president, in title and in powers, when the occupant of the White House has died or resigned.

But if vice presidents frequently acquire office because of death, they rarely acquire it by election. Since the earliest period of the Founding, when John Adams and Thomas Jefferson were each elected president after having first served as vice president under their predecessors, there have been only three occasions when a vice president was later able to win the presidency without the president having died in office. One was in 1836, when Martin Van Buren was elected president after having served as Andrew Jackson's vice president. The second was in 1968, when Richard Nixon became president after having served as Dwight Eisenhower's vice president from 1953 to 1961. The third was in 1988, when George Bush succeeded Ronald Reagan. Many vice presidents who entered the Oval Office because their predecessors died were subsequently elected to terms in their own right—Theodore Roosevelt, Calvin Coolidge, Harry Truman, and Lyndon Johnson. But no one who wishes to become president should assume that to become vice president first is the best way to get there.

The vice-presidency is just what so many vice presidents have complained about its being: a rather empty job. John Adams described it as "the most insignificant office that ever the invention of man contrived or his imagination conceived," and most of his successors would have agreed. Thomas Jefferson, almost alone, had a good word to say for it: "The second office of the government is honorable and easy, the first is but a splendid misery." [62] Daniel Webster rejected

Policy Dynamics: Inside/Outside the Box | The Sequester: Entrepreneurial or Majoritarian Politics?

In the spring of 2013, federal spending cuts took effect because the White House and Congress did not reach a budget agreement. The cuts, known as the "sequester," were part of the 2011 agreement to increase the debt ceiling, which stated that if the federal government did not enact a plan to cut $1.5 trillion in spending over 10 years, then automatic spending reductions, divided evenly between domestic and defense spending, would be enacted.

Republican leaders in Congress presented the sequester as entrepreneurial politics. Those directly affected by the spending cuts—furloughed government employees, participants in public tours of the White House (which were halted after the sequester began)—would pay, but the public as a whole would benefit from trimming the budget deficit and achieving more moderate and sustainable federal spending of public dollars over the next decade.

The Obama White House criticized the spending cuts as draconian efforts to limit short-term government spending at the expense of our long-term economic health. The president's economic advisers defined budgetary battles as majoritarian politics: everyone would pay for deficit spending now, which would lead to greater and more sustained economic productivity, lower unemployment, and reduced budget deficits in the future. The sequester did not cut wasteful government spending, according to the White House, but cut preschool and after-school educational opportunities in the Head Start program, halted meals for senior citizens, and reduced funds for first responders nationwide. Those who most needed assistance from the federal government were harmed most by the sequester, with significant consequences for curtailing their educational and economic opportunities in the future.

In 2019, the White House and Congress reached a two-year budget deal to raise the debt ceiling and increase both defense and domestic spending. The agreement greatly decreased the likelihood of the United States defaulting on its debt or facing another government shutdown. But many lawmakers and analysts raised concerns about the lack of fiscal discipline with the spending increases, and questioned how to develop a budget plan that would address this issue in coming years.

How do you think the White House and Congress should decide on immediate and long-term spending priorities? What does the United States need to do in the coming years to reduce budget deficits and the national debt? And how should proposals be presented to maximize public support?

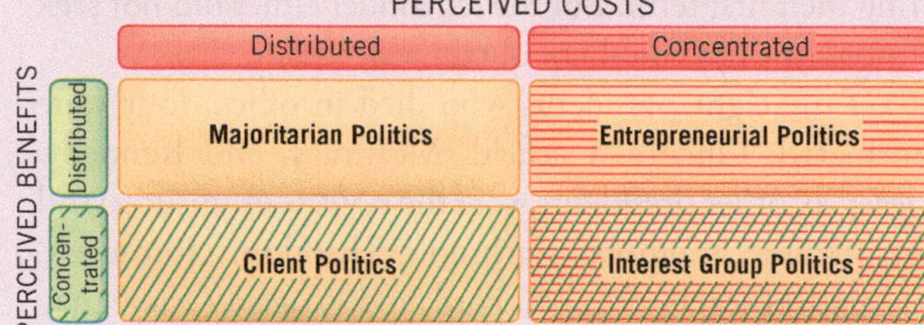

Sources: Dylan Matthews, "The Sequester: Absolutely Everything You Could Possibly Need to Know," *Washington Post*, 1 March 2013; White House, "What You Need to Know About the Sequester," https://obamawhitehouse.archives.gov/issues/sequester; Ylan Mui, Jacob Pramuk, and Mallika Mitra, "White House, Congress Strike a Two-Year Debt Ceiling and Budget Deal," www.cnbc.com, 22 July 2019.

a vice-presidential nomination in 1848 with the phrase, "I do not choose to be buried until I am really dead."[63] (Had he taken the job, he would have become president after Zachary Taylor died in office, thereby achieving a remarkable secular resurrection.) For all the good and bad jokes about the vice-presidency, however, candidates still struggle mightily for it. John Nance Garner gave up the speakership of the House to become Franklin Roosevelt's vice president (a job he later cuttingly valued as "not worth a pitcher of warm spit"*), and Lyndon Johnson gave up the majority leadership of the Senate to become Kennedy's. Truman, Nixon, Humphrey, Mondale, and Gore all left reasonably secure Senate seats for the vice-presidency.

*The word he actually used was a good deal stronger than *spit*, but historians are decorous.

The only official task of the vice president is to preside over the Senate and to vote in case of a tie. (Vice President Mike Pence did this in early 2017 for Secretary of Education Betsy DeVos's confirmation vote.) Even this is scarcely time-consuming, as the Senate chooses from among its members a president pro tempore, as required by the Constitution, who (along with others) presides in the absence of the vice president. The vice president's leadership powers in the Senate are weak, especially when the vice president is of a different party from the majority of the senators. But on occasion the vice president can become very important. Right after the terrorists attacked the United States in 2001, President Bush was in his airplane while his advisers worried that he might be attacked next. Vice President Cheney was quickly hidden away in a secret, secure location so he could run the government if anything happened to President Bush. And for many months thereafter, Cheney stayed in this location in case he suddenly became president. But absent a crisis, the vice president is, at best, only an adviser to the president.

Problems of Succession

If the president should die in office, the right of the vice president to assume that office has been clear since the time of John Tyler. But two questions remain: What if the president falls seriously ill, but does not die? And if the vice president steps up, who then becomes the new vice president?

The first problem has arisen on a number of occasions. After President James A. Garfield was shot in 1881, he lingered through the summer before he died. President Woodrow Wilson collapsed from a stroke in 1919, became a virtual recluse for several months, and then sharply curtailed activity for the rest of his term. Eisenhower had three serious illnesses while in office; Reagan was shot during his first term and hospitalized during his second.

The second problem has arisen on eight occasions when the vice president became president owing to the death of the incumbent. In these cases, no elected person was available to succeed the new president, should he die in office. For many decades, the problem was handled by law. The Succession Act of 1886, for example, designated the secretary of state as next in line for the presidency should the vice president die, followed by the other cabinet officers in order of seniority. But this meant that a vice president who became president could pick a successor by choosing the secretary of state. In 1947, the law was changed to make the Speaker of the House and then the president pro tempore of the Senate next in line for the presidency. But that created still other problems: a Speaker or a president pro tempore is likely to be chosen because of seniority, not executive skill, and in any event might well be of the party opposite to that occupying the White House.

Both problems were addressed in 1967 by the Twenty-fifth Amendment to the Constitution. It deals with the disability problem by allowing the vice president to serve as "acting president" whenever the president declares an inability to discharge the powers and duties of the office, or whenever the vice president and a majority of the cabinet declare that the president is incapacitated. If the president disagrees with the opinion of the vice president and a majority of the cabinet, then Congress decides the issue. A two-thirds majority is necessary to confirm that the president is unable to serve.

The amendment deals with the succession problem by requiring a vice president who assumes the presidency (after a vacancy is created by death or resignation) to nominate a new vice president. This person takes office if the nomination is confirmed by a majority vote of both houses of Congress. When there is no vice president, then the 1947 law governs: next in line are the Speaker, the Senate president, and the 15 cabinet officers, beginning with the secretary of state.

impeachment *Charges against a president approved by a majority of the House of Representatives.*

The disability problem has not arisen since the adoption of the amendment, but the succession problem has. In 1973, Vice President Spiro Agnew resigned, having pleaded no contest to criminal charges. President Nixon nominated Gerald Ford as vice president, and after extensive hearings he was confirmed by both chambers of Congress and sworn in. Then on August 9, 1974, Nixon resigned the presidency—the only president to do so—and Ford became president. He nominated as his vice president Nelson Rockefeller, who was confirmed by both houses of Congress—again, after extensive hearings—and was sworn in on December 19, 1974. For the first time in history, the two principal executive officers of the nation had not been elected to either the presidency or the vice-presidency. It is a measure of the legitimacy of the Constitution that this arrangement caused no crisis in public opinion.

Impeachment

A president can leave office early one other way—besides death, disability, or resignation—and that is by impeachment. Not only the president and vice president but also all "civil officers of the United States" can be removed by being impeached and convicted. As a practical matter civil officers—cabinet secretaries, bureau chiefs, and the like—are not subject to impeachment because the president can remove them at any time and usually will if their behavior makes them a serious political liability. Federal judges, who serve during "good behavior"† and who are constitutionally independent of the president and Congress, have been the most frequent objects of impeachment.

An **impeachment** is like an indictment in a criminal trial: a set of charges against somebody, voted by (in this case) the House of Representatives. To be removed from office, the impeached officer must be convicted by a two-thirds vote of the Senate, which sits as a court, is presided over by the Chief Justice, hears the evidence, and makes its decision under whatever rules it wishes to adopt. Twenty people have been impeached by the House, and eight have been convicted by the Senate. The last conviction was in 2010, when a federal judge was removed from office.

Only three presidents have ever been impeached—Andrew Johnson in 1868, Bill Clinton in 1998, and Donald Trump in 2019. (Richard Nixon likely would have been

†"Good behavior" means judges can stay in office until they retire or die, unless they are impeached and convicted.

impeached in 1974, had he not resigned after the House Judiciary Committee voted to recommend impeachment.) The Senate did not convict Johnson, Clinton, or Trump by the necessary two-thirds vote. The case against Johnson was primarily political—radical Republicans wanted to punish the South after the Civil War, and were angry with Johnson, a Southerner, for his more lenient policies on having the Confederate states rejoin the Union. The Senate vote was one short of the two-thirds required for conviction.[64]

The case against Clinton was more serious. The House Judiciary Committee, relying on the report of independent counsel Kenneth Starr, charged Clinton with perjury (lying under oath about his sexual affair with a White House intern), obstruction of justice (trying to block the Starr investigation), and abuse of power (making false written statements to the Judiciary Committee). The vote to impeach was passed by the House along party lines. The Senate vote fell far short of the two-thirds required for conviction.

Why did Clinton survive? There were many factors. The public disliked his private behavior, but did not think it amounted to an impeachable offense. (In fact, right after the affair became public, Clinton's standing in opinion polls went up.) The economy was strong and the nation was at peace. Clinton was a centrist Democrat whose private behavior may have offended voters, but whose public policies still had broad support.

One casualty of the entire episode was the death of the law creating the office of the Independent Counsel. Passed in 1978 by a Congress that was upset by the Watergate crisis, the law directed the attorney general to ask a three-judge panel to appoint an independent counsel whenever a high official is charged with serious misconduct. (In 1993, when the 1978 law expired, President Clinton asked that it be passed again. It was.) Eighteen people were investigated by various independent counsels from 1978 to 1999. In about half the cases, no charges were brought to court.

For a long time, Republicans disliked the law because the counsels were investigating them. After Clinton came to office, the counsels started investigating him and his associates, and so the Democrats began to oppose it. In 1999, when the law expired, it was not renewed. The U.S. attorney general may still appoint an independent counsel to lead a criminal investigation if having the Justice Department investigate presents a conflict of interest. A problem remains, however. How will any high official, including the president, be investigated when the attorney general, who does most investigations, is part of the president's team? One answer is to let Congress do it, but Congress may be controlled by the president's party. No one has yet solved this puzzle.

For example, the news that several advisers to the Trump campaign had met with the Russian ambassador to the United States during the 2016 presidential campaign and transition period sparked controversy because of U.S. intelligence reports that Russia had tried to influence the presidential election. Attorney General Jeff Sessions announced in March 2017 that he would recuse himself from any investigation because he had met with the Russian ambassador during the campaign, when Sessions was a member of the Senate Armed Services Committee and a supporter of Trump's candidacy. A few weeks later, President Trump dismissed his Federal Bureau of Investigation (FBI) Director James B. Comey, prompting allegations that the president was trying to halt any investigation of possible connections between the Trump campaign and Russian officials. The Justice Department then appointed former FBI Director Robert S. Mueller to serve as special counsel to investigate possible campaign ties. After a nearly two-year investigation, Mueller submitted a 400-page report to Attorney General William Barr, who released a redacted version a few weeks later. The report found no evidence of conspiracy or coordination between the Trump campaign and Russia during the 2016 election, though it stopped short of clearing the president of obstruction of justice.[65]

While the Trump White House and critics disagreed over whether the Mueller report identified impeachable offenses by the president, another controversy soon arose that did lead to impeachment. In the summer of 2019, an unnamed government official filed a whistleblower complaint with the intelligence community about President Trump. The complaint identified a July phone call in which President Trump allegedly asked Ukrainian President Volodymyr Zelensky to investigate claims of corruption against former Vice President Joe Biden, who was running against Trump in the 2020 presidential race, and his son Hunter. News of the complaint also revealed that the president had discussed withholding U.S. military aid to Ukraine to pressure the country to pursue the investigation. In late September, House Speaker Nancy Pelosi announced that the House would begin a formal impeachment inquiry into President Trump's actions (a process that she previously had rejected for other allegations as too divisive for the country). After nearly three months of hearings, the House voted on an almost entirely party-line vote (two Democrats voted with Republicans against impeachment) to impeach President Trump for abuse of power and obstruction of Congress. The Senate conducted a trial for almost three weeks, hearing from House impeachment managers but calling no witnesses, and then voted to acquit Trump, again on an almost fully party-line vote. (Republican U.S. Senator and former presidential candidate Mitt Romney voted to convict Trump on the obstruction of Congress charge.[66])

Some Founders may have thought that impeachment would be used frequently against presidents, but as a practical matter it is so complex and serious an undertaking that it has been reserved for grave allegations of presidential misconduct.

No one quite knows what a high crime or misdemeanor is, but most scholars agree that the charge must involve something illegal or unconstitutional, not just unpopular. Apart from impeachment, many experts believe the president and vice president are not liable to prosecution while in office. (No one is certain, because the question has never been tested.) President Ford's pardon of Richard Nixon meant that he could not be prosecuted under federal law after leaving the White House for alleged actions while in office.

Students may find the occasions of misconduct or disability remote and the details of succession or impeachment tedious. But the problem is not remote—succession has occurred nine times and disability at least twice—and what may seem tedious goes, in fact, to the heart of the presidency. The first and fundamental problem is to make the office legitimate. That was the great task George Washington set himself, and that was the substantial accomplishment of his successors.

Despite bitter and sometimes violent partisan and sectional strife, beginning almost immediately after Washington stepped down, U.S. presidential succession has always occurred peacefully, without a military coup or a political plot. For centuries, in the bygone times of kings as well as in the present times of dictators and juntas, peaceful succession has been a rare event among the nations of the world. Many of the critics of the Constitution believed in 1787 that peaceful succession would not happen in the United States either: somehow the president would connive to hold office for life or to handpick a successor. Their predictions were wrong, though their fears are understandable.

14-6 How Powerful Is the President Today?

Just as members of Congress bemoan their loss of power, so presidents bemoan theirs. Can both be right?

In fact, they can. If Congress is less able to control events than it once was, that does not mean the president is thereby more able to exercise control. The federal government *as a whole* has become more constrained, so it is less able to act decisively. The chief source of this constraint is the greater complexity of the issues that Washington must address.

It was one thing to pass the Social Security Act in 1935; it is quite another thing to keep the Social Security system adequately funded. It was one thing for the nation to defend itself when attacked in 1941; it is quite another to maintain a constant military preparedness while simultaneously exploring possibilities for arms control. It was not hard to give pensions to veterans; it seems almost impossible today to determine how to address such highly controversial issues as illegal immigration and reducing annual budget deficits and the ballooning national debt.

In the face of modern problems, all branches of government, including the presidency, seem both big and ineffectual. Furthermore, increased participation in politics by organized interests, as discussed in Chapter 11, raises additional issues for elected officials to contend with in policymaking. Add to this continuous, and often highly critical, media coverage (see Chapter 12), and it is small wonder that both presidents and members of Congress view their offices today as less powerful than in the past.

To address this problem for the presidency, some scholars recommend changing the institution in fundamental ways. One proposal is to give the president "fast-track" authority to propose legislation to Congress, which would have to approve or reject initiatives without amendments and within a fixed timetable.[67] Another proposal is to create a constitutional provision for special elections, for the president and Congress, if the public demonstrates a lack of confidence in both institutions. (This would be comparable to a no-confidence vote in parliamentary systems for the prime minister, though finding an acceptable measure for public confidence in the United States would be difficult.) Special elections could further test prospects for presidential influence, but they also could give the president a mandate to govern in a time of crisis.[68] Apart from the substantive debates, though, prospects for either proposal to be enacted are slim, as they likely would require a constitutional amendment.

Nevertheless, despite institutional constraints, presidents do have significant constitutional and political powers that enable them to set the direction of the country in domestic, economic, and foreign policy. (See Chapters 17, 18, 19 for a discussion of each policy area.) The rise of the modern presidency, as discussed earlier in this chapter, means that presidents are expected to lead the country and direct the national policy agenda, even if their ability to do so is constrained by other institutions and political actors. Consequently, presidents have come to acquire certain rules of thumb for addressing political expectations and challenges. Among them are these:

- *Move it or lose it.* A president who wants to get something done should do it early in the term, before political influence erodes.
- *Avoid details.* President Carter's lieutenants regret having tried to do too much. Better to have three or four top priorities and forget the rest.
- *Cabinets don't get much accomplished; people do.* Find capable White House subordinates and give them well-defined responsibility; then watch them closely.[69]

These informal guides to action illustrate well how presidents must operate quickly once in office to achieve as many of their goals as possible within a fixed time period of four or eight years.[70]

What Would You Do? | Will You Support the Budget Plan Proposed by Congress?

To: *President Lucy Barr*
From: *Talya Potter, Director, Office of Legislative Affairs*
Subject: *Passing budget bills under divided government*

With the opposition party in control of Congress, media pundits and other commentators are calling for the president to accept the other party's agenda for the next round of budget bills.

To Consider:

In the latest budget battle between the White House and Congress, the pressure on the president to accept a compromise with political opponents is great, given the looming threat of not only a government shutdown but also a debt default by the United States for the first time in the history of the American republic.

Arguments for:

1. With a reelection battle around the corner, the president cannot afford to get caught up in a budget battle with Congress.
2. The president's ability to gain public support for policy proposals is limited, and even increased public support will not improve leverage with Congress.
3. The president should defer to Congress as the primary representative of the people in American politics.

Arguments against:

1. American politics is guided too often by campaigns, and the president will build support for reelection by acting presidential—that is, by setting the agenda for the budget and not backing down.
2. The president can build public support through speeches and other forms of communication, and this support can be used as political capital to negotiate with Congress.
3. The president is the only nationally elected official in American politics (other than the vice president), and therefore is responsible for identifying and promoting public priorities, even if this means legislative battles with Congress.

What Will You Decide? Enter **MindTap** to make your choice.

Your decision: ☐ Favor plan ☐ Oppose plan

Learning Objectives

14-1 Explain how presidents differ from prime ministers and discuss the evolution of divided government in the United States.

Unlike prime ministers, American presidents are elected independently of Congress, which gives them both more independence in governing and more challenges in building political coalitions. Divided government has become much more common in the United States since the mid-20th century, with mixed consequences for policymaking.

14-2 Summarize how the constitutional and political powers of the presidency have evolved from the founding of the United States to the present.

The Framers developed the Constitution with the expectation that Congress would be the most important institution in the national government. And it was, with a few exceptions, until the 20th century. Today, presidential power has grown significantly from its constitutional origins. Since the 1930s, the president has become the central figure in American politics, even though the president's ability to achieve political success remains highly dependent on other individuals and institutions.

14-3 Discuss how modern presidents influence policymaking.

To make policy, a president must work closely with advisers and Congress while being attentive to political party and public expectations. A president needs to show why policy proposals are in their interest in order to win the support of advisers, political party members, Congress, and the public. Presidents additionally may influence policymaking in other ways, including through vetoes, executive privilege, impoundment of funds, executive orders, and signing statements.

14-4 Explain why presidential character and organization matter for policymaking.

A president's personality influences how White House advisors convey and evaluate information as well as how executive offices are organized. Many offices, within the White House as well as cabinet departments and executive agencies, influence the president's policy program.

14-5 Describe presidential transitions and their consequences for executive power.

The Constitution provides limited guidance on presidential transitions, creating four-year terms as well as the office of vice president and establishing the procedure of impeachment. Subsequently, Congress has passed legislation on executive succession, and constitutional amendments have limited a president to two terms of office and addressed the possibility of presidential disability. All of these provisions affect a president's ability to develop and enact a policy agenda.

14-6 Evaluate how powerful U.S. presidents are today.

The increasing complexity of policy challenges today make U.S. national political institutions seem ill-equipped to address public needs. Proposals to change the U.S. presidency, such as fast-track authority for legislation, or a provision for special elections (that would apply to Congress as well) are unlikely to be enacted because they would require a constitutional amendment. Still, the rise of the modern presidency does give the chief executive clear opportunities to govern, provided that the president is willing to take quick, decisive action in a limited time period.

To Learn More

Official White House blog: **www.whitehouse.gov**

Studies of presidents:

Miller Center of Public Affairs, University of Virginia: **https://millercenter.org/president**

The American Presidency Project, University of California at Santa Barbara: **www.presidency.ucsb.edu**

Cohen, Jeffrey E. *Going Local: Presidential Leadership in the Post-Broadcast Age*. New York: Cambridge

University Press, 2010. Study of how party polarization and an increasingly decentralized media have led presidents to target their public communications to local audiences over the national arena.

Corwin, Edward S. *The President: Office and Powers.* 5th ed. New York: New York University Press, 1985. Constitutional, historical, and legal development of the office.

Cronin, Thomas E., Michael A. Genovese, and Meena Bose. *The Paradoxes of the American Presidency.* 5th ed. New York: Oxford University Press, 2018. Concise study of contradictory expectations for presidential leadership in American politics.

Edwards, George C. III. *On Deaf Ears: The Limits of the Bully Pulpit.* New Haven, CT: Yale University Press, 2006. Analysis of the limits of presidential speeches for influencing public opinion polls.

Greenstein, Fred I. *The Presidential Difference: Leadership Style from FDR to Barack Obama.* 3rd ed. Princeton, NJ: Princeton University Press, 2009. Assessment of how, independent of other influences, modern presidents' leadership styles account for consequential changes in policymaking.

Howell, William G. *Power Without Persuasion: The Politics of Direct Presidential Action.* Princeton, NJ: Princeton University Press, 2003. Model of how presidents may use tools such as executive orders to enact policy initiatives independent of other political institutions.

Kernell, Samuel. *Going Public: New Strategies of Presidential Leadership.* 4th ed. New Haven, CT: Yale University Press, 2007. Analysis of how modern presidents develop policies with a focus on how to communicate with multiple public audiences.

Mayer, Kenneth. *With the Stroke of a Pen: Executive Orders and Presidential Power.* Princeton, NJ: Princeton University Press, 2002. Study of unilateral presidential policymaking through executive orders.

Neustadt, Richard E. *Presidential Power and the Modern Presidents: The Politics of Leadership from Roosevelt to Reagan.* New York: The Free Press, 1990 (original edition published in 1960). Study of how presidents try to acquire and hold political power in the competitive world of official Washington, by a man who was both a scholar and an insider.

Peterson, Mark A. *Legislating Together: The White House and Congress from Eisenhower to Reagan.* Cambridge, MA: Harvard University Press, 1990. Analysis of bargaining and cooperation between Congress and the executive branch.

Polsby, Nelson W., Aaron Wildavsky, Steven E. Schier, and David A. Hopkins. *Presidential Elections: Strategies and Structures of American Politics.* 15th ed. New York: Rowman & Littlefield, 2019. Systematic overview of how U.S. presidents win election.

Skowronek, Stephen. *Presidential Leadership in Political Time: Reprise and Reappraisal*. 2nd ed. rev. and exp. Lawrence: University Press of Kansas, 2011. Examination of how a president's political environment affects prospects for leadership and action.

Tulis, Jeffrey K. *The Rhetorical Presidency.* Princeton, NJ: Princeton University Press, 1987. Study of how once-powerful constitutional customs that proscribed presidents rallying the public for political support on a routine basis changed in the early 20th century.

Wayne, Stephen J. *The Road to the White House 2020.* 11th ed. Boston, MA: Cengage, 2020. Comprehensive study of the evolution of U.S. presidential selection and the modern process from nomination to election.

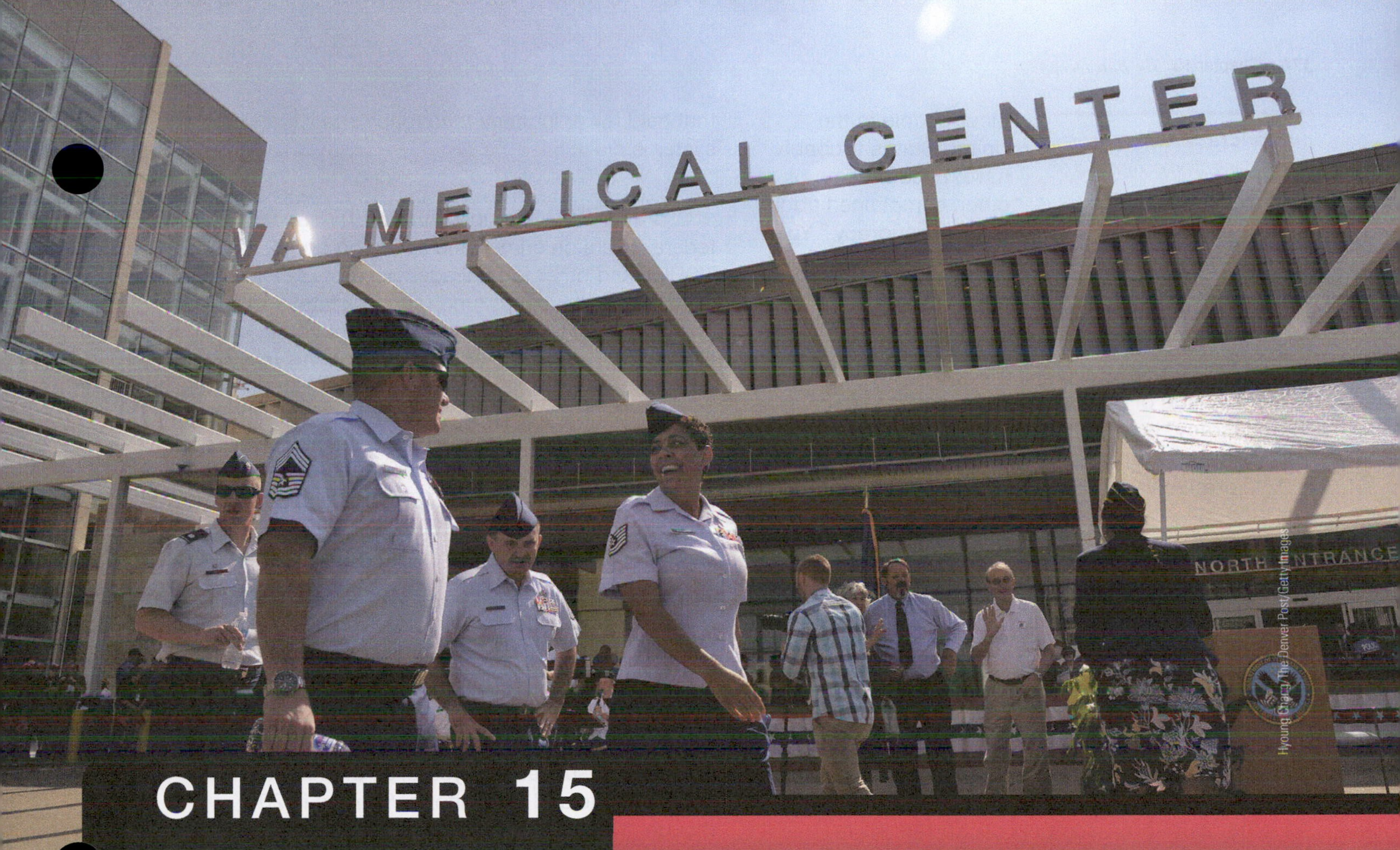

Hyoung Chang/The Denver Post/Getty Images

CHAPTER 15

The Bureaucracy

Learning Objectives

15-1 Discuss the unique features of the American federal bureaucracy.

15-2 Explain the evolution of the federal bureaucracy.

15-3 Summarize how the federal bureaucracy functions today.

15-4 Discuss checks on and problems with the federal bureaucracy, and possibilities for reform.

bureaucracy *A large, complex organization composed of appointed officials*

Most people in the United States probably have, at some time or other, complained about "the bureaucracy." Your birthday card did not reach your grandparent in time? The Internal Revenue Service (IRS) took months to process your tax refund? The Defense Department paid $400 for a hammer? The Occupational Safety and Health Administration (OSHA) said you installed the wrong kind of portable toilet for employees? The "bureaucracy" is to blame.

For most people and politicians, bureaucracy is a pejorative word implying waste, confusion, red tape, and rigidity. But for scholars—and for bureaucrats themselves—*bureaucracy* is a word with a neutral, technical meaning. A **bureaucracy** is a large, complex organization composed of appointed officials. By complex, we mean that authority is divided among several managers; no one person is able to make all the decisions. A large corporation is a bureaucracy; so also are a big university and a government agency. With its sizable staff, even Congress has become, to some degree, a bureaucracy.

What is it about complex organizations in general, and government agencies in particular, that leads so many people to complain about them? In part, the answer is to be found in their very size and complexity. But in large measure the answer is to be found in the political context within which such agencies must operate. If we examine that context carefully, we will discover that many of the problems that we blame on "the bureaucracy" are in fact the result of what Congress, the courts, and the president do. And, if we dig just a bit deeper, we will also discover that behind just about every government bureaucracy is some set of new or old public demands. Consider, for example, how Washington bureaucracies work to keep people safe from street criminals, clean up toxic waste sites, and make sure all children have nutritious school lunches.

« Then The U.S. Department of Justice (USDOJ—this is bureaucracy, so enjoy all the alphabet soup) was established in 1789, but until several federal "crime bills" were enacted beginning in the 1960s, it had only an incidental role in crime control. For the most part, the Justice Department neither funded nor worked at all closely with state and local criminal justice agencies. A USDOJ subunit, the Federal Bureau of Prisons (FBOP), was a tiny agency that held fewer inmates than many small state prison systems did.

*** Now** With public support for successive federal "wars on crime" and "wars on drugs," the USDOJ and other federal agencies now spend billions of dollars each year to fund federal, state, and local agencies engaged in combating street crime, and the FBOP now runs one of the largest prison systems in the world.

« Then Before the Environmental Protection Agency (EPA) was launched in 1970, the federal government's environmental protection activities were virtually nonexistent.

*** Now** The media stories and public outcries that accompanied the discovery of lethal toxic waste sites in and around New York's Love Canal area led in 1978 to the creation of the so-called Superfund program. To administer Superfund, the EPA expanded in 1980, and federal environmental protection efforts increased in subsequent years, as did federally directed state and local efforts. Starting in 2017, though, the Trump administration began curtailing environmental initiatives and regulations from the previous administration, leading many veteran staffers to resign or retire from the agency.

« Then The first federal law providing for subsidized school lunches was passed in 1946, but it was not until the 1960s that Washington began expanding its programs in this area to include ever-greater numbers of children eligible for both free (or reduced-price) breakfasts and lunches.

*** Now** It was only in 2010 that the U.S. Department of Agriculture (USDA)—created in 1862, made into a cabinet department in 1889, and long concerned mainly with the nation's farms and agri-businesses—was mandated by law to work with local school districts and other organizations to make nutritious meals (breakfasts, lunches, and snacks) available to children in low-income households year-round, including in the summer months when school is out. The Trump administration modified nutrition regulations such as the amount of whole-grain products and sodium content to include in these meals, to give schools more flexibility.

Whatever else it may be, bureaucracy is an outgrowth of representative democracy. If people demanded that government do less or do nothing, in due course public laws would change and the agencies that exist to translate those laws into administrative action would dissolve. But that has rarely happened in the United States. Instead, 6 of the federal government's 15 cabinet agencies were created after 1964. This includes the second and third largest agencies: the Department of Veterans Affairs, created in 1989, and the Department of Homeland Security, created in 2002. (The largest federal agency, the Department of Defense, dates back to 1947 and was predated by the Department of War, which was one of the original cabinet departments created in 1789.)

15-1 Distinctiveness of the American Bureaucracy

As you might expect, much the same can be said for the growth of bureaucracy in other democratic nations. Indeed, bureaucratic government has become an obvious feature of all modern societies, democratic and nondemocratic alike.

American Constitutionalism and the Federal Bureaucracy

In the United States, however, three aspects of our constitutional system and political traditions give to the bureaucracy a distinctive character. First, political authority over the bureaucracy is not in one set of hands but is shared among several institutions. In a parliamentary regime, such as in the United Kingdom, the appointed officials of the national government work for the cabinet ministers, who are in turn dominated by the prime minister. In theory, and to a considerable extent in practice, British bureaucrats report to and take orders from the ministers in charge of their departments, do not deal directly with Parliament, and rarely give interviews to the press. In the United States, the Constitution permits both the president and Congress to exercise authority over the bureaucracy. Every senior appointed official has at least two masters: one in the executive branch and the other in the legislative branch. Often there are many more than two: Congress, after all, is not a single organization but a collection of committees, subcommittees, and individuals. This divided authority encourages bureaucrats to play one branch of government against the other and to make heavy use of the media.

Second, most of the agencies of the federal government share their functions with related agencies in state and local governments. Though some federal agencies deal directly with American citizens—the Internal Revenue Service collects taxes from them, the Federal Bureau of Investigation looks into crimes for them, the Postal Service delivers mail to them—many agencies work with other organizations at other levels of government. For example, the Department of Education gives money to local school systems; the Centers for Medicare and Medicaid Services in the Department of Health and Human Services reimburse states for money spent on health care for the poor through Medicaid and other programs; the Department of Housing and Urban Development gives grants to cities for community development; and the Employment and Training Administration in the Department of Labor supplies funds to local governments so that they can run job-training programs. In France, by contrast, government programs dealing with education, health, housing, and employment are centrally run, with little or no control exercised by local governments.

Third, the institutions and traditions of American life have contributed to the growth of what some writers have described as an "adversary culture," in which the definition and expansion of personal rights, and the defense of rights and claims through lawsuits as well as political action, are given central importance. A government agency in this country operates under closer public scrutiny and with a greater prospect of court challenges to its authority than in almost any other nation. Virtually every important decision of the Occupational Safety and Health Administration or of the Environmental Protection Agency is likely to be challenged in the courts or attacked by an affected party; in Sweden the decisions of similar agencies go largely uncontested.

The scope as well as the style of bureaucratic government differ. In many Western European nations, national governments owned and operated large parts of the economy, including banks, cigarettes, railways, and telecommunications, for much of the 20th century. In the 1970s, for example, publicly operated enterprises accounted for about 12 percent of all employment in France but less than 3 percent in the United States.[1] In the 21st century, advanced industrialized countries have shifted away from state ownership of companies, though governments still play a large part in many industries. In the United States, the federal government regulates privately owned enterprises to a degree not found in many other countries. Why we should prefer regulation to ownership or management as the proper government role is an interesting question to which we return.

government by proxy
Washington pays state and local governments and private groups to staff and administer federal programs.

Proxy Government

Much of our federal bureaucracy operates on the principle of **government by proxy**.[2] In every representative government, the voters elect legislators who make the laws, but in this country the bureaucrats often pay other people to do the work. These "other people" include state and local governments, business firms, and nonprofit organizations.

Among the programs run this way are Social Security, Medicare, much environmental protection, and the collection of income taxes by withholding money from your paycheck. Even many military duties are contracted out.[3] In the first Gulf War in 1991, American soldiers outnumbered private contractors in the region by 60 to 1. But in 2006, there were nearly as many private workers as soldiers in Iraq. One company was paid $7.2 billion to get food and supplies to U.S. troops there.[4]

When Hurricane Katrina made landfall on the Gulf Coast in the late summer of 2005 (followed by Hurricane Rita), the nation's response was managed by a small and weak group, the Federal Emergency Management Agency (FEMA). When the levees broke, FEMA had only about 2,600 full-time staff; most of the help it was to provide came through "partners," such as state and local agencies, and some of these were not very competent (see our discussion of this disaster in Chapter 3).[5] Twelve years later, FEMA faced criticism again for inadequate disaster assistance in response to Hurricanes Harvey, Irma, and Maria, which devastated areas in Florida, Texas, Puerto Rico, and the U.S. Virgin Islands.[6]

Critics of our government-by-proxy system argue that it does not keep track of how the money we send to public and private agencies is used. Congress, of course, could change matters around, but it has an interest in setting policies and defining goals, not in managing the bureaucracy or levying taxes. Moreover, the president and Congress like to keep the size of the federal bureaucracy small by giving jobs to people not on the federal payroll.[7]

Defenders of government by proxy claim that the system produces more flexibility, takes advantage of private and nonprofit skills, and defends the principle of federalism embodied in our Constitution. The defenders make fair points, but the system does produce certain everyday oddities, such as the fact that many average citizens receive costly federal government services over long periods of time without ever directly interacting with civil servants. Donald F. Kettl, a political scientist and professor at the University of Maryland, dubbed this the "Mildred Paradox": In her last several years of life, his aged and ill mother-in-law, Mildred, applied successfully for multiple federal health insurance programs and received several years' worth of different types of expensive institutional care and top-quality medical treatment—all at government expense—but without ever actually encountering a single government worker.[8]

Jeff Greenberg/Universal Images Group/Getty Images

Image 15.1 The national government provides assistance to states for disaster-related needs, such as rebuilding after hurricanes or wildfires, through the Federal Emergency Management Agency (FEMA).

Or look a bit closer at what we noted above regarding the U.S. Department of Agriculture (USDA). As a result of federal law (the Healthy, Hunger-Free Kids Act of 2010), the USDA is required to expand and improve its "food security" programs by, among other measures, seeing to it that all eligible low-income children have daily access to free meals (breakfast or lunch plus a snack) during the summer months when school is out. The law, however, did not even begin to specify just how the USDA and its scores and scores of state and local government proxy agencies (not to mention their tens of thousands of administrative partners) are to accomplish that objective. For example, after the law passed in 2010, Philadelphia developed one of the largest USDA-funded summer food programs in the country (almost 4 million meals served each summer through more than 1,000 local "sites" including churches, recreation centers, and private homes on streets closed off for the purpose by local police). But the city's summer participation rate among eligible children was about 50 percent. Given this complex web of administration, perhaps it is a surprise that the program works as well as it does.

15-2 Evolution of the Federal Bureaucracy

The Constitution made scarcely any provision for an administrative system other than to allow the president to appoint, with the advice and consent of the Senate, "ambassadors, other public ministers and consuls, judges of the Supreme Court, and all other officers of the United States whose appointments are not herein otherwise provided for, and which shall be established by law."[9] Departments and bureaus were not mentioned.

In the first Congress in 1789, James Madison introduced a bill to create a Department of State to assist the new secretary of state, Thomas Jefferson, in carrying out his duties. People appointed to this department were to be nominated by the president and approved by the Senate, but they were "to be removable by the president" alone. These six words, which would confer the right to fire government officials, occasioned six days of debate in the House. At stake was the locus of power over what was to become the bureaucracy. Madison's opponents argued that the Senate should consent to the removal of officials as well as their appointment. Madison responded that, without the unfettered right of removal, the president would not be able to control his subordinates, and without this control he would not be able to discharge his constitutional obligation to "take care that the laws be faithfully executed."[10] Madison won, 29 votes to 22. When the issue went to the Senate, another debate resulted in a tie vote, broken in favor of the president by Vice President John Adams. The Department of State, and all cabinet departments subsequently created, would be run by people removable only by the president.

That decision did not resolve the question of who would really control the bureaucracy, however. Congress retained the right to appropriate money, to investigate the administration, and to shape the laws that would be executed by that administration—more than ample power to challenge any president who claimed to have sole authority over his subordinates. And many members of Congress expected the cabinet departments, even though headed by people removable by the president, to report to Congress.

The government in Washington was at first minuscule. The State Department started with only nine employees; the War Department did not even have 80 civilian employees until 1801. Only the Treasury Department, concerned with collecting taxes and finding ways to pay the public debt, had much power, and only the Post Office Department provided any significant service.

Appointment of Officials

Small as the bureaucracy was, people struggled, often bitterly, over who would be appointed to it. From George Washington's day to modern times, presidents have found appointment to be one of their most important and difficult tasks. The officials they select affect how the laws are interpreted (thus the political ideology of the job holders is important), what tone the administration will display (thus personal character is important), how effectively the public business is discharged (thus competence is important), and how strong the political party or faction in power will be (thus party affiliation is important). Presidents trying to balance the competing needs of ideology, character, fitness, and partisanship have rarely pleased most people. As John Adams remarked, every appointment creates one ingrate and 10 enemies.

Because Congress, during most of the 19th and 20th centuries, was the dominant branch of government, congressional preferences often controlled the appointment of officials. And because Congress was, in turn, a collection of people who represented local interests, appointments were made with an eye toward rewarding the local supporters of members of Congress or building up local party organizations. These appointments made on the basis of political considerations—patronage—would later become a major issue. They galvanized various reform efforts that sought to purify politics and to raise the level of competence of the public service. Many of the abuses the reformers complained about were real enough, but patronage served some useful purposes as well. It gave the president a way to ensure that subordinates were reasonably supportive of administration policies, it provided a reward the president could use to induce recalcitrant members of Congress to vote for programs, and it enabled party organizations to grow to perform the necessary functions of nominating candidates and getting out the vote.

Though at first there were not many jobs to fight over, by the middle of the 19th century, there were a lot. From 1816 to 1861, the number of federal employees increased eightfold. This expansion was not, however, the result of the government taking on new functions, but simply a result of the increased demands on its traditional functions. The Post Office alone accounted for 86 percent of this growth.[11]

The Civil War was a great watershed in bureaucratic development. Fighting the war led, naturally, to hiring many new officials and creating many new offices. Just as important, the Civil War revealed the administrative weakness of the federal government and led to demands by the civil service reform movement for an improvement in the quality and organization of federal employees. And finally, the war was followed by a period of rapid industrialization and the emergence of a national economy. The effects of these developments could no longer be managed by state governments acting alone. With the creation of a nationwide network of railroads, commerce among the states became increasingly important. The constitutional powers of the federal government to regulate interstate commerce, long dormant for want of much commerce to regulate, now became an important source of controversy.

laissez-faire *An economic theory that government should not regulate or interfere with commerce.*

A Service Role

From 1861 to 1901, new agencies were created, many to deal with particular sectors of society and the economy. More than 200,000 new federal employees were added, with only about half of this increase in the Post Office. The rapidly growing Pension Office began paying benefits to Civil War veterans; the Department of Agriculture was created in 1862 to help farmers; the Department of Labor was founded in 1882 to serve workers; and the Department of Commerce was organized in 1903 to assist businesspeople. Many more specialized agencies, such as the National Bureau of Standards, also came into being.

These agencies had one thing in common: Their role was primarily to serve, not to regulate. Most did research, gathered statistics, dispensed federal lands, or passed out benefits. Not until the Interstate Commerce Commission (ICC) was created in 1887 did the federal government begin to regulate the economy (other than by managing the currency) in any meaningful way. Even the ICC had, at first, relatively few powers.

Federal officials primarily performed a service role for several reasons. The values that had shaped the Constitution were still strong; these included a belief in limited government, the importance of states' rights, and the fear of concentrated discretionary power. The proper role of government in the economy was to promote, not to regulate, and a commitment to **laissez-faire**—a freely competitive economy—was strong. But just as important, the Constitution said nothing about giving any regulatory powers to bureaucrats. It gave to *Congress* the power to regulate commerce among the states. Now, obviously, Congress could not make the necessary day-to-day decisions to regulate, for example, the rates that interstate railroads charged to farmers and other shippers. Some agency or commission comprising appointed officials and experts would have to be created to do that. For a long time, however, the prevailing interpretation of the Constitution was that no such agency could exercise such regulatory powers unless Congress first set down clear standards that would govern the agency's decisions. As late as 1935, the Supreme Court held that a regulatory agency could not make rules on its own; it could only apply the standards enacted by Congress.[12] The Court's view was that the legislature may not delegate its powers to the president or to an administrative agency.[13]

These restrictions on what administrators could do were set aside in wartime. During World War I, for example, President Woodrow Wilson was authorized by Congress to fix prices, operate the railroads, manage the communications system, and even control the distribution of food.[14] This kind of extraordinary grant of power usually ended with the war.

Some changes in the bureaucracy did not end with the war. During the Civil War, World War I, World War II, the Korean War, and the Vietnam War, the number of civilian (as well as military) employees of the government rose sharply. These increases were not simply in the number of civilians needed to help serve the war effort; many of the additional people were hired by agencies, such as the Treasury Department, not obviously connected with the war. Furthermore, the number of federal officials did not return to prewar levels after each war. Though there was some reduction, each war left the number of federal employees larger than before.[15]

It is not hard to understand how this happens. During wartime, almost every government agency argues that its activities have *some* relation to the war effort, and few legislators want to be caught voting against something that may help that effort. Hence in 1944, the Reindeer Service in Alaska, an agency of the Interior Department, asked for more employees because reindeer are "a valued asset in military planning."

A Change in Role

Today's bureaucracy is largely a product of two events: the Great Depression of the 1930s (and the concomitant New Deal program of President Franklin Roosevelt) and World War II. Though many agencies have been added since then, the basic features of the bureaucracy were set mainly as a result of changes in public attitudes and in constitutional interpretation that occurred during these periods. The government was now expected to play an active role in dealing with economic and social problems. In the late 1930s, the Supreme Court reversed its earlier decisions (see Chapter 16) on the question of delegating legislative powers to administrative agencies and upheld laws by which Congress merely instructs agencies to make decisions that serve "the public interest" in some area.[16] As a result, it was possible for President Nixon to set up in 1971 a system of price and wage controls based on a statute that simply authorized the president "to issue such orders and regulations as he may deem appropriate to stabilize prices, rents, wages, and salaries."[17] The Cost of Living Council and other agencies that Nixon established to carry out this order were run by appointed officials who had the legal authority to make sweeping decisions based on general statutory language.

World War II was the first occasion during which the government made heavy use of federal income taxes—on individuals and corporations—to finance its activities. Between 1940 and 1945, total federal tax collections increased from about $5 billion to nearly $44 billion. The end of the war brought no substantial tax reduction: The country believed that a high level of military preparedness continued to be necessary and that various social programs begun before the war should enjoy the heavy funding made possible by wartime taxes. Tax receipts continued, by and large, to grow. Before 1913, when the Sixteenth Amendment to the Constitution was passed, the federal government could not collect income taxes at all (it financed itself largely from customs duties and excise taxes). From 1913 to 1940, income taxes were small (in 1940, the average American paid only $7 in federal income taxes). World War II created the first great financial boom for the government, permitting the sustained expansion of a wide variety of programs and thus entrenching a large number of administrators in Washington.[18]

A third event—the September 11, 2001, terrorist attacks on the United States—may have affected bureaucracy as profoundly as the depression of the 1930s and World War II. A law creating a massive new cabinet agency, the Department of Homeland Security (DHS), was passed in late 2002. Within two years of its creation, the DHS had consolidated under its authority 22 smaller federal agencies with nearly 180,000 federal employees (third behind the Departments of Defense and Veterans Affairs) and over $40 billion in budgets (fourth behind the Departments of Defense, Health and Human Services, and Education). In addition, dozens of intergovernmental grant-making programs came under the authority of the DHS.

In late 2004, Congress passed another law that promised, over time, to centralize under a single director of national intelligence the work of the more than 70 federal agencies authorized to spend money on counterterrorist activities. But even after related reforms in 2006, dozens of different agencies were still authorized to spend money on counterterrorism activities. In 2013, the DHS faced sharp questioning from the House Subcommittee on Oversight and Management Efficiency, and the Government

Constitutional Connections | Beyond Checks and Balances?

The Framers of the Constitution did not envision anything akin to today's federal bureaucracy, with its several million full-time employees and its millions more part-time employees. But far more surprising to the Framers than the sheer size of today's federal bureaucracy (after all, the country and its population have grown, too) would be its scope: cabinet departments, bureaus, independent agencies, government corporations, and regulatory commissions touching virtually every facet of the nation's economic, social, and civic life-trade, banking, labor, environmental protection, broadcasting, transportation, human services, health, housing, education, energy, space exploration, national parks, homeland security, and more. Beyond the contemporary federal bureaucracy's size and scope, the Framers might be mystified by the "proxy government" system described earlier in the chapter, and by how so many "federal" programs are actually jointly funded and administered by federal, state, and local governments in conjunction with for-profit firms and nonprofit organizations.

But would the Framers, in turn, view today's federal bureaucracy not only as a "fourth branch" of American national government but one that operates outside their system of separated powers and checks and balances, and that has transformed federalism (see Chapter 3) into Washington-controlled "intergovernmental administration"?

Some think so. They argue that federal agencies, including the Internal Revenue Service, the Environmental Protection Agency, and many others, routinely exercise not only executive powers but also lawmaking and judicial powers as well, and that state governments are required to fund or co-fund and administer many federal programs including large ones such as Medicaid. Moreover, they claim, Congress now commonly passes long and complicated laws and leaves it almost entirely to the discretion of federal bureaucrats to decide what the laws mean, how to apply them, and even in some cases how much to spend on them.

Others, however, think not. They argue that through federal laws that set boundaries on administrators' authority (like the Administrative Procedures Act of 1946), routine oversight of federal agencies by congressional committees and subcommittees, and federal court decisions limiting how far Washington can go in requiring state governments to fund or administer its programs, the federal bureaucracy's powers and the discretion exercised by Washington's appointed officials normally remain duly limited. We share this view: the "fourth branch" is far bigger and broader than the Framers could ever have envisioned, but most federal government agencies most of the time are checked and balanced by Congress and by other means.

discretionary authority
The extent to which appointed bureaucrats can choose courses of action and make policies not spelled out in advance by laws.

Accountability Office once again ranked the DHS, which by then employed more than 220,000 employees, among those agencies with serious management problems.[19]

15-3 The Federal Bureaucracy Today

Presidents do not want to admit that they have increased the size of the bureaucracy. They can avoid saying this by pointing out that the number of civilians working for the federal government, excluding postal workers, has not increased significantly in recent years and is about the same today (2 million persons) as it was in 1960, and less than it was during World War II. This explanation is true but misleading, for it neglects the roughly 13 million people who work *indirectly* for Washington as employees of private firms and state or local agencies that are largely, if not entirely, supported by federal funds. Nearly three persons earn their living indirectly from the federal government for every one who earns it directly. While federal employment has remained quite stable, employment among federal contractors and consultants and in state and local governments has mushroomed. Indeed, most federal bureaucrats, like most other people who work for the federal government, live outside Washington, D.C.

As Figure 15.1 shows, from 1990 to 2018, several federal executive departments reduced their workforce. The Department of Defense cut its civilian employees by almost one-third. Other departments, including Agriculture and Treasury, also have fewer employees. The Department of Veterans Affairs expanded after 2007 as veterans from the wars in Iraq and Afghanistan began to return home. High growth also was evident in the U.S. Department of Justice (DOJ). This growth is explained mainly by the growth in just one DOJ unit— and one of the few federal agencies anywhere in the bureaucracy that was slow to join the trend toward what we described earlier in this chapter as government by proxy—the Federal Bureau of Prisons (BOP). The BOP administers nearly 200 facilities, from maximum-security prisons to community corrections centers, all across the country. Between 1990 and 2013, its staff doubled to nearly 39,000, while the prisoner populations these federal workers supervised more than doubled to about 276,000.[20]

The power of the federal bureaucracy cannot be measured by the number of employees, however. A bureaucracy of 5 million persons would have little power if each employee did nothing but type letters or file documents, whereas a bureaucracy of only 100 persons would have awesome power if each member were able to make arbitrary life-and-death decisions affecting the rest of us. The power of the bureaucracy depends on the extent to which appointed officials have **discretionary authority**—that is, the ability to choose courses of action and to make policies not spelled

Figure 15.1 **Federal Civilian Employment, 1990–2018**

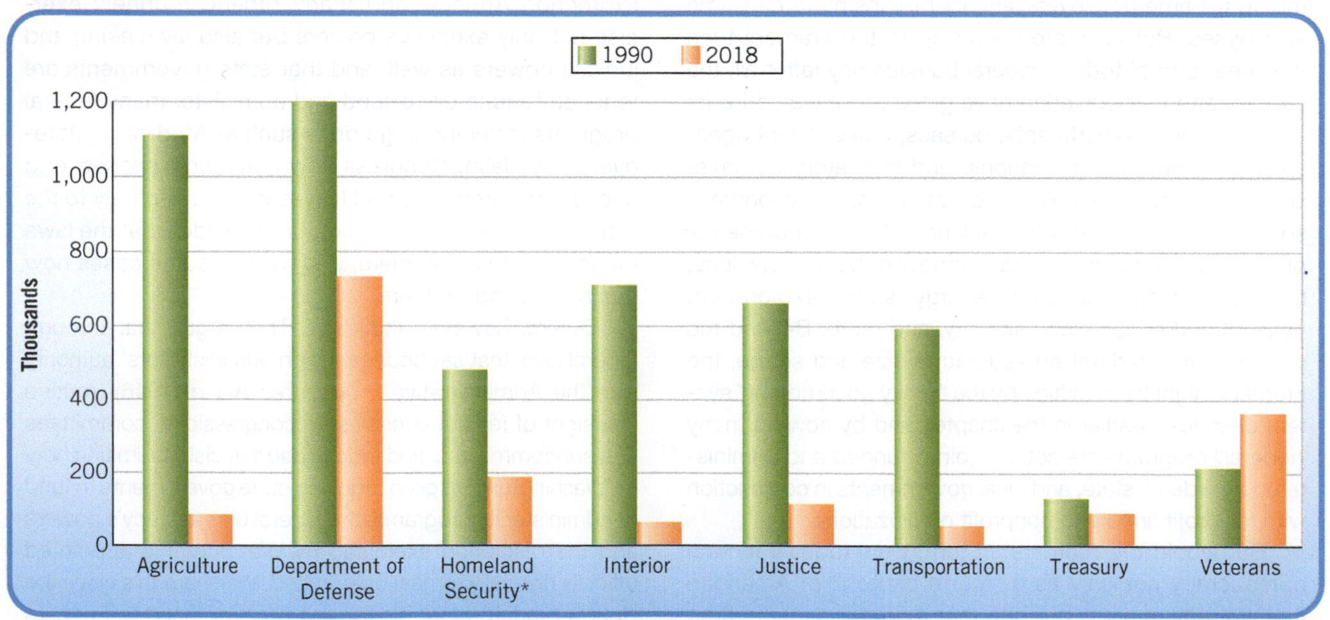

*Homeland Security previously referred to 22 different federal agencies, which became part of a single cabinet department in 2002.

Source: Office of Management and Budget, *Fiscal Year 2020 Historical Tables: Budget of the U.S. Government*, Table 16.1, "Total Executive Branch Civilian Full-Time Equivalent Employees, 1981–2020." NOTE: 2018 figures are used for comparison because 2019 and 2020 data are estimates.

What might explain why federal civilian employment has decreased in almost all Cabinet departments (except Veterans Affairs) from the late twentieth century to the present?

Figure 15.2 **The Growth of the Federal Government in Money, People, and Rules, 1940–2018**

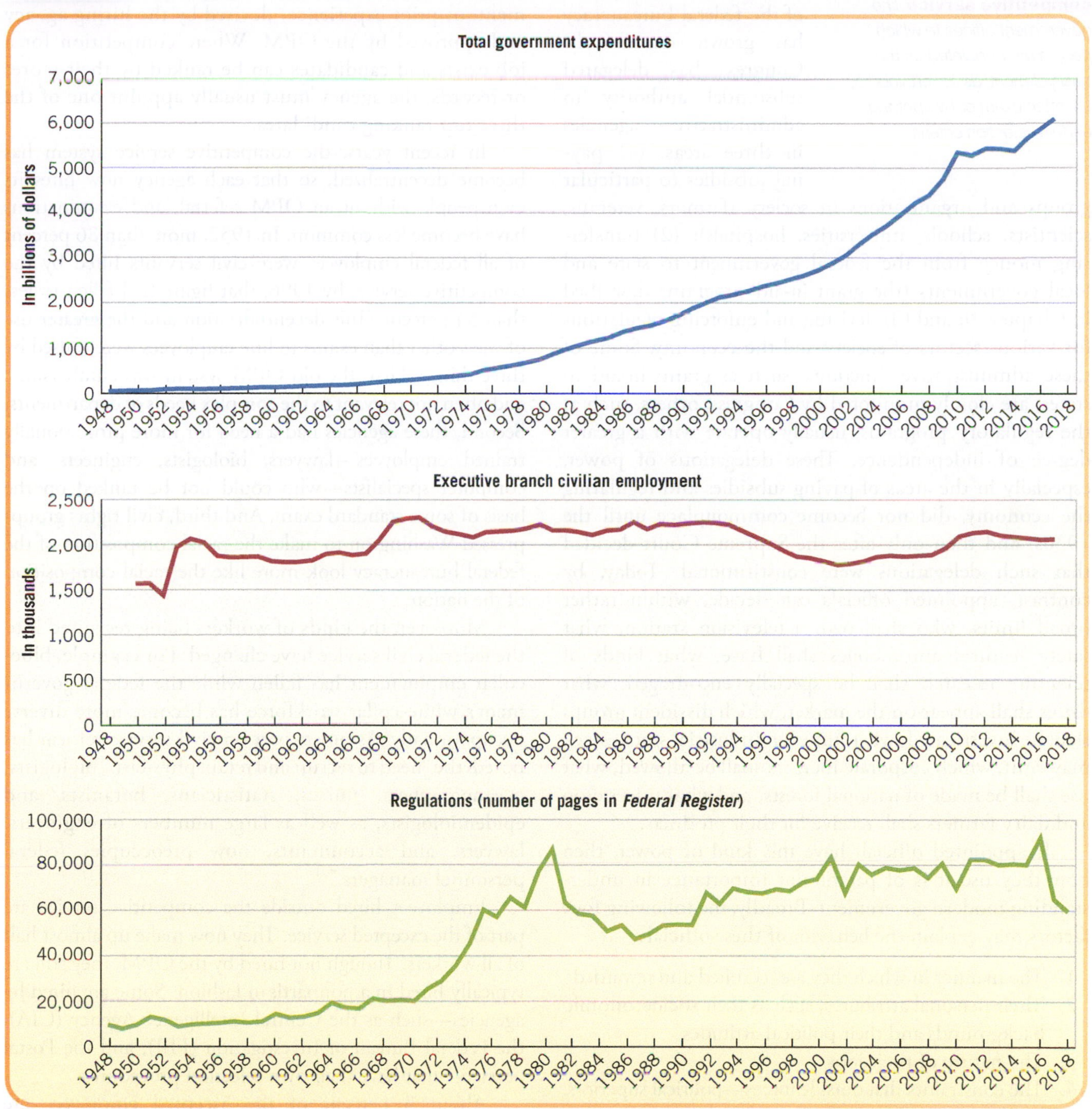

Sources: Office of Management and Budget, *Fiscal Year 2020: Historical Tables: Budget of the U.S. Government*, Table 14.4, "Total Government Expenditures by Major Category of Expenditure, 1948–2018"; Office of Personnel Management, *Data, Analysis, & Documentation: Federal Employment Reports, Historical Federal Workforce Tables*, "Executive Branch Civilian Employment Since 1940"; Office of Management and Budget, *Fiscal Year 2020 Historical Tables: Budget of the U.S. Government*, Table 16.1, "Total Executive Branch Civilian Full-Time Equivalent Employees: 1981–2020"; Congressional Research Service, "Counting Regulations: An Overview of Rulemaking, Types of Federal Regulations, and Pages in the *Federal Register*," Updated September 3, 2019, pp. 17–19; Caitlin Styrsky, "Federal Register Weekly Update; 2019 Page Total Surpasses 70,000 Pages," *Ballotpedia News*, 26 December 2019.

out in advance by laws. As Figure 15.2 shows, the volume of regulations issued after World War II increased much faster than the rate of government spending (relative to gross domestic product) and the number of federal employees who write the regulations and spend the money (federal employees who, as we have explained, often work mainly through state and local government employees and other administrative proxies). This trend shifted in the first two years of the Trump administration, when the number of pages in the *Federal Register* dropped by approximately one-third.

competitive service The government offices to which people are appointed on the basis of merit, as ascertained by a written exam or by applying certain selection criteria.

By this test, the power of the federal bureaucracy has grown enormously. Congress has delegated substantial authority to administrative agencies in three areas: (1) paying subsidies to particular groups and organizations in society (farmers, veterans, scientists, schools, universities, hospitals); (2) transferring money from the federal government to state and local governments (the grant-in-aid programs described in Chapter 3); and (3) devising and enforcing regulations for various sectors of society and the economy. Some of these administrative functions, such as grants-in-aid to states, are closely monitored by Congress; others, such as the regulatory programs, usually operate with a greater degree of independence. These delegations of power, especially in the areas of paying subsidies and regulating the economy, did not become commonplace until the 1930s, and then only after the Supreme Court decided that such delegations were constitutional. Today, by contrast, appointed officials can decide, within rather broad limits, who shall own a television station, what safety features automobiles shall have, what kinds of scientific research shall be specially encouraged, what drugs shall appear on the market, which dissident groups shall be investigated, what fumes an industrial smokestack may emit, which corporate mergers shall be allowed, what use shall be made of national forests, and what prices crop and dairy farmers shall receive for their products.

If appointed officials have this kind of power, then how they use it is of paramount importance in understanding modern government. Broadly, the following four factors may explain the behavior of these officials:

1. The manner in which they are recruited and rewarded
2. Their personal attributes, such as their socioeconomic backgrounds and their political attitudes
3. The nature of their jobs
4. The constraints that outside forces—political superiors, legislators, interest groups, journalists—impose on their agencies

Recruitment and Retention

The federal civil service system was designed to recruit qualified people on the basis of merit, not political patronage, and to retain and promote employees on the basis of performance, not political favoritism. Many appointed federal officials belong to the **competitive service**. This means they are appointed only after they have passed a written examination administered by the Office of Personnel Management (OPM) or met certain selection criteria (such as training, educational attainment, or prior experience) devised by the hiring agency and approved by the OPM. Where competition for a job exists and candidates can be ranked by their scores or records, the agency must usually appoint one of the three top-ranking candidates.

In recent years, the competitive service system has become decentralized, so that each agency now hires its own people without an OPM referral, and examinations have become less common. In 1952, more than 86 percent of all federal employees were civil servants hired by the competitive service; by 1996, that figure had fallen to less than 54 percent. This decentralization and the greater use of ways other than exams to hire employees were caused by three things. First, the old OPM system was cumbersome and often not relevant to the complex needs of departments. Second, these agencies had a need for more professionally trained employees—lawyers, biologists, engineers, and computer specialists—who could not be ranked on the basis of some standard exam. And third, civil rights groups pressed Washington to make the racial composition of the federal bureaucracy look more like the racial composition of the nation.

Moreover, the kinds of workers being recruited into the federal civil service have changed. For example, blue-collar employment has fallen while the federal government's white-collar workforce has become more diverse occupationally. As one expert on civil service reform has noted, the "need to recruit and retain physicists, biologists, oceanographers, nurses, statisticians, botanists, and epidemiologists, as well as large numbers of engineers, lawyers, and accountants, now preoccupies federal personnel managers."[21]

Employees hired outside the competitive service are part of the excepted service. They now make up almost half of all workers. Though not hired by the OPM, they still are typically hired in a nonpartisan fashion. Some are hired by agencies—such as the Central Intelligence Agency (CIA), the Federal Bureau of Investigation (FBI), and the Postal Service—that have their own selection procedures.

About 3 percent of the excepted employees are appointed on grounds other than or in addition to merit. These legal exceptions exist to permit presidents to select, for policymaking and politically sensitive posts, people who agree with their policy views. Such appointments are generally of three kinds:

1. Presidential appointments authorized by statute (cabinet and subcabinet officers, judges, U.S. marshals and U.S. attorneys, ambassadors, and members of various boards and commissions).
2. "Schedule C" appointments to jobs described as having a "confidential or policy-determining

character" below the level of cabinet or subcabinet posts (including executive assistants, special aides, and confidential secretaries).

3. Noncareer executive assignments given to high-ranking members of the regular competitive civil service or to persons brought into the civil service at these high levels. These people are deeply involved in the advocacy of presidential programs or participate in policymaking.

These three groups of excepted appointments constitute the patronage available to a presidential administration. When President Kennedy took office in 1961, he had 451 political jobs to fill. When President Trump took office in 2017, he had more than four times that number, including nearly double the number of top cabinet posts, and he had filled fewer spots one month into his term than his recent predecessors.[22] And this was no short-term challenge; as of early 2020, nearly one-quarter of key executive branch positions requiring Senate confirmation were vacant with no nominee in place. Furthermore, more than three-quarters of senior White House positions had experienced turnover, with almost one-third doing so multiple times.[23]

Scholars disagree over whether this proliferation of political appointees has improved or worsened Washington's performance, but one thing is clear: widespread presidential patronage is hardly unprecedented. In the 19th century, practically every federal job was a patronage job. For example, when Grover Cleveland, a Democrat, became president in 1885, he replaced some 40,000 Republican postal employees with Democrats.

Ironically, two years earlier, in 1883, the passage of the Pendleton Act had begun a slow but steady transfer of federal jobs from the patronage to the merit system. It may seem strange that a political party in power (the Republicans) would be willing to relinquish its patronage in favor of a merit-based appointment system. Two factors made it possible for the Republicans to pass the Pendleton Act: (1) public outrage over the abuses of the spoils system, highlighted by the assassination of President James Garfield by a man always described in the history books as a "disappointed office seeker" (*lunatic* would be a more accurate term); and (2) the fear that if the Democrats came to power on a wave of antispoils sentiment, existing Republican officeholders would be fired. (The Democrats won anyway.)

The merit system spread to encompass most of the federal bureaucracy, generally with presidential support. Though presidents may have liked in theory the idea of hiring and firing subordinates at will, most felt that the demands for patronage were impossible either to satisfy or to ignore. Furthermore, by increasing the coverage of the merit system, a president could "blanket in" patronage appointees already holding office, thus making it difficult or impossible for the next administration to fire them.

U.S. COAST GUARD/UPI/Newscom

Image 15.2 In 2010, fire erupted from an offshore oil rig operated by BP in the Gulf of Mexico near American land, creating an environmental disaster and requiring a federal investigation and response.

name-request job *A job filled by a person whom an agency has already identified.*

The Buddy System

The actual recruitment of civil servants, especially in mid-and upper-level jobs, is somewhat more complicated, and slightly more political, than the laws and rules might suggest. Though many people enter the federal bureaucracy by learning of a job, filling out an application, perhaps taking a test, and being hired, many also enter on a "name-request" basis. A **name-request job** is one that is filled by a person whom an agency has already identified. In this respect, the federal government is not so different from private business. A person learns of a job from somebody who already has one, or the head of a bureau decides in advance whom to hire. The agency must still send a form describing the job to the OPM, but it also names the person whom the agency wants to appoint. Sometimes the job is even described in such a way that the person named is the only one who can qualify for it. Occasionally, this tailor-made name-request job is offered to a person at the insistence of a member of Congress who wants a political supporter taken care of; more often it is made available because the bureaucracy itself knows whom it wishes to hire and wants to circumvent an elaborate search. This is the "buddy system."

The buddy system does not necessarily produce poor employees. Indeed, it is frequently a way of hiring people known to the agency as capable of handling the position. It also opens up the possibility of hiring people whose policy views are congenial to those already in office. Such networking is based on shared policy views, not (as once was the case) on narrow partisan affiliations. For example, bureaucrats in consumer protection agencies recruit new staff from private groups with an interest in consumer protection, such as the various organizations associated with Ralph Nader, or from academics who have a pro-consumer inclination.

There has always been an informal "old boys' network" among those who move in and out of high-level government posts; with the increasing appointment of women to these jobs, there has begun to emerge an old girls' network as well.[24] In a later section, we consider whether, or in what ways, these recruitment patterns make a difference.

Firing a Bureaucrat

The great majority of bureaucrats who are part of the civil service and who do not hold presidential appointments have jobs that are, for all practical purposes, beyond reach. An executive must go through elaborate steps to fire, demote, or suspend a civil servant. (See Table 15.1.) Realistically, this means no one is fired or demoted unless their superior is prepared to invest a great deal of time and effort in the attempt. In 1987, about 2,600 employees who had completed their probationary period were fired for misconduct or poor performance. That is about one-tenth of 1 percent of all federal employees. It is hard to believe that a large private company would fire only one-tenth of 1 percent of its workers in a given year. It's also impossible to believe that, as is often the case in Washington, it would take a year to fire anyone. To cope with this problem, federal executives have devised a number of strategies for bypassing or forcing out civil servants with whom they cannot work—denying them promotions, transferring them to undesirable locations, or assigning them to meaningless work.

With the passage of the Civil Service Reform Act of 1978, Congress recognized that many high-level positions in the civil service have important policymaking responsibilities and that the president and his cabinet officers ought to have more flexibility in recruiting, assigning, and paying such people. Accordingly, the act created the Senior Executive Service (SES), about 8,000 top federal managers who can (in theory) be hired, fired, and transferred more easily than ordinary civil servants. Moreover, the act stipulated that members of the SES would be eligible for substantial cash bonuses if they performed their duties well. (To protect the rights of SES members, anyone who is removed from the SES is guaranteed a job elsewhere in government.)

Things did not work out quite as the sponsors of the SES had hoped. Though most eligible civil servants joined it, the proportion of higher-ranking positions increased only modestly in agencies that were filled by transfer from another agency; the cash bonuses did not prove to be an important incentive (perhaps because the base salaries of top bureaucrats did not keep up with inflation); and hardly any member of the SES was actually fired. Two years after the SES was created, less than one-half of 1 percent of its members had received an unsatisfactory rating, and none had been fired. Nor does the SES give the president a large opportunity to make political appointments: only 10 percent of the SES can be selected from outside the existing civil service. And no SES member can be transferred involuntarily.

The Agency's Point of View

When one realizes that most agencies are staffed by people recruited by those agencies, sometimes on a name-request basis, and are virtually immune from dismissal, it becomes clear that the recruitment and retention policies of the civil service work to ensure that most bureaucrats will have an "agency" point of view. Even with the encouragement for transfers created by the SES, most government agencies are dominated by people who have not served in any other agency and who have been in government service most of their lives. This fact has some advantages: It means that most top-tier bureaucrats are experts in the procedures and policies of their agencies and that there will be a substantial degree of continuity in agency behavior no matter which political party happens to be in power.

But the agency point of view has its costs as well. A political executive entering an agency with responsibility for shaping its direction will soon discover the need to carefully win the support of career subordinates. A subordinate has an infinite capacity for discreet sabotage and can make life miserable for a political superior by delaying action, withholding information, following the rule book with literal exactness, or making an "end run" around a superior to mobilize members of Congress sympathetic to the bureaucrat's point of view. For instance, a political executive who wanted to downgrade a bureau within a department found, naturally, that the bureau chief was opposed. The bureau chief spoke to some friendly lobbyists and a key member of Congress. When the political executive asked the

TABLE 15.1 | Firing a Bureaucrat

To fire or demote members of the competitive civil service, these procedures must be followed:

1. Employees must be given written notice at least 30 days in advance that they will be fired or demoted for incompetence or misconduct.
2. The written notice must contain a statement of reasons, including specific examples of unacceptable performance.
3. Employees have the right to an attorney and to reply, orally or in writing, to the charges.
4. Employees have the right to appeal any adverse action to the Merit Systems Protection Board (MSPB), a three-person, bipartisan body appointed by the president with the consent of the Senate.
5. The MSPB must grant employees a hearing, at which employees have the right to have an attorney present.
6. Employees have the right to appeal the MSPB decision to a U.S. court of appeals, which can hold new hearings.

member of Congress if there was a problem with the proposed reorganization, the member of Congress replied, "No, you have the problem, because if you touch that bureau, I'll cut your job out of the budget."[25]

Personal Attributes

Another factor that may shape the way a bureaucrat uses power is personal attributes. These include social class, education, and personal political beliefs. The federal civil service as a whole looks very much like a cross section of American society in the education, sex, race, and social origins of its members (see Figure 15.3). But as with many other employers, African Americans and other minorities are most likely heavily represented in the lowest grade levels and tend to be underrepresented at the executive level. At the higher-ranking levels, where the most power is found—say, in the supergrade ranks of GS 16 through GS 18—the typical civil servant is a middle-aged white man with a college degree whose father was somewhat more advantaged than the average citizen. In the great majority of cases, this individual is in fact very different from the typical American in both background and personal beliefs.

Because political appointees and career bureaucrats are not representative of the average American, and because of their supposed occupational self-interest, some critics have speculated that the people holding these jobs think about politics and government in ways very different from the public at large. Some surveys do find that career bureaucrats are more likely than other people to hold liberal views, to trust government, and to vote for Democrats.[26]

It is important, however, not to overgeneralize from such differences. For example, whereas Obama appointees (virtually all of them strong Democrats) were likely more liberal than average citizens, George W. Bush appointees (virtually all of them loyal Republicans) were undoubtedly more conservative than average citizens; the same is probably true of those appointed by President Trump. Likewise, career civil servants are more pro-government than the public at large, but on most specific policy questions, federal bureaucrats do not have extreme positions. Still, those employed in "activist" agencies such as the Federal Trade Commission, Environmental Protection Agency, and Food and Drug Administration tend to have more liberal views than those who work for the more "traditional" agencies such as the Departments of Agriculture, Commerce, and the Treasury. Even when the bureaucrats come from roughly the same social backgrounds, their policy views seem to reflect the type of government work that they do. For example, studies dating back decades have found that Democrats and people with liberal views tend to be overrepresented in social service agencies, whereas Republicans and people with conservative views tend to be overrepresented in defense agencies.[27] But it is not clear whether such differences in attitudes are produced by the jobs that people hold or whether certain jobs attract people with certain beliefs. Probably both forces are at work.

Nick Suydam/Alamy Stock Photo

Image 15.3 Amtrak passenger trains bring long-distance travel to many small towns in the United States. Amtrak service costs the federal government much more than the trains earn in fares.

Figure 15.3 **Characteristics of Federal Civilian Employees, 1960 and 2017**

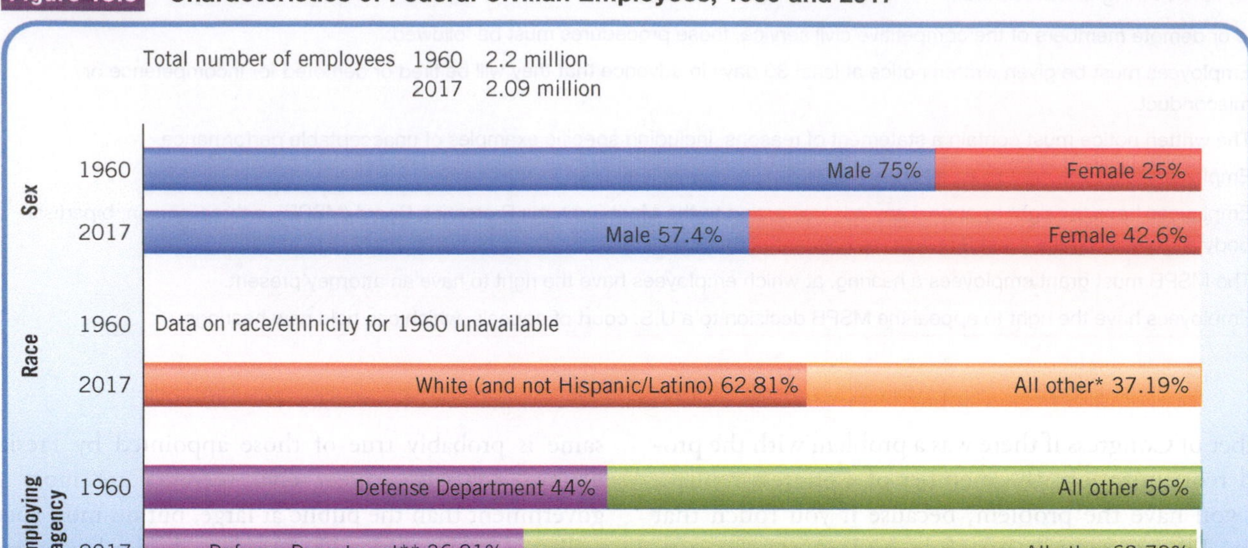

*Includes Asian, Black/African American, Hispanic/Latino, Native American, and Pacific Islander employees

**Includes Departments of the Air Force, Navy, and Army.

Source: *Statistical Abstract of the United States*, 1961, pp. 392–394; Office of Personnel Management, *Common Characteristics of the Government Fiscal Year 2017*.

Kumar Sriskandan/Alamy Stock Photo

Image 15.4 In addition to mail delivery, the U.S. Postal Service performs other functions, such as assistance with passport applications.

Do Bureaucrats Sabotage Their Political Bosses?

Because it is so hard to fire career bureaucrats, it is often said that these people will sabotage any actions by their political superiors with whom they disagree. And since civil servants tend to have liberal views, it has been conservative presidents and cabinet secretaries who have usually expressed this worry.

Some bureaucrats will no doubt drag their heels if they don't like their bosses, and a few will block actions they oppose. However, most bureaucrats try to carry out the policies of their superiors even when they personally disagree with them. When David Stockman was director of the OMB, he set out to make sharp cuts in government spending programs in accordance with the wishes of his boss, President Ronald Reagan. He later published a book complaining about all the people in the White House and Congress who worked against him.[28] But nowhere in the book is there any major criticism of the civil servants at the OMB. It seems that whatever these people thought about Stockman and Reagan, they loyally tried to carry out Stockman's policies.

Bureaucrats tend to be loyal to political superiors who deal with them cooperatively and constructively. An agency head who tries to ignore or discredit them can be in for a tough time, however. The powers of obstruction available to aggrieved bureaucrats are formidable. Such people can leak embarrassing stories to Congress or to the media, help interest groups mobilize against the agency head, and discover a thousand procedural reasons why a new course of action won't work.

The exercise of some of those bureaucratic powers is protected by the Whistle Blower Protection Act. Passed in 1989, the law created the Office of Special Counsel, charged with investigating complaints from bureaucrats that they were punished after reporting to Congress about waste, fraud, or abuse in their agencies.

It may seem odd that bureaucrats, who have great job security, would not always act in accordance with their personal beliefs instead of in accordance with the wishes of their bosses. Bureaucratic sabotage, in this view, ought to be very common. But bureaucratic cooperation with superiors is not odd, once you take into account the nature of a bureaucrat's job.

If you are a voter at the polls, your beliefs will clearly affect how you vote (see Chapters 7 and 10). But if you are the second baseman for the Boston Red Sox, your political beliefs, social background, and education will have nothing to do with how you field ground balls. Sociologists like to call the different things that people do in their lives "roles" and to distinguish between roles that are loosely structured (such as the role of voter) and those that are highly structured (such as that of second baseman). Personal attitudes greatly affect loosely structured roles and only slightly affect highly structured ones. Applied to the federal bureaucracy, this suggests that civil servants performing tasks that are routinized (such as filling out forms), tasks that are closely defined by laws and rules (such as issuing welfare checks), or tasks that are closely monitored by others (supervisors, special-interest groups, the media) will probably perform them in ways that can be explained only partially, if at all, by their personal attitudes. Civil servants performing complex, loosely defined tasks that are not closely monitored may carry out their work in ways powerfully influenced by their attitudes.

Among the loosely defined tasks are those performed by professionals, and so the values of these people may influence how they behave. An increasing number of lawyers, economists, engineers, and physicians are hired to work in federal agencies. These men and women have received extensive training that produces not only a set of skills, but also a set of attitudes as to what is important and valuable. For example, the Federal Trade Commission (FTC), charged with preventing unfair methods of competition among businesses, employs two kinds of professionals: lawyers, organized into a Bureau of Competition, and economists, organized into a Bureau of Economics. Lawyers are trained to draw up briefs and argue cases in court and are taught the legal standards by which they will know whether they have a chance of winning a case. Economists are trained to analyze how a competitive economy works and what costs consumers must bear if the goods and services are produced by a monopoly (one firm controlling the market) or an oligopoly (a small number of firms dominating the market).

Because of their training and attitudes, lawyers in the FTC prefer to bring cases against a business firm that has done something clearly illegal, such as attending secret meetings with competitors to rig the prices that will be charged to a purchaser. These cases appeal to lawyers because there is usually a victim (the purchaser or a rival company) who complains to the government, the illegal behavior can be proved in a court of law, and the case can be completed rather quickly.

Economists, on the other hand, are trained to measure the value of a case not by how quickly it can be proved in court, but by whether the illegal practice imposes large or small costs on the consumer. FTC economists often dislike the cases that appeal to lawyers. The economists argue that the amount of money that such cases save the consumer is often small and that the cases are a distraction from the major issues—such as whether Samsung or Apple unfairly dominates the smartphone market, or whether General Motors is too large to be efficient. Lawyers, in turn, are leery of big cases, because the facts are hard to prove and they may take forever to decide (one blockbuster case can drag through the courts for 10 years). In many federal agencies, divergent professional values such as these help explain how power is used.

Culture and Careers

Unlike the lawyers and economists working in the FTC, the government bureaucrats in a typical agency don't have a lot of freedom to choose a course of action. Their jobs are spelled out not only by the laws, rules, and routines of their agency, but also by the informal understandings among fellow employees as to how they are supposed to act. These understandings are the *culture* of the agency.[29]

If you belong to the air force, you can do a lot of things, but only one thing really counts: flying airplanes, especially advanced jet fighters and bombers. The culture of the air force is a pilots' culture. If you belong to the navy, you have more choices: fly jet aircraft or operate nuclear submarines. Both jobs provide status and a chance for promotion to the highest ranks. By contrast, sailing minesweepers or transport ships (or worse, having a desk job and not sailing anything at all) may not be a very rewarding job. The culture of the CIA emphasizes working overseas as a clandestine agent; staying in Washington as a report writer is not as good for your career. The culture of the State Department rewards skill in political negotiations; being an expert on international economics or embassy security is much less rewarding.

You can usually tell what kind of culture an agency has by asking an employee, "If you want to get ahead here, what sort of jobs should you take?" The jobs that are career enhancing are part of the culture; the jobs that are not career enhancing ("NCE," in bureaucratic lingo) are not part of it.

Being part of a strong culture is good—to a point. It motivates employees to work hard in order to win the respect of their coworkers and the approval of their bosses. But a strong culture also makes it hard to change an agency. FBI agents for many years resisted getting involved in civil rights or organized crime cases, and diplomats in the State Department didn't pay much attention to embassy security. These important jobs were not a career-enhancing part of the culture.

Constraints

The biggest difference between a government agency and a private organization is the vastly greater number of constraints on the agency. Unlike a business firm, the typical government bureau cannot hire, fire, build, or sell without going through procedures set down in laws. How much money it pays its members is determined by statute, not by the market. Not only the goals of an agency, but often its exact procedures, are spelled out by Congress.

At one time, the Soil Conservation Service was required by law to employ at least 14,177 full-time workers. The State Department has been forbidden by law from opening a diplomatic post in Antigua and Barbuda but forbidden from closing a post anywhere else. The Agency for International Development (which administers our foreign-aid program) has been given by Congress 33 objectives and 75 priorities and must send to Congress 288 reports each year. When it buys military supplies, the Department of Defense must give a "fair proportion" of its contracts to small businesses, especially those operated by "socially and economically disadvantaged individuals," and must buy from American firms even if, in some cases, buying abroad would be cheaper. Some of the more general constraints include the following:

- *Administrative Procedure Act (1946).* Before adopting a new rule or policy, an agency must give notice, solicit comments, and (often) hold hearings.
- *Freedom of Information Act (1966).* Citizens have the right to inspect all government records except those containing military, intelligence, or trade secrets or those revealing private personnel actions.
- *National Environmental Policy Act (1969).* Before undertaking any major action affecting the environment, an agency must issue an environmental impact statement.
- *Privacy Act (1974).* Government files about individuals, such as Social Security and tax records, must be kept confidential.
- *Open Meeting Law (1976).* Every part of every agency meeting must be open to the public unless certain matters (e.g., military or trade secrets) are being discussed.

One of the biggest constraints on bureaucratic action is that Congress rarely gives any job to a single agency. Stopping drug trafficking is the task of the Customs Service, the FBI, the Drug Enforcement Administration, the Border Patrol, and the Defense Department (among others). Disposing of the assets of failed savings-and-loan associations was the job of the Resolution Funding Corporation, Resolution Trust Corporation, Federal Housing Finance Board, Office of Thrift Supervision in the Treasury Department, Federal Deposit Insurance Corporation, Federal Reserve Board, and Justice Department (among others). Similarly, in the aftermath of the 2007 financial crisis, many different agencies were involved in the Troubled Asset Relief Program, the bailouts, and the programs to help homeowners who could no longer afford their homes.

The effects of these constraints on agency behavior are not surprising.

- The government will often act slowly. (The more constraints that must be satisfied, the longer it will take to get anything done.)
- The government will sometimes act inconsistently. (What is done to meet one constraint—for example, freedom of information—may endanger another constraint—for example, privacy.)
- It will be easier to block action than to take action. (The constraints ensure that lots of voices will be heard; the more voices heard, the more they may cancel each other out.)
- Lower-ranking employees will be reluctant to make decisions on their own. (Having many constraints means having many ways to get into trouble; to avoid trouble, let your boss make the decision.)
- Citizens will complain of red tape. (The more constraints to serve, the more forms to fill out.)

These constraints do not mean government bureaucracy is powerless, only that, however great its power, it tends to be clumsy. That clumsiness arises not from the fact that the people who work for agencies are dull or incompetent, but from the complicated political environment in which that work must be done.

Policy Dynamics: Inside/Outside the Box | Postal Service Reform: Client Politics?

Article I, section 8 of the Constitution authorized the Congress to "establish Post Offices." Today's United States Postal Service (USPS) is the second largest employer in the nation (behind Walmart). It is not taxpayer-funded and generates more than $70 billion a year in revenue from its services. It has close to 500,000 career employees. It has mail routes that cover every square mile of the nation. It delivers mail to more than 158 million addresses each week. It handles about 146 billion pieces of mail each year. It has more retail outlets than the number of McDonald's, Starbucks, and Walmart stores combined. Millions of people (especially older people) and many businesses (not only "junk mail" purveyors) continue to rely heavily on "snail mail." And certain legal documents still normally get sent in paper envelopes via "regular mail."

But the USPS is in trouble. In 2018, the volume of mail delivered by the USPS declined 31 percent from its peak of 213 billion pieces in 2006, even as its number of delivery points reached a record of more than 158 million. In the 2018 fiscal year, the USPS had a net loss of nearly $4 billion. Facebook, email, texting, and other means of electronic communications have increasingly displaced both routine and episodic communications that once started with dropping paper into the old metal mailbox on the street corner. Meanwhile, for-profit shipping businesses like United Parcel Service (UPS) and Federal Express have expanded. They carry substantial portions of all "door-to-door" mail, including express or "overnight" envelopes, packages, and boxes.

In recent years, Congress has considered numerous proposals to "save" or "streamline" the USPS. For instance, in 2012, Postmaster General Patrick Donahoe proposed reducing mail delivery to five days a week (eliminating most Saturday deliveries), restructuring payments for postal worker retiree health benefits, consolidating mail processing centers, and reducing "window hours" in about half of the roughly 26,000 post offices around the country. The USPS receives no taxpayer funding. In 2012, the Senate passed a bill that would have pumped billions of tax dollars into the USPS, but the House rejected the measure. In 2013, the USPS announced that it would end most Saturday deliveries effective August of that year, but Congress refused to let it do so.

Some have characterized battles over USPS reform as, in effect, examples of client politics. Supposedly, the issue pits the labor union representing most postal workers (the American Postal Workers Union of the AFL-CIO) against a broad, bipartisan coalition, backed by majority public opinion, that favors closing more postal offices and accelerating workforce reductions. But that view is at odds with at least two facts: First, many members of Congress, both Democrats and Republicans, have opposed sweeping reforms to the USPS. (During the coronavirus crisis in the spring of 2020, President Trump called for USPS to increase its prices, but critics said that would be disastrous for the postal service's competitiveness with private shipping services.) Second, as revealed in a major survey commissioned by the USPS Office of the Inspector General in early 2013, most Americans, including young Americans, oppose such reforms, too:

- Although three-quarters of people erroneously assume that the USPS is taxpayer-funded, four-fifths still say they want the USPS to serve all citizens in all locations even if it means that the USPS loses money.
- Three-quarters are opposed to reducing postal service hours, and three-quarters also oppose plans for three-day delivery schedules.
- Even 95 percent of young adults, a population that relies largely on online communications, say they would be adversely affected if the USPS went out of business anytime soon.

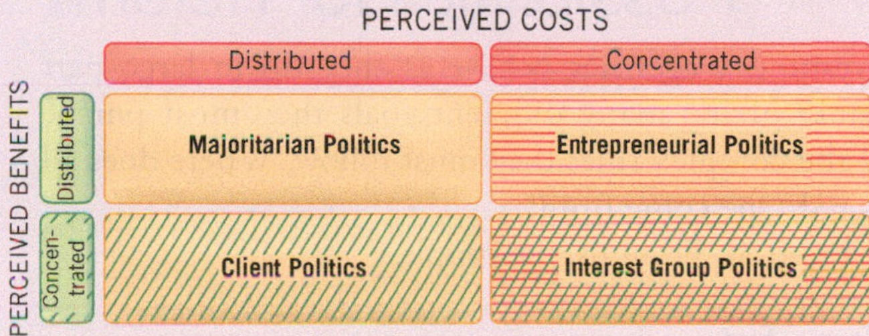

Sources: United States Postal Service, "A Decade of Facts and Figures," https://facts.usps.com/table-facts/#nav; Coalition for a Twenty-First Century Postal Service, "A Postal Primer: The Basic and Pivotal Issues Affecting the Future of the United States Postal Service," 16 April 2019; "U.S. Postal Service Reports Fiscal Year 2018 Results," 14 November 2018; Julia Ziegler, "Postmaster General Urges Quick Action in Lame Duck Session," Federal News Radio, 1 November 2012; American Postal Workers Union, "Survey Says: Most Americans Oppose Plant Closures," 4 June 2013. www.apwu.org.

AP Images/Gregory Bull

Image 15.5 Every ten years, the United States is constitutionally required to count the population, which means that some census takers will visit remote areas of the country, such as rural Alaska.

iron triangle *A close relationship between an agency, a congressional committee, and an interest group.*

The moral of the story: the next time you get mad at a bureaucrat, ask yourself, why would a rational, intelligent person behave that way? Chances are you will discover good reasons for that action. You might well behave the same way if you were working for the same organization.

15-4 Checks, Problems, and Possibilities for Reform

Government agencies behave as they do in large part because of the many different goals they must pursue and the complex rules they must follow. Where does all this red tape come from?

From us. From us, the people.

Checks

Every goal, every constraint, every bit of red tape, was put in place by Congress, the courts, the White House, or the agency itself responding to the demands of some influential faction. Civil rights groups want every agency to hire and buy from women and minorities. Environmental groups want every agency to file environmental impact statements. Industries being regulated want every new agency policy to be formulated only after a lengthy public hearing with lots of lawyers present. Labor unions also want those hearings so that they can argue against industry lawyers. Everybody who sells something to the government wants a "fair chance" to make the sale, and so everybody insists that government contracts be awarded only after complex procedures are followed. A lot of people don't trust the government, and so they insist that everything it does be done in the sunshine—no secrets, no closed meetings, no hidden files.

If we wanted agencies to pursue their main goal with more vigor and less encumbering red tape, we would have to ask Congress, the courts, or the White House to repeal some of these constraints. In other words, we would have to be willing to give up something we want in order to get something else we want even more. But politics does not encourage people to make these trade-offs; instead, it encourages us to expect to get everything—efficiency, fairness, help for minorities—all at once.

Agency Allies

Despite these constraints, government bureaucracies are not powerless. In fact, some of them actively seek certain constraints. They do so because it is a way of cementing a useful relationship with a congressional committee or an interest group.

At one time scholars described the relationship between an agency, a committee, and an interest group as an **iron triangle** (see Figure 15.4). For example, the Department of Veterans Affairs, the House and Senate committees on veterans' affairs, and veterans' organizations (such as the American Legion) would form a tight, mutually advantageous alliance. The department would do what the committees wanted and in return get political support and budget appropriations; the committee members would do what the veterans' groups wanted and in return get votes and campaign contributions. Iron triangles are examples of what are called *client politics* (see our discussion of client politics in Chapter 1 for more details).

Many agencies still have important allies in Congress and the private sector, especially those bureaus that serve the needs of specific sectors of the economy or regions of the country. The Department of Agriculture works closely with farm organizations, the Department of the Interior with groups interested in obtaining low-cost irrigation or grazing rights, and the Department of Housing and Urban Development with mayors and real-estate developers.

Sometimes these allies are so strong that they can defeat a popular president. For years, President Reagan tried to abolish the Small Business Administration (SBA), arguing that its program of loans to small firms was wasteful and ridden with favoritism. But Congress, reacting to pressures from small-business groups, rallied to the SBA's defense. As a result, Reagan had to oversee an agency that he didn't want.

But iron triangles are much less common today than once was the case. Politics of late has become far more complicated. For one thing, the number and variety of

Figure 15.4 Iron Triangle

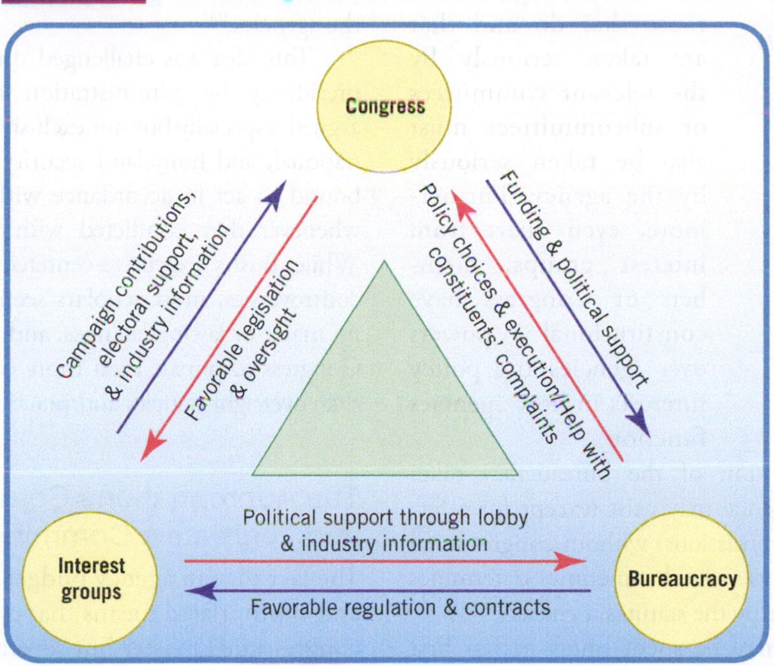

interest groups have increased so much in recent years that scarcely any agency is not subject to pressures from several competing interests instead of from only one powerful interest. For another, the growth of subcommittees in Congress has meant most agencies are subject to control by many different legislative groups, often with very different concerns. Finally, the courts have made it much easier for all kinds of individuals and interests to intervene in agency affairs.

As a result, nowadays government agencies face a bewildering variety of competing groups and legislative subcommittees that constitute not a loyal group of allies, but a fiercely contentious collection of critics. The Environmental Protection Agency is caught between the demands of environmentalists and those of industry organizations, the Occupational Safety and Health Administration between the pressures of labor and those of business, and the Federal Communications Commission between the desires of broadcasters and those of cable television companies. Even the Department of Agriculture faces not a unified group of farmers, but many different farmers split into rival groups, depending on the crops they raise, the regions in which they live, and the attitudes they have toward the relative merits of farm subsidies or free markets.

Political scientist Hugh Heclo has described the typical government agency today as being embedded not in an iron triangle, but in an **issue network**.[30] These issue networks consist of people in Washington-based interest groups, on congressional staffs, in universities and think tanks, and in the mass media who regularly debate government policy on a certain subject—say, health care or auto safety. The networks are contentious, split along political, ideological, and economic lines. When presidents take office, they often recruit key agency officials from those members of the issue network who are most sympathetic to their views.

issue network *A network of people in Washington, D.C.-based interest groups, on congressional staffs, in universities and think tanks, and in the mass media, who regularly discuss and advocate public policies.*

When Jimmy Carter, a Democrat, became president, he appointed to key posts in consumer agencies people who were from that part of the consumer issue network associated with Ralph Nader. Ronald Reagan, a conservative Republican, filled these same jobs with people who were from that part of the issue network holding free-market or antiregulation views. When George Bush the elder, a more centrist Republican, took office, he filled these posts with more centrist members of the issue network. Bill Clinton brought back the consumer activists. George W. Bush reversed Clinton, and Barack Obama reversed Bush, and (not surprisingly) Trump reversed Obama.

Congressional Oversight

The main reason why some interest groups are important to agencies is that they are important to Congress. Not every interest group in the country has substantial

authorization legislation *Legislative permission to begin or continue a government program or agency.*

appropriation *A legislative grant of money to finance a government program or agency.*

trust funds *Funds for government programs collected and spent outside the regular government budget.*

access to Congress, but those that do and that are taken seriously by the relevant committees or subcommittees must also be taken seriously by the agency. Furthermore, even apart from interest groups, members of Congress have constitutional powers over agencies and policy interests in how agencies function.

Congressional supervision of the bureaucracy takes several forms. First, no agency may exist (except for a few presidential offices and commissions) without congressional approval. Congress influences—and sometimes determines precisely—agency behavior by the statutes it enacts.

Second, no money may be spent unless it has first been authorized by Congress. **Authorization legislation** originates in a legislative committee (such as Agriculture, Education and Labor, or Public Works) and states the maximum amount of money that an agency may spend on a given program. This authorization may be permanent, it may be for a fixed number of years, or it may be annual (i.e., it must be renewed each year, or the program or agency goes out of business).

Third, even funds that have been authorized by Congress cannot be spent unless (in most cases) they are also appropriated. Appropriations usually are made annually, and they originate not with the legislative committees but with the House Appropriations Committee and its various (and influential) subcommittees. An **appropriation** (money formally set aside for a specific use) may be, and often is, for less than the amount authorized. The Appropriations Committee's action thus tends to have a budget-cutting effect. Some funds can be spent without an appropriation, but in virtually every part of the bureaucracy, each agency is keenly sensitive to congressional concerns at the time that the annual appropriations process is going on.

But is the constitutional principle of separation of powers (see Chapter 2) challenged when Congress engages in oversight of agencies that are in the executive branch? Members of Congress themselves once debated that issue, but the aforementioned Administrative Procedure Act of 1946 and a dozen subsequent laws that built on it (the latest being the Data Quality Act of 2000, and all upheld when challenged in the courts) are predicated on the idea that agencies are "adjuncts for legislative functions. . . . Congress lacks the capacity to legislate on all matters it touches and perforce must delegate a great deal of legislative authority to the agencies."[31]

This idea was challenged during the George W. Bush presidency by administration officials and others who argued, especially but not exclusively with respect to military, national, and homeland security issues, that agencies were bound to act in accordance with the president's directives whenever they conflicted with directives from Congress. While Bush's executive-centered approach sparked many controversies, most scholars seem to think that it effected no major or lasting changes, and some suggest that it stirred Congress to pursue even more comprehensive (and aggressive) oversight policies and practices.[32]

The Appropriations Committee and Legislative Committees

The fact that an agency budget must be both authorized and appropriated means that each agency serves not one congressional master but several, and that these masters may be in conflict. The real power over an agency's budget is exercised by the Appropriations Committee; the legislative committees are especially important when a substantive law is first passed or an agency is first created, or when an agency is subject to annual authorization. In the past, the power of the Appropriations Committee was rarely challenged; from 1947 through 1962, fully 90 percent of the House Appropriations Committee's recommendations on expenditures were approved by the full House without change.[33] Furthermore, the Appropriations Committee tends to recommend less money than an agency requests (though some specially favored agencies, such as the FBI, the Soil Conservation Service, and the Forest Service, have tended to get almost everything that they have asked for). Finally, the process of "marking up" (revising, amending, and approving) an agency's budget request gives to the Appropriations Committee, or one of its subcommittees, substantial influence over the policies that the agency follows. Of late, the appropriations committees have lost some of their great power over government agencies. This has happened in three ways. First, Congress has created trust funds to pay for the benefits many people receive. The Social Security trust fund is the largest of these. For many years, Social Security had more funds in reserve than it spent, but in 2020, government projections indicated that the program's total cost would exceed its total income for the first time in almost 40 years. (In Chapter 17, we examine the creation of Social Security and its burgeoning costs in the 21st century.) Several other trust funds also exist. **Trust funds** operate outside the regular government budget, and the appropriations committees have no control over these expenditures. They are automatic.

Second, Congress has changed the authorization of many programs from permanent or multiyear to annual authorizations. This means that every year the legislative committees, as part of the reauthorization process, get to set limits on what these agencies can spend. This limits the ability of the appropriations committees to determine the spending limits. Before 1959, most authorizations were permanent or multiyear. Now a long list of agencies must be reauthorized every year—the State Department, NASA, military procurement programs of the Defense Department, the Justice Department, the Energy Department, and parts or all of many other agencies.

Third, the existence of huge budget deficits during the 1980s and the 2000s has meant that much of Congress's time has been taken up with trying (usually not very successfully) to keep spending down. As a result, there has rarely been much time to discuss the merits of various programs or how much ought to be spent on them; instead, attention has been focused on meeting a target spending limit. In 1981, the budget resolution passed by Congress mandated cuts in several programs before the appropriations committees had even completed their work.[34] In addition to the power of the purse, Congress can control the bureaucracy through informal ways. An individual member of Congress can call an agency head on behalf of a constituent. Most such calls merely seek information, but some result in, or attempt to obtain, special privileges for particular people. Congressional committees may also obtain the right to pass on certain agency decisions. This is called **committee clearance**, and though it usually is not legally binding on the agency, few agency heads will ignore the expressed wish of a committee chair to be consulted before certain actions (such as transferring funds) are taken.

The Legislative Veto

For many decades, Congress made frequent use of the legislative veto to control bureaucratic or presidential actions. A **legislative veto** is a requirement that an executive decision must lie before Congress for a specified period (usually 30 or 90 days) before it takes effect. Congress could then veto the decision if a resolution of disapproval was passed by either house (a "one-house veto") or both houses (a "two-house veto"). Unlike laws, such resolutions were not signed by the president. Between 1932 and 1980, about 200 laws were passed providing for a legislative veto, many of them involving presidential proposals to sell arms abroad.

But in June 1983, the Supreme Court declared the legislative veto to be unconstitutional. In the *Chadha* case, the Court held that the Article I of the Constitution clearly requires that "every order, resolution, or vote to which the concurrence of the Senate and House of Representatives may be necessary" (with certain minor exceptions) "shall be presented to the President of the United States," who must either approve it or return it with his veto attached. In short, Congress cannot take any action that has the force of law unless the president concurs in that action.[35] With a stroke of the pen, parts of 200 laws suddenly became invalid. At least that happened in theory. In fact, since the *Chadha* decision, Congress has passed a number of laws that contain legislative vetoes, despite the Supreme Court having ruled against them! (Someone will have to go to court to test the constitutionality of these new provisions.)

committee clearance *The ability of a congressional committee to review and approve certain agency decisions in advance and without passing a law.*

legislative veto *The authority of Congress to block a presidential action after it has taken place. The Supreme Court has held that Congress does not have this power.*

Opponents of the legislative veto hope future Congresses will have to pass laws that state much more clearly than before what an agency may or may not do. But it is just as likely that Congress will continue to pass laws stated in general terms and require that agencies implementing those laws report their plans to Congress, so that it will have a chance to enact and send to the president a regular bill disapproving the proposed action. Or Congress may rely on informal (but scarcely weak) means of persuasion, including threats to reduce the appropriations of an agency that does not abide by congressional preferences.

Congressional Investigations

Perhaps the most visible and dramatic form of congressional supervision of an agency is the investigation. Since 1792, when Congress investigated an army defeat by a Native American tribe, congressional investigations of the bureaucracy have been a regular feature—sometimes constructive, sometimes destructive—of legislative-executive relations. The investigative power is not mentioned in the Constitution, but it has been inferred from the power to legislate. The Supreme Court has consistently upheld this interpretation, though it has also said that such investigations should not be solely for the purpose of exposing the purely personal affairs of private individuals and must not operate to deprive citizens of their basic rights.[36] Congress may compel a person to attend an investigation by issuing a subpoena; anyone who ignores the subpoena may be punished for contempt. Congress can

red tape Complex bureaucratic rules and procedures that must be followed to get something done.

vote to send the person to jail or can refer the matter to a court for further action. As explained in Chapter 14, the president and his principal subordinates have refused to answer certain congressional inquiries on grounds of "executive privilege."

Although many areas of congressional oversight—budgetary review, personnel controls, investigations—are designed to control the exercise of bureaucratic discretion, other areas are intended to ensure the freedom of certain agencies from effective control, especially by the president. In dozens of cases, Congress has authorized department heads and bureau chiefs to operate independent of presidential preferences. Congress has resisted, for example, presidential efforts to ensure that policies to regulate pollution do not impose excessive costs on the economy, and interest groups have brought suit to prevent presidential coordination of various regulatory agencies. If the bureaucracy sometimes works at cross-purposes, it usually is because Congress—or competing committees in Congress—wants it that way.

Bureaucratic "Pathologies"

Everyone complains about bureaucracy in general (though rarely about bureaucratic agencies that everyone believes are desirable). This chapter should persuade you that it is difficult to say anything about bureaucracy "in general"; there are too many different kinds of agencies, kinds of bureaucrats, and kinds of programs to label the entire enterprise with a single adjective. Nevertheless, many people who recognize the enormous variety among government agencies still believe they all have some general features in common and suffer from certain shared problems or pathologies.

This is true enough, but the reasons for it—and the solutions, if any—are often not understood. Bureaucracies experience five major (or at least frequently mentioned) problems: red tape, conflict, duplication, imperialism, and waste. **Red tape** refers to the complex rules and procedures that must be followed to get something done. (As early as the 7th century, legal and government documents in England were bound together with a tape of pinkish-red color. Since then *red tape* has come to mean "bureaucratic delay or confusion," especially that accompanied by unnecessary paperwork.[37]) *Conflict* exists because some agencies seem to be working at cross-purposes with other agencies. (For example, the Agricultural Research Service tells farmers how to grow crops more efficiently, while the Agricultural Stabilization and Conservation Service pays farmers to grow fewer crops or to produce less.) *Duplication* (usually called "wasteful duplication") occurs when two government agencies seem to be doing the same thing, as when the Customs Service and the Drug Enforcement Administration both attempt to intercept illegal drugs being smuggled into the country. *Imperialism* refers to the tendency of agencies to grow without regard to the benefits that their programs confer or the costs that they entail. *Waste* means spending more than is necessary to buy some product or service.

These problems all exist, but they do not necessarily exist because bureaucrats are incompetent or power-hungry. Most exist because of the very nature of government itself. Take red tape: We encounter cumbersome rules and procedures in part because any large organization, governmental or not, must have some way of ensuring that one part of the organization does not operate out of step with another. Business corporations have red tape also; it is to a certain extent a consequence of bigness. But a great amount of governmental red tape is also the result of the need to satisfy legal and political requirements. Government agencies must hire on the basis of "merit," must observe strict accounting rules, must supply Congress with detailed information on their programs, and must allow for citizen access in countless ways. Meeting each need requires rules; enforcing the rules requires forms. As described by political scientist Herbert Kaufman, "One person's 'red tape' may be another's treasured safeguard."[38]

Or take conflict and duplication: They do not occur because bureaucrats enjoy conflict or duplication. (Quite the contrary!) They exist because Congress, in as a quote setting up agencies and programs, often wants to achieve a number of different, partially inconsistent goals or finds that it cannot decide which goal it values the most. Congress has 535 members and little strong leadership; it should not be surprising that 535 people will want different things and will sometimes succeed in getting them.

Imperialism results in large measure from government agencies seeking goals so vague and so difficult to measure that it is hard to tell when they have been attained. When Congress is unclear as to exactly what an agency is supposed to do, the agency will often convert that legislative vagueness into bureaucratic imperialism by taking the largest possible view of its powers. It may do this on its own; more often it does so because interest groups and judges rush in to fill the vacuum left by Congress. As we saw in Chapter 3, the 1973 Rehabilitation Act was passed with a provision barring discrimination against people with disabilities in any program receiving federal aid. Under pressure from people with disabilities, that ambitious, yet vague, goal was converted by the Department of Transportation into a requirement that virtually every big-city bus must have a device installed to lift people in wheelchairs onboard.

Image 15.6 At one of the world's busiest border crossings, cars line up to enter the United States from Tijuana, Mexico, where passengers must first meet strict immigration requirements overseen by the U.S. Border Patrol.

GUILLERMO ARIAS/AFP/Getty Images

Waste is probably the biggest criticism that people have of the bureaucracy. Everybody has heard stories of the Pentagon's paying $91 for screws that cost 3 cents in the hardware store. President Reagan's "Private Sector Survey on Cost Control," generally known as the Grace Commission (after its chairman, J. Peter Grace), publicized these and other tales in a 1984 report. No doubt there is waste in government. After all, unlike a business firm worried about maximizing profits, in a government agency there are only weak incentives to keep costs down. A business employee who cuts costs often receives a bonus or raise, and the firm gets to add the savings to its profits. A government official who cuts costs receives no reward, and the agency cannot keep the savings—they go back to the Treasury.

But many of the horror stories are either exaggerations or unusual occurrences.[39] Most of the screws, hammers, and light bulbs purchased by the government are obtained at low cost by means of competitive bidding among several suppliers. When the government does pay outlandish amounts, the reason typically is that it is purchasing a new or one-of-a-kind item not available at your neighborhood hardware store—for example, a new bomber or missile.

Even when the government is not overcharged, it still may spend more money than a private firm in buying what it needs. The reason is red tape—the rules and procedures designed to ensure that when the government buys something, it will do so in a way that serves the interests of many groups. For example, it often must buy from American rather than foreign suppliers, even if the latter charge a lower price; it must make use of contractors that employ minorities; it must hire only union laborers and pay them the "prevailing" (i.e., the highest) wage; it must allow public inspection of its records; it frequently is required to choose contractors favored by influential members of Congress; and so on. Private firms do not have to comply with all these rules and thus can buy for less.

From this discussion, it should be easy to see why these five basic bureaucratic problems are so hard to correct. To end conflicts and duplication, Congress would have to make some policy choices and set some clear priorities, but with all the competing demands that it faces, Congress finds it difficult to do that. You make more friends by helping people than by hurting them, and so Congress is more inclined to add new programs than to cut old ones, whether or not the new programs conflict with existing ones. To check imperialism, some way would have to be found to measure the benefits of government, but that is often impossible; government exists in part to achieve precisely those goals—such as national defense—that are least measurable. Furthermore, what might be done to remedy some problems would make other problems worse. If you simplify rules and procedures to cut red tape, you are also likely to reduce the coordination among agencies and thus to increase the extent to which duplication or conflict occurs. If you want to reduce waste, you will have to have more rules and inspectors—in short, more red tape. The problem of bureaucracy is inseparable from the problem of government generally.

Just as people are likely to say they dislike Congress but like their own member of Congress, they are inclined to express hostility toward "the bureaucracy" but goodwill for that part of the bureaucracy with which they have dealt personally. While most Americans have unfavorable impressions of government agencies and officials in general, they have quite favorable impressions about government agencies and officials with whom they have had direct contact or about which they claim to know something specific.

For example, Figure 15.5 shows that wide majorities have very or somewhat favorable impressions of diverse federal government agencies. Surveys dating back decades suggest that, despite persistent public complaints about "the bureaucracy," most Americans have judged, and continue to judge, each federal agency to be fair and useful.[40]

This finding helps explain why government agencies are rarely reduced in size or budget: whatever the popular feelings about the bureaucracy, any given agency tends to have many friends. Even the much-criticized FEMA, viewed unfavorably by half the public, was able to fend off budget cuts in the several years following its failed response to Hurricane Katrina.

Figure 15.5 **How the Public Views Particular Federal Agencies**

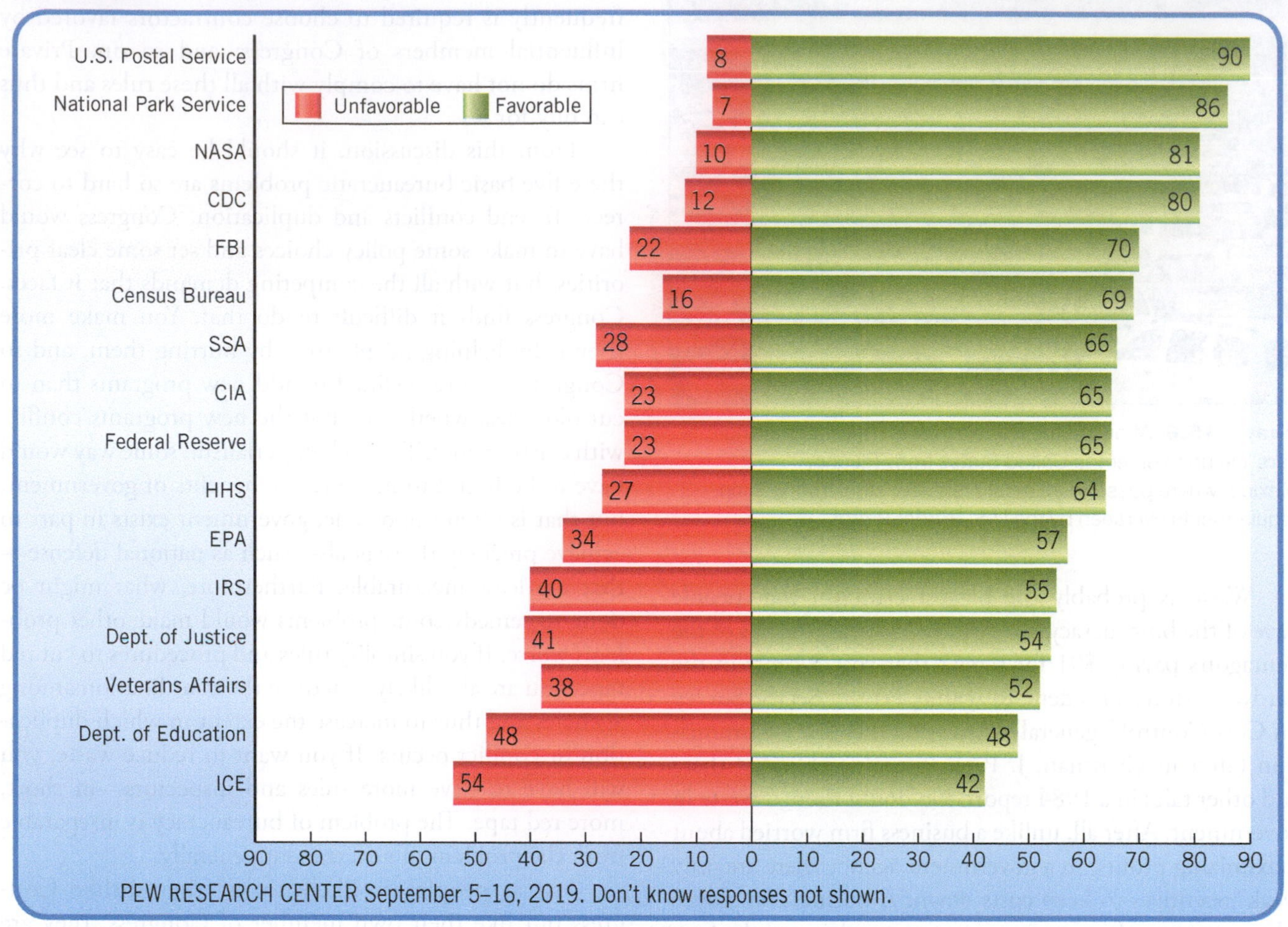

Source: Pew Research Center, "Public Expresses Favorable Views of a Number of Federal Agencies," 1 October 2019.

Q Why do you think the public views some federal agencies, such as the U.S. Postal Service, much more favorably than others, such as U.S. Immigration and Customs Enforcement or the U.S. Department of Education?

Reforming the Bureaucracy

The history of American bureaucracy has been punctuated with countless efforts to make it work better and cost less. There were 11 major attempts in the 20th century alone. The latest was the National Performance Review (NPR)—popularly called the plan to "reinvent government"—led by Vice President Al Gore.

The NPR differed from many of the preceding reform efforts in one important way. Most of the earlier ones suggested ways of increasing central (i.e., presidential) control of government agencies: the Brownlow Commission (1936–1937) recommended giving the president more assistants, the First Hoover Commission (1947–1949) suggested ways of improving top-level management, and the Ash Council (1969–1971) called for consolidating existing agencies into a few big "super departments." The intent was to make it easier for the president and his cabinet secretaries to run the bureaucracy. The key ideas were efficiency, accountability, and consistent policies.

The NPR, by contrast, emphasized customer satisfaction (the "customers" in this case being the citizens who come into contact with federal agencies). To the authors of the NPR report, the main problem with the bureaucracy was that it had become too centralized, too rule-bound, too little concerned with making programs work, and too much concerned with avoiding scandal. The NPR report contained many horror stories about useless red tape, excessive regulations, and cumbersome procurement systems that make it next to impossible for agencies to do what they were created to do. (For example, when smoking was permitted in federal office buildings, the General Services Administration issued a nine-page document that described an ashtray and specified how many pieces it must break into, should it be hit with a hammer.[41])

To solve these problems, the NPR called for less centralized management and more employee initiative, fewer detailed rules and more emphasis on customer satisfaction. It sought to create a new kind of organizational culture in government agencies, one more like that found in innovative, quality-conscious American corporations. The NPR was reinforced legislatively by the Government Performance and Results Act (GPRA) of 1993, which required agencies "to set goals, measure performance, and report on the results."

President George W. Bush built on the Clinton–Gore NPR efforts and the GPRA using the Performance Assessment Rating Tool (PART). The main goal of the PART was to link management reform to the budget process. During the 2008 presidential campaign, Barack Obama harkened back to the Clinton–Gore NPR but also pledged to keep but improve Bush's PART. By Obama's second term, however, administrative reform was not widely mentioned among main priorities or accomplishments in office. The Trump administration declared that the federal bureaucracy was too large and imposed burdensome requirements on individuals and companies, so it drastically cut staffs in several executive agencies, and it issued executive orders to limit bureaucratic power.[42]

Reforming the bureaucracy is easier said than done. Most of the rules and red tape that make it hard for agency heads to do a good job are the result either of the struggle between the White House and Congress for control over the agencies or of the agencies' desire to avoid irritating influential voters. Silly as the rules for ashtrays may sound, they were written so that the government could say it had an "objective" standard for buying ashtrays. If it simply had bought ashtrays at a department store the way ordinary people do, it would have risked being accused by Ashtray Company One of buying trays from its competitor, Ashtray Company Two, because of political favoritism.

The rivalry between the president and Congress for control of the bureaucracy makes bureaucrats nervous about irritating either branch, and so they issue rules designed to avoid trouble, even if these rules make it hard to do their job. Matters become even worse during periods of divided government, when different parties control the White House and Congress. As we saw in Chapter 14, divided government may not have much effect on *making* policy, but it can have a big effect on *implementing* it. Presidents of one party have tried to increase political control over the bureaucracy ("executive micromanagement"), and Congresses of another party have responded by increasing the number of investigations and detailed rule-making ("legislative micromanagement"). Divided government intensifies the cross fire between the executive and legislative branches, making bureaucrats dig into even deeper layers of red tape to avoid getting hurt.

This does not mean that reform is impossible, only that it is very difficult. For example, despite a lack of clear-cut successes in other areas, the NPR's procurement reforms stuck: government agencies can now buy things costing as much as $100,000 without following any complex regulations. Still, the main effect of the NPR, the GPRA, and the PART was to get federal agencies to collect far more information than in the past concerning what they do, without, however, using the information to improve the way they do it.

It might be easier to make desirable changes if the bureaucracy were accountable to only one person or institution—say, the president—instead of to several. But that situation, which exists in many parliamentary democracies, creates its own problems. When the bureaucracy has but one master, it often ends up having none; it becomes so powerful that it controls the prime minister and no longer listens to citizen complaints. A weak, divided bureaucracy, such as exists in the United States, may strike us as inefficient, but that very inefficiency may help protect our liberties.

John Moore/Getty Images News/Getty Images

Image 15.7 The Transportation Security Administration (TSA) screens passengers and their luggage at U.S. airports.

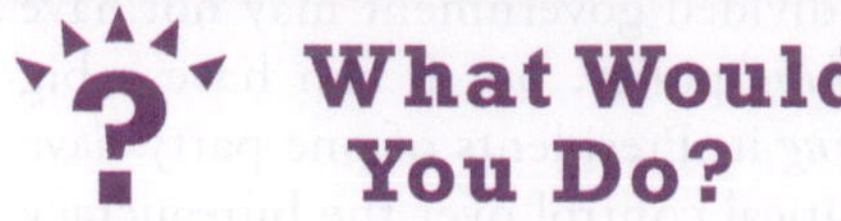

What Would You Do? | Will You Become the Assistant Secretary of Defense?

To: *Dr. Leah Titanium, president of Cybersystems Engineering*
From: *Colin Rob, secretary of defense*
Subject: *Becoming an assistant secretary of defense*

As both secretary and a dear old college buddy of yours, I write again to express my hope that you will accept the president's call to service. We all desperately want you aboard. Yes, conflict-of-interest laws will require you to sell your stock in your present company and drop out of its generous pension plan. No, the government won't even pay moving costs. And once you leave office, you will be barred for life from lobbying the executive branch on matters in which you were directly involved while in office, and you will be barred for two years from lobbying on matters that were under your general official authority. Your other concerns have merit, too, but let me help you weigh your options.

To Consider:

Four months into the new administration, hundreds of assistant secretary and deputy assistant secretary positions remain unfilled. In 1960, the total number of presidential political appointees was just 450. Today the total is closer to 3,000, but sheer growth is not the whole story. Rather, say experts on federal bureaucracy, plum public service posts go unfilled because the jobs have become so unrewarding, even punishing.

Arguments for:

1. I hate to preach, but it is one's duty to serve one's country when called. Your sacrifice would honor your family and benefit your fellow Americans for years to come.
2. As an accomplished professional and the head of a company that has done business with the government, you could help the president succeed in reforming the department so that it works better and costs less.
3. Despite the restrictions, you could resume your career once your public service was complete.

Arguments against:

1. Since you will have to be confirmed by the Senate, your life will be put under a microscope, and everything (even some of our old college mischief together) will be fair game for congressional staffers and reporters.
2. You will face hundreds of rules telling you what you can't do and scores of members of Congress and their staffs telling you what you should do. Longtime friends will get mad at you for not doing them favors. The president will demand loyalty. The press will pounce on your every mistake, real or imagined.
3. Given the federal limits on whom in the government you can deal with after you leave office, your job at Cybersystems may well suffer.

What Will You Decide? Enter **MindTap** to make your choice.

Your decision: ☐ Accept position ☐ Reject position

Learning Objectives

15-1 Discuss the unique features of the American federal bureaucracy.

A bureaucracy is a large, complex organization composed of appointed officials. American bureaucracy is distinctive in three ways: political authority over the bureaucracy is shared by several institutions; most national government agencies share their functions with state and local government agencies; and government agencies are closely scrutinized and frequently challenged by both individuals and nongovernmental groups.

15-2 Explain the evolution of the federal bureaucracy.

The Constitution made no provision for an administrative system other than to allow the president to appoint, with the advice and consent of the Senate, ambassadors, Supreme Court judges, and "all other officers . . . which shall be provided by law." By the early 20th century, however, Washington's role in making, administering, and funding public policies had already grown far beyond what the Framers had contemplated. Two world wars, the New Deal, and the Great Society each left the government with expanded powers and requiring new batteries of administrative agencies to exercise them.

Still, the president, cabinet secretaries, and thousands of political appointees are ultimately bosses of these administrative agencies. And Congress and the courts have ample, if imperfect, means of checking and balancing even the biggest bureaucracy, old or new.

15-3 Summarize how the federal bureaucracy functions today.

Today, the federal bureaucracy is as vast as most people's expectations about Washington's responsibility for every public concern one can name. It is the appointed officials—the bureaucrats—not the elected officials or policymakers, who command the troops, deliver the mail, audit the tax returns, run the federal prisons, decide who qualifies for public assistance, and do countless other tasks. Unavoidably, many bureaucrats exercise discretion in deciding what public laws and regulations mean and how to apply them.

Discretionary authority refers to the extent to which appointed bureaucrats can choose courses of action and make policies not spelled out in advance by laws. It is impossible for Congress to specify every detail about how a law will be implemented. Many laws are administered by persons with special information and expertise, and many private citizens administer public laws by working as government contractors or grantees.

15-4 Discuss checks on and problems with the federal bureaucracy, and possibilities for reform.

Congress exerts control over the bureaucracy in many different ways. It decides whether an agency may exist and how much money an agency spends. It can hold oversight hearings and launch investigations into just about any aspect of agency decision making or operations it chooses. And it traditionally has enjoyed wide latitude from the president in exercising its oversight functions.

Numerous efforts have tried to make the bureaucracy work better and cost less, including 11 presidential or other major commissions in the 20th century. Among the latest was the National Performance Review (NPR), popularly called the plan to "reinvent government." Vice President Gore led the NPR during the two terms of the Clinton administration. The NPR was predicated on the view that bureaucracy had become too centralized, too rule-bound, too little concerned with program results, and too much concerned with avoiding scandal.

In the end, the NPR produced certain money-saving changes in the federal procurement process (how government purchases goods and services from private contractors), and it also streamlined parts of the federal personnel process (how Washington hires career employees). Most experts, however, gave the NPR mixed grades. The Bush administration abolished the NPR but began the Performance Assessment Rating Tool (PART). Most experts judged the PART to be only mildly successful.

All large organizations, including business firms, have some complex rules and procedures, or red tape. Some red tape in government agencies is silly and wasteful (or worse), but try imagining government without any red tape at all. Imagine no rules about hiring on the basis of merit, no strict financial accounting procedures, and no regulations concerning citizen access to information or public record-keeping. As Yale political scientist Herbert Kaufman once quipped, one citizen's "red tape" often is another's "treasured safeguard."

To Learn More

For addresses and reports of various cabinet departments: **www.whitehouse.gov**

Office of Personnel Management: **www.opm.gov**

National Partnership for Reinventing Government: govinfo.library.unt.edu/npr/index.htm

A few specific websites of federal agencies:

Department of Defense: **www.defense.gov**

Department of Education: **www.ed.gov**

Department of Health and Human Services: **www.hhs.gov**

Department of State: **www.state.gov**

Federal Bureau of Investigation: **www.fbi.gov**

Department of Labor: **www.dol.gov**

Burke, John P. *Bureaucratic Responsibility*. Baltimore: Johns Hopkins University Press, 1986. Examines the problem of individual responsibility—for example, when to be a whistle blower—in government agencies.

Carpenter, Daniel. *The Forging of Bureaucratic Autonomy: Reputations, Networks, and Policy Innovation in Executive Agencies, 1862–1928.* Princeton: Princeton University Press, 2001. A systematic study of the evolution of administrative agencies in the United States.

Downs, Anthony. *Inside Bureaucracy*. Boston: Little, Brown, 1967. An economist's explanation of why bureaucrats and bureaus behave as they do.

Durant, Robert F., ed. *The Oxford Handbook of American Bureaucracy*. New York: Oxford University Press, 2012. Thirty-three academic essays covering just about every facet of the subject.

Halperin, Morton H. *Bureaucratic Politics and Foreign Policy.* Washington, D.C.: Brookings Institution, 1974. Insightful account of the strategies by which diplomatic and military bureaucracies defend their interests.

Heclo, Hugh. *A Government of Strangers*. Washington, D.C.: Brookings Institution, 1977. Analyzes how political appointees attempt to gain control of the Washington bureaucracy and how bureaucrats resist those efforts.

Kettl, Donald F. *Government by Proxy (Mis?Managing Federal Programs)*. Washington, D.C.: Congressional Quarterly Press, 1988. An account of how the federal government pays others to staff and run its programs.

Kettl, Donald F. *The Next Government of the United States: Why Our Institutions Fail Us and How to Fix Them.* New York: W. W. Norton, 2008. A masterful study of how proxy government functions and often fails today, and what might be done to remedy its worst failures.

Mettler, Suzanne. *The Submerged State: How Invisible Government Policies Undermine American Democracy.* Chicago: University of Chicago Press, 2011. A detailed and instructive analysis of how federal policies that provide benefits through subsidies or incentives receive limited public visibility as government programs.

Moore, Mark H. *Creating Public Value: Strategic Management in Government.* Cambridge, MA: Harvard University Press, 1995. A thoughtful account of how wise bureaucrats can make government work better.

Parkinson, C. Northcote. *Parkinson's Law*. Boston: Houghton Mifflin, 1957. Half-serious, half-joking explanation of why government agencies tend to grow.

Wilson, James Q. *Bureaucracy: What Government Agencies Do and Why They Do It.* New York: Basic Books, 1989. A comprehensive review of what we know about bureaucratic behavior in the United States.

CHAPTER 16

The Judiciary

Learning Objectives

16-1 Explain the concept of judicial review.

16-2 Summarize the development of the federal courts.

16-3 Discuss the structure, jurisdiction, and operation of the federal courts.

16-4 Explain how the federal courts exercise power and the checks on judicial power.

« Then When the states were debating the ratification of the Constitution, Alexander Hamilton wrote in Federalist No. 78 that the new system of federal courts would be "the least dangerous" branch of government because, unlike the president, it would not command the sword and, unlike Congress, it would not control the purse strings. The courts, he argued, could take "no active resolution whatever." Nowhere in the Constitution was the Supreme Court given the right to declare laws of Congress or decisions of the president to be unconstitutional, though Hamilton argued that such a power was necessary. That document was our fundamental law and expressed the will of the people, and so it ought to be preferred to a law passed by Congress if there were an "irreconcilable variance between the two."

*** Now** Within a few years after the Constitution was ratified, the Supreme Court took Hamilton's position by asserting that the Court could decide whether a law was unconstitutional. A dozen years later, the same Court said that Congress could not only pass laws on the basis of powers explicitly given it by the Constitution, but also do things that were "necessary and proper" in order to implement those powers. By the middle of the 19th century, the Supreme Court had begun to declare many federal and scores of state laws to be unconstitutional, and this practice has continued into the present.

As a result of its newfound powers in the 19th century, justices began serving on the Supreme Court for much longer periods. The 11 justices nominated by President George Washington served, on average, 7 years, while the 5 nominated 40 years later by President Andrew Jackson served on average 20 years. The Court had become not the least dangerous branch, but a powerful one.

In recent years, the political identity of judicial nominees has become a major issue in confirmation hearings. From the end of World War II to the mid-1980s, the Senate approved most federal judicial nominees without controversy (though there were some important exceptions, particularly for Supreme Court candidates). Since then, however, judicial nominations have had a less certain reception in the Senate. When President Ronald Reagan nominated Antonin Scalia for the Supreme Court, he was confirmed by the Senate in 1986 by a vote of 98 to 0. But one year later, when President Reagan nominated Robert Bork, he was rejected by the Senate. Four years after that, Clarence Thomas barely survived a confirmation vote (52 to 48). In 2006, President George W. Bush's nominee Samuel Alito won confirmation by a vote of 58 to 42 after Senate Democrats tried to block the vote by means of a filibuster.

Both of President Barack Obama's nominees were confirmed, but in each case, many Republicans voted against the nominee. And after Justice Scalia's death in early 2016, Republican Majority Leader Mitch McConnell declared that the Senate would not hold confirmation hearings until the next president made a nomination. President Donald Trump's nomination of Judge Neil Gorsuch in 2017 to fill the spot won Senate approval by a 54–45 vote. But his nomination of Judge Brett Kavanaugh in 2018 became far more contentious after an allegation of sexual assault during Kavanaugh's high-school years became public. The news prompted a national outcry and a special Senate hearing for the accuser and nominee. Ultimately, Kavanaugh was confirmed 50–48 on an almost fully party-line vote. (One Democrat voted for confirmation.)

In U.S. District and Appeals (Circuit) Courts—the lower levels of the federal court system below the Supreme Court—the confirmation process has slowed considerably in the past thirty years. From 1945 until 1970, almost every federal court nominee was confirmed, but in the George H. W. Bush administration, the number dropped to just under 80 percent of nominees. As Figure 16-1 shows, the appellate court confirmation rate dropped further under Clinton and George W. Bush, and then moved above 80 percent in the Obama administration.[1] In contrast, District Court confirmations improved under Clinton and George W. Bush, and then fell to about 80 percent in the Obama years. As of mid-2019, more than 90 percent of the Trump administration's appeals court nominees had been confirmed, though the percentage for district court nominees was lower, at about 70 percent. Of particular concern was the length of time from nomination to confirmation, which more than quintupled from Reagan to Obama; as Figure 16-2 shows, the median number of days needed in the Reagan area was 45, but under Obama, it increased to 229.[2]

Why the changes? A major reason is that the federal judiciary has played an increasingly important role in making public policy. It, and not Congress, decided that abortions should be legal, settled the closely contested 2000 presidential election, and allowed private homes to be seized in order to build a residential hotel and other private structures aimed at affluent clientele. In these and many other cases, the federal courts have become major political actors; as a result, Congress has become concerned about who will be federal judges. Especially during certain periods of divided government (see Chapter 14), the increased partisan polarization in Congress (see Chapter 13) has made its mark on the Senate's

Figure 16.1 Federal District and Appeals Court Appointments, 1981–2019

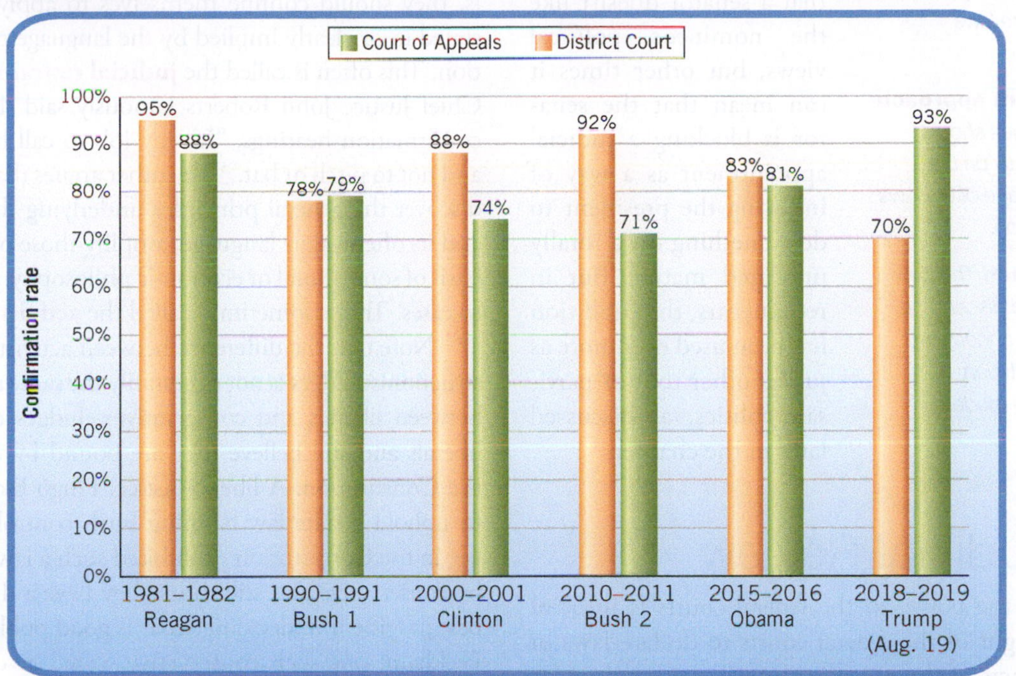

Source: Russell Wheeler, "Trump's Judicial Appointments Record at the August Recess: A Little Less Than Meets the Eye," *Brookings*, 8 August 2019.

Figure 16.2 Federal Court Appointments, Time from Nomination to Confirmation

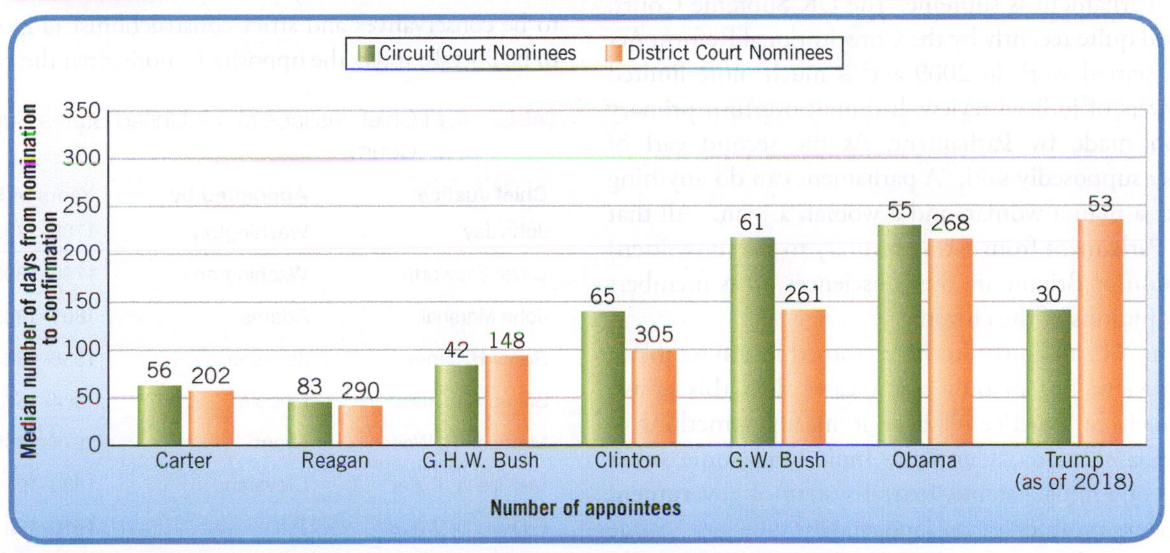

Source: Adapted from Congressional Research Service, "Judicial Nomination Statistics and Analysis: U.S. District and Circuit Courts, 1977–2018," 21 March 2019, Table 7, pp. 13–14.

Q **Why has the time period for confirmation of federal judicial nominees increased so much in recent years, and what are the consequences for American governance?**

confirmation process. For example, during President Bill Clinton's first two years in office, a period of unified government, 86 percent of his nominees for the U.S. Court of Appeals were confirmed; however, during his second two years in office, a period of divided government, the confirmation rate dropped to 55 percent.[3]

As federal judges make more policy decisions, and as partisan rancor over those decisions rises, the process by which the Senate considers nominees for the federal bench has become longer, more ideologically charged, and less certain to result in confirmations. By long-standing tradition, senators from the home state of an appeals court nominee are allowed to file a private objection—what is called registering a negative "blue slip" complaint. If filed by a Judiciary Committee member, this will prevent a hearing on the nominee from being held. Sometimes

judicial review *The power of courts to declare laws unconstitutional.*

judicial restraint approach *The view that judges should decide cases strictly on the basis of the language of the laws and the Constitution.*

activist approach *The view that judges should discern the general principles underlying laws or the Constitution and apply them to modern circumstances.*

these blue slips indicate that a senator doesn't like the nominee's political views, but other times it can mean that the senator is blocking a judicial appointment as a way of inducing the president to do something on a totally unrelated matter. But in recent years, that tradition has been used ever more as just another tool of partisan politics, as discussed later in the chapter.

16-1 Judicial Review

One aspect of the power of the federal courts is **judicial review**—the right of the federal courts to declare laws of Congress and acts of the executive branch void and unenforceable if they are judged to be in conflict with the Constitution. Since 1789, the Supreme Court has declared more than 160 federal laws to be unconstitutional. In Britain, by contrast, Parliament is supreme. The UK Supreme Court, established quite recently by the Constitutional Reform Act of 2005, started work in 2009 and is much more limited in its powers of judicial review. It cannot overturn primary legislation made by Parliament. As the second earl of Pembroke supposedly said, "A parliament can do anything but make a man a woman and a woman a man." All that prevents Parliament from acting contrary to the (unwritten) constitution of Britain are the consciences of its members and the opinions of the citizens.

About 60 nations do have something resembling judicial review, but in only a few cases does this power mean much in practice. Where it means something—in Australia, Canada, Germany, India, and some other nations—one finds a stable, federal system of government with a strong tradition of an independent judiciary.[4] Some other nations—France, for example—have special councils, rather than courts, that can under certain circumstances decide that a law is not authorized by the constitution.

Judicial review is the federal courts' chief weapon in the system of checks and balances on which the American government is based. Today, few people would deny to the courts the right to decide that a legislative or executive act is unconstitutional, though once that right was controversial. What remains controversial is the method by which such review is conducted.

Two competing views exist, each ardently pressed during the fight to confirm Clarence Thomas, as well as subsequent justices. The first holds that judges should only judge—that is, they should confine themselves to applying those rules stated in or clearly implied by the language of the Constitution. This often is called the **judicial restraint approach**. As Chief Justice John Roberts famously said during his 2005 confirmation hearings, "It's my job to call balls and strikes and not to pitch or bat."[5] The other argues that judges should discover the general principles underlying the Constitution and its often vague language, amplify those principles on the basis of some moral or economic philosophy, and apply them to cases. This is sometimes called the **activist approach**.

Note that the difference between activist and strict constructionist judges is not necessarily the same as the difference between liberals and conservatives. Judges can be political liberals and still believe they are bound by the language of the Constitution. A liberal justice, Hugo Black, once voted to uphold a state law banning birth control because nothing in the Constitution prohibited such a law. Or judges can be conservative and still think they have a duty to use their best judgment in deciding what is good public policy. Rufus Peckham, one such conservative, voted to overturn a state law setting maximum hours of work because he believed the Fourteenth Amendment guaranteed something called "freedom of contract," even though those words are not in the amendment. Seventy years ago, judicial activists tended to be conservatives and strict constructionist judges tended to be liberals; today the opposite is more often the case.

TABLE 16.1 | Chief Justices of the United States Supreme Court.

Chief Justice	Appointed by	Years of Service
John Jay	Washington	1789–1795
Oliver Ellsworth	Washington	1796–1800
John Marshall	Adams	1801–1835
Roger B. Taney	Jackson	1836–1864
Salmon P. Chase	Lincoln	1864–1873
Morrison R. Waite	Grant	1874–1888
Melville W. Fuller	Cleveland	1888–1910
Edward D. White	Taft	1910–1921
William Howard Taft	Harding	1921–1930
Charles Evans Hughes	Hoover	1930–1941
Harlan Fiske Stone	F. Roosevelt	1941–1946
Fred M. Vinson	Truman	1946–1953
Earl Warren	Eisenhower	1953–1969
Warren E. Burger	Nixon	1969–1986
William H. Rehnquist	Reagan	1986–2005
John G. Roberts, Jr.	Bush	2005–present

Note: *Omitted is John Rutledge, who served for only a few months in 1795 and who was not confirmed by the Senate.*

16-2 Development of the Federal Courts

Most of the Founders probably expected the Supreme Court to have the power of judicial review (though they did not say that in so many words in the Constitution), but they did not expect federal courts to play so large a role in making public policy. The traditional view of civil courts was that they judged disputes between people who had direct dealings with each other—they had entered into a contract, for example, or one had dropped a load of bricks on the other's toe—and decided which of the two parties was right. The court then supplied relief to the wronged party, usually by requiring the other person to pay money ("damages").

This traditional understanding was based on the belief that judges would find and apply existing law. The purpose of a court case was not to learn what the judge believes but what the law requires. The later rise of judicial activism occurred when judges questioned this traditional view and argued instead that judges do not merely find the law, they make the law.

The view that judges interpret the law, not make policy, made it easy for the Founders to justify the power of judicial review. It also led them to predict that the courts would play a relatively neutral, even passive, role in public affairs. Alexander Hamilton, writing in *Federalist* No. 78, described the judiciary as the branch "least dangerous" to political rights. The president is commander-in-chief and thus holds the "sword of the community"; Congress appropriates money and thus "commands the purse" as well as decides what laws shall govern. But the judiciary "has no influence over either the sword or the purse" and "can take no active resolution whatever." It has "neither force nor will but merely judgment," and thus is "beyond comparison the weakest of the three departments of power." As a result, "liberty can have nothing to fear from the judiciary alone." Hamilton went on to state clearly that the Constitution intended to give to the courts the right to decide whether a law is contrary to the Constitution. But this authority, he explained, was designed not to enlarge the power of the courts but to confine that of the legislature.

Obviously, things have changed since Hamilton's time. The evolution of the federal courts, especially the Supreme Court, toward the present level of activism and influence has been shaped by the political, economic, and ideological forces of three historical eras. From 1787 to 1865, nation-building, the legitimacy of the federal government, and slavery were the great issues; from 1865 to 1937, the great issue was the relationship between the government and the economy; from 1938 to the present, the major issues confronting the Court have involved personal liberty and social equality, and the potential conflict between the two. In the first period, the Court asserted the supremacy of the federal government; in the second, it placed important restrictions on the powers of that government; and in the third, it enlarged the scope of personal freedom and narrowed that of economic freedom.

National Supremacy and Slavery

A classic study of the Supreme Court describes well the primary debate about judicial power in the early American republic: "From 1789 until the Civil War, the dominant interest of the Supreme Court was in that greatest of all the questions left unresolved by the Founders—the nation–state relationship."[6] The answer the Court gave, under the leadership of Chief Justice John Marshall, was that national law was in all instances the dominant law, with state law having to give way, and that the Supreme Court had the power to decide what the Constitution meant. In two cases of enormous importance—*Marbury v. Madison* in 1803 and *McCulloch v. Maryland* in 1819–the Court, in decisions written by Marshall, held that the Supreme Court could declare an act of Congress unconstitutional; that the power granted by the Constitution to the federal government flows from the people and thus should be generously construed (and thus any federal laws that are "necessary and proper" to the attainment of constitutional ends are permissible); and that federal law is supreme over state law, even to the point that a state may not tax an enterprise (such as a bank) created by the federal government.[7]

The supremacy of the federal government was reaffirmed by other decisions as well. In 1816, the Supreme Court rejected the claim of the Virginia courts that the Supreme Court could not review the decisions of state courts. The Virginia courts were ready to acknowledge the supremacy of the U.S. Constitution but believed they had as much right as the U.S. Supreme Court to decide what the Constitution meant. The Supreme Court felt otherwise, and in this case and another like it, the Court asserted its own broad powers to review any state court decision if that decision seemed to violate federal law or the federal Constitution.[8]

The power of the federal government to regulate commerce among the states was also established. When New York gave to Robert Fulton, the inventor of the steamboat, the monopoly right to operate his steamboats on the rivers of that state, the Marshall Court overturned the license because the rivers connected New York and New Jersey and thus trade on those rivers would involve *inter*state commerce, and federal law in that area was supreme. Because there was a conflicting federal law on the books, the state law was void.[9]

All of this may sound rather obvious today, when the supremacy of the federal government is largely unquestioned. In the early 19th century, however, these were almost revolutionary decisions. The Jeffersonian Republicans were in power and had become increasingly devoted to states' rights; they were aghast at the Marshall decisions. President Andrew Jackson attacked the Court bitterly for defending the right of the federal government to create a national bank and for siding with the Cherokee Indians in a dispute with Georgia. In speaking of the latter case, Jackson is supposed to have remarked, "John Marshall has made his decision; now let him enforce it!"[10]

Though Marshall seemed to have secured the supremacy of the federal government over the state governments, another even more divisive issue had arisen; that, of course, was slavery. (See Table 16.1 on p. 406 for a list of all the chief justices of the U.S. Supreme Court.) Roger B. Taney succeeded Marshall as chief justice in 1836. He was deliberately chosen by President Jackson because he was an advocate of states' rights, and he began to chip away at federal supremacy, upholding state claims that Marshall would have set aside. But the decision for which he is famous—or infamous—came in 1857 when, in the *Dred Scott* case, he wrote perhaps the most disastrous judicial opinion ever issued. A slave, Dred Scott, had been taken by his owner to a territory (near what is now St. Paul, Minnesota) where slavery was illegal under federal law. Scott claimed that since he had resided in a free territory, he was now a free man. Taney held that African Americans were not citizens of the United States and could not become so, and that the federal law—the Missouri Compromise—prohibiting slavery in Northern territories was unconstitutional.[11] The public outcry against this view was enormous, and the Court and Taney were discredited, at least in the North. The Civil War was ultimately fought over what the Court mistakenly had assumed was a purely legal question.

Government and the Economy

The supremacy of the federal government may have been established by John Marshall and the Civil War, but the scope of the powers of that government or even of the state governments was still to be defined. During the period from the end of the Civil War to the early years of the New Deal, the dominant issue the Supreme Court faced was deciding when the economy would be regulated by the states and when by the nation.

The Court revealed a strong though not inflexible attachment to private property. In fact, that attachment had always been there: the Founders thought political and property rights were inextricably linked, and Marshall certainly supported the sanctity of contracts. But now, with the muting of the federal supremacy issue and the rise of a national economy with important unanticipated effects, the property question became the dominant one. In general, the Court developed the view that the Fourteenth Amendment, adopted in 1868 primarily to grant citizenship to African Americans and provide protection from hostile state action, also protected private property and corporations from unreasonable state action. The crucial phrase was this: no state shall "deprive any person of life, liberty, or property, without due process of law." Once it became clear that a "person" could be a firm or a corporation as well as an individual, business and industry began to flood the courts with cases challenging various government regulations.

The Court quickly found itself in a thicket: it began ruling on the constitutionality of virtually every effort by any government to regulate any aspect of business or labor, and its workload increased sharply. Judicial activism was born in the 1880s and 1890s as the Court set itself up as the arbiter of what kind of regulation was permissible. In the first 75 years of this country's history, only two federal laws were held to be unconstitutional; in the next 75 years, 71 were.[12] Of the roughly 1,300 state laws held to be in conflict with the federal Constitution since 1789, about 1,200 were overturned after 1870. In one decade alone—the 1880s—5 federal and 48 state laws were declared unconstitutional.

Many of these decisions provided clear evidence of the Court's desire to protect private property: it upheld the use of injunctions to prevent labor strikes,[13] struck down the federal income tax,[14] sharply limited the reach of the antitrust law,[15] restricted the powers of the Interstate Commerce Commission to set railroad rates,[16] prohibited the federal government from eliminating child labor,[17] and prevented the states from setting maximum hours of work.[18] In 184 cases between 1899 and 1937, the Supreme Court struck down state laws for violating the Fourteenth Amendment, usually by economic regulation.[19]

But the Court also rendered decisions that authorized various kinds of regulation. It allowed states to regulate businesses "affected with a public interest,"[20] changed its mind about the Interstate Commerce Commission and allowed it to regulate railroad rates,[21] upheld rules requiring railroads to improve their safety,[22] approved state antiliquor laws,[23] approved state mine safety laws,[24] supported state workers' compensation laws,[25] allowed states to regulate fire-insurance rates,[26] and in time upheld a number of state laws regulating wages and hours. Indeed, between 1887 and 1910, in 558 cases involving the Fourteenth Amendment, the Supreme Court upheld state regulations over 80 percent of the time.[27]

To characterize the Court as pro-business or antiregulation is both simplistic and inexact. More accurate, perhaps, is to characterize it as supportive of the rights of private property but unsure how to draw the lines that distinguish "reasonable" from "unreasonable" regulation. Nothing in the Constitution clearly differentiates reasonable from unreasonable regulation, and the Court has been able to invent no consistent principle of its own to make this determination. For example, what kinds of businesses are "affected with a public interest"? Grain elevators and railroads are, but are bakeries? Sugar refineries? Saloons? And how much of commerce is "interstate"—anything that moves? Or only something that actually crosses a state line (recall our discussion of this point in Chapter 3)? The

Court found itself trying to make detailed judgments that it was not always competent to make and to invent legal rules where no clear legal rules were possible.

In one area, however, the Supreme Court's judgments were clear: the Fourteenth and Fifteenth Amendments were construed so narrowly as to give African Americans only the most limited benefits of their provisions. In a long series of decisions, the Court upheld segregation in schools and on railroad cars and permitted African Americans to be excluded from voting in many states.

Government and Political Liberty

After 1936, the Supreme Court stopped imposing any serious restrictions on state or federal power to regulate the economy, leaving such matters in the hands of the legislatures. From 1937 to 1974, the Supreme Court did not

Marbury v. Madison

The story of *Marbury v. Madison* is often told, but it deserves another telling because it illustrates so many features of the role of the Supreme Court–how apparently small cases can have large results, how the power of the Court depends not simply on its constitutional authority but also on its acting in ways that avoid a clear confrontation with other branches of government, and how the climate of opinion affects how the Court goes about its task.

When President John Adams lost his bid for reelection to Thomas Jefferson in 1800, he—and all members of his party, the Federalists—feared that Jefferson and the Republicans would weaken the federal government and turn its powers to what the Federalists believed were wrong ends, such as states' rights, an alliance with the French, and hostility toward business. As his hours in office came to an end, Adams worked feverishly to pack the judiciary with 59 loyal Federalists by giving them so-called midnight appointments before Jefferson took office.

John Marshall, as Adams's secretary of state, had the task of certifying and delivering these new judicial commissions. In the press of business, he delivered all but 17; these he left on his desk for the incoming secretary of state, James Madison, to send out. Jefferson and Madison, however, were furious at Adams's behavior and refused to deliver the 17. William Marbury and three other Federalists who had been promised these commissions hired a lawyer and brought suit against Madison to force him to produce the documents. The suit requested the Supreme Court to issue a writ of mandamus (from the Latin, "we command") ordering Madison to do his duty. The right to issue such writs had been given to the Court by the Judiciary Act of 1789.

Marshall, the man who had failed to deliver the commissions to Marbury and his friends in the first place, had become the chief justice and was now in a position to decide the case. These days, any justices who had been involved in an issue before it came to the Court would probably recuse themselves, but Marshall had no intention of letting others decide this question. He faced, however, not simply a partisan dispute over jobs but what was nearly a constitutional crisis. If he ordered the commission delivered, Madison might still refuse, and the Court had no way—if Madison was determined to resist—to compel him. The Court had no police force, whereas Madison had the support of the president of the United States. And if the order were given, whether or not Madison complied, the Jeffersonian Republicans in Congress would probably try to impeach Marshall. On the other hand, if Marshall allowed Madison to do as he wished, the power of the Supreme Court would be seriously reduced.

Marshall's solution was ingenious. Speaking for a unanimous Court, he announced that Madison was wrong to withhold the commissions, that courts could issue writs to compel public officials to do their prescribed duty—*but* that the Supreme Court had no power to issue such writs in this case because the law (the Judiciary Act of 1789) giving it that power was unconstitutional. The law said the Supreme Court could issue such writs as part of its "original jurisdiction"—that is, persons seeking such writs could go *directly* to the Supreme Court with their request (rather than go first to a lower federal court and then, if dissatisfied, appeal to the Supreme Court). Article III of the Constitution, Marshall pointed out, spelled out precisely the Supreme Court's original jurisdiction; it did not mention issuing writs of this sort and plainly indicated that on all matters not mentioned in the Constitution, the Court would have only appellate jurisdiction. Congress may not change what the Constitution says; hence, the part of the Judiciary Act attempting to do this was null and void.

The result was that a showdown with the Jeffersonians was avoided—Madison was not ordered to deliver the commissions—but the power of the Supreme Court was unmistakably clarified and enlarged. As Marshall wrote, "It is emphatically the province and duty of the judicial department to say what the law is." Furthermore, "a law repugnant to the Constitution is void."

overturn a single federal law designed to regulate business but did overturn 36 congressional enactments that violated personal political liberties. It voided as unconstitutional laws that restricted freedom of speech,[28] denied passports to communists,[29] permitted the government to revoke a person's citizenship,[30] withheld a person's mail,[31] or restricted the availability of government benefits.[32]

This new direction began when one justice changed his mind, and it continued as the composition of the Court changed. At the outset of the New Deal, the Court was by a narrow margin dominated by justices who opposed the welfare state and federal regulation based on broad grants of discretionary authority to administrative agencies. President Franklin Roosevelt, who was determined to get just such legislation implemented, found himself powerless to alter the composition of the Court during his first term (1933–1937); because no justice died or retired, he had no vacancies to fill. After his overwhelming reelection in 1936, he moved to remedy this problem by "packing" the Court.

Roosevelt proposed a bill that would have allowed him to appoint one new justice for each one over the age of 70 who refused to retire, up to a total membership of 15. Since six men in this category were then on the Supreme Court, he would have been able to appoint six new justices, enough to ensure a comfortable majority supportive of his economic policies. A bitter controversy ensued, but before the bill could be voted on, the Supreme Court, perhaps reacting to Roosevelt's big win in the 1936 election, changed its mind. While it had been striking down several New Deal measures by votes of five to four, now it started approving them by the same vote. One justice, Owen Roberts, had switched his position. This was called the "switch in time that saved nine," but in fact Roberts had changed his mind *before* FDR's plan was announced.

The "Court-packing" bill was not passed, but it was no longer necessary. Justice Roberts had yielded to public opinion in a way that Chief Justice Taney a century earlier had not, thus forestalling an assault on the Court by the other branches of government. Shortly thereafter, several justices stepped down, and Roosevelt was able to make his own appointments (he filled seven seats during his four terms in office). From then on, the Court turned its attention to new issues—political liberties and, in time, civil rights.

With the arrival in office of Chief Justice Earl Warren in 1953, the Court began its most active period yet. Activism now arose to redefine the relationship of citizens to the government and especially to protect the rights and liberties of citizens from governmental trespass. Although the Court has always seen itself as

Constitutional Connections | The "Exceptions" Clause

Article III, Section II of the Constitution provides that "the Supreme Court shall have appellate Jurisdiction, both as to Law and Fact, with such Exceptions, and under such Regulations as the Congress shall make." In the 1868 case of *Ex parte McCardle*, the Court unanimously agreed that the "Exceptions" clause gives Congress the power to restrict the Court's appellate jurisdiction. Since then, many noted jurists and scholars have taken serious issue with that interpretation, but the prevailing view is that, at least on an issue-by-issue basis, the exceptions clause gives Congress broad, if not unlimited, power to prohibit the federal courts, including the Supreme Court, from exercising judicial review.

Over the past several decades, each session of Congress has witnessed proposals to deny the federal courts appellate jurisdiction. There have been such proposals on abortion rights, busing to achieve racial balance in schools, school prayer, prisoners' rights, same-sex marriage, and many other issues. Some exception clause proposals have become bills and made it into federal law; for example, the Illegal Immigration Reform and Immigrant Responsibility Act of 1996 prohibited the federal courts from hearing appeals regarding certain decisions by the U.S. Immigration and Naturalization Service.

Typically, however, even exception clause—related bills that come to a vote never make it into law. For example, in each of several sessions after 2000, the House approved a bill prohibiting federal courts from exercising appellate jurisdiction in cases involving the invocation of "under God" in the Pledge of Allegiance. But none of these bills made it through the Senate. Likewise, in 2011, Rep. Ron Paul (R-TX) sponsored the Sanctity of Life Act, which would have stripped the federal courts of the authority to hear abortion cases; but that was just the latest in a series of such exception clause bills on abortion that were much debated but never enacted.

Power of the Supreme Court

- ***Marbury v. Madison* (1803):** Upheld judicial review of congressional acts.
- ***Martin v. Hunter's Lessee* (1816):** The Supreme Court can review the decisions of the highest state courts if they involve a federal law or the federal Constitution.
- ***McCulloch v. Maryland* (1819):** Ruled that creating a federal bank, though not mentioned in the Constitution, was a "necessary and proper" exercise of the government's right to borrow money.
- ***Ex parte McCardle* (1869):** Allowed Congress to change the appellate jurisdiction of the Supreme Court.

protecting citizens from arbitrary government, before 1937 that protection was of a sort that conservatives preferred; after 1937, it was of a kind that liberals preferred. (Figure 16.3 shows how the Supreme Court shifted focus in the 20th century from overturning laws on economic regulation to reversing restrictions on civil liberties.)

The Revival of State Sovereignty

For many decades, the Supreme Court allowed Congress to pass almost any law authorized by the Constitution, no matter how it affected the states. As we saw in Chapter 3, the Court had long held that Congress could regulate almost any activity if it affected interstate commerce, and in the Court's opinion virtually every activity did affect it. The states were left with few rights to challenge federal power. But since around 1992, the Court has backed away from this view. By narrow majorities, it has begun to restore the view that states have the right to resist some forms of federal action.

When Congress passed a bill that forbade anyone from carrying a gun near a school, the Court held that carrying guns did not affect interstate commerce, and so the law was invalid.[33] One year later, it struck down a law that allowed Indian tribes to sue the states in federal courts, arguing that Congress lacks the power to ignore the "sovereign immunity" of states—that is, the right, protected by the Eleventh Amendment, not to be sued in federal court. (It has since upheld that view in two more cases.) And the next year, it held that the Brady gun control law could not be used to require local law enforcement officers to do background checks on people trying to buy weapons.[34] These cases are all hints that the supremacy of the federal government has some real limits created by the existence and powers of the several states.

Figure 16.3 Economics and Civil Liberties Laws Overturned by the U.S. Supreme Court, by Decade, 1900–2014

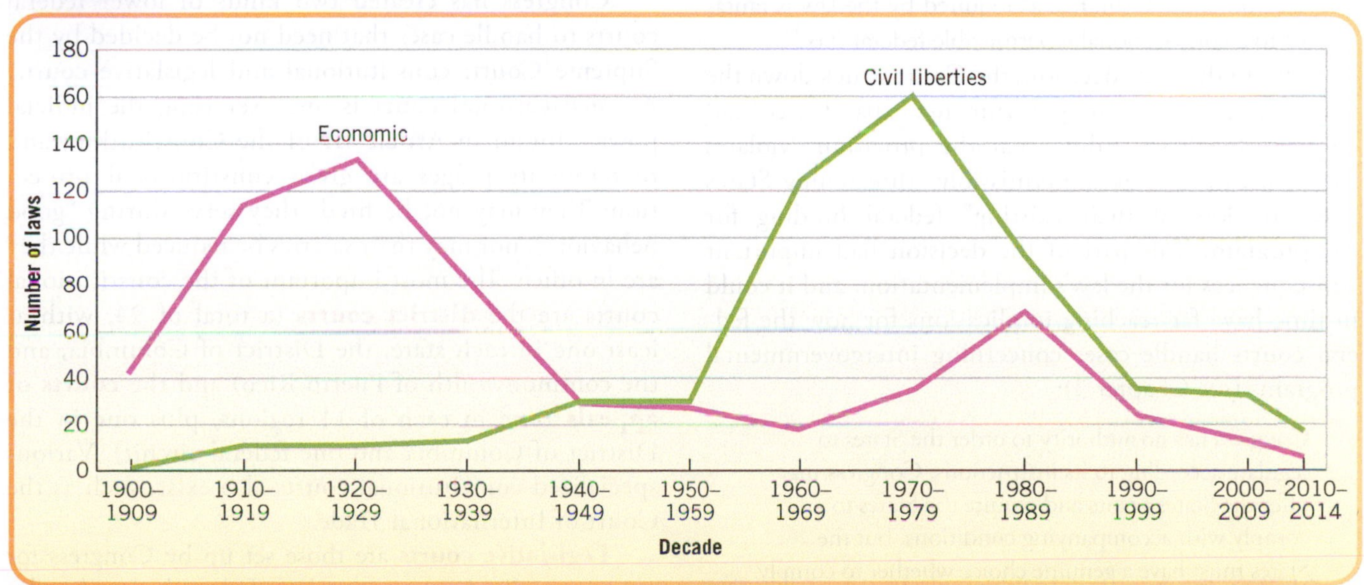

Note: The Civil liberties category does not include laws supportive of civil liberties. Laws include federal, state, and local.

Source: Harold W. Stanley and Richard G. Niemi, *Vital Statistics on American Politics, 2015–2016* (Washington, D.C.: Congressional Quarterly Press, 2015), Figure 7.4.

constitutional court A federal court, authorized by Article III of the Constitution, that keeps judges in office during good behavior and prevents their salaries from being reduced. They include the Supreme Court (created by the Constitution) and appellate and district courts created by Congress.

district courts The lowest federal courts; federal trials can be held only here.

courts of appeals Federal courts that hear appeals from district courts; no trials.

legislative courts Courts created by Congress for specialized purposes, whose judges do not enjoy the protections of Article III of the Constitution.

After the enactment of President Obama's health care plan in 2010, several states argued that its requirement that everyone purchase health insurance was unconstitutional. Some district courts agreed with the claims and others disagreed. The issue was whether Congress's authority to levy taxes or to regulate interstate commerce gave it the right to require citizens to purchase a product. In addition, some state officials questioned the constitutionality of provisions requiring state governments to expand health care coverage for low-income citizens via the federal–state Medicaid program or risk losing all existing federal funding for that program.

In *National Federation of Independent Business v. Sebelius* (2012), the Supreme Court decided these issues. It upheld the law's "individual mandate" to purchase "minimum essential" health insurance, ruling that the monetary "penalty" to be levied by the Internal Revenue Service on anyone that does not purchase insurance as required by the law is tantamount to a constitutionally permissible federal "tax."

But, in the same decision, the Court struck down the law's mandate that state governments expand Medicaid coverage by 2014, ruling that the provision "violates the Constitution" by impermissibly "threatening States with the loss of their existing" federal funding for the program. This part of the decision had important consequences for the law's implementation, and it could in time have far-reaching implications for how the federal courts handle cases concerning intergovernmental programs (see Chapter 3):

> Congress has no authority to order the States to regulate according to its instructions. Congress may offer the States grants and require the States to comply with accompanying conditions, but the States must have a genuine choice whether to comply.

Debate over the federal government's appropriate role in health care continues. In 2015, the Supreme Court ruled six to three in *King v. Burwell* that the Affordable Care Act permits the federal government to provide subsidies for people to buy health insurance through the federal exchange if their state does not have its own exchange for comparing and purchasing health-care plans. Opponents had insisted the law allowed subsidies only for plans purchased through state exchanges; if that view had prevailed, then more than 6 million Americans in 34 states likely would no longer be able to afford health insurance. By upholding subsidies for the federal exchange, the Court ensured the viability of the health-care law for the foreseeable future, barring legislative or executive action to modify it.[35] More recently, several states have argued that with the 2017 tax law's elimination of the federal tax penalty for not having health insurance, the Affordable Care Act is unconstitutional, and the Supreme Court agreed in the spring of 2020 to hear this case.

16-3 The Structure, Jurisdiction, and Operation of the Federal Courts

The only federal court the Constitution requires is the Supreme Court, as specified in Article III. All other federal courts and their jurisdictions are creations of Congress. Nor does the Constitution indicate how many justices shall be on the Supreme Court (there were originally six, now there are nine) or what its appellate jurisdiction shall be.

Congress has created two kinds of lower federal courts to handle cases that need not be decided by the Supreme Court: constitutional and legislative courts. A **constitutional court** is one exercising the judicial powers found in Article III of the Constitution, and therefore its judges are given constitutional protection: They may not be fired (they serve during "good behavior"), nor may their salaries be reduced while they are in office. The most important of the constitutional courts are the **district courts** (a total of 94, with at least one in each state, the District of Columbia, and the commonwealth of Puerto Rico) and the **courts of appeals** (one in each of 11 regions, plus one in the District of Columbia and one federal circuit). Various specialized constitutional courts also exist, such as the Court of International Trade.

Legislative courts are those set up by Congress for some specialized purpose and staffed with people who have fixed terms of office and can be removed or have their salaries reduced. Legislative courts include the Court of Military Appeals and the territorial courts.

Map 16.1 U.S. District and Appellate Courts

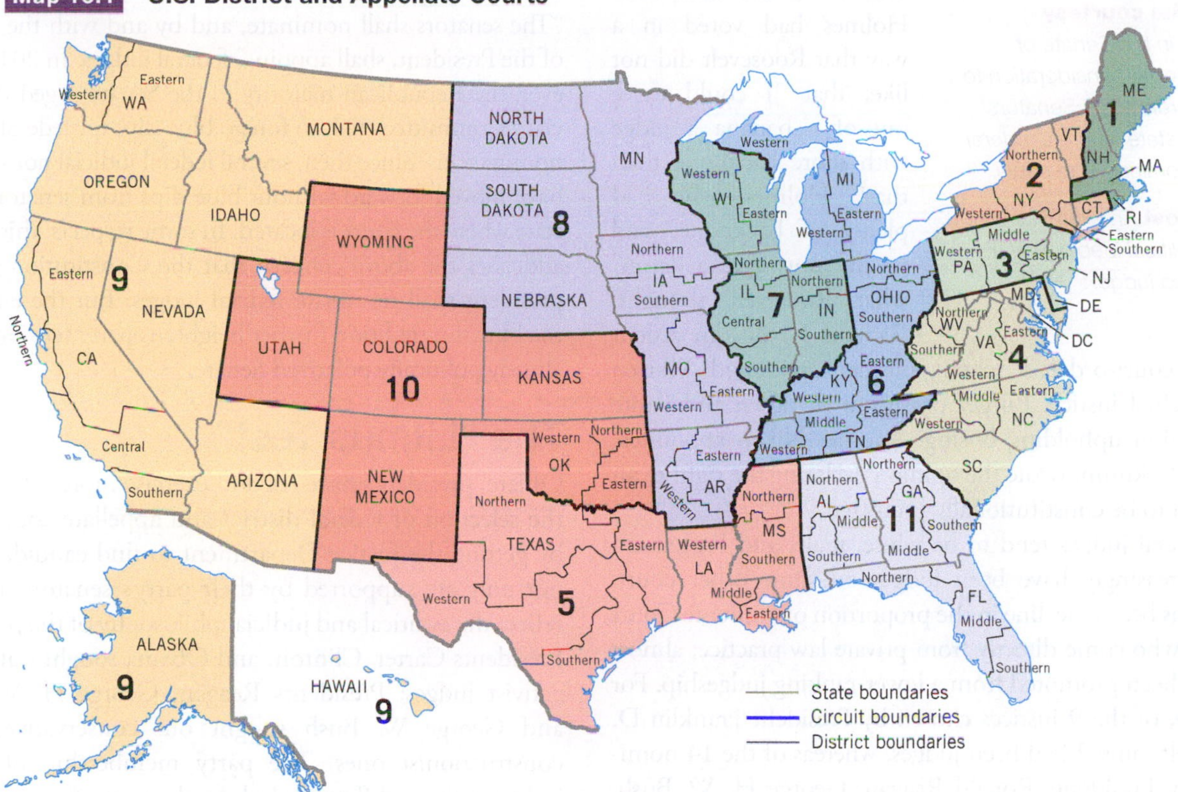

Note: Washington, DC, is in a separate court. Puerto Rico is in the first circuit; the Virgin Islands are in the third; Guam and the Northern Mariana Islands are in the ninth. The Court of Appeals for the Federal Circuit, located in Washington, DC, is a Title 3 court that hears appeals regarding patents, trademarks, international trade, government contracts, and from civil servants who claim they were unjustly discharged.

Source: Administrative Office of the United States Courts.

Selecting Judges

Party background makes a difference in how judges behave. Researchers have analyzed more than 80 studies of the link between party and either liberalism or conservatism among state and federal judges in cases involving civil liberties, criminal justice, and economic regulation. It shows that judges who are Democrats are more likely to make liberal decisions and Republican judges are more likely to make conservative ones.* The party effect is not small.[36] We should not be surprised by this, since we have already seen that among political elites (and judges are certainly elites), party identification influences personal ideology.

But ideology does not entirely determine behavior. So many other things shape court decisions— the facts of the case, prior rulings by other courts, the arguments presented by lawyers—that there is no reliable way of predicting how judges will behave in all matters. Presidents sometimes make the mistake of thinking they know how their appointees will behave, only to be surprised by the facts. Theodore Roosevelt appointed Oliver Wendell Holmes to the Supreme Court,

*A "liberal" decision is one that favors a civil right, a criminal defendant, or an economic regulation; a "conservative" one opposes the right or the regulation, or supports the criminal prosecutor.

Image 16.1 Louis Brandeis, creator of the "Brandeis Brief" that developed court cases based on economic and social more than legal arguments, became the first Jewish Supreme Court justice. He served on the Court from 1916 until 1939.

senatorial courtesy *Tradition in the Senate of giving special consideration to the preferences of Senators from the state where a federal judicial nominee is to serve.*

litmus test *An examination of the political ideology of a nominated judge.*

only to remark later, after Holmes had voted in a way that Roosevelt did not like, that "I could carve out of a banana a judge with more backbone than that!" Holmes, who had plenty of backbone, said he did not "give a damn" what Roosevelt thought. Richard Nixon, an ardent foe of court-ordered school busing, appointed Warren Burger chief justice. Burger promptly sat down and wrote the opinion upholding busing. Another Nixon appointee, Harry Blackmun, wrote the opinion declaring the right to an abortion to be constitutionally protected.

Federal judges tend to be white, male, and Protestant, and increasingly have been judges on some other court. There has been a decline in the proportion of Supreme Court justices who come directly from private law practice; almost all have been promoted from a lower-ranking judgeship. For example, of the 9 justices chosen by President Franklin D. Roosevelt, only 2 had been judges, whereas of the 14 nominated by Presidents Ronald Reagan, George H. W. Bush, Bill Clinton, George W. Bush, Barack Obama, and Donald Trump, 12 had been judges. Sex, race, and ethnicity also have become important factors in selecting judges. As is evident in Figure 16.4, Democratic presidents since President Lyndon Johnson have appointed higher percentages of women, African Americans, and Hispanics than Republican presidents have, including a record-shattering fraction of female appointees during the Obama presidency.

Senatorial Courtesy

In theory, the president nominates a "qualified" person to be a judge, and the Senate approves or rejects the nomination based on those "qualifications." In fact, the tradition of **senatorial courtesy** has, until recently, given heavy consideration to the preferences of the senators from the state where a federal judge is to serve. Ordinarily, the Senate will not confirm a district or appeals court judge if the senior senator from the state where the court is located objects (if the senator is of the president's party). The senator can exercise this veto power by means of the "blue slip"—a blue piece of paper on which the senator is asked to record views on the nominee. A negative opinion, or even failure to return the blue slip, usually kills the nomination. This means that as a practical matter the president nominates only persons recommended by that key senator.

With respect to district and appeals court judges, the constitutional process appears to have been reversed for many years. To reflect political reality through 2016, Article II, section 2 might have been more accurate if written as follows: "The senators shall nominate, and by and with the consent of the President, shall appoint" federal judges. In 2017, however, the Republican majority in the Senate urged the Judiciary Committee chair to forego blue slips for federal judicial nominations. Since then, several federal judicial nominations have moved forward without blue slips from senators of the state where the court is located. In some respects, this reversal addresses the above concern that the Constitution says the president shall nominate federal judges. But the ending of the blue slip tradition further heightens party tensions in the already politically polarized Senate.[37]

The "Litmus Test"

Of late, presidents have tried to exercise more influence on the selection of federal district and appellate court judges by getting the Justice Department to find candidates who not only are supported by their party's senators, but also reflect the political and judicial philosophy of the president. Presidents Carter, Clinton, and Obama sought out liberal, activist judges; Presidents Reagan, George H. W. Bush, and George W. Bush sought out conservative, strict-constructionist ones. The party membership of federal judges makes a difference in how they vote.[38]

Because different courts of appeals have different combinations of judges, some will be more liberal than others. For example, more liberal judges are in the court of appeals for the ninth circuit (which includes most of the far western states) and more conservative ones are in the fifth circuit (Texas, Louisiana, and Mississippi). The ninth circuit takes liberal positions, the fifth more conservative ones. Because the Supreme Court does not have time to settle every disagreement among appeals courts, different interpretations of the law may exist in different circuits. In the fifth, for instance, it was for a while unconstitutional for state universities to have affirmative action programs, but in the ninth circuit that was permitted.

These differences make some people worry about the use of a political **litmus test**—a test of ideological purity—in selecting judges. When conservatives are out of power, they complain about how liberal presidents use such a test; when liberals are out of power, they complain about how conservative presidents use it. Many people would like to see judges picked on the basis of professional qualifications, without reference to ideology, but the courts are now so deeply involved in political issues that it is hard to imagine what an ideologically neutral set of professional qualifications might be.

A judicial nominee's view on abortion is the chief motive for using the litmus test. Because it is easy to mount a filibuster and it takes 60 votes to end one, a nominee usually must be assured of 60 Senate votes to be confirmed. But the Senate may adopt a rule preventing filibusters of nominations, as it has done in the 21st century. In 2005, a group of

Figure 16.4 **Gender, Race, and Ethnicity in Federal Judicial Appointments, 1980–2018.**

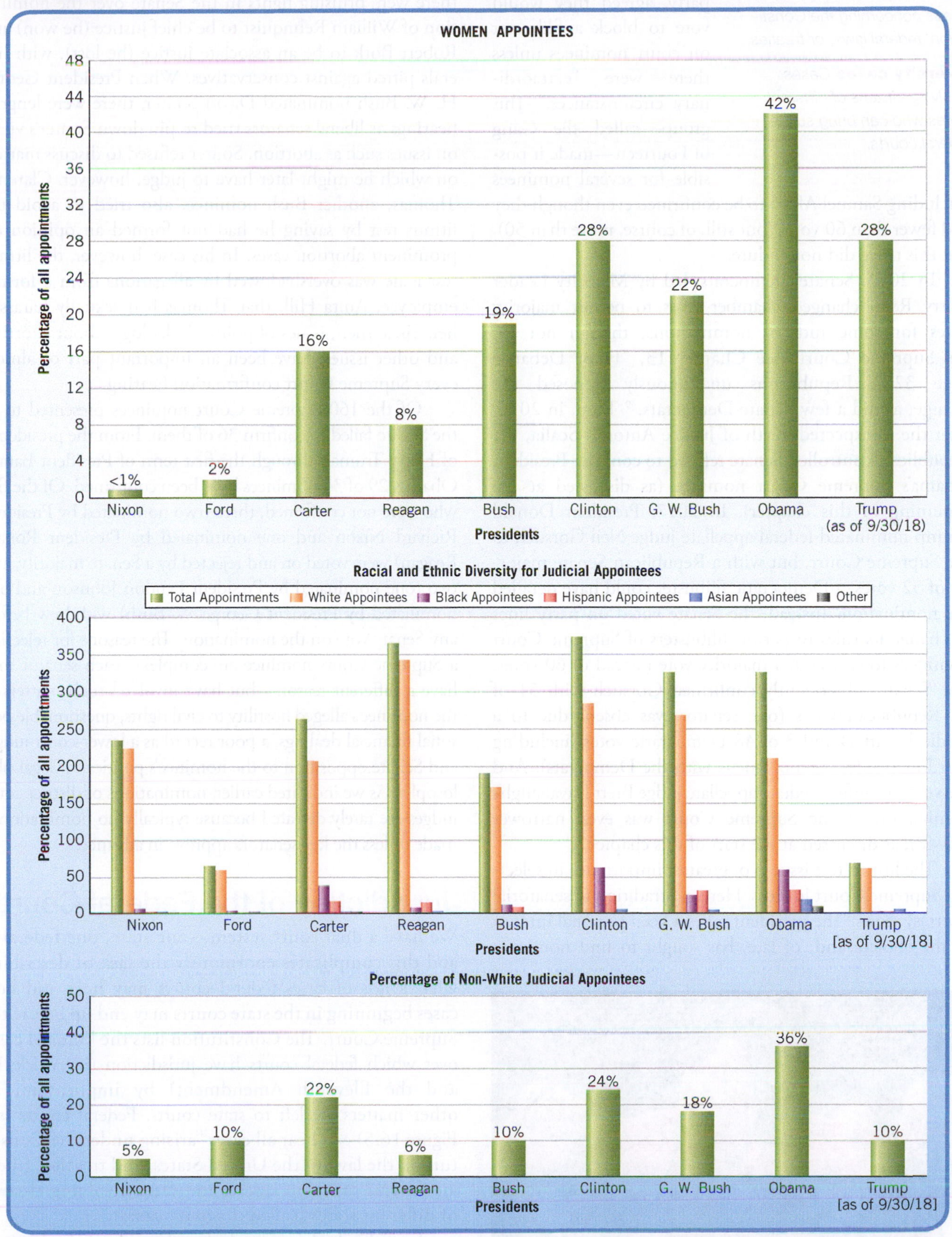

Source: John Gramlich, "Trump Has Appointed a Larger Share of Female Judges Than Other GOP Presidents, But Lags Obama," Pew Research Center, 2 October 2018.

federal-question cases *Cases concerning the Constitution, federal laws, or treaties.*

diversity cases *Cases involving citizens of different states who can bring suit in federal courts.*

14 senators, half from each party, agreed they would vote to block a filibuster on court nominees unless there were "extraordinary circumstances." This group—called the Gang of Fourteen—made it possible for several nominees (including Samuel Alito) to be confirmed even though they had fewer than 60 votes (but still, of course, more than 50). But this truce did not endure.

In 2013, Senate Democrats, led by Majority Leader Harry Reid, changed chamber rules to permit majority votes for some judicial nominations, though not for the Supreme Court (see Chapter 13, "Floor Debate," page 325). Republicans unanimously opposed the change, as did a few Senate Democrats.[39] Then, in 2016, after the unexpected death of Justice Antonin Scalia, the Republican-controlled Senate refused to consider President Obama's Supreme Court nominee (as discussed at the beginning of this chapter). In 2017, President Donald Trump nominated federal appellate judge Neil Gorsuch to the Supreme Court, but with a Republican Senate majority of 52 votes, a Democratic filibuster could have derailed the nomination. Instead, the Senate voted on party lines to change its rules to permit filibusters of Supreme Court nominees to end with a majority vote instead of 60 votes. The Senate subsequently confirmed Gorsuch with 51 of 52 Republican votes (one senator was absent due to a medical matter) and 3 of 48 Democratic votes (including two Independents who caucus with the Democrats). And the vote to confirm federal appellate judge Brett Kavanaugh's nomination to the Supreme Court was even narrower (50-48), as discussed at the start of this chapter.

The litmus test issue is of greatest importance in selecting Supreme Court justices. Here, no tradition of senatorial courtesy exists. The president takes a keen personal interest in the choices and, of late, has sought to find nominees who share his philosophy. In the Reagan administration, there were bruising fights in the Senate over the nomination of William Rehnquist to be chief justice (he won) and Robert Bork to be an associate justice (he lost), with liberals pitted against conservatives. When President George H. W. Bush nominated David Souter, there were lengthy hearings as liberal senators tried to pin down Souter's views on issues such as abortion. Souter refused to discuss matters on which he might later have to judge, however. Clarence Thomas, another Bush nominee, also tried to avoid the litmus test by saying he had not formed an opinion on prominent abortion cases. In his case, however, the litmus test issue was overshadowed by allegations from a former employee, Anita Hill, that Thomas had sexually harassed her. Since then, issues of political ideology, about abortion and other issues, have been an important part of almost every Supreme Court confirmation hearing.

Karen Bleier/AFP/Getty Images

Image 16.2 In 2009, Sonia Sotomayor answered questions in Senate confirmation hearings to become a Supreme Court justice.

Of the 160 Supreme Court nominees presented to it, the Senate failed to confirm 36 of them. From the presidency of Harry Truman through the first term of President Barack Obama, 29 of 34 nominees have been confirmed. Of the five who were not confirmed, three (two nominated by President Richard Nixon and one nominated by President Ronald Reagan) were voted on and rejected by a Senate majority, and two (one nominated by President Lyndon Johnson and one nominated by President George W. Bush) withdrew before any Senate vote on the nomination. The reasons for rejecting a Supreme Court nominee are complex—each senator may have a different reason—but have involved such matters as the nominee's alleged hostility to civil rights, questionable personal financial dealings, a poor record as a lower-court judge, and Senate opposition to the nominee's political or legal philosophy. As we indicated earlier, nominations of district court judges are rarely defeated because typically no nomination is made unless the key senators approve in advance.

Jurisdiction of the Federal Courts

We have a dual court system—one state, one federal—and this complicates enormously the task of describing what kinds of cases federal courts may hear and how cases beginning in the state courts may end up before the Supreme Court. The Constitution lists the kinds of cases over which federal courts have jurisdiction (in Article III and the Eleventh Amendment) by implication; all other matters are left to state courts. Federal courts (see Figure 16.5) can hear all cases "arising under the Constitution, the laws of the United States, and treaties" (these are **federal-question cases**), and cases involving citizens of different states (called **diversity cases**).

Some kinds of cases can be heard in either federal or state courts. For example, if citizens of different states wish to sue one another and the matter involves more than $75,000, they can do so in either a federal or a state court. Similarly, if people

Figure 16.5 The Jurisdiction of the Federal Courts

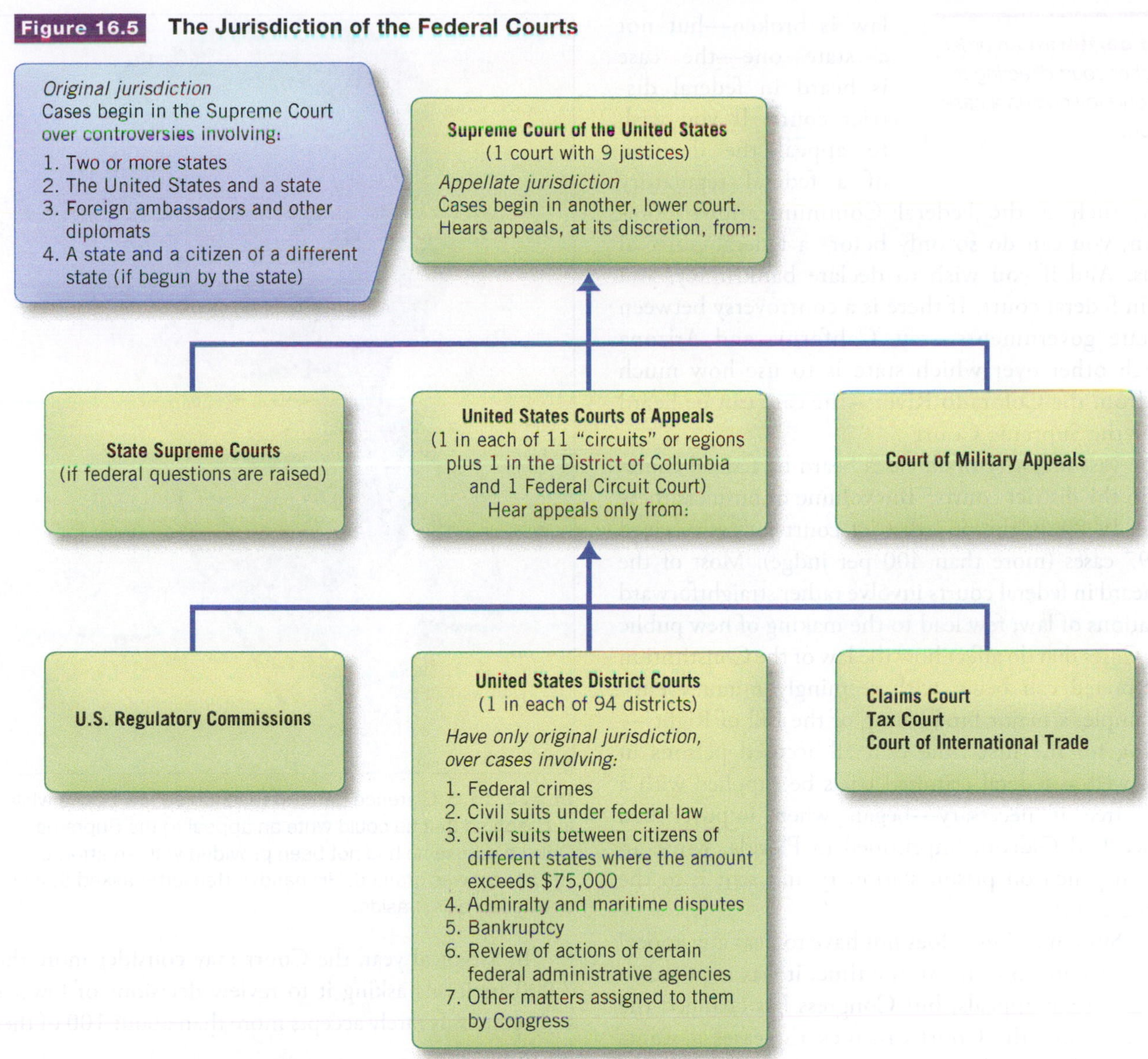

rob a federally insured bank, they have broken both state and federal law and thus can be prosecuted in state or federal courts, or both. Lawyers have become quite sophisticated in deciding whether, in a given civil case, their clients will get better treatment in a state or federal court. Prosecutors often send a person who has broken both federal and state law to whichever court system is likelier to give the toughest penalty.

Sometimes defendants may be tried in both state and federal courts for the same offense. In 1992, four Los Angeles police officers accused of beating Rodney King were tried in a California state court and acquitted of assault charges. They were then prosecuted in federal court for violating King's civil rights. This time, two of the four were convicted. Under the dual sovereignty doctrine, state and federal authorities can prosecute the same person for the same conduct. The Supreme Court has upheld this doctrine on two grounds. First, each level of government has the right to enact laws serving its own purposes.[40] As a result, federal civil rights charges could have been brought against the officers even if they had already been convicted of assault in state court (though as a practical matter this would have been unlikely). Second, neither level of government wants the other to be able to block prosecution of an accused person who has the sympathy of the authorities at one level. For example, when certain Southern state courts were in sympathy with white individuals who had lynched African Americans, the absence of the dual sovereignty doctrine would have meant that a trumped-up acquittal in state court would have barred federal prosecution.

Furthermore, a matter that is exclusively within the province of a state court—for example, a criminal case in which the defendant is charged with violating only a state law—can be appealed to the U.S. Supreme Court under certain circumstances. Thus federal judges can overturn state court rulings even when they had no jurisdiction over the original matter. Under what circumstances this should occur has been the subject of longstanding controversy between the state and federal courts.

Some matters, however, are exclusively under the jurisdiction of federal courts. When a federal criminal

writ of certiorari *An order by a higher court directing a lower court to send up a case for review.*

law is broken—but not a state one—the case is heard in federal district court. If you wish to appeal the decision of a federal regulatory agency, such as the Federal Communications Commission, you can do so only before a federal court of appeals. And if you wish to declare bankruptcy, you do so in federal court. If there is a controversy between two state governments—say, California and Arizona sue each other over which state is to use how much water from the Colorado River—the case can be heard only by the Supreme Court.

The vast majority of all cases heard by federal courts begin in the district courts. The volume of business there is huge. In 2009, the 667 district court judges received 276,397 cases (more than 400 per judge). Most of the cases heard in federal courts involve rather straightforward applications of law; few lead to the making of new public policy. Cases that do affect how the law or the Constitution is interpreted can begin with seemingly minor events. For example, a major broadening of the Bill of Rights—requiring for the first time that all accused persons in *state* as well as federal criminal trials be supplied with a lawyer, free if necessary—began when impoverished Clarence Earl Gideon, imprisoned in Florida, wrote an appeal in pencil on prison stationery and sent it to the Supreme Court.[41]

The Supreme Court does not have to hear any appeal it does not want to hear. At one time, it was required to listen to certain appeals, but Congress has changed the law so that now the Court can pick the cases it wants to consider. It does this by issuing a **writ of certiorari**. *Certiorari* is a Latin word meaning, roughly, "made more certain"; lawyers and judges have abbreviated it to *cert*. It works this way: The Court considers all the petitions it receives to review lower-court decisions; if four justices agree to hear a case, cert is issued and the case is scheduled for a hearing.

In deciding whether to grant certiorari, the Court tries to reserve its time for cases decided by lower federal courts or by the highest state courts in which a significant federal or constitutional question has been raised. For example, the Court often will grant certiorari when one or both of the following is true:

- Two or more federal circuit courts of appeals have decided the same issue in different ways.
- The highest court in a state has held a federal or state law to be in violation of the Constitution or has upheld a state law against the claim that it is in violation of the Constitution.

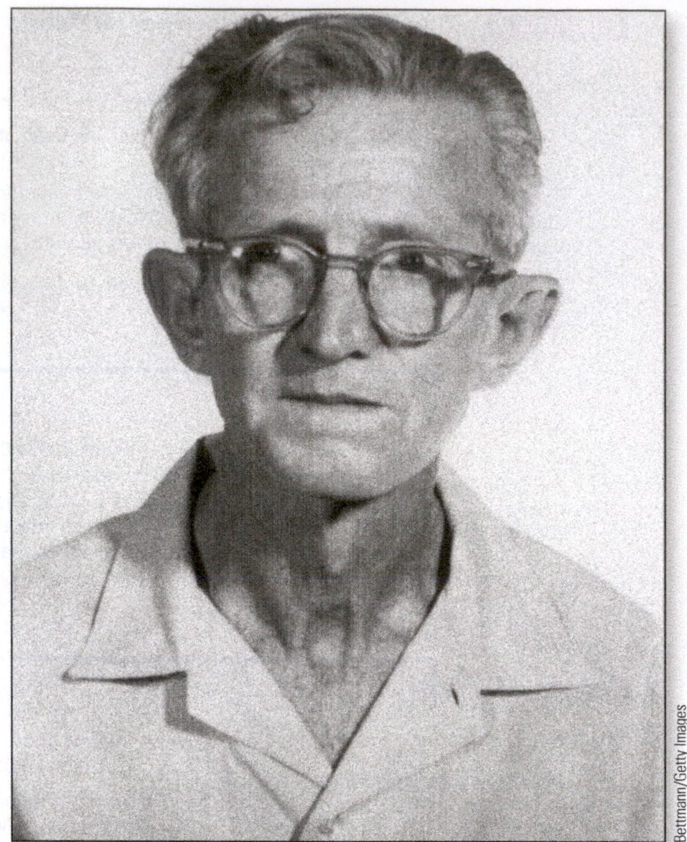

Bettmann/Getty Images

Image 16.3 Clarence Earl Gideon studied law books while in prison so that he could write an appeal to the Supreme Court because he had not been provided with an attorney. His appeal was granted. His handwritten letter asked that his conviction be set aside.

In a typical year, the Court may consider more than 7,000 petitions asking it to review decisions of lower or state courts. It rarely accepts more than about 100 of them for full review.

In exercising its discretion in granting certiorari, the Supreme Court is on the horns of a dilemma. If it grants it frequently, it will be inundated with cases. As it is, the Court's workload has quintupled in the past 50 years. If, on the other hand, the Court grants certiorari only rarely, then the federal courts of appeals have the last word on the interpretation of the Constitution and federal laws, and since there are 12 of these, staffed by about 167 judges, they may well be in disagreement. In fact, this has already happened: Because the Supreme Court reviews only about 1 or 2 percent of appeals court cases, applicable federal law may be different in different parts of the country.[42] One proposal to deal with this dilemma is to devote the Supreme Court's time entirely to major questions of constitutional interpretation and to create a national court of appeals that would ensure that the 12 circuit courts of appeals are producing uniform decisions.[43]

Because the Supreme Court has a heavy workload, the influence wielded by law clerks has grown. These clerks—recent graduates of law schools who are hired by the justices—play a big role in deciding which cases should be heard under a writ of certiorari. Indeed, some of the opinions written by the justices are drafted by the clerks. Because the reasons for a decision may be as important as the decision itself, and because these reasons are sometimes created by the clerks, the power of the clerks can be significant.

Getting to Court

In theory, the courts are the great equalizer in the federal government. To use the courts to settle a question, or even to fundamentally alter the accepted interpretation of the Constitution, one need not be elected to any office, have access to the mass media, be a member of an interest group, or be otherwise powerful or rich. Once the contending parties are before the courts, they are legally equal.

It is too easy to believe this theory uncritically or to dismiss it cynically. In fact, it is hard to get before the Supreme Court: It rejects over 96 percent of the applications for certiorari that it receives. And the costs involved in getting to the Court can be high. To apply for certiorari costs only $300 (plus 40 copies of the petition), but if certiorari is granted and the case is heard, the costs—for lawyers and for copies of the lower-court records in the case—can be very high. And by then one has already paid for the cost of the first hearing in the district court and probably one appeal to the circuit court of appeals. Furthermore, the time it takes to settle a matter in federal court can be quite long.

But there are ways to make these costs lower. If you are indigent—without funds—you can file and be heard as a pauper for nothing; about half the petitions arriving before the Supreme Court are **in forma pauperis** (such as the one from Gideon, described earlier). If your case began as a criminal trial in the district courts and you are poor, the government will supply you with a lawyer at no charge. If the matter is not a criminal case and you cannot afford to hire a lawyer, interest groups representing a wide spectrum of opinions sometimes are willing to take up the cause if the issue in the case seems sufficiently important. The American Civil Liberties Union (ACLU), a liberal group, represents some people who believe their freedom of speech has been abridged or their constitutional rights in criminal proceedings have been violated. The Center for Individual Rights, a conservative group, represents some people who feel that they have been victimized by racial quotas.

But interest groups do much more than just help people pay their bills. Many of the most important cases decided by the Court got there because an interest group organized the case, found the plaintiffs, chose the legal strategy, and mobilized legal allies. The NAACP has brought many key civil rights cases on behalf of individuals. Although in the past most such cases were brought by liberal interest groups, in the past few decades, conservative interest groups have entered the courtroom on behalf of individuals. One helped sue CBS for televising a program that allegedly libeled General William Westmoreland, once the American commander in Vietnam. (Westmoreland lost the case.) Other conservative groups have supported challenging affirmative action programs in colleges and universities (some of which have survived, some of which have not; see Chapter 6). And many important issues are raised by attorneys representing state and local governments. Several price-fixing cases have been won by state attorneys general on behalf of consumers in their states.

in forma pauperis *A method whereby a poor person can have their case heard in federal court without charge.*

Fee shifting *A rule that allows a plaintiff to recover costs from the defendant if the plaintiff wins.*

plaintiff *The party that initiates a lawsuit.*

Fee Shifting

Unlike what happens in most of Europe, each party to a lawsuit in this country must pay its own way. (In England, by contrast, if you sue someone and lose, you pay the winner's costs as well as your own.) But various laws have made it easier to get someone else to pay. **Fee shifting** enables the **plaintiff** (the party that initiates the suit) to collect its costs from the defendant if the defendant loses, at least in certain kinds of cases. For example, if a corporation is found to have violated the antitrust laws, it must pay the legal fees of the winner. If an environmentalist group sues the Environmental Protection Agency (EPA) and wins, it can get the EPA to pay the group's legal costs. Even more important to individuals, Section 1983 of Chapter 42 of the *United States Code* allows a citizen to sue a state or local government official—say, a police officer or a school superintendent—who has deprived the citizen of some constitutional right or withheld some benefit to which the citizen is entitled. A citizen who wins can collect money damages and lawyers' fees from the government. Citizens, more aware of their legal rights, have become more litigious, and a flood of such "Section 1983" suits has burdened the courts. The Supreme Court has restricted fee shifting to cases authorized by statute,[44] but it is clear that the drift of policy has made it cheaper to go to court—at least for some cases.

standing *A legal rule stating who is authorized to start a lawsuit.*

sovereign immunity *The rule that a citizen cannot sue the government without the government's consent.*

class-action suit *A case brought by someone to help both him-or herself and all others who are similarly situated.*

Standing

There is, in addition, a nonfinancial restriction on getting into federal court. To sue, one must have **standing**, a legal concept that refers to who is entitled to bring a case. It is especially important in determining who can challenge the laws or actions of the government itself. A complex and changing set of rules governs standings; some of the more important ones are these:

- An actual controversy must exist between real adversaries. (You cannot bring a "friendly" suit against someone, hoping to lose in order to prove your friend right. You cannot ask a federal court for an opinion on a hypothetical or imaginary case or ask it to render an advisory opinion.)
- You must show that you have been harmed by the law or practice about which you are complaining. (It is not enough to dislike what the government or a corporation or a labor union does; you must show that you were actually harmed by that action.)
- Merely being a taxpayer does not ordinarily entitle you to challenge the constitutionality of a federal governmental action. (You may not want your tax money to be spent in certain ways, but your remedy is to vote against the politicians doing the spending; the federal courts will generally require that you show some other personal harm before you can sue.)

Congress and the courts have recently made it easier to acquire standing. It has always been the rule that a citizen could ask the courts to order federal officials to carry out some act that they were under a legal obligation to perform or to refrain from some action that was contrary to law. A citizen can also sue a government official personally to collect damages if the official acted contrary to law. For example, it was long the case that if an FBI agent broke into your office without a search warrant, you could sue the agent and, if you won, collect money. However, you cannot sue the government itself without its consent. This is the doctrine of **sovereign immunity**. For instance, if the army accidentally kills your cow while testing a new cannon, you cannot sue the government to recover the cost of the cow unless the government agrees to be sued. (Since testing cannons is legal, you cannot sue the army officer who fired the cannon.) By statute, Congress has given its consent for the government to be sued in many cases involving a dispute over a contract or damage done as a result of negligence (e.g., the dead cow). Over the years, these statutes have made it easier to take the government into court as a defendant.

Even some of the oldest rules defining standing have been liberalized. The rule that merely being a taxpayer does not entitle you to challenge in court a government decision has been relaxed where the citizen claims that a right guaranteed under the First Amendment is being violated. The Supreme Court allowed a taxpayer to challenge a federal law that would have given financial aid to parochial (or church-related) schools on the grounds that this aid violated the constitutional requirement of separation between church and state. On the other hand, another taxpayer suit to force the CIA to make public its budget failed because the Court decided that the taxpayer did not have standing in matters of this sort.[45]

Class-Action Suits

Under certain circumstances, a citizen can benefit directly from a court decision even without going directly to court. This can happen by means of a **class-action suit**, a case brought into court not only on behalf of the person filing suit, but also for all other people in similar circumstances. Among the most famous of these was the 1954 case in which the Supreme Court found that Linda Brown, a young African American student in a Topeka, Kansas, public school, was denied the equal protection of the laws (guaranteed under the Fourteenth Amendment) because the schools in Topeka were segregated. The Court did not limit its decision to Linda Brown's right to attend an unsegregated school but extended it—as Brown's lawyers from the NAACP had asked—to cover all "others similarly situated."[46] It was not easy to design a court order that would eliminate segregation in the schools, but the principle was clearly established in this class action.

Since the *Brown* case, many other groups have been quick to take advantage of the opportunity created by class-action suits. By this means, the courts could be used to give relief not simply to a particular person but to all those represented in the suit. A landmark class-action case challenged the malapportionment of state legislative districts (see Chapter 13).[47] There are thousands of class-action suits in the federal courts involving civil rights, the rights of prisoners, antitrust suits against corporations, and other matters. These suits became more common partly because people were beginning to have new concerns that were not being met by Congress and partly because some class-action suits became quite profitable. The NAACP got no money from Linda Brown or from the Topeka Board of Education in compensation for its long and expensive labors, but, beginning in the 1960s, court rules were changed to make it financially attractive for lawyers to bring certain kinds of class-action suits.

Suppose, for example, you think your cell phone company overcharged you by $50. You could try to hire a lawyer to get a refund, but not many lawyers would take the case

Image 16.4 Linda Brown was refused admission to a white elementary school in Topeka, Kansas. On her behalf, the NAACP brought a class-action suit that resulted in the 1954 landmark Supreme Court decision *Brown v. Board of Education*.

because there would be no money in it. Even if you were to win, the lawyer would stand to earn no more than perhaps one-third of the settlement, or less than $20. Now suppose you bring a class action against the company on behalf of everybody who was overcharged. Millions of dollars might be at stake; lawyers would line up eagerly to take the case because their share of the settlement, if they won, would be huge. The opportunity to win profitable class-action suits, combined with the possibility of having the loser pay the attorneys' fees, led to a proliferation of such cases.

In response to the increase in its workload, the Supreme Court decided in 1974 to drastically tighten the rules governing these suits. It held that it would no longer hear (except in certain cases defined by Congress, such as civil rights matters) class-action suits seeking monetary damages unless each and every ascertainable member of the class was individually notified of the case. To do this often is prohibitively expensive (imagine trying to find and send a letter to every customer who may have been overcharged by the cell phone company!), and so the number of such cases declined and the number of lawyers seeking them out dropped.[48]

But it remains easy to bring a class-action suit in most state courts. State Farm automobile insurance company was told by a state judge in a small Illinois town that it must pay over $1 billion in damages on behalf of a "national" class, even though no one in this class had been notified. Big class-action suits powerfully affect how courts make public policy. Such suits have forced into bankruptcy companies making asbestos and silicone breast implants and have threatened to put out of business tobacco companies and gun manufacturers. (Ironically, in some of these cases, such as the one involving breast implants, there was no scientific evidence showing that the product was harmful.) Some class-action suits, such as the one ending school segregation, are good, but others are frivolous efforts to get companies to pay large fees to the lawyers who file the suits.

brief *A written statement by an attorney that summarizes a case and the laws and rulings that support it.*

In sum, getting into court depends on having standing and having resources. The rules governing standing are complex and changing, but generally they have been broadened to make it easier to enter the federal courts, especially for the purpose of challenging the actions of the government. Obtaining the resources is not easy, but it has become easier because in some cases laws now provide for fee shifting, private interest groups are willing to finance cases, and it is sometimes possible to bring a class-action suit that lawyers find lucrative.

16-4 The Supreme Court in Action

If your case should find its way to the Supreme Court—and of course the odds are that it will not—you will be able to participate in one of the more impressive, sometimes dramatic ceremonies of American public life. The Court is in session in its white marble building for 36 weeks of each year, from early October until the end of June. The nine justices (see Table 16.2 on p. 422 for a list of the current Supreme Court justices) read briefs in their individual offices, hear oral arguments in the stately courtroom, and discuss their decisions with one another in a conference room where no outsider is ever allowed. (In the spring of 2020, due to the coronavirus pandemic, the Supreme Court heard arguments for the first time through teleconferencing. The Court also released live audio recordings of its hearings, giving the public a unique opportunity to listen to debates that only people fortunate enough to get one of the few public seats in the courtroom previously had heard.)

Most cases, as we have seen, come to the Court on a writ of certiorari. The lawyers for each side may then submit their briefs. A **brief** is a document that sets forth the facts of the case, summarizes the lower-court decision, gives the arguments for the side represented by the lawyer who wrote the brief, and discusses the other cases that the Court has decided bear on the issue. Then the lawyers are allowed to present their oral arguments in open court. They usually summarize their briefs or emphasize particular points

amicus curiae *A brief submitted by a "friend of the court."*

per curiam opinion *A brief, unsigned court opinion.*

opinion of the Court *A signed opinion of a majority of the Supreme Court.*

concurring opinion *A signed opinion in which one or more members agree with the majority view but for different reasons.*

in them, and they are strictly limited in time—usually to no more than a half hour. (The lawyer speaks from a lectern that has two lights on it. When the white light goes on, the attorney has five minutes remaining; when the red flashes, the attorney must stop—instantly.) The oral arguments give the justices a chance to question the lawyers, sometimes searchingly.

Since the federal government is a party—as either plaintiff or defendant—to about half the cases that the Supreme Court hears, the government's top trial lawyer, the solicitor general of the United States, appears frequently before the Court. The solicitor general is the third-ranking officer of the Department of Justice, right after the attorney general and deputy attorney general. The solicitor general decides what cases the government will appeal from lower courts and personally approves every case the government presents to the Supreme Court. In recent years, the solicitor general often has been selected from the ranks of distinguished law school professors.

In addition to the arguments made by lawyers for the two sides in a case, written briefs and even oral arguments may also be offered by a "friend of the court," or **amicus curiae**. An amicus brief is from an interested party not directly involved in the suit. For example, when Allan Bakke complained that he had been the victim of "reverse discrimination" when he was denied admission to a University of California medical school, 58 amicus briefs were filed supporting or opposing his position. Before such briefs can be filed, both parties must agree or the Court must grant permission. Though these briefs sometimes offer new arguments, they are really a kind of polite lobbying of the Court that declare which interest groups are on which side. The ACLU, the NAACP, the AFL-CIO, and the U.S. government itself have been among the leading sources of such briefs.

These briefs are not the only source of influence on the justices' views. Legal periodicals such as the *Harvard Law Review* and the *Yale Law Journal* are frequently consulted, and citations to them often appear in the Court's decisions. Thus the outside world of lawyers and law professors can help shape, or at least supply arguments for, the conclusions of the justices.

The justices retire every Friday to their conference room, where in complete secrecy they debate the cases they have heard. The chief justice speaks first, followed by the other justices in order of seniority. After the arguments they vote, traditionally in reverse order of seniority: the newest justice votes first, the chief justice last. By this process an able chief justice can exercise considerable influence—in guiding or limiting debate, in setting forth the issues, and in handling sometimes temperamental personalities. In deciding a case, a majority of the justices must be in agreement: If there is a tie, the lower-court decision is left standing. (There can be a tie among nine justices if one is ill or decides not to participate because of prior involvement in the case.)

Though the vote is what counts, by tradition the Court usually issues a written opinion explaining its decision. Sometimes the opinion is brief and unsigned (called a **per curiam opinion**); sometimes it is quite long and signed by the justices agreeing with it. If in the majority, then the chief justice will either write the opinion or assign the task to a justice who agrees. If the chief justice is in the minority, the senior justice on the winning side will decide who writes the Court's opinion. There are three kinds of opinions—an **opinion of the Court** (reflecting the majority's view), a **concurring opinion** (an opinion

TABLE 16.2 | Supreme Court Justices in Order of Seniority

Name (Birth Date)	Home State	Prior Experience	Appointed by (Year)
John G. Roberts, Jr., Chief Justice (1955)	Maryland	Federal judge	G. W. Bush (2005)
Clarence Thomas (1948)	Georgia	Federal judge	G. H. W. Bush (1991)
Ruth Bader Ginsburg (1933)	New York	Federal judge	Clinton (1993)
Stephen Breyer (1938)	Massachusetts	Federal judge	Clinton (1994)
Samuel Alito, Jr. (1950)	New Jersey	Federal judge	G. W. Bush (2006)
Sonia Sotomayor (1954)	New York	Federal judge	Obama (2009)
Elena Kagan (1960)	New York	Law school dean	Obama (2010)
Neil Gorsuch (1967)	Colorado	Federal judge	Trump (2017)
Brett Kavanaugh (1965)	Maryland	Federal judge	Trump (2018)

by one or more justices who agree with the majority's conclusion but for different reasons that they wish to express), and a **dissenting opinion** (the opinion of the justices on the losing side). Justices each have three or four law clerks to help them review the many petitions the Court receives, study cases, and write opinions.

Many Supreme Court decisions, perhaps two-fifths of them, are decided unanimously. In these cases, the law is clear and no difficult questions of interpretation exist. But for the remaining ones, there seem to be two main blocs on today's Court (Justices Gorsuch and Kavanaugh are not included because they joined so recently, so we need to see more of their rulings to identify a pattern):

- A conservative bloc of Samuel Alito, John Roberts, and Clarence Thomas.
- A liberal bloc of Stephen Breyer, Ruth Bader Ginsburg, Elena Kagan, and Sonia Sotomayor.

The Power of the Federal Courts

The great majority of the cases heard in the federal courts have little or nothing to do with changes in public policy: people accused of bank robbery are tried, disputes over contracts are settled, personal-injury cases are heard, and patent law is applied. In most instances, the courts are simply applying a relatively settled body of law to a specific controversy.

The Power to Make Policy

The courts make policy whenever they reinterpret the law or the Constitution in significant ways, extend the reach of existing laws to cover matters not previously thought to be covered by them, or design remedies for problems that involve the judges' acting in administrative or legislative ways. By any of these tests the courts have become exceptionally powerful.

dissenting opinion *A signed opinion in which one or more justices disagree with the majority view.*

stare decisis *"Let the decision stand"; allowing prior rulings to control a current case.*

One measure of that power is the fact that more than 160 federal laws have been declared unconstitutional. And as we shall see, on matters where Congress feels strongly, it can often get its way by passing slightly revised versions of a voided law.

Another measure, and perhaps a more revealing one, is the frequency with which the Supreme Court changes its mind. An informal rule of judicial decision making has been **stare decisis**, meaning "let the decision stand." It is the principle of precedent: A court case today should be settled in accordance with prior decisions on similar cases. (What constitutes a similar case is not always clear; lawyers are especially gifted at finding ways of showing that two cases are different in some relevant way.) Precedent is important for two reasons. The practical reason should be obvious: If the meaning of the law continually changes, if the decisions of judges become wholly unpredictable, then human affairs affected by those laws and decisions become chaotic. A contract signed today might be invalid tomorrow. The other reason is at least as important: If the principle of equal justice means anything, it means that similar cases should be decided in

Kevin Dietsch/Pool via CN/ dpa picture alliance/Alamy Stock Photo

Image 16.5 The nine members of the U.S. Supreme Court in the 2019-20 term were: Front row—Justices Stephen Breyer and Clarence Thomas, Chief Justice John Roberts, Justices Ruth Bader Ginsberg and Samuel Alito Jr; second row—Justices Neil Gorsuch, Sonia Sotomayor, Elena Kagan, and Brett Kavanaugh.

political question *An issue the Supreme Court will allow the executive and legislative branches to decide.*

remedy *A judicial order enforcing a right or redressing a wrong.*

a similar manner. On the other hand, times change, and the Court can make mistakes. As Justice Felix Frankfurter once said, "Wisdom too often never comes, and so one ought not to reject it merely because it comes late."[49]

However compelling the arguments for flexibility, the pace of change can become dizzying. By one count, the Court has overruled its own previous decisions in more than 260 cases since 1810.[50] In fact, it may have done it more often, because sometimes the Court does not say that it is abandoning a precedent, claiming instead that it is merely distinguishing the present case from a previous one.

A third measure of judicial power is the degree to which courts are willing to handle matters once left to the legislature. For example, the Court refused for a long time to hear a case about the size of congressional districts, no matter how unequal their populations.[51] The determination of congressional district boundaries was regarded as a **political question**—that is, as a matter that the Constitution left entirely to another branch of government (in this case, Congress) to decide for itself. Then, in 1962, the Court decided that it was competent after all to handle this matter, and the notion of a "political question" became a much less important (but by no means absent) barrier to judicial power.[52]

By all odds the most powerful indicator of judicial power can be found in the kinds of remedies that the courts will impose. A **remedy** is a judicial order setting forth what must be done to correct a situation that a judge believes to be wrong. In ordinary cases, such as when one person sues another, the remedy is straightforward: The loser must pay the winner for some injury that was caused, the loser must agree to abide by the terms of a contract that was broken, or the loser must promise not to do some unpleasant thing (such as dumping garbage on a neighbor's lawn).

Today, however, judges design remedies that go far beyond what is required to do justice to the individual parties who actually appear in court. The remedies now imposed often apply to large groups and affect the circumstances under which thousands or even millions of people work, study, or live. For example, when a federal district judge in Alabama heard a case brought by a prison inmate in that state, he issued an order not simply to improve the lot of that prisoner but to revamp the administration of the entire prison system. The result was an improvement in the living conditions of many prisoners, at a cost to the state of an estimated $40 million a year. Similarly, a person who feels entitled to welfare payments that have been denied them may sue in court to get the money, and the court order will in all likelihood affect all welfare recipients. In one case certain court orders made an additional 100,000 people eligible for welfare.[53]

The basis for sweeping court orders can sometimes be found in the Constitution; the Alabama prison decision, for example, was based on the judge's interpretation of the Eighth Amendment, which prohibits "cruel and unusual punishments."[54] Others are based on court interpretations of federal laws. The Civil Rights Act of 1964 forbids discrimination on grounds of "race, color, or national origin" in any program receiving federal financial assistance. The Supreme Court interpreted that as meaning the San Francisco school system was obliged to teach English to

dpa/dpa picture alliance/Alamy Stock Photo

Image 16.6 Justice Amy Coney Barrett was appointed to the Supreme Court in the fall of 2020 following the death of Justice Ginsburg.

Chinese students unable to speak it.[55] Since a Supreme Court decision is the law of the land, the impact of that ruling was not limited to San Francisco. Local courts and legislatures elsewhere decided that that decision meant that classes must be taught in Spanish for Hispanic children. What Congress meant by the Civil Rights Act is not clear; it may or may not have believed that teaching Hispanic children in English rather than Spanish was a form of discrimination. What is important is that it was the Court, not Congress, that decided what Congress meant.

Views of Judicial Activism

Judicial activism has, of course, been controversial. Those who support it argue that the federal courts must correct injustices when the other branches of the federal government, or the states, refuse to do so. The courts are the institution of last resort for those without the votes or the influence to obtain new laws, and especially for the poor and powerless. After all, Congress and the state legislatures tolerated segregated public schools for decades. If the Supreme Court had not declared segregation unconstitutional in 1954, it might still be law today.

Those who criticize judicial activism rejoin that judges usually have no special expertise in matters of school administration, prison management, environmental protection, and so on; they are lawyers, expert in defining rights and duties but not in designing and managing complex institutions. Furthermore, however desirable court-declared rights and principles may be, implementing those principles means balancing the conflicting needs of various interest groups, raising and spending tax monies, and assessing the costs and benefits of complicated alternatives. Finally, federal judges are not elected; they are appointed and are thus immune to popular control. As a result, if they depart from their traditional role of making careful and cautious interpretations of what a law or the Constitution means and instead begin formulating wholly new policies, they become unelected legislators.

Some people think we have activist courts because we have so many lawyers. The more we take matters to courts for resolution, the more likely it is that the courts will become powerful. It is true that we have more lawyers in proportion to our population than most other nations. There is one lawyer for every 325 Americans, but only one for every 970 Britons, every 1,220 Germans, and every 8,333 Japanese.[56] But that may well be a symptom, not a cause, of court activity. As we suggested in Chapter 4, we have an adversary culture based on an emphasis on individual rights and an implicit antagonism between the people and the government. In general, lawyers do not create cases; contending interests do, thereby generating a demand for lawyers.[57] Furthermore, we had more lawyers in relation to our population in 1900 than in 1970, yet the courts at the turn of the 20th century were far less active in public affairs. In fact, in 1932 there were more court cases per 100,000 people than there were in 1972.

A more plausible reason for activist courts is the developments discussed earlier in this chapter that have made it easier for people to get standing in the courts, to pay for the costs of litigation, and to bring class-action suits. The courts and Congress have gone a long way toward allowing private citizens to become "private attorneys general." Making it easier to get into court increases the number of cases being heard. For example, in 1961, civil rights cases, prisoners' rights cases, and cases under the Social Security laws were relatively uncommon in federal court. Between 1961 and 1990, the increase in the number of such matters was phenomenal: the number of civil rights cases rose more than 60-fold and prisoners' petitions increased more than 40-fold. Such matters are the fastest-growing portion of the courts' civil workload.

Legislation and the Courts

An increase in cases by itself will not lead to sweeping remedies. For that to occur, the law must be sufficiently vague to permit judges wide latitude in interpreting it, and the judges must want to exercise that opportunity fully. The Constitution is filled with words of seemingly ambiguous meaning—"due process of law," "equal protection of the laws," the "privileges or immunities of citizens." Such phrases may have been clear to the Framers, but to the Supreme Court they have become equivocal or elastic. How the Court has chosen to interpret such phrases has changed greatly over the past two centuries in ways that can be explained in part by the personal political beliefs of the justices.

Increasingly, Congress has passed laws that also contain vague language, thereby adding immeasurably to the courts' opportunities for designing remedies. Various civil rights acts outlaw discrimination but do not say how one is to know whether discrimination has occurred or what should be done to correct it if it does occur. That is left to the courts and the bureaucracy. Various regulatory laws empower administrative agencies to do what the "public interest" requires but say little about how the public interest is to be defined. Laws intended to alleviate poverty or rebuild neighborhoods speak of "citizen participation" or "maximum feasible participation" but do not explain who the citizens are that should participate, or how much power they should have.

In addition to laws that require interpretation, other laws induce litigation. Almost every agency that regulates business will make decisions that cause the agency to be challenged in court—by business firms if the regulations go too far, by consumer or labor organizations if they do not go far enough.

One study showed that the federal courts of appeals heard more than 3,000 cases in which they had to review the decision of a regulatory agency. In two-thirds of them, the agency's position was supported; in the other third, the agency was overruled.[58] Perhaps one-fifth of these cases arose out of agencies or programs that did not even exist in 1960. The federal government today is much more likely to be on the defensive in court than it was 20 or 30 years ago.

Finally, the attitudes of the judges powerfully affect what they will do, especially when the law gives them wide latitude. Their decisions and opinions have been extensively analyzed—well enough, at least, to know that different judges often decide the same case in different ways. Conservative Southern federal judges in the 1950s, for example, often resisted plans to desegregate public schools, while judges with a different background authorized bold plans.[59] Some of the greatest disparities in judicial behavior can be found in the area of sentencing criminals.[60]

Checks on Judicial Power

No institution of government, including the courts, operates without restraint. The fact that judges are not elected does not make them immune to public opinion or to the views of the other branches of government. How important these restraints are varies from case to case, but in the broad course of history they have been significant.

One restraint exists because of the very nature of courts. Judges have no police force or army; decisions that they make can sometimes be resisted or ignored, *if* the person or organization resisting is not highly visible and is willing to run the risk of being caught and charged with contempt of court. For example, long after the Supreme Court's controversial decisions that school-organized prayer and Bible reading could not take place in public education,[61] schools all over the country still allowed prayers and Bible reading.[62] Years after the Court declared segregated schools to be unconstitutional, scores of school systems remained segregated. On the other hand, when a failure to comply is easily detected and punished, the courts' power is usually unchallenged. When the Supreme Court declared the

Telecommunications and "Decency": Interest-Group Politics

In the more than six decades that separated the Communications Act of 1934 from the Telecommunications Act of 1996, radio, television, and the Internet became everyday features of American life. The 1996 overhaul of the 1934 law was a clear-cut case of interest-group politics. The politically pitched battles over the bills that preceded the 1996 act were fought out mainly among and between economically self-interested groups. For instance, television broadcasters fought cable companies over who may send what kinds of signals to which homes. Telephone companies fought firms in other industries as well as each other.

As is often the case with interest-group politics, the telecommunications policy debates involved issues that most average citizens did not understand (in this case, "spectrum allotment," "intramodal competition," and others) but which interest-group members lived and breathed. When the interest-group politics dust settled, the complex law deregulated the industry and fostered competition, but it also made possible cross-media mega-corporations like those that now dominate cable broadcasting and telecommunications services in many regions.

In the mid-1990s, the general public and the media focused less on how an overhaul of the 1934 law might affect most people as consumers and more on Title V of the 1996 bill, which sought to restrict Internet and cable television pornography. The bill's "communications decency" provisions made it into law; but, a year later, in *Reno v. ACLU* (1997), the Supreme Court declared that the provisions were unconstitutional.

In 2008, the Federal Communications Commission launched investigations into the pricing policies of cable television companies. The effort resulted in few changes to industry practices. In 2012, an interfaith coalition of religious leaders publicly petitioned five leading national hotel chains to stop offering on-demand "adult" cable service. None complied. Since then, telecommunications companies have contributed millions of dollars to candidates of both parties; they also have maintained a huge lobbying presence on Capitol Hill and skirmished with each other over proposed tweaks to this or that provision of the 1996 law.

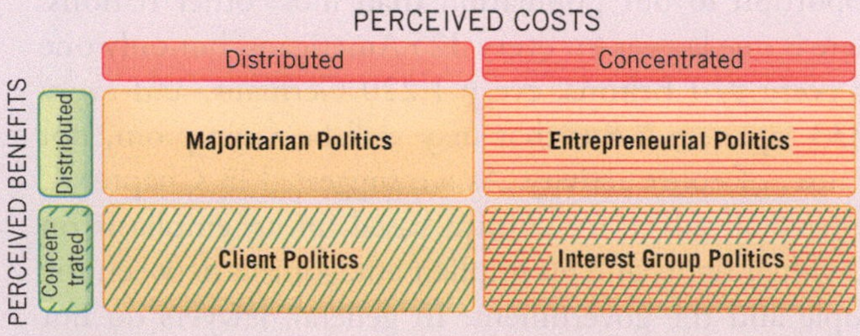

income tax to be unconstitutional in 1895, income tax collections promptly ceased. When the Court in 1952 declared illegal President Harry Truman's effort to seize steel mills in order to stop a strike, the management of the mills was immediately returned to their owners.

Congress and the Courts

Congress has a number of ways of checking the judiciary. It can gradually alter the composition of the judiciary by the kinds of appointments the Senate is willing to confirm, or it can impeach judges it does not like. Fifteen federal judges have been the object of impeachment proceedings in our history, and nine others have resigned when such proceedings seemed likely. Of the 15 who were impeached, 8 were convicted by the Senate, 4 were acquitted, and 3 resigned before trial. In 2009, Samuel Kent resigned from the U.S. District Court for the Southern District of Texas, and in 2010, Thomas Porteous was convicted by the Senate and removed from office.[63] In practice, however, confirmation and impeachment proceedings do not make much of an impact on the federal courts because simple policy disagreements are not generally regarded as adequate grounds for voting against a judicial nominee or for starting an impeachment effort.

Congress can alter the number of judges, though, and by increasing the number sharply, it can give a president a chance to appoint judges to his liking. As described above, a "Court-packing" plan was proposed (unsuccessfully) by Franklin Roosevelt in 1937 specifically to change the political persuasion of the Supreme Court. In 1978, Congress passed a bill creating 152 new federal district and appellate judges to help ease the workload of the federal judiciary. This bill gave President Carter a chance to appoint over 40 percent of the federal bench. In 1984, an additional 84 judgeships were created; by 1988, President Reagan had appointed about half of all federal judges. In 1990, an additional 72 judges were authorized. During and after the Civil War, Congress may have been trying to influence Supreme Court decisions when it changed the size of the Court three times in six years (raising it from 9 to 10 in 1863, lowering it again from 10 to 7 in 1866, and raising it again from 7 to 9 in 1869).

Congress and the states can also undo a Supreme Court decision interpreting the Constitution by amending that document. This happens, but rarely: The Eleventh Amendment was ratified to prevent a citizen from suing a state in federal court; the Thirteenth, Fourteenth, and Fifteenth were ratified to undo the *Dred Scott* decision regarding slavery; the Sixteenth was added to make it constitutional for Congress to pass an income tax; and the Twenty-sixth was added to give the vote to 18-year-olds in state elections.

On more than 30 occasions, Congress has merely repassed a law that the Court has declared unconstitutional. In one case, a bill to aid farmers, voided in 1936, was accepted by the Court in slightly revised form three years later.[64] (In the meantime, of course, the Court had changed its collective mind about the New Deal.)

One of the most powerful potential sources of control over the federal courts, however, is the authority of Congress, given by the Constitution, to decide what the entire jurisdiction of the lower courts and the appellate jurisdiction of the Supreme Court shall be. In theory, Congress could prevent matters on which it did not want federal courts to act from ever coming before the courts. This happened in 1868. A Mississippi newspaper editor named McCardle was jailed by federal military authorities who occupied the defeated South. McCardle asked the federal district court for a writ of habeas corpus to get him out of custody; when the district court rejected his plea, he appealed to the Supreme Court. Congress at that time was fearful that the Court might find the laws on which its Reconstruction policy was based (and under which McCardle was in jail) unconstitutional. To prevent that from happening, it passed a bill withdrawing from the Supreme Court appellate jurisdiction in cases of this sort. The Court conceded that Congress could do this and thus dismissed the case because it no longer had jurisdiction.[65]

Congress has threatened to withdraw jurisdiction on other occasions, and the mere existence of the threat may have influenced the nature of Court decisions. In the 1950s, for example, congressional opinion was hostile to Court decisions in the field of civil liberties and civil rights, and legislation was proposed that would have curtailed the Court's jurisdiction in these areas. It did not pass, but the Court may have allowed the threat to temper its decisions.[66] On the other hand, as congressional resistance to the Roosevelt Court-packing plan shows, the Supreme Court enjoys a good deal of prestige in the nation, even among people who disagree with some of its decisions, and so passing laws that would frontally attack it would not be easy except perhaps in times of national crisis.

Furthermore, laws narrowing jurisdiction or restricting the kinds of remedies that a court can impose often are blunt instruments that might not achieve the purposes of their proponents. Suppose that you, as a member of Congress, would like to prevent the federal courts from ordering schoolchildren to be bused for the purpose of achieving racial balance in the schools. If you denied the Supreme Court appellate jurisdiction in this matter, you would leave the lower federal courts and all state courts free to do as they wished, and many of them would go on ordering busing. If you wanted to attack that problem, you could propose a law that would deny to all federal courts the right to order busing as a remedy for racial imbalance. But the courts would still be free to order busing (and of course a lot of busing goes on even without court orders), provided that they did not say that it was for the purpose of achieving racial balance. (It could be for the purpose of "facilitating desegregation" or making possible "redistricting.") Naturally, you could always make it illegal for children to enter a school bus for any reason, but then many children would not be able to get to school at all. Finally, the Supreme Court might well decide that if busing were essential to achieve a constitutional right, then any congressional law prohibiting such busing would itself be unconstitutional. Trying to think through how *that* dilemma would be resolved is like trying to visualize two kangaroos simultaneously jumping into each other's pouches.

Public Opinion and the Courts

Though they are not elected, judges read the same newspapers as members of Congress, and thus they, too, are aware of public opinion, especially elite opinion. Though it may be going too far to say the Supreme Court follows the election returns, it is nonetheless true that the Court is sensitive to certain bodies of opinion, especially of those elites—liberal or conservative—to whom its members happen to be attuned. The justices will keep in mind historical cases in which their predecessors, by blatantly disregarding public opinion, very nearly destroyed the legitimacy of the Court itself. This was the case with the *Dred Scott* decision, which infuriated the North and was widely disobeyed. No such crisis exists today, but it is altogether possible that changing political moods affect the kinds of remedies that judges will think appropriate.

Opinion not only restrains the courts; it may also energize them. The most activist periods in Supreme Court history have coincided with times when the political system was undergoing profound and lasting changes. The assertion by the Supreme Court, under John Marshall's leadership, of the principles of national supremacy and judicial review occurred at the time when the Jeffersonian Republicans were coming to power and their opponents, the Federalists, were collapsing as an organized party. The pro-slavery decisions of the Taney Court came when the nation was so divided along sectional and ideological lines as to make almost any Court decision on this matter unpopular. Supreme Court review of economic regulation in the 1890s and 1900s came at a time when the political parties were realigning and the Republicans were acquiring dominance that would last for several decades. The Court decisions of the 1930s corresponded to another period of partisan realignment. (The meaning of a realignment period was discussed in Chapter 10.)

Pollsters have measured changes in public perceptions of how well the Supreme Court is handling its job. The results are shown in Figure 16.6. The percentage of people who say that they approve of how the Court is handling its job has fluctuated in recent years. In the 21st century, public approval of the Court's performance has been as low as 42 percent (in 2005) and as high as 61 percent (in 2009). These movements do not reflect any obvious swings in how the public perceives the Court's ideological tilt. Gallup polls and other opinion surveys indicate that, for most of the past decade, about half to four-fifths of the public thought the Court was neither too liberal nor too conservative, about a third thought the Court was too liberal, and about a fifth thought it was too conservative. Rather, the shifts in opinion seem to reflect the public's reaction not only to what the Court does but also to what the government as a whole is doing. An upturn in public approval of the Supreme Court in the early 1970s was probably caused by the Watergate scandal, an episode that simultaneously discredited the presidency and boosted the stock of those institutions (such as the courts) that seemed to be checking the abuses of the White House. And a gradual upturn in the 1980s may have reflected a general restoration of public confidence in government during that decade.[67]

Figure 16.6 **Public Approval of the Supreme Court's Performance, 2000–2019**

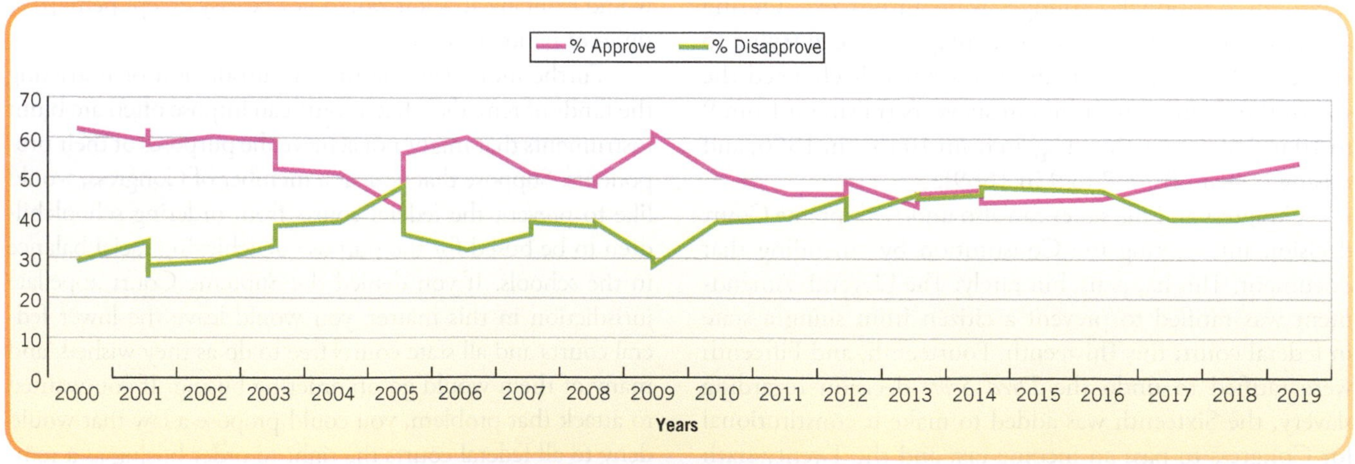

Source: Gallup, "Job Approval: Supreme Court," Gallup website, www.gallup.com/poll/4732/supreme-court.aspx.

Q What patterns do you see in public opinion about the Supreme Court in the 21st century, and what factors might explain those patterns?

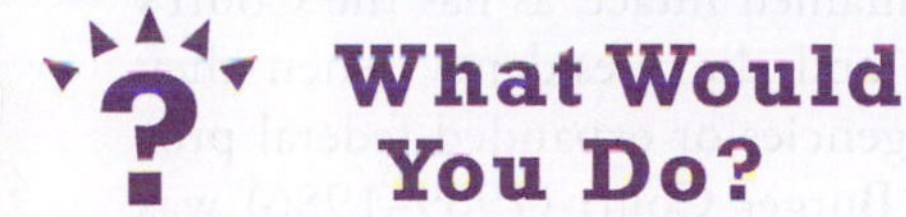

What Would You Do? | Will You Support the Data Surveillance Program?

To: *Senator Xabi Brian*
From: *Amaia Lucy, chief of staff*
Subject: *Internet surveillance*

In 2007, the National Security Agency (NSA) and the Federal Bureau of Investigation (FBI) created a secret surveillance program, code-named PRISM, that—in conjunction with British intelligence agencies—gathered, tracked, and analyzed massive amounts of "private" data (audio and video chats, emails, and more) by directly searching the central servers of Microsoft, Yahoo, Google, Facebook, PalTalk, AOL, Skype, YouTube, and Apple. NSA contractor Edward Snowden leaked classified information about the program to journalists in 2013, and some people questioned whether it intruded upon American civil liberties.[68] Should the program be continued?

To Consider:

Congress is discussing whether to continue a secret surveillance program that gathers data from Internet companies as part of the federal government's counter-terrorism strategy.

Arguments for:

1. Broad data collection is necessary to fight terrorists, who rely almost exclusively on electronic communications.
2. Although the program was secret, some members of Congress were aware of, and approved, the surveillance for national security.
3. In the interest of national security, some civil liberties must be curtailed to keep the United States safe.

Arguments against:

1. Data collection will not substitute for human intelligence gathering, and this program diverts much-needed resources from the latter.
2. Congress has deferred too much to the executive branch in combating terrorism and needs to scrutinize surveillance programs much more carefully.
3. While civil liberties are not absolute, especially when national security is at stake, this program is unnecessarily broad in scope and allows the federal government to collect data without sufficient justification for intruding upon constitutionally guaranteed protections.

What Will You Decide? Enter **MindTap** to make your choice.

Your decision: ☐ Support the program ☐ Oppose the program

Though popular support for the Court sometimes declines, these drops have so far not resulted in any legal checks placed on it. As explained in this chapter's Constitutional Connections feature (see page 410), each Congress witnesses many proposals that restrict the jurisdiction of federal courts and prohibit them from exercising judicial review in relation to given issues, but these proposals almost never become bills that make their way into law. The changes that have occurred in the Court have been caused by changes in its personnel. Presidents Nixon and Reagan attempted to produce a less activist Court by appointing justices who were more inclined to be strict constructionists and conservatives. To some extent, they succeeded: Justices Kennedy, O'Connor, Rehnquist, and Scalia were certainly less inclined than Justice Thurgood Marshall to find new rights in the Constitution or to overturn the decisions of state legislatures. But as of yet, there has been no wholesale retreat from the positions staked out by the Warren Court. As noted above, a Nixon appointee, Justice Blackmun, wrote the decision making antiabortion laws unconstitutional; and another Nixon appointee, Chief Justice Burger, wrote the opinion upholding court-ordered school busing to achieve racial integration. A Reagan appointee, Justice O'Connor, voted to uphold a right to an abortion. The Supreme Court has become somewhat less willing to impose restraints on police practices, and it has not blocked the use of the death penalty.

But in general, the major features of Court activism and liberalism during the Warren years—school integration, sharper limits on police practice, greater freedom of expression—have remained intact, as has the Court's deference to Congress and the presidency when they have established new agencies or expanded federal programs. The Warren E. Burger Court (1969–1986) was succeeded by courts with conservative Chief Justices, namely William H. Rehnquist (1986–2005) and John G. Roberts (2005–present). The aforementioned 2012 Court decision upholding the constitutionality of all (save the Medicaid expansion provision) of the 2010 health care reform law was written by Chief Justice Roberts.

The reasons for the growth in court activism are clear. One is the sheer increase in the size and scope of the government as a whole. The courts have come to play a larger role in our lives because Congress, the bureaucracy, and the president have come to play larger ones as well. In 1890, hardly anybody would have thought of asking Congress—much less the courts—to make rules governing the participation of women in college sports or the district boundaries of state legislatures. Today such rules are commonplace, and the courts are inevitably drawn into interpreting them. And when the Court decided how the vote in Florida would be counted during the 2000 presidential election, it created an opportunity in the future for scores of new lawsuits challenging election results.

The other reason for increased activism is the acceptance by a large number of judges, conservative as well as liberal, of the activist view of the function of the courts. If courts once existed solely to "settle disputes," today they also exist in the eyes of their members to "solve problems."

PAUL J. RICHARDS/AFP/Getty Images

Image 16.7 When the Supreme Court heard arguments about the constitutionality of same-sex marriage in 2015, demonstrators expressed their views outside the building.

Though the Supreme Court is the pinnacle of the federal judiciary, most decisions, including many important ones, are made by the several courts of appeals and the 94 district courts. The Supreme Court can control its own workload by deciding when to grant certiorari. It has become easier for citizens and groups to gain access to the federal courts (through class-action suits, by amicus curiae briefs, by laws that require government agencies to pay legal fees). At the same time, the courts have widened the reach of their decisions by issuing orders that cover whole classes of citizens or affect the management of major public and private institutions. However, the courts can overstep the bounds of their authority and bring upon themselves a counterattack from both the public and Congress. Congress has the right to control much of the courts' jurisdiction, but it rarely does so. As a result, the ability of judges to make law is only infrequently challenged directly.

Hank Walker/The LIFE Picture Collection/Getty Images

Image 16.8 Thurgood Marshall was the first African American Supreme Court justice. As chief counsel for the NAACP, Marshall argued the 1954 *Brown v. Board of Education* case in front of the Supreme Court. He was appointed to the Court in 1967 and served until 1991.

Learning Objectives

16-1 Explain the concept of judicial review.

Nowhere in the Constitution does it say that the Supreme Court has the power of judicial review. The Constitution is silent on this matter, but the Court has asserted, and almost every scholar has agreed, that our system of separated powers means that the Court must be able to defend the Constitution. Otherwise, Congress and the president would be free to ignore it.

16-2 Summarize the development of the federal courts.

The federal courts have focused on different issues in American history depending on major political debates at the time. From the founding through the Civil War, the courts made significant decisions on nation-building, the legitimacy of the federal government, and slavery. From the end of the Civil War to the 1930s, the courts decided key cases on how government may be involved in the economy. Since the 1930s, the courts have concentrated on issues of personal liberty and social equality, and potential conflicts between the two concepts.

16-3 Discuss the structure, jurisdiction, and operation of the federal courts.

Article III of the Constitution guarantees federal judges that they can serve during good behavior. The Supreme Court, courts of appeal, and all district courts are all Article III courts. Original jurisdiction refers to a trial held before a court; appellate jurisdiction refers to an appeal a court hears from a trial in another court. Even the Supreme Court has original jurisdiction. For example, it will hear a trial involving ambassadors or a controversy between two or more states.

Strictly speaking, federal judges serve during "good behavior," but that means they would have to be impeached and convicted in order to be removed. The reason for this protection is clear: The judiciary cannot be independent of the other two branches of government if judges could be removed easily by the president or Congress, and this independence ensures that they are a separate branch of government.

16-4 Explain how the federal courts exercise power and the checks on judicial power.

Though the Constitution does not explicitly give federal courts the power of judicial review, they have acquired it on the reasonable assumption that the Constitution would become meaningless if the president and Congress could ignore its provisions. The Constitution, after all, states that it shall be the "supreme law of the land."

The federal courts rarely think their decisions create entirely new laws, but in fact their interpretations sometimes come close to just that. One reason is that many provisions of the Constitution are vague. What does the Constitution mean by "respecting an establishment of religion," the "equal protection of the law," or a "cruel and unusual punishment"? The courts must give concrete meaning to these phrases. But another reason is the personal ideology of judges. Some think a free press is more important than laws governing campaign finance, while others think a free press must give way to such laws. Some believe the courts ought to use federal law to strike down discrimination, but judges disagree about what types of affirmative action programs must be put in place. Congress can check the courts through nominations and the size of the judiciary, and public opinion also serves as a check on the courts over time. Still, the judicial power is highly significant for policymaking in American politics.

To Learn More

Federal courts: **www.uscourts.gov**—Administrative and information website of the judicial branch of the United States.

Federal Judicial Center: **www.fjc.gov**—Research agency of the judicial branch of the United States.

FindLaw: **www.findlaw.com**—Legal information website for individuals and small businesses.

Legal Information Institute: **www.law.cornell.edu**—Website of federal laws, commentary, and related information.

Oyez: **www.oyez.org**—Multimedia archive of Supreme Court decisions, audio recordings, and history of Supreme Court justices.

Abraham, Henry J. *The Judicial Process*. 7th ed. New York: Oxford University Press, 1998. An excellent, comprehensive survey of how the federal courts are organized and function.

Abraham, Henry J., and Barbara A. Perry. *Freedom and the Court: Civil Rights and Liberties in the United States*. 8th ed. Lawrence, KS: University Press of Kansas, 2010. Careful summary of civil liberties and civil rights cases.

Cardozo, Benjamin N. *The Nature of the Judicial Process*. New Haven, CT: Yale University Press, 1921. Important statement of how judges make decisions, by a former Supreme Court justice.

Ely, John Hart. *Democracy and Distrust*. Cambridge, MA: Harvard University Press, 1980. Effort to create a theory of judicial review that is neither strict constructionist nor activist.

Greenburg, Jan Crawford. *Supreme Conflict*. New York: Penguin, 2007. A fascinating journalistic account of how the Supreme Court operates.

Hall, Kermit L., and James W. Ely Jr., eds. *The Oxford Guide to United States Supreme Court Decisions*. 2nd ed. New York: Oxford University Press, 2009. Summarizes the 440 most important decisions of the Supreme Court and includes a comprehensive bibliography of books about the Court.

Lasser, William. *The Limits of Judicial Power*. Chapel Hill, NC: University of North Carolina Press, 1988. Shows how the Court throughout history has withstood the political storms created by its more controversial decisions.

McCloskey, Robert G. *The American Supreme Court*. 6th ed. Revised by Sanford Levinson. Chicago, IL: University of Chicago Press, 2016. Superb brief history of the Supreme Court, updated by one of McCloskey's former students, who teaches law at the University of Texas.

Rabkin, Jeremy. *Judicial Compulsions*. New York: Basic Books, 1989. Explains (and argues against) the extensive Court intervention in the work of administrative agencies.

Wolfe, Christopher. *The Rise of Modern Judicial Review*. New York: Basic Books, 1986 (revised edition published by New York: Rowman & Littlefield, 1994). An excellent history of judicial review from 1787 to the late 20th century.

PART 4

Public Policy and American Democracy

In the extended republic of the United States, and among the great variety of interests, parties, and sects, which it embraces, a coalition of a majority of the whole society could seldom take place on any other principles than those of justice and the general good.

— *FEDERALIST NO. 51*

The Asahi Shimbun/Getty Images

CHAPTER 17

Domestic Policy

Learning Objectives

17-1 Explain how America's social welfare policies differ from those of many other modern democracies, and why some programs are politically protected while others are politically imperiled.

17-2 Discuss how government regulations on certain big businesses have been imposed over the objections of those industries.

17-3 Explain why environmental policies are designed and enforced differently in America than in other industrialized nations, and describe the politics that drive environmental programs.

17-4 Discuss the difficulty with changing policies—domestic, economic, and foreign—or developing new programs in the United States today.

As we explained in Chapter 1, understanding any political system means being able to give reasonable answers to each of two separate but related questions about it: Who governs, and to what ends? The preceding chapters should be especially helpful in discovering "who governs," while this chapter and the next three chapters should be especially helpful in discerning "to what ends."

The primary puzzles about public policy in America concern the nation's political agenda (see pages 9–11). How do people come to believe that certain issues require governmental action? What explains why some issues are on the political agenda while others are not? Why are some issues more prominent on today's political agenda than they were either in previous historical periods or just a few years ago, and why are other issues less prominent than they once were? Why do elected officials sometimes suddenly shift attention away from some issues and toward others? What explains the timing and character of government action (or inaction) on any given issue?

The causes, contours, and consequences of government action or inaction on any given issue or any class of issues (domestic policy, economic policy, or foreign policy) are not easily explained. What at first glance may appear to be simple and stable policymaking patterns often, upon closer inspection, turn out to be more complex and dynamic than they seemed. For instance, consider what has happened in each of three domestic policy domains: social welfare policy, business regulation policy, and environmental protection policy.

Social Welfare Policy

« Then Before the 1960s, neither most Washington lawmakers nor most citizens believed that the federal government should ensure that all retirees, whatever their work history, have enough money to live on; that all veterans of foreign wars are given grants for college and subsidized medical care for life; that all poor children are guaranteed free or reduced-price meals in schools and during summers; that all physically, mentally, or developmentally disabled people, like all people with life-threatening medical maladies, are insured for hospital stays and treatment, including long-term nursing care; that all low-wage workers receive tax credits that effectively boost their wages; that all citizens who may need it have access to affordable housing; that all low-income children are able to attend preschools; that all special needs children receive special education; and that all full-time workers who lose their jobs receive unemployment benefits and (in many cases) job training. If they existed at all, national laws touching on these social welfare matters were few and narrow, and federal departments, bureaus, or programs to fund or administer such social welfare benefits were virtually nonexistent.

*** Now** Washington sets, funds, and implements policies on all these social welfare matters. Today, nearly half of the federal budget goes to two broad classes of social welfare spending: social security and health care spending (encompassing Medicare, Medicaid, the State Children's Health Insurance Program, and the health exchange subsidies provided by the Affordable Care Act). And other social welfare programs exist, many of them either established or expanded after 1965. The U.S. Department of Health and Human Services and the U.S. Department of Veterans Affairs are two of the main bureaucracies responsible for federal social welfare policies and programs, but benefits also emanate from several other federal departments. For instance, the U.S. Department of Justice has supported myriad programs for "at-risk youth," including ones that provide mentors to the children of prisoners and "second-chance" job training to young adult ex-prisoners. But, in recent years, as policymakers have struggled with big annual budget deficits and a growing national debt (see Chapter 18), the future of many social welfare policies and programs, including the largest entitlement programs such as Social Security and Medicare, may be—for the first time in more than a generation—placed in some serious doubt.

Business Regulation Policy

« Then Big oil companies were once able to persuade the government to sharply restrict the amount of foreign oil imported into the United States, to give them preferential tax treatment, and to permit them to drill for new oil just about anywhere they liked. Automobile manufacturers once faced virtually no federal controls on the products they manufactured. Well into the 1990s, communications and broadcasting companies were regulated under a 1934 federal law that was debated and developed at a time when most Americans neither owned radios nor had ever even heard of television. Certain telephone companies were free to function as monopolies.

*** Now** Today, the restrictions on foreign oil imports have ended, the tax breaks the oil companies enjoyed have been reduced considerably (though they still exist), and the freedom of oil companies to drill in certain places, particularly offshore locations, has been restricted. Auto companies are heavily regulated regarding the safety of the vehicles they make, and two of them (GM and Chrysler) were briefly partially owned by the federal government following the 2008 financial crisis. A new federal communications act took effect in 1996, and the industry now features not only more broadcasting companies, stricter rules governing what cable service providers can charge, and no telephone company monopolies, but also fewer regulations to keep corporate conglomerates from dominating these markets.

Environmental Policy

« Then Environmental policies in the United States gained widespread public attention in the 1960s and 1970s, when reports of water and air pollution, pesticide use, and other threats to natural resources prompted the passage of legislation to control such activity. The Environmental Protection Agency (EPA) was created in 1970 to set standards for environmental safety, track violations, and enforce compliance. Since then, the field has expanded to encompass concerns about broader national and international environmental issues such as global warming.

*** Now** President Barack Obama enacted several new policies to protect the environment. While little such legislation was passed during his tenure, policies were put in place via executive or agency actions. For example, during Obama's tenure, the EPA issued new rules on power plant emissions, wetlands protection, and hydraulic fracturing (better known as "fracking"). In 2015, President Obama signed the historic Paris Agreement on climate change, a plan among the world's nations to reduce greenhouse gases and fight climate change. Since taking office, President Donald Trump has rolled back some of Obama's environmental regulations, including withdrawing the United States from the Paris Climate Accord.[1]

The shift between Presidents Obama and Trump also reflects the divide between the mass parties on environmental issues. Overall, while Democrats and Republicans both support efforts to help the environment, a large gap exists—and is growing—between the parties, with Democrats being far more likely to support such policies. In a 2020 study by the Pew Research Center, 85 percent of Democrats—but only 39 percent of Republicans—said the environment should be a top priority for the president and Congress.[2] As we will see later in the chapter, Democrats are also much more likely to express concern about climate change and to support efforts to address it.

To begin to understand policy dynamics, in order to help explain both short-term shifts and long-term trends in what issues are on the political agenda and how government acts on these issues (or doesn't), we need some theory of policymaking. After defining key terms ranging from *politics* to *representative democracy* (see pages 4 and 5, respectively) and explaining five different views of "power in America" (see pages 6–8), the first chapter of this book outlined a theory of policymaking involving four different types of politics: majoritarian, client, interest group, and entrepreneurial (see pages 12–15, as well as Figure 17.1 below). Each chapter also includes a Policy Dynamics feature that applies the theory and its key terms to a current policy debate.

This chapter elaborates and applies the theory of policymaking outlined in Chapter 1 to domestic policy dynamics on issues in social welfare policy, business regulation policy, and environmental policy. Each area of domestic policy has issues and policy dynamics all its own. But in social welfare, business regulation, and environmental policy, as in education, housing,

Figure 17.1 A Way of Classifying and Explaining the Politics of Different Policy Issues

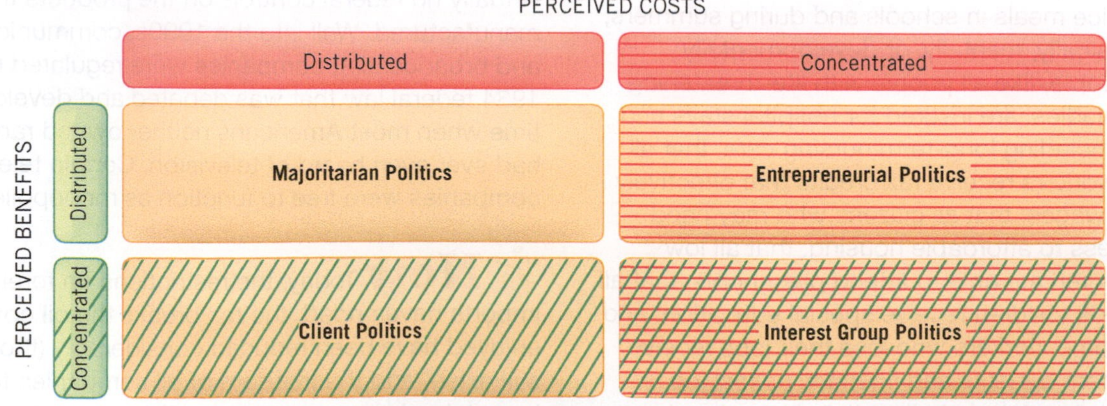

homeland security, transportation, and other domestic policy domains, each of the four types of policymaking politics can be found. In Chapter 18, we will explore the politics of economic policy, and in Chapter 19 we will examine the politics of foreign and military policy.

17-1 Social Welfare Policy

Among the reasons given in the Preamble to the U.S. Constitution for establishing the national government is a desire to "promote the general Welfare." Article I, section 8 of the Constitution states the power of Congress to "provide for the . . . general Welfare."

From the first, however, the Constitution's defenders disagreed about what the phrase was supposed to mean. Some, like James Madison, argued that it was meant to restrict Congress to taxing and spending only for things that the Constitution specifically empowered Congress to do (like regulating interstate commerce or maintaining the military). Others, like Alexander Hamilton, argued for a broader meaning that would allow Congress to tax and spend for things that it was not specifically empowered by the Constitution to do, but which might reasonably be expected to meet national needs and benefit some or all citizens.

In the 1930s, asserting a constitutional authority to advance the "general welfare," Congress enacted a host of new national policies and programs in response to the economic hardships wrought by the Great Depression. The biggest was the Social Security Act of 1935. Among other provisions, the law created a national system of old-age pensions and, to pay for it, imposed an income tax on workers that was deducted from their wages and paid by their employers.

In 1937, in the case of *Helvering v. Davis*, the U.S. Supreme Court upheld the constitutionality of that provision, ruling that Congress has broad discretion to tax and spend "in aid of the 'general welfare,'" including policies and programs designed to ease the "plight of men and women" who lose their jobs and to provide for others who are either temporarily or permanently "needy and dependent." Nobody, however, foresaw just how far Congress would go in exercising that power, or where doing so would lead.

From the New Deal to the Affordable Care Act

The first major steps toward today's social welfare policies and programs were taken after the election of 1932. Hardly any state had a systematic program for supporting the unemployed, though many states provided some kind of help if it was clear that individuals were out of work through no fault of their own.

When the economy suddenly ground to a near standstill and the unemployment rate rose to include one-fourth of the workforce, private charities and city relief programs nearly went bankrupt. With so many Americans in dire need of assistance, the popular 1931 song "Brother, Can You Spare a Dime?" aptly encapsulated public opinion. But, with families, neighbors, local churches, charities, and city

The State of the Union and Presidential Agenda-Setting

The Framers of the Constitution drafted Article I about Congress because they expected that the legislature would be the primary branch of government. Congress would introduce, consider, and vote on legislation, which the president would sign or veto. Article II of the Constitution discusses the executive branch and says the president "shall from time to time" report to Congress on the state of union, but does not provide more specifics on the president's role in policymaking.

Over time, this requirement evolved into the modern State of the Union Address. While George Washington and John Adams delivered their addresses in person, Thomas Jefferson decided in 1801 that addressing Congress in person seemed too monarchical, and instead he submitted a written text. Throughout the 19th and early 20th centuries, presidents continued to submit written remarks to Congress. Woodrow Wilson revived the practice of delivering an in-person address in 1913, and subsequent presidents have followed suit.

Especially in more recent decades, the address has become an important mechanism for the president to present a policy agenda to Congress and the public. Scholars have shown that the topics the president discusses in the speech influence the political debate in the days and weeks following the address.[3] Somewhere between one-quarter and one-half of policy proposals in the address are at least partially enacted, and presidents have used the address to expound on some of the most significant policy proposals, such as when President Johnson launched his "war on poverty" in his 1964 address.[4]

Federal Laws about "General Welfare"

- ***United States v. Butler* (1936):** Found particular federal regulations on agricultural production to be unconstitutional, but proclaimed that Congress has wide power to tax and spend for whatever it deems to be for the "general welfare."
- ***Helvering v. Davis* (1937):** Upheld key provisions of the Social Security Act of 1935, and declared that Congress has broad discretion to tax and spend "in aid of the 'general welfare.'"
- ***South Dakota v. Dole* (1987):** Ruled that Washington could condition the receipt of federal highway funds on a state's compliance with a 21-year-old drinking age, and declared that Congress's power to define the "general welfare" and to spend in pursuit of it is virtually unlimited.

insurance program *A self-financing government program based on contributions that provide benefits to unemployed or retired persons.*

assistance program *A government program financed by general income taxes that provides benefits to poor citizens without requiring contributions from them.*

agencies all unable to meet the economic crisis despite their best efforts, on the eve of the 1932 presidential election, ever more citizens decided it was time for Uncle Sam to lend a hand.

That election produced an overwhelming congressional majority for the Democrats and placed Franklin D. Roosevelt in the White House. Almost immediately, Washington enacted a number of emergency measures to cope with the depression by supplying federal cash to bail out state and local relief agencies and by creating public works jobs under federal auspices. These measures were recognized as temporary expedients, however, and were unsatisfactory to those who believed the federal government had a permanent and major responsibility for welfare.

Topham/The Image Works

Image 17.1 In 1932, unemployed workers line up at a soup kitchen during the Great Depression.

Roosevelt created the Cabinet Committee on Economic Security to consider long-term policies. The committee drew heavily on the experience of European nations and on the ideas of various American scholars and social workers, but it understood that it would have to adapt these proposals to the realities of American politics. Chief among these was the widespread belief that any direct federal welfare program might be unconstitutional. The Constitution nowhere explicitly gave to Congress the authority to set up an unemployment compensation or old-age retirement program. And even if a welfare program were constitutional, many believed it would be wrong because it violated the individualistic creed that people should help themselves unless they were physically unable to do so.

But Roosevelt's supporters were concerned that White House failure to produce a comprehensive social security program might make the president vulnerable in the 1936 election to the leaders of various radical social movements. Huey Long of Louisiana proposed a "Share Our Wealth" plan; Upton Sinclair ran for governor of California on a platform calling for programs to "End Poverty in California"; and Dr. Francis E. Townsend lead an organization of hundreds of thousands of older adults on whose behalf he demanded government pensions of $200 a month (or slightly less than $3,700 in today's dollars).

The plan that emerged from the cabinet committee was carefully designed to meet popular demands within the framework of constitutional understandings. It called for two kinds of programs: (1) an **insurance program** for the unemployed and elderly, to which workers would contribute and from which they would benefit when they became unemployed or retired; and (2) an **assistance program** for blind people, dependent children, and the aged. (Giving assistance as well as providing "insurance" for the aged was necessary because for the first few years the insurance program would not pay out any benefits.)

The federal government would use its power to tax in order to provide the funds, but all of the programs (except for old-age insurance) would be administered by the states. Everybody, rich or poor, would be eligible for the insurance programs. Only the poor, as defined by a means test (a measure to determine that incomes are below a certain level), would be eligible for the assistance programs. Though bitterly opposed by some, the resulting Social Security Act passed swiftly and virtually unchanged through Congress. It was introduced in January 1935 and signed by President Roosevelt in August of that year.

The Social Security Act became a cornerstone of Roosevelt's New Deal. But many of the act's supporters also wanted Washington to guarantee all citizens, including the elderly and the poor, a certain minimum level of health care. The idea of having the government pay the medical and hospital bills of the elderly and the poor had been discussed in Washington since the drafting of the Social Security Act. President Roosevelt and his Committee on Economic Security sensed that medical care would be very controversial, and so health programs were left out of the 1935 bill in order not to jeopardize its chances of passage.[5]

The proponents of the idea did not abandon it, however. Working mostly within the executive branch, they continued to press—sometimes publicly, sometimes behind the scenes—for a national health care plan. Democratic presidents, including Truman, Kennedy, and

Image 17.2 In 1934, Huey Long, the popular governor of Louisiana, claimed that Roosevelt was not doing enough to help the common man. But before he could become a serious threat to Roosevelt in the 1936 election, Long was assassinated in 1935.

Johnson, favored it; Republican President Eisenhower opposed it; Congress was deeply divided on it. The American Medical Association attacked it as "socialized medicine." For 30 years, key policy entrepreneurs, such as the former Social Security director Wilbur Cohen, worked to find a formula that would produce a congressional majority.

The first and highest hurdle to overcome, however, was not Congress as a whole but the House Ways and Means Committee, especially its powerful chairman from 1958 to 1975, Wilbur Mills of Arkansas. A majority of the committee members opposed a national health care program. Some members believed it wrong in principle; others feared that adding a costly health component to the Social Security system would jeopardize the financial solvency and administrative integrity of one of the most popular government programs. By the early 1960s, a majority of the House favored a health care plan, but without the approval of Ways and Means it would never reach the floor.

The 1964 elections changed all that. The Johnson landslide produced such large Democratic majorities in Congress that the composition of the committees changed. In particular, the membership of the Ways and Means Committee was altered. While before it had three Democrats for every two Republicans, after 1964 it had two Democrats for every one Republican. The House leadership saw to it that the new Democrats on the committee were strongly committed to a health care program. Suddenly, the committee had a majority favorable to such a plan, and Mills, realizing that a bill would pass and wanting to help shape its form, changed his position and became a supporter of what was to become Medicare.

Medicare became a cornerstone of Johnson's Great Society. The policy entrepreneurs in and out of the government who drafted the Medicare plan attempted to anticipate the major objections to it. First, the bill would apply only to the aged—those eligible for Social Security retirement benefits. This would reassure legislators worried about the cost of providing tax-supported health care for everybody. Second, the plan would cover only hospital expenses, not doctors' bills. Since doctors were not to be paid by the government, they would not be regulated by it; thus, presumably, the opposition of the American Medical Association would be blunted.

Unexpectedly, however, the Ways and Means Committee broadened the coverage of the plan beyond what the administration had thought was politically feasible. It added sections providing medical assistance, called Medicaid, for the poor (defined as those already getting public assistance payments) and payment of doctors' bills for the aged (a new part of Medicare). The new, much-enlarged bill passed both houses of Congress with ease. The key votes pitted a majority of the Democrats against a majority of the Republicans.

Image 17.3 President Lyndon Johnson signs the Medicare Act in 1965.

Image 17.4 President Barack Obama signs the Affordable Health Care for America Act in 2010.

Johnson's Great Society programs and "war on poverty" went far beyond Roosevelt's New Deal programs. But neither the chief political architects of Social Security in 1935 nor the main political movers behind Medicare and Medicaid in 1965 ever envisioned scores of millions of Americans, including middle-and upper-income Americans, receiving food, money, medicine, and other benefits through programs funded largely by the federal government. Yet that day arrived long ago. By 2018 (the last year for which data are available), 60 million Americans were enrolled in Medicare, and more than 74.6 million Americans were enrolled in Medicaid (or in the Children's Health Insurance Program; this number has increased sharply in recent years as a result of the expansion of Medicaid under the Affordable Care Act).[6] Similarly, approximately 64 million Americans today receive benefits from Social Security.

The two largest federal social welfare programs, Social Security and Medicare, are bound for big increases in beneficiaries over the next several decades as the primary beneficiary population each program serves, persons aged 65 and older, continues to grow. Likewise Medicaid, for several decades now the largest program co-funded by the federal government and the states, has grown rapidly as many states expanded the program under the Affordable Care Act (see the discussion in Chapter 3).

As discussed in several previous chapters, one of the most heated political controversies of recent years concerned social welfare policy, namely, the passage of the Patient Protection and Affordable Care Act of 2010. Dubbed by certain of its critics (and eventually called by President Obama himself) "Obamacare," the bill was passed by the House and Senate without a single Republican vote. 34 Democrats in the House and three in the Senate voted against it.[7]

Obamacare made several important changes to health insurance in America. It required all Americans to have health care or to pay a penalty (the individual mandate, though the 2017 Tax Cut and Jobs Act removed this penalty), but it also expanded Medicaid, created health insurance exchanges to serve as marketplaces where people could buy coverage, and offered subsidies to many Americans to help them purchase insurance policies. It also set new rules for health insurance plans, requiring that children be allowed to remain on their parents' plans until the age of 26, removed bans on denying insurance to individuals because of preexisting conditions, and required insurance plans to cover a variety of preventive screenings and procedures.

The effects of Obamacare have been mixed. The uninsured rate has dropped dramatically: before Obamacare, about 18.5 percent of the population did not have health insurance, and that figure dropped to 8.5 percent in 2018; such changes have been especially large for low-income Americans.[8] That said, premiums increased under Obamacare, and one of the main reasons people remain uninsured is that they cannot afford an insurance plan, even with government subsidies.[9]

Since its passage, public opinion has been deeply divided on Obamacare. Overall support has fluctuated, but most Republicans have opposed—and most Democrats have supported—the act (Independents have been somewhere in the middle). That said, while overall support for the law remains divided by party, both Democrats and Republicans alike support many of the specific policies enacted by the law (e.g., allowing young adults to remain on their parents' health insurance until age 26).[10]

President Trump and congressional Republicans campaigned on a promise to repeal and replace Obamacare, and they began to lay the groundwork to do so shortly after President Trump's inauguration in 2017. First the House, then the Senate, took up bills designed to repeal and replace the Affordable Care Act. Much of the debate centered around how exactly to do that: which parts of the 2010 law should be left in place, and which parts should be repealed and replaced with a new law. Paralleling 2009, when citizens packed town halls to protest the enactment of Obamacare, in 2017, citizens packed town halls to protest its repeal, especially the parts they favored. While the House passed legislation that would have repealed and replaced much of the Affordable Care Act, efforts in the Senate failed in July 2017 when 3 Republicans joined Democrats in voting down the bill. Opponents of the health care law did achieve some of their goals with the Tax Cut and Jobs Act of 2017, which repealed the penalties associated with the individual mandate. Beginning in 2019, individuals will not be penalized for failing to purchase insurance. The remainder of the law, however, remains intact, though several cases challenging the law are being litigated in the courts. The law—and the debate over the future of health care—will continue to be one of the central issues in American politics for years to come.

Two Kinds of Social Welfare Programs

Today, some eight decades after Social Security was first debated, two kinds of social welfare programs exist in this country: those that benefit most or all of the people and those that help only a small number of them. In the first category are Social Security and Medicare, programs that provide retirement benefits or medical assistance to almost every citizen who has reached a certain age. In the second are programs such as Temporary Assistance to Needy Children (TANF) and the Supplemental Nutrition Assistance Program (SNAP, which encompasses food stamps) that offer help only to people with low incomes. In Table 17.1, we outline several

TABLE 17.1 | Major Social Welfare Programs

Insurance, or "Contributory," Programs	Assistance, or "Noncontributory," Programs
Old Age, Survivors, and Disability Insurance (OASDI) • Monthly payments to retired or disabled people and to surviving members of their families. • This program, popularly called Social Security, is paid for by a payroll tax on employers and employees. *No means test.*	**Unemployment Insurance (UI)** • Weekly payments to workers who have been laid off and cannot find work. • Benefits and requirements determined by states. • Paid for by taxes on employers. • *No means test.*
Medicare • Federal government pays for part of the cost of medical care for retired or disabled people covered by Social Security. • Paid for by payroll taxes on employees and employers. *No means test.*	**Temporary Assistance for Needy Families (TANF)** • Payments to needy families with children. • Replaced the old AFDC program. • Partially paid for by block grants from the federal government to the states. • *Means test.*
	Supplemental Security Income (SSI) • Cash payments to aged, blind, or disabled people whose income is below a certain amount. • Paid for from general federal revenues. • *Means test.*
	Food Stamps (now part of the **Supplemental Nutrition Assistance Program [SNAP]**) • Vouchers, given to people whose income is below a certain level, that can be used to buy food at grocery stores. • Paid for out of general federal revenues. • *Means test.*
	Medicaid • Pays medical expenses of certain low-income persons. • *Means test.*
	Earned Income Tax Credit • Pays cash or tax credit to poor working families. • *Means test.*

means test *An income qualification program that determines whether one is eligible for benefits under government programs reserved for lower-income groups.*

different types of social welfare programs, differentiating them using this classification.

Legally, the difference between the two kinds of social welfare programs is that the first have no **means test** (they are available to everyone without regard to income) while the second are *means tested* (you must fall below a certain income level to enjoy them). Politically, the programs differ in how they get money from the government. The first kind of welfare program represents majoritarian politics: nearly everyone benefits, nearly everyone pays. The second kind represents client politics: a (relatively) small number of people benefit, but almost everyone pays (for more discussion of majoritarian and client politics generally, see Chapter 1). The biggest problem facing majoritarian welfare programs is their cost: who will pay, and how much will they pay? The biggest problem facing client-oriented programs is their legitimacy: who should benefit, and how should they be served?

This political difference between these programs has a huge impact on how the government acts in regard to them. Social Security and Medicare are sacrosanct. The thought of making any changes that might reduce the benefits these programs pay is so politically risky that most politicians never even discuss them. As we discuss in the next section, because of growing senior citizen populations, increasing expenses, and rising demands for more benefits, Medicare and Social Security will both face considerable financial pressures in the years ahead. No politician wants to raise taxes or cut benefits, so they adopt a variety of halfhearted measures (like slowly increasing the age at which people can get these benefits) designed to postpone the tough decisions until they are out of office.

Client-based welfare programs—those that are means tested—are a very different matter. Like many other client-based programs, their political appeal changes as popular opinion about them changes. Take the old Aid to Families with Dependent Children (AFDC) program. When it was started in 1935, people thought of it as a way of helping poor women whose husbands had been killed in war or had died in mining accidents. The goal was to help these women support their children, who had been made fatherless by death or disaster. Most people thought of these women as the innocent victims of a tragedy. No one thought that they would take AFDC for very long. It was a program to help smooth things over for them until they could remarry.

About 30 years later, however, the public's opinion of AFDC had begun to change. People started to think AFDC was paying money to women who had never married and had no intention of marrying. The government, according to this view, was subsidizing single-parent families, encouraging out-of-wedlock births, and creating social dependency. From the mid-1960s through the mid-1990s, these views became stronger. AFDC had lost the legitimacy it needed, as a client program, to survive politically. As we discuss in more detail later in this chapter, even though it never accounted for as much as 1 percent of total federal spending, in 1996, AFDC suffered a fate that few decades-old federal programs of any type ever do, and that far more costly majoritarian social welfare programs never do: it was abolished.

Now, however, let's take a closer look at Washington's two biggest social welfare programs, Social Security and Medicare, and how the majoritarian politics surrounding each program helps to explain what federal policymakers are (or, more to the point, are not) doing as each program faces severe financial stresses.

Social Security and Medicare: *Majoritarian Politics*

When Social Security began in 1935 and Medicare in 1965, many people benefited and the cost was small. In the late 1930s, an old-age check for a retired person receiving Social Security was paid for by taxes levied on 42 workers; today, only about 3 workers pay for each retired program beneficiary, and that figure is expected to fall to 2.3 workers per beneficiary by 2030.[11] The current Social Security tax is 12.4 percent of a person's earnings (half of this is paid by the employer). This money is used to make payments to current retirees, and the leftover funds are invested in government bonds owned by the Treasury Department (this is known as the Social Security trust fund).

But that system is breaking down as the baby boomer generation (Americans born between 1946 and 1964) retires and begins collecting their Social Security benefits. By 2030, nearly one in five Americans will be age 65 or older; each day, about 10,000 Americans turn 65. For many years, the government took in more in Social Security payroll taxes than it paid out in benefits, but that is changing. In 2020, the Social Security trustees (the group overseeing the program) estimated that for the first time in a generation, the total cost of the program will exceed its income, and the government will need to begin spending down the trust fund to pay out current benefits. The Social Security Administration estimates suggest that the trust fund will be exhausted in 2035, at which point it will only be able to pay 79 percent of promised benefits.[12] Some claim, however, that even this forecast is too optimistic, and the program may have to reduce benefits before then.[13]

Still, the program's prospects for remaining solvent are pretty good for at least three reasons. First, Social Security is well run, costing less than 1 percent of total annual expenditures to administer. Second, the program remains highly popular with the public, and most people are aware that it faces a solvency problem. Third, and most important, Congress, as it has done in the past when the program's finances were faltering, will almost certainly act before 2035 to increase future funding so that all scheduled benefits get paid.

Like Social Security, Medicare is a widely popular program. Medicare, however, poses a more formidable financial challenge than Social Security does. In 1965, supporters of Medicare said it would not cost more than $8 billion a year. Today, Medicare costs more than $740 billion a year. Even when adjusted for inflation (a dollar in 1965 bought what about $8.12 did in 2019), that is almost 90 times what the program cost when it started. Medicare now has more than 60 million beneficiaries, and that number is expected to grow dramatically in the near term as the baby boomers qualify for the program. If anything, the fiscal health of Medicare is more dire than that of Social Security, as its main trust fund is set to expire in 2026.[14]

As presently structured, Medicare allows beneficiaries to visit the doctor or go to the hospital pretty much whenever they feel they need to do so. The doctor or hospital is paid a fee for each visit. This creates three problems: some people use medical services when they don't really need them; some doctors and hospitals overcharge the government for their services; and doctors and hospitals are paid on the basis of a government-approved payment plan that can change whenever the government wants to save money. Various laws—including Obamacare—have included provisions to make Medicare most cost-efficient. That said, while there have been some successes, fully constraining the growth of these programs has been difficult.

Federal policymakers at both ends of Pennsylvania Avenue and in both parties have struggled to solve each major social welfare program's problems. For example, President George W. Bush proposed partially privatizing Social Security, allowing individuals to invest part of their payroll taxes in private accounts, but the proposal never gained traction with the public or Congress. Republican House member Paul Ryan and Democratic Senator Ron Wyden introduced a Medicare reform bill in 2011 that featured a "premium support" (voucher-type) option under which beneficiaries could choose either a traditional Medicare plan or a Medicare-approved private plan, but the plan did not become law. Other efforts to change these programs have similarly come up short.

Facing these fiscal challenges, you might expect that Americans would support dramatic challenges to these programs to ensure their long-term survival. But you would be wrong. As we show in Figure 17.2, many Americans anticipate that Social Security will not be able to pay all of its promised benefits when they go to retire. Nevertheless, Americans do not support cuts to these programs—indeed, in that same study, half of Americans supported increased spending on both Medicare and Social Security! If faced with a choice, most Americans say we should increase taxes rather than cutting benefits, though as we will see in the next chapter, many assume that taxes should be raised on someone else, not themselves.

Figure 17.2 **Public Opinion on Medicare and Social Security**

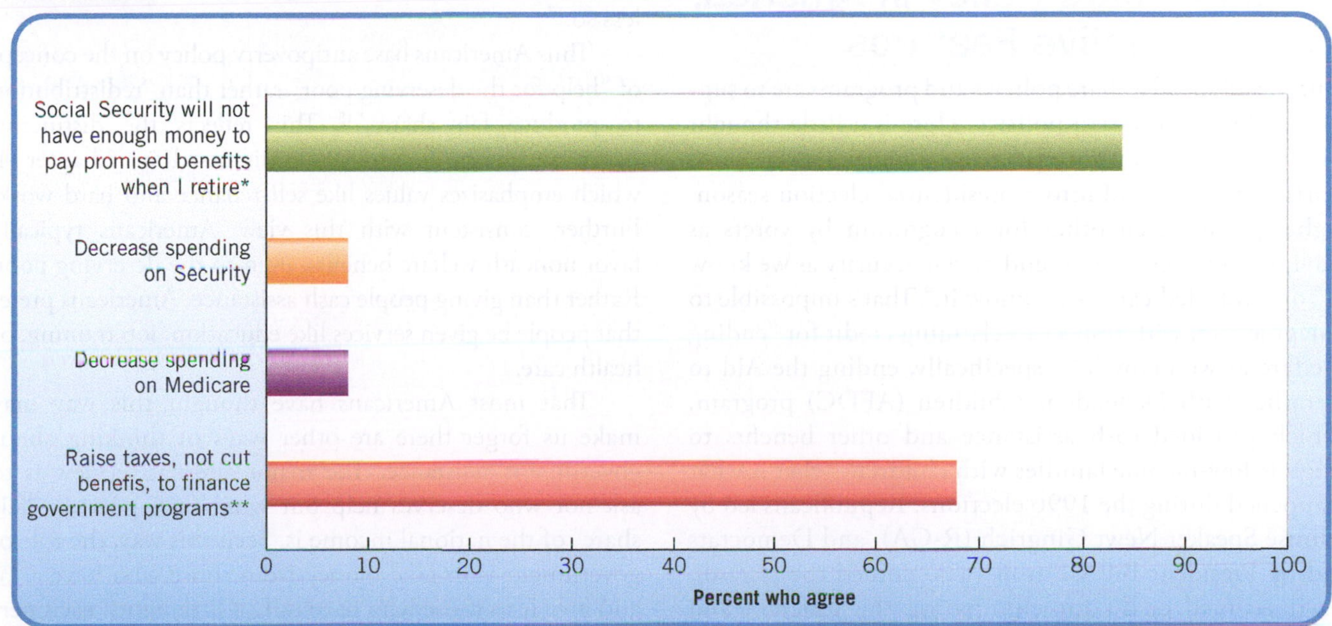

Source: Pew Research Center, "Little Public Support for Reduction in Federal Spending," April 2019; Pew Research Center, "Looking to the Future, The Public Sees a Decline on Many Fronts," March 2019,** NPR/PBS News Hour Poll, 2018.

Looking at public opinion on this topic, what would you recommend to those wanting to reform Social Security?

It may be tempting to see the politics of Social Security and Medicare as a species of client politics in which older citizens benefit and young and middle-aged citizens pay. But resist that temptation. It is true that older citizens vote at higher rates than young ones do. It is also true that interest groups like AARP that advocate or lobby for older adults and retirees have great influence in Washington. But as Figure 17.2 shows, Americans—young and old alike—support the programs; and most oppose trimming benefits and tinkering too much with how the programs presently work. Each program is widely perceived as one into which all people pay and from which all people can and should benefit. The fact that many people receive more in benefits than they ever pay in, and that the programs' massive unfunded liabilities do not fall equally on people of all ages (and will also be borne by citizens yet to be born), seem to have little bearing on popular attitudes toward these highly popular programs.

Apparently, most federal policymakers share those public attitudes; regardless, even those who may view the long-term costs differently know that they would court real reelection troubles if they publicly prescribed deep cuts in benefits or steep tax increases for either program. For instance, the first lines of the aforementioned Wyden-Ryan Medicare reform plan read like a majoritarian politics rhapsody: the goal was to "strengthen Medicare and health security for all," with "no changes for those in or near retirement," and guaranteeing that Americans age 56 and older "would see no changes to the structure of their benefits" save any changes they might voluntarily opt to make.

Social Welfare Policy in America: Four Distinctive Features

But not all social welfare policies and programs are so supported by majoritarian politics. Here is a little thought experiment: Try imagining federal policymakers in both parties, as they head into a presidential election season, fighting with each other for recognition by voters as having led the charge to "end Social Security as we know it" or "end Medicare as we know it." That's impossible to imagine. Yet, with respect to claiming credit for "ending welfare as we know it"—specifically, ending the Aid to Families with Dependent Children (AFDC) program, which provided cash assistance and other benefits to eligible low-income families with children—that is what happened during the 1996 elections. Republicans led by House Speaker Newt Gingrich (R-GA), and Democrats led by President Bill Clinton (who coined the phrase), each claimed credit for eliminating the program and replacing it with a "work-based welfare" program, Temporary Assistance to Needy Families (TANF).

Before describing the particular client politics that led to AFDC's demise and TANF's rise, it is first necessary to understand that social welfare policy in the United States, most especially as it relates to antipoverty programs designed primarily to benefit low-income children and families, is shaped by four factors that make it different from what exists in many other nations.

The first distinctive feature of the American welfare state involves who benefits. The way most Americans have seen it, who benefits has been a question of who *deserves* to benefit. Americans usually have insisted that public support be given only to those who cannot help themselves. Social welfare policy since the 1930s has been fundamentally shaped by how Americans and their elected leaders have separated the "deserving" from the "undeserving" poor.

But which poor people deserve government assistance? The answer has changed somewhat over time, but survey data suggest that several groups are currently seen as deserving: the elderly, the blind/disabled, veterans, and children. In contrast, working-age adults, even if they have young children, are not seen as deserving of assistance—Americans consistently believe they should support themselves through hard work.[15] While Americans support doing more to help the poor, they want that support to be directed to those who are most deserving of it—if individuals are seen as deserving, Americans typically support welfare benefits for those individuals.[16] Over time, American welfare policy has directed a larger and larger share of funds toward those groups seen as most deserving, and a shrinking share to those considered less so.[17]

Thus Americans base antipoverty policy on the concept of "help for the deserving poor" rather than "redistribution to produce fair shares."[18] This reflects the distinctive American political culture we discussed in Chapter 4, which emphasizes values like self-reliance and hard work. Further, consistent with this view, Americans typically favor noncash welfare benefits, even to the deserving poor. Rather than giving people cash assistance, Americans prefer that people be given services like education, job training, or health care.

That most Americans have thought this way may make us forget there are other ways of thinking about government assistance. The major alternative view is to ask not who deserves help but what each person's "fair share" of the national income is. Seen this way, the role of government is to take money from those who have a lot and give it to those who have only a little, until each person has, if not the same amount, then at least a fair share. In some nations—Sweden is an example—government policy is aimed at redistributing income from better-off to not-so-well-off persons, without regard to who "deserves" the money.

If Americans believed success at work was a matter of luck rather than effort or was dictated by forces over which they had no control, they might support a different approach, one closer to that followed in many European democracies. The very title of the 1996 federal law that abolished AFDC reflects Americans' rejection of this redistributionist approach, however. It was named "The Personal Responsibility and Work Opportunity Reconciliation Act," reflecting instead our belief in hard work and individual responsibility.

The second striking fact about American social welfare policy is how late in our history it arrived (at least at the national level) compared with other nations. By 1935, when Congress passed the Social Security Act, at least 22 European nations already had similar programs, as did Australia and Japan.[19] Germany was the first to create a nationwide social security program when it developed sickness and maternity insurance in 1883. Six years later, it added old-age insurance, and then in 1927, it enacted unemployment insurance.

The United Kingdom offers perhaps the clearest contrast with the United States. In 1908, a national system of old-age pensions was set up, followed three years later by a plan for nationwide health and unemployment insurance.[20] The United Kingdom had a parliamentary regime in which a political party with liberal sentiments and a large majority had come to power. With authority concentrated in the hands of the prime minister and his cabinet, there was virtually no obstacle to instituting measures, such as welfare programs, that commended themselves to party leaders on grounds of either principle or party advantage. Furthermore, the British Labour party was then beginning to emerge. Though the party was still small (it had only 30 seats in Parliament in 1908), its leaders included people who had been influential in formulating social welfare programs that the leaders of the dominant Liberal party backed. And once these programs were approved, they were in almost all cases nationally run: there were no state governments to which authority had to be delegated or whose different experiences had to be accommodated.

Moreover, the British in 1908 were beginning to think in terms of social classes, to accept the notion of an activist government, and to make welfare the central political issue. Americans at that time also had an activist leader, Theodore Roosevelt; there was a progressive movement; and labor was well along in its organizing drives. But the issues were defined differently in the United States. Progressives, or at least most of them, emphasized the reform of the political process—by eliminating corruption, by weakening the parties, and by improving the civil service—and attacked bigness by breaking up industrial trusts.

Though some progressives favored the creation of a welfare state, they were a distinct minority. They had few allies in organized labor (which was skeptical of public welfare programs) and could not overcome the general distrust of big government and the strong preference for leaving matters of welfare in state hands. In sum, what ordinary politics brought to England in 1908–1911, only the crisis politics of 1935 would bring to the United States. But once started, the programs grew. By 1983, almost one-third of all Americans received benefits from one or more social welfare programs, and today some argue that the fraction is even larger.

The third factor involves the degree to which federalism has shaped national social welfare policy. Since the Constitution was silent on whether Congress had the power to spend money on welfare and since powers not delegated to Congress were reserved to the states, it was not until the constitutional reinterpretation of the 1930s (see Chapter 16) that it became clear that the federal government could do anything in the area of social policy. At the same time, federalism meant that any state so inclined could experiment with welfare programs. Between 1923 and 1933, 30 states enacted some form of an old-age pension. By 1935 all but two states had adopted a "mother's pension"—a program whereby a widow with children was given financial assistance, provided that she was a "fit mother" who ran a "suitable home." The poor were given small doles by local governments, helped by private charities, or placed in almshouses. Only one state, Wisconsin, had an unemployment insurance program.

Politically the state programs had a double-edged effect: they provided opponents of a federal welfare system with an argument (the states were already providing welfare assistance), but they also supplied a lobby for federal financial assistance (state authorities would campaign for national legislation to help them out). Some were later to say that the states were the laboratories for experimentation in welfare policy. When the federal government entered the field in 1935, it did so in part by spending money through the states, thereby encouraging the formation in the states of a strong welfare bureaucracy whose later claims would be difficult to ignore.

A fourth distinctive feature of social welfare policy in the United States is that much of it is administered via grants and contracts to nongovernmental institutions, both for-profit firms and nonprofit organizations. For example, many large national nonprofit organizations—such as Big Brothers Big Sisters of America, Youth Build,

charitable choice *Name given to four federal laws passed in the late 1990s specifying the conditions under which nonprofit religious organizations could compete to administer certain social service delivery and welfare programs.*

the Jewish Federation, and Catholic Charities—have received large federal grants and long participated in the administration of federal social welfare programs.

The 1996 law that abolished the AFDC program contained a provision (Section 104) directing that religious nonprofit organizations, including small community-based groups, be permitted to compete for government grants with which to administer federal welfare-to-work and related policies. The provision, known as **charitable choice**, enjoyed bipartisan support. The provision prohibited religious organizations from using any public funds for proselytizing, religious instruction, or worship services, but it also prohibited the government from requiring them to remove religious art or iconography from buildings where social service delivery programs funded in whole or in part by Washington might be administered.

In 2001, President Bush created a White House "faith-based" office with centers in five cabinet agencies. In 2009, President Obama renamed but retained that White House office and expanded its centers to all federal cabinet agencies as well as the Corporation for National and Community Services (the agency responsible for most national service programs funded by Washington). The Trump White House renamed the office again and focused efforts on having staff in cabinet agencies oversee existing faith-based programs and services.

From AFDC to TANF: Client Politics

All four distinctive features of social welfare policy in the United States are evident in the story of what came to be called Aid to Families with Dependent Children (AFDC). The program began as part of the Social Security Act of 1935. It was scarcely noticed at the time. In response to the Great Depression, the federal government promised to provide aid to states that in many cases were already running programs to help poor children who lacked a father.

Because AFDC involved giving federal aid to existing state programs, it allowed the states to define what constituted "need," to set benefit levels, and to administer the program. Washington did, however, set (and, over the years, continued to increase) a number of rules governing how the program would work. Washington told the states how to calculate applicants' incomes and, after 1965, required the states to give Medicaid to AFDC recipients (a fact that we return to in the next section when we parse Medicaid's policy dynamics). The states had to establish mandatory job-training programs for many AFDC recipients and to provide child care programs for working parents receiving aid under AFDC. Washington also required that women on AFDC identify their children's fathers. In addition to the growing list of requirements, Washington created new programs for which AFDC recipients were eligible, such as food stamps, the Earned Income Tax Credit (a cash grant to poor parents who work), free school meals, various forms of housing assistance, and certain other benefits. But while all this was happening, public opinion moved against the AFDC program.

Kevork Djansezian/Getty Images News/Getty Images

Image 17.5 People rally against funding cuts for the Supplemental Nutrition Assistance Program.

By the time abolishing AFDC was being debated in Congress, opinion surveys found more than 70 percent of the public agreed that people "abuse the system by staying on too long," more than 60 percent agreed that the system "gives people benefits without requiring them to do work" and also permits people "to cheat and commit fraud to get welfare benefits," and about 60 percent agreed that the program encourages out-of-wedlock births.[21] The combination of souring public opinion, increasing federal regulations, and a growing roster of benefits produced a program that lost many who at one time supported it.

The states disliked having to conform to a growing list of federal regulations. The public disliked the program because over time it came to be viewed as weakening the family by encouraging out-of-wedlock births (since AFDC recipients received additional benefits for each new child). The public worried that AFDC recipients were working covertly on the side; the data proved that this was true of at least half of them in several large cities. AFDC recipients saw that the actual (inflation-adjusted) value of their AFDC checks was going down. Critics countered that if you added together all the benefits they were receiving (Food Stamps, Medicaid, housing assistance, etc.), benefit levels were actually going up. Politicians complained that healthy parents were living off AFDC instead of working.

The AFDC law was revised many times, including in 1988 (just eight years before AFDC was abolished). But the program was never revised in a way that satisfied all, or even most, of its critics. Though AFDC recipients were only a small fraction of all Americans, they had become a large political problem.

What made the political problem worse was that the composition of the people in the program had changed. In 1970, about half of the mothers on AFDC were there because their husbands had died or divorced them; only a quarter had never been married. By 1994, the situation had changed dramatically: Only about a quarter of mothers on AFDC were widowed or divorced, and over half had never been married at all. And though most women on AFDC for the first time got off it after just a few years, almost two-thirds of the women on AFDC at any given moment had been on it for eight years or more.

These facts, combined with the increased proportion of out-of-wedlock births in the country as a whole, made it virtually impossible to sustain political support for what had begun as a noncontroversial client program. AFDC was abolished in 1996. It was replaced by Temporary Assistance for Needy Families (TANF), a block grant program that set strict federal requirements about work and limited how long families can receive federally funded benefits.

Now, more than 20 years later, what are the effects of welfare reform? First, on the positive side, welfare rolls have decreased dramatically, from about 12.5 million in 1996 to about 3.1 million people in 2018.[22] Childhood poverty has experienced an especially sharp decline: 13.1 percent of children were living in poverty in 1996, but that figure fell to 7.8 percent by 2014. This happened because policymakers made a special effort to reduce childhood poverty rates, even beyond welfare reform, by creating programs for children's health insurance and strengthening free and reduced-price school lunch programs. Further, there was also some success at helping single mothers enter the workforce, though some of those gains have evaporated in recent years.[23]

Welfare reform had more mixed effects on other areas. While childhood poverty has declined sharply, overall poverty may or may not have declined; the debate largely centers on the correct measure of poverty, and how to calculate the value of different types of aid.[24] And welfare reform has at least one notable failure: its inability to fight deep poverty. One study suggests that the number of families living in deep poverty, defined as living on less than $2 per day, nearly doubled from 1996 to 2011.[25] Scholars continue to debate overall whether the program was a success; your answer to that question depends on how you view the weight one should attach to these different outcomes.

Medicaid: Client and Majoritarian

At first glance, Medicaid may seem closer to the old AFDC program and the present TANF program than it does to Social Security and Medicare. As explained earlier in this chapter, in 1965, Medicaid was enacted into law in the 11th hour of Medicare's approval so that at least some low-income persons who were not Medicare-eligible senior citizens might receive some health care coverage. Indeed, the program was initially considered so insignificant that, when it was passed, *The New York Times* story about the bill did not even mention Medicaid, it focused only on Medicare, which the *Times*—like most political observers—thought was the only important program.[26]

But today, no one would argue that Medicaid is irrelevant. Medicaid is still a means-tested program that pays the medical expenses of persons receiving TANF payments, mainly TANF-eligible low-income adults and their dependent children. But that is not all it covers. Medicaid also pays medical expenses of persons receiving Social Security benefits, including senior citizens that have spent down their life savings and require long-term medical care, people with permanent or total disabilities, and others, including certain *Medicare* enrollees. Medicaid now covers about 74 million Americans—almost one in five Americans receives some benefits from the program.

It is true that about two-thirds of all Medicaid beneficiaries are low-income children plus nondisabled low-income adults; the other third are nonelderly disabled adults plus low-income or disabled senior citizens. But it is also true that about two-thirds of Medicaid dollars are spent on the one-third of the Medicaid beneficiaries who are elderly or disabled. The other third or so of Medicaid dollars are spent on the roughly two-thirds of the Medicaid beneficiaries who are TANF-eligible nondisabled, low-income adults or low-income children. The average annual per capita Medicaid expenditure for disabled and elderly beneficiaries has been more than four times the average annual per capita Medicaid expenditure for nondisabled adult or low-income child beneficiaries.

In the mid-1990s, when AFDC was being dismantled, more than five times as much public money was being spent on Medicaid as was being spent on AFDC, and a majority of Medicaid beneficiaries were also AFDC beneficiaries. But Medicaid has had, and continues to have, a beneficiary population that AFDC did not, namely, senior citizens and disabled persons. Today, just as it was some two decades ago when Congress was about the business of ending AFDC, Medicaid is the main source of public funding for long-term care, accounting for more than half of all government spending on nursing homes, intermediate-care facilities, and medical home-care services. In Congress as well as in state legislatures, Medicaid has had political support from interest groups beyond those advocating directly for its various beneficiaries, namely, the for-profit firms and nonprofit organizations that receive billions of dollars each year to supply nursing-home care and other services.

Thus it is that the policy dynamics surrounding Medicaid mix client politics with majoritarian politics. Over the past few decades, most proposals to "cut Medicaid" have actually been proposals to trim program benefits for the program's TANF-eligible non-disabled adult populations. For example, in 2018, the Trump administration allowed states to impose work requirements for able-bodied adults to receive Medicaid.[27] Almost nobody thinks of poor senior citizens, poor children, or disabled persons as "undeserving." Since the late 1990s, while Medicaid benefits for TANF-eligible adults have remained flat or been reduced in some states, Medicaid benefits for the program's youngest and oldest beneficiaries, as well for its disabled beneficiaries, have remained stable or grown just about everywhere, including through related policies and programs such as the State Children's Health Insurance Program, known as SCHIP.

In sum, because of its client politics components, Medicaid is not as politically sacrosanct as either Social Security or Medicare; but, because of its majoritarian politics components, Medicaid, unlike AFDC, has survived every major push for program-wide cuts while preserving most benefits for TANF-eligible nondisabled adults and expanding benefits for low-income children. And there is not now nor has there ever been any politically significant constituency for "ending Medicaid as we know it."

17-2 Business Regulation Policy

Efforts by government to regulate business not only illustrate the four kinds of policymaking politics but also shed light on a facet of political life that many people think is fundamental to understanding who governs and to what ends—namely, the relationship between wealth and power.

To some observers, the very existence of large corporations is a threat to popular rule. Economic power will dominate political power, they believe, for one or more of three reasons: first, because wealth can be used to buy influence; second, because politicians and business leaders have similar class backgrounds and thus similar beliefs about public policy; and third, because elected officials must defer to the preferences of business so as to induce corporations to keep the economy healthy and growing. Karl Marx, of course, proposed the most sweeping version of the view that economics controls politics; for him, the state in a capitalist society was nothing more than the executive committee of the propertied classes.[28] But there are other non-Marxist or neo-Marxist versions of the same concern.[29]

To other observers, politics, far from being subordinate to economic power, is a threat to the very existence of a market economy and the values—economic growth, private property, personal freedom—that they believe such an economy protects. In this view, politicians will find it in their interest, in their struggle for votes, to take the side of the nonbusiness majority against that of the business minority. The heads of large corporations, few in number but great in wealth, fear that they will be portrayed as a sinister elite on whom politicians can blame war, inflation, unemployment, and pollution. Defenders of business worry that corporations will be taxed excessively to pay for social programs that in turn will produce more votes for politicians. Just as bad, in this view, is the tendency of universities (on which corporations must rely for technical experts) to inculcate antibusiness values in their students.[30]

As the theory of the policymaking process presented in this book should suggest, neither of these two extreme views of business–government relations is entirely correct. These relations depend on many things, including the *kind* of business regulation policy proposed. Instead of clenching our fists and shouting pro-business or anti-business slogans at each other, we should be able, after applying this theory to the available facts, to make more careful and exact statements of the following sort: "If certain conditions exist, then business regulation policy will take certain forms."

Antitrust Laws: Majoritarian Politics

Not all efforts to regulate business pit one group against another. From time to time, laws are passed that reflect the views of a majority of voters and that neither impose its will on a hostile business community nor accede to the desires of a privileged industry.

Much of the antitrust legislation passed in this country—including the Sherman Act (1890), parts of the Federal Trade Commission Act (1914), and the Clayton Act (1914)—has been the result of majoritarian politics. Toward the end of the 19th century there arose a broadly based criticism of business monopolies (then called trusts) and, to a lesser extent, of large corporations, whether or not they monopolized trade. The Grange, an organization of farmers, was especially outspoken in its criticism, and popular opinion generally—insofar as we can know it in an era without pollsters—seems to have been indignant about trusts and in favor of "trust-busting." Newspaper editorials and magazine articles frequently dwelt on the problem.[31]

But though antitrust feeling was strong, it was also relatively unfocused: No single industry was the special target of this criticism (the oil industry, and especially the Standard Oil Company, came as close as any), and no specific regulation was proposed. In fact, no general agreement existed about how to define the problem: for some it was monopoly, for others sheer bigness, and for still others the legal basis of the modern corporation. The bill proposed by Senator John Sherman did not clarify matters much: While it made it a crime to "restrain" or "monopolize" trade, it did not define these terms, nor did it create any new regulatory agency charged with enforcing the law.[32]

No doubt some large corporations worried about what all this would mean for them, but few felt sufficiently threatened to try very hard to defeat the bill. It passed the Senate by a voice vote and the House by a vote of 242 to 0.

Laws do not execute themselves, and vague laws are especially likely to lie dormant unless political leaders work hard at bringing them to life. For the first decade or so after 1890, only one or two antitrust cases a year were filed in the courts. In 1904, President Theodore Roosevelt persuaded Congress to provide enough money to hire five full-time lawyers, and soon the number of prosecutions increased to about seven a year. Then, in 1938, President Franklin Roosevelt appointed as head of the Antitrust Division of the Justice Department a vigorous lawyer named Thurman Arnold, who began bringing an average of 50 cases a year.[33] Today, more than 400 lawyers in the division sift through complaints alleging monopolistic or other unfair business practices. Though controversy exists over the kinds of cases that should be brought, neither politicians nor business leaders make any serious effort to abandon the commitment to a firm antitrust policy, the strongest such policy found in any industrial nation.

The antitrust laws were strengthened in 1914 by bills that created the Federal Trade Commission and made (via the Clayton Act) certain specific practices, such as price discrimination, illegal. As with the earlier Sherman Act, the advocates of these measures had a variety of motives. Some proponents favored these laws because they would presumably help consumers (by preventing unfair business practices); other proponents supported them because they might help business (by protecting firms against certain tactics that competitors might use).

President Woodrow Wilson endorsed both of these bills and helped create a broad coalition on behalf of the legislation; the Federal Trade Commission Act and the Clayton Act passed Congress by lopsided majorities.[34]

As with the Sherman Act, controversy has continued about how these laws should be administered. But this controversy, like the debate over the initial passage of the laws, has not been dominated by interest groups.[35] The reason for the relative absence of interest-group activity is that these laws do not divide society into permanent and identifiable blocs of proponents and opponents. Any given business firm can be either helped or hurt by the enforcement of the antitrust laws. One year, the XYZ Widget Company might be sued by the government to prevent it from unfairly advertising its widgets, and the next year the same XYZ Company might ask the government to prosecute its competitor for trying to drive XYZ out of business by selling widgets at prices below cost.

The amount of money the federal government devotes to antitrust enforcement and the direction those enforcement efforts take are determined more by the political ideology and personal convictions of the administration in power, as well as the specifics of the particular deal, than by interest-group pressures. For example, the Reagan administration chose not to break up IBM, but it did break up American Telephone and Telegraph (AT&T), making the local phone companies independent of AT&T and forcing AT&T to compete with other long-distance service providers. More recently, President Obama pursued a more vigorous anti-trust enforcement policy, blocking proposed mergers between Comcast and Time Warner, Sprint and T-Mobile, as well as Pfizer and Allegran.[36] Given some of President Trump's populist rhetoric during the 2016 campaign, some thought that he might pursue a similar anti-trust enforcement strategy. His administration, however, has supported some mergers, while opposing others. The Trump administration's Department of Justice opposed the AT&T–Time Warner merger (though it lost its lawsuit to block this merger),[37] and announced that it would review previous technology mergers to search for potential antitrust violations.[38] That said, the Trump administration did allow other mergers, such as when Aetna bought CVS, and when Sprint and T-Mobile merged.[39]

Labor and Occupational Health and Safety: Interest-Group Politics

Organized interest groups are very powerful, however, when the regulatory policies confer benefits on a particular group and costs on another, equally distinct group.

In 1935, labor unions sought government protection for their right to organize, to bargain collectively with industry, and to compel workers in unionized industries to join the unions. Business firms opposed these plans. The struggle was fought out in Congress, where the unions won. The Wagner Act, passed that year, created the National Labor Relations Board (NLRB) to regulate the conduct of union-organizing drives and to hear complaints of unfair labor practices brought by workers against management.

But the struggle was far from over. In 1947, management sought to reverse some of the gains won by unions by pressing for a law (the Taft-Hartley Act) that would make illegal certain union practices (such as the closed shop and secondary boycotts) and would authorize the president to obtain a court order blocking for up to 80 days any strike that imperiled "national health or safety." Business won.

Business and labor fought round three in 1959 over a bill (the Landrum-Griffin Act) intended to prevent corruption in unions, to change the way in which organizing drives were carried out, and to prohibit certain kinds of strikes and picketing. Business won.

In each of these cases, the struggle was highly publicized. The winners and losers were determined by the partisan composition of Congress (Republicans and Southern Democrats tended to support business, Northern Democrats to support labor) and by the existence of economic conditions (a depression in 1935, revelations of labor racketeering in 1959) that affected public opinion on the issue.

But the interest-group struggle did not end with the passage of the laws; it continued throughout their administration. The NLRB, comprising five members appointed by the president, had to adjudicate countless disputes between labor and management over the interpretation of these laws. The losing party often appealed the NLRB decision to the courts, where the issue was fought out again. Moreover, each president has sought to tilt the NLRB in one direction or another by means of whom he appoints to it. Democratic presidents favor labor and thus tend to appoint pro-union board members; Republican presidents favor business and thus tend to appoint pro-management members. Because NLRB members serve five-year terms, a new president cannot immediately appoint all of the board's members; thus the board is often split between two factions.

But one vote can make a difference. When President Obama appointed a Democrat to the NLRB, it acquired a Democratic majority. The Board then issued an order that would prevent Boeing from building its 787 aircraft in South Carolina, a state with a "right to work" law that prevents workers from being required to join a union. The issue was, of course, appealed. In December 2011, the NLRB rescinded the order after the Machinists Union ratified a new contract with Boeing.

A similar pattern of interest-group influence is revealed by the history of the Occupational Safety and Health Act, passed in 1970. Labor unions wanted a strict bill with tough standards set by a single administrator; business organizations wanted a more flexible bill with standards set by a commission that would include some business representatives. After a long struggle, labor prevailed, and the Occupational Safety and Health Administration (OSHA), headed by a single administrator, was set up inside the Department of Labor.

Image 17.6 Construction workers and laborers rally for safer workplace conditions in New York City in early 2017.

As with the NLRB, conflict did not end with the passage of the law, and OSHA decisions were frequently appealed to the courts. The politics swirling about OSHA were all the more contentious because of the vast mandate of the agency; it is supposed to determine the safe limits for worker exposure to hundreds of chemicals and to inspect tens of thousands of workplaces to see whether they should be cited for violating any standards.

Agriculture Subsidies: Client Politics

Many people suppose that when government sets out to regulate business, the firms that are supposed to be regulated will in fact "capture" the agency that is supposed to do the regulating. But as we have already seen, certain kinds of policies—those that give rise to majoritarian and interest-group politics—do not usually lead to capture because the agency either faces no well-organized, enduring opponent (as with majoritarian politics) or is caught in a crossfire of competing forces (as with interest-group politics).

But when a policy confers a benefit on one group at the expense of many other people, client politics arises, and so agency "capture" is likely. More precisely, nothing needs to be captured at all, since the agency will have been created from the outset to serve the interests of the favored group. We sometimes think regulations are always resisted. But a regulation need not be a burden; it can be a great benefit.

How this works can be seen close to home. State and city laws regulate the practice of law and medicine as well as a host of other occupations—barbers, beauticians, plumbers, dry cleaners, taxi drivers, and undertakers. These regulations are sometimes designed and always defended as ways of preventing fraud, malpractice, and safety hazards. But they also have the effect of restricting entry into the regulated occupation, thereby enabling its members to charge higher prices than they otherwise might.[40] Ordinarily, citizens do not object to this, in part because they believe, rightly or wrongly, that the regulations in fact protect them, and in part because the higher prices are spread over so many customers as to be unnoticed.

Much the same thing can be found at the national level. In the early 1930s, the American dairy industry was suffering from rapidly declining prices for milk. As the farmers' incomes fell, many could no longer pay their bills and were forced out of business. Congress responded with the Agricultural Adjustment Act, which authorized an agency of the Department of Agriculture to regulate the milk industry. This agency, the Dairy Division of the Agricultural Marketing Service, would issue "market orders" that had the effect of preventing price competition among dairy farmers and thus kept the price of milk up. If this guaranteed minimum price leads to the production of more milk than people want to drink, then another part of the Agriculture Department—the Commodity Credit Corporation—stands ready to buy up the surplus with tax dollars.[41]

Consumers wind up paying more for milk than they otherwise would, but they have no way of knowing the difference between the regulated and unregulated prices of milk.[42] The same is true of other agricultural goods that have similar programs behind them. Such programs are very costly—by one estimate, all farm subsidies (not just those for milk) cost nearly $20 billion per year.[43] But because the cost is spread across so many consumers, no one has much incentive to organize against them.

From time to time, various officials attempt to change the regulations that benefit a client group. But they must confront some sobering political facts. Farmers are found scattered through scores of congressional districts, and they play key roles in many states crucial to presidential elections, such as Iowa, Wisconsin, Pennsylvania, and Ohio. While Congress has reformed these programs over time, they have not been completely repealed.

Client politics has become harder to practice in this country unless a group is widely thought to be a "deserving" client. Dairy farmers, sugar producers, and tobacco growers struggle (sometimes successfully, sometimes unsuccessfully) to keep their benefits, but the struggle relies on "insider politics"—that is, on dealing with key Washington decision makers and not on building widespread public support. By contrast, when a devastating flood, tornado, earthquake, or hurricane strikes a community, the victims are thought to be eminently deserving of help. After all, people say, it was not their fault that their homes were destroyed. (In some cases, they had built homes in areas they knew were at high risk for hurricanes or floods.) They receive client benefits.

Bob Mahoney/The Image Works

Image 17.7 Dairy farmers get government subsidies for their milk production.

Although client politics for "special interests" seems to be on the decline, that is true mostly for programs that actually send certain groups money. Pietro Nivola reminds us of a different form of client politics: using regulations instead of cash to help groups. For example, regulations encourage the use of ethanol (a kind of alcohol made from corn) in gasoline, which benefits corn farmers and ethanol manufacturers. Clients that might not be thought legitimate increasingly get their way by means of regulations rather than subsidies.[44]

But regulation that starts out by trying to serve a client can end up hurting it. Radio broadcasters supported the creation of the Federal Communications Commission (FCC), which would, broadcasters and telephone companies thought, bring order and stability to their industries. It did. But then it started doing a bit more than the industries had hoped for. It began reviewing efforts by companies to merge. When one telephone company tried to merge with another, the FCC said it would have to review the consolidation even though the law did not give it the power to do so. After long (and secret) negotiations, it extracted concessions from the companies as a condition of their merger. Because no law required such concessions, the firms accepted them "voluntarily." But if they had not agreed, they would have been in deep trouble with the FCC in the future.

Regulatory agencies created to help clients can become burdens to those clients when the laws the agencies enforce are sufficiently vague so as to provide freedom of action by the people who run them. For a long time, most of these laws were hopelessly vague. The FCC, for example, was told to award licenses as "the public interest, convenience, and necessity" required. In time, such language can give an agency powers that are wide and undefined.

Consumer and Environmental Protection: Entrepreneurial Politics

During the 1960s and 1970s some two dozen consumer and environmental protection laws were passed, including laws that regulated the automobile industry, oil companies, toy manufacturers, poultry producers, the chemical industry, and pharmaceutical companies.[45]

When measures such as these become law, it is often because a policy entrepreneur has dramatized an issue, galvanized public opinion, and mobilized congressional support. Sometimes that entrepreneur is in the government (a senator or an outspoken bureaucrat); sometimes that entrepreneur is a private person (one of the best known is Ralph Nader). The motives of such entrepreneurs can be either self-serving or public-spirited; the policies they embrace may be either good or bad. (Just because someone succeeds in regulating business does not mean that the public will necessarily benefit; by the same token, just because business claims that a new regulation will be excessively costly does not mean that business will in fact have to pay those costs.)

An early example of a policy entrepreneur inside the government was Dr. Harvey Wiley, a chemist in the Department of Agriculture, who actively campaigned for what was to become the Pure Food and Drug Act of 1906. Later, Senator Estes Kefauver held hearings that built support for the 1962 drug laws (and incidentally for his presidential bid), and Senator Edmund Muskie called attention to the need for air and water pollution control legislation (and incidentally to his own 1972 presidential aspirations).

When policy entrepreneurs are outside the government, they will need a sympathetic ear within it. Occasionally, the policy needs of the entrepreneur and the political needs of an elected official coincide. When Ralph Nader was walking the corridors of the Capitol looking for someone interested in auto safety, he found Senators Abraham Ribicoff and Warren Magnuson, who themselves were looking for an issue with which they could be identified.

The task of the policy entrepreneur is made easier when a crisis or scandal focuses public attention on a problem. Upton Sinclair's book *The Jungle*[46] dramatized the frightful conditions in meat-packing plants at the turn of the century and helped pave the way for the Meat Inspection Act of 1906. The stock market collapse of 1929 helped develop support for the Securities and Exchange Act. When some people who had taken a patent medicine (elixir of sulfanilamide) died as a result, the passage of the 1938 drug laws became easier. Oil spilled on the beaches of Santa Barbara, California, drew attention to problems addressed by the Water Quality Improvement Act of 1970.

The dramatic event need not be an actual crisis; in some cases, a political scandal will do. Highway fatalities were not a matter of great concern to most citizens when Congress began considering an auto safety act in 1965–1966, but support for the bill grew when it was revealed that General Motors had hired a private detective who made a clumsy effort to collect (or manufacture) gossip harmful to Ralph Nader, whose 1965 book, *Unsafe at Any Speed: The Designed-In Dangers of the American Automobile*,[47] had criticized the safety of certain GM cars.

In some cases, no dramatic event at all is required for entrepreneurial politics to succeed. Most of the air and water pollution control bills were passed despite the absence of any environmental catastrophe.[48] Support for such measures was developed by holding carefully planned committee hearings that were closely followed

Policy Dynamics: Inside/Outside the Box | The First Step Act: Bipartisan Entrepreneurial Politics

As we discussed in Chapter 13, we often think that partisanship rules the contemporary Congress. On some issues—like the Tax Cut and Jobs Act or the Affordable Care Act—that is correct. But on other pieces of legislation, it does not, and a broad bipartisan coalition carries the day. One such example is the 2018 First Step Act, which made two significant changes to federal criminal justice policy. First, the law shortens prison sentences, by, for example, allowing judges to waive mandatory minimum sentences for some offenses, such as drug crimes. Second, it helps inmates reenter society better prepared to succeed by giving them incentives to enroll in vocational and rehabilitative programs.

The bill was supported by a variety of groups from across the ideological spectrum and had over 30 co-sponsors from both parties, including liberal Democrats like Dick Durbin of Illinois and conservative Republicans like Mike Lee of Utah.

This type of criminal justice reform is best thought of as entrepreneurial politics. The costs of this type of reform would be concentrated among those who benefit from more prisoners, such as private prison firms, prison guards (and their unions), and firms that use prison labor. The benefits would flow to two groups. First, there are prisoners themselves, but because they cannot vote (except in a few states), they are not the main politically relevant group. Instead, the main beneficiary of such support would be society as a whole, given lower costs (since incarceration in incredibly expensive) and lower levels of recidivism (given more vocational and rehabilitative programming).

In this sort of concentrated cost, dispersed benefits scenario, a policy entrepreneur is needed. This was especially true here, because President Trump had campaigned on a "tough on crime" policy in 2016, and initially did not seem likely to support this bill or similar reforms. Two broad sets of entrepreneurs were vital to the success of this legislation. First, some conservatives had grown increasingly skeptical of the harsh sentencing policies of the 1990s, and had begun to argue that prisons were another example of government growth that needed to be restrained. Groups like the Charles Koch Foundation, and Republican politicians like former Texas governor Rick Perry, worked together to pass legislation in the states that reduced harsh sentences and still kept crime rates low. Given these successes, many Republicans argued that comparable federal legislation was needed. Such Republican support was essential given that Republicans controlled both chambers of Congress in 2018 when the bill was working its way through the legislative process (while Democrats won control of the House in the 2018 elections, they would not assume control until the new Congress convened in January 2019).

But that was not all it took. For the bill to become law, Jared Kushner, the president's son-in-law and advisor, also needed to become involved. Prison reform is personal for Kushner, as his father was incarcerated for more than a year in federal prison for witness tampering, tax evasion, and making illegal campaign contributions. Not only did Kushner work to build the legislative coalition, he also worked to persuade President Trump to support the bill. He even had celebrities Kanye West and Kim Kardashian West, both of whom are prison reform advocates, make the case to the president. In the end, Kushner, and the broad bipartisan coalition, convinced the president, who signed the bill into law in December 2018.

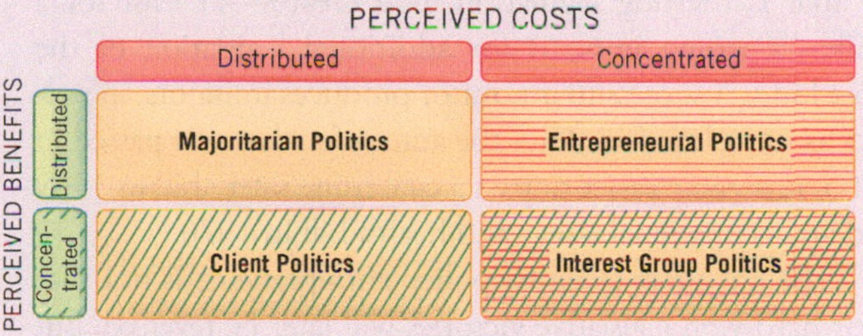

Source: John Wagner, "Trump Signs Bipartisan Criminal Justice Bill Amid Partisan Rancor over Stopgap Spending Measure," *The Washington Post*, 21 December 2018; German Lopez, "The First Step Act, Explained," Vox, 5 February 2019; David Dagan and Steve Teles, *Prison Break: Why Conservatives Turned Against Mass Incarceration* (New York: Oxford University Press, 2016).

by the media. For example, by drawing attention to the profits of the pharmaceutical companies, Senator Kefauver was able to convince many people that these firms were insensitive to public needs. By drawing on information made available to him by environmentalists, Senator Muskie was able to capitalize on and help further a growing perception in the country during the early 1970s that nature was in danger.

Because political resistance must be overcome without the aid of a powerful economic interest group, policy entrepreneurs seeking to regulate an industry often adopt a moralistic tone, portraying their opponents as devils, viewing their allies with suspicion, and fiercely resisting compromises. When Senator Muskie was drafting an air pollution bill, Ralph Nader issued a highly publicized report *attacking* Muskie, his nominal ally, for not being tough enough. This strategy forced

Bettmann/Getty Images

AP Images

Images 17.8 and 17.9 Entrepreneurial politics: Upton Sinclair's book *The Jungle*, published in 1906, shocked readers with its description of conditions in the meat-packing industry and helped bring about passage of the Meat Inspection Act of 1906.

Muskie—who wanted acclaim, not criticism, for his efforts—to revise the bill so that it imposed even more stringent standards.[49] Other allies of Nader, such as Dr. William Haddon, Jr., and Joan Claybrook, got the same treatment when they later became administrators of the National Highway Traffic Safety Administration. They came under attack not only from the auto industry, for designing rules that the companies thought were too strict, but also from Nader, for devising rules that he thought were not strict enough.

Once a policy entrepreneur manages to defeat an industry that is resisting regulation, that creates—at least for a while—a strong impetus for additional legislation of the same kind. A successful innovator produces imitators, in politics as in rock music. After the auto safety law was passed in 1966, it became easier to pass a coal mine safety bill in 1969 and an occupational safety and health bill in 1970.

The great risk faced by policy entrepreneurs is not that their hard-won legislative victories will later be reversed, but that the agency created to do the regulating will be captured by the industry it is supposed to regulate. The Food and Drug Administration (FDA), which regulates the pharmaceutical industry, has during much of its history fallen victim to precisely this kind of capture. Once the enthusiasm of its founders had waned and public attention had turned elsewhere, the FDA seemed to develop a cozy and rather uncritical attitude toward the drug companies. (In 1958, the head of the Pharmaceutical Manufacturers' Association received an award from the FDA.)[50] In the mid-1960s, under the spur of renewed congressional and White House attention, the agency was revitalized. During the Reagan administration, and later during the Trump administration, environmentalists worried that the leadership of the Environmental Protection Agency had been turned over to persons who were unduly sympathetic to polluters.

The consumer and environmental protection agencies may not, however, be as vulnerable to capture as some critics contend, for at least five reasons. First, these agencies often enforce laws that impose specific standards in accordance with strict timetables, and so they have relatively little discretion. (The Environmental Protection Agency, for example, is required by law to reduce certain pollutants by a fixed percentage within a stated number of years.) Second, the newer agencies, unlike the FDA, usually regulate many different industries and so do not confront a single, unified opponent. The Occupational Safety and Health Administration, for example, deals with virtually every industry. Third, the very existence of these agencies has helped strengthen the hand of the "public-interest" lobbies that initially demanded their creation. Fourth, these lobbies can now call upon many sympathetic allies in the media who will attack agencies thought to have a pro-business bias.

Finally, as explained in Chapter 16, it has become easier for groups to use the federal courts to put pressure on regulatory agencies. These groups do not have to be large or broadly representative of the public; all they need are the services of one or two able lawyers. If the Environmental Protection Agency (EPA) issues a rule disliked by a chemical company, the company would probably promptly sue the EPA; if it issues a ruling that pleases the company, the Environmental Defense Fund may sue.

17-3 Environmental Policy

Since 1963, more than three dozen major federal environmental laws have been enacted. When an offshore well spewed thousands of gallons of oil onto the beaches of Santa Barbara, California, at the very time (January 1969) when protest politics was in the air, it became difficult or impossible for the government or business firms to resist the demand that threats to our natural surroundings be curtailed. The emerging environmental movement created an occasion—Earth Day, first celebrated April 22, 1970—to commemorate its beginning.

The movement was hugely successful. In 1970, President Nixon created the EPA and Congress toughened the existing Clean Air Act and passed the Water Quality Improvement Act. Two years later, it passed laws designed to clean up the water; three years later, it adopted the Endangered Species Act. New laws were passed right into the 1990s. Existing environmental organizations grew in size, and new ones were formed. Public opinion rallied around environmental issues.

The Politics of Global Warming

Of course, as on virtually all other issues, public sentiments on environmental policy are not perfectly stable, and they have fluctuated over time. Still, overall, most Americans are now environmentalists first, including on the single most interesting and important environmental policy issue of our time: global warming, which is also known as climate change.

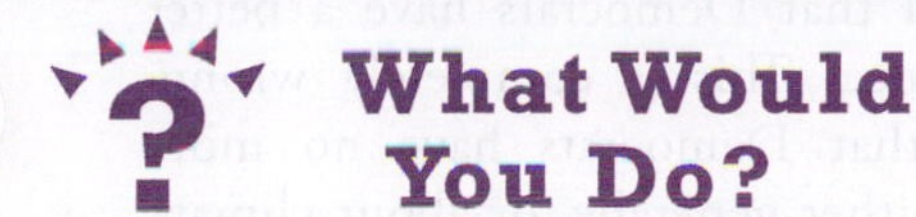

Will You Support Efforts to "Go Green"?

To: *President Brian Barr*
From: *Paul Anthony, Legislative Liaison*
Subject: *Climate Change and Energy Policy*

Scientists are nearly unanimous that to address the threat of climate change, America—and countries around the world—must curb their greenhouse gas emissions. One of the major causes of such emissions is electricity production: much of the U.S.'s energy production uses coal and natural gas, which produce greenhouse gases. To address this issue, some have proposed that the U.S. require that all electricity be produced by 100 percent renewable sources by 2050, such as solar, wind, and nuclear power.

To Consider:

The president will make a major announcement about efforts to address climate change in the 2021 State of the Union message next week.

Arguments for:

1. If the United States and other countries do not do more to reduce their greenhouse gas emissions, global temperatures will increase, causing wide-spread environmental destruction.
2. Such investment will generate new jobs in renewable energy technologies, and will also spur on new technological advances in this area.
3. Given that the United States makes up about five percent of the world's population but uses nearly a quarter of the world's energy, it should take the lead in using renewable resources to limit its carbon footprint.

Arguments against:

1. This will disproportionately hurt workers in areas where coal and natural gas are plentiful, including key swing states like Pennsylvania and Ohio. This makes the proposal very politically risky.
2. In Vermont, where they passed a similar bill, experts estimate that the cost will be at least $33 billion, and it would be much more expensive on a national scale.
3. To achieve the goal on this timeline, the U.S. would need to expand its use of nuclear power, which carries its own risks.

What Will You Decide? Enter **MindTap** to make your choice.

Your decision: ☐ Approve ☐ Oppose

Global warming occurs when gases, such as carbon dioxide, produced by people when they burn fossil fuels—wood, oil, or coal—get trapped in the atmosphere and cause the earth's temperature to rise. When the temperature goes up, bad things happen—floods on coastal areas as the polar ice caps melt, wilder weather as more storms are created, and tropical diseases spread throughout the world. Scientists are nearly unanimous that global warming is real, is caused by human activity, and poses significant risks to the planet and to mankind.[51]

In most countries around the world, there is broad agreement with this scientific consensus, but the United States is an exception. Here, we find sharp differences by party and ideology, as we see in Figure 17.3. Democrats, especially liberal Democrats, tend to believe climate change is occurring as a result of human activity, that climate scientist agree with this assessment and are trustworthy, and that climate change will have negative effects on the planet in the years to come. Republicans—especially conservative Republicans—are much less likely to believe this.

What explains this sharp polarization? Democrats often suggest that this is because Democrats are smarter than Republicans, and that Democrats have a better understanding of science. This is completely wrong. Studies have shown that Democrats have no more scientific knowledge (either generally, or about climate change specifically) than Republicans do.[52] For example, Democrats and Republicans are just about equally likely to know that greenhouse gases increase global temperatures.[53] This difference cannot be explained by how much the two parties know.

Instead, two other factors drive this effect. First, as we discussed in Chapter 12, the mass media reports on this issue in a way that downplays the scientific consensus on this topic. By wanting to include both the consensus scientific view and the opposing viewpoint, they make both seem equally likely, when in fact the consensus viewpoint is much more widely shared in the scientific community.[54] But even more important is the behavior of political elites. As we discussed in Chapter 7, when party leaders divide on an issue, so do their rank-and-file members.

Many Republican politicians have questioned global warming, while few prominent Democrats have, and

Figure 17.3 **Partisan/Ideological Divides on Global Warming**

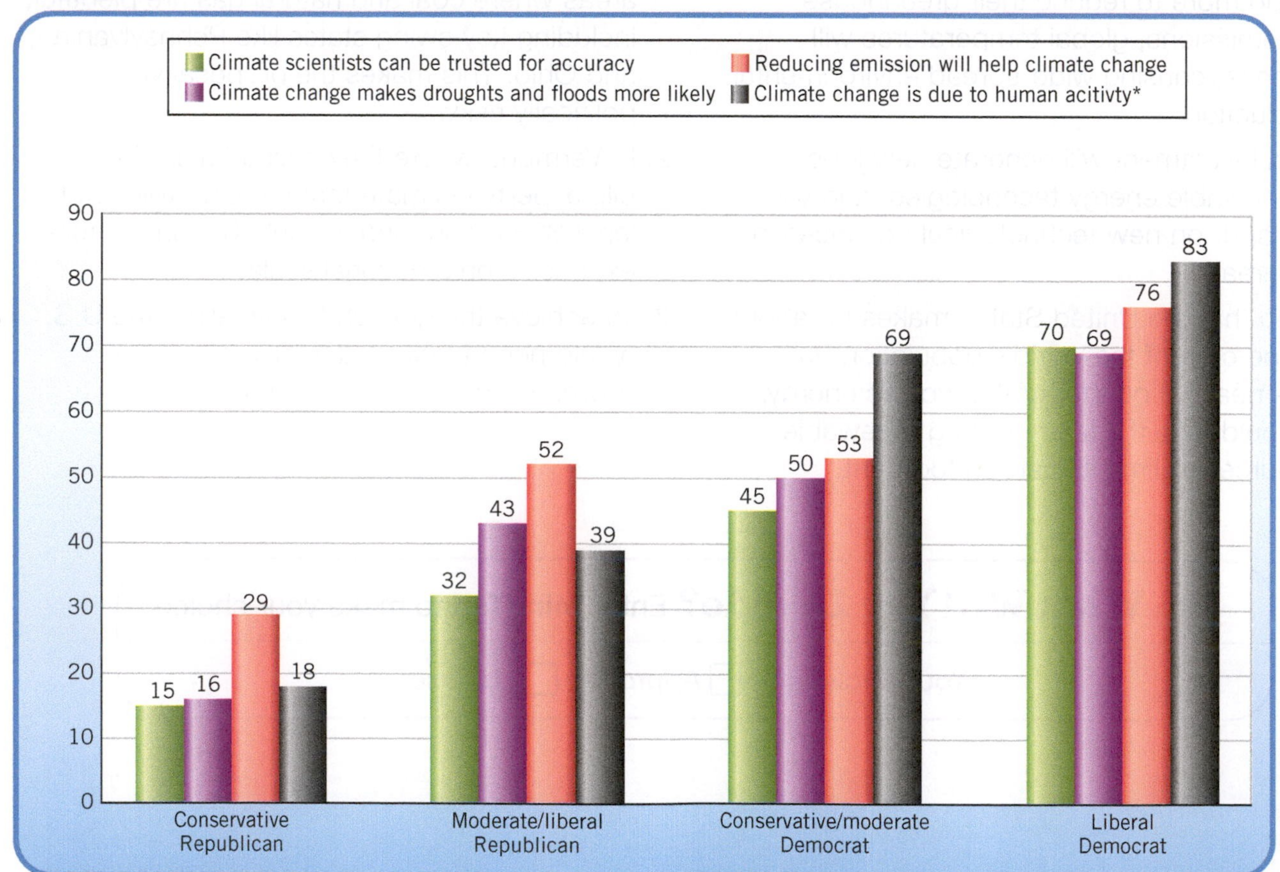

Source: Cary Funk and Brian Kennedy, "The Politics of Climate," Pew Research Center, 4 October 2016; *from Pew Research Center, "Majorities See Government Efforts to Protect the Environment as Insufficient," 14 May 2018.

Q **What do these differences across these different partisan and ideological groups suggest about the contours of future debates over global warming?**

the issue therefore has become politicized. For example, Oklahoma Republican Senator James Inhofe authored a book on global warming called *The Greatest Hoax*, and in a 2012 tweet President Trump called global warming a hoax invented by the Chinese.[55] By contrast, many Democratic elites have been strong supporters of climate change. For example, the leading candidates for the Democratic nomination in both 2016 and 2020 argued that we needed to take action to fight global warming. As a result of these elite divisions, we see similar divides among the public.[56]

Despite the partisan divide, a bipartisan group in Congress did try to pass legislation on this issue. For example, in 2009 the House of Representatives passed the American Clean Energy and Security Act, though the bill failed in the Senate. The bill represented perhaps the most ambitious legislative attempt to curb greenhouse gas emissions to date. It featured a "cap-and-trade" provision that would set maximum emissions of carbon dioxide for most large firms. The emissions allowed by these caps would decline as the years passed. If a firm produced less than the maximum emissions, it could sell part of its permit to another firm. The theory was that firms would take the least costly way to meet the standards: either reducing their emissions or, if that was too expensive, buying an additional permit from another firm. A similar system was used to cap emissions from sulfur dioxide that were linked to acid rain.

Despite the efforts of a small bipartisan group of senators, the bill did not come to a vote in their chamber. The White House was focused on passing health care reform, and the president's advisers were divided over how much the president should engage in the legislative negotiations about the environmental bill. Then the Senate majority leader, Democrat Harry Reid of Nevada, declared that immigration reform needed to pass before environmental reform—an effort to win support from immigration activists in his home state, where he faced a tough though ultimately successful reelection campaign. Finally, the disastrous oil spill in the Gulf of Mexico doomed any prospects of passing legislation that had promised, with White House support, an expansion of offshore oil drilling in return for capping carbon emissions.[57]

After his failure to make headway on one of his signature campaign issues, President Obama pursued environmental reforms through regulation instead of legislation. For example, the EPA tightened regulations on coal power plants, which produce large amounts of greenhouse gases. President Trump pledged to roll back many of these Obama era regulations, and many of his supporters hoped this would mark a new era of deregulation. The Trump administration was successful in some cases—for example, they successfully rolled back high-profile Obama regulations like the Clean Power Plant Rule, the Waters of the U.S. Rule, and Obama-era increases to automobile fuel efficiency standards. Indeed, according to an analysis by the *New York Times*, as of May 2020, President Trump had fully rolled back 64 such rules, and another 34 rollbacks are currently in progress.[58] But many others have been overturned or blocked by the courts, often due to failure to follow proper procedures, making the Trump administration's record more mixed than many initially expected it to be.[59]

U.S. leaders—including President Obama and Secretary of State John Kerry—also pushed for new global agreements, including the landmark 2015 Paris Climate Accords, which pledge nations around the world to slow the growth of greenhouse gas emissions. In November 2016, enough nations signed on to the Paris Climate Accords that the agreement went into effect. In 2019, however, President Trump officially began the process to withdraw the United States from this agreement.

Over the past four decades, the United States has constructed the most comprehensive and complicated body of environmental laws and regulations in the world. On such issues as endangered species (entrepreneurial), auto pollution (majoritarian), acid rain (interest group), and agricultural pesticides (client), environmental policies arose, persisted, and changed through one or more of the four types of politics we have been discussing; we outline some major environmental laws in Table 17.2 (see page 458).

Spencer Platt/Getty Images News/Getty Images

Image 17.10 U.S. Secretary of State John Kerry addresses world leaders while negotiating the Paris Climate Accords.

TABLE 17.2 | Major Environmental Laws

Smog	Clean Air Act (passed in 1970; amended in 1977 and 1990)
Stationary sources	EPA sets national air quality standards; states must develop plans to attain them. If the state plan is inadequate, EPA sets a federal plan. Local sources that emit more than a certain amount of pollutants must install pollution-control equipment.
Gasoline-powered vehicles	Between 1970 and 1990, pollution from cars was cut by between 60 and 80 percent. Between 1991 and 1998 another 30 percent reduction occurred. All states must have an auto pollution inspection system.
Cities	Classifies cities in terms of how severe their smog problem is and sets deadlines for meeting federal standards.
Water	Clean water acts of various years state that there is to be no discharge of wastewater into lakes and streams without a federal permit; to get a permit, cities and factories must meet federal discharge standards.
Toxic wastes	EPA is to clean up abandoned dump sites with money raised by a tax on the chemical and petroleum industries and from general revenues. (Many thousands of such sites exist.)
Environmental impact statements	Since 1969, any federal agency planning a project that would significantly affect the human environment must prepare in advance an environmental impact statement.
Acid rain	The Clean Air Act of 1990 requires a reduction of 10 million tons of sulfur dioxide (mostly from electric-generating plants that burn coal) by 1995. The biggest sources must acquire government allowances (which can be traded among firms) setting emission limits.

Environmental Policy in America: Three Distinctive Features

First, environmental policymaking in the United States is much more adversarial than it is in most European nations. In this country, bitter and lasting conflicts have ensued over the contents of the Clean Air Act. Minimum auto emissions standards are uniform across the nation, regardless of local conditions (states can set higher standards if they wish). Many rules for improving air and water quality have strict deadlines and require expensive technology. Hundreds of inspectors enforce these rules, and hundreds of lawyers bring countless lawsuits to support or challenge this enforcement. Government and business leaders have frequently denounced each other for being unreasonable or insensitive. So antagonistic are the interests involved in environmental policy that it took 13 years, from 1977 to 1990, to agree on a congressional revision of the Clean Air Act.

In the United Kingdom, by contrast, rules designed to reduce air pollution were written by government and business leaders acting cooperatively. The rules are neither rigid nor nationally uniform; they are flexible and allow plenty of exceptions to deal with local variations in business needs. Compliance with the rules depends mostly on voluntary action, not formal enforcement. Lawsuits are rare. You might think all this sweetness and light were the result of having meaningless rules, but not so. As David Vogel has shown, by the early 1980s the British government had implemented an impressive and effective array of regulations intended to improve the nation's air and water quality.[60]

Second, environmental policy here, as in so many other policy areas, depends heavily on the states. Though uniform national air quality standards exist, how those standards are achieved is left to the states (subject to certain federal controls). Though sewage treatment plants are in large measure paid for by Washington, they are designed, built, and operated by state and local governments.

Though the federal government decrees that radioactive waste must be properly disposed of somewhere, the states have a big voice in where that is. Federalism reinforces adversarial politics: one of the reasons environmental issues are so contentious in this country is that cities and states fight over what standards should apply where.

Third, the separation of powers guarantees that almost anybody who wants to wield influence over environmental policy will have an opportunity to do so. In the United Kingdom and in most European nations, the centralized, parliamentary form of government means that the opponents of a policy have less leverage. Here, environmental pressures are brought by interest groups; in Europe, where such groups have less influence, environmentalists form political parties, such as the Green party, so as to be represented in the legislature.

Image 17.11 An EPA environmental scientist surveys a Superfund site in Houston, Texas, where bacteria are used to clean up toxic industrial waste.

The distinctive features of environmental policy in America are evident in the policy dynamics history of each of four different issues: endangered species, pollution from automobiles, acid rain, and agricultural pesticides.

Endangered Species: Entrepreneurial Politics

Passed in 1973, the Endangered Species Act (ESA) forbids buying or selling a bird, fish, animal, or plant the government regards as "endangered"—that is, likely to become extinct unless it receives special protection—or engaging in any economic activity (such as building a dam or running a farm) that would harm an endangered species. More than 600 species have been on the protected list; about half are plants. The regulations forbid not only killing a protected species but also adversely affecting its habitat.

The ESA is run by the Fish and Wildlife Service and the National Oceanic and Atmospheric Administration. They can add species to the endangered or threatened list on their own accord or in response to a private petition. Trafficking in an endangered species can lead to criminal penalties; fines may be imposed for managing private land in ways that might harm a species. Several species (such as bald eagles, grizzly bears, gray wolves, and sea otters) have increased in number since being listed and a few (such as bald eagles and gray wolves) have been taken off the list.

Firms and government agencies that wish to build a dam, bridge, factory, or farm in an area where an endangered species lives must comply with federal regulations. The complaints of such clients about these regulations are outweighed by the public support for the law. Sometimes the law preserves a creature, such as the bald eagle, that almost everyone admires; sometimes it protects a creature, such as the snail darter, that almost no one has ever heard of.

Wood product companies and loggers want access to forests under the control of the U.S. Forest Service. Though only a small fraction of all cut timber comes from these forests and most of the U.S. forest system is already off-limits to logging, environmentalists want further restrictions, especially to prevent clear-cutting (cutting down all the trees in a given area) and to prevent harvesting trees from the old-growth forests of Oregon and Washington. But Congress has generally supported the timber industry, ordering the Forest Service to sell harvesting rights at below-market prices, in effect subsidizing the industry. Some activists have worked to convert this client politics into entrepreneurial politics by demanding that clear-cutting in certain forests be stopped in order to protect endangered species, such as the spotted owl.

In 2019, the Trump administration revised the rules governing how the Endangered Species Act is applied. The changes to the rules will, generally speaking, make it easier to approve new projects in areas where endangered species live.[61] Nevertheless, the act survives and continues to be an important part of U.S. environmental policymaking.

Pollution from Automobiles: Majoritarian Politics

The Clean Air Act of 1970 imposed tough restrictions on the amount of pollutants that could come out of automobile tailpipes. Indeed, most of the debate over that bill centered on this issue.

Initially, the auto emissions control rules followed the pattern of entrepreneurial politics: an aroused public with media support demanded that automobile companies be required to make their cars less polluting. It seemed to be "the public" against "the interests," and the public won: By 1975, new cars would have to produce 90 percent less of two pollutants (hydrocarbons and carbon monoxide), and by 1976 achieve a 90 percent reduction in another (nitrous oxides). This was a tall order. There was no time to redesign automobile engines or to find an alternative to the internal combustion engine; it would be necessary to install devices (called catalytic converters) on exhaust pipes that would transform pollutants into harmless gases.

But a little-noticed provision in the 1970 law soon shoved the battle over automobile pollution into the arena of majoritarian politics. That provision required states to develop land-use and transportation rules to help attain air quality standards. What that meant in practice was that in any area where smog was still a problem, even after emission controls had been placed on new cars, there would have to be rules restricting the public's use of cars. There was no way for cities such as Denver, Los Angeles, and New York to get rid of smog just by requiring people to buy less-polluting cars—the increase in the number of cars

environmental impact statement (EIS) *A report required by federal law that assesses the possible effect of a project on the environment if the project is subsidized in whole or part by federal funds.*

or in the number of miles driven in those places outweighed the gain from making the average car less polluting. That meant the government would have to impose such unpopular measures as bans on downtown parking, mandatory use of buses and carpools, and even gasoline rationing. But efforts to do this failed. Popular opposition to such rules was too great, and the few such rules put into place didn't work. Congress reacted by postponing the deadlines by which air quality standards in cities would have to be met; the EPA reacted by abandoning any serious effort to tell people when and where they could drive.[62]

Even the effort to clean up the exhausts of new cars ran into opposition. Some people didn't like the higher cost of cars with catalytic converters; others didn't like the loss in horsepower these converters caused (many people disconnected them). The United Auto Workers union began to worry that antismog rules would hurt the U.S. auto industry and cost them their jobs. Congress took note of these complaints and decided that despite a lot of effort, new cars could not meet the 90 percent emission reduction standard by 1975–1976, and so in 1977 it amended the Clean Air Act to extend these deadlines by up to six years.

The Clean Air Act, when revised again in 1990, set new, tougher auto emission control standards—but it pushed back the deadline for compliance. It reiterated the need to get rid of smog in the smoggiest cities and proposed a number of ways to do it—but it set the deadline for compliance in the worst area (Los Angeles) at 20 years in the future. That said, over time, these laws have dramatically reduced emissions from vehicles, improving overall air quality and public health.[63]

Most clean-air laws passed since 1990 have targeted particular industries. For example, in 2004 the Bush administration approved a new measure to dramatically reduce emissions from heavy-use diesel engines used in construction, agricultural, and other industrial machinery. The public will support such tough environmental laws when somebody else pays or when the costs are hidden (as in the price of a car); it will not give as much support when it believes it is paying, especially when the payment takes the form of changing how and when it uses the family car. Here are more examples of each kind of majoritarian politics.

Majoritarian Politics when People Believe the Costs Are Low

The National Environmental Policy Act (NEPA), passed in 1969, contained a provision requiring that an **environmental impact statement (EIS)** be written before any federal agency undertakes an activity that will "significantly" affect the quality of the human environment. (Similar laws have been passed in many states, affecting not only what government does but also what private developers do.) Because it required only a "statement" rather than some specific action and because it was a pro-environment law, NEPA passed by overwhelming majorities.

As it turned out, the EIS provision was hardly innocuous. Opponents of virtually any government-sponsored project have used the EIS as a way of blocking, changing, or delaying the project. Hundreds of lawsuits have been filed to challenge this or that provision of an EIS or to claim that a project was not supported by a satisfactory EIS. In this way, environmental activists have challenged the Alaska pipeline, a Florida canal, and several nuclear power plants, as well as countless dams, bridges, highways, and office buildings. Usually the agency's plan is upheld, but this does not mean the EIS is unimportant: an EIS induces the agency to think through what it is doing, and it gives critics a chance to examine, and often to negotiate, the content of those plans.

Despite the grumbling of many people adversely affected by fights over an EIS (someone once complained that Moses would never have been able to part the Red Sea if he had had to file an EIS first), popular support for it remains strong because the public at large does not believe it is paying a high price and does believe it is gaining a significant benefit.

Majoritarian Politics when People Believe the Costs Are High

From time to time, someone proposes that gasoline taxes be raised sharply. Such taxes would discourage driving, and this not only would conserve fuel but also would reduce smog. Indeed, many economists argue that higher gas taxes should be how the U.S. fights smog and other pollutants. Almost everyone would pay, but almost everyone would benefit. However, it is only with great difficulty that the public can be persuaded to support such taxes. The reason is that the people pay the tax first, and the benefit, if any, comes later, and may be a general, rather than individual, result. Unlike Social Security, where the taxes we pay now support cash benefits we get later, gasoline taxes support noncash benefits (cleaner air, less congestion) that many people doubt will ever appear or, if they do, may not be meaningful to them.[64]

When gasoline taxes have been raised, it has usually been because the politicians did not push the tax hike as an environmental measure. Instead, they promised that

Government and the Environment

- ***Union Electric Co. v. Environmental Protection Agency* (1976):** EPA rules must be observed without regard to their cost or technological feasibility.
- ***Chevron v. National Resources Defense Council* (1984):** States should comply with EPA decisions, even if not explicitly authorized by statute, provided they are reasonable efforts to attain the goal of the law.
- ***Whitman v. American Trucking Associations* (2001):** Allows Congress to delegate broad authority to regulatory agencies.
- ***Massachusetts v. Environmental Protection Agency* (2007):** The EPA must hear a petition asking it to regulate greenhouse gases.

in return for paying higher taxes the public would receive some concrete benefits—more highways, more buses, or a reduction in the federal deficit (as happened with the gas tax hike of 1990 and again in 1993).

Since it cannot easily cut gasoline use by raising taxes, the government has turned to other approaches. One is to provide tax breaks and other incentives to companies that seek to develop alternative energy sources. Another is to offer incentives to car manufacturers to build vehicles that consume less fuel by relying in whole or in part on electricity.

Acid Rain: Interest-Group Politics

Sometimes the rain, snow, or dust particles that fall onto the land are acidic. This is called *acid rain*. In the 1970s, policymakers began to debate policies to deal with it. As everyone acknowledged, one source of acid precipitation is burning fuel such as certain types of coal that contain a lot of sulfur. Some of the sulfur (along with nitrogen) will turn into sulfuric (or nitric) acid as it comes to earth. Steel mills and electric power plants that burn high-sulfur coal are concentrated in the Midwest and Great Lakes regions of the United States. The prevailing winds tend to carry those sulfurous fumes eastward, where some fall to the ground.

That much was certain. Everything else about the issue, however, was surrounded by controversy. Many lakes and rivers in the eastern United States and in Canada had become more acidic, and some forests in these areas had died back. Some part of this was the result of acid rain caused by industrial smokestacks, but some part of it was also the result of naturally occurring acids in the soils and rainfall. How much of the acidification is man-made and how much is a result of the actions of Mother Nature was a matter of dispute. Some lakes were not affected by acid rain; some were. Why were some affected more than others? Each side in the debate mustered its favorite experts. They provided some support for each side in what became a fierce interest-group battle. Residents of Canada and New England have complained bitterly of the loss of forests and the acidification of lakes, blaming it on Midwestern smokestacks. Midwestern businesses, labor unions, and politicians denied that their smokestacks were the major cause of the problem (if, indeed, there was a problem) and argued that, even if they were the cause, they shouldn't have to pay the cost of cleaning up the problem.

An attempt to deal with the issue in 1977 reflected the kind of bizarre compromises that sometimes result when politically opposed forces have to be reconciled. There were essentially two alternatives. One was to require power plants to burn low-sulfur coal. This would undoubtedly cut back on sulfur emissions, but it would cost money because low-sulfur coal is mined mostly in the West, hundreds of miles away from the Midwestern coal-burning industries. The other way would be to require power plants to install scrubbers—complicated and very expensive devices that would take sulfurous fumes out of the gas before it came out of the smokestack. In addition to their cost, the trouble with scrubbers was that they didn't always work and that they generated a lot of unpleasant sludge that would have to be hauled away and buried somewhere. Their great advantage, however, was that they would allow Midwestern utilities to continue their practice of using cheap, high-sulfur coal.

Congress voted for the scrubbers for all new coal-burning plants, even if they burned low-sulfur coal. In the opinion of most economists, this was the wrong decision,[65] but it had four great political advantages. First, the jobs of miners in high-sulfur coal mines would be protected. They had powerful allies in Congress. Second, environmentalists liked scrubbers, which they seemed to regard as a definitive, technological "solution" to the problem, an approach far preferable to relying on incentives to induce power plants to buy low-sulfur coal. Third, scrubber manufacturers liked the idea, for obvious reasons. Finally, some eastern governors liked scrubbers because if all new plants had to have them, it would be more costly, and thus less likely, for existing factories in their states to close down and move to the West.

The 1977 law in effect required scrubbers on all new coal-burning plants—even ones located right next to mines where they could get low-sulfur coal. As two scholars later described the law, it seemed to produce "clean coal and dirty air."[66] The 1977 bill did not solve much. Many of the scrubbers, as predicted, didn't work very well. Eventually, President George H. W. Bush worked out a compromise that gradually reduced sulfur emissions in several steps; a key component was the creation of a system of sulfur dioxide allowances that could be bought and sold was established. This compromise became part of the Clean Air Act of 1990.

Over time, this system has been shown to be a success: while the issue has not been completely resolved, longitudinal data from the national program that monitors the composition of precipitation showed that significant progress has been made. The data indicate that, between 1994 and 2010, acid rain falling in the parts of the country where the problem had been most severe had dramatically decreased, and that decrease was achieved largely without the adverse economic and other impacts that the critics had been predicting since the 1977 law took effect.[67]

Agricultural Pesticides: Client Politics

Some client groups have so far escaped this momentum. One such group is organized farmers, who have more or less successfully resisted efforts to restrict the use of pesticides or to control the runoff of pesticides from farmlands.

For a while, it seemed as though farmers would also fall before the assaults of policy entrepreneurs. When Rachel Carson published *Silent Spring* in 1962,[68] she set off a public outcry about the harm to wildlife caused by the indiscriminate use of DDT, a common pesticide. In 1972, the EPA banned the use of DDT.

That same year, Congress directed the EPA to evaluate the safety of *all* pesticides (herbicides, insecticides, fungicides, and others) on the market; unsafe ones were to be removed. However, that was easier said than done. By the late 1970s, more than 50,000 pesticides were in use, with 5,000 new ones introduced every year.[69] Testing all of these chemicals proved to be a huge, vastly expensive, and very time-consuming job, especially since any health effects on people could not be observed for several years. Pesticides have many beneficial uses; therefore, the EPA had to balance the gains and the risks of using a given pesticide and compare the relative gains and risks of two similar pesticides.

In 2004, Congress directed the EPA to expand and improve its pesticides regulation. Again, that would be a tall order. As summarized in a 2011 EPA report, today in America there are some 112 pesticides producers and about 13,000 pesticides distributors; and about $12 billion a year is spent on pesticides by about 78 million households and 1.2 million farms.[70]

The client politics of the issue makes the EPA's huge regulatory task even harder. American farmers are the most productive in the world, and most of them believe they cannot achieve that output (and thus their present incomes) without using pesticides. These farmers are well organized to express their interests and well represented in Congress (especially on the House and Senate Agricultural Committees). Complicating matters is the fact that the subsidies the taxpayers give to farmers often encourage them to produce more food than they can sell and thus to use more pesticides than they really need. Though many of these chemicals do not remain in the crops harvested, large amounts sink into the soil, contaminating water supplies. But these problems are largely invisible to the public and are much harder to dramatize than the discovery of a toxic waste dump like that at Love Canal, New York.

Though opposed by environmental organizations, farm groups have been generally successful at practicing client politics. Even with the aforementioned 2004 mandate to expand and improve pesticides regulation, now, as when the effort began, the EPA's budget for reviewing pesticides has been kept small. Very few pesticides have been taken off the market, and those that have been removed have tended to be ones that, because they were involved in some incident receiving heavy media coverage (such as the effect of DDT on birds), were decided through entrepreneurial politics.

17-4 Beyond Domestic Policy

Challenge yourself to learn more about some or all of the various domestic issues, policies, and programs discussed in this chapter. In each case, ask yourself about the type (or types) of policymaking politics that is (or was) most important to whether, when, and how government acted (or failed to act). Once a policy is in place, political support for keeping it typically can mobilize more forcefully than proposals to change or replace it.

The next chapter explores economic policy and examines which type of politics has mattered most on such issues as what to do about budget deficits and the public debt. Economic policy is sometimes discussed as if it were all about political battles among and between competing, economically self-interested groups, suggesting it is dominated by interest-group politics. Chapter 19 explores foreign and military policy and examines which type of politics has mattered most on such issues as international trade and decisions to commit troops abroad. Foreign and military policy is sometimes discussed as if it were all about majoritarian politics that "stops at the water's edge." But, as we shall see, economic policy is hardly all about interest-group politics, foreign and military policy is far from uniformly majoritarian, and both "who governs" and "to what ends" vary a lot from issue to issue. And, as with domestic policy, existing programs are easier to keep than to change or replace with new policies.

Learning Objectives

17-1 Explain how America's social welfare policies differ from those of many other modern democracies, and why some programs are politically protected while others are politically imperiled.

America's social welfare programs differ in four main ways. First, Americans have taken a more restrictive view of who is entitled to or "deserves" to benefit from government assistance. Second, America was slower to embrace the need for the "welfare state" and, in turn, slower to adopt and enact relevant policies and programs.

Third, state governments have played a large role in administering or co-funding many "national" social welfare measures (e.g., Medicaid). Fourth, nongovernmental organizations, both for-profit firms and nonprofit groups (secular as well as religious), have played a large role in administering Washington's social welfare initiatives. Political support for social welfare programs depends primarily on who benefits directly, or who is perceived to benefit directly.

For example, Social Security and Medicare benefit almost all people who have reached a certain age, whereas the Food Stamps program—like the old AFDC program's successor, TANF—benefits only people with low incomes. The first type of social welfare program has no means test (they are available to everyone without regard to income), whereas the second type is means tested (only people who fall below a certain income level are eligible). The first type represents majoritarian politics and is almost always politically protected; the second type represents client politics and is often politically imperiled. Medicaid, the federal–state health program, is means tested, but it has as beneficiaries not only low-income persons but also the aged and the disabled. It mixes majoritarian and client politics, making it less politically sacrosanct than Social Security or Medicare, but more so than the Food Stamps program, TANF, and other means-tested programs.

17-2 Discuss how government regulations on certain big businesses have been imposed over the objections of those industries.

Several reasons explain the passage of government regulations on industries, but the most important ones have to do with entrepreneurial politics. Starting in the 20th century, consumer advocates and environmental activists began to challenge big oil companies, auto manufacturing companies, drug companies, pesticides producers, and other corporations that once had, or were perceived to have, cozy relationships with government. Policy entrepreneurs outside government, like Ralph Nader and Rachel Carson, dramatized how existing public policies and programs helped the companies to profit but hurt most people in the pocketbook, jeopardized public health and safety, or both.

By the 1970s and 1980s, policy entrepreneurs inside government, like those at the Environmental Protection Agency (founded in 1970), began regulating businesses even more closely than they had in the past. Although business regulation policy still generates much controversy and many debates over its cost-effectiveness, most people now favor diverse regulations on big oil companies and other large-scale businesses.

17-3 Explain why environmental policies are designed and enforced differently in America than in other industrialized nations, and describe the politics that drive environmental programs.

The adversarial nature of American politics, as well as the system of federalism, complicates policymaking in America, as illustrated by efforts to pass and enforce legislation on automobile emissions, clean air and water, and other environmental issues. While entrepreneurial politics figure prominently in environmental policy dynamics, including on an issue like protecting endangered species, environmental issues are included in each "box," like pollution from automobiles (majoritarian politics), acid rain (interest-group politics), and agricultural pesticides (client politics). The same can be said for social welfare, business regulation, and other domestic policies and programs.

17-4 Discuss the difficulty with changing policies—domestic, economic, and foreign—or developing new programs in the United States today.

The fundamental challenge with changing existing policies is the persistent public majority opposed to making either major or minor cuts to a program. Even the ostensibly far-reaching, bipartisan plans offered in recent sessions of Congress have been predicated on preserving (or expanding) all extant benefits to all present-day and near-term beneficiaries without raising taxes and without reducing services. For good or for ill, their majoritarian politics forbid any truly far-reaching reforms, and consequently leave scarce resources for developing new programs.

To Learn More

Nonpartisan reviews of public policy issues:

Public Agenda: **www.publicagenda.org**

Pew Research Center: **www.people-press.org**

Selected social welfare programs:

Social Security: **www.ssa.gov**

Medicare and Medicaid: **www.cms.gov**

TANF: **www.acf.hhs.gov/programs/ofa**

Selected federal agencies:

Environmental Protection Agency: **www.epa.gov**

National Labor Relations Board: **www.nlrb.gov**

Occupational Safety and Health Administration: **www.osha.gov**

Allen, Will. *The Good Food Revolution: Growing Healthy Food, People, and Communities*. New York: Gotham, 2012. Account by a former professional basketball player and fast-food executive who built an "urban farm" program that applies sustainable food cultivation strategies, creates local jobs, promotes healthier eating habits, and has been replicated in many cities all across the country.

Derthick, Martha. *Policymaking for Social Security*. Washington, D.C.: Brookings Institution, 1979. A detailed analysis of how the Social Security program grew during its first four decades.

Heclo, Hugh. *Modern Social Politics in Britain and Sweden*. New Haven, CT: Yale University Press, 1974. Classic comparative analysis of how social welfare programs came to Britain and Sweden.

Kingdon, John W. *Agendas, Alternatives, and Public Policies*. Boston, MA: Little, Brown, 1984. An insightful account of how domestic issues, especially those involving health and transportation, get on (or drop off) Washington's political agenda.

Mead, Lawrence M. *From Prophecy to Charity: How to Help the Poor*. Washington, D.C.: American Enterprise Institute, 2011. Argues that the work-based welfare reform programs that succeeded AFDC have been largely successful and prescribes more "paternalistic programs" plus a wider role for charities in administering antipoverty policies.

Monsma, Stephen V. *Putting Faith in Partnerships: Welfare-to-Work in Four Cities*. Ann Arbor: University of Michigan Press, 2004. Careful study of the six different types of organizations that administer welfare-to-work programs in big cities.

Rosenbaum, Walter A. *Environmental Politics and Policy*. 11th ed. Washington, D.C.: Congressional Quarterly Press, 2019. Analyses of the politics of air and water pollution, the use of chemicals, and other environmental issues.

Stokes, Leah. 2020. *Short-Circuiting Policy: Interest Groups and the Battle over Clean Energy and Climate Policy in the United States*. New York: Oxford University Press. A careful study of the debates over clean energy policy, focusing on the role of interest groups. It also highlights the importance of federalism to contemporary environmental politics.

Vogel, David. *National Style of Regulation: Environmental Policy in Great Britain and the United States*. Ithaca, NY: Cornell University Press, 1986. An explanation of why environmental politics in America tends to be adversarial.

Washington Post Staff. *Landmark: The Inside Story of America's New Health Care Law and What It Means for All of Us*. New York: Public Affairs, 2010. A lively journalistic account of the politics that produced the Patient Protection and Affordable Care Act of 2010.

Wilson, James Q., ed. *The Politics of Regulation*. New York: Basic Books, 1980. Analyzes regulatory politics in nine agencies and provides a more detailed statement of the theory of policymaking politics presented in this text.

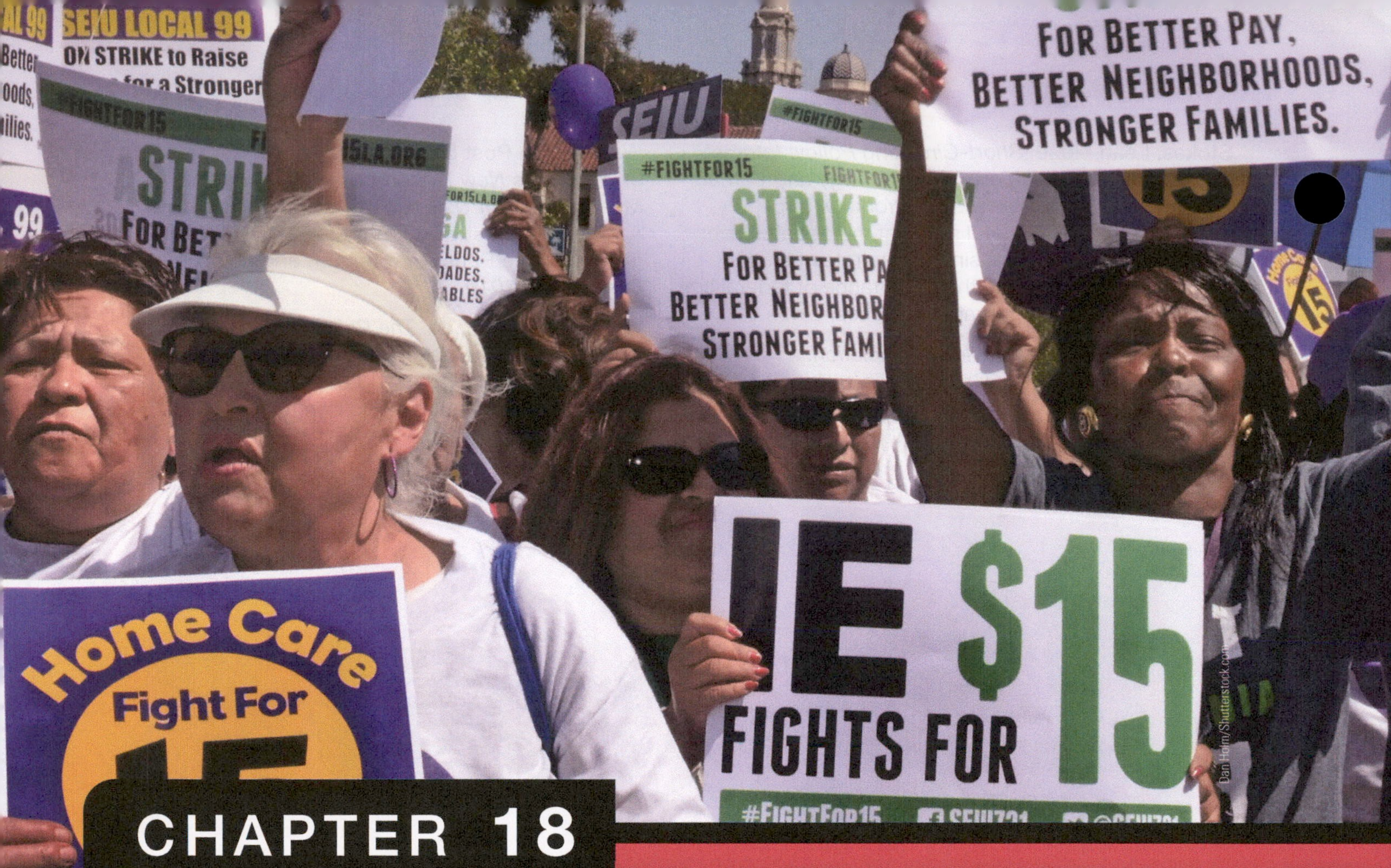

Dan Holm/Shutterstock.com

CHAPTER 18

Economic Policy

Learning Objectives

18-1 Summarize how politics and public opinion shape economic policy.

18-2 Summarize four main theories of economic policymaking.

18-3 Describe how American institutions work to set economic policy.

18-4 Explain the budget process and discuss why cutting spending or increasing taxes is difficult.

18-5 Summarize the debates over globalization and income inequality and how they fit within our broader framework for understanding policy issues.

Like most Americans, you probably think about the way the government spends its money the same way you think about how you ought to spend yours. You look at your income, and you look at your expenses, and you make a **budget** to determine how much you can spend on each item that you need for your household: we can spend so much on rent, so much on groceries, and so forth. If you spend more than you earn, then you will have to borrow money and pay it back to the bank with interest, so you only do that when you are buying something of long-term value, like a home, a car, or a college education. If you run up so many charges that you max out your credit card, then you won't be able to charge anything more. If you keep spending more than you earn, then you may have to declare bankruptcy.

Surely, the government ought to work the same way: it should spend no more than it makes from taxes, and borrow only when it is buying items of real value. But it doesn't. As we discuss later in the chapter, the federal government makes its budget differently: it decides how much to spend on various programs with little reference to how much money it takes in via taxes. Indeed, in almost every year since 1960, the government has spent more money than it earned. The amount it spends in excess of what it takes in each year is called the **deficit** (see Figure 18.1). In 2019, that deficit was $892.3 billion, and the original budget for 2020 had it increasing to $961.3 billion. But then the COVID-19 pandemic hit, and just through May of 2020, the deficit for 2020 was $1.88 trillion. Once the full cost of the COVID-19 pandemic is known, this deficit will likely be substantially higher.[1]

To finance that deficit, the government needs to borrow money from someone. To do that, it sells government bonds, issued by the Treasury Department, to Americans and foreigners. When you buy a bond, including a savings bond, you are making a loan to the U.S. government: you are giving the government money now in exchange for being paid back, with interest, in the future.

Because of this yearly deficit spending, the federal government's **national debt** has risen rapidly. The total amount of all deficits is the national debt. In 2019, the national debt rose to over $22 trillion, and given the costs of responding to the COVID-19 pandemic, it will increase even more in the years to come.

For the past four decades, the government in Washington has gotten away with routine deficit spending and non-stop increases in the national debt. At certain points, Congress becomes concerned with its spending and makes cuts, as it did in the wake of the great recession in 2008 and the rise of the Tea Party (see our discussion

budget *A document that states income, spending levels, and the allocation of spending among purposes.*

deficit *The result of the government in one year spending more money than it takes in from taxes.*

national debt *The total deficit from the first presidency to the present.*

Figure 18.1 **Federal Budget Deficit or Surplus, Fiscal Years (FY) 1940–2020, in Billions of Constant FY2012 Dollars**

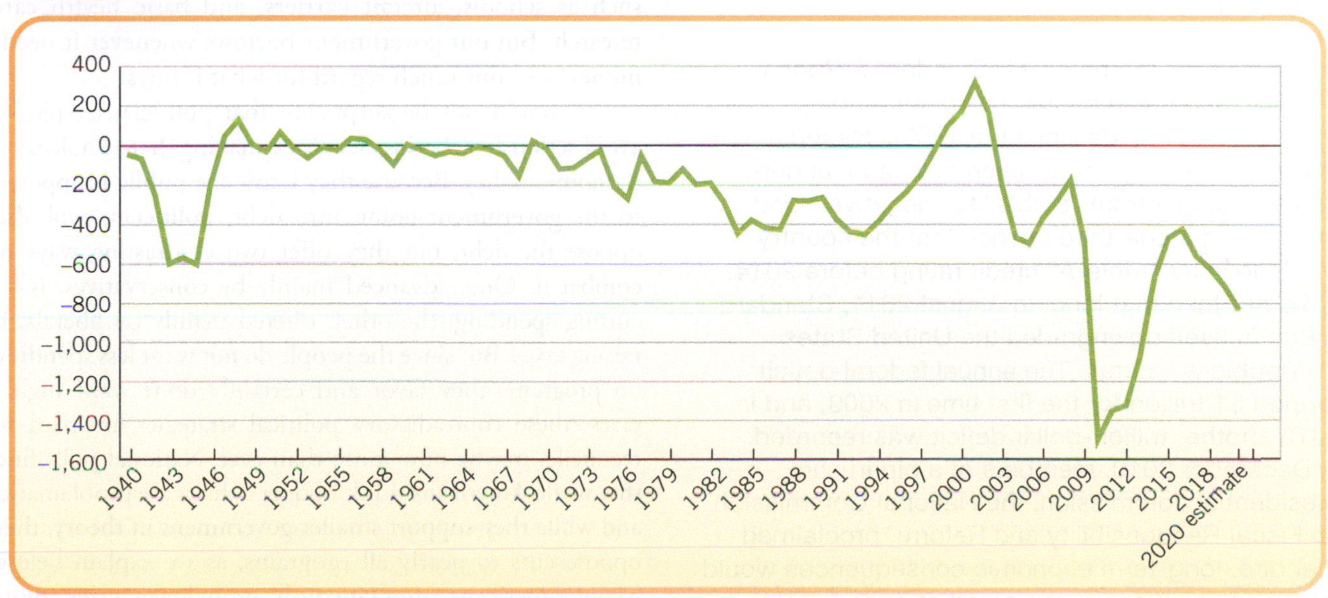

Source: Office of Management and Budget, Historical Tables (Table 1.3).

Q **Study the over-time trends in the nation's budget deficit. What trends stand out to you? How do those trends correspond to other developments in American politics?**

gross domestic product
The total of all goods and services produced in an economy during a given year.

in Chapter 9). But in the last few years, the will to do so has evaporated for both Democrats and Republicans in Congress.

« Then Deficits that result in debt are important economically only insofar as the government cannot make the payments on its bonds in a currency that people regard as stable and valuable. Happily, almost everybody around the world has regarded the American dollar as stable and valuable. As a result, people have lined up to buy U.S. Treasury bonds whenever they are sold. But to keep our currency stable, people must believe that the dollar will always be valuable and that the government is not borrowing more than it can pay back. Before 1980, annual deficit spending was relatively minor and large deficits occurred only during wartime. Washington began its deficit spending and debt accumulation spree in the mid-1970s, interrupted only by several years during the 1990s when the government ran surpluses. Despite the huge deficits and mounting debt, most people, including most major domestic and foreign investors and public finance experts, nonetheless considered America to be a good credit risk. In particular, concerns about "too much debt" were often dismissed as unduly alarmist, and presidents and congressional leaders in both parties quietly and consistently increased the national debt ceiling so that Washington could keep right on spending and borrowing.

*** Now** In April 2011, Standard & Poor's, a credit rating agency that has been grading U.S. Treasury bonds since the 1930s, issued a first-ever warning about America's national debt, downgrading it from "stable" to "negative," and forecasting a one-third chance that the country would lose its "triple-A" credit rating before 2014. It did not take that long. In August 2011, Standard & Poor's itself downgraded the United States to "double-A" status. The annual federal deficit topped $1 trillion for the first time in 2009, and in 2010 another trillion-dollar deficit was recorded. In December 2010, members of a bipartisan presidential commission, the National Commission on Fiscal Responsibility and Reform, proclaimed that dire, long-term economic consequences would follow unless Washington acted at once to rein in deficit spending and slow debt accumulation. For example, the total value of all the goods and services the nation produces each year is called **gross domestic product**, or GDP. The Commission warned that the national debt would soon exceed the nation's annual GDP, and that annual interest payments on the national debt could rise to almost 4 percent of GDP (from about 2.3 percent of GDP in 2012) over the next decade, crowding out other types of spending.

In 2011, as part of the deal to raise the debt ceiling (the federal government's borrowing limit established by Congress), Congress passed the Budget Control Act of 2011, which included the Congressional Joint Select Committee on Deficit Reduction (better known as the "super committee"). This committee was charged with finding $1.5 trillion dollars in additional debt reduction; if they did not (or if Congress rejected their plan), then across-the-board spending cuts would go into effect. They failed to agree on a plan, but members of Congress used various measures to block the "automatic" cuts. Since then, the debt limit has continued to be a political football, and Congress has shown little initiative to reducing spending.

The core reason why ongoing debates over economic policy are so divisive is that people disagree, often fundamentally, not so much over the sheer size of our national debt, but over what we buy with all this borrowed money. Most families borrow to buy long-lasting items, such as a home, a new car, or a college education. We don't really know what the federal debt is used for. It would be nice if we knew that we borrowed only to pay for long-lasting programs that enhance security and economic growth, such as schools, aircraft carriers, and basic health care research. But our government borrows whenever it needs money, without much regard for what it buys.

It should not be surprising that politicians typically avoid seriously debating, let alone making, hard choices on economic policy. Because they know the public is opposed to the government going into debt, politicians will also oppose the debt, but they offer two contrasting ways to combat it. One, advanced mainly by conservatives, is by cutting spending; the other, offered mainly by liberals, is raising taxes. But since the people do not want less spending on programs they favor and certainly don't want higher taxes, these contradictory political strategies are hard to reconcile, maybe now more than ever. National polls find that while Americans think budget deficits are problematic, and while they support smaller government in theory, they oppose cuts to nearly all programs, as we explain below. Many Americans simultaneously want lower taxes, more spending, and minimal debt, which is not possible in the long term. Thus, any truly far-reaching fiscal reforms will require politicians in both parties to win back public trust while telling the people what few care to hear.

18-1 The Economy and Elections

In more normal economic times, however, economic policy is not nearly so hard for politicians to fashion without fighting big legislative battles or risking public ire. The health of the American economy creates majoritarian politics. Hardly anyone wants inflation or unemployment; everyone wants rapid increases in income and wealth. But this fact is a bit puzzling. You might think that people would care about their own jobs and worry only about avoiding their own unemployment. If that were the case, they would vote for politicians who promise to award contracts to firms that would hire them or who would create programs that would benefit them, regardless of how well other people were getting along. In fact, though, people see connections between their own well-being and that of the nation, and they tend to hold politicians responsible for the state of the country.

As we discussed in Chapter 10, the health of the overall economy strongly shapes presidential elections. But when people evaluate "the economy," what do they consider? Do they look at their own economic fortunes, labeled "pocketbook voting"? Or do they instead look to the health of the nation's economy as a whole, labeled "sociotropic (other-regarding) voting"?

People do, to some degree, look to their own economic circumstances. Those who think their own economic circumstances have deteriorated are more likely to vote against the incumbent party.[2] For example, in the 2020 election, 41 percent of Americans thought their family's financial situation had improved during President Trump's tenure in office, while 20 percent thought it had gotten worse. 73 percent of the former, but only 27 percent of the latter, voted to reelect President Trump.[3]

But people do not simply vote with their own pocketbooks. Instead, they look more at the overall health of the economy when casting a ballot for president. When assessing "the economy," they consider the national economy: Did unemployment go up or down? Did inflation increase or decrease? They use these national-level indicators to assess the economy, and they reward the incumbent president (and that party) accordingly.[4] In presidential elections, those who think national economic trends are bad are much more likely to vote against the incumbent, *even when* their own personal finances have not worsened.[5]

In technical language, voting behavior and economic conditions are strongly correlated at the national level but not at the individual level, and this is true both in the United States and in Europe.[6] Such voters are behaving in an "other-regarding" or "sociotropic" way. In ordinary language, voters seem to respond more to the condition of the national economy than to their own personal finances.

It is not hard to understand why this might be true. A big part of the explanation is that people understand what government can and cannot be held accountable for. If you lose your job at an aircraft manufacturing plant because the government has not renewed the plant's contract, then you will be more likely to hold the government responsible than if you lose your job because you were always showing up late or because the plant moved out of town.[7]

Another part of the explanation is that people see general economic conditions as having indirect effects on them even when they are still doing pretty well. They may not be unemployed, but they may have friends who are, and they may worry that if unemployment grows worse, they will be next to lose their jobs.

What Politicians Try to Do

Elected officials, who have to run for reelection every few years, are strongly tempted to take a short-run view of the economy and to adopt those policies that will best satisfy the self-regarding voter. They would dearly love to produce low unemployment rates and rising family incomes just before an election. Some think that they do just this.

Since the 19th century, the government has used money to affect elections. At first this mostly took the form of patronage passed out to the party faithful and money benefits given to important blocs of voters. The massive system of Civil War pensions for Union army veterans was run in a way that did no harm to the political fortunes of the Republican Party. After the Social Security system was established, Congress voted to increase the benefits in virtually every year in which there was an election until such adjustments were made automatic in 1975 (see Chapter 17).

But it is by no means clear that the federal government can or will do whatever is necessary to reduce unemployment, cut inflation, lower interest rates, and increase incomes just to win an election. For one thing, the government does not know how to produce all of these desirable outcomes. Moreover, achieving one outcome often may be possible only at the cost of not doing another. For example, reducing inflation can, in many cases, require the government to raise interest rates, and this in turn can slow the economy by making it harder to sell houses, automobiles, and other things purchased with borrowed money.

If it were easy to stimulate the economy just before an election, practically every president would serve two full terms. But because of the uncertainties and complexities of the economy, presidents can lose elections over economic issues they do not manage to the satisfaction of voters. Ford lost in 1976, as did Carter in 1980, George H. W. Bush in 1992, and Trump in 2020. In all cases, economic conditions played a major role.

All this means that politicians must make choices about economic policy—choices affected by uncertainty and ignorance. No one knows how perfectly to balance unemployment and inflation, how to set the ideal tax rate, and so forth. Thus, the political debate on these policies continues.

Public Opinion and Government Spending

Of course, presidents and other actors do not operate in a vacuum. The policies they pursue are constrained and shaped by what the public wants. People want prosperity, but they also want no tax increases, no government deficit, and continued (or higher) government spending on the things they like, such as education, health care, the environment, and retirement benefits. Politicians confront two inconsistent kinds of majoritarian politics: everybody wants general prosperity, and large majorities want more government spending on popular programs. But the more the government spends on popular programs, the more money it requires, and the more it takes in, the less that is left over for private investment that produces prosperity. In short, public opinion supports a conundrum: Americans want more spending without more taxes or bigger government.[8]

Figure 18.2 illustrates this general tendency: Americans claim to not like big government in principle, but they certainly seem to like it in practice. The figure shows the percentage of all Americans, as well as of Democrats and Republicans, who support cuts to spending across various federal programs. In all cases, there is very little public support for spending cuts, especially in areas like Social Security, Medicare, public education, and veterans' benefits. Indeed, there is no majority support for cutting spending in any of these policy areas. This is not just an artifact of using this one data source from the Pew Research Center, we can find the same pattern again and again in many different policy areas and on many different surveys. Americans might say they want smaller government in *theory*, but in practice, they want government to expand.

The same thing is true of members of both parties. The overwhelming majority of Democrats oppose spending cuts in all areas. The highest Democratic support for spending cuts is for defense spending, and even there, only 31 percent support reductions from our current spending levels. While Republicans are generally more supportive of spending cuts, even here, a minority supports cutting spending in almost every area. There is only one exception—spending on aid to

Figure 18.2 **Support for Spending Cuts**

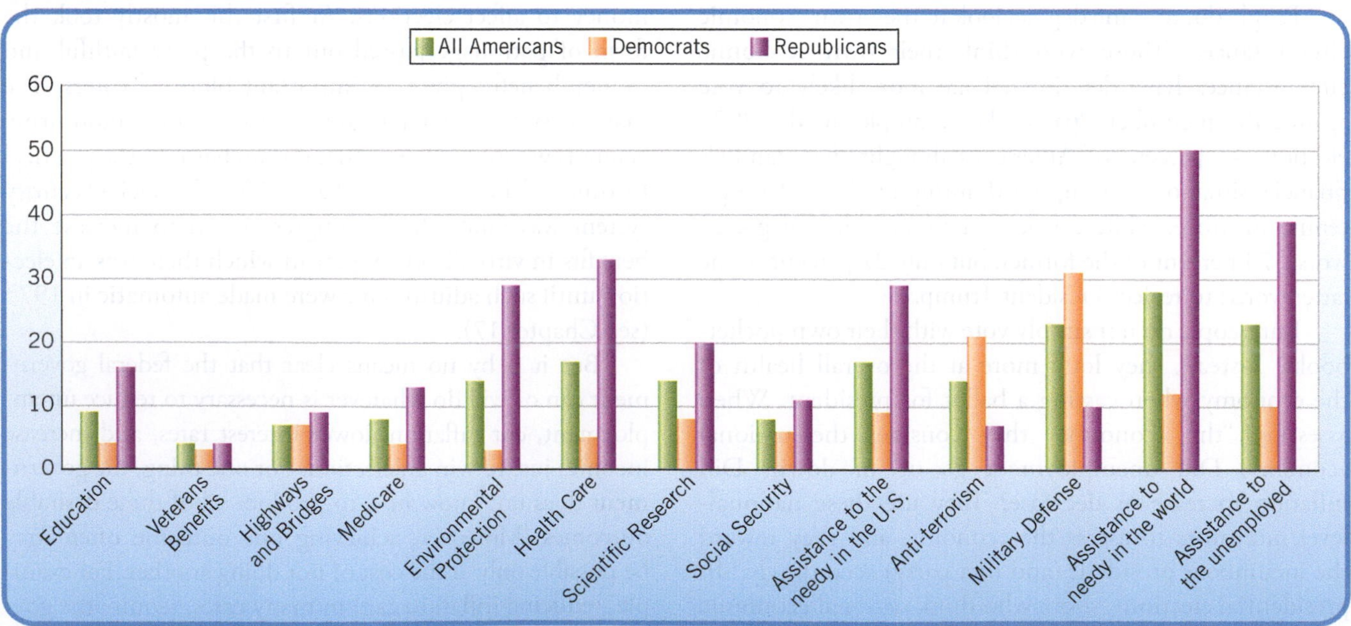

Source: Pew Research Center, "Little Public Support for Reductions in Federal Spending," April 2019.

Q **Looking across these different areas, what partisan differences, if any, stand out? What does that tell you about the possibility of changes to government spending in these areas?**

the needy around the world, better known as foreign aid. But foreign aid is such a small part of the federal budget—less than 1 percent—that cutting foreign aid would generate no real savings. The major government expenses—programs such as Social Security, Medicare, defense spending, and so forth (see Figure 18.4)—are popular, and the public opposes cuts in these areas.

Such opposition to spending cuts is not problematic if the public is also willing to support increased taxes. Unfortunately, they are not. Figure 18.3 shows support for various tax increases. In general, the American public is very hostile toward creating new taxes, such as a national sales tax, or increasing existing taxes, like the gasoline tax. Furthermore, they are also strongly opposed to eliminating popular tax deductions, such as the deduction for home mortgage interest, or increasing fees for government programs, such as the premiums seniors pay for Medicare. The Gallup polling firm has since the late 1950s been asking Americans whether they think the amount they pay in taxes is too high. Every time the question has been asked, a majority or near majority (at least 45 percent) say their taxes are too high.[9] Many Americans from across the political spectrum agree with the slogan of the Tea Party that was active during the Obama administration (see Chapter 9): they think they are Taxed Enough Already.

Americans support increasing taxes in one area, however: when someone else pays them. In Figure 18.3, we can see majority support for increasing taxes when it comes to taxes paid by the wealthy and corporations. Americans think their taxes are too high, but they consistently think that the wealthy (defined in various ways) and large corporations should pay more in taxes.

Not only the rich and big corporations are the object of such targeted tax increases. For example, the State Children's Health Insurance Program (SCHIP) is partially funded through cigarette taxes.[10] The SCHIP subsidizes health insurance for low-income children and has remained popular since its inception in the 1990s. Using cigarette taxes is a way of keeping such a program popular, as smokers represent a minority, whereas nearly everyone supports health insurance for children. In short, if you want to raise taxes, it would behoove you to paint it as a tax increase on some unpopular group.

Most voters would like to have lower taxes, less debt, and new (or expanded) programs. Unfortunately, this is logically impossible. We cannot have lower taxes, no debt, and higher spending on politically popular programs such as health care, education, the environment, and retirement benefits. If we have more spending, then we have to pay for it, either with higher taxes or with more borrowing.

Figure 18.3 **Support for Tax Increases**

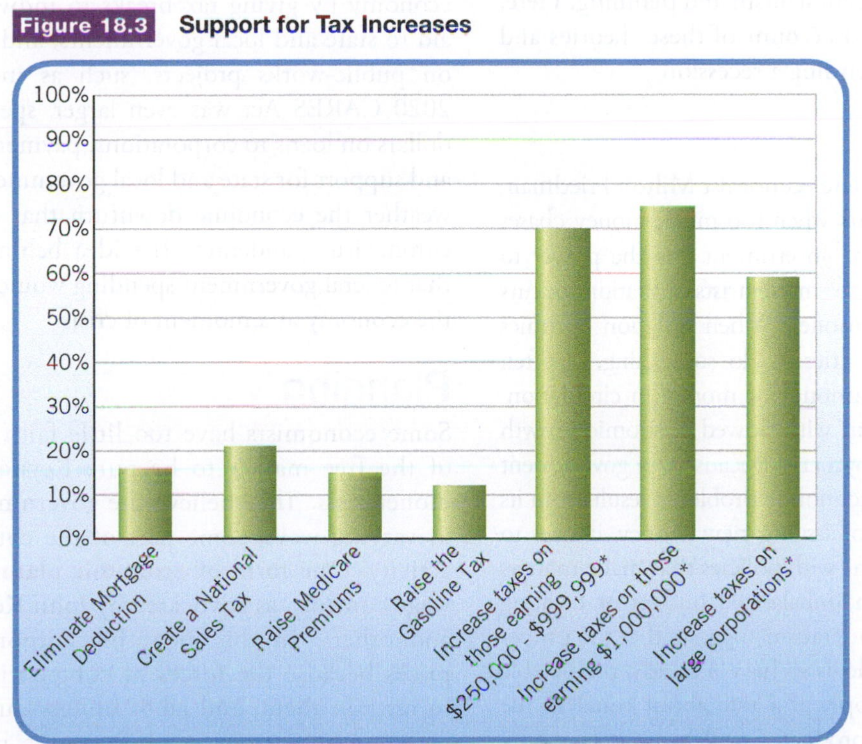

Source: Author's analysis of the Pew Research Center's December 2010 political survey; * United States Tax Policy, Ipsos Poll Conducted for NPR [National Public Radio], April 2017.

monetarist *One who believes that inflation occurs when too much money is chasing too few goods.*

Keynesianism *The belief the government must manage the economy by spending more money when in a recession and cutting spending when inflation occurs.*

economic planning *The belief that government plans, such as wage and price controls or the direction of investment, can improve the economy.*

Given public opinion on taxes and spending, therefore, the solution is that American politicians deficit-spend. Americans support increased spending on a wide variety of programs, but not a commensurate increase in taxes (or really any increase in taxes, except for someone else). The end result is that politicians grow the size of the deficit over time. This delays the difficult decision—cutting spending or raising taxes—until some point in the future.

18-2 Economic Theories and Political Needs

Four main theories exist about how to improve the economy, and many of the economists picked by presidents represent one or more of these theories. In general, conservative economists tend to support monetarism and supply-side economics, whereas liberal economists are more likely to embrace Keynesianism and planning. Here, we give a highly simplified account of these theories and what each implies about ending a recession.

Monetarism

A **monetarist**, such as the late economist Milton Friedman, believes that inflation occurs when too much money chases too few goods. The federal government has the power to create money; according to monetarists, inflation occurs when it prints too much money. When inflation becomes rampant and government tries to do something, it often cuts back sharply on the amount of money in circulation. Then a recession will occur, with slowed economic growth and an increased unemployment. Because the government does not understand that economic problems result from its own start-and-stop habit of issuing new money, it tries to cure some of these problems with policies that make matters worse—such as having an unbalanced budget or creating new welfare programs. Monetarism suggests that the proper thing for government to do is to have a steady, predictable increase in the money supply at a rate about equal to the growth in the economy's productivity. When the economy goes into a recession, however, many monetarists think the Federal Reserve Bank should cut interest rates to make it easier for people and businesses to borrow money. That is what the Fed did during 2008, and again in the spring of 2020 as the coronavirus pandemic slowed the U.S. economy.

Keynesianism

John Maynard Keynes, an English economist who died in 1946, believed that a market will not automatically operate at a full-employment, low-inflation level. Its health depends on the fraction of people's incomes being saved or spent. If people save too much, demand will be too low, production will decline, and unemployment will rise. If they spend too much, demand will rise too fast, prices will go up, and shortages will develop. According to **Keynesianism**, the key is to create the right level of demand. This is the task of government. When demand is too low, the government should pump more money into the economy (by spending more than it collects in taxes and by creating public-works programs). When demand is too great, the government should take money out of the economy (by increasing taxes or cutting federal expenditures). The government's budget does not need to be balanced on a year-to-year basis; what counts is the performance of the economy.

The American Recovery and Reinvestment Act of 2009 (more commonly known as the stimulus bill) and the CARES Act of 2020 (the government's first bill to address the COVID-19 pandemic) are both examples of Keynesian thinking. The 2009 stimulus spent approximately $800 billion of federal money to help jump-start the economy by giving tax breaks to individuals, providing aid to state and local governments, and spending money on public-works projects, such as infrastructure. The 2020 CARES Act was even larger, spending $2 trillion dollars on loans to corporations, payments to individuals, and support for state and local governments, to help them weather the economic downturn that accompanied the coronavirus pandemic. The idea behind both bills was that federal government spending would help to shore up the economy at a moment of crisis.

Planning

Some economists have too little faith in the workings of the free market to be pure Keynesians, much less monetarists. They believe the government should plan, in varying ways, some part of the country's economic activity. One form of **economic planning** is price and wage controls, as advocated by John Kenneth Galbraith and others. In this view, big corporations can raise prices because the forces of competition are too weak to restrain them, and labor unions can force up wages because management finds it easy to pass the increases along to consumers in the form of higher prices. Thus, during periods of inflation, the government should

Federal Laws about Commerce

- ***Lochner v. New York* (1905):** A New York law limiting the number of hours that may be worked by bakers; was struck down as unconstitutional.
- ***Muller v. Oregon* (1980):** An Oregon law limiting the number of hours worked by women, which was upheld as constitutional; in effect, it overruled the *Lochner* decision.
- ***West Coast Hotel Co. v. Parrish* (1937):** A Washington State minimum wage law for women; upheld as constitutional.
- ***Youngstown Sheet & Tube Co. v. Sawyer* (1952):** The president does not have the authority to seize private steel mills even in wartime.

regulate the maximum prices that can be charged and wages that can be paid, at least in the larger industries.

Planning has never been popular in America, but when the Troubled Asset Relief Program began investing in banks, some people began to suggest that perhaps the government should own the banks. That way, they said, the government might get back some of the money it had spent on assisting the banks during the 2008 financial crisis. The government was already the largest single stockholder in Bank of America and Citigroup (though in each case it owned less than half the available stock). Such plans were never put into place, and the government has largely ended its stake in the banks (as expected).

Supply-Side Economics

Exactly the opposite remedy for declining American productivity is suggested by people who call themselves supply-siders. The view of economists such as Arthur Laffer and Paul Craig Roberts is that the market, far from having failed, has not been given an adequate chance. According to **supply-side theory**, what is needed is not more planning but less government interference. In particular, sharply cutting taxes will increase people's incentive to work, save, and invest. Greater investments will then lead to more jobs, and if the earnings from these investments and jobs are taxed less, it will lessen the tendency of many individuals to shelter their earnings from the tax collector by taking advantage of various tax loopholes or cheating on their income tax returns. The greater productivity of the economy will produce more tax revenue for the government. Even though tax *rates* will be lower, the total national income to which these rates are applied will be higher.

Politicians looking to cut taxes have frequently invoked supply-side arguments. For example, in the 1980s, Ronald Reagan and his economic advisers used supply-side logic to justify his tax cuts, as have more contemporary Republicans, such as President Trump with the 2017 Tax Cut and Jobs Act.

supply-side theory *The belief that lower taxes and fewer regulations will stimulate the economy.*

Unfortunately, economists give no definitive answer as to which theory—monetarism, Keynesianism, planning, or supply-side economics—actually works the best in practice. Such an answer likely does not exist even in theory, as the "best" theory likely depends a great deal on the particular circumstances. As a result, the debate among economists—and politicians—will continue into the future.

18-3 The Machinery of Economic Policymaking

Predicting what will happen to the economy is extraordinarily difficult. Because the U.S. economy is complex and depends on so many variables, even the smartest economists often miss the mark in their economic forecasts. Few economists, for example, foresaw the recession that began in 2007. Furthermore, even if economists could perfectly predict the economy, that does not mean the president could necessarily respond to their predictions. The machinery for making decisions about economic matters is complex and not under the president's full control. Within the executive branch, three people other than the president are of special importance. Sometimes called the troika,* these are the chairman of the Council of Economic Advisers (CEA), the director of the Office of Management and Budget (OMB), and the secretary of the treasury.

The CEA, comprising several professional economists plus a small staff, has existed since 1946. In theory, it is an impartial group of experts responsible for forecasting economic trends, analyzing economic issues, and helping

*From the Russian word for a carriage pulled by three horses.

monetary policy *Managing the economy by altering the supply of money and interest rates.*

to prepare the economic report that the president submits to Congress each year. Though quite professional in tone, the CEA is not exactly impartial in practice, since each president picks members sympathetic to his point of view. Obama picked Keynesians; Bush picked supply-siders and monetarists, as has Trump. But whatever its philosophical tilt, the CEA is seen by other executive agencies as the advocate of the opinion of professional economists, who despite their differences generally tend to favor reliance on the market.

The OMB originally was the Bureau of the Budget, which was created in 1921 and made part of the Executive Office of the President in 1939; in 1970 it was renamed the Office of Management and Budget. Its chief function is to prepare estimates of the amount that will be spent by federal agencies, to negotiate with other departments over the size of their budgets, and to make certain (insofar as it can) that the legislative proposals of these other departments are in accord with the president's program. Of late it has acquired something of a split personality; it is in part an expert, nonpartisan agency that analyzes spending and budget patterns and in part an activist, partisan organization that tries to get the bureaucracy to carry out the president's wishes.

The secretary of the treasury often is close to or drawn from the world of business and finance and is expected to argue the point of view of the financial community. (Because its members do not always agree, this is not always easy.) The secretary provides estimates of the revenue that the government can expect from existing taxes and what will be the result of changing tax laws, and represents the United States in its dealings with the top bankers and finance ministers of other nations.

A good deal of pulling and hauling takes place among members of the troika, but if that were the extent of the problem, presidential leadership would be fairly easy. The problem is far more complex. Dozens, if not hundreds, of parts of the government contribute to economic policy. They regulate business, make loans, and supply subsidies. For example, because international trade is important to the U.S. economy, the secretary of state (among many others) has acquired an interest in economic policy, and the Export-Import Bank has also become more important as well (we discuss this feature in the Policy Dynamics: Inside/Outside the Box feature on page 478).

The Federal Reserve System

Among the most important of these other agencies is the board of governors of the Federal Reserve Bank (the "Fed"). Its seven members are appointed by the president, with the consent of the Senate, for non-renewable 14-year terms, and they may not be removed except for cause. (No member has been removed since it was created in 1913.) The chairperson serves four years. In theory, and to some degree in practice, the Fed is independent of both the president and Congress. Its most important function is to regulate, to the extent possible, the supply of money (both in circulation and in bank deposits) and the price of money (in the form of interest rates). The Fed sets **monetary policy**, that is, the effort to shape the economy by controlling the amount of money and bank deposits and the interest rates charged for money. The Fed primarily does this in three ways:

1. **Buying and selling federal government securities** (bonds, Treasury notes, and other pieces of paper

Keystone-France/Gamma-Keystone/Getty Images

Image 18.1 Milton Friedman

Tim Gidal/Picture Post/Getty Images

Image 18.2 John Maynard Keynes

Hulton Archive/Archive Photos/Getty Images

Image 18.3 John Kenneth Galbraith

Walter Bennett/The LIFE Picture Collection/Getty Images

Image 18.4 Arthur B. Laffer

that constitute government IOUs). When the Fed buys securities, it in effect puts more money into circulation and takes securities out of circulation. With more money available, interest rates tend to drop, and more money is borrowed and spent. When the Fed sells government securities, it in effect takes money out of circulation, causing interest rates to rise and making borrowing more difficult.

2. **Regulating the amount of money that a member bank must keep on hand as reserves** to back up the customer deposits it holds. A bank lends out most of the money deposited with it. If the Fed says the bank must keep in reserve a larger portion of its deposits, then the amount it can lend decreases, loans become harder to obtain, and interest rates rise.
3. **Changing the interest charged to banks** that want to borrow money from the Federal Reserve System. Banks borrow from the Fed to cover short-term needs. The interest that the Fed charges for this is called the *discount rate*. The Fed can raise or lower that rate, which has an effect, though usually a rather small one, on how much money the banks will lend.

All of these are powerful tools for setting monetary policy, and the Fed regularly uses all three. For example, the Fed routinely adjusts interest rates to keep the economy growing, but not too quickly (which would result in inflation). For example, when the economy is slowing down—as it was in 2001, in 2007–2008, and in 2020, the Fed lowers rates to try and boost economic growth. But when the economy is expanding, as it was from 2004 to 2006, and from 2015 to 2018, it raises rates to prevent the economy from overheating. The Fed routinely monitors and adjusts this rate to keep economic growth in line with its targets.[11]

Just how independent the Fed is can be a matter of dispute. For example, the Nixon administration pressured Fed chairman Arthur Burns to expand the money supply in 1971 and 1972 (to benefit Nixon in the 1972 election), and many argue this created inflation later in the decade.[12] This suggests that the Fed is not terribly independent of the administration, but other examples suggest otherwise. For example, the Fed's policies in the late 1970s and early 1980s to tighten the money supply were unpopular at the time, but they worked to solve persistently high inflation. While political leaders and the Fed both desire the same outcome—a healthy economy—how best to get there is often in dispute.

Congress

fiscal policy *Managing the economy through the use of tax and spending laws.*

The most important part of the economic policymaking machinery, of course, is Congress. It must approve all taxes and almost all expenditures; there can be no wage or price controls without its consent; and it has the ability to alter the policy of the nominally independent Federal Reserve Board by threatening to pass laws that would reduce its powers. And Congress itself is fragmented: the members of key committees wield great influence, especially the House and Senate Budget Committees, the House and Senate Appropriations Committees, the House Ways and Means Committee, and the Senate Finance Committee. The decisions Congress makes about how high taxes should be and how much money the government should spend create the nation's **fiscal policy**.

In sum, no matter what economic theory the president may support, if he is to put that theory into effect he needs the assistance of many agencies within the executive branch, of independent agencies such as the Federal Reserve Board, and of the various committees of Congress. Though members of the executive and legislative branches are united by their common desire to get reelected (and thus their common interest in producing sound economic growth), each part of this system may also be influenced by different economic theories and be motivated by the claims of interest groups.

The effect of these interest-group claims is clearly shown in the debate over trade restriction. The economic health of the nation usually affects everyone in pretty much the same way—we are all hurt by inflation or helped by stable prices; the incomes of all of us tend to grow (or remain stagnant) together. In these circumstances, the politics of economic health is majoritarian.

Suppose, however, that most of us are doing pretty well, but that the people in a few industries or occupations are suffering. That is sometimes the result of foreign competition. In many countries, labor costs are much lower than in the United States. That means these countries can ship to American buyers goods—such as shoes, textiles, and beef—that sell at much lower prices than American producers can afford to charge. By contrast, if the price of a product is based chiefly on having advanced technology rather than low labor costs, American manufacturers can beat almost any foreign competitor.

When Congress passes laws governing foreign trade, it is responding to interest group politics. Industries that find it easy to sell American products abroad want free trade—that is, they want no taxes or restrictions on international exchanges. Industries that find it hard to compete with foreign imports oppose free trade—that is, they want tariffs and other limitations on imports.

Policy Dynamics: Inside/Outside the Box | The Export-Import Bank: Interest Group and Entrepreneurial Politics

In 1934, President Franklin Delano Roosevelt established the Export-Import Bank to help American companies sell their goods and services abroad. The bank serves as a guarantor to help foreign companies obtain loans to buy U.S. goods. For example, the bank helps foreign airlines buy Boeing airliners, such as the Boeing Dreamliner. Because new airplanes cost hundreds of millions of dollars, even wealthy airlines can have trouble obtaining private financing for them. To help them purchase such expensive goods, the bank (and therefore implicitly the U.S. government) serves as a loan guarantor, making it much easier for foreign companies to buy U.S. goods. In 2015, the Bank's authorization was set to expire, and a vigorous political battle ensued.

The bank and its loan guarantees can be seen as interest-group politics. While the bank benefits many companies, none benefit more so than Boeing, because Boeing's airplanes are so expensive. The benefits of the bank ensue primarily to a concentrated constituency—namely, Boeing and its employees and shareholders. One interpretation of the costs is that domestic airlines pay them. Because they cannot get Export-Import Bank loan guarantees, they argue that this creates an unfair advantage for foreign airlines. The loan guarantees allow foreign airlines to pay lower interest rates on their loans for new jets, which reduces their borrowing costs, which means they can pass on cheaper ticket prices to consumers. For example, Delta Airlines has advanced this position, claiming that the Export-Import Bank loan guarantees allow foreign competitors like Emirates or Air India to undercut it on profitable international flight routes.

But Delta and other domestic airlines are not the only ones working against the bank. Many fiscal conservatives, and allied interest groups such as the Club for Growth and Freedom Partners, are also working to eliminate the bank. Such calls are an example of entrepreneurial politics: eliminating loan guarantees would impose concentrated costs on Boeing and other exporters, but give dispersed benefits to all Americans in the form of lower federal spending and debt. These groups are trying to raise the salience of the issue by launching a media campaign depicting the bank as an example of crony capitalism, with large manufacturers like Boeing benefitting at the expense of ordinary Americans. These groups are willing to pay the price of being an entrepreneur because of their ideological position: they believe in smaller government, so they want to eliminate the Export-Import Bank and other entities like it. Given this contentious politics, the bank's authorization lapsed for a brief period in 2015, before being approved later in the year. These same issues resurfaced when the bank's charter came up for renewal in 2019, but Congress agreed to extend the bank's charter for seven years as part of a year-end spending deal.

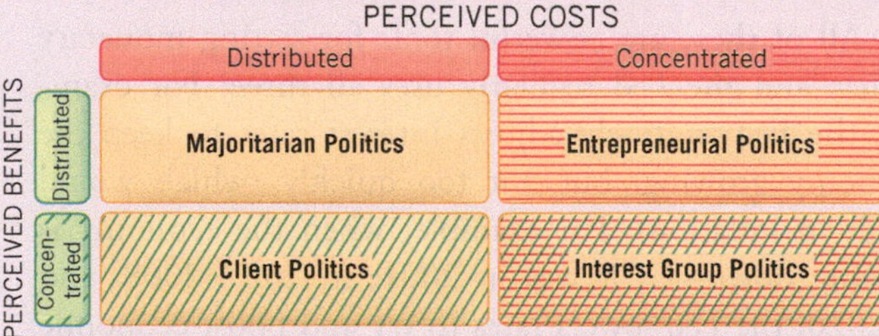

Source: Jonathan Weisman and Eric Lipton, "Air Skirmish in War over Ex-Im Bank," *New York Times*, 7 April 2015.

When the North American Free Trade Agreement (NAFTA) was passed by Congress in 1993, the free traders won, and tariffs on our commerce with Canada and Mexico were largely abolished (as we discuss below, NAFTA was revised somewhat with the USMCA, but the basic structure of NAFTA remains in place). But when the government later suggested creating free trade with all of Latin America, the critics of free trade opposed the idea, and it died. This is a good example of how people who bear the costs of a policy are often much more effective in influencing the votes on it than are those who stand to benefit from it. Indeed, the politics of free trade has continued to be contentious, as we discuss below in the context of globalization.

Ron Sachs/Consolidated News Photos/Ron Sachs -CNP/dpa/Alamy Live News/Alamy Stock Photo

Image 18.5 Jerome Powell, Chair of the Federal Reserve Board of Governors, testifies before Congress.

18-4 The Budget, Spending, and Taxes

As we said at the outset of the chapter, a budget is a document that announces how much the government will collect in taxes and spend in revenues and how those expenditures will be allocated among various programs. Each of the federal government's budgets covers a **fiscal year**, which runs from October 1 of one year through September 30 of the next. A fiscal year is named after the year in which it **ends:** thus, "fiscal 2021" or "FY2021" means the year ending on September 30, 2021.

In theory, the federal budget should be based on *first* deciding how much money the government is going to spend and *then* allocating that money among different programs and agencies. That is the way a household makes up its budget: "We have this much in the paycheck, and so we will spend X dollars on rent, Y dollars on food, and Z dollars on clothing, and what's left over on entertainment. If the amount of the paycheck goes down, we will cut something out—probably entertainment."

But as we noted at the start of the chapter, that is decidedly *not* how the federal government behaves. In fact, the federal budget is a list of everything the government is going to spend money on, with only slight regard (or often, no regard at all) for how much money is available to be spent. Instead of being a way of *allocating* money to be spent on various purposes, it is a way of *adding up* what is being spent.

Indeed, there was no federal budget at all before 1921, and there was no unified presidential budget until the 1930s. Even after the president began submitting a single budget, the committees of Congress acted on it separately, adding to or subtracting from the amounts he proposed. (Usually they followed his lead, but they were certainly free to depart from it as they wished.) If one committee wanted to spend more on housing, no effort was made to take that amount away from the committee that was spending money on health (in fact, there was no machinery for making such an effort).

The Congressional Budget Act of 1974 changed this somewhat. Now after the president submits his budget in February, two budget committees—one in the House, one in the Senate—study the overall package and obtain an analysis of it from the Congressional Budget Office. Each committee then submits to its chamber a **budget resolution** that proposes a total budget ceiling and a ceiling for each of several spending areas (such as health or defense). Each May, Congress is supposed to adopt, with some modifications, these budget resolutions, intending them to be targets to guide the work of each legislative committee as it decides what should be spent in its area. During the summer Congress then takes up the specific appropriations bills, informing its members as it goes along whether or not the spending proposed in these bills conforms to the May budget resolution. The object, obviously, is to impose some discipline on the various committees. After each committee approves its appropriations bill and Congress passes it, the president then signs (or vetoes) the resolution.

These appropriations bills, however, can rarely make big changes in government spending. Much of what the government spends is **mandatory**—that is, the money goes to people who are entitled to it. **Entitlements** include Social Security and Medicare payments, veterans' benefits, food stamps, and money the government owes investors who have bought Treasury bonds (i.e., the interest on the national debt). For mandatory spending programs, the federal government does not decide to increase or decrease the amount of money spent on these programs. The amount spent is determined by the eligibility rules and on who chooses to apply. For example, Congress does not decide how much to spend on food stamps. The amount spent is based on the number of people who qualify for these benefits and choose to comply. To control the amount spent on food stamps, the federal government would have to change the eligibility rules or benefits levels (as they did in 2008).

Other spending is **discretionary**—that is, the amount of spending that is not mandated by law, but is instead set by Congress through the appropriations process. Discretionary spending is all of the remaining nonmandatory spending: defense, housing and community development, transportation, education, and so forth. In FY2019, mandatory spending including interest payments was $2.735 trillion, versus about only $1.336 trillion for discretionary spending.[13] Because of how the federal government calculates discretionary spending, even much of that discretionary spending could not really be cut without a political outcry; for example, health benefits for

fiscal year *For the federal government, October 1 through the following September 30.*

budget resolution *A congressional decision that states the maximum amount of money the government should spend.*

mandatory spending *Money that the government is required to spend by law.*

entitlements *A claim for government funds that cannot be changed without violating the rights of the claimant.*

discretionary spending *Spending that is not required to pay for contracts, interest on the national debt, or entitlement programs such as Social Security.*

debt ceiling *A limit on how much money the federal government can borrow (by limiting the amount of debt it can issue).*

veterans and military personnel are discretionary spending, but are quite popular.[14] As a result, what can be cut is a rather modest share of the budget, and as we will see below, and even cutting this would be quite challenging.

Over time, mandatory spending has expanded dramatically. In the 1960s, discretionary spending accounted for two-thirds of federal spending, but today, mandatory spending makes up that much of the budget.[15] Much of this is because of the growth of entitlement programs, predominantly Social Security, Medicaid, and Medicare (and other health care–related spending). As we see in the right-hand panel of Figure 18.4, in 2019, Social Security ate up approximately one-quarter of federal spending, with health care spending consuming almost another quarter. The lion's share of this spending on health care goes to Medicare, which alone accounts for nearly 17 percent of federal outlays.

As we see in Figure 18.5, these programs have, over time, come to make up a larger share of U.S. GDP. In 1970, Medicare was less than 1 percent of U.S. GDP, but today it is almost 4 percent, and that figure is expected to rise to over 6 percent by 2050 with a rapidly aging population; the figures for Social Security show a similar, albeit less dramatic, rise. Over time, the growth in these programs will make it even more difficult to restrain the overall increase of government spending (we return to this point below).

When we look at the revenue side of Figure 18.4, we see that the U.S. government funds itself through three main sources: individual income taxes, corporate income taxes, and a set of miscellaneous taxes and fees (largely excise taxes on items like alcohol and tobacco). Looking at the amounts, it is clear that the U.S. is quite dependent on individual income taxes: just about one-half of federal revenues come from the income taxes paid by individual Americans.

You will no doubt note that we've ignored the second biggest category here—payroll taxes. Payroll taxes are the taxes individuals and their employers pay for Social Security and Medicare, which account for a bit over 35 percent of total revenues. But these taxes go to fund these programs, not the rest of the government. As we discussed in Chapter 17, as the baby boom generation retires, these programs are becoming ever-more expensive, and their costs exceed the amount of these taxes. So soon, these programs will require either changes to the programs or general revenue transfers, making the budget puzzle even more complicated moving forward.

As we noted at the outset of the chapter, year in and year out, the U.S. spends more than it takes in from taxes: in 2019, we spent almost $1 trillion (technically, "only" $892 billion, see Figure 18.1) more than we took in from taxes. So to finance this, the federal government has to sell bonds (i.e., borrow money).

Before the 20th century, Congress individually approved the duration, amount, and interest rate of each bond, typically issuing bonds to fund a particular project, such as the Panama Canal. But during World War I, this simply became too time-intensive given the amount of money that needed to be raised to fund the overseas military campaigns.

To help expedite funding the war effort, Congress delegated the power to issue bonds and other debt instruments to the Treasury Department. But because some feared that this was abrogating Congress's power of the purse, in 1917 Congress imposed a limit on how much debt the Treasury department was authorized to sell: the federal **debt ceiling**.[16] This freed Congress from the

Figure 18.4

Federal Revenues in 2019

Other Revenue 7.9%
Individual Income Taxes 49.6%
Payroll Taxes 35.9%
Corporate Taxes 6.6%

Source: Office of Management and Budget, Historical Tables (Table 2.2).

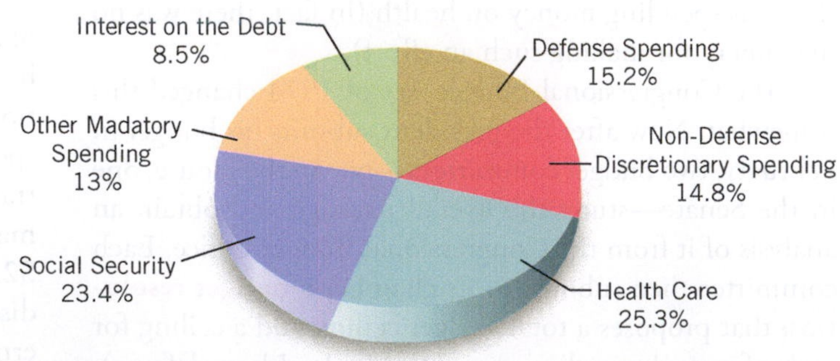

Source: Congressional Budget Office, The Budget and Economic Outlook, 2020 to 2030, Historical Budget Data Appendix.

Figure 18.5 **Social Security and Medicare Costs as a Percentage of GDP**

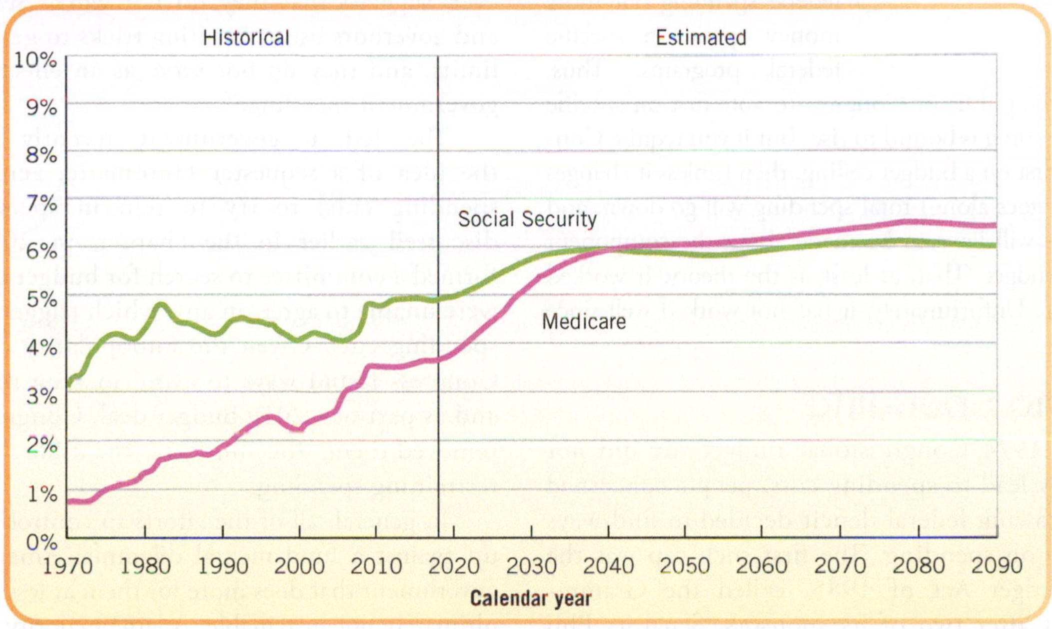

Source: "A Summary of the 2019 Annual Reports," Social Security Administration, www.ssa.gov/oact/trsum/.

responsibility of having to approve each bond individually, but gave it some control over how much debt was issued by the federal government. Note, however, that the debt ceiling is separate from decisions about taxation and spending: Congress approves those separately; the debt ceiling simply is a limit on how much debt the U.S. Treasury is authorized to sell at any given point in time.

For much of the 20th century, the debt ceiling was largely uncontroversial. Between 1962 and 2012, Congress voted 74 times to raise the debt ceiling, including 16 times between 1993 and 2010, and 10 times between 2001 and 2010. In 2011, with the rise of the Tea Party, the debate over raising the debt ceiling became contentious, and resulted in the automatic spending cuts (somewhat) going into effect. Contentious debates also occurred in 2013, 2014, 2015, and will likely continue into the future.

The debate over the debt ceiling shows how controversial tax and spending decisions have become. Many popular programs exist, and not many have an appetite for increasing taxes, so debates of this type are likely to continue. But even setting aside the debt ceiling, a big loophole can be found in the current budget process: nothing in the process requires Congress to tighten the government's financial belt. It can pass a budget resolution authorizing spending that is more or less than what the president has proposed. Nonetheless, the process has made a difference. Congress is now conscious of how its spending decisions match up with estimates of tax revenues.

When President Reagan took office, he and his allies in Congress took advantage of the Congressional Budget Act to start the controversial process of cutting federal spending. The House and Senate budget committees, with the president's support, used the first budget resolution in May 1981 not simply to set a budget ceiling that, as in the past, looked pretty much like the previous year's budget, but to direct each committee of Congress to make cuts—sometimes deep cuts—in the programs for which it was responsible. These cuts were to be made in the authorization legislation (see Chapter 13) as well as in the appropriations.

The object was to get members of Congress to vote for a total package of cuts before they could vote on any particular cut. Republican control of the Senate and an alliance between Republicans and conservative Southern Democrats in the House allowed this strategy to succeed. The first budget resolution ordered Senate and House committees to reduce federal spending during fiscal year 1982 by about $36 billion—less than the president had first asked, but a large sum nonetheless. Then the individual committees set to work trying to find ways of making these cuts.

Note how the procedures used by Congress can affect the *policies* it adopts. If the Reagan plan had been submitted in the old piecemeal way, it is unlikely that cuts of this size would have occurred so quickly, or at all. The reason is not that Congress would have wanted to ignore the president, but that, then as now, Congress reflects public opinion on economic policy. As stated at the beginning of the chapter,

sequester Automatic spending cuts.

the public wants less total federal spending but more money spent on specific federal programs. Thus, if you allow the public or Congress to vote first on specific programs, spending is bound to rise. But if you require Congress to vote first on a budget ceiling, then (unless it changes its mind as it goes along) total spending will go down, and tough choices will have to be made about the component parts of the budget. That, at least, is the theory. It worked once, in 1981. Unfortunately, it has not worked well since then.

Reducing Spending

Because the 1974 Congressional Budget Act did not automatically lead to spending cuts, people concerned about the growing federal deficit decided to find ways to put a cap on spending. The first such cap was the Balanced Budget Act of 1985, called the Gramm-Rudman Act after two of its sponsors, Senators Phil Gramm (R-TX) and Warren Rudman (R-NH). The law required that each year from 1986 to 1991 the budget would automatically be cut until the federal deficit had disappeared. What made the cuts automatic, its authors hoped, was a provision in the bill, called a **sequester**, that required across-the-board percentage cuts in all federal programs (except for entitlements) if the president and Congress failed to agree on a total spending level that met the law's targets.

But nobody much liked the idea, and the plan failed. Congress and the president found ways to get new spending that was higher than the targeted amounts (largely through budgetary accounts and tricks; some were valid, others less so). By 1990, it was evident that a new strategy was needed if the government was going to help eliminate the deficit.

That strategy had two parts. First, Congress voted for a tax increase. Second, it passed the Budget Enforcement Act of 1990 that set limits on discretionary spending. According to the 1990 act, if Congress were to spend more on a discretionary program, it would have to cut spending on another discretionary program or raise taxes. The law expired in 2001, and it has not been put back in place (though we discuss other efforts below).

Various proposals have been put forth about how to restrain federal government spending. One popular idea is a balanced budget amendment, which would prohibit the government from spending more money than it takes in from taxes and fees (i.e., the government could not deficit-spend). Such proposals have been implemented in a number of states, and have been proposed multiple times at the federal level. The evidence, however, suggests that they do not work. State legislators and governors use accounting tricks to get around their limits, and they do not serve as an effective check on government spending.[17]

The federal government recently returned to the idea of a sequester (automatic, across-the-board spending cuts) to try to rein in spending. As we discussed earlier in the chapter, in 2011 Congress formed a committee to search for budget cuts, but they were unable to agree on any, which triggered automatic spending cuts. Given the unpopularity of these cuts, Congress found ways to avoid making most of them, and as part of a 2019 budget deal, Congress effectively removed them. This illustrates the difficulty of actually restraining spending.

In general, all of the efforts to control spending run up against a fundamental dilemma: Americans want a government that does more for them at less cost, which is ultimately not sustainable. A large majority of Americans wants more generous social spending on a variety of programs, but they don't want a bigger government or higher taxes. Furthermore, as we explained in Chapter 8, because programs create constituencies who lobby for their continuation and expansion, once programs are in place, they are difficult to remove.

Restraining spending is effectively entrepreneurial politics. The benefits of spending on any given program are relatively concentrated, while the benefits are dispersed to the public as a whole (in the form of a more balanced budget). An entrepreneur needs to take up the cause, and few members of Congress have been willing in recent years to do this, though 2012 vice presidential candidate and former House Speaker Paul Ryan is an example of one such individual. So far, they have not been successful, though that may, of course, change at some point in the future.

Of course, if we cannot restrain spending, another alternative exists: raising taxes. Below, we consider the feasibility of this option.

Levying Taxes

Tax policy reflects a mixture of majoritarian politics ("What is a 'fair' tax law?") and client politics ("How much is in it for me?"). In the United States, a fair tax law generally has been viewed as one that keeps the overall tax burden rather low, requires everyone to pay something, and requires those who are better off to pay at a higher rate than those who are less well-off. The law, in short, was viewed as good if it imposed modest burdens, prevented cheating, and was mildly progressive.

Americans have had their first goal satisfied. The tax burden in the United States is lower than it is in most other democratic nations. Some evidence shows that they have also had their second goal met—there is reason to believe that Americans evade their income taxes less than do citizens of, say, France or Italy. (That is one reason why many nations rely more on sales taxes than we do—they are harder to evade.) And federal income taxes here are progressive: The bottom 50 percent of earners paid about 3 percent of income taxes, but the top 10 percent paid about 68 percent of taxes.[18]

Keeping the burden low and the cheating at a minimum are examples of majoritarian politics: most people benefit, most people pay. The loopholes, however, are another matter—all manner of special interests can get some special benefit from the tax law that the rest of us must pay for, but, given the complexity of the law, rarely notice. Loopholes are client politics *par excellence.*

Because of that, hardly any scholars believed tax reform (dramatically reducing the loopholes) was politically possible. Every interest that benefited from a loophole—and these included not just corporations but universities, museums, states, cities, and investors—would lobby vigorously to protect it.

Nevertheless, in 1986 a sweeping tax reform act was passed. Many of the most cherished loopholes were closed or reduced. What happened? It is as if scientists who had proved that a bumblebee could not fly got stung by a flying bumblebee.

The Rise of the Income Tax

To understand what happened in 1986, one must first understand the political history of taxation in the United States. Until almost the end of the 19th century, there was no federal income tax (except for a brief period during the Civil War). The money the government needed came mostly from tariffs (i.e., taxes on goods imported into this country). And when Congress did enact a peacetime income tax, the Supreme Court in 1895 struck it down as unconstitutional.[19] To change this, Congress proposed, and in 1913 the states ratified, the Sixteenth Amendment, which authorized such a tax.

For the next 40 years or so, tax rates tended to go up during wartime and down during peacetime (see Figure 18.6). The rates were progressive—that is, the wealthiest individuals paid at a higher rate than the less affluent. For example, during World War II, incomes in the highest bracket were taxed at a rate of 94 percent.

The Power to Tax and Spend

"The Congress shall have Power to lay and collect Taxes, Duties, Imposts and Excises, to pay the Debts and provide for the common Defence and general Welfare of the United States...." (Article I, Section 8)

The clause above is the source of the federal government's ability to tax and to spend money. But what exactly does that power entail? Even the Founding Fathers disagreed over this. Some—most notably Alexander Hamilton—supported a more expansive interpretation, which would strengthen the government's ability to tax and spend (see his discussion in *Federalist* No. 30). Others—such as James Madison—thought the federal government's powers in this area should be more strictly limited to those defined in the Constitution: to pay the government's debts and provide for the common defense and general welfare. Hamilton, in short, wanted a broad reading, giving rise to a stronger federal government, whereas Madison wanted a narrow reading, giving rise to a more constrained federal government.

In general, in the early decades of the new government, the more limited view reigned. For example, in 1822, President James Monroe vetoed a bill to fund improvements on the Cumberland Road on the grounds that it was primarily a state, not a national, project—Congress could only provide for the general (i.e., national) welfare, not fund more local projects.

In the 20th century, however, the power to tax and spend took on a more expansive connotation. The modern interpretation begins with *United States v. Butler* (1936), in which the Supreme Court held that Congress could spend money as long as it was in the general welfare of the nation. But because the Court gave Congress wide latitude in determining the general welfare, this greatly expanded the tax and spending powers of the federal government. Subsequent court decisions, most notably *South Dakota v. Dole* (1987), have furthered this logic, and allow the federal government very broad latitude to tax and spend for a wide variety of purposes.

Figure 18.6 **Federal Taxes on Income, Top Percentage Rates, 1913–2019**

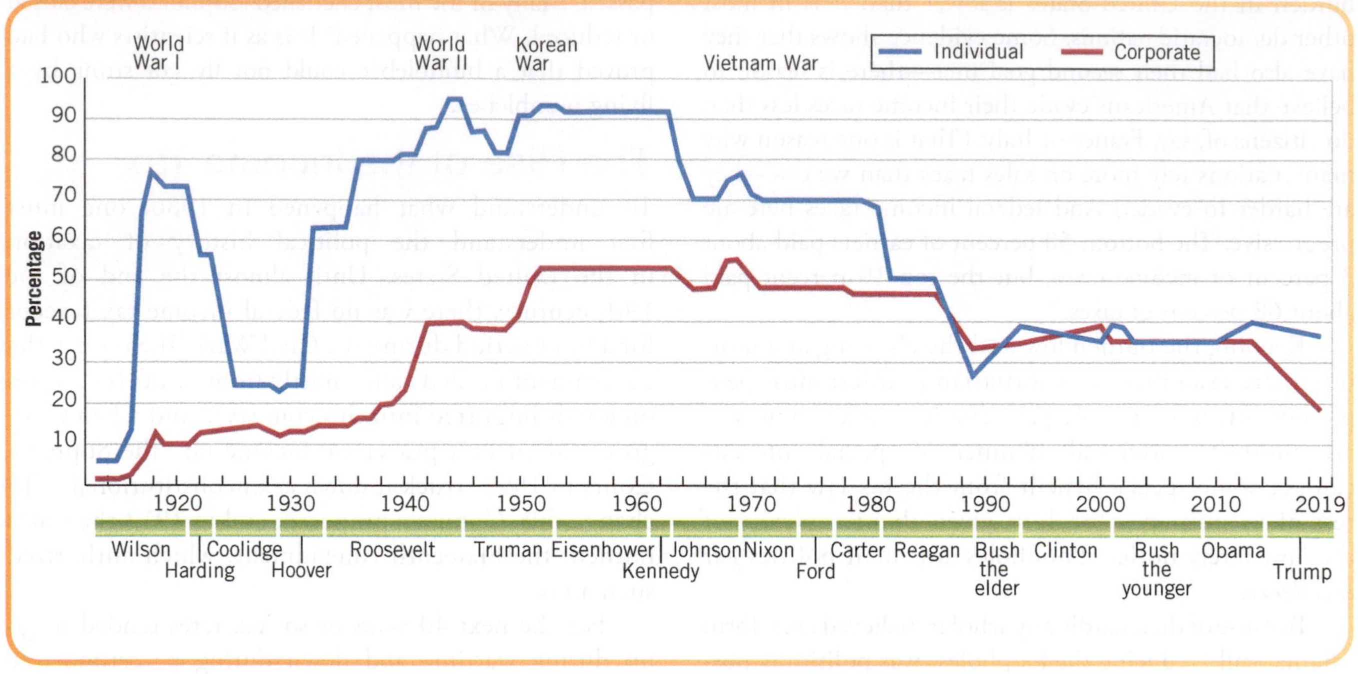

Source: Internal Revenue Service, Tax Tables, 2019.

Economists call the key tax rate the "marginal rate." This is the percentage of the last dollar you earn that must be paid out in taxes.

An income tax offers the opportunity for majoritarian politics to become class politics. The majority of the citizenry earn average incomes and control most of the votes. In theory, nothing can prevent the mass of people from voting for legislators who will tax only the rich, who, as a minority, will always be outvoted. During the early decades of the 20th century, that is exactly what the rich feared would happen. Because the highest marginal tax rate was 94 percent, you might think that is in fact what did happen.

You would be wrong. Offsetting the high rates were the deductions, exemptions, and exclusions by which people could shelter some of their income from taxation. These loopholes were available for everyone, but they particularly helped the well-off. In effect, a political compromise was reached during the first half of the 20th century. The terms were these: the well-off, generally represented by the Republican Party, would drop their bitter opposition to high marginal rates provided that the less-well-off, generally represented by the Democratic Party, would support a large number of loopholes. The Democrats (or more accurately, the liberals) were willing to accept this compromise because they feared that if they insisted on high rates with no loopholes, the economy would suffer as people and businesses lost their incentive to save and invest.

For at least 30 years after the adoption of the income tax in 1913, only a small number of high-income people paid any significant amount in federal income taxes. The average citizen paid very little in such taxes until World War II. After the war, taxes did not fall to their prewar levels.

Most people did not complain too much because they, too, benefited greatly from the loopholes. They could deduct from their taxable income the interest they paid on their home mortgages, the state and local taxes they paid, much of what they paid in medical insurance premiums, and the interest they paid on consumer loans (such as those used to buy automobiles). On the eve of the Tax Reform Act of 1986, an opinion poll showed that more people favored small cuts in tax rates coupled with many large deductions than favored big cuts in tax rates coupled with fewer and smaller deductions.[20]

Interest groups organized around each loophole. Homebuilders organized to support the mortgage-interest deduction; universities supported the charitable-contribution deduction; insurance companies supported the deduction for medical insurance premiums; and automakers supported the deduction for interest on consumer loans.

In addition to these well-known loopholes, countless others—not so well known and involving much less money—were defended and enlarged through the efforts of other interest groups. For instance, oil companies supported the deduction for drilling costs, heavy industry supported the investment tax credit, and real estate developers supported special tax write-offs for apartment and office buildings.

Until 1986, the typical tax fight was less about rates than about deductions. Rates were important, but not as important as tax loopholes. "Loophole politics" was client politics. When client groups pressed for benefits, they could take advantage of the decentralized structure of Congress to find well-placed advocates who could advance these interests through low-visibility bargaining. In effect, these groups were getting a subsidy from the federal government equal to the amount of the tax break. However, the tax break was even better than a subsidy because it did not have to be voted on every year as part of an appropriations bill: once part of the tax code, it lasted for a long time, and given the length and complexity of that code, scarcely anyone would notice it was there.

Then the Tax Reform Act of 1986 turned the decades-old compromise on its head: Instead of high rates with big deductions, we got low rates with much smaller deductions. The big gainers were individuals; the big losers were businesses.

Since then, Congress has both raised and lowered taxes at different points in time. While President George H. W. Bush famously said "Read my lips, no new taxes," he signed a tax increase during his presidency as part of a broader budget deal. President Clinton also raised marginal rates, especially for higher-income Americans, in 1993. President George W Bush lowered taxes in 2001 and 2003, but many of those tax provisions expired in 2010. After much debate, Congress first temporarily extended all of the tax cuts until 2012, and in that year, made the tax cuts for all but the wealthiest Americans permanent (the wealthiest Americans saw their tax rates return to the pre-Bush levels set by President Clinton). The Tax Cut and Jobs Act of 2017 reduced the top marginal tax rate, but it also eliminated some deductions.

Moving forward, it is unclear what will happen with future tax rates. While increasing spending is popular, increasing taxes is not. And unlike in 1986, the deductions that are worth significant money are all considered sacrosanct by middle-class and upper-middle class Americans: the home mortgage interest deduction, employer-sponsored health insurance, and so forth. Cutting these policies would be extremely difficult indeed. And given the parties' very different visions for governmental priorities in the decades ahead, little progress has been made.

This puts American fiscal policy in a difficult position. As Americans age, the costs of Social Security and Medicare will continue to rise beyond what they bring in from payroll taxes. As the non-partisan Congressional Budget Office estimates, these programs will eat up an increasing share of the budget in the years to come, and will require additional borrowing. Of course, borrowing more money means that the government will owe even more in interest payments, requiring further cuts to other types of spending.[21] This harkens back to the fundamental dilemma noted earlier: generally speaking, it is not possible to have both higher spending and lower taxes in the long run.

globalization *The growing integration of the economies and societies of the world.*

18-5 Contemporary Debates about Economic Policy

As you've seen throughout the chapter, debates over taxation and spending might seem dull and abstract, but they are anything but that in reality: they cut to the very heart of what government does. We close this chapter by considering two of the most contentious economic policy issues from recent years: debates over globalization and income inequality.

Globalization

As we discussed earlier in the chapter, free trade has long been a contentious issue in American politics. Such tensions have been especially acute in recent years as part of a rising concern around **globalization**, the growing integration of the economies and societies of the world. We all experience globalization in our everyday lives. If your computer develops a problem and you call technical support, you are likely to speak with a technician based in India or the Philippines. If you go to a shopping mall and buy a new shirt, it was likely made not in America, but in Bangladesh or Vietnam. Your cell phone or computer may have been made in China or Taiwan. All of these are examples of globalization.

Supporters of globalization argue that it has increased the income, literacy, and standard of living of people in almost every country involved in the worldwide process of economic growth. These supporters favor free trade because it makes products cheaper. For example, they have pushed for free trade agreements with Central America (enacted 2005), Panama, Colombia, and South Korea (all enacted in 2011).

Opponents of globalization make several different and not always consistent arguments. Some (such as labor union leaders) argue that free trade undercuts the wages of American workers, as less expensive foreign workers make products that are sold here. Others argue that globalization is driven by selfish corporate interests that exploit people in poor countries when they work for American firms. Still others contend that

income inequality *The extent to which income is unevenly distributed throughout society.*

globalization means imposing one culture on everyone in ways that hurt local cultures.

President Trump has pushed back against globalization, especially with respect to free trade. President Trump has consistently critiqued the politics of free trade, dating back to the start of his 2016 campaign. After assuming office, President Trump withdrew from the Trans-Pacific Partnership (a new trade deal not yet fully implemented), and renegotiated NAFTA into a new trade agreement, known as the U.S. Mexico Canada Agreement (USMCA), which was ratified into law in early 2020.[22]

He also imposed tariffs on a number of products where he said foreign manufacturers were competing unfairly with domestic producers, such as solar panels, steel and aluminum, as well as many products made in China. In response, other countries imposed retaliatory tariffs on American goods, or cut back on buying American products—most notably, the Chinese stopped purchasing as many soybeans from American farmers. To protect farmers, President Trump authorized the Agriculture Department to spend $28 billion in payments to farmers to make up for these lost sales.[23] There is little mystery why Trump gave this aid to farmers: they are a key voting bloc in several swing states, and he was worried that they would not support him in the 2020 elections. This incident reminds us that most of the debates about international economics, free trade, and tariffs are really—at their core—arguments about domestic politics.

Indeed, we can use our same policymaking framework from earlier chapters to understand many of these debates about globalization. For example, some of these debates are largely about interest group politics. For example, when President Trump—or President George W. Bush—imposed tariffs on imported steel, this is interest group politics. The debate here is between domestic producers of steel (steel mills), who want tariffs to prevent foreign steel manufacturers from selling cheap steel here, versus companies who use steel, such as auto manufacturers, who want the cheapest steel possible. The battle may play out publicly because both groups are important electoral constituencies, but the debate is primarily about the costs and benefits to these groups. In contrast, President Trump's decision to subsidize farmers hurt by his trade policy is classic client politics: the farmers receive the concentrated benefits from the payments, all Americans pay the higher costs needed to offset them.

The spread of COVID-19 also influenced this debate as well. For example, many of the necessary medical testing supplies are not made in the U.S., but in overseas markets, and the same is true in many European nations as well. Given this, some have called for globalization to be scaled back, though whether that will actually come to pass remains to be seen.[24]

Income Inequality

But globalization is not the only contentious economic issue in the contemporary United States. In recent years, debates over **income inequality** have also entered the public sphere. For example, the Congressional Budget Office calculates that since 1979, the incomes of the top 1 percent have increased by 174 percent, while the incomes of the bottom 80 percent only increased 16 percent—the top 1 percent saw their incomes increase 11 times faster than the vast majority of Americans.[25] This is true not just in terms of income, but also of wealth (all assets, including homes, cars, stocks, etc.): the richest 1 percent of Americans have more wealth than the middle 60 percent of Americans (i.e., the middle class).[26] No matter what statistics one uses, the conclusion is clear: The economic gains of recent decades have accrued primarily to those at the very top of the economic ladder.[27]

The causes of inequality are quite complex, and economists have put forth a number of different explanations, including the rising premium attached to higher education and higher-skilled jobs,[28] the substitution of higher-wage jobs in manufacturing with lower-wage jobs in the service industry,[29] and the decline of unions.[30] However, part of the explanation stems from shifts in government policy as well, particularly tax and spending policies that tend to favor the well-off.[31] This becomes a particular political concern, especially in light of the finding that policy is more responsive to the most affluent (see Chapter 7). In particular, many fear that rising inequality helps to perpetuate itself: those at the top do well by virtue of being born at the top, whereas those at the bottom struggle even if they have considerable talent.[32]

In response to such concerns, income inequality has become a hot political issue. The most visible example of this trend was the Occupy Wall Street movement in 2011 and its slogan "We are the 99 Percent." The slogan highlighted the trend seen in the previous paragraph: Many of the benefits of the economy accrued to those at the top (the 1 percent), rather than to most Americans (the 99 percent). While the movement did not change policy, it did bring the issue of income inequality into active public discussion, a theme that politicians—such as Senators Bernie Sanders and Elizabeth Warren, both of whom sought the 2020 Democratic nomination—have picked up in their rhetoric.

As a result, there has been more debate in recent years about policies that would ameliorate this inequality. One striking example is the debate over the minimum wage (whether minimum wage laws help or hurt poor workers

Pacific Press/LightRocket/Getty Images

Image 18.6 As income inequality has increased in recent years, many have debated various solutions to address it.

is the subject of debate among economists).[33] While the federal minimum wage has been constant at $7.25 since 2009, many states and localities have increased their minimum wage since then, often as the result of ballot initiatives. Indeed, 29 states and the District of Columbia now have state-level minimum wages above the federal one, and across the United States, the average minimum wage in 2019 was $11.80, 62 percent above the federal minimum.[34] The fact that these proposals passed in both Republican and Democratic states underscores that such policies are popular across party lines, a fact also borne out by public opinion data. For example, two-thirds of Americans—and even 43 percent of Republicans—support a $15 per hour federal minimum wage.[35] You can consider the effect such minimum wage increases have on inequality more in the What Would You Do? box on page 488.

Of course, raising the minimum wage is not the only policy scholars and politicians have proposed to reduce the growing levels of economic inequality. For example, in the 2020 Democratic nomination campaign, both Senators Bernie Sanders and Elizabeth Warren made inequality a key theme of their respective campaigns, and proposed a number of different policies, including efforts to forgive student debt, make public colleges tuition-free, fund early childhood education, and so forth. But perhaps most notably, both proposed a wealth tax, an idea favored by some economists as a mechanism for reducing income disparities. A wealth tax is a tax on all assets, not just the income one earns.[36] Economists are deeply divided on the feasibility of such taxes, and whether or not they actually work to reduce income inequality; there is also the question of whether such a tax is even constitutional (since the 16th Amendment allows for an income tax, not necessarily a wealth tax).[37] But the fact that such issues are receiving serious discussion as part of a U.S. presidential campaign shows how much the issue has seeped into the public consciousness.

Our policy dynamics framework also helps us to understand the politics of these issues. Some policies to reduce inequality can be seen as majoritarian politics, such as universal pre-K for young children. These are policies where everyone pays, and everyone benefits, much like Social Security. Such efforts can also be framed as promoting equality of opportunity, rather than equality of outcomes. As we discussed in Chapter 4, in the United States, unlike many European countries, there is much stronger support for equality of opportunity (making sure everyone has similar opportunities to succeed) than there is for equality of outcomes (making sure everyone ends up in a similar place). Such policies are therefore more likely to garner the support of many Americans.

Other policies to reduce inequality fit better in the entrepreneurial politics category. Many policy solutions to income inequality—like a wealth tax—redistribute from the richer to the poorer parts of society. This means that the wealthy—who are heavily advantaged in terms of political and economic resources—pays the concentrated costs, and society at large receives the benefits. Such policies are therefore likely to require a dedicated policy entrepreneur—someone like Senators Sanders or Warren—as well as considerable media attention to succeed. The debate over these policies will no doubt continue into the future, but the framework we have developed throughout the text will help you to understand them.

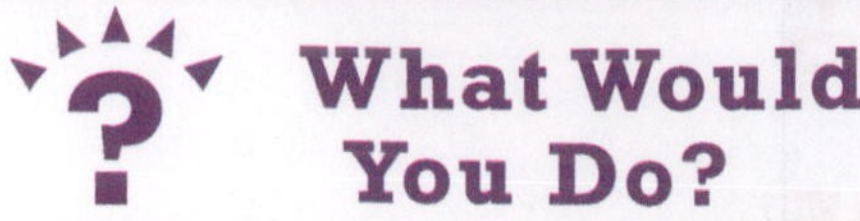

What Would You Do? | Will You Raise the Minimum Wage?

To: *Ben Brian, White House Chief of Staff*
From: *Dillon Jake, Chair, Council of Economic Advisers*
Subject: *Raise the minimum wage*

As the president requested, here is the council's evaluation of the proposal to increase the federal minimum wage to $15 per hour, indexed to inflation.

To Consider:

Presidential candidate Lily Luke declared yesterday that she would seek to raise the minimum wage to $15 per hour over the next few years. Her proposal would also index the minimum wage to increase with inflation.

Arguments for:

1. A higher minimum wage benefits those at the bottom of the economic ladder, helping them to meet their basic needs. Studies suggest that a higher minimum wage reduces poverty.
2. Minimum-wage earners are no longer teenagers with summer jobs. Their average age is 35; most work full time; more than one-fourth are parents; and, on average, they earn half of their families' total income. They need this boost just to make ends meet.
3. Over time, inflation eats away at the minimum wage if it is not indexed to rise as costs rise. Adjusted for inflation, the minimum wage from 1969 ($1.60) would be $11.58 today, far above the current $7.25 per hour federal minimum wage.

Arguments against:

1. It will likely reduce employment, especially for unskilled workers, according to the Congressional Budget Office.
2. A higher minimum wage results in higher prices, which are then passed on to consumers.
3. A higher minimum wage keeps people in minimum-wage jobs longer, blocking younger workers with fewer skills from entry-level positions.

Source: "The Effects of a Minimum Wage Increase on Employment and Family Income," Congressional Budget Office, 18 February 2014, www.cbo.gov/publication/44995; Mike Konczal, "Economists Agree: Raising the Minimum Wage Reduces Poverty," *Washington Post*, 4 January 2014.

What Will You Decide? Enter **MindTap** to make your choice.

Your decision: ☐ Support ☐ Oppose

Learning Objectives

18-1 Summarize how politics and public opinion shape economic policy.

The politics of taxing and spending are so difficult mainly because most people don't like being taxed but do value government spending on a wide variety of government programs. Most voters want lower taxes, less debt, and new programs, but if we spend more, we have to pay for it, either through higher taxes or by borrowing more (hence accumulating more, not less, debt).

18-2 Summarize four main theories of economic policymaking.

The four main theories of economic policy are monetarism (inflation occurs when too much money chases too few goods), Keynesianism (the government should spend more money when there is a recession and less when the economy is doing well), economic planning (the government should actively plan the economy), and supply-side economics (lower taxes will stimulate economic growth). Unfortunately, no consensus exists among economists about which one is best.

18-3 Describe how American institutions work to set economic policy.

The difficulty is that many different actors play a role: the president, Congress, the Federal Reserve System, the Council of Economic Advisors, the secretary of the treasury, and hundreds of other agencies all contribute to economic policy. All of these actors have very imperfect control of the economy.

18-4 Explain the budget process and discuss why cutting spending or increasing taxes is difficult.

Restraining spending or raising taxes are difficult for several reasons. First, most government spending is mandatory spending required by law. Second, the general public and members of Congress like government spending and dislike taxes. Given this, restraining the growth of government is quite complicated.

18-5 Summarize the debates over globalization and income inequality and how they fit within our broader framework for understanding policy issues.

Globalization focuses on the increasing integration of the global economy, and primarily plays out in U.S. politics surrounding debates over free trade. Economic inequality, the gap between the rich and the poor, plays out in a variety of debates about how best to address this problem. Both sets of debates can be understood through the policy dynamics framework developed in the text.

To Learn More

Internal Revenue Service: **www.irs.gov**

Tax Foundation: **www.taxfoundation.org**

Hutchins Center on Fiscal and Monetary Policy at Brookings: **https://www.brookings.edu/center/the-hutchins-center-on-fiscal-and-monetary-policy/**

Birnbaum, Jeffrey H., and Alan S. Murray. *Showdown at Gucci Gulch.* New York: Random House, 1987. Lively journalistic account of the passage of the Tax Reform Act of 1986.

Cogan, John. 2017. *The High Costs of Good Intentions: A History of U.S. Federal Entitlement Programs.* Stanford, CA: Hoover Institution Press. A lucid history of various entitlement programs, explaining why they almost always expand over time.

Kiewiet, D. Roderick. *Macroeconomics and Micropolitics: The Electoral Effects of Economic Issues.* Chicago: University of Chicago Press, 1983. Argues that citizens vote on the basis of their estimate of national economic conditions as well as their own financial circumstances.

Morgenson, Gretchen and Joshua Rosner. *Reckless Endangerment: How Outside Ambition, Greed, and Corruption Led to Economic Armageddon.* New York: Times Books/Henry Holt, 2011. The subtitle says it all.

Samuelson, Robert J. *The Good Life and Its Discontents.* New York: Times Books/Random House, 1995. A readable, intelligent account of American economic life since World War II.

Schick, Allen. *The Federal Budget.* Washington, D.C.: Brookings Institution, 2000. Excellent overview of how Washington allocates money.

Sorkin, Andrew Ross. *Too Big to Fail: The Inside Story of How Wall Street and Washington Fought to Save the Financial System—and Themselves.*

New York: Viking, 2009. The captivating tale of how certain top Washington officials and Wall Street leaders reacted to the near-collapse of the financial system.

Stimson, James. *Tides of Consent: How Public Opinion Shapes American Politics.* 2nd ed. New York: Cambridge University Press, 2015. Lucid account of public opinion, especially the desire to spend without offset tax cuts.

Wessel, David. *Red Ink: Inside the High-Stakes Politics of the Federal Budget.* New York: Crown Business, 2013. A readable account of the budget process and challenges facing the budget.

CHAPTER 19

Foreign and Military Policy

Learning Objectives

19-1 Summarize the different types of politics involved in American foreign policy.

19-2 Discuss the constitutional and legal contexts for making American foreign policy.

19-3 Explain how political elites and public opinion influence American foreign policy.

19-4 Explain the key challenges that the United States faces in foreign affairs and defense politics today.

Every American knows we struggle against terrorists—that is, against private groups that attack unarmed civilians. But this is not a recent development.

« Then Between 1801 and 1805, President Thomas Jefferson sent our navy to fight the Barbary Pirates who operated out of various North African countries against merchant shipping in the Mediterranean. They were sponsored by the Ottoman Empire, which was based in Turkey. In the 19th century, American warships did battle with pirates in the Caribbean and along our Atlantic coast. Some terrorists operated inside the country. John Brown fought against slavery by raiding the supplies of the American military at Harper's Ferry. One might sympathize with his antislavery views, but he and his followers killed innocent civilians. He was caught and hanged.

After the Civil War, the Ku Klux Klan (KKK) was formed to block the emancipation of African Americans by lynching them and shooting into their homes as well as those of sympathetic white supporters. The first KKK, created in the 19th century, was replaced by a second one created in the 20th; each of them enrolled several million members and continued the policy of harassment and murder. To defeat the Klan, Congress passed a law in 1871 that gave the president power to suspend the writ of habeas corpus in any state where ordinary law enforcement procedures were unavailable, and afforded people the right to sue officials who violated their rights.

In the 1960s and 1970s, the Weather Underground, a radical leftist organization, bombed police stations, the Pentagon, and a townhouse; threw Molotov cocktails through a judge's window; and robbed a Brink's armored car. Though several of its leaders have abandoned radical action and taken respectable jobs, they denounce conservatives in and out of government in the strongest language.

*** Now** The 9/11 attacks in which hijacked aircraft crashed into the World Trade Center and the Pentagon represented more widespread destruction through terrorism than the United States had encountered in decades. This attack, as well as the 1998 bombing of two American embassies and the 2000 attack on the *USS Cole*, were carried out by al Qaeda, a radical Islamic group founded by Osama bin Laden and his colleagues. (*Al Qaeda* means "the base" in Arabic.) But these attacks were different from that on Pearl Harbor: the latter attack had, so to speak, a return address—we knew who did it and where they lived. But 9/11 had no return address; it was a terrorist attack waged by small groups that could be located anywhere.

In response, the United States launched an attack on Afghanistan, where the ruling party, the Taliban, had supported and helped train al Qaeda, and passed the Patriot Act, which improved cooperation among intelligence and law enforcement agencies. The federal government amended the Foreign Intelligence Surveillance Act to make it possible for the government to eavesdrop on communications that cross our national borders. In 2011, Osama bin Laden, the founder of al Qaeda, was found in Pakistan and killed by American special forces operatives. Nine years later, the United States signed an agreement with the Taliban establishing a roadmap for ending

Aamir Qureshi/AFP/Getty Images

Image 19.1 In May 2011, Osama bin Laden was killed by U.S. special forces in the house behind this wall, located in Abbottabad, Pakistan.

the war and withdrawing American military forces after almost two decades of military conflict. But in the spring of 2020, prospects for implementing the agreement were tenuous at best.

Such choices must be made in a democracy, and some observers think democratic politics make managing foreign and military policy harder. Tocqueville said the conduct of foreign affairs requires precisely those qualities most lacking in a democratic nation: "A democracy can only with great difficulty regulate the details of an important undertaking, persevere in a fixed design, and work out its execution in spite of serious obstacles. It cannot combine its measures with secrecy or await their consequences with patience."[1] In plain language, a democracy is forced to play foreign policy poker with its cards turned up. As a result, aggressors the likes of Adolf Hitler and Saddam Hussein can bluff a democracy, but the reverse is far more difficult.

Other writers, however, disagree with Tocqueville. To them, the strength of democracy is that, though it rarely if ever wages an unjustified war on another country, its people, when mobilized by the president, will support overseas engagements even when many deaths occur.[2] In this chapter, we consider how the U.S. democracy makes foreign policy, and what implications that process has for our nation.

19-1 Kinds of Foreign Policy

The majoritarian component of foreign policy includes those decisions (and nondecisions) perceived to confer widely distributed benefits and impose widely distributed costs. The decision to go to war is an obvious example of this type of policymaking. So, too, are the establishment of military alliances with Western Europe, the negotiation of a nuclear test ban treaty or a strategic arms limitation agreement, the response to the placement of Soviet offensive missiles in Cuba, and the opening of diplomatic relations with the People's Republic of China. These may be good or bad policies, but the benefits and costs accrue to the nation as a whole.

Some argue that the costs of many of these policies are in fact highly concentrated—for example, soldiers bear the burden of a military operation—but on closer inspection that turns out not to shape the positions that people take on issues of war and peace. Though soldiers and their immediate families bear the costs of war to an especially high degree, public opinion surveys taken during the Vietnam War showed that having a family member in the armed forces did not significantly affect how people evaluated the war.[3] There is a sense that during wartime, we are all in it together.

Foreign policy decisions also may reflect interest-group politics. Tariff decisions confer benefits on certain business firms and labor unions and impose costs on other firms and unions. (See our discussion in Chapter 18.) If the price of foreign steel imported into this country is increased by tariffs, quotas, or other devices, this helps the American steel industry and the United Steel Workers of America. On the other hand, it hurts those firms (and associated unions) that had been purchasing the once-cheap foreign steel.

Examples of client politics also occur in foreign affairs. Washington often provides aid to American corporations doing business abroad because the aid helps those firms directly without imposing any apparent costs on an equally distinct group in society. Another example of client politics is foreign aid. The United States has been a steadfast ally of Israel since its creation in 1948, and numerous interest groups, such as the American Israel Public Affairs Committee, advocate to maintain that alliance. Other countries that have received large sums of U.S. foreign aid in the 21st century, primarily military or security funds, include Afghanistan, Egypt, Iraq, and Jordan.[4]

Who has power in foreign policy depends very much on what kind of foreign policy we have in mind. Where it is of a majoritarian nature, the president is clearly the dominant figure, and much, if not everything, depends on the president's beliefs and skills, as well as those of top advisers. Public opinion will ordinarily support, but not guide, this presidential leadership. Woe to the president who forfeits that trust through questionable actions.

When interest-group or client politics is involved, Congress plays a much larger role. Although Congress has a subsidiary role in the conduct of foreign diplomacy, the decision to send troops overseas, or the direction of intelligence operations, it has a large one in decisions involving foreign economic aid, the structure of the tariff system, the shipment of weapons to foreign allies, the creation of new weapons systems, and the support of Israel and other allies.

And Congress is the central political arena on those occasions when entrepreneurial politics shapes foreign policy. If a multinational corporation is caught in a scandal, congressional investigations shake the usual indifference of politicians to the foreign conduct of such corporations. If presidential policies abroad lead to reversals—as in 1986, when presidential aides sought to trade arms for U.S. hostages in Iran and then use some profits from the arms sales to support the anti-Marxist contras fighting in Nicaragua—Congress becomes the forum for investigations and criticism. At such moments Congress often seeks to expand its power over foreign affairs.

In this chapter, we are chiefly concerned with foreign policy insofar as it displays the characteristics of majoritarian politics. Limiting the discussion in this way

XINHUA/Gamma-Rapho/Getty Images

Image 19.2 A nuclear power plant in Iran raises concerns for the United States about potential threats to regional and international security.

permits us to focus on the grand issues of foreign affairs—war, peace, and global diplomacy. It allows us to see how choices are made in a situation in which public majorities support but do not direct policy, in which opinion tends to react to events, and in which interest groups are less important than in other types of policies.

19-2 The Constitutional and Legal Contexts

The Constitution defines the authority of the president and of Congress in foreign affairs in a way that, as Edward Corwin put it, is an "invitation to struggle."[5] The president is commander-in-chief of the armed forces, but Congress must authorize and appropriate money for those forces. The president appoints ambassadors, but they must be confirmed by the Senate. The president may negotiate treaties, but the Senate must ratify these by a two-thirds vote. Only Congress may regulate commerce with other nations and "declare" war. (In an early draft of the Constitution, the Framers gave Congress the power to "make" war but changed this to "declare" so that the president, acting without Congress, could take military measures to repel a sudden attack.) Because power over foreign affairs is shared by the president and Congress, conflict between them is to be expected.

Yet Americans typically think instinctively that the president is in charge of foreign affairs, and what popular opinion supposes, the historical record confirms. Presidents have asserted the right to send troops abroad on their own authority in more than 125 instances. Only five of the more than one dozen major wars that this country has fought have followed a formal declaration of war by Congress.[6] The State Department, the Central Intelligence Agency, and the National Security Agency are almost entirely "presidential" agencies, with clear congressional control in theory, but more limited exercise in practice. The Defense Department, though keenly sensitive to congressional views on weapons procurement and the location of military bases, is very much under the control of the president on matters of military strategy. While the Senate has since 1789 ratified well over 1,000 treaties signed by the president, the president during this period also has signed around 7,000 executive agreements with other countries that did not require Senate ratification and yet have the force of law.[7]

Presidential Box Score

When presidents seek congressional approval for foreign policy matters, they tend to win more often than when they ask for support on domestic matters. One student of the presidency, Aaron Wildavsky, concluded that the American political system has "two presidencies"—one in domestic affairs that is relatively weak and closely checked, and another in foreign affairs that is quite powerful.[8] As we shall see, this view considerably overstates presidential power in certain areas.

When it comes to international diplomacy and the use of American troops, the president is indeed strong—much stronger than the Framers may have intended and certainly stronger than many members of Congress would prefer. Examples abound:

- 1861: Abraham Lincoln blockaded southern ports and declared martial law.
- 1940: Franklin D. Roosevelt sent 50 destroyers to England to be used against Germany, with which we were then technically at peace.
- 1950: Harry Truman sent American troops into South Korea to help repel a North Korean attack on that country.
- 1960s: John F. Kennedy and Lyndon Johnson sent American forces into South Vietnam without a declaration of war.
- 1983: Ronald Reagan sent troops to overthrow a pro-Castro regime in Grenada.
- 1989: George H. W. Bush ordered the U.S. invasion of Panama to depose dictator Manuel Noriega.
- 1990: Bush ordered troops to Saudi Arabia in response to Iraq's invasion of Kuwait.
- 1999: Bill Clinton ordered the military to attack, with bombs and cruise missiles, Serbian forces that were trying to control Kosovo.
- 2001: George W. Bush sent U.S. troops to liberate Afghanistan from the Taliban, a regime supportive of Osama bin Laden, the architect of the September 11 terrorist attacks.
- 2003: Bush, with some allied nations, invaded Iraq.
- 2011: Barack Obama secured a UN Security Council resolution (but not congressional authorization) to give military support to rebels in Libya, who successfully overturned the repressive regime of Muammar Gaddafi.
- 2017 (and 2018): Donald J. Trump authorized U.S. air strikes in Syria in response to the government's use of chemical weapons in the country's civil war.

However, by the standards of other nations, even other democratic ones, the ability of an American president to act decisively often seems rather modest. The United Kingdom was dismayed at the inability of Woodrow Wilson in 1914–1915 and Franklin Roosevelt in 1939–1940 to enter into an alliance when the British were engaged in a major war with Germany. After the war, Wilson was unable to bring the United States into the League of Nations. In the 1970s, Gerald Ford could not intervene covertly in Angola in support of an anti-Marxist faction. Ronald Reagan was heavily criticized in Congress in the 1980s for sending 55 military advisers to El Salvador and a few hundred Marines to Lebanon. After George H. W. Bush sent U.S. troops to the Persian Gulf in 1990, he began a long debate with Congress over whether he would need a formal declaration of war before the troops were sent into combat. George W. Bush's decision to invade Iraq in 2003 became bitterly controversial in the 2004, 2006, and 2008 elections.

Furthermore, a treaty signed by the president is little more than a promise to try to get the Senate to go along.

Sending U.S. Troops Abroad

The Constitution divides responsibility for sending U.S. forces abroad between Congress and the president. Article I, section 8, states, "The Congress shall have Power ... To declare War," while Article II, section 2, says, "The President shall be Commander in Chief of the Army and Navy of the United States, and of the Militia of the several States, when called into the actual Service of the United States." In *Federalist* No. 69, Alexander Hamilton contrasted this power with that of the British king, saying the executive power would "be much inferior. . . . It would amount to nothing more than the supreme command and direction of the military and naval forces."

In practice, though, American presidents have sent troops abroad on many occasions without a declaration of war (which Congress has issued in just five cases—the War of 1812, the Mexican-American War of 1848, the Spanish-American War of 1898, World War I, and World War II). After the undeclared wars of Korea and Vietnam, Congress passed the War Powers Resolution over President Richard M. Nixon's veto to ensure that the president would not send troops abroad indefinitely without legislative approval. But every president has said the War Powers Resolution is unconstitutional, and the issue almost certainly will not be decided in the courts, as that would require an actual test of the law with Congress ordering the president to bring troops home from a conflict or cutting off funding (both of which would risk danger on the battlefield). Since the ending of the Cold War, presidents have secured joint resolutions of support from Congress for the use of military force in some, though not all, conflicts. But the Framers of the Constitution called for a much more active congressional role in deciding when to send troops abroad than has happened in practice. Achieving the Framers' vision likely will require political will from both the legislative and executive branches.

Sources: Alexander Hamilton, *The Federalist Papers*: No. 69, "The Real Character of the Executive," 14 March 1788; Louis Fisher, *Presidential War Power*. 3rd rev. ed. Lawrence: University Press of Kansas, 2013.

The president can sign executive agreements without Senate consent, but most of these are authorized in advance by Congress.[9]

By contrast, the leaders of other democratic nations (to say nothing of totalitarian ones) often are able to act with much greater freedom. While Reagan was arguing with Congress over whether we should assign any military advisers to El Salvador, the president of France, François Mitterrand, ordered 2,500 combat troops to Chad with scarcely a ripple of opposition. A predecessor of Mitterrand, Charles de Gaulle, brought France into the European Common Market over the explicit opposition of the French Assembly and granted independence to Algeria, then a French colony, without seriously consulting the Assembly.[10] British Prime Minister Edward Heath brought his country into the Common Market (the predecessor of the European Union) despite popular opposition, and the prime minister can declare war without the consent of Parliament.[11]

Evaluating the Power of the President

Whether you think the president is too strong or too weak in foreign affairs may depend not only on a specific policy debate but also on whether you agree or disagree with a president's policies. Historian Arthur M. Schlesinger, Jr., thought that President Kennedy exercised commendable presidential vigor when he made a unilateral decision to impose a naval blockade on Cuba to induce the Soviets to remove missiles installed there. However, Schlesinger viewed President Nixon's decision to extend U.S. military action in Vietnam into neighboring Cambodia as a deplorable example of the "imperial presidency."[12] To be sure, there were important differences between these two actions, but that is precisely the point: An office strong enough to do something that one thinks proper is also strong enough to do something that one finds wrong.

The Supreme Court has fairly consistently supported the view that the federal government has powers in the conduct of foreign and military policy beyond those specifically mentioned in the Constitution. An often-cited decision, rendered in 1936, holds that the right to carry out foreign policy is an inherent attribute of any sovereign nation:

> The power to declare and wage war, to conclude peace, to make treaties, to maintain diplomatic relations with other sovereignties, if they had never been mentioned in the Constitution, would have vested in the Federal Government as necessary concomitants of nationality.[13]

Moreover, the Supreme Court has been reluctant to intervene in disputes over the conduct of foreign affairs.

Image 19.3 In 1962, President Kennedy forced the Soviet Union to withdraw missiles it had placed in Cuba, just 90 miles from the Florida coast.

When various members of Congress brought suit challenging the right of President Nixon to enlarge the war in Vietnam without congressional approval, the court of appeals essentially refused to resolve the issue. The court said it was a matter for the president and Congress to decide and that if Congress was unwilling to cut off the money to pay for the war, it should not expect the courts to do the job for it.[14]

The Supreme Court upheld the extraordinary measures taken by President Lincoln during the Civil War and refused to interfere with the conduct of the Vietnam War by Presidents Johnson and Nixon.[15] After Iran seized American hostages in 1979, President Carter froze Iranian assets in this country. To win the hostages' freedom, the president later agreed to return some of these assets and to nullify claims on them by American companies. The Court upheld the nullification because it was necessary for the resolution of a foreign policy dispute.[16]

How great the deference to presidential power may be is vividly illustrated by the actions of President Franklin Roosevelt in ordering the army to move more than 100,000 Japanese Americans—the great majority of them born in this country and citizens of the United States—from their homes on the West Coast to inland "relocation centers" for the duration of World War II. Though this action was a wholesale violation of the constitutional rights of U.S. citizens and was unprecedented in American history, the Supreme Court decided that with the West Coast vulnerable to attack by Japan, the president was within his rights to declare that people of Japanese ancestry might pose a threat to internal security; thus the relocation order was upheld. (No Japanese American was ever found guilty of espionage or sabotage.) One of the few cases in which the Court denied the president broad wartime powers occurred in 1952, when it decided, six to three, to reverse President Truman's seizure of steel mills—a move that he had made in order to avert a strike that, in his view, would have imperiled the war effort in Korea.[17]

Checks on Presidential Power

If there is a check on the powers of the federal government or the president in foreign affairs, it is chiefly political rather than constitutional. The most important check is Congress's control of the purse strings. In addition, Congress has imposed three important kinds of restrictions on the president's freedom of action, all since Vietnam.

Limitations on the President's Ability to Give Military or Economic Aid to Other Countries

Between 1974 and 1978, the president could not sell arms to Turkey because of a dispute between Turkey and Greece over control of the island of Cyprus. The pressure on Congress from groups supporting Greece was much stronger than that from groups supporting Turkey. In 1976, Congress prevented President Ford from giving aid to the pro-Western faction in the Angolan civil war. Until the method was declared unconstitutional, Congress for many years could use a legislative veto, a resolution disapproving of an executive decision (see Chapter 15), to block the sale by the president of arms worth more than $25 million to another country.

The War Powers Act

Passed in 1973 over a presidential veto, this law placed the following restrictions on the president's ability to use military force:

- The president must report in writing to Congress within 48 hours after introducing U.S. troops into areas where hostilities have occurred or are imminent.
- Within 60 days after troops are sent into hostile situations, Congress must, by declaration of war or other specific statutory authorization, provide for the continuation of hostile action by U.S. troops.
- If Congress fails to provide such authorization, the president must withdraw the troops (unless Congress has been prevented from meeting as a result of an armed attack).
- If Congress passes a concurrent resolution (which the president may not veto) directing the removal of U.S. troops, the president must comply.

Until recently the War Powers Act has had very little influence on American military actions. Since its passage, every president—Ford, Carter, Reagan, George H. W. Bush, Clinton, George W. Bush, Obama, and Trump—has sent American forces abroad without explicit congressional authorization. (George H. W. Bush asked for and received congressional support just before the 1991 Persian Gulf War, as did George W. Bush a few months

National Archives and Records Administration

Image 19.4 Following the attack on Pearl Harbor, in 1942 President Roosevelt ordered that all Japanese Americans living on the West Coast be interned in prison camps.

before the 2003 Iraq War.) No president has acknowledged that the War Powers Act is constitutional. In its 1983 decision in the *Chadha* case, the Supreme Court struck down the legislative veto, which means that this section of the act is already in constitutional trouble.[18]

Even if the act is constitutional, politically it is all but impossible to use. Few members of Congress would challenge a president who carried out a successful military operation (e.g., those in Grenada, Panama, and at least initially in Afghanistan). More might challenge the president if, after a while, the military action were in trouble, but the easiest way to do that would be to cut off funding for the operation. But even during the Vietnam War, a conflict that preceded the War Powers Act, Congress, though it had many members who were critics of U.S. policy, never stopped military appropriations.

In 2011, however, after the United States, working with the North Atlantic Treaty Organization (NATO), used military resources in support of rebels attacking the despotic regime of Muammar Gaddafi in Libya, Republicans in Congress (who in the past had shown little interest in the War Powers Act) attacked President Obama over his failure to comply with the 1973 law. Then in 2013, after Syria used chemical weapons against opposition rebel forces, President Obama said he would not authorize military action without congressional support, but Congress demurred. During the Trump presidency, the Senate for the first time invoked the War Powers Act to vote to block a president's use of military force abroad, doing so three times between 2018 and2020. Although none of the measures became law (due either to a presidential veto or a failure to pass in the House), the chamber's Republican majority in all three cases made the bipartisan rebuke especially significant.[19]

Intelligence Oversight

Owing to the low political stock of President Nixon during the Watergate scandal and the revelations of illegal operations by the Central Intelligence Agency (CIA) within the United States, Congress required that the CIA notify appropriate congressional committees about any proposed covert action (between 1974 and 1980 it had to notify *eight* different committees). Today it must keep two groups, the House and the Senate Intelligence Committees, "fully and currently informed" of all intelligence activities, including covert actions. The committees do not have the authority to disapprove such actions.

However, from time to time Congress will pass a bill blocking particular covert actions. This happened when the Boland Amendment (named after its sponsor, Representative Edward Boland) was passed on several occasions between 1982 and 1985. Each version of the amendment prevented, for specifically stated periods, intelligence agencies from supplying military aid to the Nicaraguan contras.

The 9/11 terrorist attacks left everyone wondering why our intelligence agencies had not foreseen them. After the attacks, there was an investigation to find out why the CIA had not warned the country of this risk. In an effort to improve matters, Congress passed and President Bush signed a law creating the Office of the Director of National Intelligence (DNI). It was designed to coordinate the work of the CIA, the FBI, the Defense Intelligence Agency, and the intelligence units of several other government agencies. The DNI also replaced the director of the CIA as the president's chief adviser. How much real coordination takes place is difficult to assess and presents a challenge because the DNI's office is another large bureaucracy placed on top of other big ones.

19-3 Making Foreign Policy

From the time that Thomas Jefferson took the job in Washington's first administration until well into the 20th century, foreign policy typically was made and carried out by the secretary of state. No more. When America became a major world power during and after World War II, our commitments overseas expanded dramatically. With that expansion two things happened. First, presidents began to put foreign policy at the top of their agenda and to play a larger role in directing it. Second, that policy was shaped by the scores of agencies (some brand new) that had acquired overseas activities. While presidents and executive agencies now set the direction for American foreign policy, public opinion also shapes the broad outlines of American interests and priorities.

Political Elites

Today, Washington, D.C., has one official State Department and many other departments and agencies that participate in diplomacy. The Defense Department has military bases and military advisers abroad. The CIA has intelligence officers abroad, most of them assigned to "stations" that are part of the American embassy but not under the full control of the American ambassador there. The Departments of Agriculture, Commerce, and Labor have missions abroad. The Federal Bureau of Investigation and the Drug Enforcement Administration have agents abroad. The Agency for International Development has offices to dispense foreign aid in host countries. The U.S. Information Agency runs libraries, radio stations, and educational programs abroad.

New secretaries of state typically announce that they will "coordinate" and "direct" this enormous foreign policy establishment. In practice, they never do. The reason is partly that the job is too big for any one person and partly that most of these agencies owe no political or bureaucratic loyalty to the secretary of state. If anyone is to coordinate them, it will have to be the president. But the president cannot keep track of what all these agencies are doing in the more than 190 nations and 50 international organizations where we have representatives, or in the more than 800 international conferences in which the United States participates each year.

So the president now has a staff to coordinate foreign policy. That staff is part of the National Security Council (NSC), created by law in 1947 and chaired by the president. Since its inception, the NSC has been composed of the vice president and the secretaries of state and defense, along with several other top executive officials. Depending on the president, the NSC can be an important forum in which to hammer out foreign policy. Attached to it is a staff headed by the national security adviser, a position created in the Eisenhower administration (with the official title then of special assistant to the president for national security affairs) that does not require Senate confirmation and reports directly to the president. The NSC policy staff can be (again, depending on the president) an enormously powerful instrument for formulating and directing foreign policy.[20]

Presidents Truman and Eisenhower made only limited use of the NSC staff, but beginning with President Kennedy it has grown greatly in influence. Its head, the national security adviser, has come to rival the secretary of state for foreign policy leadership, especially when the adviser is a powerful personality such as Henry Kissinger in the Nixon administration.

President Reagan attempted to downgrade the importance of the national security adviser, but ironically it was one of his relatively low-visibility advisers, Admiral John Poindexter, and his subordinate, Lieutenant Colonel Oliver North, who precipitated the worst crisis of the Reagan presidency when, allegedly without informing the president, they tried to use cash realized from the secret sale of arms to Iran to finance guerrillas fighting against the Marxist government of Nicaragua. The sale and the diversion became known, North was fired, a congressional investigation ensued, criminal charges were filed against Poindexter and North, and the president's political position was weakened. But even in ordinary times the NSC staff has been the rival of the secretary of state, except during a period in the Ford administration when Henry Kissinger held *both* jobs.

The way in which the machinery of foreign policymaking operates has two major consequences for the substance of that policy. First, as former secretary of state George Shultz asserted, "It's never over." Foreign policy issues are endlessly agitated, rarely settled. The reason is that the rivalries *within* the executive branch intensify the rivalries *between* that branch and Congress. In ways already described, Congress has steadily increased its influence over the conduct of foreign policy. Anybody in the executive branch who loses out in a struggle over foreign policy can take the matter case (usually by means of a well-timed leak) to a sympathetic member of Congress, who then can make a speech, hold a hearing, or introduce a bill.

Second, the interests of the various organizations making up the foreign policy establishment profoundly affect the positions that they take. Because the State Department has a stake in diplomacy, it tends to resist bold or controversial new policies that might upset established relationships with other countries. Part of the CIA has a stake in gathering and analyzing information; that part tends to be skeptical of the claims of other agencies that their overseas

Foreign Affairs

- ***Curtiss-Wright Export Corp. v. United States* (1936):** American foreign policy is vested entirely in the federal government, where the president has plenary power.
- ***Korematsu v. United States* (1944):** Sending Japanese Americans to relocation centers during World War II was based on an acceptable military justification.
- ***Youngstown Sheet & Tube Co. v. Sawyer* (1952):** The president may not seize factories during wartime without explicit congressional authority, even when they are threatened by a strike.
- ***Hamdi v. Rumsfeld* (2004):** An American citizen in jail because he allegedly joined the Taliban extremist group should have access to a "neutral decision maker."
- ***Rasul v. Bush* (2004):** Foreign nationals held at Guantanamo Bay because they are believed to be terrorists have a right to bring their cases before an American court.
- ***Hamdan v. Rumsfeld* (2006):** The executive branch cannot unilaterally set up military commissions to try suspected terrorists; Congress must authorize their creation.
- ***Boumedine v. Bush* (2008):** Congress may not suspend the writ of habeas corpus for suspected terrorists held at Guantanamo Bay.

operations are succeeding. Another part of the CIA conducts covert operations abroad; it tends to resent or ignore skepticism from intelligence analysts. The air force flies airplanes and so tends to be optimistic about what can be accomplished through the use of air power in particular and military power in general; the army, on the other hand, which must fight in the trenches, is often dubious about such prospects for military success. During the American-led war in Iraq, comparable conflicts between the CIA and the Defense Department became evident when people on both sides leaked information to the media.

Americans often worry that their government is keeping secrets from them. In fact, there are no secrets in Washington—at least not for long.

Public Opinion

World War II was the great watershed event in American foreign policy. Before that time, a clear majority of the American public opposed active involvement in world affairs. The public saw the costs of such involvement as being substantially in excess of the benefits, and only determined, skillful leaders were able, as was President Roosevelt during 1939–1940, to affect in even a limited fashion the diplomatic and military struggles then convulsing Europe and Asia.

In 1937, 94 percent of the American public preferred the policy of doing "everything possible to keep out of foreign wars" to the policy of doing "everything possible to prevent war, even if it means threatening to fight countries that fight wars." In 1939, after World War II had begun in Europe but before Pearl Harbor was attacked, only 13 percent of Americans polled thought that we should enter the war against Germany. Just a month before Pearl Harbor, only 19 percent felt that the United States should take steps, at the risk of war, to prevent Japan from becoming too powerful.[21] Congress reflected the noninterventionist mood of the country: in the summer of 1941, with war breaking out almost everywhere, the proposal to continue the draft passed the House of Representatives by only one vote.

The Japanese attack on Pearl Harbor on December 7 changed all that. Not only was the American war effort supported almost unanimously, not only did Congress approve the declaration of war with only one dissenting vote, but World War II—unlike World War I—produced popular support for an active assumption of international responsibilities that continued after the war had ended.[22] Although after World War I a majority opposed U.S. entry into the League of Nations, after World War II a clear majority favored our entry into the United Nations.[23]

This willingness to see the United States remain a world force persisted. Even during the Vietnam War, the number of people thinking that we should "keep independent" in world affairs as opposed to "working closely with other nations" rose from 10 percent in 1963 to only 22 percent in 1969.[24] In 1967, after more than two years of war in Vietnam, 44 percent of Americans believed that this country had an obligation to "defend other Vietnams if they are threatened by communism."[25]

Before 9/11, hardly any American thought we should fight a war in Afghanistan, but after that attack we fought exactly that war in order to get rid of the Taliban regime. The Taliban, a group of radical young Muslims, had taken control of that country and allowed Osama bin Laden, the head of al Qaeda, to use the nation as a place to train and direct terrorists. Though al Qaeda designed and carried out the 9/11 attacks on America, it is not a single organization located in one place and is therefore very difficult to defeat. It is instead a network of terrorist cells found all over the world that is allied with other terrorist groups. Even though its leader was killed in 2011, al Qaeda continues to operate in many nations around the world (though its power has been reduced).[26]

But the support for an internationalist American foreign policy was, and is, highly general and heavily dependent on the phrasing of poll questions, the opinions expressed by popular leaders, and the impact of world events. Public opinion, while more internationalist than once was the case, is both mushy and volatile. Just prior to President Nixon's decision to send troops into Cambodia, only 7 percent of the people said they supported such a move. After the troops were sent and Nixon made a speech explaining his move, 50 percent of the public said they supported it.[27] Similarly, only 49 percent of the people favored halting the American bombing of North Vietnam before President Johnson ordered such a halt in 1968; afterward 60 percent of the people said they supported such a policy.[28]

Backing the President

Much of this volatility in specific opinions (as opposed to general mood) reflects the already mentioned deference to the "commander-in-chief" and a desire to support the United States when it confronts other nations. Figure 19.1 shows the proportion of people who said that they approved of the way the president was doing his job before and after various major foreign policy events from the Cold War to the first decade after the 9/11 terrorist attacks. Almost every foreign crisis increased the level of public approval of the president, often dramatically. The most vivid illustration of this was the Bay of Pigs fiasco: An American-supported, American-directed invasion of Cuba by anti-Castro Cuban emigres was driven back into the sea. President Kennedy accepted responsibility for the aborted project. His popularity *rose*. (Comparable data for domestic crises tend to show no similar effect.)

This tendency to "rally 'round the flag" operates for some but not all foreign military crises.[29] The rally not only

Figure 19.1 **Popular Reactions to Foreign Policy Crises**

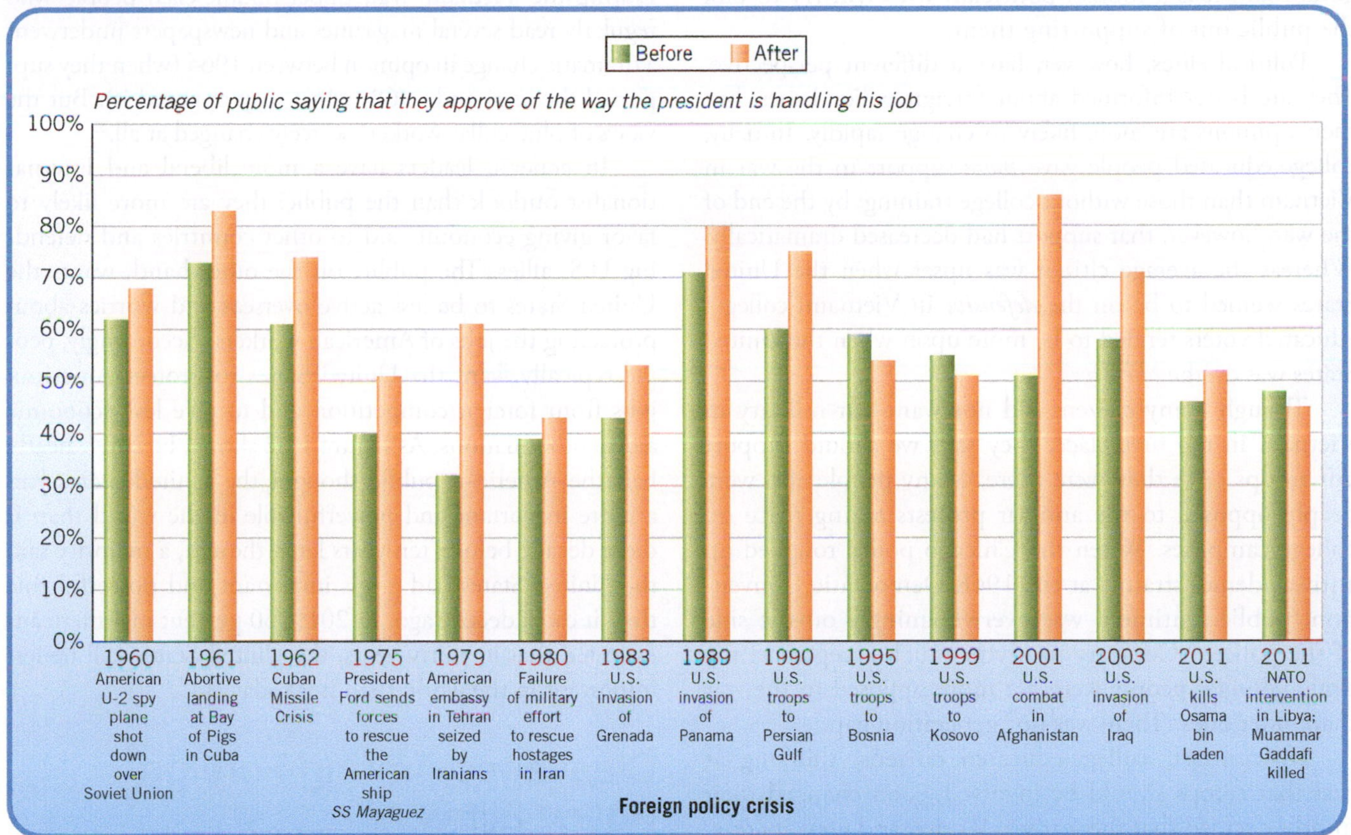

Source: Updated from Theodore J. Lowi, *The End of Liberalism* (New York: Norton, 1969), 184. Poll data are from Gallup and www.realclearpolitics.com. The time lapse between "before" and "after" samplings of opinion was in no case more than one month.

helped Kennedy after the Bay of Pigs, but it also helped Ronald Reagan when he invaded Grenada and George H. W. Bush when he sent troops to move Iraqi forces out of Kuwait. But it did not help Bill Clinton when he sent forces to Bosnia or launched bombing attacks on Iraq. If there is an attack on America, then the public typically unites in support of the president. Just before September 11, 2001, George W. Bush's favorability rating was 51 percent; just after the attack, it was 86 percent.

Sometimes people argue that whatever support a president gets during a military crisis will disappear when American soldiers are killed in battle. But a close study of how casualty rates affect public opinion showed that although deaths tend to reduce how "favorable" people are toward a war, what they then support is not withdrawal but an *escalation* in the fighting so as to defeat the enemy more quickly.[30] This was true during the wars in Korea, Vietnam, and the Persian Gulf in 1991.

In sum, people tend to be leery of overseas military expeditions by the United States—until they start. Then they support them and want to win, even if it means more intense fighting. When Americans began to dislike U.S. involvement in Korea and Vietnam, they did not conclude that we should pull out; they concluded instead that we should do whatever was necessary to win.[31] The 2003 invasion of Iraq did not raise large questions for many Americans until terrorist attacks on the American military continued after the Iraqi army had been defeated.

Despite the tendency for most Americans to rally around the flag, some public opposition exists for almost any war in which the United States participates. About one-fifth of Americans opposed the 2003 invasion of Iraq, which is close to the level of opposition to the wars in Korea and Vietnam. Opposition has generally been highest among Democrats, African Americans, and people with a postgraduate degree.[32] For the U.S. intervention in Libya in 2011, just 47 percent of Americans approved of this military action, with 37 percent in opposition.[33]

Mass Versus Elite Opinion

The public is poorly informed about foreign affairs. People generally have a vague idea of basic facts such as where Afghanistan and Iraq are on a map, or why Palestinians and Israelis disagree about the future of Israel. But that is to be expected. Foreign affairs are, well, foreign. They do not have much to do with the daily lives of American citizens, except during wartime. But since World War II, the public has consistently said the United States should play an important international role.[34] And if our troops go abroad, it is a foolish politician who will try to talk the public out of supporting them.

Political elites, however, have a different perspective. They are better informed about foreign policy issues, but their opinions are more likely to change rapidly. Initially, college-educated people gave *more* support to the war in Vietnam than those without college training; by the end of the war, however, that support had decreased dramatically. Whereas the average citizen was upset when the United States seemed to be on the *defensive* in Vietnam, college-educated voters tended to be more upset when the United States was on the *offensive*.[35]

Though many citizens did not want our military in Vietnam in the first place, they said we should support our troops once they were there. Many people also were deeply opposed to the antiwar protests taking place on college campuses. When the Chicago police roughed up antiwar demonstrators at the 1968 Democratic Convention, public sentiment was overwhelmingly on the side of the police.[36] Contrary to myths much accepted at the time, younger people were *not* more opposed to the war than older ones. There was no "generation gap."

By contrast, college-educated citizens, thinking at first that troops should be involved, soon changed their minds, decided that the war was wrong, and grew increasingly upset when the United States seemed to be enlarging the war (by invading Cambodia, for example). College students protested against the war largely on moral grounds, and their protests received more support from college-educated adults than from other citizens.

Elite opinion changes more rapidly than public opinion. During the Vietnam War, upper-middle-class people who regularly read several magazines and newspapers underwent a dramatic change in opinion between 1964 (when they supported the war) and 1968 (when they opposed it). But the views of blue-collar workers scarcely changed at all.[37]

In general, leaders have a more liberal and internationalist outlook than the public: they are more likely to favor giving economic aid to other countries and defending U.S. allies. The public, on the other hand, wants the United States to be less active overseas and worries about protecting the jobs of American workers. Accordingly, people typically want the United States to protect American jobs from foreign competition and to give less economic aid to other nations. As Figure 19.2 shows, in 2004, nearly half the American public thought the United States had a more important and powerful role in the world than it did a decade before; ten years later, though, a majority said the United States had a less important and powerful role than it did a decade ago. In 2019, 60 percent of Americans expected that in thirty years, the United States will be less important in the world than it is today.[38]

Cleavages Among Foreign Policy Elites

As we have seen, public opinion on foreign policy is permissive and a bit mushy: It supports presidential action without giving much direction. Elite opinion therefore acquires extraordinary importance. Of course, events and world realities are also important, but since events

Figure 19.2 **Public's View of America as a World Leader**

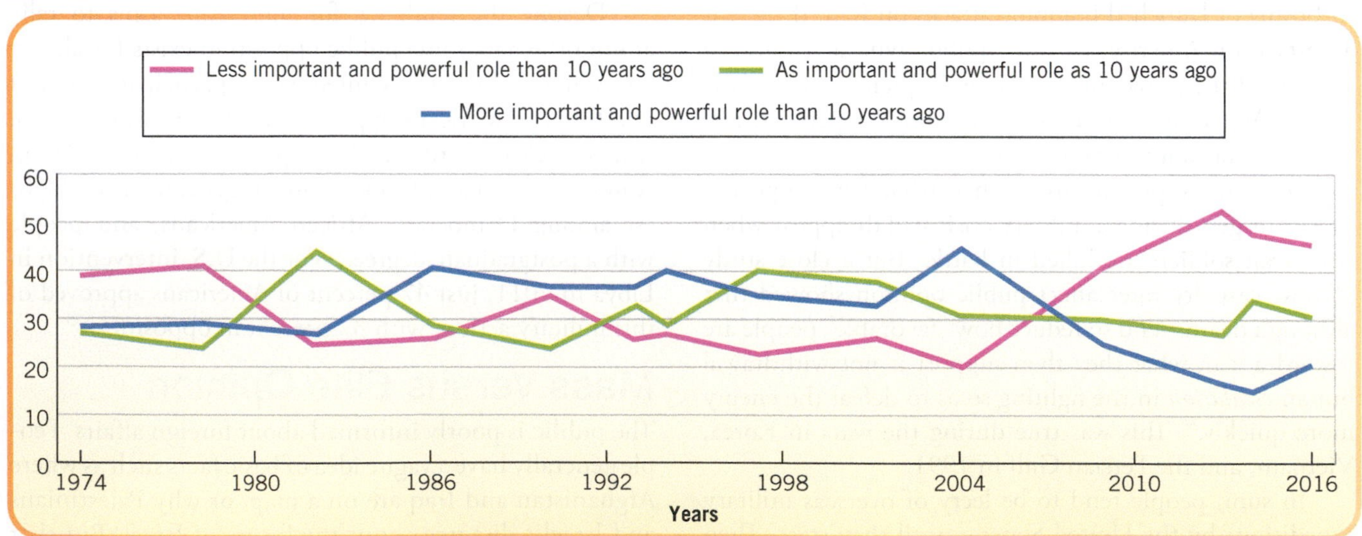

Source: Pew Research Center, "Public Uncertain, Divided Over America's Place in the World," 5 May 2016. www.people-press.org.

Q What are some reasons why the public's view of the U.S. role in the world has changed from the 1970s to the 21st century (with major shifts in the past two decades)?

have no meaning except as they are perceived and interpreted by people who must react to them, the attitudes and beliefs of people in and out of government who are actively involved in shaping foreign policy often assume decisive importance.

Contrary to the views of people who think that some shadowy, conspiratorial group of insiders runs American foreign policy, the foreign policy elite in this country is deeply divided. That elite consists not only of those people with administrative positions in the foreign policy field—senior State Department officials and NSC staff—but also members and staffs of key congressional committees concerned with foreign affairs (chiefly the Senate Foreign Relations Committee and the House Foreign Affairs Committee) and various private organizations that help shape elite opinion, such as members of the Council on Foreign Relations and editors of two important publications, *Foreign Affairs* and *Foreign Policy*. To these must be added influential columnists and editorial writers whose work appears regularly in the national media. One could extend the list by adding ever-wider circles of people with some influence (lobbyists, professors, leaders of veterans' organizations); this would complicate without changing the central point: Elite beliefs are probably more important in explaining foreign policy than in accounting for decisions in other policy areas.

How a Worldview Shapes Foreign Policy

These beliefs can be described in simplified terms as **worldviews** (or, as some social scientists put it, as *paradigms*)—more or less comprehensive mental pictures of the critical problems facing the United States in the world and of the appropriate and inappropriate ways of responding to these problems. The clearest, most concise, and perhaps most influential statement of one worldview that held sway for many years was in an article published in 1947 in *Foreign Affairs*, titled "The Sources of Soviet Conduct."[39] Written by a "Mr. X" (later revealed to be George F. Kennan, director of the Policy Planning Staff of the State Department and thereafter ambassador to Moscow), the article argued that the Russians were pursuing a policy of expansion that could only be met by the United States applying "unalterable counterforce at every point where they show signs of encroaching upon the interests of a peaceful and stable world." This he called the strategy of "containment," and it became the governing principle of American foreign policy for at least two decades.

There were critics of the containment policy at the time—Walter Lippmann, in his book *The Cold War*, argued against it in 1947[40]—but the criticisms were less influential than the doctrine. A dominant worldview is important precisely because it prevails over alternative views. One reason why it prevails is that it is broadly consistent with the public's mood. In 1947, when Kennan wrote, popular attitudes toward the Soviet Union—favorable during World War II when Russia and America were allies—had turned quite hostile. In 1946, less than one-fourth of the American people believed Russia could be trusted to cooperate with this country,[41] and by 1948 over three-fourths were convinced the Soviet Union was trying not simply to defend itself, but to become the dominant world power.[42]

worldviews *Comprehensive opinions of how the United States should respond to world problems.*

isolationism *The belief that the United States should withdraw from world affairs.*

containment *The belief that the United States should resist the expansion of aggressive nations, especially the former Soviet Union.*

Such a worldview was also influential because it was consistent with events at the time: Russia had occupied most of the previously independent countries of Eastern Europe and was turning them into puppet regimes. When governments independent of both the United States and the Soviet Union attempted to rule in Hungary and Czechoslovakia, they were overthrown by Soviet-backed coups. A worldview also becomes dominant when it is consistent with prior experiences of people holding it.

Four Worldviews

Every generation of political leaders comes to power with a foreign policy worldview shaped, in large measure, by the real or apparent mistakes of the previous generation.[43] This pattern can be traced back, some have argued, to the very beginnings of the nation. One scholar traces the alteration since 1776 between two national "moods" that favored first "extroversion" (or an active, internationalist policy) and then "introversion" (a less active, even isolationist, posture).[44]

Since the 1920s, American elite opinion has moved through four dominant worldviews: isolationism, containment (or antiappeasement), disengagement, and human rights. **Isolationism** was the view adopted as a result of our unhappy experience in World War I. Our efforts to help European allies had turned sour: Thousands of American troops had been killed in a war that had seemed to accomplish little and certainly had not made the world, in Woodrow Wilson's words, "safe for democracy." As a result, in the 1920s and 1930s elite opinion (and popular opinion) opposed U.S. involvement in European wars.

The **containment** (or antiappeasement) paradigm was the result of World War II. Pearl Harbor was the death knell for isolationism. Senator Arthur H. Vandenberg of Michigan, a staunch isolationist before the attack, became

disengagement *The belief that the United States was harmed by its war in Vietnam and so should avoid supposedly similar events.*

an ardent internationalist not only during but after the war. He later wrote of the Japanese attack on Pearl Harbor on December 7, 1941, "that day ended isolationism for any realist."[45] At a conference in Munich, efforts of British and French leaders to satisfy Hitler's territorial demands in Europe had led not to "peace in our time," as British Prime Minister Neville Chamberlain had claimed, but to ever-greater territorial demands and ultimately to world war. This crisis brought to power men determined not to repeat their predecessors' mistakes: *Munich* became a synonym for weakness, and leaders such as Winston Churchill made antiappeasement the basis of their postwar policy of resisting Soviet expansionism. Churchill summed up the worldview that he had acquired from the Munich era in a famous speech delivered in 1946 in Fulton, Missouri, in which he coined the term *iron curtain* to describe Soviet policy in Eastern Europe.

The events leading up to World War II were the formative experiences of those leaders who came to power in the 1940s, 1950s, and 1960s. What they took to be the lessons of Pearl Harbor and Munich were applied repeatedly—in building a network of defensive alliances in Europe and Asia during the late 1940s and 1950s, in operating an airlift to aid West Berlin when road access to it was cut off by the Russians, in coming to the aid of South Korea, and finally in intervening in Vietnam. Most of these applications of the containment worldview were successful in the sense that they did not harm American interests, they proved welcome to allies, or they prevented a military conquest.

Historical/Corbis Historical/Getty Images

Image 19.5 A meeting that named an era: In Munich in 1938, British Prime Minister Neville Chamberlain attempted to appease the territorial ambitions of Hitler. Chamberlain's failure brought World War II closer.

The **disengagement** (or "Vietnam") view resulted from the experience of the younger foreign policy elite that came to power in the 1970s. Unlike previous applications of the antiappeasement view, our entry into Vietnam had led to a military defeat and a domestic political disaster. That crisis could be interpreted in three ways: (1) we applied the correct worldview in the right place but did not try hard enough; (2) we had the correct worldview but tried to apply it in the wrong place under the wrong circumstances; or (3) the worldview itself was wrong. By and large, the critics of our Vietnam policy tended toward the third conclusion, and thus when they supplanted in office the architects of our Vietnam policy, they inclined toward a worldview based on the slogan "no more Vietnams." Critics of this view called it the "new isolationism," arguing that it would encourage Soviet expansion.

The debates over the Vietnam War colored many subsequent discussions of foreign policy. Almost every military initiative since then has been debated in terms of whether it would lead us into "another Vietnam": sending the Marines to Lebanon, invading Grenada, dispatching military advisers to El Salvador, supporting the contras in Nicaragua, helping South American countries fight drug producers, and sending troops to invade Iraq.

How elites thought about Vietnam affected their foreign policy views for many years. If they thought the war was "immoral," they were reluctant to see American military involvement elsewhere. These elites played a large role in the Carter administration but were replaced by rival elites—those more inclined to a containment view—during the Reagan presidency.[46] When George H. W. Bush sought to expel Iraqi troops from Kuwait, the congressional debate pitted those committed to containment against those who believed in disengagement. The Senate vote on Bush's request for permission to use troops was narrowly carried by containment advocates.

After Bush lost reelection in 1992, Bill Clinton entered the White House with less interest in foreign policy than his predecessor, combined with an advisory team that largely (though not entirely) favored the disengagement approach. Clinton's strongest congressional supporters were those who had argued against the Gulf War. But then a remarkable change occurred. When Slobodan Milošević, the Serbian leader, sent troops into neighboring Kosovo to suppress the ethnic Albanians living there, the strongest voices for American military intervention came from those who once advocated disengagement. During the Gulf War, 47 Senate Democrats voted to oppose U.S. participation. A few years later, 42 Senate Democrats voted to support U.S. military action in Kosovo.

What had happened? The change was inspired by the view that helping the Albanians was required by the doctrine of **human rights**. Liberal supporters of U.S. air attacks on Serbian forces argued that the United States was helping Albanians escape mass killing. By contrast, many conservative members of Congress who had followed a containment policy in the Gulf War now felt that disengagement ought to be followed in Kosovo. Of course, politics also mattered. Clinton was a Democratic president; Bush had been a Republican one.

But politics was not the whole story. Advocates of intervention declared that the attack in Kosovo resembled the genocide—that is, the mass murder of people because of their race or ethnicity—that Jewish people had suffered in Nazi Germany. They held that we must "never again" permit a whole people to be killed. Anti-interventionists said if American foreign policy were guided by human rights, then the United States would have to send troops to many places. How would military action resolve a conflict that had gone on for centuries? Policymakers wrestled with bringing together American principles and American interests, a challenge that became especially pressing after mass atrocities in ethnic conflicts around the globe in the 1990s.

In Rwanda, for example, a civil war between ethnic Hutus and Tutsis resulted in the deaths of 800,000 people in just a few months in 1994. The Canadian government subsequently convened an international commission in 2001 to develop guidelines for states to prevent such crimes against humanity in the future. The panel's report, "Responsibility to Protect," declared that state sovereignty includes an affirmative responsibility to protect citizens from large-scale human rights violations, such as genocide or war crimes, and that states may take action (political or economic, with military force as a last resort) to ensure that other states uphold that responsibility. The United Nations adopted the "R2P" doctrine in 2005, though states differ sharply on where and how implementation is needed.[47] The UN Security Council used R2P language in 2011 for resolutions calling for protection of civilians in the violent civil war in Libya. But those resolutions said Libya, not the international community, was responsible for providing that protection. The international community also did not apply the R2P doctrine to protect civilians in Syria from mass atrocities in that country's civil war. (See discussion of Syria below on p. 510).[48]

Political Polarization

American public opinion historically has been slow to favor military action overseas in the abstract but quick to give support once it begins. However, that pattern ended with the 2003 invasion of Iraq. Public opinion became deeply divided about that war, with most Democrats strongly opposing it and most Republicans favoring it.

U.S. Navy

Image 19.6 Japanese warplanes attacked U.S. naval forces at Pearl Harbor on December 7, 1941.

human rights *The belief that we should try to improve the lives of people in other countries.*

That was not how things worked out during U.S. wars in Korea and Vietnam. The Korean War produced angry divisions in Congress, especially after General Douglas MacArthur, the allied commander in Korea, was fired in 1951 for having disobeyed the president. Yet he received a hero's welcome when he returned to this country and gave an emotional speech to a joint session of Congress. Many Republicans demanded that President Truman be impeached. Despite this public support for MacArthur and these angry congressional words, the country was not split along partisan lines. Slightly more Republicans than Democrats said the war was a mistake (roughly half of each party), but the differences between these voters was not great.

The war in Vietnam split American political elites even more deeply. Journalists and members of Congress took sharply opposing sides, and some Americans traveled to North Vietnam to express their support for the Communist cause. When the North Vietnamese launched a major offensive to destroy American and South Vietnamese troops during the Tet holidays in 1968, it failed, but the American press reported it as a Communist victory, and demands to bring U.S. troops home were raised during the presidential campaign that year. But public opinion did not divide along party lines; in 1968,

polarization A deep and wide conflict over some government policy.

military-industrial complex An alleged alliance between military leaders and corporate leaders.

bipolar world A political landscape with two superpowers.

unipolar world A political landscape with one superpower.

Democratic and Republican voters had just about the same views (a little over half thought the war was a mistake, about a third thought it wasn't).

The U.S. invasion of Iraq in 2003 was more divisive for the American public. From the start, Democratic voters strongly opposed it and Republican voters favored it. By 2006, 76 percent of Democrats said the United States should have stayed out of Iraq, whereas 71 percent of Republicans said that the invasion was the right thing to do.[49]

American public opinion has become increasingly polarized on foreign policy. **Polarization** means a deep and wide conflict, usually along party lines, over some government policy (recall our discussion in Chapter 7). It has replaced the bipartisan foreign policy of World War II and the modest differences in public opinion during Korea and Vietnam.[50]

Figure 19.3 shows that what political party we belong to is strongly linked to our views on foreign policy. The public is deeply divided about these matters, and so, we think, will be the people for whom they vote. But this does not mean the American public has deeply divided views about foreign policy aims.

All Americans—Democrats and Republicans alike—want peace, prosperity, and security, and they support troops that are deployed.[51] Americans tend to divide along party lines on conflicts like Iraq when elites divide along party lines. As we learned in Chapter 7, ordinary voters take their cues from elites from their political party, and divisions on foreign policy reflect divisions among congressional elites. While elites were divided on Vietnam, that division existed within both parties in Congress, and so public opinion was less polarized by party during those conflicts.[52] Whether the public is divided along party lines in future conflicts depends a great deal on how elites divide on those conflicts.

19-4 The Politics of Foreign Affairs: Military Action, Defense Policy, and the Future

Using the policy-making classification from Chapter One, we see two views about the role of the military in American life. One is majoritarian: The military exists to defend the country or to help other nations defend themselves. When troops are used, almost all Americans benefit and almost all pay the bill. (Some Americans, such as those who lose a loved one in war, pay much more than the rest of the population.) The president is the commander-in-chief, and Congress plays a largely supportive role.

Although the other view does not deny the primary role of the armed forces in protecting U.S. national security, it focuses on the extent to which the military is a large and powerful client. The real beneficiaries of military spending are the generals and admirals, as well as the big corporations and members of Congress whose districts get fat defense contracts. Everyone pays, but these clients get most of the benefits. What we spend on defense is shaped by the **military-industrial complex**, a supposedly unified bloc of Defense Department leaders and military manufacturers. From this perspective, there are two key issues in national defense: how much money we spend and how it is divided up. The first reflects majoritarian politics, the second, interest-group bargaining.

Military Action

Foreign policy takes many forms—discussions are held, treaties are signed, organizations are joined—but in many cases it depends on the ability to use military force. Troops, ships, and aircraft are not the only ways to influence other countries; international trade and foreign aid are also useful. But in modern times, as in the past, the nations of the world know the difference between a "great power" (i.e., a heavily armed one) and a weak nation.

During the Cold War, distinctions between nations were relatively easy. For a half century, each American president, operating through the National Security Council, made clear that our chief goal was to prevent the Soviet Union from overrunning Western Europe, bombing the United States, or invading other nations. But since the Soviet Union has disappeared, no other nation has acquired the power to take its place. During the Cold War, we lived in a **bipolar world** made up of two superpowers. Now we live in a **unipolar world** with the United States as the only superpower, though elites and the public alike express ambivalence today over how to employ that power abroad.[53]

With the collapse of the Soviet Union and the end of the Cold War, one might think that military power is less important than in the 20th century. But it remains as important as ever. Since the Soviet Union was dissolved and the Berlin Wall came down in 1989, the United States has used military force to attack Iraq, maintain order in Bosnia, defend Kosovo, and go to war in Afghanistan. Various rogue nations, such as Iran and North Korea, have acquired or are about to acquire long-range rockets and weapons of mass destruction (i.e., nuclear, chemical, and biological arms). Many nations, such as China, India, Pakistan, and Israel, that perceive threats from neighbors have nuclear bombs.

Figure 19.3 Foreign Policy Goals

Percentage of people surveyed who say the issue should be a top U.S. foreign policy priority (Data listed by party support and overall support for issue.)

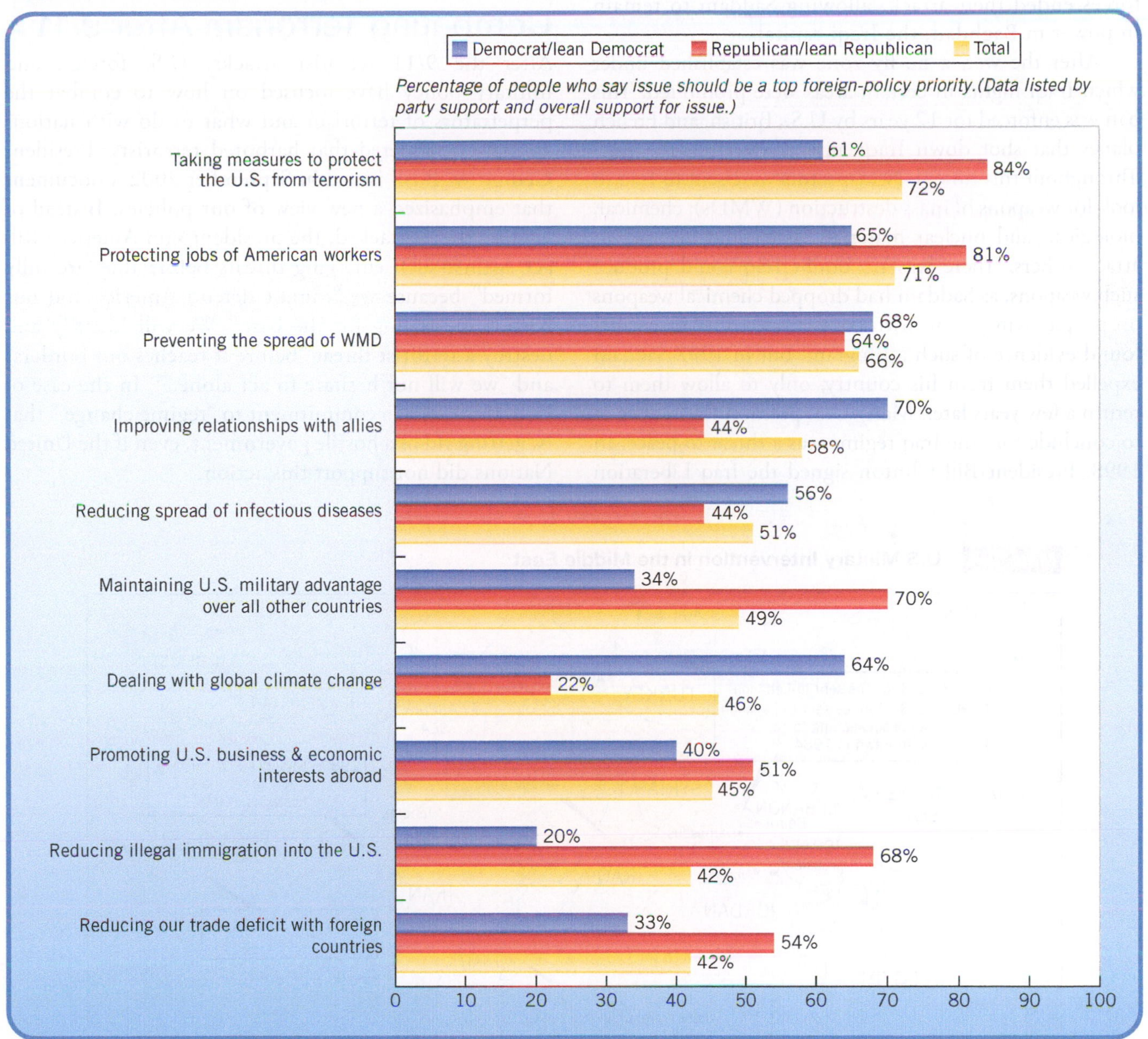

Source: Pew Research Center, "Conflicting Partisan Priorities for U.S. Foreign Policy," 29 November 2018.

Q **"What might be the sources of partisan differences on U.S. foreign policy goals?"**

And Russia still has many of the nuclear weapons that the Soviet Union built. As the events of the 1990s and the early 21st century make clear, by no means has the end of the Cold War meant the end of war.

The Post–Cold War Era and the Persian Gulf War

Although the Soviet Union did not formally dissolve until the end of 1991, the ending of the Cold War became clear when the two superpowers worked together to resolve an international conflict. In the summer of 1990, the Iraqi army under Saddam Hussein invaded neighboring Kuwait. Calling for Iraq to withdraw, President George H. W. Bush declared that nations uniting to oppose the invasion were creating a "new world order.... A world where the rule of law supplants the rule of the jungle.... A world where the strong respect the rights of the weak."[54] The United Nations (UN) Security Council subsequently passed a resolution demanding that Iraq withdraw and authorizing force to expel it. In January 1991, the United States led a coalition of forces from several nations that attacked Iraq; within 100 days, the Iraqi army had retreated from Kuwait and fled home. The U.S.-led military forces ended their attack, allowing Saddam to remain in power in Baghdad, the Iraqi capital.

After the war, a no-fly zone was established under which Iraqi flights in certain areas were prohibited. This ban was enforced for 12 years by U.S., British, and French planes that shot down Iraqi aircraft violating the rule. Throughout this time, UN inspectors were sent to Iraq to look for weapons of mass destruction (WMDs): chemical, biological, and nuclear materials that could be used to attack others. There was no doubt Iraq could produce such weapons, as Saddam had dropped chemical weapons on people living in his own country. The UN inspectors found evidence of such a program, but in 1997 Saddam expelled them from his country, only to allow them to return a few years later. Many U.S. political leaders began to conclude that the Iraq regime was a threat to peace. In 1998, President Bill Clinton signed the Iraq Liberation Act, which called for new leadership in Iraq. But how this change would be achieved was unclear.

Combating Terrorism After 9/11

After the 9/11 terrorist attacks, U.S. foreign and military policy have focused on how to combat the perpetrators of terrorism and what to do with nations we have conquered that harbored terrorists. President George W. Bush issued in September 2002 a document that emphasized a new view of our policies. Instead of waiting to be attacked, the president said America "will act against such emerging threats before they are fully formed" because we "cannot defend America and our friends by hoping for the best." We will identify and destroy a terrorist threat "before it reaches our borders" and "we will not hesitate to act alone."[55] In the case of Iraq, this meant a commitment to "regime change," that is, getting rid of a hostile government, even if the United Nations did not support this action.

Map 19.1 **U.S Military Intervention in the Middle East**

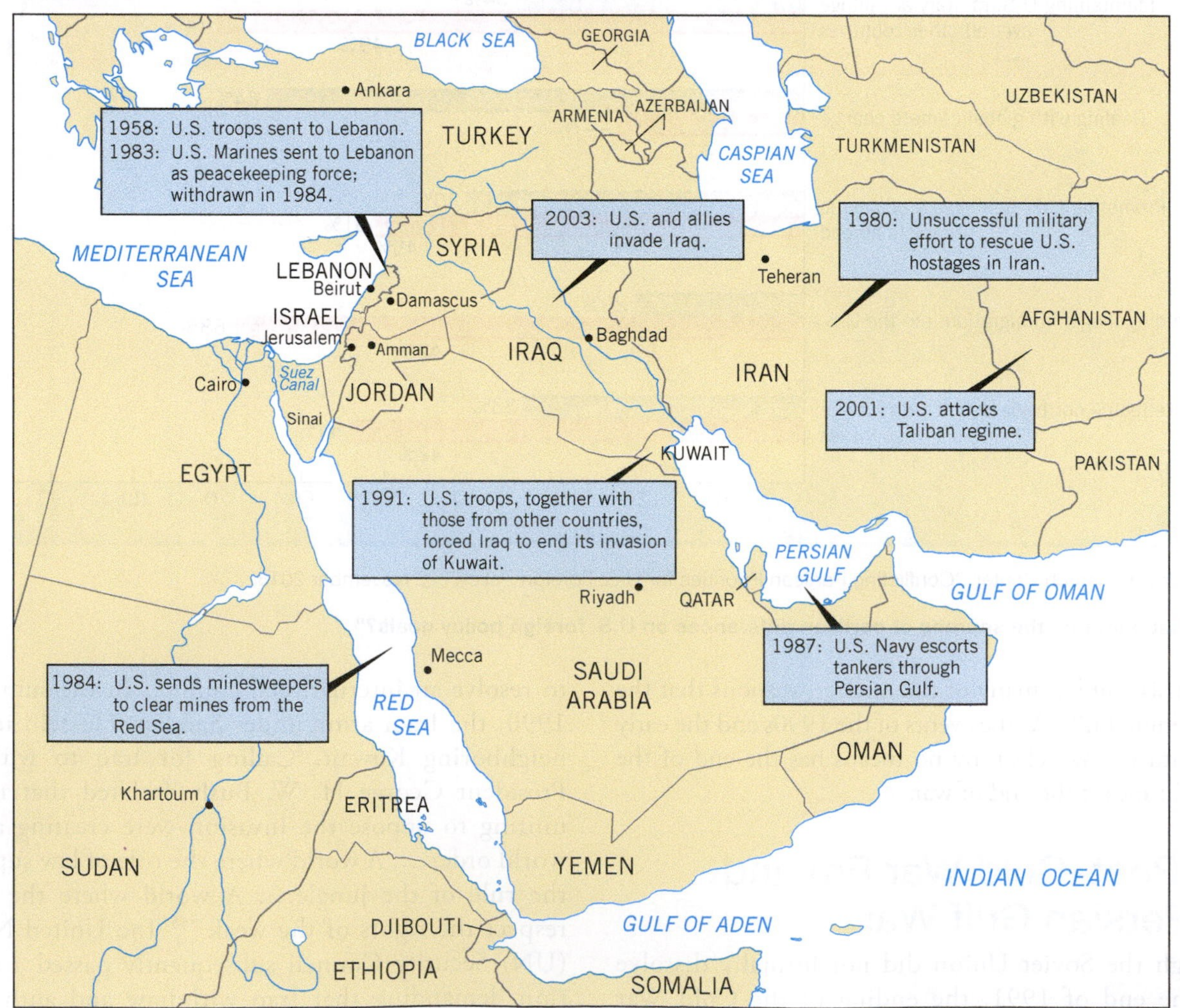

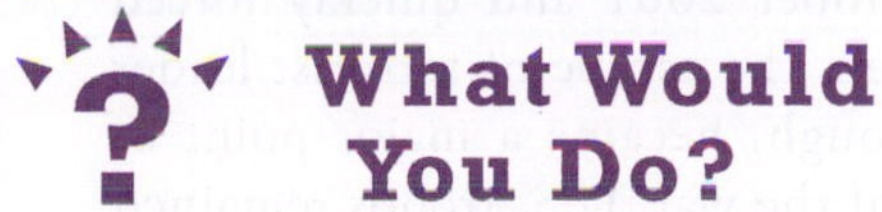

Will You Negotiate a Hostage Release?

To: *President Amaia Xabi*
From: *Arjun Luce, national security adviser*
Subject: *Hostages*

The six Americans held hostage in the Middle East are beginning their second year of captivity. One, a CIA officer, has been tortured. This administration has a declared policy of not negotiating with terrorists, but hostage families and their sympathizers are highly critical of this stance. A moderate government in the region has secretly indicated that, in exchange for military supplies, it may be able to help win the release of "some" hostages.

To Consider:

The families of the six American hostages held captive in the Middle East today criticized the president for failing to win their release. Public opinion also favors a negotiated solution, and members of Congress have called for the White House to deliver results through diplomacy or possibly military action.

Arguments for:

1. Public sympathy for the hostages and their families is increasing, and people are highly critical of the administration for failing to free captive Americans.
2. The White House is pursuing the possibility of a secret arms deal in exchange for the release of Americans. If these negotiations succeed, then we will secure the hostages' freedom and perhaps earn the goodwill of moderates in the region, thereby increasing our influence.
3. If negotiations fail, then we will have a strong case, with congressional and public support, for taking military action to free the hostages.

Arguments against:

1. Our "no-negotiations" policy remains credible and will deter other terrorist groups from thinking they may win concessions by capturing Americans.
2. Negotiations to provide arms in exchange for the hostages' release have no guarantee that the former will lead to the latter. Furthermore, if those secret negotiations become public, then the administration will be widely criticized for abandoning longstanding U.S. policy.
3. U.S. military leaders are not optimistic about finding and freeing the hostages, who are being kept in hidden, scattered sites, without grave risk to their lives.

What Will You Decide? Enter **MindTap** to make your choice.

Your decision: ☐ Support ☐ Oppose

This has been called a doctrine of preemption, that is, of attacking a determined enemy before it can launch an attack against us or an ally. In fact, it is not really new. President Bill Clinton launched cruise missile strikes against training camps that followers of Osama bin Laden were using in the aftermath of their bombing of American embassies in Kenya and Tanzania in 1998. President George W. Bush elevated the policy of preemption into a clearly stated national doctrine.

Afghanistan and Iraq

The United States did not use preemption in Afghanistan in 2001, as Congress's September 18 joint resolution authorized the use of military force against the perpetrators of the 9/11 terrorist attacks as well as nations that had aided or harbored them.[56] The United States and Great Britain commenced air strikes in Afghanistan in October 2001 and quickly forced the Taliban from power. The escape of terrorist leader Osama bin Laden, though, became a major point of contention for critics of the war. U.S. troops remained in Afghanistan, and in 2003, NATO sent peacekeeping forces to the country.[57]

Congress also passed a joint resolution in October 2002 authorizing the use of force in Iraq if Saddam Hussein did not comply with weapons inspections. The following month, the United Nations Security Council unanimously passed a resolution that gave Iraq one final opportunity to provide a full accounting of its WMD programs or face "serious consequences." But when Iraq did not comply, the Security Council lacked consensus on whether the November 2002 resolution authorized military force, and U.S. efforts to secure another resolution explicitly granting that authorization were unsuccessful.[58]

The Iraq War: Majoritarian or Client Politics?

The George W. Bush administration sent U.S. forces into Iraq in the spring of 2003 to depose Iraqi leader Saddam Hussein, who had failed repeatedly to comply with United Nations inspections of Iraqi facilities to ensure that Iraq was no longer producing weapons of mass destruction (WMDs). President Bush declared that the Iraq invasion was necessary to keep the United States and the world safe from potential attack, making his case through majoritarian politics—everyone would bear the cost of war to ensure global security. As he said at the outset of the invasion in March 2003, "The people of the United States and our friends and allies will not live at the mercy of an outlaw regime that threatens the peace with weapons of mass murder."[59]

The United States succeeded quickly in toppling Saddam Hussein's regime, but it did not find the expected WMD stockpiles in Iraq.[60] Nevertheless, the Bush White House said the possible existence of these programs justified intervention. Furthermore, on humanitarian grounds, removing from power a brutal dictator who had committed atrocities against his own people provided strong justification for intervention, as did the prospect of bringing democracy to Iraq. President Bush provided a strong defense of the war in his memoirs: "America is safer without a homicidal dictator pursuing WMD and supporting terror at the heart of the Middle East. The region is more hopeful with a young democracy setting an example for others to follow. And the Iraqi people are better off with a government that answers to them instead of torturing and murdering them."[61]

But humanitarian intervention and democracy promotion often are viewed as client politics—Americans as a whole pay for people in another nation to benefit. Making a case for the legitimacy of such interventions is more difficult than with majoritarian politics. With the security threat of possible WMD, the Bush administration made a strong case for invading Iraq in 2003 (though the decision was still highly contentious in the United States and around the globe).[62] The subsequent focus on humanitarian and political arguments, and the challenges with establishing a stable democratic regime in Iraq, led to diminished public support for the war by the end of the Bush administration. One of Democratic presidential candidate Barack Obama's major campaign promises in the 2008 election was to bring home U.S. military forces in Iraq (which Obama did as president in 2011, as discussed below).

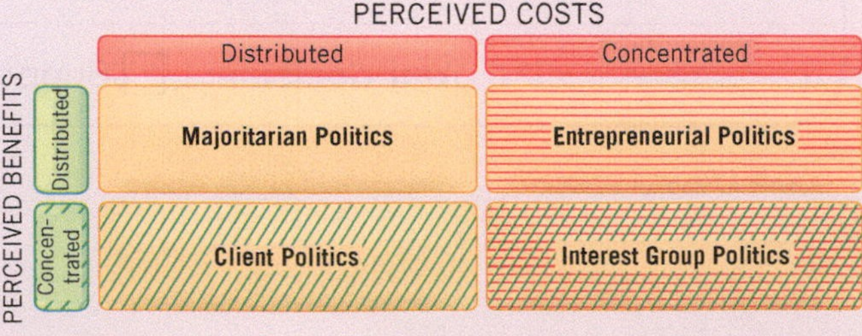

Unable to convince the United Nations to support a war, the United States, the United Kingdom, and other countries decided to act alone. On March 30, 2003, they invaded Iraq in a campaign called Operation Iraqi Freedom; within about six weeks, the Iraqi army was defeated and the American-led coalition occupied all of the country. After the war, a large group of inspectors toured Iraq looking for WMDs, but they found virtually none. Later, a bipartisan commission concluded that Saddam had apparently cancelled his WMD program, but had told hardly any of his own military leaders about this.[63]

The newly freed Iraqi people voted first for an interim parliament, then for a new constitution, and finally for a regular government. But this process was offset by the terrorist activities of various insurgents, first aimed at American troops and later at Iraqi civilians, killing several tens of thousands of them. The situation in Iraq became a major American political issue, contributing to the loss of the Republican congressional majority in the 2006 elections.

After conquering Afghanistan and Iraq, the United States faced the problem of rebuilding these nations. The United States has had a lot of experience, some good and some bad, with this problem. It helped put Germany and Japan back on their feet after World War II. From 1992 to 1994, It tried to bring peace among warring factions to Somalia. From 1994 to 1996, the United States worked to install a democratically elected president and rebuild the local police force in the Caribbean country of Haiti. Starting in 1995, the United States worked with European allies to restore order to Bosnia and Kosovo, located in what used to be Yugoslavia. In 2001, the United States began helping Afghans create a new government and economy, and in 2003 it started to do the same in Iraq. The United States succeeded in Germany and Japan, failed in Somalia and Haiti, and made progress in Bosnia and Kosovo.[64]

After easily defeating the Iraqi army in 2003, the United States tried to bring stability and democracy to the country in mistaken ways. It abolished the Iraqi army (and so had no native defense force), relied on too few American troops (and so could not pacify the country), and kept these troops when they were not fighting in American compounds (thus leaving Iraqi civilians unprotected). Iran funneled arms and terrorists into the country to help attack American soldiers. Public opinion in that country, though deeply divided along party lines, became hostile to U.S. efforts there.

To deal with this problem, President Bush (over the objections of many subordinates) announced a new strategy. The United States would send another 30,000 troops to Iraq (the "surge") and instruct these troops to work in Iraqi neighborhoods and build alliances with local groups. He assigned General David Petraeus to be the military leader.

The surge worked. Deaths of American forces and Iraqi civilians fell dramatically, an elected Iraqi government began to function effectively, and new Iraqi elections in 2009 were held peacefully. The American government negotiated an agreement with Iraqi leaders that called for withdrawing most American troops from the country by 2011. Because of this progress and because the U.S. economy went into a recession, the American public began to lose interest in Iraq. This changed a few years later with the rise of militant groups in the Middle East, as discussed below.

Afghanistan is a more difficult problem. Unlike Iraq, it has never been a unified nation and lacks a large middle class or many populous cities. The United States easily defeated the Taliban regime and managed to put in office a moderate leader. Troops from other nations arrived to help. But creating an effective central government in a country that has rarely had one and ending terrorist attacks have proved to be difficult assignments. During the 2008 presidential campaign, Barack Obama promised to send more forces to that country, and beginning in 2009 he did so. By the middle of the year, 60,000 U.S. troops were deployed there, but they were not enough.

In 2009, the general leading U.S. forces in Afghanistan asked President Obama for another 40,000 troops; the president sent 30,000. In 2011, the Obama administration began to draw down its "surge" in Afghanistan, with fewer than 10,000 troops there at the end of Obama's second term. At the start of the Trump presidency, the U.S. commander in Afghanistan requested additional forces to advise Afghan troops and combat insurgents, and the White House approved an increase of 3,000–5,000 troops in the summer of 2017. But in December 2018, President Trump declared that the United States would prepare to draw down about half of its 14,000 troops in Afghanistan, prompting the resignation of Defense Secretary and former U.S. Marine Corps General James Mattis, who disagreed with the plan as well as with the president's decision to withdraw U.S. troops from Syria. Uncertainty about continued U.S. involvement raised concerns about prospects for long-term stability in both countries, particularly as the war in Afghanistan became the longest military intervention in U.S. history in Obama's second term. In late 2019, top-secret government documents were revealed to show that U.S. officials had expressed deep concerns about the prospect for victory in Afghanistan for many years since the war began in 2001.[65]

Building Support for U.S. Military Action

Supporters of Bush's preemption strategy hailed it as a positive step to defeat terrorists abroad before they could attack the United States at home. Critics attacked the argument as justifying preemptive and possibly unjust wars and abandoning the United Nations. This debate has divided Congress in a way that puts an end to the old adage that partisanship ends at the water's edge.

Since the end of the Cold War, the United States has not had a common enemy that, in the opinion of critics of U.S. overseas efforts, should justify a nonpartisan view. As noted earlier (see pages 503–504), most liberal Democrats opposed both the U.S. effort to get Iraq out of Kuwait in 1991 and the U.S. invasion of Iraq in 2003; most Republicans supported both efforts.[66] But when President Clinton launched attacks on hostile forces in Kosovo, he was supported by many liberal Democrats and opposed by many conservative Republicans.[67] Party differences and political ideology now make a big difference in foreign policy.

In the 20th century, the United States sometimes sought and obtained United Nations support, as with going to war in Korea (1950) and in launching the military effort to force Iraqi troops out of Kuwait (1991). The United States did not have UN authorization to fight against North Vietnam (in the 1960s), occupy Haiti (1994), or assist friendly forces in Bosnia (1994) or Kosovo (1999). In the aftermath of 9/11, policymakers are divided over whether the United States should "go it alone" against its enemies abroad, or do so only on the basis of a broad coalition of supporting nations. The first President Bush assembled just such a coalition to force Iraq out of Kuwait, but the second President Bush acted without UN support in invading Afghanistan and later Iraq, though he received crucial support from the United Kingdom, Australia, and Poland.

The Obama administration had many disputes with Congress in foreign affairs. In 2012, Obama said use of chemical weapons by Syria would cross a "red line" that could prompt military intervention, but when Syria gassed its own people one year later, the president said he would act only with legislative authorization, which Congress did not grant.[68] (The United States and Russia ultimately negotiated a deal with Syria to destroy its chemical weapons.)

In the summer of 2014, Obama approved air strikes against Islamic militants in the Middle East (known as ISIS, the Islamic State of Iraq and Syria, or ISIL, the Islamic State of Iraq and the Levant) without congressional approval. He did request a resolution afterward authorizing the use of force, saying it was not necessary for him to act but would demonstrate American unity.[69] The Obama administration also pursued discussions with Iran to end its nuclear program, but in the face of strong legislative opposition, the president agreed in the spring of 2015 that Congress would have a formal say in any accord.[70] When the administration announced an agreement a few months later, many legislators—primarily Republicans, but also some Democrats—declared that the deal would endanger U.S. national security.[71]

In 2016, Republican presidential candidate Donald Trump campaigned strongly against the Obama administration's agreement with Iran. As president, Trump initially called for a review of the nuclear deal, but in 2018, he announced that the United States would withdraw from the agreement and reimpose economic sanctions upon Iran. President Trump pursued a different strategy for addressing North Korea's nuclear program, holding a summit meeting in 2018 with North Korean leader Kim Jong Un in Singapore, and then holding a second meeting in Vietnam in 2019 that ended early when the two sides could not reach agreement on denuclearization plans for North Korea.

During the campaign, Trump also said the United States should stay out of the civil war in Syria. But after government forces there attacked rebels and civilians with chemical weapons, the president authorized U.S. air strikes in Syria in 2017 and 2018. Then in late 2018, President Trump issued a surprise announcement that the approximately 2,000 U.S. troops in Syria would return soon, declaring that the mission of combating terrorists there had been achieved. Advisers, members of Congress—including several Republicans—and U.S. allies expressed deep concern about having troops depart precipitously, and as discussed earlier, Defense Secretary Mattis resigned over the decision.[72]

These strong public conflicts between the executive and legislative branches in the 21st century illustrate that the Cold War consensus in foreign affairs (though certainly not as cohesive as sometimes suggested) no longer guides decision making. And the increased divisiveness in domestic deliberations about American foreign policy choices constrains prospects for U.S. global leadership.

Defense Policy

Throughout most of our history the United States has not maintained large military forces during peacetime. For instance, the percentage of the gross national product spent on defense in 1935, on the eve of World War II, was about the same as it was in 1870, when we were on the eve of nothing in particular. We armed when a war broke out, then we disarmed when the war ended.

But all of that changed after World War II, when defense spending declined sharply but did not return to its prewar levels. And in 1950, our defense expenditures soared again. In that year, we rearmed to fight a war in Korea, but when it was over, we did not completely disarm. The reason was our containment policy toward the Soviet Union. For about 40 years—from the outbreak of the Korean War in 1950 to the collapse of the Soviet Union in 1991—American military spending was driven by our desire to contain the Soviet Union and its allies. The Soviet Union had brought under its control most of Eastern Europe; would it also invade Western Europe? Russia had always wanted access to the oil and warm-water ports of the Middle East; would the Soviets someday invade or subvert Iran or Turkey? The Soviet Union was willing to help North Korea invade South Korea and North Vietnam to invade South Vietnam; would it next use an ally to threaten the United States? Soviet leaders supported "wars of national liberation" in Africa and Latin America; would they succeed in turning more and more nations against the United States?

To meet these threats, the United States built up a military system designed to repel a Soviet invasion of Western Europe and at the same time help allies resist smaller-scale invasions or domestic uprisings. Figure 19.4 shows U.S. military spending from World War II to the present. It illustrates that even after we decided to keep a large military force after World War II, there have been many ups and downs in the actual level of spending. After the Korean War was over, we spent less; when we became involved in Vietnam, we spent more; when the Soviet Union invaded Afghanistan and we invaded Iraq, we spent more again. These changes in spending tended to reflect changes in public opinion about the defense budget.

As Figure 19.5 shows, a majority of Americans have said that our defense program is either "about right" or "not strong enough," but other studies show that popular support for spending more money on defense changes from year to year.

The collapse of the Soviet Union ushered in a major debate about U.S. defense strategy. Liberals demanded sharp cuts in defense spending, weapons procurement, and military personnel, arguing that with the Soviet threat ended, it was time to collect our "peace dividend" and divert funds from the military to domestic social programs. Conservatives agreed that some military cuts were in order, but they argued that the world was still a dangerous place and therefore that a strong (and well-funded) military remained essential to the nation's defense. This disagreement reflected different predictions about what the future would be like. Many liberals (and some conservatives, such as Pat Buchanan, who believed that America should "stay at home") argued that we could not afford to be the "world's policeman." Many conservatives (and some liberals) responded by saying that Russia was still a military powerhouse that might once again fall under the control of ruthless leaders and that many other nations hostile to the United States (such as North Korea, Iran, and Iraq) were becoming potential adversaries as they tried to build or acquire nuclear weapons and missile systems.

Figure 19.4 **Trends in National Defense Spending**

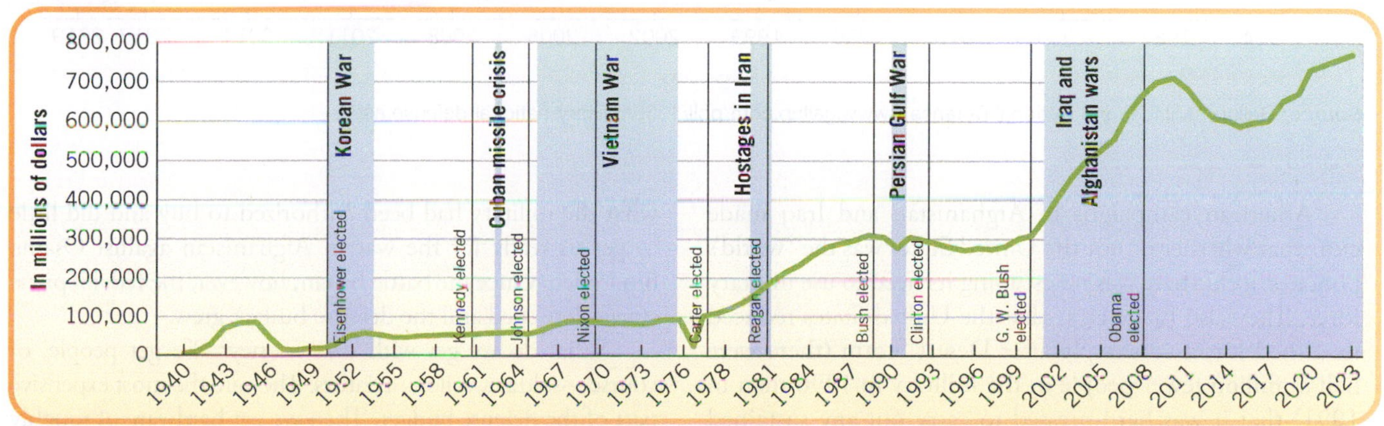

Note: Last data point is an estimated cost.

Source: Office of Management and Budget, *A Budget for a Better America: Promises Kept. Taxpayers First. Fiscal Year 2020 Budget of the U.S. Government* (Washington, D.C.: U.S. Government Printing Office, 2020), Historical Tables, Table 3.1, "Outlays by Super Function and Function, 1940–2025."

Map 19.2 **U.S. Military Intervention in Central America and the Caribbean Since 1950**

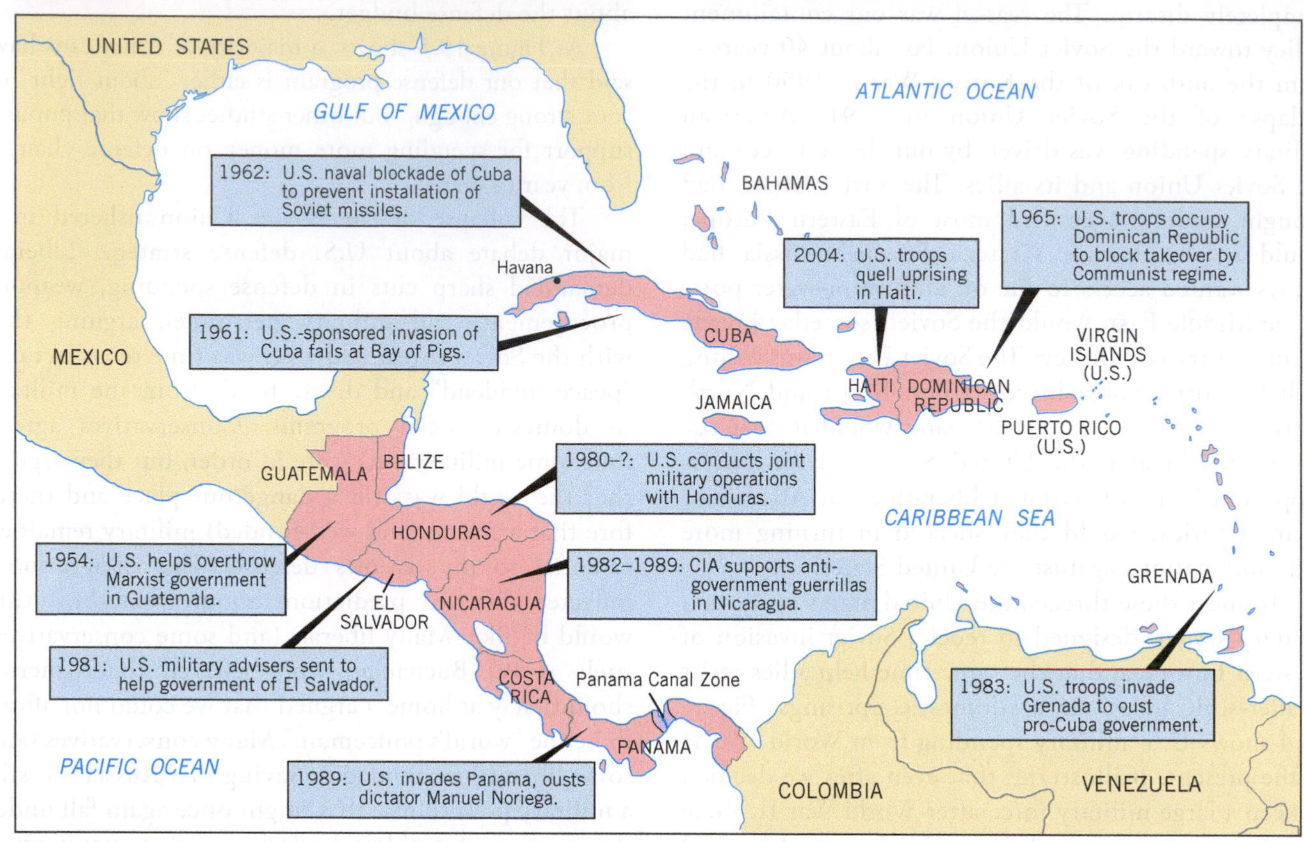

Figure 19.5 **Most Americans Think National Defense Is Either "About Right" or "Not Strong Enough"**

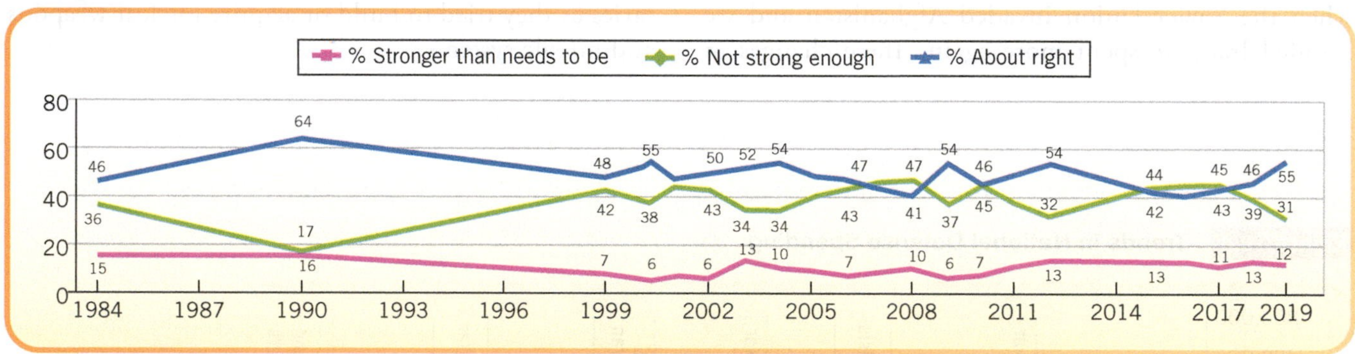

Source: Gallup, "Military and National Defense," www.gallup.com/poll/1666/military-national-defense.aspx.

American campaigns in Afghanistan and Iraq made clear that whether or not the United States was the "world's police officer," there was no escaping its need to use military force. They also made clear that the United States reduced its armed forces so sharply after Desert Storm (there were half a million fewer people in the military in 1996 than in 1991) that it was hard-pressed to carry out any sustained military campaign (see Table 19.1).

After the national budget deficit was eliminated in 1998, both President Clinton and the Republican Congress did call for more military spending. But that increase did not pay for what the military had been authorized to buy and did little to get us ready for the war in Afghanistan against Osama bin Laden. Once the battle began, however, the federal purse strings loosened and the defense budget grew.

What do we get with that money? We get people, of course—soldiers, sailors, aviators. They are the most expensive part of the defense budget. Then we get hardware of roughly two kinds: big-ticket items, like aircraft carriers and bombers, and small-ticket items, like hammers and screwdrivers. Each of these kinds of hardware has its own politics. Finally, we get "readiness": training, supplies, munitions, fuel, and food.

TABLE 19.1 | U.S. Military Forces Before and After the Breakup of the Soviet Union

Service	Before 1991	End FY 1998
Army		
Active divisions	18	10
National Guard divisions	10	8
Navy		
Aircraft carriers	15	11
Training carriers	1	2
Ships	546	346
Air Force		
Active fighter wings	24	13
Reserve fighter wings	12	7
Marine Corps		
Active divisions	3	3
Reserve divisions	1	1
Strategic Nuclear Forces		
Ballistic missile submarines	31	18
Strategic bombers	324	182
ICBMs	1,000	550

ICBM, intercontinental ballistic missile

Source: *Statistical Abstract of the United States, 1998*, 363.

Personnel

Efforts to develop our military forces before World War II reflected the considerable American discomfort with a strong central government. The United States did not institute a peacetime draft until 1940, when the rest of the world was already at war, and the draft was renewed the following year (only a few months before Pearl Harbor) by only a one-vote margin in the House. Until 1973, the United States relied on the draft to obtain military personnel. Then, at the end of the Vietnam War, it replaced the draft with the all-volunteer force (AVF). After getting off to a rocky start, the AVF began to improve due to increases in military pay and rising civilian unemployment from the mid-1970s into the early 1980s. Abolishing the draft was politically popular: people did not like being ordered to serve, particularly when they did not agree with the war. Since then, even in congressional districts that otherwise are staunch supporters of a strong defense, voters often tell elected officials that they do not want to return to the draft (and many military leaders agree). All men between the ages of 18 and25 must register for Selective Service (women do not have to register, even after the Pentagon opened all combat positions to women in 2015).[73] Legislation would be required to reinstate a draft—which some people have advocated to share the responsibility of military service across society, but that proposal has not gained widespread popular support to date.[74]

The percentage of women in the military has steadily increased. (In 2017, they constituted approximately 16 percent of the total active-duty force.)[75] For a long time, however, women were barred by law from serving in combat roles. (What constitutes a "combat role" is a bit difficult to say, since even personnel far from the main fighting can be hit by an enemy bomb or artillery shell.) In 1993, Congress ended the legal ban on assigning women to navy combat ships and air force fighter jets, and soon women were serving on three aircraft carriers. Twenty years later, the Pentagon lifted its official ban on women serving in combat. The military's rules on sexual orientation and military service also have changed significantly in the past two decades. Until 1993, it was the long-standing policy of the U.S. armed forces to bar LGBTQ+ soldiers from entering the military and to discharge them if they were discovered when serving. LGBTQ+ rights organizations had long protested this exclusion. In 1993, a LGBTQ+ soldier won a lawsuit against the army for having discharged him; he settled for back pay and retirement benefits in exchange for a promise not to reenlist. In 1993, a judge ordered the navy to reinstate a discharged sailor who had revealed his LGBTQ+ sexual orientation on national television.

In 1992, presidential candidate Bill Clinton promised that as president, he would lift the official ban on soldiers with same-sex orientations serving in the military. Once in office, he discovered it was not that easy. Many members of the armed forces believed that knowingly serving alongside and living in close quarters with individuals with same-sex orientations would create unnecessary tension and harm military morale and troop solidarity. The Joint Chiefs of Staff opposed lifting the ban, and several key members of Congress said they would try to pass a law reaffirming it. President Clinton was forced to settle

Michael Fitzsimmons/Shutterstock.com

Image 19.7 The U.S. defense budget funds military hardware such as this unmanned aerial vehicle, or surveillance drone.

cost overruns *When the money actually paid to military suppliers exceeds the estimated costs.*

gold plating *The tendency of Pentagon officials to ask weapons contractors to meet excessively high requirements.*

for a compromise: "Don't ask, don't tell." Under this policy, persons entering or serving in the military would not be asked about their sexual orientation and would be allowed to serve, provided they did not reveal their sexual orientation, if it was same-sex. If a person did do so, that would not be automatic grounds for discharge, but it might be grounds for launching an investigation to determine whether rules against same-sex conduct had been violated.

In 1994, the new Pentagon rules designed to implement "don't ask, don't tell" went into effect, but challenges of implementation soon prompted calls for ending altogether the prohibition on some soldiers revealing their sexual orientation. President Obama signed a law repealing "don't ask, don't tell" in 2010 with the strong support of his secretary of defense and chairman of the Joint Chiefs, who said this would not harm military readiness.

In 2016, the Obama administration announced that transgender individuals could serve openly in the military, but the Trump administration reversed the policy. The Supreme Court ruled in early 2019 that the reversal could be implemented while the policy was challenged in court.

Big-Ticket Items

Whenever the Pentagon buys a new submarine, airplane, or missile, we hear about **cost overruns**. In the 1950s, actual costs were three times greater than estimated costs; by the 1960s, things were only slightly better—actual costs were twice estimated costs.

There are five main reasons for these overruns. First, it is hard to know in advance what something that has never existed before will cost once you build it. People who have remodeled their homes know this all too well. So do government officials who build new subways or congressional office buildings. It is no different with a B-2 bomber.

Second, people who want to persuade Congress to appropriate money for a new airplane or submarine have an incentive to underestimate the cost. To get the weapon approved, its sponsors tell Congress how little it will cost; once the weapon is under construction, the sponsors go back to Congress for additional money to cover "unexpected" cost increases.

Third, the Pentagon officials who decide what kind of new aircraft they want are drawn from the ranks of those who will fly it. These officers naturally want the best airplane (or ship or tank) that money can buy. As Air Force General Carl "Tooey" Spaatz once put it, "A second-best aircraft is like a second-best poker hand. No damn good."[76] But what exactly is the "best" airplane? Is it the fastest one? Or the most maneuverable one? Or the most reliable one? Or the one with the longest range? Pentagon officials have a tendency to answer, "All of the above." Of course, trying to produce all of the above is incredibly expensive (and sometimes impossible). But asking for the expensive (or the impossible) is understandable, given that the air force officers who buy it will also fly it. This tendency to ask for everything at once is called **gold plating**.

Fourth, many new weapons are purchased from a single contractor. This is called sole-sourcing. A contractor is hired to design, develop, and build an airplane. As a result there is no competition, and so the manufacturer has no strong incentive to control costs. And if the sole manufacturer gets into financial trouble, the government, seeking to avoid a shutdown of all production, has an incentive to bail the company out.

Fifth, when Congress wants to cut the military budget, it often does so not by canceling a new weapons system but by stretching out the number of years during which it is purchased. Say that Congress wants to buy 100 F-22s, 25 a year for four years. To give the appearance of cutting the budget, it will decide to buy only 15 the first year and take five years to buy the rest. Or it will authorize the construction

Photo 12/Alamy Stock Photo

Image 19.8 General Colin Powell served as Chairman of the Joint Chiefs of Staff during the George Bush presidency and the first year of the Clinton presidency. He later served as Secretary of State for President George W. Bush.

of 20 now and then ask again next year for the authority to build more. But start-and-stop production decisions and stretching out production over more years drives up the cost of building each unit. If General Motors or Toyota built cars this way, they would go broke.

There are ways to cope with four of these five problems. You cannot do much about the first, ignorance, but you can do something about low estimates, gold plating, sole-sourcing, and stretch-outs. If the Pentagon would give realistic cost estimates initially (perhaps verified by another agency); if it would ask for weapons that meet a few critical performance requirements instead of every requirement that can be thought of; if two or more manufacturers were to compete in designing, developing, and manufacturing new weapons; and if Congress were to stop trying to "cut" the budget using the smoke-and-mirrors technique of stretchouts, then we would hear a lot less about cost overruns.

Some of these things are being done. There is more competition and less sole-sourcing in weapons procurement today than once was the case. But the political incentives to avoid other changes are very powerful. Pentagon officers will always want "the best." They will always have an incentive to understate costs. Congress will always be tempted to use stretch-outs as a way of avoiding hard budget choices.

Readiness

Presumably, we have a peacetime military so that we will be ready for wartime. Presumably, therefore, the peacetime forces will devote a lot of their time and money to improving their readiness.

Not necessarily. The politics of defense spending is such that readiness often is given a very low priority. Here is why.

Client politics influences the decision. In 1990, Congress was willing to cut almost anything, provided it wasn't built or stationed in some member's district. That doesn't leave much. Plans to stop producing F-14 fighters for the navy were opposed by members from Long Island, where the Grumman manufacturing plant was located. Plans to kill the Osprey aircraft for the Marines were opposed by members from the places where it was to be built. Plans to close bases were opposed by all members with a base in their district.

That leaves training and readiness. These things, essential to military effectiveness, have no constituencies and hence few congressional defenders. When forced to choose, the services themselves often prefer to allocate scarce dollars to developing and buying new weapons than to spending for readiness. Moreover, the savings from buying less fuel or having fewer exercises shows up right away, while the savings from canceling an aircraft carrier may not show up for years. Not surprisingly, training and readiness are usually what get the ax.

WDC Photos/Alamy Stock Photo

Image 19.9 The repeal of the "Don't Ask, Don't Tell" policy in the Obama administration ended restrictions on people in the U.S. military making their sexual orientation public.

Bases

At one time, the opening and closing of military bases was pure client politics, which meant that a lot of bases were opened and hardly any were closed. Most members of Congress fought to get a base in their district, and every member fought to keep an existing base open. Even the biggest congressional critics of the U.S. military, people who would vote to take a gun out of a soldier's hand, would fight hard to keep bases in their districts open and operating.

In 1988, Congress finally concluded that no base would ever be closed unless the system for making decisions was changed. It created the Commission on Base Realignment and Closure (BRAC), consisting of private citizens (originally 12, later 8) who would consider recommendations from the secretary of defense. By law, Congress would have to vote within 45 days for or against the commission's list as a whole, without having a chance to amend it. Five BRAC reports have been issued since 1998. Congress approved each one, resulting in the closing of more than 350 bases.

Congress, it seems, has finally figured out how to make some decisions that most members know are right but that each member individually finds it politically necessary to oppose.

The Structure of Defense Decision Making

The formal structure within which decisions about national defense are made was in large part created after World War II, but it reflects concerns that go back at least to the time of the Founding. Chief among these is the persistent desire by citizens to ensure civilian control over the military.

The National Security Act of 1947 and its subsequent amendments created the Department of Defense. It is headed by the secretary of defense, under whom serve the secretaries of the army, the air force, and the navy as well as the Joint Chiefs of Staff. The secretary of defense, who must be a civilian (though one former general, George C. Marshall, was allowed by Congress to be the secretary), exercises, on behalf of the president, command authority over the defense establishment. The secretary of the army, the secretary of the navy (who manages two services, the Navy and the Marine Corps), and the secretary of the air force also are civilians and are subordinate to the secretary of defense. Unlike their boss, they do not attend cabinet meetings or sit on the National Security Council. In essence, they manage the "housekeeping" functions of the various armed services, under the general direction of the secretary of defense and deputy and assistant secretaries of defense.

The four armed services are separate entities; by law, they cannot be merged or commanded by a single military officer, and each has the right to communicate directly with Congress. There are two reasons for having separate uniformed services functioning within a single department: the fear of many citizens that a unified military force might become too powerful politically, and the desire of each service to preserve its traditional independence and autonomy. The result, of course, is a good deal of interservice rivalry and bickering, but this is precisely what Congress intended when it created the Department of Defense. Rivalry and bickering, it was felt, would ensure that Congress would receive the maximum amount of information about military affairs and would enjoy the largest opportunity to affect military decisions.

Since the end of World War II, Congress has aimed both to retain a significant measure of control over the military's decision making and to ensure the adequacy of the nation's defenses. Congress does not want a single military command headed by an all-powerful general or admiral, but neither does it want the services to be so autonomous nor their heads so equal that coordination and efficiency suffer. In 1986, Congress passed and the president signed a defense reorganization plan known as the Goldwater-Nichols Act, which increased the power of the officers who coordinate the activities of the different services. The 1947 structure was left in place, but with revised procedures.

Joint Chiefs of Staff

The Joint Chiefs of Staff (JCS) is a committee consisting of the uniformed heads of each of the military services (the army, navy, air force, and Marine Corps), plus a chairman and a (nonvoting) vice chairman, also military officers, who are appointed by the president and confirmed by the Senate. The JCS does not have command authority over troops, but it plays a key role in national defense planning. Since 1986, the chairman of the joint chiefs has been designated the president's principal military adviser, in an effort to foster more influence over the JCS.

Assisting the JCS is the Joint Staff, consisting of several hundred officers from each of the four services. The staff draws up plans for various military contingencies. Before 1986, staff members were loyal to the service whose uniform they wore. As a result, the staff was often "joint" in name only, since few members were willing to take a position opposed by their service for fear of being passed over for promotion. The 1986 law changed this in two ways. First, it gave the chairman of the JCS control over the Joint Staff; now they work for the chairman, not for the JCS as a group. Second, it required the secretary of defense to establish guidelines to ensure that officers assigned to the Joint Staff (or to other interservice bodies) are promoted at the same rate as officers whose careers are spent entirely with their own services.

The Services

Each military service is headed by a civilian secretary— one for the army, the navy (including the Marine Corps), and the air force—plus a senior military officer: the chief of staff of the army, the chief of naval operations, the commandant of the Marine Corps, and the chief of staff of the air force. The civilian secretaries are in charge of purchasing, auditing, congressional relations, and public affairs. The military chiefs oversee the discipline and training of their uniformed forces and in addition represent their services on the JCS.

The Chain of Command

Under the Constitution the president is the commander-in-chief of the armed forces. The chain of command runs from the president to the secretary of defense (also a civilian), and then to the various unified and specified commands. These orders may be transmitted through the Joint Chiefs of Staff or its chairman, but by law the chairman of the JCS does not have command authority over the combat forces. Civilians are in charge at the top to protect against excessive concentration of power.

Analysts debate the effects of the 1986 changes, though many viewed the quick victory in the 1991 Persian Gulf War as evidence of their success. Critics of the Pentagon have been urging changes along these lines at least since 1947. But others say that unless the armed services are actually merged, interservice rivalry will continue. Still others argue that even the coordination achieved by the 1986 act is excessive. The country, in their view, is better served by having wholly autonomous services. What is striking is that so many members of Congress who once would have insisted on the anticoordination view voted for the 1986 law, thereby indicating a greater willingness to permit some degree of central military leadership.

The Future of American Foreign Policy

In the 21st century, American foreign policy continues to face overarching questions about the U.S. role in the world as well as more specific debates about defense programs, spending, and national decision making. Politically, the president leads foreign policymaking, but the Constitution divides power between Congress and the president, and some members of Congress have recently become more assertive in criticizing executive actions abroad. As the United States determines how it will engage with other nations, and where it will seek to exercise influence abroad, executive–legislative cooperation—with some guidance from public opinion—will be essential for pursuing American goals and interests.

Learning Objectives

19-1 Summarize the different types of politics involved in American foreign policy.

American foreign policy typically involves majoritarian, interest-group, or client politics. Decisions about going to war largely raise questions about majoritarian politics, trade and defense spending issues often incorporate interest-group politics, and foreign-aid debates usually present concerns in client politics.

19-2 Discuss the constitutional and legal contexts for making American foreign policy.

The Constitution states that the president is commander-in-chief of the military, and the Supreme Court generally has endorsed broad executive power in foreign affairs, particularly for military intervention. The president often has sent troops to fight without a declaration of war, but Congress almost always supports military action. The president is supposed to get Congress's approval under the War Powers Resolution, but if U.S. troops are already fighting, then Congress will face great difficulty in trying to reverse executive action.

19-3 Explain how political elites and public opinion influence American foreign policy.

Elite views matter greatly because most Americans pay little attention to foreign affairs most of the time. And on many key issues, the public disagrees with elites. But when the president sends troops overseas to fight, the public will rally in support.

19-4 Explain the key challenges that the United States faces in foreign affairs and defense politics today.

In the 21st century, the United States faces the challenges of protecting American national security, combating terrorism, and exercising global leadership to advance American ideals and interests. To achieve these goals, the United States must maintain a sufficient defense budget and a well-organized decision-making structure for military choices.

To Learn More

U.S. Army: **www.army.mil**

U.S. Air Force: **www.af.mil**

U.S. Navy: **www.navy.mil**

Central Intelligence Agency: **www.cia.gov**

Department of State: **www.state.gov**

Allison, Graham T. *Essence of Decision: Explaining the Cuban Missile Crisis*. Boston, MA: Little, Brown, 1971 (2nd ed with Philip Zelikow, New York: Pearson: 1999). Classic study of presidential leadership and diplomacy that shows how organizational and bureaucratic factors shaped crisis decision making in U.S. foreign policy.

Barnett, Thomas P. M., *The Pentagon's New Map: War and Peace in the Twenty-First Century*. New York: Berkley Books, 2004. Analysis of U.S. foreign and military priorities in the global war against terror in the early 21st century.

Bremmer, Ian. *Superpower: Three Choices for America's Role in the World.* New York: Portfolio/Penguin, 2015. Succinct overview of three choices for how the United States can lead in the world in the 21st century.

Commission on the Intelligence Capabilities of the United States Regarding Weapons of Mass Destruction. *Report to the President of the United States*. Washington, D.C.: Government Printing Office, 2005. Bipartisan panel examines why American intelligence agencies did not understand Iraq's WMD efforts.

Fisher, Louis. *Presidential War Power*. 3rd rev. ed. Lawrence, KS: University Press of Kansas, 2013. Detailed historical and institutional study of the evolution of executive power in foreign and military affairs from the founding of the American republic to current debates on combating terrorism in the 21st century.

Kissinger, Henry. *White House Years*. Boston, MA: Little, Brown,1979. A brilliant insider's account of the art of diplomacy, including policy strategies and tactics, during the Nixon administration.

Mead, Walter Russell. *Special Providence: American Foreign Policy and How It Changed the World*. New York: Knopf, 2001. Major synthesis of American foreign policy from the founding to the present that explains how four key schools of thought have shaped decisions about the U.S. role in the world.

Mueller, John E. *War, Presidents, and Public Opinion.* New York: Wiley, 1973. Classic study of how public opinion views presidential foreign policy decisions.

KAMIL KRZACZYNSKI/AFP/Getty Images

CHAPTER 20

American Democracy, Then and Now

Learning Objectives

20-1 Contrast three features of the Old System versus the New System of American government.

20-2 Discuss how the structure and policies of the American political system have influenced the growth of the federal government, and the consequences of that growth.

20-3 Summarize the key challenges for American democracy in the 21st century.

Like most Americans, you probably worry about social problems. These might include abortion, crime, drug abuse, civil rights, education, gun control, or homelessness. Maybe you have argued about these matters with your friends, discussing what Washington should do to address these issues. While you deliberate, remember this: Until the mid-20th century, all of this talk would have seemed unnecessary to most people in the United States. None of these issues were policy areas that people believed the federal government could or should address.

« Then: RESTRAINTS ON THE GROWTH OF GOVERNMENT When Dwight Eisenhower was president, none of these issues except civil rights was even thought to be a matter for federal policy, and on civil rights Congress didn't do very much. Our national political agenda was very short. During the Eisenhower administration, we decided to build an interstate highway system, admit Alaska and Hawaii into the union, and fight over the power of labor unions. For *eight years*, these were the major domestic political issues. The rest of the time, Washington focused on foreign policy and the U.S. role in the world.

This was about what the Founders had expected, though many of them would have objected to certain policy actions in the Eisenhower administration. Some would have thought Washington should not build highways because the Constitution did not authorize Congress to make laws about such matters. The federal government, in their view, should limit itself to war, peace, interstate commerce, establishing a national currency, and delivering mail. And for a long time, the prevailing interpretation of the Constitution sharply limited what policies the federal government could adopt. The Supreme Court restricted the government's authority to regulate business and prevented it from levying an income tax. Most important, the Supreme Court refused, with some exceptions, to allow the delegation of broad discretionary power to administrative agencies.

The Supreme Court could not have maintained this position for as long as it did if it had faced sustained popular opposition. But popular opinion was also against the growth of government. The public largely did not view federal intervention in the economy as legitimate (even the American Federation of Labor, led by Samuel Gompers, resisted federal involvement in labor-management issues). The public also did not advocate strongly for the federal government to end racial segregation as it was practiced in both the North and the South. Constitutional amendments were needed to persuade Congress that it had the authority to levy an income tax or to prohibit the sale of alcoholic beverages. Even in the 1930s, public opinion polls showed that as many as half of voters were skeptical of a federal unemployment compensation program.

*** Now: RELAXING THE RESTRAINTS** That was the Old System. Today, under the New System, federal politics is not about some small list of problems thought to be truly national; it is about practically everything. It is almost impossible to think of a problem about which Washington has no policy at all or around which it does not carry on intense debates. Listen to radio talk shows, watch television news, read digital news content, or scroll through social media, and you will find heated debate about national politics and policy making on just about every conceivable issue.

What is puzzling about this change from the Old System to the New System is that the Constitution is filled with arrangements designed to make it difficult, not easy, for the federal government to act. The separation of powers permits the president, Congress, and the courts to check one another; federalism guarantees that states will have an important role to play; and the division of legislative authority between the House and the Senate ensures that each body will be inclined to block the other. Passing a law requires approval from many political actors; to block legislation, just one congressional committee must be convinced.

That system made the national government relatively unimportant for many decades. Until well into the 20th century, some governors and mayors were more important than the president for influencing people's lives through policy decisions. Most members of Congress did not serve more than one or two terms in Washington; there didn't seem to be much point in becoming a career legislator because Congress didn't do much, didn't pay much, and wasn't in session for very long.

As we have said, the constraints on federal action have now weakened or disappeared altogether.

First, the courts have altered their interpretation of the Constitution in ways that have not only permitted but sometimes even required government action. The Bill of Rights has been extended so that almost all its important provisions are now regarded as applying to the states (by having been incorporated into the due process clause of the Fourteenth Amendment). This means that a citizen can use the federal courts to alter state policy to a greater degree than ever before. (Overturning state laws that banned abortions or required racially separate schools are two important examples of this change.) The special protection the courts once granted property rights has been substantially reduced so that business can be regulated to a greater degree than previously. The Court has permitted Congress to give broad discretionary powers to administrative agencies, allowing bureaucrats to make decisions that once only Congress could make.

Second, public opinion has changed in ways that support an expanded role for the federal government. The public demanded action to deal with the Great Depression (the programs that resulted, such as Social Security, survived in part because the Supreme Court changed its mind about the permissible scope of federal action). Political elites changed their minds faster than the average citizen. Well-educated, politically active people began demanding federal policies regarding civil rights, public welfare, environmental protection, consumer safety, and foreign aid well before the average citizen became concerned with such things.

Once in place, most of these programs proved popular, so their continuance was supported by mass as well as elite opinion. The cumulative effect of this process was to blur, if not erase altogether, the line that once defined what the government had the authority to do. At one time, a new proposal was debated in terms of whether it was *legitimate* for the federal government to do it all. Federal aid to education, for example, usually was opposed because many people feared it would lead to national control of local schools. But after passage of many programs (including federal aid to education), people stopped arguing about whether a certain policy was legitimate and argued instead about whether it was *effective*.

Third, political resources have become more widely distributed. The number and variety of interest groups have increased enormously. The funds available from foundations for organizations pursuing specific causes have grown. It is now easier to get access to the federal courts than formerly was the case, and once in the courts, plaintiffs are more likely to encounter judges who believe that the law and the Constitution should be interpreted broadly to permit particular goals (e.g., prison reform) to be attained by legal rather than legislative means. Numerous media outlets provide policy information to particular groups focused on those areas. The techniques of mass protest, linked to the desire of news organizations to show visually interesting accounts of social conflict, have been perfected in ways that convey the beliefs of a few into the living rooms of millions.

Campaign finance laws and court rulings have given legal status and constitutional protection to thousands of political action committees (PACs) that raise and spend tens of millions of dollars from contributors that include wealthy donors as well as contributors who give much smaller sums. College education, once the privilege of a tiny minority, has become the common experience of millions of people, so that the effects of college—in encouraging political participation and in shaping political beliefs (sometimes, but not always, in a liberal direction)—are now widely shared. The ability of candidates to win nomination for office no longer depends on their ability to curry favor with a few powerful bosses; it now reflects their skill at raising money, mobilizing friends and activists, cultivating a media image, and winning enough delegates to secure their party's nomination.

Constitutional Connections | Amending the Constitution

When the Framers drafted the Constitution in the summer of 1787, they expected that it would be an evolving document. Article V of the Constitution specifically provides for two ways of amending the Constitution—amendments may be introduced by a two-thirds vote in Congress or a special convention proposed by two-thirds of the states (the second has never been used), and then must be ratified by three-fourths of the state legislatures or three-fourths of the states at special ratifying conventions (the second has been used just one time, for repealing Prohibition with the Twenty-First Amendment in 1933). In his first inaugural address, President George Washington referred to the amendment process as an "occasional power," to be used sparingly in "pursuit of the public good."[1]

As President Washington recommended, the amendment power has been used infrequently: In more than 225 years, 27 amendments have been added to the Constitution, and only a handful of those have changed the structure of the political process. For example, the Seventeenth Amendment gave voters—not state legislatures—the power to elect senators, and the Twenty-Second Amendment limited the president to two terms. But even without constitutional amendments, the American political system has undergone significant political changes, as this chapter's discussion of the Old System versus the New System explains.

20-1 The Old Versus the New System

So great have been the changes in the politics of policymaking in this country starting in the 1930s that we can refer, with only slight exaggeration, to one policymaking system having been replaced by another (see Table 20.1).

The Old System

The Old System had a small agenda. Though people voted at a high rate and often took part in torchlight parades and other mass political events, political leadership was professionalized in the sense that the leadership circle was small, access to it was difficult, and the activists in social movements generally were kept out. Only a few major issues were under discussion at any time. A member of Congress had a small staff (if any at all), dealt with colleagues on a personal basis, deferred to the prestige of House and Senate leaders, and tended to become part of some stable coalition (the farm bloc, the labor bloc, the Southern bloc) that persisted across many issues.

When someone proposed adding a new issue to the public agenda, a major debate often arose over whether it was legitimate for the federal government to act at all on the matter. A dominant theme in this debate was the importance of "states' rights." Except in wartime, or during a very brief period when the nation expressed interest in acquiring new states or territories, the focus of policy debate was on domestic affairs. Members of Congress saw these domestic issues largely in terms of their effect on local constituencies. The presidency was small and somewhat personal; there was only a rudimentary White House staff. The president would cultivate the press, but there was a clear understanding that what was said in a news conference was never to be quoted directly.

For the government to take bold action under this system, the nation usually had to be facing a crisis. War presented such crisis, and so the federal government

TABLE 20.1 | How American Politics Has Changed

Old System		New System
	Congress	
Chairs relatively strong		Chairs relatively weak
Small staffs		Large staffs
Few subcommittees		Many subcommittees
	Interest Groups	
A few large blocs (farmers, business, labor)		Many diverse interests that form ad hoc coalitions
Rely on "insider" lobbying		Mobilize grassroots
	Presidency	
Small staff		Large staff
Reaches public via news conferences		Reaches public via radio, television, and social media
	Courts	
Allow government to exercise few economic powers		Allow government to exercise broad economic power
Take narrow view of individual freedoms		Take broad view of individual freedoms
	Political Parties	
Dominated by state and local party leaders meeting in national party conventions		Dominated by activists participating in primaries and caucuses
	Policy Agenda	
Brief		Lengthy
	Key Question	
Should the federal government enter a new policy area?		How can the federal government fix or modify, as well as pay, for an existing or new policies?
	Key Issue	
Would a new federal program abridge states' rights?		Would a new federal program prove popular?

Q How might the New System change in the 21st century? Are changes possible within the current constitutional structure, or are more fundamental reforms needed?

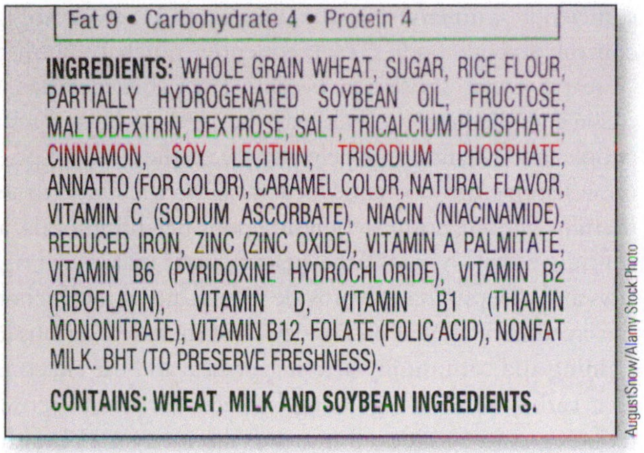

AugustSnow/Alamy Stock Photo

Image 20.1 Food products now contain health notifications, such as this package containing wheat, milk, and soybean ingredients, which can pose allergy risks.

during the Civil War and World Wars I and II acquired extraordinary powers to conscript soldiers, control industrial production, regulate the flow of information to citizens, and restrict the scope of personal liberty. Each succeeding crisis left the government bureaucracy somewhat larger than it had been before, but when the crisis ended, the exercise of extraordinary powers ended. Once again, the agenda of political issues became small, and legislators argued about whether it was legitimate for the government to enter some new policy area, such as civil rights or industrial regulation.

The New System

The New System began in the 1930s but did not take its present form until the 1970s. It is characterized by a large policy agenda, the end of the debate over the legitimacy of government action (except in the area of First Amendment freedoms), the diffusion and decentralization of power in Congress, and the multiplication of interest groups. The government has grown so large that it has a policy on almost every conceivable subject, and so the debate in Washington is less often about whether it is right and prudent to take some bold new step and more often about how the government can best cope with the strains and problems that arise from implementing existing policies. To some, the federal government today may appear more concerned with managing than with ruling.

For example, in 1935 Congress debated whether the nation should have a Social Security system at all; in the 1980s, it debated whether the system could best be kept solvent by raising taxes or by cutting benefits; in 2004 and 2005, it debated whether some part of each person's Social Security payments could be invested in the stock market. In the 1960s, Congress argued over whether there should be any federal civil rights laws at all; by the 1980s and 1990s, it was arguing over whether those laws should be administered by eliminating legal barriers to equal opportunity for racial minorities, or by compensating through affirmative action programs for disadvantages that historically have burdened some groups of Americans. As late as the 1950s, the president and Congress argued over whether it was right to adopt a new program if the government would have to borrow money to pay for it. As late as the 1960s, many members of Congress believed the federal government had no business paying for the health care of its citizens; in the 21st century, hardly anyone argues against having Medicare, but a major public debate is underway over how best to control its rising cost.

The differences between the Old and New Systems should not be exaggerated. The Constitution still enables Congress to block the proposals of the president, or for some committee of Congress to defeat the preferences of the majority of Congress, than in almost any other democratic government. The system of checks and balances operates as before. The essential differences between the Old and the New Systems are these:

1. Under the Old System, the checks and balances made *starting* a new program difficult for the federal government, and so the government remained relatively small. Under the New System, these checks and balances have presented obstacles to *changing* what the government is already doing, and so the government has remained large.
2. Under the Old System, power was *somewhat centralized* in the hands of party and congressional leaders. Plenty of political conflict existed among these leaders, but the number of people who had to agree before something could be done was not large. Under the New System, power is much more *decentralized*, and so resolving conflict is much tougher because so many more people— party activists, interest group leaders, individual members of Congress, heads of government agencies—must agree.

The transition from the Old to the New System occurred chiefly during two periods in American politics. The first was in the early 1930s, when a catastrophic depression led the government to explore new ways of helping the needy, regulating business, and preventing a recurrence of the disaster. Franklin D. Roosevelt's New Deal was the result. The huge majorities enjoyed by the Democrats in Congress, coupled with popular demands to solve the problem, led to a vast outpouring of new legislation and the creation of dozens of new government agencies. Though initially the Supreme Court struck down some of these measures as unconstitutional, a key member of the Court eventually changed his mind, and then others retired from the bench; by the late 1930s, the Court had virtually ceased opposing any economic legislation.

The second period was in the mid-1960s, a time of prosperity. There was no crisis akin to the Great Depression or World War II, but two events helped change the face of American politics. One was an intellectual and popular ferment that we now refer to as the spirit of "the sixties"—a strong civil rights movement, student activism on college campuses aimed at resisting the Vietnam War, growing concern about threats to the environment, the popular appeal of public advocates such as Ralph Nader and his consumer protection movement, and optimism among many political and intellectual leaders that the government could solve whatever problems it was willing to address. The other was the 1964 election that returned Lyndon Johnson to the presidency with a larger share of the popular vote than any other president in modern times. Johnson swept into office, and with him came liberal Democratic majorities in both the House and Senate.

The combination of organized demands for new policies, elite optimism about the likely success of those policies, and extraordinary majorities in Congress meant that President Lyndon Johnson was able, for a few years, to get almost any program he wanted enacted into law. So large were his majorities in Congress that the conservative coalition of Republicans and Southern Democrats was no longer large enough to block action; Northern Democratic liberals were sufficiently numerous in the House and Senate to take control of both bodies. Consequently, much of Johnson's "Great Society" legislation became law. This included the passage of Medicare (to help pay the medical bills of retired people) and Medicaid (to help pay the medical bills of people on welfare); greatly expanded federal aid to the states (to assist them in fighting crime, rebuilding poor neighborhoods, and running transit systems); the enactment of major civil rights laws and of a program to provide federal aid to local schools; the creation of a "War on Poverty" that included various job-training and community-action agencies; and the enactment of a variety of laws regulating business for the purpose of reducing auto fatalities, improving the safety and health of industrial workers, cutting back on pollutants entering the atmosphere, and safeguarding consumers from harmful products.

These two periods—the early 1930s and the mid-1960s—changed the political landscape in America. Of the two, the latter was perhaps more important, for not only did it witness the passage of so much unprecedented legislation, but also it saw major changes in patterns of political leadership. During this time, the great majority of the members of the House of Representatives came to enjoy relatively secure seats, primary elections came to supplant party conventions as the decisive means of selecting presidential candidates, interest groups increased greatly in number, and television and subsequent other media technologies began to play an important role in shaping the political agenda and influencing the kinds of candidates nominated.

Bill Pugliano/Getty Images News/Getty Images

Image 20.2 The federal government bailed out the U.S. automobile industry in 2009 to help companies avoid bankruptcy.

20-2 Government Growth: Influences and Consequences

The enormous expansion of the scope and goals of the federal government has not been random or unguided. The government has tended to enlarge its powers more in some directions than in others; certain kinds of goals have been served more frequently than others. Though many factors shape this process of selection, two are of special importance: our constitutional structure and our political culture.

The Influence of Structure

To see the influence of structure, it is necessary to perform a mental experiment. Suppose the Founders had adopted a centralized, parliamentary regime instead of a decentralized, congressional one. They had the British model right before their eyes. Every other European democracy adopted it. What difference would it have made had we followed the British example?

No one can be certain, of course, because the United States and the United Kingdom differ in many ways and not just in their political forms. At best, our mental experiment will be an educated guess. But the following possibilities seem plausible.

A parliamentary regime of the British sort centralizes power in the hands of an elected prime minister with a disciplined partisan majority in the legislature and freedom from most of the constraints created by independent congressional committees or independent, activist courts. Had the Framers adopted a parliamentary system, we might see these features in the political life of the United States today:

- *Quicker adoption of majoritarian policies, such as those in the area of social welfare.* Broad popular desires would be translated sooner into national policy when they are highly salient and conform to the views of party leaders.
- *More centralization of bureaucratic authority—more national planning and less local autonomy.* More decisions would be made bureaucratically, both because bureaucracies would be proportionately larger and because they would have wider discretionary authority delegated to them. (If prime ministers head *both* the executive branch and the legislature, then they may see no reason why decisions cannot be made as easily in one place as the other.) Local authorities would not have been able to prevent groups of citizens (such as African Americans) from voting or otherwise participating in public life by maintaining segregated facilities at the local level.
- *Fewer opportunities for citizens to challenge or block government policies of which they disapprove.* Without independent and activist courts, without local centers (state and city) of autonomous power, U.S. citizens would have fewer chances to organize to stop a highway or an urban-renewal project, for example, and hence fewer citizen organizations with these and similar purposes would exist.
- *Greater executive control of government.* If a situation like Watergate occurred, we might never know about it. No legislative investigating committees would be sufficiently independent of executive control to be able to investigate claims of executive wrongdoing.
- *Similar foreign policy.* We probably would have fought in about the same number of wars and under pretty much the same circumstances.
- *Higher and more centralized taxation.* Taxes would be higher, and a larger share of our tax money would be collected at the national level. Thus we would find it harder to wage a "tax revolt," as Californians did in the 1970s (since it is easier to block local spending decisions than national ones).

If this list of guesses is even approximately correct, it means that you would get more of some things that you want and less of others. In general, it would be easier for temporary majorities to govern and harder for individuals and groups to protect their interests.

The Founders would probably not be surprised at this list of differences. Though they could not have foreseen all the events and issues that would have led to these outcomes, they would have understood them because they thought they were creating a system designed to keep central power weak and to enhance local and citizen power. They would have been amazed, of course, at the extent to which central power has been enhanced and local power

AP Images/Rebecca F. Miller/The Gazette

Image 20.3 To contain the spread of the COVID-19 pandemic in 2020, the Centers for Disease Control and Prevention recommended the use of face coverings and social distancing.

Q What policies should the federal government enact to protect the American public from another crisis like the COVID-19 pandemic that started in 2020?

weakened in the United States, but if they visited Europe, they would learn that, by comparison, American politics typically remains far more sensitive to local concerns than does politics abroad.

The Influence of Ideas

The broadly shared political culture of Americans has also influenced the policies adopted by the U.S. government. Paramount among these attitudes is the preoccupation with rights. More than the citizens of perhaps any other nation, Americans define their relations with one another and with political authority in terms of rights. The civil liberties protected by the Bill of Rights have been assiduously defended and their interpretation significantly broadened even while the power of government has been growing.

For example, we expect that the groups affected by any government program will have a right to play a role in shaping and administering that program. In consequence, interest groups have proliferated. We think citizens should have the right to select the nominees of political parties as well as to choose between the parties. Hence, primary elections have largely replaced party conventions in selecting candidates. Individual members of Congress assert their rights, and thus the power of congressional leaders and committee chairs has steadily diminished. We probably use the courts more frequently than the citizens of any other nation to make or change public policy; in doing so, we are asserting one set of rights against a competing set. The procedural rules that set forth how government is to act—the Freedom of Information Act, the Privacy Act, the Administrative Procedure Act—are more complex and demanding than the rules under which any other democratic government must operate. Each rule exists because it embodies what somebody has claimed to be a right: the right to know information, to maintain one's privacy, to participate in making decisions, and to bring suit against rival parties.

The more vigorously we assert our rights, the harder making government decisions or managing large institutions becomes. We recognize this when we grumble about red tape and bureaucratic confusion, but we rarely give much support to proposals to centralize authority or simplify decision making. We seem to accept costs in efficiency or effectiveness in order to maintain the capacity for asserting our rights.

We do not always agree on which rights are most important, however. In addition to the widely shared commitment to rights generally, government is also shaped by the views that certain political elites have about which rights ought to be given the highest priority. Elite opinion in the United States historically has favored freedom of expression over freedom to manage or dispose of property. Mass opinion, though it has changed a good deal in the past few decades, is less committed to the preferred position of freedom of expression. Rank-and-file citizens often complain that what the elite calls essential liberty should instead be regarded as excessive permissiveness. People who own or manage property often lament the extent to which the rights governing its use have declined.

Changes in the relative security of personal and property freedom are linked to a fundamental and enduring tension in American thought. Tocqueville said it best: Americans, he wrote, "are far more ardently and tenaciously attached to equality than to freedom." Though democratic communities have a "natural taste for freedom," that freedom is hard to preserve because its excesses are immediate and obvious and its advantages are remote and uncertain. The advantages of equality, on the other hand, are readily apparent, and its costs are obscure and deferred.[2] For example, Americans believe in free speech, but most of us rarely take advantage of that right and notice the problem only when somebody says something we don't like. We have to remind ourselves that freedom has to be protected even when it does not help us directly. By contrast, we notice equality immediately, as when everybody of a certain age gets Social Security even when they are already rich. Equality makes us comfortable, even if some people hardly need the benefits they receive.

Tocqueville, however, may have underestimated the extent to which political liberties would endure because he did not foresee the determination of the courts to resist, in the long run if not the short, the passions of temporary majorities seeking to curtail such liberties. But he did not underestimate the extent to which in the economic and social realms Americans would decide that improving the conditions of life would justify restrictions on the right to dispose of property and to manage private institutions. At first, the conflict was between liberty and equality of opportunity; more recently it has become a conflict—among political elites if not within the citizenry itself—between equality of opportunity and equality of results.

The fact that decisions can be influenced by opinions about rights indicates that decisions can be influenced by opinions generally. As the political system has become more fragmented and more individualized as a result of our collective assertion of rights, it has come more under the sway of ideas. When political parties were strong and congressional leadership was centralized (as in the latter part of the 19th and the early part of the 20th centuries), gaining access to the decision-making process in Washington was difficult, and the number of new ideas that stood a chance of adoption was small. However, proposals that could command leadership support were more easily adopted: though there were powerful organizations that could say no, those same organizations could also say yes.

Today, these and other institutions are fragmented and in disarray. Individual members of Congress are far more important than congressional leaders. Political parties no longer control nominations for office: candidates have direct access to voters through social media and other resources, and campaign finance laws restrict, but by no means eliminate, the influence of interest groups, particularly by spending money. Forming new, issue-oriented lobbying groups is much easier today than it was formerly, thanks to micro-targeting strategies that use demographic and other data to identify people's interests and concerns.

These idea-based changes in institutions affect how policy is made. When there is widespread enthusiasm for an idea—especially among political elites but also in the public at large—new programs can be formulated and adopted with great speed. This happened when Lyndon Johnson's Great Society legislation was proposed, when the environmental and consumer protection laws first arrived on the public agenda, and when campaign finance reform was proposed in the wake of Watergate. So long as such symbols have a powerful appeal, so long as a consensus persists, change is possible. But when these ideas lose their appeal—or are challenged by new ideas—the competing pressures make change extremely difficult. Proposals to protect the environment are challenged by concerns about creating jobs and economic growth; social legislation is challenged by skepticism about its effectiveness and concern over its cost; campaign finance reforms are, to some critics, merely devices for protecting incumbents.

This may all seem obvious to a reader raised in the world of contemporary politics. But it is different in degree if not in kind from the way in which politics was once carried out. In the 1920s, the 1930s, the 1940s, and even the 1950s, people described politics as a process of bargaining among organized interests, or "blocs," representing business, farming, labor, ethnic, and professional groups. With the expansion of the scope of government policy, there are no longer a few major blocs that sit astride the policy process. Instead, thousands of highly specialized interests and constituencies seek above all to protect whatever benefits, intangible as well as tangible, they get from government.

Consequences of Government Growth

One way of describing the New System is to call it an "activist" government. It is tempting to make a sweeping judgment about such a government, either praising it because it serves a variety of popular needs or condemning it because it is a bureaucratic affliction. Such generalizations are not entirely empty, but neither are they very helpful. The worth of any given program, or of any collection of programs, can be assessed only by a careful consideration of its costs and benefits, of its effects and side effects. But we may discover some general political consequences of the enlarged scope of government activity.

First, as the government gets bigger, public officials must spend more time managing the consequences—intended and unintended—of existing programs and less time debating at length new ideas. As a result, all parts of the government, not just executive agencies, become more bureaucratized. The White House Office and the Office of Management and Budget grow in size and influence, as do the staffs of Congress. At the same time, private organizations (corporations, unions, universities) that deal with the government must also become more bureaucratic. The government hires more people when it is running 80 programs concerned with employment than when it is running 2. By the same token, private employers will hire (and give power to) more people when they are complying with 80 sets of regulations than when they are complying with 2.

Second, the more government does, the more it will seem to act in inconsistent, uncoordinated, and cumbersome ways. When people complain of red tape, bureaucracy, stalemates, and confusion, they often assume these irritants are caused by incompetent or self-seeking public officials. There is incompetence and self-interest in government just as in every other part of society, but these character traits are not the chief cause of the problem. As citizens, we want many different and often conflicting goals. The result is the rise of competing policies, the division of labor among separate administrative agencies, the diffusion of accountability and control, and the multiplication of paperwork. And because Americans are especially energetic about asserting their rights, we must add to the above list of problems the regular use of the courts to challenge policies that we do not like.

Third, an activist government is less susceptible to control by electoral activity than a passive one. When the government in Washington did little, elections made a larger difference in policy than when the government began to do a lot. We have pointed out in this book the extent to which both political parties and voter turnout declined in the late 20th century, and their limited resurgence to date in the 21st century. This has occurred for many reasons, but an important one often is forgotten. If elections make less of a difference—because the few people for whom one votes can do little to alter the ongoing programs of government—then it may make sense for people to spend less time on party or electoral activities and more on interest-group activities aimed at specific agencies and programs.

The rapid increase in the number and variety of interest groups and their enlarged role in government are not pathological. They are a rational response to the fact that elected officials can tend to only a few matters, and therefore we must direct our energies at appointed officials (and judges) who tend to all other government matters. Every president tries to accomplish more, usually by trying to reorganize the executive branch. But no president and no reorganization plan can affect more than a tiny fraction of the millions of federal employees and thousands of government programs. "Coordination" from the top can at best occur selectively, for a few issues of exceptional importance.

Ronald Reagan learned this when he took office in 1981 after promising to reduce the size of government. He did persuade Congress to cut taxes and increase defense spending, but his plans to cut domestic spending resulted in only small declines in some programs and actual increases in many others. Though some programs, such as public housing, were significantly affected, most were not, and agricultural subsidies increased dramatically.

When George W. Bush became president in 2001, his philosophy was summarized by the phrase "compassionate conservatism," words that implied that, though he was a conservative, he was not much interested in simply cutting the size of the federal government. And while in office, he proposed policies that would increase spending on many programs. His actions suggest a fact: cutting down on what Washington does is virtually impossible because people want so much of what it does.

Finally, the more government tries to do, the more it will be held responsible for and the greater the risk of failure. At various times in the 19th century, the business cycle made many people unhappy with the federal government—recall the rise of various protest parties—though then the government did very little. If federal officials were lucky, popular support increased as soon as economic conditions improved. If they were unlucky and a depression lasted into the election campaign, they were thrown out of office. Today, however, the government—and the president in particular—is held responsible for crime, drug abuse, abortion, civil rights, the environment, the elderly, the status of women, the decay of central cities, the price of gasoline, and international tensions in half a dozen places around the globe.

No government and no president can do well on all or even most of these matters most of the time. Indeed, most of these problems, such as crime, may be totally beyond the reach of the federal government, no matter what its policy. It should not be surprising, therefore, that opinion surveys taken since the early 1960s have shown a steep decline in public confidence in government. There is no reason to believe that this represents a loss of faith in our form of government or even in the design of its institutions, but it clearly reflects a disappointment in, and even cynicism about, the performance of government.

It is too soon to know which direction public sentiment about the performance of government will take in the third decade of the 21st century, or whether the public will demand more action from government or possibly even institutional change. In response to the 2007–2008 economic crisis, Washington expanded government activity faster than it has grown in any periods since the late 1930s and the mid-1960s. President Barack Obama proposed a budget for fiscal year 2012 that contemplated a deficit of $1.645 trillion. Congressional Republicans, who won control of the House in 2010, objected, and threatened not to increase the debt ceiling. After long negotiations with the White House, the two sides agreed on a compromise that made some cuts in spending and raised the debt ceiling. The United States did not default on its financial obligations, thus averting a potential global economic disaster.

But two years later, when the White House and Congress could not reach a budget agreement, automatic spending cuts known as the "sequester" went into effect. (These automatic cuts, which proved to be unpopular, were effectively eliminated in 2019). Later, in 2013, the U.S. government shut down for the first time in almost 18 years because the two branches could not complete a budget deal. The government reopened after 16 days, but public confidence in Congress dropped into the single digits in the next few years. (It has risen slightly, to 11–12 percent, since 2017.[3]) And prospects for long-term executive-legislative fiscal planning have dimmed after the five-week government shutdown from late December 2018 into January 2019—the longest ever—which resulted from a dispute between the Trump White House and the partially divided 116th Congress (Democratic House and Republican Senate) over border security and the president's insistence on funding for a wall between the United States and Mexico.

Spending battles, however, are only half the story. The other half concerns the federal government taking on new responsibilities and challenges. For a time, it was the majority stockholder in what was once the world's largest automotive company, General Motors; it has more closely controlled dozens of other companies and diverse financial markets; and it oversees a large, government-regulated health care system.

Political scientist Donald F. Kettl has argued that the "financial meltdown accelerated our expectations that government will keep us safe ... We've gone from debates over privatizing the public sector to big steps toward governmentalizing the private sector."[4] The far-reaching changes include "more public money in the private economy, more rules to shape how the private sector behaves, and more citizen expectations that government will manage the risks we face."[5] Similar actions occurred in response to the coronavirus pandemic. As the economy faltered in the spring of 2020, the federal government once again stepped in to shore up many private industries, from banking, to airlines, to many others.[6]

We cannot yet say whether multitrillion-dollar budget deficits and policies that represent government-guaranteed corporate capitalism will persist in the years to come. But it seems a fair bet that the New System is entering a new era of expansion that, not unlike the one that began in the late 1930s, has been fueled by economic problems that have afflicted or threatened most Americans. The coronavirus pandemic in the spring of 2020 accelerated that expansion significantly, with the federal government approving more than $3 trillion in spending to assist individuals and businesses facing severe economic crisis through cash relief, expanded unemployment insurance, the Paycheck Protection Program, and more.[7]

It also seems likely that, if anything, public disenchantment with government performance will continue to grow along with government's role in people's lives. Such disenchantment is hardly unique to the United States; it seems to be a feature of almost every democratic political system. The disenchantment is in fact probably greater elsewhere. Americans who complain of high taxes might feel somewhat differently if they lived in Sweden, where taxes are nearly twice as high as here. Those who criticize U.S. bureaucracy likely have never dealt with the massive, centralized bureaucracies of Italy or France. People who are annoyed by congestion, pollution, and inflation should consider conditions in Beijing, Mexico City, or Tokyo. However frustrating private life and public affairs may be in this country, every year thousands living in other nations seek to immigrate to this country. Few Americans choose to emigrate to other places.

20-3 American Democracy—Then, Now, and Next

We have a large government—and large expectations about what it can achieve. But the government finds it increasingly difficult to satisfy those expectations. The public's acceptance of a larger and larger role for government has been accompanied by a decline in public confidence in those who lead and manage that government. We expect more and more from government but are less and less certain that we will get it, or get it in a form and at a cost that we find acceptable. This perhaps constitutes the greatest challenge to political leadership in the years ahead: to find a way to serve the true interests of the people while restoring and retaining their confidence in the legitimacy of government itself. We might begin by challenging the increasingly popular notion that present-day American democracy's problems are so deep because its political leaders are so shallow, not least by comparison to the nation's first leaders.

Then

When the Constitution was created and ratified, national leaders beholden only to their own consciences could meet in secret to debate and decide even the most controversial and consequential questions about government. They could belittle, berate, or battle each other one day and beseech, bargain, or broker deals with each other the next day, all without their words or deeds (or misdeeds) being a matter of public record or widely known at all.

Now

In stark contrast, the political leaders that today hold office under the terms of that same Constitution, amended only 27 times in more than 225 years, must deliberate and legislate while the whole world—friend and foe alike—is listening and watching. Contemporary presidents and members of Congress face the challenge of leading a large and diverse population, coping with an all-pervasive mass communications media, and steering a federal government that is far bigger, and administered in a way that is far more complicated, than any of the Constitution's authors ever envisioned.

As a class, today's elected officials at both ends of Pennsylvania Avenue and in both parties are often much maligned, not only, at times, by each other and by their other respective partisan and ideological opponents, but also by the public at large, with majorities disparaging the "politicians" about as readily as they denounce the "bureaucrats." But now reflect seriously on questions like the following:

- How do you suppose James Madison, George Washington, or the other authors of the Constitution would have fared if they had led not a slave-holding society of barely 4 million people, but a demographically diverse and free society of more than 300 million people?
- How do you think the nation's early political leaders, bitterly divided over the Constitution as they were (see Chapter 2), would have held up had they faced anything like the incessant public stare and media glare that national political leaders such as Mitch McConnell, Nancy Pelosi, Barack Obama, and Donald Trump routinely have faced in their public offices in the 21st century, even when not battling with each other?
- Do you believe that American democracy's first generation of leaders would in our present-day context come any closer than today's leaders have come to forging a national consensus and getting decisive action on difficult issues like the federal government's annual budget deficits and the growing national debt?
- As contentious and complicated as the debates over federalism (see Chapter 3) were when the republic was founded, do you think that those who forged the compromises that then defined federal-state relations would be significantly more effective than today's federal, state, and local public officials are when it comes to ensuring that the more than $600 billion a year that Washington now spends on grants to state and local governments for social welfare (see Chapter 17) and other public purposes is all money well spent?
- And do you suppose that earlier generations of leaders would be any more adept than today's leaders when it comes to ensuring that the private, for-profit firms and nonprofit organizations that are a big part of today's proxy-government system of public administration (see Chapter 15) serve the public well?

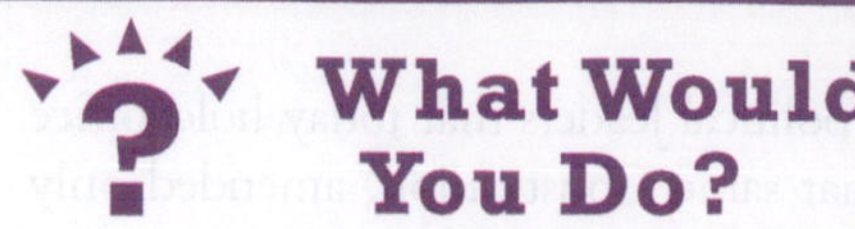

What Would You Do? | Will You Support a New Constitutional Convention?

To: *Senator Romy Jasper Mocha*
From: *Lucy Talya Ili, chief of staff*
Subject: *A new constitutional convention?*

With the continuing stalemate in Washington, many members of Congress say a new constitutional convention is needed to change the governing process. While the opposition party, which controls both chambers, is calling for the convention to impose restrictions on executive power, members of your party say a convention will permit much-needed changes in how the legislature functions.

To Consider:

Party leaders urge the president to support the opposition party's proposed constitutional convention measure so they may pursue needed reforms to prevent a tyranny of the minority from obstructing progress in Washington.

Arguments for:

1. After 230 years, public expectations for the national government have expanded greatly, and the political structure is not designed to meet those expectations swiftly or effectively.
2. Washington needs to move to a four-year electoral system, with no midterm elections, and advocates for a convention support this reform.
3. A constitutional convention today will have extensive public input and deliberation in the media, both of which will improve our democratic process.

Arguments against:

1. A constitutional convention risks changing all that works well with the current American political structure, with no guarantee of achieving desired reforms.
2. Ending midterm elections removes an important check in the political process, and supporters of this change seek to avoid accountability at the polls and losing their majority in Congress.
3. The impossibility of having secrecy in convention proceedings today virtually ensures that a new Constitution will not be improved; too much democracy will undo the entire system, as James Madison warned in *Federalist* No. 10.

What Will You Decide? Enter **MindTap** to make your choice.

Your decision: ☐ Approve ☐ Oppose

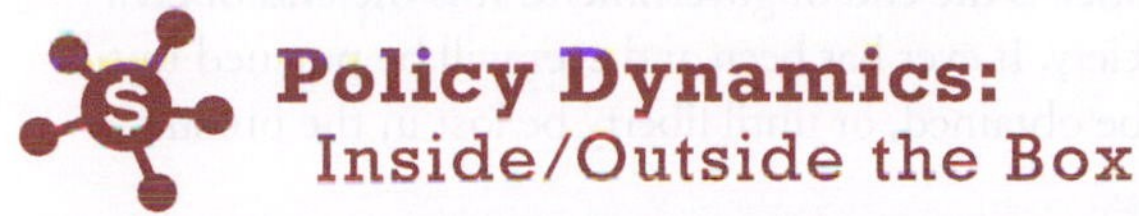

Policy Dynamics: Inside/Outside the Box | Drafting a New Constitution: Majoritarian or Interest-Group Politics?

In the late 1980s, James L. Sundquist, a noted Brookings Institution scholar, published a critique of the political structure and process that the Framers designed in the Constitution. Whatever the Constitution's virtues, argued Sundquist in *Constitutional Reform and Effective Government*, the separation of powers system had by the late 20th century saddled the nation with a Congress that could not plan, could not act quickly, and could not solve major problems of all sorts. Far-reaching constitutional change was needed, Sundquist argued, making an argument grounded in majoritarian politics—everyone would bear the cost of redesigning the American political system, and then the American public as a whole would benefit from more efficient and effective government. (Nearly 25 years later, political scientists William G. Howell and Terry M. Moe presented a similar critique of the applicability of Madisonian democracy in the 21st century in *Relic: How Our Constitution Undermines Effective Government*. See Chapter 14, p. 371, for a discussion of their proposal to increase presidential power.)

Sundquist favored replacing the Congress and the Constitution with a parliamentary system like that in the United Kingdom, but he reckoned that no such radical reform was politically possible. Instead, he advocated a host of institutional and other reforms that would bring parliamentary features to American democracy. These proposals, which would require constitutional amendments, included eliminating congressional midterm elections, so elected officials would have more time to govern between campaigns; offering the opportunity for "special elections" for the president and Congress if the public approval of the government fell below a certain level; requiring party-ticket voting, so the president would have a guaranteed majority in Congress; and permitting members of Congress to serve in the Cabinet, so they could facilitate enactment and execution of the president's agenda.

If these proposed reforms passed and achieved the goals of increased efficiency and effectiveness, then the promise of majoritarian politics would indeed be fulfilled. But skeptics of constitutional reform raise several concerns about the merits of the proposals and about whether a constitutional convention would devolve into interest-group politics. Even though many more people are eligible to participate in politics today than in 1787, the people who would exercise most influence in a convention likely would be those who have the greatest stake in protecting certain interests. Consequently, constitutional battles would be waged between elites competing against each other for scarce political resources, with limited effect on the broader public.

Without broad agreement on who governs and to what ends in a new political system, presenting constitutional reform as majoritarian politics becomes difficult.

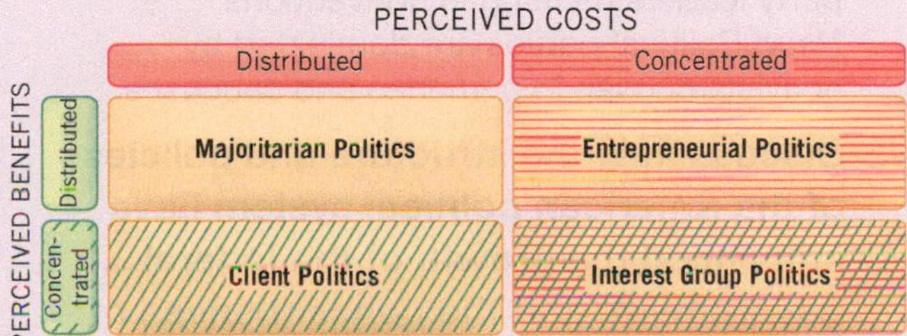

Sources: James L. Sundquist, *Constitutional Reform and Effective Government* (Washington, D.C.: Brookings Institution Press, 1986; rev. ed. 1992); William G. Howell and Terry M. Moe, *Relic: How Our Constitution Undermines Effective Government – And Why We Need a More Powerful Presidency* (New York: Basic Books, 2016).

We suspect that Madison himself, if he were returned to our political moment in time, might conclude that exercising effective leadership now is even harder than it was then.

Regardless, the next chapters in the still-unfolding story of American democracy remain to be written by the nation's next generation of leaders, including, we hope, some students whose interest in politics, government, and public policy was stirred in part by this book.

- At each level of government, whatever one's party or policy preferences, to be a public-spirited "politician" who wins elected office and participates in the democratic legislative process, or to be a judge responsible for interpreting and applying laws, including in cases that involve civil liberties (see Chapter 5) and civil rights (see Chapter 6), is to live a truly noble calling.
- To be a "bureaucrat"—a career public servant— who serves the public by responsibly translating democratically enacted laws on health, housing, trade, transportation, education, environmental protection, nuclear energy, or any other policy area into administrative action is a truly noble calling, too.
- And, for those who, like most people, are called instead to careers in business, the arts, or other fields, to yet be an engaged citizen of American democracy, to seek to know ever more about American government, political institutions, and public policies, is a most worthy intellectual and civic pastime.

So, we end with words from *Federalist* No. 51 that should remind us all why the subject you have been studying with the aid of this book is so important:

> Justice is the end of government. It is the end of civil society. It ever has been and ever will be pursued until it be obtained, or until liberty be lost in the pursuit.

Learning Objectives

20-1 Contrast three features of the Old System versus the New System of American government.

Old: Congress had strong committee chairpersons, small staffs, and few subcommittees.
New: Congress has weak committee chairpersons, large staffs, and many subcommittees.

Old: The courts allowed government to exercise few economic powers and took a narrow view of individual freedoms.
New: The courts allow the government many economic powers and take a broad view of individual freedoms.

Old: Political parties were dominated by local party leaders meeting in conventions.
New: Political parties are dominated by activists chosen in primaries and caucuses.

20-2 Discuss how the structure and policies of the American political system have influenced the growth of the federal government, and the consequences of that growth.

The separation of powers in American politics means that the enactment of major policy changes that take place with expansion of the federal government typically takes much longer than in parliamentary democracies. Furthermore, the wide range of governmental and nongovernmental actors who participate in policymaking brings many different, often competing, ideas for policy change, which complicates consensus-building. As the federal government expands, it also becomes more complex and bureaucratic.

20-3 Summarize the key challenges for American democracy in the 21st century.

Unlike the authors of the Constitution and most other previous generations of political leaders, today's presidents and members of Congress make important decisions under intense public scrutiny. They lead a demographically diverse and free society of more than 300 million citizens, with a government that constitutes a much larger share of the nation's economy than any of the Framers ever envisioned, and that touches virtually every facet of contemporary economic, social, and civic life.

Appendixes

The Declaration of Independence

In Congress, July 4, 1776

The Unanimous Declaration of the Thirteen United States of America

When, in the course of human events, it becomes necessary for one people to dissolve the political bands which have connected them with another, and to assume, among the powers of the earth, the separate and equal station to which the laws of nature and of nature's God entitle them, a decent respect to the opinions of mankind requires that they should declare the causes which impel them to the separation.

We hold these truths to be self-evident: That all men are created equal; that they are endowed by their Creator with certain unalienable rights; that among these are life, liberty, and the pursuit of happiness; that, to secure these rights, governments are instituted among men, deriving their just powers from the consent of the governed; that whenever any form of government becomes destructive of these ends, it is the right of the people to alter or to abolish it, and to institute new government, laying its foundation on such principles, and organizing its power in such form, as to them shall seem most likely to effect their safety and happiness. Prudence, indeed, will dictate that governments long established should not be changed for light and transient causes; and accordingly all experience hath shown that mankind are more disposed to suffer, while evils are sufferable, than to right themselves by abolishing the forms to which they are accustomed. But when a long train of abuses and usurpations, pursuing invariably the same object, evinces a design to reduce them under absolute despotism, it is their right, it is their duty, to throw off such government, and to provide new guards for their future security. Such has been the patient sufferance of these colonies; and such is now the necessity which constrains them to alter their former systems of government. The history of the present King of Great Britain is a history of repeated injuries and usurpations, all having in direct object the establishment of an absolute tyranny over these states. To prove this, let facts be submitted to a candid world.

He has refused to assent to laws, the most wholesome and necessary for the public good.

He has forbidden his governors to pass laws of immediate and pressing importance, unless suspended in their operation till his assent should be obtained; and, when so suspended, he has utterly neglected to attend to them.

He has refused to pass other laws for the accommodation of large districts of people, unless those people would relinquish the right of representation in the legislature, a right inestimable to them, and formidable to tyrants only.

He has called together legislative bodies at places unusual, uncomfortable, and distant from the depository of their public records, for the sole purpose of fatiguing them into compliance with his measures.

He has dissolved representative houses repeatedly, for opposing, with manly firmness, his invasions on the rights of the people.

He has refused for a long time, after such dissolutions, to cause others to be elected; whereby the legislative powers, incapable of annihilation, have returned to the people at large for their exercise; the state remaining, in the mean time, exposed to all dangers of invasions from without and convulsions within.

He has endeavored to prevent the population of these states; for that purpose obstructing the laws for naturalization of foreigners; refusing to pass others to encourage their migration hither, and raising the conditions of new appropriations of lands.

He has obstructed the administration of justice, by refusing his assent to laws for establishing judiciary powers.

He has made judges dependent on his will alone, for the tenure of their offices, and the amount and payment of their salaries.

He has erected a multitude of new offices, and sent hither swarms of officers to harass our people, and eat out their substance.

He has kept among us, in times of peace, standing armies, without the consent of our legislatures.

He has affected to render the military independent of, and superior to, the civil power.

He has combined with others to subject us to a jurisdiction foreign to our constitution, and unacknowledged by our laws, giving his assent to their acts of pretended legislation:

For quartering large bodies of armed troops among us:

For protecting them, by a mock trial, from punishment for any murders which they should commit on the inhabitants of these states;

For cutting off our trade with all parts of the world;

For imposing taxes on us without our consent;

For depriving us, in many cases, of the benefits of trial by jury;

For transporting us beyond seas, to be tried for pretended offenses;

For abolishing the free system of English laws in a neighboring province, establishing therein an arbitrary government, and enlarging its boundaries, so as to render it at once an example and fit instrument for introducing the same absolute rule into these colonies;

For taking away our charters, abolishing our most valuable laws, and altering fundamentally the forms of our governments;

For suspending our own legislatures, and declaring themselves invested with power to legislate for us in all cases whatsoever.

He has abdicated government here, by declaring us out of his protection and waging war against us.

He has plundered our seas, ravaged our coasts, burned our towns, and destroyed the lives of our people.

He is at this time transporting large armies of foreign mercenaries to complete the works of death, desolation, and tyranny already begun with circumstances of cruelty and perfidy scarcely paralleled in the most barbarous ages, and totally unworthy the head of a civilized nation.

He has constrained our fellow-citizens, taken captive on the high seas, to bear arms against their country, to become the executioners of their friends and brethren, or to fall themselves by their hands.

He has excited domestic insurrection among us, and has endeavored to bring on the inhabitants of our frontiers the merciless Indian savages, whose known rule of warfare is an undistinguished destruction of all ages, sexes, and conditions.

In every stage of these oppressions we have petitioned for redress in the most humble terms; our repeated petitions have been answered only by repeated injury. A prince, whose character is thus marked by every act which may define a tyrant, is unfit to be the ruler of a free people.

Nor have we been wanting in our attentions to our British brethren. We have warned them, from time to time, of attempts by their Legislature to extend an unwarrantable jurisdiction over us. We have reminded them of the circumstances of our emigration and settlement here. We have appealed to their native justice and magnanimity; and we have conjured them, by the ties of our common kindred, to disavow these usurpations, which would inevitably interrupt our connections and correspondence. They, too, have been deaf to the voice of justice and of consanguinity. We must, therefore, acquiesce in the necessity which denounces our separation, and hold them, as we hold the rest of mankind, enemies in war, in peace friends.

We, therefore, the representatives of the United States of America, in General Congress assembled, appealing to the Supreme Judge of the world for the rectitude of our intentions, do, in the name and by the authority of the good people of these colonies, solemnly publish and declare, that these United Colonies are, and of right ought to be, FREE AND INDEPENDENT STATES; that they are absolved from all allegiance to the British crown, and that all political connection between them and the state of Great Britain is, and ought to be, totally dissolved; and that, as free and independent states, they have full power to levy war, conclude peace, contract alliances, establish commerce, and do all other acts and things which independent states may of right do. And for the support of this declaration, with a firm reliance on the protection of Divine Providence, we mutually pledge to each other our lives, our fortunes, and our sacred honor.

John Hancock [*President*]
[*and fifty-five others*]

The Constitution of the United States

Preamble

We the People of the United States, in Order to form a more perfect Union, establish Justice, insure domestic Tranquility, provide for the common defence, promote the general Welfare, and secure the Blessings of Liberty to ourselves and our Posterity, do ordain and establish this Constitution for the United States of America.

Article I.

Bicameral Congress

Section 1. All legislative Powers herein granted shall be vested in a Congress of the United States, which shall consist of a Senate and House of Representatives.

Membership of the House

Section 2. The House of Representatives shall be composed of Members chosen every second Year by the People of the several States, and the Electors in each State shall have the Qualifications requisite for Electors of the most numerous Branch of the State Legislature.

No person shall be a Representative who shall not have attained to the age of twenty five Years, and been seven Years a Citizen of the United States, and who shall not, when elected, be an Inhabitant of that State in which he shall be chosen.

Representatives and direct Taxes shall be apportioned among the several States which may be included within this Union, according to their respective Numbers, which shall be determined by adding to the whole Number of free Persons, including those bound to Service for a Term of Years, and excluding Indians not taxed, three fifths of all other Persons.[1] The actual Enumeration shall be made within three Years after the first Meeting of the Congress of the United States, and within every subsequent Term of ten Years, in such Manner as they shall by Law direct. The Number of Representatives shall not exceed one for every thirty Thousand, but each State shall have at Least one Representative; and until such enumeration shall be made, the State of New Hampshire shall be entitled to chuse three, Massachusetts eight, Rhode-Island and Providence Plantations one, Connecticut five, New-York six, New Jersey four, Pennsylvania eight, Delaware one, Maryland six, Virginia ten, North Carolina five, South Carolina five, and Georgia three.

When vacancies happen in the Representation from any State, the Executive Authority thereof shall issue Writs of Election to fill such Vacancies.

Power to impeach

The House of Representatives shall chuse their Speaker and other Officers; and shall have the sole Power of Impeachment.

Membership of the Senate

Section 3. The Senate of the United States shall be composed of two Senators from each State, *chosen by the Legislature thereof*[2], for six Years; and each Senator shall have one Vote.

Immediately after they shall be assembled in Consequence of the first Election, they shall be divided as equally as may be into three Classes. The Seats of the Senators of the first class shall be vacated at the Expiration of the second Year, of the second Class at the Expiration of the fourth Year, and of the third Class at the Expiration of the sixth Year, so that one third may be chosen every second Year; *and if Vacancies happen by Resignation, or otherwise, during the Recess of the Legislature of any State, the Executive thereof may make temporary Appointments until the next Meeting of the Legislature, which shall then fill such Vacancies.*[3]

No Person shall be a Senator who shall not have attained to the Age of thirty Years, and been nine Years a Citizen of the United States, and who shall not, when elected, be an Inhabitant of that State for which he shall be chosen.

NOTE: The topical headings are not part of the original Constitution. Excluding the Preamble and Closing, those portions set in italic type have been superseded or changed by later amendments.

[1]*Changed by the Fourteenth Amendment, section 2.*

[2]*Changed by the Seventeenth Amendment.*

[3]*Changed by the Seventeenth Amendment.*

The Vice President of the United States shall be President of the Senate, but shall have no Vote, unless they be equally divided.

The Senate shall chuse their other Officers, and also a President pro tempore, in the Absence of the Vice President, or when he shall exercise the Office of President of the United States.

Power to try impeachments

The Senate shall have the sole Power to try all Impeachments. When sitting for that Purpose, they shall be on Oath or Affirmation. When the President of the United States is tried the Chief Justice shall preside: And no Person shall be convicted without the Concurrence of two thirds of the Members present.

Judgment in Cases of Impeachment shall not extend further than to removal from Office, and disqualification to hold and enjoy any Office of honor, Trust or Profit under the United States: but the Party convicted shall nevertheless be liable and subject to Indictment, Trial, Judgment and Punishment, according to Law.

Laws governing elections

Section 4. The Times, Places and Manner of holding Elections for Senators and Representatives, shall be prescribed in each State by the Legislature thereof; but the Congress may at any time by Law make or alter such Regulations, except as to the Places of chusing Senators.

The Congress shall assemble at least once in every Year, and such Meeting shall be on the *first Monday in December, unless they shall by Law appoint a different Day.*[4]

Rules of Congress

Section 5. Each House shall be the Judge of the Elections, Returns and Qualifications of its own Members, and a Majority of each shall constitute a Quorum to do Business; but a smaller number may adjourn from day to day, and may be authorized to compel the Attendance of absent Members, in such Manner, and under such Penalties as each House may provide.

Each House may determine the Rules of its Proceedings, punish its Members for disorderly Behaviour, and, with the Concurrence of two thirds, expel a Member.

Each House shall keep a Journal of its Proceedings, and from time to time publish the same, excepting such Parts as may in their Judgment require Secrecy; and the Yeas and Nays of the Members of either House on any question shall, at the Desire of one fifth of those Present, be entered on the Journal.

Neither House, during the Session of Congress, shall, without the Consent of the other, adjourn for more than three days, nor to any other Place than that in which the two Houses shall be sitting.

Salaries and immunities of members

Section 6. The Senators and Representatives shall receive a Compensation for their Services, to be ascertained by Law, and paid out of the Treasury of the United States. They shall in all Cases, except Treason, Felony and Breach of the Peace, be privileged from Arrest during their Attendance at the Session of their respective Houses, and in going to and returning from the same; and for any Speech or Debate in either House, they shall not be questioned in any other Place.

Bar on members of Congress holding federal appointive office

No Senator or Representative shall, during the Time for which he was elected, be appointed to any civil Office under the Authority of the United States, which shall have been created, or the Emoluments whereof shall have been encreased during such time; and no Person holding any Office under the United States, shall be a Member of either House during his Continuance in Office.

Money bills originate in House

Section 7. All Bills for raising Revenue shall originate in the House of Representatives; but the Senate may propose or concur with Amendments as on other Bills.

Procedure for enacting laws; veto power

Every Bill which shall have passed the House of Representatives and the Senate, shall, before it become a Law, be presented to the President of the United States; If he approve he shall sign it, but if not he shall return it, with Objections to that House in

---

[4]*Changed by the Twentieth Amendment, section 2.*

which it shall have originated, who shall enter the Objections at large on their Journal, and proceed to reconsider it. If after such Reconsideration two thirds of that House shall agree to pass the Bill, it shall be sent, together with the Objections, to the other House, by which it shall likewise be reconsidered, and if approved by two thirds of that House, it shall become a Law. But in all such Cases the Votes of both Houses shall be determined by yeas and Nays, and the Names of the Persons voting for and against the Bill shall be entered on the Journal of each House respectively. If any Bill shall not be returned by the President within ten Days (Sundays excepted) after it shall have been presented to him, the Same shall be a Law, in like Manner, as if he had signed it, unless the Congress by their Adjournment prevent its Return, in which Case it shall not be a Law.

Every Order, Resolution, or Vote to which the Concurrence of the Senate and House of Representatives may be necessary (except on a question of Adjournment) shall be presented to the President of the United States; and before the Same shall take Effect, shall be approved by him, or being disapproved by him, shall be repassed by two thirds of the Senate and House of Representatives, according to the Rules and Limitations prescribed in the Case of a Bill.

Powers of Congress—taxes

Section 8. The Congress shall have Power To lay and Collect Taxes, Duties, Imposts and Excises, to pay the Debts and provide for the common Defence and general Welfare of the United States; but all Duties, Imposts and Excises shall be uniform throughout the United States.

—borrowing

To borrow Money on the credit of the United States;

—regulation of commerce

To regulate Commerce with foreign Nations, and among the several States, and with the Indian Tribes;

—naturalization and bankruptcy

To establish an uniform Rule of Naturalization, and uniform Laws on the subject of Bankruptcies throughout the United States;

—money

To coin Money, regulate the Value thereof, and of foreign Coin, and fix the Standard of Weights and Measures;

—counterfeiting

To provide for the Punishment of counterfeiting the Securities and current Coin of the United States;

—post office

To establish Post Offices and post Roads;

—patents and copyrights

To promote the Progress of Science and useful Arts, by securing for limited Times to Authors and Inventors the exclusive Right to their respective Writings and Discoveries;

—create courts

To constitute Tribunals inferior to the Supreme Court;

—punish piracies

To define and punish Piracies and Felonies committed on the high Seas, and Offences against the Law of Nations;

—declare war

To declare War, grant Letters of Marque and Reprisal, and make Rules concerning Captures on Land and Water;

—create army and navy

To raise and support Armies, but no Appropriation of Money to that Use shall be for a longer Term than two Years;

To provide and maintain a Navy;

To make Rules for the Government and Regulation of the land and naval Forces;

—call the militia

To provide for calling forth the Militia to execute the Laws of the Union, suppress Insurrections and repel Invasions;

To provide for organizing, arming, and disciplining, the Militia, and for governing such Part of them as may be employed in the Service of the United States, reserving to the States respectively, the Appointment of the Officers, and the Authority of training the Militia according to the discipline prescribed by Congress;

—govern District of Columbia

To exercise exclusive Legislation in all Cases whatsoever, over such District (not exceeding ten Miles square) as may, by Cession of Particular States, and the Acceptance of Congress, become the Seat of the Government of the United States, and to exercise like Authority over all Places purchased by the Consent of the Legislature of the State in which the Same shall be, for the Erection of Forts, Magazines, Arsenals, dock-Yards and other needful Buildings;—And

—"necessary-and-proper" clause

To make all Laws which shall be necessary and proper for carrying into Execution the foregoing Powers, and all other Powers vested by this Constitution in the Government of the United States, or in any Department or Officer thereof.

Restrictions on powers of Congress—slave trade

Section 9. The Migration or Importation of such Persons as any of the States now existing shall think proper to admit, shall not be prohibited by the Congress prior to the Year one thousand eight hundred and eight, but a Tax or duty may be imposed on such Importation, not exceeding ten dollars for each Person.

—habeas corpus

The Privilege of the Writ of Habeas Corpus shall not be suspended, unless when in Cases of Rebellion or Invasion the public Safety may require it.

—no bill of attainder or ex post facto law

No bill of Attainder or ex post facto Law shall be passed.

No Capitation, or other direct, Tax shall be laid, *unless in Proportion to the Census or Enumeration herein before directed to be taken.*[5]

—no interstate tariffs

No Tax or Duty shall be laid on Articles exported from any State.

—no preferential treatment for some states

No Preference shall be given by any Regulation of Commerce or Revenue to the Ports of one State over those of another; nor shall Vessels bound to, or from, one State, be obliged to enter, clear or pay Duties in another.

—appropriations

No Money shall be drawn from the Treasury, but in Consequence of Appropriations made by Law; and a regular Statement and Account of the Receipts and Expenditures of all public Money shall be published from time to time.

—no titles of nobility

No Title of Nobility shall be granted by the United States: And no Person holding any Office of Profit or Trust under them, shall, without the Consent of the Congress, accept of any present, Emolument, Office, or Title, of any kind whatever, from any King, Prince, or foreign State.

Restrictions on powers of states

Section 10. No State shall enter into any Treaty, Alliance, or Confederation; grant Letters of Marque and Reprisal; coin Money; emit Bills of Credit; make any Thing but gold and silver Coin a Tender in Payment of Debts; pass any Bill of Attainder, ex post facto Law, or Law impairing the Obligation of Contracts, or grant any Title of Nobility.

No State shall, without the Consent of Congress, lay any Imposts or Duties on Imports or Exports, except what may be absolutely necessary for executing its inspection Laws; and the net Produce of all Duties and Imposts, laid by any State on Imports or Exports, shall be for the Use of the Treasury of the United States; and all such Laws shall be subject to the Revision and Controul of the Congress.

No State shall, without the Consent of Congress, lay any Duty of Tonnage, keep Troops, or Ships of War in time of Peace, enter into any Agreement or Compact with another State, or with a foreign Power, or engage in War, unless actually invaded, or in such imminent Danger as will not admit of delay.

Article II.

Office of president

Section 1. The executive Power shall be vested in a President of the United States of America. He shall hold his Office during the Term of four Years, and, together with the Vice President, chosen for the same Term, be elected, as follows:

Election of president

Each State shall appoint, in such Manner as the Legislature thereof may direct, a Number of Electors, equal to the whole Number of Senators and Representatives to which the State may be entitled in the Congress: but no Senator or Representative, or Person holding an Office of Trust or Profit under the United States, shall be appointed an Elector.

The Electors shall meet in their respective States, and vote by Ballot for two Persons, of whom one at least shall not be an Inhabitant of the same State with themselves. And they shall make a List of all the Persons voted for, and of the Number of Votes for each; which List they shall sign and certify, and transmit sealed to the Seat of the Government of the United States,

---

[5]*Changed by the Sixteenth Amendment.*

directed to the President of the Senate. The President of the Senate shall, in the Presence of the Senate and House of Representatives, open all the Certificates, and the Votes shall then be counted. The Person having the greatest Number of Votes shall be the President, if such Number be a Majority of the whole Number of Electors appointed; and if there be more than one who have such Majority, and have an equal Number of Votes, then the House of Representatives shall immediately chuse by Ballot one of them for President; and if no Person have a Majority, then from the five highest on the List said House shall in like Manner chuse the President. But in chusing the President, the Votes shall be taken by States, the Representation from each State having one Vote; a quorum for this Purpose shall consist of a Member or Members from two thirds of the States, and a Majority of all the States shall be necessary to a Choice. In every Case, after the Choice of the President, the Person having the greatest Number of Votes of the Electors shall be the Vice President. But if there should remain two or more who have equal Votes, the Senate shall chuse from them by Ballot the Vice President.[6]

The Congress may determine the Time of chusing the Electors, and the Day on which they shall give their Votes, which Day shall be the same throughout the United States.

Requirements to be president

No Person except a natural born Citizen, or a Citizen of the United States, at the time of the Adoption of this Constitution, shall be eligible to the Office of President; neither shall any person be eligible to that Office who shall not have attained to the Age of thirty five Years, and been fourteen Years a Resident within the United States.

In Case of the Removal of the President from Office, or of his Death, Resignation, or Inability to discharge the Powers and Duties of the said Office, the Same shall devolve on the Vice President, and the Congress may by Law provide for the Case of Removal, Death, Resignation or Inability, both of the President and Vice President, declaring what Officer shall then act as President, and such Officer shall act accordingly, until the Disability be removed, or a President shall be elected.[7]

Pay of president

The President shall, at stated Times, receive for his Services, a Compensation, which shall neither be increased nor diminished during the Period for which he shall have been elected, and he shall not receive within that Period any other Emolument from the United States, or any of them.

Before he enter on the Execution of his Office, he shall take the following Oath or Affirmation:—"I do solemnly swear (or affirm) that I will faithfully execute the Office of President of the United States, and will to the best of my Ability preserve, protect and defend the Constitution of the United States."

Powers of president
—commander in chief
—pardons

Section 2. The President shall be Commander in Chief of the Army and Navy of the United States, and of the Militia of the several States, when called into the actual Service of the United States; he may require the Opinion, in writing, of the principal Officer in each of the executive Departments, upon any Subject relating to the Duties of their respective Offices, and he shall have Power to grant Reprieves and Pardons for Offences against the United States, except in Cases of Impeachment.

—treaties and appointments

He shall have Power, by and with the Advice and Consent of the Senate, to make Treaties, provided two thirds of the Senators present concur; and he shall nominate, and by and with the Advice and Consent of the Senate, shall appoint Ambassadors, other public Ministers and Consuls, Judges of the supreme Court, and all other Officers of the United States, whose Appointments are not herein otherwise provided for, and which shall be established by Law: but the Congress may by Law vest the Appointment of such inferior Officers, as they think proper, in the President alone, in the Courts of Law, or in the Heads of Departments.

[6] *Superseded by the Twelfth Amendment.*
[7] *Modified by the Twenty-fifth Amendment.*

The President shall have Power to fill up all Vacancies that may happen during the Recess of the Senate, by granting Commissions which shall expire at the End of their next Session.

Relations of president with Congress

Section 3. He shall from time to time give to the Congress Information of the State of the Union, and recommend to their Consideration such Measures as he shall judge necessary and expedient; he may, on extraordinary Occasions, convene both Houses, or either of them, and in Case of Disagreement between them, with Respect to the Time of Adjournment, he may adjourn them to such Time as he shall think proper; he shall receive Ambassadors and other public Ministers; he shall take Care that the Laws be faithfully executed, and shall Commission all the Officers of the United States.

Impeachment

Section 4. The President, Vice President and all civil Officers of the United States, shall be removed from Office on Impeachment for, and Conviction of, Treason, Bribery, or other high Crimes and Misdemeanors.

Article III.

Federal courts

Section 1. The judicial Power of the United States, shall be vested in one supreme Court, and in such inferior Courts as the Congress may from time to time ordain and establish. The Judges, both of the supreme and inferior Courts, shall hold their Offices during good Behaviour, and shall, at stated Times, receive for their Services, a Compensation, which shall not be diminished during their Continuance in Office.

Jurisdiction of courts

Section 2. The judicial Power shall extend to all Cases, in Law and Equity, arising under this Constitution, the Laws of the United States, and Treaties made, or which shall be made, under their Authority;—to all Cases affecting Ambassadors, other public Ministers and Consuls;—to all Cases of admiralty and maritime Jurisdiction;—to Controversies to which the United States shall be a Party;—to Controversies between two or more States;—*between a State and Citizens of another State*;[8]—between Citizens of different States;—between Citizens of the same State claiming Lands under Grants of different States, and between a State, or the Citizens thereof, and foreign States, Citizens or Subjects.

—original

In all Cases affecting Ambassadors, other public Ministers and Consuls, and those in which a State shall be Party, the supreme Court shall have original Jurisdiction. In all the other Cases before mentioned, the supreme Court shall have appellate Jurisdiction, both as to Law and Fact, with such Exceptions, and under such Regulations as the Congress shall make.

—appellate

The Trial of all Crimes, except in Cases of Impeachment, shall be by Jury; and such Trial shall be held in the State where the said Crimes shall have been committed; but when not committed within any State, the Trial shall be at such Place or Places as the Congress may by Law have directed.

Treason

Section 3. Treason against the United States, shall consist only in levying War against them, or in adhering to their Enemies, giving them Aid and Comfort. No Person shall be convicted of Treason unless on the Testimony of two Witnesses to the same overt Act, or on Confession in open Court.

The Congress shall have Power to declare the Punishment of Treason, but no Attainder of Treason shall work Corruption of Blood, or Forfeiture except during the Life of the Person attainted.

Article IV.

Full faith and credit

Section 1. Full Faith and Credit shall be given in each State to the public Acts, Records, and judicial Proceedings of every other State. And the Congress may by general Laws prescribe the Manner in which such Acts, Records and Proceedings shall be proved, and the Effect thereof.

---

[8]*Modified by the Eleventh Amendment.*

Privileges and immunities

Section 2. The Citizens of each State shall be entitled to all Privileges and Immunities of Citizens in the several States.

Extradition

A person charged in any State with Treason, Felony, or other Crime, who shall flee from Justice, and be found in another State, shall on Demand of the executive Authority of the State from which he fled, be delivered up, to be removed to the State having Jurisdiction of the Crime.

No Person held to Service or Labour in one State, under the Laws thereof, escaping into another, shall, in Consequence of any Law or Regulation therein, be discharged from such Service or Labour, but shall be delivered up on Claim of the Party to whom such Service or Labour may be due.[9]

Creation of new states

Section 3. New States may be admitted by the Congress into this Union; but no new State shall be formed or erected within the Jurisdiction of any other State; nor any State be formed by the Junction of two or more States, or Parts of States, without the Consent of the Legislatures of the States concerned as well as of the Congress.

Governing territories

The Congress shall have Power to dispose of and make all needful Rules and Regulations respecting the Territory or other Property belonging to the United States; and nothing in this Constitution shall be so construed as to Prejudice any Claims of the United States, or of any particular State.

Protection of states

Section 4. The United States shall guarantee to every State in this Union a Republican Form of Government, and shall protect each of them against Invasion; and on Application of the Legislature, or of the Executive (when the Legislature cannot be convened) against domestic Violence.

Article V.

Amending the Constitution

The Congress, whenever two thirds of both Houses shall deem it necessary, shall propose Amendments to this Constitution, or, on the Application of the Legislatures of two thirds of the several States, shall call a Convention for proposing Amendments, which, in either Case, shall be valid to all Intents and Purposes, as Part of this Constitution, when ratified by the Legislatures of three fourths of the several States, or by Conventions in three fourths thereof, as the one or the other Mode of Ratification may be proposed by the Congress; Provided that no Amendment which may be made prior to the Year One thousand eight hundred and eight shall in any Manner alter the first and fourth Clauses in the Ninth Section of the first Article; and that no State, without its Consent, shall be deprived of its equal Suffrage in the Senate.

Article VI.

Assumption of debts of Confederation

All Debts contracted and Engagements entered into, before the Adoption of this Constitution, shall be as valid against the United States under this Constitution, as under the Confederation.

Supremacy of federal laws and treaties

This Constitution, and the Laws of the United States which shall be made in Pursuance thereof; and all Treaties made, or which shall be made, under the Authority of the United States, shall be the Supreme Law of the Land; and the Judges in every State shall be bound thereby, any Thing in the Constitution or Laws of any State to the Contrary notwithstanding.

No religious test

The Senators and Representatives before mentioned, and the Members of the several State Legislatures, and all executive and judicial Officers, both of the United States and of the several States, shall be bound by Oath or Affirmation, to support this Constitution; but no religious Test shall ever be required as a Qualification to any Office or public Trust under the United States.

---

[9]*Changed by the Thirteenth Amendment.*

Article VII.

Ratification procedure

The Ratification of the Conventions of nine States, shall be sufficient for the Establishment of this Constitution between the States so ratifying the Same.

Done in Convention by the Unanimous Consent of the States present the Seventeenth Day of September in the Year of our Lord one thousand seven hundred and Eighty seven and of the Independence of the United States of America the Twelfth In witness whereof We have hereunto subscribed our Names,

G. Washington — *Presidt. and deputy from Virginia*

New Hampshire
- J. LANGDON
- N. GILMAN

Massachusetts
- N. GORHAM
- R. KING

New Jersey
- W. LIVINGSTON
- D. BREARLEY
- W. PATERSON
- J. DAYTON

Pennsylvania
- B. FRANKLIN
- T. MIFFLIN
- R. MORRIS
- G. CLYMER
- T. FITZSIMONS
- J. INGERSOLL
- J. WILSON
- G. MORRIS

Connecticut
- W. JOHNSON
- R. SHERMAN

New York
- A. HAMILTION

Maryland
- J. McHENRY
- D. OF ST. T. JENIFER
- D. CARROLL

Virginia
- J. BLAIR—
- J. MADISON JR.

North Carolina
- W. BLOUNT
- R. DOBBS SPAIGHT
- H. WILLIAMSON

South Carolina
- J. RUTLEDGE
- C. COTESWORTH PINCKNEY
- C. PINCKNEY
- P. BUTLER

Delaware
- G. READ
- G. BEDFORD JUN
- J. DICKINSON
- R. BASSETT
- J. BROOM

Georgia
- W. FEW
- A. BALDWIN

AMENDMENT I.

Freedom of religion, speech, press, assembly

Congress shall make no law respecting an establishment of religion, or prohibiting the free exercise thereof, or abridging the freedom of speech, or of the press; or the right of the people peaceably to assemble, and to petition the Government for a redress of grievances.

AMENDMENT II.

Right to bear arms

A well regulated Militia, being necessary to the security of a free State, the right of the people to keep and bear Arms, shall not be infringed.

AMENDMENT III.

Quartering troops in private homes

No Soldier shall, in time of peace be quartered in any house without the consent of the Owner, nor in time of war, but in a manner to be prescribed by law.

AMENDMENT IV.

Prohibition against unreasonable searches and seizures

The right of the people to be secure in their persons, houses, papers, and effects, against unreasonable searches and seizures, shall not be violated, and no Warrants shall issue, but upon probable cause, supported by Oath or affirmation, and particularly describing the place to be searched, and the persons or things to be seized.

AMENDMENT V.

Right when accused; "due-process" clause

No person shall be held to answer for a capital, or otherwise infamous crime, unless on a presentment or indictment of a Grand Jury, except in cases arising in the land or naval forces, or in the Militia, when in actual service in time of War or public danger; nor shall any person be subject for the same offence to be twice put in jeopardy of life or limb; nor shall be compelled in any criminal case to be a witness against himself, nor be deprived of life, liberty, or property, without due process of law, nor shall private property be taken for public use, without just compensation.

AMENDMENT VI.

Rights when on trial

In all criminal prosecutions, the accused shall enjoy the right to a speedy and public trial, by an impartial jury of the State and district wherein the crime shall have been committed, which district shall have been previously ascertained by law, and to be informed of the nature and cause of the accusation; to be confronted with the witnesses against him; to have compulsory process for obtaining witnesses in his favor, and to have the Assistance of Counsel for his defence.

AMENDMENT VII.

Common-law suits

In Suits at common law, where the value in controversy shall exceed twenty dollars, the right of trial by jury shall be preserved, and no fact tried by a jury, shall be otherwise reexamined in any Court of the United States, than according to the rules of the common law.

AMENDMENT VIII.

Bail; no "cruel and unusual" punishments

Excessive bail shall not be required, nor excessive fines imposed, nor cruel and unusual punishments inflicted.

AMENDMENT IX.

Unenumerated rights protected

The enumeration in the Constitution, of certain rights, shall not be construed to deny or disparage others retained by the people.

AMENDMENT X.

Powers reserved for states

The powers not delegated to the United States by the Constitution, nor prohibited by it to the States, are reserved to the States respectively, or to the people.

AMENDMENT XI.

[Ratified in 1795.]

Limits on suits against states

The Judicial power of the United States shall not be construed to extend to any suit in law or equity, commenced or prosecuted against one of the United States by Citizens of another state, or by Citizens or Subjects of any Foreign State.

AMENDMENT XII.

[Ratified in 1804.]

Revision of electoral-college procedure

The Electors shall meet in their respective states and vote by ballot for President and Vice President, one of whom, at least, shall not be an inhabitant of the same state with themselves; they shall name in their ballots the person voted for as President, and in distinct ballots the person voted for as Vice President, and they shall make distinct lists of all persons voted for as President, and of all persons voted for as Vice President, and of the number of votes for each, which lists they shall sign and certify, and transmit sealed to the seat of government of the United States, directed to the President of the Senate;—The President of the Senate shall, in the presence of the Senate and House of Representatives, open all the certificates and the votes shall then be counted;—The person having the greatest number of votes for President, shall be the President, if such number be a majority of the whole number of Electors appointed; and if no person have such majority, then from the persons having the highest numbers not exceeding three on the list of those voted for as President, the House of Representatives shall choose immediately, by ballot, the President. But in choosing the President, the votes shall be taken by states, the representation from each state having one vote; a quorum for this purpose shall consist of a member or members from two-thirds of the states, and a majority of all the states shall be necessary to a choice. *And if the House of Representatives shall not choose a President whenever the right of choice shall devolve upon them, before the fourth day of March next following, then the Vice President shall act as President, as in the case of the death or other constitutional disability of the President.*—[10] The person having the greatest number of votes as Vice President, shall be the Vice President, if such number be a majority of the whole number of Electors appointed, and if no person have a majority, then from the two highest numbers on the list, the Senate shall choose the Vice President; a quorum for the purpose shall consist of two-thirds of the whole number of Senators, and a majority of the whole number shall be necessary to a choice. But no person constitutionally ineligible to the office of President shall be eligible to that of Vice President of the United States.

AMENDMENT XIII.

[Ratified in 1865.]

Slavery prohibited

Section 1. Neither slavery nor involuntary servitude, except as a punishment for crime whereof the party shall have been duly convicted, shall exist within the United States, or any place subject to their jurisdiction.

Section 2. Congress shall have power to enforce this article by appropriate legislation.

---

[10]*Changed by the Twentieth Amendment, section 3.*

AMENDMENT XIV.

[Ratified in 1868.]

Ex-slaves made citizens "Due-process" clause applied to states "Equal-protection" clause

Section 1. All persons born or naturalized in the United States and subject to the jurisdiction thereof, are citizens of the United States and of the State wherein they reside. No State shall make or enforce any law which shall abridge the privileges or immunities of citizens of the United States; nor shall any State deprive any person of life, liberty, or property, without due process of law; nor deny to any person within its jurisdiction the equal protection of the laws.

Reduction in congressional representation for states denying adult males the right to vote

Section 2. Representatives shall be apportioned among the several States according to their respective numbers, counting the whole number of persons in each State, excluding Indians not taxed. But when the right to vote at any election for the choice of electors for President and Vice President of the United States, Representatives in Congress, the Executive and Judicial officers of a State, or the members of the Legislature thereof, is denied to any of the male inhabitants of such State, being *twenty-one*[11] years of age and citizens of the United States, or in any way abridged, except for participation in rebellion, or other crime, the basis of representation therein shall be reduced in the proportion which the number of such male citizens shall bear to the whole number of male citizens twenty-one years of age in such State.

Southern rebels denied federal office

Section 3. No person shall be a Senator or Representative in Congress, or elector of President and Vice President, or hold any office, civil or military, under the United States, or under any State, who, having previously taken an oath, as a member of Congress, or as an officer of the United States, or as a member of any State legislature, or as an executive or judicial officer of any State, to support the Constitution of the United States, shall have engaged in insurrection or rebellion against the same, or given aid or comfort to the enemies thereof. But Congress may by a vote of two-thirds of each House, remove such disability.

Rebel debts repudiated

Section 4. The validity of the public debt of the United States, authorized by law, including debts incurred for payment of pensions and bounties for services in suppressing insurrection or rebellion, shall not be questioned. But neither the United States nor any State shall assume or pay any debt or obligation incurred in aid of insurrection or rebellion against the United States, or any claim for the loss or emancipation of any slave; but all such debts, obligations and claims shall be held illegal and void.

Section 5. The Congress shall have power to enforce, by appropriate legislation, the provisions of this article.

AMENDMENT XV.

[Ratified in 1870.]

Blacks given right to vote

Section 1. The right of citizens of the United States to vote shall not be denied or abridged by the United States or by any State on account of race, color, or previous condition of servitude.

Section 2. The Congress shall have power to enforce this article by appropriate legislation.

---

[11] *Changed by the Twenty-sixth Amendment.*

AMENDMENT XVI.

[Ratified in 1913.]

Authorizes federal income tax

The Congress shall have power to lay and collect taxes on incomes, from whatever source derived, without apportionment among the several States, and without regard to any census or enumeration.

AMENDMENT XVII.

[Ratified in 1913.]

Requires popular election of Senators

The Senate of the United States shall be composed of two Senators from each State, elected by the people thereof, for six years; and each Senator shall have one vote. The electors in each State shall have the qualifications requisite for electors of the most numerous branch of the State legislatures.

When vacancies happen in the representation of any State in the Senate, the executive authority of such State shall issue writs of election to fill such vacancies: Provided, That the legislature of any State may empower the executive thereof to make temporary appointments until the people fill the vacancies by election as the legislature may direct.

This amendment shall not be so construed as to affect the election or term of any Senator chosen before it becomes valid as part of the Constitution.

AMENDMENT XVIII.

[Ratified in 1919.]

Prohibits manufacture and sale of liquor

Section 1. After one year from the ratification of this article the manufacture, sale, or transportation of intoxicating liquors within, the importation there-of into, or the exportation thereof from the United States and all territory subject to the jurisdiction thereof for beverage purposes is hereby prohibited.

Section 2. The Congress and the several States shall have concurrent power to enforce this article by appropriate legislation.

Section 3. This article shall be inoperative unless it shall have been ratified as an amendment to the Constitution by the legislatures of the several States, as provided in the Constitution, within seven years from the date of the submission hereof to the States by the Congress.[12]

AMENDMENT XIX.

[Ratified in 1920.]

Right to vote for women

The right of citizens of the United States to vote shall not be denied or abridged by the United States or by any State on account of sex.

Congress shall have power to enforce this article by appropriate legislation.

AMENDMENT XX.

[Ratified in 1933.]

Federal terms of office to begin in January

Section 1. The terms of the President and Vice President shall end at noon on the 20th day of January, and the terms of Senators and Representatives at noon on the 3d day of January, of the years in which such terms would have ended if this article had not been ratified; and the terms of their successors shall then begin.

---

[12]*Repealed by the Twenty-first Amendment.*

Section 2. The Congress shall assemble at least once in every year, and such meeting shall begin at noon on the 3d day of January, unless they shall by law appoint a different day.

Emergency presidential succession

Section 3. If, at the time fixed for the beginning of the term of the President, the President elect shall have died, the Vice President elect shall become President. If a President shall not have been chosen before the time fixed for the beginning of his term, or if the President elect shall have failed to qualify, then the Vice President elect shall act as President until a President shall have qualified; and the Congress may by law provide for the case wherein neither a President elect nor a Vice President elect shall have qualified, declaring who shall then act as President, or the manner in which one who is to act shall be selected, and such person shall act accordingly until a President or Vice President shall have qualified.

Section 4. The Congress may by law provide for the case of the death of any of the persons from whom the House of Representatives may choose a President whenever the right of choice shall have devolved upon them, and for the case of the death of any of the persons from whom the Senate may choose a Vice President whenever the right of choice shall have devolved upon them.

Section 5. Sections 1 and 2 shall take effect on the 15th day of October following the ratification of this article.

Section 6. This article shall be inoperative unless it shall have been ratified as an amendment to the Constitution by the legislatures of three-fourths of the several States within seven years from the date of its submission.

AMENDMENT XXI.

[Ratified in 1933.]

Repeals Prohibition

Section 1. The eighteenth article of amendment to the Constitution of the United States is hereby repealed.

Section 2. The transportation or importation into any State, Territory, or possession of the United States for delivery or use therein of intoxicating liquors, in violation of the laws thereof, is hereby prohibited.

Section 3. This article shall be inoperative unless it shall have been ratified as an amendment to the Constitution by conventions in the several States, as provided in the Constitution, within seven years from the date of submission hereof to the States by the Congress.

AMENDMENT XXII.

[Ratified in 1951.]

Two-term limit for president

Section 1. No person shall be elected to the office of the President more than twice, and no person who has held the office of President, or acted as President, for more than two years of a term to which some other person was elected President shall be elected to the office of President more than once. But this Article shall not apply to any person holding the office of President when this Article was proposed by the Congress, and shall not prevent any person who may be holding the office of President, or acting as President, during the term within which this Article becomes operative from holding the office of President or acting as President during the remainder of such term.

Section 2. This Article shall be inoperative unless it shall have been ratified as an amendment to the Constitution by the legislatures of three-fourths of the several States within seven years from the date of its submission to the States by the Congress.

AMENDMENT XXIII.

[Ratified in 1961.]

Right to vote for president in District of Columbia

Section 1. The District constituting the seat of Government of the United States shall appoint in such manner as the Congress may direct:

A number of electors of President and Vice President equal to the whole number of Senators and Representatives in Congress to which the District would be entitled if it were a State, but in no event more than the least populous State; they shall be in addition to those appointed by the States, but they shall be considered, for the purposes of the election of President and Vice President, to be electors appointed by a State; and they shall meet in the District and perform such duties as provided by the twelfth article of amendment.

Section 2. The Congress shall have power to enforce this article by appropriate legislation.

AMENDMENT XXIV.

[Ratified in 1964.]

Prohibits poll taxes in federal elections

Section 1. The right of citizens of the United States to vote in any primary or other election for President or Vice President, for electors for President or Vice President, or for Senator or Representative in Congress, shall not be denied or abridged by the United States or any State by reason of failure to pay any poll tax or other tax.

Section 2. The Congress shall have the power to enforce this article by appropriate legislation.

AMENDMENT XXV.

[Ratified in 1967.]

Presidential disability and succession

Section 1. In case of the removal of the President from office or of his death or resignation, the Vice President shall become President.

Section 2. Whenever there is a vacancy in the office of the Vice President, the President shall nominate a Vice President who shall take office upon confirmation by a majority vote of both Houses of Congress.

Section 3. Whenever the President transmits to the President pro tempore of the Senate and the Speaker of the House of Representatives his written declaration that he is unable to discharge the powers and duties of his office, and until he transmits to them a written declaration to the contrary, such powers and duties shall be discharged by the Vice President as Acting President.

Section 4. Whenever the Vice President and a majority of either the principal officers of the executive departments or of such other body as Congress may by law provide, transmit to the President pro tempore of the Senate and the Speaker of the House of Representatives their written declaration that the President is unable to discharge the powers and duties of his office, the Vice President shall immediately assume the powers and duties of the office as Acting President.

Thereafter, when the President transmits to the President pro tempore of the Senate and the Speaker of the House of Representatives his written declaration that no inability exists, he shall resume the powers and duties of his office unless the Vice President and a majority of either the principal officers of the executive department[s] or of such other body as Congress may by law provide, transmit within four days to the President pro tempore of the Senate and the Speaker of the House of Representatives their written declaration that the President is unable to discharge the powers and duties of his office. Thereupon Congress shall decide the issue, assembling within forty-eight hours for that purpose if not in session. If the Congress, within twenty-one days after receipt of the latter written declaration, or, if Congress is not in session, within twenty-one days after Congress is required to assemble, determines by two-thirds vote of both Houses that the President is unable to discharge the powers and duties of his office, the Vice President shall continue to discharge the same as Acting President; otherwise, the President shall resume the powers and duties of his office.

AMENDMENT XXVI.

[Ratified in 1971.]

Voting age lowered to eighteen

Section 1. The right of citizens of the United States, who are eighteen years of age or older, to vote shall not be denied or abridged by the United States or by any State on account of age.

Section 2. The Congress shall have power to enforce this article by appropriate legislation.

AMENDMENT XXVII.

[Ratified in 1992.]

Congressional pay raises

No law varying the compensation for the services of the Senators and Representatives shall take effect, until an election of Representatives shall have intervened.

A Brief Guide to Reading the *Federalist* Papers

In 1787, to help win ratification of the new Constitution in the New York state convention, Alexander Hamilton decided to publish a series of articles defending and explaining the document in the New York City newspapers. He recruited John Jay and James Madison to help him, and the three of them, under the pen name "Publius," wrote 85 articles that appeared from late 1787 through 1788. The identity of the authors was kept secret at the time, but we now know that Hamilton wrote 51 of them, Madison 26, and Jay five, and that Hamilton and Madison jointly authored three.

The *Federalist* papers probably played only a small role in securing ratification. Like most legislative battles, this one was not decisively influenced by philosophical writings. But these essays have had a lasting value as an authoritative and profound explanation of the Constitution. Though written for political purposes, the *Federalist* has become the single most important piece of American political philosophy ever produced. Ironically, Hamilton and Madison were later to become political enemies; even at the Philadelphia convention they had different views of the kind of government that should be created. But in 1787–1788, they were united in the belief that the new constitution was the best that could have been obtained under the circumstances.

Although Hamilton wrote most of the *Federalist* papers, Madison wrote the two most famous articles—Nos. 10 and 51, reprinted here in the Appendix. On your first reading of the papers, you may find Madison's language difficult to understand and his ideas overly complex. The following pointers will help you decipher his meaning.

In *Federalist* No. 10, Madison begins by stating that "a well constructed Union" can "break and control the violence of faction." He goes on to define a *faction* as any group of citizens who attempt to advance their ideas or economic interests at the expense of other citizens, or in ways that conflict with "the permanent and aggregate interests of the community" or "public good." Thus what Madison terms "factions" are what we today call "special interests."

One way to defeat factions, according to Madison, is to remove whatever causes them to arise in the first place. This can be attempted in two ways. First, government can deprive people of the liberty they need to organize: "Liberty is to faction what air is to fire." But that is surely a cure "worse than the disease." Second, measures can be taken to make all citizens share the same ideas, feelings, and economic interests. However, as Madison observes, some people are smarter or more hardworking than others, and this "diversity in the faculties" of citizens is bound to result in different economic interests as some people acquire more property than others. Consequently, protecting property rights, not equalizing property ownership, "is the first object of government." Even if everyone shared the same basic economic interests, they would still find reasons "to vex and oppress each other" rather than cooperate "for their common good." Religious differences, loyalties to different leaders, even "frivolous and fanciful distinctions" (not liking how other people dress or their taste in music) can be fertile soil for factions. In Madison's view, people are factious by nature; the "causes of faction" are "sown" into their very being.

Madison thus proposes a second and, he thinks, more practical and desirable way of defeating faction. The way to cure "the mischiefs of faction" is not by removing its causes but by "controlling its effects." Factions will always exist, so the trick is to establish a form of government that is likely to serve the public good through the even-handed "regulation of these various and interfering interests." Wise and public-spirited leaders can "adjust these clashing interests, and render them all subservient to the public good," but, he cautions, "Enlightened statesmen will not always be at the helm." (Madison implies that "enlightened statesmen"—such as himself, Washington, and Jefferson—were at the "helm" of government in 1787.)

Madison's proposed cure for the evils of factions is in fact nothing other than a republican form of government. Use the following questions to guide your own analysis of Madison's ideas. Why does Madison think the problem of a "minority" faction is easy to handle? Conversely, why is he so troubled by the potential of a majority faction? How does he distinguish direct democracy from republican government? What is he getting at when he terms elected representatives "proper guardians of the public weal," and why does he think that "extensive republics" are more likely to produce such representatives than small ones?

When you are finished with *Federalist* No. 10, try your hand at *Federalist* No. 51. You will find that the ideas in the former paper anticipate many of those in the latter. And you will find many points on which you may or may not agree with Madison. For example, do you agree with his assumption that people—even your best friends or college roommates—are factious by nature? Likewise, do you agree with his view that government is "the greatest of all reflections on human nature"?

By attempting to meet the mind of James Madison, you can sharpen your own mind and deepen your understanding of American government.

The *Federalist* No. 10

November 22, 1787

James Madison

To the People of the State of New York.

Among the numerous advantages promised by a well-constructed Union, none deserves to be more accurately developed than its tendency to break and control the violence of faction. The friend of popular governments, never finds himself so much alarmed for their character and fate, as when he contemplates their propensity to this dangerous vice. He will not fail therefore to set a due value on any plan which, without violating the principles to which he is attached, provides a proper cure for it. The instability, injustice and confusion introduced into the public councils, have in truth been the mortal diseases under which popular governments have every where perished; as they continue to be the favorite and fruitful topics from which the adversaries to liberty derive their most specious declamations. The valuable improvements made by the American Constitutions on the popular models, both ancient and modern, cannot certainly be too much admired; but it would be an unwarrantable partiality, to contend that they have as effectually obviated the danger on this side as was wished and expected. Complaints are everywhere heard from our most considerate and virtuous citizens, equally the friends of public and private faith, and of public and personal liberty; that our governments are too unstable; that the public good is disregarded in the conflicts of rival parties; and that measures are too often decided, not according to the rules of justice, and the rights of the minor party; but by the superior force of an interested and over-bearing majority. However, anxiously we may wish that these complaints had no foundation, the evidence of known facts will not permit us to deny that they are in some degree true. It will be found indeed, on a candid review of our situation, that some of the distresses under which we labor, have been erroneously charged on the operation of our governments; but it will be found, at the same time, that other causes will not alone account for many of our heaviest misfortunes; and particularly, for that prevailing and increasing distrust of public engagements, and alarm for private rights, which are echoed from one end of the continent to the other. These must be chiefly, if not wholly, effects of the unsteadiness and injustice, with which a factious spirit has tainted our public administrations.

By a faction I understand a number of citizens, whether amounting to a majority or minority of the whole, who are united and actuated by some common impulse of passion, or of interest, adverse to the rights of other citizens, or to the permanent and aggregate interests of the community.

There are two methods of curing the mischiefs of faction: the one, by removing its causes; the other, by controlling its effects.

There are again two methods of removing the causes of faction: the one by destroying the liberty which is essential to its existence; the other, by giving to every citizen the same opinions, the same passions, and the same interests.

It could never be more truly said than of the first remedy, that it is worse than the disease. Liberty is to faction, what air is to fire, an aliment without which it instantly expires. But it could not be a less folly to abolish liberty, which is essential to political life, because it nourishes faction, than it would be to wish the annihilation of air, which is essential to animal life, because it imparts to fire its destructive agency.

The second expedient is as impracticable, as the first would be unwise. As long as the reason of man continues fallible, and he is at liberty to exercise it, different opinions will be formed. As long as the connection subsists between his reason and his self-love, his opinions and his passions will have a reciprocal influence on each other; and the former will be objects to which the latter will attach themselves. The diversity in the faculties of men from which the rights of property originate, is not less an insuperable obstacle to a uniformity of interests. The protection of these faculties is the first object of Government. From the protection of different and unequal faculties of acquiring property, the possession of different degrees and kinds of property immediately results: and from the influence of these on the sentiments and views of the respective proprietors, ensues a division of the society into different interests and parties.

The latent causes of faction are thus sown in the nature of man; and we see them every where brought into different degrees of activity, according to the different circumstances of civil society. A zeal for different opinions concerning religion, concerning Government and many other points, as well of speculation as of practice; an attachment to different leaders ambitiously contending for pre-eminence and power; or to persons of other descriptions whose fortunes have been interesting to the human passions, have in turn divided mankind into parties, inflamed them with mutual animosity, and rendered them much more disposed to vex and oppress each other, than to cooperate for their common good. So strong is this propensity of mankind to fall into mutual animosities, that where no substantial occasion presents itself, the most frivolous and fanciful distinctions have been sufficient to kindle their unfriendly passions, and excite their most violent conflicts. But the most common and durable source of factions, has been the various and unequal distribution of property. Those who hold, and those who are without property, have ever formed distinct interests in society. Those who are creditors, and those who are debtors, fall under a like discrimination. A landed interest, a manufacturing interest, a mercantile interest, a monied interest, with many lesser interests, grow up of necessity in civilized nations, and divide them into different classes, actuated by different sentiments and views. The regulation of these various and interfering interests forms the principal task of modern Legislation, and involves the spirit of party and faction in the necessary and ordinary operations of Government.

No man is allowed to be judge in his own cause; because his interest would certainly bias his judgment, and, not improbably, corrupt his integrity. With equal, nay with greater reason, a body of men, are unfit to be judges and parties, at the same time; yet, what are many of the most important acts of legislation, but so many judicial determinations, not indeed concerning the rights of single persons, but concerning the rights of large bodies of citizens, and what are the different classes of legislators, but advocates and parties to the causes which they determine? Is a law proposed concerning private debts? It is a question to which the creditors are parties on one side, and the debtors on the other. Justice ought to hold the balance between them. Yet the parties are and must be themselves the judges; and the most numerous party, or, in other words, the most powerful faction must be expected to prevail. Shall domestic manufactures be encouraged, and in what degree, by restrictions on foreign manufactures? are questions which would be differently decided by the landed and the manufacturing classes; and probably by neither, with a sole regard to justice and the public good. The apportionment of taxes on the various descriptions of property, is an act which seems to require the most exact impartiality; yet, there is perhaps no legislative act in which greater opportunity and temptation are given to a predominant party, to trample on the rules of justice. Every shilling with which they over-burden the inferior number, is a shilling saved to their own pockets.

It is in vain to say, that enlightened statesmen will be able to adjust these clashing interests, and render them all subservient to the public good. Enlightened statesmen will not always be at the helm: Nor, in many cases, can such an adjustment be made at all, without taking into view indirect and remote considerations, which will rarely prevail over the immediate interest which one party may find in disregarding the rights of another, or the good of the whole.

The inference to which we are brought, is, that the *causes* of faction cannot be removed; and that relief is only to be sought in the means of controlling its *effects*.

If a faction consists of less than a majority, relief is supplied by the republican principle, which enables the majority to defeat its sinister views by regular vote: It may clog the administration, it may convulse the society; but it will be unable to execute and mask its violence under the forms of the Constitution. When a majority is included in a faction, the form of popular government on the other hand enables it to sacrifice to its ruling passion or interest, both the public good and the rights of other citizens. To secure the public good, and private rights, against the danger of such a faction, and at the same time to preserve the spirit and the form of popular government, is then the great object to which our inquiries are directed: Let me add that it is the great desideratum, by which alone this form of government can be rescued from the opprobrium under which it has so long labored, and be recommended to the esteem and adoption of mankind.

By what means is this object attainable? Evidently by one of two only. Either the existence of the same passion or interest in a majority at the same time, must be prevented; or the majority, having such co-existent passion or interest, must be rendered, by their number and local situation, unable to concert and carry into effect schemes of oppression. If the impulse and the opportunity be suffered to coincide, we well know that neither moral nor religious motives can be relied on as an adequate control. They are not found to be such on the injustice and violence of individuals, and lose their efficacy in proportion to the number combined together; that is, in proportion as their efficacy becomes needful.

From this view of the subject, it may be concluded, that a pure Democracy, by which I mean, a Society, consisting of a small number of citizens, who assemble and administer the Government in person, can admit of no cure for the mischiefs of faction. A common passion or interest will, in almost every case, be felt by a majority of the whole; a communication and concert results from the form of Government itself; and there is nothing to check the inducements to sacrifice the weaker party, or an obnoxious individual. Hence it is, that such Democracies have ever been spectacles of turbulence and contention; have ever been found incompatible with personal security, or the rights of property; and have in general been as short in their lives, as they have been violent in their deaths. Theoretic politicians, who have patronized this species of Government, have erroneously supposed, that by reducing mankind to a perfect equality in their political rights, they would, at the same time, be perfectly equalized and assimilated in their possessions, their opinions, and their passions.

A republic, by which I mean a government in which the scheme of representation takes place, opens a different prospect, and promises the cure for which we are seeking. Let us examine the points in which it varies from pure democracy, and we shall comprehend both the nature of the cure and the efficacy which it must derive from the union.

The two great points of difference, between a democracy and a republic, are, first, the delegation of the government, in the latter, to a small number of citizens, elected by the rest; second, the greater number of citizens, and greater sphere of country, over which the latter may be extended.

The effect of the first difference is, on the one hand, to refine and enlarge the public views, by passing them through the medium of a chosen body of citizens, whose wisdom may best discern the true interest of their country, and whose patriotism and love of justice, will be least likely to sacrifice it to temporary or partial considerations.

Under such a regulation, it may well happen, that the public voice, pronounced by the representatives of the people, will be more consonant to the public good, than if pronounced by the people themselves, convened for the purpose. On the other hand, the effect may be inverted. Men of factious tempers, of local prejudices, or of sinister designs, may by intrigue, by corruption, or by other means, first obtain the suffrages, and then betray the interest of the people. The question resulting is, whether small or extensive republics are most favorable to the election of proper guardians of the public weal, and it is clearly decided in favor of the latter by two obvious considerations.

In the first place, it is to be remarked that, however small the republic may be, the representatives must be raised to a certain number, in order to guard against the cabals of a few; and that however large it may be, they must be limited to a certain number, in order to guard against the confusion of a multitude. Hence, the number of representatives in the two cases not being in proportion to that of the constituents, and being proportionally greatest in the small republic, it follows, that if the proportion of fit characters be not less in the large than in the small republic, the former will present a greater option, and consequently a greater probability of a fit choice.

In the next place, as each Representative will be chosen by a greater number of citizens in the large than in the small Republic, it will be more difficult for unworthy candidates to practise with success the vicious arts, by which elections are too often carried; and the suffrages of the people being more free, will be more likely to center on men who possess the most attractive merit, and the most diffusive and established characters.

It must be confessed, that in this, as in most other cases, there is a mean, on both sides of which inconveniences will be found to lie. By enlarging too much the number of electors, you render the representatives too little acquainted with all their local circumstances and lesser interests; as by reducing it too much, you render him unduly attached to these, and too little fit to comprehend and pursue great and national objects. The Federal Constitution forms a happy combination in this respect; the great and aggregate interests being referred to the national, the local and particular, to the state legislatures.

The other point of difference is, the greater number of citizens and extent of territory which may be brought within the compass of Republican, than of Democratic Government; and it is this circumstance principally which renders factious combinations less to be dreaded in the former, than in the latter. The smaller the society, the fewer probably will be the distinct parties and interests composing it; the fewer the distinct parties and interests, the more frequently will a majority be found of the same party; and the smaller the number of individuals composing a majority, and the smaller the compass within which they are placed, the more easily they will concert and execute their plans of oppression. Extend the sphere, and you take in a greater variety of parties and interests; you make it less probable that a majority of the whole will have a common motive to invade the rights of other citizens; or if such a common motive exists, it will be more difficult for all who feel it to discover their own strength, and to act in unison with each other. Besides other impediments, it may be remarked, that where there is a consciousness of unjust or dishonorable purposes, communication is always checked by distrust, in proportion to the number whose concurrence is necessary.

Hence it clearly appears, that the same advantage, which a Republic has over a Democracy, in controlling the effects of factions, is enjoyed by a large over a small Republic—is enjoyed by the Union over the States composing it. Does this advantage consist in the substitution of Representatives, whose enlightened views and virtuous sentiments render them superior to local prejudices, and to schemes of injustice? It will not be denied, that the Representation of the Union will be most likely to possess these requisite endowments. Does it consist in the greater security afforded by a greater variety of parties, against the event of any one party being able to out-number and oppress the rest? In an equal degree does the increase variety of parties, comprised within the Union, increase this security? Does it, in fine, consist in the greater obstacles opposed to the concert and accomplishment of the secret wishes of an unjust and interested majority? Here, again, the extent of the Union gives it the most palpable advantage.

The influence of factious leaders may kindle a flame within their particular States, but will be unable to spread a general conflagration through the other States: a religious sect, may degenerate into a political faction in a part of the Confederacy but the variety of sects dispersed over the entire face of it, must secure the national Councils against any danger from that source: a rage for paper money, for an abolition of debts, for an equal division of property, or for any other improper or wicked project, will be less apt to pervade the whole body of the Union, than a particular member of it; in the same proportion as such a malady is more likely to taint a particular county or district, than an entire State.

In the extent and proper structure of the Union, therefore, we behold a Republican remedy for the diseases most incident to Republican Government. And according to the degree of pleasure and pride, we feel in being Republicans, ought to be our zeal in cherishing the spirit, and supporting the character of Federalists.

PUBLIUS

The *Federalist* No. 51

February 6, 1788

James Madison

To the People of the State of New York.

To what expedient then shall we finally resort for maintaining in practice the necessary partition of power among the several departments, as laid down in the constitution? The only answer that can be given is, that as all these exterior provisions are found to be inadequate, the defect must be supplied, by so contriving the interior structure of the government, as that its several constituent parts may, by their mutual relations, be the means of keeping each other in their proper places. Without presuming to undertake a full development of this important idea, I will hazard a few general observations, which may perhaps place it in a clearer light, and enable us to form a more correct judgment of the principles and structure of the government planned by the convention.

In order to lay a due foundation for that separate and distinct exercise of the different powers of government, which to a certain extent, is admitted on all hands to be essential to the preservation of liberty, it is evident that each department should have a will of its own; and consequently should be so constituted, that the members of each should have as little agency as possible in the appointment of the members of the others. Were this principle rigorously adhered to, it would require that all the appointments for the supreme executive, legislative, and judiciary magistracies, should be drawn from the same fountain of authority, the people, through channels, having no communication whatever with one another. Perhaps such a plan of constructing the several departments would be less difficult in practice than in it may in contemplation appear. Some difficulties however, and some additional expense, would attend the execution of it. Some deviations therefore from the principle must be admitted. In the constitution of the judiciary department in particular, it might be inexpedient to insist rigorously on the principle; first, because peculiar qualifications being essential in the members, the primary consideration ought to be to select that mode of choice, which best secures these qualifications; secondly, because the permanent tenure by which the appointments are held in that department, must soon destroy all sense of dependence on the authority conferring them.

It is equally evident that the members of each department should be as little dependent as possible on those of the others, for the emoluments annexed to their offices. Were the executive magistrate, or the judges, not independent of the legislature in this particular, their independence in every other would be merely nominal.

But the great security against a gradual concentration of the several powers in the same department, consists in giving to those who administer each department, the necessary constitutional means, and personal motives, to resist encroachments of the others. The provision for defense must in this, as in all other cases, be made commensurate to the danger of attack. Ambition must be made to counteract ambition. The interest of the man must be connected with the constitutional right of the place. It may be a reflection on human nature, that such devices should be necessary to control the abuses of government. But what is government itself but the greatest of all reflections on human nature? If men were angels, no government would be necessary. If angels were to govern men, neither external nor internal controls on government would be necessary. In framing a government which is to be administered by men over men, the great difficulty lies in this: You must first enable the government to control the governed; and in the next place, oblige it to control itself. A dependence on the people is no doubt the primary control on the government; but experience has taught mankind the necessity of auxiliary precautions.

This policy of supplying by opposite and rival interests, the defect of better motives, might be traced through the whole system of human affairs, private as well as public. We see it particularly displayed in all the subordinate distributions of power; where the constant aim is to divide and arrange the several offices in such a manner as that each may be a check on the other; that the private interest of every individual, may be a sentinel over the public rights. These inventions of prudence cannot be less requisite in the distribution of the supreme powers of the state.

But it is not possible to give each department an equal power of self defense. In republican government the legislative authority, necessarily, predominates. The remedy for this inconvenience is, to divide the legislative into different branches; and to render them by different modes of election, and different principles of action, as little connected with each other, as the nature of their common functions, and their common dependence on the society, will admit. It may even be necessary to guard against dangerous encroachments by still further precautions. As the weight of the legislative authority requires that it should be thus divided, the weakness of the executive may require, on the other hand, that it should be fortified. An absolute negative, on the legislature, appears at first view to be the natural defense with which the executive magistrate should be armed. But perhaps it would be neither altogether safe, nor alone sufficient. On ordinary occasions, it might not be exerted with the requisite firmness, and on extraordinary occasions, it might be prefidiously abused. May not this defect of an absolute negative be supplied, by some qualified connection between this weaker department, and the weaker branch of the stronger department, by which the latter may be led to support the constitutional rights of the former, without being too much detached from the rights of its own department?

If the principles on which these observations are founded be just, as I persuade myself they are, and they be applied as a criterion, to the several state constitutions, and to the federal constitution, it will be found, that if the latter does not perfectly correspond with them, the former are infinitely less able to bear such a test.

There are moreover two considerations particularly applicable to the federal system of America, which place the system in a very interesting point of view.

First. In a single republic, all the power surrendered by the people, is submitted to the administration of a single government; and usurpations are guarded against by a division of the government into distinct and separate departments. In the compound republic of America, the power surrendered by the people, is first divided between two distinct governments, and then the portion allotted to each, subdivided among distinct and separate departments. Hence a double security arises to the rights of the people. The different governments will control each other; at the same time that each will be controlled by itself.

Second. It is of great importance in a republic, not only to guard the society against the oppression of its rulers; but to guard one part of the society against the injustice of the other part. Different interests necessarily exist in different classes of citizens. If a majority be united by a common interest, the rights of the minority will be insecure. There are but two methods of providing against this evil: The one by creating a will in the community independent of the majority, that is, of the society itself, the other by comprehending in the society so many separate descriptions of citizens, as will render an unjust combination of a majority of the whole, very improbable, if not impracticable. The first method prevails in all governments possessing an hereditary or self appointed authority. This at best is but a precarious security; because a power independent of the society may as well espouse the unjust views of the major, as the rightful interests, of the minor party, and may possibly be turned against both parties.

The second method will be exemplified in the federal republic of the United States. While all authority in it will be derived from and dependent on the society, the society itself will be broken into so many parts, interests and classes of citizens, that the rights of individuals or of the minority, will be in little danger from interested combinations of the majority. In a free government, the security for civil rights must be the same as for religious rights. It consists in the one case in the multiplicity of interests, and in the other, in the multiplicity of sects. The degree of security in both cases will depend on the number of interests and sects; and this may be presumed to depend on the extent of country and number of people comprehended under the same government. This view of the subject must particularly recommend a proper federal system to all the sincere and considerate friends of republican government: Since it shows that in exact proportion as the territory of the union may be formed into more circumscribed confederacies or states, oppressive combinations of a majority will be facilitated, the best security under the republican form, for the rights of every class of citizens, will be diminished; and consequently, the stability and independence of some member of the government, the only other security, must be proportionally increased. Justice is the end of government. It is the end of civil society. It ever has been, and ever will be pursued, until it be obtained, or until liberty be lost in the pursuit. In a society under the forms of which the stronger faction can readily unite and oppress the weaker, anarchy may as truly be said to reign, as in a state of nature where the weaker individual is not secured against the violence of the stronger: And as in the latter state even the stronger individuals are prompted by the uncertainty of their condition, to submit to a government which may protect the weak as well as themselves: So in the former state, will the more powerful factions or parties be gradually induced by a like motive, to wish for a government which will protect all parties, the weaker as well as the more powerful. It can be little doubted, that if the state of Rhode Island was separated from the confederacy, and left to itself, the insecurity of rights under the popular form of government within such narrow limits, would be displayed by such reiterated oppressions of factious majorities, that some power altogether independent of the people would soon be called for by the voice of the very factions whose misrule had proved the necessity of it. In the extended republic of the United States, and among the great variety of interests, parties and sects which it embraces, a coalition of a majority of the whole society could seldom take place on any other principles than those of justice and the general good; and there being thus less danger to a minor from the will of the major party, there must be less pretext also, to provide for the security of the former, by introducing into the government a will not dependent on the latter; or in other words, a will independent of the society itself. It is no less certain than it is important, notwithstanding the contrary opinions which have been entertained, that the larger the society, provided it lie within a practicable sphere, the more duly capable it will be of self government. And happily for the *republican cause*, the practicable sphere may be carried to a very great extent, by a judicious modification and mixture of the *federal principle*.

PUBLIUS

Presidents and Congresses, 1789–2017

Year	President and Vice President	Party of President	Congress	House		Senate	
				Majority Party	Minority Party	Majority Party	Minority Party
1789–1797	**George Washington**	None	1st	38 Admin	26 Opp	17 Admin	9 Opp
	John Adams		2d	37 Fed	33 Dem-Rep	16 Fed	13 Dem-Rep
			3d	**57 Dem-Rep**	**48 Fed**	17 Fed	13 Dem-Rep
			4th	54 Fed	52 Dem-Rep	19 Fed	13 Dem-Rep
1797–1801	**John Adams**	Federalist	5th	58 Fed	48 Dem-Rep	20 Fed	12 Dem-Rep
	Thomas Jefferson		6th	64 Fed	42 Dem-Rep	19 Fed	13 Dem-Rep
1801–1809	**Thomas Jefferson**	Dem-Rep	7th	69 Dem-Rep	36 Fed	18 Dem-Rep	13 Fed
	Aaron Burr–(to 1805)		8th	102 Dem-Rep	39 Fed	25 Dem-Rep	9 Fed
	George Clinton		9th	116 Dem-Rep	25 Fed	27 Dem-Rep	7 Fed
	(to 1809)		10th	118 Dem-Rep	24 Fed	28 Dem-Rep	6 Fed
1809–1817	**James Madison**	Dem-Rep	11th	94 Dem-Rep	48 Fed	28 Dem-Rep	6 Fed
	George Clinton (to 1813)		12th	108 Dem-Rep	36 Fed	30 Dem-Rep	6 Fed
	Elbridge Gerry		13th	112 Dem-Rep	68 Fed	27 Dem-Rep	9 Fed
	(to 1817)		14th	117 Dem-Rep	65 Fed	25 Dem-Rep	11 Fed
1817–1825	**James Monroe**	Dem-Rep	15th	141 Dem-Rep	42 Fed	34 Dem-Rep	10 Fed
	Daniel D. Tompkins		16th	156 Dem-Rep	27 Fed	35 Dem-Rep	7 Fed
			17th	158 Dem-Rep	25 Fed	44 Dem-Rep	4 Fed
			18th	187 Dem-Rep	26 Fed	44 Dem-Rep	4 Fed
1825–1829	**John Quincy Adams**	Nat-Rep	19th	105 Admin	97 Jack	26 Admin	20 Jack
	John C. Calhoun		20th	**119 Jack**	**94 Admin**	**28 Jack**	**20 Admin**
1829–1837	**Andrew Jackson**	Democrat	21st	139 Dem	74 Nat Rep	26 Dem	22 Nat Rep
	John C. Calhoun (to 1833)		22d	141 Dem	58 Nat Rep	25 Dem	21 Nat Rep
	Martin Van Buren (to 1837)		23d	147 Dem	53 AntiMas	20 Dem	20 Nat Rep
1837–1841	**Martin Van Buren**	Democrat	25th	108 Dem	107 Whig	30 Dem	18 Whig
	Richard M. Johnson		26th	124 Dem	118 Whig	28 Dem	22 Whig
1841	**William H. Harrison** *	Whig					
	John Tyler						
1841–1845	**John Tyler**	Whig	27th	133 Whig	102 Dem	28 Whig	22 Dem
	(VP vacant)		28th	**142 Dem**	**79 Whig**	28 Whig	25 Dem
1845–1849	**James K. Polk**	Democrat	29th	143 Dem	77 Whig	31 Dem	25 Whig
	George M. Dallas		30th	**115 Whig**	**108 Dem**	36 Dem	21 Whig
1849–1850	**Zachary Taylor***	Whig	31st	**112 Dem**	**109 Whig**	**35 Dem**	**25 Whig**
	Millard Fillmore						
1850–1853	**Millard Fillmore**	Whig	32d	**140 Dem**	**88 Whig**	**35 Dem**	**24 Whig**
	(VP vacant)						

NOTES: Only members of two major parties in Congress are shown; omitted are independents, members of minor parties, and vacancies. Party balance as of beginning of Congress.

Congresses in which one or both chambers are controlled by the president's party show the major-party distribution for the chamber(s) in color.

During administration of George Washington and (in part) John Quincy Adams, Congress was not organized by formal parties; the split shown is between supporters and opponents of the administration.

ABBREVIATIONS: **Admin** = Administration supporters; **AntiMas** = Anti-Masonic; **Dem** = Democratic; **Dem-Rep** = Democratic-Republican; **Fed** = Federalist; **Jack** = Jacksonian Democrats; **Nat Rep** = National Republican; **Opp** = Opponents of administration; **Rep** = Republican; **Union** = Unionist; **Whig** = Whig.

*Died in office.

Year	President and Vice President	Party of President	Congress	House		Senate	
				Majority Party	Minority Party	Majority Party	Minority Party
1853–1857	**Franklin Pierce** William R. King	Democrat	33d 34th	159 Dem **108 Rep**	71 Whig **83 Dem**	38 Dem 40 Dem	22 Whig 15 Rep
1857–1861	**James Buchanan** John C. Breckinridge	Democrat	35th 36th	118 Dem **114 Rep**	92 Rep **92 Dems**	36 Dem 36 Dem	20 Rep 26 Rep
1861–1865	**Abraham Lincoln*** Hannibal Hamlin (to 1865) Andrew Johnson (1865)	Republican	37th 38th	105 Rep 102 Rep	43 Dem 75 Dem	31 Rep 36 Rep	10 Dem 9 Dem
1865–1869	**Andrew Johnson** (VP vacant)	Republican	39th 40th	149 Union 143 Rep	42 Dem 49 Dem	42 Union 42 Rep	10 Dem 11 Dem
1869–1877	**Ulysses S. Grant** Schuyler Colfax (to 1873) Henry WIlson (to 1877)	Republican	41st 42d 43d 44th	149 Rep 134 Rep 194 Rep **169 Dem**	63 Dem 104 Dem 92 Dem **109 Rep**	56 Rep 52 Rep 49 Rep 45 Rep	11 Dem 17 Dem 19 Dem 29 Dem
1877–1881	**Rutherford B. Hayes** William A. Wheeler	Republican	45th 46th	**153 Dem** **149 Dem**	**140 Rep** **130 Rep**	39 Rep 42 Dem	36 Dem 33 Rep
1881	**James A. Garfield*** Chester A. Arthur	Republican	47th	147 Rep	135 Dem	37 Rep	37 Dem
1881–1885	**Chester A. Arthur** (VP vacant)	Republican	48th	197 Dem	118 Rep	38 Rep	36 Rep
1885–1889	**Grover Cleveland** Thomas A. Hendricks	Democrat	49th 50th	183 Dem 169 Dem	140 Rep 152 Rep	**43 Rep** **39 Rep**	**34 Dem** **37 Dem**
1889–1893	**Benjamin Harrison** Levi P. Morton	Republican	51st 52d	166 Rep **235 Dem**	159 Dem **88 Rep**	39 Rep 47 Rep	37 Dem 39 Dem
1893–1897	**Grover Cleveland** Adlai E. Stevenson	Democrat	53d 54th	218 Dem **244 Rep**	127 Rep **105 Dem**	44 Dem **43 Rep**	38 Rep **39 Dem**
1897–1901	**William McKinley*** Garret A. Hobart (to 1901) Theodore Roosevelt (1901)	Republican	55th 56th	204 Rep 185 Rep	113 Rep 163 Rep	47 Rep 53 Rep	34 Dem 26 Dem
1901–1909	**Theodore Roosevelt** (VP vacant, 1901–1905) Charles W. Fairbanks (1905–1909)	Republican	57th 58th 59th 60th	197 Rep 208 Rep 250 Rep 222 Rep	151 Dem 178 Dem 136 Dem 164 Dem	55 Rep 57 Rep 57 Rep 61 Rep	31 Dem 33 Dem 33 Dem 31 Dem
1909–1913	**William Howard Taft** James S. Sherman	Republican	61st 62d	219 Rep **228 Dem**	172 Dem **161 Rep**	61 Rep 51 Rep	32 Dem 41 Dem
1913–1921	**Woodrow Wilson** Thomas R. Marshall	Democrat	63d 64th 65th **66th**	291 Dem 230 Dem 216 Dem **240 Rep**	127 Rep 196 Rep 210 Rep **190 Dem**	51 Dem 56 Dem 53 Dem **49 Rep**	44 Rep 40 Rep 42 Rep **47 Dem**
1921–1923	**Warren G. Harding*** Calvin Coolidge	Republican	67th	301 Rep	131 Dem	59 Rep	37 Dem

*Died in office.

Year	President and Vice President	Party of President	Congress	House		Senate	
				Majority Party	Minority Party	Majority Party	Minority Party
1923–1929	**Calvin Coolidge**	Republican	68th	225 Rep	205 Dem	51 Rep	43 Dem
	(VP vacant, 1923–1925)		69th	247 Rep	183 Dem	56 Rep	39 Dem
	Charles G. Dawes (1925–1929)		70th	237 Rep	195 Dem	49 Rep	46 Dem
1929–1933	**Herbert Hoover**	Republican	71st	267 Rep	167 Dem	56 Rep	39 Dem
	Charles Curtis		72d	**220 Dem**	**214 Rep**	48 Rep	47 Dem
1933–1945	**Franklin D. Roosevelt***	Democrat	73d	310 Dem	117 Rep	60 Dem	35 Rep
	John N. Garner (1933–1941)		74th	319 Dem	103 Rep	69 Dem	25 Rep
			75th	331 Dem	89 Rep	76 Dem	16 Rep
	Henry A. Wallace (1941–1945)		76th	261 Dem	164 Rep	69 Dem	23 Rep
			77th	268 Dem	162 Rep	66 Dem	28 Rep
	Harry S. Truman (1945)		78th	218 Dem	208 Rep	58 Dem	37 Rep
1945–1953	**Harry S. Truman**	Democrat	79th	242 Dem	190 Rep	56 Dem	38 Rep
	VP vacant, 1945–1949		80th	**245 Rep**	**188 Dem**	**51 Rep**	**45 Dem**
	Alben W. Barkley (1949–1953)		81st	263 Dem	171 Rep	54 Dem	42 Rep
			82d	234 Dem	199 Rep	49 Dem	47 Rep
1953–1961	**Dwight D. Eisenhower**	Republican	83d	221 Rep	211 Dem	48 Rep	47 Dem
	Richard M. Nixon		84th	**232 Dem**	**203 Rep**	**48 Dem**	**47 Rep**
			85th	**233 Dem**	**200 Rep**	**49 Dem**	**47 Rep**
			86th	**283 Dem**	**153 Rep**	**64 Dem**	**34 Rep**
1961–1963	**John F. Kennedy***	Democrat	87th	263 Dem	174 Rep	65 Dem	35 Rep
	Lyndon B. Johnson						
1963–1969	**Lyndon B. Johnson**	Democrat	88th	258 Dem	177 Rep	67 Dem	33 Rep
	(VP vacant, 1963–1965)		89th	295 Dem	140 Rep	68 Dem	32 Rep
	Hubert H. Humphrey (1965–1969)		90th	247 Dem	187 Rep	64 Dem	36 Rep
1969–1974	**Richard M. Nixon**†	Republican	91st	**243 Dem**	**192 Rep**	**57 Dem**	**43 Rep**
	Spiro T. Agnew††		92d	**254 Dem**	**180 Rep**	**54 Dem**	**44 Rep**
	Gerald R. Ford§						
1974–1977	**Gerald R. Ford**	Republican	93d	**239 Dem**	**192 Rep**	**56 Dem**	**42 Rep**
	Nelson A. Rockefeller		94th	**291 Dem**	**144 Rep**	**60 Dem**	**37 Rep**
1977–1981	**Jimmy Carter**	Democrat	95th	292 Dem	143 Rep	61 Dem	38 Rep
	Walter Mondale		96th	276 Dem	157 Rep	58 Dem	41 Rep

*Died in office. †*Resigned from the presidency* ††*Resigned from the vice presidency.* §*Appointed vice president.*

Year	President and Vice President	Party of President	Congress	House		Senate	
				Majority Party	Minority Party	Majority Party	Minority Party
1981–1989	**Ronald Reagan** George Bush	Republican	97th 98th 99th 100th	**243 Dem** **269 Dem** **253 Dem** **257 Dem**	**192 Rep** **165 Rep** **182 Rep** **178 Rep**	53 Rep 54 Rep 53 Rep **54 Dem**	46 Dem 46 Dem 47 Dem **46 Rep**
1989–1993	**George Bush** Dan Quayle	Republican	101st 102d	**262 Dem** 267 Dem	**173 Rep** 167 Rep	**55 Dem** 56 Dem	**45 Rep** 44 Rep
1993-2001	**Bill Clinton** Albert Gore, Jr.	Democrat	103d 104th 105th 106th	258 Dem 230 Rep 228 Rep 223 Rep	176 Rep **204 Dem** **206 Dem** **211 Dem**	57 Dem **53 Rep** **55 Rep** **54 Rep**	43 Rep **47 Dem** **45 Dem** **46 Dem**
2001-2009	**George W. Bush** Dick Cheney	Republican	107th 108th 109th 110th	220 Rep 229 Rep 233 Rep **229 Dem**	215 Dem 204 Dem 206 Dem **196 Rep**	50 Rep 51 Rep 55 Rep **51 Dem**	50 Dem 48 Dem 44 Dem **49 Rep**
2009–2017	**Barack Obama** Joe Biden	Democrat	111th 112th 113th** **114th*****	256 Dem **242 Rep** **234 Rep** **246 Rep**	179 Rep **193 Dem** **201 Dem** **188 Dem**	60 Dem 51 Dem 45 Rep **54 Rep**	40 Rep 47 Rep 53 Dem **44 Dem**
2017–2021	**Donald Trump** Mike Pence	Republican	**115th** 116th****	**241 Rep** 235 Dem	**194 Dem** 198 Rep	**52 Rep** **47 Dem**	**46 Dem** **53 Rep**
2021–	**Joe Biden** Kamala Harris	Democrat	117th	222D	205R (8 races not yet called)*****	50R	48D (2 races not yet called)*****

***In the 113th through 117th Congresses, there were 2 Independents in the Senate that caucused with Democrats.*
****In 2015, there was one vacancy in the House.*
*****In the early 116th Congress, there were two vacancies in the House.*
******As of late November 2020.*

Glossary

501(c)4 group A social welfare organization that can devote no more than 50 percent of its funds to politics. Sometimes referred to as "dark money" groups because they do not have to disclose their donors.

527 organizations Organizations under section 527 of the Internal Revenue Code that raise and spend money to advance political causes.

Activist approach The view that judges should discern the general principles underlying laws or the Constitution and apply them to modern circumstances.

Activists People who tend to participate in all forms of politics.

Ad hoc structure Several subordinates, cabinet officers, and committees report directly to the president on different matters.

Adversarial press The tendency of the national media to be suspicious of officials and eager to reveal unflattering stories about them.

Affective polarization Tendency of partisans to dislike and distrust those from the other party.

Affirmative action Laws or administrative regulations that require a business firm, government agency, labor union, school, college, or other organization to take positive steps to increase the number of African Americans, other minorities, or women in its membership.

Agenda-setting (gatekeeping) The ability of the news media, by printing stories about some topics and not others, to shape the public agenda.

Amicus curiae A brief submitted by a "friend of the court."

Antifederalists Those who favor a weaker national government.

Appropriation A legislative grant of money to finance a government program or agency.

Articles of Confederation A weak constitution that governed America during the Revolutionary War.

Assistance program A government program financed by general income taxes that provides benefits to poor citizens without requiring contributions from them.

Australian ballot A government-printed ballot of uniform dimensions to be cast in secret that many states adopted around 1890 to reduce voting fraud associated with party-printed ballots cast in public.

Authority The right to use power.

Authorization legislation Legislative permission to begin or continue a government program or agency.

Battleground states The most competitive states in the presidential election that either candidate could win; also called swing states.

Benefit A satisfaction that people believe they will enjoy if a policy is adopted.

Bicameral legislature A lawmaking body made up of two chambers or parts.

Bill of attainder A law that declares a person, without a trial, to be guilty of a crime.

Bill of Rights First 10 amendments to the Constitution.

Bipolar world A political landscape with two superpowers.

Brief A written statement by an attorney that summarizes a case and the laws and rulings that support it.

Budget A document that states income, spending levels, and the allocation of spending among purposes.

Budget resolution A congressional decision that states the maximum amount of money the government should spend.

Bully pulpit The president's use of prestige and visibility to guide or mobilize the American public.

Bureaucracy A large, complex organization composed of appointed officials.

Bureaucratic view View that the government is dominated by appointed officials.

Cabinet The heads of the 15 executive branch departments of the federal government.

Categorical grants Federal grants for specific purposes, such as building an airport.

Caucus (Political Parties) A meeting of party followers in which party delegates are selected.

Caucus (Congress) An association of congressional members created to advance a political ideology or a regional, ethnic, or economic interest.

Charitable choice Name given to four federal laws passed in the late 1990s specifying the conditions under which nonprofit religious organizations could compete to administer certain social service delivery and welfare programs.

Checks and balances Constitutional ability of multiple branches of government to limit each other's power.

Circular structure Several of the president's assistants report directly to him.

Civic competence A belief that one can affect government policies.

Civic duty A belief that one has an obligation to participate in civic and political affairs.

Civil disobedience Opposing a law one considers unjust by peacefully disobeying it and accepting the resultant punishment.

Civil forfeiture A procedure in which law-enforcement officers take assets from people who are suspected of illegal activity, but have not been charged with a crime.

Civil liberties Rights—chiefly, rights to be free of government interference—accorded to an individual by the Constitution: free speech, free press, and so on.

Civil rights The rights of people to be treated without unreasonable or unconstitutional differences.

Civil society Voluntary action that makes cooperation easier.

Class-action suit A case brought by someone to help both him-or herself and all others who are similarly situated.

Class-consciousness A belief that one is a member of an economic group whose interests are opposed to people in other such groups.

Class view View that the government is dominated by capitalists.

Clear-and-present-danger test Law should not punish speech unless there was a clear and present danger of producing harmful actions.

Client politics A policy in which one small group benefits and almost everybody pays.

Closed primary A primary election where only registered party members may vote for the party's nominee.

Closed rule An order from the House Rules Committee that sets a time limit on debate; forbids a bill from being amended on the floor.

Cloture rule A rule used by the Senate to end or limit debate.

Coalition An alliance of groups.

Coattails The tendency of candidates to win more votes in an election because of the presence at the top of the ticket of a better-known candidate, such as the president.

Committee clearance The ability of a congressional committee to review and approve certain agency decisions in advance and without passing a law.

Competitive service The government offices to which people are appointed on the basis of merit, as ascertained by a written exam or by applying certain selection criteria.

Concurrent powers Powers shared by the national and state governments.

Concurrent resolution An expression of opinion without the force of law that requires the approval of both the House and the Senate, but not the president.

Concurring opinion A signed opinion in which one or more members agree with the majority view but for different reasons.

Conditions of aid Terms set by the national government that states must meet if they are to receive certain federal funds.

Confederation or confederal system A system of government where state governments are sovereign, and the national government can do only what the states permit.

Conference committee Joint committees appointed to resolve differences in the Senate and House versions of the same bill.

Congressional campaign committee A party committee in Congress that provides funds to members and would-be members.

Conservative coalition An alliance between Republicans and conservative Democrats.

Constitutional Convention A meeting in Philadelphia in 1787 that produced a new constitution.

Constitutional court A federal court, authorized by Article III of the Constitution, that keeps judges in office during good behavior and prevents their salaries from being reduced. They include the Supreme Court (created by the Constitution) and appellate and district courts created by Congress.

Containment The belief that the United States should resist the expansion of aggressive nations, especially the former Soviet Union.

Cooperative federalism Idea that the federal and state governments share power in many policy areas.

Cost A burden that people believe they must bear if a policy is adopted.

Cost overruns When the money actually paid to military suppliers exceeds the estimated costs.

Courts of appeals Federal courts that hear appeals from district courts; no trials.

Creedal passion view View that morally impassioned elites drive important political changes.

Critical or realignment periods A period when a major, lasting shift occurs in the popular coalition supporting one or both parties.

Debt ceiling A limit on how much money the federal government can borrow (by limiting the amount of debt it can issue).

De facto segregation Racial segregation that occurs not as a result of the law, but as a result of patterns of residential settlement.

Deficit The result of the government in one year spending more money than it takes in from taxes.

De jure segregation Racial segregation that is required by law.

Democracy The rule of the many.

Descriptive representation When citizens are represented by elected officials from their same racial/ethnic background.

Devolution The transfer of power from the national government to state and local governments.

Direct or participatory democracy A government in which all or most citizens participate directly.

Discharge petition A device by which any member of the House, after a committee has had the bill for 30 days, may petition to have it brought to the floor.

Discretionary authority The extent to which appointed bureaucrats can choose courses of action and make policies not spelled out in advance by laws.

Discretionary spending Spending that is not required to pay for contracts, interest on the national debt, or entitlement programs such as Social Security.

Disengagement The belief that the United States was harmed by its war in Vietnam and so should avoid supposedly similar events.

Dissenting opinion A signed opinion in which one or more justices disagree with the majority view.

District courts The lowest federal courts; federal trials can be held only here.

Diversity cases Cases involving citizens of different states who can bring suit in federal courts.

Divided government One party controls the White House and another party controls one or both houses of Congress.

Divided government One political party controls the White House and another political party controls one or both chambers of Congress.

Division vote A congressional voting procedure in which members stand and are counted.

Double tracking A procedure to keep the Senate going during a filibuster in which the disputed bill is shelved temporarily so that the Senate can get on with other business.

Dual federalism Doctrine holding that the national government is supreme in its sphere, the states are supreme in theirs, and the two spheres should be kept separate.

Due process of law Denies the government the right, without due process, to deprive people of life, liberty, and property.

Earmark A provision in a law that provides a direct benefit to a client without the benefit having been reviewed on the merits by all of Congress.

Echo chamber Media environment in which people only hear messages they already agree with; they are also called filter bubbles.

Economic planning The belief that government plans, such as wage and price controls or the direction of investment, can improve the economy.

Electoral College The people chosen to cast each state's votes in a presidential election. Each state can cast one electoral vote for each senator and representative it has. The District of Columbia has three electoral votes, even though it cannot elect a representative or senator.

Elite Persons who possess a disproportionate share of some valued resource, such as money, prestige, or expertise.

Entitlements A claim for government funds that cannot be changed without violating the rights of the claimant.

Entrepreneurial politics A policy in which almost everybody benefits and a small group pays.

Enumerated powers Powers given to the national government alone.

Environmental impact statement (EIS) A report required by federal law that assesses the possible effect of a project on the environment if the project is subsidized in whole or part by federal funds.

Equality of opportunity Giving people an equal chance to succeed.

Equality of results Making certain that people achieve the same result.

Equal protection of the laws A standard of equal treatment that must be observed by the government.

Equal time rule An FCC rule that if a broadcaster sells time to one candidate, it must sell equal time to other candidates.

Establishment clause First Amendment ban on laws "respecting an establishment of religion."

Exclusionary rule Improperly gathered evidence may not be introduced in a criminal trial.

Executive order A presidential directive that calls for action within the executive branch.

Exit polls Polls based on interviews conducted on election day with randomly selected voters.

Ex post facto law A law that makes an act criminal even though the act was legal when it was committed.

Fact checking Efforts by news organizations to evaluate the veracity of statements by politicians and other public actors

Faction A group with a distinct political interest.

Fake news Manufactured stories typically designed to support a particular point of view or candidate.

Federal-question cases Cases concerning the Constitution, federal laws, or treaties.

Federalism Government authority shared by national and local governments.

Federalism Government authority shared by national and local governments.

Federalists Those who favor a stronger national government.

Federal system A system of government where the national and state governments share sovereignty.

Fee shifting A rule that allows a plaintiff to recover costs from the defendant if the plaintiff wins.

Filibuster An attempt to defeat a bill in the Senate by talking indefinitely, thus preventing the Senate from taking action on the bill.

Fiscal policy Managing the economy through the use of tax and spending laws.

Fiscal year For the federal government, October 1 through the following September 30.

Framing The way in which the news media, by focusing on some aspects of an issue, shapes how people view that issue.

Franking privilege The ability of members to mail letters to their constituents free of charge by substituting their facsimile signature for postage.

Free-exercise clause First Amendment requirement that law cannot prevent free exercise of religion.

Freedom of expression Right of people to speak, publish, and assemble.

Freedom of religion People shall be free to exercise their religion, and government may not establish a religion.

Free rider problem The tendency of individuals to avoid contributing to public goods.

Game frame The tendency of media to focus on political polls and strategy rather than on the issues.

Gender gap Difference in political views between men and women.

Gerrymandering Drawing the boundaries of legislative districts in bizarre or unusual shapes to favor one party.

Globalization The growing integration of the economies and societies of the world.

Gold plating The tendency of Pentagon officials to ask weapons contractors to meet excessively high requirements.

Good faith exception An error in gathering evidence sufficiently minor that it may be used in a trial.

Government by proxy Washington pays state and local governments and private groups to staff and administer federal programs.

Grandfather clause A clause in registration laws allowing people who do not meet registration requirements to vote if they or their ancestors had voted before 1867.

Grants-in-aid Money given by the national government to the states.

Grassroots lobbying Using the general public (rather than lobbyists) to contact government officials about a public policy.

Great Compromise Plan to have a popularly elected House based on state population and a state-selected Senate, with two members for each state.

Gridlock The inability of the government to act because rival parties control different parts of the government.

Gross domestic product The total value of all goods and services produced in an economy during a given year.

Habeas corpus An order to produce an arrested person before a judge.

Heuristics Informational shortcuts used by voters to make a decision.

Horse-race (scorekeeper) journalism News coverage that focuses on who is ahead rather than on the issues.

Human rights The belief that we should try to improve the lives of people in other countries.

Ideological interest groups Political organizations that attract members by appealing to their political convictions or principles.

Impeachment Charges against a president approved by a majority of the House of Representatives.

Impressionable years hypothesis Argument that political experiences during the teens and early 20s powerfully shape attitudes for the rest of the life cycle.

Incentive Something of value one cannot get without joining an organization.

Income inequality The extent to which income is unevenly distributed throughout society.

Incumbency advantage The tendency of incumbents to do better than otherwise similar challengers, especially in congressional elections.

Incumbent The person already holding an elective office.

Independent expenditures Spending by political action committees, corporations, or labor unions to help a party or candidate but done independent from the party or candidate.

Inevitable discovery The police can use evidence if it would inevitably have been discovered.

In forma pauperis A method whereby a poor person can have their case heard in federal court without charge.

Initiative Process that permits voters to put legislative measures directly on the ballot.

Insurance program A self-financing government program based on contributions that provide benefits to unemployed or retired persons.

Interest group An organization of people sharing a common interest or goal that seeks to influence public policy.

Interest group politics A policy in which one small group benefits and another small group pays.

Invisible primary Process by which candidates try to attract the support of key party leaders before an election begins.

Iron triangle A close relationship between an agency, a congressional committee, and an interest group.

Isolationism The belief that the United States should withdraw from world affairs.

Issue A conflict, real or apparent, between the interests, ideas, or beliefs of different citizens.

Issue network A network of people in Washington, D.C.-based interest groups, on congressional staffs, in universities and think tanks, and in the mass media, who regularly discuss and advocate public policies.

Joint committees Committees on which both senators and representatives serve.

Joint resolution A formal expression of congressional opinion that must be approved by both houses of Congress and by the president; constitutional amendments need not be signed by the president.

Judicial restraint approach The view that judges should decide cases strictly on the basis of the language of the laws and the Constitution.

Judicial review The power of courts to declare laws unconstitutional.

Judicial review The power of the courts to declare laws unconstitutional.

Keynesianism The belief the government must manage the economy by spending more money when in a recession and cutting spending when inflation occurs.

Laboratories of democracy Idea that different states can implement different policies, and the successful ones will spread.

Laissez-faire An economic theory that government should not regulate or interfere with commerce.

Legislative courts Courts created by Congress for specialized purposes, whose judges do not enjoy the protections of Article III of the Constitution.

Legislative veto The authority of Congress to block a presidential action after it has taken place. The Supreme Court has held that Congress does not have this power.

Legitimacy Political authority conferred by law or by a state or national constitution.

Libel Writing that falsely injures another person.

Line-item veto An executive's ability to block a particular provision in a bill passed by the legislature.

Literacy test A requirement that citizens show that they can read before registering to vote.

Litmus test An examination of the political ideology of a nominated judge.

Lobbyist A person who tries to influence legislation on behalf of an interest group.

Log-rolling A legislator supports a proposal favored by a colleague with reciprocal support for a proposal endorsed by the legislator.

Majoritarian politics A policy in which almost everybody benefits and almost everybody pays.

Majority-minority districts Congressional district where a majority of voters are racial/ethnic minorities.

Majority leader The legislative leader elected by party members holding the majority of seats in the House or the Senate.

Mandates Terms set by the national government that states must meet whether or not they accept federal grants.

Mandatory spending Money that the government is required to spend by law.

Marginal districts Districts in which candidates elected to the House of Representatives win in close elections (typically, less than 55 percent of the vote).

Material incentives Money or things valued in monetary terms.

Means test An income qualification program that determines whether one is eligible for benefits under government programs reserved for lower-income groups.

Military-industrial complex An alleged alliance between military leaders and corporate leaders.

Minority leader The legislative leader elected by party members holding a minority of seats in the House or the Senate.

Momentum The boost that a candidate gains in future contests after an election victory (especially an upset win). Sometimes also called the bandwagon effect.

Monetarist One who believes that inflation occurs when too much money is chasing too few goods.

Monetary policy Managing the economy by altering the supply of money and interest rates.

Mugwumps or progressives Republican Party faction of the 1890s to the 1910s, comprising reformers who opposed patronage.

Name-request job A job filled by a person whom an agency has already identified.

National chair Day-to-day party manager elected by the national committee.

National committee Delegates who run party affairs between national conventions.

National convention A meeting of party delegates held every four years, which nominates the party's candidate for president.

National debt The total deficit from the first presidency to the present.

"Necessary and proper" clause Section of the Constitution allowing Congress to pass all laws "necessary and proper" to its duties, and that has permitted Congress to exercise powers not specifically given to it (enumerated) by the Constitution.

New Jersey Plan Proposal to create a weak national government.

Nullification The doctrine that a state can declare null and void a federal law that, in the state's opinion, violates the Constitution.

Open primary A primary election where all voters (regardless of party membership) may vote for the party's nominee.

Open rule An order from the House Rules Committee that permits a bill to be amended on the floor.

Opinion of the Court A signed opinion of a majority of the Supreme Court.

Orthodox A belief that morality and religion ought to be of decisive importance.

Partisan identification A voter's long-term, stable attachment to one of the political parties.

Partisan polarization Heightened conflict between elected Democrats and Republicans

Partisanship An individual's identification with a party; whether they consider themselves a Democrat, Republican, or an Independent. Also called partisan identity.

Party sorting The alignment of partisanship and issue positions so that Democrats tend to take more liberal positions and Republicans tend to take more conservative ones.

Party vote A vote where most Democrats are on one side of the bill, and most Republicans are on the other.

Per curiam opinion A brief, unsigned court opinion.

Plaintiff The party that initiates a lawsuit.

Pluralist view View that competition among all affected interests shapes public policy.

Plurality system An electoral system in which the winner is the person who gets the most votes, even without receiving a majority; used in almost all American elections.

Pocket veto A bill fails to become law because the president did not sign it within 10 days before Congress adjourns.

Polarization A deep and wide conflict over some government policy.

Police powers State power to effect laws promoting health, safety, and morals.

Policy entrepreneurs Activists in or out of government who pull together a political majority on behalf of unorganized interests.

Political action committees (PACs) Committees set up by a corporation, labor union, or interest group that raise and spend campaign money from voluntary donations.

Political agenda Issues that people believe require governmental action.

Political cue A signal telling a legislator what values are at stake in a vote, and how the issue fits into the legislator's own political views or party agenda.

Political culture A patterned and sustained way of thinking about how political and economic life ought to be carried out.

Political elites Persons with a disproportionate share of political power.

Political ideology A more or less consistent set of beliefs about what policies government ought to pursue.

Political machines A party organization that recruits members by dispensing patronage.

Political participation The many different ways that people take part in politics and government.

Political party A group that seeks to elect candidates to public office.

Political question An issue the Supreme Court will allow the executive and legislative branches to decide.

Political socialization Process by which one's family influences one's political views.

Politics The activity by which an issue is agitated or settled.

Poll A survey of public opinion.

Poll tax A requirement that citizens pay a tax in order to register to vote.

Pork-barrel legislation Legislation that gives tangible benefits to constituents in several districts or states in the hope of winning their votes in return.

Positional issues Issues in which rival candidates have opposing views and that also divide voters.

Power elite view View that the government is dominated by a few top leaders, most of whom are outside of government.

Power The ability of one person to get another person to act in accordance with the first person's intentions.

Primary elections An election held to determine the nominee from a particular party.

Priming The ability of the news media to influence the factors individuals use to evaluate political elites.

Prior restraint Censorship of a publication.

Probable cause Reasonable cause for issuing a search warrant or making an arrest; more than mere suspicion.

Progressive A belief that personal freedom and solving social problems are more important than religion.

Prospective voting Voting for a candidate because you favor their ideas for handling issues.

Public-interest lobby A political organization whose goals will principally benefit nonmembers.

Public good Something of value that all individuals share, whether or not they contribute to it (such as clean air or water).

Public opinion How people think or feel about particular things.

Public safety exception The police can question a non-Mirandized suspect if there is an urgent concern for public safety.

Purposive incentive A benefit that comes from serving a cause or principle.

Pyramid structure A president's subordinates report to him through a clear chain of command headed by a chief of staff.

Question wording The way in which survey questions are phrased, which influences how respondents answer them.

Quorum The minimum number of members who must be present for business to be conducted in Congress.

Random sampling Method of selecting from a population in which each person has an equal probability of being selected.

Ratings Assessments of a representative's voting record on issues important to an interest group.

Recall Procedure whereby voters can remove an elected official from office.

Red tape Complex bureaucratic rules and procedures that must be followed to get something done.

Referendum Procedure enabling voters to reject a measure passed by the legislature.

Remedy A judicial order enforcing a right or redressing a wrong.

Representative democracy A government in which leaders make decisions by winning a competitive struggle for the popular vote.

Republic A government in which elected representatives make the decisions.

Reserved powers Powers given to the state government alone.

Restrictive rule An order from the House Rules Committee that permits certain kinds of amendments but not others to be made to a bill on the floor.

Retrospective voting Voting for a candidate because you like their past actions in office.

Riders Amendments on matters unrelated to a bill that are added to an important bill so that they will "ride" to passage through the Congress. When a bill has many riders, it is called a Christmas-tree bill.

Roll-call vote A congressional voting procedure that consists of members answering "yea" or "nay" to their names.

Safe districts Districts in which incumbents win by a comfortable margin.

Sampling error The difference between the results of random samples taken at the same time.

Search warrant A judge's order authorizing a search.

Select committees Congressional committees appointed for a limited time and purpose.

Selective exposure Consuming only those news stories with which one already agrees.

Selective incorporation process The process whereby the Court has applied most, but not all, parts of the Bill of Rights to the states.

Senatorial courtesy Tradition in the Senate of giving special consideration to the preferences of Senators from the state where a federal judicial nominee is to serve.

Separate-but-equal doctrine The doctrine established in *Plessy v. Ferguson* (1896) that African Americans could constitutionally be kept in separate but equal facilities.

Separation of powers Sharing of constitutional authority by multiple branches of government.

Sequester Automatic spending cuts.

Shays's Rebellion A 1787 rebellion in which ex-Revolutionary War soldiers attempted to prevent foreclosures of farms as a result of high interest rates and taxes.

Signing statement A presidential document that reveals what the president thinks of a new law and how it ought to be enforced.

Simple resolution An expression of opinion either in the House or Senate to settle procedural matters in either body.

Social movement A widely shared demand for change in some aspect of the social or political order.

Soft money Funds obtained by political parties that are spent on party activities, such as get-out-the-vote drives, but not on behalf of a specific candidate.

Solidary incentives The social rewards (sense of pleasure, status, or companionship) that lead people to join political organizations.

Sovereign immunity The rule that a citizen cannot sue the government without the government's consent.

Sovereignty The ultimate political author in a system.

Speaker The presiding officer of the House of Representatives and the leader of the majority party in the House.

Standing A legal rule stating who is authorized to start a lawsuit.

Standing committees Permanently established legislative committees that consider and are responsible for legislation within a certain subject area.

Stare decisis "Let the decision stand"; allowing prior rulings to control a current case.

Strict scrutiny The standard by which "suspect classifications" are judged. To be upheld, such a classification must be related to a "compelling government interest," be "narrowly tailored" to achieve that interest, and use the "least restrictive means" available.

Substantive representation Ability of citizens to elect officials who will enact into law policies that the citizens favor.

Super-delegates Party leaders and elected officials who become delegates to the national convention without having to run in primaries or caucuses.

Super PAC A group that raises and spends unlimited amounts of money from corporations, unions, and individuals but cannot coordinate its activities with campaigns in any way.

Supply-side theory The belief that lower taxes and fewer regulations will stimulate the economy.

Surge and decline Tendency for the president's party to do better in presidential election years when the president is at the top of the ticket (the surge), but to do worse in midterm election years when the president is not because many voters are less enthusiastic and stay home (the decline).

Suspect classification Classifications of people based on their race or ethnicity; laws so classifying people are subject to "strict scrutiny."

Symbolic speech An act that conveys a political message.

Teller vote A congressional voting procedure in which members pass between two tellers, the "yeas" first and the "nays" second.

Trial balloon Information leaked to the media to test public reaction to a possible policy.

Trust funds Funds for government programs collected and spent outside the regular government budget.

Two-party system An electoral system with two dominant parties that compete in national elections.

Unalienable A human right based on nature or God.

Unified government The same political party controls the White House and both chambers of Congress.

Unipolar world A political landscape with one superpower.

Unitary system A system of government where sovereignty is fully vested in the national government, not the states.

Valence issue An issue on which everyone agrees, but the question is whether the candidate embraces the same view.

Veto Literally, "I forbid"; it refers to the power of a president to disapprove a bill, and may be overridden by a two-thirds vote of each house of Congress.

Veto message A message from the president to Congress stating that that a bill passed in both chambers will not be signed. Must be produced within 10 days of the bill's passage.

Virginia Plan Proposal to create a strong national government.

Voice vote A congressional voting procedure in which members shout "yea" in approval or "nay" in disapproval, permitting members to vote quickly or anonymously on bills.

Voter identification laws Laws requiring citizens to show a government-issued photo ID in order to vote.

Voting-age population (VAP) Residents who are eligible to vote after reaching the minimum age requirement.

Voting-eligible population (VEP) Residents who have reached the minimum age to be eligible to vote, excluding those who are not legally permitted to cast a ballot.

Waiver A decision by an administrative agency granting some other party permission to violate a law or rule that would otherwise apply to it.

Wall of separation Court ruling that government cannot be involved with religion.

Watchdog The press's role as an overseer of government officials to ensure they act in the public interest.

Whip A senator or representative who helps the party leader stay informed about what party members are thinking.

White primary The practice of keeping African Americans from voting in the southern states' primaries through arbitrary use of registration requirements and intimidation.

Worldviews Comprehensive opinions of how the United States should respond to world problems.

Writ of certiorari An order by a higher court directing a lower court to send up a case for review.

Notes

Chapter 1

1. *Federalist* No. 45.
2. Patrick Henry, Virginia Convention, June 12, 1788, in *The Debate on the Constitution*, Part Two, ed. Bernard Bailyn (New York: The Library of America, 1993), 683.
3. Office of Management and Budget, *A Budget for America's Future: Fiscal Year 2021—Budget of the U.S. Government,* "Summary Tables," S-1: Budget Totals; S-10: Federal Government Financing and Debt. https://www.whitehouse.gov/wp-content/uploads/2020/02/budget_fy21.pdf
4. Martin Meyerson and Edward C. Banfield, *Politics, Planning, and the Public Interest* (New York: Free Press, 1955), 304.
5. Ibid.
6. Henry Milner, *The Internet Generation: Engaged Citizens or Political Dropouts* (Medford, MA: Tufts University Press, 2010).
7. Jane Eisner, *Taking Back the Vote: Getting American Youth Involved in Our Democracy* (Boston: Beacon Press, 2004).
8. Martin P. Wattenberg, *Is Voting for Young People?*, 3rd ed. (Boston: Pearson, 2012). Wattenberg proposes compulsory voting.
9. David E. Campbell, *Why We Vote: How Schools and Communities Shape Our Civic Life* (Princeton, NJ: Princeton University Press, 2006). Campbell proposes enhanced civic education in high schools.
10. Aristotle, *Politics,* IV.4.
11. Joseph A. Schumpeter, *Capitalism, Socialism, and Democracy*, 3rd ed. (New York: Harper Torchbooks, 1950), 269. First published in 1942.
12. Samuel P. Huntington, *The Third Wave: Democratization in the Late Twentieth Century* (Norman: University of Oklahoma Press, 1993), 7.
13. Ibid.
14. Ibid., 12–13.
15. Karl Marx and Friedrich Engels, "The Manifesto of the Communist Party," in *The Marx-Engels Reader*, 2nd ed., ed. Robert C. Tucker (New York: Norton, 1978), 469–500.
16. C. Wright Mills, *The Power Elite* (New York: Oxford University Press, 1956).
17. H. H. Gerth and C. Wright Mills, eds. *From Max Weber: Essays in Sociology* (London: Routledge and Kegan Paul, 1948), 232–35.
18. David B. Truman, *The Governmental Process: Political Interests and Public Opinion* (New York: Knopf, 1951).
19. Samuel P. Huntington, *American Politics: The Promise of Disharmony* (Cambridge, MA: Harvard University Press, 1981).
20. David O. Sears and J. B. McConahay, *The Politics of Violence* (Boston: Houghton Mifflin, 1973).
21. Daniel Patrick Moynihan, *Maximum Feasible Misunderstanding* (New York: Free Press, 1969), chap. 2.
22. Nelson W. Polsby, "Goodbye to the Senate's Inner Club," in *Congress in Change: Evolution and Reform,* ed. Norman J. Ornstein (New York: Praeger, 1975), 208–15.
23. Jack L. Walker, "Setting the Agenda in the U.S. Senate: A Theory of Problem Selection," *British Journal of Political Science* 7 (1977): 434, 439, 441.
24. James Q. Wilson, *Political Organizations* (New York: Basic Books, 1973), chap. 16; and *The Politics of Regulation* (Basic Books, 1980), 367–72. Public policies can be classified in other ways, notably that of Theodore J. Lowi, "American Business, Public Policy, Case Studies, and Theory," *World Politics* 16, no. 4 (July 1964): 677–715.
25. Donald F. Kettl, *Sharing Power: Public Governance and Private Markets* (Washington, D.C.: Brookings Institution, 1993); Lawrence J. Hajna, "Superfund: Costly Program Under Fire," *Courier-Post*, February 13, 1994, 6A.
26. Pew Research Center, "Changing Attitudes on Gay Marriage," 24 September 2014.
27. Aristotle, *The Niomachean Ethics*, I.3.

Chapter 2

1. Quoted in Bernard Bailyn, *The Ideological Origins of the American Revolution* (Cambridge, MA: Harvard University Press, 1967), 61n6.
2. Ibid., 135–37.
3. Ibid., 77.
4. Ibid., 160.
5. *Federalist* No. 37.
6. Gordon S. Wood, *The Creation of the American Republic* (Chapel Hill: University of North Carolina Press, 1969). See also *Federalist* No. 49.
7. Letter from George Washington to Henry Lee (October 31, 1787), in *Writings of George Washington*, vol. 29, ed. John C. Fitzpatrick (Washington, D.C.: Government Printing Office, 1939), 34.
8. Letters from Thomas Jefferson to James Madison (January 30, 1787) and to Colonel William S. Smith (November 13, 1787), in *Jefferson Himself*, ed. Bernard Mayo (Boston: Houghton Mifflin, 1942), 145.
9. Thomas Hobbes, *Leviathan* (Oxford, UK: Basil Blackwell, 1957). First published in 1651; John Locke, *Second Treatise of Civil Government* (New York: Hafner Publishing Co., 1956). First published in 1690.

10. *Federalist* No. 51.
11. *Federalist* No. 48.
12. James Madison, May 31,1787, in *The Records of the Federal Convention of 1787,* ed. Max Farrand (New Haven: Yale University Press, 1911). Vol. 1.
13. *Federalist* No. 51.
14. Ibid.
15. Ibid.
16. "The Address and Reasons of Dissent of the Minority of the State of Pennsylvania to Their Constituents," in *The Anti-Federalist,* ed. Cecelia Kenyon (Indianapolis, IN: Bobbs-Merrill, 1966), 39.
17. Max Farrand, *The Framing of the Constitution of the United States* (New Haven, CT: Yale University Press, 1913), 185.
18. See, for example, John Hope Franklin, *Racial Equality in America* (Chicago: University of Chicago Press, 1976), chap. 1, esp. 12–20.
19. Max Farrand, *The Records of the Federal Convention of 1787,* 4 vols. (New Haven, CT: Yale University Press), 1911–37.
20. Theodore J. Lowi, *American Government: Incomplete Conquest* (Hinsdale, IL: Dryden Press, 1976), 97.
21. Article I, section 2, para. 3.
22. *Gary Wills, "Negro President": Jefferson and the Slave Power (Boston: Houghton Mifflin,* 2003).
23. Article I, section 9, para. 1.
24. Article IV, section 2, para. 3.
25. Charles A. Beard, *An Economic Interpretation of the Constitution* (New York: Macmillan, 1913), esp. 26–51, 149–51, 324–25.
26. Forrest McDonald, *We the People* (Chicago: University of Chicago Press, 1958); Robert E. Brown, *Charles Beard and the Constitution* (Princeton, NJ: Princeton University Press, 1956).
27. Robert A. McGuire, "Constitution Making: A Rational Choice Model of the Federal Convention of 1787," *American Journal of Political Science* 32 (May 1988): 483–522. See also Forrest McDonald, *Novus Ordo Seclorum* (Lawrence, KS: University of Kansas Press, 1985), 221.
28. McDonald, *Novus Ordo Seclorum,* 202–21.
29. Robert A. McGuire and Robert L. Ohsfeldt, "Economic Interests and the American Constitution: A Quantitative Rehabilitation of Charles A. Beard," *Journal of Economic History* 44 (June 1984): 509–19.
30. Lloyd N. Cutler, "To Form a Government," *Foreign Affairs* (Fall 1980): 126–43; James L. Sundquist, *Constitutional Reform and Effective Government,* rev. ed. (Washington, D.C.: Brookings Institution Press, 1992).

Chapter 3

1. Nicholas Jacobs, Desmond King, and Sidney Milkis. 2019. "Building a Conservative State: Partisan Polarization and the Redeployment of Administrative Power." *Perspectives on Politics* 17(2): 453–469.
2. Kaiser Family Foundation, "State Health Insurance Marketplace Types, 2020."
3. Woodrow Wilson, *Constitutional Government in the United States* (New York: Columbia University Press, 1961), 173. First published in 1908.
4. Martin Diamond, "The Federalists' View of Federalism," in *Essays in Federalism,* ed. George C. S. Benson (Claremont, Calif.: Institute for Studies in Federalism, 1961), 21–64; Samuel H. Beer, "Federalism, Nationalism, and Democracy in America," *American Political Science Review* 72 (March 1978): 9–21.
5. *United States v. Sprague,* 282 U.S. 716 (1931).
6. *Garcia v. San Antonio Metropolitan Transit Authority,* 105 S. Ct. 1005 (1985), overruling *National League of Cities v. Usery,* 426 U.S. 833 (1976).
7. *McCulloch v. Maryland,* 17 U.S. 316 (1819).
8. *Pollock v. Farmers' Loan & Trust Co.,* 157 U.S. 429 (1895); *South Carolina v. Baker,* No. 94 (1988).
9. *Texas v. White,* 74 U.S. 700 (1869).
10. *Champion v. Ames,* 188 U.S. 321 (1903).
11. *Hoke v. United States,* 227 U.S. 308 (1913).
12. *Clark Distilling Co. v. Western Maryland Ry. Co.,* 242 U.S. 311 (1917).
13. *Hipolite Egg Co. v. United States,* 220 U.S. 45 (1911).
14. *United States v. E. C. Knight Co.,* 156 U.S. 1 (1895).
15. *Paul v. Virginia,* 75 U.S. 168 (1869).
16. *Veazie Bank v. Fenno,* 75 U.S. 533 (1869).
17. *Brown v. Maryland,* 25 U.S. 419 (1827).
18. *Wickard v. Filburn,* 317 U.S. 111 (1942); *NLRB v. Jones & Laughlin Steel Corp,* 301 U.S. 58 (1937).
19. *Kirschbaum Co. v. Walling,* 316 U.S. 517 (1942).
20. Jacob Grumach. 2018. "From Backwaters to Major Policymakers: Policy Polarization in the States, 1970–2014." *Perspectives on Politics* 16(2): 416–35.
21. David B. Truman, "Federalism and the Party System," in *Federalism: Mature and Emergent,* ed. Arthur McMahon (Garden City, N.Y.: Doubleday, 1955), 123.
22. Harold J. Laski, "The Obsolescence of Federalism," *New Republic* (May 3, 1939): 367–69.
23. William H. Riker, *Federalism: Origin, Operation, Significance* (Boston, MA: Little, Brown, 1964), 154.
24. Daniel J. Elazar, *American Federalism: A View from the States* (New York: Crowell, 1966), 216.
25. *New State Ice Co. v. Liebmann,* 285 U.S. 262 (1932).
26. Jack Walker, "The Diffusion of Innovations among the American States," *American Political Science Review* 63 , no. 3 (September 1969): 880–889; Craig Volden, "States as Policy Laboratories: Emulating Success in the Children's Health Insurance Program," *American Journal of Political Science* 50, no. 2 (April 2006): 294–312.
27. Office of Management and Budget, FY2021 Budget, Historical Tables, Table 12.1—Summary Comparison of Total Outlays

for Grants to State and Local Governments, 1940–2025.

28. Martha Derthick, *Keeping the Compound Republic: Essays on American Federalism* (Washington, D.C.: Brookings Institution, 2001), 140.
29. Donald F. Kettl, ed., *The Department of Homeland Security's First Year: A Report Card* (New York: Century Foundation Report, 2004), 18, 102.
30. Julie Bosman and Matt Apuzzo, "In Wake of Clashes, Calls to Demilitarize Police," *New York Times,* August 15, 2014.
31. Adam Goldman, "Trump Reverses Restrictions on Military Hardware for Police," *New York Times,* 28 August 2017.
32. U.S. Census Bureau, Annual Survey of State and Local Government Finances, 2017 Tables.
33. Office of Management and Budget, FY2021 Budget, Historical Table 12.1, Summary Comparison of Total Outlays for Grants to State and Local Governments: 1940–2025 (in Current Dollars, as Percentages of Total Outlays, as Percentages of GDP, and in Constant (FY2012) Dollars).
34. Samuel H. Beer, "The Modernization of American Federalism," *Publius: The Journal of Federalism* 3 (Fall 1973): esp. 74–79; and Beer, "Federalism," 18–19.
35. Center for Responsive Politics, "Influence and Lobbying: Industry: Civil Servants/Public Officials," https://www.opensecrets.org/federal-lobbying/industries/summary?cycle=2019&id=W03, Accessed April 2020.
36. Congressional Budget Office, *Federal Constraints on State and Local Government Actions* (Washington, D.C.: Government Printing Office, 1979).
37. William T. Gormley, Jr., "Money and Mandates: The Politics of Intergovernmental Conflict," *Publius: The Journal of Federalism* 36 (Fall 2006): 527.
38. Ibid., 535–37.
39. U.S. Advisory Commission on Intergovernmental Relations, *Federally Induced Costs Affecting State and Local Governments,* September 1994.
40. Office of Management and Budget, FY2020 Budget, Historical Table 1.1, Summary of Receipts, Outlays and Surpluses or Deficits, 1789–2024; U.S. Census Bureau, Historical Household Tables, HH-1, Households by Type, 1940–Present.
41. U.S. Census Bureau, State and Local Government Finance Data, Summary Tables, 2017.
42. Abby Goodnough, "Trump Administration Unveils a Major Shift in Medicaid," *New York Times,* 30 January 2020.
43. Paul Teske, *Regulation in the States* (Washington, D.C.: Brookings Institution, 2004).
44. *Massachusetts v. Environmental Protection Agency,* 549 U.S. 497 (2007).
45. Center for Budget and Policy Priorities, "Chart Book: TANF at 18," August 2014. www.cbpp.org/cms/index.cfm?fa=view&id=3566.
46. Stephen V. Monsma, *Putting Faith in Partnerships: Welfare-to-Work in Four Cities* (Ann Arbor: University of Michigan Press, 2004).
47. Sarah Anzia and Terry Moe, "Public Sector Unions and the Costs of Government," *Journal of Politics* 77, no. 1 (January 2015): 114–27.
48. Mike Macaig, "Report: 21 States' Pension Systems Not Fiscally Sound," *Governing* 29 (November 2012).
49. Government Accountability Office, "2019 Annual Report: Additional Opportunities to Reduce Fragmentation, Overlap and Duplication and Achieve Billions in Financial Benefits," GAO-19-285SP, Published 21 May 2019. Available online at: https://www.gao.gov/products/GAO-19-285SP, accessed January 2020.
50. Congressional Budget Office, "Federal Grants to State and Local Governments," Publication No. 4472, March 2013.

Chapter 4

1. Alexis de Tocqueville, "Principal Causes Which Tend to Maintain the Democratic Republic in the United States," in *Democracy in America,* vol. 1, ed. Phillips Bradley (New York: Knopf, 1951). First published in 1835.
2. *The Public Perspective* (November/December 1991): 5, 7, reporting survey data from the Roper Center for Public Opinion Research.
3. Fred I. Greenstein, "The Benevolent Leader Revisited: Children's Images of Political Leaders in Three Democracies," *American Political Science Review* 69 (December 1975): 1387.
4. de Tocqueville, *Democracy in America,* 1:288.
5. Donald J. Devine, *The Political Culture of the United States* (Boston, MA: Little, Brown, 1972), 185; Herbert McClosky and John Zaller, *The American Ethos: Public Attitudes Toward Capitalism and Democracy* (Cambridge, MA: Harvard University Press, 1984), chap. 3, esp. 74–75; Sidney Verba, Kay Lehman Schlozman, and Henry E. Brady, *Voice and Equality: Civic Voluntarism in American Politics* (Cambridge, Ma.: Harvard University Press, 1995).
6. McClosky and Zaller, *The American Ethos,* 74–77.
7. Ibid., 66.
8. Gunnar Myrdal, *An American Dilemma: The Negro Problem in Modern Democracy* (New York: Harper, 1944), introduction and chap. 1.
9. Frank R. Westie, "The American Dilemma: An Empirical Test," *American Sociological Review* 30, no. 4 (August 1965): 536–37.
10. Samuel P. Huntington, *American Politics* (Cambridge, MA: Harvard University Press, 1983), 202.
11. Eric L. McKitrick, "Party Politics and the Union and Confederate War Efforts," in *The American Party Systems,* 2nd ed., eds. William Nisbet Chambers and Walter Dean Burnham (New York: Oxford University Press, 1975), 117–21.

12. Russell J. Dalton, *The Good Citizen* (Washington, D.C.: Congressional Quarterly Press, 2008), 38, 71, 168–71.
13. McClosky and Zaller, *The American Ethos*, 174.
14. Sidney Verba and Gary R. Orren, *Equality in America: The View from the Top* (Cambridge, MA: Harvard University Press, 1985), 146–47.
15. McClosky and Zaller, *The American Ethos*, 82–84, 93, 95.
16. Verba and Orren, *Equality in America*, 72, 254.
17. Donald Kinder and David Sears, "Prejudice and Politics: Symbolic Racism Versus Racial Threats to the Good Life," *Journal of Personality and Social Psychology* 40, no. 3 (1981): 414–31.
18. Paul M. Sniderman and Michael Gray Hagen, *Race and Inequality: A Study in American Values* (Chatham, NJ: Chatham House, 1985), 111.
19. Ibid., 37–38.
20. Frank Newport, "Inequality as a Voter Concern in 2020," *Gallup: Polling Matters,* 31 July 2019, https://news.gallup.com/opinion/polling-matters/262439/inequality-voter-concern-2020.aspx; Chris Edwards and Ryan Bourne, "Exploring Wealth Inequality," *The Cato Institute,* 5 November 2019, https://www.cato.org/publications/policy-analysis/exploring-wealth-inequality. Accessed February 2020.
21. Theodore Caplow and Howard M. Bahr, "Half a Century of Change in Adolescent Attitudes: A Replication of a Middletown Survey by the Lynds," *Public Opinion Quarterly* 43 (1979): 1–17, table 1.
22. Juliana Menasce Horowitz, Ruth Igielnik, and Rakesh Kochhar, "Most Americans Say There Is Too Much Economic Inequality in the U.S., but Fewer Than Half Call It a Top Priority," *Pew Research Center*, 9 January 2020, https://www.pewsocialtrends.org/2020/01/09/most-americans-say-there-is-too-much-economic-inequality-in-the-u-s-but-fewer-than-half-call-it-a-top-priority/.
23. Thomas J. Anton, "Policy-Making and Political Culture in Sweden," *Scandinavian Political Studies* 4 (1969): 88–100; M. Donald Hancock, *Sweden: The Politics of Post-Industrial Change* (Hinsdale, *IL*: Dryden Press, 1972); Richard Scarse, ed., *Readings in the Swedish Class Structure: Readings in Sociology* (New York: Pergamon Press, 1976); Steven J. Kelman, *Regulating America, Regulating Sweden: A Comparative Study of Occupational Safety and Health Policy* (Cambridge, MA: MIT Press, 1981), 118–23.
24. Lewis Austin, *Saints and Samurai: The Political Culture of American and Japanese Elites* (New Haven, CT: Yale University Press, 1975).
25. Gabriel Almond and Sidney Verba, *The Civic Culture* (Princeton, NJ: Princeton University Press, 1963), 169, 185. See also Gabriel Almond and Sidney Verba, eds., *The Civic Culture Revisited* (Boston, MA: Little, Brown, 1980).
26. Sidney Verba et al., *Voice and Equality: Civic Voluntarism in American Politics* (Cambridge, MA: Harvard University Press, 1995), 69, 70.
27. Elizabeth J. Zeichmeister, ed., *The Political Culture of Democracy in the Americas, 2014: Democratic Governance Across 10 Years of the Americas Barometer* (Washington, D.C.: United States Agency for International Development, 2014), 194.
28. Zeichmeister, *The Political Culture of Democracy in the Americas,* 193; Amy Erica Smith, "Do Americans Still Believe in Democracy?" *Washington Post*, April 9, 2016.
29. James Davison Hunter and Carl Desportes Bowman, "The Vanishing Center of American Democracy," University of Virginia Institute for Advanced Studies in Culture, 2016, iasculture.org/research/publications/vanishing-center.
30. Verba and Orren, *Equality in America*, 255.
31. Pippa Norris and Ronald Ingelhart, *Sacred and Secular: Religion and Politics Worldwide* (Cambridge, UK: Cambridge University Press, 2004); George Gallup Jr. and Thomas Jones, *The Next American Spirituality* (Colorado Springs, CO: Cook, 2000).
32. Arthur C. Brooks, *Who Really Cares: The Surprising Truth about Compassionate Conservatism—America's Charity Divide: Who Gives, Who Doesn't, and Why It Matters* (New York: Basic Books, 2006), chap. 2; Ram A. Cnaan, *The Other Philadelphia Story: How Local Congregations Support Quality of Life in Urban America* (Philadelphia, PA: University of Pennsylvania Press, 2006).
33. "In U.S., Decline of Christianity Continues at Rapid Pace," *Pew Research Center on Religion & Public Life*, October 17, 2019, https://www.pewforum.org/2019/10/17/in-u-s-decline-of-christianity-continues-at-rapid-pace/. Accessed February 2020.
34. Max Weber, *The Protestant Ethic and the Spirit of Capitalism*, trans. Talcott Parsons (New York: Scribner's, 1930). First published in 1904.
35. Erik H. Erikson, *Childhood and Society* (New York: Norton, 1950), chap. 8.
36. James Davison Hunter, *Culture Wars: The Struggle to Define America* (New York: Basic Books, 1991); and Hunter, *Before the Shooting Begins* (New York: Macmillan, 1994).
37. Morris P. Fiorina, *Culture War? The Myth of a Polarized America,* 3rd ed. (New York: Pearson, 2010); Morris P. Fiorina and Matthew S. Levendusky, "Disconnected: The Political Class versus the People," in *Red and Blue Nation? Characteristics and Causes of America's Polarized Politics*, eds. Pietro S. Nivola and David W Brady (Washington, D.C.: Brookings Institution, 2006), 49–71.
38. Alan I. Abramovitz, "Comment" and "Rejoinder," in Nivola and Brady, *Red and Blue Nation?*, 72–85, 111–14; Gary C. Jacobson, "Comment," in Nivola and Brady, *Red and Blue Nation?*, 85–95.
39. Philip D. Zelikow and David C. King, eds., *Why People Don't Trust*

Government (Cambridge, MA: Harvard University Press, 1997).

40. "Public Trust in Government: 1958–2019," Pew Research Center, U.S. Politics and Policy, 11 April 2019, https://www.people-press.org/2019/04/11/public-trust-in-government-1958-2019/.
41. Matthew MacWilliams, "The One Weird Trait That Predicts Whether You're a Trump Supporter," *The Atlantic,* January 17, 2016.
42. Wendy Rahn and Eric Oliver, "Trump's Voters Aren't Authoritarians, New Research Says. So What Are They?" *Washington Post*, March 9, 2016.
43. Marc J. Hetherington, *Why Trust Matters* (Princeton, NJ: Princeton University Press, 2005).
44. Robert D. Putnam, *Bowling Alone: The Collapse and Revival of American Community* (New York: Simon & Schuster, 2000); and Robert D. Putnam et al., *Better Together: Report of the Saguaro Seminar on Civic Engagement in America* (Cambridge, MA: Kennedy School of Government, Harvard University, 2001).
45. Associated Press, "Young Adult Americans Committed to Volunteering, Poll Finds," Washington Post, 29 December 2014.
46. James Q. Wilson, "Bowling with Others," *Commentary*, October 1, 2007, 30–33.
47. Thomas H. Sander and Robert D. Putnam, "Still Bowling Alone?: The Post-9/11 Split," *Journal of Democracy* 21, no. 1 (January 2010): 9–16. Quotation is on p. 13.
48. Robert D. Putnam, *Our Kids: The American Dream in Crisis* (New York: Simon & Schuster, 2015).
49. James W. Prothro and Charles M. Grigg, "Fundamental Principles of Democracy: Bases of Agreement and Disagreement," *Journal of Politics* 22, no. 2 (Spring 1960): 275–94.
50. John L. Sullivan, James Piereson, and George F. Marcus, *Political Tolerance and American Democracy* (Chicago, IL: University of Chicago Press, 1982), 194–202.

Chapter 5

1. Paul Leicester Ford, ed., *Works of Thomas Jefferson,* vol. 9 (New York: G.P. Putnam's Sons, 1905), 449.
2. *Zamora v. Pomeroy,* 639 F.2d 662 (1981); *Goss v. Lopez,* 419 U.S. 565 (1975); *Tinker v. DesMoines Community School District,* 393 U.S. 503 (1969); *Smith v. Goguen,* 415 U.S. 566 (1974); *New Jersey v. T.L.O.,* 469 U.S. 325 (1985); *Morse v. Frederick,* No. 06–278 (2007).
3. *Snyder v. Phelps,* 131 S. Ct. 1207 (2011); *New York Times Co. v. United States,* 403 U.S. 713 (1971); *Kunz v. New York,* 340 U.S. 290 (1951).
4. *Barron v. Baltimore*, 7 Pet. 243 (1833).
5. *Chicago, Burlington, and Quincy Railroad Co. v. Chicago*, 166 U.S. 226 (1987); *Gitlow v. New York, 268 U.S.* 652 (1925); *Palko v. Connecticut*, 302 U.S. 319 (1937).
6. *District of Columbia v. Heller,* 554 U.S. 570 (2008); *McDonald v. Chicago,* 130 S. Ct. 3020 (2010).
7. Adam Liptak, "After Long Gap, Supreme Court Poised to Break Silence on Gun Rights," *New York Times,* 2 December 2019.
8. William Blackstone, *Commentaries*, vol. 4 (1765), 151–52.
9. Jefferson's remarks are from a letter to Abigail Adams (quoted in Walter Berns, *The First Amendment and the Future of American Democracy* [New York: Basic Books, 1976], 82), and from a letter to Thomas McKean, governor of Pennsylvania, February 19, 1803 (Paul L. Ford, ed., *The Writings of Thomas Jefferson: 1801–1806,* vol. 8 [New York: Putnam, 1897], 218).
10. *Schenck v. United States,* 249 U.S. 47 (1919), p. 52.
11. *Gitlow v. New York,* 268 U.S. 652 (1925), p. 666.
12. *Fiske v. Kansas,* 274 U.S. 380 (1927); *Stromberg v. California,* 283 U.S. 359 (1931); *Near v. Minnesota,* 283 U.S. 697 (1931); *De Jonge v. Oregon,* 299 U.S. 353 (1937).
13. *Dennis v. United States,* 341 U.S. 494 (1951), 510ff. The test was first formulated by Judge Learned Hand of the court of appeals: see *Dennis v. United States,* 183 F.2d 201 (1950), p. 212.
14. *Yates v. United States*, 354 U.S. 298 (1957).
15. *Brandenburg v. Ohio*, 395 U.S. 444 (1969).
16. *Chaplinsky v. New Hampshire,* 315 U.S. 568 (1942); David L. Hudson, Jr., "Fighting Words Case Still Making Waves in First Amendment Jurisprudence," *Newseum Institute,* 9 March 2012.
17. *Village of Skokie v. National Socialist Party,* 432 U.S. 43 (1977); 366 N.E.2d 349 (1977); and 373 N.E.2d 21 (1978).
18. *R.A.V. v. City of St. Paul,* 112 S. Ct. 2538 (1992).
19. *Wisconsin v. Mitchell,* No. 92–515 (1993).
20. C. Herman Pritchett, *Constitutional Civil Liberties* (Englewood Cliffs, NJ: Prentice Hall, 1984), 100.
21. *New York Times v. Sullivan, 376 U.S. 254 (1964); but compare Time, Inc. v. Firestone, 424 U.S.* 448 (1976).
22. Henry J. Abraham, *Freedom and the Court,* 4th ed. (New York: Oxford University Press, 1982), 193, fn 189.
23. Justice Stewart's famous remark was made in his concurring opinion in *Jacobellis v. Ohio,* 378 U.S. 184 (1964), p. 197.
24. *Miller v. California,* 413 U.S. 15 (1973).
25. *Jenkins v. Georgia*, 418 U.S. 153 (1974).
26. *Schad v. Borough of Mt. Ephraim,* 452 U.S. 61 (1981).
27. *Barnes v. Glen Theatre*, 111 S. Ct. 2456 (1991).
28. *American Booksellers Association v. Hudnut,* 771 F.2d 323 (1985), affirmed at 475 U.S. 1001 (1986).
29. *Renton v. Playtime Theatres,* 475 U.S. 41 (1986). *See also Young v. American Mini-Theatres, Inc.*, 427 U.S. 50 (1976).
30. *Reno v. American Civil Liberties Union,* 521 U.S. 844 (1997); *Ashcroft v. Free Speech Coalition,* 122 S. Ct. 1389 (2002).

31. *United States v. O'Brien,* 391 U.S. 367 (1968).
32. *Texas v. Johnson,* 109 S. Ct. 2533 (1989).
33. *United States v. Eichman,* 496 U.S. 310 (1990).
34. *First National Bank of Boston v. Bellotti,* 435 U.S. 765 (1978); *Federal Election Commission v. Massachusetts Citizens for Life, Inc.,* 479 U.S. 238 (1986).
35. *44 Liquormart v. Rhode Island,* 517 U.S. 484 (1996); *Greater New Orleans Broadcasting Association v. United States,* 527 U.S. 173 (1999).
36. *Pacific Gas and Electric Co. v. Public Utilities Commission,* 475 U.S. 1 (1986). Some limitations on corporate speech have been upheld, including a state law prohibiting a firm from spending money on candidates for elective office. *Austin v. Michigan Chamber of Commerce,* 100 S. Ct. 1391 (1990).
37. *Board of Trustees of the State University of New York v. Fox,* 492 U.S. 469 (1989).
38. *Bates v. State Bar of Arizona,* 433 U.S. 350 (1977); *Edenfield v. Bane,* 113 S. Ct. 1792 (1993).
39. *McConnell v. Federal Election Commission,* 124 S. Ct. 619 (2003); *Federal Election Commission v. Wisconsin Right to Life,* No. 06–969 (2007).
40. *Hazelwood School District v. Kuhlmeier et al.,* 484 U.S. 260 (1988).
41. *Murdock v. Pennsylvania,* 319 U.S. 105 (1943).
42. *Church of the Lukumi Babalu Aye v. City of Hialeah,* 508 U.S. 520 (1993).
43. *Reynolds v. United States,* 98 U.S. 145 (1878).
44. *Jacobson v. Massachusetts,* 197 U.S. 11 (1905).
45. *Employment Division, Department of Human Resources of Oregon v. Smith,* 110 S. Ct. 1595 (1990).
46. *Society for Krishna Consciousness v. Lee,* 112 S. Ct. 2701 (1992).
47. *City of Boerne v. Flores,* 521 U.S. 507 (1997).
48. *Burwell v. Hobby Lobby Stores, Inc.,* 573 U.S. (2014).
49. Kimberly Leonard, "After Hobby Lobby, A Way to Cover Birth Control," *U.S. News & World Report,* July 10, 2015.
50. *Welsh v. United States, 398 U.S. 333 (1970); Pritchett, Constitutional Civil Liberties,* 140–41.
51. *Sherbert v. Verner,* 374 U.S. 398 (1963); *Wisconsin v. Yoder,* 406 U.S. 205 (1972); *Hobbie v. Unemployment Appeals Commission of Florida,* 480 U.S. 136 (1987); *Estate of Thornton v. Caldor, Inc.,* 472 U.S. 703 (1985).
52. *Berns, The First Amendment.*
53. *Pritchett, Constitutional Civil Liberties,* 145–47.
54. *Everson v. Board of Education,* 330 U.S. 1 (1947).
55. *Engel v. Vitale,* 370 U.S. 421 (1962).
56. *Lubbock Civil Liberties Union v. Lubbock Independent School District,* 669 F .2d 1038 (1982).
57. *School District of Abington Township v. Schempp,* 374 U.S. 203 (1963).
58. *Lee v. Weisman,* 112 S. Ct. 2649 (1992); *Santa Fe Independent School District v. Jane Doe,* 530 U.S. 290 (2000).
59. *Ahlquist v. City of Cranston,* C.A. no. 11–138L (2012).
60. *Epperson v. Arkansas,* 393 U.S. 97 (1968); *McLean v. Arkansas Board of Education,* 529 F. Supp. 1255 (1982).
61. *McCollum v. Board of Education,* 333 U.S. 203 (1948); *Zorach v. Clauson,* 343 U.S. 306 (1952).
62. *Tilton v. Richardson,* 403 U.S. 672 (1971).
63. *Board of Education v. Allen,* 392 U.S. 236 (1968).
64. *Walz v. Tax Commission,* 397 U.S. 664 (1970).
65. *Mueller v. Allen,* 463 U.S. 388 (1983).
66. *Zobrest v. Catalina Foothills School District,* 509 U.S. 1 (1993); *Mitchell v. Helms,* 2000 Lexis 4485.
67. *Lemon v. Kurtzman,* 403 U.S. 602 (1971).
68. *Committee for Public Education v. Nyquist,* 413 U.S. 756 (1973).
69. *Meek v. Pittenger,* 421 U.S. 349 (1975); *Wolman v. Walter,* 433 U.S. 229 (1977).
70. *Edwards v. Aguillard,* 482 U.S. 578 (1987); *Board of Education of Kiryas Joel Village School v. Louis Grumet,* 114 S. Ct. 2481 (1994).
71. *Agostini v. Felton,* 521 U.S. 203 (1997), overruled *Aguilar v. Felton,* 473 U.S. 402 (1985).
72. *Zelman v. Simmons-Harris,* 536 U.S. 639 (2002).
73. *Lemon v. Kurtzman,* 403 U.S. 602 (1971).
74. *Lynch v. Donelly,* 465 U.S. 668 (1984); *Allegheny v. ACLU,* 109 S. Ct. 3086 (1989).
75. *McCreary County, Kentucky, v. ACLU,* 125 S. Ct. 2722 (2005); *Van Orden v. Perry,* 125 S. Ct. 2854 (2005).
76. *Marsh v. Chambers,* 492 U.S. 573 (1983).
77. *Town of Greece v. Galloway,* 572 U.S. Town of Greece v. Galloway, 572 U.S. 565 (2014).
78. Yale Kamisar, "Does (Did) (Should) the Exclusionary Rule Rest on a 'Principled Basis' Rather Than an 'Empirical Proposition'?" *Creighton Law Review* 16 (1982–1983): 565–667.
79. *Wolf v. Colorado,* 338 U.S. 25 (1949).
80. John J. Dilulio, Jr., *Godly Republic: A Centrist Blueprint for America's Faith-Based Future* (Berkeley: University of California Press, 2007), 31.
81. White House, "Executive Order on the Establishment of a White House Faith and Opportunity Initiative," 3 May 2018; Emma Green, "Trump Creates a Not-So-New Faith Office in the White House," *The Atlantic,* 3 May 2018.
82. *Mapp v. Ohio,* 367 U.S. 643 (1961).
83. *Chimel v. California,* 395 U.S. 752 (1969).
84. *Washington v. Chrisman,* 455 U.S. 1 (1982).
85. *Oliver v. United States,* 466 U.S. 170 (1984).
86. *Arkansas v. Sanders,* 442 U.S. 753 (1979); *Robbins v. California,* 453 U.S. 420 (1981).
87. *United States v. Ross, 456 U.S. 798 (1982); Maryland v. Dyson,* 199 S. Ct. 2013 (1999); *Wyoming v. Houghton,* 119 S. Ct. 1297 (1999); *Whren v. United States,* 517 U.S. 806 (1996).

88. *Winston v. Lee,* 470 U.S. 753 (1985).
89. *South Dakota v. Neville,* 459 U.S. 553 (1983); *Schmerber v. California,* 384 U.S. 757 (1966).
90. *United States v. Dunn,* 480 U.S. 294 (1987); *California v. Ciraolo,* 476 U.S. 207 (1986); *California v. Carney,* 471 U.S. 386 (1985).
91. *O'Connor v. Ortega,* 480 U.S. 709 (1987).
92. *Escobedo v. Illinois,* 378 U.S. 478 (1964); *Miranda v. Arizona,* 384 U.S. 436 (1966).
93. *Malloy v. Hogan,* 378 U.S. 1 (1964).
94. *Miranda v. Arizona,* 384 U.S. 436 (1966).
95. *Gilbert v. California,* 388 U.S. 263 (1967); *Kirby v. Illinois,* 406 U.S. 682 (1972).
96. *Estelle v. Smith,* 451 U.S. 454 (1981).
97. *Brewer v. Williams,* 430 U.S. 387 (1977).
98. *Illinois v. Perkins,* 496 U.S. 292 (1990).
99. *Missouri v. Seibert,* 542 U.S. 600 (2004).
100. *Dickerson v. United States,* 530 U.S. 428 (2000).
101. *Fare v. Michael C.,* 442 U.S. 707 (1979).
102. *United States v. Leon,* 468 U.S. 897 (1984); *Massachusetts v. Sheppard,* 468 U.S. 981 (1984); *Herring v. United States,* No. 07–513 (2008).
103. *New York v. Quarles,* 467 U.S. 649 (1984); *Arizona v. Fulminante,* 499 U.S. 279 (1991); *Kentucky v. King,* No. 09–1272 (2011).
104. *Nix v. Williams,* 467 U.S. 431 (1984).
105. Michael Sallah et al., "Stop and Seize," *Washington Post,* September 6, 2014; Sarah Stillman, "Taken," *New Yorker,* August 12–19, 2013.
106. Jason M. Breslow, "With or Without the Patriot Act, Here's How the NSA Can Still Spy on Americans," *Frontline,* June 1, 2015; Justin Elliott, "Remember When the Patriot Act Debate Was All About Library Records?" *ProPublica,* June 17, 2013.
107. James Risen and Eric Lichtbau, "Bush Lets U.S. Spy on Callers Without Courts," *New York Times,* December 16, 2005; James Risen, *State of War: The Secret History of the CIA and the Bush Administration* (New York: Free Press, 2006).
108. *In re Sealed Case, Foreign* Intelligence Review Court, No. 02–001 (2002); David Cole and Martin S. Lederman, "The National Security Agency's Domestic Spying Program: Framing the Debate," *The Scholarly Commons,* Georgetown University Law Center, 2006 (see p. 1357); Ellen Nakashima, "Legal Memos Released on Bush-Era Justification for Warrantless Wiretapping," *Washington Post,* September 6, 2014.
109. "FISA Amendments Act of 2008," *Wall Street Journal,* June 19, 2008.
110. "Debate: Was Edward Snowden Justified?" *National Public Radio,* February 18, 2014; Bryan Burrough, Sarah Ellison, and Suzanna Andrews, "The Snowden Saga: A Shadowland of Secrets and Light," *Vanity Fair,* May 2014.
111. "Obama Signs Bill Reforming Surveillance Program," *New York Times,* June 2, 2015; Jeremy Diamond, "NSA Surveillance Bill Passes After Weeks-Long Showdown," www.cnn.com, June 2, 2015.
112. *Ex parte Quirin,* 317 U.S. 1 (1942).
113. President George W. Bush, Military Order of November 13, 2001 (Federal Register 66, no. 222); *Hamdi v. Rumsfeld,* 542 U.S. 507 (2004); *Rasul v. Bush,* 542 U.S. 466 (2004).
114. *Hamdan v. Rumsfeld,* 548 U.S. 557 (2006).
115. Military Commissions Act, Public Law 109–366 (2006). www.mc.mil, accessed May 15, 2017.
116. *Boumedine v. Bush,* 553 U.S. 723 (2008).
117. Congressional Research Service, "The Military Commissions Act of 2009 (MCA 2009): Overview and Legal Issues, August 4, 2014.
118. Connie Bruck, "Why Obama Has Failed to Close Guantanamo," *New Yorker,* August 1, 2016; CNN Library, "Guantanamo Bay Naval Station Fast Facts," updated March 7, 2017, www.cnn.com; "Inside Obama's Final Push to Transfer Guantanamo Detainees," *PBS NewsHour,* December 20, 2016, www.pbs.org/newshour/.

Chapter 6

1. *United States v. Carolene Products Co.,* 304 U.S. 144 (1938); *San Antonio Independent School District v. Rodriguez,* 411 U.S. 1 (1973).
2. Gunnar Myrdal, *An American Dilemma* (New York: Harper, 1944), chap. 27.
3. Richard Kluger, *Simple Justice* (New York: Random House/Vintage Books, 1977), 89–90.
4. Paul B. Sheatsley, "White Attitudes Toward the Negro," in *The Negro American,* ed. Talcott Parsons and Kenneth B. Clark (Boston, MA: Houghton Mifflin, 1966), 305, 308, 317.
5. CNN Editorial Research "Controversial Police Encounters Fast Facts," www.cnn.com, 4 June 2020.
6. *Strauder v. West Virginia,* 100 U.S. 303 (1880).
7. *Civil Rights Cases,* 109 U.S. 3 (1883).
8. *Plessy v. Ferguson,* 163 U.S. 537 (1896).
9. *Cumming v. Richmond County Board of Education,* 175 U.S. 528 (1899).
10. *Missouri ex rel. Gaines v. Canada,* 305 U.S. 337 (1938).
11. *Sipuel v. Board of Regents of the University of Oklahoma,* 332 U.S. 631 (1948).
12. *Sweatt v. Painter,* 339 U.S. 629 (1950); *McLaurin v. Oklahoma State Regents for Higher 3 Education,* 339 U.S. 637 (1950).
13. *Brown v. Board of Education of Topeka,* 347 U.S. 483 (1954).
14. *Brown v. Board of Education of Topeka,* 349 U.S. 294 (1955). This case is often referred to as *Brown II.*
15. Frederick S. Mosteller and Daniel P. Moynihan, eds., *On Equality of Educational Opportunity* (New York: Random House, 1972), 60–62.
16. *Brown v. Board of Education of Topeka,* 347 U.S. 483 (1954).
17. C. Herman Pritchett, *Constitutional Civil Liberties* (Englewood Cliffs, NJ: Prentice Hall, 1984), 250–251, 261.

18. *Green et al. v. County School Board of New Kent County*, 391 U.S. 430 (1968).
19. *Swann v. Charlotte-Mecklenburg Board of Education*, 402 U.S. 1 (1971).
20. Busing within the central city was upheld in *Armour v. Nix*, 446 U.S. 930 (1980); *Keyes v. School District No. 1, Denver*, 413 U.S. 189 (1973); *Milliken v. Bradley*, 418 U.S. 717 (1974); *Board of School Commissioners of Indianapolis v. Buckley*, 429 U.S. 1068 (1977); *and School Board of Richmond v. State Board of Education*, 412 U.S. 92 (1972). *Busing across city lines was upheld in Evans v. Buchanan*, 423 U.S. 963 (1975), *and Board of Education v. Newburg Area Council*, 421 U.S. 931 (1975).
21. *Pasadena City Board of Education v. Spangler*, 427 U.S. 424 (1976).
22. See, for example, Herbert Mc-Closky and John Zaller, *The American Ethos* (Cambridge, MA: Harvard University Press, 1984), 92, 100.
23. NES, 1952–1990 Cumulative Data File; 1992 NES Pre/Post Election Study (1992).
24. *Freeman v. Pitts*, 112 S. Ct. 1430 (1992); *Parents v. Seattle School District*, No. 05-908 (2007).
25. Robert S. Erikson and Norman R. Luttbeg, *American Public Opinion* (New York: Wiley, 1973), 49; Hazel Erskine, "The Polls: Demonstrations and Race Riots," *Public Opinion Quarterly* 31, no. 4 (Winter 1967–1968): 655–77.
26. Howard Schuman, Charlotte Steeh, and Lawrence Bobo, *Racial Attitudes in America* (Cambridge, MA: Harvard University Press, 1985), 69, 78–79.
27. Ibid., 102, 110, 127–135.
28. *Grove City College v. Bell*, 465 U.S. 555 (1984).
29. *Shelby County v. Holder*, 570 U.S. Shelby County v. Holder, 570 U.S. 529 (2013).
30. J. Ginsburg, dissenting opinion, *Shelby County v. Holder*, 37; Adam Liptak, "Supreme Court Invalidates Key Part of Voting Rights Act," *New York Times*, June 25, 2013.
31. "Statement by the President on the Supreme Court Ruling on *Shelby County v. Holder*," June 25, 2013.
32. Jaime Fuller, "How Has Voting Changed Since *Shelby County v. Holder*?" *Washington Post*, July 7, 2014; J. Gerald Hebert and Danielle Lang, "Courts Are Finally Pointing Out the Racism Behind Voter ID Laws," *Washington Post*, August 3, 2016.
33. *Mueller v. Oregon*, 208 U.S. 412 (1908).
34. Equal Pay Act of 1963; Civil Rights Act of 1964, Title VII, and 1978 amendments thereto; Education Amendments of 1972, Title IX.
35. *Reed v. Reed*, 404 U.S. 71 (1971).
36. *Frontiero v. Richardson*, 411 U.S. 677 (1973).
37. 111th Congress Public Law 2, "Lilly Ledbetter Fair Pay Act of 2009."
38. "U.S. Departments of Justice and Education Release Joint Guidance to Help Schools Secure the Civil Rights of Transgender Students," May 13, 2016; Liam Stack, "Trump Drops Defense of Obama Guidelines on Transgender Students," *New York Times*, February 11, 2017; Daniel Trotta, "Trump Revokes Obama Guidelines on Transgender Bathrooms," *Reuters*, February 23, 2017; Matt Stevens, "Transgender Student in Bathroom Dispute Wins Court Ruling," *New York Times*, May 22, 2018.
39. Robert Barnes and Moriah Balingit, "Supreme Court Leaves in Place Pennsylvania Policy Supporting Transgender Students," *Washington Post*, May 28, 2019.
40. "Equal Rights Amendment: Frequently Asked Questions," Alice Paul Institute, Mount Laurel, NJ, www.equalrightsamendment.org, accessed February 2020.
41. Bill Chappell, "Virginia Ratifies the Equal Rights Amendment, Decades After the Deadline," www.npr.org, 15 January 2020.
42. *Stanton v. Stanton*, 421 U.S. 7 (1975).
43. *Craig v. Boren*, 429 U.S. 190 (1976).
44. *Dothard v. Rawlinson*, 433 U.S. 321 (1977).
45. *Cleveland Board of Education v. LaFleur*, 414 U.S. 632 (1974).
46. *Fortin v. Darlington Little League*, 514 F. 2d 344 (1975).
47. *Roberts v. United States Jaycees*, 468 U.S. 609 (1984); *Board of Directors Rotary International v. Rotary Club of Duarte*, 481 U.S. 537 (1987).
48. *Arizona Governing Committee for Tax Deferred Annuity and Deferred Compensation Plans v. Norris*, 463 U.S. 1073 (1983).
49. *EEOC v. Madison Community Unit School District No. 12*, 818 F.2d 577 (1987).
50. *MichaelM. v. Superior Court*, 450 U.S. 464 (1981).
51. *Vorchheimer v. School District of Philadelphia*, 430 U.S. 703 (1977).
52. *Kahn v. Shevin*, 416 U.S. 351 (1974).
53. *Schlesinger v. Ballard*, 419 U.S. 498 (1975).
54. *Bennett v. Dyer's Chop House*, 350 F. Supp. 153 (1972); *Morris v. Michigan State Board of Education*, 472 F.2d 1207 (1973); *Fitzgerald v. Porter Memorial Hospital*, 523 F.2d 716 (1975); *Kruzel v. Podell*, 226 N.W.2d 458 (1975).
55. *United States v. Virginia*, 116 S. Ct. 2264 (1996).
56. *Rostker v. Goldberg*, 453 U.S. 57 (1981).
57. *Gebser v. Lago Vista School District*, 118 S. Ct. 1989 (1998); *Faragher v. Boca Raton*, 118 S. Ct. 2275 (1998); *Burlington Industries v. Ellerth*, 118 S. Ct. 2257 (1998).
58. "Harvey Weinstein Timeline: How the Scandal Unfolded," *BBC News*, January 7, 2020; Dan Corey, "A Growing List of Men Accused of Sexual Misconduct Since Weinstein," *NBC News*, November 8, 2017; Cara Kelly and Aaron Hegarty, "#MeToo Was a Culture Shock. But Changing Laws Will Take More Than a Year," *USA Today*, October 5, 2018.
59. *Griswold v. Connecticut*, 381 U.S. 479 (1965).
60. *Roe v. Wade*, 410 U.S. 113 (1973).
61. Though the constitutionality of the Hyde Amendment was upheld

in *Harris v. McRae,* 448 U.S. 297 (1980), other limitations on access to abortions were struck down in *Planned Parenthood Federation of Central Missouri v. Danforth,* 428 U.S. 52 (1976); *Akron v. Akron Center for Reproductive Health,* 462 U.S. 416 (1983); and *Thornburgh v. American College of Obstetricians and Gynecologists,* 476 U.S. 747 (1986).

62. *Planned Parenthood v. Casey,* 112 S. Ct. 2791 (1992).
63. *Gonzales v. Carhart,* Gonzales v. Carhart, 550 U.S. 124 (2007).
64. Heather Boonstra and Elizabeth Nash, "A Surge of State Abortion Restrictions Put Providers—And the Women They Serve—in the Crosshairs," *Guttmacher Policy Review* 17 (Winter 2014): 9–15.
65. Adam Liptak, "Supreme Court to Consider Limits on Contraception Coverage," *New York Times,* 17 January 2020.
66. Robert D. McFadden, "Norma McCorvey, 'Roe' in *Roe v. Wade,* Is Dead at 69," *New York Times,* February 18, 2017.
67. For an argument in support of a color-blind Constitution, see Andrew Kull, *The Color-Blind Constitution* (Cambridge, MA: Harvard University Press, 1992).
68. *Regents of the University of California v. Bakke,* 438 U.S. 265 (1978).
69. *Fullilove v. Klutznick,* 448 U.S. 448 (1980).
70. *City of Richmond v. J.A. Croson Co.,* 488 U.S. 469 (1989).
71. *Metro Broadcasting v. FCC,* 497 U.S. 547 (1990).
72. *Northeastern Florida Contractors v. Jacksonville,* 508 U.S. 656 (1993).
73. *Firefighters Local Union No. 1784 v. Stotts,* 467 U.S. 561 (1984); *Wygant v. Jackson Board of Education,* 476 U.S. 267 (1986); *City of Richmond v. J.A. Croson Co.,* 488 U.S. 469 (1989).
74. *Local No. 28 of the Sheet Metal Workers' International Association v. Equal Employment Opportunity Commission,* 478 U.S. 421 (1986); *Wards Cove Packing Co. v. Atonio,* 490 U.S. 642 (1989); *Price Waterhouse v. Hopkins,* 490 U.S. 228 (1989). (Note: the Wards Cove and Price decisions were both superseded in part by the Civil Rights Act of 1991.)
75. *Fullilove v. Klutznick,* 448 U.S. 448 (1980); *Metro Broadcasting v. FCC,* 497 U.S. 547 (1990).
76. *United Steelworkers of America v. Weber,* 443 U.S. 193 (1979); *Johnson v. Santa Clara County Transportation Agency,* 480 U.S. 616 (1987).
77. *Wygant v. Jackson Board of Education,* 476 U.S. 267 (1986); *United States v. Paradise,* 480 U.S. 149 (1987).
78. Seymour Martin Lipset and William Schneider, "An Emerging National Consensus," *The New Republic,* October 15, 1977, 8–9.
79. John R. Bunzel, "Affirmative Re-Actions," *Public Opinion* (February/March 1986): 45–49; Sam Howe Verhovek, "In Poll, Americans Reject Means But Not Ends of Racial Diversity," *New York Times,* December 14, 1997.
80. *Adarand Constructors v. Pena,* 515 U.S. 200 (1995).
81. *Hopwood v. Texas,* 78 F.3d 932 (1996).
82. *Gratz v. Bollinger,* 539 U.S. 244 (2003).
83. *Grutter v. Bollinger,* 539 U.S. 306 (2003).
84. *Schuette v. Coalition to Defend Affirmative Action, 572* U.S. Schuette v. Coalition to Defend Affirmative Action, 572 U.S. 291 (2014).
85. *Bowers v. Hardwick,* 478 U.S. 186 (1986).
86. *Romer v. Evans,* 517 U.S. 620 (1996).
87. *Lawrence v. Texas,* 539 U.S. 558 (2003).
88. *Goodridge v. Department of Public Health,* 440 Mass. 309 (2003) and 440 Mass. 1201 (2004).
89. *Boy Scouts of America v. Dale,* 530 U.S. 640 (2000).
90. Adam Liptak, "Civil Rights Law Protects Gay and Transgender Workers, Supreme Court Rules," *New York Times,* 15 June 2020.

Chapter 7

1. *Federalist* No. 50.
2. *Federalist* No. 63.
3. Annenberg Public Policy Center of the University of Pennsylvania, "Americans' Civics Knowledge Increases But Still Has a Long Way to Go [press release]," September, 12, 2019. Available online at: https://www.annenbergpublicpolicycenter.org/americans-civics-knowledge-increases-2019-survey/, Accessed January 2020.
4. George W. Bishop, Alfred Tuchfarber, and Robert Oldendick, "How Much Can We Manipulate and Control People's Answers to Public Opinion Surveys?" Paper delivered at the 1984 annual meeting of the American Political Science Association; Howard Schuman and Stanley Presser, *Questions and Answers in Attitude Surveys* (New York: Academic Press, 1981).
5. For example, see Bernard Berelson et al., *Voting: A Study of Opinion Formation in a Presidential Campaign* (Chicago: University of Chicago Press, 1954); and Phillip E. Converse, "The Nature of Belief Systems in Mass Publics," in *Ideology and Discontent,* ed. David E. Apter (New York: Free Press, 1964).
6. For example, see V. O. Key, *The Responsible Electorate* (Cambridge, MA: Harvard University Press, 1966); Samuel Popkin, *The Reasoning Voter: Communication and Persuasion in Presidential Campaigns* (Chicago: University of Chicago Press, 1991); Benjamin I. Page and Robert Y. Shapiro, *The Rational Public: Fifty Years of Trends in Americans' Policy Preferences* (Chicago: University of Chicago Press, 1992).
7. Terry M. Moe, *Schools, Vouchers, and the American Public* (Washington, D.C.: Brookings Institution, 2001), 253.
8. Neil Malhotra and Jon A. Krosnick, "The Effect of Survey Mode and Sampling on Inferences about Political Attitudes and Behavior: Comparing the 2000 and 2004 ANES to Internet Surveys with Non-Probability Samples," *Political Analysis* 15, no. 3 (2007): 286–323; David Yeager et al., "Comparing the Accuracy of RDD Telephone Surveys and Internet Surveys Conducted with Probability and Non-Probability Samples," *Public Opinion Quarterly* 75, no. 4 (2011): 709–47.

9. Tom Smith, "That Which We Call Welfare By Any Other Name Would Smell Sweeter: An Analysis of the Impact of Question Wording on Response Patterns," *Public Opinion Quarterly* 51, no. 1 (1987): 75–83.
10. Greg Huber and Celia Paris, "Assessing the Programmatic Equivalence Assumption in Question Wording Experiments: Understanding Why Americans Like Assistance to the Poor More than Welfare," *Public Opinion Quarterly* 77, no. 1 (2013): 385–97.
11. Public Religion Research Institute, Religion & Politics Tracking Survey, J anuary 2013. Retrieved January 2015 from the iPOLL Databank, the Roper Center for Public Opinion Research, University of Connecticut.
12. Morris Fiorina, Samuel Abrams, and Jeremy Pope, *Culture War?: The Myth of a Polarized America* (New York: Pearson Longman, 2005).
13. David Moore, "Revisiting Gay Marriage vs. Civil Unions," Gallup, 2014, www.gallup.com/poll/11662/revisiting-gay-marriage-vs-civil-unions.aspx, accessed January 2015.
14. Howard Schuman and Stanley Presser, *Questions and Answers in Attitude Surveys* (New York: Academic Press, 1981).
15. M. Kent Jennings and Richard G. Niemi, "The Transmission of Political Values from Parent to Child," *American Political Science Review* 62, no. 1 (March 1968): 173; Robert D. Hess and Judith V. Tomey, *The Development of Political Attitudes in Children* (Chicago, IL: Aldine, 1967), 90.
16. John Alford, Carolyn Funk, and John Hibbing, "Are Political Orientations Genetically Transmitted?" *American Political Science Review*, 99, no. 1 (2005): 153–67.
17. Evan Charney and William English, "Genopolitics and the Science of Genetics," *American Political Science Review* 107, no. 2 (2013): 382–95.
18. M. Kent Jennings, Laura Stoker, and Jake Bowers, "Politics across Generations: Family Transmission Reexamined," *Journal of Politics* 71, no. 3 (2009): 782–99.
19. Jon Krosnick and Duane Alwin, "Age and Susceptibility to Attitude Change," *Journal of Personality and Social Psychology* 57, no. 3 (1989): 416–25.
20. Yair Ghitza and Andrew Gelman, "The Great Society, Reagan's Revolution, and Generations of Presidential Voting," unpublished manuscript, Columbia University, 2014.
21. Pew Research Center, "The Generation Gap in American Politics," March 2018.
22. Pew Research Center, "Early Benchmarks Show 'Post-Millennials' On Track to Be Most Diverse, Best-Educated Generation Yet," November 2018.
23. Pew Research Center, "Looking to the Future, Public Sees an America in Decline on Many Fronts," March 2019.
24. Stella Rouse and Ashley Ross. 2018. *The Politics of Millennials: Political Beliefs and Policy Preferences of America's Most Diverse Generation*. Ann Arbor: University of Michigan Press.
25. National Public Radio, "Millennials Are No More Liberal on Gun Control than their Elders, Polls Show," 24 February 2018.
26. Janna Riess, "Same-Sex Marriage Has Support among Most American Religious Groups, Study Shows," *National Catholic Reporter*, 1 May 2018.
27. Robert Shapiro and Harpreet Mahajan, "Gender Differences in Public Preferences: A Summary of Trends from the 1960s to the 1980s," *Public Opinion Quarterly* 50, no. 1 (1986): 42–61.
28. John Aldrich, Jamie Carson, Brad Gomez, and David Rohde, *Change and Continuity in the 2016 Elections* (Washington, D.C.: Congressional Quarterly Press, 2018).
29. Pew Research Center, "Fact Sheet: Attitudes on Same-Sex Marriage," May 2019.
30. Pew Research Center, "Two-Thirds of Americans Support Marijuana Legalization," November 2019
31. "The Black and White of Public Opinion," Pew Research Center for the People & the Press, October 31, 2005.
32. Drew Desilver, "Can We All Get Along?: For Most, the Answer Is Yes," Pew Research Center, August 26, 2013.
33. Mark Peffley and Jon Hurwitz, *Justice in America: The Separate Realities of Blacks and Whites* (New York: Cambridge University Press, 2010).
34. Emily Guskin, Scott Clement, and Dan Balz, "Americans Support Black Lives Matter But Resist Shifts of Police Funds or Removal of Statues of Confederate Generals or Presidents Who Were Enslavers," The Washington Post, 21 July 2020; Nate Cohn and Kevin Quealy, "How Public Opinion Has Moved on Black Lives Matter," New York Times, 10 June 2020.
35. Marisa Abrajano and R. Michael Alvarez, "Hispanic Public Opinion and Partisanship in American," *Political Science Quarterly* 126, no. 2 (2011): 255–85.
36. Ted Jelen, "Religion and American Public Opinion: Social Issues," in *The Oxford Handbook of Religion and American Politics*, eds. Corwin Smidt, Lyman Kellstedt, and James Guth, pp. 217–42 (New York: Oxford University Press, 2009).
37. Frank Newport and Lydia Saad, "Religion, Politics Inform Americans' Views on Abortions," Gallup, April 2006.
38. Pew Research Center, "Religion and the Issues: Few Say Religion Shapes Immigration, Environment Views," September 2010.
39. David Campbell, Geoffrey Layman, and John Green, "A Jump to the Right, A Step to the Left: Religion and Public Opinion," in *New Directions in Public Opinion*, ed. Adam Berinsky, pp. 168–92 (New York: Routledge, 2012).
40. Southern Baptist Convention, "On the Gulf of Mexico Catastrophe," www.sbc.net/resolutions/1207/on-the-gulf-of-mexico-catastrophe. Accessed January 2015.
41. David Kirkpatrick, "The Evangelical Crackup," *New York Times*, October 28, 2007.

42. V. O. Key, Jr., *Public Opinion and American Democracy* (New York: Knopf, 1961), 122–38.
43. Richard E. Dawson, *Public Opinion and Contemporary Disarray* (New York: Harper & Row, 1973), chap. 4.
44. Stuart Soroka and Christopher Wlezien, "On the Limits to Inequality in Representation," *PS: Political Science and Politics* 41, no. 2 (2008): 319–27.
45. Benjamin Page, Larry Bartels, and Jason Seawright, "Democracy and the Policy Preferences of Wealthy Americans," *Perspectives on Politics* 18, no. 1 (2013): 51–73.
46. Alan Gerber, Gregory Huber, and Ebonya Washington, "Party Affiliation, Partisanship, and Political Beliefs: A Field Experiment," *American Political Science Review* 104, no. 4 (2010): 720–44.
47. John Zaller, *The Nature and Origins of Mass Opinion* (New York: Cambridge University Press, 1992); Gabriel Lenz, *Follow the Leader? How Voters Respond to Politicians' Policies and Performance* (Chicago: University of Chicago Press, 2012).
48. W Lance Bennett, "Toward a Theory of Press-State Relations in the United States," *Journal of Communication* 40 , no. 2 (1990): 103–27.
49. Nolan McCarty, Keith Poole, and Howard Rosenthal, *Polarized America* (Cambridge, MA: MIT Press, 2006).
50. Morris Fiorina, Samuel Abrams, and Jeremy Pope, *Culture War? The Myth of a Polarized America* (New York: Pearson Longman, 2005).
51. Matthew Levendusky, *The Partisan Sort: How Liberals Became Democrats and Conservatives Became Republicans (Chicago, IL: University of Chicago Press,* 2009).
52. Levendusky, *The Partisan Sort.*
53. Alan Abramowitz, *The Disappearing Center: Engaged Citizens, Polarization, and American Democracy* (New Haven, CT: Yale University Press, 2010).
54. Shanto Iyengar, Yph Lelkes, and Gaurav Sood. "Affect, Not Ideology: A Social Identity Perspective on Polarization." *Public Opinion Quarterly* 76, no. 3 (2012): 405–31; Shanto Iyengar et al., "The Origins and Consequences of Affective Polarization in the United States," *Annual Review of Political Science* 22, no. 1 (2019): 129–46.
55. Pew Research Center, "Partisanship and Political Animosity in 2016," June 2016.
56. Gregory Huber and Neil Malhotra. "Political Homophily in Social Relationships: Evidence from Online Dating Behavior." *Journal of Politics* 79, no. 1 (2017): 269–83.
57. Karen Gift and Thomas Gift. "Does Politics Influence Hiring? Evidence from a Randomized Experiment." *Political Behavior* 37, no. 3 (2015): 653–75; Christopher McConnell et al. "The Economic Consequences of Partisanship in a Polarized Era," *American Journal of Political Science* 62, no. 1 (2018): 5–18.
58. Jamie Settle and Taylor Carlson. "Opting Out of Political Discussions." *Political Communication* 36, no. 3 (2019): 476–96.
59. James Druckman and Matthew Levendusky. "What Do We Measure When We Measure Affective Polarization?" *Public Opinion Quarterly* 83, no. 1 (2019): 114–22.
60. Samara Klar, Yanna Krupnikov, and John Barry Ryan. "Affective Polarization or Partisan Disdain? Untangling a Dislike for the Opposing Party from a Dislike of Partisanship." *Public Opinion Quarterly* 82, no. 2 (2018): 379–90; James Druckman et al. 2019. "The Illusion of Affective Polarization." Manuscript: Northwestern University.
61. Pew Research Center, "Wide Gender Gap, Growing Educational Divide in Voters' Party Identification," March 2018.
62. Christopher Ellis and James Stimson, *Ideology in America* (New York: Cambridge University Press, 2012).
63. Donald Kinder and Nathan Kalmoe, *Neither Liberal Nor Conservative: Ideological Innocence in the American Public* (Chicago: University of Chicago Press, 2017).
64. Pew Research Center, "Political Typology Reveals Deep Fissures on the Right and the Left," October 2017, p.13.
65. Alexander Agadjanian and G. Elliot Morris, "The Twitter Bot that Defies Polarization." *The New York Times*, 20 January 2020.
66. *Zaller, The Nature and Origins of Mass Opinion.*
67. Michael Delli-Carpini and Scott Keeter, *What Americans Know about Politics and Why It Matters* (New Haven, CT: Yale University Press, 1996).
68. Arthur Lupia, "Shortcuts Versus Encyclopedias: Information and Voting Behavior in California Insurance Reform Elections," *American Political Science Review* 88, no. 1 (1992): 63–76.
69. Richard Lau, David Andersen, and David Redlawsk, "An Exploration of Correct Voting in Recent U.S. Presidential Elections," *American Journal of Political Science* 52, no. 2 (2008): 395–411.
70. Henry Brady and Paul Sniderman, "Attitude Attribution: A Group Basis for Political Reasoning," *American Political Science Review* 79, no. 4 (1985): 1061–78.
71. Larry Bartels, "Uninformed Votes: Information Effects in Presidential Elections," *American Journal of Political Science* 40, no. 1 (1996): 194–230; Richard Lau and David Redlawsk, "Advantages and Disadvantages of Cognitive Heuristics in Political Decision-Making," *American Journal of Political Science* 45, no. 4 (2001): 951–71.
72. Nicholas Carnes and Meredith Sadin, "The 'Mill Worker's Son' Heuristic: How Voters Perceive Politicians from Working-Class Families—and How They Really Behave in Office," *Journal of Politics* 77, no. 1 (2015): 285–98.
73. Larry Bartels, "Homer Gets a Tax Cut: Inequality and Public Policy in the American Mind," *Perspectives on Politics* 3, no. 1 (2005): 15–31.

74. Martin Gilens, "Political Ignorance and Collective Policy Preferences," *American Political Science Review* 95, no. 2 (2001): 379–96.
75. Benjamin Page and Robert Shapiro, "Effects of Public Opinion on Policy," *American Political Science Review* 77, no. 1 (1983): 175–90.
76. Pew Research Center, "Broad Support for Renewed Background Checks Bill, Skepticism about Its Chances," May 23, 2013.
77. Matt Grossman, *The Not-So-Special Interests: Interest Groups, Public Representation, and American Governance* (Stanford, CA: Stanford University Press, 2012).
78. Martin Gilens, *Affluence and Influence* (Princeton, NJ: Princeton University Press, 2012); Larry Bartels, *Unequal Democracy* (Princeton, NJ: Princeton University Press, 2008).
79. Kay Schlozman, Sidney Verba, and Henry Brady, *The Unheavenly Chorus* (Princeton, NJ: Princeton University Press, 2012).

Chapter 8

1. New York Times Editorial Board, "The Worst Voter Turnout in 72 Years," *New York Times*, November 11, 2014.
2. Michael McDonald and Samuel L. Popkin, "The Myth of the Vanishing Voter," *American Political Science Review* 95, no. 4 (December 2001): 963–74.
3. U.S. Census Bureau, Voting and Registration in the Election of November 2016, Table 1.
4. U.S. Census Bureau, Voting and Registration in the Election of November 2016, Table 10.
5. Paul LeBlanc, "Virginia Governor Makes Election Day a Holiday and Expands Early Voting," CNN. Com, 12 April 2020.
6. Miles Parks, "Seattle-Area Voters to Vote By Smartphone In 1st For U.S. Elections," *NPR*, 22 January 2020.
7. Alan Gerber, Gregory Huber, and Seth Hill, "Identifying the Effect of All-Mail Elections on Turnout: Staggered Reform in the Evergreen State," *Political Science Research and Methods* 1, no. 1 (June 2013): 91–116; Matthew R. Knee and Donald P. Green, "The Effects of Registration Laws on Voter Turnout: An Updated Assessment," in *Facing the Challenges of Democracy*, eds. Paul M. Sniderman and Benjamin Highton, pp. 312–28 (Princeton, NJ: Princeton University Press, 2011).
8. Kate Rabinowitz and Brittaqny Renee Mayes, "At Least 83% of American Voters Can Cast Ballots by Mail in the Fall," The Washington Post, 20 August 2020.
9. Daniel Thompson et al., "Universal Vote by Mail Has No Impact on Partisan Turnout or Vote Share," PNAS, Forthcoming; Reid Epstein and Stephanie Saul, "Does Vote-by-Mail Favor Democrats? No, It's a False Argument by Trump," *The New York Times*, 10 April 2020.
10. Drew Desilver, "U.S. Trails Most Developed Countries in Voter Turnout," Pew Research Center Fact Tank, 21 May 2018.
11. Raymond Wolfinger and Jonathan Hoffman, "Registering and Voting with Motor Voter," *PS: Political Science and Politics* 34, no. 1 (March 2001): 90.
12. David Nickerson, "Do Voter Registration Drives Increase Participation? For Whom and When?" *Journal of Politics* 77, no. 1 (January 2015): 88–101.
13. Niraj Chokshi, "Automatic Voter Registration a 'Success' in Oregon," *New York Times*, December 2, 2016.
14. Nathaniel Rakich, "What Happened When 2.2 Million People Were Automatically Registered to Vote," *FiveThirtyEight.com*, 10 October 2019. Available online at: https://53eig.ht/3ajQJfq.
15. Donald Green and Alan Gerber, *Get Out the Vote: How to Increase Voter Turnout* (Washington, D.C.: Brookings Institution Press, 2008).
16. Alan S. Gerber, Donald P. Green, and Christopher W. Larimer, "Social Pressure and Voter Turnout: Evidence from a Large-Scale Field Experiment," *American Political Science Review* 102, no. 1 (February 2008): 33–48.
17. Elizabeth McKenna and Hahrie Han, *Groundbreakers: How Obama's 2.2 Million Volunteers Changed Campaigning in America* (New York: Oxford University Press, 2015).
18. Ryan Enos and Anthony Fowler, "Aggregate Effects of Large-Scale Campaigns on Voter Turnout," *Political Science Research and Methods* 6, no. 4 (October 2018): 733–51.
19. McKenna and Han, *Groundbreakers.*
20. Joshua Darr, "Abandoning the Ground Game? Field Organization in the 2016 Election," *Presidential Studies Quartrerly*, Forthcoming.
21. Ryan Enos, Anthony Fowler, and Lynn Vavreck, "Increasing Inequality: The Effect of GOTV Mobilization on the Composition of the Electorate," *Journal of Politics* 76, no. 1 (January 2014): 273–88.
22. Melissa Michelson and Lisa Garcia Bedolla, *Mobilizing Inclusion: Redefining Citizenship through Get-Out-the-Vote Campaigns* (New Haven, CT: Yale University Press, 2012).
23. Morton Keller, *Affairs of State* (Cambridge, MA: Harvard University Press, 1977), 523.
24. *United States v. Reese*, 92 U.S. 214 (1876); *United States v. Cruikshank*, 92 U.S. 556 (1876); and *Ex Parte Yarbrough*, 110 U.S. 651 (1884).
25. *Guinn and Beall v. United States*, 238 U.S. 347 (1915).
26. 25 *Smith v. Allright*, 321 U.S. 649 (1944).
27. *Schnell v. Davis*, 336 U.S. 993 (1949).
28. Sophie Schuit and Jon Rogowski, "Race, Representation, and the Voting Rights Act," *American Journal of Political Science* 61 (July 2017), 513–526; Charles Bullock and Ronald Keith Gaddie, *The Triumph of Voting Rights in the South* (Norman, OK: University of Oklahoma Press, 2009).
29. U.S. Commission on Civil Rights, "An Assessment of Minority Voting Rights Access in the United States: 2018 Statutory Report." Available online at: https://www.usccr.gov/pubs/2018/Minority_Voting_Access_2018.pdf

30. Figures on 2020 turnout come from the Center for Information and Research on Civic Learning and Engagement, "Youth Voter Turnout Increased in 2020," November 2020.
31. U.S. Census Bureau, *Historical Statistics of the United States: Millennium Edition Online*, Cambridge University Press, Table Eb114–112, "Voter Turnout in Presidential and Congressional Elections: National, South, and non-South, 1824–1998," pp. 5-169–5-170. Data from 2000 forward come from the U.S. Election Project, www.electproject.org.
32. Walter Dean Burnham, "The Changing Shape of the American Political Universe," *American Political Science Review* 59, no. 1 (March 1965): 11; Michael McDonald, "National General Election VEP Turnout Rates, 1789–Present," U.S. Elections Project.
33. Burnham, "The Changing Shape"; E. E. Schattschneider, *The Semi-Sovereign People* (New York: Holt, Rinehart & Winston, 1960), chaps. 5, 6.
34. Philip E. Converse, "Change in the American Electorate," in *The Human Meaning of Social Change*, ed. Angus Campbell and Philip E. Converse, 263–338 (New York: Russell Sage Foundation, 1972).
35. National Conference of State Legislatures, "Voter Identification Requirements," January 2020.
36. Nathaniel Persily et al., "The American Voting Experience: Report and Recommendations of the Presidential Commission on Election Administration," Presidential Commission on Election Administration, January 2014; John Ahlquist, Ken Mayer, and Simon Jackman, "Alien Abduction and Voter Impersonation in the 2012 Election: Evidence from a Survey List Experiment," *Election Law Journal: Rules, Politics, and Policy* 13, no. 4 (December 2014): 460–75; Sharad Goel et al. "One Person, One Vote: Estimating the Prevalence of Double Voting in U.S. Presidential Elections," *American Political Science Review*, Forthcoming.
37. Nick Corasaniti, Reid Epstein, and Jim Rutenberg, "The Times Called Officials in Every State: No Evidence of Voter Fraud," *New York Times*, 10 November 2020; David Cottrell, Michael Herron, and Sean Westwood, "An Exploration of Donald Trump's Allegations of Massive Voter Fraud in the 2016 General Election," *Electoral Studies* 51 (February 2018): 123–42.
38. Keesha Gaskins and Sundeep Iyer, "The Challenge of Obtaining Voter Identification," Report of the Brennan Center for Justice, July 2012; "Issues Related to State Voter Identification Laws," GAO Report 14–634.
39. Rachel Cobb, James Greiner, and Kevin Quinn, "Can Voter ID Laws Be Administered in a Race-Neutral Manner? Evidence from the City of Boston in 2008," *Quarterly Journal of Political Science* 7, no. 1 (January 2012): 1–33; Ariel White, Noah Nathan, and Julie Faller, "What Do I Need to Vote? Bureaucratic Discretion and Discrimination by Local Election Officials," *American Political Science Review* 109, no. 1 (February 2015): 129–42.
40. *Crawford v. Marion County Election Board*, 553 U.S. 181 (2008).
41. "Issues Related to State Voter Identification Laws."
42. Darron Shaw and John Petrocik, *The Turnout Myth: Voting Rates and Partisan Outcomes in American National Elections* (New York: Oxford University Press, 2020); Jack Citrin, Erik Schickler, and John Sides, "What if Everyone Voted? Simulating the Impact of Increased Turnout in Senate Elections," *American Journal of Political Science* 47, no. 1 (January 2003): 75–90; Ben Highton and Raymond E. Wolfinger, "The Political Implications of Higher Turnout," *British Journal of Political Science* 31, no. 1 (January 2001): 179–223.
43. Cindy Kam and Maggie Deichert, "Boycotting, Buycotting, and the Psychology of Political Consumerism," *Journal of Politics*, 82 (January 2020): 72–88; Costas Panagopolous et al., "Political Consumerism: Experimental Tests of Consumer Reactions to Corporate Political Activity," *Journal of Politics*, forthcoming.
44. Data come from the American National Election Studies Guide to Public Opinion and Election Behavior, https://electionstudies.org/resources/anes-guide/, accessed February 2020.
45. Sidney Verba, Kay Schlozman, and Henry Brady, *Voice and Equality* (Cambridge, MA: Harvard University Press, 1995).
46. Sidney Verba and Norman Nie, *Participation in America: Political Democracy and Social Equality* (New York: Harper and Row, 1972).
47. Verba et al., *Voice and Equality.*
48. Rodney Hero and Anne Campbell, "Understanding Latino Political Participation: Exploring the Evidence from the Latino National Political Survey," *Hispanic Journal of Behavioral Sciences* 18, no. 2 (May 1996): 129–41.
49. Cindy Kam, Elizabeth Zechmeister, and Jennifer Wilking, "From the Gap to the Chasm: Gender and Participation among Non-Hispanic Whites and Mexican Americans," *Political Research Quarterly* 61, no. 2 (June 2008): 205–18.
50. Verba et al., *Voice and Equality.*
51. Dave Campbell, *Why We Vote: How Schools and Communities Shape Our Civic Life* (Princeton, NJ: Princeton University Press, 2006); Josh Pasek et al., "Schools as Incubators of Democratic Participation: Building Long-Term Political Efficacy with Civic Education," *Applied Development Science* 12, no. 1 (January 2008): 26–37.
52. Steven Rosenstone and John Mark Hansen, *Mobilization, Participation, and Democracy in America* (New York: Macmillan, 1993).
53. Robert Putnam and David Campbell, *American Grace: How Religion Divides and Unites Us* (New York: Simon and Schuster, 2010).
54. Catherine Wilson, *The Politics of Latino Faith: Religion, Identity, and Urban Community (New York:* New York University Press, 2008).

55. Alan Gerber, Donald Green, and Ron Shachar, "Voting May Be Habit-Forming: Evidence from a Randomized Field Experiment," *American Journal of Political Science* 47, no. 3 (September 2003): 540–50.
56. Marc Meredith, "Persistence in Political Participation," *Quarterly Journal of Political Science* 4, no. 3 (September 2009): 187–209.
57. John Aldrich, Jacob Montgomery, and Wendy Wood, "Turnout as a Habit," *Political Behavior* 33, no. 4 (December 2011): 535–63.
58. Hahrie Han, *Moved to Action: Motivation, Participation, and Inequality in American Politics* (Stanford, CA: Stanford University Press, 2009).
59. Andrea Campbell, *How Policies Make Citizens: Senior Political Activism and the American Welfare State* (Princeton, NJ: Princeton University Press, 2005).
60. Cliff Zukin et al., *A New Engagement? Political Participation, Civic Life, and the Changing American Citizen* (New York: Oxford University Press, 2006); Jane Eisner, *Taking Back the Vote: Getting American Youth Involved in Our Democracy* (Boston, MA: Beacon Press, 2006).

Chapter 9

1. Gallup Inc., Party Affiliation, https://news.gallup.com/poll/15370/party-affiliation.aspx, last accessed April 2020.
2. "Washington's Farewell Address, 1796," Avalon Project, Yale Law School, avalon.law.yale.edu/18th_century/washing.asp. Accessed May 9, 2017.
3. Leon D. Epstein, "Political Parties," in *Handbook of Political Science*, eds. Fred I. Greenstein and Nelson W Polsby (Reading, MA: Addison-Wesley, 1975), vol. 4, 230.
4. V.O. Key, *Politics, Parties, and Pressure Groups* (New York: Crowell, 1942).
5. Quoted in Henry Adams, *History of the United States of America during the Administrations of Jefferson and Madison*, ed. Ernest Samuels, abridged ed. (Chicago, IL: University of Chicago Press, 1967), 147.
6. Martin Wattenberg, *The Decline of American Political Parties, 1952–1980* (Cambridge, MA: Harvard University Press, 1984).
7. Edward Carmines and James Stimson, *Issue Evolution: Race and the Transformation of American Politics* (Princeton, NJ: Princeton University Press, 1989).
8. Martin Cohen et al., *The Party Decides: Presidential Nominations Before and After Reform* (Chicago, IL: University of Chicago Press, 2008).
9. "Toward a More Responsible Two-Party System," *American Political Science Review* 44 (September 1950, Supplement).
10. Matthew Levendusky, *The Partisan Sort* (Chicago, IL: University of Chicago Press, 2009).
11. Walter Dean Burnham, *Critical Elections and the Mainsprings of American Politics* (New York: Norton, 1970), 10.
12. David Mayhew, *Electoral Realignments: A Critique of an American Genre* (New Haven, CT: Yale University Press, 2002).
13. Carmines and Stimson, *Issue Evolution*.
14. Geoffrey Layman and Thomas Carsey, "Party Polarization and 'Conflict Extension' in the American Electorate," *American Journal of Political Science* 46, no. 4 (October 2002): 786–802.
15. David Broockman, "Mobilizing Candidates: Political Actors Strategically Shape the Candidate Pool with Personal Appeals," *Journal of Experimental Political Science* 1, no. 2 (Winter 2014): 104–19.
16. Naftali Bendavid, *The Thumpin': How Rahm Emanuel and the Democrats Learned to Be Ruthless and Ended the Republican Revolution* (New York: Doubleday, 2007).
17. James Dao and Adam Nagourney, "They Served, and Now They're Running," *New York Times*, February 16, 2006; Emmarie Huettman, "Democrats Court Military Veterans in Effort to Reclaim House," *New York Times*, July 5, 2017.
18. Seth Masket and Boris Shor, "Polarization without Parties: Term Limits and Legislative Partisanship in Nebraska's Unicameral Legislature," *State Politics and Policy Quarterly* 15, no. 1 (March 2015).
19. Priscilla Southwell, "Open versus Closed Primaries: The Effect on Strategic Voting and Candidate Fortunes," *Social Science Quarterly* 72, no. 4 (1991): 789–96.
20. Will Bullock and Josh Clinton, "More a Molehill than a Mountain: The Effects of the Blanket Primary on Elected Officials' Behavior from California," *Journal of Politics* 73, no. 3 (July 2011): 915–30; Eric McGhee et al., "A Primary Cause of Partisanship?: Nomination Systems and Legislator Ideology," *American Journal of Political Science* 58, no. 2 (April 2014): 337–51.
21. Astead Herndon, "Democrats Overhaul Controversial Superdelegate System," *New York Times*, 25 August 2018.
22. Geoffrey Layman et al., "Activists and Conflict Extension in American Party Politics," *American Political Science Review* 104, no. 2 (May 2010): 324–46.
23. *Cohen et al., The Party Decides;* Hans Hassell, "Party Control of Party Primaries: Party Influence in Nominations for the U.S. Senate," *Journal of Politics* 78 (January 2016): 75–87.
24. Brian Brox, *Back in the Game: Political Party Campaigning in an Era of Reform* (Albany: State University of New York Press, 2013).
25. Federal Election Commission, "Statistical Summary of 24-Month Campaign Activity of the 2017–2018 Cycle [Press Release]," 15 March 2019. Available online at: https://www.fec.gov/updates/statistical-summary-24-month-campaign-activity-2017-2018-cycle/
26. Douglas Roscoe and Shannon Jenkins, "Changes in Local Party Structure and Activity, 1980–2008," in *The State of the Parties: The Changing Role of Contemporary American Parties,* 7th ed., eds. Jon Green, Daniel Coffey, and David Cohen, pp. 287–302 (Lanham,

MD: Rowman and Littlefield, 2014).

27. Morton Keller, *Affairs of State* (Cambridge, MA: Harvard University Press, 1977), 239.
28. Quoted in Keller, *Affairs of State*, 256.
29. Martin Shefter, "Parties, Bureaucracy, and Political Change in the United States," in *The Development of Political Parties, Sage Electoral Studies Yearbook*, vol. 4, ed. Louis Maisel and Joseph Cooper (Beverly Hills, CA: Sage, 1978).
30. David Mayhew, *Placing Parties in American Politics* (Princeton, NJ: Princeton University Press, 1986).
31. James Q. Wilson, *The Amateur Democrat: Club Politics in Three Cities* (Chicago, IL: University of Chicago Press, 1962).
32. Nicholas Confessore, "A National Party Strategy Funds State Political Monopolies," *New York Times*, January 11, 2014; Brox, *Back in the Game*.
33. Roscoe and Jenkins, Changes in Local Party Structure and Activity; John Aldrich, "Southern Parties in State and Nation," *Journal of Politics* 62, no. 3 (2000): 643–70.
34. Richard Niemi and M. Kent Jennings, "Issues and Inheritance in the Formation of Party Identification," *American Journal of Political Science* 35, no. 4 (November 1991): 970–88.
35. Angus Campbell et al., *The American Voter* (Chicago, IL: University of Chicago Press, Midway Reprints, 1980).
36. Donald Green, Bradley Palmquist, and Eric Schickler, *Partisan Hearts and Minds* (New Haven, CT: Yale University Press, 2002).
37. Morris Fiorina, *Retrospective Voting in American National Elections* (New Haven, CT: Yale University Press, 1981).
38. Eitan Hersh, "The Long-Term Effect of September 11 on the Political Behavior of Victims' Families and Neighbors," *Proceedings of the National Academy of Sciences* 110, no. 52 (2013): 20959–63.
39. Carmines and Stimson, *Issue Evolution*; Ilyana Kuziemko and Ebonya Washington, "Why Did Democrats Lose the South? Bringing New Data to an Old Debate," *American Economic Review*, 108, no. 10 (2018): 2830–67.
40. Gallup: Party Affiliation, available online at: https://news.gallup.com/poll/15370/party-affiliation.aspx, Accessed February 2020.
41. Bruce Keith et al., *The Myth of the Independent Voter* (Berkeley, CA University of California Press, 1992).
42. Jack Dennis, "Political Independence in America, Part II: Towards a Theory," *British Journal of Political Science* 18, no. 2 (April 1988): 197–219; Jack Dennis, "Political Independence in America, Part I: On Being an Independent Partisan Supporter," *British Journal of Political Science* 18, no. 1 (January 1988): 77–109; Samara Klar and Yanna Krupnikov, *Independent Politics: How American Disdain for Parties Leads to Political Inaction* (New York: Cambridge University Press, 2016).
43. See, for example, the data from Gallup: https://news.gallup.com/poll/15370/party-affiliation.aspx, or from the Pew Research Center: https://www.people-press.org/2018/03/20/party-identification-trends-1992-2017/.
44. Authors analysis of the Views of the Electorate Research (VOTER) Survey Data.
45. Patrick Tucker, Jacob Montgomery, and Steven Smith, "Party Identification in the Age of Obama: Evidence on the Sources of Stability and Systematic Change in Party Identification from a Long-Term Panel Survey," *American Politics Research* 72 (June 2019): 309–28; Phillip Converse and Gregory Markus, "Plus Ca Change: The New CPS Election Study Panel," *American Political Science Review* 73 (March 1979): 32-49.
46. Larry Bartels, "Partisanship and Voting Behavior, 1952–1996," *American Journal of Political Science* 44, no. 1 (January 2000): 35–50.
47. Justin McCarthy and Jeffrey Jones, "U.S. Economic Confidence Surges After Election," Gallup, November 15, 2016, www.gallup.com/poll/197474/economic-confidence-surges-election.aspx.
48. Alan Gerber and Greg Huber, "Partisanship, Political Control, and Economic Assessments," *American Journal of Political Science* 54, no. 1 (January 2010): 153–73.
49. Brendan Nyhan, "The Partisan Divide on Ebola Preparedness," *New York Times,* October 16, 2014.
50. Luke Keele, "The Authorities Really Do Matter: Party Control and Trust in Government," *Journal of Politics* 67, no. 3 (August 2005): 873–86.
51. Bureau of Labor Statistics, Historical Unemployment Rate, data.bls.gov/timeseries/LNU04000000?years_option=all_years&periods_option=specific_periods&periods=Annual+Data. Accessed February 2015.
52. The World Bank, "Inflation, Consumer Prices," data.worldbank.org/indicator/FP.CPI.TOTL.ZG, accessed February 2015.
53. Larry Bartels, "Beyond the Running Tally: Partisan Bias in Political Perceptions," *Political Behavior* 24, no. 2 (June 2002): 117–50.
54. Congressional Quarterly, "Browse by Party System," in *Political Handbook of the World,* last modified 2014, library.cqpress.com /phw/toc.php?source =PoliticalHandbook+of+the+World+2014&mode=phw-partysystem&level=1&values=&sort=Party+System. Accessed May 2015.
55. Stephen Ansolabehere, Jonathan Rodden, and James Snyder, "Purple America," *Journal of Economic Perspectives* 20, no. 2 (Spring 2006): 97–118.
56. Lee Drutman, *Breaking the Two-Party Doom Loop: The Case for Multiparty Democracy in America* (New York: Oxford University Press, 2020).
57. Lee Drutmn, William Galston, and Tod Lindberg. "Spoiler Alert: Why Americans' Desires for a Third Party Are Unlikely to Come True," Voter Study Group, Available online: https://www.voterstudygroup.org/publication/spoiler-alert, Accessed February 2020.

58. Drutman et al., Spoiler Alert
59. Levendusky, *The Partisan Sort.*
60. John Petrocik, "Issue Ownership in Presidential Elections, with a 1980 Case Study," *American Journal of Political Science* 40, no. 4 (August 1996): 825–50.
61. *Williams v. Rhodes*, 393 U.S. 23 (1968).
62. Vanessa Willamson and Theda Skocpol, *The Tea Party and the Remaking of American Conservatism* (New York: Oxford University Press, 2012).
63. Jeremy W. Peters, "The Tea Party Didn't Get What It Wanted, But It Did Unleash the Politics of Anger," *New York Times*, 30 August 2019.
64. Bryan Gervais and Irwin Morris, *Reactionary Republicanism: How the Tea Party Paved the Way for Trump's Election* (New York: Oxford University Press, 2018).
65. Gervais and Morris, *Reactionary Republicanism*; Pew Research Center, "Trump's Staunch GOP Supporters Have Roots in the Tea Party," 16 May 2019.

Chapter 10

1. Federal Elections Commission, 12 Month Data Summary for the 2019–2020 Election Cycle.
2. Christopher Karpowitz and Jeremy Pope, "Who Caucuses?: An Experimental Approach to Institutional Design and Electoral Participation," *British Journal of Political Science*, 45 (April 2015): 329–51.
3. Nate Cohn, "How the New Primary Calendar Changes the Contest for Democrats," *New York Times*, 11 December 2019.
4. John Sides and Lynn Vavreck, *The Gamble: Choice and Chance in the 2012 Presidential Election* (Princeton, NJ: Princeton University Press, 2013), especially chaps. 2 and 3.
5. Larry Bartels, *Presidential Primaries* (Princeton, NJ: Princeton University Press, 1985).
6. Philip Bump, "Ted Cruz Did Steal Ben Carson's Votes. But He Did It in November." *Washington Post*, February 3, 2016.
7. Larry Bartels, "Messages Received: The Political Impact of Media Exposure," *American Political Science Review* 87, no. 2 (June 1993): 267–85.
8. Nicholas Confessore and Karen Yourish, "Measuring Donald Trump's Mammoth Advantage in Free Media," *New York Times*, March 15, 2016; Nate Silver, "How Trump Hacked the Media," *FiveThirtyEight.com*, March 30, 2016.
9. Bartels, *Presidential Primaries;* Brian Knight and Nathan Schiff, "Momentum and Social Learning in Presidential Primaries," *Journal of Political Economy* 118, no. 6 (December 2010): 1110–50.
10. Mark Wattier, "Presidential Primaries and Frontloading: An Empirical Polemic," Paper presented at the "State of the Party: 2004 and Beyond" Conference, Akron, OH, October 5–7, 2005.
11. Paul Abramson et al., *Change and Continuity in the 2012 Elections* (Thousand Oaks, CA: Sage, 2015), 20–22.
12. Jonathan Martin, "Republicans Vote to Streamline Nomination Process," *New York Times*, January 24, 2014.
13. Trip Gabriel, "Donald Trump Finds an Ally in Delegate Selection System, Much to G.O.P.'s Chagrin," *New York Times*, February 29, 2016.
14. Lonna Rae Atkeson and Cherie Maestas, "Racing to the Front: The Effects of Frontloading on Presidential Primary Turnout," Paper presented at the Reforming the Presidential Nomination Process Conference, Iowa City, IA, January 3–4, 2008.
15. James Gimpel, Karen Kaufmann, and Shana Pearson-Merkowitz, "Battleground States versus Blackout States: The Behavioral Implications of Modern Presidential Campaigns." *Journal of Politics* 69, no. 3 (2007): 786–97.
16. Lynn Vavreck, *The Message Matters* (Princeton, NJ: Princeton University Press, 2009).
17. Morris P. Fiorina, *Retrospective Voting in American National Elections* (New Haven, CT: Yale University Press, 1981).
18. John Sides, Lynn Vavreck, and Michael Tessler, *Identity Crisis: The 2016 Presidential Campaign and the Battle for the Meaning of America* (Princeton, NJ: Princeton University Press, 2018); Diana Mutz, "Status Threat, Not Economic Hardship, Explains the 2016 Presidential Vote," *Proceedings of the National Academy of Sciences*, 115, no. 19: E4330-9.
19. Vavreck, *The Message Matters,* table 3.1, 29.
20. "Economy Is Dominant Issue for Americans as Election Nears," Gallup, October 2012.
21. Thomas Holbrook, "Campaigns, National Conditions, and U.S. Presidential Elections," *American Journal of Political Science* 38, no. 4 (November 1994): 973–98.
22. James Campbell, "When Have Presidential Campaigns Decided Election Outcomes?" *American Politics Research* 29, no. 5 (September 2001): 437–60.
23. James Campbell, "Presidential Election Campaigns and Partisanship," in *American Political Parties: Decline or Resurgence,* eds. Jeffrey Cohen, Richard Fleishner, and Paul Kantor (Washington, D.C.: Congressional Quarterly Press, 2001), 12.
24. Corwin Smidt, "Dynamics in Partisanship During American Presidential Campaigns," *Public Opinion Quarterly* 78, no. S1 (2014): 303–29.
25. John Petrocik, "Issue Ownership in Presidential Elections, with a 1980 Case Study," *American Journal of Political Science* 40, no. 3 (August 1996): 825–50.
26. Nate Cohn, "A 2016 Review: Turnout Wasn't the Driver of Clinton's Defeat," *New York Times*, 28 March 2017.
27. Andrew Gelman and Gary King, "Why Are American Presidential Campaign Polls So Variable When Votes Are So Predictable?" *British Journal of Political Science* 23, no. 4 (October 1993): 409–51.
28. Carolyn Funk, "Bringing the Candidate into Models of Candidate Evaluation," *Journal of Politics* 61, no. 3 (August 1999): 700–20.

29. Lynn Vavreck, "Why This Election Was Not about the Issues," *New York Times: The Upshot*, November 23, 2016.
30. 2016 Exit Polls as reported by Fox News, www.foxnews.com/politics/elections/2016/exit-polls.
31. Funk, "Bringing the Candidate into Models of Candidate Evaluation."
32. Donald Stokes, "Spatial Models of Party Competition," *American Political Science Review* 57, no. 2 (June 1963): 368–77.
33. Dan Hopkins, "Voters Really Did Switch to Trump at the Last Minute," *FiveThirtyEight.com*, December 20, 2016.
34. Ted Brader, *Campaigning for Hearts and Minds* (Chicago, IL: University of Chicago Press, 2006).
35. Ibid., 140–43.
36. Erika Franklin Fowler, Travis Ridout, and Michael Franz, "Political Advertising in 2016: The Presidential Election as Outlier?" *The Forum* 14, no. 4 (2016): 445–69.
37. Kathleen Hall Jamieson, Paul Waldman, and Susan Sherr, "Eliminate the Negative?: Categories of Analysis for Political Advertisements," in *Crowded Airwaves: Campaign Advertising in Elections,* eds. James Thurber, Candice Nelson, and David Dulio, pp. 44–64 (Washington, D.C.: Brookings Institution Press, 2000).
38. Erika Franklin Fowler, Michael Franz, and Travis Ridout, *Political Advertising in the United States* (Boulder, CO: Westview Press, 2016).
39. John Geer, *In Defense of Negativity* (Chicago, IL: University of Chicago Press, 2006).
40. Jonathan Krasno and Donald Green, "Do Televised Presidential Ads Increase Voter Turnout? Evidence from a Natural Experiment," *Journal of Politics* 70, no. 1 (January 2008): 245–61.
41. Martin Gilens, Lynn Vavreck, and Martin Cohen, "The Mass Media and the Public's Assessments of Presidential Candidates, 1952–2000," *Journal of Politics* 69, no. 4 (November 2007): 1160–75.
42. Gregory Huber and Kevin Arceneaux, "Identifying the Persuasive Effects of Presidential Advertising," *American Journal of Political Science* 51, no. 4 (October 2007): 957–77.
43. Seth Hill et al., "How Quickly We Forget: The Duration of Persuasion Effects from Mass Communication," *Political Communication* 30, no. 4 (Winter 2013): 521–47.
44. John Zaller, "The Myth of Massive Media Impact Revisited," in *Political Persuasion and Attitude Change*, eds. Diana Mutz, Paul Sniderman, and Richard Brody, pp. 17–78 (Ann Arbor, MI: University of Michigan Press, 1996).
45. Thomas Holbrook, *Do Campaigns Matter?* (Thousand Oaks, CA: Sage, 1996).
46. Thomas Holbrook, "Bump Time," Politics by the Numbers, August 23, 2012. politics-by-the-numbers.blogspot.com/2012/08/bump -time.html. Accessed February 2015.
47. Kim Fridkin et al., "Capturing the Power of a Campaign Event: The 2004 Presidential Debate in Tempe," *Journal of Politics* 69, no. 3 (August 2007): 770–85.
48. Diana Owen, *Media Messages in American Presidential Elections* (New York: Greenwood Press, 1991).
49. *Holbrook, Do Campaigns Matter?*
50. Sides and Vavreck, *The Gamble*, 155–61.
51. Ibid., 1.
52. Gary Jacobson, "It's Nothing Personal: The Decline of the Incumbency Advantage in U.S. House Elections," *Journal of Politics* 77, no. 3 (2015): 861–73.
53. Bruce Cain, John Ferejohn, and Morris Fiorina, *The Personal Vote* (Cambridge, MA: Harvard University Press, 1987).
54. Alan Abramowitz, Brad Alexander, and Matthew Gunning, "Incumbency, Redistricting, and the Decline of Competition in U.S. House Elections," *Journal of Politics* 68, no. 1 (February 2006): 75–88.
55. Marc Meredith, "Exploiting Friends-and-Neighbors to Estimate Coattail Effects," *American Political Science Review* 107, no. 4 (November 2013): 742–65.
56. Angus Campbell, "Surge and Decline: A Study of Electoral Change," *Public Opinion Quarterly* 24, no. 3 (Autumn 1960): 397–418; James Campbell, "The Revised Theory of Surge and Decline," *American Journal of Political Science* 31, no. 4 (November 1987): 965–79.
57. Philip Bump, "How the 2014 Electorate Compares to 2010 and 2012, in One Chart," *Washington Post,* November 4, 2014.
58. Federal Election Commission, "Statistical Summary of the 24-Month Campaign Activity of the 2017–2018 Cycle," March 15, 2019.
59. Robert Maguire, "$1.4 Billion and Counting in Spending by Super PACs, Dark Money Groups," Open Secrets [Press Release], 9 November 2016.
60. Campaign Finance Institute, Table 2-8: House Receipts from Individuals, PACs, and Others, All General Election Candidates, 1999–2018.
61. Campaign Finance Institute, Table 2-9: Senate Receipts from Individuals, PACs, and Others, All General Election Candidates, 1999–2018.
62. Stephen Ansolabehere, John De Fugueiredo, and James Snyder, "Why Is There So Little Money in U.S. Politics?" *Journal of Economic Perspectives* 17, no. 1 (Winter 2003): 105–30.
63. Center for Responsive Politics, Candidate Profiles, Hillary Clinton and Donald Trump.
64. R. Michael Alvarez, Jonathan Katz, and Seo-Young Silvia Kim, "Hidden Donors: The Censoring Problem in U.S. Federal Campaign Finance Data," *Election Law Journal*, Forthcoming.
65. Nicholas Confessore and Sarah Cohen, "How Jeb Bush Spent $130 Million Running for President With Nothing to Show for It," *New York Times,* 22 February 2016.
66. Alan Gerber, "Does Campaign Spending Work?: Field Experiments Provide Evidence and Suggest New Theory," *American Behavioral Scientist* 47 (January 2004): 541–74.

67. National Conference of State Legislatures, "Overview of State Laws on Public Financing," January 2013, www.ncsl.org/research/elections-and-campaigns/public-financing-of-campaigns-overview.aspx.
68. Michael Miller, *Subsidizing Democracy: How Public Financing Changes Elections and How It Can Work in the Future* (Ithaca, NY: Cornell University Press, 2013).
69. Gerald Pomper, *Elections in America* (New York: Dodd, Mead, 1971); Tracy Sulkin, *The Legislative Legacy of Congressional Campaigns* (New York: Cambridge University Press, 2011).
70. *Kathleen Hall Jamieson, Everything You Think You Know about Politics . . . And Why You're Wrong* (New York: Basic Books, 2000).
71. Benjamin Ginsberg, "Elections and Public Policy," *American Political Science Review* 70 (March 1976): 41–49.

Chapter 11

1. Lee Drutman, *The Business of America Is Lobbying* (New York: Oxford University Press, 2015).
2. The Norris-LaGuardia Act of 1932 restricted the use of injunctions in labor disputes; the Wagner Act of 1935 guaranteed rights to collective bargaining and to the union shop.
3. U.S. Census Bureau, *Historical Statistics of the United States, Colonial Times to 1970, vol. 1* (Washington, D.C.: Government Printing Office, 1975), Series H 751–765, "Institutions of Higher Education—Degrees Conferred, by Sex: 1870 to 1970," pp. 385–86.
4. Beth Leech, Frank Baumgartner, Timothy LaPira, and Nicholas Semanko. "Drawing Lobbyists to Washington: Government Activity and the Demand for Advocacy," *Political Research Quarterly* 58 (March 2005): 19–30.
5. Timothy LaPira, "Lobbying after 9/11: Policy Regime Emergence and Interest Group Mobilization," *Policy Studies Journal* 42 (May 2014): 226–51.
6. Dana Priest and William M. Arkin, "A Hidden World, Growing Beyond Control" and "National Security Inc.," *Washington Post,* July 19–21, 2010.
7. Timothy P. Carney, "The TSA and the Full-Body Scanner Lobby," *Washington Examiner*, December 29, 2009; Kimberly Kindy, "Ex-Homeland Security Chief Head Said to Abuse Public Trust by Touting Body Scanners," *Washington Post,* January 1, 2010.
8. The distinction is drawn from Kay Lehman Schlozman and John T. Tierney, *Organized Interests and American Democracy* (New York: Harper and Row, 1985).
9. Center for Responsive Politics, "Lobbying: Top Spenders"; data available by year at www.opensecrets.org.
10. Gabriel A. Almond and Sidney Verba, *The Civic Culture* (Princeton, NJ: Princeton University Press, 1963), 194.
11. Robert D. Putnam, *Bowling Alone: The Collapse and Revival of American Community* (New York: Simon and Schuster, 2001); and Robert D. Putnam and David Campbell, *American Grace: How Religion Unites and Divides Us* (New York: Simon and Schuster, 2010).
12. Mancur Olson Jr., *The Logic of Collective Action* (Cambridge, MA: Harvard University Press, 1965), 153–57.
13. Joel Lovell, "Can the ACLU Become the NRA for the Left?" *New York Times*, 2 July 2018.
14. Joanne Miller and Jon Krosnick, "Threat as a Motivator of Political Activism: A Field Experiment," *Political Psychology* 25, no. 4 (August 2004): 507–23.
15. Derek C. Bok and John T. Dunlop, *Labor and the American Community* (New York: Simon and Schuster, 1970), 134.
16. Drutman, *The Business of America Is Lobbying.*
17. Frank Baumgartner et al., *Lobbying and Policy Change: Who Wins, Who Loses, and Why* (Chicago, IL: University of Chicago Press, 2009).
18. Daniel Gillion, *The Loud Minority: Why Protests Matter in American Democracy.* (Princeton, NJ: Princeton University Press, 2020).
19. Walter A. Rosenbaum, *Environmental Politics and Policy*, 8th ed. (Washington, D.C.: Congressional Quarterly College Press, 2010).
20. Anne Barnard and James Baron, "Climate Strike N.Y.C.: Young Crowds Demand Action, Welcome Greta Thunberg," *New York Times*, 20 September 2019.
21. Jane Mansbridge, *Why We Lost the ERA* (Chicago, IL: University of Chicago Press, 1986), chap. 10.
22. Ibid.
23. Heidi Przybyla and Fredreka Schouten, "At 2.6 Million Strong, Women's Marches Crush Expectations," *USA Today,* January 21, 2017.
24. Drew DeSilver, "A Record Number of Women Will Be Serving in the New Congress," Pew Research Center, December 18, 2018.
25. Anna North, "The Women's Marches Are Shrinking. Their Influence Isn't," *Vox*, 17 January 2020.
26. Bureau of Labor Statistics, Union Membership (Annual) News Release, Economic News Release USDL-20-0108, 22 January 2020.
27. 138 S. Ct. 2448; 201 L. Ed. 2d 924
28. Rebecca Rainey and Ian Kulgren, "1 Year after Janus, Unions are Flush," *Politico*, 15 May 2019.
29. Anthony Nownes, *Total Lobbying: What Lobbyists Want (And How They Try to Get It)* (New York: Cambridge University Press, 2006).
30. Kevin Easterling, *The Political Economy of Expertise: Information and Efficiency in American Politics* (Ann Arbor, MI: University of Michigan Press, 2004).
31. John Mark Hansen, *Gaining Access: Congress and the Farm Lobby, 1919–1981* (Chicago, IL: University of Chicago Press, 1991).
32. Frank Baumgartner and Beth Leech, "Interest Niches and Policy Bandwagons: Patterns of Interest Group Involvement in National Politics," *Journal of Politics* 63, no. 4 (November 2001): 1191–213.
33. Baumgartner and Leech, "Interest Niches and Policy Bandwagons."
34. James M. Snyder, Jr., "Artificial Extremism in Interest Group Ratings," *Legislative Studies Quarterly* 17 (August 1992): 319–45.

35. Robert Kaiser, *So Damn Much Money: The Triumph of Lobbying and the Corrosion of American Government* (New York: Knopf, 2009).
36. Ron Nixon, "Special Funds in Congress Called New Earmarks," *New York Times,* February 6, 2012; David Joachim, "With Stealth, Congressional Spending on Pet Projects Persist, Report Says," *New York Times,* May 7, 2014.
37. Ken Kollman, *Outside Lobbying. Public Opinion and Interest Group Strategies* (Princeton, NJ: Princeton University Press, 1998).
38. Jeff Zeleny, "Thousands Rally in Capital to Protest Big Government," *New York Times*, September 13, 2009.
39. Eric Heberlig, Marc Hetherington, and Bruce Larson, "The Price of Leadership: Campaign Money and the Polarization of Congressional Parties," *Journal of Politics* 68, no. 4 (November 2006): 992–1005.
40. John Wright, *Interest Groups and Congress: Lobbying, Contributions, and Influence* (Boston, MA: Allyn & Bacon, 1996); Hansen, Gaining Access.
41. David Broockman and Joshua Kalla, "Campaign Contributions Facilitate Access to Congressional Officials: A Randomized Field Experiment," *American Journal of Political Science* 60, no. 3 (July 2016): 545–58.
42. Janet Grenzke, "PACs and the Congressional Supermarket: The Currency Is Complex," *American Journal of Political Science* 33, no. 1 (February 1989) : 1–24; Anthony Fowler, Haritz Garro, and Jörg Spenkuch, "Quid Pro Quo? Corporate Returns to Campaign Contributions," Journal of Politics, Forthcoming.
43. Richard Hall and Alan Deardorff, "Lobbying as Legislative Subsidy," *American Political Science Review* 100, no. 1 (February 2006): 69–84.
44. Rui de Figueiredo and Geoff Edwards, "Does Private Money Buy Public Policy? Campaign Contributions and Regulatory Outcomes in Telecommunications," *Journal of Economics and Management Strategy* 16, no. 3 (February 2007): 547–76; Amy McKay, "Buying Amendments? Lobbyists' Campaign Contributions and Microlegislation in the Creation of the Affordable Care Act," *Legislative Studies Quarterly*, Forthcoming.
45. Kimberly Kindy, "Ex-Homeland Security Chief Head Said to Abuse Public Trust by Touting Body Scanners," *Washington Post*, January 1, 2010.
46. Robert O'Harrow and Scott Higham, "Report Finds DHS Lax on Contracting Procedures," *Washington Post*, November 22, 2006.
47. Susan Weaver, *Decision to Prosecute: Organization and Public Policy in the Antitrust Division* (Cambridge, MA: MIT Press, 1977), 154–63.
48. Michael Schmidt and Eric Lipton, "Trump Toughens Some Facets of Lobbying Ban and Weakens Others," *New York Times,* January 28, 2017.
49. Adreas Madestam et al., "Do Political Protests Matter? Evidence from the Tea Party Movement," *Quarterly Journal of Economics* 128, no. 4 (September 2013): 1633–85; Daniel Gillion, *The Political Power of Protests: Minority Activism and Shifts in Public Policy* (New York: Cambridge University Press, 2013).
50. Baumgartner et al., *Lobbying and Policy Change.*
51. James Surowiecki, "Masters of Main Street," *The New Yorker,* July 12, 2010.
52. Neil Haggerty, "Trump Makes Repeal of CFPB Auto Lending Rule Official," *American Banker*, 21 May 2018.
53. Matthew Grossman, *The Not-So-Special Interests: Interest Groups, Public Representation, and American Governance* (Stanford, CA: Stanford University Press, 2012).
54. Baumgartner et al., *Lobbying and Policy Change.*
55. *United States v. Harris,* 347 U.S. 612 (1954).
56. U.S. Code, Title 26, section 501(c) (3).

Chapter 12

1. Craig Silverman, "This Analysis Shows How Viral Fake Election News Stories Outperformed Real News on Facebook," *Buzzfeed News,* November 16, 2016.
2. See "The Watergate Story," *Washington Post.* Available at www.washingtonpost.com/watergate/.
3. Michael Shear et al, "How Trump Reshaped the Presidency in Over 11,000 Tweets," *New York Times,* 2 November 2019.
4. Julia Hirschfield Davis, "House Condemns Trump's Attack on Four Congresswomen as Racist," *New York Times*, 16 July 2019.
5. Frank Newport, "Deconstructing Trump's Use of Twitter," Gallup, 16 May 2018.
6. David E. Butler, "Why America's Political Reporting Is Better than England's," *Harper's,* May 1963, 15–25.
7. Gerard Alexander, "Illiberal Europe," *Weekly Standard,* April 10, 2006.
8. Maria Petrova, "Newspapers and Parties: How Advertising Revenues Created an Independent Press," *American Political Science Review* 105 (November 2011): 790–808.
9. Quoted in Frank Luther Mott, *American Journalism: A History, 1690–1960,* 3rd ed. (New York: Macmillan, 1962), 529.
10. David Mindich, *Just the Facts: How "Objectivity" Came to Define American Journalism* (New York: New York University Press, 1998).
11. Jeremy Padget, Johanna Dunaway, and Joshua Darr, "As Seen on TV? How Gatekeeping Makes the U.S. House Seem More Extreme," *Journal of Communication* 69 (December 2019): 696–719.
12. Pew Research Center, "State of the News Media 2012" and "State of the News Media 2019"
13. Matthew Hindman, *The Myth of Digital Democracy* (Princeton, NJ: Princeton University Press, 2009).
14. Hindman, *The Myth of Digital Democracy, 61.*
15. Seth Flaxman, Sharad Goel, Justin Rao, "Filter Bubbles, Echo Chambers, and Online News Consumption," *Public Opinion Quarterly* 80 (Special Issue 2016): 298–320.

16. Daniela Dimitrova et al., "The Effects of Digital Media on Political Knowledge and Participation in Election Campaigns: Evidence from Panel Data," *Communications Research* 41, no. 1 (January 2014): 95–118; Kate Kenski and Natalie Jomini Stroud, "Connections Between Internet Use and Political Efficacy, Knowledge, and Participation," *Journal of Broadcasting and Electronic Media* 50, no. 2 (June 2006): 173–92.
17. Markus Prior, *Post-Broadcast Democracy* (New York: Cambridge University Press, 2006).
18. Matthew Baum and Samuel Kernell, "Has Cable Ended the Golden Age of Presidential Television?" *American Political Science Review* 93, no. 1 (March 1999): 99–114.
19. Prior, *Post-Broadcast Democracy.*
20. Pew Research Center, "Amid Criticisms, Support for Media's 'Watchdog' Role Stands Out," August 2013.
21. James Druckman, "Media Matter: How Newspapers and Television News Cover Campaigns and Influence Voters," *Political Communication* 22, no. 4 (Fall 2005): 463–81.
22. Newspaper Association of America, "Newspaper Circulation Volume"; Pew Research Center's Project for Excellence in Journalism, "State of the News Media 2016."
23. Pew Research Center, "America's Shifting Statehouse Press: Can New Players Compensate for Lost Legacy Reporters?" July 2014.
24. Matthew Hindman, "More of the Same: The Lack of Local News on the Internet," Report to the FCC, 2011.
25. Sam Schulfofer-Wohl and Miguel Carrido, "Do Newspapers Matter? Short-Run and Long-Run Evidence from the Closure of the Cincinnati Post," *Journal of Media Economics* 26, no. 2 (January 2013): 60–81; Danny Hayes and Jennifer Lawless, "As Local News Goes, So Goes Citizen Engagement: Media, Knowledge, and Participation in U.S. House Elections," *Journal of Politics* 77, no. 2 (April 2015): 447–62; Danny Hayes and Jennifer Lawless, "The Decline of Local News and Its Effects: New Evidence from Longitudinal Data," *Journal of Politics* 80 (January 2018): 332–36.
26. David Karpf, *The MoveOn Effect: The Unexpected Transformation of American Political Advocacy* (New York: Oxford University Press, 2012).
27. Robert Bond et al., "A 61-Million-Person Experiment in Social Influence and Political Mobilization," *Nature 489* (13 September 2012): 295–98.
28. Allison Dale and Aaron Strauss, "Don't Forget to Vote: Text Message Reminders as a Mobilization Tool," *American Journal of Political Science* 53, no. 4 (October 2009): 787–804.
29. Cathy Cohen et al., "Participatory Politics: New Media and Youth Political Action," McArthur Research Network on Youth and Participatory Politics, July 2012.
30. Niraj Chokshi, "How #BlackLivesMatter Came to Define a Movement," *New York Times*, August 22, 2016.
31. Kathleen Hall Jamieson and Joseph Cappella, *Echo Chamber* (New York: Oxford University Press, 2008); Natalie Stroud, *Niche News* (New York: Oxford University Press, 2011); Matthew Levendusky, *How Partisan News Polarizes America* (Chicago, IL: University of Chicago Press, 2013).
32. Diana Mutz, *Hearing the Other Side: Deliberative versus Participatory Democracy* (New York: Cambridge University Press, 2006).
33. Pew Research Center, "Polarization and Media Habits," October 2014.
34. Eric Lawrence, John Sides, and Henry Farrell, "Self-Segregation or Deliberation? Blog Readership, Participation, and Polarization in American Politics," *Perspectives on Politics* 8 (March 2010): 141–57.
35. Stroud, *Niche News.*
36. Matthew Gentzkow and Jesse Shapiro, "Ideological Segregation Online and Offline," *Quarterly Journal of Economics* 126 (December 2011): 1799–839
37. Seth Flaxman et al., "Filter Bubbles, Echo Chambers, and Online News Consumption"; Jacob Nelson and James Webster, "The Myth of Partisan Selective Exposure: A Portrait of the Online Political News Audience," *Social Media and Society*, https://doi.org/10.1177/2056305117729314.
38. Gregory Eady et al., "How Many People Live in Political Bubbles on Social Media? Evidence from Linked Survey and Twitter Data," *SAGE Open* 2019 (January–March): 1–21.
39. Jamie Settle, *Frenemies: How Social Media Polarizes America* (New York: Cambridge University Press, 2018); Michael Scharkow et al., "How Social Network Sites and Other Online Intermediaries Increase Exposure to News," *Proceedings of the National Academy of Sciences*, 117 (February 11, 2020): 2761–63; Flaxman et al., "Filter Bubbles, Echo Chambers, and Online News Consumption."
40. Eytan Bakshy, Solomon Messing, and Lala Adamic, "Exposure to Ideologically Diverse News and Opinion on Facebook," *Science* 328(5 June 2015): 1130–32.
41. Andrew Guess, "(Almost) Everything in Moderation: New Evidence on Americans' Online Media Diets." Manuscript: Princeton University.
42. Guess, "(Almost) Everything in Moderation,"; Nate Cohn and Kevin Quealy, "The Democratic Electorate on Twitter Is Not the Democratic Electorate in Real Life," *New York Times*, 9 April 2019.
43. David Lazer et al., "The Science of Fake News" *Science* 359 (9 March 2018): 1094–96.
44. Ethan Porter and Thomas Wood, *False Alarm: The Truth about Political Mistruths in the Trump Era* (New York: Cambridge Elements, Cambridge University Press, 2019), 32.
45. Silverman, "This Analysis Shows How Viral Fake Election News Stories Outperformed Real News on Facebook."

46. Nir Grinberg et al., "Fake News on Twitter during the 2016 U.S. Presidential Election," *Science* 363 (25 January 2019): 374–78; Andrew Guess, Jonathan Nagler, and Joshua Tucker, "Less than You Think: Prevalence and Predictors of Fake News Dissemination on Facebook," *Science Advances* 5 (9 January 2019): DOI: 10.1126/sciadv.aau4586.
47. Andrew Guess, Brendan Nyhan, and Jason Reifler, "Exposure to Untrustworthy Websites in the 2016 U.S. Presidential Election," *Nature Human Behavior*,2020, DOI: 10.1038/s41562-020-0833-x; Christopher Bail et al., "Assessing the Russian Internet Research Agency's Impact on the Political Attitudes and Behaviors of American Twitter Users in Late 2017," *Proceedings of the National Academy of Sciences* 117 (January 2020): 243–50.
48. Hunt Allcott and Matthew Gentzkow, "Social Media and Fake News in the 2016 Election," *Journal of Economic Perspectives* 31, no. 2 (2017): 211–36; Jennifer Allen et al., "Evaluating the Fake News Problem at the Scale of the Information Ecosystem," *Science Advances*, 6, no. 14 (1 April 2020): eaay3539.
49. Pew Research Center, "Many Americans Believe Fake News Is Sowing Confusion," December 2016.
50. Mark Jurkowitz and Amy Mitchell, "An Oasis of Bipartisanship: Republicans and Democrats Distrust Social Media Sites for Political and Election News," Pew Research Center, 29 January 2020.
51. David Karpf, "On Digital Disinformation and Democratic Myths," Social Science Research Council, Media Well Blog, https://mediawell.ssrc.org/expert-reflections/on-digital-disinformation-and-democratic-myths/, 10 December 2019.
52. Mike Isaac, "Facebook Mounts Effort to Limit Tide of Fake News," *New York Times,* December 15, 2016.
53. Hunt Allcott, Matthew Gentzkow, and Chuan Yu, "Trends in the Diffusion of Misinformation on Social Media." *Research and Politics* (2019): https://doi.org/10.1177/2053168019848554
54. Katherine Clayton et al., "Real Solutions for Fake News? Measuring the Effectiveness of General Warnings and Fact-Check Tags in Reducing Belief in False Stories on Social Media," *Political Behavior*, Forthcoming.
55. Matt Apuzzo and Sharon LaFraniere, "13 Russians Indicted as Mueller Reveals Effort to Aid Trump Campaign," *New York Times*, 16 February 2018.
56. Maggie Miller, "FBI Director Says Foreign Disinformation Campaigns 'Never Stopped' after 2016 Elections," *The Hill*, 5 February 2020.
57. Michael Grynbaum, "After Another Year of Trump Attacks, 'Ominous Signs' for the American Press," *New York Times*, 30 December 2019.
58. Chris Wells et al., "How Trump Drove Coverage to the Nomination: Hybrid Media Campaigning," *Political Communication* 33, no. 4 (October 2016): 669–76.
59. Maxwell McCombs and Donald Shaw, "The Agenda Setting Function of Mass Media," *Public Opinion Quarterly* 36, no. 2 (Summer 1972): 176–87.
60. Dorris Graber, *Mass Media and American Politics*, 8th ed. (Washington, D.C.: Congressional Quarterly Press, 2010), chap. 4.
61. Joanne Miller and Jon Krosnick, "News Media Impact on the Ingredients of Presidential Evaluations: Politically Knowledgeable Citizens Are Guided by a Trusted Source," *American Journal of Political Science* 44, no. 2 (April 2000): 301–15.
62. Jon Krosnick and Donald Kinder, "Altering the Foundations of Support for the President through Priming," *American Political Science Review* 84, no. 2 (June 1990): 497–512.
63. Joshua Darr et al., "Collision with Collusion: Partisan Reaction to the Trump-Russia Scandal," *Perspectives on Politics* 17 (September 2019): 772–87.
64. Shanto Iyengar, *Media Politics: A Citizen's Guide,* 2nd ed. (New York: W.W. Norton, 2011).
65. Miller and Krosnick, "News Media Impact on the Ingredients of Presidential Evaluations."
66. Tom Nelson, Rosalee Clawson, and Zoe Oxley, "Media Framing of a Civil Liberties Conflict and Its Effect on Tolerance," *American Political Science Review* 91, no. 3 (September 1997): 567–83.
67. Dennis Chong and James Druckman, "Framing Public Opinion in Competitive Democracies," *American Political Science Review* 101 (November 2007): 301–15.
68. Douglas McLeod and Dhavan Shah, *News Frames and National Security: Covering Big Brother* (New York: Cambridge University Press, 2015).
69. Martin Gilens, *Why Americans Hate Welfare: Race, Media, and the Politics of Antipoverty Policy* (Chicago, IL: University of Chicago Press, 1999).
70. Pew Research Center, "Americans' Attitudes about the News Media Deeply Divided along Partisan Lines," 10 May 2017.
71. Rick Hasen, "Why Isn't Congress More Corrupt?" *Fordham Law Review* 84, no. 2 (2015): 101–15.
72. Brendan Nyhan and Jason Reifler, "The Effect of Fact-Checking on Elites: A Field Experiment on U.S. State Legislators," *American Journal of Political Science* 59 (July 2015): 628–40.
73. Nathan Walter et al., "Fact-Checking: A Meta-Analysis of What Works and For Whom," *Political Communication*, Forthcoming.
74. James Snyder and David Stromberg, "Press Coverage and Political Accountability," *Journal of Political Economy* 110, no. 2 (April 2010): 355–408; R. Douglas Arnold, *Congress, the Press, and Political Accountability* (Princeton, NJ: Princeton University Press, 2004).
75. Martin Gilens, Lynn Vavreck, and Martin Cohen, "The Mass Media and the Public's Assessments of Presidential Candidates, 1952–2000," *Journal of Politics* 69, no. 4 (November 2007): 1160–75.

76. Thomas Patterson, *Out of Order* (New York: Knopf, 1993).
77. Thomas E. Patterson, "News Coverage of the 2016 Presidential Primaries: Horse Race Reporting Has Consequences," Shorenstein Center on Media, Politics, and Public Policy, July 11, 2016.
78. Thomas E. Patterson, "News Coverage of the 2016 General Election: How the Press Failed the Voters," Shorenstein Center on Media, Politics, and Public Policy, December 7, 2016.
79. Margaret Sullivan, "Waiter, Where's Our (Political) Spinach?" *New York Times,* March 5, 2016.
80. Shanto Iyengar, Helmut Norpoth, and Kyu Hahn, "Consumer Demand for Election News: The Horserace Sells," *Journal of Politics* 66, no. 1 (February 2004): 157–75.
81. Toril Aalberg, Jesper Stromback, and Claes de Vreese, "The Framing of Politics as a Strategy and Game: A Review of Concepts, Operationalizations and Key Findings," *Journalism* 13, no. 2 (February 2012): 162–78.
82. John Zaller, "A Theory of Media Politics" (Unpublished manuscript, University of California, Los Angeles, 2001).
83. Joseph N. Cappella and Kathleen Hall Jamieson, *Spiral of Cynicism: The Press and the Public Good* (New York: Oxford University Press, 1997).
84. Thomas Patterson, "Bad News, Period," *PS: Political Science and Politics* 29, no. 1 (March 1996): 17–20.
85. Patterson, "News Coverage of the 2016 General Election."
86. Patterson, "News Coverage of the 2016 General Election."
87. *Kathleen Hall Jamieson, Everything You Think You Know about Politics … And Why You're Wrong* (New York: Basic Books, 2000); Tracy Sulkin, *The Legislative Legacy of Congressional Campaigns* (New York: Cambridge University Press, 2011).
88. "Tracking Obama's Promises," Politifact.www.politifact.com /truth-o-meter/promises /obameter/.
89. Michael Robinson, "Public Affairs Television and the Growth of Political Malaise: The Case of 'The Selling of the Pentagon,'" *American Political Science Review* 70, no. 2 (June 1976): 409–32.
90. Larisa Bomlitz and Mayer Brezis, "Misrepresentation of Health Risks by Mass Media," *Journal of Public Health* 30, no. 2 (June 2008): 202–04.
91. Paul Vettehen, Koos Nuijten, and Allerd Peeters, "Explaining Effects of Sensationalism on Liking of Television News Stories: The Role of Emotional Arousal," *Communication Research* 35, no. 3 (June 2008): 319–38.
92. Jennifer Jerit et al., "Differences between National and Local Media in News Coverage of the Zika Virus," *Health Communication* v34, n19 (2019): 1816–23.
93. Larry Bartels, "Messages Received: The Political Impact of Media Exposure," *American Political Science Review* 87, no. 2 (June 1993): 267–85.
94. CNN. CNN Poll, Jan, 2020 [survey question]. 31117011.00016. SSRS [producer]. Cornell University, Ithaca, NY: Roper Center for Public Opinion Research, iPOLL [distributor], accessed Feb 7, 2020.
95. W. Lance Bennett, "Toward a Theory of Press-State Relations in the United States," *Journal of Communication* 40, no. 2 (January 1990): 103–27; Dan C. Hallin, "The Media, the War in Vietnam, and Political Support: A Critique of the Thesis of Oppositional Media," *Journal of Politics* 46, no. 1 (February 1984): 2–24.
96. Megan Brenan, "American's Trust in Media Edges Down to 41%," Gallup, 26 September 2019.
97. Andrew Danniler et al., "Measuring Trust in the Press in a Changing Media Environment," *Communication Methods and Measures* 11 (January 2017): 76–85.
98. Pew Research Center, "U.S. Media Polarization and the 2020 Election: A Nation Divided," 24 January 2020.
99. Jonathan Ladd, *Why Americans Hate the Media and How It Matters* (Princeton, NJ: Princeton University Press, 2012).
100. "Amid Criticism, Support for Media's 'Watchdog' Role Stands Out," Pew Research Center, August 8, 2013.
101. Jeffrey Gottfried et al, "Partisans Remain Sharply Divided in their Attitudes about the News Media," Pew Research Center, 25 September 2018.
102. S. Robert Lichter, Stanley Rothman, and Linda S. Lichter, *The Media Elite* (Bethesda, MD: Adler and Adler, 1986); Stanley Rothman and Amy Black, "Elites Revisited: American Social and Political Leadership in the 1990s," *International Journal of Public Opinion Research* 11, no. 2 (1999): 169–95; William Schneider and I.A. Lewis, "Views on the News," *Public Opinion* (August/September 1985): 7.
103. Megan Brenan, "Local News Media Considered Less Biased Than National News," Gallup, 8 November 2019.
104. Joe Concha, "Poll: Public Overwhelmingly Believes Media Is in the Tank for Clinton," *The Hill,* October 31, 2016.
105. Hans Hassell, John Holbein, and Matthew Miles, "There Is No Liberal Media Bias in the News Political Journalists Choose to Cover," *Science Advances,* 6, no. 14 (1 April 2020): eaay9344.
106. Jamieson*, Everything You Think You Know about Politics.*
107. Tim Groseclose, *Left Turn* (New York: St. Martin's Press, 2012), especially chap. 16.
108. Dave D'Alessio and Mike Allen, "Media Bias in Presidential Elections: A Meta-Analysis," *Journal of Communication* 50, no. 4 (December 2000): 133–56; Jamieson, *Everything You Think You Know about Politics.*
109. David Niven, "Objective Evidence of Media Bias: Newspaper Coverage of Congressional Party Switchers," *Journalism and Mass Communication Quarterly* 80, no. 2 (Summer 2003): 311–26.

110. Stephen Ansolabehere, Rebecca Lessem, and James Snyder, "The Orientation of Newspaper Endorsements in U.S. Elections, 1940–2002," *Quarterly Journal of Political Science* 1, no. 4 (2006): 393–404.
111. Kim Fridkin Kahn and Patrick Kenney, "The Slant of the News: How Editorial Endorsements Influence Campaign Coverage and Citizens' Views of Candidates," *American Political Science Review* 96, no. 2 (June 2002): 381–94; James Druckman and Michael Parkin, "The Impact of Media Bias: How Editorial Slant Affects Voters," *Journal of Politics* 67, no. 4 (November 2005): 1030–49.
112. Thomas Rosensteil, "Comment: Two Alternative Perspectives," in *Red and Blue Nation? Volume 1: Characteristics and Causes of America's Polarized Politics,* eds. Pietro Novla and David Brady (Washington, D.C.: Brookings Institution Press, 2006), 249–54.
113. James T. Hamilton, *All the News that's Fit to Sell: How the Market Transforms Information into News* (Princeton, NJ: Princeton University Press, 2004).
114. *Near v. Minnesota*, 283 U.S. 697 (1931).
115. *New York Times v. United States*, 403 U.S. 713 (1971).
116. *New York Times v. Sullivan*, 376 U.S. 254 (1964).
117. *Miami Herald Publishing Co. v. Tornillo*, 418 U.S. 241 (1974).
118. *Yates v. United States*, 354 U.S. 298 (1957).
119. *Branzburg v. Hayes*, 408 U.S. 665 (1972).
120. *Zurcher v. Stanford Daily*, 436 U.S. 547 (1978), overturned by the Privacy Protection Act of 1980 (P.L. 96–440).
121. Josh Dawsey, Tara Palmeri, Eli Stokols, and Shane Goldmarcher, "Distrust in Trump's White House Spurs Leaks, Confusion," *Politico*, February 2, 2017.
122. Letter from Thomas Jefferson to Edward Carrington, January 16, 1787, collected in *The Jefferson Monticello: Jefferson Quotes and Family Letters,* tjrs.monticello.org/letter/1289/.
123. Claire Cain Miller and Kevin Quealy, "Democracy in America: How Is It Doing?" *The New York Times: The Upshot,* February 23, 2017.
124. Matthew Nussbaum, "Pence: Trump White House Supports Free and Independent Press," *Politico*, February 2, 2017.
125. The relevant information is at www.fcc.gov/guides/review-broadcast-ownership-rules. James Stewart, "When Media Mergers Limit More than Competition," *New York Times,* July 25, 2014.
126. Stewart, "When Media Mergers Limit More than Competition."
127. Matthew Gentzkow and Jesse M. Shapiro, "What Drives Media Slant?: Evidence from U.S. Newspapers," *Econometrica* 78, no. 1 (January 2010): 35–71; though for an exception, see Gregory Martin and Joshua McCrain, "Local News and National Politics," *American Political Science Review* 113 (May 2019): 372–84.
128. Martin Gilens and Craig Hertzman, "Corporate Ownership and News Bias: Newspaper Coverage of the 1996 Telecommunications Bill," *Journal of Politics* 62, no. 2 (May 2000): 369–86; Catie Snow Bailard, "Corporate News Ownership and News Bias Revisited: Newspaper Coverage of the Supreme Court's *Citizens United* Ruling," *Political Communication* 33, no. 4 (October 2016): 583–604.
129. Jeffrey Berry and Sarah Sobieraj, *The Outrage Industry: Political Opinion Media and the New Incivility* (New York: Oxford University Press, 2014).
130. Matthew Rosenberg et al., "How Trump Consultants Exploited the Facebook Data of Millions," *New York Times*, 17 March 2018.
131. Federal Trade Commission, "FTC Imposes $5 Billion Penalty and Sweeping New Privacy Restrictions on Facebook" [Press Release], 24 July 2019.
132. Jason Lynch, "Advertisers Spent $5.25 Billion on the Midterm Election, 17% More Than in 2016," Kantar Media, 15 November 2018.
133. Kate Conger, "What Ads Are Political? Twitter Struggles with a Definition," *New York Times*, 15 November 2019.
134. Nick Corasaniti and Matthew Rosenberg, "Campaigns Say Google Ad Policy Sidesteps Problem of Disinformation," *New York Times*, 21 November 2019.
135. Bill Chappell, "FEC Commissioner Rips Facebook Over Political Ad Policy: This Will Not Do," National Public Radio, 9 January 2020.

Chapter 13

1. Thomas E. Mann and Norman J. Ornstein, *The Broken Branch: How Congress Is Failing America and How to Get It Back on Track*, 2nd ed. (New York: Oxford University Press 2008). Also see Richard F. Fenno, "If as Ralph Nader Says Congress Is the 'Broken Branch,' How Come We Love Our Congressmen So Much More than Our Congress?" in *Congress in Change: Evolution and Reform,* ed. Norman J. Ornstein, pp. 277–87 (New York: Praeger, 1975).
2. Fenno, "If as Ralph Nader Says," 286.
3. Norman J. Ornstein and Thomas E. Mann, *Vital Statistics on Congress, 1995–1996* (Washington, D.C.: Congressional Quarterly Press 1996), 199–200.
4. "A Polarized Congress," *National Journal,* January 21, 2006, 21; reporting data compiled by David Rhode and John Aldrich.
5. Ibid.
6. Congressional Quarterly, "History: Party Unity Votes," 25 February 2019.
7. *Federalist* No. 10.
8. Ibid.
9. Data for the 116th Congress available from the House Press Gallery, https://pressgallery.house.gov/member-data/demographics
10. Jane Mansbridge, "Should Blacks Represent Blacks and Women Represent Women? A Contingent 'Yes,'" *Journal of Politics* 61, no. 3 (August 1999): 628–57.

11. L. Martin Overby and Kenneth Cosgrove, "Unintended Consequences? Racial Redistricting and the Representation of Minority Interests," *Journal of Politics* 58, no. 2 (May 1996): 540–50.
12. Charles Cameron, David Epstein, and Sharyn O'Halloran, "Do Majority-Minority Districts Maximize Substantive Black Representation in Congress?" *American Political Science Review* 90, no. 4 (December 1996): 794–812.
13. Kevin Hill, "Does the Creation of Majority Black Districts Aid Republicans? An Analysis of the 1992 Congressional Elections in Eight Southern States," *Journal of Politics* 57, no. 2 (May 1995): 384–401.
14. Maggie Astor, "'It Can't Be Worse:' How Republican Women are Trying to Rebuild," *New York Times*, 9 July 2019.
15. H. Douglas Price, "Careers and Committees in the American Congress," in *The History of Parliamentary Behavior,* ed. William O. Aydelotte, pp. 28–62 (Princeton, NJ: Princeton University Press, 1977); John F. Bibby et al., *Vital Statistics on Congress, 1980* (Washington, D.C.: American Enterprise Institute, 1980), 53–54.
16. *U.S. Term Limits, Inc v. Thornton*, 514 U.S. 779 (1995).
17. Scott Wong, "Right Renews Push for Term Limits as Trump Takes Power," *The Hill,* January 15, 2017.
18. Quinnipiac University Polling Institute. Quinnipiac University Poll, November, 2016 [survey question]. USQUINN.112316. R45. Quinnipiac University Polling Institute [producer]. Cornell University, Ithaca, NY: Roper Center for Public Opinion Research, iPOLL [distributor]. Accessed January 17, 2019.
19. Elizabeth Garrett, "Term Limits and the Myth of the Citizen-Legislator," *Cornell Law Review* 81, no. 3 (March 1996): 623–97.
20. John Carey et al., "The Effects of Term Limits on State Legislatures: A New Survey of the 50 States," *Legislative Studies Quarterly* 31, no. 1 (February 2006): 105–34.
21. William T. Egar and Amber Hope Wilhelm, "Congressional Careers: Service Tenure and Patterns of Member Service, 1789–2019," Congressional Research Service, January 3, 2019.
22. David Mayhew, *Congress: The Electoral Connection* (New Haven, CT: Yale University Press, 1974).
23. "As Midterms Near, GOP Leads on Key Issues, Democrats Have a More Positive Image," Pew Research Center, October 23, 2014.
24. Norman Orenstein et al., *Vital Statistics on Congress*, Table 2-14. www.brookings.edu/vitalstats/.
25. Orenstein et al., *Vital Statistics on Congress*, Table 2-12. www.brookings.edu/vitalstats/.
26. Mayhew, *Congress;* Morris Fiorina, *Congress: Keystone of the Washington Establishment* (New Haven, CT: Yale University Press, 1977).
27. Bruce Cain, John Ferejohn, and Morris Fiorina, *The Personal Vote: Constituency Service and Electoral Independence* (Cambridge, MA: Harvard University Press, 1990).
28. Anthony King, *Running Scared: Why America's Politicians Campaign Too Much and Govern Too Little* (New York: Free Press, 1997).
29. Nicholas Goedert, "Gerrymandering or Geography? How Democrats Won the Popular Vote but Lost the Congress in 2012," *Research & Politics* 1, no. 1 (April 2014); Jonathan Kastellec, Andrew Gelman, and Jamie Chandler, "Predicting and Dissecting the Seats-Votes Curve in the 2006 U.S. House Election," *PS: Political Science and Politics* 41, no. 1 (April 2008): 139–45.
30. Michael Peress and Yangzi Zhao, "How Many Seats in Congress Is Control of Redistricting Worth?" *Legislative Studies Quarterly*, Forthcoming.
31. See, for example, *White v. Weiser,* 412 U.S. 783, 790 (1973).
32. Gary Jacobson, "It's Nothing Personal: The Decline of the Incumbency Advantage in US House Elections," *Journal of Politics* 77, no. 3 (July 2015): 861–63; Jowie Chen and Jonathan Rodden, "Unintentional Gerrymandering: Political Geography and Electoral Bias in Legislatures," *Quarterly Journal of Political Science* 8, no. 3 (2013): 239–69; Jonathan Rodden, *Why Cities Lose* (New York: Basic Books, 2019).
33. Morris Fiorina, *Representatives, Roll Calls, and Constituencies* (Boston, MA: Lexington Books, 1974).
34. Daniel Butler and David Nickerson, "Can Learning Constituency Opinion Affect How Legislators Vote? Results from a Field Experiment," *Quarterly Journal of Political Science* 6, no. 1 (2011): 55–83.
35. Richard Fenno, *Home Style: House Members in Their Districts* (Boston, MA: Little Brown, 1978).
36. Brandice Canes-Wrone, David Brady, and John Cogan, "Out of Step, Out of Office: Electoral Accountability and House Members' Voting," *American Political Science Review* 96, no. 1 (March 2002): 127–40.
37. Brendan Nyhan et al. "One Vote Out of Step? The Effects of Salient Roll Call Votes in the 2010 Election," *American Politics Research* 40, no 5. (2012): 844–79.
38. Gary Cox and Mathew McCubbins, *Legislative Leviathan* (Berkeley: University of California Press, 1993).
39. Nolan McCarty, Keith Poole, and Howard Rosenthal, "The Hunt for Party Discipline in Congress," *American Political Science Review* 95, no. 3 (2001): 673–87.
40. Laurel Harbridge and Neil Malhotra, "Electoral Incentives and Partisan Conflict in Congress: Evidence from Survey Experiments," *American Journal of Political Science* 55, no. 3 (2011): 494–510.
41. Alan Abramowitz, *The Disappearing Center* (New Haven, CT: Yale University Press, 2010).
42. Morris Fiorina and Samuel Abrams, *Disconnect: The Breakdown of Representation in American Politics* (Norman, OK: University of Oklahoma Press, 2011).
43. Richard F. Fenno, *Congressmen in Committees* (Boston, MA: Little, Brown, 1973).

44. Barry Weingast and William Marshall, "The Industrial Organization of Congress; Or, Why Legislatures, Like Firms, Are Not Organized as Markets," *Journal of Political Economy* 96, no. 1 (1988): 132–63.
45. *Vital Statistics on Congress, Table* 5-1, www.brookings.edu/vitalstats.
46. Bibby et al., *Vital Statistics on Congress*, 60.
47. Michael J. Malbin, "Delegation, Deliberation, and the New Role of Congressional Staff," in *The New Congress*, eds. Thomas E. Mann and Norman J. Ornstein (Washington, D.C.: American Enterprise Institute, 1981), 134–77, esp. 170–71.
48. Sarah Binder, "Dis-Charge! Historical Data and Prospects for Success," The Monkey Cage, *Washington Post*, October 7, 2013.
49. Gregory Koger, *Filibustering: A Political History of Obstruction in the House and Senate* (Chicago, IL: University of Chicago Press, 2010).
50. *Vital Statistics on Congress*, Table 6-7, www.brookings.edu/vitalstats.
51. Matt Flegenheimer, "Senate Republicans Deploy 'Nuclear Option' to Clear Path for Gorsuch," *New York Times*, April 6, 2017.
52. Malcolm E. Jewell and Samuel C. Patterson, *The Legislative Process in the United States*, 3rd ed. (New York: Random House, 1977), 349.
53. Mann and Ornstein, *The Broken Branch*; Joshua Clinton and John Lapinski, "Measuring Legislative Accomplishment," *American Journal of Political Science* 50, no. 1 (2006): 232–49; J. Tobin Grant and Nathan J. Kelly, "Legislative Productivity of the U.S. Congress," *Political Analysis* 16, no. 3 (2008): 303–23.
54. Daniel Newhauser, "No, The 113th Congress Wasn't the Least Productive Ever," *National Journal*, December 23, 2014.
55. David Mayhew, *Divided We Govern: Party Control, Lawmaking, and Investigations* (New Haven, CT: Yale University Press, 1991); Grant and Kelly, "Legislative Productivity."
56. Kevin Kossar, "How to Strengthen Congress," *National Affairs*, 25 (Fall 2015).
57. Lee Drutman and Steven Teles, "Congressional Reform Should Start with Professional Staff," *The Atlantic*, March 10, 2015.
58. Continuity of Government Commission, "Preserving Our Institutions: The Continuity of Congress-First Report," (Washington, D.C.: American Enterprise Institute & The Brookings Institution, June 3, 2003): 3–4.
59. *The 9/11 Commission Report: Final Report of the National Commission on Terrorist Attacks Upon the United States* (New York: W.W. Norton, 2004).
60. Matthew Glassman, "Franking Privilege: Historical Development and Options for Change," Congressional Research Service, RL34274, April 22, 2015.
61. Diana Evans, *Greasing the Wheels: The Use of Pork Barrel Projects to Build Majority Coalitions in Congress* (New York: Cambridge University Press, 2004).
62. John Heltman, "27th Amendment or Bust," *The American Prospect*, May 30, 2012.

Chapter 14

1. Anu Narayanswamy, Darla Cameron, and Matea Gold, "Election 2016: Money Raised as of December 31," *Washington Post*, February 1, 2017.
2. Jean Blondel, *An Introduction to Comparative Government* (New York: Praeger, 1969), as cited in Nelson W. Polsby, "Legislatures," in *Handbook of Political Science*, eds. Fred I. Greenstein and Nelson W. Polsby (Reading, MA: Addison-Wesley, 1975), 5:275; Drew DeSilver, "Among Democracies, U.S. Stands Out in How It Chooses Its Head of State," Pew Research Center, 22 November 2016.
3. Donald F. Kettl, *Deficit Politics: Public Budgeting in Its Institutional and Historical Context* (New York: Macmillan, 1992), 13.
4. Morris P. Fiorina, *Divided Government* (New York: Macmillan, 1992), 86–111.
5. *David Mayhew, Divided We Govern: Party Control, Lawmaking, and Investigations, 1946–1990* (New Haven, CT: Yale University Press, 1993), 76.
6. Woodrow Wilson, *Congressional Government* (New York: Meridian Books, 1956), 167–68, 170. First published in 1885.
7. Gouverneur Morris, Constitutional Convention Debates, July 24, 1787, cited in "Notes on the Debates in the Federal Convention." Available through The Avalon Project: Documents in Law, History and Diplomacy, Yale University, at www.avalon.yale.edu.
8. For more details, see the National Popular Vote's website at https://www.nationalpopularvote.com/. Accessed July 2020.
9. Fred I. Greenstein, "Toward a Modern Presidency," in *Leadership in the Modern Presidency*, ed. Fred I. Greenstein (Cambridge, MA.: Harvard University Press, 1988), 1–6.
10. Mark A. Peterson, *Legislating Together: The White House and Congress from Eisenhower to Reagan* (Cambridge, MA: Harvard University Press, 1990).
11. Richard E. Cohen, *Washington at Work: Back Rooms and Clean Air* (New York: Macmillan, 1992), 154–55.
12. Ibid., 169.
13. Kettl, *Deficit Politics*, 138.
14. Richard E. Neustadt, *Presidential Power and the Modern Presidents: The Politics of Leadership from Roosevelt to Reagan* (New York: Free Press, 1990), chap. 4.
15. Gerhard Peters, "Presidential News Conferences," *The American Presidency Project*, ed. John T. Woolley and Gerhard Peters (Santa Barbara, CA: University of California). Available online: https://www.presidency.ucsb.edu/node/323900. Accessed July 2020.
16. Rob Crilly, "Trump Kills the White House Press Briefing, 50 Years After It Was Born," *Washington Examiner*, 4 September 2019.
17. Neustadt, *Presidential Power and the Modern Presidents*, 84.

18. Samuel Kernell, *Going Public: New Strategies of Presidential Leadership*, 4th ed. (Washington, D.C.: Congressional Quarterly Press, 2007); Jeffrey K. Tulis, *The Rhetorical Presidency* (Princeton, NJ: Princeton University Press, 1987); Mary E. Stuckey, *The President as Interpreter-in-Chief* (Chatham, NJ: Chatham House, 1991); Karlyn Kohrs Campbell and Kathleen Hall Jamieson, *Presidents Creating the Presidency: Deeds Done in Words* (Chicago, IL: University of Chicago Press, 2008).
19. George C. Edwards III, *On Deaf Ears: The Limits of the Bully Pulpit* (New Haven, CT: Yale University Press, 2003); Jeffrey E. Cohen, *Going Local: Presidential Leadership in the Post-Broadcast Age* (New York: Cambridge University Press, 2010).
20. U.S. House of Representatives, "Presidential Vetoes," https://history.house.gov/Institution/Presidential-Vetoes/Presidential-Vetoes/.
21. United States Senate, "Vetoes by President Donald J. Trump," https://www.senate.gov/legislative/vetoes/TrumpDJ.htm .
22. *Marbury v. Madison,* 1 Cranch 137 (1803).
23. *United States v. Nixon*, 418 U.S. 683 (1974).
24. *Clinton v. Jones*, 520 U.S. 681 (1997); *In re Grand Jury Subpoena Duces Tecum*, 112 F.3d 910 (1997); *In re Sealed Case*, 121 F.3d 729 (1997).
25. Richard Lempert, "All the President's Privileges," The Brookings Institution, 19 December 2019, https://www.brookings.edu/research/all-the-presidents-privileges/; Spencer S. Hsu and Ann E. Marimow, "Former White House Counsel Don McGahn Does Not Have to Testify to House, Appeals Court Finds," *Washington Post,* 28 February 2020.
26. Kenneth Mayer, *With the Stroke of a Pen: Executive Orders and Presidential Power* (Princeton, N.J.: Princeton University Press, 2001), 4–5.
27. *Mayer, With the Stroke of a Pen,* 5–7; Phillip J. Cooper, *By Order of the President: The Use and Abuse of Executive Direct Action*, 2nd ed., rev. and exp. (Lawrence: University Press of Kansas, 2014).
28. Gerhard Peters and John T. Woolley, "Executive Orders," *The American Presidency Project,* ed. John T. Woolley and Gerhard Peters (Santa Barbara, CA: University of California, 1999–2017). www.presidency.ucsb.edu/data/orders.php.
29. Kristen Bialik, "Obama Issued Fewer Executive Orders on Average Than Any President Since Cleveland," Pew Research Center Fact Tank, January 23, 2017. www.pewresearch.org/fact-tank/2017/01/23/obama-executive-orders/.
30. Mark Hugo Lopez and Jens Manuel Krogstad, "5 Facts About the Deferred Action for Childhood Arrivals Program," Pew Research Center Fact Tank, August 15, 2014. www.pewresearch.org/fact-tank/2014/08/15/5-facts-about-the-deferred-action-for-childhood-arrivals-program/.
31. "2014 Executive Actions on Immigration," U.S. Citizenship and Immigration Services, April 15, 2015; Haeyoun Park and Alicia Parlapiano, "Supreme Court's Decision on Immigration Case Affects Millions of Unauthorized Immigrants," *New York Times*, June 23, 2016.
32. Adam Liptak and Michael D. Shear, "Trump's Travel Ban Is Upheld by Supreme Court," *New York Times,* 26 June 2018.
33. Christopher S. Kelley, "A Comparative Look at the Constitutional Signing Statement," paper presented at the Midwest Political Science Association meeting, Chicago, IL, April 2003; Christopher S. Kelley, "To Be (Unitarian) or Not to Be (Unitarian): Presidential Power in the George W. Bush Administration," *White House Studies* 10, no. 2 (2010): 115–29.
34. John Woolley and Gerhard Peters, "Presidential Signing Statements: Hoover-Obama," *The American Presidency Project*, ed. Woolley and Peters (Santa Barbara, CA: University of California, Los Angeles 1999–2017). www.presidency.ucsb.edu/signingstatements.php.
35. Walter Dellinger, "Memorandum for Bernard N. Nussbaum, Counsel to the President," Office of Legal Counsel, U.S. Department of Justice, November 3, 1993.
36. *Chevron v. NRDC,* 467 U.S. 837 (1984).
37. Edwin S. Corwin, *The Presidency: Office and Powers* (New York: New York University Press, 1957), 171.
38. Stephen E. Ambrose, *Eisenhower*, 2 vols. (New York: Simon & Schuster, 1984); Fred I. Greenstein, *The Hidden-Hand Presidency: Eisenhower as Leader* (New York: Basic Books, 1982).
39. Lewis J. Paper, *The Promise and the Performance: The Leadership of John F. Kennedy* (New York: Crown, 1975); Meena Bose, *Shaping and Signaling Presidential Policy: The National Security Decision Making of Eisenhower and Kennedy* (College Station: Texas A&M University Press, 1998).
40. Doris Kearns Goodwin, *Lyndon Johnson and the American Dream* (New York: Harper and Row, 1976); Robert Dallek, *Lyndon B. Johnson: Portrait of a President* (New York: Oxford University Press, 2005).
41. Melvin Small, *The Presidency of Richard Nixon* (Lawrence: University Press of Kansas, 1999); Richard Reeves, *President Nixon: Alone in the White House* (New York: Simon & Schuster, 2007).
42. John Robert Greene, *The Presidency of Gerald R. Ford* (Lawrence: University Press of Kansas, 1994).
43. Peter G. Bourne, *Jimmy Carter: A Comprehensive Biography from Plains to Post-Presidency* (New York: Scribner, 1997); Randall Balmer, *Redeemer: The Life of Jimmy Carter* (New York: Basic Books, 2014).
44. Lou Cannon, *President Reagan: The Role of a Lifetime* (New York: Simon & Schuster, 1991); H.W. Brands, *Reagan: The Life* (New York: Doubleday, 2015).

45. David Mervin, *George Bush and the Guardianship Presidency* (New York: Palgrave Macmillan, 1996); Lori Cox Han, *A Presidency Upstaged: The Public Leadership of George H.W. Bush* (College Station: Texas A&M University Press, 2011).
46. David Maraniss, *First in His Class: A Biography of Bill Clinton* (New York: Simon & Schuster, 1995); Joe Klein, *The Natural: The Misunderstood Presidency of Bill Clinton* (New York: Doubleday, 2002).
47. Robert Draper, *Dead Certain: The Presidency of George W. Bush* (New York: Free Press, 2007); Ivo H. Daalder and James M. Lindsay, *America Unbound: The Bush Revolution in Foreign Policy* (Washington, D.C.: Brookings Institution Press, 2003).
48. David Remnick, *The Bridge: The Life and Rise of Barack Obama* (New York: Knopf, 2010); Stanley A. Renshon, *Barack Obama and the Politics of Redemption* (New York: Routledge, 2011).
49. James P. Pfiffner, *The Modern Presidency*, 6th ed. (Boston, MA: Wadsworth/Cengage Learning, 2011), 99.
50. Stephen Hess, *Organizing the Presidency* (Washington, D.C.: Brookings Institution, 1976), 3; R.W. Apple, "Clinton's Refocusing," *New York Times*, May 6, 1993, A22; Michael K. Frisby, "Power Switch," *Wall Street Journal*, March 26, 1993, A1, A7.
51. Kathryn Dunn Tenpas, "Tracking Turnover in the Trump Administration," Brookings Institution, February 2020, https://www.brookings.edu/research/tracking-turnover-in-the-trump-administration/.
52. Meena Bose and Andrew Rudalevige, eds., *Executive Policymaking: The Role of the OMB in the Presidency* (Washington, D.C.: Brookings Institution Press, forthcoming).
53. U.S. Department of Health and Human Services, "Fiscal Year 2016 Budget in Brief."
54. David T. Stanley et al., *Men Who Govern* (Washington, D.C.: Brookings Institution, 1967), 41–42, 50.
55. Daniel J. Elazar, "Which Road to the Presidency?" in *The Presidency*, ed. Aaron Wildavsky (Boston, MA: Little, Brown, 1969), 340.
56. William E. Leuchtenberg, *Franklin D. Roosevelt and the New Deal, 1932–1940* (New York: Harper & Row, 1963); Doris Kearns Goodwin, *No Ordinary Time: Franklin and Eleanor Roosevelt, the Home Front in World War II* (New York: Simon & Schuster, 1994).
57. Michael R. Beschloss, *The Crisis Years: Kennedy and Khrushchev 1960–1963* (New York: Harper Collins, 1991.)
58. Robert A. Caro, *The Years of Lyndon Johnson*, 4 vols. (New York: Alfred A. Knopf, 1982–2012).
59. Stephen E. Ambrose, *Nixon*, 3 vols. (New York: Simon & Schuster, 1987–1991).
60. Herbert C. Parmet, *George Bush: The Life of a Lone Star Yankee* (New York: Scribner, 1997); Jon Meacham, *Destiny and Power: The American Odyssey of George Herbert Walker Bush* (New York: Random House, 2015).
61. Jean Edward Smith, *Bush* (New York: Simon & Schuster, 2016).
62. Marcus Cunliffe, *American Presidents and the Presidency* (New York: American Heritage Press/ McGraw-Hill, 1972), 63, 65.
63. Ibid., 214.
64. Andrew Johnson National Historic Site, "Why Was Andrew Johnson Impeached?" National Park Service, https://www.nps.gov/articles/why-was-andrew-johnson-impeached.htm.
65. Philip Ewing, "The Mueller Report Is Getting a Lot of Attention. Here's How We Got Here," *NPR*, 22 March 2019; Tara Law, "Here Are the Biggest Takeaways From the Mueller Report," *Time*, 19 April 2019; Special Counsel Robert S. Mueller, III, "Report on the Investigation Into Russian Interference In the 2016 Presidential Election," 2 vols., https://www.justice.gov/storage/report.pdf.
66. Eric Lipton, Maggie Haberman, and Mark Mazzetti, "Behind the Ukraine Aid Freeze: 84 Days of Conflict and Confusion," *New York Times*, 29 December 2019; Nicholas Fandos, "Nancy Pelosi Announces Formal Impeachment Inquiry of Trump," *New York Times*, 24 September 2019; Joe Heim, "Nancy Pelosi on Impeaching Trump: 'He's Just Not Worth It'," *Washington Post Magazine*, 11 March 2019; Rebecca Ballhaus and Natalie Andrews, "Senate Acquits Trump on Both Impeachment Articles," *Wall Street Journal*, 5 February 2020.
67. William G. Howell and Terry M. Moe, *Relic: How Our Constitution Undermines Effective Government-And Why We Need a More Powerful Presidency* (New York: Basic Books, 2016).
68. James L. Sundquist, *Constitutional Reform and Effective Government*, rev. ed. (Washington, D.C.: Brookings Institution Press, 1992).
69. Adapted from Paul C. Light, *The President's Agenda* (Baltimore, MD: Johns Hopkins University Press, 1982), 217–25.
70. For an analysis of how U.S. presidents may achieve results quickly in office, see James P. Pfiffner, *The Strategic Presidency: Hitting the Ground Running*, 2nd ed. rev. (Lawrence, KS: University Press of Kansas, 1996).

Chapter 15

1. Charles E. Lindblom, *Politics and Markets* (New York: Basic Books, 1977), 114.
2. Donald F. Kettl, *Government by Proxy (Mis?) Managing Federal Programs* (Washington, D.C.: Congressional Quarterly Press, 1988); John J. DiIulio Jr., "Government by Proxy: A Faithful Overview," *Harvard Law Review* 116, no. 5 (March 2003): 1272–84.
3. Mark Hemmingway, "Warriors for Hire," *Weekly Standard*, December 18, 2006, 25.
4. Ibid., 26.
5. *The Federal Response to Hurricane Katrina: Lessons Learned* (February 2006), Chapter 2: "National Preparedness—A Primer," https://georgewbush-whitehouse.archives.gov/reports/katrina-lessons-learned/appendix-e.html#chapter2. accessed July 2020.

6. Emily Atkin, "The Troubling Failure of America's Disaster Response," *The New Republic,* 17 July 2018; FEMA, *2017 Hurricane Season FEMA After-Action Report,* 12 July 2018.
7. Martha Derthick, *Keeping the Compound Republic: Essays on American Federalism* (Washington, D.C.: Brookings Institution, 2001), 63.
8. Donald F. Kettl, *The Next Government of the United States: Why Our Institutions Fail Us and How to Fix Them* (New York: W.W. Norton, 2008), 1–14.
9. Article II, section 2, para. 2.
10. Article II, section 3.
11. Calculated from data in U.S. Census Bureau, *Historical Statistics of the United States: Colonial Times to 1970, volume 2* (Washington, D.C.: Government Printing Office, 1975), "Series Y: 308–317: Paid Civilian Employment of the Federal Government, 1816–1970," pp. 1102–3.
12. *Panama Refining Co. v. Ryan*, 293 U.S. 388 (1935).
13. *Hampton Jr. & Co. v. United States*, 276 U.S. 394 (1928).
14. Edward S. Corwin, *The Constitution and What It Means Today,* 13 th ed., edited by Harold W. Chase and Craig R. Ducat (Princeton, NJ: Princeton University Press, 1973), 151.
15. Bruce D. Porter, "Parkinson's Law Revisited: War and the Growth of American Government," *Public Interest* (Summer 1980): 50–68.
16. See the cases cited in Corwin, *The Constitution*, 8.
17. *U.S. Statutes*, vol. 84, sec. 799 (1970).
18. U.S. Census Bureau, *Historical Statistics of the United States, volume 2* (Washington, D.C.: Government Printing Office, 1975), "Series Y 358–373: Internal Revenue Collections: 1863–1970," p. 1107.
19. Department of Homeland Security, Hearings Before the Subcommittee on Oversight and Management Efficiency, Committee on Homeland Security, U.S. House of Representatives, 113th, 1st Sess. (2013); U.S. Government Accountability Office, *Key Issues: DHS Implementation and Transformation*, 2013; *also see Kettl, The Next Government of the United States*, 52.
20. Federal Bureau of Prisons Weekly Population Report and Quick Facts.
21. Donald F. Kettl et al., *Civil Service Reform: Building a Government That Works* (Washington, D.C.: Brookings Institution, 1996), 15.
22. Aaron Kessler and Tal Kopan, "Trump Still Has to Fill Nearly 2,000 Vacancies," www.cnn.com, February 25, 2017.
23. "Tracking How Many Key Positions Trump Has Filled So Far," *The Washington Post* in collaboration with the Partnership for Public Service, February 3, 2020; Kathryn Dunn Tenpas, "Tracking Turnover in the Trump Administration," Brookings Institution, February 3, 2020; Dareh Gregorian, " 'Off the Charts': White House Turnover is Breaking Records," *NBC News,* September 23, 2019.
24. Hugh Heclo, "Issue Networks and the Executive Establishment," in *The New American Political System*, ed. Anthony King (Washington, D.C.: American Enterprise Institute, 1978), 87–124.
25. Quoted in Hugh Heclo, *A Government of Strangers* (Washington, D.C.: Brookings Institution, 1977), 225.
26. Alexis Simendinger, "Of the People, for the People," *National Journal*, April 18, 1998, 852–55. Data from the Pew Charitable Trusts Research Center for the People and the Press.
27. Kenneth Meier and Lloyd Nigro, "Representative Bureaucracy and Policy References: A Study of the Attitudes of Federal Executives," *Public Administration Review* 36 (July/August 1976): 458–67; Bernard Mennis, *American Foreign Policy Officials* (Columbus: Ohio State University Press, 1971).
28. David Stockman, *The Triumph of Politics* (New York: Harper and Row, 1986).
29. James Q. Wilson, *Bureaucracy* (New York: Basic Books, 1989), chap. 6.
30. Heclo, "Issue Networks and the Executive Establishment," 87–124.
31. David H. Rosenbloom, "Reevaluating Executive-Centered Public Administrative Theory," in *The Oxford Handbook of American Bureaucracy*, ed. Robert F. Durant (New York: Oxford University Press, 2010), 114.
32. Ibid., 121–22.
33. Richard F. Fenno, Jr., *The Power of the Purse* (Boston, MA: Little, Brown, 1966), 450, 597.
34. John E. Schwartz and L. Earl Shaw, *The United States Congress in Comparative Perspective* (Hinsdale, IL: Dryden Press, 1976), 262–63; Richard E. Cohen, "Budget Express Leaving the Station Without Appropriations Committees," *National Journal,* July 4, 1981, 1211–14.
35. *Immigration and Naturalization Service v. Chadha*, 462 U.S. 919 (1983); *Maine v. Thiboutot*, 448 U.S. 1 (1980).
36. See cases cited in Corwin, *The Constitution*, 22.
37. William Safire, *Safire's Political Dictionary* (New York: Random House, 1978).
38. Herbert Kaufman, *Red Tape: Its Origins, Uses, and Abuses* (Washington, D.C.: The Brookings Institution, 1977; republished in 2015), p. 1.
39. Steven Kelman, "The Grace Commission: How Much Waste in Government?" *Public Interest* 78 (Winter 1985): 62–87.
40. Daniel Katz et al., *Bureaucratic Encounters: A Pilot Study in the Evaluation of Government Services* (Ann Arbor: Survey Research Center, University of Michigan, 1975), 63–69, 118–20, 184–88.
41. U.S. Government Accountability Office, "Government Performance Lessons Learned," GAO Report, July 24, 2008, as cited in Kettl, *The Next Government of the United States*, 173, 255.
42. Michael Knowles, "Trump Slashes Federal Bureaucracy: Morale Has Never Been Lower," www.dailywire.com, 12 January 2018; Jared Serbu, "Trump

Administration Issues Orders To Combat 'Bureaucratic Abuse' by 'Rogue Agencies'," *Federal News Network,* 9 October 2019.

Chapter 16

1. Russell Wheeler, "Trump's Judicial Appointments Record at the August Recess: A Little Less Than Meets the Eye," *Brookings,* 8 August 2019.
2. Congressional Research Service, "Judicial Nomination Statistics and Analysis: U.S. District and Circuit Courts, 1977–2018," 21 March 2019, Table 7, pp. 13–14; Jasmine C. Lee, "President Trump Could 'Flip' the Supreme Court. His Impact on the Lower Courts Is Less Clear." *New York Times,* 4 September 2018.
3. Russell Wheeler, "Judicial Nominations and Confirmations In Obama's First Term," Brookings Institution, December 13, 2012. www.brookings.edu/research/judicial-nominations-and-confirmations-in-obamas-first-term/. Accessed July 2020.
4. Henry J. Abraham, *The Judicial Process,* 3rd ed. (New York: Oxford University Press, 1975), 279–80.
5. www.cnnpolitics.com, 12 September 2005 .
6. Robert G. McCloskey, *The American Supreme Court* (Chicago, IL: University of Chicago Press, 1960), 27.
7. *Marbury v. Madison*, 5 U.S. 137 (1803); and *McCulloch v. Maryland*, 17 U.S. 316 (1819).
8. *Martin v. Hunter's Lessee,* 14 U.S. 304 (1816); and *Cohens v. Virginia*, 19 U.S. 264 (1821).
9. *Gibbons v. Ogden,* 22 U.S. 1 (1824).
10. Quoted in Albert J. Beveridge, *The Life of John Marshall* (Boston, MA: Houghton Mifflin, 1919), 4:551.
11. *Dred Scott v. Sandford,* 60 U.S. 393 (1857).
12. *Abraham, The Judicial Process*, 286.
13. 13 *In re Debs,* 158 U.S. 564 (1895).
14. *Pollock v. Farmers' Loan & Trust Co.*, 157 U.S. 429 (1895).
15. *United States v. Knight*, 156 U.S. 1 (1895).
16. *Cincinnati, N.O. &T.P. Railway Co. v. Interstate Commerce Commission*, 162 U.S. 184 (1896).
17. *Hammer v. Dagenhart*, 247 U.S. 251 (1918).
18. *Lochner v. New York,* 198 U.S. 45 (1905).
19. *McCloskey, The American Supreme Court,* 151.
20. *Munn v. Illinois,* 94 U.S. 113 (1877).
21. *Dayton-Goose Creek Railway Co. v. United States*, 263 U.S. 456 (1924).
22. *Atchison, Topeka, and Santa Fe Railroad Co. v. Matthews*, 174 U.S. 96 (1899).
23. *Mugler v. Kansas,* 123 U.S. 623 (1887).
24. *St. Louis Consolidated Coal Co. v. Illinois*, 185 U.S. 203 (1902).
25. *New York Central Railroad Co. v. White*, 243 U.S. 188 (1917).
26. *German Alliance Insurance Co. v. Lewis*, 233 U.S. 389 (1914).
27. Morton Keller, *Affairs of State* (Cambridge, MA: Harvard University Press, 1977), 369. See also Mary Cornelia Porter, "That Commerce Shall Be Free: A New Look at the Old Laissez-Faire Court," in *The Supreme Court Review*, ed. Philip B. Kurland (Chicago: University of Chicago Press, 1976), 135–59.
28. *Chief of Capitol Police v. Jeannette Rankin Brigade*, 409 U.S. 972 (1972).
29. *Aptheker v. Secretary of State*, 378 U.S. 500 (1964).
30. *Trop v. Dulles,* 356 U.S. 86 (1958); *Afroyim v. Rusk*, 387 U.S. 253 (1967); and *Schneider v. Rusk,* 377 U.S. 163 (1964).
31. *Lamont v. Postmaster General,* 381 U.S. 301 (1965); and *Blount v. Rizzi,* 400 U.S. 410 (1971).
32. *Richardson v. Davis, 409 U.S.* 1069 (1972); *U.S. Department of Agriculture v. Murry*, 413 U.S. 508 (1973); *Jimenez v. Weinberger,* 417 U.S. 628 (1974); and *Washington v. Legrant*, 394 U.S. 618 (1969).
33. *United States v. Lopez, 514 U.S.* 549 (1995).
34. *Seminole Tribe of Florida v. Florida*, 517 U.S. 44 (1996); *Aden v. Maine*, 527 U.S. 706 (1999); *Florida v. College Savings Bank*, 527 U.S. 627 (1999).
35. Adam Liptak, "Supreme Court Allows Nationwide Health Care Subsidies," *New York Times,* June 25, 2015.
36. Daniel R. Pinello, "Linking Party to Judicial Ideology in American Courts: A Meta-Analysis," *Justice System Journal* 20 (1999): 219–54.
37. "Blue Slip (Federal Judicial Nominations)," *Ballotpedia,* https://ballotpedia.org/Blue_slip_(federal_judicial_nominations); American Bar Association, "Judicial Vacancies—116th Congress: Significant Events and Issues," updated 26 June 2020, https://www.americanbar.org/advocacy/governmental_legislative_work/priorities_policy/independence_of_the_judiciary/judicial_vacancies/. Accessed July 2020.
38. An opinion survey of federal judges shows how party affects ideology: see Althea K. Nagai, Stanley Rothman, and S. Robert Lichter, "The Verdict on Federal Judges," *Public Opinion* 10, no. 4 (November/December 1987): 52–56.
39. Susan Davis and Richard Wolf, "U.S. Senate Goes 'Nuclear,' Changes Filibuster Rules," *USA Today*, November 21, 2013.
40. *United States v. Lanza*, 260 U.S. 377 (1922). *Cf. Abbate v. United States,* 359 U.S. 187 (1959), and *Bartkus v. Illinois,* 359 U.S. 121 (1989).
41. *Gideon v. Wainwright*, 372 U.S. 335 (1963). The story is told in Anthony Lewis, *Gideon's Trumpet* (New York: Random House, 1964).
42. Erwin Griswold, "Rationing Justice: The Supreme Court's Case Load and What the Court Does Not Do," *Cornell Law Review* 60 (1975): 335–54.
43. Joseph Weis, Jr., "Disconnecting the Overloaded Circuits—A Plan for a Unified Court of Appeals," *St. Louis University Law Journal* 39 (1995): 455.
44. *Alyeska Pipeline Service Co. v. Wilderness Society*, 421 U.S. 240 (1975).
45. *Flast v. Cohen,* 392 U.S. 83 (1968), which modified the earlier *Frothingham v. Mellon*, 262 U.S. 447 (1923); *United States v. Richardson,* 418 U.S. 166 (1947).

46. *Brown v. Board of Education of Topeka*, 347 U.S. 483 (1954).
47. *Baker v. Carr*, 369 U.S. 186 (1962).
48. See Louise Weinberg, "A New Judicial Federalism?" *Daedalus* 107, no. 1 (Winter 1978): 129–41.
49. Quoted in Abraham, *The Judicial Process*, 330.
50. Carolyn D. Richmond, "The Rehnquist Court: What Is in Store for Constitutional Precedent?" *New York Law Review* 39 (1994): 511.
51. *Colegrove v. Green*, 328 U.S. 549 (1946).
52. The Court abandoned the "political question" doctrine in *Baker v. Carr*, 369 U.S. 186 (1962), and began to change congressional district apportionment in *Wesberry v. Sanders*, 376 U.S. 1 (1964).
53. Donald L. Horowitz, *The Courts and Social Policy* (Washington, D.C.: Brookings Institution, 1977), 6.
54. *Gates v. Collier*, 349 F. Supp. 881 (1972).
55. *Lau v. Nichols*, 414 U.S. 563 (1974).
56. Jane Burnbaum, "Guilty!: Too Many Lawyers and Too Much Litigation," *Business Week*, April 13, 1992, 60–61.
57. Joel B. Grossman and Austin Sarat, "Litigation in the Federal Courts: A Comparative Perspective," *Law and Society Review* 9 (Winter 1975): 321–46.
58. Administrative Office of the U.S. Courts, *Annual Report*, 1988, 109.
59. Jack W. Peltason, *Fifty-Eight Lonely Men: Southern Federal Judges and School Desegregation* (New York: Harcourt Brace, 1961).
60. Anthony Partridge and William B. Eldridge, *The Second Circuit Sentencing Study* (Washington, D.C.: Federal Judicial Center, 1974).
61. *Abington School District v. Schempp*, 374 U.S. 203 (1963).
62. Robert H. Birkby, "The Supreme Court and the Bible Belt: Tennessee Reaction to the 'Schempp' Decision," *Midwest Journal of Political Science* 10, no. 3 (August 1966): 304–19.
63. *"Impeachment of Federal Judges," Ballotpedia: An Interactive Almanac of U.S. Politics.*
64. *United States v. Butler*, 297 U.S. 1 (1936).
65. *Ex parte McCardle*, 74 U.S. 506 (1869).
66. Walter F. Murphy, *Congress and the Court* (Chicago, IL: University of Chicago Press, 1962); and C. Herman Pritchett, *Congress Versus the Supreme Court* (Minneapolis: University of Minnesota Press, 1961).
67. Gregory A. Caldeira, "Neither the Purse nor the Sword: Dynamics of Public Confidence in the U.S. Supreme Court," *American Political Science Review* 80 (1986): 1209–26. See also Joseph T. Tannenhaus and Walter F. Murphy, "Patterns of Public Support for the Supreme Court: A Panel Study," *Journal of Politics* 43 (1981): 24–39.
68. Barton Gellman and Laura Poitras, "U.S. British Intelligence Mining Data from Nine U.S. Internet Companies in Broad Secret Program," *Washington Post*, 6 June, 2013.

Chapter 17

1. Lisa Friedman, "Trump Serves Notice to Quit Paris Climate Agreement," *New York Times*, 4 November 2019.
2. Pew Research Center, "As Economic Concerns Recede, Environmental Protection Rises on the Public's Policy Agenda," 13 February 2020.
3. Jeffrey Cohen, "Presidential Rhetoric and the Public Agenda," *American Journal of Political Science* 39, no. 1 (1995): 87–107.
4. Danielle Kurtzleben, "How Much Gets Done from the State of the Union Speeches?" NPR Politics, January 12, 2016.
5. Theodore Marmor, "Doctors, Politics, and Health Insurance for the Aged: The Enactment of Medicare," in *Cases in Contemporary American Government*, ed. Allan Sindler (Boston, MA: Little, Brown, 1969).
6. Center for Medicare and Medicaid Services, CMS Fast Facts, November 2019.
7. Staff of the *Washington Post*, *Landmark: The Inside Story of America's New Health Care Law and What It Means for All of Us* (New York: Public Affairs, 2010).
8. Phil Galewitz, "Breaking A 10-Year Streak, The Number Of Uninsured Americans Rises," Kaiser Health News, 10 September 2019.
9. "Key Facts about the Uninsured Population," Henry J. Kaiser Family Foundation, September 29, 2016.
10. Kristen Bialik and Abagail Geiger, "Republicans, Democrats Find Common Ground on Many Provisions of Health Care Law," Pew Research Center Fact Tank, December 8, 2016.
11. "Fact Sheet: Social Security," Social Security Administration, 2016.
12. Status of the Social Security and Medicare Programs, Social Security and Medicare Board of Trustees, 2019. Available online at: https://www.ssa.gov/oact/trsum/. Accessed February 2020.
13. Konstantin Kashin, Gary King, and Samir Soneji, "Explaining Systematic Bias and Nontransparency in the US Social Security Administration Forecasts," *Political Analysis* 23, no. 3 (2015): 336–62.
14. Status of the Social Security and Medicare Programs, Social Security and Medicare Board of Trustees, 2019. Available online at: https://www.ssa.gov/oact/trsum/, accessed February 2020.
15. Kristina Cooke, David Rohde, and Ryan McNeil, "The Undeserving Poor," *The Atlantic*, December 20, 2012.
16. Michael Bang Peterson et al., "Who Deserves Help? Evolutionary Psychology, Social Emotions, and Public Opinion about Welfare," *Political Psychology* 33, no. 3 (2012): 395–418; Lauren Applebaum, "The Influence of Perceived Deservingness on Policy Decisions Regarding Aid to the Poor," *Political Psychology* 22, no. 3 (2001): 419–42.
17. Robert Moffitt, "The Deserving Poor, the Family, and the U.S. Welfare System," *Demography* 52, no. 3 (2015): 729–49.
18. Charles E. Gilbert, "Welfare Policy," in *Handbook of Political*

Science, eds. Fred I. Greenstein and Nelson W. Polsby (Reading, MA: Addison-Wesley, 1975), vol. 6, chap. 4; Lawrence M. Mead, *From Prophecy to Charity: How to Help the Poor* (Washington, D.C.: American Enterprise Institute, 2011), 14–18.

19. Congressional Quarterly, *Congress and the Nation, 1945–1964* (Washington, D.C.: Congressional Quarterly Service, 1965), 1225.
20. Harold E. Raynes, *Social Security in Britain: A History* (London: Pitman, 1960), chap. 18; Hugh Heclo, *Modern Social Politics in Britain and Sweden* (New Haven, CT: Yale University Press, 1974).
21. *The Values We Live By: What Americans Want from Welfare Reform* (New York: Public Agenda Foundation, 1996): 42.
22. Max Ehrenfreund, "How Welfare Reform Changed American Poverty in 9 Charts," *Washington Post Wonkblog,* August 22, 2016; "Temporary Assistance for Needy Families (TANF) Block Grant: Responses to Frequently Asked Questions," Congressional Research Service, December 30, 2019
23. Ehrenfreund, *"How Welfare Reform Changed American Poverty in 9 Charts."*
24. Christopher Jencks, "The War on Poverty: Was It Lost?" *New York Review of Books,* April 2, 2015.
25. H. Luke Shaefer and Kathryn Edin, "Extreme Poverty in the United States, 1996 to 2011," National Poverty Center, Policy Brief #28, February 2012.
26. Kate Kzernike, Abby Goodnough, and Pam Belluck, "In Health Bill's Defeat, Medicaid Comes of Age," *New York Times*, 29 March 2017.
27. Robert Pear, "Trump Administration Says States May Impose Work Requirements for Medicaid," *New York Times*, 11 January 2018.
28. Edward S. Greenberg, *Serving the Few: Corporate Capitalism and the Bias of Government Policy* (New York: Wiley, 1974).
29. Charles E. Lindblom, *Politics and Markets: The World's Political-Economic Systems* (New York: Basic Books, 1977).
30. Joseph Schumpeter, *Capitalism, Socialism, and Democracy* (New York: Harper and Row, 1950).
31. Louis Galambos, *The Public Image of Big Business in America, 1880–1940* (Baltimore, MD: Johns Hopkins University Press, 1975).
32. Suzanne Weaver, *Decision to Prosecute: Organization and Public Policy in the Antitrust Division* (Cambridge, MA: MIT Press, 1977); Robert H. Bork, *The Antitrust Paradox* (New York: Basic Books, 1977).
33. Richard A. Posner, *Antitrust Law: An Economic Perspective* (Chicago, IL: University of Chicago Press, 1976), 25.
34. Alan L. Seltzer, "Woodrow Wilson as 'Corporate-Liberal': Toward a Reconsideration of Left Revisionist Historiography," *Western Political Quarterly* 30 (June 1977): 183–212.
35. Weaver, *Decision to Prosecute;* Robert A. Katzmann, *Regulatory Bureaucracy: The Federal Trade Commission and Antitrust Policy* (Cambridge, MA: MIT Press, 1980).
36. "Has Antitrust Enforcement Been Reinvigorated Under Obama?" *National Law Review,* October 27, 2015; Steve Mufson and Renae Merle, "As Obama's Term Winds Down, Crackdowns on Mergers Speed Up," *Washington Post,* May 2, 2016.
37. Edmund Lee and Cecelia Kang, "U.S. Loses Appeal Seeking to Block AT&T-Time Warner Merger," *New York Times*, 26 February 2019.
38. Tony Romm, "FTC Will Review Past Mergers by Facebook, Google, and Other Big Tech Companies," *Washington Post,* 11 February 2020.
39. Drew Fitzgerald et al, "T-Mobile, Sprint Deal Wins Approval, Reshaping Industry," *Wall Street Journal*, 11 February 2020.
40. Charles R. Plott, "Occupational Self-Regulation: A Case Study of the Oklahoma City Dry Cleaners," *Journal of Law and Economics* 8 (October 1965): 195–222.
41. Paul H. MacAvoy, ed. *Federal Milk Marketing Orders and Price Supports* (Washington, D.C.: American Enterprise Institute, 1977).
42. Ibid.
43. "Milking Taxpayers," *The Economist,* February 12, 2015.
44. Pietro Nivola, "The New York Pork Barrel," *Brookings Review* (Winter 1998): 6–13.
45. The list would include the following laws: the 1962 amendments to the Pure Food and Drug Act, the Motor Vehicle Air Pollution Control Act of 1965, the National Traffic and Motor Vehicle Safety Act of 1966, the Wholesome Poultry Act of 1968, the Children's Protection and Toy Safety Act of 1969, the Clean Air Act of 1970, and the Toxic Substances Control Act of 1976.
46. Upton Sinclair, *The Jungle* (New York: Doubleday and Company, 1906).
47. Ralph Nader, *Unsafe at Any Speed: The Designed-In Dangers of the American Automobile* (New York: Grossman, 1965).
48. Mark V. Nadel, *The Politics of Consumer Protection* (Indianapolis, IN: Bobbs-Merill, 1971): 143–44.
49. Alfred A. Marcus, *Promise and Performance: Choosing and Implementing an Environmental Policy* (Westport, CT: Greenwood Press, 1980).
50. Nadel, *The Politics of Consumer Protection*, 66–68.
51. William Anderegg et al., "Expert Credibility in Climate Change," *Proceedings of the National Academy of Sciences* 107, no. 27 (2010): 12107–9.
52. Cary Funk and Brian Kennedy, "The Politics of Climate," Pew Research Center, October 4, 2016; Dan Kahan et al., "The Polarizing Impact of Science Literacy and Numeracy on Perceived Climate Change Risks," *Nature Climate Change* 2 (2012): 732–35.
53. Dan Kahan, "Climate-Science Communication and the Measurement Problem," *Advances in Political Psychology* 36, no. S1 (2015): 1–43.

54. Ariel Malka et al., "Featuring Skeptics in News Media Stories about Global Warming Reduces Public Beliefs in the Seriousness of Global Warming" (unpublished manuscript, Stanford University, June 2009); Maxwell Boykoff and Jules Boykoff, "Balance as Bias: Global Warming and the U.S. Prestige Press," *Global Environmental Change* 14, no. 2 (2004): 125–36.
55. Louis Jacobsen, "Yes, Donald Trump Did Call Climate Change a Chinese Hoax," Politifact, June 3, 2016; Senator James Inhofe, *The Greatest Hoax: How the Global Warming Conspiracy Threatens Your Future* (Medford, OR: WND Books, 2012).
56. Dan Kahan, "Ideology, Motivated Reasoning, and Cognitive Reflection: An Experimental Study," *Judgment and Decision Making* 8 (2013): 407–24; Eric Merkley and Dominik Stecula, "Party Cues in the News: Democratic Elites, Republican Backlash, and the Dynamics of Climate Skepticism," *British Journal of Political Science*, Forthcoming.
57. Ryan Lizza, "As the World Burns," *New Yorker*, October 22, 2010.
58. Nadja Popovich, Livia Albeck-Rivka, Kendra Pierre-Louis, "The Trump Administration Is Reversing Nearly 100 Environmental Rules. Here's the Full List," *New York Times*, 6 May 2020.
59. Keith Belton and John Graham, "Trump's Deregulation Record: Is It Working?" *Administrative Law Review* volume 71, number 4 (2019): 803–80; Stuart Shapiro, "Making Sense of the Trump Administration's Regulatory Numbers," *The Regulatory Review*, 14 January 2020.
60. David Vogel, *National Styles of Regulation* (Ithaca, NY: Cornell University Press, 1986), 19–30.
61. Lisa Friedman, "U.S. Significantly Weakens Endangered Species Act," *New York Times*, 12 August 2019.
62. R. Shep Melnick, *Regulation and the Courts: The Case of the Clean Air Act* (Washington, D.C.: Brookings Institution Press, 1983), chap. 9.
63. Adam Isen, Maya Rossin-Slater, and W. Reed Walker, "Every Breath You Take—Every Dollar You'll Make: The Long-Term Consequences of the Clean Air Act of 1970," *Journal of Political Economy* 125, no. 3 (June 2017): 848–902.
64. Pietro S. Nivola, *The Politics of Energy Conservation* (Washington, D.C.: Brookings Institution Press, 1986), 11–12, 244–47.
65. Robert W. Crandall, "Pollution, Environmentalists, and the Coal Lobby," in *The Political Economy of Deregulation*, eds. Roger G. Noll and Bruce M. Own (Washington, D.C.: American Enterprise Institute, 1983), 83–84; Robert W. Crandall, *Controlling Industrial Pollution* (Washington, D.C.: American Enterprise Institute, 1983.
66. Bruce A. Ackerman and William T. Hassler, *Clean Coal/Dirty Air: or How the Clean Air Act Became a Multibillion-Dollar Bail-Out for High-Sulfur Coal Producers and What Should Be Done about It* (New Haven, CT: Yale University Press, 1981).
67. Bill Chalmeides, "U.S. Acid Rain Regulations: Did They Work?," *Huffington Post,* May 5, 2012, www.huffingtonpost.com/bill-chameides/us-acid-rain-regulations_b_1507392.html. accessed February 2020.
68. Rachel Carson, *Silent Spring* (New York: Houghton Mifflin, 1962).
69. Robert Dorfman, "Lessons from Pesticide Regulation," in *Reform of Environmental Regulation,* ed. Wesley A. Magat (Cambridge, MA: Ballinger, 1982), 13–30.
70. Arthur Grube et al., *Pesticide Industry Sales and Usage 2006 and 2007: Market Estimates* (Washington, D.C.: U.S. Environmental Protection Agency, 2011).

Chapter 18

1. D. Roderick Kiewiet, *Macroeconomics and Micropolitics: The Electoral Effect of Economic Issues* (Chicago, IL: University of Chicago Press, 1983).
2. Donald Kinder and D. Roderick Kiewiet, "Sociotropic Politics: The American Case" British Journal of Political Science 11, no. 2 (April 1981): 129–61.
3. 2020 Exit Polls, as reported by NBC News, https://www.nbcnews.com/politics/2020-elections/exit-polls?icid=election_nav
4. Kiewiet, *Macroeconomics and Micropolitics.*
5. Michael S. Lewis-Beck, "Comparative Economic Voting: Britain, France, Germany, Italy," *American Journal of Political Science* 30, no. 2 (May 1986): 315–46.
6. Gerald Kramer, "The Ecological Fallacy Revisited: Aggregate-versus Individual-Level Findings on Economics and Elections, and Sociotropic Voting," *American Political Science Review* 77, no. 1 (March 1983): 92–111.
7. James Stimson, *Tides of Consent: How Public Opinion Shapes American Politics* (New York: Cambridge University Press, 2004).
8. Gallup, "Taxes," www.gallup.com/poll/1714/taxes.aspx. accessed February 2020.
9. Centers for Disease Control and Prevention (CDC), "Federal and State Cigarette Excise Taxes—United States, 1995–2009," *MMWR Weekly* 58, no. 19 (2009): 524–27.
10. For a listing of recent changes to the federal funds rate, see www.federalreserve.gov/monetarypolicy/openmarket.htm.
11. Andrew Healey and Gabriel Lenz, "Substituting the End for the Whole: Why Voters Respond Primarily to the Election-Year Economy," *American Journal of Political Science* 58, no. 1 (January 2014): 31.
12. Congressional Budget Office, "The Budget and Economic Outlook: 2020 to 2030," January 2020.
13. D. Andrew Austin, "The Budget Control Act and Trends in Discretionary Spending," Congressional Research Service, RL34424.
14. Ibid.
15. D. Andrew Austin and Mindy Levit, "The Debt Limit: History and Recent Increases," Congressional Research Service Report RL31967, 2012; Robert Smith, "The History of the Debt Ceiling,"

National Public Radio, May 16, 2011.

16. Thad Kousser, Mathew McCubbins, and Ellen Moule, "For Whom the TELL Tolls: Can State Tax and Expenditure Limits Effectively Reduce Spending?" *State Politics and Policy Quarterly* 8, no. 4 (2008): 331–61.
17. "Top 10 Percent of Earners Paid 68 Percent of Federal Income Taxes," 2015 Federal Budget in Pictures, The Heritage Foundation.
18. *Pollock v. Farmers' Loan & Trust Co.,* 157 U.S. 429, affirmed at 158 U.S. 601 (1895).
19. NBC News/ *Wall Street Journal* poll, as reported in *National Journal* (July 12, 1986): 1741.
20. Congressional Budget Office, The Budget and Economic Outlook: 2020 to 2030, January 2020.
21. Ana Swanson and Emily Cochran, "Trump Signs Trade Deal with Canada and Mexico," *New York Times*, 29 January 2020.
22. Alan Rappeport, "U.S. Watchdog to Investigate Trump's Farm Bailout Program," *New York Times*, 14 February 2020.
23. "Has COVID-19 Killed Gloablisation?" *The Economist,* 14 May 2020.
24. "The Distribution of Household Income and Federal Taxes, 2011," Congressional Budget Office, November 12, 2014. See in particular figure 8.
25. Isabel Sawhill and Christopher Pulliam, "Six Facts about Wealth in the United States," The Brookings Institution, 25 June 2019.
26. Thomas Piketty, *Capital in the Twenty-First Century* (Cambridge, MA: Belknap Press of Harvard University Press, 2014).
27. David Autor, "Skills, Education, and the Rise of Earnings Inequality among the 'Other 99 Percent,'" *Science* 344, no. 6186 (2014): 843–51.
28. David Autor and David Dorn, "The Growth of Low-Skill Service Jobs and the Polarization of the U.S. Labor Market," *American Economic Review* 103, no. 5 (2013): 1553–97.
29. David Card, "The Effects of Unions on Wage Inequality in the U.S. Labor Market," *Industrial and Labor Relations Review* 54 (January 2001).
30. Joseph Stiglitz, *The Great Divide: Unequal Societies and What We Can Do About Them* (New York: W.W. Norton, 2015); Larry Bartels, *Unequal Democracy: The Political Economy of the New Gilded Age* (Princeton, NJ: Princeton University Press, 2008).
31. Robert Putnam, *Our Kids: The American Dream in Crisis* (New York: Simon and Schuster, 2014); Raj Chetty et al., "The Fading American Dream: Trends in Absolute Income Mobility Since 1940," *Science* 356 (28 April 2017): 398–406.
32. For the competing perspectives, see: Thomas MaCurdy, "How Effective is the Minimum Wage at Supporting the Poor?" *Journal of Political Economy* 123, no. 2 (2015): 497–545; David Card, "Do Minimum Wages Reduce Employment? A Case Study of California, 1987–1989," *Industry and Labor Relations Review* 46, no. 1 (1992): 38–54.
33. Ernie Tedeschi, "Americans Are Seeing Highest Minimum Wages in History (Without Federal Help)," *New York Times*, 24 April 2019.
34. Leslie Davis and Hannah Hartig, "Two-Thirds of Americans Favor Raising Federal Minimum Wage to $15 Per Hour," Pew Research Center Fact Tank, 30 July 2019.
35. Emanuel Saez and Gabriel Zucman, *The Triumph of Injustice: How the Rich Dodge Taxes and How to Make Them Pay* (New York: W.W. Norton, 2019).
36. For a cogent breakdown of these issues, see Greg Rosalsky, "If a Wealth Tax Is Such a Good Idea, Why Did Europe Kill Theirs?" *NPR: Planet Money,* 26 February 2019.

Chapter 19

1. Alexis de Tocqueville, *Democracy in America*, vol. 1, ed. Phillips Bradley (New York: Knopf, 1951), 235.
2. See Victor Davis Hanson, *Carnage and Culture* (New York: Anchor Books, 2002); Hanson, *The Soul of Battle* (New York: Free Press, 1999).
3. Richard Lau, Thad A. Brown, and David O. Sears, "Self-Interest and Civilians' Attitudes Toward the Vietnam War," *Public Opinion Quarterly* 42 (1978): 464–81.
4. James McBride, "How Does the U.S. Spend Its Foreign Aid?" *Council on Foreign Relations Backgrounder,* 1 October 2018; George Ingram, "What Every American Should Know About U.S. Foreign Aid," *Brookings Policy 2020: Voter Vitals,* 15 October 2019.
5. Edward S. Corwin, *The President: Office and Powers* (New York: New York University Press, 1940), 200.
6. Louis W. Koenig, *The Chief Executive,* 6th ed. (Fort Worth, TX: Harcourt Brace, 1992), 216.
7. Louis Fisher, *President and Congress* (New York: Free Press, 1972), 45; *United States v. Belmont*, 301 U.S. 324 (1937).
8. Aaron Wildavsky, "The Two Presidencies," in *The Presidency,* ed. Aaron Wildavsky (Boston, MA: Little, Brown, 1969), 231.
9. Loch Johnson and James M. McCormick, "The Making of International Agreements: A Reappraisal of Congressional Involvement," *Journal of Politics* 40 (1978): 468–78.
10. Bernard E. Brown, "The Decision to End the Algerian War," in *Cases in Comparative Politics*, ed. James B. Christoph (Boston, MA: Little, Brown, 1965), 154–80; Roy C. Macridis, "De Gaulle and NATO," in *Modern European Governments*, ed. Roy C. Macridis (Englewood Cliffs, NJ: Prentice-Hall, 1968), 92–115; and John E. Schwartz and L. Earl Shaw, *The United States Congress in Comparative Perspective* (Hinsdale, IL: Dryden Press, 1976), 235–36.
11. Peter G. Richards, *Parliament and Foreign Affairs* (London: George Allen & Unwin, 1967), 37–38; Schwartz and Shaw, *The United States Congress in Comparative Perspective,* 235.

12. Arthur M. Schlesinger Jr., *A Thousand Days: John F. Kennedy in the White House* (Boston, MA: Houghton Mifflin, 1965), chaps. 30 and 31. Schlesinger described Kennedy's actions as a "brilliantly controlled," "matchlessly calibrated" combination of "nerve and wisdom" (841). His view of Nixon's actions was a good deal less charitable; see Schlesinger, *The Imperial Presidency* (Boston, MA: Houghton Mifflin, 1974), chap. 7.
13. *United States v. Curtiss-Wright Export Co.*, 299 U.S. 304 (1936).
14. *Mitchell v. Laird,* 488 F.2d 611 (1973).
15. *Prize Cases*, 67 U.S. 635 (1863); *Mora v. McNamara*, 389 U.S. 934 (1964); *Massachusetts v. Laird,* 400 U.S. 886 (1970).
16. *Dames and Moore v. Regan,* 435 U.S. 654 (1981).
17. *Youngstown Sheet & Tube Co. v. Sawyer*, 343 U.S. 579 (1952).
18. *Immigration and Naturalization Service v. Chadha*, 103 S. Ct. 2764 (1983).
19. Sarah Binder, "The Republican Senate Just Rebuked Trump Using the War Powers Act – For the Third Time. That's Remarkable," *Washington Post,* 14 February 2020.
20. Richard A. Best Jr., "The National Security Council: An Organizational Assessment," Congressional Research Service, December 28, 2011; Nahal Toosi, "Trump's Plan to Shrink NSC Staff Draws Fire," *Politico,* 11 November 2019.
21. Robert S. Erikson and Norman R. Luttbeg, *American Public Opinion* (New York: Wiley, 1973), 50–51.
22. William R. Caspary, "The 'Mood Theory': A Study of Public Opinion and Foreign Policy," *American Political Science Review* 64 (June 1970): 536–47.
23. Erikson and Luttbeg, *American Public Opinion*, 52.
24. John E. Mueller, *War, Presidents, and Public Opinion* (New York: Wiley, 1973), 110.
25. Ibid., 112.
26. Bruce Riedel, "Al-Qaida Today, 18 Years After 9/11," *Brookings,* 10 September 2019.
27. Milton J. Rosenberg, Sidney Verba, and Philip E. Converse, *Vietnam and the Silent Majority* (New York: Harper and Row, 1970), 26–27.
28. Erikson and Luttbeg, *American Public Opinion*, 155.
29. John R. Oneal and Brad Lian, "Presidents, the Use of Military Force, and Public Opinion," Working Papers in International Security I–92–8, Hoover Institution, Stanford, CA (July 1992).
30. Benjamin C. Schwarz, *Casualities, Public Opinion, and U.S. Military Intervention* (Santa Monica, CA: RAND, 1994).
31. Mueller, *War, Presidents, and Public Opinion*, 45–47, 169.
32. James Q. Wilson and Karlyn Bowman, "Defining the Peace Party," *The Public Interest* (Fall 2003): 69–78.
33. Jeffrey M. Jones, "Americans Approve of Military Action Against Libya, 47% to 37%," *Gallup Politics,* March 22, 2011. www.gallup.com.
34. Everett Carll Ladd, "Since World War II, Americans Have Persistently Looked Outward," *The Public Perspective* (August/ September 1997): 5–34.
35. Howard Schuman, "Two Sources of Antiwar Sentiment in America," *American Journal of Sociology* 78 (1973): 513–36.
36. Philip E. Converse, Warren E. Miller, Jerrold G. Rusk, and Arthur C. Wolfe, "Continuity and Change in American Politics," *American Political Science Review* 63 (December 1969): 1083–105; John P. Robinson, "Public Reaction to Political Protest: Chicago, 1968," *Public Opinion Quarterly* 34 (Spring 1970): 1–9.
37. James D. Wright, "Life, Time, and the Fortunes of War," *Transaction* 9, no. 3 (January 1972): 42–52.
38. Kim Parker, Rich Morin, and Juliana Horowitz, "Looking to the Future, Public Sees An America In Decline on Many Fronts," *Pew Research Center,* 21 March 2019.
39. X, "The Sources of Soviet Conduct," *Foreign Affairs* 25 (July 1947): 566.
40. Walter Lippmann, *The Cold War* (New York: Harper Brothers, 1947).
41. Erikson and Luttbeg, *American Public Opinion*, 52.
42. Mueller, *War, Presidents, and Public Opinion*, 40.
43. Michael Roskin, "From Pearl Harbor to Vietnam: Shifting Generational Paradigms and Foreign Policy," *Political Science Quarterly* 89 (Fall 1974): 567.
44. Frank L. Klingberg, "The Historical Alternation of Moods in American Foreign Policy," *World Politics* 4 (1952): 239–73.
45. Roskin, "From Pearl Harbor to Vietnam," 567.
46. *American Public Opinion and U.S. Foreign Policy, 1987* (Chicago, IL: Chicago Council on Foreign Relations, 1987), 33.
47. Gareth Evans and Mohamed Sahnoun, "The Responsibility to Protect," *Foreign Affairs* 81, no. 6 (November/December 2002); Charles Homans, "Responsibility to Protect: A Short History," *Foreign Policy,* October 11, 2011.
48. Mark Kersten, "The Responsibility to Protect Doctrine Is Faltering. Here's Why," *Washington Post,* 8 December 2015.
49. Carl M. Cannon, "Comment," in *Red and Blue Nation?,* eds. Pietro S. Nivola and David W. Brady (Washington, D.C.: Brookings Institution, 2006), 168; and Cannon, "Administration: A New Era of Partisan War," *National Journal,* March 18, 2006.
50. For a lively debate over the extent of political polarization, see Morris Fiorina and Matthew S. Levendusky, "Disconnected: The Political Class Versus the People"; Alan I. Abramowitz, "Comment"; and Gary C. Jacobson, "Comment," all in Nivola and Brady, eds., *Red and Blue Nation?*
51. Peter Beinart, "When Politics No Longer Stops at the Water's Edge," in Nivola and Brady, eds., *Red and Blue Nation?,* vol. 2.
52. John Zaller, *The Nature and Origins of Mass Opinion* (New York: Cambridge University Press, 1992), esp. chap. 9.

53. Ian Bremmer, *Superpower: Three Choices for America's Role in the World* (New York: Portfolio/Penguin, 2015).
54. George H. W Bush, "Address Before a Joint Session of Congress," September 11, 1990.
55. *The National Security Strategy of the United States of America*, September 2002, cover letter and 6.
56. The White House, "President Bush Addresses the Nation," March 19, 2003.
57. National Public Radio, "Iraq WMD Timeline: How the Mystery Unraveled," November 15, 2005.
58. George W. Bush, *Decision Points* (New York: Crown Publishers, 2010), 267.
59. "Joint Resolution: To Authorize the Use of United States Armed Forces Against Those Responsible for the Recent Attacks Launched Against the United States," 107th Congress, Public Law 107–40, September 18, 2001.
60. "The War in Afghanistan: A Timeline," *CBS News,* December 1, 2009. www.cbsnews.com.
61. Meena Bose, "Who Makes U.S. Foreign Policy?: Presidential Leadership in Gulf Wars I and II," in *The Presidency and the Challenge of Democracy,* eds. Michael A. Genovese and Lori Cox Han (New York: Palgrave Macmillan, 2006), 139–58.
62. Kenneth M. Pollack, *The Threatening Storm: The Case for Invading Iraq* (New York: Random House, 2002).
63. Commission on the Intelligence Capabilities of the United States Regarding Weapons of Mass Destruction, *Report to the President* (Washington, D.C.: Government Printing Office, 2005), 243–49.
64. James Dobbins et al., *America's Role in Nation Building: From Germany to Iraq* (Santa Monica, CA: RAND, 2003).
65. Paul Sonne, Josh Dawsey, and Missy Ryan, "Mattis Resigns After Clash With Trump Over Troop Withdrawal From Syria and Afghanistan," *Washington Post*, 20 December 2018; Craig Whitlock, "The Afghanistan Papers: A Secret History of the War," *Washington Post,* 9 December 2019.
66. The vote on the Persian Gulf War as reported in *Congress and the Nation*, vol. 8 (Washington, D.C.: Congressional Quarterly Press, 1993), 310; the vote on the war in Iraq as reported in *New York Times*, October 12, 2002, A11.
67. No congressional votes were taken on U.S. military efforts in Bosnia and Kosovo, but speeches supporting them were made by (among others) Democratic Senators Barbara Boxer, Carl Levin, and Paul Wellstone and Representative David Bonior; speeches opposing them were made by (among others) Republican Senators Don Nickles and John Warner and by Representatives Robert Barr and Dan Burton. In the vote on the invasion of Iraq, each group took the opposite position.
68. James Ball, "Obama Issues Syria a 'Red Line' Warning on Chemical Weapons," *Washington Post*, August 20, 2012; Michael D. Shear, "History Aside, Obama Bets on Congress," *New York Times*, September 1, 2013.
69. Alexis Simendinger and James Arkin, "Approval of War Authorization Against ISIL Uncertain in Congress," February 12, 2015, www.realclearpolitics.com. Accessed July 2020.
70. Jonathan Weisman and Peter Baker, "Obama Yields, Allowing Congress Say on Iran Nuclear Deal," *New York Times*, April 14, 2015.
71. Jethro Mullen and Nic Robertson, "Landmark Deal Reached on Iran Nuclear Program," *CNN Politics,* July 14, 2015, www.cnn.com/politics; Manu Raju and Burgess Everett, "Key Democrats Skeptical of Iran Deal," *Politico*, July 14, 2015. Accessed July 2020.
72. Kevin Liptak, "In Syria Withdrawal, Trump Discards Advice from Allies and Officials," www.cnnpolitics.com, 20 December 2018; Helene Cooper, "Jim Mattis, Defense Secretary, Resigns In Rebuke of Trump's Worldview," *New York Times*, 20 December 2018.
73. Sarah Mervosh, "Will There Be a Draft? Young People Worry After Military Strike," *New York Times,* 3 January 2020.
74. Martin Matishak, "Rangel: Reinstate the Draft," *The Hill,* 19 March 2015.
75. Amanda Barroso, "The Changing Profile of the U.S. Military: Smaller in Size, More Diverse, More Women in Leadership," Pew Research Center, 10 September 2019.
76. Quoted in Robert J. Art, *The TFX Decision* (Boston, MA: Little, Brown, 1968), 126.

Chapter 20

1. National Archives and Records Administration, "Washington's Inaugural Address of 1789," April 30, 1789.
2. Alexis de Tocqueville, *Democracy in America*, vol. 2, ed. Phillips Bradley (New York: Knopf, 1951), book 2, chap. 1.
3. Gallup, "Confidence in Institutions," https://news.gallup.com/poll/1597/confidence-institutions.aspx.
4. Donald F. Kettl, "Heading for Disaster," *Government Executive*, February 1, 2009.
5. Ibid.
6. Matt Philips, "Too Big to Fail: The Entire Private Sector," *New York Times*, May 19, 2020.
7. Kelsey Snell, "Here's How Much Congress Has Approved for Coronavirus Relief So Far and What It's For," *National Public Radio,* May 15, 2020.

Index

E

F

J

K

N

O

P

S

T

U

Y

Z